LATIN LOANWORDS IN ANCIENT GREEK

Why, when, and how did speakers of ancient Greek borrow words from Latin? Which words did they borrow? Who used Latin loanwords, and how? Who avoided them, and why? How many words were borrowed, and what kind of word? How long did the loanwords survive? Until now, attempts to answer such questions have been based on incomplete and often misleading evidence, but this study offers the first comprehensive collection of evidence from papyri, inscriptions, and literature from the fifth century BC to the sixth century AD. That collection – included in the book as a lexicon of Latin loanwords – is examined using insights from linguistic work on modern languages to provide new answers that often differ strikingly from earlier ones. The analysis is accessibly presented, and the lexicon offers a firm foundation for future work in this area.

ELEANOR DICKEY is Professor of Classics at the University of Reading and a Fellow of the British Academy. She has published more than a hundred scholarly works on Latin, Greek, and how both languages have been used, taught, and understood through the ages, including *Learning Latin the Ancient Way* (2016), *Ancient Greek Scholarship* (2007), *Introduction to the Composition and Analysis of Greek Prose* (2016), *The Colloquia of the Hermeneumata Pseudodositheana* (2012–15), *Latin Forms of Address* (2002), and *Greek Forms of Address* (1996).

LATIN LOANWORDS
IN ANCIENT GREEK

A LEXICON AND ANALYSIS

ELEANOR DICKEY

University of Reading

CAMBRIDGE
UNIVERSITY PRESS

CAMBRIDGE
UNIVERSITY PRESS

University Printing House, Cambridge CB2 8BS, United Kingdom

One Liberty Plaza, 20th Floor, New York, NY 10006, USA

477 Williamstown Road, Port Melbourne, VIC 3207, Australia

314–321, 3rd Floor, Plot 3, Splendor Forum, Jasola District Centre, New Delhi – 110025, India

103 Penang Road, #05–06/07, Visioncrest Commercial, Singapore 238467

Cambridge University Press is part of the University of Cambridge.

It furthers the University's mission by disseminating knowledge in the pursuit of education, learning, and research at the highest international levels of excellence.

www.cambridge.org
Information on this title: www.cambridge.org/9781108841009
DOI: 10.1017/9781108888387

First published 2023

Printed in the United Kingdom by TJ Books Limited, Padstow Cornwall

A catalogue record for this publication is available from the British Library.

A Cataloging-in-Publication data record for this book is available from the Library of Congress

ISBN 978-1-108-84100-9 Hardback

Dedicated to the memory of

M. L. West,

with gratitude for all his help on this and many other projects

CONTENTS

FIGURES

ACKNOWLEDGEMENTS

A century ago, Bernhard Meinersmann set out to produce a book about the phonology and morphology of Latin loanwords in Greek papyri. As a necessary preliminary he gathered a list of loanwords, which grew much larger than he had anticipated and eventually occupied almost all the space in his book, leaving fewer than twenty pages for the analysis originally intended. Reading his sad explanation of this situation (Meinersmann 1927: 103), I should have been warned. And yet I was as surprised as Meinersmann when my own Lexicon expanded exponentially and threatened to eliminate the analysis. My first thanks, therefore, go to Cambridge University Press for being willing to publish a ridiculously oversized book and therefore making it possible to include both lexicon and analysis after all. I am also grateful to all my predecessors working on Latin loanwords in Greek, particularly Hugh Mason (to whose 1974 book *Greek terms for Roman institutions: a lexicon and analysis* my title pays homage), Sergio Daris, Herbert Hofmann, and Irene-Maria Cervenka-Ehrenstrasser: without their work, mine would have been impossible, and if I sometimes express disagreement with them, that is because their views are always worthy of serious consideration.

My own work on Latin loanwords began in 2008 and could never have been completed without a great deal of help and support from many different sources. Chief among these is the Leverhulme Trust, whose generous funding provided essential time to work on the project. The Department of Classics at the University of Reading generously offered further research leave that made it possible to complete the work, and a period as Spinoza Visiting Scholar at the University of Leiden was of considerable assistance.

Numerous individuals were generous with their expertise, thus greatly improving the final product. Philomen Probert read endless drafts, corrected countless mistakes, provided good solid common-sense advice, and offered moral support when I despaired; the task would have been impossible without her help. M. L. West asked hard questions that shaped the work at its early stages, as well as bringing to my attention material that I might otherwise have missed. Hélène Cuvigny searched her unpublished ostraca for Latinisms and allowed me to use the results (all references to unpublished Eastern Desert ostraca are due to her, with many thanks). Stephanie Roussou provided extensive help with modern Greek and allowed me to use her work on Ps.-Arcadius before publication. Panagiotis Filos allowed me to use his unpublished dissertation and gave further help with modern Greek. Andreas Gavrielatos also helped with modern Greek. Giuliano Sidro identified numerous errors and omissions in early versions of the Lexicon and shared insights from his own forthcoming work; when his ideas are not mentioned in this book it does not imply that I disagree with them, only that they are his to publish. Amin Benaissa drew my attention to several important points that greatly enriched the final work. Jan Joosten must be acknowledged for the considerable help he provided with words alleged to occur in the Septuagint. Michele Pedone not only drew my attention to scholarly works that I did not know about, but also enabled me to access those works during lockdown. Michele Bianconi read a draft and found numerous errors. J. N. Adams pointed out many things that I would otherwise have missed. John Blundell and Adam Gitner helped me understand the background to material in *TLL* entries, and Samantha Schad helped me with data from the *OED*. Klaus-Dietrich Fischer assisted me with the Hippiatrica and with Galen's work, and Philippa Townsend with understanding Χριστιανός. Angelos Chaniotis alerted me to epigraphic evidence that I might otherwise have missed. Nigel Wilson allowed me to use his work before publication. Richard Ashdowne advised me on points of medieval Latin. Emanuele Zimbardi kindly pointed out a misuse of Ephraem Syrus. John Taylor discussed Acts with me. Alessia Pezzella and Simon Korneev very kindly checked references in the Lexicon, making significant improvements in the accuracy of the final result. Generous help with proofreading and fact-checking was provided by Annette Copping, Costas Panayotakis, Adrienne Gould, and Lisa Rengo George. My copyeditor Jane Burkowski was not only amazingly good, but also amazingly patient. And Michael Sharp at Cambridge University Press was unfailingly prompt and helpful in response to an endless stream of queries and requests; this is the eighth book of mine that Michael has published, and he has not once lost his temper with me, despite considerable provocation.

1

INTRODUCTION

Athenaeus' *Deipnosophistae* depicts a guest at a Greek banquet reacting with anger upon hearing a fellow diner use the Latin-derived word δηκόκτα (*decocta* 'decoction'): it offends his Atticist sensibilities. But the speaker, Cynulcus, defends his word choice on the grounds that he lives in Rome (where the banquet is held) and therefore uses 'the local speech', as is normal.

1 Ἐπὶ τούτοις λεχθεῖσιν ὁ Κύνουλκος πιεῖν ᾔτησε δηκόκταν, δεῖν λέγων ἁλμυροὺς λόγους γλυκέσιν ἀποκλύζεσθαι νάμασι. πρὸς ὃν ὁ Οὐλπιανὸς σχετλιάσας καὶ τύψας τῇ χειρὶ τὸ προσκεφάλαιον ἔφη· Μέχρι πότε βαρβαρίζοντες οὐ παύσεσθε; ἢ ἕως ἂν καταλιπὼν τὸ συμπόσιον οἴχωμαι, πέττειν ὑμῶν τοὺς λόγους οὐ δυνάμενος; καὶ ὅς· Ἐν Ῥώμῃ τῇ βασιλευούσῃ διατρίβων τὰ νῦν, ὦ λῷστε, ἐπιχωρίῳ κέχρημαι κατὰ τὴν συνήθειαν φωνῇ. καὶ γὰρ παρὰ τοῖς ἀρχαίοις ποιηταῖς καὶ συγγραφεῦσι τοῖς σφόδρα ἑλληνίζουσιν ἔστιν εὑρεῖν καὶ Περσικὰ ὀνόματα κείμενα διὰ τὴν τῆς χρήσεως συνήθειαν, ὡς τοὺς παρασάγγας καὶ τοὺς ἀστάνδας ἢ ἀγγάρους καὶ τὴν σχοῖνον ἢ τὸν σχοῖνον· μέτρον δ᾽ ἐστὶ τοῦτο ὁδοῦ μέχρι νῦν οὕτως παρὰ πολλοῖς καλούμενον. μακεδονίζοντάς τ᾽ οἶδα πολλοὺς τῶν Ἀττικῶν διὰ τὴν ἐπιμιξίαν. (Athenaeus 3.121e–122a)

When these things had been said Cynulcus asked to drink δηκόκτα, saying that it was necessary to purify himself from the salty words by means of sweet streams. Ulpian reacted indignantly, struck the cushion with his hand, and said, 'How long will it be until you stop speaking like a barbarian? Until I leave the symposium and go away, being unable to stomach your words?' And he said, 'My good man, since I am now spending time in Rome, the city that rules the world, I use the local speech, as is the normal practice. For even in the works of the ancient poets and of the writers who use the purest Greek it is possible to find Persian words established by the normal practice of usage, like παρασάγγαι and ἀστάνδαι or ἄγγαροι and σχοῖνος, which can be either feminine or masculine (it is a measure of distance and still called that by many people today). And I know that many of the Attic writers use Macedonian words on account of their interactions with them.'[1]

What does Cynulcus mean by 'the local speech'? At first glance it seems obvious that the local speech of Rome must have been Latin, with the implication that δηκόκτα was a codeswitch, a bilingual speaker's brief use of one language in the midst of an utterance in another language. But Cynulcus then goes on to argue that his word choice was Classical in spirit, for the Classical Athenian writers used foreign words in their Greek once such words had become established parts of normal Greek usage. This argument suggests that δηκόκτα was not a codeswitch but an established part of normal Greek usage, in other words a loanword. Cynulcus' point cannot be that Classical Athenians learned foreign languages and therefore regularly codeswitched when speaking or writing Greek; Athenaeus' readers were well aware that most Athenians did not learn foreign languages and that therefore codeswitching would have been met with incomprehension in Athens. Rather, the point seems to be that certain foreign terms became loanwords in Classical Attic owing to the Athenians' extended interactions with speakers of other languages, and that these words were then used by monolingual Greek writers.

If that is the argument, 'the local speech' referred to by Cynulcus must be not Latin, but the Greek spoken in Rome c. AD 200, in which (Cynulcus seems to be arguing) δηκόκτα was a loanword just as 'parasang' was a loanword in Classical Attic. This interpretation, however, only raises more questions: was there in fact a distinctive variety of Greek spoken in Rome? Was

[1] Translations are my own unless otherwise noted.

1

δηκόκτα in fact a loanword, in the Greek of Rome or in any other variety? Did the diner who objected, the bearer of a conspicuously Roman name, react particularly to the acceptance of a loanword as part of Greek, or would he have been equally upset at a codeswitch marked by a qualification like 'as the Romans say'? Why does Cynulcus point out that Rome rules the world – is that actually relevant to the question at hand? And was Cynulcus' argument actually supposed to be as internally consistent as this interpretation suggests?[2]

Such questions are not easily answered by the type of work that has so far been done on Latin loanwords in Greek. That work has often not distinguished between loanwords and codeswitches, lumping together words attested only once with those found thousands of times and paying little or no attention to the difference between words that Greek writers explicitly labelled as Latin and those that they treated as Greek. It has rarely looked for regional variation in the use of loanwords. And it has often been fragmented, with different studies usually focussed on particular types of evidence, such as papyri or inscriptions or individual literary authors; different questions are asked of different types of evidence and different assumptions made in answering them, making it difficult to gain an overall picture by combining the answers.

Nevertheless, some overall conclusions about Latin loanwords in Greek have become generally accepted: that Greek speakers began borrowing Latin words relatively late in the history of contact between speakers of the two languages; that Greek speakers were resistant to using loanwords, especially in the higher, more literary registers; and that in the long run Latin loanwords tended not to survive.[3] Other common generalizations are that there were thousands of Latin loanwords; that most loanwords were confined to the semantic fields of law, government, and the military; that most borrowing occurred in late antiquity, subsequent to (though perhaps not caused by) the administrative reforms of Diocletian c. AD 300; and that only nouns were borrowed, never verbs

or adjectives.[4] But none of these generalizations is entirely right, at least as regards loanwords as opposed to codeswitches, and some are seriously wrong. Of the more than 3,500 words that have been or could be claimed as Latin loanwords in ancient Greek, only 820 are verifiable as being simultaneously ancient, Latin, and loanwords in Greek (§8.1) – and fewer than half of those belong to the semantic fields of law, government, and the military (§10.2.3). Greek speakers began borrowing Latin words very early (§8.1.2), the period of greatest borrowing activity was in or before the second century AD (§8.1.1), and many Greek speakers were not at all resistant to using loanwords (§9.5). Not only are loanwords common in papyri, but they are reasonably frequent in many types of literature – in fact more loanwords are attested in literature than in papyri (§9.1). Verbs and adjectives were indeed borrowed (§10.3.1), and most of the ancient loanwords survived the end of antiquity (§8.2.2), with many having descendants in the mainstream vocabulary of modern Greek (§8.2.3).

The main reason so many misconceptions about Latin loanwords have persisted among scholars is the lack of a complete list of Latin words occurring in Greek and accurate information on their attestation.[5] The present study, therefore, has as its main component a lexicon (§3.2) including not only all (I hope) Latin loanwords, but also the vast majority of the words that have been or could plausibly be claimed as Latin loanwords, so that readers can evaluate for themselves the reasoning behind the decisions for classifying each word. In addition to the 820 verifiable loanwords, the Lexicon includes entries

[4] E.g. Filos (2014: 321), Kaczko (2016: 393), Dietrich (1995: 45), Biville (1992: 234), Daris (1991a: 17–18), Brixhe (1987: 107), Cadell (1974), Viscidi (1944: 2, 43, 49–50, 56–7), Reichmann (1943: 2), Chantraine (1937: 88), Costas (1936: 50), Meillet (1930: 304–5). Hemer (1989: 212) puts a borrowing peak in the third century AD, inferring it from less definite statements by Mason (1974: 3, 11).

[5] Viscidi (1944: 2) and Diethart (2008: 16) claim to have collected c. 2,900 and c. 2,700 Latin words respectively, but neither lists the words concerned. The largest published list, that of Hofmann (1989), contains c. 1,730 words, many of them clearly codeswitches; Daris (1991a: 17) lists c. 800 words attested in papyri, some of which could be codeswitches.

[2] The last of these questions may be unanswerable, but for the others see §9.3, §9.4, §10.1, and §3.2 *s.v.* δηκόκτα.

[3] E.g. Coleman (2007: 799), Deroy (1956: 35).

for 1,002 possible loanwords, i.e. words that are rarely attested and therefore are more likely to be codeswitches (§2.2.1), 847 ancient words of (at least partial) Latin origin that are definitely not loanwords (§2.2),[6] 476 that are not (or are probably not) ancient, 243 that do not (or may not) derive from Latin (cf. §2.1), and 221 that do not (or may not) exist at all; there are also more than a thousand variant spellings of loanwords, some of which have sometimes been considered separate words. The Lexicon includes evidence from papyri, inscriptions, and literature and provides the dates of attestations whenever these can be ascertained. It aims not only to provide a solid evidence base for the conclusions drawn in §4–11, but also to give future research on Latin loanwords in Greek a firmer footing than previous research has enjoyed.

Another reason for the current poor understanding of Latin loanwords is that the findings of linguists' work on language contact in modern times have not sufficiently informed work on ancient loanwords. The most obvious manifestation of this problem is the frequent conflation of loanwords and codeswitches, a conflation that can lead scholars drawing generalizations about how Greek speakers used Latin to base them primarily on words that monolingual Greek speakers never used. In addition to helping separate loanwords from codeswitches, linguistic work on modern languages can be useful by helping to sift out extraneous material that is neither loanword nor codeswitch, by providing typological parallels against which to test theories about Greek, and by supplying explanations for borrowing patterns and for peculiar aspects of the spelling and inflection of Latin loanwords. The reason Classicists have tended to neglect this work is no doubt that linguistics is a completely different academic discipline from Classics and as such can be challenging for outsiders to access, not only because of technical terminology but also because of a focus on different questions from the ones that interest Classicists and debates framed in terms

of unfamiliar theories. The present study, being heavily informed by linguistics, is in principle of interest to both disciplines, but no research can be effectively presented to two such different audiences at the same time. Therefore this presentation is aimed at Classicists, and the linguistic background is discussed in terms designed to be accessible to that audience, avoiding – as much as possible – both linguistic terminology and theoretical debates that do not contribute to an understanding of Greek or its speakers.[7] Nevertheless linguistic terminology is unavoidable when it describes a relevant and otherwise unnamed phenomenon, as in the case of 'codeswitch'.

A third problem affecting much previous work on Latin loanwords is insufficient attention to Latin. Hundreds of the words formerly claimed as Latin loanwords may not come from Latin at all, and significant numbers of the remainder probably do not come from the particular Latin words usually said to be their sources. In some cases the Latin words alleged as sources never existed. The valuable resources offered by the *Thesaurus Linguae Latinae*, which often provides excellent information on the Greek derivatives of Latin words, have been generally neglected, as has the information in etymological dictionaries. Therefore this study is also based on a complete re-examination of the etymology of each alleged 'Latin' word found in Greek.

A further difficulty faced by some earlier work on loanwords was attempts to make the linguistic findings fit particular theories about the world in which the loanwords were borrowed. Of course, aspects of culture are reflected in vocabulary, and it was the human interaction between Greek speakers and Latin speakers that led each language to leave visible traces on the other. And since the historical and linguistic facts can shed light on each other, neither can be examined in isolation. Nevertheless, there is a real risk of distortion when one tries to force linguistic data into theories about culture and history, and that problem has led to some of the incorrect generalizations that are so common about Latin loanwords in Greek. The present study attempts to deal with this hazard by using established historical facts

---

[6] I.e. 766 that are always marked as foreign (§2.2.3), 57 that appear only as proper names (§12.2.2), and 24 semantic extensions (§2.3); words in these categories were not systematically collected and have been included only when there is a special reason to do so, such as when they have been considered loanwords by previous scholars.

[7] The findings likely to be of greatest interest to linguists have been published as Dickey (2018).

where relevant but avoiding taking any position on the historical questions that loanwords are often invoked to solve. Accordingly it does not address issues such as the relationship between language and identity in the Roman world, whether Diocletian (or other emperors) had a language policy, whether Egypt was governed differently from the rest of the Roman empire, or whether the relationship between Latin and Greek can accurately be described as an antagonistic struggle. Nor does it attempt to make contributions on questions such as the extent of bilingualism during the Empire, which Greek speakers learned Latin, or why they learned it. Such questions cannot be answered from loanword data alone and in any case have been extensively studied elsewhere; this study takes as a basis the generally accepted answers that there was considerable bilingualism, both from Latin speakers learning Greek (often because knowledge of Greek was useful to pass as an educated aristocrat) and from Greek speakers learning Latin (often because knowledge of Latin was useful for a career in law, government, or the army).[8]

Scholars have so far asked many different questions about Latin loanwords. How many were borrowed at which dates, and how long did they last? Which semantic fields and parts of speech did the borrowings fall into? What types of text used loanwords, and what were the differences in loanword use between different text types, registers, genres, and authors? How were Latin words spelled in Greek, and what do those spellings tell us about the pronunciations of Latin and Greek

at different periods? How were Latin words adapted to the complex Greek inflectional system, and how did those adaptations change over time? When and why was Latin script used in the midst of Greek texts? How were Latin words accented in Greek? These are all good questions, and most do not have simple answers; an attempt to answer them fully would require far more space than is available even in this somewhat oversized volume. Therefore all that is attempted here is an outline of the main answers to each, not detailed studies of any; some related questions, such as the factors governing the choices made by speakers between loanwords and native Greek words expressing the same or similar ideas, are hardly addressed at all. It is hoped that this study will serve not as a definitive set of answers to all previous questions about Latin loanwords, but as a catalyst for further work on the topic: those who find the answers offered in this study insufficient will be able to use the data in the Lexicon to do their own further research and provide more complete and nuanced answers.

Some questions that have not traditionally been asked about Latin loanwords also turn out to offer promising routes towards insight into the language(s) of ancient Greek speakers, and into their ways of thinking. Were there regional differences in the use of Latin loanwords, and if so, what were they? Why did Greek writers sometimes treat well-established loanwords as foreign words? Why were some Latin loanwords specifically seen as medical terminology, if the language of ancient medicine was emphatically Greek? Why does the New Testament's Acts of the Apostles use much more Latin than the Gospel of Luke, if the two books were written by the same person? These questions are also addressed here (§9.2, §9.5.4, §9.5.3, §9.3), but they too are treated in far less depth than they deserve. It is hoped that the information collected in the Lexicon will allow further work to be undertaken on them as well – and on other questions about Latin loanwords that have not yet been asked.

---

[8] See e.g. Rochette (1997, 2010, 1996, 1998, 2000, 2007), J. N. Adams (2003), Kearsley and Evans (2001), Binder (2000: 21–48), Rizakis (1995, 2008), Holford-Strevens (1993), Petersmann (1992), Dubuisson (1981, 1992a, 1992b), Millar (2006a: 84–93), Mullen (2011), Garcea (2019), Fournet (2019), Rapp (2019), Nocchi Macedo (2019), Pellizzari (2019), Rhoby (2019), Ghiretti (1996), García Domingo (1983), Zgusta (1980), Kaimio (1979a, 1979b), Hahn (1906), Mullen and James (2012), Stein (1915: 132–86).

2

THE PARAMETERS OF THIS STUDY

One reason for the huge disparities between different scholars' statements about the number and types of Latin loanwords in ancient Greek is that 'Latin', 'loanword', and 'ancient Greek' are all terms that can be used in multiple ways.[1] How does this study use them?

2.1 LATIN AND ANCIENT GREEK

For the purposes of this study, 'ancient Greek' means texts in Greek produced before AD 600, regardless of where they come from, and the Byzantine period is considered to start in AD 600.[2] The distinguishing characteristic of a Greek text is its language, not its script, and therefore Latin texts written in the Greek alphabet are excluded.[3] Texts in Coptic, Aramaic, or other languages are also excluded.[4]

'Latin' means the language originally spoken in Latium, excluding other languages of ancient Italy (Oscan, Umbrian, Etruscan, etc.). Greek speakers also borrowed words from these other languages, and some other work on Latin loanwords includes those borrowings, in part because they are difficult to distinguish from Latin loans. The difficulty comes not only from the fact that the non-Latin languages of ancient Italy are now poorly preserved, making it challenging to recognize words that ought to come from them, but also from the way that ancient writers such as Hesychius identified loanwords. They sometimes specified the source of a loanword as Ἰταλοί, Ἰταλιῶται, or Ἰταλικός 'Italian(s)', terms that could encompass any or all of the ancient peoples of Italy, including Latin speakers.[5] This problem is confined to early loanwords; words borrowed during the Empire and labelled 'Italian' normally do come from Latin, since by that time the other languages of Italy had largely disappeared.

---

[1] E.g. Viscidi (1944: 1–2) claims c. 2,900 Latin words attested in Greek up to AD 1100; Diethart (2008: 16) c. 2,700 Latin words attested in ancient and Byzantine Greek; Hofmann (1989: i) c. 1,730 words from Latin or other languages of ancient Italy attested in Greek up to AD 600; Daris (1991a: 17) c. 800 Latin words attested in Greek papyri up to AD 800; and Meyer (1895) c. 300 'ancient' Latin borrowings surviving into modern Greek. See also Filos (2014: 321). Rochette (2010: 292) appears to claim that I (Dickey 2003: 256) found 3,365 'Latin borrowings' in fourth-century papyri, but this was my estimate for the total number of *occurrences* of Latin words, not the number of different words in use (in linguistic terms, I was counting tokens rather than types).

[2] This date is the latest plausible one for the end of antiquity; one could put the cutoff earlier, for example at the sack of Rome in AD 410, but that event did not put an abrupt end to the ancient world (especially not from a Greek perspective). Contact with the West was maintained, and in the sixth century the Constantinople-based emperor Justinian even reconquered a substantial portion of Italy. Around AD 600, however, contact between East and West was significantly reduced and the teaching and use of Latin declined in the East; moreover (around this time, probably as a gradual process) the breakup of Latin into the Romance languages meant that such Western contact as still took place did not necessarily involve Latin *per se*. Therefore it is common to use AD 600 as a cutoff point: cf. e.g. *TLL*, J. N. Adams (2007), Souter (1949).

[3] For these see e.g. J. N. Adams (2003: 40–63).

[4] This exclusion is not as obvious as it sounds, since such texts often contain Latin loanwords. Because speakers of Coptic, Aramaic, and some Slavic languages had more contact with Greek speakers than with Latin speakers, it is likely that their Latin borrowings came via Greek, even when the loanwords in question are not attested in Greek at all (cf. e.g. Rosén 1980: 230–3; Orioles 1974: 121–3). Attestation in such languages is therefore sometimes used as indirect evidence of a Latin word's existence in Greek, and in general this is no doubt a reasonable argument. In each specific case, however, it is difficult to prove that the borrowing could not have come directly from Latin and bypassed Greek (see e.g. Hörn 1984: 1373–4).

[5] For example, Hesychius α 3137 reads ἄλλην· λάχανον, Ἰταλοί, meaning effectively "Ἄλλην is an Italian word for "vegetable"'; this could be a reference to Latin *alium* 'garlic' or to a related word in an Italic language such as Oscan.

5

Most of the 'Italian' loanwords borrowed into Greek at a very early period are unlikely to come from Latin. These loanwords were borrowed in Magna Graecia, the areas of Italy and Sicily where Greek colonists came into contact with speakers of a wide variety of 'Italian' languages, ranging from non-Indo-European ones markedly different from Latin to Italic ones very similar to Latin.[6] Some of the Greek settlements in this area go back to the eighth century BC and were located far from Latium, which at the time of their foundation was small and insignificant; it is *a priori* unlikely that at that stage Greek speakers borrowed from Latin speakers words that they could have got instead from larger, more important groups living closer to them. Thus at the earliest period one needs to exercise great caution about ascribing Latin origins even to words for which Latin is a perfectly plausible source on linguistic grounds, such as Ἰταλία 'Italy'.

The result of excluding loanwords that probably come from other languages of ancient Italy is therefore to exclude Ἰταλία and some other important early words. Studies that include such loanwords have significantly more early material at their disposal than this one, but they suffer from some disadvantages avoided here. Latin is the only 'Italian' language whose relationship with Greek we can hope to understand in any detail, and an admixture of data from other languages could jeopardise that understanding: any attempt to illuminate the influence of one language on another inevitably becomes murky when evidence pertaining to other languages is mixed in.

Even when one excludes words that may go back to other languages of ancient Italy, it is not entirely obvious what 'Latin etymology' means, for some words have complex histories. For example, there are words that come originally from Celtic, Germanic, or other languages, whence they were borrowed by Latin speakers who eventually passed them on to Greek speakers. Thus Latin *veredus* 'fast horse', originally borrowed from

Celtic, later became Greek βέρεδος 'fast horse'; similarly a Germanic word borrowed into Latin produced *sapo* 'soap', which then became Greek σάπων 'soap'. Such words are included in this study, since they show Latin influence on Greek.[7]

Greek was one of the languages from which Latin speakers borrowed words, and therefore words of Greek etymology could become Latin loanwords in Greek by being borrowed into Latin and then back into Greek. For example ὀψωνέω 'buy food' was borrowed into Latin as *obsono* 'buy food', which produced the derivative *obsonator* 'caterer', which was then borrowed into Greek as ὀψωνάτωρ 'caterer'. Likewise κοχλίας 'snail' was borrowed into Latin as *cochlea* 'snail', which produced *cochlear* 'spoon for eating snails', which was borrowed back into Greek as κοχλιάριον 'spoon'.[8] It is even possible for a single Latin loanword to combine multiple non-Latin sources, as with κλιβανάριος from *clibanarius*, which has a Greek source in one of its meanings and a Persian source in another.

It is not always possible to determine a word's etymology with complete confidence. Where scholars disagree about whether a word comes from Latin, I have examined the evidence and tried to find a convincing solution one way or the other; if none could be found, I have not counted the word as Latin.[9] No doubt the result of such

---

6 For the complex linguistic situation of ancient Italy, see e.g. Bourdin (2012: esp. 46–51); for contact between Greek and 'Italian' languages other than Latin e.g. J. N. Adams (2003: 148–50, 165–6), McDonald (2015); for the long-term survival of early Sicilian borrowings e.g. Cassio (2014: 42–5).

7 In studying loanwords it is common to attribute borrowings to their immediate source rather than to their ultimate source; see e.g. Grant (2009: 368). In studying borrowings from particular languages it is also possible to include both words whose ultimate source is outside those languages but whose immediate source is within them, and words whose immediate source is outside but whose ultimate source is within (cf. Stolz 2008: 8–11 pointing out that 'Romanicisation' involves both direct borrowings from Romance and borrowings from other languages of words derived ultimately from Romance). This second group is not relevant for this study, for I know of no Latin words that entered Greek via a third language. In the study of Latin loanwords in Greek there is a long tradition of including words that were originally borrowed into Latin from a third language, while acknowledging their complex etymologies: see e.g. Triandaphyllidis (1909: 170).

8 Other probable examples of borrowing back into Greek include ἀβερτή, ἀνισᾶτος, and δρακονάριος. Gusmani (1981–3: 1.91–3) discusses the phenomenon more generally.

9 Famous loanwords excluded for this reason include μαῦρος 'black', which has been argued to be a borrowing

decisions has been to exclude from consideration some genuine loanwords, but in attempting to make generalizations about a group of words the danger of distortion from including some data that do not belong is much greater than that from excluding some data that do belong. The excluded words can be found in the Lexicon (§3.2) with a discussion of their etymologies, but they do not form part of the evidence on which the discussion in §4–10 is based.

2.2 DISTINGUISHING LOANWORDS FROM CODESWITCHES

Most linguists distinguish between two ways that words originating in one language may be used by speakers of another language. Some such words are used only rarely and by bilingual speakers; these are known as 'codeswitches' because a speaker who uses one effectively switches into his or her other language briefly to do so. Other words of foreign origin are more common and used even by monolingual speakers; these are known as 'loanwords' or 'borrowings'.[10] There is no firm dividing line between the two, and a word that starts off as a codeswitch may become a loanword over time.[11] Nevertheless the distinction is an important one, because the two types of foreign word are used very differently. An English speaker who utters a sentence containing French loanwords such as 'chair', 'beef', 'demand', or 'garage' is simply engaging in normal monolingual communication, whereas one who utters a

sentence containing French codeswitches such as *selle*, *vache*, or *étable* is doing something special, and most listeners will appreciate the distinction and react accordingly.

What features distinguish the loanword from the codeswitch? Some linguists argue that the key difference is frequency: 'chair' is often used in English, and *selle* is not.[12] Others argue that it is integration: 'chair' is pronounced with English sounds, forms an English plural 'chairs', is not distinguished by italics, etc.[13] Still others maintain that both frequency and integration are important.[14] Other considerations (which are sometimes subsumed under 'integration') include diachronic stability, use by monolingual speakers, establishment as the only or main term for the concept it represents, and whether the word is explicitly labelled by users as foreign.[15]

2.2.1 Frequency

How frequent does a word need to be in order to count as a loanword, and how is frequency measured? These questions are surprisingly difficult to answer, and not only because frequency is obviously a continuum on which any simple cutoff point would be arbitrary.[16] In order to measure frequency with complete accuracy, one would need an ideal corpus consisting of all the words spoken and/or written in a particular language over a defined period. Even the best linguistic corpora of the best-studied modern languages are far from that ideal and insufficient to capture fine frequency distinctions between rare words –

---

of *Maurus* 'Moorish' but may instead have a Greek derivation from ἀμαυρός 'dark', and βάνδον 'military standard', which must derive ultimately from Gothic *bandwa* but could either have come via Latin *bandum* 'standard' or be a parallel borrowing.

[10] For the distinction see e.g. Thomason (2001: 131–6), Nivens (2002), Clyne (2003: 142–52), Winford (2003: 42–51, 107–10), Myers-Scotton (2002, 2006: 253–60), Matras (2020: 107–208), Haspelmath (2009: 40–3), Odlin (2009), Gardner-Chloros (2009: 30–3, 2010: 195–7), Manfredi, Simeone-Senelle, and Tosco (2015), Hadei (2016). Both phenomena certainly existed in antiquity; for codeswitches between Latin and Greek see e.g. J. N. Adams (2003: 297–416), Swain (2002), and Dubuisson (2005).

[11] This change is a gradual process, though it may happen faster with some words than with others and indeed faster for some speakers than for others: Thomason (2003: 696), Ashdowne and White (2017: 28).

[12] E.g. Backus (2014: 29).

[13] E.g. Heath (1989: 23–5).

[14] E.g. Haspelmath (2009: 41).

[15] Some linguists (e.g. Poplack 2018: 6; Zenner and Kristiansen 2014: 4) use inclusion in a dictionary as a measure of a loanword's establishment, and that measure probably works well for languages like English – but it does not work for Greek. Greek dictionaries compiled by modern scholars often include all words that appear in the texts on which the dictionary is based, while Greek dictionaries compiled by ancient scholars often focus specifically on unfamiliar words, including ones the compilers perceived as foreign while excluding well-established loanwords.

[16] In practice some linguists imply a key division as falling between words that are attested only once in their corpus and those that occur more than once (cf. Poplack 2018: 6, 122–40), but this is not claimed to be the cutoff point between codeswitches and loanwords.

and it is precisely those distinctions that matter for this question.[17] Moreover, to be really useful a measurement of frequency would need to be more than a simple number of occurrences in any corpus, even an ideal one. A meaningful evaluation of frequency would include numbers of users as well as numbers of attestations, for ten uses by a single individual clearly indicate a different type of establishment from one use each by ten different individuals.[18]

Codeswitching may be rare in a language as a whole without being at all rare in particular settings or among particular individuals. Indeed codeswitching is the norm in some settings, even in largely monolingual cultures like those of many English speakers today; for example English-language explanations of French grammar often include terms like *imparfait*, *conditionnel*, and *passé composé*, and discussions of Spartan education may use words such as εἴρην or *eiren* and μελλείρην or *melleiren*. Such words may even be common in the English spoken in French classes or academic conferences about Sparta, but they are nevertheless codeswitches and very rarely appear in other contexts. Frequency, therefore, needs to be evaluated in a way that takes into account distribution as well as absolute numbers of both forms and users.

In dealing with ancient Greek there is also the problem that the surviving texts are not representative of the language as a whole. We have only written varieties of the language, and primarily varieties produced by adult males with above-average educational attainment and social standing. If there were loanwords used only in completely unwritten varieties of Greek, or only by women, children, farm workers, sailors, or slaves, they are probably now lost beyond recall; we need to start by accepting that a study of the ancient Greek language is really a study of particular varieties of that language. (Of course, even a study of a modern language is really a study of particular varieties, for most natural language corpora do not capture all varieties of the language in question. But the varieties available to study are more restricted in the case of ancient Greek.)

Moreover, some highly prolific writers are disproportionately represented in surviving literature, and some of those writers may have been idiosyncratic in their use of Latin: Plutarch and Dionysius of Halicarnassus, for example, sometimes use particular Latin words more often than other writers, even other writers dealing with Roman matters. Care must be taken to prevent the idiosyncrasies of individual writers from distorting the results.

Despite these drawbacks, however, the corpus of surviving ancient Greek also has some advantages. If one includes all surviving texts produced within our chronological range – literature, inscriptions, and documents – it is a much larger corpus than those normally used to study loanwords in modern languages, and it is publicly available so that claims made about it can be checked and challenged.[19] It is also diverse chronologically, geographically, and in terms of genre.

How can this corpus best be utilized to establish the frequency of potential loanwords? The obvious way to start is by attempting to locate all surviving examples of each term, both via electronic searches of the three main databases and via hand searches for material not included in those databases, and by presenting the attestations in a way that makes each word's distribution clear and minimizes the distorting effect of prolific individuals.[20] But that process still does

---

[17] See e.g. Backus (2014: 30–2), Haspelmath and Tadmor (2009: 15), Thomason (2001: 134).

[18] Cf. Backus (2014: 27).

[19] For centuries relevant to this study, we have searchable online corpora of literature (over 50 million words from more than a thousand different authors within our period), documentary papyri (c. 4.5 million words from thousands of individual writers), and inscriptions: see §9.1 notes 1–6. Although the exact size of the inscriptional corpus has not been calculated, the word καί 'and' (common in Greek of all regions and dates) occurs 225,909 times in the inscriptional database and 31,132 times in the documentary one, suggesting that there are seven times as many words in the former as in the latter; the inscriptional database is therefore likely to contain around 30 million words of Greek, composed by thousands of writers. These three databases together therefore probably contain more than 80 million words of Greek composed by many thousands of writers. By contrast the largest modern-language corpus used for a loanword study appears to be Poplack's (2018: 33, 35) corpus of c. 2,500,000 words of Canadian French from 120 different speakers, followed by Backus's (2014: 31) corpus of c. 500,000 words of Turkish.

[20] My method of operation was first to collect from reference

not provide frequency data that can be evaluated on a purely quantitative basis, because examples differ significantly in quality. A good example, broadly speaking, is one that certainly contains the word in question, treats it as a Greek word, can definitely be dated to our period, and is independent of other examples of the same word. A word with at least three good examples can confidently be taken to be a loanword, at least in the varieties of Greek represented by those examples. Two good examples may also indicate a loanword if corroborated by additional evidence, such as survival into the Byzantine period, but one or two good examples unsupported by additional evidence are not enough, since even a good example could be an unmarked codeswitch. One must therefore reserve judgement in the case

works all words claimed as Latin loans, and then to search the databases (for which see §9.1 notes 1–3) not for the words themselves but for their Latin roots, in all likely variant spellings; the purpose of that system was to find all Greek words formed from each root. Most data were collected between January 2014 and July 2015, going through the Lexicon roughly in alphabetical order; although there was a major change to the *TLG* search interface during that period, I was a beta tester for the newer version and therefore all data were collected using that version. (All three databases are problematic in various ways, but I took precautions to prevent those problems from distorting the data; for example dates given by the *TLG* have been modified to reflect the likely composition date of the words in a text rather than the lifetime of the author to whom the ideas are attributed.) If the database searches did not find all the examples listed in the reference works from which I had started, I checked those examples by hand; that process identified a set of texts particularly likely to contain Latinisms not picked up by database searches (usually because they were not included in the databases or contained words in Latin script, which are usually not picked up by such searches), so I next searched those texts by hand. This method has, I hope, produced complete information on all words identified as ancient loanwords by Cervenka-Ehrenstrasser (1996, 2000), Daris (1991a), Mason (1974), Hofmann (1989), Avotins (1989, 1992), Zilliacus (1935a, 1937), Cameron (1931), Immisch (1885), Sophocles (1887), and the LSJ supplement, as well as many other Latin words occurring in Greek texts. (However, as the focus of this project is on loanwords rather than codeswitches, obvious codeswitches that no scholar has ever claimed as loanwords have not been deliberately sought out: thus no mention is made of many Latin words quoted by Plutarch, nor of many Latin plant names in Ps.-Dioscorides.) For the arrangement of the data see §3.1.

of words for which good examples exist but not in sufficient quantity to meet the frequency criterion; in the present study they are referred to as 'rare words' and treated separately from the established loanwords.

Examples that do not meet this definition of 'good' cannot always be discarded, because they may provide useful information, but they need to be evaluated with an awareness of the risks they pose. One common hazard is a lack of certainty about whether the example even exists: many words occurring in papyri and inscriptions are doubtful readings or supplements, and some in literature are editorial emendations. Generally agreed emendations can usually be accepted as secure, but contested emendations, doubtful readings of papyri and inscriptions, and partial supplements have to be given less weight than secure attestations. And no faith at all can be placed in complete supplements, generally rejected emendations, or former readings of papyri and inscriptions that have since been re-edited. Unfortunately, many previous discussions of Latin loanwords have relied heavily on examples that are doubtful or inadmissible on these grounds: more than 200 words previously claimed as loanwords actually have no secure attestations at all.[21]

Even among examples that certainly contain the word in question, some are of dubious value. For example, the use of a word as a lemma in an ancient Greek–Greek lexicon such as that of Hesychius does not constitute evidence that it was part of Greek; in fact, since ancient monolingual lexica were much more likely to list obscure words than well-known ones, the appearance of a word as a lemma may indicate that it was infrequent and unfamiliar. Likewise a word's appearance as a lemma in a commentary or other exegetical work usually indicates unfamiliarity rather than familiarity; as both lexica and commentaries tend to repeat material from other works of the same genre, some words occur dozens of times in such contexts, a distribution pattern that must not be confused with genuine frequency.

But lexica and commentaries cannot be set aside entirely; in fact the use of a word as a gloss

---

[21] E.g. ἀννωνεακόν, βελλικός, γουβερνάριος. These are marked 'non-existent' in the Lexicon.

in such a work can be a sign that it was familiar to readers and thus constitute a particularly good example. Likewise an ancient writer's mention of a word as being in common use is an especially good example. Such mentions can be made even when there is little other surviving evidence that the word existed and thus provide precious access to varieties of Greek now largely lost. For example, there are only three ancient attestations of ὀψωνάτωρ 'caterer', but one of them is a comment that ἐκάλουν δὲ καὶ ἀγοραστὴν τὸν τὰ ὄψα ὠνούμενον, νῦν δ' ὀψωνάτωρα 'and they also used to call a person who buys food an ἀγοραστής, but now they call him an ὀψωνάτωρ' (Athenaeus 4.171a). Σιτλίον 'little bucket' is likewise attested only three times in antiquity, but one of those occurrences is a gloss in a lexicon. Φεμινάλια 'trousers' appears in only three datable sources, but one of those is Hesychius, where it twice occurs as a gloss; therefore it must have been reasonably well known to the compiler(s) of that lexicon.

Use as a gloss does not, however, always demonstrate that a word was familiar. Ancient lexica were occasionally expanded by reversing the entries so that the glosses became additional lemmata, with the original lemmata acting as their glosses; such glosses are potentially misleading, but fortunately they can be identified fairly easily. More care is needed with the few glosses that are problematic for other reasons. For example, φουρνοπλάστης 'potter' occurs only once, as a gloss in a lexicon – but the lemma is ἰπνοπλάθης, of which φουρνοπλάστης is probably an explanatory calque coined by the lexicographer (ἰπνός = φοῦρνος 'oven' + the agent noun from πλάσσω 'form', 'mould'). More difficult is χειρομάνικον 'sleeve', whose only ancient occurrence is likewise a gloss; although this time there is nothing suspicious about the lexicon entry itself,[22] it is nevertheless notable that most of the word's few Byzantine attestations are lexicon entries apparently derived from this one. Such a pattern raises suspicions about the original creation of the gloss: we cannot be sure that it derives from a native Greek speaker and has not been corrupted in transmission. No individual example can ever

be good enough to prove that a word was a loanword in the absence of any confirming evidence.

As this last example shows, the independence of examples is also an important consideration; a passage derived from another example does not constitute a separate good attestation of a potential loanword. And dependence takes many forms beside verbatim repetition. Literary authors (especially commentators) who do not quote a passage verbatim may nevertheless be heavily dependent on a source and take from it vocabulary that they would not otherwise have used. Composers of inscriptions may recycle standard formulae containing words they hardly understand. Such situations do not justify simply discarding evidence, but they mean that some of the evidence is of reduced value.[23]

The reason frequency indicates establishment of a loanword is that repeated use of a foreign word is normally caused by that word's circulation within the borrowing language: a frequently used Latin word is a loanword because Greek speakers transmit it to each other rather than taking it independently from Latin each time it is used. But of course multiple independent codeswitches are also possible, and care must be taken to identify repetition that arises from such a cause and is therefore not evidence of an established loanword. When there are significant differences (e.g. in date, in form, or in usage) between individual occurrences of a Latin word, with no intermediaries to bridge the gap, it may be suspected that the occurrences are independent rather than offering combined evidence of the word's establishment as a loan. For example, πίλα 2 'pier' seems to have been borrowed in the second century AD, despite a single appearance in the first century BC, and βέρνακλος (a term for members of a Jewish community in Rome) seems never to have been borrowed at all despite numerous occurences, for it appears in diverse forms suggesting multiple independent adaptations from Latin.

---

[22] Orion, *Etymologicum* p. 192.39 Sturz: χειρὶς χειρίδος· σημαίνει δὲ τὸ χειρομάνικον 'χειρίς, genitive χειρίδος; and it means χειρομάνικον'.

[23] Viscidi (1944: 9) argued that frequent occurrence in papyri is of greater value than frequency in literature and inscriptions, and broadly speaking he was right. But even papyri can be problematic; they too contain formulae that are often repeated. And when documents are fragmentary it can be difficult to tell whether they were composed by native speakers of Greek.

2.2.2 *Integration*

Integration is a complex process that varies greatly according to the characteristics of the words borrowed and the needs of the borrowing language. Some words can be taken over by some languages with few or no changes, while others going into other languages are so altered as to become unrecognizable to speakers of the language from which they came. Perhaps as a result, integration tends to be described rather differently by linguists working on different languages. A good general description is that of Clyne, who distinguishes several variables:[24]

A) Type of integration. Integration can be morphological (when a word alters its form to fit the structure of, and takes inflections from, the borrowing language, as with 'demand', which has an English past participle 'demanded'; for our purposes 'morphological' is equivalent to 'inflectional'), phonological (when a word is pronounced with sounds usual in the borrowing language rather than ones usual in the source language, as with 'garage', which English speakers pronounce with an English *r* rather than a French one), prosodic (e.g. when the syllable on which a word is stressed fits the patterns of the borrowing rather than the source language, as with 'garage' in British English, which has a stressed first syllable, though the French original did not), graphemic (when a word is written according to the conventions of the borrowing rather than the source language, e.g. in a different alphabet), or semantic (when a word's meaning is different in the borrowing language from in the source language, as with 'beef' referring only to a kind of meat whereas Old French *boef* referred both to a living animal and to the meat from that animal). A word can be integrated in some of these respects but not in others.

B) Degree of integration. Many types of integration can fall on a continuum from completely unintegrated to fully integrated. For example,

phonological integration can be not only absent (when a word is pronounced exactly as in the source language) or complete (when a word is pronounced entirely according to the phonology of the borrowing language), but partial to varying degrees (when some of the sounds in the word are pronounced as in one language and some as in the other, or when an individual sound is partially adapted so that it falls somewhere in between the ways it would be pronounced in each of the two languages).

What type and degree of integration shows that a word is a loan rather than a codeswitch? There is significant disagreement on this point. For example, one of the simplest and clearest types of integration is inflectional: a foreign word inflected like a native one is clearly being treated differently from a foreign word that retains its foreign inflection or remains uninflected in contexts where a native word would be inflected. Many linguists therefore assert that codeswitches are inflectionally unintegrated and loanwords inflectionally integrated,[25] but there is good evidence that speakers of some languages normally integrate foreign words completely into the grammar of their own languages, including inflecting them like native words, even on the first occasion that these foreign words are used.[26] Greek speakers appear to fall into this category: full inflectional integration is the norm for Latin words used singly, even if they are clearly labelled as foreign. The attachment of a Greek ending to a Latin word therefore does not indicate that it is an established loanword, but the retention of a Latin ending usually indicates that it is a codeswitch (though there exceptions: see §7.2).

---

[25] E.g. Haspelmath (2009: 41).

[26] E.g. Poplack (2018: 50–6, 80–121), Nivens (2002: 125), Heath (1989: 41), and Miller (1997: 238), who argues that English is one of the languages that do this, since any new verb, regardless of its source, can automatically form a past tense in '-ed'. Poplack uses this evidence to argue for a category of 'nonce borrowings' encompassing what others would call single-word codeswitches, but this category has not been generally accepted (e.g. Haspelmath 2009: 41). Most other linguists who observe such rapid integration argue instead that speakers of certain languages simply apply morphological integration to single-word codeswitches; cf. e.g. Clyne (2003: 142–3), Gardner-Chloros (2009: 31–2).

[24] Clyne (2003: 142–6), cf. Myers-Scotton (2006: 219–31), Haspelmath (2009: 42–3), Gusmani (1981–3: I.21–71). Clyne also includes a third variable, 'centrality and stability in the system of the recipient language', encompassing several factors that many other scholars see as criteria separate from integration; these are discussed separately in §2.2.3.

Phonological integration is not a feature to which we have much access in the case of ancient Greek,[27] so it is perhaps fortunate that linguists are sceptical of its diagnostic value. Poplack presents extensive data showing that phonological integration is unpredictably distributed: it does not correlate with morphological or syntactic integration, frequency, period of time for which a word has been present in a language, number of words in a codeswitch, speakers' fluency in the source language, or other features with which correlation might be expected.[28] Although many studies assume a correlation between established loanwords and phonological integration, many scholars note exceptions to it,[29] and I am not aware of any studies systematically demonstrating such a correlation the way that Poplack demonstrates a lack of it.

Prosodic integration has not been much studied. For Greek, the only prosodic feature of loanwords for which we have any information is the position of the accent – and even for that, evidence is preserved only for established loanwords (§5). Most of these words were prosodically integrated, but some retained Latin accents that ran counter to Greek accentual tendencies (§5.3.2). But the lack of any information on the prosody of codeswitches in Greek means that we cannot use prosodic integration to evaluate loanword status.

Graphemic integration is clearly visible in English, where writers mark foreign words by putting them in italics; words from a language with a different alphabet can also be marked by leaving them in the foreign alphabet. Both these choices signal that the writer considers the word in question to be not merely of foreign origin, but synchronically still a foreign word: a Greek word borrowed into English, such as 'philosophy', would not normally receive either of these treatments, whereas one not borrowed, such as δίκη or *dikē* 'justice', would. And words on the borderline of integration, such as 'peplos', are graphemically marked in some books and not others, giving a clear signal of their ambiguous status even if within any given work any given word is either consistently marked or consistently unmarked.[30] Such a practice in Greek could potentially be of great use in distinguishing loanwords from codeswitches, since Latin and Greek use different alphabets; indeed Greek codeswitches in Latin are often marked by the use of Greek script. But in practice this feature is of less use than one might hope, because until the sixth century Greek writers rarely used Latin script even for clear codeswitches (§4.1). When Latin script does appear it is very often, but not always, applied to codeswitches (§7.1).

Semantic integration (shift in meaning) is not a necessary or even a normal part of the borrowing process, typologically speaking: although some loanwords end up with different meanings in their new languages, many well-established loans keep their original meanings. The preservation of a word's original meaning is therefore no indication that it is not an established loanword.[31] A new meaning maintained consistently across numerous occurrences is a clear sign of a loanword, but rarer words cannot be demonstrated to have consistent new meanings, since mistakes are common among codeswitchers with limited competence in one of their languages: such speakers

---

[27] Spelling can be used as a rough guide, and some previous studies of Latin loanwords have stressed its importance for determining integration (e.g. Viscidi 1944: 6), but in practice ancient spelling is highly variable and may depend on factors other than contemporary pronunciation; see §4.1.

[28] Poplack (2018: 56–8, 158–85). One potentially relevant factor that Poplack did not investigate is speakers' identity construction: do speakers sometimes pronounce foreign words in a more foreign way in order to signal their own closeness to the culture from which those words come, and sometimes pronounce foreign words in a less foreign way in order to signal their distance from the other culture? Nevertheless, Poplack's finding that the same speaker could display considerable variation in phonetic integration on different occasions suggests that if identity construction is a factor, its application is variable (perhaps with reference to different audiences).

[29] E.g. Thomason (2001: 134) observes apparently random fluctuation in the phonological integration even of established loanwords. Haugen (1953: 392–6) offers a good presentation of the earlier view of phonological integration.

[30] For example, 'peplos' is italicized in Loraux (1995: 126), but not in Nagy (2010: 271).

[31] In fact some linguists consider preservation of the original meaning to be the default state for loanwords and classify as 'pseudo-loans' borrowings in which the meaning of a word is significantly altered, as when the English adjective 'handy' became a German noun meaning 'mobile telephone' (e.g. Matras 2020: 191).

may simply misunderstand words and so misuse them. In Greek, many Latin words retain their Latin meanings, but some established Latin loanwords have new meanings, and some probable codeswitches seem to include mistakes.[32] In many cases, however, we cannot be sure exactly what a word meant in Greek; scholars normally start from the assumption that loanwords keep their original meanings, and a new meaning can be detected only if the Greek word occurs in a context where the Latin meaning does not fit.

The idea that there are criteria by which the integration of loanwords can be measured is not in itself a recent one; indeed some of the earliest scholars to work on Latin loanwords in Greek attempted to distinguish loanwords from codeswitches and discussed the criteria usable for this purpose.[33] Some of their criteria effectively matched ones just discussed: use of Greek endings (morphological integration), sound changes peculiar to Greek (phonological integration), and development of new meanings (semantic integration). These scholars also considered frequency a criterion of loanword status, along with long-term survival (§2.2.3) – and some criteria that for good reason are no longer considered usable, such as the formation of derivatives and compounds (§2.4). But some of their suggestions are worthy of serious consideration even if absent from the linguistic literature. For example, Viscidi must be right that (consistent) change of gender indicates integration as a loanword, for such a change shows a clear difference from the source language that could only be maintained by internal Greek transmission.[34] Although consistent change of gender is rare for Latin words in Greek, it does occur (§4.2.3–5) and usually correlates with other features suggesting loanword status. Another criterion suggested in the early studies of Latin loanwords is alteration by folk

etymology (§4.4); here again consistent change is rare, and some of the words involved probably should not be considered loanwords. But when the Greek version of a word consistently has a different form from its Latin original, in respects going beyond the use of Greek script and attachment of Greek endings, that different form is itself evidence of integration. Unfortunately, the need for evidence of consistency here means that this criterion can only be used with words that already occur often enough to count as loanwords on the basis of frequency.

In sum, therefore, integration can only rarely be useful for distinguishing loanwords from codeswitches in Greek: the few words that consistently have a form (apart from the ending), gender, or meaning different from the Latin are likely to be loanwords, while words that do not have Greek endings and/or do not appear in the Greek alphabet are probably codeswitches (but note §7.1, §7.2.2). Neither the presence of a Greek ending nor the use of the Greek alphabet shows that a word is a loan rather than a codeswitch, and we have too little information on accentuation to use it for this purpose.

2.2.3 Other criteria

Another criterion that can be used to judge the extent to which a word has become part of a language is its long-term survival (diachronic stability). This criterion has been heavily employed by previous scholars working on loanwords in ancient Greek, particularly in the form of considering whether loanwords survive into modern Greek (§8.2.3). It is less often used by linguists, though they sometimes note in passing that diachronic stability is an important indication of loanword status.[35] The difficulty is that words' survival or lack thereof is often due to other factors; that is why many words of impeccably native etymology eventually die out. The question of long-term survival cannot be ignored, but it needs a more careful and nuanced consideration than it has so far received (see §8.2–3).

The use of a foreign word by monolingual speakers of the borrowing language is generally

[32] E.g. βέρρης (*verres*), which in Latin refers to an uncastrated boar, is said by Plutarch (*Cicero* 7.6) to be a Roman word for a castrated pig.

[33] E.g. Viscidi (1944: 5–10), Zilliacus (1935a: 99), Cameron (1931: 232–3), Meinersmann (1927: 120–1), Hahn (1906: 231–2). The abandonment of this distinction may have been due to the accumulation of more and more data in loanword studies: the more examples you have, the harder it is to look at each one in detail.

[34] Viscidi (1944: 7).

[35] E.g. Backus (2014: 29); note also the interesting diachronic work of Poplack (e.g. 2018: 122–40).

agreed to be a key criterion, arguably the key criterion, indicating that it is a loanword rather than a codeswitch.[36] Bilingual speakers can use both codeswitches and loanwords, but people who do not know a second language cannot codeswitch into it, so any foreign word they use must be an established loan. In practice, however, use by monolingual speakers is rarely employed as a diagnostic criterion, because it is too difficult to tell whether particular speakers are completely monolingual. This problem is even greater in dealing with ancient Greek; although some writers were clearly not monolingual, and others are very likely to have been monolingual, it is almost never possible to state with certainty that the composer of a given Greek text had no knowledge of Latin at all.

Another criterion difficult to apply to ancient Greek is words' place in the vocabulary of the borrowing language. A single language does not normally have multiple words with exactly the same meaning (if one defines 'meaning' to include register and connotation as well as simple denotation), but two different languages very often do have words with the same meaning. For this reason it is often argued that a word of foreign origin is more likely to be a loanword if its meaning is different from that of any native words in the language, while foreign words duplicating the meanings of native words are more likely to be codeswitches.[37] Of course, a word with a meaning different from that of native words may also be a codeswitch; indeed codeswitching is often triggered by the need to express ideas for which the speaker's native language has no suitable words. But a loanword does normally seem to have a specific, consistent place in the vocabulary of the borrowing language, in which place it is the normal word to use; if speakers borrow a word that does not express a new concept, it typically either replaces the native word originally used for that concept or restricts the native term's meaning or register.[38] English speakers mentioning the

meat of an ox, for example, regularly refer to it as 'beef' rather than 'ox', but there was a time when 'ox' was the normal term for the meat as well as the animal; the borrowing of 'beef' has led to a change in the meaning of 'ox', which is now restricted to living animals in order to, as it were, make room for the loanword.

In practice, however, this criterion is rarely used, since it is very difficult to ascertain whether the meanings of two words are indeed exactly the same.[39] That difficulty is even greater in ancient Greek, where rare words are particularly likely to be poorly understood. In Greek it is also difficult to ascertain whether a native word was replaced, for Classical Greek words were often employed in literature long after they had disappeared from the conversational register.

A more useful criterion for our purposes is speakers' marking of words as foreign.[40] Such marking can be conveyed either by an overt statement or by extra-linguistic cues indicating language switch.[41] Words thus marked are not always counted by linguists as codeswitches, since they do not fit the usual pattern of codeswitching. That pattern involves two bilingual speakers; a typical codeswitch would be something like 'I'd use the *passé composé* there if I were you', directed at someone who knew enough French to understand it. By contrast an utterance specifically marking the word as French, like 'The French call that the *passé composé*', would probably be used to someone who did not know French. Although utterances of the latter type are not typical codeswitches, they have even less in common with loanwords and thus tend to be grouped with codeswitches by scholars working on loanwords: as long as one operates with the traditional binary distinction between codeswitches and loanwords, words marked as foreign must in principle fall into the former category.[42]

---

[36] Cf. Matras (2020: 117–18), Thomason (2001: 133), Haspelmath (2009: 40), Zenner and Kristiansen (2014: 4), Myers-Scotton (2006: 259–60).

[37] E.g. Naiditch (2000: 278).

[38] Cf. e.g. Clyne (2003: 145–6), Matras (2020: 118, 162), Gardner-Chloros (2010: 196–7), Gusmani (1981–3: I.157–67), Weinreich (1953: 53–6).

[39] Nivens (2002: 71–2).

[40] This criterion is the only one besides frequency used by the *Oxford English Dictionary* to determine whether words should count as English: Latin words retaining unadapted Latin morphology are included in the dictionary if sufficiently frequent in English contexts, but Latin words explicitly flagged as Latin are excluded regardless of frequency (Durkin and Schad 2017: 330).

[41] Cf. Naiditch (2000: 277–8).

[42] Poplack (2018: 41) tried to get around this problem by

The situation is complicated by a number of factors, however. One is variation: a word marked as foreign by one writer may be an established loanword for another, especially if the second writer is later. Another is that Greek speakers recognized several different levels of foreignness and tailored their marking accordingly. For example, the five underlined words in passage 2 are all of Latin origin, all written in Greek script, all furnished with Greek endings, and all included in major Greek dictionaries,[43] but the writer divides them into three groups in terms of markedness. Two (Καπιτώλιον and Ῥωμαίοις) are neither flagged nor explained but simply treated like Greek words, implying that the writer expected them to be familiar to his readers. Two (τραβέας and ἄπικας) are both flagged with forms of καλέω 'call' and explained, implying that the writer expected them to be unfamiliar to his readers. One (Μαρτίῳ) is flagged but not explained, suggesting an intermediate status. And in fact, if one examines other evidence for the attestation of these words, one finds that the two unmarked ones had both been borrowed into Greek by the time this text was written (first century BC), the two that are flagged and explained are completely unattested before this text (and for some time after it), and the intermediate word is first attested elsewhere around the time of this text. In other words, at the time this text was written the first two were loanwords, the second two were codeswitches, and the last was in the process of being borrowed. Thus the way in which these words are marked here corresponds exactly to what their loanword or non-loanword status

probably was, on the basis of other evidence – but the distinction is not simply a binary one.

2 Ἑορτὴ δ' αὐτῶν ἐστι περὶ τὰ Παναθήναια ἐν τῷ καλουμένῳ <u>Μαρτίῳ</u> μηνὶ δημοτελὴς ἐπὶ πολλὰς ἡμέρας ἀγομένη, ἐν αἷς διὰ τῆς πόλεως ἄγουσι τοὺς χοροὺς εἴς τε τὴν ἀγορὰν καὶ τὸ <u>Καπιτώλιον</u> καὶ πολλοὺς ἄλλους ἰδίους τε καὶ δημοσίους τόπους, χιτῶνας ποικίλους χαλκαῖς μίτραις κατεζωσμένοι καὶ τηβέννας ἐμπεπορπημένοι περιπορφύρους φοινικοπαρύφους, ἃς καλοῦσι <u>τραβέας</u> (ἔστι δ' ἐπιχώριος αὕτη Ῥωμαίοις ἐσθὴς ἐν τοῖς πάνυ τιμία) καὶ τὰς καλουμένας <u>ἄπικας</u> ἐπικείμενοι ταῖς κεφαλαῖς, πίλους ὑψηλοὺς εἰς σχῆμα συναγομένους κωνοειδές, ἃς Ἕλληνες προσαγορεύουσι κυρβασίας. (Dionysius of Halicarnassus, *Antiquitates Romanae* 2.70.2)

The festival [of the *Salii*] is around the time of the Panathenaea, in the month called <u>March</u>, and it is celebrated at public expense over many days, in which they lead their dances through the city to the Forum and the <u>Capitol</u> and many other public and private places, wearing multicoloured tunics fastened with bronze belts and fastening over them with brooches robes with purple borders and red stripes, which they call *trabeae* (and this garment native to the <u>Romans</u> is a mark of great honour), and having on their heads the so-called *apices*, high caps contracted into a cone shape, which the Greeks call κυρβασίαι.

The situation is further complicated by the fact that Greek speakers, like those of many modern languages, were sometimes aware of, and commented on, the origins of long-established loanwords.[44] For example, in passage 3 the fifth-century AD writer Orion correctly identifies as Latin a word borrowed in or before the first century BC, commonly used in the intervening

---

excluding such words from her data completely: 'Excluded from ensuing quantitative analyses were words in the context of perceptible hesitations, false starts, reported speech, meta-linguistic commentary, flagging, or other indications of awareness on the part of the speaker of their L_D [donor language] provenance.' This policy may have contributed to Poplack's finding that the foreign words used by her informants were always morphologically and syntactically integrated, whether they were loanwords or codeswitches; indeed it would be difficult to define 'indications of awareness on the part of the speaker of their donor language provenance' so as to exclude the use of donor language morphology and syntax. As this example illustrates, excluding words marked as foreign from one's data can jeopardize the validity of one's conclusions.

[43] The first four appear in LSJ and the fifth in LSJ suppl.

[44] In a study of Moroccan Arabic, Heath (1989: e.g. 158–9) found that speakers were generally aware of which words came from which languages, even in the case of long-established borrowings from languages those speakers did not know; he inferred that some information about these words' histories must have been transmitted in the Arabic-speaking community. (Such information is not always correct, however: Heath's speakers occasionally made mistakes, either by attributing borrowings to the wrong source language or by claiming foreign origin for words that probably did not have it.) I have myself observed Latinless speakers of both English and German correctly identifying established loanwords in their languages as coming from Latin.

centuries, and morphologically integrated – in fact more integrated than Orion realized, since ξέστης actually comes from *sextarius*.

> 3   Ξέστης· Ῥωμαϊκόν ἐστι τὸ ὄνομα. τὸ γὰρ παρ' ἡμῖν ἓξ ἀριθμὸν αὐτοὶ λέγουσι σέξ, καὶ μέτρου τινὸς παρ' αὐτοῖς τὸ ἕκτον λέγεται σέξτον· διὰ δὲ εὐφωνίας τὸ σέξτης λέγεται ξέστης, μεταθέσει τοῦ ξ. (Orion, *Etymologicum* p. 112.6–9 Sturz, citing Philoxenus)

> Ξέστης: the word is Latin. For they say *sex* for the number that is ἓξ for us, and the sixth part of a measure is called *sextum* among them; but through euphony *sextes* is pronounced ξέστης, with metathesis of the ξ.

Therefore one cannot simply assume that any word marked as Latin was not an established loanword in the Greek of the writer who so marked it; the marking has to be taken in conjunction with other evidence. This is particularly true for writers who had literary motivations for marking words as Latin.[45] And unmarked usage is not always an indication that a word was familiar to readers, for writers did not necessarily mark foreign words every single time they used them. For example, Plutarch uses δεκίης 'million' without marking or explanation at *Antony* 4.9, but only because he explained the term at *Antony* 4.8; as these two passages are the word's only occurrences in Greek it was clearly not a loanword. A very few words, such as τόγα 'toga', are not rare but nevertheless regularly marked as foreign; these were probably not loanwords, but it is difficult to be certain. The most difficult cases are those in which a late Greek writer who attributes a word to Ῥωμαῖοι 'Romans' may be using Ῥωμαῖοι to refer to Greek speakers (§10.4.1), as with βάνδον 'military standard', 'troop'.

2.2.4 Conclusions

Overall, frequency (at least three good examples) is the best indication of loanword status in ancient Greek. Any consistent difference from the Latin original in form (apart from the ending), gender, or meaning is also likely to indicate loanword status, but in practice these criteria are of little use since in order to demonstrate such consistency the word needs to be frequent. The best evidence against loanword status is usually writers' marking words as foreign, lack of inflectional integration, and appearance in Latin script.

2.3 OTHER BORROWING PHENOMENA RELATED TO LOANWORDS

Words of entirely native etymology can sometimes be influenced by foreign words so as to become in some sense lexical borrowings. For example, in calques (also called loan translations), the structure of a phrase, compound, or morphologically complex word is replicated in the borrowing language using native words and/or native affixes. Examples include English 'cornerstone' for French *pierre angulaire* and 'almighty' for Latin *omnipotens*, German *Wolkenkratzer* for English 'skyscraper', Latin *compassio* for Greek συμπάθεια, and Latin *qualitas* for Greek ποιότης.[46] There are also semantic extensions (also called semantic loans), in which an existing word extends its meaning under the influence of a word in another language that already matches some of its meanings; for example the extension of Latin *casus* 'fall' to mean 'grammatical case' under the influence of Greek πτῶσις, which meant both 'fall' and 'grammatical case'.[47] Sometimes, as in this example, the two words involved sound completely different from one another, but semantic extension can also occur with words that resemble each other in sound as well as in meaning. For example, Spanish *registrarse* originally could be used in some of the meanings of English 'register', but not in the sense 'register for class', which was expressed with *matricularse*; under the influence

---

[45] For Atticist writers with these motivations see §9.4. Later authors may have sometimes followed the Atticists in this respect: see Hahn (1906: 250, 1907: 712) on Plutarch's and Procopius' marking of well-known Latin words, and Zilliacus (1937: 327) on marking of long-established words in the tenth century.

[46] Miller (2012: 172), Durkin (2014: 164), Gusmani (1981–3: ii.3–70, 1987: 106–7), Weinreich (1953: 50–1).

[47] For these see e.g. Durkin (2009: 136–7), who uses the term 'semantic loan', Langslow (2000: 140–205), who uses the term 'semantic extension', Gusmani (1981–3: ii.3–70), and Nicolas (1996), who (writing in French) uses the term *calque sémantique*; Nicolas discusses *casus* and πτῶσις on pp. 93–117.

of English, some Spanish speakers living in the United States extended the meaning of *registrarse* to replace *matricularse*.[48] It is also possible for a word in one language to pick up a new meaning from a word in another language that resembles it in sound but not in meaning.[49]

These phenomena are of considerable interest in their own right,[50] but they are not normally considered loanwords,[51] since that term tends to be restricted to borrowings resulting in the presence of identifiably foreign words or parts of words in the vocabulary of the borrowing language. In an influential classification of types of lexical borrowing, Einar Haugen coined the term 'loanshift' as a cover term for the phenomena discussed above and in general for any type of borrowing that appears only as a change in the use of native words (or parts of words).[52] In many circles this term is still used in this sense (e.g. Haspelmath 2008: 47), but historical linguists often use it as a synonym for 'semantic extension'.[53] There is therefore no longer an available cover term for the phenomena discussed in the preceding paragraph, at least not one that can be used without danger of confusion in work likely to be consulted by historical linguists.

Some other phenomena result in words that are partly foreign and partly native. One of these is the 'loanblend', in which a word is borrowed as a whole but part of it is replaced by an element native to the borrowing language. For example, English has borrowed French *neurotiser* 'to provide with new nerve fibres or nerves' but substituted the English suffix '-ize' for the *-iser*, producing 'neurotize'.[54] Most linguists consider loanblends to be a type of loanword, but some treat them as a separate category.[55]

All the phenomena just mentioned occur between Latin and Greek: which should count as loanwords? Everyone agrees that calques and semantic extensions in which there is no resemblance in sound between the Latin and Greek words are separate phenomena from loanwords, but there is some debate about the classification of words in which an original resemblance in sound has contributed to the borrowing outcome. For example θρίαμβος, originally meaning 'hymn to Dionysus', acquired the additional meaning 'triumphal procession' from *triumphus* (itself originally a borrowing of θρίαμβος, via Etruscan); ἀήρ 'air' probably acquired the additional meaning 'space over a grave' from *area* 'open space', and the plant name βολβός could be used to mean 'bulb' under the influence of *bulbus* 'bulb'. For this reason ἀήρ and βολβός (but not, as far as I know, θρίαμβος) have been called loanwords in Greek: the idea is that *area* and *bulbus* were actually borrowed but changed their forms to match pre-existing Greek words. Such changes are often called 'folk etymology' or 'popular etymology', whether they affect whole words (as in these examples) or only part of a word, as in the loanblend διπλοκάριος, a variant of δουπλικάριος 'soldier receiving double pay' (from *duplicarius*) affected by association with Greek διπλόος 'double'.[56]

It is difficult to know exactly where the line between loanwords and non-loanwords should be drawn, particularly in the absence of any

---

[48] Backus and Dorleijn (2009: 83).

[49] Haugen (1950: 219), with examples from Portuguese spoken by immigrants to the United States: *grosseria* 'rude remark' acquired the additional meaning 'grocery' from English, and *livraria* 'bookstore' aquired the additional meaning 'library'. Cf. Gusmani (1981–3: 1.93–9, 139–56).

[50] See e.g. J. N. Adams (2003: 459–68, 522–3).

[51] They are explicitly excluded from loanword studies by e.g. Poplack (2018: 41) and Haspelmath (2009: 38–40).

[52] Haugen (1950: especially 219–20, 1953: 390–1, 400–3). Originally (1950: 214–15, 218–20) Haugen proposed a three-way classification into loanwords, loanshifts, and loanblends (for which see next paragraph), but later (1953: 391, 396–403) he opted for a two-way classification into loanwords and loanshifts, with loanblends as a subcategory of loanwords.

[53] See Burton (2002: 409) for an investigation of the way different historical linguists have used the term 'loanshift'; to this could be added its use for semantic extensions by Coleman (1975: 106), Hock (1986: 398–9), and J. N. Adams (2003: 461–2). But Nicolas (1996: 61–3) uses 'loanshift' in Haugen's sense.

[54] Durkin (2009: 138), Haugen (1950: 218–19, cf. 1953: 391, 397–9, 402), Weinreich (1953: 51–2).

[55] Haugen himself changed his mind on this point (see n. 52). More recent linguists treating loanblends as a type of loanword include Winter-Froemel (2011: 66 n. 4) and Winford (2010: 172); linguists treating them as a separate category include Haspelmath (2009: 39) and Treffers-Daller (2010: 22).

[56] For folk etymology see e.g. Michel (2015), Durkin (2009: 202–5), Panagl (2005), Gusmani (1981–3: 1.61–6), Weinreich (1953: 49–53). For its effect on Latin loanwords in Greek, see §4.4.

information on what speakers thought they were doing: did Greeks who used βολβός to mean 'bulb' think that they were using Latin *bulbus* with a Greek spelling, or did they think of the meaning 'bulb' as an additional sense of the plant name βολβός?[57] And did the different speakers who used such forms all think of them the same way? Nevertheless an opportunity to make a distinction using criteria accessible to us arises from the fact that in the case of θρίαμβος, ἀήρ, and βολβός the form of the resulting word is purely Greek; only its usage is Latinate. These borrowings therefore belong in the category that Haugen called 'loanshifts' and can be excluded from a study of loanwords. On the other hand διπλοκάριος is at least partially a loanword; it contains recognizable Latin elements, and those who consider loanblends a type of loanword would no doubt consider διπλοκάριος a loanword. We can therefore draw the line so as to include διπλοκάριος in this study (for discussion and more examples see §4.4) and to exclude ἀήρ etc.

But folk etymology was not always needed to make a Latin borrowing resemble a native Greek word: there are some words for which the expected form of a Latin borrowing happens to exactly match a pre-existing Greek word. For example ταλάριον 'sandal fastened at the ankles' is thought to be a borrowing of *talaris* 'of the ankles'; is the existence of ταλάριον 'small basket' relevant to this situation? What about μέταλλον 'marble paving-slab': can that be a borrowing of *metallum* 'mosaic work', or is it an extension of μέταλλον 'mine'? Is Γραικός 'Greek' a borrowing of *Graecus* 'Greek' (or a related word in another Italic language), or an extension of the original use of Γραικός for a particular subset of Greeks?[58]

It is not feasible to include in a loanword study all the words in this category, as there would be no clear dividing line between them and ordinary semantic extension (of which there are many, many examples). But excluding words like ταλάριον, in which the new word has a meaning completely unrelated to the native word, is also unwarranted: it is highly unlikely that Greek speakers would have consistently failed to distinguish the two ταλάριον words (cf. §12.2.1). Therefore this study includes borrowings like ταλάριον that happened to resemble a Greek word from which they probably remained distinct, but excludes ones like Γραικός that probably merged with a Greek word of related meaning.

2.4 DERIVATIVES AND COMPOUNDS FORMED FROM LOANWORDS

Derivatives and compounds formed from loanwords within the borrowing language were labelled 'creations' as part of the same classification that produced the terms 'loanshifts' and 'loanblends';[59] the term is now little used, and the concept itself not much studied. The phenomenon is common, however; for example English 'quorate' and 'inquorate' are derivatives of the loanword 'quorum', and 'armchair' is a compound formed from the loanword 'chair'. Linguists are divided on how to treat these words; some studies of loanwords exclude them and others include them.[60] Whether included or not, they are often used as evidence for the solid establishment of the original loanwords from which they were formed.[61]

At first glance the point that derivatives and compounds provide evidence of the integration of the loanword they include seems a strong one: Latin *quorum*, originally a genitive plural pronoun meaning 'of which', could not possibly have taken the affixes '-ate' or 'in-' and had

---

[57] One word in this category does provide some information on what its users were thinking: *poena* 'penalty' appears in Latin script in legal writers (see §3.2 *s.v.* ποῖνα), who thus seem to distinguish it from native ποινή 'penalty'. But the same writers also used ποινή, apparently without any distinction in meaning from *poena*, leading one to wonder whether *poena* might be (at least in part) a Latinization of the familiar Greek term – a process the opposite of folk etymology.

[58] Other examples include λάκκος, μηλωτή, πιλίον, πῖλος 1, προοίμιον, τέτριξ, τρίβολος, τρίβος. There are also words that have been erroneously placed in this category when they actually have no connection with Latin, such as αἴθριον, and ones whose Latin connection is uncertain, such as λυγγούριον.

[59] Haugen (1950: 220–2, though he later used the term 'creation' differently, to designate a kind of loanshift: 1953: 391, 402); cf. Haspelmath (2009: 39–40).

[60] They are excluded e.g. by Haspelmath and Tadmor (2009: 13) and included e.g. by Muysken (2000: 70).

[61] E.g. Muysken (2000: 72–3). For application of this criterion to Greek see e.g. Meinersmann (1927: 120), Cameron (1931: 232), Viscidi (1944: 7–8), Browning (1983: 40).

to undergo significant changes in meaning and grammar before English speakers could attach those affixes. Likewise 'armchair' could only have been formed once English speakers were familiar enough with the term 'chair' to want to identify an armchair as a particular kind of chair. But the rule does not always hold, as 'stratigraphy' and 'arachnophobia' demonstrate. These compounds made of Greek elements were formed within English rather than being borrowed from Greek, but they do not prove that 'strati' and 'arachno' (or any variants thereof) had already been established as loanwords in English at the time the compounds were formed. The second halves of both compounds were indeed already established, but the first halves were borrowed directly from Greek to form the compounds – and such borrowing is not uncommon.[62] In fact the only way to know whether the component parts of a word formed within the borrowing language had previously been borrowed is to find out whether they were previously attested in that language: it is impossible to tell simply from the compound or derivative itself.

Greek has many derivatives and compounds formed from Latin words (§4.3, §4.5, §4.6). Some of these are clearly formed from previously established loanwords, such as κουρατορεύω 'act as curator' from κουράτωρ 'curator' (from *curator*) + -εύω, πωμαρίτης 'fruiterer' from πωμάριον 'orchard' (from *pomarium* 'orchard') + -ίτης, λωροτόμος 1 'strap-cutter' from λῶρος 'strap' (from *lorum/lorus* 'leather strap') + -τόμος, or φιλορώμαιος 'friend of the Romans' from φιλο- +

Ῥωμαῖος 'Roman' (from *Roma* via Ῥώμη 'Rome' + -αῖος). Others are equally clearly formed directly from Latin, without an intermediate loanword: for example ἐξπελλεύω 'collect taxes' from *expello* 'drive out' + -εύω, βαστέρνιον 'enclosed litter' from *basterna* 'enclosed litter' + -ιον, προμάξιμον (a garment) from πρό 'before' + *maximum* 'greatest', and ὁλοκόττινος (a coin) from ὅλος 'whole' + *coctum* (*aurum*) 'smelted gold' + -ινος. Often we cannot be sure how a word was originally formed; given the limited evidence surviving, the fact that an intermediary loanword is not attested earlier than a derivative does not absolutely prove that the derivative was not formed from an intermediary.

Scholars working on Latin loanwords in Greek generally include derivatives and compounds formed from pre-existing loanwords, not only because it is so difficult to separate them from directly borrowed words but also because they provide important information about the extent of Latinization of Greek. A loanword study that excludes derivatives of loanwords offers only partial information about the impact of the source language on the borrowing one. For example, a recent study of loanwords in English which excludes derivatives and compounds of pre-existing loanwords finds that 41% of English words are borrowings from other languages.[63] This might seem to indicate that 59% of the vocabulary of English descends from Anglo-Saxon, which is far from being the case: only about 27% of the words in the *Shorter Oxford English Dictionary* have Anglo-Saxon etymologies.[64] Therefore omission of derivatives and compounds from the present study would seriously diminish the usefulness of the results.

---

[62] Cf. Winter-Froemel (2011: 36). Haspelmath and Tadmor (2009: 15) include such words in their study, despite excluding derivatives of established loanwords. It is disputed whether such forms can be created spontaneously by codeswitching within a word (e.g. could an English-speaking Latin teacher whose students did not like the verb *capio* talk to another Latin teacher about their 'capiophobia'?), but evidence has been produced in favour of this possibility (e.g. Thomason 2001: 135).

[63] Grant (2009: 370).

[64] Finkenstaedt and Wolff (1973: 121), though exact figures for the amount of 'borrowed' and 'native' vocabulary in English vary from study to study (cf. e.g. Durkin 2014: 24, 37; Miller 2012: 230).

3

LEXICON

3.1 PRELIMINARY INFORMATION

Entries are divided into two types; although alphabetized together for ease of reference these are constructed very differently.

- Entries for words that appear to have been genuine Latin loanwords in ancient Greek indicate in the margin the type of loanword ('Direct loan', 'Deriv. of loan', etc.) and then provide detailed information on the word's etymology and usage, including at least one example per century from each text type.
- Entries for words that have been or might be suggested as Latin loanwords in ancient Greek, but for which convincing evidence of loanword status cannot be found, indicate in the margin the reason why the word is not classified as a loanword ('rare', 'not Latin', 'not ancient', etc.) and then offer a brief discussion of the relevant evidence. In these entries examples of the word's use are provided only if pertinent to that discussion. For these entries inflectional and gender information is given only if it is both known and not obvious from the nominative singular. 'No examples' and 'no ancient examples' mean that I have located the example cited by previous scholars and verified that it is a superseded reading or the text is not ancient. 'No certainly ancient examples' means that I have located the example but am not sure whether the text is ancient. 'I can find no examples' and 'I can find no ancient examples' mean that I do not think I have found the attestation that caused previous scholars to cite the word.

Lemmata: These give all the different spellings in which the word occurs in ancient texts and modern editions thereof (and many spellings found only in lexica), except that the very common alternation between -ιον and -ιν in neuter nouns and between -ιος and -ις in masculines is not specifically indicated, nor are differences consisting only of accentuation. Variants found in Byzantine manuscripts and post-antique papyri are not systematically included. The first form given for each lemma (including its accentuation) normally comes from the most reputable lexicon to contain the word, except that demonstrably incorrect forms (e.g. plurals where the singular is attested, accentuation contradicting ancient evidence) have been corrected. Because spellings in lexica are included, not all spellings given here are attested in ancient sources. Lemmata are in Greek script if the word is ever found in Greek script (even if only in modern scholarship); words found only in Latin script remain in Latin and are alphabetized under the most likely sixth-century Greek spelling (i.e. *h* is ignored, *e* and *ē* alphabetize as ε, *o* and *ō* alphabetize as ο, *u* alphabetizes as ου, *c* and *q* alphabetize as κ, and *v* alphabetizes as β). A few lemmata are presented as phrases rather than single words; because the word division is editorial, the spaces are ignored for alphabetization purposes.

Latin: Unless otherwise noted, information is taken from the *Oxford Latin Dictionary* with vowel quantities from Pinkster (2014). When another source is cited, some information may still come from the *OLD* and quantities may still come from Pinkster. When two Latin forms are separated with /, both appear in the dictionary specified and the first is the citation form. Meanings given are those most relevant to the Greek usage, not necessarily the best attested in Latin. Latin words said to be unattested are not in the *OLD*, *TLL*, or any of the dictionaries in Brepols' *Database of Latin Dictionaries* (www.brepolis.net).

Examples: All examples cited have been verified to be genuine occurrences in (probably) ancient Greek texts; editorial supplements and most examples not verifiable as ancient are omitted, and references to occurrences that I cannot find are listed separately as 'unverified'. 'Perhaps' before a reference indicates that the reading is doubtful, usually because a significant part of it is a modern supplement. For loanwords, examples are divided by the text types of the sources (for the precise definitions of 'documents', 'inscriptions', and 'literature' used here, see §9.1 with notes 1–3); when one of these categories is missing, I have been unable to find any examples in that text type. Normally one reference is provided for every writer who used the word, with 'etc.' after the reference when further (certain or doubtful) examples occur in the same document, inscription, or author. When only a selection of examples is provided, that is signalled by 'common, e.g.' (usually indicating more than 50 examples) or 'e.g.' (usually indicating fewer than 50 examples); in those entries the presence of additional examples from the same writer is not signalled. When a selection of examples is given, an effort has been made to provide at least one good example per century; if no example is given for a particular century I was unable to find one, and if only a poor example is given (e.g. one marked 'perhaps' or with doubtful dating), I was unable to find a good one. Examples are dated whenever possible; the dates are those of the text, not the life of the author, and thus often differ from dates in the *TLG Canon*. When no date is given I consider the text undatable but potentially ancient. Examples are arranged chronologically, by centuries only. 'Marked' indicates that the word is treated as unfamiliar in that example. Examples are in Greek script unless stated otherwise.

Post-antique: This section does not offer the same kind of overview of the word's usage as is provided for usage up to AD 600, only a rough indication of the amount of survival. Changes in meaning are not noted unless significant (e.g. suggesting a lack of continuity). Modern usage is mentioned only when I consider it a continuation or revival of ancient usage; for example modern λίβρα 'pound' is not cited in connection with the occasional ancient use of λίβρα as a transliteration of *libra* 'pound', since the large chronological gap and rarity of ancient λίβρα mean that the ancient and modern words are unlikely to be directly connected.

Notes: This section includes references to selected treatments of the lemma in modern scholarship, starting with those offering substantial discussions of that particular word and discussions in unexpected places, then works focussing on Latin loanwords, etymological dictionaries, works on Byzantine and modern Greek, Latin lexica and grammars, Greek grammars, and lastly mainstream lexica of ancient Greek (*DGE*, LSJ, LSJ suppl.). Editors' commentaries on specific occurrences of the word are cited only when they are more useful than one would expect; otherwise it is assumed without discussion that information can often be found in editions of epigraphic and documentary occurrences. This section also serves as an index to the work as a whole by indicating which other Lexicon entries and which sections in the rest of the text concern the word at hand; such references are in bold if they provide significant information beyond what is in the Lexicon entry.

When words or passages are quoted, brackets, dots, and other editorial symbols are not normally included; readers needing to know exactly which letters are securely attested are advised to check the editions.

Marginal notations:

'Direct loan' indicates a word with Latin etymology probably borrowed into Greek.

'With univerbation' indicates that the original Latin was a phrase rather than a single word (§4.5).

'With suffix' indicates that a Greek suffix was added as part of the original borrowing process (§4.3).

'With influence' indicates that the word's form was influenced by pre-existing Greek words (§4.4).

'Loan compound' indicates a compound containing one or more elements that seem to have been taken directly from Latin and combined in Greek (§4.5); for example a Latin word combined with a Greek word, a Greek prefix (but not a Greek suffix), or another Latin word (but not when the two Latin words formed a compound or phrase already in Latin).

'Deriv(ative) of loan' indicates a word formed within Greek (by affixation, compounding, or any other derivation process) using a Latin word that had previously been borrowed into Greek (§4.6).

'Rare' indicates a word with Latin etymology for which at least one apparently integrated occurrence in an ancient Greek text (other than as a name) can be verified, but such occurrences are too few to demonstrate borrowing (§2.2.1).

'Foreign' indicates a word with Latin etymology for which at least one occurrence in an ancient Greek text (other than as a name) can be verified, but all such occurrences are marked as foreign by the writers (§2.2.3). Since there is a huge number of such words, not all are included here, only those previously claimed as loanwords and those that I happened to find while looking for loanwords.

'Name' indicates a word with Latin etymology that occurs in ancient Greek texts only as a proper name (§12.2.2); out of the many Latin names in Greek, only the ones previously claimed as loanwords are included here.

'Semantic extension' indicates a word of Greek etymology whose meaning has been influenced by Latin (§2.3); out of the many semantic extensions in Greek, only the ones previously claimed as loanwords are included here.

'Not Latin' and 'not Latin?' indicate a word for which a Latin etymology has been claimed but is not completely persuasive (cf. §2.1). Some words in this category are also of dubious antiquity.

'Not ancient' and 'not ancient?' indicate a word for which examples exist, but I cannot find any that are definitely datable to earlier than AD 600; the former is used only when I have been able to trace and date all attestations previously claimed to be ancient. Words appearing only in undated texts normally fall into this category. Some words in this category also have a dubious connection to Latin.

'Non-existent' and 'non-existent?' indicate a word for which I cannot find any certain attestation in Greek texts; the former is used only when I have been able to trace all attestations previously claimed to exist. Partial supplements have not been counted as certain attestations unless most of the word is visible; 'perhaps' usually means that an editor reads the word but a significant number of its letters are restored. Some words in this category also have a dubious connection to Latin.

For symbols and abbreviations see the list at the end of the volume.

3.2 LEXICON

A

non-existent	**ἀ, ἀβ**, cited as borrowing of Latin *ā, ab* 'from' by Mason (1974: 19): probably does not exist independently (cf. Cameron 1931: 257–8). For use as part of univerbations see *s.vv.* ἀβάκτης, Ἀβοριγῖνες, ἀβρέβις, ἀκομενταρήσιος, ἀννούμερος, ἀ πιγμέντις, ἀ σαβάνις, ἀσηκρῆτις. In Latin script as part of legal phrases (probably univerbations in legal Greek): e.g. Antec. 4.1.2 *a fraude*, 2.20.20 *a morte testatoris, ab adita hereditate*, 4.18.5 *a sica*, 3.15.pr. *a stipe* (VI AD). For *a* in Latin titles see *TLL* (*s.v. ā, ab* 22.81–23.46), Väänänen (1977).
Direct loan with univerbation IV AD – Byz.	**ἀβάκτης, ἀβάκτις, ἀβ ἄκτις** (-ου or indeclinable, ὁ) 'registrar', from *ab āctīs* 'registrar' (*TLL s.v. ago* 1410.17–35, cf. *s.v. ā, ab* 23.18). Documents: e.g. *P.Herm.Landl.* 2.509 etc. (IV AD); *SB* 9106.3 (V AD); *P.Mich.* XI.624.10 (VI AD). Literature: Nil. 2.207 (V AD); Lyd. *Mag.* p. 162.13 etc., marked (VI AD). Post-antique: survives. *LBG*. Notes: Cervenka-Ehrenstrasser (1996: 39–40), Filos (2006: 47–8, 2010: 251), Daris (1991a: 25), Hofmann (1989: 1), Cavenaile (1952: 193), Viscidi (1944: 19, 22), Zilliacus (1935a: 172–3), Meinersmann (1927: 5), Lampe (1961), *DGE*, LSJ suppl. See §4.2.3.2, §4.5, §9.5.5 passage 75, §10.2.1, §10.2.2 D, §12.2.1.
not Latin	**ἀββᾶ, ἀββᾶς** 'father', 'abbot', originally Semitic, may have been borrowed directly or via Latin (cf. *TLL s.v. abbās*). Triantaphyllides (1892: 255), Kriaras (1968–), *DGE*, LSJ suppl.
foreign	**ἄβεις** 'you have', probably from *habēs*, second person singular of *habeō* 'have': Hesych. as lemma α 102 (V/VI AD). Pisani (1955: 279), Immisch (1885: 350), Frisk (1954–72: III.15), Beekes (2010), Sophocles (1887), *DGE*. See §9.5.4.
foreign	***habeō*** 'have': Antec. 3.29.1 *habeo, habesne* (VI AD).
Direct loan III AD – Byz.	**ἀβερτή, ἀβερτά, ἀβερτής, ἀβελτής, βέρτα** (-ῆς?, ἡ or -οῦ?, ὁ) 'backpack', from *averta* 'backpack' (*TLL*), itself from ἀορτή. Documents: *P.Mich.* IX.576.4 (III AD); *P.Coll.Youtie* II.84.8 (IV AD). Inscriptions: Edict.Diocl. 10.1a (IV AD). Literature: with *liba* in Gloss. Ps.-Philox. 122.33; with *averta* in Gloss. Serv. 517.25. Post-antique: survives. *Suda* α 2850 (and elsewhere): ἀορτήν· λέγουσιν οἱ πολλοὶ νῦν ἀβερτήν. Μακεδονικὸν δὲ καὶ τὸ σκεῦος καὶ τὸ ὄνομα. *LBG*. Notes: Cervenka-Ehrenstrasser (1996: 40), Diethart (1993: 226, 1998: 165), Hofmann (1989: 1), *DGE* (*s.v.* ἀβέρτα), LSJ suppl. See §2.1 n. 8, §4.2.3.1, §10.2.1, §10.2.2 H.
not ancient	**ἀβῆνα** transliterating *avēna* 'oat': interpolation in Dsc. 4.137 RV. Sophocles (1887), *DGE*.
not ancient?	**ἀβῆνα** 'thong', from *habēna* 'strap': scholion to Ar. *Eq.* 767b; often in Byzantine texts. Zilliacus (1935a: 226–7), *LBG*, Triandaphyllidis (1909: 123), Lampe (1961), *DGE* (*s.v.* ἀβῆναι).

foreign   ἀβιτατίων, ναβιτατίων 'right to dwell in a particular place', from *habitātiō* 'residence': Antec. in Latin script 2.5.2 *habitationa* etc. (VI AD); later in Greek script. Replacement of Latin H by Greek N is post-antique graphic confusion. Hofmann (1989: 1), Zilliacus (1935a: 190–1), *LBG*. See §9.5.6 n. 68.

rare   ἀβιτώριον 'latrine', apparently from unattested *abitōrium* (from *abeō* 'go away'): inscription *I.Histria* 363.7 (III AD). Wilhelm (1928b: 229), Hofmann (1989: 1), Beekes (2010), *DGE*, LSJ suppl.

ἀβολεῖς: see ἀβόλλης.

rare   ἀβολιτίων, ἀβουλητίων 'withdrawal of a charge', from *abolitiō* 'withdrawal of a charge': Pall. *V.Chrys.* 85.22 (IV/V AD); often in Byzantine texts. Hofmann (1989: 2, suggesting that the spelling with -ου- is influenced by ἀβουλέω 'be unwilling'), Zilliacus (1935a: 172–3), *LBG*, Lampe (1961), *DGE*.

Direct loan
I–IV AD   ἀβόλλης, ἀβόλλα (-ου?, ὁ or -ης?, ἡ) 'thick woollen cloak', probably from *abolla* 'cloak'.

         Documents: e.g. *P.Oslo* III.150.17 (I AD); *P.Oxy.* 2593.24 (II AD); *BGU* III.814.8 (III AD); *SB* 9834b.5 (III/IV AD).

         Literature: *Periplus Maris Erythraei* e.g. 6.47 Casson (I/II AD); with *toga* and *vestimentum* in *Glossae Laudunenses*, *CGL* II.553.56 n. 1.

         Notes: Sicilian ἀβολεῖς or ἀβολλεῖς, lemma in Hesych. α 162 (V/VI AD), may be the same word (Willi 2008: 28; Campanile 1969: 309; Immisch 1885: 328–9). Cervenka-Ehrenstrasser (1996: 41–2), Diethart (1993: 221, 1998: 165–6), Schirru (2013: 304–5, 320), Murri (1943: 106–10), Palmer (1945: 67–8), *DÉLG*, Frisk (1954–72: 1.4 *s.vv.* ἀβολεῖς, ἀβόλλης), Beekes (2010 *s.vv.* ἀβολεῖς, ἀβόλλης), Daris (1991a: 25), Hofmann (1989: 2), Meinersmann (1927: 5), *DGE*, LSJ suppl. (replacing LSJ *s.v.* ἀβόλλα). See §4.2.3.1, §10.2.1, §10.2.2 H.

Direct loan
II? BC – modern   Ἀβοριγῖνες, Ἀβορήγινες, Ἀβωριγῖνες, Ἀβωριγῆνες, Ἀβοριγῖναι, Βορείγονοι (-ων, οἱ) 'original inhabitants of Italy', from *Aborīginēs* 'original inhabitants of Italy'.

         Literature: perhaps Hellanicus no. 4 frag. 79b Jacoby (V BC); perhaps Myrsilus no. 477 frag. 8 Jacoby (III BC); Lycophron, *Alexandra* 1253 (II BC?); DH *AR* 1.10.1 etc. (I BC); Strabo 5.3.2 etc. (I BC/AD); Juba, *FHG* III frag. 1 etc. (I BC/AD); App. *Basilica* 1.1 etc. (I/II AD); perhaps Hdn. *Pros. Cath.* III.1.18.2 etc. (II AD); Eus. *PE* 4.16.15 etc. quoting DH (IV AD); Stephanus of Byzantium α 10 (VI AD); Lyd. *Mag.* p. 36.14, marked (VI AD); Evagr.Schol. *HE* 218.21, marked (VI AD).

         Post-antique: survives despite absence from lexica. Modern use not independent of Latin: Babiniotis (2002 *s.v. ab origine*).

         Notes: inflection of Ἀβοριγῖνες disputed in antiquity; see Stephanus of Byzantium α 10. Hofmann (1989: 2), *DGE* (*s.vv.* Ἀβοριγῖνες, Βορείγονοι), LSJ. See §4.2.5, **§4.4**, **§8.1.3**, §10.2.1, §10.2.2 N.

ἀβουλητίων: see ἀβολιτίων.

foreign   ἀβούνκολος 'maternal uncle', from *avunculus* 'maternal uncle': Antec. in Latin script 3.6.3 *avunculus* (VI AD). Zilliacus (1935a: 174–5). See §7.1.1, §7.2.1.

Loan compound
IV AD

ἀβρέβις, ἀβρέβεις (indeclinable, ὁ), a title, from *ā* 'from' (*TLL s.v. ā, ab* 22.81–23.46) + *breve* 'summary' (see *s.v.* βρέβιον), combined within Greek. Documents: e.g. *BGU* XIX.2776.B27 (IV AD); *Stud.Pal.* XX.85v.2.26 (IV AD). Notes: all provenanced examples come from Hermopolis and its environs. Cervenka-Ehrenstrasser (1996: 42–3), Filos (2006: 48–9, 2008: 432–5, 2010: 251), Diethart (1998: 166), Daris (1991a: 25), Zilliacus (1935a: 172–3), Meinersmann (1927: 5), *DGE*. See §4.2.3.2 n. 47, **§4.5**, §9.2, §10.2.1, §10.2.2 D, §10.2.3; cf. βρέβιον.

foreign

ἀβσολουτίων 'acquittal', from *absolūtiō* 'acquittal': Antec. in Latin script 4.12.2 *absolutionos* etc. (VI AD); later in Greek script. Zilliacus (1935a: 172–3), *LBG*.

foreign

absolūtōrius 'favouring acquittal': Antec. 4.12.2 *absolutoria* (VI AD). Zilliacus (1935a: 172–3).

foreign

ἀβστινατεύω 'disinherit', 'refuse an inheritance', from *abstineō* 'keep off' (pf. part. is *abstentus*, so apparently formed by adding -ευω to imaginary pf. part. *abstinātus* created on analogy of first-conjugation participles such as *lēgātus* from *lēgō*, which became ληγατεύω in Greek; cf. οὐσουκαπιτεύω, προνερεδεγεριτεύω): papyrus *P.Ant.* III.153 frag. 8a.5 in Latin script (V AD); Just. *Nov.* in Latin script 89.3.pr. (VI AD); Antec. in Latin script 2.19.5 *abstinateusas* etc. (VI AD); later in Greek script. Cervenka-Ehrenstrasser (1996: 43–4), Diethart (1998: 166, 2008: 34), Burgmann (1991: 68), Hofmann (1989: 3 *s.v. abstinatíων*), Viscidi (1944: 26), Zilliacus (1935a: 172–3), *LBG*, LSJ suppl. See §9.5.6 n. 68.

rare

ἀβστινατίων 'act of disinheriting', 'refusal of an inheritance', from *abstineō* 'keep off' + -ατίων or via the type of derivation used for ἀβστινατεύω (derivation from unattested *abstinātiō* is unlikely: Cervenka-Ehrenstrasser 1996: 45): papyrus *P.Cair.Masp.* 67097v.D82 (VI AD); Antec. in Latin script 2.19.5 *abstinationa* etc. (VI AD). Cervenka-Ehrenstrasser (1996: 44–5), Daris (1991a: 25, with derivation from *abstentiō* 'abstention', *TLL*), Hofmann (1989: 3), Viscidi (1944: 26), Zilliacus (1935a: 172–3), Meinersmann (1927: 5), *DGE*, LSJ suppl. See §6.10.

Ἀβωριγῖνες: see Ἀβοριγῖνες.

not Latin

ἀγγαρ(ε)ία, ἀνγαρ(ε)ία, ἐγγαρ(ε)(ι)α, ἐνγαρ(ε)ία 'requisitioning for the public service', probably not from *angāria* 'compulsory services' but *vice versa*. Brust (2005: 21), Mason (1974: 19 *s.v.* ἀγγαρεῖος), Zilliacus (1935a: 174–5), Meinersmann (1927: 9 *s.v.* αγγαριας), *DÉLG* (*s.v.* ἄγγαρος), Beekes (2010: *s.v.* ἄγγαρος), Lampe (1961), *DGE*, LSJ, LSJ suppl.

not Latin

ἀγγαρεύω, ἀνγαρεύω, ἐγγαρεύω, ἐνγαρεύω 'requisition', probably from ἄγγαρος, borrowed from Persian or another Iranian language, not from *angarius* 'messenger' (*TLL*), itself from ἄγγαρος '(Persian) mounted courier'. Brust (2005: 20–1), Hofmann (1989: 3 *s.v.* ἄγγάριος), *DÉLG* (*s.v.* ἄγγαρος), Frisk (1954–72: I.7–8, III.16), Beekes (2010 *s.v.* ἄγγαρος), Meinersmann (1927: 9 *s.v.* αγγαριας), Lampe (1961), *DGE*, LSJ (*s.vv.* ἀγγαρεύω, ἐγγαρεύω).

not Latin   **ἀγγαριεύω** 'requisition' is a variant of ἀγγαρεύω (*q.v.*), perhaps influenced by Latin *angāriō* 'requisition'. Cervenka-Ehrenstrasser (1996: 45–6), Gonis (1998: 217), *DGE*, LSJ suppl.

not Latin?   **ἀγγάριος** 'impressed for public service', as masc. subst. 'workman', perhaps from *angarius* 'messenger' (*TLL*), itself from ἄγγαρος '(Persian) mounted courier' (a Latinate status for this word is more plausible than for other words on this stem, see *s.v.* ἀγγαρεύω, but still doubtful): papyri *P.Cair.Isid.* 72.3.23, 73.12 (both IV AD); probably not *O.Claud.* 1.142.7 (II AD), cf. commentary *ad loc.* Hofmann (1989: 3), *DGE*, LSJ suppl.

not Latin?   **ἀγγλάριον, ἀνγλάριον**, perhaps a vessel-name from *angulāris* 'having corners': inscription *I.Cret.* III.III.7.13 (II AD). *DGE*, LSJ suppl.

rare   **ἀγεντισηρίβους** 'government agents', from *agentēs in rēbus* 'those who act in affairs': Athan. *Apol.Const.* 10.3 (IV AD). Paschoud (1983: 232–4), Hofmann (1989: 3), Sophocles (1887 *s.v.* ἀγεντησιρῆβους), Lampe (1961), *DGE*.

foreign   **ἄγεστα, ἀγέστον, ἔγεστα** 'bank of earth used in siege warfare', from *aggestus, -ūs* 'bank of earth' or neut. pl. of *aggestus*, pf. part. of *aggerō* 'heap up': Evagr. Schol. *HE* 175.1, 175.22, 176.2, marked (VI AD); Procop. *Bell.* 2.26.29, marked (VI AD); occasional Byzantine texts. *Suda* (α 203, α 840, ε 52). Binder (2000: 251), Hofmann (1989: 3), Viscidi (1944: 12), *LBG* (*s.vv.* ἀγέστα, ἄκεσσα), Sophocles (1887), Lampe (1961 *s.v.* ἀγέστον), *DGE*, LSJ suppl.

non-existent   **ἀγκέντουμ**, plant name allegedly from unattested plant name **ancentum*: variant reading in interpolation in Dsc. 4.150 RV. Sophocles (1887), *TLL* (*s.v.* *ancentum*). See §8.1.7 n. 34.

foreign   **ἀγκίλιον, ἀγκύλιον** 'small shield shaped like a figure 8', from *ancīle* 'small shield shaped like a figure 8': Plut. *Numa* 13.9, marked (I/II AD); Lyd. *Mag.* p. 22.10 etc., marked (VI AD). Strobach (1997: 194), *LBG*, *DGE*, LSJ (*s.v.* ἀγκύλιον).

foreign   **ἀγκίλλα** transliterating *ancilla* 'female slave': Lyd. *Mag.* p. 22.12 (VI AD). *LBG*.

not ancient   **ἀγκλία** 'hollow gourd used for bailing', perhaps from *anclō* 'serve (wine)': no ancient examples. Meyer (1895: 9).

ἀγνατ-: see ἀδγνατ-.

ἀγουστ-: see αὐγουστ-.

Deriv. of loan
IV–VI AD   **ἀγραρεύω** 'lie in garrison', from *agrāria*, a type of guard duty (*TLL*) via ἀγραρία + -εύω.

     Documents: *SB* 10930.9 (IV AD); *P.Münch.* 1.16.11 (V AD); *P.Cair.Masp.* 67009r.21, 67022r.8 (both VI AD); *P.Grenf.* II.95.2 (VI AD); *SB* 7656.8 (VI AD).

     Literature: Hesych. as lemma α 759 (V/VI AD).

     Notes: Cervenka-Ehrenstrasser (1996: 46–7), Daris (1970: 37, 1991a: 25), Hofmann (1989: 4 *s.v* αγραρια), Mandilaras (1973: 67), Zilliacus (1935a: 216–17), Meinersmann (1927: 5), Immisch (1885: 364), *DGE*, LSJ suppl. See §4.6.1 n. 91, §10.2.2 C.

**Direct loan
V AD – Byz.**   **ἀγραρία, ἀγραρέα** (-ας, ἡ) 'garrison', from *agrāria*, a type of guard duty
(*TLL*).
Documents: *P.Bingen* 121.5 etc. (IV/V AD); *P.Herm.* 75.2 (V AD); *P.Ross.Georg.*
v.30 *passim* (V AD); *P.Lond.* v.1889r.12 (VI AD).
Post-antique: survives despite absence from lexica.
Notes: forms derivative ἀγραρεύω, therefore is probably older than it
looks. Ἀγραρία as cult title for Mother of the Gods on inscription *IGR*
1.92.2 probably comes independently from *agrārius* 'of land'. Cervenka-
Ehrenstrasser (1996: 47–8), Daris (1991a: 25), Hofmann (1989: 4),
Zilliacus (1935a: 216–17), Meinersmann (1927: 5), *DGE*, LSJ suppl. See
§4.2.3.1, §6.2, §10.2.1, §10.2.2 C.

non-existent?   **ἀγριλάρια, ἀριλάρια, αὐριολάρια,** plant name allegedly from unattested
agrilāria or *auriolāria*: interpolation in Dsc. 4.56 RV, where αὐριολάρια
is emendation for manuscripts' ἀριλάρια and αἰλάρια. *TLL* (*s.v. agrilaria*),
Hofmann (1989: 28). See §8.1.7 n. 34.

   ἀγτουάριος: see ἀκτουάριος.

**semantic
extension**   **ἄγω** 'lead', in principle a Greek word, can be used for *agō* 'pursue a case', and
impersonal *agitur* appears as ἄγεται in papyri *P.Yadin* 1.28.7, 29.7 (both II
AD); these are semantic extensions. Borrowing/codeswitch: Antec. in Latin
script 3.17.2 *agere* as legal term for going through another person's land with
an animal, 4.15.7 *agitur* as part of phrase (VI AD). Cervenka-Ehrenstrasser
(1996: 48).

foreign   *ad* 'to': Antec. as part of phrases e.g. 1.14.3 *ad certum tempus*, 2.1.29 *ad exhibendum*,
1.3.4 *ad pretium participandum* (VI AD). See §7.3 passage 33.

non-existent?   **ἀδβενδιτίων,** meaning uncertain, from unattested *advenditiō*: cited as an ancient
loan by Zilliacus (1935a: 172–3), but I can find no examples.

foreign   **ἀδβεντίκιος** 'alien', from *adventīcius* 'alien': *Schol.Sinai.* in Latin script 33
adventician etc. (V/VI AD); Just. *Nov.* in Latin script 91.2 (VI AD); later in
Greek script. Zilliacus (1935a: 172–3), *LBG* (*s.v.* ἀδβεντίτζιος). See §7.1.2,
§9.5.6 n. 56.

not ancient   **ἀδβοκᾶτος** 'advocate', from *advocātus* 'advocate': no ancient examples. Hofmann
(1989: 4), Lampe (1961).

rare   **ἀ(δ)γνατικός, ἀδνατικός** 'of a relative on the father's side' (esp. in neut. pl. of
the rights derived from that relationship), from *agnātus* 'relative on the
father's side' via ἀδγνᾶτος + -ικός: Ath.Schol. 9.10 (VI AD); Antec. in Latin
script 3.2.4 *adgnaticn* etc. (VI AD); Just. *Nov.* in Latin script 118.5 (VI
AD); occasionally later. Hofmann (1989: 4 *s.v.* ἀδγνάτος), Zilliacus (1935a:
174–5), *LBG*, Triantaphyllides (1892: 255), Lampe (1961 *s.vv.* ἀγνατικός,
ἀδνατικά), *DGE* (*s.v.* ἀγνατικός). See §7.1.3.

foreign   **ἀδ(γ)νατίων** 'relationship on the father's side', from *agnātiō/adgnātiō*
'relationship on the father's side': Antec. in Latin script 1.10.1 *adgnationa*
etc. (VI AD); later in Greek script. Zilliacus (1935a: 174–5), *LBG*.

rare   ἀ(δ)γνᾶτος, ἀδνᾶτος 'relative on the father's side', from *agnātus/adgnātus* 'relative on the father's side': Just. *Nov.* 115.3.14 = p. 543.1, but in Latin script 89.4 etc. (VI AD); Antec. in Latin script 1.10.1 *adgnatoi* etc. (VI AD); Ath.Schol. in Latin script 9.10.5 (VI AD); later often in Greek script. Forms derivative ἀδγνατικός. Avotins (1992), Hofmann (1989: 4), Zilliacus (1935a: 174–5), *LBG*, Lampe (1961 *s.v.* ἀδνᾶτος). See §9.5.6 n. 68.

     ἀδγνούμιον: see ἀδνούμιον.

foreign   ἀδεμπτεύω 'revoke (a legacy)', from *adimō* 'take away' or *adēmptiō* 'revocation (of a legacy)' via ἀδεμπτίων: Antec. in Latin script 2.20.36 *adempteuthē* etc. (VI AD); later in Greek script. Hofmann (1989: 5 *s.v.* ἀδεμπίων), *LBG*. See §9.5.6 n. 68.

foreign   ἀδεμπτίων 'revocation (of a legacy)', from *adēmptiō* 'revocation (of a legacy)': Antec. in Latin script 2.21.pr. *ademptiona* etc. (VI AD); later in Greek script. Hofmann (1989: 5), Zilliacus (1935a: 172–3), *LBG*. See §7.1.1 passage 19.

foreign   *adeō* 'approach': Antec. 1.2.7 *adire* (VI AD).

rare   ἀδεφένδευτος (-ον) 'undefended (in a legal case)', calque of *indēfēnsus* 'undefended' formed from ἀ- 'not' + *dēfendō* 'defend' (via διφηνδεύω?) + -τος: Just. *Nov.* 155.1 (VI AD); Byzantine legal texts. Avotins (1992), Hofmann (1989: 5), Zilliacus (1935a: 190–1), *LBG*, Lampe (1961), *DGE*, LSJ suppl. See §9.5.6 n. 68.

rare   ἀδηληγάτευτος (-ον), ἀδηλεγάτευτος (-ον), ἀδηληγάτευτον (-ου, τό) '(tax) not forming part of the *dēlēgātiō*', from ἀ- 'not' + the Latin source of δηληγατεύω via δηληγατεύω: papyri *P.Oxy.* 3424.5 (IV AD); *SB* 13252.12 (IV AD); perhaps *P.Flor.* 1.95.39 (IV AD). Cervenka-Ehrenstrasser (1996: 49–50), Diethart (1998: 166), Filos (2010: 249), Daris (1991a: 25), LSJ suppl.

not ancient   ἀδιοβάντης 'helpers', from *adiuvantēs*, pres. part. pl. of *adiuvō* 'help': no ancient examples. Cervenka-Ehrenstrasser (1996: 50), Binder (2000: 151, 264), Daris (1991a: 25), Hofmann (1989: 5), *DGE*, LSJ suppl.

foreign   ἀδιουδικατεύω 'adjudicate', from *adiūdicātus* (pf. part. of *adiūdicō* 'adjudicate', *TLL*) + -εύω: Antec. in Latin script 4.17.5 *adiudicateuestho* etc. (VI AD); later in Greek script. Hofmann (1989: 5 *s.v.* ἀδιουδικατίων), Zilliacus (1935a: 172–3), *LBG*.

foreign   ἀδιουδικατίων 'adjudication', from *adiūdicātiō* 'adjudication' (*TLL*): Antec. in Latin script 4.17.7 *adiudicationos* etc. (VI AD); later in Greek script. Hofmann (1989: 5), Zilliacus (1935a: 172–3), *LBG*. See §9.5.6 n. 68.

Direct loan
II AD – Byz.   ἀδιούτωρ, ἀδιούτορ, ἀϊούτωρ (-ορος/-ωρος, ὁ), a title, from *adiūtor* 'helper'.
Documents: e.g. *P.Ross.Georg.* II.26.2.8 (II AD); *Stud.Pal.* III.315v.1 (V/VI AD); *PSI* XV.1569.16 (VI AD).
Inscriptions: perhaps *SEG* XXXII.1554.A11 etc. (VI AD).
Literature: Nil. 2.287.1 (V AD); Lyd. *Mag.* p. 136.16 etc., marked (VI AD).
Post-antique: survives in papyri.
Notes: spelled ἀϊούτωρ on unpublished ostracon O.Dios inv. 687.12 (II AD). Cervenka-Ehrenstrasser (1996: 50–1), Daris (1991a: 25), Mason (1974: 5, 19), Hofmann (1989: 6), Zilliacus (1935a: 216–17), Meinersmann (1927: 5), Lampe (1961), *DGE*, LSJ suppl. See §4.2.5, §10.2.1, §10.2.2 D.

foreign	*adipīscor* 'achieve': Antec. 4.15.2 *adipiscendae* etc. (VI AD). *adīre*: see *adeō*.
Direct loan with suffix VI AD – Byz.	ἀδιτεύω 'take possession of an inheritance', from *aditus* (pf. part. of *adeō* 'take possession of an inheritance', *TLL s.v.* 627.84–628.17) + -εύω. Literature: Ath.Schol. 9.1.1 etc. (VI AD); Antec. in Latin script 2.20.33 *aditeusai, aditeuon, aditeusantos, aditeusei*, 3.4.4 ἠ*diteusan*, etc. (VI AD). Post-antique: common in legal texts. *LBG*. Notes: Hofmann (1989: 7 *s.v.* ἀδιτίων), Zilliacus (1935a: 172–3), Lampe (1961), *DGE*. See §4.3.1, **§9.5.6**, §10.2.1, §10.2.2 B, §10.3.1.
Direct loan VI AD – Byz.	ἀδιτίων (-ονος, ἡ) 'act of taking possession of an inheritance', from *aditiō* 'act of taking possession of an inheritance'. Literature: Just. *Nov.* in Latin script 1.1.4 etc. (VI AD); Ath.Schol. 9.1.2 etc. (VI AD); Antec. in Latin script 2.19.4 *aditionos* etc. (VI AD). Post-antique: common. *LBG*. Notes: Hofmann (1989: 7), Zilliacus (1935a: 172–3), Lampe (1961), *DGE*. See §4.2.5, §9.5.6 n. 68, §10.2.1, §10.2.2 B.
rare	ἀδμινιστρατίων, ἀδμινουστρατίων 'official rank or function', from *administrātiō* 'administration': Just. *Codex* 6.48.1.10 (VI AD); Byzantine texts. Avotins (1989), Zilliacus (1935a: 172–3), *LBG*, LSJ suppl. See §9.5.6 n. 68.
rare	ἀδμισσάριος 'for breeding' (of animals), from *admissārius* 'for breeding': Edict. Diocl. 32.4 (IV AD). Considered noun by LSJ suppl. and *DGE*, but acts like adjective. Hofmann (1989: 7).
rare	ἀδμισσιονάλιος, ἀμισσιωνάλιος, an official at the imperial court, from *admissionālis*, an official concerned with imperial audiences (*TLL*): Lyd. *Mag.* p. 110.14 (VI AD). Binder (2000: 222), *LBG*, Sophocles (1887). ἀδνατ-: see ἀδγνατ-.
Direct loan V–VI AD	ἀδνοτατίων, ἀδνωτατίων, ἀδνουτατίων (-ονος/-ωνος, ἡ) 'imperial decision on a petition', from *adnotātiō* 'note'. Documents: *SB* 9763.34 (V AD); *P.Münch.* 1.14.85 (VI AD); *P.Petra* III.29.155 (VI AD). Notes: Cervenka-Ehrenstrasser (1996: 51–2), Daris (1991a: 26), Zilliacus (1935a: 172–3), Meinersmann (1927: 6), *DGE*, LSJ suppl. See §4.2.5, §10.2.1, §10.2.2 A.
rare	ἀδνούμιον, ἀδνοῦμεν, ἀδγνούμιον 'muster', 'levy', probably from *ad nōmen* (*respondeō*) '(answer) to one's name', though some scholars (e.g. *TLL s.v. agnōmen* 1353.28, Lampe 1961) derive it from *agnōmen* 'surname' or from unattested **adnumium* 'muster' (Du Cange 1883–7): Ath.Schol. 4.11.2 (VI AD); common in Byzantine texts including papyri (with derivatives ἀδνουμεύω 'check', ἀδνουμιάζω 'muster', ἀδνουμιαστής 'inspector of troops'). Probably source of ἐνεραδνούμιον. Cervenka-Ehrenstrasser (1996: 52), Binder (2000: 222), Filos (2010: 251), Diethart (1998: 166), Daris (1991a: 26), Hofmann (1989: 4), Sophocles (1887), Triandaphyllidis (1909: 126), *LBG*, Kriaras (1968– *s.v.* ἀδνούμιν), *DGE*. ἀδνουτατίων, ἀδνωτατίων: see ἀδνοτατίων.

foreign	ἀδοπτίων 'adoption', from *adoptiō* 'adoption': Antec. in Latin script 1.11.1 *adoptiona* etc. (VI AD); later in Greek script. Hofmann (1989: 7), Zilliacus (1935a: 172–3), *LBG*, Triantaphyllides (1892: 256).
non-existent?	ἀδουέρτωρ, meaning uncertain, from unattested *advertor: cited as an ancient loan by Zilliacus (1935a: 174–5), but I can find no examples.
not ancient	ἀδουλτέριος 'adulterer', 'adulterous', from *adulter* 'adulterer': no ancient examples. Zilliacus (1935a: 172–3), *LBG* (*s.vv.* ἀδουλτερίη, ἀδουλτέριον).
rare	ἀδρεσπόνσουμ, ἀδρεσπόνσον, a title, from *ad respōnsum* (a title): Just. *Edict* 13.2 = p. 781.9 (VI AD); Ath.Schol. in Latin script 4.4.1 (VI AD). Lampe (1961) incorrectly defines it as 'machinery of torture'. Avotins (1992), Burgmann (1991: 69), Hofmann (1989: 8), *DGE*, LSJ suppl.
Direct loan **II–III AD**	Ἀδριανός (-οῦ, ὁ) 'Hadrian' (an Egyptian month), from the name *Hadriānus*. Documents: e.g. *BGU* I.88(p.106).2 (II AD); *BGU* I.275.5 (III AD). Inscriptions: *I.Thèbes Syène* 328.15 (II AD); *IGR* I.1204.7 (II AD). Notes: Scott (1931: 261–2), Bagnall (2009: 181), *DGE*, LSJ suppl. See §4.2.4.1 n. 51, §10.2.1, §10.2.2 E.
foreign	ἀδρογατίων, a type of adoption, from *arrogātiō/adrogātiō* 'adoption of a man not under a father or guardian's power': Antec. in Latin script 1.11.1 *adrogationa* etc. (VI AD); later in Greek script. Zilliacus (1935a: 172–3), *LBG*. See §9.5.6 n. 68.
foreign	ἀδρογάτωρ 'adopter by *arrogatio*', from *arrogātor/adrogātor* 'adopter by *arrogatio*': Antec. in Latin script 1.11.3 *adrogatora* etc. (VI AD); later in Greek script. Zilliacus (1935a: 172–3), *LBG*. See §9.5.6 n. 68.
foreign	*adsertor*, champion (*OLD s.v. assertor*): Antec. 4.10.pr. *adsertor* (VI AD).
	ἀδσηκρῆτις: see ἀσηκρῆτις.
foreign	ἀδσιγνατεύω 'designate a particular person to inherit the patronage of a freedman', from *assignātus* (pf. part. of *assignō/adsignō* 'assign') + -εύω: Antec. in Latin script 3.8.2 *adsignateuein* etc. (VI AD); later in Greek script. Zilliacus (1935a: 172–3), *LBG*. See §9.5.6 n. 68.
foreign	ἀδσιγνατίων 'designation of a particular person to inherit the patronage of a freedman', from *assignātiō/adsignātiō* 'assignment': Antec. in Latin script 3.8.pr. *adsignationos* etc. (VI AD); later in Greek script. Zilliacus (1935a: 172–3), *LBG*.
rare	ἀδωράτωρ 'retired soldier', from unattested *adōrātor: Lyd. *Mag.* p. 74.12, 14 (VI AD). Zilliacus (1935a: 216–17), *LBG*, *TLL* (*s.v.* 1. *adōrātor*). See §8.1.7.
foreign	ἀδωρέα transliterating *adōria/adōrea* 'glory': Lyd. *Mag.* p. 74.15 (VI AD). *LBG*.
foreign	*aeditor* 'person in charge of a temple' (rare; cf. *TLL s.v. aeditumor*): Antec. 1.13.2 *aeditores* (VI AD).
rare	ἀειουτώρειν 'medicine', from *adiūtōrium* 'medicine' (*TLL s.v.* 717.39–51) with influence from ἀεί 'always': ostracon *O.Claud.* II.408.5 (II AD).
semantic extension?	ἀερικόν 'tax on lights' may be connected to *ārea* 'open space' via ἀήρ. Hofmann (1989: 8 *s.v.* αηρ), Cameron (1931: 238), *LBG*, LSJ.

ἀεστιματίων: see αἰστιματίων.

semantic extension	**ἀήρ** 'air' is purely Greek in form, but the meaning 'space over a grave' may be influenced by *ārea* 'open space'. Drew-Bear (1972: 61–2), Hofmann (1989: 8), Cameron (1931: 238), *DÉLG*, Beekes (2010), LSJ, LSJ suppl. See §2.3.
Direct loan **II AD**	**αἶγροι** (-ων, οἱ) 'ill', from *aegrī*, nom. pl. of *aeger* 'ill'. Documents: *O.Claud.* IV.697.10, 698.15, 699.14 (all I/II AD); *O.Claud.* II.191.1, IV.721.7, probably II.192.1 (all II AD). Notes: only at Mons Claudianus. J. N. Adams (2003: 458, 607). See §4.2.4.1, §9.2, §10.2.1, §10.2.2 C.
foreign	**αἴδης** 'temple(s)', from *aedēs* 'temple': Lyd. *Mag.* p. 52.27, marked (VI AD); Antec. in Latin script 1.2.7 *aedes* (VI AD).
foreign	**αἰδίλης** 'aedile', from *aedīlis* 'aedile': inscriptions perhaps *SEG* VI.555.8 (II AD); restored on *I.North Galatia* 414.6 (III AD); Antec. in Latin script 1.2.7 *aediles* etc. (VI AD). Mason (1974: 6, 20), Hofmann (1989: 9), Zilliacus (1935a: 174–5), *DGE*, LSJ suppl.
rare	**αἰδιλίκιος** 'of the aediles', 'of the rank of aedile', from *aedīlicius* 'connected with aediles': Eutropius 5.9 (IV AD); Antec. in Latin script 3.18.2 *aediliciae* etc. (VI AD); occasionally later. Triantaphyllides (1892: 256) and Zilliacus (1935a: 174–5) incorrectly cite it as αἰδιλίτια with derivation from unattested *aedīlitia. LBG.*
not Latin	**αἴθριον** 'space open to the sky' (with diminutive **αἰθρίδιον**) is often claimed to be an adaptation of *ātrium* 'atrium' (LSJ and LSJ suppl. *s.v.* αἴθριος, Frisk 1954–72: 1.37, Beekes 2010 *s.v.* αἰθήρ, Filos 2019: 176, Hofmann 1989: 9, Sophocles 1887 *s.v.* αἴθριος), but since it occurs from III BC, it is probably neut. subst. of αἴθριος 'clear' without Latin influence: Chantraine (1964), Husson (1983: 30), Cervenka-Ehrenstrasser (1996: 117), *DGE*. See §2.3 n. 58; cf. ἄτριον.
foreign	**αἶκον** transliterating *aequum* 'level ground': DH *AR* 12.4.6 (I BC). Hofmann (1989: 9).

ἀϊούτωρ: see ἀδιούτωρ.

Direct loan **I–VI AD**	**αἰράριον, ἀράριον, ἐράριον** (-ου, τό) 'public treasury', from *aerārium* 'public treasury'. Documents: Pintaudi and Soldati 2021 line 3v (VI AD). Inscriptions: common, e.g. *Agora* XVI.337.10 etc. (I AD); *I.Ephesos* 5102.9 (II AD); *IG* XIV.911.B5 (III AD); *TAM* V.I.776.12 (IV AD). Notes: García Domingo (1979: 286), Mason (1974: 5, 12, 20, 138), Hofmann (1989: 118), *DGE*, LSJ suppl. See §4.1.1, §4.2.4.1 n. 54, §6.3 n. 22, §10.2.1, §10.2.2 D.
rare	**αἰράριος** 'citizen of the lowest class', from *aerārius* 'citizen of the lowest class': Dio Cassius 17.57.71 (II/III AD). Freyburger-Galland (1997: 216), Mason (1974: 20, with different definition), *DGE*, LSJ suppl.
rare	**αἰρίσφλως** and **χαλκοῦ φλοῦς** (in gen. χαλκοῦ φλοός), for *aeris flos* 'impure cuprous oxide' (*OLD s.v. flos* 4): *Hippiatr.Par.* (Apsyrtus) 354, 534 (III/IV AD?); n.b. also ἐρίφλος and ἐρίφας in apparatus to *Hippiatr.Berl.* 11.30, 96.19 (= Hoppe and Oder 1924–7: 1.67.24, 333.7). *DGE*.

not Latin   **αἰσός** 'god', probably from Etruscan: Hesych. as lemma α 2124 (V/VI AD). Hofmann (1989: 10).

not ancient   **αἰστιματίων, αἐστιματίων** 'evaluation', from *aestimātiō* 'evaluation': no ancient examples. Zilliacus (1935a: 174–5), *LBG*.

foreign   **αἰστιματόρια**, legal cases arising from objects entrusted for sale at a specified price, from *aestimātōrius* 'concerning the valuation of property': Antec. in Latin script 4.6.28 *aestimatoria* (VI AD); later in Greek script. *LBG*.

not ancient   **αἰστιμᾶτος, αἐστιμᾶτος** 'estimated', from *aestimātus*, pf. part. of *aestimō* 'estimate': no ancient examples. Zilliacus (1935a: 174–5), *LBG*.

not Latin?   **ἄϊτυρον**, lemma glossed ὕαλλον 'crystal', 'glass' in Hesych. α 2183 (V/VI AD), may be from *vitrum* 'glass' (cf. Hofmann 1989: 10) but is probably a corruption of λίγυρον or λιγύριον, a precious stone; the entry is perhaps taken from Septuagint Exodus 28:19 (Latte *ad loc.*). LSJ.

non-existent?   **αἰωνοκολλητίων** 'permanent military policeman', from αἰών 'age' + κολλητίων (and thus ultimately from whatever that word's Latin source is): perhaps papyrus *BGU* 1.23.6 (III AD), as a one-off creation with humorous intent. Cervenka-Ehrenstrasser (1996: 53–4), Diethart (1998: 166), *DGE*.

    ἀκεισκλ-: see ἀκισκλ-.

not Latin?   **ἀκελλεά** 'they stole', lemma (corrupt?) in Hesych. α 2315 (V/VI AD), may be from *cella* 'room' (presumably via κέλλα). Immisch (1885: 307–9), LSJ (*s.v.* ἀκέλλεα⟨ν⟩).

    ἀκεπτιλατίων: see ἀκκεπτιλατίων.

    ἄκεσσα: see ἄγεστα.

    ἀκεσ(σ)ίων: see ἀκκεσσίων.

not ancient?   **ἀκία** 'battle line', from *aciēs* 'edge', 'army': probably no ancient examples. Binder (2000: 256), Hofmann (1989: 10), Viscidi (1944: 12), Zilliacus (1935a: 216–17), *LBG*.

foreign   **ἀκιδοῦκτος** 'right to divert water from another person's land', from *aquīductus, -ūs* (*TLL s.v. aquae ductus* 364.42–5), variant of *aquaeductus* 'conveyance of water': Antec. in Latin script 2.3.pr. *aquaeductus* etc. (VI AD); later in Greek script. Sophocles (1887), Triandaphyllidis (1909: 124).

not ancient   **ἀκίκουλα** transliterating *acucula/acicula*, a plant (*TLL s.v.* 456.18–21): interpolation in Dsc. 2.138 RV. Binder (2000: 163, 174), Sophocles (1887).

not Latin   **ἄκινος** 'wild basil' has been implausibly connected with *acinus* 'berry'. Hofmann (1989: 11), *DGE*, LSJ.

    ἀκιπήσιος: see ἀκκιπήσιος.

Direct loan
II AD

ἀκισκλάριος, ἀκεισκλάριος (-ου, ὁ) 'stonemason', from *acisculārius* 'worker with an adze'.
Documents: *O.Claud.* often, e.g. 1.15.3, 1.23.2, 1.132.4 (all I/II or II AD).
Notes: only at Mons Claudianus. Cervenka-Ehrenstrasser (1996: 55, but many more examples have since emerged), Diethart (1998: 166), *DGE*. See §4.2.4.1 n. 50, §9.2, §10.2.1, §10.2.2 J.

rare

ἀκίσκλη, ἀκίσκλα 'chisel' or 'adze', from *acisculus*, a cutting tool (*TLL*): papyrus *BGU* IV.1028.2.12 etc. (II AD). Perhaps a variant of or mistake for ἀκίσκλος, *q.v.* (cf. Cervenka-Ehrenstrasser 1996: 56); the feminine gender could be due to influence from ἀκίς, ἀκίδος 'pointed object', 'chisel'. Cervenka-Ehrenstrasser (1996: 54), Binder (2000: 157), Diethart (1998: 166), Daris (1991a: 26 *s.v.* ἀκίσκλον), Cavenaile (1951: 395 *s.v.* ἄκισκλον), *DGE*, LSJ, LSJ suppl.

Direct loan
II AD

ἀκίσκλος, ἀκεῖσκλος (-ου, ὁ) 'adze', 'iron part of a mill', from *acisculus*, a cutting tool (*TLL*).
Documents: meaning 'adze': *O.Claud.* IV.824.2 (I/II AD), 1.132.2 (II AD), perhaps IV.759.6 (II AD), perhaps IV.801.1 (II AD). Meaning 'iron part of a mill': *O.Krok.* 1.14.4, marked (II AD).
Notes: Cervenka-Ehrenstrasser (1996: 55–6), *O.Claud.* IV p. 251, *DGE*. See §4.1.1 n. 8, §4.2.4.1 n. 51, §9.2, §10.2.1, §10.2.2 J.

foreign

ἀκ(κ)επτιλατίων 'oral acknowledgement of receipt', from *acceptilātiō* 'formal verbal release from an obligation': Antec. in Latin script 3.29.1 *acceptilation* etc. (VI AD); often later in Greek script. Zilliacus (1935a: 172–3), *LBG*. See §7.2.2 passage 29, §9.5.6 n. 68.

rare

ἄκκεπτον 'income', from *acceptum* 'receipts': Ignat. *Ep.* 7.6.2 (I/II AD), repeated in a spurious letter. Lampe (1961 *s.v.* ἄκκεπτα) defines 'money placed to the credit of a soldier and paid out to him on discharge', but Hofmann (1989: 11) argues for 'heavenly gift'. Sophocles (1887), *DGE* (*s.v.* ἄκκεπτα).

foreign

ἀκ(κ)εσ(σ)ίων 'addition', from *accessiō* 'addition': Antec. in Latin script 3.20.5 *accession* etc. (VI AD); later in Greek script. Zilliacus (1935a: 172–3), *LBG* (*s.v.* ἀκεσίων). See §9.5.6 n. 68.

foreign

ἀκκῆσσος, ἀκκῆνσος transliterating *accēnsus* 'supernumerary' (a title): Latinate inscriptions. Mason (1974: 4, 20), Cameron (1931: 237), Hofmann (1989: 11–12), LSJ suppl.

rare

ἀκ(κ)ιπήσιος, ἀκυιπῆνσερ 'sturgeon', from *acipēnser* 'sturgeon': Athenaeus 7.294f, marked (II/III AD); Lyd. *Mag.* pp. 8.25, 232.13, marked (VI AD); with *accipiens* (for *accipenser*?) in Gloss. *Herm.M.* 186.50. Hofmann (1989: 12), *LBG*, *DGE*, LSJ.

ἀκκουβίζω: see ἀκκουμβίζω.

non-existent

ἀκκουβίκυλον 'dining room', from unattested **accubiculum*: probably not papyrus *P.Oxy.* 2058.25 (VI AD). Cervenka-Ehrenstrasser (1996: 129), Diethart (1998: 166), Daris (1991a: 26, with derivation from *cubiculum* 'bedroom'), LSJ suppl.

Direct loan
IV AD – Byz.

ἀκ(κ)ουβιτάλιον, ἀκκουβιτάριον (-ου, τό) 'couch cover', from *accubitāle* 'couch cover' (*TLL*).

Documents: *P.Oxy.* 3860.18 (IV AD); *O.Trim.* II.531.8 (IV AD); *P.Berl.Sarisch.* 21.46 (V/VI AD); *P.Berl.Zill.* 13.4 (VI AD); perhaps *SB* 15249.5 (VI AD).

Post-antique: some survival in papyri.

Notes: Cervenka-Ehrenstrasser (1996: 56), Diethart (1990b: 193–4, 1998: 166, 2002: 148), Daris (1991a: 26), *DGE* (*s.v.* ἀκκουβιτάλιος), LSJ suppl. (*s.v.* ἀκκουβιτάλια). See §4.1.1 n. 15, §4.2.5, §4.4 n. 79, §8.2.2, §9.2, §10.2.1, §10.2.2 H.

rare

ἀκκουβιτάριος, ἀκκουβιτάλιος 'of or for a couch', from *accubitālis* 'for a couch' (*TLL s.v. accubitāle*): Edict.Diocl. 19.34 (IV AD); perhaps papyrus *SB* 15249.5 (VI AD). Cervenka-Ehrenstrasser (1996: 57), Hofmann (1989: 12), *TLL* (*s.v. accubitāle*), *DGE* (*s.v.* ἀκκουβιτάλιος), LSJ suppl. (*s.v.* ἀκκουβιτᾶρις).

rare

ἀκ(κ)ουβίτιον, apparently from *accubitum* 'semi-circular dining couch' (*TLL*) via ἀκκούβιτον + -ιον: papyrus *SB* 14625.11 (V/VI AD), where Cervenka-Ehrenstrasser (1996: 57–8) suggests a meaning 'bed', 'couch'; inscription *MAMA* VI.84, where LSJ suppl. suggests a meaning 'dining room'. Diethart (1998: 166), Daris (1991a: 26), *DGE*.

Direct loan
III AD – Byz.

ἀκ(κ)ούβιτον, ἀκούμβιτον (-ου, τό) 'couch', 'dining room', 'bedroom', from *accubitum* 'semi-circular dining couch' (*TLL*).

Documents: e.g. *PSI* III.225.5 (VI AD); *P.Münch.* I.8.13 (VI AD); *P.Lond.* V.1724.30 (VI AD).

Literature: *Act.Xanth.Polyx.* 13, 17 (III AD); Ps.-Athanasius, *PG* XXVIII.805d (IV AD?); *Historia Alexandri Magni* rec. β 1.21.7 Bergson (V AD); Jo.Scholast. 3 p. 146.7 (VI AD).

Post-antique: common. Sophocles (1887), Triandaphyllidis (1909: 120).

Notes: spelling with μ (rare, only in literature) shows influence from ἀκκουμβίζω and in Byzantine texts means 'couch cover' (cf. Ps.-Zonaras α 110.22). Forms derivative ἀκκουβίτιον. Cervenka-Ehrenstrasser (1996: 58–9), Husson (1983: 36–7, 1990: 125), Diethart (1998: 166–7), Binder (2000: 140), Daris (1991a: 26), Hofmann (1989: 12–13 *s.v.* ἀκκουβιτος), Meinersmann (1927: 6), Lampe (1961), *DGE*, LSJ suppl. See §4.2.4.1 n. 55, §9.2, §10.2.1, §10.2.2 M.

rare

ἀκκούβιτος 'couch', from *accubitus, -ūs* 'couch' (*TLL*): Edict.Diocl. 19.34 (IV AD); LSJ suppl. also assigns to this heading an occurrence meaning 'bedroom' on papyrus *BGU* XII.2202.19 (VI AD), which Cervenka-Ehrenstrasser (1996: 59) and Daris (1991a: 26) take as belonging to neuter ἀκκούβιτον. Diethart (1998: 167), Hofmann (1989: 12–13), Triandaphyllidis (1909: 126), *TLL* (*s.v. accubitus* 339.6), *DGE*.

not ancient?

ἀκ(κ)ου(μ)βίζω, ἀκ(κ)ούμβω, ἀκ(κ)ουμπίζω, ἀκ(κ)ούμπω 'recline at table', from *accumbō* 'recline': *V.Aesopi* G 40 (II AD?); common in Byzantine texts. Zervan (2019: 265) dates borrowing to VII AD, but if it is source of συνακουμβίζω it is older. Modern ακουμπώ 'touch': Babiniotis (2002), Andriotis (1967). Hofmann (1989: 13), Meyer (1895: 9–10), Triandaphyllidis (1909: 123), Zervan (2019: 9), *LBG* (*s.vv.* ἀκουμβίζω, ἀκούμβω), Kriaras (1968– *s.vv.* ἀκουμπίζω, ἀκουμπῶ), Lampe (1961 *s.v.* ἀκουμβίζω), *DGE*, LSJ suppl.

rare
ἀκμινάλιον, ἀκμινάλιος 'baggage animal', from *agminālis* 'of the army' (*TLL*): papyrus *P.Oxy.* 3741v.45 (IV AD). Cervenka-Ehrenstrasser (1996: 59–60), Daris (1991a: 26), LSJ suppl.

ἀκοά: see ἄκουα.

ἀκοάριος: see ἀκουάριος.

Direct loan with univerbation and influence IV AD
ἀκομενταρήσιος, ἀκομεντανήσιος (-ου, ὁ), 'official in charge of public records', from *ā commentāriīs* 'official in charge of records' (*TLL s.v. ā, ab* 23.21) with influence from κομμενταρήσιος.
Documents: *SB* 2253.12 (III/IV AD); *O.Ashm.Shelt.* 73.2 (III/IV AD?); *P.Harr.* 1.94.7 (IV AD); *SB* 11591.26, 11592.24 (both IV AD); perhaps *CPR* VI.61.3 (IV AD).
Inscriptions: *IGR* III.1264.1.
Post-antique: no evidence unless late date accepted for *O.Ashm.Shelt.* 73 (cf. *LBG*).
Notes: common spelling ἀκομεντανήσιος shows it spread within Greek. Inscription *IGR* III.275.1 has ἀπὸ κομενταρηνσίων, a different approach to the same Latin. Cervenka-Ehrenstrasser (1996: 60–1), Filos (2006: 49–50, 2010: 252), Daris (1991a: 26, with derivation from *commentariensis*), Mason (1974: 62), *DGE*, LSJ suppl. See §4.2.3.2 n. 47, §4.4, §4.5, §6.7, §10.2.1, §10.2.2 D.

rare
ἄκουα, ἀκοά 'water', from *aqua* 'water': inscription *IG* IV².1.126.10 etc. (II AD); Lyd. *Mens.* 4.46.3–6, marked (VI AD); *aqua* in Latin script as part of legal phrases e.g. Antec. 1.16.2 *aqua et igni interdictos* 'banished man', 2.3.2 *aquaehaustum* 'right to get water on another person's land' (VI AD); Just. *Nov.* 22.13 *aqua et igni interdictiona* (VI AD). Hofmann (1989: 13), Sophocles (1887), *DGE* (*s.v.* ἀκοαί). See §7.2.1; cf. ἀκιδοῦκτος.

Direct loan II AD
ἀκο(υ)άριος (-ου, ὁ) 'water-carrier', from *aquārius* 'water-carrier'.
Documents: e.g. *O.Claud.* II.212.10, IV.708.15, IV.803.3 (all I/II or II AD).
Notes: only at Mons Claudianus. Cervenka-Ehrenstrasser (1996: 61–2, when most examples were still unknown), Diethart (1998: 167), *DGE*. See §4.2.4.1 n. 50, §8.2.1, §9.2, §10.2.1, §10.2.2 K.

ἀκουβ-: see ἀκκουβ-.

Ἄκουος: see Αὔγουστος.

Direct loan I AD – Byz.
ἄκτα (-ων, τά), **ἄκτον** (-ου, τό) 'acts', 'official records', also a title, from *āctum* 'act'.
Documents: *P.Oxy.* 2725.21 (I AD); *O.Krok.* 1.1.44 etc. (II AD); *SB* 17079.4 (II AD); *P.Yadin* 1.12.1 etc. (II AD); probably *P.Ryl.* IV.625.3 (IV AD).
Inscriptions: *I.Tralleis* 80.13 (II AD); *IG* XIV.830.20 (II AD); *I.Pergamon Asklepieion* 24.7 (II/III AD); perhaps *SEG* XXXVII.1501 (II/III AD); *TAM* IV.1.39.3 (III AD); *MAMA* VIII.584.
Literature: e.g. Justin Martyr, *Apologia prima* 35.9 Minns and Parvis (II AD); *Martyrium Apollonii* 12 in Musurillo 1972 (II–IV AD); Epiph. *Pan.* II.246.4 (IV AD); Malal. 18.29 (VI AD).
Post-antique: common. *LBG*, Triandaphyllidis (1909: 127).
Notes: Cervenka-Ehrenstrasser (1996: 62), Daris (1991a: 26), Mason (1974: 5, 8, 20, 141), Hofmann (1989: 14), Zilliacus (1935a: 172–3, 1937: 328), *DGE*, LSJ suppl. See §4.2.4.1 n. 55, §10.2.1, §10.2.2 B.

ἀκτάριος: see ἀκτουάριος.

foreign   ἀκτίων '(legal) action', from *āctiō* 'action': in Latin script in sixth-century legal texts (e.g. Just. *Nov.* 81.pr.; Antec. 4.6.pr. *actionas*); later in Greek script. Zilliacus (1935a: 172–3), *LBG*.

ἄκτον: see ἄκτα.

Direct loan
II AD – Byz.   ἀκτο(υ)άριος, ἀκτάριος, ἀκτωάριος, ἀκτούριος, ἀγτουάριος, ἀκτουάρης (-ου, ὁ) 'keeper of records', 'paymaster', from *āctuārius* 'keeper of records'.
Documents: common, e.g. *P.Berl.Leihg.* II.39r.112 (II AD); *P.Panop.Beatty* 1.46 (III AD); *P.Abinn.* 10.13 (IV AD); *SB* 16723r.4 (V AD); *P.Münch.* I.12.56 (VI AD).
Inscriptions: *SEG* XLII.649 (III AD); *IGBulg.* III.II.1835.a2 (III AD); *IGBulg.* III.II.1774.4; *SEG* XXXIV.1562c.3; *CIG* 4004.1; *I.Syringes* 1879.2.
Literature: Just. *Codex* 1.42.2.2, *Nov.* 117.11 (VI AD); Ath.Schol. 10.9.12 (VI AD).
Post-antique: common. *LBG*, Zervan (2019: 9–10), Triandaphyllidis (1909: 126).
Notes: Cervenka-Ehrenstrasser (1996: 63–6), Avotins (1989, 1992), Daris (1991a: 26–7), Mason (1974: 4, 20), Hofmann (1989: 13), Zilliacus (1935a: 172–3, 216–17), Meinersmann (1927: 6), Lampe (1961), *DGE*, LSJ suppl. See §4.2.4.1 n. 50, §10.2.1, §10.2.2 D.

foreign   ἄκτους 'right of way for a beast of burden or vehicle', from *āctus, -ūs* 'right of way': Antec. in Latin script 2.3.pr. *actus* etc. (VI AD); later in Greek script. Byzantine ἄκτος 'wagon' (*LBG*) is a separate borrowing of *āctus*. Triantaphyllides (1892: 256).

foreign   ἄκτωρ, in origin a purely Greek word meaning 'leader' (LSJ), died out and in V AD was re-created from *āctor* to mean 'plaintiff', 'person responsible for a legal action': Thüngen 2016: B11 etc. in Latin script (V AD); Antec. 4.11.3, marked, and often in Latin script, e.g. 4.6.39 *actora* (VI AD). *LBG*, Zilliacus (1935a: 172–3), Triantaphyllides (1892: 256). A different Latinate usage on inscription *I.Ephesos* 2245.2 (Mason 1974: 20, Hofmann 1989: 14; *DGE* online version only). See §9.5.6 n. 68.

ἀκυιπῆνσερ: see ἀκκιπήσιος.

not Latin?   ἀκυλεής 'eagle', perhaps from *aquila* 'eagle': Hesych. as lemma α 2687 (V/VI AD). Immisch (1885: 321), *DGE*, LSJ.

not Latin   ἀκύλινον 'abortion': probably not from *aquilīnus* 'of an eagle'. Cervenka-Ehrenstrasser (1996: 127).

non-existent?   αλ, tentatively suggested by Hofmann (1989: 14) as transcription of *al(lectus)*, pf. part. of *alliciō* 'attract': I can find no examples.

ἄλα: see ἄλη.

non-existent   ἀλάριος, from *ālārius* 'of the auxiliary cavalry': superseded reading for [σινγ]-λάριος on inscription *IG* X.II.1.583.2 (III AD). Hofmann (1989: 15).

not ancient?   ἀλβάριος 'plasterer', from *albārius* 'worker in stucco': inscription *IG* XIV.2271.3. Hofmann (1989: 15), LSJ.

foreign	**ἀλβᾶτοι** transliterating *albātī*, the 'white' circus faction: Lyd. *Mens.* 4.30.18 (VI AD). Hofmann (1989: 16), *DGE*.
not ancient	**ἀλβῖνος, ἀλβίνους** transliterating *albīnus* 'white', a plant (*TLL*): interpolation in Dsc. 3.117 RV. Sophocles (1887), *TLL* (*s.v. albīnus*).
non-existent?	**ἀλβόμαυρος** 'grey', from *albus* 'white' + μαῦρος 'black': perhaps papyrus *CPR* v.26.929 (V AD). Cervenka-Ehrenstrasser (1996: 129), Diethart (1998: 167), Daris (1991a: 27), *LBG* (*s.v.* ἀλβόμαυρον), LSJ suppl. (*s.v.* ἀλβόμαυρον).
foreign	**ἄλβον** 'edict', from *albus* 'white' (edicts being written in white): Antec. in Latin script 4.6.12 *albi, albu, albon* (VI AD); later in Greek script. Zilliacus (1935a: 174–5).
foreign	**ἄλβος** 'white (circus faction)', from *albus* 'white': curse tablet Audollent 1904: no. 235.19 etc., Latinate (II/III AD); numerous interpolations in Dsc. Hofmann (1989: 16), *LBG*.
not ancient	**ἀλβούκιουμ** transliterating *albūcum* 'asphodel': interpolations in Dsc. 1.91.6 RV, 2.169.1 RV. Sophocles (1887).
rare	**ἀλγενήσιος** 'coloured with seaweed', apparently from *algēnsis* 'living on seaweed': Edict.Diocl. 24.9 (IV AD). Lauffer (1971: 271), Sophocles (1887), *DGE*, LSJ suppl.
	ἀλειμέντα: see ἀλιμέντα.
non-existent	**ἀλεκτόριον, ἀλλεκτόριον** 'reading room', perhaps from *lēctor* 'reader', is no longer thought to exist, and ἀλεκτόριον 'poultry-yard' has a Greek etymology. Wilhelm (1928b: 229–30), Hofmann (1989: 16), LSJ, LSJ suppl.; cf. *LBG* for another meaning, 'cockerel'.
Direct loan I AD – Byz.	**ἄλη, ἄλα** (-ης, ἡ) 'squadron', from *āla* 'squadron'. Documents: e.g. *P.Lips.* II.133.4 (I AD); *BGU* I.4.10 (II AD); *BGU* II.623.5 (II/III AD); *O.Douch.* V.555.2 (IV/V AD). Inscriptions: e.g. *IG* XII.VI.II.821.3 (I AD); *I.Ephesos* 680.12 (II AD); *I.Tomis* 106.10 (III AD). Literature: Lyd. *Mag.* p. 70.5 (VI AD). Post-antique: survives. *LBG*. Notes: partly replaced by ἴλη in II AD (Ghiretti 1996: 280, 291). Cervenka-Ehrenstrasser (1996: 66–7), Diethart (1998: 167), Daris (1991a: 27), Mason (1974: 5, 20, 138), Hofmann (1989: 15), Viscidi (1944: 12), Zilliacus (1935a: 142, 216–17), Meinersmann (1927: 6), *DGE* (*s.v.* ἄλα 2), LSJ suppl. See §4.1.1, §4.2.3.1, §10.2.1, §10.2.2 C.
foreign	**ἀλιενονόμινε, ἀλιενόμινε** 'taking legal action in someone else's name', from *aliēnō nōmine* 'in someone else's name': Antec. in Latin script 4.10.pr. *alieno nomine* etc. (VI AD); later in Greek script.
not Latin?	**ἀλίκιον** is diminutive of ἄλιξ 2 (*q.v.*). Cervenka-Ehrenstrasser (1996: 127–8), LSJ suppl.
rare	**ἀλίκλα**, a garment, from *ālicula* 'light cloak' (itself from ἄλλιξ 'cloak'): papyri perhaps *SB* 15922.3 etc. (II/III AD); *SB* 9834b.10 (III/IV AD). Cervenka-Ehrenstrasser (1996: 67–8), Binder (2000: 157–8), Diethart (1998: 167), Daris (1991a: 27), Hofmann (1989: 17), *DGE*, LSJ suppl.

Direct? loan with suffix
II–III AD

ἀλίκλιον, ἀλίκλειον, ἀλλίκλιν, ἀρίκλιον (-ου, τό), a garment, from *ālicula* 'light cloak' (itself from ἄλιξ 'cloak'), perhaps via ἀλίκλα, + -ιον.
Documents: unpublished O.Xer. inv. 1076.8 (II AD); unpublished O.Xer. 97 frag. B.3 (II AD); unpublished O.Dios inv. 747.12 (II AD); perhaps *SB* 15922.3 etc. (II/III AD); *P.Col.* X.279.2 (III AD).
Notes: the examples in *SB* 15922 are abbreviated from either this or ἀλίκλα. Cervenka-Ehrenstrasser (1996: 68), Diethart (1998: 167), *DGE* (*s.v.* ἀλίκλιν). See §4.3.2 n. 69, §10.2.1, §10.2.2 H.

Direct loan
II–III AD

ἀλιμέντα, ἀλειμέντα (-ων, τά) 'provisions' (as responsibility of an official), 'maintenance allowance', from *alimenta*, plural of *alimentum* 'provisions'.
Inscriptions (meaning 'provisions'): *I.Callatis* 114.7 (II AD); *TAM* II.278.11 (I–III AD); *I.Ephesos* 805.6 (III AD).
Literature (meaning 'maintenance allowance'): Antec. in Latin script 1.26.9 *alimenta* etc. (VI AD).
Post-antique (meaning 'maintenance allowance'): common in legal texts. *LBG*.
Notes: the two meanings are probably separate borrowings. Mason (1974: 5, 20, 138), Hofmann (1989: 16), Zilliacus (1935a: 174–5), *DGE*, LSJ suppl. See §4.2.4.1 n. 55, §10.2.1, §10.2.2 I.

not ancient

ἀλιμεντάριος 'person supported by a charity', from *alimentārius* 'person supported by a charity': no ancient examples. Zilliacus (1935a: 174–5), *LBG*.

Direct loan
II AD – ?

ἄλιξ 1, ἄλ(λ)ηξ (ἄλικος/ἀλ(λ)ηκος, ὁ) 'fish sauce', from *hallēc/hallēx* 'fish sauce'.
Documents: *SB* 15453.6 (II AD); unpublished O.Max. inv. 1376.3, 1512.1 (both II AD).
Post-antique: not in lexica, but in *Geoponica* 20.46.2.
Notes: spelled ἄλιξ by modern scholars, but in documents always ἄλ(λ)ηξ. *DÉLG*, Beekes (2010), *DGE* (*s.v.* 1 ἄλιξ), LSJ suppl. (*s.v.* ἄλιξ B, replacing LSJ *s.v.* ἄλιξ II). See §4.2.5 n. 63, §10.2.1, §10.2.2 I.

not Latin?

ἄλιξ 2 'groats of rice-wheat' must be related to *alica* 'emmer groats' but need not be derived from it (despite Ps.-Herodian, *Philetaerus* 139 Dain χόνδρον οἱ Ἀττικοί· τὸ δὲ ἄλιξ Ἰταλιωτικὸν ὄνομα). Cervenka-Ehrenstrasser (1996: 127), Lauffer (1971: 216), *DÉLG*, Frisk (1954–72: 1.73), Beekes (2010), *DGE* (*s.v.* 2 ἄλιξ), LSJ, LSJ suppl. (*s.vv.* ἀλίκιον, ἄλιξ I).

non-existent

ἄλιξ 3 'water channel', perhaps from *ēlix* 'furrow made to drain off water': superseded emendation of Hesych. ι 559. Hofmann (1989: 17).

foreign

aliud 'mistaking one thing for another', from *alius* 'other': Antec. in Latin script 4.6.35 *aliud* (VI AD).

not Latin

ἀλλᾶς, a type of sausage, and derivatives ἀλλαντοειδής 'sausage-shaped', ἀλλαντοποιός 'sausage-maker', ἀλλαντοπωλέω 'sell sausages', ἀλλαντοπώλης 'sausage-seller', perhaps related to Latin *ālium* 'garlic' but probably not derived from it. Wackernagel (1916: 197), *DÉLG*, Frisk (1954–72: 1.75), Beekes (2010), Hofmann (1989: 17), *DGE*, LSJ.

rare

ἀλληλομανδάτορες 'reciprocal guarantors', from ἀλλήλων 'of each other' + *mandātor* 'guarantor' via μανδάτωρ: papyrus *P.Hamb.* I.23.7 (VI AD). Cervenka-Ehrenstrasser (1996: 68–9), Filos (2010: 249), Daris (1991a: 27), *DGE*, LSJ.

not Latin?	**ἄλλην**, a vegetable, from *ālium* 'garlic' or a related Oscan word: Hesych. α 3137 (V/VI AD), calling it Italian ('Ἰταλοί). Hofmann (1989: 18), Immisch (1885: 307), *DGE* (*s.v.* 2 ἄλλην), LSJ. See §2.1 n. 5.
	ἄλληξ: see ἄλιξ 1.
foreign	**ἀλλιγᾶρε** transliterating inf. of *alligō* 'bind': Plut. *Rom.* 26.3, *Mor.* 280a (I/II AD). Sophocles (1887), *DGE*.
not ancient	**ἄλ(λ)ιουμ** transliterating *ālium* 'garlic': interpolations in Dsc. 2.152 RV. Sophocles (1887).
foreign	**ἀλ(λ)ουβίων** 'gradual increase of land as a result of deposits from a river', from *alluviō* 'alluvial deposits': Antec. in Latin script 2.1.20 *alluvionos* etc. (VI AD); later in Greek script. Zilliacus (1935a: 174–5), *LBG*, Sophocles (1887).
not ancient?	**ἄλμα** transliterating fem. of *almus* 'nourishing': Philostorgius, *Historia ecclesiastica*, frag. ap. Photium 2.9.9 Winkelmann, frag. e vita Constantini 2.9a.38 Winkelmann. Sophocles (1887).
not ancient	**ἀλόαμ** transliterating acc. of *aloē/aloa* 'aloe' (*TLL*), itself from ἀλόη: interpolation in Dsc. 3.22 RV. Sophocles (1887 *s.v.* ἄλοα).
foreign	**ἀλοῦμεν** transliterating *alūmen*, an astringent chemical: Lyd. *Mag.* p. 48.17 (VI AD). Sophocles (1887).
foreign	**ἀλοῦμνος** and **ἀλοῦμνα** 'foster child', from *alumnus* and *alumna* 'foster child': Antec. in Latin script 1.6.5 *alumnos, alumna* (VI AD); inscriptions *IGUR* II.793.4, Latinate; *IGPorto* 28.5, Latinate; Byzantine texts. Zilliacus (1935a: 174–5), *LBG*, Triantaphyllides (1892: 256), *DGE*.
foreign	**ἀλοῦτα** transliterating *alūta* 'piece of soft leather': Lyd. *Mag.* p. 48.16 (VI AD). *LBG*.
rare	**ἀλτάριον** 'altar', from *altārium* 'altar' (*TLL s.v.* altāria 1725.24–5): Anton.Hag. *V.Sym.Styl.* 29.22 (V AD); Byzantine texts. Hofmann (1989: 19), *LBG*, Zervan (2019: 11), Lampe (1961).
non-existent	**ἀλτάριος**, from unattested *altārius 'of altars': superseded reading for ⟨σ⟩αλτάριοι on inscription *IGBulg.* IV.2319.2 (III AD). Hofmann (1989: 19).
foreign	**ἀλτερνατίων** 'alternative', from *alternātiō* 'alternative': Antec. in Latin script 4.6.33d *alternation* etc. (VI AD); later in Greek script. Zilliacus (1935a: 174–5), *LBG*. See §9.5.6 n. 68.
rare	**ἀλύσαθρον**, plant name from *holus atrum*: Hippiatr.Berl. 22.18, Appendix 8. *LBG*.
not Latin	**ἀλφός** 'white' is cited by Sophocles (1887) as from *albus* 'white' on the basis of Hesych. α 3344 (V/VI AD) ἀλφούς· λευκούς, which is probably Greek ἀλφός 'leprosy'. *DÉLG*, Beekes (2010), *DGE*, LSJ.
	ἀμαξιλλάριος: see μαξιλλάριος.
not Latin?	**ἀμᾶρον, ἀμᾶρων**, perhaps 'bitter thing', perhaps from *amārus* 'bitter': papyrus *P.Rain.UnterrichtKopt.* 256.245 (VI AD). Cervenka-Ehrenstrasser (1996: 69). Cf. μαρούλιον.

foreign	Ἀμβαρουία transliterating *Ambarvālia*, a festival: Strabo 5.3.2.65 (I BC/AD). Hofmann (1989: 19). Ἀμβιανήσιος: see Ἀνβιανήσιος.
rare	ἀμβιτεύω 'seek public service', 'solicit', 'intrigue for', from *ambitus, -ūs* 'going around' or *ambītus* (pf. part. of *ambiō* 'canvass') + -εύω: papyrus *P.Oxy.* 2110.15 (IV AD); Pall. *V.Chrys.* 61.9 (IV/V AD); occasional Byzantine texts. Cervenka-Ehrenstrasser (1996: 69–70), Brunner (1988), Mandilaras (1973: 67), Daris (1991a: 27), Hofmann (1989: 20 *s.v.* ἀμβίτους), Cavenaile (1951: 395), *LBG*, Lampe (1961), *DGE*, LSJ suppl.
non-existent	ἀμβιτιάω 'strive for an office', from *ambītus* (pf. part. of *ambiō* 'canvass') + -άω (?): probably not Hesych. as lemma α 3502 (V/VI AD). The form there is ἀμβιτιῶν, which *DGE* sees as noun ἀμβιτίων and Immisch (1885: 350) claims is evidence for unattested *ambitāre. LBG*.
rare	ἀμβιτιονάριος, ἀββιτιονάριος 'plotter', from *ambitiō* 'ambition' via ἀμβιτίων + -άριος: Harrauer and Pintaudi 2003: 140.14. Cervenka-Ehrenstrasser (1996: 71).
rare	ἀμβιτιονεύω 'strive', from *ambitiō* 'ambition' via ἀμβιτίων + -εύω: *ACO* II.I.II p. 58.26 (V AD). *LBG*.
rare	ἀμβιτίων 'ambition', from *ambitiō* 'ambition': often in records of V AD church councils (*ACO* II.I.II pp. 57.36, 58.23, 59.21, 60.19, etc.) but almost never elsewhere. Source of ἀμβιτιονάριος and ἀμβιτιονεύω. For ἀμβιτιῶν in Hesych. α 3502 see ἀμβιτιάω. Hofmann (1989: 20), *LBG*, Lampe (1961, citing letters of Cyril of Alexandria quoted in records of the church councils), *DGE* (with incorrect masculine gender).
not ancient?	ἀμβίτους 'corruption', from *ambitus, -ūs* 'going around', 'corruption': no certainly ancient examples. Hofmann (1989: 20), Zilliacus (1935a: 174–5).
foreign	ἄμβλα μοῦλα transliterating *ambulā mūla* 'go, mule!' (a veterinary treatment): *Hippiatr.Berl.* 130.13. *LBG*. Cf. μοῦλα.
rare	ἀμβλατώριος '(portico) for walking', from *ambulātōrius* 'for walking': *I.Ephesos* 437.2. Binder (2000: 186–7). ἀμβ(ο)ῦλλα: see ἀμποῦλλα.
non-existent	ἀμήνιον, suggested as from *minium* 'bright red colour' by Sophocles (1887): no convincing examples.
Direct loan **II–IV AD**	ἀμικτώριον, ἀμικτόριον, ἀμικτώρειον (-ου, τό) 'shawl', 'scarf', 'covering', from *amictorium* 'shawl', 'scarf'. Documents: *BGU* XIII.2351.7 (II AD); *P.Eleph.Wagner* 1.98.2 (II AD); *SB* 9568.2 (II/III AD); *SB* 9238.17, 12594.16 (both III AD); *P.Fay.* 103.2 (III AD); *P.Oxy.* 1535v.8 (III AD); *P.Meyer* 22.10 (III/IV AD). Notes: forms derivative λεπταμικτόριον. Cervenka-Ehrenstrasser (1996: 72), Daris (1991a: 27), Hofmann (1989: 20), Meinersmann (1927: 6), *DGE*, LSJ suppl. See §4.2.4.1 n. 54, §9.2, §10.2.1, §10.2.2 H. ἄμιουμ: see ἄμμιουμ.

foreign | ἄμιτα 'paternal aunt', from *amita* 'paternal aunt': Antec. in Latin script 1.10.5 *amitan* etc. (VI AD). Zilliacus (1935a: 174–5), Sophocles (1887). See §7.1.1.

foreign | ἀμιτῖνος 'cousin', from *amitīnus* 'cousin': Antec. in Latin script 3.6.4 *amitini* etc. (VI AD). Zilliacus (1935a: 174–5).

not ancient | ἄμ(μ)ιουμ probably transliterating *ami*, a plant: interpolation in Dsc. 3.62 RV. Sophocles (1887).

Direct loan III AD – Byz.? | ἀμπ(ο)ῦλλα, ἀμβ(ο)ῦλλα, ἀνπ(ο)ῦλλα, ἀνπύλλη, ἀμπύλλη (-ης, ἡ) 'flask', from *ampulla* 'flask'.
Documents: *P.Oxy.* 3993.8 (II/III AD); *BGU* I.40.2 (II/III AD); *P.Kellis* IV.96.1261 (IV AD).
Literature: Aëtius 7.101.15, 18 (VI AD).
Post-antique: some survival. *LBG*. Modern αμπούλα 'small bottle' is probably from a Romance language: Babiniotis (2002), Andriotis (1967), but note Meyer (1895: 10 *s.v.* ἄμουλα).
Notes: forms derivative ἀμπυλλάριον. Cervenka-Ehrenstrasser (1996: 72–3), Palmer (1945: 65), Daris (1991a: 27), Hofmann (1989: 20–1), Meinersmann (1927: 7), *DGE* (*s.v.* ἀμπύλλη), LSJ suppl. (*s.v.* ἄμπυλλα). See §4.3.2, §5.2.1, §10.2.1, §10.2.2 M.

not ancient | ἀμπουλλάκια transliterating *ampullācea*, a plant (*TLL s.v. ampullāceus*): interpolation in Dsc. 1.91 RV. Sophocles (1887), *DGE*.

Direct loan with suffix II–IV AD | ἀμπούλ(λ)ιον, ἀβούλιν (-ου, τό) 'flask', from *ampulla* 'flask' + -ιον.
Documents: *P.Lond.* II.191.16 (II AD); *P.Lund* IV.14.15 etc. (III AD); *SB* 9238.19 (III AD); *SB* 16831.6 (IV AD).
Notes: looks like diminutive of ἀμπούλλα, but attested earlier; thus probably the original loan, later replaced. Cervenka-Ehrenstrasser (1996: 74), Daris (1991a: 28), Hofmann (1989: 20 *s.v.* ἄμπουλλα), Cavenaile (1952: 196), Meinersmann (1927: 6), *DGE*, LSJ suppl. See §4.3.2, §9.2, §10.2.1, §10.2.2 M.

rare | ἀμπυλλάριον, from *ampulla* 'flask' via ἀμπούλλα + -άριον: papyrus *CPR* V.26.455. LSJ suppl. and Daris (1991a: 27) date it to IV AD and suggest meaning 'holder or container for flasks', but Cervenka-Ehrenstrasser (1996: 73–4) and Diethart (1998: 167) date it to V AD and suggest meaning 'little flask'. See §6.3 n. 21.

ἀμπύλλη: see ἀμπούλλα.

not Latin? | ἀναγλυφάριος 'sculptor in low relief' in Ps.-Macar. *Serm.* 46.2.5 (V AD?) may be from *anaglyphārius* 'sculptor' (*TLL*) or a Greek formation from ἀναγλυφή 'work in low relief' + -άριος. Hofmann (1989: 21), Lampe (1961), *DGE*.

name | Ἀνβιανήσιος, Ἀμβιανήσιος 'from Amiens', from *Ambiānēnsis* 'from Amiens' (*TLL*). Lauffer (1971: 268 on 19.72), Hofmann (1989: 21).

ἀνγαρ-: see ἀγγαρ-.

ἀνγλάριον: see ἀγγλάριον.

rare | ἄνγλος, from *angulus* 'corner': unpublished ostraca O.Dios inv. 934.7, 1302.6, 1307.4, 1310.7, 1353.2 (all II AD).

foreign   **ἀνδαβάτης**, apparently from *andabata* 'gladiator who fights blindfolded': Lyd. *Mag.* p. 70.18 (VI AD), calling it a Latin word for an armoured soldier. Hofmann (1989: 21), LSJ, LSJ suppl., *DGE* (latter two taking very different views on the meaning). See §9.5.5 n. 47.

not ancient   **ἀνήθουμ** transliterating *anēthum* 'dill': interpolation in Dsc. 3.58 RV. Sophocles (1887), *DGE* (*s.v.* ἄνηθον).

not ancient   **ἀνήσουμ** transliterating *anēsum* 'anise': interpolation in Dsc. 3.56 RV. *DGE* (*s.v.* ἄννησον), Sophocles (1887 *s.v.* ἄνισουμ).

Direct loan VI? AD – Byz.   **ἀνισᾶτος, ἀννησᾶτος** (-η?, -ον) 'flavoured with aniseed', esp. neut. sing. 'decoction of aniseed', 'wine flavoured with aniseed', from *anēsātus/anīsātus* 'flavoured with aniseed' (*TLL*), cf. *anēsum* 'anise' (itself from ἄννησον).
     Literature: Ps.-Orib. *Col.* 5.33.10 (IV AD?); Hieroph. *Nut.* 4.7, 6.5, Πῶς 462.6 (IV–VI AD); Aëtius 16.159.1 (VI AD); Alex.Trall. II.341.17, 487.13 (VI AD).
     Post-antique: survives. *LBG*.
     Notes: adj. in Hierophilus, subst. elsewhere. Hofmann (1989: 21), *DGE* (*s.v.* ἀνισᾶτον), LSJ (*s.v.* ἀνισᾶτον). See §2.1 n. 8, §4.2.2, §6.5, §10.2.1, §10.2.2 I.

Direct loan VI AD – Byz.   **ἀννάλιος** (-α, -ον) 'yearly', from *annālis* 'yearly'.
     Literature: Just. *Codex* 1.3.45.9 etc. (VI AD); Ath.Schol. 2.3.15 (VI AD); Antec. in Latin script 4.12.pr. *annaliae, annalian* (VI AD).
     Post-antique: common. *LBG*.
     Notes: Avotins (1989), Hofmann (1989: 21–2), Zilliacus (1935a: 174–5), Lampe (1961), *DGE*, LSJ suppl. See §4.2.2, §9.5.6 n. 68, §10.2.1, §10.2.2 B.

ἀννησᾶτος: see ἀνισᾶτος.

ἀννον(ν)-: see ἀννων-.

rare   **ἀνν(ο)υάλιος** 'yearly', from *annuālis* 'of the year' (*TLL*): papyri *P.Lond.* v.1706 (after line 11: see editor's note) (VI AD); *P.Rain.UnterrichtKopt.* 256.343 (VI AD). Cervenka-Ehrenstrasser (1996: 75), Daris (1991a: 28), *LBG*, *DGE*.

Loan compound IV–V AD   **ἀν(ν)ούμερος** (-ου, ὁ), a title, apparently from unattested **ā numerō* or **ā numerīs* 'functionary in charge of accounts', perhaps with influence from νούμερος.
     Documents: *O.Ashm.Shelt.* 74.2 (III/IV AD); *SB* 2253.11 (III/IV AD); *P.Mich.* XX.807.8 (IV AD); *P.Oxy.* 4612.13 (IV AD); *SB* 16204.17 (IV/V AD).
     Notes: all securely provenanced examples are from Oxyrhynchus. For this use of *ā* see *TLL* (*s.v. ā, ab* 22.81–23.46). Cervenka-Ehrenstrasser (1996: 75), Filos (2006: 50–1, 2008: 436–7, 2010: 252), Daris (1991a: 28), Hofmann (1989: 22), *DGE*. See **§4.5**, §9.2, §10.2.1, §10.2.2 D; cf. νουμεράριος.

ἀννυάλιος: see ἀννουάλιος.

Direct loan I AD – modern   **ἀν(ν)ῶνα, ἀν(ν)όν(ν)α, ἀν(ν)ώνη** (-ης/-ας, ἡ) 'grain supply', 'tax in kind', 'allowance', from *annōna* 'grain supply', 'allowance'.
     Documents: very common, e.g. *O.Wilck.* 779.9 (I AD); *PSI* VI.683.12 (II AD); *BGU* I.336.10 etc. (III AD); *P.Oxy.* 1490v.5 (IV AD); *PSI* I.43.4 (V AD); *P.Oxy.* 156.3 (VI AD); *BGU* III.836.3 etc. (VI AD).
     Inscriptions: e.g. *SEG* I.276.10 (II AD); *SEG* XX.324.59 etc. (III AD); Peek 1969: 33 no. 40.12 (III/IV AD); *SEG* XXXII.1601.13 (IV/V AD); *SEG* XXXII.1554.A4 (VI AD); *IGLS* II.262.12 (VI AD).

Literature: e.g. *ACO* I.I.VII p. 71.12 (V AD); Lyd. *Mag.* p. 180.4 (VI AD); Dor.Gaz. *Doct.Div.* 1.11.23 (VI AD); Just. *Nov.* 8.2 (VI AD); Antec. 2.11.6 (VI AD).

Post-antique: common. Zervan (2019: 14–15), Kriaras (1968–), Sophocles (1887), Triandaphyllidis (1909: 131), used as gloss in *Suda* (δ 401). Modern dialectal αννώνα(ς) 'year's supply of food' etc.: Andriotis (1974: 114).

Notes: forms derivatives ἀννωνικός, ἀννωνιακός, ἀννωνεύομαι, ἀννωναταμίας, ἀννωνέπαρχος, ἀννωνοκάπιτον, perhaps ἀννωνάριος. Cervenka-Ehrenstrasser (1996: 76–9), Avotins (1989, 1992 *s.v.* ἀννώνη), Mitthof (2001), Mason (1974: 5, 6, 22), Daris (1991a: 28–9), Hofmann (1989: 22–3), Zilliacus (1935a: 174–5, 216–17, 1937: 328), Meinersmann (1927: 7), Lampe (1961 *s.v.* ἀννώνη), *DGE*, LSJ (*s.v.* ἀννώνη), LSJ suppl. See §4.1.1 n. 9, §4.2.3.1, §4.6.1, §6.1 n. 9, §10.2.1, §10.2.2 D.

ἀννωναρία: see ἀννωνάριος.

Direct? loan **IV AD – Byz.**	**ἀννωνάριος, ἀννωννάριος, ἀννονάριος** (-ου, ὁ) 'official administering the grain supply', from *annōnārius* 'concerned with the grain supply' or perhaps *annōna* 'grain supply' via ἀννῶνα + -άριος. Documents: *P.Oxy.* 4088 *passim* (IV AD); *SB* 11592.26, 12167.7 = *P.Erl.Diosp.* 2.7 (both IV AD); perhaps *CPR* VI.61.7 (IV AD). Post-antique: numerous. *LBG*, Triandaphyllidis (1909: 128). Notes: perhaps really ἀννωναρία 'ration voucher' in *P.Oxy.* 4088 (Mitthof 2001: 506–8). Cervenka-Ehrenstrasser (1996: 79–80), Daris (1991a: 29), LSJ suppl. See §4.2.4.1 n. 50, §6.1 n. 9, §10.2.1, §10.2.2 D.
not ancient?	**ἀννωναρχέω** 'be in charge of the grain supply', from *annōna* 'grain supply' via ἀννῶνα + -αρχέω 'be in charge of' (cf. -άρχης): inscription *TAM* IV.1.189.8. Mason (1974: 22), Hofmann (1989: 23 *s.v.* ἀννώνα), *DGE*, LSJ, LSJ suppl.
rare	**ἀννωναταμίας** 'official in charge of the grain supply', a calque of *praefectus annonae* from *annōna* 'grain supply' via ἀννῶνα + ταμίας 'controller': inscription *I.Ephesos* 4330.10 (III AD). Mason (1974: 22), *DGE*, LSJ suppl.
non-existent	**ἀννωνεακόν** 'belonging to the grain supply', from *annōna* 'grain supply': superseded reading of a form of ἀννωνιακός in Lyd. *Mag.* p. 190.22 (VI AD). LSJ. See §2.2.1 n. 21.
rare	**ἀννωνέπαρχος, ἀν(ν)ονέπαρχος** 'official in charge of the grain supply', a calque of *praefectus annōnae* from *annōna* 'grain supply' via ἀννῶνα + ἔπαρχος 'person in charge': papyri *P.Flor.* I.75.20 (IV AD); perhaps *CPR* XXIV.2.9 (IV/V AD); Just. *Codex* 1.44.2.3 (VI AD); Byzantine texts. Cervenka-Ehrenstrasser (1996: 80), Filos (2010: 244, 249), Daris (1991a: 29), Hofmann (1989: 23 *s.v.* ἀννώνα), Cavenaile (1952: 199), *LBG*, *DGE*, LSJ, LSJ suppl.
Deriv. of loan **V AD – Byz.**	**ἀννωνεύομαι** 'have as an allowance', from *annōna* 'allowance' (*OLD s.v.* 2d) via ἀννῶνα + deponent version of -εύω. Documents: *CPR* VIII.54.5 (V AD); probably not *Stud.Pal.* III.95.4 (V AD). Inscriptions: *SEG* XXXII.1601.16 etc. (IV/V AD); *OGIS* 200.20 etc. (IV/V AD). Post-antique: survives. *LBG*, Triandaphyllidis (1909: 131). Notes: Cervenka-Ehrenstrasser (1996: 80–1), Mandilaras (1973: 67), Daris (1991a: 29), Hofmann (1989: 23 *s.v.* ἀννώνα), Zilliacus (1935a: 174–5), Meinersmann (1927: 7), *DGE*, LSJ. See §4.6.1 n. 91, §10.2.2 D.

Deriv. of loan
IV–VI AD

ἀν(ν)ωνιακός (-ή, -όν) 'belonging to the grain supply', from *annōna* 'grain supply' via ἀννῶνα + -ιακός.
Documents: e.g. *P.Ryl.* IV.652.9 (IV AD); *BGU* XII.2168.10 (V AD); *P.Flor.* III.377.15 (VI AD).
Literature: Lyd. *Mag.* p. 190.22 (VI AD).
Notes: LSJ suppl. and *DGE* incorrectly (see Cervenka-Ehrenstrasser) date *P.Wisc.* I.32.13 to I AD. Cervenka-Ehrenstrasser (1996: 81–3, adding that neut. subst. means 'bread'), Daris (1991a: 29), Hofmann (1989: 23 *s.v.* ἀννώνα), Cavenaile (1952: 197), Zilliacus (1935a: 174–5), *DGE*, LSJ, LSJ suppl. (adding that fem. subst. means 'corn supply'). See §4.6.1, §10.2.2 D.

Deriv. of loan
III AD – Byz.

ἀν(ν)ωνικός, ἀν(ν)ον(ν)ικός (-ή, -όν) 'concerning the grain supply', as neut. subst. 'bread', from *annōna* 'grain supply' via ἀννῶνα + -ικός.
Documents: e.g. *P.Panop.Beatty* 1.101 (III AD); *P.Oxy.* 3392.2 (IV AD); *CPR* VII.42.2 etc. (V AD); *P.Herm.* 41.4 (VI AD).
Post-antique: numerous. *LBG* (*s.v.* ἀννονικός), Kriaras (1968–).
Notes: Cervenka-Ehrenstrasser (1996: 82–3), Daris (1991a: 29), Hofmann (1989: 23 *s.v.* ἀννώνα), Cavenaile (1952: 197), Meinersmann (1927: 7), *DGE*, LSJ, LSJ suppl. See §4.6.1, §10.2.2 D.

rare

ἀννωνοκάπιτον 'grain rations', from *annōna* 'grain supply' via ἀννῶνα + *caput* 'head' via κάπιτον: papyri *P.Lond.* V.1889v.3 (VI AD); *SB* 16279.2 (VI AD); *Stud.Pal.* XX.231.23 is post-antique (*BL* X.272). Cervenka-Ehrenstrasser (1996: 83–4), Diethart (1998: 167), Filos (2010: 249).

ἀνον(ν)-, ἀνων-: see ἀννων-.

ἀνούμερος: see ἀννούμερος.

ἀνπ(ο)ῦλλα, ἀνπύλλη: see ἀμποῦλλα.

ἀντεκέσσωρ, ἀντεκήνσωρ: see ἀντικήνσωρ.

not ancient

ἀντελίνα 'horse's breast-strap', from *antilēna* 'breast-strap' (*TLL s.v. antēla*): no ancient examples. Zilliacus (1935a: 216–17), *LBG*.

rare

ἀντιδικτάτωρ 'deputy dictator', from ἀντί 'in the place of' + *dictātor* 'dictator' via δικτάτωρ: Lyd. *Mag.* p. 60.10 (VI AD). Hofmann (1989: 23), *DGE*, LSJ.

Direct loan with
influence
V AD – Byz.

ἀντικήνσωρ, ἀντικένσωρ, ἀντεκήνσωρ, ἀντεκέσσωρ (-ορος/-ωρας, ὁ) 'teacher of law', from *antecessor* 'teacher of law' (*TLL*) with influence from κήνσωρ (*q.v.*) and ἀντί 'in place of'.
Literature: Nil. 1.192.1 (V AD); Hesych. as lemma α 5421 (V/VI AD); Lyd. *Mag.* p. 174.26 (VI AD); Just. *Const. Δέδωκεν* 9, 11 (VI AD); Antec. 1.26.13 etc. (VI AD).
Post-antique: common. *LBG* (*s.v.* ἀντικένσωρ), Kriaras (1968–).
Notes: Hofmann (1989: 23), Zilliacus (1935a: 174–5, 216–17), Immisch (1885: 350–1), *TLL* (*s.v. antecessor* 146.72, 147.7–10), Lampe (1961 *s.v.* ἀντεκήνσωρ), *DGE* (*s.v.* ἀντεκήνσωρ), LSJ suppl. See §4.2.5, §4.4, §10.2.1, §10.2.2 B.

non-existent

ἀντικόμης, from ἀντί 'in the place of' + *comes* 'count' via κόμης: no examples. Cervenka-Ehrenstrasser (1996: 128).

44

rare	**ἀντικουάριος** 'copyist', from *antīquārius* 'student of the past': Lyd. *Mens.* 1.33 (VI AD); Byzantine texts. Zilliacus (1935a: 174–5), *LBG*.
rare	**ἀντικουράτωρ** 'substitute curator', from ἀντί 'in the place of' + *cūrātor* 'curator' via κουράτωρ: ostracon *SB* 16941.2 etc. (II AD). Cuvigny (2002: esp. 243).
non-existent	**ἀντιλιβράριος**, conjectured (in *BGU* 11.423v.29) as a borrowing of *librārius* 'bookseller': no examples. Cervenka-Ehrenstrasser (1996: 128).
name	**Ἀντιοχήσιος** 'from Antioch', from *Antiochēnsis* 'from Antioch'. Cervenka-Ehrenstrasser (1996: 84–5), *LBG*, *DGE*, LSJ suppl.
rare	**ἀντίπανον** 'embroidered cloth', probably from unattested **antepannus* 'embroidered cloth' with influence from ἀντί: Hesych. as gloss π 707 (V/VI AD); occasionally later. *LBG*, LSJ suppl. See §8.1.7 n. 34.
non-existent?	**ἀντισαγιττάτωρ**, perhaps 'deputy archer', from ἀντί 'in the place of' + *sagittātor* 'archer' (Souter 1949) via σαγιττάτωρ: cited as an ancient loan by Zilliacus (1935a: 234–5), but I can find no examples.
rare	**ἀντισιγνᾶνος**, from *antesignānus* 'soldier fighting in the front rank of a legion' with influence from ἀντί: inscription *IGLS* v.2132.5 (II AD). Mason (1974: 22), *DGE*.
rare	**ἀντισκρίβας**, a kind of judicial secretary, from ἀντί 'in the place of' + *scrība* 'scribe' via σκρίβας: papyri *PSI* VII.768.15 etc. (V AD); *Chrest.Mitt.* 71.11 etc. (V AD); probably *Stud.Pal.* 1 (p. 8).3.3 etc. (V AD) (see Cervenka-Ehrenstrasser 1996: 85–6). LSJ suppl. defines it 'deputy scribe'. Filos (2010: 249), Daris (1991a: 29), Hofmann (1989: 403 *s.v.* σκριβα), *DGE*.
rare	**Ἀντίφορος**, the name of a square in a suburb of Antioch, from *ante forum* 'before the forum' with influence from ἀντί: Malal. 16.6.43 (VI AD); Simplicius, *In Aristotelis quattuor libros de caelo commentaria* p. 156.20 Heiberg (VI AD); Evagr.Schol. *HE* 124.22, marked (VI AD); Procop. *Aed.* 2.7.6, marked (VI AD); occasionally later. Hofmann (1989: 23), Lampe (1961).
Direct loan with suffix **II–III AD**	**Ἀντώνεια, Ἀντώνια, Ἀντωνήα, Ἀντωνειν(ε)ῖα, Ἀντωνῖνα** (-ων, τά) 'Antonine festival', from the name *Antōnius/Antōnīnus* + -ειος. Inscriptions: e.g. *IG* II/III².II.2068.122 (II AD); *IG* II/III².II.2193.23 (II/III AD); *IG* II/III².II.2235.47 (III AD); *IG* II/III².II.2239.181 (III AD). Coins: ΑΝΤΩΝΕΙΝΙΑ at Laodiceia, Head 1911: 679 (I–III AD). Notes: spellings derived from *Antōnīnus* now perhaps unattested on inscriptions due to re-readings. Drew-Bear (1972: 185), *DGE* (*s.vv.* Ἀντώνια, Ἀντωνίνεια), LSJ suppl. (*s.vv.* Ἀντώνεια, Ἀντωνεινεῖα). See §4.3.2, §9.1 n. 4, §10.2.1, §10.2.2 F.
name	**Ἀντωνεῖνος, Ἀντωνίνειος** 'Antonine', from *Antōnīnus* 'Antonine'. Drew-Bear (1972: 185), Hofmann (1989: 24, 344), *DGE* (*s.v.* Ἀντωνίνειοι). Cf. ψευδαντωνῖνος.
rare	**Ἀντωνινεῖον** 'tomb of the Antonines', from *Antōnīnus* 'Antonine' + -(ε)ῖος in the neuter: Dio Cassius 76.15.4, 78.9.1 (II/III AD). *DGE*.
name	**Ἀντωνινιανός** 'Antonine', from *Antōnīniānus* 'Antonine'. Mason (1974: 23).

not ancient?   **ἄξαμος**, a measure, perhaps from *exāminō* 'weigh': probably no ancient examples. Meyer (1895: 10), *LBG* (*s.v.* ἔξαμος 'standard measure').

ἀξουγγία, ἀξούγγιον, ἀξύγγιον: see ὀξύγγιον.

ἀορδινάριος: see ὀρδινάριος 2.

Ἀούγουστος, Ἄουστος: see Αὔγουστος.

ἀουκτώριτας: see αὐκτώριτας.

ἀουνδίκιος: see οὐνδίκιος.

Direct loan
VI AD – modern   **ἀπαλαρέα, ἀπαλαρία, ἐπουλαρία, ἐπουλαρέα** (-ας, ἡ) 'bread-basket', 'dish', from *epulāris* 'of feasts' (not a noun **epulāria*: Cervenka-Ehrenstrasser 1996: 87).
Documents: *SB* 14530.2 (VI AD).
Literature: Lyd. *Mens.* 1.29.2–4 (VI AD).
Post-antique: numerous. *LBG*, Kriaras (1968–), Triandaphyllidis (1909: 121). Modern dialectal ἀπαλαρέα 'dish' etc.: Andriotis (1974: 125).
Notes: integrated only in form ἀπαλαρέα. Forms derivative κυθραπαλαρία. Cervenka-Ehrenstrasser (1996: 87), Diethart (1998: 167), Hofmann (1989: 117), *LBG* (*s.v.* ἐπουλαρία), *TLL* (*s.v.* *epulāria*). See §4.2.3.1 n. 38, §4.2.5, §8.1.7, **§9.5.5** passage 73, §10.2.1, §10.2.2 I.

not ancient   **ἀπιάστρουμ** transliterating *apiastrum* 'balm', a plant: interpolations in Dsc. 3.103 RV, 104 RV. Sophocles (1887).

rare   **ἀπιᾶτον** 'wine flavoured with celery', from *apiātum*, neuter of *apiātus* 'flavoured with celery' (*TLL*): Aëtius 16.162.1 (VI AD); Alex.Trall. 11.341.16, 457.13 (VI AD); occasionally later. Hofmann (1989: 24), *DGE*, LSJ. See §6.5 with n. 31.

foreign   **ἀ πιγμέντις**, apparently from an unknown *ā pigmentīs* 'functionary concerned with ingredients': explained by Lyd. *Mag.* p. 162.15 (VI AD) as title of official in charge of perfumes. See §9.5.5 passage 75.

foreign   **ἄπικας** 'conical hats', from *apicēs*, acc. pl. of *apex* 'mitre': DH *AR* 2.70.2, marked (I BC). Hofmann (1989: 24), *DGE* (*s.v.* ἄπικες), LSJ suppl. (*s.v.* ἄπικες). See **§2.2.3** with passage 2.

rare   **Ἀπίκια**, name for kinds of cake, from personal name *Apicius*: Athenaeus 1.7a (II/III AD); as lemma in Byzantine lexica drawing on Athenaeus. *DGE*.

foreign   **Ἀπικιανόν**, cake name from personal name *Apicius* + *-iānus*: Athenaeus 14.647c, marked (II/III AD), with a set of similarly formed cake names (Κρασσιανόν, Τουτιανόν, Ἰουλιανόν, Μοντιανόν, κλοῦστρον Φαβωνιανόν, Παυλινιανόν), none of which is attested of cakes in Latin (cf. Hauri-Karrer 1972: 120). *DGE*. See §9.4 passage 61.

rare   **ἄπιον, ἄποιον** 'celery', from *apium* 'celery': Orib. *Ecl.* 51.1 (IV AD), with feminine gender; as part of ἀπιουσῆμεν 'celery seed', *Hippiatr.Par.* (Apsyrtus) 63, marked (III/IV AD?); perhaps elsewhere (certainty is impossible because of the word's similarity to ἄπιον 'pear'). Hofmann (1989: 24), *DGE* (*s.v.* ἀπιουσῆμεν), LSJ suppl. (with additional post-antique reference).

rare	**ἀπληκεύω, ἀπ(π)λικεύω** 'encamp', 'lodge', from (*castra*) *applicō* 'make camp' (*TLL s.v. applico* 297.28–47) + -εύω: Malal. 13.24, 14.10, 18.50 (VI AD); common in Byzantine texts. Modern dialectal απλικεύω 'come', 'live': Meyer (1895: 11). Petersmann (1992: 227–8), Hofmann (1989: 24), Viscidi (1944: 9, 12), Zilliacus (1935a: 216–17), *LBG*, Kriaras (1968– s.v. ἀπλικεύω), Triandaphyllidis (1909: 130), Lampe (1961), LSJ suppl.
	ἄπληκτον: see ἀπλίκιτον.
rare	**ἀπλικιτάριος**, title of an official responsible for arrests, probably from *applicitum* (via ἀπλίκιτον?) + -άριος, though unattested **applicitārius* has also been suggested: papyri perhaps *BGU* XIX.2773.8 (V AD); perhaps *P.Cair.Masp.* 67287.4.1 (VI AD); Lyd. *Mag.* pp. 142.1, 158.9 (VI AD); occasionally later. Cervenka-Ehrenstrasser (1996: 88), Kramer (1998c, 2011: 165–73), Binder (2000: 204), Daris (1991a: 29), Hofmann (1989: 25), Zilliacus (1935a: 174–5, 216–17), Meinersmann (1927: 7), *LBG* (s.v. ἀπληκτάριος), *TLL* (s.v. *applicitārius*), *DGE*, LSJ (s.v. ἀπλίκιτον). See §8.1.7.
rare	**ἀπλίκιτον** 'camp-prison', from *applicitum*, pf. part. neut. of (*castra*) *applicō* 'make camp' (*TLL s.v. applico* 297.28–47): papyrus *P.Lond.* VI.1914.44 (IV AD). Probably does not survive in Byzantine ἄπ(π)ληκτον, ἄπ(π)λικτον 'camp' (with modern dialectal αμπλίτσι 'hut', απλίκιν 'dwelling': Andriotis 1974: 129; Meyer 1895: 11), which may be a reborrowing of the same Latin or a formation from ἀπληκεύω. Cervenka-Ehrenstrasser (1996: 88–9), Binder (2000: 203–4), Mihăescu (1993: 347), Kramer (1998c, 2011: 165–73), Diethart (1992: 240), Daris (1991a: 29), Zilliacus (1935a: 216–17), *LBG* (s.v. ἄπληκτον), Kriaras (1968– s.v. ἀπλίκιν), Lampe (1961 s.v. ἄπληκτον), *DGE* (s.vv. ἄπληκτον, ἀπλίκιτον), LSJ, LSJ suppl. (s.v. ἄπληκτον). See §5.2.1.
not ancient	**ἀπλοπάλλιον** 'simple mantle', from ἁπλοῦς 'simple' + *pallium* 'mantle' via πάλλιον: no ancient examples. Cervenka-Ehrenstrasser (1996: 90), Diethart (1986: 89, 1988: 54–5), Filos (2010: 249), Daris (1991a: 29), LSJ suppl.
rare	**ἀποδρακωνάριος** 'former standard-bearer', 'person belonging to the class of standard-bearers', from ἀπό 'former', 'belonging to the class of' (§4.6.2) + *dracōnārius* 'standard-bearer' (*TLL*) via δρακονάριος: papyrus *P.Amst.* I.45.7 (VI AD). Cervenka-Ehrenstrasser (1996: 90), Filos (2010: 249), Daris (1991a: 29), LSJ suppl. See §4.6.2 n. 95.
not Latin?	**ἀποθηκάρ(ι)ος, ἀποθεκάριος, ἀποθικάριος** 'storekeeper' may be from *apothēcārius* 'storekeeper' (*TLL*) or a Greek formation from ἀποθήκη 'storehouse' + -άριος. Robert (1965: 332–6), Coleman (2007: 796), *DGE*, LSJ suppl.
	ἄποιον: see ἄπιον.
rare	**ἀποκαισαρόομαι** 'assume the monarch', from ἀπό 'from' + *Caesar* via Καῖσαρ + a deponent version of -όω: Marc.Aurel. 6.30.1 (II AD). Mason (1974: 6, 24), LSJ.
not Latin?	**ἀποκελλέρω** 'steal', perhaps from ἀπό 'away from' + *cella* 'room' via κέλλα: as ἀπεκέλλερεν, Hesych. as lemma α 5923 (V/VI AD). Hofmann (1989: 167 s.v. κέλλη), Immisch (1885: 307–8), LSJ (s.v. ἀπεκέλλερεν).

non-existent	**ἀποκομερκίων** on papyrus *SB* 13930.1 (VI/VII AD), claimed by Zilliacus (1935a: 172–3), Meinersmann (1927: 7), and Hofmann (1989: 25) to be from *ā commerciīs* 'functionary concerned with trade': superseded reading (*BL* X.224). Cf. κομμέρκιον.
rare	**ἀποκόμης** 'former count', from ἀπό 'former' (§4.6.2) + *comes* 'count' via κόμης: papyrus *CPR* XXIV.8.1 (V AD). Cervenka-Ehrenstrasser (1996: 91), Filos (2010: 249). See §4.6.2 n. 95.
not Latin?	**ἀποκρισ(ι)άριος, ἀποκρεισιάριος** 'agent', 'envoy' may be from *apocris(i)ārius* 'envoy' (*TLL*) or a Greek formation from ἀπόκρισις 'answer' + -άριος; it first appears in IV AD in both languages. Coleman (2007: 796), Cavenaile (1952: 202), Zilliacus (1935a: 174–5, 216–17), *LBG*, Kriaras (1968–), Lampe (1961), *DGE* (with definitions significantly different from mine), LSJ suppl. (replacing LSJ). See §6.1.
	ἀπομακκόω: see μακκοάω.
non-existent?	**ἀπονουμεράριος** 'former accountant' on papyrus *P.Oxy.* 2004.2 (V AD), from ἀπό 'former' (§4.6.2) + *numerārius* 'accountant' (L&S) via νουμεράριος, is cited by Daris (1991a: 29, with derivation from *numerus*), Hofmann (1989: 25 *s.v.* απονομιραριος), Zilliacus (1935a: 224–5), *DGE*, LSJ suppl., but Cervenka-Ehrenstrasser (1996: 129) argues that it is two words. Diethart (1998: 168).
non-existent?	**ἀποπραιπόσιτος** 'former *praepositus*', 'person belonging to the class of *praepositi*', from ἀπό 'former', 'belonging to the class of' (§4.6.2) + *praepositus* 'person in charge' via πραιπόσιτος, is cited by LSJ suppl. with a number of examples (cf. Daris 1991a: 30, Filos 2010: 249, *DGE*), but Cervenka-Ehrenstrasser (1996: 91) argues that only one is valid, an undated Coptic papyrus (Crum 1905: 167 no. 355).
non-existent?	**ἀποπραίτωρ** 'former praetor', from ἀπό 'former' (§4.6.2) + *praetor* 'praetor' via πραίτωρ, is cited by Daris (1991a: 30), but Cervenka-Ehrenstrasser (1996: 130) argues that it is two words.
rare	**ἀποπροτήκτωρ** 'former protector', 'person belonging to the class of protectors', from ἀπό 'former', 'belonging to the class of' (§4.6.2) + *prōtēctor* 'guardian' via προτήκτωρ: papyri *P.Abinn.* 55.1 (IV AD); probably *P.Oxy.* 4367.2 (IV AD). Cervenka-Ehrenstrasser (1996: 92), Gonis (1998: 217), Filos (2010: 249), Diethart (1998: 168), Daris (1991a: 30). See §4.6.2 n. 95.
rare	**ἀποσκουτλόω** 'deprive of its paving', from ἀπό 'away from' + *scutula* 'diamond shape' via σκουτλόω: inscriptions *IG* II/III².III.13209.7, 13210.11 (both II AD). *DGE*, LSJ.
non-existent?	**ἀποτριβοῦνος** 'former tribune', from ἀπό 'former' (§4.6.2) + *tribūnus* 'tribune' via τριβοῦνος: only in Coptic. Cervenka-Ehrenstrasser (1996: 92), Filos (2010: 249), Gonis (1998: 218).
	ἄππληκτον, ἄππλικτον: see ἀπλίκιτον.
	ἀππλικεύω: see ἀπληκεύω.
not ancient	**ἀπραίδευτος** 'not plundered', from the Latin source of πραιδεύω via πραιδεύω: no ancient examples. *LBG*, *DGE*, LSJ suppl.

Direct loan
I BC – modern

Ἀπρίλιος, Ἀπρίλ(λ)(ε)ιος, Ἀπρείλ(λ)(ε)ος (-α, -ον or -ου, ὁ) 'April', from *Aprīlis* 'April'.

Documents: e.g. *P.Oxy.* 3361.7 (II AD); *O.Cret.Chers.* 10.1, 38.1, 61.1 (all II/ III AD); *P.Mich.* XX.816.7 (IV AD); *SB* 16521.6 (IV/V AD); *P.Eirene* II.16.3 (V/VI AD); *P.Petra* III.32.4 (VI AD).

Inscriptions: e.g. Sherk 1969: no. 18.20 (I BC); *IG* XIV.757.2 (I AD); *MAMA* VIII.418c.39 (II AD); *IG* XII.VII.240.35 (III AD); *SEG* XXX.585 (IV AD); *I.Mylasa* 612.8 (V AD); *I.Chr.Bulgarien* 87.4 (VI AD).

Literature: common, e.g. Jos. *AJ* 14.219 (I AD); Plut. *Rom.* 23.7 (I/II AD); Dio Cassius 76.17.4 (II/III AD); Hippolytus, *Commentarium in Danielem* 4.23.3 (III AD); Epiph. *Pan.* II.246.1 (IV AD); Soz. 7.18.14 (V AD); Aëtius 3.164.10 (VI AD).

Post-antique: common. *LBG* (*s.v.* Ἀπρίλλιος), Kriaras (1968–), Sophocles (1887). Modern Απρίλιος, Ἀπρίλης, Ἀπρίλις: Babiniotis (2002), Andriotis (1967), Meyer (1895: 11).

Notes: Cervenka-Ehrenstrasser (1996: 93–4), Solin (2008), Sijpesteijn (1979), García Domingo (1979: 318), Avotins (1992 *s.v.* Ἀπρίλλιος), Strobach (1997: 194), Hofmann (1989: 26), Meinersmann (1927: 7), Lampe (1961), *DGE*, LSJ suppl. See §4.1.1 n. 9, **§4.2.1**, §4.2.2, §8.2.3 n. 51, §10.2.1, §10.2.2 E.

not Latin

ἄρακος 'hawk', stated by Hesych. α 6954 (V/VI AD) to be Etruscan. Hofmann (1989: 26), LSJ.

ἀράριον: see αἰράριον.

non-existent

αρατιον, cited as from *arō* 'plough' (Hofmann 1989: 26 *s.v.* ἀρᾶν): probably not inscription *IG* IX.II.1229.10 (II BC), where these letters occur but need not make a full word.

not Latin

Ἀράτυος, a Locrian month, cited as from *arō* 'plough' (Hofmann 1989: 26 *s.v.* ἀρᾶν), probably has a Greek source: Schwyzer (1922: 1–2), *DÉLG*, Frisk (1954–72: I.129), *DGE*, LSJ.

not Latin?

ἀράω 'plough', cited as from *arō* 'plough' by Hofmann (1989: 26) following a tentative remark of Schwyzer (1922: 1–2); the connection is uncertain, but the context (*IG* XIV.645.i.133, an early inscription from Italy) makes Latin influence possible. LSJ.

Ἀρβᾶλις: see Ἀρουᾶλις.

not Latin?

ἀρβίννη, ἀρβέννη 'meat', related to *arvīna* 'fat', 'lard': Hesych. as lemma α 6999 (V/VI AD), called Sicilian (Σικελοί). Willi (2008: 28), Campanile (1969: 318–19), Hofmann (1989: 26–7), Immisch (1885: 322), *DÉLG*, Frisk (1954–72: I.130), Beekes (2010), *DGE*, LSJ.

foreign

ἀρβιτράριος 'dependent on the discretion of the judge', from *arbitrārius* 'discretionary': Antec. in Latin script 4.6.31 *arbitrarias* (VI AD); later in Greek script. Zilliacus (1935a: 174–5), *LBG*. See §9.5.6 n. 68.

not ancient

ἀρβίτριον 'verdict', from *arbitrium* 'judgement': no ancient examples. Zilliacus (1935a: 174–5), *LBG*.

not ancient

ἄρβιτρος 'arbitrator', from *arbiter* 'arbitrator': no ancient examples. Zilliacus (1935a: 174–5), *LBG*.

rare   **ἀργενταρία** 'box of silver', from *argentāria* (*cista*) '(chest) for silver' or *argentum* 'silver' + -αρία: Pall. *H.Laus.* 10.2.5 (IV/V AD); papyrus *P.Oxy.* 1923.24 (V/VI AD). Cervenka-Ehrenstrasser (1996: 94), Diethart (1998: 168), Daris (1991a: 30), Hofmann (1989: 27, two entries), Lampe (1961), *DGE*. See §6.2.

rare   **ἀργεντάριον** 'bank', 'casket for silver/money', from *argentārium* 'chest for silver': Ps.-Herodian, *Philetaerus* 194 Dain ἀργυροθήκη, τὸ νῦν ἀργεντάριον καλούμενον (II–IV AD?); perhaps inscription *SEG* 11.421; Byzantine texts. *LBG, DGE*.

Direct loan   **ἀργεντάριος** (-ου, ὁ) 'banker', from *argentārius* 'banker'.
II AD – Byz.   Documents: *BGU* III.781.vi.8 (I/II AD); perhaps *O.Trim.* 1.413.3 (IV AD); *PSI* VIII.957.3 (VI AD). But *P.Ital.* 11.30.92 (VI AD) is Latin in Greek script.
         Inscriptions: perhaps *SEG* 11.421.
         Post-antique: common. *LBG, Stud.Pal.* X.249.1 (VII AD).
         Notes: *SEG* 11.421 accepted by LSJ suppl., but *DGE* puts it under ἀργεντάριον and Hofmann (1989: 27) under αργενταρια. Cervenka-Ehrenstrasser (1996: 95) provides a Coptic example. Bogaert (1997: 92) argues that it sometimes means a kind of goldsmith. Daris (1991a: 30), Meinersmann (1927: 7). See §4.2.4.1 n. 50, §10.2.1, §10.2.2 G.

not ancient   **ἀργενταρίτης** 'cashier', from *argentārius* 'banker' (via ἀργεντάριος?) + -ίτης or *argentārium* 'chest for silver' via ἀργεντάριον + -ίτης: no ancient examples. Cervenka-Ehrenstrasser (1996: 95–6), Daris (1991a: 30), LSJ suppl.

rare   **ἀργέντινος** (-ον or -η, -ον) 'silvery', 'made with silver thread', from *argenteus* 'silvery' + -ινος: papyri *SB* 16645.32 (II/III AD); *P.Oxy.* 1273.12 (III AD). Cervenka-Ehrenstrasser (1996: 96), Daris (1991a: 30), Hofmann (1989: 27–8 *s.v.* ἀργέντιος), Meinersmann (1927: 7), *DGE*, LSJ, LSJ suppl.

rare   **ἀργέντιος**, perhaps 'silvery', from *argenteus/argentius* 'silvery' (*TLL*): papyrus *P.Oxy.* 1310 (III AD). Cervenka-Ehrenstrasser (1996: 96–7), Daris (1991a: 30), Hofmann (1989: 27–8), *DGE*, LSJ (*s.v.* ἀργέντινος).

not ancient   **ἀργεντός** 'ash grey', from *argenteus* 'silvery': no ancient examples. Meyer (1895: 11).

Direct loan   **ἀρῆνα** (-ης, ἡ) 'arena', from *harēna/arēna* 'arena'.
II AD – Byz.   Inscriptions: perhaps *SEG* XXXIX.1339.12 (II AD).
         Literature: *Acta Pauli et Theclae* 36 = Lipsius 1891: 262.6 (II AD); Ps.-Basil Seleuciensis, *De vita et miraculis sanctae Theclae* 2.34.41 Dagron (V AD). Unverified examples (II and IV AD) in Zilliacus (1937: 322–3, 328).
         Post-antique: common. *LBG*.
         Notes: Hofmann (1989: 28), Zilliacus (1937: 328), Lampe (1961), *DGE*. See §10.2.1, §10.2.2 F.

     ἀριλάρια: see ἀγριλάρια.

not Latin?   **ἄριλλα**, meaning uncertain, perhaps from *āreola/āriola* 'open courtyard', 'garden plot': inscription *IGR* IV.1349.18 (II/III AD). Hofmann (1989: 28), Beekes (2010), *DGE*, LSJ.

not Latin   **ἄριμος** 'ape' is stated by Strabo (13.4.6, cf. Hesych. α 7228) to be an Etruscan word. Hofmann (1989: 28), *DGE*, LSJ.

Direct loan   **ἄρκα, ἄρκη** (-ης, ἡ) 'chest', 'coffin', 'state treasury', from *arca* 'chest', 'coffin',
III AD – modern   'treasury'.

    Documents: perhaps *SB* 12667.5 (III AD).

    Inscriptions: *TAM* v.11.913.a16, 935.4 (both III AD); *IG* XIV.2327.4 (V AD).

    Literature: Just. *Nov.* 128.1 (VI AD).

    Post-antique: common. *LBG*, Triandaphyllidis (1909: 125). Modern dialectal ἄρκα 'grave', etc.: Andriotis (1974: 153), Meyer (1895: 11).

    Notes: may form derivative ἄρκος. Cervenka-Ehrenstrasser (1996: 97–8), Drew-Bear (1972: 187), Avotins (1992), Diethart (1998: 168), Mason (1974: 5, 25, 143), Hofmann (1989: 28–9), Viscidi (1944: 23), Zilliacus (1935a: 174–5), Lampe (1961), *DGE*, LSJ (*s.v.* ἄρκη), LSJ suppl. See §10.2.1, §10.2.2 M.

non-existent?   **ἀρκαρικάριος**, title of a tax-collecting official, from *arcārius* 'treasurer': papyrus *P.Oxy.* 126.15 (VI AD). This reading is accepted by Cervenka-Ehrenstrasser (1996: 98, with arguments) and *LBG*, but not by the editor, who corrects to ἀρκαρίῳ (and is followed therein by LSJ and *DGE*). Cavenaile (1952: 202) sees a Greek formation in -άριος based on ἀρκαρικός from *arcārius*. Daris (1991a: 30) cites a second example no longer believed to exist.

Deriv. of loan   **ἀρκαρικός** (-ή, -όν) 'of the treasurer', as neut. subst. a tax, from *arcārius* 'treasurer'
VI AD   via ἀρκάριος + -ικός.

    Documents: *P.Oxy.* 126.14 etc., 2020.9 etc. (both VI AD); *P.Flor.* III.377.2 (VI AD).

    Literature: Just. *Edict* 13.20 = p. 791.3 (VI AD).

    Notes: Cervenka-Ehrenstrasser (1996: 99–100), Avotins (1992), Daris (1991a: 30), Hofmann (1989: 29), Cavenaile (1952: 197), Meinersmann (1927: 8), *DGE*, LSJ, LSJ suppl. See §4.6.1, §10.2.2 G.

Direct loan   **ἀρκάριος** (-ου, ὁ) 'treasurer', from *arcārius* 'treasurer'.
I AD – Byz.   Documents: perhaps *P.Oxy.* 126.15 (VI AD), see above on ἀρκαρικάριος.

    Inscriptions: *TAM* v.1.692.4 (I AD); *I.Pergamon Asklepieion* 125.9 (I/II AD); *TAM* v.1.713.8 (II AD); perhaps *SEG* XXXVI.970.56 (III AD); *I.Pergamon Asklepieion* 99.1; *SEG* 11.421; perhaps *I.Ephesos* 809.1.

    Literature: Artemios in Papadopulos-Kerameus 1909: 21.23, 24 (IV AD?); Just. *Codex* 1.2.24.16, *Nov.* 147.2, *Edict* 13.11 = p. 786.16 (VI AD).

    Post-antique: survives. *LBG*.

    Notes: forms derivative ἀρκαρικός. Avotins (1992), Mason (1974: 4, 25), Hofmann (1989: 29–30), Zilliacus (1935a: 174–5), Lampe (1961), *DGE*, LSJ, LSJ suppl. See §4.2.4.1 n. 50, §4.6.1, §6.1, §10.2.1, §10.2.2 G.

not ancient?   **ἀρκᾶτος** 'archer', from *arcus, -ūs* 'bow' (not *arcātus*, which is a rare variant of *arcuātus* 'bow-shaped', 'jaundice': *TLL*): probably no ancient examples. Hofmann (1989: 30), Zilliacus (1935a: 216–17), *LBG*, Andriotis (1974: 153).

    ἄρκη: see ἄρκα.

not ancient   **ἄρκιον** 'little chest', from *arca* 'chest': no ancient examples. Cervenka-Ehrenstrasser (1996: 100), *LBG*.

not ancient?   **ἄρκλα** 'chest', 'hut', from *arcula/arcla* 'casket': scholion to Ar. *Pl.* 807 as
gloss; Byzantine texts. Zervan (2019: 16) argues that it must have
been the source of ἀρκλαρία and therefore borrowed before VI AD, but
relationship with ἀρκλαρία is uncertain. Avotins (1992) suggests that it
may occur in Just. *Nov.* 128.1 (VI AD). Modern ἄρκλα 'chest': Andriotis
(1967), Meyer (1895: 11). Binder (2000: 167–8), Hofmann (1989: 30),
Viscidi (1944: 23), *LBG*, Kriaras (1968–), Triandaphyllidis (1909: 120,
125), Lampe (1961).

rare   **ἀρκλαρία** 'money chest', from unattested **arclāria* or *arcula/arcla* 'casket' + -αρία:
Narratio de rebus Persicis 214a, 245a (= Bratke 1899: 11.5, 44.6) (V/VI AD).
Hofmann (1989: 30), Lampe (1961). See §6.2.

non-existent?   **ἀρκλόλιγκλα, ἀρκλόλαγκλα**, a piece of kitchen equipment apparently
compounded from *arcula* (via ἄρκλα) and *ligula* (via λίγλα) or *lanc(u)la* (via
λάγκλα): perhaps unpublished papyrus P.Vindob. G 29.938 (VI AD), in
Diethart and Hasitzka (2001: 33–4).

rare   **ἄρκος** 'coffin' (feminine, *pace* LSJ suppl.: see Diethart 1998: 168), from *arca*
'coffin' perhaps via ἄρκα: *IG* XIV.2325.4, 2326.4, 2328.5, 2334.6, all from
one place (all V AD). Drew-Bear (1972: 187–8), *DGE* (*s.v.* 2 ἄρκος), LSJ
suppl. (*s.v.* ἄρκος C).

foreign   **ἀρκουάριος** transliterating *arcuārius* 'bow-maker': Lyd. *Mag.* p. 72.19 (VI AD).
Hofmann (1989: 30), *LBG*.

foreign   **ἀρκύτης** transliterating *arquitēs* 'archers': Lyd. *Mag.* p. 70.20 (VI AD). Hofmann
(1989: 30), Sophocles (1887 *s.v.* ἀρκύτεις).

Direct loan   **ἄρμα** (-ματος, τό) 'weapons', 'armed men', 'monk's habit', from *arma, -ōrum*
V AD – modern   'weapons'.
    Documents: part of ἰν ἄρμις (*in armis*), *P.Col.* VIII.221.5 (II AD).
    Literature: e.g. *V.Dan.Styl.* A. 84.12 (V AD); Malal. 12.49, 16.4 (VI AD).
    Post-antique: common, forming derivatives ἀρματοποιός 'weapons-maker',
    ἀρματόω 'arm', etc. *LBG*, Kriaras (1968–), Triandaphyllidis (1909:
    129). Modern ἄρματα 'weapons': Babiniotis (2002 *s.v.* ἄρμα – ἄρματα –
    αρματολός), Andriotis (1967), Meyer (1895: 11–12).
    Notes: Daris (1991a: 30), Hofmann (1989: 31), Zilliacus (1935a: 216–17),
    Zervan (2019: 16–17), Lampe (1961), *DGE* (*s.v.* 2 ἄρμα). See §4.2.5, §6.11,
    §10.2.1, §10.2.2 C.

not Latin   **ἀρμάδα** 'naval force', cited as a Latin loan by Hofmann (1989: 31) but probably
from Venetian *armada*, itself originally from Latin *armātus* 'furnished
with weapons': no ancient examples. Hofmann (1989: 31), Meyer (1895:
12), Andriotis (1967), Zervan (2019: 17–18), Kriaras (1968–), *LBG* (*s.v.*
ἀρμάδια), Lampe (1961).

    ἀρμαλαύσιον: see ἀρμελαύσιον.

not ancient?   **ἀρμαμεντάριον** 'arsenal', from *armāmentārium* 'arsenal': probably no ancient
examples. Hofmann (1989: 32), *LBG*.

rare   **ἀρμαμέντον** 'arsenal', 'arms', from *armāmenta/armāmentum* 'equipment': bronze label *SEG* XLII.1756.1 (VI AD); Just. *Nov.* 85.1 etc. (VI AD). Cervenka-Ehrenstrasser (1996: 100–1) cites meaning 'ship's rigging' from a later papyrus. Avotins (1992), Daris (1991a: 30), Hofmann (1989: 32), Zilliacus (1935a: 216–17), Triandaphyllidis (1909: 129, 131), Lampe (1961), *DGE*, LSJ suppl.

     ἀρμαραύσιον: see ἀρμελαύσιον.

Direct loan   **ἀρμάριον** (-ου, τό) 'chest', 'wardrobe', 'safe', from *armārium* 'cabinet'.
III AD – modern   Documents: *P.Brookl.* 84.10 (II/III AD).
     Literature: *Coll.Herm.* H 25d (II–IV AD); Cyr.S. *Vit.Eu.* 69.14–22 etc. (VI AD); Antec. 2.1.25 (VI AD). Unverified example (IV AD) in Zilliacus (1937: 323, 328).
     Post-antique: common. *Etymologicum Magnum* 146–7: Ἀρμάριον· ὅτι τὰ λεγόμενα παρ' ἡμῖν ἀρμάρια, ἑρμάρια ὀφείλουσι λέγεσθαι, ὡς εὗρον ἐν τοῖς σχολίοις τοῦ ἁγίου Διονυσίου, ἀρχῇ τοῦ θ' κεφαλαίου περὶ τῶν Θείων Ὀνομάτων. οἱ γὰρ Ἕλληνες οἷα τινὰς ἀνδριάντας ἐποίουν, μήτε χεῖρας μήτε πόδας ἔχοντας· τούτους δὲ Ἑρμᾶς ἐκάλουν· οὗ ὑποκοριστικὸν, ἑρμάριον. ἐποίουν δὲ αὐτοὺς διακένους, θύρας ἔχοντας καθάπερ τοιχοπυργίσκους· καὶ ἔσωθεν αὐτῶν ἐτίθουν ἀγάλματα ὧν ἔσεβον θεῶν· ἔξωθεν δὲ ἀπέκλειον τοὺς ἑρμᾶς. Kriaras (1968–), Triandaphyllidis (1909: 120), Sophocles (1887). Modern ερμάριο, αρμάρι 'wardrobe': Babiniotis (2002), Andriotis (1967), Meyer (1895: 12).
     Notes: forms derivative ἀρμαρίτης. Cervenka-Ehrenstrasser (1996: 101), Daris (1991a: 30), Hofmann (1989: 32), Zilliacus (1935a: 174–5, 1937: 328), Meinersmann (1927: 8), Lampe (1961), *DGE*, LSJ suppl. See §4.2.4.1 n. 54, §10.2.1, §10.2.2 M.

rare   **ἀρμαρίτης** 'bank manager', from *armārium* 'cabinet' via ἀρμάριον + -ίτης: Just. *Edict* 9.2 = p. 773.27 (VI AD); Byzantine texts. *LBG*, *DGE*, LSJ, LSJ suppl.

not ancient   **ἀρμαστατίων, ἀρμοστατίων** 'muster', from *arma* 'weapons' via ἄρμα + *statiō* 'state of standing still': no ancient examples. Zilliacus (1935a: 216–17), *LBG*, Lampe (1961).

not ancient?   **ἀρμᾶτος** 'armed man', from *armātus* 'armed man': probably no ancient examples. Hofmann (1989: 32), Zilliacus (1935a: 216–17), *LBG*, Triandaphyllidis (1909: 128).

Direct loan   **ἀρματοῦρα** (only nom. attested, ὁ or ἡ) 'person skilled in the use of the
IV–V AD?   sword', 'military training', 'formation (of troops)', from *armātūra* (fem.) 'armament'.
     Documents: *O.Douch.* III.226.1, perhaps I.17.6, perhaps IV.431.2 (all IV/V AD).
     Inscriptions: *SEG* XXXVIII.1776.6 (IV AD); *I.Syringes* 317.2.
     Literature: Lyd. *Mag.* p. 72.10–11, marked (VI AD).
     Notes: fem. only in Lydus, who suggests that it had died out by VI AD. Sometimes claimed to be a name in *I.Syringes* 317. Attested elsewhere as a place name, leading to misunderstanding in Hofmann (1989: 32–3). Cervenka-Ehrenstrasser (1996: 101–3, with discussion of the meaning and additional, undated examples), Daris (1991a: 30), Zilliacus (1935a: 216–17), Meinersmann (1927: 8). See §4.2.3.1 n. 42, §6.11, §10.2.1, §10.2.2 C; cf. σχολὰ ἀρματούρων.

not Latin?   ἀρμελαύσ(ι)ον, ἀρμαλαύσιον, ἀρμαραύσιον, ἑρμελαύσιον, related to *armilausa*, a short, sleeveless garment (*TLL*): ultimately Germanic, may have entered Greek directly or via Latin. Kramer (1996a: 113–15, 2011: 39–41), Cervenka-Ehrenstrasser (1996: 103–4), editor of *P.Münch.* III.I.142.3 *ad loc.*, Zilliacus (1935a: 216–17), *DGE*, LSJ suppl. (*s.v.* ἀρμαραύσιον).

not ancient?   ἀρμεντάριον, meaning uncertain, from *armentārius* 'in charge of a herd': no certainly ancient examples. Hofmann (1989: 33), *LBG*, Lampe (1961).

rare   ἀρμίγερος, ἑρμίγερος 'squire', from *armiger* 'squire' (i.e. armour-bearer): papyri *P.Oxy.* 1888.2 (V AD); *P.Laur.* IV.177v.9 in Sijpesteijn 1984 (V AD); Lyd. *Mag.* p. 72.1, marked (VI AD). Cervenka-Ehrenstrasser (1996: 104), Daris (1991a: 31), Hofmann (1989: 33), *DGE* (*s.v.* ἀρμίγεροι), LSJ suppl. (*s.v.* ἀρμίγεροι).

Direct loan with suffix
II–IV AD   ἀρμικούστωρ, -ορ, ἀρμοκ-, ἑρμοκ-, ἀρμορο(μ)κ-, ἀρμωρωκ-, ἀρμόρου κούστωρ, ἀρμώρων κούστωρ (-ορος/-ωρος, ὁ) 'person in charge of weapons', from *armicustōs/armōrum custōs* 'person in charge of weapons' (*TLL*) + -τωρ.
    Documents: *P.Hamb.* I.88v.2 (II AD); *ChLA* XLII.1207.17 (II AD); perhaps *Pap.Choix* 6.5 (II AD); perhaps *P.Mich.* VIII.466.17 (II AD); *Rom.Mil.Rec.* 78 no. 39.5, no. 71.1 (both II/III AD); perhaps *BGU* I.344.14 (II/III AD); *P.Erl.Diosp.* 1.356 (IV AD).
    Inscriptions: *SB* 7979.2 (II AD); *SB* 6146.3, 6147.3.
    Notes: all examples found in Egypt. Cervenka-Ehrenstrasser (1996: 104–5), Filos (2010: 232, 252), Olsson (1926: 112), Daris (1991a: 31), Hofmann (1989: 34, 214), Cavenaile (1952: 201), Meinersmann (1927: 8), *DGE*, LSJ (*s.v.* κούστωρ), LSJ suppl. (*s.v.* ἀρμοροκούστωρ). See §4.3.2, §6.8, §9.2, §10.2.1, §10.2.2 C.

foreign   ἀρμιλλίγεροι, designation of military rank apparently transliterating unattested *armilliger 'wearing armbands': Lyd. *Mag.* p. 70.26 (VI AD). *LBG*, *TLL* (*s.v.* *armilliger*), LSJ suppl. See §8.1.7.

foreign   ἀρμιλούστριον transliterating *armilūstrium* 'ceremony of purifying the arms': Plut. *Rom.* 23.3 (I/II AD); Lyd. *Mens.* 4.34.29 (VI AD). Sophocles (1887), *DGE*.

foreign   ἀρμοράκιον transliterating *armoracia/armoracium* 'wild radish': Dsc. 2.112.2 (I AD). Hofmann (1989: 33–4; two entries, the first a ghost reference), *DGE*.

    ἀρμοροκούστωρ: see ἀρμικούστωρ.

    ἀρμοστατίων: see ἀρμαστατίων.

rare   ἄρον (or ἰάριον) Γαλλικόν, a plant, for *aurum Gallicum*, a plant: *Hippiatr.Par.* (Pel.) 142 (V AD?); *Hippiatr.Berl.* 64.1. Editor *ad locc.*, index of Hoppe and Oder 1924–7: II.344.

rare   Ἀρουᾶλις, Ἀρβᾶλις, title indicating membership of a priestly college, from *Arvālis* 'Arval': as ἀδελφὸς Ἀρουᾶλις, Augustus, *Res gestae* 7.6 Volkmann (I AD); on other inscriptions as φράτρεμ Ἀρουᾶλεμ, e.g. *I.Pergamon* II.440.5 (II AD) and φρᾶτρεμ Ἀρβᾶλεμ, *I.Didyma* 151.2 (II AD). Mason (1974: 4, 7, 26, 117), Hofmann (1989: 34), LSJ suppl. (*s.v.* ἀρουᾶλος). See **§7.3** passage 32.

not ancient?	**ἄρουλ(λ)α** 'brazier', from *ārula* 'little altar': scholion to Ar. *Ach.* 888a, "ἐσχάραν" τὴν νῦν καλουμένην ἄρουλαν; common in Byzantine texts. Cervenka-Ehrenstrasser (1996: 106), Diethart (1995a: 81, 1998: 168), Hofmann (1989: 35), *LBG*, Triandaphyllidis (1909: 120), Lampe (1961), *DGE*, LSJ suppl.
not Latin	**ἀρουρατίων, ἀρουρατείων** 'tax assessed in proportion to area of land': Greek formation from ἄρουρα 'land' + -*ātiō*, though -*ātiō* is not normally productive in Greek. Cervenka-Ehrenstrasser (1996: 106–7), Palmer (1945: 120), Frisk (1954–72: 1.147), *DGE*, LSJ suppl. See §6.10.
foreign	**ἀρούσπεξ** (in acc. ἀρούσπικα) transliterating *haruspex*, a type of diviner: DH *AR* 2.22.3 (I BC). Vaahtera (2001: 75–8), Mason (1974: 6, 26), Hofmann (1989: 35), *DGE*.
	ἀρχεδεκανός: see δεκανός.
not ancient?	**ἀρχιβαλιστάριος** 'chief catapult operator', from ἀρχι- 'chief' + *ballistārius* 'catapult operator' (*TLL*) via βαλλιστάριος: inscription *SEG* VII.989.2. Hofmann (1989: 47 *s.v.* βαλλιστ(ρ)αριος), *DGE*.
	ἀρχιδεκανός: see δεκανός.
	ἀρχιεβδομ(αδ)άριος: see ἑβδομαδάριος.
not ancient?	**ἀρχισαγιττάτωρ** 'chief archer', from ἀρχι- 'chief' + *sagittātor* 'archer' (Souter 1949) via σαγιττάτωρ: no certainly ancient examples. Hofmann (1989: 35), Zilliacus (1935a: 234–5), Cameron (1931: 256), *LBG*.
Deriv. of loan V AD – Byz.	**ἀρχισταβλίτης** (-ου, ὁ) 'chief stableman', from ἀρχι- 'chief' + *stabulum* 'stable' via σταβλίτης. Documents: *SB* 12252.10 etc. (V AD); *SB* 16856.4 (VI AD); *P.Princ.* III.145.11 (VI AD). Post-antique: numerous in papyri. Notes: Cervenka-Ehrenstrasser (1996: 107–8), Filos (2010: 249), Daris (1991a: 31), Cavenaile (1952: 199), *LBG*, *DGE*, LSJ suppl. See §4.6.2, §4.6.3, §8.2.2, §9.2, §10.2.2 K.
rare	**ἀρχιστάτωρ** 'chief usher' (title of the leader of the military police), from ἀρχι- 'chief' + *stator* 'official messenger' via στάτωρ: papyri *P.Oxy.* 294.17 etc. (I AD); *P.Oxy.* 2754.9 (II AD). Perhaps reborrowed into Latin as *archistator* (not in lexica): Pflaum (1959), Gilliam (1961), *AE* 1958 no. 156.9. Cervenka-Ehrenstrasser (1996: 108), Filos (2010: 226, 249), Daris (1991a: 31), Mason (1974: 6, 26, 114), Cavenaile (1952: 199), *DGE*, LSJ.
rare	**ἀρχιστράτωρ**, title of an equestrian official, from ἀρχι- 'chief' + *strātor* 'groom' via στράτωρ: inscription *TAM* III.1.52.8 (II AD); probably a name in Galen XIII.835.8 Kühn. Mason (1974: 6, 26, 114), *DGE*, LSJ suppl.
rare	**ἀρχιταβλάριος** 'chief keeper of records', from ἀρχι- 'chief' + *tabulārius* 'bookkeeper' via ταβλάριος: inscription *ILS* 8846.6 (II AD). Filos (2010: 249), Daris (1991a: 31 *s.v.* ἀρχιταβουλάριος), Mason (1974: 6, 26, 114), *DGE*, LSJ.
foreign	***as*** 'complete inheritance': Antec. 2.14.5 (VI AD). See §7.1.1 passage 18.

foreign	ἀ σαβάνις, explained by Lyd. *Mag.* p. 162.18 (VI AD) as title of official in charge of baths, appears to be from unattested title *ā sabanīs* 'from towels'. Sophocles (1887 *s.v.* ἀσαβάνις); for this use of *a* in titles *TLL* (*s.v. ā, ab* 22.81–23.46). See §9.5.5 passage 75.
	ἀσάριον: see ἀσσάριον.
Direct loan with univerbation **V AD – Byz.**	ἀσηκρῆτις, ἀσηκρήτης, ἀδσηκρῆτις, ἀ σηκ- (usually indeclinable but sometimes -ου, ὁ) 'imperial secretary', from *ā sēcrētīs* 'imperial secretary'. Documents: none. Ἀσυνκρίτου in *P.Hamb.* 1.54.i.17 is not a variant of ἀσηκρῆτις (*pace* Zervan 2019: 18; Binder 2000: 88) but from ἀσύγκριτος 'incomparable'. Inscriptions: *IGLS* IV.1809.5 (VI AD); Calder 1912b: 260 no. 21.17 (VI AD). Literature: e.g. *V.Dan.Styl.* A. 84.1 (V AD); Malal. 18.141.28 (VI AD); Procop. *Bell.* 2.7.15.4, marked (VI AD); Lyd. *Mag.* p. 146.24: οὔπω γὰρ ἦν τὸ τῶν ἄρτι παραφυέντων ἀ σηκρήτις ὄνομα, 162.13–18 (VI AD). Post-antique: common, forming derivative πρωτοασηκρήτης 'chief secretary'. *LBG*, Zervan (2019: 18–19), Binder (2000: 87–8), Kriaras (1968–), Triandaphyllidis (1909: 126). Notes: for this use of *a* in titles see *TLL* (*s.v. ā, ab* 22.81–23.46). Binder (2000: 97, 228–9), Hofmann (1989: 35–6), Viscidi (1944: 19), Lampe (1961), *DGE*, LSJ suppl. See §4.2.3.2, §4.5, **§9.5.5** passage 75, §10.2.1, §10.2.2 D, §12.2.1.
not ancient?	ἄσκλα 'splinter', from *assula* 'splinter': probably no ancient examples. Binder (2000: 180), Meyer (1895: 12).
not Latin?	ἀσκλατάριος, cited by LSJ suppl. as perhaps related to medieval *sclata* 'shingle', 'slate' (*DMLBS*, Du Cange 1883–7), and by Cavenaile (1952: 201) as Greek derivative in -άριος: probably a name at *SB* 6951v.34 = *SB* 12521.6 (II AD). Diethart (1998: 168), Meinersmann (1927: 8).
rare	ἀσπράτουρα 'unworn coin', from *asprātūra* 'unworn coin' (?) (*TLL*) or perhaps *asper* 'rough' (via ἄσπρος?): inscription *IGR* IV.352.25 (II AD). Schwyzer (1931: 29), Hofmann (1989: 36), *DÉLG* (*s.v.* ἄσπρος), *DGE*, LSJ.
rare	ἀσπροειδής 'tending to whiteness', from *asper* 'rough' via ἄσπρος + -ειδής 'looking' (cf. εἶδος 'form'): Damigeron, Mesk 1898: 319.6 (II AD), repeated by Socrates and Dionysius 26.10 = Halleux and Schamp 1985: 166. *DGE*, LSJ suppl.
rare	ἀσπρομαυροπολυποίκιλος 'white-black-much-variegated', from *asper* 'rough' via ἄσπρος + μαῦρος 'black' + πολυποίκιλος 'much-variegated': *Physiologus* 21 Sbordone (II–IV AD).
not ancient	ἄσπρον, ἄσπρος 'white metal', 'tin', from *asper* 'rough' via ἄσπρος: probably no ancient examples. Cervenka-Ehrenstrasser (1996: 109), Diethart (1998: 168), *LBG*, Kriaras (1968–), *DGE* (*s.v.* ἀσπρός).
Direct loan **IV AD – modern**	ἄσπρος (-α/-η, -ον) 'white', as neut. subst. 'egg white', from *asper* 'rough'. Documents: *PSI* XIV.1427.19 etc. (VI AD); perhaps *Stud.Pal.* XX.245.4 (VI AD). Inscriptions: *IG* XII.VIII.568.4. Literature: Aelian, *De natura animalium* 1.25, marked (II/III AD); *Physiologus* 19 Sbordone (II–IV AD); Hieroph. Πῶς 462.16, 462.18 (IV–VI AD); Malal. 12.7 etc. (VI AD); Cyr.S. *Vit.Eu.* 35.22 (VI AD). Meaning 'egg white': Ps.-Galen XIV.560.5 Kühn.

Post-antique: common, forming derivatives ἀσπρίζω 'make white', ἀσπρότης 'whiteness', etc. *LBG* (*s.vv.* ἄσπρον, ἄσπρος), Kriaras (1968–), Triandaphyllidis (1909: 131), Zervan (2019: 19), Shipp (1979: 110). Modern ἄσπρο, ἄσπρος 'white' and derivatives: Babiniotis (2002), Andriotis (1967), Meyer (1895: 12).

Notes: the shift from 'rough' to white' occurred via use for new silver coins, which appeared light-coloured and rough compared to the tarnished, smoothly worn condition of older coins (convincingly argued by Psichari 1889: 312–15, with a less convincing claim that the form comes from neuter *asprum* = ἄσπρον: the neuter is usually *asperum*). Meaning 'egg white' apparently only in Ps.-Galen. Forms derivatives ἀσπροειδής, ἀσπρομαυροπολυποίκιλος, ἀσπροφορέω, perhaps ἀσπράτουρα. Cervenka-Ehrenstrasser (1996: 109–10), Schwyzer (1931: 28–40), Hofmann (1989: 36–7), Viscidi (1944: 31), *DÉLG*, Beekes (2010), Lampe (1961), *DGE* (*s.vv.* ἀσπρός, ἄσπρος), LSJ, LSJ suppl. See §4.2.2, §8.2.3, §10.2.1, §10.2.2 O.

not ancient?	**ἀσπρόσαρκος** 'with white flesh', from *asper* 'rough' via ἄσπρος + σαρκος (cf. σάρξ 'flesh'): *Passio Bartholomaei* 2 = Bonnet 1898: 131.19. Hofmann (1989: 37 *s.v.* ἄσπρος), Lampe (1961), *DGE*.
rare	**ἀσπροφορέω** 'wear white', from *asper* 'rough' via ἄσπρος + φορέω 'wear': Dan. Sket. *M.* 58, *AA* 169 (VI AD). Hofmann (1989: 37 *s.v.* ἄσπρος), *LBG*, Kriaras (1968– *s.v.* ἀσπροφορῶ), Lampe (1961).
not ancient?	**ἀσπρόχρους** 'white-coloured', from *asper* 'rough' via ἄσπρος + χρους (cf. χρώς 'flesh'): probably no ancient examples. Hofmann (1989: 37 *s.v.* ἄσπρος), *LBG*, *DGE*, LSJ suppl.
rare	**ἀσσαριαῖος** '(interest) at the rate of 12 asses per denarius per month', from *assārius* 'penny' via ἀσσάριον + -αῖος: inscription *I.Ephesos* 27.66 (II AD). Hofmann (1989: 37 *s.v.* ἀσσάριον), *DGE*, LSJ.
Direct loan **II BC – Byz.**	**ἀσ(σ)άριον** (-ου, τό) 'penny' (as a coin with a small value and as a small weight), in μέχρι ἀσσαρίου ἑνός 'to the last penny' a legal phrase meaning 'entirely', from *assārius* (*nummus*) 'penny'.

Documents: *PSI* XIII.1325.10 (II AD); *SB* 17156.7 (II/III AD); *P.Oxy.* 3756.12 etc. (IV AD); *P.Oxy.* 3758.11 etc. (IV AD); *P.Oxy.Hels.* 44.13 (IV AD); *P.Iand.* VI.126.7 (IV AD); *SB* 8265.15 (IV AD); *SB* 11075.14 (V AD); perhaps *Stud.Pal.* I p. 6 no. 1.13 (V AD); *P.Köln* III.155.16 (VI AD); *P.Cair.Masp.* 67151.93, 67154r.16, 67154v.9, 67312.47, 67313.9, 67353v.A13 (all VI AD).

Inscriptions: common, e.g. *I.Délos* 1439.Bbc.ii.91 (II BC); *I.Délos* 1442.B51 etc. (II BC); *I.Cret.* II.XI.3.21 etc. (I BC); *I.Cos Segre* ED10.6 (I BC/AD); *IG* X.II. II.325.i.9 etc. (I AD); *IG* XII.V.I.663.18 etc. (II AD); *SEG* XXXII.512.8 (II/III AD); *IG* XII.V.I.329.10 (III AD).

Coins: often in imperial period, Head 1911: 413, 479, 492, 601.

Literature: common, e.g. DH *AR* 9.27, 10.49 (I BC); NT Matthew 10:29, Luke 12:6 (I AD); Dsc. *Eup.* 1.235.1 (I AD); Plut. *Cam.* 13.1 (I/II AD); Athenaeus 15.701b (II/III AD); Jul.Afric. *Cest.* 4.1.46 (II/III AD); Gregorius Nazianzenus, *PG* XXXV.861c (IV AD); the frequent later examples are all commentary on the biblical passages or explanations of the word, e.g. Hesych. α 7646 (V/VI AD).

Post-antique: survives. *LBG*, Kriaras (1968–).

Notes: in inscriptions and literature means 'penny', but in papyri almost always 'entirely' (exception: *SB* 17156). Forms derivatives: see §4.6.2 Figure 1, and ἀσσαριαῖος. Cervenka-Ehrenstrasser (1996: 110–11), Diethart (1998: 169), Daris (1991a: 31, with derivation from neuter of *assārius*: see *TLL s.v.*), Hofmann (1989: 37), Viscidi (1944: 29–30), Meinersmann (1927: 8), Immisch (1885: 366), *DGE*, LSJ. See §4.2.4.1, §4.3.2 n. 75, §4.6.2, §6.3 n. 22, §8.1.4, §9.1 n. 4, §9.3 nn. 21 and 23, §10.2.1, §10.2.2 G.

ἀσσεδάριος, ἀσσιδάριος: see ἐσσεδάριος.

rare **ἀστατaρία** 'candlestick', from *statārius* 'stationary': papyrus *SB* 14528.4 (V/VI AD); occasional Byzantine texts. Cervenka-Ehrenstrasser (1996: 112–14, with multiple Latin source words), Daniel (1986: 60, with a different Latin etymology), Daris (1991a: 31, with a different Latin etymology), LSJ suppl. Cf. στατάριον 1.

Direct loan
II–III AD **ἀστᾶτος** (-ου, ὁ), a military rank, from *hastātus*, a military rank (*OLD s.v. hastātus²* 2).

Documents: *P.Rain.Cent.* 69.9 (III AD).

Inscriptions: *SEG* XXXIII.1195.2 (I/II AD); *IGLS* IV.1804.3 (II AD); *IGR* III.1206.

Literature: Polybius 6.23.1 etc., marked (II BC); Lyd. *Mag.* p. 72.12, marked (VI AD).

Notes: accent is disputed; I follow Cervenka-Ehrenstrasser (1996: 114). Dubuisson (1985: 21), Diethart (1998: 169), Daris (1991a: 31), Mason (1974: 4, 27), Hofmann (1989: 37), *DGE*, LSJ (*s.v.* ἄστατοι), LSJ suppl. (*s.v.* ἄστατοι). See §4.2.4.1 n. 51, §6.6 n. 40, §8.1.3 n. 17, §10.2.1, §10.2.2 C.

Direct loan
II AD – Byz. **ἄστη, ἄστα** (-ης, ἡ) 'spear', 'auction', from *hasta* 'spear'.

Documents: *P.Panop.Beatty* 2.138 etc. (III/IV AD).

Inscriptions: *I.Ephesos* 680.16 (I/II AD).

Post-antique: survives. *LBG*, Triandaphyllidis (1909: 129).

Notes: may form derivative ἀστιάριος. Cervenka-Ehrenstrasser (1996: 112, citing an additional unpublished papyrus), Turner (1961: 167), Daris (1991a: 31), Zilliacus (1935a: 226–7), *DGE*, LSJ suppl. See §6.1 n. 9, §10.2.1, §10.2.2 C.

ἀστιάριος: see ὀστιάριος.

Direct? loan
IV AD **ἀστιάριος** (-ου, ὁ), a military position, from barely attested *hastiārius* 'one who fights with a spear' (*TLL*) or *hasta* 'spear' via ἄστη + -άριος.

Documents: *BGU* IV.1024.5.8 (IV AD); *P.Herm.Landl.* 2.518 (IV AD); *SB* 11591.17, 11592.17 (both IV AD).

Notes: probably all examples are from Hermopolis and its environs. Cervenka-Ehrenstrasser (1996: 114–15), Daris (1991a: 32), *DGE* (with definition 'armourer specialising in the repair of spears'), LSJ suppl. (with definition 'grade of cavalry officer'). See §4.2.4.1 n. 50, §6.1 n. 9, §9.2, §10.2.1, §10.2.2 C.

Direct loan **II AD – Byz.**	**ἀστίλιον, ἀστίλλιον** (-ου, τό) 'shaft', 'spear', from *hastīle* 'spear-shaft'. Documents: *SB* 9017.9.7 (I/II AD); *SB* 11641.10 (II AD). Inscriptions: Edict.Diocl. 14.4 etc. (IV AD). Post-antique: occasional examples. *LBG*. Notes: Cervenka-Ehrenstrasser (1996: 115–16), Daris (1991a: 32), Hofmann (1989: 38), Cavenaile (1951: 395), Zilliacus (1935a: 226–7), *DGE*, LSJ suppl. See §4.2.5, §10.2.1, §10.2.2 C.
rare	**ἀστλῶσος** 'crumbly', from *assulōsus/astulōsus* 'crumbly' (*TLL*): Hippiatr.Berl. 130.187. *LBG*, *DGE* (*s.v.* ἀστλῶσα).
rare	**ἀστούργων** 'Asturian horse', from *asturcō* 'Asturian horse': *P.Sijp.* 29.32 etc. (II AD). Editor *ad loc.*
Direct loan **II BC – II AD**	**ἄτριον, ἀτρεῖον** (-ου, τό) 'entrance hall', 'courtyard' (esp. in name of *Atrium Magnum* in Alexandria), from *ātrium* 'entrance hall', 'courtyard'. Documents: *SB* 8247.15 (I AD); *P.Fouad* 21.4 (I AD); *P.Oxy.* 2406 (II AD). Inscriptions: *Syll.*³ 656.26 (II BC); *I.Stratonikeia* 15.7, 664.4 (both I AD); *I.Portes du désert* 70.3 (II AD); *IGR* 1.1048.3 (II AD). Literature: Teucer, Boll 1908: 202.23 (I AD?). Notes: perhaps spelled ἄτρεον in *Syll.*³ 656. Cervenka-Ehrenstrasser (1996: 116–17, but note that *SB* 8815 and 8283 are inscriptions: *I.Portes du désert* 70, *IGR* 1.1048), Chantraine (1964: 13–14), Daris (1991a: 32), Hofmann (1989: 38), Cavenaile (1951: 395), Meinersmann (1927: 8), *DGE* (*s.v.* 2 ἄτριον), LSJ suppl. (*s.v.* ἄτριον B). See §4.2.4.1 n. 54, §4.3.2 n. 75, **§8.1.4**, §10.2.1, §10.2.2 J.
not ancient	**ἀτρίπλικεμ** transliterating acc. of *ātriplex* 'orach' (a plant): interpolation in Dsc. 2.119 RV. Sophocles (1887 *s.v.* ἀτριπλεξ).
rare	**ἀτταγήνα, ἀτταγήνη** 'female francolin', apparently from *attagēna* 'female francolin': Edict.Diocl. 4.30 (IV AD). Döttling (1920: 12), *DGE* (*s.v.* ἀτταγήνη), LSJ suppl. (*s.v.* ἀτταγήνη).
foreign	**ἀττένδερε** transliterating inf. of *attendō* 'pay attention': Lyd. *Mag.* p. 26.3 (VI AD), arguing that *attendere* means 'engage in rivalry'. Sophocles (1887).
foreign	**ἀττηνσίων** 'service', from *attentiō* 'attention': Lyd. *Mag.* pp. 4.20, 24.25, marked (VI AD). Binder (2000: 232), Hofmann (1989: 38), *LBG*.
foreign	**ἀττῆνσος** transliterating *attentus* 'attentive': Lyd. *Mag.* p. 26.1 (VI AD). *LBG*.
	Αὔγοστος: see Αὔγουστος.
Direct loan **I–II AD?**	**αὖγο(υ)ρ, αὖγυρ** (-ος, ὁ) 'augur', from *augur* 'augur'. Inscriptions: e.g. *IG* II/III².III.4115.5 (I AD?); *IG* II/III².III.4102.4 (I/II AD?); *IG* XIV.1125.5 (II AD); Lane 1971: no. 164.4. Literature: DH *AR* 2.64.4, marked (I BC); Augustus, *Res gestae* 7.5 Volkmann (I AD); Plut. e.g. *Aem.* 3.2, often marked (I/II AD). Notes: Vaahtera (2001: esp. 65–7), Binder (2000: 215–16), García Domingo (1979: 326), Mason (1974: 4, 27–8, 116), Hofmann (1989: 38), *DGE*. See §4.2.5, §10.2.1, §10.2.2 D.

Direct loan
III AD – Byz.

Α(ὐ)γοῦστα (-ης, ἡ) 'empress' (for fem. of adj. see Αὔγουστος 2), from *Augusta* 'empress'.

Documents: *CPR* V.18.4 (VI AD).

Inscriptions: common esp. in III AD, e.g. *I.Tomis* 83.9 (II/III AD); *IGBulg.* III.II.1710.6 (III AD); *IGBulg.* IV.2009.5 (III AD); *IG* XII.V.1.748.4 (III AD); *I.Aphrodisias Late Ant.* 23.2 (IV AD); *SEG* XXXII.1502 (V AD).

Literature: common, e.g. Dio Cassius 56.46.2 (II/III AD); Eus. *VC* 3.43.4 (IV AD); Marc.Diac. 38.17 (V AD); Evagr.Schol. *HE* 85.28 (VI AD). Also Choeroboscus (VIII/IX AD) probably following Herodian (II AD): Hdn. Κλισ.Ὀνομ. III.II.752.34–753.13.

Post-antique: common, forming derivatives αὐγουστιακός 'of the empress', αὐγουστικός 'of the empress', etc. Zervan (2019: 20), Kriaras (1968–), Triandaphyllidis (1909: 126), Sophocles (1887 *s.v.* αὔγουστος), *LBG* (*s.v.* ἀγοῦστα).

Notes: Cervenka-Ehrenstrasser (1996: 117–18), Lampe (1961), *DGE*, LSJ suppl. (*s.v.* αὔγουστος). See **§4.2.3.1** with passage 4 and n. 36, §4.6.1, §10.2.1, §10.2.2 A.

Αὐγουσταῖον: see Αὐγουστεῖον.

Αὐγουσταλειανός: see Αὐγουσταλιανός.

Αὐγουστάλης: see Αὐγουστάλιος.

rare

Αὐγουστάλια 'imperial games', 'festival in honour of Augustus', from *Augustālia* 'festival in honour of Augustus': Augustus, *Res gestae* 11.8 Volkmann (I AD); Dio Cassius 56.47.2 etc. (II/III AD). García Domingo (1979: 327), Hofmann (1989: 39–40), *DGE*, LSJ (*s.v.* αὔγουστος).

Direct loan
V–VI AD

Α(ὐ)γουσταλιανός, Α(ὐ)γουσταλειανός (-ή, -όν) 'of the Augustalis (of Egypt)', as masc. subst. 'functionary in the office of the Augustalis', as neut. subst. 'court of the Augustalis', from *Augustāliānus* 'of the Augustalis (of Egypt)' (*TLL*).

Documents, adj.: *P.Oxy.* 4394.21 etc. (V AD); *P.Oxy.* 4395.14 etc. (V AD); *CPR* VIII.54.7 (V AD); *P.Oxy.* 1882.4 etc. (VI AD); *P.Wash.Univ.* 1.6.4 etc. (VI AD); *P.Gascou* 34.9 (VI AD). Masc. subst.: *P.Oxy.Hatz.* 13.15, quoted by Cervenka-Ehrenstrasser 1996: 118 (VI AD). Neut. subst.: *P.Princ.* II.82.9 (V AD); perhaps *PSI* IV.301.17 (V AD).

Literature, adj.: Just. *Edict* 13.2 = p. 781.11 etc. (VI AD). Masc. subst.: Just. *Edict* 13.2 = p. 781.12 etc. (VI AD).

Notes: Cervenka-Ehrenstrasser (1996: 118–19), Gonis (1998: 217–18), Avotins (1992 *s.v.* αὐγουσταλειανός), Daris (1991a: 32 *s.vv.* αὐγουσταλιανόν, αὐγουσταλιανός), Hofmann (1989: 39), Cavenaile (1951: 395), *TLL* (*s.v.* *Augustus* 1408.54–61), *DGE*, LSJ suppl. See §4.2.2, §10.2.1, §10.2.2 D.

Direct loan
I AD – Byz.

Α(ὐ)γο(υ)στάλιος, Αὐγουστάλης, Αὐγουστᾱλις (-α, -ον) 'of Augustus', as masc. subst. the title *Augustālis* (esp. of the prefect of Egypt, but also of a priest in the cult of Augustus, a subset of the *exceptores*, and a military rank), from *Augustālis* 'of Augustus'.

Documents, adj.: perhaps *PSI* IV.301.17 (V AD); *P.Cair.Masp.* 67002.1.18 (VI AD). Masc. subst.: common (esp. in VI AD), e.g. *P.Oxy.* 4382.7 (IV AD); *P.Münch.* I.15.25 (V AD); *P.Flor.* III.293.1 (VI AD).

Inscriptions, masc. subst. only: ending -ιος: e.g. *IG* v.ii.151.13 (ii ad); perhaps *IGR* iii.1152.3 (iii ad?); *SEG* xxviii.1454.4 (iv ad); *I.Philae* 216.6 (vi ad). Ending -ις: *I.Ephesos* 17.2, part of σωδᾶλις αὐγουστᾶλις = *sodālis augustālis* (i ad); *IG* xiv.157.2; *IGUR* ii 766.4. Ending (implying) -ης: *I.Prusa* 77.2 (ii ad); *SEG* lii.606.3 (iii ad); *SEG* xxix.614.4.

Literature, adj.: Just. *Edict* 13.24 = p. 793.2 (vi ad). Masc. subst.: common from v/vi ad, e.g. Pall. *H.Laus.* 46.3, *V.Chrys.* 39.4 (iv/v ad); Malal. 11.23 (vi ad); Lyd. *Mag.* p. 86.26 (vi ad); Just. *Nov.* 7.ep. (vi ad). Unverified example (iv ad) in Zilliacus (1937: 322, 328).

Post-antique: numerous, forming derivative αὐγουσταλικός 'of the Augustalis' (*LBG*). Kriaras (1968–), Zervan (2019: 20), Sophocles (1887), Triandaphyllidis (1909: 125, 126, 131).

Notes: variants Αὐγουστάλης and Αὐγουστᾶλις occur only in inscriptions: αὐγουστάλ(οις) in papyrus *P.Princ.* iii.139v.2.12 (v/vi ad) should be αὐγουσταλ(ίοις) (Cervenka-Ehrenstrasser 1996: 120). Cervenka-Ehrenstrasser (1996: 119–22), Avotins (1992), Daris (1991a: 32, two entries), Mason (1974: 28, 117), Hofmann (1989: 39–40), Zilliacus (1935a: 216–17, 1937: 328), Meinersmann (1927: 8), *TLL* (*s.v. Augustus* 1403.4–1409.11), Lampe (1961), *DGE*, LSJ (*s.v.* αὔγουστος), LSJ suppl. (*s.vv.* Αὐγουστάλης, Αὐγουστάλιος). See §4.2.2 with n. 34, §10.2.1, §10.2.2 D.

name

Αὐγουσταμνική, an Egyptian region, from *Augustus* 'Augustus'. Meinersmann (1927: 8–9), *DGE*, Lampe (1961).

not ancient

αὐγουστέα 'sweet violet', probably ultimately from *Augustus*: interpolation in Dsc. 3.123 RV. Hofmann (1989: 41 *s.v.* αυγουστιον), *DGE*.

Αὐγούστεια (τά): see Αὐγούστειος.

Direct loan (with influence?)
i–iii ad and vi ad – Byz.

Αὐγουστ(ε)ῖον, Αὐγουστῆον, Αὐγουσταῖον, Ἀουσταῖον (-ου, τό) 'Augusteum', from *Augustēum* 'temple of Augustus' (in Rome), 'building containing the imperial memorials' (in Constantinople) (*TLL*), perhaps with influence from Greek -εῖον suffix used for temples and other places (Chantraine 1933: 61).

Documents: unpublished O.Claud. inv. 7250.6 (ii ad).

Inscriptions: *I.Ephesos* 412.5 (i ad).

Literature: Dio Cassius 57.10.2, 60.5.2 (ii/iii ad); Malchus, *Testimonia* 1.4 Cresci (v/vi ad?); Malal. 18.85 (vi ad); Hesychius Illustrius, *Patria Constantinopoleos* 40 in Preger 1901, marked (vi ad); Lyd. *Mens.* 4.138 (vi ad); Procop. *Aed.* 1.2.1, 1.10.5, marked (vi ad).

Post-antique: survives.

Notes: early examples refer to Rome and later ones to Constantinople. Hofmann (1989: 40–1), *TLL* (*s.v. Augustus* 1410.23–37), Lampe (1961 *s.v.* Αὐγουσταῖον), *DGE* (*s.v.* αὐγουστεῖος), LSJ (*s.v.* αὔγουστος). See §4.4, §8.2.1, §10.2.1, §10.2.2 A, §12.2.2; cf. αὐγουστεών, which may be the same word.

Direct loan with influence
ii–iii ad

Αὐγούστειος (-α, -ον) 'of Augustus', 'in honour of Augustus', as neut. pl. subst. 'festival of Augustus' (including athletic games), from *Augustēus* 'Augustan' with influence from -ειος.

Inscriptions, adj.: common, e.g. *MAMA* viii.521.26 etc. (ii/iii ad); *TAM* v.ii.1019.7 (iii ad). Neut. pl. subst.: common, e.g. *I.Tralleis* 136.16 (ii ad); *F.Delphes* iii.iv.476.Bb.1 (ii/iii ad); *IG* ii/iii².iii.3169/70.27 (iii ad).

Coins: neut. pl. subst. e.g. Head 1911: 658, 661, 702 (i–iii ad).

Literature, adj.: Dio Cassius 55.23.7 etc. (II/III AD).

Notes: traditionally considered two-termination, but feminine probably occurs. Mason (1974: 6, 28), Hofmann (1989: 40, giving Αὐγούστειοι a separate entry and putting Αὐγούστεια under Αὐγουστάλιος), *TLL* (*s.v. Augustus* 1409.63–1410.23), *DGE* (*s.vv.* αὐγούστεια, αὐγούστειοι, αὐγουστεῖος), LSJ (*s.v.* αὔγουστος). See §4.4, §9.1 n. 4, §10.2.1, §10.2.2 F.

Αὐγουστέσιοι: see Αὐγουστήσιοι.

rare   **Αὐγουστεών, Αὐγουστιών**, a forum in Constantinople, ultimately from *Augustus* 'Augustus', probably immediately from *Augustēum* 'temple of Augustus' + -ων: Malal. 13.8, 18.94 (VI AD); Byzantine texts. May have been the same word as Αὐγουστεῖον (*q.v.*) for some speakers. Hofmann (1989: 40–1 *s.v.* Αὐγουστεῖον), *LBG*, Lampe (1961), *DGE*.

Αὐγουστῆον: see Αὐγουστεῖον.

Direct loan
III/IV AD   **Αὐγουστήσιοι, Αὐγουστέσιοι** (-ων, οἱ), a Jewish group in Rome, from *Augustēnsis* 'Augustan' (*TLL s.v. Augustus* 1409.54–63, 1419.32–8).

Inscriptions: *I.Jud.Western Europe* II.96.3, 189.4, 194.5, 542.4, perhaps 169.3 (all III/IV AD).

Notes: found only in Rome. This meaning is not attested for the Latin. *TLL* (*s.v. Augustus* 1409.61–3, 1419.37–8), *DGE*. See §4.2.5, §6.7 n. 45, §9.2, §10.2.1, §10.2.2 N.

non-existent   **Αὐγούστιον**, cited as a unit of measurement from *Augustēus* 'Augustan' (Lampe 1961, Hofmann 1989: 41, *DGE*): superseded reading of inscription *I.Chr.Asie Mineure* I.290.5 (IV AD). Cuvigny (2017: 102).

Αὐγουστιών: see Αὐγουστεών.

Direct loan
I AD – Byz.   **Α(ὔ)γο(υ)στος 1, Ἄγυστος, Ἄκουος, Ἀούγουστος, Ἄουστος, Αὔουστος** (-ου, ὁ) 'Augustus', 'emperor', from *Augustus* 'Augustus' (*OLD s.v. Augustus²*).

Documents: very common (esp. from IV AD onwards), e.g. *BGU* VII.1655.3.55 (II AD); *SB* 16169.5 (III AD); *P.Oxy.* 4085.3 (IV AD); *SB* 15801.12 (V AD); *P.Oxy.* 4350.2 (VI AD).

Inscriptions: common, e.g. *IGBulg.* I².58.7 (I AD); *IG* IV.588.11 (II AD); *IG* VII.2500.4 (II/III AD); *IGBulg.* III.II.1559.3 (III AD); *IG* XII.VIII.244b.7 (IV AD); *IG* V.I.451.6 (IV AD); *SEG* XXXIX.1004.10 (V AD); *I.Chr. Bulgarien* 231.11 (VI AD).

Literature: very common, e.g. NT Luke 2:1 (I AD); Pausanias 4.31.1 (II AD); Hippolytus, *Commentarium in Danielem* 4.23.3 (III AD); Eus. *HE* 10.5.4 (IV AD), Soz. 6.4.7 (V AD); Evagr.Schol. *HE* 105.3 (VI AD).

Post-antique: common, forming derivatives αὐγουσταδέλφη 'emperor's sister', αὐγουστόδοξος 'with honourable reputation', etc. (*LBG*). Kriaras (1968–), Sophocles (1887), Triandaphyllidis (1909: 126).

Notes: used like a name for the first emperor in literature until IV AD. Forms derivative τρισαυγούστιον. Cervenka-Ehrenstrasser (1996: 123–4), Menci (2000: 280–1), Binder (2000: 215), Leclercq (1997: 294), Freyburger-Galland (1992: 241–3), Mason (1974: 9, 12, 28), Hofmann (1989: 41–2), Zilliacus (1937: 328), Meinersmann (1927: 8), Lampe (1961), *DGE*, LSJ, LSJ suppl. See §4.1.1, §4.2.4.1 n. 51, §5.2.1, §5.2.2 n. 10, §8.1.1 n. 3, §9.3 nn. 21 and 23, §10.2.1, §10.2.2 A, §12.2.1, §12.2.2.

Direct loan
I BC – modern

Α(ὔ)γ(ο)υστος 2, Ἄγοστος, Ἀούγουστος, Ἄουστος (-η, -ον) 'of Augustus', 'imperial', esp. of military units, also of month 'August' (in this meaning often substantivized), from *Augustus* 'of Augustus' (*OLD s.v. Augustus*³).

Documents: 'imperial': *P.Hamb.* 1.1.8 (I AD); *O.Claud.* IV.775.8, 776.11 (both I/II AD); *O.Claud.* III.540.2, 541.3 (both II AD); *P.Stras.* V.340.12 (II AD); *BGU* III.741.7, perhaps 709.2 (both II AD); perhaps *O.Krok.* 1.59.3 (II AD); *SB* 16735.4 (III AD).   'August': e.g. *BGU* IV.1032.5 (II AD); *P.Panop.Beatty* 1.25 (III AD); *PSI* XII.1264.14 (IV AD); *SB* 8028.9 (VI AD).

Inscriptions: 'imperial', 'of Augustus': e.g. *SEG* VII.970.4 (I AD); Bosch 1967: 136 no. 113.5 (I/II AD); *SEG* XVIII.557.6 (II AD); *I.Tomis* 85.9 (II/III AD); *IGBulg.* V.5891.5 (III AD).   'August': e.g. *I.Cret.* II.XI.3.14 etc. (I BC); *IG* IV².1.88.20 (II AD); *IGBulg.* II.669.5 (III AD); *SEG* XXX.585 (IV AD); *SEG* XXXIX.1016.4 (V AD); *IG* II/III².V.13521.7 (VI AD).

Literature: 'imperial': Dio Cassius 54.10.6, 54.11.5 (II/III AD), perhaps others.   'August': e.g. *Jubil.* frag. x'14 (I BC?); Plut. *Rom.* 15.7 (I/II AD); Ostanes, Berthelot and Ruelle 1888: 261.16 (I/II AD); Polyaenus, *Strategemata* 8.10.3 (II AD); *Act.Scillit.* 113.2 (II/III AD); Eus. *HE* 10.5.23 (IV AD); Socr. 7.39.26 (IV/V AD); Malal. 7.13 (VI AD); Cyr.S. *Vit.Eu.* 9.13 (VI AD).

Post-antique: common in meaning 'August'. *LBG* (*s.v.* Ἄγουστος), Kriaras (1968–). Modern Αὔγουστος: Babiniotis (2002), Andriotis (1967), Meyer (1895: 12).

Notes: Cervenka-Ehrenstrasser (1996: 122–3), Solin (2008), Menci (2000: 280–1), Binder (2000: 215), Avotins (1992), Sijpesteijn (1979), Hofmann (1989: 41–2), Meinersmann (1927: 8), Lampe (1961), *DGE*, LSJ, LSJ suppl. See **§4.2.1**, §4.2.2, §8.1.1 n. 3, **§8.1.5**, §8.2.3 n. 51, §10.2.1, §10.2.2 E.

rare

αὐδιτώριον, αὐδειτώριον, αὐδιτόριον (-ου, τό) 'hall of justice', from *audītōrium* 'hall': inscription *I.Ephesos* 3009.3 (II/III AD); Just. *Nov.* 50.pr. (VI AD); occasional Byzantine texts. Avotins (1992 *s.v.* αὐδειτώριον), Hofmann (1989: 42), Zilliacus (1935a: 174–5), *LBG*, *DGE*, LSJ suppl.

foreign

αὔκτωρ transliterating *auctor* 'person with authority': inscription *I.Leukopetra* 51.3 (III AD). On tablet *I.Dacia Rom.* 1.38 (in margin) it is Latin in Greek script.

foreign

αὐκτώριτας transliterating *auctōritās* 'authority': Dio Cassius 55.3.4 (II/III AD). Freyburger-Galland (1992: 239–41, 1997: 28, 215–16, 1998: 141), Mason (1974: 6, 12, 28), Sophocles (1887 *s.v.* ἀουκτώριτας), *DGE*. See **§9.5.2** passage 62.

rare

αὐξιλιάριος, αὐσιλιάριος 'auxiliary', from *auxiliārius* 'auxiliary' and perhaps *auxiliāris* 'auxiliary': perhaps papyrus *BGU* I.316.8 (IV AD); for auxiliary troops, Lyd. *Mag.* pp. 72.4 (marked), 136.10 (VI AD); as epithet of Athena, Ps.-Plut. *Mor.* 308c. Cervenka-Ehrenstrasser (1996: 124–5), Diethart (1998: 169), Binder (2000: 228), Daris (1991a: 32), Hofmann (1989: 43), Meinersmann (1927: 9), *DGE*.

Direct loan
VI AD?

αὐράριος (-ου, ὁ) 'goldsmith', 'supporter', from *aurārius* 'goldsmith' (*TLL s.v.* 1. *aurārius* 1481.40) and *aurārius* 'supporter' (*TLL s.v.* 2. *aurārius*).

Inscriptions: perhaps *I.Perinthos* 49B.3 (II AD); *IG* XII.V.1.712.67.5; *I.Aphrodisias Performers* 45.39; *MAMA* I.214.6, 215.2, 281.7, 281a.5; *MAMA* III.254, 348b, 413; *MAMA* VII.87.2.

Literature: Unverified example (III AD) in Zilliacus (1937: 323, 328).
Notes: although all secure examples are undated, derivative πρωταυράριος (VI AD) provides a *terminus ante quem*. Hofmann (1989: 43), Zilliacus (1937: 328), Lampe (1961), *LBG, DGE* (s.v. 1 αὐράριος), LSJ suppl. See §4.2.4.1 n. 50, §10.2.1, §10.2.2 F; cf. πρωταυράριος.

foreign	**αὐρίγαμμος** 'adorned with a golden gamma', from *aurum* 'gold' + γάμμα 'gamma': Lyd. *Mag.* p. 88.16, marked (VI AD). *DGE*, LSJ.
foreign	**αὐρικαίσωρ** 'gold-beater', from unattested **auricaesor*: in unassimilated Latin dat. pl. αὐρικαισωρίβους or αὐρικαεσωρίβους, Edict.Diocl. 30.4 (IV AD). Lauffer (1971: 279), Hofmann (1989: 43), *TLL* (s.v. *auricaesor*), *DGE*. See §5.2.3 n. 17, §8.1.7, §9.5.1.

αὐριολάρια: see ἀγριλάρια.

rare	**αὐροχάλκειος** 'of orichalcum', either from *orichalcum/aurichalcum* 'orichalcum' + -ειος or variant of ὀρείχαλκος/ὀρειχάλκινος 'of orichalcum' influenced by *aurum* 'gold': inscription *CISemiticarum* II.III.3914.6 (II AD); occasional Byzantine texts. Hofmann (1989: 43 s.v. αὐρόχαλκος), *LBG, DGE*, LSJ suppl.
rare	**αὐρόχαλκος** 'of aurichalcum', 'of gilded bronze', either from *orichalcum/ aurichalcum* 'orichalcum' or variant of ὀρείχαλκος/ὀρειχάλκινος 'of orichalcum' influenced by *aurum* 'gold': inscriptions *I.Ephesos* 3015.3 (III AD); Edict.Diocl. 15.63a (IV AD); with *aurichalcum* in Gloss. Ps.-Cyril. 251.20. Hofmann (1989: 43), *TLL* (s.v. *aurichalcum*, esp. 1494.4–5), *DGE*, LSJ suppl.

αὐσιλιάριος: see αὐξιλιάριος.

foreign	**αὖσπεξ** (in acc. pl. αὖσπικας) transliterating *auspex* 'bird-diviner': Plut. *Mor.* 281a (I/II AD). Vaahtera (2001: 76–7), Mason (1974: 6, 28), Hofmann (1989: 44), *DGE* (s.v. αὖσπιξ).
foreign	**αὐσπίκειον** transliterating *auspicium* 'augury from birds': Eutropius 2.26 (IV AD). *LBG*.
not Latin	**ἀφρᾶτον**, a kind of foam, cited by LSJ as from *afratum* 'soufflé': see *TLL* (s.v. *afrutum*), *DGE* (s.vv. ἀφράτος, ἄφρατος).
name	**Ἀφρικανός** 'African', from *Āfricānus* 'African'. *DGE*.
name	**Ἀφρική** 'Africa', from *Āfrica* 'Africa'. Hofmann (1989: 44), *DGE*.

ἀχαόμαυρος: see μαῦρος.

ἀψινθάτιον: see ἀψινθᾶτος.

Direct loan **II AD – Byz.**	**ἀψινθᾶτος, ἀψινθιᾶτος** (-η, -ον) 'flavoured with wormwood', esp. neut. subst. 'wine flavoured with wormwood', 'potion made with wormwood', probably from *apsinthiātum/absentātum* 'wine flavoured with wormwood' (*TLL*) and/ or *absinthiātus* 'containing wormwood' (L&S); they are from *apsinthium* 'wormwood', itself from ἀψίνθιον. Documents, subst.: *P.Lond.* III.1259r.32 (IV AD); *P.Ryl.* IV.639.73 (IV AD); Andorlini 2001: no. 15.4 (VI AD). Inscriptions, subst.: Edict.Diocl. 2.18 (IV AD).

Literature, adj.: Aelius Promotus, Περὶ τῶν ἰοβόλων θηρίων 59.8 Ihm (II AD); Orib. *Eun.* 3.7.18 (IV AD). Subst.: Ps.-Orib. *Col.* 5.33.13 (IV AD?); Hieroph. *Nut.* 9.5 (IV–VI AD); Aëtius 3.71.1 etc. (VI AD); Alex.Trall. 1.543.27 etc. (VI AD); Simplicius, *In Aristotelis categorias commentarium* p. 413.9 Kalbfleisch (VI AD).

Post-antique: survives. *LBG.*

Notes: Maravela-Solbakk (2010: 257–8, 265) and Chantraine (*DÉLG s.v.* ἄψινθος) see neuter ἀψινθᾶτον not as a loanword but as a Greek formation (later borrowed into Latin) from ἄψινθος or ἀψίνθιον 'wormwood' + -ᾶτον. *P.Lond.* III.1259 has ἀψινθάτιον, which LSJ considers a mistake for ἀψινθιᾶτον (found in Alex.Trall. II.487.13) but Frisk (1954–72: I.204) and Maravela-Solbakk (2010: 257) consider a diminutive in -ιον. Andorlini (2001: 168–9), Hofmann (1989: 45), Beekes (2010 *s.v.* ἀψίνθιον), *DGE* (*s.v.* ἀψινθᾶτον), LSJ and LSJ suppl. (*s.v.* ἀψινθᾶτον). See §4.2.2, **§6.5**, §6.6, §10.2.1, §10.2.2 I, §10.3.2.

B

not ancient? βαβοῦλι 'bud', perhaps from *valvolī* 'husks of beans': no certainly ancient examples. Meyer (1895: 12), Kriaras (1968–).

not ancient? βαγεύω 'wander', from *vagor* 'wander' + -εύω: no certainly ancient examples. Zilliacus (1935a: 214–15, 238–9), *DGE*, LSJ suppl. (*s.v.* βαγεύει).

rare βαγινάριος 'scabbard-maker', apparently from medieval *vāgīnārius* 'scabbard-maker' (Du Cange 1883–7): inscription *SEG* XL.552 (V/VI AD); Lyd. *Mag.* p. 72.18, marked (VI AD). Zilliacus (1935a: 238–9), *DGE*, LSJ suppl.

βάδα: see οὐάδα.

not Latin βαδιάζω 'go', suggested as from *vador* 'to accept sureties from (the other party) for his appearance in court' by Zilliacus (1935a: 214–15), is probably from Classical βαδίζω 'go'. *LBG.*

rare βάδιλλος 'shovel', from *batillum/batillus* 'shovel' (L&S): papyrus *P.Oxy.* 521.13 (II AD). Cervenka-Ehrenstrasser (2000: 133), Schirru (2013: 315), Daris (1991a: 32), Hofmann (1989: 45), *DGE*, LSJ.

not Latin? βαΐα 'nurse', perhaps from *bāiula* 'nurse' (*TLL s.v. baiulus* 1687.53–6): inscription *SEG* XLIV.584 (VI AD); perhaps several papyri; probably not Strabo, *Chrestomathia* 5.39 (Radt 2010: 267.34). Chantraine (*DÉLG*), Frisk (1954–72: I.208), and Beekes (2010) consider it to have no etymology; Chantraine and Beekes also say it means 'grandmother', which does not fit the context. Wilhelm (1928a: 277), Sophocles (1887), Meyer (1895: 12–13 *s.v.* βαΐλας), *DGE*, LSJ, LSJ suppl.

rare βάιουλος 'porter', 'tutor', from *bāiulus* 'porter': with uncertain meaning (LSJ suppl., though *DGE* uses 'porter') on inscription *I.Prusias* 72.11 (II AD); meaning 'porter' perhaps in Hesych. as gloss α 423 (V/VI AD); scholion to Sophocles, *Ajax* 551 is probably not ancient (not included by Christodoulou 1977). Common in Byzantine texts, meaning 'tutor' and being an official title: *LBG*, Zervan (2019: 20–1), Kriaras (1968–), Triandaphyllidis (1909: 123). Hofmann (1989: 45), Meyer (1895: 12–13 *s.v.* βαΐλας), *DGE*, LSJ suppl.

not Latin?   βακάϊον, a measure, perhaps from *bacarium*, a vessel for water (*TLL*): Hesych. as gloss β 105 (V/VI AD). Immisch (1885: 360–1), LSJ.

rare   βακάντιβος 'absentee bishop', from *vacantīvus* 'not at work' (Du Cange 1883–7): Syn.Cyr. *Ep.* 66.324 (IV/V AD); Byzantine texts. Hofmann (1989: 45–6), *LBG*, Lampe (1961), *DGE*.

foreign   βακάντιος 'unclaimed' (of inheritances), from *vacantia* 'vacant estates', pres. part. neut. pl. of *vacō* 'be vacant' (L&S *s.v. vaco*, section on *vacans* A): Antec. in Latin script 2.6.9 *vacantia* etc. (VI AD); later in Greek script. Zilliacus (1935a: 214–15) cites both this and a different βακάντιος (a variant of βακάντιβος), for which I can find no ancient examples. *LBG*. See §9.5.6 n. 68.

foreign   βακατίων 'grace period', from *vacātiō* 'respite': Antec. in Latin script 1.25.2 *vacationa* (VI AD). Zilliacus (1935a: 214–15).

Deriv. of loan
V AD – modern   βακλίζω 'beat', from *baculum* 'staff' via βάκλον + -ίζω.
  Documents: *P.Herm.* 48.2 (V AD); *P.Cair.Masp.* 67005.18 (VI AD); *SB* 9616r.5 (VI AD).
  Literature: with *fustigo* in Gloss. Ps.-Philox. 74.57.
  Post-antique: numerous. *LBG*. Modern βακλίζω: Kahane and Kahane (1972–6: 534–5).
  Notes: Cervenka-Ehrenstrasser (2000: 134–5), Binder (2000: 168), Daris (1991a: 32), Hofmann (1989: 46 *s.v.* βάκλον), Lampe (1961), *DGE*, LSJ (*s.v.* βάκλον). See §4.6.1, §9.2, §10.2.2 O.

rare   βάκλιον 'stick', from *baculum* 'staff' via βάκλον: *Apophth.Patr.* 18.51.5 (V AD); with *bacillum* in Gloss. Ps.-Cyril. 255.27.

Direct loan
III AD – modern   βάκλον, βάκιλον (-ου, τό) 'stick', 'cudgel', from *baculum* 'staff', perhaps with influence from *bacillum* 'small staff' for βάκιλον.
  Documents: none. *DGE* cites *P.Prag.* 1.90.12, but see Cervenka-Ehrenstrasser (2000: 272).
  Literature: Plut. *Rom.* 26.3, marked (I/II AD); *V.Secundi* 68.7 (II/III AD); Agath. *Arm.* 31.3 (V AD); *ACO* II.I.I p. 75.14 etc. (V AD); Thdr.Anag. *HE* 4.483.5 (V/VI AD); EphraemSyr. VII pp. 191.8, 363.11 (V/VI AD); Hesych. as gloss α 3857 (V/VI AD); Malal. 7.12.21, 18.132.20 (VI AD); Cyr.S. *Vit.Eu.* 70.4 (VI AD); Romanus Melodus, *Cantica genuina* 58.17.10 Maas and Trypanis (VI AD); Aesop, *Fabulae* 93.2b.24 Hausrath and Hunger; scholion to Ar. *Pl.* 476; with *fustis* in Gloss. Ps.-Philox. 74.56. Unverified examples (III, IV, and VI AD) in Zilliacus (1937: 322, 328).
  Post-antique: common. *LBG*, Triandaphyllidis (1909: 122). Modern dialectal βάκλο etc. 'stick', 'tail': Andriotis (1974: 171), Meyer (1895: 13).
  Notes: forms derivative βακλίζω. Cervenka-Ehrenstrasser (2000: 135 *s.v.* βακλίζω), Binder (2000: 168, 251), Strobach (1997: 194), Daris (1991a: 32), Hofmann (1989: 46), Viscidi (1944: 40), Zilliacus (1937: 328), Immisch (1885: 368), *DGE*, LSJ. See §4.2.4.1 n. 55, §4.6.1, §9.2, §10.1, §10.2.1, §10.2.2 M.

βαλανείων: see ἐπὶ βαλανείων.

foreign   βάλεας 'may you fare', from *valeas*, subjunctive of *valeō* 'be well': in Latin script as part of *bene baleas* (= *bene valeas* 'farewell'), papyrus *P.Münch.* 1.2.21 etc. (VI AD); not in *P.Münch.* 1.14.111 (VI AD). Daris (1991a: 33), Meinersmann (1927: 9).

Βαλεντινιανοί: see Οὐαλεντινιανοί.

foreign | **βαλῆρε** transliterating inf. of *valeō* 'be well': Zosimus, *Historia nova* 2.3.2 Paschoud (v AD?). Sophocles (1887 *s.v.* οὐαλῆρε).

Direct loan
IV AD – Byz. | **βαλ(λ)ιστάριος, βαλ(λ)ιστράριος** (-ου, ὁ) 'catapult operator', from *ballistārius/ ballistrārius* 'catapult operator' (*TLL*).

Inscriptions: *SEG* VII.154 (IV AD); *CIG* 8621.7 (VI AD); perhaps *MAMA* III.93.

Literature: Just. *Nov.* 85.2 etc. (VI AD); Ath.Schol. 23.21 (VI AD); Lyd. *Mag.* p. 72.23, marked (VI AD).

Post-antique: numerous. *LBG*, Triandaphyllidis (1909: 128).

Notes: Avotins (1992), Hofmann (1989: 47), Zilliacus (1935a: 218–19), *TLL* (*s.v. ballistārius* 1702.24, 36, 44), Lampe (1961), *DGE*, LSJ suppl. (citing an unverified example that could be another inscription). See §4.2.4.1 n. 50, §10.2.1, §10.2.2 C; cf. ἀρχιβαλιστάριος.

rare | **βαλ(λ)ίστρα** 'catapult', from *ballista/bālista/ballistra* 'catapult' (*TLL*): Ps.-Macar. *Hom.* 52.2.7 (V AD?); Procop. *Bell.* 5.21.14 etc., marked (VI AD); with *tormentum murale* in Gloss. Ps.-Cyril. 255.44; common in Byzantine texts (with derivatives βαλλιστροφόρος 'catapult-bearing' (*LBG*) and τοξοβαλλίστρα/ τοξοβολίστρα 'engine for shooting darts' (Sophocles 1887)). Shipp (1960: 151, with good explanation of etymology), Hofmann (1989: 46), Zilliacus (1935a: 218–19), Sophocles (1887), Triandaphyllidis (1909: 129), *TLL* (*s.v. ballista*, observing that the Latin seems to be derived from unattested *βαλλιστής), Lampe (1961), *DGE*, LSJ.

βαλ(λ)ιστράριος: see βαλλιστάριος.

rare | **βαλν-** in words pertaining to baths can indicate borrowing or at least influence from Latin, since Greek βαλανεῖον 'bath' etc. gave Latin (*balineum* and) *balneum* 'bath' etc.: the loss of the second vowel occurred in Latin. Such spelling occurs in βαλνε(υτικόν) in *O.Wilck.* 583.3 (II AD), βαλνωνο in *P.IFAO* III.36.14 (III AD), and βαλνίου in *SB* 15865.6 (III AD) – but also βαλνηω(ν) in *O.Wilck.* 318.2 (II BC). Binder (2000: 206), *LBG*, Triandaphyllidis (1909: 124).

rare | **βαλνικάριος** 'bath attendant', apparently from *balneum* 'bath' + -ικός + -άριος (**balnicārius* is unattested): inscriptions *Corinth* VIII.III.534.5, probably 547.3 (both V/VI AD). *LBG*, *DGE*, LSJ suppl. See §6.1 n. 8.

Direct loan
I AD – Byz. | **βάλτιον, βάλτεον, βάλτις, βάλτεος** (-ου, τό or ὁ), 'belt', 'sword-belt', from *balteus/ balteum* 'sword-belt'.

Documents: *P.Mich.* VIII.464.18 (I AD); *P.Mich.* VIII.474.8 (II AD); *P.Oxy.* 3616.4 (III AD?); *P.Mich.* III.217.19 (III AD); *P.Col.* VII.188.18 (IV AD).

Inscriptions: Edict.Diocl. 10.8 etc. in *SEG* XXXVII.335.iii.17 etc. (IV AD).

Literature: Antiochus, Boll 1908: 127.27, of a constellation (I BC/AD); Lyd. *Mag.* p. 104.16, marked (VI AD); Aëtius 2.126.8 (VI AD).

Post-antique: survives only in Byzantine derivative βαλτίδι(ο)ν. *LBG*, Lampe (1961), Triandaphyllidis (1909: 121).

Notes: originally means 'sword-belt', adds civilian uses in III AD. Cavenaile (1952: 196) derives βάλτιον from *balteus* + -ιον, but *balteum* with change of *e* to ι is more likely. Masculine only on Edict of Diocletian: the use there may come directly from Latin. Cervenka-Ehrenstrasser (2000: 135–6), Diethart (1999: 177), Daris (1991a: 33), Hofmann (1989: 47), Cavenaile (1951: 395), *DGE*, LSJ suppl. (*s.vv.* βάλτιον, βάλτιος). See §4.2.4.1 n. 58, §9.5.1, §10.1, §10.2.1, §10.2.2 C.

not Latin? βάνδον, βάνδα (both neuter) 'military standard' or 'troop' (with derivative βανδοφόρος 'standard-bearer' and perhaps μονόβανδον, but see *LBG s.v.*) is often said to be from *bandum* 'standard' (*TLL*) on the basis of Procopius saying it was used by 'Romans' (*Bell.* 4.2.1 τὸ σημεῖον, ὃ δὴ βάνδον καλοῦσι Ῥωμαῖοι; also *Bell.* 4.10.4 ὃν δὴ βανδοφόρον καλοῦσι Ῥωμαῖοι). But Kramer (1996a: 115–16, 2011: 41) argues that by 'Romans' Procopius meant 'Byzantine Greeks' (cf. §10.4.1) and that the source was Gothic *bandwa*, probably not via Latin *bandum*, which is attested considerably later than the Greek. Cervenka-Ehrenstrasser (2000: 272), Binder (2000: 249–50), Drew-Bear (1972: 189), Daris (1991a: 33), Hofmann (1989: 47–8), Viscidi (1944: 13), Zilliacus (1935a: 145, 218–19), Immisch (1885: 359–60), Zervan (2019: 22–3), *LBG* (*s.vv.* βάνδα, βάνδον, βάνδος, etc.), Kriaras (1968–), *TLL* (*s.v. bandum*), Lampe (1961), *DGE*, LSJ suppl. See §2.1 n. 9, §2.2.3.

rare βανιάριον 'baths', from *balneārium* 'baths' (*OLD s.v. balneārius*) with influence from βαλανεῖον 'bath' (which is ultimately the ancestor of the Latin): Malal. 9.14 (VI AD); Byzantine texts. Hofmann (1989: 48), *LBG*, Lampe (1961), *DGE*.

not ancient βανιάτωρ 'bath attendant', from *balneātor* 'bath attendant' with influence from βαλανεῖον 'bath' (which is ultimately the ancestor of the Latin): no ancient examples, since *Stud.Pal.* VIII.980.6 has been redated to VII AD. Cervenka-Ehrenstrasser (2000: 137–8), Diethart (1998: 169), Daris (1991a: 33), Hofmann (1989: 48), Meinersmann (1927: 9), *LBG* (*s.v.* βαλνίτωρ), LSJ suppl.

not Latin? βαννάται 'slanting roads', lemma in Hesych. β 194 (V/VI AD), was suggested by Immisch (1885: 309) as from a Latin word in *band*-, perhaps the root of the names *Bandusia* and *Bantius* (*TLL*); *DÉLG* does not see a Latin source, and Beekes (2010) considers the etymology uncertain. LSJ.

not ancient βάρβα transliterating *barba* 'beard' (part of a plant name): interpolation in Dsc. 4.55 RV. Sophocles (1887).

Direct loan
IV AD – Byz. βαρβαρικάριος (-ου, ὁ) 'brocade-maker', from *barbaricārius* 'one who weaves with gold' (*TLL*).
Documents: *SB* 11982.5 (VI AD).
Inscriptions: Edict.Diocl. 20.5 etc. (IV AD); *I.Tyr* 122, 123; perhaps *MAMA* III.266.
Post-antique: survives. *LBG*.
Notes: Cervenka-Ehrenstrasser (2000: 138–9), *I.Tyr* pp. 157–8, Diethart (1998: 169), Hofmann (1989: 48), *TLL* (*s.v. barbaricārius* 1731.32–6), *DGE*, LSJ suppl. See §4.2.4.1 n. 50, §8.2.2, §10.2.1, §10.2.2 H.

name	**Βαρβᾶτος** 'bearded', from *barbātus* 'bearded': only a name in antiquity, though later a common noun with multiple meanings. *LBG*, Kriaras (1968–), Triandaphyllidis (1909: 131), Sophocles (1887), Meyer (1895: 13), Andriotis (1967), Lampe (1961), *DGE*. See §6.6 n. 40.
foreign	**βάρδοι** 'bards', ultimately Celtic but probably via *bardī*, plural of *bardus* 'bard' (*TLL*): Diodorus Siculus 5.31.2, marked (I BC); Strabo 4.4.4, marked (I BC/AD); Athenaeus 6.246d, marked (II/III AD); Hesych. as lemma β 225 (V/VI AD). Sophocles (1887), *DGE*, LSJ, LSJ suppl.
foreign	**βάρκα** 'small boat', from *barca* 'small boat': Lyd. *Mag.* p. 106.9, marked: βάρκας αὐτάς, ἀντὶ τοῦ δρόμωνας, πατρίως ἐκάλεσαν οἱ παλαιότεροι καὶ κέλωκας, οἷον ταχινάς, ὅτι κέλερ κατ' αὐτοὺς ὁ ταχὺς λέγεται, καὶ σαρκιναρίας, ἀντὶ τοῦ ὁλκάδας, ὅτι σάρκινα κατ' αὐτοὺς τὸ ἄχθος καλεῖται (VI AD). Borrowed into Byzantine Greek, survives into modern period: Zervan (2019: 23–4), Bartoli (1912: 995–6), Kriaras (1968–), *LBG*, Meyer (1895: 13), Babiniotis (2002).
	βαρυγαύδης: see παραγαύδης.
non-existent	**βαρών** 'blockhead', from *bārō* 'blockhead': superseded reading of papyrus *BGU* III.836.1 (VI AD). Byzantine βάρωνες 'barons' (*LGB*, Triandaphyllidis 1909: 132, Andriotis 1967 *s.v.* βαρῶνος) is a separate borrowing from a much later Latin usage of *bārō* (*TLL*, noting that *bārō* 'baron' may not even be the same word) or from French *baron*; cf. its standard form μπαρόνος (*LBG*, Zervan 2019: 120). Cervenka-Ehrenstrasser (2000: 270), Diethart (1999: 178), Hofmann (1989: 49), Meinersmann (1927: 9), *DGE*, LSJ suppl.
rare	**βασκαύλης**, a vessel, probably from *bascauda*, a vessel (*TLL*), perhaps via unattested variant **bascaula*: papyrus *P.Oxy.* 109.22 (III/IV AD). Cervenka-Ehrenstrasser (2000: 139–40), Kramer (1983: 117–18, 2009, 2011: 185–94), Daris (1991a: 33, with derivation from *vasculum*), Hofmann (1989: 49), Meinersmann (1927: 9–10), *DÉLG*, Frisk (1954–72: 1.224), Beekes (2010), *TLL* (*s.v. bascauda* 1760.7), *DGE*, LSJ, LSJ suppl.
rare	**βασκαύλιον**, **πασκαύλιον**, a vessel, from *bascauda*, a vessel (*TLL*) (via βασκαύλης?) + -ιον: papyrus *P.Cair.Isid.* 137.3 (III/IV AD); perhaps *P.Oxy.* 3998.36 (IV AD). Cervenka-Ehrenstrasser (2000: 140), Kramer (1983: 117, 2009, 2011: 185–94), Daris (1991a: 33, with derivation from *vasculum*), *DGE*.
rare	**βασκέλ(ε)ιον** 'little vessel', from *vāscellum* 'small vase' or perhaps *vāsculum* 'little vessel' + -ιον: papyrus *P.Coll.Youtie* II.84.10 (IV AD). Cervenka-Ehrenstrasser (2000: 140–1), Diethart (1998: 169), Daris (1991a: 33), *DGE*, LSJ suppl.
rare	**βάσκυλον** 'little vessel', from *vāsculum* 'little vessel': papyrus *P.Ryl.* IV.627.82 (IV AD). Cervenka-Ehrenstrasser (2000: 141–2), Kramer (1983: 117, with derivation from unattested **bascaula*), Daris (1991a: 33), Hofmann (1989: 49), *DGE* (*s.v.* βάσκυλα), LSJ suppl. (*s.v.* βάσκυλα).
not Latin	**βαστά**, cited by Hesych. β 310 (V/VI AD) as Italian (Ἰταλιῶται) word for 'sandals', is probably not related to *fascis* 'bundle'. Hofmann (1989: 49), *DÉLG*, Frisk (1954–72: 1.225), Beekes (2010), *DGE*, LSJ.

not Latin	**βασταγάριος** 'transport worker' is probably not from *vastō* 'plunder' + *agrōs* 'fields' + -άριος but from βαστάζω 'carry'. Meinersmann (1927: 10), Lampe (1961), *DGE*, LSJ.
rare	**βαστερνάριος**, from *basternārius* 'person responsible for transport in a litter' (*TLL*) and therefore probably meaning 'litter-bearer' or 'bier-bearer': inscriptions *IG* II/III².III.13224.7 (III/IV AD); *IG* II/III².V.13380.7 (V/VI AD). Wilhelm (1928b: 230), Hofmann (1989: 50), *DGE*, LSJ (*s.v.* βαστέρνιον).
Direct loan with suffix **V AD – Byz.**	**βαστέρνιον** (-ου, τό) 'enclosed litter', 'covered passage', from *basterna* 'enclosed litter' (*TLL*) + -ιον.

Documents: *SB* 15297.2 (VI AD).
Literature: John Chrysostom, *PG* LX.320.7 (IV/V AD); *V.S.Aux.* 28.2 etc. (VI AD); Just. *Codex* 8.10.12.4a: τούτων, ἃ καλοῦσιν οἱ πολλοὶ βαστέρνια (VI AD).
Post-antique: numerous; both senses survive. *LBG*, Kriaras (1968–).
Notes: Cervenka-Ehrenstrasser (2000: 142–3), Avotins (1989), Diethart (1998: 169), Hofmann (1989: 50), *TLL* (*s.v. basterna* 1782.81–2), *DGE*, LSJ, LSJ suppl. See §2.4, §4.3.2, §10.2.1, §10.2.2 K.

rare	**βαστέρνος** 'enclosed litter', from *basterna* 'enclosed litter' (*TLL*): cited as a Greek word by Herodian (II AD) in the palimpsest fragment (Hunger 1967: 26). *DGE*, LSJ suppl.
	βαστιλᾶς: see παστιλλᾶς.
	βατάνη, βατάνια, βατάνιον: see πατάνη.
	βατελλ-: see πατελλ-.
	βατρανός: see οὐετερανός.
	βατριμούνιον: see πατριμώνιον.
	βεβράϊνος, βέβρανος, βέβρινος: see μεμβράϊνος.
	βεικήσιμον: see βικήσιμον.
	βεῖκον, βεῖκος: see βῖκος.
rare	**βεΐκουλον, οὐεΐκουλον**, from *vehiculum* 'vehicle': inscription *I.Cos Paton* 102.12 (III AD). Mason (1974: 72), LSJ suppl.
	βείνετος: see βένετος.
	βείριον: see βίρριον.
	βειρόν, βείρρος: see βίρρος.
not ancient	**βεκτιγάλιον** 'tax', from *vectīgal* 'tax': no ancient examples. Zilliacus (1935a: 214–15), *LBG* (*s.v.* βεκτιγάλιος).
rare	**βεκτοῦρα** 'transport', from *vectūra* 'transport': Edict.Diocl. 17.1–5 (IV AD). *DGE*, LSJ suppl.
non-existent	**βελλικός**, cited by Hofmann (1989: 50) as from *bellus* 'pretty': superseded reading of Athenaeus 14.647d. See §2.2.1 n. 21.

not ancient   **βελόκιον**, a fruit, from *vēlox* 'swift': no ancient examples. Cervenka-Ehrenstrasser (2000: 147), Diethart (1998: 169), *LBG*, *DGE*.

not ancient   **βενάλιος** 'saleable', from *vēnālis* 'saleable': no ancient examples. Zilliacus (1935a: 214–15), *LBG*.

foreign   **βενδιτίων** 'sale', from *venditiō* 'sale': Antec. in Latin script e.g. 3.12.pr. *venditiones* as part of *bonōrum venditiō* (VI AD). Zilliacus (1935a: 214–15).

foreign   **βένε** 'well', from *bene*: in Latin script as part of *bene baleas* (= *bene valeas* 'farewell') in papyrus *P.Münch.* I.2.21 etc. (VI AD); superseded reading of *P.Münch.* I.14.111 (VI AD). Daris (1991a: 33), Meinersmann (1927: 9).

        Βένερις: see Βένους.

rare   **βενέτειος** 'of the blue faction', from *venetus* 'blue' via βένετος + -ειος: Procop. *Bell.* 1.24.49 (VI AD). *DGE*, LSJ (*s.v.* βένετος).

Direct loan
II–III AD   **βενετιανός**, **ούενετιανός** (-οῦ, ὁ) 'supporter of the blue circus faction', from *venetiānus* 'supporter of the blue circus faction'.
        Documents: Audollent 1904: no. 237.6 etc. (II/III AD).
        Inscriptions: *IGUR* II.443.7.
        Literature: Marc.Aurel. 1.5.1 (II AD).
        Notes: eventually replaced by βένετος (Cameron 1976: 78). Hofmann (1989: 50, 303), *DÉLG* (*s.v.* βένετος), Beekes (2010 *s.v.* βένετος), LSJ (*s.vv.* βενετιανός, ούένετος). See §4.2.4.1 n. 51, §6.4, §10.2.1, §10.2.2 F.

not ancient   **βενετίζω** 'support the blue faction', 'be bluish', from *venetus* 'blue' via βένετος + -ίζω: no ancient examples. Hofmann (1989: 50 *s.v.* βένετοι, citing an example no longer thought to exist), *LBG*, Lampe (1961).

Direct loan
III AD – modern   **βένετος**, **ούένετος**, **βείνετος**, **βέναιτος** (-η, -ον and -ου, ὁ) 'blue', 'belonging to the blue circus faction', from *venetus* 'blue'.
        Documents: Audollent 1904: no. 234.5 etc., 238.8 etc., 241.18 etc. (all II/III AD); *SEG* LII.988.1 etc., Latinate (IV AD?); *P.Oxy.* 2480.10 etc. (VI AD); *PSI* VIII.953.42 (VI AD).
        Inscriptions: *SEG* VIII.213 (V AD); common at Aphrodisias and Tyre in V/VI AD, e.g. *I.Aphrodisias Late Ant.* 180.iii, 181.iii, 181.vii; Rey-Coquais 2002 nos 1, 6, 7; at other sites often present but undatable.
        Literature: e.g. Malal. 7.5 (VI AD); *Anthologia Graeca* 15.46.5 (VI AD); Lyd. *Mens.* 4.30 (VI AD); Procop. *Bell.* 1.24.2 (VI AD). But Vet.Val. *App.* 2.7 is probably interpolated.
        Post-antique: survives, forming derivatives βενετοπράσινος 'of the blues and greens', βενετοφορέω 'wear blue', etc. (*LBG*). Kriaras (1968–), Triandaphyllidis (1909: 131). Modern dialectal βένετος 'blue', βενετιάζω 'turn blue' etc.: Andriotis (1974: 175).
        Notes: integrated for the faction, but not as a colour term. The factions became widespread in the East in V AD (Cameron 1976: 193). Also means 'Venetian'. Forms derivative βενέτειος. Hofmann (1989: 50, 303–4), Meinersmann (1927: 10), *DÉLG*, Beekes (2010), *DGE*, LSJ (*s.vv.* βένετος, ούένετος). See §4.2.2, §8.2.2, §10.2.1, §10.2.2 F, §12.2.1; cf. ούενέτιος.

Direct loan
I BC – Byz.

βενεφικ(ι)άριος, βενεφικ(ι)άλιος, βενεφικειάρις, βενεψικιάριος, μενεπικιάριος (-ου, ὁ), a title, a provider of medical aid for veterans, or a type of criminal; primarily from *beneficiārius*, a soldier attendant on an officer or a minister attendant on a magistrate (*TLL*); in meaning 'criminal' (only in Justinian) from *venēficus* 'poisoner'.

Documents: common, e.g. *SB* 11953.11 (I BC); perhaps *P.Oxy.Hels.* 11.7 (I AD); *BGU* I.241.35 (II AD); *P.Lond.* III.1157va.4 (III AD); *Chrest.Mitt.* 78.3 (IV AD); perhaps *Stud.Pal.* XX.117.3 (V AD); *P.Oxy.* 1917.63 (VI AD?).

Inscriptions: common, e.g. perhaps Bosch 1967: 59 no. 65.11 (I AD); *TAM* II.485.7 (I/II AD); *SEG* XL.1162.3 (II AD); *IGBulg.* I².24bis.4 (III AD).

Literature: Eus. *HE* 9.9a.7 (IV AD); Didymus Caecus, *Commentarii in Psalmos 35–9* 245.33 Gronewald (IV AD); *Martyrium Agapae etc.* 3.1 in Musurillo 1972 (IV AD?); Just. *Nov.* 13.4.pr. (VI AD); Lyd. *Mag.* p. 70.24, marked (VI AD).

Post-antique: numerous. *LBG* (s.v. βενεφικιάλιος), Zervan (2019: 25–6).

Notes: Cervenka-Ehrenstrasser (2000: 147–51), Bartalucci (1995: 107–9), Avotins (1992 *s.v.* βενεφικιάλιος), Daris (1991a: 33–4), Mason (1974: 4, 9, 30, 170), Hofmann (1989: 51), Zilliacus (1935a: 174–5, 218–19), Meinersmann (1927: 10), Sophocles (1887), *TLL* (s.v. *beneficiārius* 1878.14–28), *DGE* (s.v. βενεφικιάριος), LSJ suppl. (*s.vv.* βενεφικιάλιος A and B, βενεφικιάριος). See §4.2.4.1 n. 50, §6.1, §8.1.5, §10.2.1, §10.2.2 D.

Direct loan
V AD? – Byz.

βενεφίκιον, βενιφίκιον (-ου, τό) 'gift', 'favour', from *beneficium* 'benefit', 'kindness'.

Documents: *P.Flor.* III.296.49 (VI AD).

Literature: *Acta Phileae* 11.3 in Musurillo 1972 (IV AD?); Gel.Cyz. 2.32.12 (V AD); *ACO* II.I.III p. 95.3 (V AD); Just. *Edict* 4.1 = p. 762.6, marked (VI AD); Jo.Scholast. 3 p. 101.3 (VI AD).

Post-antique: survives. *LBG*, Triandaphyllidis (1909: 128).

Notes: Cervenka-Ehrenstrasser (2000: 151), Avotins (1992), Daris (1991a: 34), Hofmann (1989: 51), Zilliacus (1935a: 174–5), Meinersmann (1927: 10), Sophocles (1887), Lampe (1961), *DGE*, LSJ suppl. See §4.2.4.1 n. 54, §10.2.1, §10.2.2 O.

name

Βένους (gen. Βένερις) 'Venus', from *Venus, Veneris* 'Venus'. Sophocles (1887).

βεξιλ-: see βηξιλ-.

rare

βεραιδαρικός 'typical of a courier', 'swift', from *verēdārius* 'messenger of the imperial post' via βερεδάριος + -ικός: Lyd. *Mens.* 1.32: βῆλωξ, ὀξύς, ὃς καὶ βεραιδαρικὸς ἔτι καὶ νῦν λέγεται (VI AD). Hofmann (1989: 51 *s.v.* βερεδάριος), Sophocles (1887), *DGE*, LSJ suppl.

βέραιδος: see βέρεδος.

not ancient

βεράτρουμ transliterating *verātrum* 'hellebore': interpolation in Dsc. 4.148 RV. Sophocles (1887).

not ancient

βερβάσκ(λ)ουμ transliterating *verbascum*, a plant: interpolation in Dsc. 4.103 RV. Sophocles (1887 *s.v.* βερβάσκουμ).

not ancient?

βερβελιά 'dung of sheep and goats', from *vervella*, diminutive of *vervex* 'wether': probably no ancient examples. Meyer (1895: 13–14), Andriotis (1967).

non-existent	**βερβενᾶκα**, plant name from *verbēnāca* 'vervain': variant reading in interpolation in Dsc. (not in Wellmann; see Kühn's edition, apparatus to 4.61). Sophocles (1887).
Direct loan **VI AD – Byz.**	**βέρβον** (-ου, τό) 'word', from *verbum* 'word' (in legal senses: Berger 1953 *s.v. verba*). Documents: *P.Stras.* v.494.8 (VI AD); *P.Petra* III.29.155 (VI AD); *P.Münch.* I.14.71 (VI AD); *P.Gen.* IV.187.3.7 has been redated to post-antique. Literature: Antec. in Latin script as *verbis* 'by formal expressions', 'orally', 3.15. pr. etc. (VI AD). Post-antique: survives only in legal texts. Notes: Cervenka-Ehrenstrasser (2000: 152), Daris (1991a: 34), Zilliacus (1935a: 214–15), Meinersmann (1927: 10), *DGE*. See §4.2.4.1 n. 55, **§7.2.2** with passage 29, §10.2.1, §10.2.2 B.
rare	**βέργα** 'rod', 'blow from a rod', from *virga* 'rod': Dan.Sket. *Eu.* 156 (V AD); martyr-legend in Angelide 1977: 153.10 (V AD?); often in Byzantine texts. Binder (2000: 122), Zilliacus (1935a: 238–9), Zervan (2019: 26), *LBG*, Kriaras (1968–), *DGE* (*s.v.* βέργαι).
not ancient?	**βέργιον** 'staff', from *virga* 'rod' via βέργα: no certainly ancient examples. Zilliacus (1935a: 238–9), *LBG*, Kriaras (1968–).
non-existent?	**βέρε** 'truly', from *vērē* 'truly': perhaps inscription *SEG* LXVI.509.2 (II AD). Chaniotis *ad loc.*
	βερεδαρικός: see βεραιδαρικός.
Direct loan **III AD – Byz.**	**βερεδάριος, βεριδάριος, βερηδάριος, βηριδάριος, οὐερεδάριος, οὐεριδάριος** (-ου, ὁ) 'courier', from *verēdārius* 'messenger of the imperial post'. Documents: *P.Oxy.* 3758.120 (IV AD). Inscriptions: *SEG* LXV.1408.C13, transliterating Latin (V/VI AD). Literature: Secundus, *Sententiae* 15.1 Perry (II/III AD); Athan. *Apol.Sec.* 77.5, 78.5 (IV AD); Hesych. o 1601 (V/VI AD); Procop. *Bell.* 3.16.12, *Aed.* 5.3.3, both marked (VI AD); old scholia to Aeschines 2.130, 277b: οἵτινες διὰ τοῦ δρόμου καὶ τοῦ τάχους δύνανταί τινα ἀγγεῖλαι, ὡς νῦν καλοῦμεν τοὺς βερεδαρίους. Unverified example (II AD) in Zilliacus (1937: 322, 328). Post-antique: survives. Sophocles (1887 *s.v.* βερηδάριος), Triandaphyllidis (1909: 123). Notes: forms derivative βεραιδαρικός. Cervenka-Ehrenstrasser (2000: 152–4), Paschoud (1983: 238–43), Diethart (1998: 170), Daris (1991a: 34, 79), Hofmann (1989: 51), Zilliacus (1935a: 238–9, 1937: 328), Meinersmann (1927: 10), Immisch (1885: 359), Lampe (1961 *s.v.* βεριδάριος), *DGE*, LSJ (*s.v.* βέρεδος), LSJ suppl. (*s.vv.* βεριδάριος, οὐεριδάριος). See §4.2.4.1 n. 50, **§9.5.4**, §10.2.1, §10.2.2 K.
Direct loan **IV AD – Byz.**	**βέρεδος, βέρετος, βέριδος, βέρηδος, βήριδος, βέραιδος** (-ου, ὁ) 'fast horse', 'post-horse', from *verēdus* 'fast horse'. Documents: *P.Fouad* 87.27 (VI AD). Literature: e.g. Dor.Poet. *Visio* 310 (III/IV AD); Callin. *V.Hypat.* 21.2 (V AD); Malal. 15.2 (VI AD); Procop. *Bell.* 2.20.20, marked (VI AD); Lyd. *Mens.* 1.32.2–5: βέραιδους δὲ Ἰταλοῖς εἶναι δοκεῖ τοὺς ὑποζυγίους ἵππους … ὅπερ ἐστίν, ἕλκειν τὸ ὄχημα (VI AD); with *veredus* in Gloss. Ps.-Cyril. 257.17.

Post-antique: survives, forming derivative βερηδεύω 'run away'. Triandaphyllidis
(1909: 119), Sophocles (1887 *s.v.* βέρηδος).

Notes: Cervenka-Ehrenstrasser (2000: 155), O'Callaghan (1970: 57–9),
Diethart (1998: 170), Daris (1991a: 34), Hofmann (1989: 51), Lampe
(1961 *s.v.* βέρεδον), *DGE*, LSJ. See §2.1, §4.2.4.1 n. 51, §10.2.1, §10.2.2 K; cf.
παραβέρεδος.

βερεκόκκιον: see πραικόκκιον.

βερηδ-, βεριδ-: see βερεδ-.

βερικόκκιον, βερίκοκκον: see πραικόκκιον.

βερναΐς: see βέρνας.

foreign   **βέρνακλος, ούέρνακλος** 'public slave', or in plural designating the members of a
Jewish community in Rome, from *vernāculus/vernāclus* 'domestic', 'native':
in inscriptions of III/IV AD with wide variety of gen. pl. endings suggesting
independent adaptation from Latin: βερνακλώρω *I.Jud.Western Europe*
II.114.4, βερνακλησίων 106.3, βερνάκλων 117.3 and 540.4 (all III/IV AD);
cf. also *I.Kibyra* 82.1. In literature usually marked: Marc.Aurel. 1.16.4 (II
AD); Malal. 7.12.21 (VI AD); Lyd. *Mag.* p. 66.16, *Mens.* 4.30.1 (VI AD).
Minimal post-antique survival: *LBG*, Triandaphyllidis (1909: 123). Binder
(2000: 160), Rochette (2008: 281), Mason (1974: 72), Hofmann (1989:
52), Lampe (1961), *DGE*. See §2.2.1.

Direct loan
II AD – ?   **βέρνα(ς), ούέρνα(ς)** (-α, ὁ) 'home-born slave', from *verna* 'home-born slave'.
Inscriptions: e.g. *I.North Galatia* 34.10 (II AD); *CIG* 3095.2 (II AD?); *SEG*
XXXIV.1374.2 (II AD?); *SEG* IV.594.3; *I.Ephesos* 2210.11; *MAMA* I.26.2,
27.2; *MAMA* VII.135.2.
Notes: died out during antiquity, but end date uncertain. A feminine βερναΐς
seems to occur on *I.Cret.* I.XVIII.147. Robert and Robert (1969: 499–500
no. 474), Mason (1974: 5, 72), Hofmann (1989: 304), Cameron (1931:
261), LSJ suppl. (*s.v.* ούέρνας). See **§4.2.3.2 with n. 45**, §10.2.1, §10.2.2 N.

βερόκκιον: see πραικόκκιον.

Βεροκόσσος: see Βερρουκῶσος.

foreign   **βερουτάριος**, apparently from *verūtum* 'short throwing-spear' + -άριος: glossed with
δισκοβόλος 'discus-thrower' by Lyd. *Mag.* p. 72.21, where a military term is
expected (VI AD). Forcellini *et al.* (1864–1926) hypothesizes *verūtārius* on
this basis. Zilliacus (1935a: 238–9), Sophocles (1887), *LBG*. See §9.5.5 n. 47.

foreign   **βέρρης** transliterating *verrēs* 'boar': Plut. *Cicero* 7.6, with incorrect definition:
βέρρην γὰρ οἱ Ῥωμαῖοι τὸν ἐκτετμημένον χοῖρον καλοῦσιν (I/II AD). Strobach
(1997: 194), Sophocles (1887). See §2.2.2 n. 32.

βερρόν: see βίρρος.

name   **Βερρουκῶσος, Βεροκόσσος**, from *verrūcōsus* 'covered with warts'. Strobach (1997:
194), Sophocles (1887).

foreign   **βέρσον** 'expenditure', from *versum*, pf. part. neut. of *vertō* 'turn': Antec. in Latin
script 4.7.4 *verson* etc. (VI AD); later in Greek script. Zilliacus (1935a:
214–15), *LBG* (*s.v.* βέρσος 'used'). See §9.5.6 n. 68.

βέρτα: see ἀβερτή.

foreign *bēs* 'two thirds (of an inheritance)': Antec. 2.14.5 (VI AD). See §7.1.1 passage 18.

βεσίλεκτος: see βισήλεκτος.

rare **βέστα, βέστη** 'garment', 'clothing' (not to be confused with Βέστα 'Vesta'), from *vestis* 'clothes': papyrus *P.Ryl.* IV.639.17 (IV AD); Byzantine texts. Cervenka-Ehrenstrasser (2000: 156), Daris (1991a: 34), *LBG* (*s.v.* βέστη), Kriaras (1968–, with Venetian derivation), *DGE* (*s.v.* βέστη).

non-existent? **βεστάριον, οὐεστάριον** 'clothes-chest': perhaps papyrus *P.Cair.Masp.* 67340v.41 (VI AD); perhaps lead weight *IG* XIV.2416.6. Ultimately related to *vestis* 'clothes', but exact source uncertain: Cervenka-Ehrenstrasser (2000: 156–7) rejects Cameron's (1931: 261) *vestiārium* 'wardrobe' (L&S *s.v. vestiārius*) in favour of a poorly attested variant *vestārium* or even *vestis* 'clothes' itself (Daris 1991a: 80).

not ancient **βεστάρχης**, a title from *vestis* 'clothes' (via βέστα?) + -άρχης: no ancient examples. Zervan (2019: 26–7), Viscidi (1944: 33), Cameron (1931: 261), *LBG*, Kriaras (1968–).

βέστη: see βέστα.

βεστήτωρ: see βεστίτωρ.

rare **βεστιάριον, βεστειάριον, βιστιάριον, βεστηάριον** 'clothing', 'wardrobe', from *vestiārius* 'concerned with clothes': meaning 'clothing', Modestinus in Just. *Dig.* 34.1.4.pr. (III AD), perhaps papyrus *PSI* III.196.2 (VI AD); meaning 'wardrobe', Hesych. as lemma β 636 (V/VI AD). Common in Byzantine texts, with additional meaning 'treasury' and derivative βεστιαρικός 'of the treasury'. Andriotis (1967) sees modern βεστιάριο as a recent reborrowing; cf. Babiniotis (2002). Cervenka-Ehrenstrasser (2000: 157), Hofmann (1989: 52), Immisch (1885: 358), Zervan (2019: 27), *LBG*, Kriaras (1968–), Lampe (1961), *DGE*, LSJ suppl. See §9.5.6 nn. 55 and 58.

not ancient? **βεστιάριος, υεστιάριος** (-ου, ὁ) 'clothes-dealer', later an official title ('keeper of the wardrobe'), from *vestiārius* 'dealer in clothes': only secure and potentially ancient example is undated inscription *IG* XIV.1686.5. Perhaps also in inscriptions *MAMA* III.287 and 735a, and papyri *SB* 10793.2 (I AD) and *P.Oxy.* 3867.22 (VI AD), but when abbreviated may be βεστιαρίτης; superseded reading in *Stud.Pal.* III.50.1 (VI AD). Common in Byzantine period, forming derivative πρωτοβεστιάριος 'chief wardrobe-keeper'. Cervenka-Ehrenstrasser (2000: 158), Daris (1991a: 34), Hofmann (1989: 52), Zilliacus (1935a: 214–15), Zervan (2019: 27–8), *LBG*, Kriaras (1968–), Lampe (1961), *DGE*, LSJ suppl.

Direct? loan with suffix
VI AD – Byz. **βεστιαρίτης, βηστιαρίτης** (-ου, ὁ) 'clothes-person' (in Byzantine period a title), from *vestiārius* 'concerned with clothes' (via βεστιάριον?) + -ίτης. Documents: *CPR* VIII.56.15 (V/VI AD); *Stud.Pal.* XX.157.2 (VI AD). Post-antique: numerous, forming derivatives βεστιαρίτισσα 'wife of a βεστιαρίτης', πρωτοβεστιαρίτης 'first βεστιαρίτης'. *LBG*, Kriaras (1968–).

Notes: Almost all the examples traditionally read as βεστιάριος (*q.v.*) may in fact be this. Cervenka-Ehrenstrasser (2000: 158–9), Daris (1991a: 34), Hofmann (1989: 52 *s.v.* βεστιάριος), Cavenaile (1952: 193), Meinersmann (1927: 10), Zervan (2019: 28), *DGE*, LSJ suppl. See §4.3.2, §4.6.1 n. 86, §10.2.1, §10.2.2 D.

non-existent? **βεστικός** 'person knowledgeable about clothing', from *vestis* 'clothes' via βεστίον + -ικός: manuscript of Hesych. β 539 (V/VI AD), reading accepted by LSJ but neither recent editor.

Direct loan with suffix **βεστίον** (-ου, τό) 'clothes', 'wardrobe', from *vestis* 'clothes' + -ιον.
IV AD – Byz. Documents: *P.Oxy.* 3860.25 (IV AD); *P.Lond.* v.1654.7 etc. (V/VI AD); *P.Jena* II.27.4 (V/VI AD); *P.Bad.* IV.95.108 etc. (VI AD); *P.Lond.* v.1708.150 etc. (VI AD); *P.Stras.* 1.40.46 (VI AD); *PSI* III.196.2 (VI AD).
Literature: Malal. 13.9 (VI AD).
Post-antique: numerous, with additional meaning 'treasury' and derivatives βεστιοπρατεῖον 'trade in clothing', βέστης 'treasurer', etc.; note distinction from βέστιον 'wild beast' (also a Latin borrowing, from *bestia*: *LBG*). *LBG*, Triandaphyllidis (1909: 94, 121).
Notes: Cervenka-Ehrenstrasser (2000: 159–60), Daris (1991a: 35), Hofmann (1989: 52), Cavenaile (1952: 196), Meinersmann (1927: 10), Lampe (1961), *DGE*, LSJ, LSJ suppl. See §4.3.2 n. 69, §10.2.1, §10.2.2 H.

not ancient? **βεστίτωρ, βεστήτωρ**, official title evidently from *vestītor* 'maker of clothes': undated Coptic text cited by Cervenka-Ehrenstrasser (2000: 161); Byzantine texts. Diethart (1998: 170), Viscidi (1944: 33), *LBG*, Lampe (1961 *s.v.* βεστήτωρ).

foreign **βέστον, βέττον** 'clothing', from *vestis* 'clothes': Hesych. as lemma β 539 (V/VI AD). Cervenka-Ehrenstrasser (2000: 160 *s.v.* βεστίον), *DGE*, LSJ.

βέτα: see βῆτα.

βετερανός: see οὐετερανός.

foreign **βέτερες** transliterating pl. of *vetus* 'old', part of σκάλας βέτερες (*scalas veteres*): Procop. *Bell.* 4.17.3 (VI AD). *LBG* (*s.v.* βέτερος). Cf. οὐέτερεμ.

βετονική: see βεττονική.

not ancient? **βετοῦλι** 'kid', from *vitulus* 'calf': probably no ancient examples. Meyer (1895: 14), Andriotis (1967).

βετρανός: see οὐετερανός.

βέττον: see βέστον.

Direct loan **βετ(τ)ονική** (-ῆς, ἡ), a plant, from *vettōnica* 'betony' (*OLD s.v. vettōnicus*).
I AD – Byz. Literature: Dsc. *Eup.* 1.78.2 etc., but marked 4.1.1 etc. (I AD); Galen XIV.178.3 etc. Kühn, but marked XII.23.17 (II AD); Orib. *Col.* 11.β.8 etc., but marked 15.1:10.40 (IV AD); *Hippiatr.Berl.* (Pel.) 4.13 (V AD?); Aëtius 1.72.1 etc., but marked 1.196.1 (VI AD).
Post-antique: numerous, forming derivative βετονικέσπορον 'seed of betony'. *LBG*, Kriaras (1968–).
Notes: Hofmann (1989: 52), *DÉLG*, Beekes (2010), *DGE*, LSJ. See §4.2.3.1, §9.5.3, §10.2.1, §10.2.2 L.

βηκάρηος, **βηκάριος**: see βικάριος.

βηλαρικός: see βιλλαρικός.

Direct loan **IV AD – modern**	**βηλάριον**, **οὐηλάριον**, **εὐηλάριον** (-ου, τό) 'curtain', from *vēlārium* 'curtain'. Documents: *P.Oxy.* 1684.11 (IV AD); *P.Princ.* II.82.39 (V AD); *Chrest.Wilck.* 135.16 (V/VI AD); *P.Prag.* II.178.1.8 (V/VI AD). Post-antique: numerous. *LBG*, Kriaras (1968– *s.v.* βηλάρι), Daris (1991a: 81). Modern dialectal βηλάρι etc. 'whole piece of cloth': Andriotis (1974: 175), Kahane and Kahane (1972–6: 535). Notes: Daris (1991a: 81), Hofmann (1989: 305), Meinersmann (1927: 42), LSJ suppl. (*s.v.* οὐηλάριον). See §4.1.1, §4.2.4.1 n. 54, §9.2, §10.2.1, §10.2.2 H.
foreign	**βηλατούρα** 'ferrying across', from *vēlātūra* 'the business of a carrier': Plut. *Rom.* 5.5, marked (I/II AD). Hofmann (1989: 53).
Deriv. of loan **VI AD – Byz.**	**βηλόθυρον**, **οὐηλόθυρον**, **βιλόθυρον** (-ου, τό) 'curtain at door', from *vēlum* 'curtain' via βῆλον + θύρα 'door'. Documents: *Chrest.Wilck.* 135.14 (V/VI AD); *P.Prag.* II.178.1.10 (V/VI AD). Literature: probably none. Scholion to Ar. *Ra.* 938a is probably not ancient. Post-antique: numerous. *LBG*, Kriaras (1968–), *DGE*, Daris (1991a: 81). Notes: derived by Meinersmann (1927: 42) from medieval *velothyrum* 'curtain at door' (Du Cange 1883–7), but the compound was probably formed in Greek, where it is far better attested than in Latin. Filos (2010: 244, 250), Daris (1991a: 81), Hofmann (1989: 54 *s.v.* βῆλον), Cavenaile (1952: 199), *DGE*, LSJ, LSJ suppl. See §4.6, §4.6.2, §9.2, §10.2.2 H.
Direct loan **II AD – Byz.**	**βῆλον**, **οὐῆλον**, **οὐῖλον** (-ου, τό) 'covering', 'cloth', 'sail', 'awning', 'curtain', 'banner', 'signal', 'processional division', from *vēlum* 'sail', 'awning', 'curtain', 'cloth'. Documents: *P.Oxy.* 2128.8 (II AD); *SB* 16922.4 etc. (IV/V AD); *SB* 14211.14 (V AD). Inscriptions: *TAM* II.408.15 (II AD); Edict.Diocl. 19.56 (IV AD); *I.Aphrodisias Performers* 52.B8. Literature: e.g. Plut. *Rom.* 5.5, marked (I/II AD); *Testamentum Iobi* 25.2 Brock (II/III AD); *Acta Thomae* 98 = Bonnet 1903: 211.5 (III AD); Epiph. *Theod.* 23.2 (IV AD); Athan. *H.Ar.* 56.1 (IV AD); Ps.-John Chrysostom, *De cruce et latrone* 11.1 Wenger: τί ἐστιν τὸ καταπέτασμα; οἷον ἐὰν εἴπωμεν ἡμεῖς βῆλον (IV/V AD); Malal. 15.5.29 (VI AD); Cyr.S. *Vit.Sab.* 142.17 (VI AD); as gloss in old scholia to Ar. *Ra.* 938. Post-antique: common. Zervan (2019: 28–9), *LBG*, Kriaras (1968–), Triandaphyllidis (1909: 94, 98, 120, 125, 129), Sophocles (1887). Notes: forms derivative βηλόθυρον. Daris (1991a: 81), Hofmann (1989: 54), Cavenaile (1951: 399), Cameron (1931: 234–5, 261), Lampe (1961), *DGE*, LSJ suppl. See §4.1.1, §4.2.4.1 n. 55, §4.6, §4.6.2, §10.2.1, §10.2.2 H; cf. οὐηλάριος.
foreign	**βήλωξ** transliterating *vēlox* 'swift': Lyd. *Mens.* 1.32 (VI AD), quoted *s.v.* βεραιδαρικός. Sophocles (1887); see Cervenka-Ehrenstrasser (2000: 147) for lack of connection to βελόκιον.

Direct loan
VI AD – Byz.

βήναβλον, βήναυλον, μέναυλον (-ου, τό) 'hunting-spear', from *vēnābulum* 'hunting-spear'.

> Literature: EphraemSyr. I p. 216.9 (V/VI AD); Malal. 6.19.15 (VI AD); scholion to Luc. *D.Meretr.* 13.3 as gloss; with *venabulum* in Gloss. Ps.-Cyril. 257.20; with *laga* (for *lancea*?) in Gloss. *Herm.M.* 173.38.

> Post-antique: numerous, forming derivatives μεναύλιον 'throwing-spear', μεναυλάτος 'spear-thrower'. *LBG* (*s.v.* μέναυλον), Triandaphyllidis (1909: 129).

> Notes: Viscidi (1944: 6–7) considers the phonetic differences between the Latin and μέναυλον evidence of integration in Greek. Binder (2000: 187), Hofmann (1989: 54), Lampe (1961 *s.vv.* βήναβλον, μέναυλος), *DGE*. See §4.1.1, §4.2.4.1 n. 55, §10.2.1, §10.2.2 C, §12.2.1.

rare

βηνάτωρ, ουηνάτωρ 'hunter', from *vēnātor* 'hunter': unpublished ostracon O.Max. inv. 1229.9 (II AD); EphraemSyr. I p. 216.10 (V/VI AD); Rhetor. *Cap.* 216.1 (VI AD); occasional Byzantine texts. *LBG.*

Direct loan
I–VI AD

βηξιλλάριος, ουηξιλλάριος, ουιξιλλάριος (-ου, ὁ), a military rank, from *vexillārius* 'standard-bearer', 'troops serving in a special detachment'.

> Documents: e.g. *SB* 13303.8 (I AD); *O.Did.* 386.13 (II AD); perhaps *O.Did.* 84.6 (III AD); perhaps *P.Stras.* III.131.3 (IV AD); *SB* 11358.1 (V/VI AD).

> Inscriptions: e.g. Ruppel 1930: 62 no. 82.a.3 (II AD); *I.Portes du désert* 85.10 (III AD).

> Literature: Lyd. *Mag.* p. 70.13 as lemma (VI AD).

> Notes: Binder (2000: 127), Daris (1991a: 81), Mason (1974: 4, 72), Hofmann (1989: 305–6). See §4.2.4.1 n. 50, §6.1, §6.10, §10.2.1, §10.2.2 C.

Direct loan
II AD – Byz.

βηξιλ(λ)ατίων, βεξ-, βιξ-, ουηξ-, ουεξ-, ουιξ-, -ξελ-, -ξαλ- (-ωνος/-ονος, ἡ) 'troop', 'squadron', from *vexillātiō* 'detachment'.

> Documents: e.g. *P.Dura* 32.5 (III AD); *P.Abinn.* 42.12 (IV AD); *SB* 14704.5 (V/VI AD); *P.Laur.* III.111.12 (VI AD).

> Inscriptions: e.g. *I.Hatshepsout* 126.2 (I/II AD); *I.Ephesos* 737.8 (III AD); *I.Portes du désert* 91.4 (IV AD).

> Literature: Lyd. *Mag.* p. 70.1, 6, *Mens.* 41.1 (VI AD); with *vexillatio* in Gloss. Ps.-Cyril. 257.13.

> Post-antique: survives. *LBG* (*s.v.* βηξιλλατίων).

> Notes: Cervenka-Ehrenstrasser (2000: 163), Binder (2000: 127), Daris (1991a: 79, 81), Mason (1974: 5, 7, 9, 72), Hofmann (1989: 306), Zilliacus (1935a: 143, 238–9), Meinersmann (1927: 11, 42), *LBG* (*s.v.* ουηξιλλατίων), LSJ suppl. (*s.vv.* βιξιλλατίων, ουιξιλλατίων). See §4.2.5, §6.10, §10.2.1, §10.2.2 C.

rare

βηξιλλιφόρος, βηξιλλοφόρος, βεξιλλοφόρος 'standard-bearer', from *vexillifer* 'standard-bearing' (L&S): spelled βεξ-, with *vexillifer* in Gloss. Ps.-Cyril. 257.14; spelled βηξ-, supplement to ostracon *O.Bodl.* II.1676.1 (II AD), suggested in Cervenka-Ehrenstrasser (2000: 164), Filos (2010: 249). The supplement is unlikely, because words on this stem are normally spelled with ου- rather than β- in papyri and ostraca, and as the β is partially preserved ου- is not possible here.

Direct loan
I AD – Byz.

βήξιλλον, οὐήξιλλον, οὐιξίλλον (-ου, τό) 'cavalry standard', 'detachment of troops', from *vexillum* 'military standard', 'detachment of troops'.
 Documents: *SB* 16941.4 (II AD).
 Inscriptions: e.g. *IG* XII.VI.II.821.4 (I AD); *Agora de Palmyre* IA.04.5, p. 153 (II AD); *I.Ephesos* 680.16 (II AD); Merkelbach and Şahin 1988: 115 no. 22.7 (III AD).
 Literature: Methodius Olympius, *PG* XVIII.400c, marked (IV AD?); Lyd. *Mag.* p. 18.24 etc., *Mens.* 41.2 (VI AD).
 Post-antique: survives. Sophocles (1887).
 Notes: Cuvigny (2002: 246), Mason (1974: 5, 72), Hofmann (1989: 54–5), Zilliacus (1935a: 238–9), Lampe (1961), LSJ suppl. (*s.v.* οὐιξίλλον). See §4.2.4.1 n. 55, §6.1, §6.10, §10.2.1, §10.2.2 C.

βηριδ-: see βερεδ-.

βῆρος: see βίρρος.

not ancient?

βηρύττα 'short throwing-spear', from *verutum* 'short throwing-spear': probably no ancient examples. Zilliacus (1935a: 238–9).

not ancient?

βησαλικόν 'brickwork', from *bessālis* 'two thirds' via βήσαλον + -ικός: Her.Mech. *Stereom.* 1.76a.1 etc. (lived I AD, but the words are probably not his). Hofmann (1989: 55 *s.v.* βήσσαλον), *DGE*, LSJ (*s.v.* βήσαλον).

Direct loan
VI AD – modern

βήσαλον, βίσαλον, βήσσαλον (-ου, τό) 'brick', from *bessālis* 'two thirds', as masc. subst. 'brick two-thirds of a foot long' (*TLL*).
 Literature: Moses, Berthelot and Ruelle 1888: 300.13 (I/II AD?); Alex.Trall. II.407.28 (VI AD); Antec. 2.1.29 (VI AD); Her.Mech. *Mens.* 51.1; *Hippiatr. Berl.* 129.56; bilingual glossaries e.g. Gloss. Ps.-Cyril. 257.22, 23.
 Post-antique: numerous, forming derivative βησαλόκτιστος 'made of brick'. *LBG*, Kriaras (1968–), Triandaphyllidis (1909: 124). Modern βήσ(σ)αλο 'brick': Andriotis (1967, 1974: 175), Meyer (1895: 14).
 Notes: Hofmann (1989: 55), Viscidi (1944: 40), *TLL* (*s.v.* bessalis 1933.68–9), Lampe (1961), *DGE*, LSJ, LSJ suppl. See §4.2.5, §10.2.1, §10.2.2 J.

not ancient

βησσαλωτός, βισαλωτόν 'brick-paved road', from *bessālis* 'two thirds' via βήσαλον: no ancient examples. Hofmann (1989: 55 *s.v.* βήσσαλον), *LBG* (*s.v.* βισαλωτόν).

βηστιαρίτης: see βεστιαρίτης.

not ancient

βῆτα, βέτα transliterating *bēta* 'beet': interpolations in Dsc. 2.123 RV, 167 RV. *LBG* (*s.v.* βητά), Sophocles (1887 *s.v.* βέτα).

foreign

βῑ 'by force', from *vī*, abl. of *vīs* 'force': Antec. in Latin script as part of phrases 4.2.pr. *vi bonorum raptorum*, 2.6.2 *vi possesson*, etc. (VI AD); later in Greek script.

foreign

βία 'right of way', from *via* 'road': Antec. in Latin script 2.3.pr. *via* etc. (VI AD). Meyer (1895: 14) suggests βία from *via* 'road' also in παράβια 'insanities'; I can find no ancient examples. Zilliacus (1935a: 214–15). Cf. οὐιάρουμ.

not Latin   βίαρχος 'commissary-general', suggested as borrowing of title *biarchus* (*TLL*) but probably from βίος 'livelihood' + -αρχος (cf. ἄρχω 'rule'). Although treated as unfamiliar by Lyd. *Mens.* 1.40 (VI AD), it is unmarked earlier, e.g. Athan. *Apol.Sec.* 76.1 (IV AD). Zilliacus (1935a: 218–19), Meinersmann (1927: 10–11), *DGE*, LSJ, LSJ suppl.

Direct loan II–III AD   βιατικόν, οὐιατικόν (-ου, τό) 'journey money', from *viāticum* 'provision for a journey'.

> Documents: *P.Cair.Goodsp.* 30.41.18 (II AD); *Chrest.Wilck.* 480.9 (II AD); perhaps *SB* 12035.4 etc. (II AD); *PSICongr.XXI* 13.3.13 (III AD).
>
> Notes: Cervenka-Ehrenstrasser (2000: 165), Daris (1991a: 35), Hofmann (1989: 55), Meinersmann (1927: 11), *DGE*, LSJ suppl. See §4.2.4.1 n. 55, §10.2.1, §10.2.2 G.

Direct loan I AD – ?   βιάτωρ, οὐιάτωρ (-ορος/-ωρος, ὁ) 'agent (for magistrate)', 'traveller' (in verse inscriptions), from *viātor* 'traveller'.

> Inscriptions: *IGR* I.1075.5 (I AD); *I.Ephesos* 1544.9, 1545.3, both Latinate (both I/II AD); *MAMA* I.243.3; *IGBulg.* III.II.1713.a2 (verse); Greek appendage to *ILS* 1920.
>
> Notes: to be distinguished from βιάτωρ 'small spoon' in Hesych. (β 593) and LSJ. Probably died out during antiquity, but end date uncertain. Diethart (1999: 181), Daris (1991a: 81), Mason (1974: 4, 72), Hofmann (1989: 55), Lampe (1961), LSJ suppl. (*s.v.* οὐιάτωρ). See §4.2.5, §6.8, §10.2.1, §10.2.2 N.

name   Βιβάριον, a place name, from *vīvārium* 'place where living creatures are kept'. Zilliacus (1935a: 214–15), Meyer (1895: 14), *DGE*, Kriaras (1968–), Andriotis (1967 *s.v.* βιβάρι).

rare   βιβερατικόν 'tip', apparently from unattested **biberaticum* 'tip': *V.Dan.Styl. Sec.* 44 (VI AD?). McCormick (1981). See §8.1.7 n. 34.

not Latin?   βιβλιοθηκάριος 'librarian', perhaps from *bibliothēcārius* 'librarian' (thus Coleman 2007: 796), or a Greek formation from βιβλιοθήκη + -άριος (thus Zilliacus 1937: 334): no ancient examples. *LBG*. See §6.1 n. 10.

non-existent?   βιβραδικός 'vibratory', probably from *vibrātus* (pf. part. of *vibrō* 'move rapidly to and fro') + -ικός: perhaps papyrus *P.Ryl.* IV.627.165 (IV AD). Hofmann (1989: 55), *DGE*, LSJ suppl.

foreign   βίγα transliterating *bīgae/bīga* 'two-horse chariot': Lyd. *Mens.* 1.12.90 (VI AD). Hofmann (1989: 55), *LBG*, Triandaphyllidis (1909: 125).

foreign   βιγάριος transliterating *bīgārius* 'driver of a two-horse chariot': Lyd. *Mens.* 1.12.91 (VI AD). Hofmann (1989: 55), *LBG*, Triandaphyllidis (1909: 125).

non-existent?   βιγᾶτος, from *bīgātus* 'stamped with the image of a two-horse chariot': cited as loanword by *DGE* and Hofmann (1989: 56) on the basis of καροῦχα βιγᾶτα in the Geronthrae copy of *Edict.Diocl.* 15.37 (IV AD). But the two other copies of the Edict in which this passage is preserved have καροῦχον βιτωτόν and καροῦχον βισατόν, and βιτωτός (*q.v.*) makes most sense in context (Lauffer 1971: 145). *TLL* (*s.v. bīgātus* 1983.52–3).

not ancient	**βίγλα, βίκλα** 'watch', 'watch post', from *vigilia* 'watch' (or *vigilō* 'stay awake' via unattested **viglō*): no ancient examples, but common in Byzantine texts (with derivatives βιγλατόριον 'watchtower', βιγλάτωρ 'watchman', etc.). Modern βίγλα 'lookout post': Babiniotis (2002), Andriotis (1967), Meyer (1895: 14–15). Cervenka-Ehrenstrasser (2000: 165–6), Eideneier (1971: 58–9), Binder (2000: 205–6), Diethart (1998: 170), Hofmann (1989: 56 *s.v.* βιγλεύειν), Viscidi (1944: 13), Zilliacus (1935a: 238–9), *LBG*, Zervan (2019: 29), Kriaras (1968–), Triandaphyllidis (1909: 130), Lampe (1961), *DGE* (*s.v.* βίκλα), LSJ suppl. (*s.v.* βίκλα).
rare	**βιγλεύω** 'watch', 'be awake', from *vigilia* 'watch' (via βίγλα?) or *vigilō* 'stay awake' + -εύω: Philogelos 56 (IV AD); Byzantine texts. Hofmann (1989: 56), Viscidi (1944: 13), Zilliacus (1935a: 238–9), *LBG*, *DGE*.
rare	**βίγλης** and **οὐίγλης**, from *vigilēs*, plural of *vigil* 'sentry': ostraca *O.Claud.* II.335.2, 336.1 (both II AD). Cervenka-Ehrenstrasser (2000: 165–6). See §9.2 n. 19; cf. οὐίγουλ.
rare	**βιγλίον** 'watch', 'guard post', from *vigilia* 'watch' (via βίγλα?) (not *vigilium* 'action of keeping watch') + -ιον: ostracon *O.Claud.* II.356.1 etc. (II AD). Cervenka-Ehrenstrasser (2000: 167).
	βίγουλ: see οὐίγουλ.
	βιδίκτα: see βινδίκτα.
rare	**βικαρᾶτος**, meaning uncertain, related to medieval *vicāriātus, -ūs* 'office of deputy' (*DMLBS*) or another word in the *vicārius* family: inscription *CIG* 8621.7 (VI AD). Hofmann (1989: 57), *LBG*.
Direct loan **V AD – Byz.**	**βικαρία** (-ας, ἡ) 'office of deputy', from *vicāria* 'office of deputy' (L&S *s.v. vicārius* II.B.2). Inscriptions: *I.Salamine* 207.2 (V/VI AD). Literature: Pall. *H.Laus.* 62.1 (IV/V AD); Just. *Nov.* 8.1 (VI AD). Post-antique: survives. *LBG*, Kriaras (1968–). Notes: Hofmann (1989: 57), Lampe (1961), *DGE*, LSJ suppl. See §4.2.3.1, §6.2, §10.2.1, §10.2.2 D.
rare	**βικαριανός** 'of the *vicarius*', from *vicāriānus* 'of a deputy' (L&S): Just. *Nov.* 26.2.2 etc. (VI AD); perhaps abbreviated in papyri of VI AD, but the abbreviations may be for βικάριος (Cervenka-Ehrenstrasser 2000: 168–9, 273). Avotins (1992), Daris (1991a: 35), Hofmann (1989: 57), Meinersmann (1927: 11), *LBG*, *DGE*, LSJ suppl.
Direct loan **I AD – modern**	**βικάριος, βηκάρηος, βηκάριος, βικέριος, οὐ(ε)ικάριος** (-ου, ὁ) 'deputy', 'substitute officer', title of the governor of a diocese, 'slave belonging to another slave', from *vicārius* 'deputy', 'substitute'. Documents: e.g. perhaps *SB* 12169.5 (I AD); *P.Oxy.* 1436.40 (II AD); *PSI* VII.830.14 (IV AD); *PSI* XIII.1366.4 (IV/V AD); *P.Lund* II.5.12 (V/VI AD); *P.Oxy.* 1883.2 (VI AD). Inscriptions: e.g. *MAMA* IV.73.2 (I AD); *TAM* II.186.3 (IV AD); *MAMA* III.155.4 (IV–VI AD); *I.Chr.Bulgarien* 171.9 (VI AD).

Literature: common, e.g. Basil Caesariensis, *Epistulae* 117.1, 226.2 Courtonne
(IV AD); Nil. 2.220.1 (V AD); Just. *Nov.* 8.2 (VI AD); Antec. in Latin script
2.20.17 *vicarion* etc. (VI AD). Unverified example (III AD) in Zilliacus
(1937: 323, 328).

Post-antique: numerous. *LBG*, Zervan (2019: 29–30), Kriaras (1968–),
Triandaphyllidis (1909: 126), Sophocles (1887 *s.v.* οὐικάριος). Modern
βικάριος 'deputy bishop': Babiniotis (2002), Andriotis (1967).

Notes: claimed by Avotins (1992) to be an adjective in Just. *Nov.* 8.1, but that is
βικαρία (*q.v.*). Cervenka-Ehrenstrasser (2000: 167–9), Avotins (1989), Daris
(1991a: 35, 81–2), Mason (1974: 4, 72), Hofmann (1989: 58), Zilliacus
(1935a: 214–15, 238–9, 1937: 328), Meinersmann (1927: 42), Lampe
(1961 *s.vv.* βικάριος, οὐικάριος), *DGE*, LSJ suppl. (*s.vv.* βικάριος, οὐικάριος).
See §4.2.4.1 n. 50, §6.1, §10.2.1, §10.2.2 D.

rare   **βίκειος, βίκκειος** 'with vetch', from *vicia* 'vetch' via βικίον + -ειος: *Hippiatr.Berl.*
(Eumelos) 103.4 (III AD?). Hofmann (1989: 58 *s.v.* βικία), LSJ (*s.v.* βικίον).

rare   **βικεννάλια, οὐικεννάλια** 'celebration of a twenty-year anniversary', from *vīcennālia*
'festival on the twentieth anniversary of an emperor's reign' (L&S *s.v.*
vīcennālis): papyri *P.Stras.* III.138.12 (IV AD); *P.Oxy.* 2187.21 (IV AD);
perhaps Eusebius, *PG* XIX.588n. (IV AD). Distinct from Byzantine βικιναλία
(ὁδός) 'shared road' (*LBG*), from *vīcīnālis* 'for the use of the locals'.
Cervenka-Ehrenstrasser (2000: 169–70), Daris (1991a: 35, 82), Cavenaile
(1951: 395), Lampe (1961), *DGE* (*s.v.* βικεννάλιον), LSJ suppl. (*s.v.*
οὐικεννάλια).

βικέριος: see βικάριος.

rare   **βικήσιμον, βεικήσιμον, οὐικήσιμον** 'twentieth part', from *vīcēsimus* 'twentieth':
papyri *Chrest.Mitt.* 91.i.7 (II AD); *P.Oxy.* 2022.2 etc. (VI AD); perhaps
others. Cervenka-Ehrenstrasser (2000: 170–1), Daris (1991a: 35, 82),
Mason (1974: 6, 72), Hofmann (1989: 306), Meinersmann (1927: 42),
LBG, LSJ suppl. (*s.v.* οὐικήσιμα).

βικία: see βικίον.

foreign   **βικινάλιος** 'of a village', presumably from *vīcīnālis* 'of the local community'
(**vīcīnālius* is not attested): Antec. in Latin script 4.3.5 *vicinalia* etc.
(VI AD). Zilliacus (1935a: 214–15), *LBG* (*s.v.* βικιναλία).

Direct loan   **βικίον** (-ου, τό), **βικία** (-ας, ἡ), and **βίκος** (-ου, ὁ) 'vetch' (a plant), from *vicia*
II AD – modern   'vetch'.

Inscriptions: Edict.Diocl. 1.30 etc. (IV AD).

Literature: Galen VI.550.15 etc. Kühn (II AD); *Hippiatr.Par.* (Apsyrtus)
22 (III/IV AD?); Orib. *Col.* 1.34.t etc. (IV AD); *Hippiatr.Berl.* (Pel.) 4.6
(V AD?); Aëtius 2.246.9 (VI AD); elsewhere in *Hippiatr.*; with *vicia* in
glossaries e.g. Gloss. *Herm.Mp.* 299.61.

Post-antique: survives. *LBG* (*s.vv.* βικίον, βίκος). Modern dialectal βικία 'vetch':
Meyer (1895: 15).

Notes: the first ι is short, distinguishing it from βικίον, diminutive of βῖκος 'jug'.
Forms derivative βίκειος. Hofmann (1989: 58), *DÉLG* (*s.v.* βικία), Beekes
(2010 *s.v.* βικία), *DGE* (*s.vv.* 2 βικίον, 2 βῖκος), LSJ, LSJ suppl. (*s.vv.* βικία,
βικίον). See §4.2.3.1, §9.5.3, §10.2.1, §10.2.2 I, §12.2.1.

βίκλα: see βίγλα.

βίκος: see βικίον.

rare

βῖκος, οὐῖκος, βεῖκος (traditionally cited as **βεῖκον**, but clearly masc. acc.) 'village', from *vīcus* 'village': inscriptions *IGUR* IV.1659.2 (II AD); perhaps *I.Smyrna* 204.11 (II AD), unless the word there is from βῖκος 'jar' and means 'jar market' (*DGE s.v.* 1 βῖκος 3); Plut. *Luc.* 37.6, marked (I/II AD); Antec. in Latin script 4.3.5 *vicus* (VI AD); with *vicus* in Gloss. Ps.-Cyril. 257.41. Mason (1974: 6, 72–3), Hofmann (1989: 50, 306), Meinersmann (1927: 11), *LBG*, *DGE* (*s.v.* 3 βῖκος).

rare

βιλλαρικός, βηλαρικός on papyrus *P.Oxy.* 1026.12 (V AD) is probably a Latinism, but its etymology and meaning are disputed: Eideneier (1971: 55–8) derives it from *vēlāris* 'used for curtains', Diethart in Cervenka-Ehrenstrasser from *vīllāris* 'belonging to a farmyard', and LSJ from *vīllāticus* 'belonging to a farmstead'. LSJ suppl. does not specify a Latin source word but translation 'used for screening or veiling' implies *vēlāris*. Cervenka-Ehrenstrasser (2000: 161–2), Daris (1991a: 35), Hofmann (1989: 58), Meinersmann (1927: 11), Kriaras (1968– *s.vv.* βηλαρικός, βιλλαρικός), *DGE*.

βιλόθυρον: see βηλόθυρον.

βίνδεξ: see βίνδιξ.

foreign

βινδικατίων, a type of legacy, from *vindicātiō* 'action of suing for possession': Antec. in Latin script 2.20.2 *vindicationos* etc. (VI AD). Zilliacus (1935a: 214–15).

foreign

vindicō 'assert a legal claim': Antec. 2.20.2 *vindicare* (VI AD).

Direct loan
II AD – Byz.

βι(ν)δίκτα, οὐι(ν)δίκτα (-ης?, ἡ), a type of manumission, from *vindicta*, a type of manumission.

Documents: *P.Diog.* 7.20, perhaps 6.21 (both II AD); *BGU* V.1210.64 (II AD); perhaps *P.Oxy.* 2937.ii.14 (III AD).

Inscriptions: *SEG* XXXV.1167.8 (III AD).

Literature: Plut. *Publ.* 7.8: ἡ δὲ παντελὴς ἀπελευθέρωσις ἄχρι νῦν οὐινδίκτα λέγεται δι' ἐκεῖνον ὥς φασι τὸν Οὐινδίκιον (I/II AD); Antec. in Latin script 1.5.3 *vindicta* etc. (VI AD); as plant name in interpolation in Dsc. 4.19 RV, marked.

Post-antique: survives, with οὐίνδικτον used as part of a gloss in *Suda* ο 836. *LBG* (*s.vv.* βινδίκτα, οὐινδίκτα).

Notes: Strobach (1997: 197), Daris (1991a: 82), Mason (1974: 5, 73), Hofmann (1989: 306–7), Zilliacus (1935a: 214–15), Meinersmann (1927: 43), LSJ suppl. (*s.v.* οὐι(ν)δίκτα). See §10.2.1, §10.2.2 B; cf. οὐινδικτάριος, οὐινδικᾶτος, οὐνδίκιος.

Direct loan
V AD – Byz.

βίνδιξ, βίνδεξ (-ικος, ὁ), an official concerned with tax collection, 'solicitor', from *vindex* 'defender'.

Literature: e.g. Nil. 2.282.1 (V AD); Malal. 16.12, marked (VI AD); Cyr.S. *Vit. Sab.* 145.22 (VI AD); Just. *Nov.* 128.5 (VI AD).

Post-antique: minimal survival. Zervan (2019: 30), Triandaphyllidis (1909: 128).

Notes: Avotins (1992), Hofmann (1989: 59), Zilliacus (1935a: 214–15), Lampe (1961), LSJ suppl. See §4.2.5, §10.2.1, §10.2.2 D.

foreign βινεάριοι, a kind of soldier, is glossed with τειχομάχοι 'wall-fighters' by Lyd. *Mag.* p. 72.25 (VI AD); *LBG* derives it from *vīnea*, a shelter used by soldiers attacking walls, and Sophocles (1887) from *vīneārius* 'connected with vine-growing'. Zilliacus (1935a: 238–9).

βιξιλ-: see βηξιλ-.

Direct loan
II–III AD?
βιόκουρος, οὐιόκουρος, ἰόκουρος (-ου, ὁ) 'person in charge of roads', from *viocūrus* 'one who has charge of roads'.
 Inscriptions: e.g. *SEG* VI.555.12 (II AD); *I.Ephesos* 3085.9 (III AD); perhaps *IGBulg.* III.1.884.8 (III AD).
 Notes: Mason (1974: 6, 8, 73), Hofmann (1989: 59), *DGE*, LSJ (*s.vv.* βιόκουρος, ἰόκουρος), LSJ suppl. (*s.vv.* βιόκουρος, οὐιόκουρος). See §4.2.4.1 n. 51, §10.2.1, §10.2.2 D.

not ancient βιόλα transliterating *viola* 'violet': interpolations in Dsc. 3.123 RV etc. *LBG*, Kriaras (1968–), Meyer (1895: 15), Andriotis (1967).

non-existent? βιοφύλαξ, cited by Diethart and Grassien (2004: 86) as perhaps from *via* 'road': only in Coptic.

not ancient βιπεράλις transliterating *vīperālis* 'good against the bite of vipers' (L&S): interpolation in Dsc. 4.87 RV. Sophocles (1887).

rare βιπίννιον 'small double-bladed axe', from *bipennis* 'double-bladed axe': Edict. Diocl. 7.36 (IV AD). Hofmann (1989: 59–60), LSJ, LSJ suppl.

foreign βίριδες, βίρηδες 'green circus faction', from pl. of *viridis* 'green': Lyd. *Mens.* 4.30.19, marked (VI AD). Hofmann (1989: 60), Sophocles (1887).

rare βιρίδιος, βυρίτιος 'green', from *viridis* 'green': papyrus *P.Wash.Univ.* 1.58.3 (V AD). Cervenka-Ehrenstrasser (2000: 171–2), Diethart (1998: 170), Schirru (2013: 315).

βίροτος: see βίρωτος.

Deriv. of loan
III AD – Byz.
βίρ(ρ)ιον, βείριον, βύρριον (-ου, τό) 'hooded cloak', from *birrus* 'hooded cloak' (*TLL*) via βίρρος + -ιον.
 Documents: *BGU* II.449.8 (II/III AD); *P.Giss.Univ.* III.32.17 (III/IV AD); *SB* 9570.9 (IV/V AD); *CPR* XIX.62.8 etc. (V AD).
 Literature: *Coll.Herm.* S 9b (I–IV AD); Pall. *H.Laus.* 63.2.3 (IV/V AD).
 Post-antique: common. *LBG*.
 Notes: Cervenka-Ehrenstrasser (2000: 172), Mihăescu (1981), Hofmann (1989: 60 *s.v.* βίρρος), Cavenaile (1952: 196), *DÉLG* (*s.v.* βίρρος), *TLL* (*s.v.* 1. *birrus* 2006.44), Lampe (1961 *s.v.* βιρίν), *DGE*, LSJ suppl. See §4.6.1 n. 83, §10.2.2 H.

βίρρον: see βίρρος.

Direct loan
II AD – Byz.
βίρ(ρ)ος, βείρρος, βῆρος, βύρ(ρ)ος (-ου, ὁ) 'hooded cloak', from *birrus* 'hooded cloak' (*TLL*).
 Documents: *BGU* III.845.13 (II AD); *P.Giss.Apoll.* 28.4 (II AD); perhaps *P.Iand.* II.9.31 (II AD); *P.Harr.* I.105.11 (III AD?); *BGU* III.814.8 etc. (III AD); *P.Oxy.* 1741.13 (IV AD); *PSI* XV.1564.11 (IV AD); *P.Ryl.* IV.627.7 (IV AD); probably *SB* 14211.10 (V AD).

Inscriptions: Edict.Diocl. 7.42 etc. (IV AD); *SEG* VII.431.15.

Literature: Artemidorus, *Onirocriticon* 2.3.71, marked (II AD); *Coll.Herm.* C 13b (I–IV AD); perhaps Dositheus, *Ars grammatica* VII.435.24 Keil (IV AD); Philogelos 99 (IV AD); Concilium Gangrense, *canones* 12 = Lauchert 1896: 82.9 (IV AD); with *birrus* in Gloss. Ps.-Cyril. 257.45, cf. 440.27.

Post-antique: survives mainly on papyrus. Sophocles (1887 *s.vv.* βίρρον, βίρρος).

Notes: neuter βίρρον is mentioned in *Suda* and probably underlies plural οουηρα in *SB* 14211.10. Immisch (1885: 330) argues that βειρόν and βερρόν, which appear as lemmata in Hesych. (β 464, 534, both with definition 'thick'), are also forms of βίρρος. Forms derivatives βίρριον, βιρροφόρος, σαγόβυρος. Cervenka-Ehrenstrasser (2000: 173–5 *s.vv.* βίρρον, βίρρος), Diethart (1990a: 101, 1998: 170), Mihăescu (1981), Murri (1943: 115–18), Hofmann (1989: 60), Meinersmann (1927: 11), *DÉLG*, Frisk (1954–72: 1.239, III.52), Beekes (2010), *TLL* (*s.v. birrus*), Lampe (1961 *s.v.* βῆρος), *DGE*, LSJ, LSJ suppl. (*s.vv.* βίρρος, βυρρός, βύρρος). See §4.1.1, §4.2.4.1 n. 51, §4.6.1 n. 83, §8.2.2, §10.2.1, §10.2.2 H.

rare | **βιρροφόρος, βυρροφόρος** 'wearer of a hooded cloak', from *birrus* 'hooded cloak' (*TLL*) via βίρρος + -φορος (cf. φορέω 'wear'): Pall. *H.Laus.* 37.6.2 (IV/V AD). Sophocles (1887 *s.v.* βυρροφόρος), Lampe (1961), *DGE*.

non-existent | **βίρωτος, βίροτος** 'for two-wheeled carts', from *birotus* 'of two-wheeled carts' (*TLL*): variant at Edict.Diocl. 15.34–6 (IV AD), where βιτωτός 'with tyres' (*q.v.*) is a better reading. Hofmann (1989: 60), Sophocles (1887 *s.v.* βίροτος).

not ancient? | **βισάκκι** 'coat-bag', from *bisaccium* 'double bag': probably no ancient examples. Meyer (1895: 15–16).

βίσαλον: see βήσαλον.

βισαλωτόν: see βησσαλωτός.

rare | **βίσεξτον** 'intercalary period', from *bisextum* 'intercalary period': Malal. 9.3 (VI AD); Lyd. *Mens.* 3.7.1 (marked), 3.10.123 (VI AD). Hofmann (1989: 61), Zilliacus (1935a: 176–7), Lampe (1961 *s.v.* βίσεξτος), *DGE* (*s.v.* βίσεξτος). For Byzantine and modern occurrences (often spelled βίσεκτος, βίσεκστος) Kriaras (1968– *s.v.* βίσεξτος), Sophocles (1887), Triandaphyllidis (1909: 120, 131), Andriotis (1974: 176), Meyer (1895: 15 *s.v.* βίσεκτος), Schwyzer (1929: 310–11).

Direct loan with univerbation | **βισήλεκτος, βισέλεκτος, βισίλεκτος, βεσίλεκτος** (-ου, ὁ), a title, from *bis* 'twice' + *ēlēctus* 'chosen'.

IV–VI AD | Documents: *SB* 14658.4, perhaps 16000.63 (both IV AD); *P.Cair.Masp.* 67057.1.6 etc., 67058.1.15, 67139.5r.4 (all VI AD); *P.Freer* 3+4.18 (VI AD).

Notes: Cervenka-Ehrenstrasser (2000: 175–6), Filos (2010: 252), Daris (1991a: 35), Zilliacus (1935a: 218–19), Meinersmann (1927: 11), *TLL* (*s.v. ēligo* 386.45–6), *DGE* (*s.v.* βισίλεκτος). See §4.1.1, §4.2.4.1 n. 51, §4.5, §9.2, §10.2.1, §10.2.2 D.

βισκάς: see βοσκάς.

foreign | **βισκᾶτος** transliterating *viscātus* 'smeared with birdlime': Plut. *Mor.* 281e (I/II AD). Hofmann (1989: 61), *DGE* (*s.v.* βισκᾶτα).

βιστιάριον: see βεστιάριον.

foreign	βίσων transliterating *bisōn* 'bison': Pausanias 10.13.1 etc. (II AD); Opp. *C.* 2.160 (II/III AD); Dio Cassius 76.1.5 (II/III AD); Timotheus of Gaza 28 in Haupt 1869: 18.26 (VI AD). Hofmann (1989: 62), *DÉLG*, Beekes (2010), Sophocles (1887), *DGE*, LSJ.
non-existent	βιτάλια 'shroud', from *vītālia* 'graveclothes' (L&S *s.v. vītālis* II.B.2): superseded reading (*BL* VI.23) of papyrus *P.Berl.Zill.* 13.4 (VI AD). Cavenaile (1951: 395), *DGE*.
not ancient	βιτᾶλις transliterating *vītālis* 'living': interpolation in Dsc. 4.89 RV. Sophocles (1887).
foreign	βίτελλος transliterating *vitellus* 'egg yolk': Lyd. *Mag.* p. 38.13 (VI AD). Sophocles (1887).
foreign	βίτιον 'taint', from *vitium* 'defect': Antec. in Latin script 2.6.3 *vition* etc. (VI AD); later in Greek script. Zilliacus (1935a: 214–15), *LBG*. See §9.5.6 n. 68.
rare	βίτος 'tyre', 'rim', from *vitus, -ūs* 'felloe of a wheel' (Souter 1949): Edict.Diocl. 15.31a (IV AD). Apparently forms derivative βιτωτός. Hofmann (1989: 62), *DÉLG*, Beekes (2010), LSJ.

βίτουλος: see οὐΐτουλος.

non-existent?	βιττιν, perhaps a container, suggested as from *buttis* (cf. *s.v.* βοῦττις), may not exist. Cervenka-Ehrenstrasser (2000: 270).
rare	βιτωτός 'with tyres', 'with rims', from *vitus, -ūs* 'felloe of a wheel' (Souter 1949) via βίτος + -ωτός: Edict.Diocl. 15.34–7 (IV AD). Hofmann (1989: 62), *DÉLG* (*s.v.* βίτος), LSJ (*s.v.* βίτος).
Direct loan **IV–VI AD**	βλάττα, βλάττη (-ης, ἡ) 'purple (wool)', from *blatta* 'purple' (*TLL s.v.* 2. *blatta*). Inscriptions: Edict.Diocl. 24.2 (IV AD). Literature: Epiph. *Gem.* 1.5 (IV AD); EphraemSyr. V p. 62.13 (V/VI AD). Post-antique: no survival. Modern βλαττίδα 'skin rash' (Babiniotis 2002) and dialectal βλάττα 'pockmark' (Andriotis 1974: 177; Meyer 1895: 16) may come independently from *blatta* 'cockroach'. Notes: forms derivatives βλαττίον, μεταξαβλάττη, ὑποβλάττα, perhaps βλαττόσημος. Cervenka-Ehrenstrasser (2000: 177), Steigerwald (1990: 224–33), Bogensperger (2017: 244–5), Hofmann (1989: 62–3), Viscidi (1944: 39), Beekes (2010), Lampe (1961), LSJ. See §10.2.1, §10.2.2 H.
rare	βλατ(τ)ίον 'purple cloth', 'purple silk', from *blatta* 'purple' (*TLL s.v.* 2. *blatta*) via βλάττα + -ιον: Lyd. *Mens.* 1.21.4 (VI AD); Byzantine texts (with derivatives βλαττικός 'of purple', βλαττοπώλης 'silk-seller', etc.). Modern βλατ(τ)ί 'red silk garment': Babiniotis (2002), Andriotis (1967). Cervenka-Ehrenstrasser (2000: 176–7), Bogensperger (2017: 245), Diethart (1998: 170), Hofmann (1989: 63 *s.v.* βλάττα), *LBG*, Zervan (2019: 32), Kriaras (1968–), Triandaphyllidis (1909: 88, 121), LSJ (*s.v.* βλάττα), LSJ suppl. (*s.v.* βλάττιος).
rare	βλάττιος 'purple', from *blatteus* 'purple' (*TLL*): papyrus *Stud.Pal.* XX.245.10 (VI AD). Cervenka-Ehrenstrasser (2000: 177–8), Bogensperger (2017: 245), Diethart (1989: 113), Daris (1991a: 35), *DGE*, LSJ suppl.

rare	**βλαττόσημος** 'having purple stripes', from *blatta* 'purple' (*TLL s.v. 2. blatta*) via βλάττα + σῆμα 'mark' or from *blattosēmus* 'having purple stripes' (*TLL*): Edict.Diocl. 29.17 etc. (IV AD). Hofmann (1989: 63 *s.v.* βλαττα), *DGE, TLL* (*s.v. blattosēmus*), LSJ suppl.
not Latin?	**βλεννός** 'drivelling', perhaps from *blennus* 'drivelling' or *vice versa*. *DÉLG* (*s.v.* βλέννα), Frisk (1954–72: 1.242–3), Beekes (2010 *s.v.* βλέννα), Immisch (1885: 275), LSJ.
not Latin?	**βλιτάς** 'worthless woman', **βλίτωνας** 'foolish', and **βλιτομάμμας** 'booby', perhaps from *bliteus* 'worthless' or *vice versa*. Campanile (1969: 304–5), Immisch (1885: 275), LSJ, LSJ suppl.
not ancient	**βλίτουμ** transliterating *blitum* 'spinach': interpolation in Dsc. 2.117 RV. Sophocles (1887).
name	**Βοάριος**, name of a forum in Rome, from *boārius* (Βοαρία ἀγορά = *forum boārium* 'cattle market'). LSJ, *DGE* (*s.v.* Βοαρία ἀγορά), Hofmann (1989: 63).
rare	**βοκάλιος** 'singer', from *vōcālis* 'vocal': papyrus *P.Oxy.* 2707.7 etc. (VI AD); Cos.Indic. 5.116, 117, marked (VI AD); Byzantine texts. Cervenka-Ehrenstrasser (2000: 178), Daris (1991a: 36), Hofmann (1989: 63), *LBG* (*s.v.* βουκάλιος), Triandaphyllidis (1909: 124), Lampe (1961), *DGE*, LSJ suppl. (*s.v.* βοκάλιοι).
	βόλβα: see βοῦλβα.
semantic extension	**βολβός** as a plant name is basically Greek, but it is used for *bulbus* 'bulb' by Galen VI.655.5 Kühn: Περὶ ὕδνων· ἐν ῥίζαις ἢ βολβοῖς ἀριθμεῖν ἀναγκαῖόν ἐστι καὶ ταῦτα … (II AD). Hofmann (1989: 63), Frisk (1954–72: 1.249–50), LSJ. See §2.3.
non-existent?	**βολλωτός, βουλλωτός** 'with knobs': perhaps papyrus *Stud.Pal.* XX.2.5 (I AD). Cervenka-Ehrenstrasser (2000: 194) derives it from *bullātus* 'ornamented with knobs' and Hofmann (1989: 64) from *bulla* 'knob'. Byzantine βουλλωτός 'with a seal' is probably an independent formation (*LBG*, Kriaras 1968–). Diethart (1998: 171), Palmer (1945: 45), Daris (1991a: 36), LSJ.
foreign	*volō* 'want': Antec. 2.24.3 *volo* (VI AD).
foreign	**βολουντάριος** 'voluntary', from *voluntārius* 'voluntary' (of heirs not obliged to accept an inheritance): Antec. in Latin script 2.19.5 *voluntarioi* etc. (VI AD); later in Greek script. Zilliacus (1935a: 214–15), *LBG, DGE*.
foreign	*voluptaria*, neut. pl. of *voluptārius* 'concerning pleasure': Schol.Sinai. 20 (V/VI AD). See §7.1.2, §9.5.6 nn. 56 and 57.
rare	**βολούπτας** 'pleasure', from *voluptās* 'pleasure': Lyd. *Mens.* 4.30.6 (VI AD). Sophocles (1887).
foreign	**βονιτάριος** 'having a particular kind of ownership (recognized by the praetor)', from unattested **bonitārius* (*TLL s.v. bonus* 2103.67, *s.v.* βονιτάριος) or from *bonus* 'good' + -άριος: Antec. in Latin script 1.5.3 *bonitarios* (VI AD). Burgmann (1991: 68), Zilliacus (1935a: 176–7), Souter (1949 *s.v. bonitarius*), *LBG*. See §8.1.7 n. 34.

Direct loan
III AD – Byz.

βόνος, βῶνος (-η, -ον) 'good', esp. in n. pl. βόνα 'goods', from *bonus* 'good'.
Documents: *P.Hamb.* 1.68r.25 (VI AD).
Inscriptions: *TAM* II.334.10 (III AD); *SEG* XLVII.1487.2, Latinate.
Literature: βόνα 'goods': Antec. 3.7.4, in Latin script as part of phrases 4.2.2 *ex bonis, in bonis*, 3.12.pr. *bonorum emption, bonorum venditiones*, 3.25.pr. *totorum bonorum*, etc. (VI AD). *Bona fide* 'in good faith': Antec. in Latin script 2.8.2 etc. (cf. Triantaphyllides 1892: 257–8). Probably a name in Isidore of Pelusium, *PG* LXXVIII.357a (V AD).
Post-antique: common in legal texts. *LBG* (*s.vv.* βόνα, βονάφιδος).
Notes: Cervenka-Ehrenstrasser (2000: 179), Daris (1991a: 36), Hofmann (1989: 76), *DGE*. See §4.2.2, **§7.3** passage 33, §9.5.6 passage 80, §10.2.1, §10.2.2 B.

βορδ-: see βουρδ-.

Βορείγονοι: see Ἀβοριγῖνες.

βορτ-: see βουρδ-.

rare

βοσκάς (or, at least in theory, **βισκάς**) 'sticky', from *viscōsus* 'sticky' (L&S): Dsc. 1.72.5 (I AD). *LBG*.

Direct loan
III AD – Byz.

βότον, βῶτον (-ου, τό) 'vow', from *vōtum* 'vow'.
Documents: *SB* 17146.6 (VI AD); *P.Cair.Masp.* 67057.1.32 (VI AD).
Coins: ΒΩΤΑ at Ephesus, Head 1911: 577 (I–III AD).
Literature: Lyd. *Mens.* 4.10.1 (VI AD).
Post-antique: common. *LBG*.
Notes: Cervenka-Ehrenstrasser (2000: 179–80), Daris (1991a: 36), *DGE*. See §4.2.4.1 n. 55, §9.1 n. 4, §10.2.1, §10.2.2 O.

rare

βότουλος 'gut', from *botulus* 'intestine' (*TLL*): scholion to Ar. *Eq.* 490a. *LBG*.

not Latin?

βόττης, a container (see *P.Berl.Sarisch.* 21.54 with commentary), is related to βοῦττις (*q.v.*). Cervenka-Ehrenstrasser (2000: 270–1).

foreign

βούβελα 'beef', from *būbula* 'beef': Hesych. as lemma β 876 (V/VI AD). Hofmann (1989: 64), Immisch (1885: 323), LSJ. See §9.5.4.

rare

βουβλάρις, a position in a synagogue, from *būb(u)lārius* 'sausage-seller' (*TLL*): inscription Negroni 2013: 303 no. 189 (III/IV AD).

name

Βουβοῦλκος, a personal name, from *bubulcus* 'ox-driver'. Strobach (1997: 194), *DGE* (*s.v.* Βουβολκοί).

rare

βοῦγλιν 'dagger', from *pūgiō* 'dagger' + -ιον: Malal. 18.141.17, 19 (VI AD). Triandaphyllidis (1909: 129), *DGE*. Cf. φουγίων.

βουκάλιος: see βοκάλιος.

βουκανάω: see βυκανάω.

βουκάνη: see βυκάνη.

βουκανίζω: see βυκινίζω.

βουκανισμός: see βυκανισμός.

rare	**βουκανιστήριον**, from *būcina* 'trumpet' apparently via βυκινίζω + -τηριον: with *bucina* and *bucinum* in glossaries, e.g. Gloss. Ps.-Cyril. 259.9. That equation suggests a meaning 'trumpet', but -τηριον is most often used for places (Buck and Petersen 1945: 47), and βουκανιστήριον looks like βουκονιστήριον (*q.v.*), a type of arena; *DGE* therefore considers βουκανιστήριον an arena. *LBG*.

βουκανιστής: see βυκανητής.

non-existent	**βούκελλα** 'small loaf', from *buccella* 'small tender loaf' (*TLL s.v.* 2227.41–52): superseded reading of papyrus *P.Flor.* 1.74.13 (II AD). Cervenka-Ehrenstrasser (2000: 271), Hofmann (1989: 65), Meinersmann (1927: 12), *DGE*, LSJ.
Direct loan **V AD – Byz.**	**βουκελ(λ)άριος, βουκκελ(λ)άριος** (-ου, ὁ) 'member of armed escort of military or civil functionary', from *buccellārius* 'privately hired soldier' (*TLL*). Documents: common, e.g. *PSI* v.481.1 (V/VI AD); *P.Vind.Sal.* 15.8 (V/VI AD); *P.Ant.* 11.103.10 (VI AD); *P.Oxy.* 2480.3 (VI AD). Inscriptions: *Corinth* VIII.1.207.5, perhaps 208.4. Literature: *V.Dan.Styl.* A. 60.22 (V AD); Aëtius 1.131.51 (VI AD). Post-antique: numerous, forming derivative βουκελλαρικός (incorrectly cited as ancient by Zilliacus 1935a: 218–19). *LBG*, Triandaphyllidis (1909: 128). Notes: Cervenka-Ehrenstrasser (2000: 181–3), Daris (1991a: 36), Hofmann (1989: 65), Zilliacus (1935a: 218–19), Meinersmann (1927: 11–12), *TLL* (*s.v. buccellārius*), *DGE*, LSJ suppl. See §4.2.4.1 n. 50, §10.2.1, §10.2.2 C.
rare	**βουκελλάτης, βουκελλατᾶς**, a type of baker, from *buccella* 'small mouthful of food': papyrus *P.Erl.* 81.49 etc. (VI AD). Cervenka-Ehrenstrasser (2000: 184), Daris (1991a: 36), *DGE*, LSJ suppl.

βουκελ(λ)ᾶτον: see βουκκελλᾶτον.

rare	**βουκέλ(λ)ιον** 'small loaf', from *buccella* 'small tender loaf' (*TLL s.v.* 2227.41–52) + -ιον: papyrus *CPR* v.26.457 etc. (V AD); Byzantine texts. Cervenka-Ehrenstrasser (2000: 185–6), Daris (1991a: 36, with derivation from *buccellum*), *LBG*, *DGE*, LSJ suppl.
rare	**βουκία**, a cake or biscuit, from *buccella* 'small mouthful of food': papyrus *P.Oxy.* 397 (I AD). Cervenka-Ehrenstrasser (2000: 186–7), Daris (1991a: 36, with derivation from *buccea*), Hofmann (1989: 65, with derivation from *buccia*), Meinersmann (1927: 12), *DGE*, LSJ suppl.

βουκίζω: see βουκκίζω.

βουκινάτωρ: see βυκινάτωρ.

βουκινίζω: see βυκινίζω.

rare	**βούκινον, β(ο)ύκ(κ)ινον** 'trumpet', from *būcinum* 'trumpet' (*TLL*) or *būcina* 'trumpet': Agath. *Greg.* 179.2 (V AD); often in Byzantine texts. Modern βούκινο 'trumpet' etc.: Babiniotis (2002), Andriotis (1967), Meyer (1895: 16). Zilliacus (1935a: 218–19), *LBG* (*s.vv.* βούκινον, βύκινον), Zervan (2019: 34), Kriaras (1968–), Triandaphyllidis (1909: 129, 168), Lampe (1961), *DGE* (*s.v.* βύκινον), LSJ suppl.

βουκίον: see βουκκίον.

βουκισμός: see βουκκισμή.

βουκίων: see βουκκίων.

not ancient

βούκκα 'cheek' and relatives, from *bucca* 'mouthful': probably no ancient examples. Meyer (1895: 16–17), Andriotis (1967 *s.v.* modern βούκα 'mouthful'), *LBG* (*s.v.* βουκίων 'biscuit'), Triandaphyllidis (1909: 103, 120), LSJ suppl. (*s.v.* βουκία).

Direct loan with suffix
IV–VI AD?

βουκ(κ)ᾶς (-ᾶ, ὁ) 'biscuit-baker', from *bucca* 'mouthful' + -ᾶς.
Documents: perhaps *O.Krok.* 1.88.9 (II AD); *P.Bad.* II.31.21 (IV AD); *Stud.Pal.* XX.148.4 (VI AD).
Notes: Diethart (1984), Cervenka-Ehrenstrasser (2000: 180–1), Daris (1991a: 36), *DGE*, LSJ suppl. See §4.3.2, §10.2.1, §10.2.2 I.

βουκκελ(λ)άριος: see βουκελλάριος.

Direct loan
V AD – Byz.

βουκ(κ)ελ(λ)ᾶτον (-ου, τό) 'flatbread', from *buccellātum* 'flatbread' (*TLL*).
Documents: *P.Oxy.* 2732.5 (VI AD?).
Literature: Pall. *H.Laus.* 18.2.3 (IV/V AD); Aëtius 3.101.1 (VI AD).
Post-antique: numerous. *LBG* (*s.v.* βουκελλᾶτον).
Notes: Cervenka-Ehrenstrasser (2000: 184–5), Daris (1991a: 36), Hofmann (1989: 65), Zilliacus (1935a: 218–19), Lampe (1961 *s.v.* βουκέλλατος), *TLL* (*s.v. buccellātum*), *DGE*. See §4.2.4.1 n. 55, §10.2.1, §10.2.2 I.

rare

βουκ(κ)ίζω, designating some type of light eating, probably ultimately from *bucca* 'mouthful' + -ίζω: with *gusto* and *iento* in Gloss. Ps.-Philox. 36.42, 75.48, 75.61. Probably source of βουκκισμή. Hofmann (1989: 66), *TLL* (*s.v. bucca* 2226.60), *DGE* (*s.v.* βουκίζω), for Byzantine survival *LBG*.

βουκκινάτωρ: see βυκινάτωρ.

βούκκινον: see βούκινον.

Direct loan with suffix
VI AD – modern?

βουκ(κ)ίον (-ου, τό), a cake or biscuit, from *bucca* 'mouthful' + -ιον.
Documents: *P.Oxy.* 155.4 (VI AD).
Literature: Barsanuph.Jo. II.II ep. 512.14, 545.10, III ep. 635.4 (VI AD); Dor. Gaz. *Doct.Div.* 11.121.37 (VI AD).
Post-antique: survives. Sophocles (1887). Perhaps modern dialectal βούκκα etc.: Meyer (1895: 16–17).
Notes: LSJ suppl. puts the *P.Oxy.* example under βουκία. Cervenka-Ehrenstrasser (2000: 189), Cavenaile (1952: 196), Lampe (1961), *DGE*. See §4.3.2 n. 69, §10.2.1, §10.2.2 I.

rare

βουκκισμή, βουκισμός 'breakfast', presumably from *bucca* 'mouthful' via βουκκίζω: with *gustarium* in Gloss. Ps.-Philox. 36.47, with *ientaculum* in Gloss. Ps.-Cyril. 259.12. Hofmann (1989: 66 *s.v.* βουκκίζειν), *TLL* (*s.v. bucca* 2226.61).

rare

βουκ(κ)ίων, meaning disputed, probably from *buccō* 'fool': with *bucco* in Gloss. Ps.-Philox. 31.37; Byzantine texts. Hofmann (1989: 66), *LBG* (*s.vv.* βουκίων, βουκκίων), *DGE*.

not Latin?   **βουκονιστήριον** on inscription *IGR* III.484.2 (II/III AD), apparently
meaning some kind of arena, might be from *būcina* 'trumpet' via βυκάνη
(Radermacher 1911: 203–4). Robert (1946: 149–50), Hofmann (1989: 74
s.v. βυκάνη), *DÉLG*, Frisk (1954–72: 1.258, III.55), Beekes (2010), *DGE*, LSJ,
LSJ suppl. Cf. βουκανιστήριον.

βούλα: see βούλλα.

Direct loan   **βοῦλβα, βόλβα** (-ης, ἡ) 'sow's womb', from *vulva* 'womb'.
IV AD – Byz.   Inscriptions: Edict.Diocl. 4.4 (IV AD).
Literature: Philogelos 103 (IV AD); Alex.Trall. 11.311.2 etc. (VI AD);
Anthologia Graeca 11.410.5, 8.
Post-antique: survives. *LBG*.
Notes: probably forms derivative βούλβιον. Binder (2000: 141), Hofmann
(1989: 66), *DGE*, LSJ (*s.v.* βόλβα), LSJ suppl. See §5.2.3, §10.2.1, §10.2.2 I.

rare   **βούλβιον** 'womb', from *vulva* 'womb' (via βοῦλβα?) + -ιον: Alex.Trall. 11.27.3 etc.
(VI AD). *LBG, DGE*.

not ancient   **βούλβους** transliterating *bulbus* 'bulb': interpolations in Dsc. 3.122 RV etc.
Sophocles (1887).

non-existent?   **βουλγαρικός**, perhaps from *vulgāris* 'ordinary': no certain examples. Cervenka-
Ehrenstrasser (2000: 189–90).

foreign   **βουλγάριος** 'common', 'ordinary', from *vulgāris* 'ordinary': Antec. in Latin script
2.16.4 *vulgarios* etc. (VI AD); later in Greek script. Zilliacus (1935a: 214–
15), *LBG*. See §10.3.1 n. 30.

foreign   **βουλγαροπουπιλλάριος** 'mixing ordinary and pupillary' (of types of substitution
of heirs), from *vulgāris* 'ordinary' and *pūpillāris* 'of a minor under care of
guardian': Antec. in Latin script 2.16.pr. *vulgaropupillarian* etc. (VI AD);
later in Greek script. The compound formation is Greek (§4.5). Zilliacus
(1935a: 214–15), *LBG*.

Direct loan   **βούλ(λ)α** (-ας/-ης, ἡ) 'Roman child's charm', 'tin', from *bulla* 'knob', 'Roman
IV? AD –   child's charm'.
modern   Documents: perhaps *P.Leipz.* 29v.i.1 (III AD); tachygraphy in Menci 2000: 281
(III/IV AD).
Literature: Plut. *Rom.* 20.4 etc., often marked (I/II AD); *Test.Sal.* p. 106*.27
etc. (III AD?); *Hippiatr.Par.* (Apsyrtus) 1026 (III/IV AD?); alchemist in
P.Leid. 10, e.g. frag. 13.5 Halleux (IV AD); alchemist in *P.Holm*, frag. 7.4
Halleux, marked (IV AD); Lyd. *Mag.* p. 84.31, marked (VI AD).
Post-antique: common, with meaning 'seal'. *LBG*, Zervan (2019: 35), Kriaras
(1968–), Triandaphyllidis (1909: 122), Daris (1991a: 36). Modern
βούλλα 'seal' and derivatives: Babiniotis (2002), Andriotis (1967), Meyer
(1895: 17).
Notes: Latin *bulla* acquires the meaning 'seal' after AD 600 (*TLL*, Du Cange
1883–7 *s.v.* p. 773 col. 2). Probably forms derivative βουλλόω. Cervenka-
Ehrenstrasser (2000: 190–2), Menci (2000: 281), Strobach (1997: 194),
Hofmann (1989: 66–7), Meinersmann (1927: 12), Lampe (1961), *DGE*,
LSJ. See §8.2.2, §8.2.3 n. 51, §10.2.1, §10.2.2 H.

not ancient | βουλλεύω 'seal', from *bulla* in its post-antique meaning 'seal' via βούλλα + -εύω: no ancient examples. Cervenka-Ehrenstrasser (2000: 192–3), Diethart (1998: 170), Daris (1991a: 37), *DGE*.

not ancient | βουλλίζω 'seal', from *bulla* in its post-antique meaning 'seal' via βούλλα + -ίζω: no ancient examples. Cervenka-Ehrenstrasser (2000: 193–4), Diethart (1998: 170), *LBG*.

rare | βουλλόω 'seal', from *bulla* in its post-antique meaning 'seal' (via βούλλα or medieval *bullō* 'seal', *DMLBS s.v. bullāre*) + -όω: *Test.Sal.* p. 106*.26 etc. (III AD?); *Historia Alexandri Magni* rec. β 1.39.2 Bergson (V AD); Byzantine texts. *LBG*, Zervan (2019: 35), Lampe (1961), *DGE*.

βουλλωτός: see βολλωτός.

rare | βουλσός 'suffering convulsions', from *vulsus*, pf. part. of *vellō* 'pluck' (L&S): *Hippiatr.Par.* (Apsyrtus) 559 (III/IV AD?); *Hippiatr.Par.* (Pel.) 503 etc. (V AD?); elsewhere in *Hippiatr. LBG, DGE*.

βουλταρίδιον: see πολταρίδιον.

rare | βουργάριος 'castle guard', from *burgārius* 'inhabitant of a castle': inscription *IGBulg.* III.II.1690.e61 (III AD). Mason (1974: 31), Hofmann (1989: 67), Kriaras (1968– *s.v.* βουργάρης), *DGE*, LSJ.

not ancient | βούργια 'sack', from *bulga* 'bag': no ancient examples. Meyer (1895: 17), Andriotis (1967).

rare | βοῦργος 'castle', from *burgus* 'castle': inscription *I.Caesarea Maritima* 57.4 (V/VI AD); Byzantine texts. Modern dialectal βουργίδι 'village': Meyer (1895: 17). *LBG*, LSJ suppl.

Direct loan
III AD – modern | βουρδών, βορδών, βουρτών (-ῶνος/-όνος, ὁ) 'mule', 'mule-tax', from *burdō* 'mule'. Documents: common, e.g. *SB* 9542.2 (III AD); *O.Bodl.* II.2064.3 (IV AD); *P.Amst.* 1.77.4 (V AD); *SB* 16746.4 (VI AD).
Inscriptions: Edict.Diocl. 14.10 etc. (IV AD).
Literature: Cyran. 2.15.t etc. (II AD?); John Chrysostom, *Epistulae ad Olympiadem* 9.3.37 Malingrey (IV/V AD); Callin. *V.Hypat.* 41.10 (V AD); Malal. 7.6.32 (VI AD); Aëtius 12.51.1 etc. (VI AD); Cyr.S. *Vit.Sab.* 134.14 (VI AD).
Post-antique: numerous. *LBG* (*s.v.* βόρδων), Triandaphyllidis (1909: 119). Modern dialectal βόρδος, βόρδως, etc.: Andriotis (1974: 180), Kahane and Kahane (1972–6: 534), Cervenka-Ehrenstrasser (2000: 197).
Notes: forms derivatives βουρδώνιον, βουρδωνάριον. Kramer (1996a: 116–19, 2011: 43–6), Cervenka-Ehrenstrasser (2000: 194–7, pointing out that the meaning 'mule-tax' is not attested for Latin), Shipp (1979: 170), Binder (2000: 141), Daris (1991a: 37), Hofmann (1989: 67), Meinersmann (1927: 12), Immisch (1885: 368), *DÉLG*, Beekes (2010), Lampe (1961), *DGE*, LSJ (*s.vv.* βουρδών, βορδών), LSJ suppl. See §4.2.5, §4.3.2, §4.6.1 n. 83, §5.2.1, §10.1, §10.2.1, **§10.2.2 K**.

rare | βουρδωνάριον 'mule', from *burdō* 'mule' via βουρδών + -άριον: papyrus *P.Ryl.* II.238.11 (III AD). Cervenka-Ehrenstrasser (2000: 197–8), Daris (1991a: 37), Cavenaile (1952: 196), *DÉLG* (*s.v.* βουρδών), LSJ (*s.v.* βουρδών). See §6.3 n. 21.

Direct loan
IV AD – modern

βο(υ)ρδωνάριος, βο(υ)ρδο(υ)νάριος, βο(υ)ρτωνάριος, βο(υ)ρτονάριος (-ου, ὁ) 'muleteer', from *burdōnārius* 'muleteer'.

Documents: perhaps *P.Oxy.* 43r.6.1 (III AD); *P.Iand.* VIII.153.19 (IV AD); *P.Iand.* VIII.154.16 (VI AD).

Inscriptions: Edict.Diocl. 7.17 (IV AD); *I.Delta* 31.2 p. 254.

Literature: Teucer, Boll 1903: 43.4 (I AD?); Cyr.S. *Vit.Sab.* 92.13, 134.9 (VI AD); old scholion to Ar. *Th.* 491 as gloss.

Post-antique: numerous. *LBG* (*s.v.* βορδονάριος), Kriaras (1968– *s.v.* βουρδωνάρης). Modern βουρδουνάρις or βορδωνάρις 'monk or servant of a monastery performing the duties of a muleteer', βορτωνάρος 'groom': Kahane and Kahane (1972–6: 533, 1982: 135).

Notes: Cervenka-Ehrenstrasser (2000: 198), Daris (1991a: 37), Hofmann (1989: 64, 67–8), Cavenaile (1951: 396), *DÉLG* (*s.v.* βουρδών), Lampe (1961), *DGE*, LSJ (*s.v.* βουρδών), LSJ suppl. See §4.2.4.1 n. 50, §10.2.1, §10.2.2 K.

Deriv. of loan
VI AD – modern

βο(υ)ρδώνιον (-ου, τό) 'mule', from *burdō* 'mule' via βουρδών + -ιον.

Documents: perhaps *P.Harr.* I.155.4 (IV AD).

Literature: Ps.-Palchus, Cumont and Boll 1904: 183.15 (V/VI AD?); Cyr.S. *Vit. Sab.* 134.10 (VI AD).

Post-antique: common. *LBG* (*s.v.* βορδόνιον), Kriaras (1968– *s.v.* βουρδώνι). Modern dialectal βορδώνι etc.: Andriotis (1974: 180–1), Kahane and Kahane (1972–6: 534).

Notes: Cervenka-Ehrenstrasser (2000: 198–9), Binder (2000: 141), Daris (1991a: 37), *DGE* (*s.v.* βουρδῶνιν), LSJ suppl. (*s.v.* βορδόνιον). See §4.3.2, §4.6.1 n. 83, §10.2.2 K.

rare

βουριχάλ(λ)ιον, βουρικάλιον, a type of cart, probably from *būricus/būrichus* 'pony' (*TLL*) or unattested **būric(h)āle* 'pony-cart': Gregorius Nazianzenus, *Testamentum*, Pitra 1868: 157.16 (IV AD); Lyd. *Mag.* p. 32.13 (VI AD); Byzantine texts. Different spellings may indicate lack of continuity. Hofmann (1989: 68), *LBG*, *TLL* (*s.v.* βουριχάλλια), Du Cange (1883–7 *s.v. buricus*), Lampe (1961), LSJ, LSJ suppl. See §8.1.7 n. 34.

not ancient?

βουριχᾶς 'pony-dealer', from *būricus/būrichus* 'pony' (*TLL*): inscription *I.Ephesos* 551.3. *DGE*, LSJ suppl.

rare

βούριχος 'pony', from *būricus/būrichus* 'pony' (*TLL*): with *mannus* in Gloss. Ps.-Philox. 127.2. *LBG*, *DGE*.

βουρτ-: see βουρδ-.

not Latin?

βούτινον, apparently a vessel, perhaps from unattested **butinum*: Hesych. as gloss ω 217 (V/VI AD). Hofmann (1989: 68), *LBG*.

not Latin?

βοῦττις, βοῦτις, βούτη, βοῦττιν, a vessel, and βουττοποιός, maker of such vessels, may be from *buttis*, a vessel (*TLL*). Binder (2000: 259), Hofmann (1989: 68), Viscidi (1944: 40), Zilliacus (1937: 328), Immisch (1885: 310), Frisk (1954–72: I.261, III.56), *LBG*, Zervan (2019: 36), Sophocles (1887), Meyer (1895: 17 *s.v.* βοῦτα), *TLL* (*s.v. buttis*), LSJ and LSJ suppl. (both *s.v.* βοῦτις). But Cervenka-Ehrenstrasser (2000: 270–1) argues that it is not from Latin; cf. *DÉLG* (*s.v.* βοῦτις), Beekes (2010), Campanile (1969: 311).

not Latin?	**βοῦφος**, nocturnal bird in Cyran. 3.8 (II AD?), may come from *būbō* 'horned owl'. *LBG*, Meyer (1895: 18–19, cf. modern μπούφος 'horned owl': Babiniotis 2002; Andriotis 1967), *DGE*, LSJ suppl.
Direct loan **IV AD – modern**	**βράκαι** (-ων, αἱ) 'trousers', from *brācae* 'trousers'.

Literature: Diodorus Siculus 5.30.1, marked (I BC); Philogelos 64 (IV AD); Epiph. *Pan.* 11.376.15, marked (IV AD); Hesych. as lemma β 1043 (V/VI AD).

Post-antique: survives. *LBG* (*s.v.* βράκα), Zervan (2019: 36–7, 263), Kriaras (1968– *s.v.* βράκα). Modern βράκα 'traditional wide trousers' and derivatives: Babiniotis (2002), Andriotis (1967), Meyer (1895: 19).

Notes: Chantraine (*DÉLG*) and Beekes (2010) see this as originally Celtic, borrowed independently into both Greek and Latin, but Kramer (1996a: 119–24, 2011: 46–51) argues more convincingly that it is originally Germanic, whence Celtic, whence Latin, whence Greek. Hofmann (1989: 69), LSJ. See §4.3.2, **§8.1.1** passages 34–5, §9.2, §10.2.1, §10.2.2 H.

rare	**βρακαρία** 'trousers', from unattested **brācāria* 'trousers' or *brācae* 'trousers' + -αρία: papyrus *P.Giss.* 90.6 (II AD). Cervenka-Ehrenstrasser (2000: 199–200), Daris (1991a: 37), Hofmann (1989: 69), Meinersmann (1927: 12), *DGE* (*s.v.* βρακαρίαι), LSJ (*s.v.* βράκαι). See §6.2.
Direct loan **IV AD – Byz.**	**βρακάριος, βρεκάριος, βρικάριος** (-ου, ὁ) 'tailor', from *brācārius* 'tailor' (*TLL*).

Documents: *P.Oxy.* 1341.1 (IV AD); allegedly *P.Lond.* inv. 2176.4, mentioned by Cervenka-Ehrenstrasser (2000: 200) (V AD).

Inscriptions: Edict.Diocl. 7.42 (IV AD); *I.Sardis* 1.167.a3 (IV AD); *I.Aphrodisias Late Ant.* 189.3 (V/VI AD); *MAMA* III.406a.4, 597.3.

Post-antique: survives. *LBG*.

Notes: Chantraine (*DÉLG s.v.* βράκαι) sees this as a Greek formation from βράκαι + -άριος, but given the respective attestations of βράκαι and βράκιον a Greek -άριος derivative should come from the latter and be βρακιάριος; a Latin borrowing is therefore more likely. D. Thomas suggests that the example in *P.Oxy.* 1341 could be a place name (in commentary on *P.Oxy.* 4535.19, another potential example). Cervenka-Ehrenstrasser (2000: 200–1), Daris (1991a: 37), Hofmann (1989: 70), Cavenaile (1952: 196), *DGE*, LSJ (*s.vv.* βράκαι, βρεκάριος), LSJ suppl. See §4.2.4.1 n. 50, §8.2.2, §10.2.1, §10.2.2 H.

rare	**βρακᾶτος** 'trouser-wearing' (and by extension of animals 'with thick fur or feathers'), from *brācātus* 'wearing trousers': papyrus *P.Sakaon* 71.8 etc. (IV AD); Hieroph. *Nut.* 1.2, 6.4 (IV–VI AD); Byzantine texts. Cervenka-Ehrenstrasser (2000: 201–2), Diethart (1998: 171), Daris (1991a: 37), *LBG*, *DGE*.
rare	**βρακέλλαι** 'trousers', from unattested **bracellae*, diminutive of *brācae* 'trousers' (thus Hofmann 1989: 70; Meinersmann 1927: 12), or *brācae* 'trousers' + -έλλα (thus Kramer 1996a: 122; Cervenka-Ehrenstrasser 2000: 202–3; Filos 2010: 226 n. 19; Daris 1991a: 37): papyrus *BGU* III.814.29 (III AD). LSJ. See **§6.13**.

Direct loan with suffix
II AD – modern

βράκιον, βράκκιον, βρέκιον, βρέκεον (-ου, τό) 'trousers', from *brācae* 'trousers' + -ιον.

Documents: *O.Florida* 23.9 (II AD); *P.Gen.* 1.80.6 (IV AD); *P.Ryl.* IV.627.33 (IV AD); *Stud.Pal.* XX.245.22 (VI AD); *P.Münch.* III.I.142.6 etc. (VI AD).

Inscriptions: Edict.Diocl. 7.46 (IV AD).

Literature: Hesych. as gloss α 4473, π 1865, σ 19 (V/VI AD); scholia to Xenophon, *Anabasis* 4.5.36 and Ar. *V.* 1087c.

Post-antique: numerous, forming derivatives βρακεώλιον 'trousers', βρακοζώνι 'belt', etc. *LBG*, Kriaras (1968–). Modern βρακί 'underpants': Babiniotis (2002), Kahane and Kahane (1972–6: 535), Meyer (1895: 19).

Notes: forms derivative κοντοβράκιον. Kramer (1996a: 119–24, 2011: 46–51), Cervenka-Ehrenstrasser (2000: 203–5), Murri (1943: 118–21), Daris (1991a: 37), Hofmann (1989: 69 *s.v.* βράκαι), Cavenaile (1952: 196), Meinersmann (1927: 12), *DGE*, LSJ (*s.v.* βράκαι), LSJ suppl. (*s.v.* βράκια). See §4.3.2, §8.2.3, §10.2.1, §10.2.2 H.

βρακτεολᾶτος: see βραττεολᾶτος.

βρακχιᾶτος: see βραχιᾶτος.

rare

βράξ (acc. βρᾶκα), from *brāx* 'trousers' (*TLL s.v. brāca*): unpublished ostracon O.Dios inv. 121.3 (II AD).

foreign

βράσκη 'cabbage', presumably from a syncopated form of *brassica* 'cabbage': Hesych. as lemma labelled 'Italian' (Ἰταλιῶται), β 1053 (V/VI AD). Hofmann (1989: 71), Immisch (1885: 330–1), *DGE*.

not ancient

βράσσικα transliterating *brassica* 'cabbage': interpolations in Dsc. 4.80 RV etc. Sophocles (1887).

foreign

βραττεολᾶτος, βρακτεολᾶτος apparently transliterating unattested **bratteolātus* 'decorated with thin gold leaf': Lyd. *Mag.* p. 88.24 (VI AD). Sophocles (1887 *s.v.* βρακτεολᾶτος), *TLL* (*s.v. bratteolātus*), *DGE*. See §8.1.7.

Direct loan
IV AD – modern

βραχιάλιον, βραχιάριον, βραχιόλιον (-ου, τό) 'bracelet', 'ring', from *brāc(c)hiāle* 'bracelet'.

Documents: *P.Abinn.* 81.5 (IV AD); *SB* 12940.6 (VI AD).

Literature: Thdt. *PG* LXXX.597b, marked (V AD); Alex.Trall. 1.571.5 (VI AD); with *viriola* in Gloss. Ps.-Cyril. 259.63, 350.14.

Post-antique: survives. *LBG*, Kriaras (1968– *s.v.* βραχιόλι), Triandaphyllidis (1909: 98, 121, 130). Modern βραχιόλι 'bracelet': Babiniotis (2002), Andriotis (1967).

Notes: βραχιόλιον is sometimes derived separately from *bra(c)chiolum* 'little arm' (*TLL*), which has the wrong meaning; Georgacas (1958: 187) claims more persuasively that βραχιόλιον comes from βραχιάλιον (and thus ultimately from *brācchiāle*), while Triandaphyllidis (1909: 103) sees it as a mixture of βραχιάλιον and βραχιόνιον, a (rare) native Greek word. Cervenka-Ehrenstrasser (2000: 205–6), Diethart (1998: 171), Daris (1991a: 37), Hofmann (1989: 71), Meinersmann (1927: 12), *DÉLG* (*s.v.* βραχίων), Frisk (1954–72: 1.264), Beekes (2010 *s.v.* βραχίων), *TLL* (*s.v.* βραχιάλιον), Lampe (1961), *DGE*, LSJ. See §4.2.5, §4.4 n. 79, §8.1.7 n. 34, §8.2.3 n. 51, §10.2.1, §10.2.2 H.

foreign   βραχιᾶτος, βρακχιᾶτος, a kind of soldier, transliterating *brāc(c)hiātus* 'wearing bracelets': inscription *SEG* LXV.1408.C26 (V/VI AD); Lyd. *Mag.* p. 70.26 (VI AD); Byzantine texts. *LBG*, Sophocles (1887), LSJ suppl. (*s.v.* βραχιᾶτοι).

βρέβειον: see βρέβιον.

βρέβεμ: see βρέβις.

rare   βρεβιατικόν, a type of fiscal revenues, from *brevia* via βρέβιον (*q.v.*), not from uncertainly attested **perviāticum* 'toll': inscription Bean and Mitford 1970: 54 no. 31.A4 etc. = *SEG* LXVI.1716 (V AD). Feissel (2016: 688–90), *TLL* (*s.v. perviāticum*), Hofmann (1989: 71), *LBG*, *DGE*. See §8.1.7.

rare   βρεβιάτωρ 'writer of a summary', from *breviātor* 'maker of a summary' (*TLL*): Just. *Nov.* 105.2.4 (VI AD). Avotins (1992), Zilliacus (1935a: 176–7), *LBG*, *TLL* (*s.v. breviātor* 2170.35–6), *DGE*.

Direct loan
III AD – Byz.   βρέβιον, βρέβειον, βρεβίων, βρέπιον, βρεπίων, βρέουιον, βρέυιον (-ου, τό) 'list', 'inventory', 'summary', from *brevia*, neut. pl. of *brevis* 'summary', 'list' (*TLL s.v. brevis* 2179.74–7, Bonneau 1984: 113–14).

Documents: common, e.g. *P.Cair.Isid.* 1.9 etc. (III AD); *P.Harr.* II.216r.21 etc. (IV AD); *CPR* IX.68.1 (V AD); *P.Bad.* IV.95.440 (VI AD).

Inscriptions: *IG* XII.IX.907.15 (IV AD).

Literature: e.g. Eus. *HE* 10.6.2 (IV AD); Pall. *V.Chrys.* 19.16 (IV/V AD); Geront. *V.Mel.* 2.35.10 (V AD); Just. *Edict* 9.2.1 = p. 773.29 (VI AD).

Post-antique: survives. *LBG* (*s.v.* βρέβαιον), Kriaras (1968–), Triandaphyllidis (1909: 128).

Notes: probably borrowed in pl. since the usual neut. sing. is *breve*. LSJ suppl. derives it from alternative neut. sing. *brevium* (which was rare at the time of borrowing) and Lampe (1961) from *breviārium* 'summary'. Bonneau (1984), Cervenka-Ehrenstrasser (2000: 207–10), Avotins (1992), Daris (1991a: 37–8), Hofmann (1989: 72), Zilliacus (1935a: 176–7), Meinersmann (1927: 12–13), *TLL* (*s.v. brevis* 2179.78–81), *DGE*, LSJ, LSJ suppl. See §4.1.1, §4.2.5, §10.1, §10.2.1, §10.2.2 O; cf. ἀβρέβις.

foreign   βρέβις (in acc. βρέβεμ) transliterating *brevis* 'short': Plut. *Mor.* 281d (I/II AD). Sophocles (1887). See §7.2.1 passage 25.

not Latin?   βρεγκάριος, perhaps 'basket-weaver' or 'water-carrier', may be related to *branca* 'paw', whose Romance descendants mean 'branch' (*TLL*). Hofmann (1989: 72), *LBG*, Lampe (1961), *DGE*.

βρεκάριος: see βρακάριος.

βρέκεον, βρέκιον: see βράκιον.

βρεκόκ(κ)ιον: see πραικόκκιον.

βρέκων: see πραίκων.

non-existent   βρέκωρ, meaning uncertain, several Latin sources suggested: superseded reading of papyrus *SB* 2254.1 (VI AD). Cervenka-Ehrenstrasser (2000: 273), Daris (1991a: 37), Zilliacus (1935a: 230–1), Meinersmann (1927: 12).

βρέουιον: see βρέβιον.

βρέπιον, βρεπίων: see βρέβιον.

βρέυιον: see βρέβιον.

βρέχων: see πραίκων.

βρικάριος: see βρακάριος.

foreign   βροῦμα transliterating *brūma* 'winter solstice': Lyd. *Mens.* 4.158.7, *Ost.* 70.41 (VI AD). Hofmann (1989: 73), for later survival *LBG*.

Direct loan βρουμάλια, βρωμμάλια (-ων, τά) 'festival of the winter solstice', apparently from
VI AD – modern   unattested festival name **Brūmālia*, neut. pl. of *brūmālis* 'of the winter solstice'.
  Documents: *P.Oxy.* 2480.37 (VI AD); perhaps *PSI* VIII.956.46 (VI AD).
  Literature: e.g. Malal. 7.7.12, marked (VI AD); Lyd. *Mens.* 4.158.8, marked (VI AD).
  Post-antique: numerous, forming derivatives βρουμαλίζω 'celebrate the festival of the winter solstice', βρουμαλιτικός 'ripening during the winter solstice', etc. *LBG* (s.vv. βρωμάλιον, βρουμάλιος), Triandaphyllidis (1909: 120). Modern dialectal Βρομαλίτης 'November', 'December': Andriotis (1974: 188).
  Notes: Cervenka-Ehrenstrasser (2000: 210–11), Daris (1991a: 38), Hofmann (1989: 73), *TLL* (s.v. *brūmālis* 2210.11–14), Lampe (1961), *DGE*. See §4.2.5, §8.1.7, §8.2.2, §10.2.1, §10.2.2 F.

foreign   βροῦτος transliterating *brūtus* 'irrational': DH *AR* 4.67.4 (I BC); Dio Cassius 2.11.10 (II/III AD). Sophocles (1887), *DGE* (s.v. βροῦτος II).

βρωμμάλια: see βρουμάλια.

rare   βυκανάω, βουκανάω 'sound the trumpet', from *būcinō* 'sound the trumpet' and/ or *būcina* 'trumpet' via βυκάνη: Polybius 6.36.1, 6.36.5 (II BC). Source of ἐμβυκανάω. Dubuisson (1985: 22), Hofmann (1989: 65), *DÉLG* (s.v. βυκάνη), Frisk (1954–72: 1.276), Beekes (2010 s.v. βυκάνη), *DGE*, LSJ. See §8.1.3 n. 17.

Direct loan with βυκάνη, βουκάνη, βυκήνη, βυκίνη (-ης, ἡ) 'trumpet', 'horn', from *būcina*
influence   'trumpet', 'horn' (with suffix alteration on the model of μηχανή vs *māchina*).
II BC – I AD   Literature: Polybius 12.4.6 etc. (II BC); DH *AR* 2.8.4 (I BC); Jos. *AJ* 9.269 etc. (I AD); with *bucinum* in Gloss. Ps.-Philox. 31.34.
  Notes: designated a specifically Roman trumpet. Died out after I AD, but not before forming derivatives βυκανητής, βυκάνημα, βυκινίζω, perhaps βυκανάω. Same or related Latin later reborrowed as βούκινον. Dubuisson (1985: 22), Famerie (1998: 102), Hofmann (1989: 74), *DÉLG*, Frisk (1954–72: 1.276), Beekes (2010), Kriaras (1968– s.v. βουκάνη), *DGE*, LSJ. See §4.2.3.1, §4.3.2 n. 75, §4.4, §4.6.1, §8.1.3, §8.1.4, §10.2.1, §10.2.2 C.

rare   βυκάνημα 'sound of the trumpet', from *būcina* 'trumpet' via βυκάνη + -μα: App. *Libyca* 87 (I/II AD). *DÉLG* (s.v. βυκάνη), Frisk (1954–72: 1.276), *DGE*, LSJ.

Deriv. of loan
II BC – II AD?

βυκανητής, βυκανίτης, βυκανιστής, βουκανιστής (-ου, ὁ) 'trumpeter', from *būcina* 'trumpet' (via βυκάνη and sometimes βυκινίζω) + -τής.

Literature: Polybius 2.29.6 etc. (II BC); DH *AR* 4.17.3 etc. (I BC); App. *Annibaica* 177, *Iberica* 85 (I/II AD); Hesych. as lemma β 1302 (V/VI AD); with *bucinator* in Gloss. Ps.-Cyril. 259.8.

Post-antique: some survival. *LBG* (*s.vv.* βυκανίτης, βουκινάτης).

Notes: in theory this ought to be two words, one from βυκάνη + -τής and one from βυκινίζω/βουκανίζω + -τής, but in practice the forms appear as variants (e.g. in Appian). Dubuisson (1985: 22), Famerie (1998: 102, 209), Hofmann (1989: 74 *s.v.* βυκάνη), *DÉLG* (*s.v.* βυκάνη), Frisk (1954–72: I.276), Beekes (2010 *s.v.* βυκάνη), *DGE* (*s.vv.* βυκανητής, βυκανιστής), LSJ and LSJ suppl. (*s.vv.* βυκανητής, βυκανιστής). See §4.6.1 n. 86, **§8.1.3** passage 40, §8.1.4, §9.5.4, §10.2.2 C.

βυκανίζω: see βυκινίζω.

rare

βυκανισμός, βουκανισμός 'deep note', from *būcina* 'trumpet' via βυκάνη or βυκινίζω + -(σ)μός: Ptol. *Harm.* 1.4.25 (II AD); Nicom. *Exc.* 4.15, marked (II AD). Hofmann (1989: 74 *s.v.* βυκάνη), *DÉLG* (*s.v.* βυκάνη), Frisk (1954–72: I.276), Beekes (2010 *s.v.* βυκάνη), *DGE*, LSJ.

βυκανιστής, βυκανίτης: see βυκανητής.

βυκήνη: see βυκάνη.

Direct loan
III AD – Byz.

βυκινάτωρ, βουκινάτωρ, β(ο)υκκινάτωρ (-ορος/-ωρος, ὁ) 'trumpeter', from *būcinātor* 'trumpeter'.

Documents: perhaps *BGU* I.344.7 etc. (II/III AD); *P.Oxy.* 1903.8 (VI AD).

Inscriptions: *IGBulg.* III.1.884.b23 (III AD); *SEG* IX.356.66 (VI AD); *I.Syria PAES* 772.1.

Literature: Lyd. *Mag.* p. 70.16, marked (VI AD).

Post-antique: numerous. *LBG* (*s.vv.* βυκινάτωρ, βουκινάτωρ), note *P.Bodl.* 145.5.

Notes: Cervenka-Ehrenstrasser (2000: 187–9), Daris (1991a: 36), Hofmann (1989: 66), Zilliacus (1935a: 218–19), *DÉLG* (*s.v.* βυκάνη), Frisk (1954–72: I.276), Beekes (2010 *s.v.* βυκάνη), *DGE* (*s.v.* βουκινάτωρ), LSJ (*s.v.* βουκινίζω). See §4.2.5, §6.9, §10.2.1, §10.2.2 C.

βυκίνη: see βυκάνη.

Direct? loan with
suffix
III AD – modern

βυκινίζω, βουκινίζω, βυκανίζω, βουκανίζω 'blow the trumpet', from *būcinō* 'sound the trumpet' or *būcina* 'trumpet' (when spelled with -α-, via or with influence from βυκάνη) + -ίζω.

Literature: Sextus Empiricus, *Adversus mathematicos* 6.24 (II/III AD); with *bucino* in Gloss. Ps.-Cyril. 260.43 and Gloss. *Herm.M.* 129.21–3.

Post-antique: survives. *LBG* (*s.vv.* βυκινίζω, βουκινίζω), Kriaras (1968– *s.v.* βουκινίζω). Modern dialectal βουκινίζω 'trumpet' with derivative βουκίνισμα 'trumpet signal': Andriotis (1974: 182).

Notes: forms derivatives βουκανιστήριον, βυκανισμός. *DÉLG* (*s.v.* βυκάνη), Frisk (1954–72: I.276), Beekes (2010 *s.v.* βυκάνη), Hofmann (1989: 74 *s.v.* βυκάνη), *DGE* (*s.v.* βουκινίζω), LSJ (*s.v.* βουκινίζω). See §4.3.1, §4.6.1, §6.9, §10.2.1, §10.2.2 C, §10.3.1.

βυκκινάτωρ: see βυκινάτωρ.

βύκ(κ)ινον: see βούκινον.

βυρίτιος: see βιρίδιος.

βύρριον: see βίρριον.

βύρ(ρ)ος: see βίρρος.

βυρροφόρος: see βιρροφόρος.

not Latin   **βυτίνη** 'flask covered with wickerwork' is said by Hesych. β 1352 (V/VI AD) to be used in Tarentum (Ταραντῖνοι); it is probably the same word as πυτίνη (with derivatives πυτιναῖος 'of a flask covered with wickerwork', πυτινοπλόκος 'maker of flasks covered with wickerwork'), which was the title of a lost play of Cratinus and therefore goes back to V BC. Whatmough (1949: 288), Hofmann (1989: 74–5), Meyer (1895: 17–18, with derivation from unattested *butina*), Immisch (1885: 309–310), *DÉLG*, Frisk (1954–72: I.278), Beekes (2010), LSJ (*s.vv.* βυτίνη, πυτίνη, πυτιναῖος, πυτινοπλόκος).

rare   **βωλητάριος** 'mushroom-shaped', from *bōlētus* 'mushroom' via βωλήτης + -άριος and/or from *bōlētar* 'vessel for holding mushrooms' + -ιος: papyri *BGU* III.781.i.1 etc. (I/II AD); *PSI* XV.1562.6 (IV AD). Cervenka-Ehrenstrasser (2000: 212–13), Helttula (1994), Hofmann (1989: 75), Meinersmann (1927: 13), *DÉLG* (*s.v.* βωλήτης), Frisk (1954–72: I.278), Beekes (2010 *s.v.* βωλήτης), LSJ (*s.v.* βωλητάρια). See §6.1.

Direct loan   **βωλήτης, βωλίτης** (-ου, ὁ), a kind of mushroom, from *bōlētus* 'mushroom'.
II AD – modern   Literature: Galen VI.655.14 Kühn (II AD); Athenaeus 3.113c (II/III AD); scholion to Nic. *Alex.* 525e as gloss; with *boletus* in glossaries, e.g. Gloss. *Herm. Mp.* 315.19.

     Post-antique: limited survival. *LBG*. Modern dialectal βωλίτης etc. 'boletus mushroom': Andriotis (1974: 190).

     Notes: forms derivatives βωλητάριος, βωλήτιον. Cervenka-Ehrenstrasser (2000: 213), Helttula (1994), Hofmann (1989: 75), *DÉLG*, Frisk (1954–72: I.278–9), Beekes (2010), *LBG*, *TLL* (*s.v. bōlētus* 2066.65, suggesting Latin borrowing from Greek), *DGE*, LSJ (*s.vv.* βωλίτης, βωλήτης). See §4.2.3.2, §10.2.1, §10.2.2 I.

foreign   **βωλητῖνος** 'mushroom-shaped', from *bōlētus* 'mushroom' (via βωλήτης + -ῖνος, or perhaps unattested *bōlētīnus*): Athenaeus 3.113c, marked (II/III AD). Cervenka-Ehrenstrasser (2000: 213), Helttula (1994), Hofmann (1989: 75–6), *DÉLG* (*s.v.* βωλήτης), Frisk (1954–72: I.278), Beekes (2010 *s.v.* βωλήτης), LSJ (*s.v.* βωλήτης).

rare   **βωλήτιον**, probably a bowl with a tall foot (i.e. mushroom-shaped), from *bōlētus* 'mushroom' via βωλήτης + -ιον: papyrus *P.Oxy.* 1657.4 (III AD). Cervenka-Ehrenstrasser (2000: 212–13), Helttula (1994), Hofmann (1989: 75 *s.v.* βωλήτης), *DÉLG* (*s.v.* βωλήτης), Frisk (1954–72: I.278), Beekes (2010 *s.v.* βωλήτης), LSJ.

βωλίτης: see βωλήτης.

βῶνος: see βόνος.

βῶτον: see βότον.

Γ

γαβάθα, γάβαθον: see κάβαθα.

γάγκελ(λ)ος: see κάγκελλος.

Direct loan with suffix
I AD

Γαιῆος or Γαίειος (-ου, ὁ) 'of Gaius' (an Egyptian month), from the name *Gāius* + -ῆος/-ειος.

Documents: e.g. *O.Bodl.* II.474.5 (I AD); *P.Oxy.* 3780.7 (I AD).

Notes: Scott (1931: 255), *DGE* (*s.v.* Γαίειος), LSJ suppl. See §4.3.2, §9.2, §10.2.1, §10.2.2 E.

foreign

Γαισᾶται, Γαισᾶτοι 'troops armed with the Gallic javelin', from *gaesātī* 'troops armed with the Gallic javelin': only as proper name and/or marked, e.g. Polybius 2.22.1 (II BC); Strabo 5.1.6 (I BC/AD); Plut. *Marc.* 3.2 (I/II AD). Dubuisson (1985: 22–3), Hofmann (1989: 76), Viscidi (1944: 13), *DÉLG* (*s.v.* γαῖσος), Frisk (1954–72: 1.283), Beekes (2010 *s.v.* γαῖσος), *TLL* (*s.v.* *gaesātī*), *DGE* (*s.v.* Γαιζήται), LSJ (Γαισᾶται *s.v.* γαῖσος). See §5.2.3, §8.1.3 n. 17, §8.1.4 n. 28.

Direct loan
II BC – Byz.

γαῖσος, γαῖσον (-ου, ὁ or τό) 'javelin', from *gaesum* 'Gallic javelin'.

Documents: *P.Tebt.* 1.230.1 (II BC).

Literature: e.g. Polybius 6.39.3 (II BC); Philo Mechanicus, *Parasceuastica et poliorcetica* 99.16 Diels and Schramm (II BC); Septuagint Joshua 8:18 (II BC?); Diodorus Siculus 13.57.3 (I BC); Septuagint Judith 9:7 (I AD?); Hdn. *Pros.Cath.* III.1.207.5 (II AD); Pollux 7.156 (II AD); Athenaeus 6.273f (II/III AD); Hesych. as lemma γ 61 (V/VI AD); *Oracula Sibyllina* 3.650 Geffcken.

Post-antique: survives. *LBG* (*s.v.* γαισσός).

Notes: originally Celtic but probably reached Greek via Latin; Latin words are not unparalleled in papyri of II BC (cf. διάριον), and since closely related Γαισᾶται is certainly from Latin it is difficult to argue for a different transmission for γαῖσος. Dubuisson (1985: 23), Viscidi (1944: 13), Hahn (1907: 707), Immisch (1885: 323–4), *DÉLG*, Beekes (2010), *DGE*; but Frisk (1954–72: 1.282–3) and LSJ have non-Latinate etymologies. See §4.2.4.1 n. 58, §4.3.2 n. 75, §5.3.2 passage 7, §8.1.3, §8.1.4, §10.2.1, §10.2.2 C.

Direct loan
II–IV AD

γάλβινος (-η, -ον) 'greenish-yellow', from *galbinus* 'greenish-yellow'.

Documents: *SB* 9273.6 (I/II AD); *O.Ashm.Shelt.* 197.4 (IV AD).

Literature: alchemist in *P.Holm.*, frag. 145.6 Halleux (IV AD).

Notes: Hofmann (1989: 77), *DGE*, LSJ (*s.v.* γάλβινα). See §4.2.2, §10.2.1, §10.2.2 O, §10.3.2.

Direct loan
I–IV AD

γαλεάριος, γαλ(λ)ιάριος, γαλλεώρ(ιος) (-ου, ὁ) 'soldier's servant', from *galeārius*/ *galiārius* 'soldier's servant' (*TLL*).

Documents: *O.Did.* 319.4 etc., perhaps 103.3, perhaps 318.4 (all I AD); perhaps *BGU* VII.1614.C5 (I AD); *O.Claud.* III.627.2 (II AD); *O.Florida* 18.7, perhaps 21.12, perhaps 23.5 (all II AD); *SB* 11581.2, 11256.5 (both II AD); *P.Lips.* 1.40.ii.10 (IV AD).

Inscriptions: *SEG* XIX.787.2.

Literature: perhaps with *calo* in *Glossae Loiselii* (*CGL* III.479.11, cf. *CGL* VI.169).

Post-antique: occasional examples that do not look as if it was actually in use. *LBG* (*s.v.* γαλιάριος).

Notes: Cervenka-Ehrenstrasser (2000: 214–15), Daris (1991a: 38), Hofmann (1989: 77), Meinersmann (1927: 13), *DGE*, LSJ suppl. (*s.vv.* γαλεάριος, γαλλεωρ; superseding LSJ *s.v.* γαλλιάριος). See §4.2.4.1 n. 50, §6.1, §10.2.1, §10.2.2 C.

non-existent?	**γαλέριον** 'fur cap', from *galērus/galērum* 'cap of untanned skin' + -ιον: perhaps papyrus *P.Naqlun* 1.11.8 (VI AD). Cervenka-Ehrenstrasser (2000: 213–14), *LBG*.

γαλιάριος: see γαλεάριος.

γαλικάριος: see καλιγάριος.

γαλλεωρ, γαλλεώριος: see γαλεάριος.

name	**Γαλλία** 'Gaul', from *Gallia* 'Gaul'. *DGE*.

γαλλιάριος: see γαλεάριος.

name	**Γαλλικός** 'Gallic', from *Gallicus* 'Gallic' or *Gallia* 'Gaul' + -ικός. Meinersmann (1927: 13), *LBG*, *DGE*, LSJ suppl.
not ancient	**γαλλινάκιος** transliterating *gallīnāceus* 'of poultry': interpolations in Dsc. 2.139 RV etc. Sophocles (1887 *s.v.* γαλλινάκεους).
non-existent?	**γάλος** 'cockerel', from *gallus* 'cockerel': perhaps papyrus *P.Giss.* 93.12 (II AD). Cervenka-Ehrenstrasser (2000: 215), Daris (1991a: 38), *DGE* (*s.v.* γάλον).

γάμπανος: see κάμπανος.

not Latin	**γαράριον** 'jar for fish sauce' is probably from γάρος 'fish sauce' + -άριον, though the *TLL* (*s.v.* γαράριον) sees it as evidence of unattested **garārium* from *garum* 'fish sauce'. *DGE*, LSJ, LSJ suppl. See §8.1.7 n. 34.
not Latin?	**γάρβολα, γάρβουλα**, apparently transliterating unattested **garbula*, a kind of boot: Lyd. *Mag.* p. 22.26 (VI AD). But *LBG* (*s.v.* γάρβολον) suggests a Greek etymology from ἀρβύλη 'strong shoe'. *TLL* (*s.v. garbula*), *DGE*. See §8.1.7.

γαστρένσιος, γαστρήσιος, γαστρίσιος: see καστρήσιος.

not Latin	**γέλα** 'hoarfrost' is implied by Stephanus of Byzantium γ 45 (VI AD) to be a Sicilian or Oscan word behind the place name Gela. Willi (2008: 28), Hofmann (1989: 77), Immisch (1885: 324–5, attempting to emend γελανδρόν in Hesych. γ 301), *DGE*, LSJ suppl.
rare	**γέμελλος** 'twin', from *gemellus* 'twin': papyrus *SB* 15465.5 (II AD). Dieterich (1901: 589) claims that modern dialectal ἴμελλα is from *gemellus* (in contrast to modern γέμελλα from Italian *gemello*). Cervenka-Ehrenstrasser (2000: 216). See §5.2.2 n. 10.
rare	**γέμινος**, epithet of Janus, from *geminus* 'twin': Dio Cassius 54.36.2 (II/III AD). Sophocles (1887), *DGE*.

Γενάρις: see Ἰανουάριος.

not ancient? γενέρωσος 'noble', from *generōsus* 'noble': inscriptions *I.Ephesos* 1540.4; perhaps *I.Perinthos* 22.1 (III AD). Wilhelm (1928b: 227–8), Drew-Bear (1972: 190), Hofmann (1989: 78), *DGE*, LSJ suppl.

foreign γένιος transliterating *genius* 'spirit': Dio Cassius 47.2.3, 50.8.2 (II/III AD); inscription *IG* XIV.2564.4. Mason (1974: 31), Sophocles (1887), *DGE*.

not Latin? γεντιανή 'gentian' (a plant), perhaps from *gentiāna* 'gentian'. Hofmann (1989: 78), Hahn (1906: 253), Immisch (1885: 341), *DÉLG*, Frisk (1954–72: I.297, III.61), Beekes (2010), *DGE*, LSJ.

rare γεντίλιος 'foreigner', from *gentīlis* 'concerning foreign peoples': inscriptions *I.Syria PAES* 223.3 (III AD); *SEG* XXVI.1374.5 (V/VI AD); John Chrysostom, *PG* LXIV.860a (IV/V AD); Malal. 13.19.17, marked (VI AD); perhaps Hesych. as lemma (conjectural replacement for γέντινοι) γ 381 (V/VI AD). Hofmann (1989: 79), Zilliacus (1937: 328, citing an unverified example from III AD), Lampe (1961 *s.v.* γεντίλιοι), *DGE* (*s.v.* γεντίλιοι), for later survival *LBG*.

γεριτεύω: see προνερεδεγεριτεύω.

Direct loan with suffix
I–III AD

Γερμανίκ(ε)ιος, Γερμανίκηος (-α?, -ον) 'of Germanicus', as masc. subst. an Egyptian month, as neut. pl. subst. a festival, from the name *Germānicus* + -ειος.
Documents: common as month, e.g. *P.Oxy.* 3051.12 (I AD); *P.Mich.* III.196.2 (II AD); *PSI* XIII.1328.67 (III AD).
Inscriptions: as festival e.g. *IG* II/III².II.2026.16, 2065.42, 2087.35 (all II AD).
Notes: the month was Pachon, differently from Γερμανικός. Scott (1931: 249–51), Bagnall (2009: 181), *DGE*, LSJ suppl. See §4.3.3, §9.2, §10.2.1, §10.2.2 E.

Direct loan
I AD

Γερμανικός (-ου, ὁ) 'Germanicus' (a month), from the name *Germānicus*.
Documents: e.g. *P.Lond.* III.900.37 (I AD); *P.Fay.* 110.33 (I AD); perhaps *BGU* I.260.13 (I AD).
Notes: in Egypt the month was usually Thoth, differently from Γερμανίκειος, but in *P.Fay.* 90.4 (III AD) it is Pachon. Scott (1931: 259–60), Bagnall (2009: 181), *DGE*, LSJ suppl. See §4.2.4.1 n. 51, §10.2.1, §10.2.2 E.

rare γερμανός 'genuine', from *germānus* 'genuine': Strabo 7.1.2, marked (I BC/AD); Plut. *Rom.* 3.6, marked (I/II AD); papyri *BGU* III.814.11 (III AD); perhaps *P.Leipz.* 29r.2.1 (III AD). Meaning 'German': paraliterary papyrus P.Sorb. inv. 2069v.123 = Dickey 2010a: 207 (III AD); Gloss. Ps.-Philox. 211.55. Also very common as personal name. Cervenka-Ehrenstrasser (2000: 216–17), Daris (1991a: 38), Hofmann (1989: 79), Kriaras (1968–), *DGE*.

Γιούλις: see Ἰούλιος.

Γιούνις: see Ἰούνιος.

γλαβαρίζω: see κλαβαρίζω.

not ancient γλαδιατώρια transliterating *gladiātōria*, a plant (*TLL s.v. gladiātōrius* 2010.29): interpolation in Dsc. 4.100 RV. Sophocles (1887), *TLL* (*s.v. gladiātōrius* 2010.29–32).

foreign	**γλαδίολον** transliterating *gladiolum*, variant of *gladiolus*, a plant: Dsc. 4.22.1 (I AD), also in form γλαδίολουμ in interpolations; Orib. *Col.* 12.xi.2 (IV AD). *LBG*, Sophocles (1887 *s.vv.* γλαδίολον, γλαδίολουμ), *TLL* (*s.v.* *gladiolus* 2010.73, 2011.29, 2011.37–9), *DGE*.
foreign	**γλάνδουλα** transliterating *glandula* 'gland', 'goitre' (*TLL*): Hippiatr. e.g. *Hippiatr. Berl.* (Eumelus) 16.4 (III AD?). *LBG*, *DGE*, *TLL* *s.v.* *glandula* 2029.79–84, 2030.40–1.
	γλέβα: see γλῆβα.
not Latin?	**γλεύδιον**, a tool ('mallet'?), perhaps from unattested **glubia* or **glubium*: Edict. Diocl. 15.43 (IV AD). Loring (1890: 313), Hofmann (1989: 79), *DGE*, LSJ suppl.
foreign	**γλῆβα, γλέβα** transliterating *gleba* 'cultivated land': Lyd. *Mag.* p. 52.9–10 (VI AD); Hesych. as lemma γ 629 (V/VI AD). Immisch (1885: 352), Sophocles (1887), *TLL* (*s.v.* *gleba* 2041.33–5, 2044.4), LSJ (*s.v.* γλέβα).
	γλόβα: see γλοῦβα.
	γλοβᾶρε: see γλουβᾶρε.
foreign	**γλοῦβα, γλόβα** transliterating a word for 'skin' (either *gluma* 'husk' or unattested **globa*): Lyd. *Mag.* p. 24.10 (VI AD). Hofmann (1989: 79), *LBG*, *TLL* (*s.v.* 1. *globa*). See §8.1.7.
foreign	**γλουβᾶρε** transliterating *glubare*, variant of *glubere*, inf. of *glubo* 'peel' (*TLL*): Lyd. *Mag.* p. 24.11 (VI AD). Sophocles (1887 *s.v.* γλοβᾶρε), *TLL* (*s.v.* *glubo* 2109.59).
foreign	**γλούττων** 'glutton', from *glutto* 'glutton': Hesych. as lemma μ 1569 (V/VI AD); variant in Pall. *H.Laus.* 21.5 (IV/V AD). Hofmann (1989: 80), Lampe (1961).
rare	**γουβε(ρ)νάριον** 'rudder', perhaps from unattested **gubernarium* but probably from *guberno* 'steer' + -άριον on the model of *gubernaculum* 'steering-oar': papyrus *P.Oxy.* 921r.3 (III AD). Cervenka-Ehrenstrasser (2000: 217–18), Palmer (1945: 13, 84), Daris (1991a: 38), Hofmann (1989: 80), *DGE*, LSJ (*s.v.* γουβενάριον). See §6.3 n. 21.
non-existent	**γουβερνάριος**, from *guberno* 'steer' or a related word: superseded reading of *CPR* x.57.11. Cervenka-Ehrenstrasser (2000: 273), Daris (1991a: 38). See §2.2.1 n. 21.
	γουγκία: see οὐγγία.
rare	**γούλα** 'gullet', from *gula* 'gullet', is mainly a Byzantine term but occasionally occurs in literature that should be ancient (though interpolation cannot be ruled out): Erot. *Voc.Hipp.* 101.16 as gloss (I AD); *Hippiatr.Par.* (Pel.) 206 (V AD?); Ps.-Galen XIV.562.15 Kühn. Hofmann (1989: 80), Lampe (1961), *DGE*, *LBG*, Kriaras (1968–), Triandaphyllidis (1909: 98, 120, 123), Meyer (1895: 19–20 with modern γούλα 'gullet', cf. Andriotis 1967).

not ancient   **γουλάρης** 'glutton', from *gula* 'gullet' via γούλα + -άρης (= -άριος); no ancient examples. Hofmann (1989: 80 *s.v.* γούλα), Meyer (1895: 19), *LBG*, Kriaras (1968–).

not ancient   **γούνα** 'fur', from *gunna* 'fur' (*TLL*): no ancient examples. Mihăescu (1981), Meyer (1895: 20), *LBG*, Kriaras (1968–), Andriotis (1967).

Direct loan   **γουνάριος, γουννάριος** (-ου, ὁ) 'furrier', from *gunnārius* 'maker of fur garments'
VI AD – modern   (*TLL*).
        Documents: perhaps *CPR* X.57.11 (VI AD).
        Inscriptions: e.g. perhaps *I.Chr.Macédoine* 34.2 (V/VI AD); *I.Chr.Bulgarien* 99.4 (VI AD); *SEG* XXXIX.699.
        Post-antique: survives, forming derivatives γουνάρια 'fur store', γουναρικός 'furrier'. *LBG* (*s.vv.* γουνάριος, γουνάρης), Zervan (2019: 40), Kriaras (1968– *s.v.* γουνάρης), Triandaphyllidis (1909: 124). Modern γουναράς 'furrier': Babiniotis (2002).
        Notes: Cervenka-Ehrenstrasser (2000: 218–19), Shipp (1979: 200), Drew-Bear (1972: 191), Mihăescu (1981: 428–30), Hofmann (1989: 81), Lampe (1961), *DGE*, LSJ suppl. See §4.2.4.1 n. 50, §8.2.3 n. 51, §10.2.1, §10.2.2 H.

        γουράτωρ: see κουράτωρ.

not ancient   **γούργουρας** 'gullet', from *gurguliō* 'gullet': no ancient examples. Meyer (1895: 20), *LBG* (*s.v.* γούργουρος), Zervan (2019: 40–1), Kriaras (1968–).

not Latin?   **γοῦρνα** 'water basin' may be from *urna* 'urn' but is probably a Greek formation. Cervenka-Ehrenstrasser (2000: 274), Daris (1991a: 38), *LBG*, *DGE*. Cf. οὖρνα.

not Latin?   **γουτάριον** 'tomb' on inscriptions Waelkens 1986: 172 no. 430.4 (III AD) and *MAMA* VI.277 might be from *gūtus* 'vase' (*TLL*) + -άριον or *gutta* 'drop' + -άριον or medieval *guttārium* 'gutter' (Du Cange 1883–7). Hofmann (1989: 81), Cameron (1931: 246–7), Beekes (2010, with a non-Latin etymology), *DGE*, LSJ suppl.

foreign   **γουττᾶτος**, adj. applied to cake, from *guttātus* 'spotted': Athenaeus 14.647c, d, marked (II/III AD). Normally cited as noun γουττᾶτον, but see *TLL* (*s.v.* *guttātus* 2373.84, 2374.6–7). Hofmann (1989: 82), *DÉLG* (*s.v.* γουττᾶτον), Frisk (1954–72: 1.322), Beekes (2010 *s.v.* γουττᾶτον), *DGE* (*s.v.* γουττᾶτον), LSJ (*s.v.* γουττᾶτον). See §5.2.1, §9.4 passage 61.

        γράβακτον: see κράββαττος.

not ancient?   **γραδικός**, apparently from *gradus, -ūs* 'step' via γράδος + -ικός: inscriptions *Spomenik* 75 (1933) 46 no. 153.15; perhaps *I.Pessinous* 83.4.

Direct loan   **γράδος** (-ου, ὁ) 'stepped pedestal', from *gradus, -ūs* 'step'.
II AD – ?   Inscriptions: e.g. *MAMA* IV.341.4 (I/II AD); *IG* X.II.1.573 (II AD); *IGBulg.* III.1.992.3.
        Notes: probably died out during antiquity, but end date uncertain. Babiniotis (2002) and Andriotis (1967) derive modern γράδο, an instrument for measuring liquid density, from Italian *grado*. Hofmann (1989: 82), Cameron (1931: 246), *DGE*, LSJ suppl. See §4.1.1, §4.2.4.2, §10.2.1, §10.2.2 J.

semantic extension	**Γραικός** 'Greek' and related words such as **γραικίζω** 'speak Greek', **γραικιστί** 'in Greek', and **Γραικίτης** 'Greek', are etymologically Greek but Latinate (or at least Italic) in meaning: the original usage of Γραικός referred to a particular local area, and the generalized meaning for Greeks in general is thought to have started in Italy, perhaps from contact with *Graecus* 'Greek' (e.g. *DÉLG s.v.*; Frisk 1954–72: 1.323). Greek speakers saw an accentual difference between the Greek word and the Latin one: Olympiodorus Philosophus, *In Aristotelis Meteora commentaria* 121.8–11 Stuve (VI AD) says Τότε μὲν Γραικοί, νῦν δὲ Ἕλληνες. Τοῦτο τὸ ὄνομα οἱ μὲν Ῥωμαῖοι παροξύνουσι "Γραίκοι" λέγοντες, ἡ δέ κοινὴ διάλεκτος ὀξύνει. Immisch (1885: 325–6), Chantraine (1956: 104 n.), *LBG*, Triandaphyllidis (1909: 169), Lampe (1961 *s.v.* Γραικιστί), *DGE*, LSJ (esp. *s.v.* γραικιστί), LSJ suppl. See §2.3.
not Latin?	**Γραικόστασις** 'Greek stand', a platform in Rome used by foreign envoys, is attested only in Latin sources, as *Graecostasis*. If it was invented by Latin speakers and then used by Greek speakers, it might in a sense be a Latin loan in Greek – but it could have been invented by the Greek-speaking envoys (the compound formation is Greek rather than Latin: §4.5), and/or used primarily in Latin. Hofmann (1989: 82), *OLD* (*s.v. Graecostasis*), *DGE*, LSJ suppl.
not ancient	**γράμεν** transliterating *grāmen* 'grass': interpolations in Dsc. 4.29 RV, 30 RV. Sophocles (1887).
not ancient?	**γρανᾶτον** 'pomegranate', from *grānātum* 'pomegranate' (*OLD s.v. grānātus¹*): anonymous commentary on Aristotle, Rabe 1896: 74.10, 176.5. Hofmann (1989: 83), Kriaras (1968–), LSJ suppl. (*s.v.* γρανᾶτα). In meaning 'granite' (not attested in Latin) may have a different source: *DGE*.
foreign	**γρατούϊτος** 'gratuitous', 'without receiving anything in exchange', from *grātuītus* 'free of charge': Antec. in Latin script 3.14.2 *gratuiton* (VI AD); later in Greek script. Zilliacus (1935a: 190–1), *LBG*. See §9.5.6 n. 68.
not Latin?	**γραφιάριον** on papyrus *P.Amh.* II.181.19 (III AD) is taken by *DGE* as substantivization of adj. γραφιάριος 'of styluses', from *graphiārius* 'of a stylus'. LSJ suppl. takes it as noun γραφιάριον, perhaps 'desk', without connection to Latin. Palmer (1945: 84) and Browning (1983: 40) take it as noun γραφιάριον 'writing tablet' with Greek root and Latin suffix *-ārium*. See §6.3.
rare	**γρέγην** 'herd of horses', from *gregem*, acc. of *grex* 'herd': curse tablet Audollent 1904: no. 160.4, with commentary p. 224. Hofmann (1989: 83).
not ancient	**γρουμπέλλα** 'snowball', perhaps from *globus* 'sphere' via unattested **globella*: no ancient examples. Meyer (1895: 20).
not ancient	**γροῦμπος** 'rounded piece', perhaps from *grūmus* 'heap': no ancient examples. Meyer (1895: 20).
not Latin?	**γωσλωάνιον**, a cake mentioned in Athenaeus 14.647d (II/III AD), has been suggested as Latin, but there is no good source word. Hofmann (1989: 83). See §9.4 passage 61.

Δ

not Latin?	**δαιμονιάριος** 'possessed man' might be from *daemoniārius* 'possessed man' (*TLL*) or a Greek formation from (e.g.) δαιμόνιος + -άριος. Hofmann (1989: 83), *LBG*, Kriaras (1968–), Lampe (1961).
	δαλματικ-: see δελματικ-.
non-existent?	**δαμνάριος**, a title on papyrus *P.Lond.* v.1711.84 (VI AD), may be Latinate, but **damnārius* is unattested; editor hypothesizes a mistake for δουκηνάριος. *DGE*.
foreign	**δαμνατίων** 'condemnation', from *damnātiō* 'condemnation': Antec. in Latin script 2.20.2 *damnationos* etc. (VI AD); later in Greek script. Zilliacus (1935a: 182–3), *LBG*.
foreign	**δαμνᾶτος** 'wrong', from *damnātus*, pf. part. of *damnō* 'judge to be at fault': Just. *Nov.* in Latin script 12.1 etc. (VI AD); later in Greek script. Zilliacus (1935a: 182–3), *LBG*.
foreign	**δάτιβος** 'deputy' (of judges), from *datīvus* 'assigned': Ath.Schol. in Latin script 7.P.1.2 (VI AD); later in Greek script. Hofmann (1989: 84), Lampe (1961), *DGE*, and for later survival *LBG*.
not ancient	**δατίων** 'giving', from *datiō* 'giving': no ancient examples. Zilliacus (1935a: 182–3).
not ancient?	**δατόν** 'gift', 'given information', from *datum*, pf. part. neut. of *dō* 'give': probably no ancient examples. Zilliacus (1935a: 182–3), *LBG*, *DGE*.
rare	**δεά** 'goddess', from *dea* 'goddess': part of gloss in Orion, *Etymologicum* p. 179.4 Sturz (V AD); Hesych. δ 342 as lemma attributed to Etruscans (V/VI AD). Hofmann (1989: 84), Immisch (1885: 278, 320), LSJ.
rare	**δεβίτωρ** 'debtor', from *dēbitor* 'debtor': Ath.Schol. 15.1.3 etc. (VI AD); Antec. in Latin script 2.8.1 *debitor* etc. (VI AD); Byzantine texts. Zilliacus (1935a: 182–3), *LBG*, Sophocles (1887), Triantaphyllides (1892: 258). See §9.5.6 n. 68.
foreign	**δεδ(ε)ιτίκιος** 'surrendered', from *dēditīcius* 'having surrendered': perhaps papyrus *P.Giss.* 40.i.9 (III AD). Mason (1974: 5, 32), *DGE* (*s.v.* [δεδ]ειτίκιοι). Effectively the same term used for the lowest class of freedmen: Antec. in Latin script 1.5.3 *dediticios* etc. (VI AD); Just. *Nov.* in Latin script 78.pr. (VI AD). Cavenaile (1951: 396), Zilliacus (1935a: 182–3), *TLL* (*s.v.* *dēditīcius* 264.17–22).
non-existent	**δεδίτιος** 'one who has surrendered': no examples. Cited by Sophocles (1887) as from unattested **dēditius*, with reference to Antec. 1.5.3 (VI AD), which probably has *dēditīcius* (see above *s.v.* δεδειτίκιος and *TLL s.v.* *dēditīcius* 264.20).
	δεῖβος: see δίβος.
	Δεκάβριος: see Δεκέμβριος.
not Latin?	**δεκακυμία** 'tenth wave', 'overwhelming wave' in Luc. *Merc.Cond.* 2 (II AD) is cited by Sophocles (1887) as a borrowing of *flūctus decimānus* 'enormous wave' (*TLL s.v.* *decimānus* 170.9–17), but LSJ prefers a Greek etymology. The context suggests some awareness of the Latin.

semantic extension	**δεκανός** 'decurion' (with derivative ἀρχιδεκανός, ἀρχεδεκανός 'chief decurion') is an extension of the meaning of δεκανός 'police officer' from contact with *decuriō* 'decurion'; it cannot be a borrowing of *decānus* 'person in charge of ten men', both because *decānus* is not attested until many centuries later than δεκανός and because δεκανικός, a derivative of δεκανός, was already in use in Egypt in III BC. Hofmann (1989: 84), Zilliacus (1935a: 222–3), Meinersmann (1927: 13), *DÉLG* (*s.v.* δέκα), Frisk (1954–72: I.359), Beekes (2010 *s.v.* δέκα), Lampe (1961), *DGE*. There is a group of related words that would also be Latin loans if δεκανός were one: δεκανία, δεκανικός, ἀρχιδεκανός, etc. (*LSJ, LBG*, Andriotis 1967 *s.v.* δεκανίκι, Meyer 1895: 20–1 *s.v.* δεκανίκι, etc.).
rare	**δεκαξεστιαῖος** 'of ten pints', from δέκα 'ten' + *sextārius* 'pint measure' via ξεστιαῖος: Philoponus, e.g. *In Aristotelis Categorias commentarium* p. 153.29 Busse (VI AD). *LBG, DGE*. See §4.6.2.
rare	**δεκαούγκιον** 'ten twelfths', from δέκα 'ten' + *ūncia* 'one twelfth' via οὐγγία: with *dextans* in Gloss. Ps.-Cyril. 267.40. *LBG, DGE*. See §4.6.2.
	δεκέμβερ: see δεκέμουιρ.
foreign	***decemviratus*** 'office of decemvir': Lyd. *Mag.* p. 66.23 (VI AD).
Direct loan **I BC – modern**	**Δεκέμβριος, Δεκένβριος, Δεκάβριος, Δεκέμπερ, Δεκένβερ** (-α, -ον or -ου, ὁ) 'December', from *December* 'December'. Documents: common, e.g. *P.Yadin* 1.16.9 etc. (II AD); *P.Oxy.* 4593.A4 (III AD); *Chrest.Wilck.* 42.6 (IV AD); *P.Cair.Masp.* 67321.A9 (VI AD). Inscriptions: common, e.g. *SEG* XLII.837.8 (I BC); *IG* V.I.1359.A3 (I AD); *I.Cret.* IV.300.B10 (II AD); *IG* XII.VII.53.39 (III AD); *IG* XIV.112.9 (IV AD); *I.Cret.* IV.495.4 (V AD); *I.Beroia* 438.3 (VI AD). Literature: common, e.g. *Jubil.* frag. x'17 (I BC?); DH *AR* 6.89.2 (I BC); Jos. *AJ* 14.145 (I AD); Plut. *Mor.* 287a (I/II AD); Dio Cassius 54.21.5 (II/III AD); *Test.Sal.* p. 99*.12 (III AD?); Julian, *Epistulae* 112 Bidez (IV AD); *V.Dan.Styl.* A. 97.13 (V AD); Hesych. as part of gloss φ 401 (V/VI AD); Cyr.S. *Vit.Sab.* 104.24 (VI AD). Post-antique: common. *LBG* (*s.v.* Δεκέβριος), Kriaras (1968–). Modern Δεκέμβριος, Δεκέμβρης, Δεκέβρις: Babiniotis (2002), Andriotis (1967), Meyer (1895: 21). Notes: Kramer (1983: 120, 2011: 37) argues for derivation from rare *Decembrius* (*TLL*). Cervenka-Ehrenstrasser (2000: 222–3), Solin (2008), Sijpesteijn (1979), Diethart (1998: 171), Hofmann (1989: 84–5), Meinersmann (1927: 13), Lampe (1961), *DGE*, LSJ suppl. See **§4.2.1**, §4.2.2, §8.2.3 n. 51, §10.2.1, §10.2.2 E.
rare	**δεκέμουιρ, δεκέμουρ, δεκύειρ**, and **δεκέμβερ** 'decemvir', from *decemvir* 'member of a board of ten': inscriptions *I.Ephesos* 215.12 (II AD); *SEG* XXXI.1300.18 (II AD); *IG* II/III².III.4071.20 (II AD); perhaps *I.Olympia* 359.2 (II AD). The divergent spellings suggest independent, repeated reference to Latin. Mason (1974: 6, 34), *DGE*.
rare	**δεκεμπεδα**, from *decempeda* 'ten-foot measuring pole': unpublished ostracon O.Claud. inv. 8661.7 (II AD).

rare   **δεκέμπριμος** 'one of the first ten' (a military and civilian title), from *decemprīmus* 'one of the ten senior members (of a group)': Nil. 1.265.1 etc. (v AD); Lyd. *Mag.* p. 70.23, marked (vi AD). Hofmann (1989: 85), Zilliacus (1935a: 222–3), Lampe (1961), *LBG, DGE*.

     Δεκένβριος: see Δεκέμβριος.

foreign   **dēcernō** 'decide': Antec. 1.2.6 *decernere* etc. (vi AD).

     δεκεσίων: see δεκισίων.

foreign   **δεκίης** transliterating *deciēs* 'million': Plut. *Ant.* 4.8, 4.9, marked (I/II AD). Sophocles (1887). See §2.2.3.

foreign   **δεκισίων, δεκεσίων** 'decision' (of the emperor in a legal dispute), from *dēcīsiō* 'agreement': Antec. in Latin script 3.23.1 *decision* etc. (vi AD); perhaps later in Greek script. Zilliacus (1935a: 182–3).

not ancient   **δεκοκτορεύω** 'misappropriate', from *dēcoquō* 'squander' (+ -τωρ? + -εύω): no ancient examples. Zilliacus (1935a: 182–3), *LBG*.

rare   **δεκουρία, δικουρία** 'class', 'division', from *decuria* 'class', 'division': Latinate inscriptions *I.Ephesos* 680.11 (II AD); *IGUR* I.206.3 (II AD); *IGR* III.778.9 (II AD); also *Hadriani Sententiae, CGL* III.34.10 (II–IV AD). Mason (1974: 34), Hofmann (1989: 85), *LBG, DGE*, LSJ suppl.

non-existent?   **δεκουριᾶλις** 'of the decuria', from *decuriālis* 'of the decuria': perhaps inscription *IGUR* I.187.2 (II AD). *DGE*.

Direct loan
I AD – Byz.   **δεκουρίων** (-ωνος, ὁ) 'decurion' (a cavalry officer or, in civilian life, member of a municipal council), 'foreman of a slave household', from *decuriō* 'decurion'.
     Documents: e.g. *SB* 13012.1 (I AD); *O.Claud.* II.383.2 (I/II AD); *O.Did.* 406.27 (II AD). But *SB* 8700 (vi AD) is an inscription.
     Inscriptions: e.g. *SEG* XXXVIII.633 (II AD); *SEG* XVIII.433.5, bilingual (III AD); *I.Philae* 216.6 (vi AD).
     Literature: Polybius 6.25.2, marked (II BC); DH *AR* 2.7.4, marked (I BC); *Hippiatr.Berl.* (Apsyrtus) 53.1 etc. (III/IV AD?); Athan. *Apol.Sec.* 56.1 (IV AD); Nil. 1.158.1 (v AD); Lyd. *Mag.* p. 20.3 (vi AD).
     Post-antique: survives. Sophocles (1887), Triandaphyllidis (1909: 129).
     Notes: Cervenka-Ehrenstrasser (2000: 223–4), Robert (1960a: 276–85), Drew-Bear (1972: 191), Dubuisson (1985: 25), Daris (1991a: 38), Mason (1974: 6, 10, 34), Hofmann (1989: 85–6), Viscidi (1944: 20), Zilliacus (1935a: 222–3), Meinersmann (1927: 14), Lampe (1961), *DGE*, LSJ suppl. See §4.1.1, §4.2.5, §8.1.3 n. 17, §10.2.1, §10.2.2 C.

Direct loan
V AD – Byz.   **δέκρετον, δέκρητον, δηκρῆτον, δίκρητον** (-ου, τό) 'decree', 'judicial decision', from *dēcrētum* 'decree', 'judicial decision'.
     Documents: *P.Lond.* v.1674.45, 1685.3 (both vi AD); *P.Cair.Masp.* 67097v.D87 (vi AD).
     Inscriptions: *SEG* LIII.1841.iii.9 etc. (v AD).
     Literature: *Carth.* 286.8 (v AD); Just. *Nov.* 7.2.1 etc. (vi AD); Antec. both in Greek (1.2.7) and Latin (1.2.6 *decreton*, etc.) script (vi AD).
     Post-antique: common. *LBG*, Zervan (2019: 41), Kriaras (1968–), Triandaphyllidis (1909: 127).

Notes: Cervenka-Ehrenstrasser (2000: 224–5), Binder (2000: 97), Avotins (1992), Daris (1991a: 39), Hofmann (1989: 86), Cavenaile (1951: 396), Zilliacus (1935a: 182–3), Lampe (1961), *DGE*, LSJ suppl. See §4.2.4.1 n. 55, §10.2.1, §10.2.2 B.

δεκύειρ: see δεκέμουιρ.

δελεγατεύω, δεληγατεύω: see δηληγατεύω.

foreign   **δελίκτον** 'offence', from *dēlictum* 'offence': Antec. in Latin script 4.1.pr. *delicton* etc. (VI AD); later in Greek script. Zilliacus (1935a: 184–5), Triantaphyllides (1892: 258), *LBG*. See §9.5.6 n. 68.

Direct loan   **δελματική, δαλματική, δερματική, τερματική** (-ῆς, ἡ) 'Dalmatian tunic', from
II–V AD   *dalmatica/delmatica* 'Dalmatian tunic' (*TLL s.v. Dalmatae* 20.79–21.42).
     Documents: e.g. *P.Oxy.* 1583.9 (II AD); *SB* 15922.22 (II/III AD); *P.Harr.* 1.105.8 (III AD); *P.Oxy.* 3776.15 (IV AD); *CPR* V.26.872 etc. (V AD).
     Inscriptions: *SEG* VII.417.14 etc., 422.2 (both III AD); perhaps *SEG* VII.419.2, 420.3 etc. (both III AD); Edict.Diocl. 19.9 etc. (IV AD); *SEG* VII.431.6.
     Literature: *Coll.Herm.* ME 1or (II–IV AD); Epiph. *Pan.* 1.209.15 (IV AD); Ps.-Epiph. *Anac.* 1.167.16 (IV AD?); bilingual glossaries, e.g. Gloss. *Herm.Mp.* 323.36.
     Notes: Gignac (1981: 8–9) considers δελματικόν a variant of this. Forms derivatives δελματίκιον, δελματικομαφόρης, δελματικομαφόρτιον, δελματικομαφόριον, perhaps δελματικόν. For the garment: Dross-Krüpe (2017: 297–8), Mossakowska-Gaubert (2017: 323–4). Cervenka-Ehrenstrasser (2000: 220–1, 225–6), O'Callaghan (1983), Gignac (1976: 106), Murri (1943: 121–7), Daris (1991a: 38, 39), Hofmann (1989: 83), Cavenaile (1951: 403), Meinersmann (1927: 13), *TLL* (*s.v. Dalmatae* 20.84–21.24), *DGE* (*s.v.* δαλματική), LSJ (*s.v.* Δαλματεῖς). See §4.2.3.1, **§4.4**, §4.6.1 n. 83, §4.6.2, §10.2.1, §10.2.2 H, §12.2.2.

Deriv. of loan   **δελματίκιον, δελματίκαιον, δερματίκιον** (-ου, τό) 'Dalmatian tunic', from
III AD – Byz.   *dalmatica/delmatica* 'Dalmatian tunic' (*TLL s.v. Dalmatae* 20.79–21.42) via δελματική + -ιον.
     Documents: e.g. *P.Tebt.* II.413.8 (II/III AD); *P.Oxy.* 3201.9 (III AD); *SB* 11575.10 (III AD); *PSI* VIII.900.7 (III/IV AD); *P.Stras.* III.131.7 (IV AD); *P.Ryl.* IV.627.11 (IV AD); *P.Princ.* II.82.38 (V AD).
     Post-antique: survives. *LBG* (*s.v.* δελματίκιν).
     Notes: for spelling with δερμ- as folk etymology from δέρμα 'skin': Cavenaile (1951: 403), Gignac (1976: 106). Cervenka-Ehrenstrasser (2000: 226–7), Murri (1943: 121–7), Daris (1991a: 39), Hofmann (1989: 83 *s.v.* δαλματικη), Cavenaile (1952: 196), *DGE*, LSJ (*s.v.* Δαλματεῖς), LSJ suppl. (*s.vv.* Δαλματεῖς, δερματίκιον). See §4.6.1 n. 83, §10.2.2 H.

Deriv. of loan   **δελματικομαφόριον, δαλματικομαφόριον** (-ου, τό) 'Dalmatian tunic with hood',
IV AD – Byz.   from *dalmatica/delmatica* 'Dalmatian tunic' (*TLL s.v. Dalmatae* 20.79–21.42) via δελματική + μαφόριον 'short cloak with hood'.
     Documents: *P.Ross.Georg.* III.28.10 (IV AD); perhaps *SB* 10988.17 (IV AD); *SB* 11075.7 etc. (V AD).
     Post-antique: survives. *LBG* (*s.v.* δαλματικομαφόριον), Cervenka-Ehrenstrasser (2000: 222).

Notes: Cervenka-Ehrenstrasser (2000: 221–2, 227–8), Daris (1991a: 39), *TLL* (*s.v. Dalmatae* 21.49–60, i.e. section on δελματικομαφέρτιον), *DGE* (*s.v.* δαλματικομαφόριον), LSJ suppl. (*s.v.* δαλματικομαφόριον). See §4.6.2, §9.2, §10.2.2 H, §12.2.1.

Deriv. of loan
III–IV AD

δελματικομαφόρτης, δαλματικομαφόρτης, δελματικομάφερτος, δελματικομάφορτος, δελματικομάφολτος (-ου, ὁ) 'Dalmatian tunic with hood', from *dalmatica/delmatica* 'Dalmatian tunic' (*TLL s.v. Dalmatae* 20.79–21.42) via δελματική + μαφόρτης 'short cloak with hood'.
Documents: *P.Oxy.* 1273.12 etc. (III AD).
Inscriptions: Edict.Diocl. 22.5 etc. (IV AD).
Notes: for the garment see Dross-Krüpe (2017: 299), Mossakowska-Gaubert (2017: 337–8). Cervenka-Ehrenstrasser (2000: 228–9), Gignac (1976: 106), Daris (1991a: 39), Hofmann (1989: 86), Filos (2010: 249), *TLL* (*s.v. Dalmatae* 21.49–60, i.e. section on δελματικομαφέρτιον), *DGE* (*s.v.* δαλματικομαφόρτης), LSJ suppl. (*s.v.* δαλματικομαφόρτης, replacing LSJ *s.v.* δαλματικομαφόρτης). See §4.6.2, §9.2, §10.2.2 H, §12.2.1.

Deriv. of loan
III–IV AD

δελματικομαφόρτιον, δαλματικομαφόρτιον, δερματικομαφόρτιον, δελματικομαφέρτιον (-ου, τό) 'Dalmatian tunic with hood', from *dalmatica/delmatica* 'Dalmatian tunic' (*TLL s.v. Dalmatae* 20.79–21.42) via δελματική + μαφόρτιον 'short cloak with hood'.
Documents: *P.Oxy.* 114.5 (II/III AD); *P.Louvre* 1.67.5 (III AD); *P.Michael.* 18.2.4 (III AD).
Inscriptions: Edict.Diocl. 19.8 etc. (IV AD).
Notes: Cervenka-Ehrenstrasser (2000: 229), Gignac (1976: 106), Filos (2010: 249), Daris (1991a: 39), *TLL* (*s.v. Dalmatae* 21.49–60, i.e. section on δελματικομαφέρτιον), *DGE*, LSJ suppl. (*s.v.* δαλματικομαφόρτιον, replacing LSJ *s.v.* δαλματικομαφόρτης). See §4.6.2, §9.2, §10.2.2 H, §12.2.1.

Direct? loan
IV? AD

δελματικόν, δερματικόν (-ου, τό), 'Dalmatian tunic', from *dalmatica/delmatica* 'Dalmatian tunic' (*TLL s.v. Dalmatae* 20.79–21.42), perhaps via δελματική.
Documents: *O.Wilck.* 1611.6 (I–IV AD); *PSI* VIII.900.7 (III/IV AD); *P.Ryl.* IV.627.4 etc. (IV AD); *P.Oxy.* 1741.15 etc. (IV AD); *P.Col.* IX.247.5 etc. (IV AD); *SB* 14661 *passim* (IV AD).
Inscriptions: *SEG* VII.431.20.
Literature: *Coll.Herm.* C 58a (II–IV AD).
Post-antique: Triandaphyllidis (1909: 121) alleges survival, but I am sceptical.
Notes: for spelling with δερμ- as folk etymology from δέρμα 'skin': Cavenaile (1951: 403). Cervenka-Ehrenstrasser (2000: 230), Gignac (1981: 9, considering it a variant of δελματική), Daris (1991a: 39), *DGE*. See §4.2.3.1, §10.2.1, §10.2.2 H.

not Latin?

δελμάτιον on papyrus *P.Oxy.* 1026.16 (V AD) may mean 'Dalmatian tunic' and come from *dalmatica/delmatica* 'Dalmatian tunic' (*TLL s.v. Dalmatae* 20.79–21.42), or it could be a Greek word from δερμ- 'skin'. Cervenka-Ehrenstrasser (2000: 230–1), Daris (1991a: 39), *DGE*, LSJ suppl. (*s.v.* Δαλμάτιον).

δεμέστιχος: see δομεστικός 1.

foreign	**δεμινουτίων** 'diminution', as part of *capitis dēminūtiō* 'loss of status': *Schol.Sinai.* in Latin script 46 *kapitis deminutiona* (V/VI AD); Antec. in Latin script 1.16. pr. *capitis deminutioni* etc. (VI AD); later in Greek script. Zilliacus (1935a: 184–5), *LBG*. See §7.1.3 n. 16, §9.5.6.
foreign	**δεμονστρατίων** 'description' (in a will, of a group to receive a legacy), from *dēmōnstrātiō* 'description': Antec. in Latin script 2.20.30 *demonstratio* etc. (VI AD); later in Greek script. Zilliacus (1935a: 184–5), *LBG*.
foreign	**δέντης** transliterating acc. pl. of *dēns* 'tooth': Plut. *Mor.* 727a (I/II AD). Strobach (1997: 194), Sophocles (1887 *s.v.* δένς). See §7.2.1.
foreign	*dēxtāns* 'five sixths of an inheritance': Antec. 2.14.5 (VI AD). See §7.1.1 passage 18.
foreign	**δέος** transliterating *deus* 'god': Hesych. as lemma δ 657 (V/VI AD). Δέῳ transliterating dat. in Σίμωνι δέῳ σάγκτῳ (*Simoni deo sancto*): Justin Martyr, *Apologia prima* 26.2 Minns and Parvis (II AD). Hofmann (1989: 86), Immisch (1885: 320), Sophocles (1887 *s.v.* δέους), LSJ (*s.v.* δεός).
foreign	*deūnx* 'eleven twelfths of an inheritance': Antec. 2.14.5 (VI AD). See §7.1.1 passage 18.
	δέους: see δέος.
foreign	**δεπορτατεύω** 'exile', from *dēportātus*, pf. part. of *dēportō* 'exile' (*TLL s.v.* 588.73–589.35) + -εύω: Antec. in Latin script 1.16.2 *deportateuθenti* etc. (VI AD); later in Greek script. Zilliacus (1935a: 184–5), *LBG*, *TLL* (*s.v.* dēporto 587.32). See §9.5.6 n. 68.
foreign	**δεπορτατίων, δηπορτατίων** 'exile', from *dēportātiō* 'deportation': Antec. in Latin script 1.12.1 *deportation* etc. (VI AD); Ath.Schol. in Latin script 10.2.11 (VI AD); later in Greek script. Hofmann (1989: 86), Zilliacus (1935a: 184–5), Sophocles (1887), *TLL* (*s.v.* dēportātio 586.78–9), Lampe (1961), *DGE* (*s.v.* δηπορτατίων). See §9.5.6 n. 68.
foreign	**δεπορτᾶτος, δηπορτᾶτος** 'exiled', from *dēportātus*, pf. part. of *dēportō* 'exile' (*TLL s.v.* 588.73–589.35): Hesych. as lemma δ 914 (V/VI AD); Antec. in Latin script 1.22.1 *deportatoi* etc. (VI AD). Zilliacus (1935a: 184–5), Immisch (1885: 353), *TLL* (*s.v.* dēporto 587.32), *DGE* (*s.v.* δηπορτᾶτος), and for later survival *LBG*.
not ancient	**δεποσιτάριος** 'depositor', from *dēpositārius* 'depositor': no ancient examples. Zilliacus (1935a: 184–5), *LBG*.
	δεπόσιτον: see δηπόσιτον.
	δεπο(υ)τᾶτος: see δηποτᾶτος.
	δεπροβατιονιβους: see προβατίων.
	δερματικ-: see δελματικ-.
	δέρμα ὀβιφέρι: see ὀβιφέρι.
	δεσέρτωρ: see δησέρτωρ.
	δεσιγνατ-: see δησιγνατ-.

not ancient	**δεστιτούτωρ** 'one who abandons a case', from *dēstitūtor* 'one who abandons a case' (*TLL*): no ancient examples. Zilliacus (1935a: 184–5), *LBG*.
non-existent?	**δεστίτωρ** 'resigner', from *dēstitor* 'one who resigns from ecclesiastical office' (*TLL*): cited as an ancient loan by Zilliacus (1935a: 184–5), but I can find no examples.
	δεφεν-: see δηφην-.
non-existent?	**δεφινιτίων** 'pronouncement', from *dēfīnītiō* 'pronouncement': cited as an ancient loan by Zilliacus (1935a: 182–3), but I can find no examples.
	δέω: see δέος.
rare	**δηκέπτος** 'unexpectedly without water', from *dēceptus*, pf. pass. part. of *dēcipiō* 'deceive', 'disappoint': ostraca Cuvigny 2019: 290 no. 7.13 (II AD); unpublished ostracon O.Claud. inv. 7558.7 (II AD). Cuvigny (2019: 291). See §9.2 n. 19.
rare	**δηκόκτα** 'decoction', 'drink made by heating and rapid cooling', from *dēcocta* 'decoction', 'drink made by rapid heating and cooling' (*TLL s.v. dēcoquo* 205.79–206.4): Galen x.467.17 Kühn, marked (II AD); Athenaeus 3.121e-f, 3.122e (II/III AD); *Hippiatr.Berl.* 129.31; Byzantine texts. Hofmann (1989: 87), *LBG*, LSJ suppl. See §1, §9.3, **§9.4** passage 57.
	δηκρῆτον: see δέκρετον.
rare	**δηλάβρα** 'winnowing-fan', from *dēlābrum* 'winnowing-fan' (*TLL*): Edict.Diocl. 15.44 (IV AD). Hofmann (1989: 87–8), *TLL* (*s.v. dēlābrum*), *DGE*, LSJ suppl.
rare	**δηλατόρευσις, δηλατώρευσις** 'denunciation', from *dēlātor* 'accuser', 'informer' via δηλατορεύω + -σις: Leontius of Constantinople, *Homiliae* 10.297 Allen and Datema (VI AD). Hofmann (1989: 88 *s.v.* δηλάτωρ), Lampe (1961), *DGE* (*s.v.* δηλατώρευσις).
Deriv. of loan IV AD – Byz.	**δηλατορεύω, δηλατωρεύω** 'accuse', 'denounce', from *dēlātor* 'accuser', 'informer' via δηλάτωρ + -εύω. Literature: Eus. *HE* 3.20.1 (IV AD); Pall. *V.Chrys.* 108.6 (IV/V AD). Post-antique: survives despite absence from lexica. Notes: forms derivative δηλατόρευσις. Hofmann (1989: 88 *s.v.* δηλάτωρ), Zilliacus (1935a: 182–3), Lampe (1961), *DGE* (*s.v.* δηλατωρεύω). See §4.6.1 n. 91, §10.2.2 O.
rare	**δηλατορία, δηλατωρία** 'accusation', from *dēlātōrius* 'of an informer' (in fem. subst.) or *dēlātor* 'informer' via δηλάτωρ + -ία: papyrus *SB* 10989.i.10 etc. (IV AD). Cervenka-Ehrenstrasser (2000: 231–2), Daris (1991a: 39), Cavenaile (1951: 396), *DGE* (*s.v.* δηλατωρία), for Byzantine use *LBG*.
Direct loan III AD – Byz.	**δηλάτωρ** (-ορος/-ωρος, ὁ) 'accuser', 'informer', from *dēlātor* 'accuser', 'informer'. Documents: Harrauer and Pintaudi 2003: 140.11 (VI AD). Inscriptions: Lemerle 1936: 337.9 (II/III AD); Kallipolitis and Lazaridis 1946: 17 no. 10.8 (III/IV AD); Lemerle 1935: 152 no. 45 (III/IV AD); Perdrizet 1900: 314 no. 5.10.

Literature: Thdt. *Ep.Sirm.* 43.16, 45.20 (V AD); Procl.Const. *Consol.* 83 (V AD); Leontius of Constantinople, *Homiliae* 10.297 Allen and Datema (VI AD); Hesych. as lemma δ 792 (V/VI AD); Lyd. *Mens.* frag. incert. 10 (VI AD); St. Gregentius, *PG* LXXXVI.I.592c (VI AD); as gloss in scholion to Demosthenes 24.323b. Unverified example (IV AD) in Zilliacus (1937: 322, 328).

Post-antique: common. *LBG*, Triandaphyllidis (1909: 124).

Notes: forms derivatives δηλατορεύω, perhaps δηλατορία. Cervenka-Ehrenstrasser (2000: 232), Hofmann (1989: 88), Zilliacus (1935a: 182–3, 1937: 328), Immisch (1885: 353), Lampe (1961), *DGE*, LSJ suppl. See §4.2.5, §10.1, §10.2.1, §10.2.2 N.

δηλατωρ-: see δηλατορ-.

Direct? loan with suffix
IV AD – Byz.

δηληγατεύω, δελεγατεύω, δεληγατεύω 'assign as tax to be paid', from *dēlēgātus*, pf. part. of *dēlēgō* 'assign', and/or from *dēlēgātiō* 'announcement of taxes' (*TLL s.v.* 2) via δηληγατίων, + -εύω.

Documents: *Chrest.Wilck.* 281.3 etc. (IV AD); *P.Oxy.* 2114.6 (IV AD); perhaps *P.Oslo* III.119.4 (IV AD); *P.Stras.* VII.695.5 etc. (V AD).

Inscriptions: *SEG* XXXII.1554.A49 etc. (VI AD).

Literature: Just. *Nov.* 130.5 (VI AD); Antec. in Latin script 3.26.2 *edelegateuon* (VI AD).

Post-antique: numerous, forming derivative δελεγάτευσις. *LBG*.

Notes: forms derivative ἀδηληγάτευτος. Cervenka-Ehrenstrasser (2000: 232–3), Avotins (1992), Mandilaras (1973: 67), Diethart (1998: 171), Daris (1991a: 40), Hofmann (1989: 88 *s.v.* δηληγατίων), Zilliacus (1935a: 182–3), Meinersmann (1927: 14), *DGE*, LSJ, LSJ suppl. See §4.3.1, §4.6.1 n. 91, §10.2.1, §10.2.2 D, §10.3.1.

Direct loan
IV AD – Byz.

δηληγατίων, δηληκατίων, δηρηγατίων (-ωνος/-ονος, ἡ) 'annual declaration by the state of the amount of tax to be paid', from *dēlēgātiō* 'announcement of taxes' (*TLL s.v.* 2).

Documents: e.g. *P.Oxy.* 2561.10 etc. (III/IV AD); *Chrest.Wilck* 281.18 (IV AD); *BGU* III.836.3 (VI AD).

Inscriptions: *SEG* IX.356.9 (VI AD).

Literature: perhaps Hesych. as lemma δ 796 (V/VI AD), though that looks like a participle of an unattested verb. Hofmann (1989: 88), Immisch (1885: 353).

Post-antique: numerous. *LBG* (*s.v.* δελεγατίων).

Notes: perhaps forms derivative δηληγατεύω. Cervenka-Ehrenstrasser (2000: 233–5), Daris (1991a: 40), Hofmann (1989: 88), Zilliacus (1935a: 182–3), Meinersmann (1927: 14), *TLL* (*s.v. dēlēgātio* 430.44), *DGE*, LSJ. See §4.2.5, §10.2.1, §10.2.2 D.

Direct loan
V AD – Byz.

δηληγάτωρ, διληγάτωρ (-ορος, ὁ), a military official, from *dēlēgātor* 'one who assigns' (*TLL*).

Literature: Nil. 2.243.1 (V AD); Malal. 13.4 (VI AD); Just. *Nov.* in Latin script 130.1 etc. (VI AD); Ath.Schol. in Latin script 20.2.1 (VI AD).

Post-antique: some survival; *Etymologicum Gudianum*, Additamenta δ p. 355.21 de Stefani: οὕτως καὶ δηληγάτωρ· Ῥωμαϊστὶ γὰρ δελεγάτωρ. Triandaphyllidis (1909: 126).

Notes: Hofmann (1989: 88–9), Zilliacus (1935a: 184–5), *LBG*, *TLL* (*s.v. dēlēgātor* 430.53), Lampe (1961), *DGE*. See §4.2.5, §10.2.1, §10.2.2 C.

non-existent? **δηλήκτωρ**, meaning uncertain, apparently from *dēlēctor* (also meaning uncertain, *TLL*): cited as an ancient loan by Zilliacus (1935a: 182–3), but I can find no examples.

rare **δηλίκιον** 'pet slave child', from (feminine) *dēlicia* 'delight', 'pet': Plut. *Ant.* 59.8, marked (I/II AD); Dor.Gaz. *Vit.Dos.* 3.1, 2 (VI AD). Hofmann (1989: 89), *DGE*.

Direct loan **δηνάριον, δινάριον, δυνάριον** (-ου, τό), a unit of value (originally a coin), from
II BC – modern *dēnārius*, a unit of value.

Documents: very common, e.g. *ChLA* XLIII.1241.L1d.7 (I BC); *SB* 9742.2 (I AD); *P.Hever* 65.7 (II AD); *P.Oxy.* 1414.8 etc. (III AD); *P.Oxy.* 5064.14 (IV AD); *PSI* VI.694.3 (V AD); *P.Vat.Aphrod.* 7.A11 (VI AD).

Inscriptions: very common (esp. I–III AD), e.g. *I.Délos* 1442.B51 (II BC); *I.Cret.* II.XI.3.5 (I BC); *IG* IV².1.27.4 (I AD); *Corinth* VIII.III.306.6 (II AD); *IG* IX.1.643.9 (III AD); *I.Stratonikeia* 310.28 (IV AD); *I.Mus.Iznik* 559.11 (V AD?).

Literature: very common, e.g. NT Matthew 18:28 (I AD); Epict. *Diss.* 1.4.16 (I/II AD); *Act.Andr.* 21.6 (II AD); *Acta Thomae* 118 = Bonnet 1903: 228.15 (III AD); Eus. *HE* 3.20.2 (IV AD); Nilus Ancyranus, Εἰς τὸ τῶν Αἰσμάτων Αἶσμα 86.4.5 Rosenbaum (V AD); Romanus Melodus, *Cantica* 24.11.9 Grosdidier de Matons (VI AD); scholia to *Od.* 2.338e.

Post-antique: survives. Kriaras (1968–), *LBG* (*s.v.* δήναρος), Zervan (2019: 43–4), Triandaphyllidis (1909: 103). Modern δηνάριο 'money', esp. of particular foreign currencies: Babiniotis (2002), Andriotis (1967, 1974: 204), Meyer (1895: 21).

Notes: forms derivative δηναρισμός. Cervenka-Ehrenstrasser (2000: 235–6), Menci (2000: 281–2), García Domingo (1979: 356), Cuvigny and Lach-Urgacz (2020: 320), Daris (1991a: 40), Hofmann (1989: 90), Cavenaile (1951: 403), Viscidi (1944: 29–30), Zilliacus (1935a: 184–5), Meinersmann (1927: 14), Immisch (1885: 340), Lampe (1961), *DGE*, LSJ, LSJ suppl. See **§4.2.4.1**, §4.3.2 n. 75, **§4.4**, §6.3 n. 22, §8.1.1 n. 3, §8.1.4, §8.1.5, §9.3 nn. 21 and 23, §10.2.1, §10.2.2 G.

rare **δηναρισμός** 'valuation in denaria', from *dēnārius* (a unit of value) via δηνάριον + -σμός: Epiph. *Mens.* 809 (IV AD). Hofmann (1989: 90 *s.v.* δηνάριον), Sophocles (1887), Lampe (1961), *DGE*.

δηπορτατ-: see δεπορτατ-.

Direct loan **δηπόσιτον, δηπόσειτον, δηπώσετον, δεπόσιτον** (-ου, τό) 'deposit', 'soldier's
II AD – Byz. savings', from *dēpositum* 'deposit'.

Documents: *P.Col.* VIII.221.4 etc. (II AD); *Rom.Mil.Rec.* 74.1.5 etc. (II AD); *P.Mich.* VIII.514.10 (III AD).

Literature: Ignat. *Ep.* 7.6.2 (I/II AD); Antec. in Latin script 3.14.3 *depositon* etc. (VI AD).

Post-antique: common, forming derivatives δεποσιτάριος 'depositor', δεποσίτωρ 'depositor', etc. *LBG* (*s.v.* δεπόσιτον).

Notes: Cervenka-Ehrenstrasser (2000: 236–7), Binder (2000: 96–7, 202), Daris (1991a: 40), Hofmann (1989: 90–1), Cavenaile (1951: 396), Zilliacus (1935a: 184–5), Lampe (1961 *s.v.* δεπόσιτον), *DGE*, LSJ suppl. See §4.2.4.1 n. 55, §10.2.1, §10.2.2 C.

δηποτατεύω: see διποτατεύω.

Direct loan
III AD – Byz.

δηποτᾶτος, δηπουτᾶτος, δεπο(υ)τᾶτος, -πωτ- (-ου, ὁ) 'deputy', 'weapons-maker', from *dēputātus*, pf. part. of *dēputō* 'delegate' (*TLL s.v.* 625.34–67).
    Documents: perhaps *P.Cair.Masp.* 67321.B10 (VI AD).
    Inscriptions: *IGR* III.28.5 (III AD); *SEG* LXV.1408.C29, transliterating Latin (V/VI AD).
    Literature: *ACO* II.I.II p. 16.2 (V AD); Lyd. *Mag.* p. 146.22 etc., marked (VI AD); Just. *Nov.* 85.1 etc. (VI AD).
    Post-antique: common, apparently splitting into various spellings and meanings. *LBG* (*s.vv.* δεποτᾶτος, δεπουτᾶτος, δηποτᾶτος, δηπουτᾶτος), Zervan (2019: 41).
    Notes: Cervenka-Ehrenstrasser (2000: 237–8), Binder (2000: 96), Caimi (1981: 334–41), Avotins (1992 *s.v.* δεπουτᾶτος), Daris (1991a: 40), Mason (1974: 4, 35), Hofmann (1989: 91), Zilliacus (1935a: 184–5, 222–3), Meinersmann (1927: 14), *TLL* (*s.v. dēputo* 625.54–66), Lampe (1961 *s.v.* δηπουτᾶτος), *DGE*, LSJ suppl. See §4.2.4.1 n. 51, §5.2.3, §10.2.1, §10.2.2 N.

δηπώσετον: see δηπόσιτον.

δηρηγατίων: see δηληγατίων.

δηριγεύω: see διριγεύω.

δησέκτωρ: see δισέκτωρ.

Direct loan
II–IV AD

δησέρτωρ, δεσέρτωρ (-ορος, ὁ) 'deserter', from *dēsertor* 'deserter'.
    Documents: *P.Flor.* III.362.3 (IV AD).
    Literature: Ignat. *Ep.* 7.6.2 (I/II AD); Basil Caesariensis, *Epistulae* 268.1.24 Courtonne (IV AD).
    Notes: Cervenka-Ehrenstrasser (2000: 238–9), Daris (1991a: 40), Hofmann (1989: 87), Meinersmann (1927: 14), Lampe (1961), *DGE*, LSJ suppl. See §4.2.5, §10.2.1, §10.2.2 C.

rare

δησιγνατεύω, δεσιγνατεύω, δισιγνατεύω 'appoint to public office', from *dēsignātus*, pf. part. of *dēsignō* 'appoint' (via δησιγνᾶτος?) + -εύω: Malal. 7.9.31, 17.8 (VI AD); Antec. in Latin script 2.20.25 *designateuesthai* (VI AD). Hofmann (1989: 94), Zilliacus (1935a: 184–5), *LBG* (*s.v.* δισιγνατεύω), Triandaphyllidis (1909: 128), Lampe (1961 *s.v.* δισιγνατεύω), *DGE*.

rare

δησιγνᾶτος, δεσιγνᾶτος, δισιγνᾶτος 'appointed to public office', from *dēsignātus* (pf. part. of *dēsignō* 'appoint'): *ACO* II.I.III pp. 120.11, 121.16, 124.22 (V AD); Olympiodorus Historicus (V AD) quoted by Photius, *Bibliotheca* codex 80.59a.36 (IX AD). May form derivative δησιγνατεύω. *LBG* (*s.v.* δεσιγνᾶτος), Sophocles (1887), *DGE*.

not ancient

δηφήνδευσις, δηφήντευσις 'defence', from *dēfendō* 'defend' via δηφηνδεύω + -σις: post-antique papyri. Cervenka-Ehrenstrasser (2000: 239), Diethart (1998: 172), Daris (1991a: 40), Cavenaile (1951: 396), *LBG* (*s.v.* δεφένδευσις), Zervan (2019: 43), Kriaras (1968– *s.v.* διαυθέντευση), *DGE*.

foreign   **δηφηνδεύω, δηφενδεύω, δηφηντεύω** 'defend', from *dēfendō* 'defend' + -εύω: Antec.
in Latin script 1.13.2 *defendeuontes* etc. (VI AD); later common in Greek
script, forming derivatives δεφένδευσις 'defence', δεφενδευτής 'defender'. If it
is source of ἀδεφένδευτος, may have been more integrated than it now looks.
Modern δεφενδεύω, διαφεντεύω 'forbid' (Meyer 1895: 21), 'defend' (Kahane
and Kahane 1972–6: 531, 1982: 135). Cervenka-Ehrenstrasser (2000: 240),
Diethart (1998: 171–2), Binder (2000: 96), Filos (2019: 160–1), Hofmann
(1989: 91), Zilliacus (1935a: 182–3, 222–3), Triantaphyllides (1892: 259),
LBG (*s.v.* δεφενδεύω), Zervan (2019: 42–3), Kriaras (1968– *s.v.* διαυθεντεύω),
Triandaphyllidis (1909: 107, 123, 128), *DGE*. See §9.5.6 n. 68.

foreign   **δηφηνσίων, δηφενσίων, δεφενσίων** 'defence', from *dēfēnsiō* 'defence': Just. *Nov.*
in Latin script 88.1 etc. (VI AD); Ath.Schol. in Latin script 6.3.2 (VI AD);
Antec. in Latin script 4.11.5 *defensioni* (VI AD); often later in Greek script.
N.B. *Etymologicum Gudianum*, Additamenta δ p. 355.21 de Stefani: Δηφενσίων·
Ῥωμαϊστὶ γὰρ δεφενσίων. Avotins (1992 *s.v.* δεφενσίων), Binder (2000:
96), Hofmann (1989: 87), Zilliacus (1935a: 182–3, 222–3), *LBG* (*s.v.*
δεφενσίων), Triandaphyllidis (1909: 128), Lampe (1961 *s.v.* δεφενσίων), *DGE*.
See §9.5.6 n. 68.

Direct loan
IV AD – Byz.   **δηφήνσωρ, δεφένσωρ, δηφένσωρ** (-ορος, ὁ), a title, from *dēfēnsor* 'protector'.
Documents: *P.Lips.* I.34.10, 35.12 (both IV AD); *P.Ross.Georg.* V.27.1 (IV AD);
P.Herm. 19.4 (IV AD); *P.Harr.* I.135.8 (V AD); *P.Herm.* 69.3 (V AD); perhaps
Chrest.Mitt. 71.15 (V AD); but *ChLA* XXIX.865.14 is Latin in Greek script.
Inscriptions: Asdracha 1995: 320 no. 146.3 (V/VI AD).
Literature: Hesych. as lemma δ 933 (V/VI AD); Just. *Nov.* 15.pr., marked
(VI AD); Antec. in Latin script 4.11.5 *defensoros* etc. (VI AD).
Post-antique: common, forming derivative δεφενσωρικός. *LBG* (*s.v.* δεφένσωρ),
Zervan (2019: 43), Kriaras (1968– *s.v.* δεφένσωρ), Triandaphyllidis (1909:
128).
Notes: Cervenka-Ehrenstrasser (2000: 240–2), Avotins (1992), Binder (2000:
96), Daris (1991a: 40), Hofmann (1989: 92), Zilliacus (1935a: 182–3,
222–3), Meinersmann (1927: 14), Immisch (1885: 353–4), *DGE*, LSJ suppl.
See §4.2.5, §6.7 n. 46, §10.2.1, §10.2.2 D.

not ancient   **δηφηνσώριος, δηφηνσόριος** 'of the protector', from *dēfēnsor* 'protector' via
δηφήνσωρ: no ancient examples. Cervenka-Ehrenstrasser (2000: 242–3),
Diethart (1998: 172), Daris (1991a: 40, with derivation from *dēfēnsōrius*),
DGE (*s.v.* δηφηνσόριος).

    δηφηντ-: see δηφηνδ-.

not Latin?   **διαιτάριος, διητάριος** 'house-steward', 'steward of the imperial household',
perhaps from *diaetārius* 'house-steward' (LSJ, Lampe 1961, Hofmann 1989:
92, *DGE*), or a Greek formation from δίαιτα 'dwelling' + -άριος (*DÉLG s.v.*
δίαιτα, Coleman 2007: 796). *DGE* considers ζητάριος (*q.v.*) a variant.

rare   **διάλι(ο)ς**, religious title from (*flāmen*) *diālis* 'priest of Jupiter at Rome': Plut.
Mor. 289e, marked (I/II AD); Dio Cassius 44.6.4, 59.28.5 (II/III AD).
Freyburger-Galland (1998: 141), Mason (1974: 6, 36), Hofmann (1989:
92), *DGE*, LSJ.

Direct loan
II BC – modern

διάριον (-ου, τό) 'daily wage', 'allowance', from *diārium* 'daily ration'.

Documents: *SB* 12375.54 (II BC); perhaps *P.Oxy.* 2908.3.17 (III AD); perhaps *P.Lond.* v.1654.7 (V/VI AD); *P.Oxy.* 1729.11 (V/VI AD); *P.Stras.* 1.40.45 (VI AD); *Stud.Pal.* III².1.87.3 (VI AD).

Inscriptions: perhaps *SEG* LIII.713.B6, see suggestion of Chaniotis p. 80 (II/III AD).

Literature: Just. *Codex* 1.2.17 (marked), *Nov.* 123.16.pr. etc. (VI AD); Barsanuph.Jo. III ep. 766.1 (VI AD); Cyr.S. *Vit.Sab.* 90.24 (VI AD); Ath. Schol. 1.2.32, 1.10 (VI AD).

Post-antique: survives. *LBG*, Cervenka-Ehrenstrasser (2000: 243). Modern dialectal δάρ 'daily ration', δαρίζω 'share out food': Kahane and Kahane (1982: 135, cf. 1972–6: 532).

Notes: Coleman (2007: 795) wrongly claims that it 'disappeared after Roman rule'. Cervenka-Ehrenstrasser (2000: 243–4), Niehoff-Panagiotidis (2019: 468), Diethart (1988: 55), Avotins (1989, 1992), Daris (1991a: 40), Hofmann (1989: 92), Zilliacus (1935a: 184–5), Meinersmann (1927: 14), Lampe (1961), *DGE*, LSJ, LSJ suppl. See §4.2.4.1 n. 54, §4.3.2 n. 75, §6.3 n. 22, **§8.1.4**, §10.2.1, §10.2.2 G.

foreign

dīvīnī iūris 'subject to divine law' (i.e. not subject to human law): Antec. 2.1.7 *divini iuris* etc. (VI AD).

non-existent?

διβινιτᾶτος, meaning uncertain, allegedly from unattested **dīvīnitātus*: cited as an ancient loan by Zilliacus (1935a: 184–5), but I can find no examples.

foreign

διβόρτιον 'divorce', from *dīvortium* 'divorce': *Schol.Sinai.* 5 in Latin script as part of *ficto diuorti* (V/VI AD); in Greek script in Byzantine texts. Zilliacus (1935a: 184–5).

rare

δίβος, δεῖβος 'divine', from *dīvus* 'god': inscription Robert and Robert 1968: 504 no. 443 (I AD); a position on a game-board, *Anthologia Graeca* 9.482.12 (VI AD). Mason (1974: 125, 37, 6), *DÉLG*, Beekes (2010), *DGE*, LSJ, LSJ suppl.

Direct loan
VI AD – Byz.

δίγεστον (-ου, τό) 'Digest' (in legal sense), from *dīgesta, -ōrum* 'abstract of a body of law arranged systematically'. In Greek usually plural, but singular also occurs.

Literature: Antec. proem. 4 (VI AD); Just. *Nov.* 18.9 etc. (VI AD).

Post-antique: common. *LBG* (s.v. δίγεστα), Kriaras (1968– s.v. δίγεστα).

Notes: Avotins (1992 s.v. δίγεστα), Triantaphyllides (1892: 259), *DGE* (s.v. δίγεστα). See §4.2.4.1 n. 55, §9.5.6 n. 68, §10.2.1, §10.2.2 B.

foreign

diēs 'day' as part of *in diem* 'on a particular date': Antec. 2.20.14 *in diem* etc. (VI AD).

διητάριος: see διαιτάριος.

foreign

δίκερε transliterating inf. of *dīcō* 'say': Plut. *Marc.* 24.12 (I/II AD).

δικουρία: see δεκουρία.

δίκρητον: see δέκρετον.

δικτατορ-: see δικτατωρ-.

foreign   δικτατοῦρα transliterating *dictātūra* 'dictatorship': Eutropius 1.12 (IV AD); Lyd.
         Mag. p. 54.6 etc. (VI AD); Byzantine texts. *LBG, DGE.*

Direct loan   δικτάτωρ (-ορος/-ωρος, ὁ) 'dictator', from *dictātor* 'dictator'.
I BC – modern   Inscriptions: e.g. *I.Cos Segre* ED7.3 (I BC); *SEG* XIV.122.3 (I BC); *IG*
         XIV.1297.i.31 (I AD).
         Literature: very common in authors discussing Roman history, e.g. Polybius
         3.87.6, marked (II BC); Diodorus Siculus 12.80.7 (I BC); DH *AR* 5.73.1,
         marked (I BC); Jos. *AJ* 14.190 (I AD); Plut. *Cam.* 1.1 (I/II AD); App. *BC*
         1.pr.3 (I/II AD); Dio Cassius 8.36.26 (II/III AD); Eutropius 1.12 (IV AD);
         Hesych. as lemma δ 1836: δικτάτωρ· ὁ διπλασίαν τὴν ἀρχὴν ἔχων (V/VI AD);
         Malal. 9.1 (VI AD); Lyd. *Mag.* p. 54.8 (VI AD).
         Post-antique: survives as term for the Republican-era Roman office. *LBG* (*s.v.*
         δικάτωρ), Zervan (2019: 45), Kriaras (1968–), Triandaphyllidis (1909: 126).
         Modern δικτάτορας 'dictator': Babiniotis (2002), Andriotis (1967).
         Notes: forms derivatives δικτατωρεία, δικτατωρεύω, ἀντιδικτάτωρ. Freyburger-
         Galland (1997: 172–4, 1998: 140), Dubuisson (1985: 26), Famerie (1998:
         110–22), García Domingo (1979: 369), Strobach (1997: 194), Mason
         (1974: 4, 6, 7, 12, 38, 118, 166), Hofmann (1989: 92–3), Viscidi (1944:
         20), Immisch (1885: 337–8), *DGE*, LSJ. See §4.2.5, §4.6.1, §6.8, **§8.1.3**
         passage 41, §8.1.4, **§8.1.5**, §8.1.7, §9.5.2, §9.5.4, §10.1 n. 2, §10.2.1,
         §10.2.2 D, §10.3.2.

Deriv. of loan   δικτατωρ(ε)ία, δικτατορ(ε)ία (-ας, ἡ) 'dictatorship', from *dictātor* 'dictator' via
I BC – IV AD   δικτάτωρ + -ία.
         Literature: writers concerned with Roman history, e.g. DH *AR* 5.73.3 (I BC);
         Plut. *Fab.* 3.7 (I/II AD); Dio Cassius 40.46.1 (II/III AD); Eutropius 2.8
         (IV AD).
         Post-antique: modern δικτατορία 'dictatorship' (Babiniotis 2002; Andriotis
         1967) is revival not survival.
         Notes: meaning perhaps linked with *dictātūra* 'dictatorship'. Freyburger-
         Galland (1997: 174), Mason (1974: 6, 38), Hofmann (1989: 93 *s.v.*
         δικτάτωρ), *DGE* (*s.v.* δικτατορία), LSJ (*s.v.* δικτάτωρ). See §4.3.2 n. 75,
         §4.6.1, §6.8 n. 57, §8.1.5, §8.2.3, §10.2.2 D, §10.3.2.

Deriv. of loan   δικτατωρεύω, δικτατορεύω 'be dictator', from *dictātor* 'dictator' via δικτάτωρ +
I BC – III AD?   -εύω.
         Literature: DH *AR* 14.5.1 (I BC); Dio Cassius 43.1.1 etc. (II/III AD).
         Post-antique: few examples, which are unmarked but because of the word's
         transparent formation could be re-creations from δικτάτωρ rather than
         survival. *LBG.* Modern δικτατορεύω 'be dictator' (Babiniotis 2002 *s.v.*
         δικτατορία) is probably re-creation or revival.
         Notes: Freyburger-Galland (1997: 174), Mason (1974: 6, 38), Hofmann (1989:
         93 *s.v.* δικτάτωρ), LSJ. See §4.6.1, §6.8 n. 57, §8.1.5, §8.2.3, §10.2.2 D,
         §10.3.2.

foreign   διλατίων 'delay', from *dīlātiō* 'delay': Antec. in Latin script 4.13.10 *dilatio*
         (VI AD); later in Greek script. *LBG.*

foreign   διλατόριος, διλατώριος 'involving delay', from *dīlātōrius* 'concerned with
         deferment': Antec. in Latin script 4.13.10 *dilatoriae* etc. (VI AD); later in
         Greek script. Zilliacus (1935a: 184–5).

διληγάτωρ: see δηληγάτωρ.

foreign διλιγεντία 'care', from *dīligentia* 'care': Antec. in Latin script 4.1.13 *diligentian* etc. (VI AD); later in Greek script. Zilliacus (1935a: 184–5), *LBG*, Kriaras (1968–). See §9.5.6 n. 68.

Direct loan δίλωρος (-ον) 'having two epaulettes', from *dilōris* 'having two epaulettes' (*TLL*).
IV–V AD? Documents: perhaps *P.Oxy.* 1737.15 (II/III AD); *Chrest.Wilck.* 186.9 (IV AD); *SB* 9305.7 (IV AD); *P.Stras.* III.131.8 (IV AD); *SB* 11075.9 (V AD); perhaps *Stud.Pal.* III.407.1 (VI AD).
Notes: not attested in feminine; LSJ infers from form that it would be two-termination. Cervenka-Ehrenstrasser (2000: 244–5), Daris (1991a: 40, 1991c: 273), Meinersmann (1927: 14), *TLL* (*s.v. dilōris* 1185.72–3), *DGE*, LSJ, LSJ suppl. See §4.2.2, §9.2, §10.2.1, §10.2.2 D.

rare διμισ(σ)ωρία 'certificate of discharge', from *dīmissōriae* (*litterae*) 'document indicating that a case has been dismissed' (*TLL s.v. dīmissōrius*): papyrus *Chrest.Wilck.* 445.13 (II/III AD). Cervenka-Ehrenstrasser (2000: 245–6), Daris (1991a: 40), Hofmann (1989: 93), Meinersmann (1927: 14), *TLL* (*s.v. dīmissōrius* 1207.44), LSJ suppl.

rare διμόδιον 'vessel holding two pecks', from δι- 'two' + *modius* 'peck' via μόδιος: inscription *I.Tomis* 388 (II/III AD); Malal. 11.14 (VI AD). *LBG*, Lampe (1961), *DGE*. See §4.6.2.

δινάριον: see δηνάριον.

rare δίξεστον 'measure of two pints', from *sextārius* 'pint measure' via ξέστης: old scholion to Ar. *Th.* 347; with *bisextum* in Gloss. Ps.-Cyril. 278.3. *DGE*, LSJ. See §4.6.2.

Deriv. of loan διούγκιον, διούγγιον, διόνκιον, διόγκιον (-ου, τό) 'two ounces', 'one sixth of an
III AD – Byz. inheritance', from δι- 'two' + *uncia* 'one twelfth' via οὐγγία.
Documents: *P.Oxy.* 2273.Ar.10 (III AD).
Inscriptions: *SEG* LV.821.A3 in Latin script.
Literature: Orib. *Ecl.* 87.4 (IV AD); Just. *Codex* 6.4.4.16c, *Nov.* 18.5 etc. (VI AD); Antec. as a gloss on *sextans*, 2.14.5 (VI AD); with *sextans* in Gloss. Ps.-Cyril. 278.37.
Post-antique: numerous, with derivatives διόγκιος 'weighing two ounces', διόγκινον 'two-ounce weight'. *LBG*.
Notes: Cervenka-Ehrenstrasser (2000: 246), Filos (2010: 244, 249), Diethart (1998: 172), Avotins (1992), Daris (1991a: 41), *DGE*, LSJ, LSJ suppl. See §4.6.2, §10.2.2 E.

διπλοκάριος, διπλουκάριος: see δουπλικάριος.

not ancient διποτατεύω, δηποτατεύω 'delegate', from *dēputō* via δηποτᾶτος + -εύω: no ancient examples. Zilliacus (1935a: 222–3), *LBG*.

rare διπούνδιον, διπούντιον, a unit of weight and value from *dupondius/dipundius* 'two asses': Lyd. *Mens.* 4.157 (VI AD); Ps.-Galen, *De ponderibus* frags 60.15, 61.12 = Hultsch 1864: 235.5, 237.15. *LBG*, *DGE* (*s.v. διπούνδιος*).

rare διπούνδιος 'new recruit', from *dupondius/dipundius* 'two asses': Lyd. *Mens.* 4.157 (VI AD). Sophocles (1887), *DGE*.

not ancient   **διρεκτάριος** 'burglar', from *dīrēctārius* 'burglar' (*TLL s.v. dē(dī)rēctārius*): no
ancient examples. Zilliacus (1935a: 184–5), *LBG* (*s.v.* δερεκτάριος).

foreign   **διρέκτος** 'direct', 'immediate', from *dīrēctus* 'direct': Antec. in Latin script
1.14.1 *directan* etc. (VI AD); later in Greek script. Zilliacus (1935a: 184–5),
Sophocles (1887), *LBG*, Kriaras (1968–). See §9.5.6 n. 68, §10.3.1 n. 30.

non-existent?   **διρέπτωρ**, from *dīreptor* 'plunderer': no certain examples. Hofmann (1989: 93),
Cameron (1931: 244).

rare   **διριβιτώριον, διριβετώριον** 'building in which ballots were sorted', from
diribitōrium 'building in which ballots were sorted': Dio Cassius 55.8.3 etc.
(II/III AD). Sophocles (1887), *DGE*.

rare   **διριγεύω, δηριγεύω** 'escort', from *dīrigō* 'direct' + -εύω: Malal. 13.8.24 (VI
AD); often in Byzantine texts. Hofmann (1989: 93), *LBG* (*s.v.* δηριγεύω),
Triandaphyllidis (1909: 128), Lampe (1961), *DGE*.

Direct loan with   **δισέκτωρ, δησέκτωρ** (-ορος, ὁ), perhaps 'quarry engineer', apparently from *dēsecō*
suffix   'remove a part' (*TLL s.v.* 669.3) + -τωρ.
III–IV AD   Documents: O.Claud. inv. 7363.7 = Cuvigny 2016: 18 (III AD); *Stud.Pal.*
XX.75.i.22 (IV AD); *P.Erl.Diosp.* 1.148 (IV AD).
Post-antique: no survival. Δισεκτορία 'desertion' (*LBG*) is a different word,
perhaps from *dēsertiō* 'desertion'.
Notes: Cuvigny (2016: 20–1), Cervenka-Ehrenstrasser (2000: 246–7), Daris
(1991a: 41, with derivation from *disiciō*), Meinersmann (1927: 14), *DGE*,
LSJ. See §4.3.2, §6.8, §10.2.1, §10.2.2 J.

    δισιγνατ-: see δησιγνατ-.

foreign   **δισιοῦνκτιμ** 'separately', from *disiūnctim* 'separately': Antec. in Latin script 2.20.8
disiunctim (VI AD); later in Greek script.

rare   **δισκουσσίων, δυσκουσσίων** 'examination', from *discussiō* 'examination' (*TLL*):
Nil. 2.22.7 (V AD); Just. *Nov.* in Latin script 147.2 etc. (VI AD); Ath.Schol.
in Latin script 20.6.2 (VI AD). Avotins (1992), Hofmann (1989: 102–3),
Zilliacus (1935a: 184–5), *LBG*.

Direct loan   **δισκούσσωρ, δισκούσστωρ, δισκούρσωρ** (-ωρος, ὁ) 'auditor', from *discussor*
IV AD – Byz.   'investigator' (*TLL*).
Documents: *P.Stras.* VIII.735.3.28 (IV AD); perhaps *P.Petra* III.34.3 (VI AD).
Inscriptions: *SEG* VIII.310.6 (VI AD).
Literature: Just. *Codex* 1.4.26.4 in Latin script (VI AD).
Post-antique: limited survival. *LBG*.
Notes: Cervenka-Ehrenstrasser (2000: 247–8), Avotins (1989), Diethart (1998:
172), Daris (1991a: 41), Hofmann (1989: 94), Zilliacus (1935a: 184–5),
Lampe (1961), *DGE*, LSJ suppl. See §4.2.5, §10.2.1, §10.2.2 G.

rare   **δισπηνσάτωρ, δισπενσάτωρ** 'steward responsible for investing his master's
money', from *dispēnsātor* 'steward': inscription *I.Ephesos* 809.2; Antec. in
Latin script 3.26.10 *dispensatora* etc. (VI AD); later in Greek script. Zilliacus
(1935a: 184–5), *LBG*, *DGE*.

not ancient   **δισποσιτίων** 'ordering', from *dispositiō* 'ordering': no ancient examples. Zilliacus
(1935a: 184–5), *LBG*.

rare	**διστριβο(ῦ)τος, διστριβοῦ(ν)τος** 'distributed', from *distribūtus*, pf. part. of *distribuō* 'distribute': papyrus *Rom.Mil.Rec.* 74.1.5 etc. (II AD). Cervenka-Ehrenstrasser (2000: 248–9), Daris (1991a: 41), Mason (1974: 4, 39), Hofmann (1989: 95), Cavenaile (1951: 396), *DGE*.
foreign	**διστριβούω** 'distribute', from *distribuō* 'distribute': Antec. in Latin script 4.7.3 *distribuere* (VI AD); later in Greek script.
not ancient?	**διτάριος** 'making rich', perhaps from *dītō* 'enrich' or a related word: no certainly ancient examples. *LBG*, *TLL* (*s.v.* διταρίοις). See §8.1.7 n. 34.
foreign	*dōdrāns* 'three quarters of an inheritance': Antec. 2.14.5 (VI AD). See §7.1.1 passage 18.
rare	**δολάβρα, δαλάββρα**, a utensil, from *dolābra* 'pick': unpublished ostraca O.Dios inv. 371.8, 988.3 (both II AD).
foreign	*dolus* 'fraud': *Schol.Sinai.* 31 *dolov* (V/VI AD); Antec. 2.8.2 *dolu* etc. (VI AD). In these authors evidently distinct from native δόλος 'trick'; for the longer-term relationship between these words see Risch (1976: 894–7). Zilliacus (1935a: 184–5, 1937: 328). See §7.1.2, §7.1.3, §9.5.6 n. 56.
foreign	**δόλων** transliterating *dolō*, a weapon: Plut. *Gracchi* 10.9 (I/II AD). But δόλων 'dagger', 'secondary mast' (with derivative δολωνικός 'of a secondary mast') is probably not from *dolō*. Commentary on *P.Lond.* VII.2139.6, Hofmann (1989: 95), *DÉLG*, Frisk (1954–72: I.408), Beekes (2010), LSJ.
Direct loan **IV AD – modern**	**δομεστικός 1, δομεστικός** (-οῦ, ὁ), a palace official, from *domesticus*, a palace official (*TLL s.v.* 1871.77–1872.75). Documents: e.g. *P.Abinn.* 25.11 (IV AD); *P.Bour.* 19.3 (V AD); *P.Berl.Cohen* 19.2 (VI AD). Inscriptions: e.g. *I.Syringes* 1254.2 (IV AD); *MAMA* v.5.3 (IV/V AD); *I.Ephesos* 1352.3 (V AD); *SEG* XXXII.1554.A24, marked (VI AD). Literature: e.g. Dor.Poet. *Visio* 18, 86 (III/IV AD); Pall. *H.Laus.* 44.1.7 (IV/V AD); Nil. 2.32.1 (V AD); Barsanuph.Jo. I ep. 213.2n (VI AD). Post-antique: common, accented δομέστικος, forming derivatives δομεστικάτον 'office of the *domesticus*', δομεστικεύω 'serve as *domesticus*', etc. *LBG*, Zervan (2019: 45–6), Kriaras (1968–). Modern δομέστικος, δεμέστιχος 'Byzantine cantor': Babiniotis (2002), Andriotis (1967), Kahane and Kahane (1972–6: 531, 1982: 135), Triandaphyllidis (1909: 107) – but Meyer (1895: 21) sees Italian influence. Notes: Cervenka-Ehrenstrasser (2000: 249–52), Avotins (1989, 1992), Diethart (1998: 172), Drew-Bear (1972: 67–8), Daris (1991a: 41), Hofmann (1989: 96–7), Zilliacus (1935a: 184–5, 222–3, 1937: 328), Meinersmann (1927: 14–15), Lampe (1961), *DGE* (*s.v.* δομεστικός 2), LSJ suppl. See §4.2.4.1 n. 51, **§4.2.6**, §5.2.1, §10.2.1, §10.2.2 A.
rare	**δομε(σ)τικός 2** 'of the household', from *domesticus* 'of the household': papyrus *SB* 15255.1 (V/VI AD). Cervenka-Ehrenstrasser (2000: 249–52), Diethart (1998: 172), *LBG*, *DGE* (*s.v.* δομεστικός 1).
not ancient	**δομικίλιον, δομιτζίλιον** 'domicile', from *domicilium* 'domicile': no ancient examples. Zilliacus (1935a: 184–5), *LBG*.

foreign	δοµινατίων transliterating *dominātiō* 'dominion': Lyd. *Mag.* p. 16.7 (VI AD). *LBG*.
not ancient?	δοµινικός, δωµενικός 'of the ruler', from *dominicus* 'of the master or mistress': inscriptions *CIG* 9207.4; *LBW* 1408. Hofmann (1989: 103), *LBG*.
foreign	δόµινος transliterating *dominus* 'master': Palladas, *Anthologia Graeca* 10.44.4 (IV AD); Lyd. *Mag.* p. 16.8 in Latin script (VI AD). Binder (2000: 207–8), Sophocles (1887); for Byzantine syncopated δόµνος Zervan (2019: 46). See §7.2.1 n. 27.

δοµιτζίλιον: see δοµικίλιον.

Direct loan **I–II AD**	**Δοµιτιανός, Δοµιττιανός** (-οῦ, ὁ) 'Domitian' (an Egyptian month), from the name *Domitiānus*. Documents: e.g. *CPR* XV.25.B16 (I AD); *P.Oxy.* 237.8.43 (II AD). Notes: Hagedorn (2007), Scott (1931: 260–1), *DGE*, LSJ suppl. See §4.2.4.1 n. 51, §9.2, §10.2.1, §10.2.2 E.
name	**Δόµνα**, from *domina* 'mistress', probably only as name. Kriaras (1968–), Sophocles (1887), Meyer (1895: 21).

δον(ν)άτιβον: see δωνατίουον.

δοπλικάρις: see δουπλικάριος.

δοράκ(ε)ι(ν)ον: see δωράκινον.

rare	δορµιτώριον, δορµειτώριον, δωρµιτώριον 'litter' (the conveyance), from *dormītōrium* 'litter' (*TLL s.v. dormītōrius* 2036.37–42): Edict.Diocl. 15.34 etc. (IV AD). Hofmann (1989: 97), *TLL* (*s.v. dormītōrius* 2036.41), *DGE*.
foreign	δοτάλιος 'forming part of a dowry', from *dōtālis* 'forming part of a dowry': *Schol. Sinai.* in Latin script 11 *dotali* (V/VI AD); Antec. in Latin script 2.8.pr. *dotalion* (VI AD); later in Greek script. Zilliacus (1935a: 184–5), *LBG*, Kriaras (1968–). See §7.1.2, §9.5.6 n. 56.
foreign	δούβιος transliterating *dubius* 'uncertain': Strabo 3.1.9 (I BC/AD). Sophocles (1887).

δούκας: see δούξ.

rare	δουκᾶτον 'dukedom', from *ducātus, -ūs* 'ducal office' (*TLL*): Cyr.S. *Vit.Sab.* 150.1, 19 (VI AD); undated texts that may be ancient; common in Byzantine texts. Modern δουκάτο 'dukedom': Babiniotis (2002), Andriotis (1967), Meyer (1895: 21), with derivation from rare medieval variant *ducātum* (Du Cange 1883–7). Hofmann (1989: 97), Diethart (2006: 14), *LBG*, Zervan (2019: 46–7), Kriaras (1968–), Lampe (1961), *DGE*.
rare	δουκάτωρ, δουκάτορ 'military leader', from *ducātor* 'leader' (*TLL*): inscription *SEG* XXXI.238.5 (III AD); possibly paraliterary papyrus P.Berol. inv. 21860.34 = Dickey 2012–15: II.281 (IV AD); Byzantine texts. *LBG*, *DGE*.

δουκενάριος: see δουκηνάριος.

Direct loan with influence
II–III AD

δουκηναρία (-ας, ἡ) 'assessment/sum of 200,000 sesterces', probably fem. subst. of *ducēnārius* 'owning or receiving 200,000 sesterces' with influence from -ία.

Documents: *P.Oxy.* 1274.14 (III AD).

Inscriptions: *I.Ephesos* 894.14 (II AD); *IGUR* II.424.2 (II/III AD).

Notes: Cervenka-Ehrenstrasser (2000: 252–3), Daris (1991a: 41), Hofmann (1989: 98), LSJ (*s.v.* δουκηνάριος). See §4.2.3.1, §4.4, §6.2, §10.2.1, §10.2.2 G.

Direct loan
II AD – Byz.

δουκηνάριος, δουκενάριος, δουκινάριος, δωκενάριος (-ου, ὁ), a title of rank (originally one with an assessment of 200,000 sesterces), from *ducēnārius* 'owning or receiving 200,000 sesterces'.

Documents: e.g. *P.Oxy.* 1711.5 (III AD); *P.Abinn.* 42.1 (IV AD).

Inscriptions: common, e.g. *SEG* XLIV.1210.7 (I/II AD); *I.Ephesos* 627.9 etc. (II AD); *I.Cos Paton* 102.14 etc. (III AD); *I.Sardis* I.170.2 (IV AD); *SEG* XXXVII.1286 (V AD); *IG* X.II.II.152.2 (V/VI AD).

Literature: Eus. *HE* 7.30.8 (IV AD); Athan. *Apol.Sec.* 76.1.3 (IV AD); Lyd. *Mag.* p. 76.24 etc. (VI AD). Unverified example (III AD) in Zilliacus (1937: 323, 328).

Post-antique: survives. *LBG* (*s.v.* δουκενάριος), Cervenka-Ehrenstrasser (2000: 253).

Notes: Cervenka-Ehrenstrasser (2000: 253–4), Daris (1991a: 41), Mason (1974: 4, 39), Hofmann (1989: 98), Zilliacus (1935a: 184–5, 222–3, 1937: 328), Meinersmann (1927: 15), Lampe (1961), *DGE*, LSJ, LSJ suppl. See §4.2.4.1 n. 50, §6.2, §10.2.1, §10.2.2 D.

Direct loan
VI AD

δουκιανός (-ή, -όν) 'of the *dux*', from *duciānus* 'of the *dux*' (*TLL*).

Documents: *P.Cair.Masp.* 67167.3, 67283.1.3 (both VI AD).

Inscriptions: *I.Philae* 216.10 (VI AD).

Notes: short-lived, more Latinate alternative to δουκικός. Cf. δουκανιός (Lampe 1961). Cervenka-Ehrenstrasser (2000: 254, but one example is not a papyrus), Daris (1991a: 41), Hofmann (1989: 98), *LBG*, *TLL* (*s.v. duciānus* 2134.78–9), LSJ suppl. See §4.2.2, §10.2.1, §10.2.2 D, **§10.3.2**.

Deriv. of loan
IV AD – Byz.

δουκικός (-ή, -όν) 'of the *dux*', from *dux* 'leader' via δούξ + -ικός.

Documents: e.g. *SB* 12854.5 (V AD); *BGU* XIX.2817.3 (V/VI AD); *P.Berl.Zill.* 6.7 (VI AD).

Inscriptions: Kaibel 1878: no. 446.6 (IV AD); *IGLS* XIII.1.9040.6 (V AD); *IGLS* XIII.1.9046.23 etc. (V/VI AD); *IGLS* XIII.1.9130.5 (VI AD); *SEG* XXXII.1554.A10 etc. (VI AD); *SEG* IX.356.7 etc. (VI AD); perhaps *IGLS* II.590.1.

Literature: Just. *Nov.* 25.1 etc. (VI AD).

Post-antique: common. *LBG*, Kriaras (1968–).

Notes: probably connected to, but not actually borrowed from, *ducālis* and *duciānus* (*TLL*). Cervenka-Ehrenstrasser (2000: 255), Avotins (1992), Daris (1991a: 41), Hofmann (1989: 99 *s.v.* δούξ), Cavenaile (1952: 197), Zilliacus (1935a: 222–3), Meinersmann (1927: 15), *TLL* (*s.v.* δουκικός), LSJ, LSJ suppl. See §4.6.1, §8.1.7 n. 34, §10.2.2 D, §10.3.2.

δουκινάριος: see δουκηνάριος.

rare   **δουκτάριον** 'rope used for hauling', from *ductārium*, neut. subst. of *ductārius* 'for hauling' (*TLL*): ostraca *O.Claud.* IV.817.2 (I/II AD), 804.2 (II AD); Edict. Diocl. 10.4 in *SEG* XXXVII.335.iii.8 (IV AD). Two independent adaptations from Latin? LSJ suppl.

not ancient   **δουλκιράδιξ** apparently transliterating unattested plant name *dulcirādīx* 'sweet root': interpolation in Dsc. 3.5 RV. *TLL* (*s.v. dulcirādix*). See §8.1.7.

non-existent   **δούλκις**, cited by Sophocles (1887) as from *dulcis* 'sweet': superseded reading for δουλκιράδιξ (*q.v.*) in Dsc. 3.5 RV.

Direct loan
III AD – modern   **δούξ** (δουκός, ὁ), a title, from *dux* 'leader' (a title in the late Empire, cf. English 'duke': *TLL s.v. dux* 2323.21–2324.49).

Documents: common, e.g. *P.Abinn.* 3.5 (IV AD); *P.Mich.* XI.611.4 (V AD); *P.Cair.Masp.* 67004.21 (VI AD). Unverified example (III AD) supposedly in Hatzitsolis (1994: no. 9.10).

Inscriptions: e.g. *SEG* XVII.770.10 (III AD); *SEG* XXXV.1537 (IV AD); *IGLS* XIII.1.9115.4 (V AD); *IGLS* XXI.II.155.2 (VI AD).

Literature: common, e.g. Athan. *Apol.Sec.* 67.3.5 (IV AD); Nil. 2.261.1 (V AD); Hesych. as lemma δ 2259 (V/VI AD); Just. *Nov.* 22.14 (VI AD). Unverified examples (III AD) in Zilliacus (1937: 322–3, 328).

Post-antique: common, forming derivatives δούκαινα/δούκισσα 'wife of the *dux*', δουκεύω 'serve as *dux*', etc. *LBG*, Zervan (2019: 47–8), Kriaras (1968–), Triandaphyllidis (1909: 126). Modern δούκας 'duke' and derivatives: Babiniotis (2002), Andriotis (1967), Meyer (1895: 21).

Notes: forms derivative δουκικός. Cervenka-Ehrenstrasser (2000: 256–60), Gonis (2003: 94), Avotins (1992), Daris (1991a: 41–2), Mason (1974: 39), Hofmann (1989: 98–9), Viscidi (1944: 13–14), Zilliacus (1935a: 222–3, 1937: 328), Meinersmann (1927: 15), Immisch (1885: 358), *TLL* (*s.v. dux* 2323.57–2324.49), Lampe (1961), *DGE*, LSJ, LSJ suppl. See §4.2.5, §4.6.1, §8.2.3 n. 51, §10.2.1, §10.2.2 D.

not ancient?   **δούπλα** 'double', 'double price', 'double penalty', from *dupla*, fem. subst. of *duplus* 'double': superseded reading of *P.Abinn.* 7.17 (IV AD); Byzantine legal texts. Hofmann (1989: 99), Meinersmann (1927: 15, 61, both *s.v.* τουπλας), *LBG*, Kriaras (1968–).

foreign   **δουπλάριος** transliterating *duplāris/duplārius* 'double' (*TLL*) and meaning 'with double pay': *SEG* LXV.1408.C23 (V/VI AD).

Direct loan
I–V AD   **δουπλικάριος, δουπλικιάριος, δουπλικίρις, δουπλεικάρειος, δουπλικιαίριος, διπλο(υ)κάρ(ι)ος, τιπλοκάριος, δοφλικάρις, δοπλικάρις** (-ου, ὁ) 'soldier receiving double pay', from *duplicārius* (with many alternative spellings) 'soldier receiving double rations or double of some other reward' (*TLL*).

Documents: e.g. *BGU* II.591.2 (I AD); *O.Claud.* II.366.1 (II AD); *BGU* IV.1021.3 (III AD); *P.Eleph.Wagner* I.100.9 (III/IV AD).

Inscriptions: e.g. *I.Portes du désert* 80.2 (II AD); *SEG* VIII.608.9 (II/III AD); *SEG* VIII.346.2 (V AD).

Notes: Cervenka-Ehrenstrasser (2000: 260–2), Diethart (2002: 150–1), Daris (1991a: 42), Mason (1974: 4, 8, 39 *s.vv.* διπλοκάρις, δουπλικάριος), Hofmann (1989: 99–100), Cavenaile (1951: 403), Meinersmann (1927: 15), *TLL* (*s.v. duplicārius* 2273.10–18), LSJ (*s.v.* διπλοκάριος) and LSJ suppl. (*s.vv.* διπλοκάριος, δουπλικάριος). See §2.3, §4.2.4.1 n. 50, **§4.4**, §6.1, §10.2.1, §10.2.2 C.

foreign | **δουπλικατίων** 'reply to a rebuttal', from *duplicātiō* 'reply to a rebuttal': Antec. in Latin script 4.14.1 *duplication* etc. (VI AD); later in Greek script. *LBG*.

rare | **δουπλικιαρία** 'rank of *duplicarius*', from *duplicārius* via δουπλικάριος (*q.v.*): in phrase ἀπὸ δουπλικιαρίας 'former *duplicarius*', *SEG* LXVI.1842.4 (III AD).

δοφλικάρις: see δουπλικάριος.

rare | **δράγλη** 'javelin', from *trāgula* 'spear with a throwing-strap': papyrus *P.Lond.* II.191.12 (II AD). Cervenka-Ehrenstrasser (2000: 262–3), Binder (2000: 194–5), Schirru (2013: 316), Daris (1991a: 42), Hofmann (1989: 100), Meinersmann (1927: 15), LSJ.

Direct loan IV AD – Byz. | **δρακονάριος, δρακωνάριος, τρακωνάριος** (-ου, ὁ) 'standard-bearer', from *dracōnārius* 'standard-bearer' (*TLL*), itself ultimately from δράκων 'serpent'.

Documents: e.g. *SB* 12844.6 (V AD); *CPR* XXIV.15.23 etc. (V/VI AD); *SB* 16043.Ar.10 (VI AD); *P.Lond.* I.113.1.74 etc. (VI AD).

Inscriptions: e.g. Ramsay 1895–7: 529 no. 373.9 (IV AD); *I.Anazarbos* 651.5 (V/VI AD); *SEG* XXXII.1554.A36 etc. (VI AD).

Literature: Thdt. *Ep.Sirm.* 59.8, 134.25 (V AD); Lyd. *Mag.* p. 72.15, marked (VI AD).

Post-antique: survives. *LBG* (*s.vv.* δρακονάριος, δρακοντάριος), Triandaphyllidis (1909: 129).

Notes: forms derivatives ἀποδρακωνάριος, πρωτοδρακωνάριος. Cervenka-Ehrenstrasser (2000: 263–4), Daris (1991a: 42), Hofmann (1989: 100–1), Zilliacus (1935a: 222–3), Meinersmann (1927: 16), *TLL* (*s.v. dracōnārius*), Lampe (1961 *s.v.* δρακονάριος), *DGE*, LSJ suppl. (*s.v.* δρακωνάριος). See §2.1 n. 8, §4.2.4.1 n. 50, §10.2.1, §10.2.2 C.

not ancient? | **δραύκιον** 'necklace', perhaps from *draucus* 'athlete', seems to appear in Gloss. Ps.-Cyril. 280.56, but δράκιον (a wearable item) is probably a better reading; δραύκιον may genuinely occur in Byzantine texts. *LBG*, *TLL* (*s.v. draukion*), *DGE* (*s.vv.* δράκιον, δραύκιον), LSJ, LSJ suppl. (*s.v.* δράκιον). See §8.1.7 n. 34.

δρόγγος: see δροῦγγος.

Direct loan II–VI? AD | **δρομεδάριος, δρομαδάριος, δρομοδάριος, δρομιδάριος, δρομιτάριος** (-ου, ὁ) 'camel-rider', 'camel', from *dromadārius* 'soldier mounted on a camel', itself from δρομάς 'running camel'.

Documents: e.g. *SB* 6221.4 (II AD); *BGU* III.827.31 (II/III AD); *P.Oxy.* 1652A.6, 1652B.6 (IV AD); *P.Kellis* I.79.7 (IV AD); *O.Douch.* IV.375.4 (IV/V AD); *P.Ness.* III.35.1 etc. (VI AD).

Inscriptions: e.g. *Agora de Palmyre* IA.05.6, p. 154 (II AD); *SEG* XXXVIII.1667 (II/III AD).

Notes: usual meaning is 'camel-rider'; only in *P.Ness.* (where it is consistently abbreviated δρο and so could be another word) does it seem to mean 'camel'. Cervenka-Ehrenstrasser (2000: 264–5), Cuvigny (2006: 343–5), Biville (1990–5: 1.39, 1992: 235), Daris (1991a: 42), Hofmann (1989: 101), Meinersmann (1927: 16), *DÉLG* (*s.v.* δραμεῖν), Frisk (1954–72: 1.419), Beekes (2010 *s.v.* δρόμος), *DGE* (*s.v.* δρομαδάριος), LSJ (*s.v.* δρομαδάριος). See §4.2.4.1 n. 50, §10.2.1, §10.2.2 C.

not Latin?	**δρομωνάριος** 'running' (of camels) is in meaning a poor match for *dromōnārius*, a rower and a ship (*TLL*), or *dromō*, a ship (*TLL*), or δρόμων, a ship. Perhaps a Greek formation from ἔδραμον, aorist of τρέχω 'run', + -άριος. Hofmann (1989: 101), *TLL* (*s.v. dromōnārius*), Lampe (1961), *DGE*.
not ancient	**δρουγγαρᾶτον**, an office in the army, from *drungus* 'troop' (*TLL*): no ancient examples. Hofmann (1989: 101), Viscidi (1944: 13), *LBG*.
not ancient	**δρουγγάριος** 'troop-leader', suggested by Cameron (1931: 245) as a borrowing of medieval *drungārius* 'troop-leader' (Du Cange 1883–7): no ancient examples. *TLL* (*s.v. drungus* 2071.9–10) considers it a VIII AD derivative of *drungus* 'troop'. Zilliacus (1935a: 222–3), *LBG*, Zervan (2019: 49), Kriaras (1968–), Lampe (1961).
not ancient	**δρουγγιστί** 'in a swarm', from *drungus* 'troop' (*TLL*) via δροῦγγος: no ancient examples. Hofmann (1989: 102 *s.v.* δροῦγγος), Zilliacus (1935a: 222–3), *LBG*.
rare	**δροῦγγος, δρόγγος** 'troop', from *drungus* 'troop' (*TLL*): John Chrysostom, *Epistulae ad Olympiadem* 9.2.30 Malingrey (IV/V AD); probably not Epiph. *Pan.* 11.239.12 (IV AD), where the meaning 'nose' suggests a different etymology; common in Byzantine texts, forming derivatives δρουγγιστί 'in a swarm', δρουγγάριος 'troop-leader', etc. Binder (2000: 141), Hofmann (1989: 102), Viscidi (1944: 13), Zilliacus (1935a: 145, 222–3; 1937: 322, 328, citing unverified example from VI AD), *LBG*, Kriaras (1968–), *TLL* (*s.v. drungus* 2071.9–10), Lampe (1961), LSJ suppl. (*s.v.* δρόγγος).
not Latin	**δροῦνα** 'beginning', said by Hesych. δ 2410 (V/VI AD) to be Etruscan. Hofmann (1989: 102), LSJ.
Direct loan with suffix **I AD**	**Δρουσιεύς** (-έως, ὁ?) 'of Drusus' (an Egyptian month), from the name *Drūsus* + -ιεύς. Documents: e.g. *Stud.Pal.* XXII.173.36 (I AD); *P.Mich.* II.121r.3.xiii (I AD). Notes: Scott (1931: 252–3), Bagnall (2009: 181), Cavenaile (1951: 396), *DGE*, LSJ suppl. See §4.3.2, §9.2, §10.2.1, §10.2.2 E.
Direct loan with suffix **I AD**	**Δρουσιλλῆος, Δρουσίλλε(ι)ος, Δρουσίλλα** (-ον or -ης) 'of Drusilla' (an Egyptian month), from the name *Drūsilla* + -ῆος/-ειος. Documents: e.g. *SB* 14632.4 (I AD); *P.Mich.* v.321.19 (I AD). Notes: Scott (1931: 245, 251–2), Cavenaile (1951: 396), *DGE* (*s.v.* Δρουσίλλειος), LSJ suppl. See §4.3.2, §9.2, §10.2.1, §10.2.2 E.

not Latin? **δρύππα**, a type of olive, and derivative δρύππιος 'planted with olive trees', perhaps from *druppa* 'almost-ripe olive', or *vice versa: Anthologia Graeca* 6.299.4 (II/I BC); Athenaeus 2.56b, marked (II/III AD). Hofmann (1989: 102), *DÉLG* (*s.v.* δρυπεπής), Beekes (2010 *s.v.* δρυπεπής), *TLL* (*s.v. druppa* 2071.11–16), Walde and Hofmann (1938–54 *s.v. druppa*), *DGE*, LSJ.

δυνάριον: see δηνάριον.

δυσκουσσίων: see δισκουσσίων.

foreign **δῶ** 'give', from *dō* 'give': Antec. in Latin script 2.21.pr. *do*, 3.17.3 *dare*, etc. (VI AD); later sometimes in Greek script.

δωκενάριος: see δουκηνάριος.

δωμενικός: see δομινικός.

δωμεστικός: see δομεστικός 1.

Direct loan
II AD – Byz. **δωνατίουον, δωνάτιβον, δον(ν)άτιβον, δωνάτιον** (-ου, τό) 'money given to soldiers as a gratuity from the emperor', from *dōnātīvum* 'money given to soldiers as a gratuity from the emperor'.
Documents: e.g. *O.Claud.* II.227.19 (II AD); *P.Vet.Aelii* 10.11 (III AD); *P.Panop.Beatty* 2.54, etc. (III/IV AD); *P.Oxy.* 1047.4 (IV AD).
Literature: unverified example (IV AD) in Zilliacus (1937: 323, 328).
Post-antique: survives. *LBG* (*s.v.* δωνατίβαι).
Notes: reversing the usual spelling changes, examples of II and III AD are spelled with β and ones of IV AD with ου. Cervenka-Ehrenstrasser (2000: 266–7), Daris (1991a: 42, 43), Hofmann (1989: 103), Zilliacus (1937: 328), Meinersmann (1927: 16), LSJ suppl. See §4.2.4.1 n. 55, §10.2.1, §10.2.2 A, §12.2.1.

Direct loan
IV AD – modern **δωράκινον, δωράκεινον, δοράκ(ε)ινον, ῥοδάκινον, δωράκιον, δοράκιον** (-ου, τό), a kind of peach, from *dūracinum*, a kind of peach (*TLL s.v. dūracinus* 2287.22–40).
Documents: *P.Mich.* XIV.680.9 (III/IV AD); *P.Ryl.* IV.630/637.342 etc. (IV AD); *SB* 15302.55 etc. (V AD).
Literature: *Coll.Herm.* ME 8c (II–IV AD); Gregorius Nyssenus, *Epistulae* 20.11 Pasquali (IV AD); Ps.-Palchus, Cumont and Boll 1904: 182.17 (V/VI AD?); Alex.Trall. 1.523.27 etc. (VI AD); Hieroph. *Nut.* 10.5, Πῶς 463.10 etc. (VI AD); scholia to Nic. *Ther.* 764a, *Alex.* 99c; with *duracina* in glossaries, e.g. Gloss. Ps.-Cyril. 282.42.
Post-antique: survives, forming derivative ῥοδακινοκόκαλον 'peach pit'. *LBG* (*s.vv.* δωράκινον, ῥοδάκινον), Triandaphyllidis (1909: 107). Modern ρωδάκινο, ροδάκινο 'peach' and derivatives: Babiniotis (2002), Andriotis (1967, 1974: 218).
Notes: the -ιον variant occurs only in the two later papyri. Forms derivatives μηλοδωράκινον, ῥοδακινέα. Cervenka-Ehrenstrasser (2000: 267–9), Volk (1991: 309–10), Shipp (1979: 225), Daris (1991a: 43), Hofmann (1989: 103–4), *DÉLG*, Beekes (2010), *TLL* (*s.v. dūracinus* 2287.24–9), *DGE*, LSJ (*s.vv.* δωράκινον 'clingstone peach', ῥοδάκινον 'nectarine'), LSJ suppl. (*s.vv.* δωράκινον, δωράκιον). See §4.2.4.1 n. 55, §8.2.3 n. 51, §10.2.1, §10.2.2 I.

δωρμιτώριον: see δορμιτώριον.

E

not Latin?	**ἑβδομαδάριος** 'deacon responsible for the weekly service' (with derivative ἀρχιεβδομ(αδ)άριος 'chief hebdomarius'), perhaps from *hebdomadārius* 'person who does something on a weekly basis' (*TLL*), but probably a Greek formation from ἑβδομάς 'week' + -άριος. Hofmann (1989: 104), *LBG* (*s.vv.* ἑβδομαδάρης, ἑβδομαδάριος), Kriaras (1968–), Lampe (1961), *DGE*, LSJ suppl. (*s.v.* ἑβδομάριος).
foreign	**ἔβεντον, εὐέντον** 'outcome', from *ēventum* 'outcome': Antec. in Latin script 1.6.3 *eventon* (VI AD); Just. *Nov.* 22.28 in Latin script (VI AD). Zilliacus (1935a: 186–7), Sophocles (1887 *s.v.* εὐέντον).
Direct loan **II AD – modern**	**ἐβίσκος, ἰβίσκος** (-ου, ἡ) 'marsh mallow' (a plant), from *hibiscum/hibiscus* 'marsh mallow' (*TLL*). Literature: Erot. *Voc.Hipp.* 113.10, marked (I AD); Dsc. 3.146.1 etc., marked (I AD); Galen XI.867.4 etc. Kühn (II AD); Orib. *Col.* 11.α.30 etc. (IV AD); *Hippiatr.* e.g. *Hippiatr.Par.* (Pel.) 142 (V AD?); Aëtius 1.96.1 etc. (VI AD). Post-antique: survives. *LBG* (*s.vv.* ἔβισκος, ἰβίσκος, βίσκος). Modern ιβίσκος 'hibiscus': Babiniotis (2002), Andriotis (1967). Notes: Binder (2000: 130), Hofmann (1989: 105), *DÉLG*, Frisk (1954–72: 1.707), Beekes (2010), *TLL* (*s.v. hibiscum* 2691.9–24), LSJ (*s.vv.* ἐβίσκος, ἰβίσκος). See §4.2.4.1 n. 58, §9.5.3 passage 63, §10.2.1, §10.2.2 L.
rare	**ἐβούλιον**, a plant, from *ebulum* 'dwarf elder' + -ιον: *Hippiatr.Berl.* (Hierocles) 87.10 (IV/V AD?).
foreign	**ἔβουλον, ἔβουλουμ, ἔβουλους** transliterating *ebulum* 'dwarf elder': *Hippiatr. Berl.* 33.22; interpolation in Dsc. 4.173.4 RV. *LBG*, Sophocles (1887 *s.v.* ἔβουλους).
	ἐγγαρ-: see ἀγγαρ-.
	ἔγεστα: see ἄγεστα.
rare	**ἐγκροστόω** 'veneer with marble', from *incrustō* 'cover with a layer of something' with influence from ἐν 'in' + -όω: inscriptions *SEG* XVII.596.7 (III AD?); perhaps *Corinth* VIII.I.318. Binder (2000: 120), Hofmann (1989: 105), Cameron (1931: 247), LSJ, LSJ suppl.
	ἐγπήτιτον: see ἐξπέδιτον.
not ancient	**ἔδερα** transliterating *hedera* 'ivy': interpolations in Dsc. 2.179 RV etc. Sophocles (1887).
foreign	**ἔδερε** transliterating inf. of *edō* 'eat' (normally *esse*, but *edere* attested: *TLL*): Plut. *Mor.* 727a (I/II AD). Strobach (1997: 195).
foreign	**ēdīcō** 'proclaim': Antec. 1.2.6 *edicere* (VI AD).
	ἔδικτον: see ἤδικτον.
	Εἰανουάριος: see Ἰανουάριος.

Direct loan
II BC – Byz.

Εἰδοί, Ἰδοί, Εἰδυοί, Εἰδυιοί (-ῶν, αἱ) 'Ides', from *Īdūs* (-*uum*, fem. pl.) 'Ides'.
  Documents: numerous but often with conversion to another dating system,
    e.g. *P.Hever* 62.a8 (II AD); *SB* 16167.5 (III AD); *P.Cair.Isid.* 117.10 (IV AD);
    P.Petra 1.2.5 (VI AD).
  Inscriptions: common, e.g. *CID* IV.119F.1 (II BC); *I.Knidos* 33.a2 (I BC); *IG*
    XII.VI.1.163.5 (I AD); Dumont and Homolle 1892: 441 no. 110b.12 (II
    AD); *IG* XII.VII.53.38 (III AD); *SEG* LI.1438.3 (IV AD); *I.Mylasa* 612.8 (V
    AD).
  Literature: common in Roman contexts, e.g. DH *AR* 10.59.1 (I BC); Jos.
    AJ 14.145 (I AD); Plut. *Rom.* 25.6 (I/II AD); Eus. *PE* 4.16.18 (IV AD);
    Hippiatr.Berl. (Theomnestus) 97.8 (IV AD?); Malal. 18.71.16 (VI AD); Lyd.
    Mens. 4.29 (VI AD).
  Post-antique: common. Triandaphyllidis (1909: 120).
  Notes: spelling with ει probably represents early Latin use of *ei* for *ī* (cf. §4.1.2).
    García Domingo (1979: 50, 97, 388), Solin (2008), Famerie (1998: 122–3),
    Strobach (1997: 195), Hofmann (1989: 105–6), Meinersmann (1927:
    16), Lampe (1961 *s.v.* ἰδοί), *DGE*, LSJ (*s.vv.* εἰδοί, εἰδυιοί). See §4.2.2 n. 32,
    §4.2.4.2, §4.3.2 n. 75, **§8.1.4**, §10.2.1, §10.2.2 E.

εἰνδικτίων: see ἰνδικτίων.

Εἰούλιος: see Ἰούλιος.

εἰσικι-: see ἰσικι-.

εἰσκότλα: see σκούτλα.

not Latin? **εἴσκυρσις**, perhaps 'attack' and if so related to *incursus, -ūs* 'attack': Isidore of
    Pelusium, *PG* LXXVIII.432a (V AD). Sophocles (1887), Lampe (1961).

not Latin? **εἰσπύλλα**, perhaps 'needle' and if so from *spīnula* 'little thorn' (L&S): inscription
    SEG VII.371.11 (II AD). Hofmann (1989: 106).

εἰσσικι-: see ἰσικι-.

non-existent? **ἐκβιργίλιος**, perhaps 'from Virgil' and if so from *Vergilius* 'Virgil': unverified
    example in Zilliacus (1937: 322, 328).

non-existent? **ἐκκεκελλήρικεν**, a (corrupt?) lemma in Hesych. ε 1428 (V/VI AD), is suggested by
    Immisch (1885: 307–8) to be from otherwise unattested ἐκ-κελληρίζω from
    cella 'room' via κέλλα. LSJ (*s.v.* ἐκ⟨κε⟩κελλήρικεν).

ἐκκουσ(σ)εύω: see ἐξκουσεύω.

ἔκκυης: see ἔκυες.

rare **ἐκλεκέβρα, ἐκλεκέβρη**, plant name from *elecebra* (*TLL s.v.* 2. *elecebra*): *Hippiatr.Par.*
    (Apsyrtus) 697 (III/IV AD?). *TLL* (*s.v.* 327.72–8), *DGE* (*s.v.* ἐλέκεβρα).

ἐκξάκτωρ: see ἐξάκτωρ.

not ancient? **ἐκουέστρης** 'equestrian', from *equester* 'equestrian': inscription *IG* V.I.1268.3.
    Mason (1974: 6, 42), *DGE* (*s.v.* ἐκουέστρις).

not ancient **ἐκουῖνος** and **ἐκυῖνος** transliterating *equīnus* 'equine': interpolations in Dsc.
    3.71 RV, 4.47 RV. Sophocles (1887).

ἐκουσ(σ)ᾶτος: see ἐξκουσᾶτος.

ἐκπελ(λ)εύω: see ἐξπελλεύω.

rare   ἐκσελλίζω 'unseat', from unattested *exsellō + -ίζω (thus *TLL s.v. exsello*) or ἐξ 'out of' + *sella* 'seat' via σέλλα + -ίζω: Malal. 4.19.17 (VI AD). Lampe (1961 *s.v.* ἐκσελλίζομαι), *DGE*, Kriaras (1968–). See §8.1.7.

non-existent?   ἐκσημιαφόρος 'former standard-bearer', apparently a calque of *ex signiferō* (*OLD s.v. ex* 13b) formed with ἐκ or *ex* + σημειοφόρος 'standard-bearer': perhaps inscription Buckler *et al.* 1924: 71 no. 103. Hofmann (1989: 108), *DGE* (*s.v.* ἐκσημειαφόρος), E. A. Barber (1968, but not in LSJ suppl.).

foreign   ἐκσκεπτάριος, ἐξκεπτάριος, a title apparently transliterating unattested *exceptārius* 'corn-receiver': Lyd. *Mag.* p. 154.2 (VI AD). Hofmann (1989: 108), *LBG*, *TLL* (*s.v. exceptārius*). See §8.1.7.

ἐκσκέπτωρ, ἐκσκέτωρ: see ἐξκέπτωρ.

ἐκσκουβιτ-: see ἐξκουβιτ-.

ἐκσπέδιτον: see ἐξπέδιτον.

ἐκσπελ(λ)ευ-, ἐκσπηλευ-: see ἐξπελλευ-.

ἐκσπούνκτωρ: see ἐξπούγκτωρ.

rare   ἔκσταβλα (neut. pl.?) 'leaving horses outside overnight', from ἐκ 'out' + *stabulum* 'stable' via στάβλον: *V.Dan.Styl. A.* 69.11 (V AD). Zilliacus (1937: 328), *LBG*.

Direct loan
III–IV AD   ἐκστρανήιος, ἐξτράνιος, ἐξτράνεος, ἐκστράνιος, ἐκτράνιος, ἐκτράνεος, ἐκτράνος (-α, -ον) 'unrelated', from *extrāneus* 'outside the family or household'.
Inscriptions: *SEG* LVII.1582.2 (II/III AD); *SEG* LVII.1624.6 (III AD?); *IG* II/III².v.13389.4 (IV AD); *TAM* III.I.481.2, 541.3, 608.3.
Literature: Antec. in Latin script 2.19.pr. *extraneoi* etc. (VI AD).
Notes: Schwyzer (1929), Hofmann (1989: 116), Zilliacus (1935a: 186–7), *DGE*, LSJ suppl. See §4.2.2, §10.2.1, §10.2.2 N.

ἐκστραορδιν-: see ἐξτραορδιν-.

ἐκσφούγκτωρ: see ἐξπούγκτωρ.

ἐκσφουνγευ-: see ἐξπουγγευ-.

ἐκτράνεος, ἐκτράνιος, ἐκτράνος: see ἐκστρανήιος.

ἐκτραορδινάριος: see ἐξτραορδινάριος.

rare   ἔκυες, ἔκυης, ἔκκυης 'knight', 'rider', from *eques* 'knight', 'rider': inscriptions *SEG* LIII.1907.5 (II/III AD); Seyrig 1941: 219 nos. 1, 3. *DGE* (*s.v.* ἔκυης).

not ancient   ἐκυινᾶλις apparently transliterating unattested *equīnālis* 'horse-tail plant': interpolation in Dsc. 4.46 RV. Sophocles (1887 *s.v.* ἐκυνᾶλις), *TLL* (*s.v. equīnālis*). See §8.1.7.

ἐκυῖνος: see ἐκουῖνος.

non-existent?	**ἐκυτᾶτος** 'mounted' (of a military unit), from *equitātus* 'provided with cavalry': perhaps inscription *SB* 4591.4 (I/II AD), but the stone has εκυτατᾳρ, perhaps for ἑκατοντράρχου. Daris (1991a: 43), Mason (1974: 6, 42), Hofmann (1989: 109), Zilliacus (1935a: 224–5), Meinersmann (1927: 16), *DGE*.
non-existent?	**ἐκύτιον**, plant name from *equisaetum* 'horse-tail plant': variant reading for σκυτίον in interpolation in Dsc. 4.47 RV. Hofmann (1989: 109), Sophocles (1887).
not Latin?	**ἐκφούγιν**, perhaps 'place of refuge' and if so from *effugium* 'means of escape': inscription *SEG* 11.727.4. Hofmann (1989: 109), Cameron (1931: 245), *DGE*, LSJ.
	ἐλέκεβρα: see ἐκλεκέβρα.
foreign	**ἐλεκτίων** 'choice', from *ēlēctiō* 'choice': Antec. in Latin script 2.20.23 *electiona* (VI AD); later in Greek script. Zilliacus (1935a: 184–5).
foreign	**ἐμαγκιπατεύω** 'emancipate' (esp. from the power of the *paterfamilias*), from *ēmancipātus* (pf. part. of *ēmancipō* 'emancipate') (via ἐμαγκιπᾶτος?) + -εύω: Antec. in Latin script 3.1.13 *emancipateutheis* etc. (VI AD); later in Greek script. Zilliacus (1935a: 184–5), *LBG*, Sophocles (1887). See §9.5.6 n. 68.
Direct loan V AD – Byz.	**ἐμαγκιπατίων, ἐμαγκηπατίων** (-ονος/-ωνος, ἡ) 'emancipation', from *ēmancipātiō* 'emancipation'. Literature: *Carth.* 256.7 (V AD); Just. *Nov.* 118.4, but in Latin script 81.pr. etc. (VI AD); Antec. in Latin script 1.12.6 *emancipationa* etc. (VI AD). Post-antique: common in legal texts. *LBG*. Notes: Avotins (1992), Zilliacus (1935a: 186–7), Triantaphyllides (1892: 260), Lampe (1961 *s.v.* ἐμαγκηπατίων), *DGE*. See §4.2.5, §8.2.2, §10.2.1, §10.2.2 B; cf. μαγκιπατίων, μαγκίπιον 2.
Direct loan V AD – Byz.	**ἐμαγκιπᾶτος, ἐμαγκηπᾶτος** (-η, -ον) 'emancipated', from *ēmancipātus*, pf. part. of *ēmancipō* 'emancipate'. Literature: *Carth.* 256.4 (V AD); *Schol.Sinai.* in Latin script 5 *emancipata* (V/VI AD); Just. *Nov.* 22.19 etc. (VI AD); Antec. in Latin script 1.10.2 *emancipatan* etc. (VI AD). Post-antique: common. *LBG*, Kriaras (1968–). Notes: Avotins (1992), Zilliacus (1935a: 186–7), Triantaphyllides (1892: 260), Lampe (1961 *s.v.* ἐμαγκήπατος), *DGE*. See §4.2.2, §7.1.2, §9.5.6 n. 56, §10.2.1, §10.2.2 B.
rare	**ἐμβυκανάω** 'blow with the trumpet', from ἐν 'in' + the Latin source of βυκανάω via βυκανάω: DH *AR* 2.8.4 (I BC). Hofmann (1989: 65 *s.v.* βουκανᾶν), *DGE*, LSJ.
	ἐμπερπερεύομαι: see πέρπερος.
not ancient	**ἔμπετος** 'attack', from *impetus, -ūs* 'attack': no ancient examples. Zilliacus (1935a: 226–7), *LBG*.
	ἐμπεφιβλωμένον: see ἐμφιβλόω.
rare	**ἐμπλούμιος** 'tapestry woven', from ἐν 'in' + *plūma* 'feather': probably papyrus *Stud.Pal.* XX.275.3 (VI AD). Diethart (1989: 114). Cf. πλουμίον, ἔμπλουμος, εὔπλουμος, ὀρθόπλουμος, πλοῦμος.

Deriv.? of loan
VI AD – Byz.

ἔμπλουμος (-ον) probably 'tapestry woven', from ἐν 'in' + *plūma* 'feather' (via πλουμίον?).

Documents: perhaps *SB* 15961.7 (V/VI AD); *Stud.Pal.* XX.245.13 etc. (VI AD); *P.Fouad* 74.6 (VI AD); perhaps *P.Cair.Masp.* 67006v.88 etc. (VI AD).

Post-antique: survives. *LBG, DGE.*

Notes: for meaning see Wild and Dross-Krüpe (2017). Not attested in feminine; LSJ infers from form that it would be two-termination. Filos (2010: 250), Daris (1991a: 43), Hofmann (1989: 333 *s.v.* πλοῦμο-), Cavenaile (1952: 199), Meinersmann (1927: 16), LSJ, LSJ suppl. See §4.5, §4.6.2, §8.2.2, §9.2, §10.2.2 H; cf. πλουμίον, ἐμπλούμιος, εὔπλουμος, ὀρθόπλουμος, πλοῦμος.

rare

ἔμπτιον, ἔμτιον 'purchase', from *ēmptiō* 'purchase': papyrus *P.Vars.* 28.2 (VI AD). Daris (1991a: 43), *LBG, DGE.*

foreign

ἐμπτίων transliterating *ēmptiō* 'purchase': papyrus *BGU* V.1210.93 (II AD). Byzantine use (*LBG*) probably unrelated.

foreign

ἔμπτωρ 'purchaser', from *ēmptor* 'purchaser': Antec. in Latin script 3.12.pr. *emptora* etc. (VI AD); later occasionally in Greek script. Zilliacus (1935a: 186–7).

ἔμτιον: see ἔμπτιον.

rare

ἐμφιβλόω 'fasten a pin into', from ἐν 'in' + *fībula* 'pin', 'brooch' via φιβλόω: Pall. *H.Laus.* 21.8 in pf. pass. ἐμπεφιβλωμένον (IV/V AD). Lampe (1961 *s.v.* ἐμφιβλόομαι), *DGE* (*s.v.* ἐμφιβλόομαι).

not Latin

ἐναράτιον, probably variant of ἐνηρόσιον 'rent for corn-land' but suggested to come from *arō* 'plough': inscription *IG* XII.I.924.20 (III BC, Rhodian). Hofmann (1989: 26 *s.v.* ἀρᾶν), LSJ.

non-existent

ἐνάρατον, cited by Schwyzer (1922: 1) without a precise reference, is probably a misquotation of ἐναράτιον (*q.v.*), *pace* Hofmann (1989: 26 *s.v.* ἀρᾶν).

ἐνγαρ-: see ἀγγαρ-.

ἐνδικτίων: see ἰνδικτίων.

rare

ἐνεραδνούμιον 'calling on the dead by name', from ἔνεροι 'those below' + *ad nōmen* 'by name' via ἀδνούμιον: papyrus *P.Cair.Masp.* 67151.168 (VI AD). Filos (2010: 250), Daris (1991a: 43), Cavenaile (1952: 199), Meinersmann (1927: 16), *DGE*, LSJ.

Deriv. of loan
VI AD – Byz.

ἐνναούγκιον (-ου, τό) 'three quarters of an inheritance', from ἐννα- 'nine' + *ūncia* 'one twelfth' via οὐγγία.

Literature: legal texts, e.g. Just. *Nov.* 18.2 (VI AD); Ath.Schol. 8.1 (VI AD).

Post-antique: survives in legal language. *LBG.*

Notes: Avotins (1992), *DGE*, LSJ suppl. See §4.6.2, §8.2.2, §9.5.6 n. 68, §10.2.2 B.

ἐνξεινπλάρεινον: see ἐξεμπλάριον.

ἐντερκλάριος: see ἰντερκαλάριος.

ἐντύβιον, ἔντυβον: see ἰντύβιον, ἴντυβον.

rare	ἐξάγιον and ἑξάγιον may be one word or two. LSJ and LSJ suppl. see two words: ἐξάγιον 'assaying, testing', a borrowing of *exagium* 'weighing' (*TLL*), and ἑξάγιον 'one sixth of one twelfth', a calque of *sextula* 'one sixth of one twelfth' (i.e. one seventy-second). But *DGE* sees one word, ἐξάγιον 'weight', 'weighing', 'one sixth of one twelfth', 'partial payment', from *exagium* (which is in fact attested in the meaning 'one sixth of one twelfth': see *TLL s.v. exagium* 1155.3–16) with frequent misapplication of aspiration on the part of editors; in the late Roman period aspiration was neither written nor pronounced, so even if the two words were originally distinct they would have merged eventually. Occurrences include (probably) papyrus *CPR* v.26.863 (v AD); inscriptions *I.Tomis* 390 = *I.Chr.Românâ* 86 (v AD) and Horsley 2007: no. 198.2 (v/vi AD); medical texts, e.g. Archigenes p. 11.18 Brescia (i/ii AD); Orib. *Ecl.* 1.3.4 (iv AD); Aëtius 8.29.50 (vi AD); Ps.-Galen xiv.327.17 Kühn; with *pensatio* in Gloss. Ps.-Cyril. 301.16; common in Byzantine texts. Most examples might be from *sextula* rather than *exagium*. Modern ξάγι, a measuring instrument: Babiniotis (2002), Andriotis (1967), Meyer (1895: 48–9). Daris (1991a: 43), Viscidi (1944: 30), *LBG*, Kriaras (1968–), Triandaphyllidis (1909: 106, 125), *DGE*, LSJ, LSJ suppl.
non-existent	ἐξάκτης, a title from *exactor* 'tax collector' via ἐξάκτωρ: superseded reading for ἐρέκτη in *SB* 12993.2. Biville (1992: 236), LSJ.
Deriv. of loan **IV–VI AD**	ἐξακτορεύω 'be tax collector', 'collect taxes', from *exactor* 'tax collector' via ἐξάκτωρ + -εύω. Documents: *CPR* xviiA.16.22 (iv AD); *P.Oxy.* 2110.18 etc. (iv AD); *P.Petra* iii.33.4 (vi AD). Notes: Daris (1991a: 43), Cavenaile (1951: 396), *TLL* (*s.v. exactor* 1137.58–61), *DGE*, LSJ suppl. See §4.6.1 n. 91, §10.2.2 D.
Deriv. of loan **IV–VI AD**	ἐξακτορία (-ας, ἡ) 'office of tax collector', 'job of tax collector', from *exactor* 'tax collector' via ἐξάκτωρ + -ία. Documents: e.g. *P.Oxy.* 4896.5 (iv AD); *P.Oxy.* 1950.2 (v AD); *P.Oxy.* 3583.4 (v AD); *P.Oxy.* 1887.3 (vi AD); *P.Petra* iii.30.187 (vi AD). Notes: occasionally neut. pl. (*TLL s.v. exactor* 1137.64). Daris (1991a: 43), Hofmann (1989: 110 *s.v.* εξακτωρ), *DGE*, *TLL* (*s.v. exactor* 1137.61–3), LSJ (*s.v.* ἐξάκτωρ). See §4.6.1, §9.2, §10.2.2 D.
rare	ἐξακτορικός 'of the tax collector', from *exactor* 'tax collector' via ἐξάκτωρ + -ικός (cf. Cavenaile 1952: 197): probably papyrus *P.Oxy.* 126.4 (vi AD); only a supplement on *P.Oxy.* 1887.2 (vi AD), *P.Warr.* 3.1 (vi AD), and *SB* 15955.3 (vi AD). Daris (1991a: 43), *TLL* (*s.v. exactor* 1137.64–5), LSJ suppl., for Byzantine survival *LBG*.
Direct loan **IV AD – Byz.**	ἐξάκτωρ, ἐκξάκτωρ (-ορος/-ωρος, ὁ) 'tax collector', from *exactor* 'tax collector'. Documents: common (esp. iv AD), e.g. perhaps *P.Ross.Georg.* v.26.12 (iii AD); *P.Oxy.* 3123.3 etc. (iv AD); *SB* 16261.A1 (v AD); *P.Stras.* v.486.6 (vi AD). Superseded reading in *P.Cair.Goodsp.* 30.42.3 (ii AD). Inscriptions: *I.Perinthos* 185.1 (iv/v AD); *I.Syringes* 1077. Literature: Athan. *Apol.Sec.* 85.7 (iv AD); Hesych. as lemma ε 3528, as gloss φ 787 (v/vi AD); Just. *Nov.* 128.5 etc. (vi AD). Post-antique: common in legal texts. *LBG*.

Notes: forms derivatives ἐξακτορεύω, ἐξακτορία, ἐξακτορικός. Nachtergael (2005: 241), Avotins (1992), Daris (1991a: 43–4), Hofmann (1989: 110), Viscidi (1944: 20), Zilliacus (1935a: 186–7), Meinersmann (1927: 17), Immisch (1885: 368–9), *TLL* (s.v. *exāctor* 1136.20–42), *DGE*, LSJ. See §4.1.1, §4.2.5, §4.6.1, §9.5.4 n. 42, §10.2.1, §10.2.2 D.

ἐξάντιον: see ἑξᾶς.

Deriv. of loan VI AD

ἐξαξεστιαῖος (-ον) 'holding six pints' or in neut. pl. 'six pints', from ἕξ 'six' + *sextārius* 'pint measure' via ξεστιαῖος.
Documents: *P.Flor.* 1.65r.6 etc. (VI AD); *P.Mich.* XIII.674.5 (VI AD); *P.Vat. Aphrod.* 12.5 etc. (VI AD).
Notes: not attested in feminine; LSJ suppl. infers from form that it would be two-termination. Filos (2010: 244, 250), Daris (1991a: 44), *DGE*. See §4.6.2, §4.6.3, §9.2, §10.2.2 E.

Deriv. of loan III–VI AD

ἐξάξεστος (-ον) 'holding six pints', in neut. pl. 'six pints', from ἕξ 'six' + *sextārius* 'pint measure' via ξέστης.
Documents: perhaps *CPR* VII.59r.2 (V/VI AD); *P.Mich.* XIII.667.17 (VI AD).
Literature: Jul.Afric. *Cest.* 4.1.79 (II/III AD); Her.Mech. *Geom.* 23.66; with *congiarium* in glossaries, e.g. Gloss. Ps.-Cyril. 301.54.
Notes: not attested in feminine; LSJ infers from form that it would be two-termination. Filos (2010: 244, 250), *DGE*, LSJ suppl. See §4.6.2, §9.2, §10.2.2 E.

Deriv. of loan VI AD – Byz.

ἐξαούγκιον, ἐξαούγγιον (-ου, τό) 'half an inheritance', 'six ounces', from ἕξ 'six' + *ūncia* 'one twelfth' via οὐγγία.
Literature: Just. *Nov.* 18.1 etc. (VI AD); Ath.Schol. 9.2 (VI AD); with *semis* in Gloss. Ps.-Cyril. 301.55.
Post-antique: common in legal language. *LBG*.
Notes: Avotins (1992), *DGE*, LSJ, LSJ suppl. See §4.6.2, §10.2.2 B.

not Latin?

ἑξᾶς, acc. ἑξᾶντα 'one sixth', a coin and a unit of measure (with diminutive ἐξάντιον), adopted by Sicilian Greeks from Italic (not necessarily Latin) *sextāns* 'one sixth'. Bellocchi (2016: 327), Willi (2008: 35), Buck and Petersen (1945: 456), Hofmann (1989: 110), *DGE*, LSJ. Cf. *sextans*.

rare

ἐξατίλιον, ἐξατίλιος, a fish, from *saxātilis* 'rockfish' (first syllable apparently interpreted as *sex* 'six', resulting in influence from ἕξ 'six'): papyrus *P.Ryl.* IV.630/637.332 etc. (IV AD). Hofmann (1989: 110), LSJ suppl.

non-existent?

ἐξεκούτωρ 'executor', from *ex(s)ecūtor* 'executor': cited by Zilliacus (1935a: 186–7), but I can find no examples.

Direct loan II AD – Byz.

ἐξεμπλάριον, ἐξομπλάριον, ἐξονπλάριον, ἐξενπλάριον, ἐξοπράρειον, ἐνξεινπλάρεινον, ἐξεμβλάριον (-ου, τό) 'sample', 'evidence', from *exemplar* 'example'.
Documents: *P.Oxy.* 1066.7 (III AD).
Inscriptions: perhaps *MAMA* IV.279.19 (II/III AD); *MAMA* IV.284.8, 285.9; *I.Smyrna* 230.b11; Ramsay 1895–7: 151 no. 47.5.
Literature: Ignat. *Ep.* 1.2.1 etc. (I/II AD); Ps.-John Chrysostom, *PG* LIX.705.19 (IV/V AD?).

Post-antique: survives.
Notes: for ἐξονπλάριν as folk etymology from ἔξον see Cavenaile (1951: 403). Daris (1991a: 44), Hofmann (1989: 111), Meinersmann (1927: 17), Lampe (1961), LSJ (*s.v.* ἐξομπλάριον). See §4.2.5, §10.2.1, §10.2.2 O, §12.2.1.

rare   **ἔξεμπλον, ἔξενπλον, ἔξομπλον** 'copy', from *exemplum* 'copy' (*OLD s.v.* 9): *Carth.* 418.14 (V AD); Hesych. as lemma ε 3935 (V/VI AD); inscription Ramsay 1895–7: 149 no. 41.8; perhaps papyrus *BGU* 11.600v.3 (II AD), where Kreller (1919: 30) suggests ἐξέμπλ(ουμ); Byzantine texts (*LBG* lists ἐξέμπλιον 'example', ἐξέμπλον 'copy', ἐξόμπλιν 'decoration', and derivatives). Modern ξόμπλι 'pattern' and derivatives: Babiniotis (2002), Andriotis (1967), Meyer (1895: 49–50). Hofmann (1989: 111), Zilliacus (1935a: 186–7), Immisch (1885: 361), Kriaras (1968– *s.v.* ξόμπλι), Triandaphyllidis (1909: 123), Lampe (1961), LSJ (*s.v.* ἔξομπλον).

      ἐξέπτωρ: see ἐξκέπτωρ.

foreign   **ἐξερεδατεύω** 'disinherit', from *exhērēdātus* (pf. part. of *exhērēdō* 'disinherit') + -εύω: Antec. in Latin script 2.13.1 *exheredateuesthai* etc. (VI AD); later in Greek script. Hofmann (1989: 111–12), Zilliacus (1935a: 186–7), *LBG*, *TLL* (*s.v. exhērēdo* 1413.7–10). See §9.5.6 n. 68.

foreign   **ἐξερεδατίων** 'act of disinheriting', from *exhērēdātiō* 'act of disinheriting': Just. *Nov.* in Latin script 1.1.4 etc. (VI AD); Antec. in Latin script 2.13.1 *exheredationa* etc. (VI AD); later in Greek script. Hofmann (1989: 112), Zilliacus (1935a: 186–7), *LBG* (*s.vv.* ἐξερεδιτατίων, ἐξνερεδατίων). See §9.5.6 n. 68.

foreign   **ἐξερεδᾶτος** 'disinherited', from *exhērēdātus*, pf. part. of *exhērēdō* 'disinherit': Just. *Nov.* in Latin script 1.1.4 (VI AD); Antec. in Latin script 2.16.4 *exheredatois* etc. (VI AD); later in Greek script. Zilliacus (1935a: 186–7), *LBG* (*s.v.* ἐξνερεδᾶτος), Triantaphyllides (1892: 260), *TLL* (*s.v. exhērēdo* 1413.5–12). See §9.5.6 n. 68.

Direct loan   **ἐξέρκετον, ἐξέρκιτον** (-ου, τό) 'army', from *exercitus, -ūs* 'army'.
V AD – Byz.   Literature: *V.Dan.Styl. A.* 56 (V AD); Malal. 16.3 etc. (VI AD); Just. *Nov.* in Latin script 41.t (VI AD). Unverified example (VI AD) in Zilliacus (1937: 322, 329).
     Post-antique: survives. *LBG* (*s.v.* ἐξέρκιτον), Triandaphyllidis (1909: 130).
     Notes: sometimes cited as ἐξέρκετος or ἐξέρκιτος, but all ancient examples are neuter or ambiguous. Diethart (2006: 14), Binder (2000: 132–3), Avotins (1992 *s.v.* ἐξέρκιτον), Daris (1991a: 44), Hofmann (1989: 112), Zilliacus (1935a: 224–5, 1937: 329), Lampe (1961), LSJ suppl. See §4.2.4.2, §10.2.1, §10.2.2 C.

foreign   **ἐξερκιτορία** 'legal case about chartering', from *exercitōria* 'concerning the operator of a business': Antec. in Latin script 4.7.2 *exercitorian* etc. (VI AD); later in Greek script. Zilliacus (1935a: 186–7 *s.v.* ἐξερκιτώριος), *LBG*. See §9.5.6 n. 68.

foreign   **ἐξερκίτωρ** 'charterer', from *exercitor* 'one who works a business': Antec. in Latin script 4.5.3 *exercitoros* etc. (VI AD); later in Greek script. Zilliacus (1935a: 186–7), *LBG*. See §9.5.6 n. 68.

ἐξερκιτώριος: see ἐξερκιτορία.

foreign   ἐξιβιτόριος, ἐξνιβιτόριος 'ordering something to be produced', from *exhibitōrius* 'connected with production in court': Antec. in Latin script 4.15.1 *exhibitoria* etc. (VI AD); later in Greek script. Zilliacus (1935a: 186–7), *LBG*. See §4.1.1 n. 23.

rare   ἐξιτίων 'expense', 'military expedition', from *exitiō* 'action of going out': papyri *P.Cair.Masp.* 67057.1.7 (VI AD); *P.Eirene* III.15.5 (VI AD). Daris (1991a: 44), Zilliacus (1935a: 186–7), Meinersmann (1927: 17), *LBG*, *TLL* (*s.v. exitio* 1527.23–5).

non-existent   ἐξκεντορικός 'of former centurions', from (the Latin source of) ἐξκεντυρίων + -ικός: superseded reading of papyrus *Stud.Pal.* XX.247.6. Hofmann (1989: 112 *s.v.* ἐξκεντυρίων).

non-existent?   ἐξκεντυρίων 'former centurion', from unattested *excenturiō* 'former centurion' (*TLL*) or *ex centuriōne* by univerbation in Greek: perhaps papyrus *Stud. Pal.* XX.109.7 (IV AD). Filos (2006: 52–3, 2010: 252), Daris (1991a: 44), Hofmann (1989: 112–13), *TLL* (*s.v. excenturio, s.v.* 2. *centurio* 844.73–9). See §4.6.2 n. 95, §8.1.7 n. 34.

ἐξκεπτάριος: see ἐξσκεπτάριος.

not ancient   ἐξκεπτορικός 'of a clerk', from *exceptor* 'copyist' via ἐξκέπτωρ + -ικός: no ancient examples. Daris (1991a: 44), Cavenaile (1952: 197), Zilliacus (1935a: 224–5).

Direct loan   ἐξκέπτωρ, ἐκσκέπτωρ, ἐξσκέπτωρ, ἐξέπτωρ, ἐκσκέτωρ (-ορος/-ωρος, ὁ) 'clerk',
III AD – Byz.   'keeper of the minutes', from *exceptor* 'copyist'.
        Documents: e.g. *P.Oxy.* 43r.2.26 (III AD); *SB* 2253.1 (III/IV AD); *P.Herm. Landl.* 1.416 (IV AD); *ChLA* XLIII.1247.6 etc. (V AD); *CPR* XIV.51.12 (VI AD).
        Inscriptions: *I.Syringes* 1415 (IV/V AD); *SEG* LIII.1841.iii.2 (V AD); *I.Aphrodisias Late Ant.* 70 (V/VI AD); *I.Syringes* 1723, 1865, 1898, perhaps 1367.
        Literature: e.g. Epiph. *Pan.* III.250.25 (IV AD); Ps.-John Chrysostom, *PG* LXI.691.76 (IV/V AD?); Nil. 2.34.1 (V AD); old scholion to Ar. *Nu.* 770: ὁ γραμματεύς· ὁ γράφων τὰ λεγόμενα ἐν ταῖς δίκαις, ὁ νῦν καλούμενος ἐξκέπτωρ. Unverified example (III AD) in Zilliacus (1937: 322, 328).
        Post-antique: survives. *LBG* (*s.v.* ἐξσκέπτωρ), Daris (1991a: 44).
        Notes: Binder (2000: 225), Daris (1991a: 44), Hofmann (1989: 108), Zilliacus (1935a: 186–7, 224–5, 1937: 328), Meinersmann (1927: 18), *TLL* (*s.v. exceptor* 1225.76–83), Lampe (1961 *s.v.* ἐξσκέπτωρ), LSJ suppl. See §4.1.1, §4.2.5, §10.2.1, §10.2.2 N.

rare   ἐξκούβιτον, ἐξκούβητον 'guarding of the imperial palace', perhaps from unattested *excubitum* or perhaps a back-formation from ἐξκουβίτωρ: *V.Dan.Styl.* A. 75.20 (V AD); tachygraphy in Menci 2000: 282 (V/VI AD); Byzantine texts. Menci (2000: 282, with different derivation), Viscidi (1944: 14, with different derivation), Zilliacus (1937: 329), *LBG*, Zervan (2019: 50), *TLL* (*s.v. excubitum*). See §8.1.7.

not ancient?	**ἐξκούβιτος, ἐκσκούβιτος, σκούβιτος** 'leader of the imperial guard', apparently from unattested *excubitus, -ī* 'member of the emperor's bodyguard' (*TLL*): probably no ancient examples. *Etymologicum Gudianum*, Additamenta ε p. 488.18 de Stefani: ἐξκούβιτος· ἐξ οὗ ἡ ζωή· βῖτα γὰρ ἡ ζωή. Binder (2000: 225, with errors), Daris (1991a: 44), Hofmann (1989: 113), Viscidi (1944: 14), Zilliacus (1935a: 224–5), *LBG, TLL* (*s.v. 2. excubitus*). See §8.1.7.
Direct loan **V AD – Byz.**	**ἐξκουβίτωρ, ἐκσκουβίτωρ, ἐξσκουβίτωρ** (-ορος/-ωρος, ὁ) 'soldier of the imperial guard', from *excubitor* 'member of the emperor's bodyguard'. Inscriptions: *SEG* XXXIV.927 in Latin script (VI AD); perhaps *Corinth* VIII. III.541.4 and/or 558.a1 etc. (both V/VI AD); *MAMA* VIII.323.4. Literature: e.g. Nil. 2.322.1 (V AD); Malal. 14.40 (VI AD); Procop. *Bell.* 4.12.17, marked (VI AD). Unverified example (IV AD) in Zilliacus (1937: 323, 329). Post-antique: common. *LBG* (*s.vv.* ἐξκουβίτωρ, σκουβίτωρ), Zervan (2019: 50–1), Triandaphyllidis (1909: 126). Notes: may be source of ἐξκούβιτον. Binder (2000: 225, with errors), Daris (1991a: 44–5), Hofmann (1989: 114), Zilliacus (1935a: 224–5, 1937: 329), Meinersmann (1927: 17), *TLL* (*s.v. excubitor* 1288.17–26), Lampe (1961 *s.v.* ἐκσκουβίτωρ), LSJ suppl. See §4.2.5, §10.2.1, §10.2.2 A.
rare	**ἐξκουσατεύω, ἐξκουσσατεύω** 'excuse (from duty or tax)', from *excūsātus* (pf. part. of *excūsō* 'excuse') + -εύω: Just. *Codex* 6.4.4.20a (VI AD); Antec. in Latin script 1.25.pr. *excusateuei* etc. (VI AD); often in Byzantine texts. Avotins (1989), Hofmann (1989: 115 *s.v.* εξκουσευειν), Viscidi (1944: 27), Zilliacus (1935a: 186–7), *LBG* (*s.v.* ἐξκουσσατεύω), Kriaras (1968–), LSJ suppl. May be a variant of ἐξκουσεύω. See §9.5.6 n. 68.
Direct loan **III AD – Byz.**	**ἐξκουσατίων** (-ονος/-ωνος, ἡ) 'grounds for being excused', 'exemption', 'immunity', from *excūsātiō* 'justification', 'exemption', 'immunity'. Literature: Modestinus in Just. *Dig.* 27.1.13.pr., but in Latin script 26.6.2.6 (III AD); *Schol.Sinai.* in Latin script 53 *excusationas* (V/VI AD); Just. *Nov.* 118.5 (VI AD); Antec. in Latin script 1.25.pr. *excusationas* etc. (VI AD). Post-antique: common. *LBG.* Notes: Avotins (1992), Hofmann (1989: 114), Zilliacus (1935a: 186–7), LSJ suppl. See §4.2.5, §7.1.2, §9.5.6 nn. 55 and 56, §10.2.1, §10.2.2 B.
rare	**ἐξκουσᾶτος, ἐξκουσσᾶτος, ἐκουσ(σ)ᾶτος, ἐξσκουσ(σ)ᾶτος** 'excused person', 'exempt person', from *excūsātus* 'admitting of excuse': papyrus *P.Ant.* 1.33v.18 (IV AD); Just. *Nov.* 59.2, marked (VI AD); often in Byzantine texts. Avotins (1992), Daris (1991a: 45), Hofmann (1989: 106–7), Zilliacus (1935a: 186–7), *LBG*, Zervan (2019: 49), Kriaras (1968–), Triandaphyllidis (1909: 128), LSJ suppl.
Direct loan with **suffix** **VI AD – Byz.**	**ἐξκουσεύω, ἐξκουσσεύω, ἐξσκουσσεύω, ἐκκουσ(σ)εύω,** 'excuse', from *excūsō* 'excuse' + -εύω. Literature: Malal. 14.8 (VI AD); Just. *Nov.* 43.t etc. (VI AD); old scholia to Hes. *Op.* 722a. Post-antique: common. *LBG* (*s.v.* ἐξκουσσεύω), Kriaras (1968–), Triandaphyllidis (1909: 128). Notes: Avotins (1992), Hofmann (1989: 115), Viscidi (1944: 27), Lampe (1961 *s.v.* ἐκκουσσεύω), LSJ suppl. See §4.3.1, §10.2.1, §10.2.2 B, §10.3.1; cf. ἐξκουσατεύω.

ἐξκουσσατ-: see ἐξκουσατ-.

ἐξνιβιτόριος: see ἐξιβιτόριος.

foreign | ἐξοδιάριος transliterating *exodiārius* 'actor (in an after-piece of a play)' (*TLL*): Lyd. *Mag.* p. 62.6 (VI AD). Zilliacus (1937: 335, with reference to a different passage of doubtful date) sees it as a Greek formation from ἐξόδιος 'after-piece' + -άριος. Sophocles (1887), *TLL* (*s.v. exodiārius* 1541.25), LSJ.

ἐξομπλ-, ἐξονπλ-: see ἐξεμπλ-.

non-existent? | ἐξουβεραντία 'excess', from *exūberantia* 'abundance': perhaps papyrus *P.Oxy.* 1660.3, abbreviated to ἐξουβερ (IV AD). Daris (1991a: 45), Meinersmann (1927: 17), *LBG*, *TLL* (*s.v. exūberantia* 2094.4–6).

Direct loan
VI AD – Byz. | ἐξπέδιτον, ἐκσπέδιτον, ἐγπήτιτον (-ου, τό) 'army camp', 'army', 'military expedition', from *expedītum* 'army', 'military expedition' (*TLL*).
Documents: *P.Ness.* III.35.15 (VI AD).
Literature: Hesych. as gloss ε 3973 (V/VI AD); Malal. 5.5.39 etc. (VI AD); Just. *Nov.* 117.11 etc. (VI AD); Antec. 2.11.pr., but in Latin script 2.13.6 *expedito* (VI AD); Ath.Schol. in Latin script 20.1.195 (VI AD).
Post-antique: survives. *LBG* (*s.v. ἐκσπέδιτον*), Zervan (2019: 51), Kriaras (1968–), Triandaphyllidis (1909: 130).
Notes: Diethart (2006: 16), Avotins (1992), Daris (1991a: 45, with derivation from *expedītiō*), Hofmann (1989: 115), Viscidi (1944: 14), Zilliacus (1935a: 186–7, 224–5), Immisch (1885: 360), *TLL* (*s.v. expedītum*), Lampe (1961). See §4.2.4.1 n. 55, §10.2.1, §10.2.2 C.

foreign | ἐξπεδῖτος transliterating *expedītus* 'ready for action': Lyd. *Mag.* p. 74.8 (VI AD). Cf. LSJ suppl. but note that Just. *Nov.* 117.11 (VI AD) is really ἐξπέδιτον.

non-existent | ἐξπεκτορικός, cited as a Latin borrowing (presumably of unattested *expectoricus*) by Schwyzer (1929: 310), Hofmann (1989: 116): no longer attested.

Deriv. of loan
VI AD – Byz. | ἐξπελλευτής, ἐξπελευ(σ)τής, ἐκσπ-, ἐξπηλευτής, ἐκσπηλευτής (-οῦ, ὁ) 'tax collector', from *expellō* 'drive out' via ἐξπελλεύω + -της.
Documents: e.g. *P.Flor.* III.291.6 (VI AD); *P.Cair.Masp.* 67054.1.2 (VI AD).
Literature: EphraemSyr. VI p. 103.6 etc., metaphorical (V/VI AD); Just. *Codex* 10.19.9.1 etc., *Nov.* 128.6 etc. (VI AD); Cyr.S. *Vit.Sab.* 163.3 etc. (VI AD); Ath.Schol. 20.1.6 (VI AD).
Post-antique: survives. *LBG* (*s.vv. ἐξπελευστής, ἐκσπιλευτής*).
Notes: probably reborrowed into Latin as *expelleuta* (*TLL s.v. ἐξπελλευστής* 1629.55–66). Palmer (1945: 7, 113), Avotins (1992), Daris (1991a: 45, with derivation from *expelleuta*), Hofmann (1989: 107 *s.v. ἐκπελεύειν*), Zilliacus (1935a: 186–7), Meinersmann (1927: 18), Lampe (1961 *s.vv. ἐκσπελλευτής, ἐξπελλευτής*), LSJ suppl. (replacing LSJ *s.v. ἐξπελευστής*). See §4.6.1 n. 86, §8.1.7 n. 34, §10.2.2 D.

Direct loan with
suffix
VI AD – Byz. | ἐξπελ(λ)εύω, ἐκσπελ(λ)εύω, ἐκπελ(λ)εύω, ἐκσπηλεύω 'collect taxes', 'drive out', from *expellō* 'drive out' + -εύω.
Documents: *SB* 9285.7 etc. (VI AD).
Literature: EphraemSyr. VII p. 396.12 (V/VI AD); Hesych. as lemma ε 1600 (V/VI AD).

Post-antique: survives. Daris (1991a: 45), *LBG* (*s.vv.* ἐκπελ(λ)εύω, ἐκσπηλεύω).
Notes: forms derivative ἐξπελλευτής. Daris (1991a: 45), Hofmann (1989: 107), Immisch (1885: 354), LSJ (*s.v.* ἐκπελεύει). See §2.4, §4.3.1, §10.2.1, §10.2.2 D, §10.3.1.

ἐξπηλευτής: see ἐξπελλευτής.

not ancient   **ἔξπληκτος** 'light-armed', from *explicitus* 'free from difficulties': no ancient examples. Zilliacus (1935a: 224–5), *LBG*.

Direct loan   **ἐξπλωράτωρ, ἐξσπλωράτωρ** (-ορος/-ωρος, ὁ) 'scout', 'spy', from *explōrātor* 'scout',
III AD – Byz.   'spy'.
Inscriptions: *IG* XIV.2433.10 (III AD); *IGBulg.* III.II.1570.14 (III AD).
Literature: Ps.-Marcus Aurelius, *Epistula ad senatum*, Otto 1876: 248.7 (after II AD?); *Historia Alexandri Magni* rec. β 1.2 Bergson, marked (V AD).
Post-antique: numerous. *LBG* (*s.v.* ἐξπλοράτωρ), Kriaras (1968– *s.v.* εξπλοράτωρ).
Notes: Zilliacus (1935a: 224–5), Sophocles (1887). See §4.2.5, §10.2.1, §10.2.2 C.

rare   **ἐξπούγγευσις, ἐξφούγγευσις, ἐκσφούγγευσις** '(military) discharge', from *expungō* 'mark off on a list' via ἐξπουγγεύω + -σις, perhaps with influence from *expūnctiō* 'military discharge': papyrus *P.Oxy.* 1204.6 (III AD). Daris (1991a: 45, with derivation from *expūnctiō*), Hofmann (1989: 117 *s.v.* ἐξφουνγευειν), *TLL* (*s.v.* expunctio 1813.18–20), LSJ suppl. (*s.v.* ἐκσφούγγευσις).

rare   **ἐξπουγγεύω, ἐξφουνγεύω, ἐκσφουνγεύω** 'discharge (from the military)', from *expungō* 'mark off on a list' + -εύω: documents *O.Claud.* II.258.4 (II AD); *P.Oxy.* 1204.19 (III AD). Apparently forms derivative ἐξπούγγευσις. Schirru (2013: 316), Daris (1991a: 45), Hofmann (1989: 117), *TLL* (*s.v.* expungo 1813.37), LSJ suppl. (*s.v.* ἐκσφουνγεύω).

rare   **ἐξπούγκερος**, perhaps 'person who discharges soldiers', apparently from *expungō* 'mark off on a list': papyrus *BGU* II.435.14 (II/III AD). Daris (1991a: 45), Hofmann (1989: 116), Meinersmann (1927: 17–18), *TLL* (*s.v.* ἐξπουγκερος). See §8.1.7 n. 34.

rare   **ἐξπούγκτωρ, ἐκσπούνκτωρ, ἐκσφούγκτωρ** 'official who discharges soldiers', from *expūnctor* 'one who deletes', 'one who pays' (*TLL*): papyri *P.Kellis* I.21.9, perhaps 77.13 (both IV AD). *LBG*.

ἐξσκέπτωρ: see ἐξκέπτωρ.

ἐξσκουβίτωρ: see ἐξκουβίτωρ.

ἐξσκουσ-: see ἐξκουσ-.

ἐξσπλωράτωρ: see ἐξπλωράτωρ.

ἐξτράνεος, ἐξτράνιος: see ἐκστρανήιος.

Direct loan   **ἐξτραορδινάριος, ἐκστραορδινάριος, ἐκτραορδινάριος** (-α, -ον) 'unusual', 'select
VI AD – Byz.   troops', from *extrāōrdinārius* 'special', 'specially selected troops'.
Documents: perhaps *P.Cair.Masp.* 67054.1 (VI AD); perhaps *SB* 16043.A3 etc. (VI AD).

Literature: Polybius 6.26.6, marked (II BC); Ath.Schol. 2.3.6 (VI AD);
Just. *Nov.* in Latin script 131.5 (VI AD); Antec. in Latin script 3.12.pr.
extraordinarion etc. (VI AD).

Post-antique: common. *LBG*.

Notes: Daris (1991a: 45), Mason (1974: 5, 42), Hofmann (1989: 116–17),
Zilliacus (1935a: 186–7), Meinersmann (1927: 16), *TLL* (*s.v. extrāordinārius*
2075.24–9), *DGE* (*s.v.* ἐκτραορδινάριος), LSJ suppl. (*s.v.* ἐκτραορδινάριοι). See
§4.2.2, §6.1 n. 11, §8.1.3 n. 17, §10.2.1, §10.2.2 C.

non-existent?	**ἔξτρα ὄρδινεμ** transliterating *extrā ōrdinem* 'extraordinary': perhaps papyrus *Chrest. Mitt.* 55.17 (IV AD). Daris (1991a: 45).
not ancient	**ἐξτραορδινεύομαι, ἐκστραορδινεύομαι** 'suffer extraordinary punishment', from *extrā ōrdinem* 'extraordinary' via ἐξτραόρδινος + a deponent version of -εύω: no ancient examples. Hofmann (1989: 108 *s.v.* ἐκστραόρδινα), *LBG*, *TLL* (*s.v. extrāordinārius* 2075.29–34).
not ancient?	**ἐξτραόρδινος, ἐκστραόρδινος**, from *extrā ōrdinem* 'extraordinary' via ὄρδινος: no securely ancient examples. *TLL* considers it Byzantine. Daris (1991a: 45), Hofmann (1989: 108), Zilliacus (1935a: 186–7), *LBG*, *TLL* (*s.v. extrāordinārius* 2075.29–34).
	ἐξφουνγευ-: see ἐξπουγγευ-.
not ancient?	**ἐξώπορτος** 'outside the door', from ἔξω 'outside' + *porta* 'door' via πόρτα: no certainly ancient examples. Hofmann (1989: 117), *LBG*, Lampe (1961 *s.v.* ἐξώπορτα).
foreign	*eō* 'go': Antec. 3.17.2 *ire* (VI AD).
	Ἐούνιος: see Ἰούνιος.
not ancient?	**ἐπενδυτοπάλλιον** 'garment worn over another garment', from ἐπενδύτης 'garment worn over another' + *pallium* 'mantle' via πάλλιον: inscription Robert 1971: 182 no. 179.6. Cameron (1931: 252), LSJ.
semantic extension	**ἐπὶ βαλανείων**, a title, is formed from Greek βαλανεῖον 'bath' on the model of the title *ā balineīs* 'from the baths' (*TLL s.v. ā, ab* 23.11). Mason (1974: 29), LSJ suppl. (*s.v.* βαλανεῖον).
rare	**ἐπισαλτικός** 'chief dancer', from ἐπί 'upon' + *salticus* 'dancing' (L&S) or another derivative of *saliō* 'leap': inscription *SB* 8697.3 (V AD). Filos (2010: 250), Daris (1991a: 45, listing the inscription as a papyrus), Hofmann (1989: 117), Meinersmann (1927: 54), *LBG*.
rare	**ἐπισέλλιον** 'saddle cover', from ἐπί 'upon' + *sella* 'seat' (via σέλλα + -ιον, or via σελλίον): with *subsellium* in Gloss. Ps.-Cyril. 310.46; Byzantine texts. Zilliacus (1935a: 236–7), *LBG*.
rare	**ἐπισηκρητεύω** 'act as secretary', from *sēcrētum* 'secret' via ἐπισήκρητος + -εύω (or 'perform secretarial duties as well', from ἐπί 'besides' + *sēcrētum* 'secret' via σήκρητον + -εύω): Lyd. *Mag.* p. 176.3 (VI AD). Hofmann (1989: 388 *s.v.* σήκρητον), LSJ.
rare	**ἐπισήκρητος** 'secretary', from ἐπί 'upon', 'over' + *sēcrētum* 'secret' via σήκρητον: Ps.-Caesarius title Riedinger (VI AD).

not ancient   **ἐπιστολάριος, ἐπιστουλάριος** 'secretary', from *epistulārius* 'secretary' (*TLL*): no ancient examples. Zilliacus (1935a: 186–7), *LBG*.

foreign   **ἔπουλαι** transliterating *epulae* 'feast': Lyd. *Mens.* 1.29.4 (VI AD). Hofmann (1989: 117), *LBG*. See §9.5.5 passage 73.

         ἐπουλαρέα, ἐπουλαρία: see ἀπαλαρέα.

rare   **ἔπουλον** 'money for a feast', from *epulum* 'public feast': papyrus *Rom.Mil.Rec.* 76.xxiv.ff.4 (II AD). Daris (1991a: 46), *LBG*.

foreign   **ἐπούλων**, nom. hypothesized from gen. pl. ἐπουλώνων and ἐπουλώνουμ: Latinate inscriptions (as part of title σεπτέμουιρ ἐπουλώνων = *septemvir epulōnum* 'board of seven men responsible for public feasts'), e.g. *MkB* 2.1 (1875–6) 18 no. 106.13 (I AD); *I.Ephesos* 3034.5 (II AD); *I.Cret.* IV.296.6 (II AD); *I.Didyma* 151.2 (II AD). Drew-Bear (1972: 197), Mason (1974: 4, 7, 49, 116), Hofmann (1989: 117), LSJ suppl. See **§7.3** passage 32.

rare   **ἑπτακελλάρ(ι)ον** 'chest with seven parts' or 'vessel holding seven units', from ἑπτά 'seven' + *cellārium* 'receptacle' (*TLL*) (via κελλάριον?): papyrus *P.Ant.* II.93.31 (IV AD). Diethart (1998: 172–3), Filos (2010: 250), Daris (1991a: 46), Hofmann (1989: 166 *s.v.* κελλάριον), LSJ suppl.

rare   **ἑπταούγκιον** 'seven twelfths', from ἑπτα- 'seven' + *ūncia* 'one twelfth' via οὐγγία: with *septunx* in Gloss. Ps.-Cyril. 313.39. LSJ. See §4.6.2.

rare   **ἐρανάριος**, a weapon, from *harēnārius* 'arena attendant': *ACO* II.I.III pp. 46.13, 47.20 (V AD). Hofmann (1989: 118), Lampe (1961).

         ἐράριον: see αἰράριον.

foreign   **ἔρβα** transliterating *herba* 'plant' as part of plant names: Galen XIII.1034.15 Kühn (II AD); interpolations in Dsc. 1.76 RV etc. Durling (1979: 220), Hofmann (1989: 119).

foreign   **ἐρβαρυβία** transliterating *herba rubia* 'madder plant': Alex.Trall. 1.457.2 (VI AD). *LBG*.

rare   **ἔρβουλον**, a plant, from *herbulum*, a plant name (*TLL*, uncertain whether it is a diminutive of *herba* 'plant' or of *ervum* 'vetch'): Edict.Diocl. 1.8a (IV AD). Lauffer (1971: 215), Hofmann (1989: 119), *TLL* (*s.v. herbulum*), LSJ suppl.

rare   **ἔρβουλος**, an Italian wine, apparently from *helvolus*, a variety of wine and of grapes: Athenaeus 1.27c (II/III AD). Sophocles (1887), LSJ suppl. (*s.v.* ἔρβουλον 2).

foreign   **ἐρεδιτάριος** 'part of an inheritance', from *hērēditārius* 'connected with inheritance': Antec. in Latin script 2.14.2 *hereditarion* etc. (VI AD); later in Greek script, sometimes as νερεδιτάριος. Zilliacus (1935a: 190–1), *LBG* (*s.vv.* ἐρεδιτάριος, νερεδιτάριος), Triantaphyllides (1892: 260). See §4.1.1 n. 23, §9.5.6 n. 68.

foreign   ***hērēs*** 'heir': Antec. 3.9.1 *heredem* etc. (VI AD). See §7.2.1; cf. προνερεδεγεριτεύω.

         ἐρμελαύσιον: see ἀρμελαύσιον.

         ἐρμίγερος: see ἀρμίγερος.

ἐρράτικους: see ἠρράτικος.

rare   ἐσκεπτώριον, from *exceptōrium* 'cistern': unpublished ostracon O.Claud. inv. 7442.4 (II AD).

name   Ἐσκυλῖνος 'Esquiline', from *Esquilīnus* 'Esquiline Hill'. Sophocles (1887).

Direct loan
II AD – ?   ἐσσεδάριος, ἀσσεδάριος, ἀσσιδάριος (-ου, ὁ) 'gladiator fighting from a chariot', from *essedārius* 'one who fights from a chariot'.
      Inscriptions: e.g. probably *SEG* XXXIX.1339.5 etc. (II AD); *I.Mylasa* 532.2; *I.Smyrna* 403.3.
      Literature: Artemidorus, *Onirocriticon* 2.32.26 (II AD).
      Notes: probably died out during antiquity, but end date uncertain. Hofmann (1989: 119), LSJ (*s.vv.* ἐσσεδάριος, ἀσσιδάριος). See §4.2.4.1 n. 50, §10.2.1, §10.2.2 F.

rare   ἔσσεδον, a vehicle, from *essedum* 'Gaulish war-chariot': papyrus *P.Lond.* III.1159.85 (II AD). Daris (1991a: 46), *LBG*.

ἐτράριος: see ἰτράριος.

εὐάστης: see οὐαστής.

εὐέντον: see ἔβεντον.

εὐηλάριον: see βηλάριον.

rare   εὔπλουμος, probably 'well-tapestry-woven', from εὖ 'well' + *plūma* 'feather': papyrus *SB* 16204.13 (IV/V AD). Wild and Dross-Krüpe (2017), Filos (2010: 250), Daris (1991a: 46), Hofmann (1989: 333 *s.v.* πλοῦμο-), Cavenaile (1952: 199), LSJ suppl. Cf. πλουμίον, ἔμπλουμος, ἐμπλούμιος, ὀρθόπλουμος, πλοῦμος.

rare   εὐρακύλων 'north-east wind' in NT Acts 27:14 (I/II AD) is often explained as a Greek hybrid compound of Εὖρος 'east wind' + *Aquilō* 'north wind', but Latin had *Eurus* 'east wind' and *Euroaquilō* 'north-east wind' (*CIL* VIII 26652); εὐρακύλων is probably from *Euroaquilō* (Bruce 1990: 518). Danker *et al.* (2000), Hemer (1989: 141–2), Leclercq (1997: 300), Blass *et al.* (1979: §5 n. 6), Hofmann (1989: 119), LSJ. See §9.3.

Z

rare   ζαβέρνα, ζάμερνα 'bag', from *zaberna* 'travelling bag' (*DMLBS*): Edict.Diocl. 11.2 etc. (IV AD); Pall. *H.Laus.* 19.4 (IV/V AD). Lauffer (1971: 250), Hofmann (1989: 119–20), Lampe (1961), LSJ suppl.

not Latin   ζάγκλον, said by Thucydides (6.4.5: τὸ δὲ δρέπανον οἱ Σικελοὶ ζάγκλον καλοῦσιν) and some later authors to be Sicilian term for 'sickle': related to *falx* 'sickle', but exact source language uncertain. Forms derivative ζαγκλαῖος. Willi (2008: 29), Simkin (2012: 167–70), Hofmann (1989: 120–1), *DÉLG* (*s.v.* ζάγκλη), Frisk (1954–72: I.606, III.98), Beekes (2010 *s.v.* ζάγκλη), LSJ.

ζάμερνα: see ζαβέρνα.

rare   **ζήστουπλομ** on papyrus *SB* 14178.22 (II AD?) seems to be from *sēscuplum*, neuter of a variant of *sēsquiplus* 'one and a half times as great'; Daris (1991a: 102) corrects it to σήστουπλουμ.

rare   **ζητάριος** 'fishmonger', from *cētārius* 'fishmonger': papyrus *P.Eirene* II.12r.9 etc. (V AD). Hofmann (1989: 121), *DGE* (interpreting this as a variant spelling of διαιτάριος, *q.v.*), LSJ suppl.

H

Direct loan
II AD – Byz.

ἠβοκᾶτος, ἠ(ο)υοκᾶτος, ἰούκατος, ἰουόκατος (-ου, ὁ) 'veteran called back into service', 'summoner', from *ēvocātus* 'veteran specially invited by a military commander to serve under him'.

Documents: none. *P.Oxy.* 33.iii.11 is literary (*Acta Alexandrinorum*, below).

Inscriptions: e.g. *I.Leukopetra* 41.3 (II AD); *I.Olbia* 45.2 (II AD); *IG* X.II. II.248.3 (II AD); *IGBulg.* III.II.1570.4 (III AD); *IGBulg.* IV.2250.2.

Literature: Hegesippus, Routh 1846: I.212.24 (II AD); *Acta Alexandrinorum* 11b.3.11 Musurillo (II/III AD); Dio Cassius 45.12.3, marked? (II/III AD); Eus. *HE* 3.20.1 (IV AD).

Post-antique: survives. Sophocles (1887 *s.v.* ἠουκᾶτος).

Notes: Freyburger-Galland (1997: 191–2), Daris (1991a: 46), Mason (1974: 5, 6, 52), Hofmann (1989: 123), Meinersmann (1927: 18), LSJ suppl. (*s.v.* ἠουοκᾶτος). See §4.2.4.1 n. 51, §10.2.1, §10.2.2 C.

rare   **ἠβωκάτωρ, ἠβοκάτωρ** 'veteran called back into service', in form apparently from *ēvocātor* 'one who orders out troops' but in meaning from *ēvocātus* 'veteran specially invited by a military commander to serve under him' (perhaps *evocatus* remodelled with -άτωρ?): papyrus *P.Ross.Georg.* III.1r.7 (III AD). Daris (1991a: 46), Hofmann (1989: 121), *LBG*. See §6.9 n. 60.

Direct loan
IV AD – modern

ἤδικτον, ἔδικτον, ἴδικτον (-ου, τό) 'edict', from *ēdictum* 'edict'.

Documents: *PSI* VI.684.3 etc. (IV AD); perhaps *CPR* XXV.6.14 (V AD); *P.Cair. Masp.* 67020r.2, 67295.1.3 etc. (both VI AD).

Inscriptions: *IG* X.II.1.22.3 (IV AD?); Bean and Mitford 1970: 57 no. 31.C11 etc. (V AD); *I.Chr.Macédoine* 85.3 (V/VI AD); *I.Sardis* I.20.27 (VI AD); *I.Ephesos* 1336.2.

Literature: common, e.g. DH *AR* 5.73.1, marked (I BC); Plut. *Marc.* 24.13, marked (I/II AD); Eutropius 8.17, marked (IV AD); *ACO* II.I.III p. 122.11 (V AD); Malal. 18.152 (VI AD); Just. *Nov.* 8 Ed.t etc. (VI AD); Cyr.S. *Vit.Sab.* 179.6 (VI AD); Antec. 1.2.3 etc., but in Latin script 1.2.6 *edicton* etc. (VI AD).

Post-antique: common. *LBG* (*s.v.* ἔδικτον), Kriaras (1968– *s.v.* ἔδικτον), Triandaphyllidis (1909: 127). Modern ἔδικτον 'edict': Babiniotis (2002).

Notes: Coleman (2007: 795) wrongly claims that it 'disappeared after Roman rule'. Binder (2000: 97), Avotins (1989, 1992), Daris (1991a: 46), Mason (1974: 6, 52), Hofmann (1989: 122), Zilliacus (1935a: 184–5), Meinersmann (1927: 16), Immisch (1885: 354), Lampe (1961 *s.vv.* ἔδικτον, ἤδικτον, ἴδικτον), LSJ suppl. See §4.2.4.1 n. 55, §10.2.1, §10.2.2 B.

ἠλεκέβρα: see ἰλλεκέβρα.

ἡμειλίτριν: see λίτρα 1.

name? ἡμέριτος 'veteran', from ēmeritus, pf. part. of ēmereō 'complete one's term in the army': usually a name, but perhaps a common noun in inscription *IGR* 1.552.2. Mason (1974: 5, 52).

rare ἡμιασσάριον 'halfpenny', from ἡμι- 'half' + assārius (*nummus*) 'penny' via ἀσσάριον: Polybius 2.15.6, marked (II BC); imperial-period coinage of Chios (Head 1911: 601); with *semis* in Gloss. Ps.-Philox. 181.54. Hofmann (1989: 37 *s.v.* ἀσσάριον), LSJ. See §4.6.2, §8.1.3 n. 17, §8.1.4, §9.1 n. 4.

rare ἡμικόγγιον 'half-congius', from ἡμι- 'half' + congius '6-pint measure': Hesych. as lemma η 494 (V/VI AD); Ps.-Galen, *De ponderibus* frag. 64.12 = Hultsch 1864: 240.19 etc. Hofmann (1989: 122), LSJ.

ἡμιλ(ε)ίτρ(ε)ιον, ἡμίλειτρον, ἡμιλιτριαῖος, ἡμιλίτριον, ἡμίλιτρον: see λίτρα 1.

not Latin? ἡμίνα 'half', perhaps from hēmīna 'half a sextarius', but probably *vice versa*. Immisch (1885: 310), *DÉLG* (*s.v.* ἡμι-), Frisk (1954–72: 1.636), Beekes (2010 *s.v.* ἡμι-), LSJ, LSJ suppl.

Deriv. of loan I AD – Byz. ἡμίξεστον (-ου, τό) 'half-pint', from ἡμι- 'half' + sextārius 'pint measure' via ξέστης.
Literature: Dsc. 1.25.1 (I AD); Jul.Afric. *Cest.* 1.12.4 etc. (II/III AD); Orib. *Syn.* 3.163.2 (IV AD); Aëtius 6.66.22 (VI AD); Ps.-Galen, *De ponderibus* frag. 55.4 = Hultsch 1864: 224.17; scholia to Ar. *Pl.* 436, 737; with *hemina* in glossaries, e.g. Gloss. Ps.-Cyril. 324.53.
Post-antique: survives.
Notes: LSJ, LSJ suppl. See §4.6.2, §10.2.2 E.

ἡμιόγκιον: see ἡμιούγκιον.

rare ἡμιουγκιαῖος 'of half an ounce', from ūncia 'one twelfth' via ἡμιούγκιον + -αῖος: with *semiuncialia* in Gloss. Ps.-Cyril. 324.61 (cf. *CGL* VII.537). Hofmann (1989: 302 *s.v.* οὐγκία), LSJ. See §4.6.2.

Deriv. of loan II AD – Byz. ἡμιούγκιον, ἡμιούγγιον, ἡμιόγκιον (-ου, τό) 'half-ounce', 'one twenty-fourth of an inheritance', from ἡμι- 'half' + ūncia 'one twelfth' via οὐγγία.
Documents: *BGU* III.781.v.17 etc. (I/II AD).
Inscriptions: *I.Ephesos* 27.466 (II AD); perhaps *I.Ephesos* 27.170 (II AD); perhaps bronze weight *IG* XIV.2417.29.
Literature: Galen XII.932.11 Kühn etc. (II AD); Ps.-Macar. *Serm.* 8.3.3 etc. (V AD?); Thdt. *PG* LXXX.556c (V AD); Just. *Nov.* 89.12.pr. etc. (VI AD); with *semiuncia* in Gloss. Ps.-Cyril. 324.60.
Post-antique: survives. *LBG*.
Notes: forms derivative ἡμιουγκιαῖος. Filos (2010: 244, 250), Cassio (2012: 259), Avotins (1992), Daris (1991a: 46), Hofmann (1989: 302 *s.v.* οὐγκία), Lampe (1961), LSJ, LSJ suppl. See §4.6.2, §9.5.3, §10.2.2 E.

ἡμ(μ)άγνιφερ: see ἰμαγίνιφερ.

ἡμφιβλατώριον: see ἰμφειβλατώριον.

ἤνουλα: see ἴνουλα.

Ἡουνουάριος: see Ἰανουάριος.

ἡουοκᾶτος: see ἡβοκᾶτος.

Ἡρακύλον: see Ἡρύκαλον.

non-existent? ἡρογατίων, perhaps 'distribution', probably from *ērogātiō* 'expenditure', 'distribution': perhaps inscription *SEG* xxxii.1554.A73 (vi AD), but the stone has ηρογαπονων.

ἡρογάτωρ: see ῥογάτωρ.

not ancient ἡρράτικος transliterating *errāticus* 'wild': interpolations in Dsc. 3.64a RV etc. Sophocles (1887 *s.v.* ἐρράτικους).

not Latin Ἡρύκαλον 'Hercules', a lemma in the manuscript of Hesych. η 855 (v/vi AD), claimed to be from *Herculēs*, is probably an error for non-Latinate Ἡρακύλον. Immisch (1885: 310–11), Latte's edition of Hesychius.

Ἡρῳδιανός: see §10.4.2.

ἤσκα: see ἴσκα.

Θ

θασσαλάριος, θεσ(σ)αλάριος, θεσσάριος: see τεσσαράριος.

foreign θῆσσα transliterating *tēnsa/thēnsa* 'wagon used to transport images of the gods': Plut. *Cor.* 25.6 (i/ii AD). Hofmann (1989: 123–4), LSJ.

semantic extension θρίαμβος 'hymn to Dionysus' acquired the meaning 'triumph' from *triumphus* 'triumph'; it then produced derivatives such as θριαμβεύω 'triumph' and θριαμβικός 'triumphal' that had only the Latin sense. Dubuisson (1985: 31–2), Versnel (1970: 11–55), Freyburger-Galland (1984: 330–3, 1997: 207–11), Blass *et al.* (1979: §5 n. 7), *DÉLG*, Frisk (1954–72: 1.682–3), Beekes (2010), Kriaras (1968–), Andriotis (1974: 277), Lampe (1961), LSJ. See §2.3.

I

rare ἰακλατόριον, ἰακλετώριον, a garment, from *iaculātōrius* 'for javelin-throwing': unpublished ostraca O.Claud. inv. 4399.6 (i/ii AD); O.Max. inv. 70.7 (ii AD); perhaps O.Xer. inv. 1016.7 (ii AD).

name Ἰανίκολον, Ἰάνικλον, Ἰανίκουλον, Ἰάνουκλον 'Janiculum', from *iāniculum* 'Janiculum Hill'. Sophocles (1887).

foreign ἰανούα transliterating *iānua* 'door': Porphyry, *De antro nympharum* 23.14 (iii AD); Lyd. *Mens.* 4.2.35 (vi AD); occasionally later. *LBG*.

Direct loan
I BC – modern Ἰανουάριος, Ἰαννουάριος, Ἰανοάριος, Εἰανουάριος, Ἡουνουάριος (-α, -ον or -ου, ὁ) 'January', from *Iānuārius* 'January'.
Documents: e.g. *SB* 9228.21 (ii AD); *SB* 12667.10 (iii AD); *P.Panop.* 15.5 etc. (iv AD); *SB* 16521.3 (iv/v AD); *P.Ness.* iii.29.2 (vi AD).
Inscriptions: e.g. Sherk 1969: no. 26.d22 (i BC); *IG* v.i.1431.42 (i AD); *Corinth* viii.iii.306.17 (ii AD); Robert and Robert 1954: 274 no. 149.24 (iii AD); *SEG* xlvi.1261.5 (iv AD); Pugliese Carratelli 1956: no. 44.6 (v AD); *SEG* viii.42.1 (vi AD).

Literature: e.g. perhaps Critolaus, *FHG* IV frag. 2.17 (II BC); perhaps
Posidonius, frag. 249.2 Theiler (II/I BC); Plut. *Marius* 12.3 (I/II AD);
Athenaeus 9.372d (II/III AD); Hippolytus, *Commentarium in Danielem*
4.23.3 (III AD); Epiph. *Pan.* II.284.12 (IV AD); Marc.Diac. 21.16 as gloss
(V AD); Antec. 2.14.9 (VI AD).

Post-antique: common. *LBG* (*s.v.* Ἰαννουάρης), Kriaras (1968–). Modern
Ιανουάριος, Γενάρης, Γενάρις: Babiniotis (2002), Andriotis (1967), Kahane
and Kahane (1972–6: 533), Meyer (1895: 19).

Notes: Solin (2008), Binder (2000: 99–100, 216, 272), Sijpesteijn (1979),
Avotins (1989, 1992), Dieterich (1898: 73), Strobach (1997: 195),
Hofmann (1989: 124), Meinersmann (1927: 19), Lampe (1961), LSJ suppl.
See **§4.2.1**, §4.2.2, §6.1, §8.2.3 n. 51, §10.2.1, §10.2.2 E, §12.2.2.

Ἰάνουκλον: see Ἰανίκολον.

ἰβίσκος: see ἐβίσκος.

not Latin?   **ἰβυκηνίζω**, lemma in Hesych. ι 135, 136 (V/VI AD), could be a variant of
βυκινίζω and therefore come ultimately from *būcina* 'trumpet'. Hofmann
(1989: 74 *s.v.* βυκάνη), Frisk (1954–72: 1.707).

not ancient   **ἰγγυνᾶλις** transliterating *inguinālis*, a plant: interpolation in Dsc. 4.119.2 RV.
Sophocles (1887).

foreign   **ἴγκερτος, ἴνκερτος** 'indeterminate', from *incertus* 'not fixed': Antec. in Latin script
2.20.25 *incerton* etc. (VI AD); later in Greek script. Zilliacus (1935a: 190–1),
LBG. See §9.5.6 n. 68.

rare   **ἴγκεστος, ἴνκεστος, ἴγκεστις, ἴνκεστις** 'incestuous', from *incestus* 'incestuous': Just.
Codex 1.3.44.3, but in Latin script *Nov.* 12.1 etc. (VI AD); Byzantine texts.
Avotins (1989, 1992), Zilliacus (1935a: 190–1), *LBG*. See §9.5.6 n. 68.

ἴγκολα(ς): see ἰνκόλας.

foreign   **ἰγκουϊλῖνος** transliterating *inquilīnus* 'lodger': App. *BC* 2.1.2 (I/II AD). Famerie
(1998: 125–7), Sophocles (1887).

rare   **ἰγκουισιτίων, ἰνκουισιτίων** 'investigation', from *inquīsītiō* 'investigation':
inscription *I.Prusias* 54.9; *Schol.Sinai.* in Latin script 46 *inquisitiona* (V/VI AD);
Antec. in Latin script 1.20.3 *inquisitiona* etc. (VI AD); Byzantine texts. Editor
of inscription *ad loc.*, Mason (1974: 5, 54), Hofmann (1989: 129), Zilliacus
(1935a: 190–1), *LBG* (*s.v.* ἰνκουισιτίων). See §7.1.2, §9.5.6 n. 56.

rare   **ἰγκρεμέντ(ι)ον, ἰγκριμέντ(ι)ον, ἰνκριμέντιον** 'additional tax', from *incrēmentum*
'addition': papyri *SB* 12215.8 (IV AD); *P.Oxy.* 3805.8 etc. (VI AD). Daris
(1991a: 46), *LBG* (*s.vv.* ἰγκριμέντιον, ἰγκρίμεντον).

ἴδικτον: see ἤδικτον.

Ἰδοί: see Εἰδοί.

foreign   **ἴλαξ** 'holm oak', from *īlex* 'holm oak': Hesych. as lemma attributed to Ῥωμαῖοι καὶ
Μακεδόνες, ι 537 (V/VI AD). Immisch (1885: 332), Sophocles (1887 *s.v.*
ἴλεξ), LSJ suppl. See §9.5.4.

foreign | ἴλιον 'female genitalia', probably from *īlia, -ium* 'groin': Hesych. as lemma ι 549, 563 (v/vi AD). Hofmann (1989: 125), *DÉLG* (s.v. ἴλια), Frisk (1954–72: 1.722), Beekes (2010 s.v. ἴλια), LSJ and LSJ suppl. (s.vv. ἴλιον, ἴλια).

not ancient? | ἰλλᾶτος, ἰνλᾶτος, from *illātus*, pf. part. of *īnferō* 'introduce': no securely ancient examples. Hofmann (1989: 125), Zilliacus (1935a: 190–1), *LBG* (s.v. ἰνλᾶτος).

foreign | ἰλλεκέβρα transliterating *illecebra* 'species of stonecrop': perhaps Dsc. 4.90.1 (but the right reading may be ἠλεκέβρα for *elecebra*: *TLL* s.v. 2. *elecebra* 327.72–8, *DGE* s.v. ἐλέκεβρα) (I AD); Galen XIX.146.11 Kühn etc. (II AD). Sophocles (1887).

non-existent? | ἰλλίκιτος 'illicit', from *illicitus* 'illicit': cited as an ancient loan by Zilliacus (1935a: 190–1), but I can find no examples.

Direct loan v AD – Byz. | ἰλ(λ)ούστριος (-α, -ον) 'noble', from *illūstris* 'distinguished'.
Documents: e.g. *Stud.Pal.* VIII.958.1 (v/vi AD); *P.Oxy.* 1913.28, 3204.4 (both VI AD); *P.Cair.Masp.* 67002.2.2 etc. (VI AD).
Inscriptions: e.g. *IGLS* V.2620.2 (V AD); *I.Sinope* 179a.10 (VI AD); *SEG* XXVII.1006.2 (VI AD).
Literature: common, e.g. Callin. *V.Hypat.* 6.4 (V AD); Nil. 1.54.1 (V AD); Just. *Nov.* 13.3.pr. (VI AD); Cyr.S. *Vit.Sab.* 172.23 (VI AD); Antec. Βασιλικῆς 3, but in Latin script 4.4.10 *illustriois* (VI AD).
Post-antique: numerous. *LBG* (s.vv. ἰλλοῦστρος, ἰλλουστρία), Triandaphyllidis (1909: 131).
Notes: Koch (1903: 34–45), Menci (2000: 282), Avotins (1989, 1992), Drew-Bear (1972: 199), Daris (1991a: 46), Hofmann (1989: 126), Zilliacus (1935a: 190–1), Meinersmann (1927: 18), Lampe (1961), LSJ suppl. See §4.2.2, §10.2.1, §10.2.2 D.

Direct loan III–IV AD | ἰμαγίνιφερ, ἰμαγινιφέρος, ἰμαγνειφερ, ἠμ(μ)άγνιφερ, μαγνιφέρ, ἰμμαγνίφερ (-ερος/-ου, ὁ), a type of standard-bearer, from *imāginifer* (gen. *imāginiferī*) 'soldier who carried a standard bearing the image of the emperor'.
Documents: perhaps *O.Did.* 180.1 (II AD); perhaps *BGU* I.344.4 etc. (II/III AD); *P.Oxy.* 3571.14, 4746.7 (both III AD); *O.Heid.* 429.3 (III/IV AD); *P.Panop.Beatty* 2.11.297 (III/IV AD).
Inscriptions: *I.Philae* 184.3 (II/III AD); *SEG* LXV.1408.C16, transliterating Latin (v/vi AD).
Literature: Lyd. *Mag.* p. 72.8, marked (VI AD).
Notes: Drew-Bear (1972: 78), Daris (1991a: 47, citing an inscription as a papyrus), Hofmann (1989: 126), Meinersmann (1927: 18), LSJ suppl. (s.v. ἰμαγινιφέρ). See §4.2.4.1, §10.2.1, §10.2.2 C.

ἰμβεντάριον: see ἰνβεντάριον.

ἰμιλίτριν: see λίτρα 1.

non-existent? | ἰμπεδιμέντον, ἰμπετιμέντον 'obstacle', from *impedīmentum* 'obstacle': perhaps papyrus *P.Cair.Masp.* 67057.3.13 (VI AD), also read as ἰμπένδια. Daris (1991a: 47), Meinersmann (1927: 18).

non-existent? ἰμπένδια 'costs', from *impendia*, plural of *impendium* 'cost': perhaps papyrus *P.Cair. Masp.* 67057.3.13 (VI AD), also read as ἰμπεδιμέντον. *LBG*.

foreign *imperāre*, inf. of *imperō* 'command': Lyd. *Mag.* p. 12.23 (VI AD).

Direct loan ἰμπεράτωρ, ἰνπεράτωρ (-ορος/-ωρος, ὁ) 'commander', 'emperor', from *imperātor*
I BC – Byz. 'commander', 'emperor'.
   Documents: none. *O.Claud.* II.331.13 (II AD) is Latin in Greek script.
   Inscriptions: Sherk 1969: no. 21.11 (I BC); *IG* V.I.1454.3 (I BC); Faraklas
      1968 (I BC); *IG* XII.I.48.6 (I BC); *IG* V.I.380.4 (II AD); perhaps *IGUR*
      I.38.4 (II/III AD).
   Coins: ΙΜΠ. ΚΑΙΣ. Μ. ΑΥΡΗ. ΑΝΤΩΝΙΝΟΣ, in *Sylloge nummorum Graecorum: the royal
      collection of coins and medals, Danish National Museum*, XIII: *Aetolia–Euboea*
      (Copenhagen 1944) no. 462 (II AD).
   Literature: e.g. perhaps Diodorus Siculus 36.14.1 (I BC); Eutropius 9.1
      (IV AD); Malal. 8.8 (VI AD); Lyd. *Mag.* p. 12.24 (VI AD).
   Post-antique: minimal survival. Triandaphyllidis (1909: 126).
   Notes: Mason (1974: 6, 7, 9, 56), Hofmann (1989: 126), Lampe (1961), LSJ
      suppl. See §4.2.5, §6.8, §8.1.5, §9.1 n. 4, §10.2.1, §10.2.2 C.

rare ἰμπέριον, ἰνπέριον, from *imperium* 'supreme power': inscription *IGR* III.481.17
      (III AD); Byzantine texts. Mason (1974: 6, 56), Hofmann (1989: 129),
      Zilliacus (1935a: 190–1), *LBG*, Kriaras (1968–).

ἰμπετιμέντον: see ἰμπεδιμέντον.

ἰμποτέστατος: see ἰνποτέστατος.

foreign ἴμφανς, ἴνφανς, ἴμφας 'infant', from *īnfāns* 'infant': Antec. in Latin script 2.19.4
      infans etc. (VI AD); later in Greek script. Zilliacus (1935a: 190–1), *LBG*. See
      §9.5.6 n. 68.

rare ἰμφειβλατώριον 'cloak fastened with a fibula', from *īnfībulātōrium* (not in
      lexica but on *T.Vindol.* III.596.3): inscription *I.Pessinous* 8.7 (II AD).
      Probably ἠμφιβλατώριον on *P.Lond.* II.191.5 (II AD). Sidro and Maravela
      (forthcoming), *SEG* LV.1399 p. 451, Hofmann (1989: 126–7), LSJ suppl. Cf.
      φιβλατώριον.

in (in phrases *in capita, in diem, in rem*): see κάπιτον, *dies*, ῥέμ.

not ancient ἴνβεκτος 'importation', from *invectus, -ūs* 'importation': no ancient examples.
      Zilliacus (1935a: 192–3), *LBG*.

rare ἰνβεντάριον, ἰμβεντάριον 'inventory of an estate', from *inventārium* 'inventory':
      papyrus *P.Petra* I.2.138 etc. (VI AD); Just. *Nov.* in Latin script 1.2.1 etc.
      (VI AD); Ath.Schol. in Latin script 7.8.8 etc. (VI AD); Antec. in Latin script
      2.19.6 *inventarion* (VI AD); Byzantine texts. Hofmann (1989: 127), Zilliacus
      (1935a: 192–3), *LBG*, Lampe (1961).

not ancient ἰνβέντον 'list', apparently from *inventum* 'invention' combined with *inventārium*
      'list': no ancient examples. Diethart (1998: 173), Hofmann (1989: 127),
      Zilliacus (1935a: 192–3), Meinersmann (1927: 16), *LBG*, *TLL* (*s.vv.*
      inventum 158.72–4, *inventārium* 151.29).

foreign *invicem* 'reciprocally': Antec. 2.15.1 *invicem* etc. (VI AD).

foreign	**ἰνδέβιτος** 'not owed', from *indēbitus* 'not owed': Antec. in Latin script 3.14.1 *indebiton* etc. (VI AD); later in Greek script. Zilliacus (1935a: 190–1), *LBG*, Lampe (1961). See §9.5.6 n. 68.
rare	**ἴνδικα** (probably acc.) on papyrus *P.Princ.* III.183.14 (IV AD) led Cavenaile (1951: 396) to cite ἴνδιξ 'informer' as a borrowing of *index* 'informer', though the context does not make the meaing clear. Cf. Byzantine ἴνδιξ 'index', *LBG*.
not Latin	**Ἰνδικός** 'Indian' and **ἰνδικόν** 'indigo': sometimes said to be from *Indicus* 'of India', but probably *vice versa* given the early attestation of Ἰνδικός (e.g. Herodotus 3.98). Hofmann (1989: 127), *LBG*, LSJ, LSJ suppl.
Direct loan **III AD – modern**	**ἰνδικτίων, εἰνδικτίων, ἐνδικτίων, ἐμδικτίων** (-ωνος/-ονος, ἡ) 'period of fifteen years', 'tax period', 'periodic tax', from *indictiō* 'indiction' (fifteen-year tax period) (*TLL*). Documents: very common, e.g. *CPR* XXIII.20.11 (III AD); *P.Oxy.* 1328 (IV AD); *SB* 14001.12 (V AD); *P.Oxy.* 3600.11 (VI AD). Inscriptions: very common, e.g. Asdracha 1998: 455 no. 196.7 (III/IV AD); *Corinth* VIII.III.522.12 (IV AD); tile stamps *SEG* XLVI.845bis (V AD); *IG* II/III².V.13362.7 (V/VI AD); *IG* X.II.II.149.C (VI AD). Literature: e.g. *Vet.Val. App.* 9.1.5 (II AD?); Epiph. *Anc.* 60.5 (IV AD); *V.Dan. Styl. A.* 97.12 (V AD); Malal. 18.87 (VI AD); Just. *Nov.* 128.1 (VI AD). Post-antique: survives. Sophocles (1887), Triandaphyllidis (1909: 120). Modern ινδικτιών 'fifteen-year period': Babiniotis (2002), Meyer (1895: 22). Notes: Binder (2000: 119–20), Avotins (1992), Drew-Bear (1972: 78), Daris (1991a: 47), Hofmann (1989: 127–8), Zilliacus (1937: 329), Meinersmann (1927: 18–19), *TLL* (*s.v. indictio* 1159.72–3, 1160.44–80), Lampe (1961), LSJ suppl. See §4.2.5, §8.1.1 n. 3, §10.2.1, §10.2.2 D.
rare	**ἰνδικτιωνάλιος** 'of an indiction or tax', from *indictiōnālis* 'of an indiction or tax' (*TLL*): Edict.Diocl. 19.2 etc. (IV AD). Hofmann (1989: 128), *TLL* (*s.v. indictiōnālis*).
rare	**ἴνδικτος** 'indiction' (fifteen-year tax period), probably a variant of ἰνδικτίων and therefore from *indictiō* 'indiction' (*TLL*), or perhaps directly from rare *indictus, -ūs* 'indiction' (*TLL s.v.* 1. *indictus*): papyrus *CPR* XXV.6.14 (V AD); Byzantine texts. Commentary *ad loc.*, *LBG*, Meyer (1895: 22), Babiniotis (2002 *s.v.* ἴνδικτος), Lampe (1961). **ἴνδιξ**: see ἴνδικα.
not ancient	**ἰνδουκέντα, ἰνδουκέντες** 'fees', related to *indūcō* 'bring in': no ancient examples. Zilliacus (1935a: 190–1, with derivation from *indūcentēs*), *LBG* (with derivation from *indūcenda*).
rare	**ἰνδουλγεντία** 'pardon', from *indulgentia* 'leniency': Malal. 12.21, 12.41, 18.132 (VI AD); occasional Byzantine texts. Hofmann (1989: 128), Zilliacus (1935a: 190–1), Triandaphyllidis (1909: 128), Sophocles (1887), Lampe (1961).
foreign	**ἰνδυστρία** transliterating *industria* 'purposeful activity': unpublished ostracon O.Max. inv. 1197.1 (I/II AD).

foreign   *inīquitās* 'injustice': Antec. 4.4.pr. *iniquitas* (VI AD).

foreign   ἰνιουρία 'injury', 'injustice', from *iniūria* 'unjust treatment' (in gen. pl. ἰνιουριάρουμ a kind of legal case): Antec. in Latin script 4.4.pr. *iniuria* etc. (VI AD); Just. *Nov.* in Latin script 71.1 (VI AD); later in Greek script. Zilliacus (1935a: 190–1), *LBG*, Kriaras (1968– *s.v.* ἰνζούρια).

foreign   *iniūstitia* 'injustice'; Antec. 4.4.pr. *iniustitia* (VI AD).

foreign   ἰνιοῦστος 'not properly done', from *iniūstus* 'unjust': Antec. in Latin script 2.17.pr. *iniusta* (VI AD); later in Greek script. *LBG*. See §9.5.6 n. 68.

          ἴνκερτος: see ἴγκερτος.

          ἴνκεστος: see ἴγκεστος.

rare   ἰνκόλας, ἴγκολα(ς) 'resident alien', from *incola* 'resident alien': Modestinus in Just. *Dig.* 27.1.13.12, 50.1.35 (III AD); Byzantine texts. Mason (1974: 12), *LBG* (*s.v.* ἴγκολος), LSJ suppl. See §9.5.6 nn. 55 and 58.

          ἰνκουισιτίων: see ἰγκουισιτίων.

          ἰνκριμέντιον: see ἰγκρεμέντιον.

          ἰνλᾶτος: see ἰλλᾶτος.

not ancient   ἴνουλα, ἤνουλα transliterating *inula*, a plant: interpolation in Dsc. 1.28 RV. Sophocles (1887 *s.v.* ἤνουλα).

foreign   ἰνούλεους 'fawn', from *hinnuleus/īnuleus* 'fawn': Hesych. as lemma ι 686 (V/VI AD). Immisch (1885: 333–4), *LBG* (*s.v.* ἰνούλεος).

          ἰνπεράτωρ: see ἰμπεράτωρ.

          ἰνπέριον: see ἰμπέριον.

foreign   ἰνποτέστατος, ἰμποτέστατος 'under the power' of a father or master, 'not emancipated', from *in potestāte* 'in (his father's) power': Antec. in Latin script 1.8.pr. *in potestate* etc. (VI AD); later in Greek script. Hofmann (1989: 129), Viscidi (1944: 27), Zilliacus (1935a: 190–1). Cf. ποτέστας.

foreign   ἴνριτος, ἴρριτος 'not valid', from *irritus* 'not valid': Antec. in Latin script 2.17.5 *irriton* etc. (VI AD); later in Greek script. Zilliacus (1935a: 192–3), *LBG*, Triantaphyllides (1892: 262 *s.v.* ἴρριτος). See §7.2.1 passage 26.

not ancient   ἰνσᾶνα transliterating *īnsāna*, a plant (*TLL s.v. īnsānus* 1834.48–50): interpolation in Dsc. 4.68 RV. Sophocles (1887).

non-existent?   ἴνσπεκτον 'inspection', 'review', from *īnspectus, -ūs* 'examination': supplement on inscription *SEG* XXVII.1139.34 (VI AD). LSJ suppl.

rare   ἰνσπέσιμον 'inspection', apparently from *īnspectiō* 'inspection' (or a related word) + -ιμος in neuter: inscription *SEG* IX.356.25 (VI AD). Oliverio (1936: 157 *ad loc.*), Hofmann (1989: 129).

foreign   ἰνστιτορία 'legal action about a slave-run business', from *īnstitōrius*, a legal action: Antec. in Latin script 4.7.2 *institoria* etc. (VI AD); later in Greek script. Zilliacus (1935a: 190–1), *LBG* (*s.v.* ἰνστιτόριος).

Direct loan **VI AD – Byz.**	**ἰνστιτοῦτα** (-ων, τά) 'introduction to Roman law', from *īnstitūta, -ōrum* 'teachings' (*OLD s.v. institūtum* 3). Literature: *Schol.Sinai.* in Latin script 35 *inst.* (V/VI AD); Antec. proem. 3 (VI AD); Just. *Nov.* 18.9 etc. (VI AD). Post-antique: survives in legal texts. *LBG* (*s.v.* ἰνστιτοῦτος), Sophocles (1887 *s.v.* ἰνστιτοῦτον). Modern ινστιτούτο 'institute' (Babiniotis 2002; Andriotis 1967) is not a direct survival. Notes: Avotins (1992). See §4.2.4.1 n. 55, §7.1.2, §8.2.2, §9.5.6 nn. 56 and 68, §10.2.1, §10.2.2 B.
foreign	**ἰνστιτουτίων** 'basic explanation of Roman law', from *īnstitūtiō* 'teaching': Antec. in Latin script 4.6.pr. *institutioni* etc. (VI AD); later in Greek script. Zilliacus (1935a: 190–1), *LBG*, Sophocles (1887). See §9.5.6 n. 68.
not ancient	**ἰνστιτουτόριος**, a legal action: no ancient examples. Zilliacus (1935a: 190–1, with derivation from *īnstitūtōrius* 'of education', *TLL*), *LBG* (*s.v.* ἰνστιτόριος, with derivation from *īnstitōrius*, a legal action).
foreign	**ἰνστιτοῦτος** 'instituted heir' (the one named in the will as the first choice), from *īnstitūtus*, pf. part. of *īnstituō* 'appoint as heir': Antec. in Latin script 2.15.4 *institutu* etc. (VI AD); later in Greek script. Zilliacus (1935a: 190–1), *LBG*. See §9.5.6 n. 68.
foreign	**ἴνστρουκτος** 'complete with facilities', 'with equipment', from *īnstrūctus* 'equipped': Antec. in Latin script 2.20.17 *instructon* (VI AD); Just. *Nov.* in Latin script 128.8 (VI AD); later in Greek script. Avotins (1992), Hofmann (1989: 129), Zilliacus (1935a: 190–1), *LBG*.
rare	**ἰ(ν)στρουμεντάριος** 'archivist', from rare medieval *īnstrūmentārius* 'documentary' (*DMLBS*), or an unattested noun of the same form (*TLL s.v. īnstrūmentārius*), or *īnstrūmentum* 'document' via ἰνστρουμέντον + -άριος: inscription *MAMA* VII.524.2 = *MAMA* I p. xiv; Lyd. *Mag.* pp. 160.29 (marked), 162.7, 164.12 (VI AD). Mason (1974: 4, 56), Hofmann (1989: 129–30), *LBG* (*s.v.* στρουμεντάριος), LSJ suppl. See §8.1.7.
rare	**ἰ(ν)στρουμέντον, στρουμέντον** 'document', 'collection of documents', 'equipment', from *īnstrūmentum* 'document': Lyd. *Mag.* p. 188.12 (VI AD); Just. *Nov.* in Latin script 128.8 (VI AD); Ath.Schol. in Latin script 20.1.8 (VI AD); Antec. in Latin script 2.20.17 *instrumenton* (VI AD); perhaps papyrus *CPR* VII.21.14 (IV AD); common in Byzantine texts. Accented recessively by most lexica but paroxytone by most editors. Binder (2000: 226), Hofmann (1989: 130), Zilliacus (1935a: 190–1), *LBG* (*s.vv.* ἰνστρούμεντον, στρουμέντον), Lampe (1961 *s.v.* στρούμεντον).
foreign	**ἰντε(ν)τίων** 'complaint', 'first part of a legal request', from *intentiō* 'statement of the charge': Antec. in Latin script 4.10.2 *intentiona* etc. (VI AD); later in Greek script. Zilliacus (1935a: 190–1), *LBG*. See §9.5.6 n. 68.
foreign	**ἰντέρβιβος** 'while alive', from *inter vīvōs* '(made) between living men': *P.Cair.Masp.* 67096.42 and 67151.130 in Latin script *inter vivos* (VI AD); Antec. in Latin script 2.7.pr. *inter vivos* etc. (VI AD); Just. *Nov.* in Latin script 22.32 (VI AD); later in Greek script. Fournet (2019: 83), *LBG*, Triantaphyllides (1892: 261).

foreign   *interdīcō* 'forbid': Antec. 4.15.1 *interdicere*, 1.16.2 *aqua et igni interdictu*, etc. (VI AD).

foreign   ἰντερδικτίων 'prohibition', from *interdictiō* 'prohibition': Just. *Nov.* in Latin script 22.13 as part of *aqua et igni interdictionα* 'banishment' (VI AD). Zilliacus (1935a: 190–1).

foreign   ἰντέρδικτον, a legal pronouncement, from *interdictum* 'injunction issued by a pro-magistrate': Antec. in Latin script 4.15.pr. *interdictois* etc. (VI AD); later in Greek script. Zilliacus (1935a: 190–1), *LBG* (s.v. ἰντέρδικτος), Sophocles (1887 s.v. ἰντερδίκτος). See §9.5.6 n. 68.

rare   ἰντερκαλάριος, ἐντερκλάριος 'intercalary', from *intercalārius* 'intercalary': inscriptions *I.Délos* 1510.18 (II BC); *I.Priene* B–M 14.71 etc. (I BC). García Domingo (1979: 419), Hofmann (1989: 130), LSJ suppl. See §8.1.4 n. 22.

not ancient   ἰντερκεδεύω 'act as surety for a debt', from *intercēdō* 'intervene' + -εύω: only in Byzantine texts, since the epitome of Ath.Schol. is not ancient. Zilliacus (1935a: 190–1), *LBG*.

foreign   ἰντερκεσ(σ)ίων 'surety', from *intercessiō* 'surety': Just. *Nov.* in Latin script 61.1.1 (VI AD); later in Greek script. Zilliacus (1935a: 190–1), *LBG*. See §9.5.6 n. 68.

foreign   ἰντέρρηξ transliterating *interrēx* 'temporary king': App. *BC* 1.11.98 (I/II AD). Famerie (1998: 130–3), Mason (1974: 6, 56).

not ancient   ἰντερρογατόριος 'concerning questioning', from *interrogātōrius* 'concerning questioning': no ancient examples. Zilliacus (1935a: 190–1), *LBG*.

not ancient   ἰντερσεδεύω 'sit among', apparently from unattested *intersedeō 'sit among' (*TLL*) + -εύω: no ancient examples. Zilliacus (1935a: 190–1). See §8.1.7.

     ἰντετίων: see ἰντεντίων.

     ἴντουβος: see ἴντυβον.

not ancient   ἴντουβουμ transliterating *intubum* 'endive', 'chicory': interpolations in Dsc. 2.132 RV etc. Cf. ἴντυβον.

rare   ἰντρόειντα, ἰντρόϊτα, ἰντρόϊτος 'entrance fee', 'receipts', from *introitus, -ūs* 'entry' and/or *introita* 'entrance fee' (*TLL* s.v. *introitum* 77.65–74): papyrus *P.Oxy.* 2024.1 (VI AD); Just. *Nov.* in Latin script 30.4 etc. (VI AD). Daris (1991a: 47, with derivation from *introeō*), Hofmann (1989: 131), Zilliacus (1935a: 190–1), Meinersmann (1927: 19), *LBG*.

rare   ἰντρόϊτον 'entrance' (to a church), from *introitus, -ūs* 'entry': *Constitutiones apostolorum* 2.57.60 Metzger (IV AD). Hofmann (1989: 131), Lampe (1961).

     ἰντρόϊτος: see ἰντρόειντα.

Direct? loan with suffix

VI AD? – Byz.   ἰντύβιον, ἐντύβιον (-ου, τό) 'endive', 'chicory', from *intubum/intibum* 'endive', 'chicory' + -ιον.

     Literature: *Praecepta salubria* 62 in Bussemaker 1862: 133 (I BC?); Hieroph. *Nut.* 6.7 (IV–VI AD); bilingual glossaries, e.g. Gloss. Ps.-Philox. 91.24.
     Post-antique: numerous. *LBG*, Kriaras (1968–).
     Notes: perhaps via ἴντυβον, but both *Praecepta salubria* and Ps.-Philoxenus are probably early enough for direct borrowing. Lampe (1961 s.v. ἐντύβιον, citing additional, unverified example from VI AD). See §4.3.2, §10.2.1, §10.2.2 I.

foreign	**ἰντυβολάχανον**, from *intubum* 'endive', 'chicory' via ἴντυβον + λάχανον 'vegetable': Ps.-Galen XIV.321.8 Kühn, marked.
Direct loan **II AD – Byz.**	**ἴντυβον, ἴντ(ο)υβος, ἔντυβον** (-ου, τό or ὁ) 'endive', 'chicory', from *intubum/intibum* 'endive', 'chicory'. Inscriptions: Edict.Diocl. 6.3 etc. (IV AD). Literature: e.g. Galen XIII.173.14 Kühn (II AD); Orib. *Col.* 2.2.1 (IV AD); Aëtius 1.168.1 (VI AD); Ps.-Hippocrates, Delatte 1939: 480.21, 489.14; with *intubum* in Gloss. Ps.-Cyril. 300.52. Post-antique: numerous. *LBG* (*s.vv.* ἴντυβον, ἴντυβος, ἐντύβι(ο)ν, ἔντυβον). Notes: Hofmann (1989: 131), *DÉLG* (*s.v.* ἔντυβον), Beekes (2010 *s.v.* ἔντυβον), LSJ (*s.vv.* ἴντυβος, ἔντυβον). See §4.2.4.1 n. 55, §10.2.1, §10.2.2 I.
	ἴνφανς: see ἴμφανς.
	ἰόκουρος: see βιόκουρος.
foreign	**ἰοῦβα** transliterating *iuba* 'crest': Lyd. *Mag.* p. 18.23 (VI AD). Hofmann (1989: 132), *LBG*.
not ancient	**Ἰουβενάλια** transliterating *Iuvenālia*, a festival (*TLL s.v. iuvenālis* 728.79–729.6): no ancient examples. Sophocles (1887).
non-existent	**ἰουγάλιον** 'land tax', cited by Sophocles (1887), Zilliacus (1935a: 192–3), and Viscidi (1944: 20) as from *iugālis* 'of a yoke' (not attested of a tax: see *TLL s.v.*): superseded conjecture for ἰουλίων in Just. *Nov.* 17.8.pr. (VI AD).
rare	**ἰουγατίων** 'land tax', from *iugātiō* 'land tax' (*TLL s.v.* 626.44–76): Thdt. *Ep.Sirm.* 42.50 (V AD); papyrus *P.Petra* I.10.10 (VI AD). Hofmann (1989: 132), Lampe (1961).
Direct loan **IV–VI AD**	**ἰούγερον** (-ου, τό), a land measurement, from *iūgerum* 'two thirds of an acre'. Documents: e.g. *P.Petra* I.5.4 etc., III.25.9 etc. (all VI AD). But *P.Ital.* II.30.92 (VI AD) is Latin in Greek script. Inscriptions: numerous in III/IV AD, e.g. *IG* XII.II.76 *passim*, *IG* XII.III.343 *passim*; perhaps also *IGNapoli* II.88.c2 (II/III AD). Literature: Hesych. as lemma ι 760 (V/VI AD); Her.Mech. *Def.* 131.1.23 etc. Notes: all documents are from Petra. Hofmann (1989: 133), Meinersmann (1927: 19), LSJ suppl. (*s.v.* ἰούγερα). See §4.2.4.1 n. 55, §10.2.1, §10.2.2 E.
Direct loan **VI AD – Byz.?**	**ἰοῦγον** (-ου, τό), a land-tax assessment unit (the unit being of a constant value and therefore consisting of more acres for poor land and fewer acres for fertile land), from *iugum* 'yoke' (also of the land-tax unit: *TLL s.v.* 641.3–17). Documents: perhaps *P.Petra* III.35.10 etc. (VI AD). Literature: Hesych. as gloss ε 132 (V/VI AD); Malal. 16.3.20 (VI AD); Just. *Nov.* 17.8.pr. etc. (VI AD). Post-antique: survival perhaps attested by Triandaphyllidis (1909: 127). Notes: Avotins (1989, 1992), Hofmann (1989: 133), Viscidi (1944: 20), Zilliacus (1935a: 192–3), Lampe (1961), LSJ suppl. See §4.2.4.1 n. 55, §5.2.3, §10.2.1, §10.2.2 D.
foreign	**ἰουδικιάλιος** 'judicial', from *iūdiciālis* 'judicial': Antec. in Latin script 3.18.1 *iudicaliae* etc. (VI AD); later in Greek script. Zilliacus (1935a: 192–3), *LBG*.

ἰούκατος: see ἠβοκᾶτος.

rare ἰουκούνδα, a type of painkiller, from *iūcundus* 'pleasant' (not a term for a particular medication, though sometimes used of medications: *TLL s.v.* 593.81–594.2): Galen XIII.94.5 Kühn (II AD). Durling (1979: 220), Hofmann (1989: 133–4), *LBG*.

foreign Ἰουλιανόν, a cake name from *Iūliānus* 'of Julius' (not attested of a cake): Athenaeus 14.647c, marked (II/III AD). Hauri-Karrer (1972: 120). See §9.4 passage 61.

rare Ἰουλιεύς 'of Julius' (an Egyptian month), from the name *Iūlius* + -ιεύς: papyri *P.Mich.* v.321.1 (I AD); *Stud.Pal.* XXII.173.16 etc. (I AD). Scott (1931: 249), Bagnall (2009: 181), Cavenaile (1951: 396), LSJ suppl.

Direct loan Ἰούλιος, Ἰουλίηος, Εἰούλιος (-α, -ον or -ου, ὁ) 'July', from *Iūlius* 'July'.
I BC – modern Documents: e.g. *P.Yadin* I.20.2 (II AD); *O.Cret.Chers.* 79.1 (II/III AD); *P.Sakaon* 17.22 etc. (IV AD); *SB* 8028.9 etc. (VI AD).
Inscriptions: e.g. *SEG* XLVI.1088.i.6 (I BC); *Agora* XXI.Hc.9, dipinto on amphora (I AD); *I.Beroia* 68.14 (III AD); *SEG* XXX.585 (IV AD); *SEG* XIX.630.9 (V AD); Mitford 1950: 129.10 (VI AD).
Literature: e.g. Plut. *Rom.* 27.4 (I/II AD); Galen XII.430.18 Kühn (II AD); *Act.Scillit.* 113.2 (II/III AD); Epiph. *Pan.* II.300.8 (IV AD); *ACO* II.I.I p. 32.19 (V AD); Lyd. *Ost.* 64.24 (VI AD).
Post-antique: common. Kriaras (1968–). Modern Ιούλιος, Γιούλις: Babiniotis (2002), Andriotis (1967), Meyer (1895: 22).
Notes: Avotins (1992) finds a different ἰούλιος or ἰούλιον, a unit of assessment (perhaps not from Latin?), in Just. *Nov.* e.g. 17.8.pr. (VI AD). Solin (2008), Sijpesteijn (1979), García Domingo (1979: 477), Hofmann (1989: 134), Meinersmann (1927: 19), Sophocles (1887), Lampe (1961), LSJ suppl. (*s.v.* Ἰουλαῖος). See §4.1.1, **§4.2.1**, §4.2.2, §8.2.1, §8.2.3 n. 51, §10.2.1, §10.2.2 E.

Direct loan Ἰούν(ι)ος, Ἐούνιος, Ἰώνιος (-α, -ον or -ου, ὁ) 'June', from *Iūnius* 'June'.
II BC – modern Documents: e.g. *P.Hamb.* I.73.16 (II AD); *P.Oxy.* 1466.6 (III AD); *P.Mert.* II.90.9 (IV AD); *P.Petra* I.1.2 (VI AD).
Inscriptions: e.g. *F.Delphes* III.II.70.4 (II BC); *IGUR* I.1.b4 (I BC); *IG* X.II.II.52.7 (II AD); *Corinth* VIII.III.646.5 (III AD); *SEG* XXX.585 (IV AD); *IG* XIV.130.3 (V AD); *IG* X.II.I.1030.7 (VI AD).
Literature: e.g. *Jubil.* frag. c56 (I BC?); DH *AR* 9.60.8 (I BC); Plut. *Numa* 19.3.2 (I/II AD); Vet.Val. *App.* 9.7.21 (II AD); Dio Cassius 57.14.4 (II/III AD); Epiph. *Pan.* II.300.9 (IV AD); *ACO* II.I.I p. 20.5 (V AD); Aëtius 12.69.18 (VI AD).
Post-antique: common. Kriaras (1968–). Modern Ιούνιος, Γιούνις: Babiniotis (2002), Andriotis (1967), Meyer (1895: 22).
Notes: Solin (2008), Sijpesteijn (1979), García Domingo (1979: 477), Avotins (1992), Strobach (1997: 195), Hofmann (1989: 134), Meinersmann (1927: 19), Lampe (1961), LSJ suppl. See **§4.2.1**, §4.2.2, **§8.1.4**, §8.2.3 n. 51, §10.2.1, §10.2.2 E.

foreign	**ἰουν(ί)ωρ** transliterating *iūnior* 'younger': Plut. *Numa* 19.3 (I/II AD); inscription *MAMA* I.167.8, spelled ἰνιώρων (IV/V AD); Eusebius, *PG* XIX.305c, d (IV AD); Lyd. *Mens.* 4.88.4 (VI AD). Hofmann (1989: 134), Sophocles (1887), Lampe (1961).
	ἰουόκατος: see ἠβοκᾶτος.
Direct loan **III–IV AD**	**ἰουράτωρ** (-ορος, ὁ) 'sworn witness', from *iūrātor* 'sworn witness'. Documents: e.g. *P.Cair.Isid.* 3.9 etc. (III AD); *P.Panop.Beatty* 2.87 etc. (III/IV AD); perhaps *Chrest.Wilck.* 230.10 (IV AD). Notes: Daris (1991a: 47), Hofmann (1989: 135), Zilliacus (1935a: 192–3), Meinersmann (1927: 19), *LBG*. See §4.2.5, §9.2, §10.2.1, §10.2.2 B.
foreign	**ἰουρίδικος** 'judge' (in Alexandria), from *iūridicus* 'judge': Antec. in Latin script 1.20.5 *iuridicu* (VI AD); later in Greek script. Zilliacus (1935a: 192–3), *LBG*, Sophocles (1887).
foreign	**ἰουρισγέντιος** '(regulated by) the law of peoples', from *iūs gentium* 'law of peoples': Antec. in Latin script 1.2.1 *iurisgentiois*, 2.1.3 *iurisgentios*, etc. (VI AD); later in Greek script. Binder (2000: 257–8), Hofmann (1989: 135), Viscidi (1944: 27), Zilliacus (1935a: 192–3), Triantaphyllides (1892: 261), *LBG*. See §9.5.6 passage 83.
foreign	**ἰουρισδικτίων** 'jurisdiction', from *iūrisdictiō* 'jurisdiction': Antec. in Latin script 1.20.4 *iurisdictiona* etc. (VI AD); later in Greek script. Zilliacus (1935a: 192–3), *LBG*, Sophocles (1887). See §9.5.6.
foreign	**ἰουρισκιβίλε** 'civil law', from *iūs cīvīle* 'civil law': Antec. in Latin script 1.2.1 *iuriscivile* etc. (VI AD). Hofmann (1989: 135), Zilliacus (1935a: 192–3), Triantaphyllides (1892: 262). See §9.5.6 passage 83.
foreign	**ἰουρισκονσοῦλτοι, ἰούρις κονσοῦλτοι** 'legal experts', from *iūris cōnsultī* 'legal experts': Antec. in Latin script 1.2.8 *iuris consulti*, marked as obsolete (VI AD). Hofmann (1989: 135), Viscidi (1944: 27), Zilliacus (1935a: 192–3). See §7.2.1 passage 27, §9.5.6.
foreign	**ἰουρισονοράριον** 'law made by aediles', from *iūs honōrārium* 'law introduced by a magistrate's edict': Antec. in Latin script 1.2.7 *iuris honorarium* etc. (VI AD). Hofmann (1989: 135), Zilliacus (1935a: 192–3).
name	**Ἰουστινιανός** 'of Justinian', from *Iustīniānus* (L&S *s.v. Justīnus*). Hofmann (1989: 135), *LBG*, LSJ suppl.
non-existent?	**ἱπποβουρδονογένεια** 'breeding of hinnies', from ἵππος 'horse' + *burdō* 'mule' via βουρδών + -γένεια (cf. γεννάω 'produce'), may not exist and is certainly not ancient; see *P.Oxy.* 1919.14, *LBG*.
non-existent?	**ἱπποβούρδων**, from ἵππος 'horse' + *burdō* 'mule' via βουρδών, may not exist and is certainly not ancient; see *P.Oxy.* 1919.14, Filos (2010: 250), Daris (1991a: 47).
foreign	**ἰπσόιουρε** 'automatically', from *ipsō iūre* 'by right itself': Antec. in Latin script 2.18.pr. *ipso iure* etc. (VI AD); later in Greek script.
	īre: see *eō*.

ἵρριτος: see ἵνριτος.

rare   ἰσικιάριον, εἰσ(σ)ικιάριον 'sausage', from *īsicium* 'minced meat' (*TLL*) via ἰσίκιον + -άριον: papyrus *P.Ryl.* IV.639.211 and perhaps 176 (IV AD). Van Minnen (1998: 132) emends 176 without seeing 211. Daris (1991a: 47). See §6.3 n. 21.

Deriv.? of loan
III–VI AD   ἰσικιάριος, ἰσσικιάριος, εἰσ(σ)ικιάριος, σικιάρος (-ου, ὁ) 'sausage-maker', from *īsicium* 'minced meat' (*TLL*) via ἰσίκιον + -άριος, or perhaps *īsiciārius* 'maker of minced meat' (*TLL*).

Documents: *P.Ryl.* IV.640.ctr.10, 641.5 etc. (both IV AD); *Stud.Pal.* XX.85r.i.29 (IV AD); *P.Oxy.* 4903.4 (V AD); *P.Stras.* I.46.10 etc. (VI AD).

Inscriptions: *SEG* XXXVI.970.51 (III AD); perhaps *SEG* XXXV.1110.6 (III AD); *MAMA* III.343, perhaps 387.

Notes: *isiciarius* is rare and later than ἰσικιάριος (*TLL*), so the suffix was probably added in Greek; cf. Beekes (2010 s.v. ἰσίκιον). Daris (1991a: 47), Hofmann (1989: 106, 136), *DÉLG* (s.v. ἰσίκιον), Lampe (1961 s.v. εἰσικάριος), LSJ, LSJ suppl. See §4.2.4.1 n. 50, §6.1 n. 9, §6.7 n. 46, §10.2.2 I.

rare   ἰσικιομάγειρος 'sausage-maker', from *īsicium* 'minced meat' (*TLL*) via ἰσίκιον + μάγειρος 'butcher', 'meat-cooker': papyri *SB* 9456.5 etc.; *SB* 14964.7 (both VI AD). Filos (2010: 250), Daris (1991a: 47), Hofmann (1989: 135–6 s.v. ἰσίκιον), Meinersmann (1927: 19), *DÉLG* (s.v. ἰσίκιον), Beekes (2010 s.v. ἰσίκιον), *TLL* (s.v. *īsicium* 492.58), LSJ suppl.

Direct loan
III AD – Byz.   ἰσίκιον, εἰσίκιον, ἴσικος (-ου, τό or ὁ) 'dish of mincemeat', from *īsicium* 'minced meat' (*TLL*).

Documents: *P.Oxy.* 1730.7 (V AD); *SB* 15302.64 etc. (V AD).

Inscriptions: Edict.Diocl. 4.13 etc. (IV AD).

Literature: Athenaeus 9.376d (II/III AD); Ps.-Alexander Aphrodisiensis, *Problemata* 1.22 = Ideler 1841: 11.16 (II/III AD); Alex.Trall. II.509.23 etc. (VI AD); Olympiodorus Philosophus, *In Platonis Gorgiam commentaria* 31.7.3 Westerink (VI AD); with *isicium* in Gloss. *Herm.Mp.* 314.47.

Post-antique: minimal survival.

Notes: had at least started to be used in Greek by I AD, when Paxamos (cited by Athenaeus) wrote. Forms derivatives ἰσικιάριον, ἰσικιομάγειρος, probably ἰσικιάριος. Daris (1991a: 47), Hofmann (1989: 135–6), *DÉLG*, Beekes (2010), *TLL* (s.v. *īsicium* 492.36–44, 57), LSJ, LSJ suppl. See §4.2.4.1 n. 54, §6.1 n. 9, §6.7 n. 46, §8.2.2, **§9.4** passage 58, §10.2.1, §10.2.2 I, §12.2.1.

not ancient   ἰσικιοπώλης 'seller of sausage meat', from *īsicium* 'minced meat' (*TLL*) via ἰσίκιον + πώλης 'seller': no ancient examples. Filos (2010: 250), Daris (1991a: 47), LSJ suppl.

ἴσικος: see ἰσίκιον.

not Latin?   ἴσκα, ὕσκα is cited as a borrowing of *ēsca* 'food' (with influence from ἰσχνός 'dry', 'thin') by Viscidi (1944: 40), Hofmann (1989: 136) and Sophocles (1887), who give the meaning 'tinder'. LSJ also links the two spellings but gives a different definition ('fungus growing on oaks and walnut-trees, used as a cautery') and sees no Latin source. For connection with a Byzantine word for a kind of fish (perhaps from *isox* 'salmon') see Volk (1991: 294–305). Meyer (1895: 21–2), Andriotis (1967 s.v. ἤσκα), Kriaras (1968–), Triandaphyllidis (1909: 122), LSJ (s.vv. ἴσκαι, ὕσκας).

ἰσκρηνάριος: see σκρινιάριος.

Deriv. of loan II–III AD	**ἰσοκαπετώλιος, ἰσοκαπιτώλιος** (-ον) 'equivalent to the Capitoline (games)', from ἴσος 'equal' + *Capitōlius* 'Capitoline' via Καπετώλια. Documents: *Pap.Agon.* 1.16 (III AD); perhaps *SB* 16959.3 (III AD). Inscriptions: *F.Delphes* III.1.555.19 (II AD); *Suppl.Rodio* 67.6 (II AD); *I.Perge* 334.4, 336.4 (both III AD). Notes: not attested in feminine; LSJ (*s.v.* ἰσοκαπιτώλιος) infers from form that it would be two-termination. Editor's comments in *Pap.Agon.* See §4.6.2, §10.2.2 F.
foreign	**ἴσοξ**, a fish, from *isox* 'salmon': Hesych. as lemma ι 972 (V/VI AD); perhaps Hdn. *Pros.Cath.* III.1.43.14 (II AD). Volk (1991: 304), Hofmann (1989: 136), LSJ.
	ἰσσικιάριος: see ἰσικιάριος.
	ἰστατιώναρις: see στατιωνάριος.
	ἰστοπένδιον: see στιπένδιον.
foreign	**ἰστρίων** transliterating *histriō* 'actor': Plut. *Mor.* 289c, d (I/II AD). Strobach (1997: 195), Hofmann (1989: 136), *LBG*.
	ἰστρουμεντ-: see ἰνστρουμεντ-.
not Latin?	**Ἰταλία** 'Italy' (and derivatives), widely attested from the Classical period onwards, is probably from a word like *Italia* in some Italic language – but probably not Latin, given its early date (cf. §2.1). Leclercq (1997: 300), Hofmann (1989: 136), LSJ. See §7.1.2 passage 24, §7.1.3, §9.5.6 n. 56.
not Latin?	**ἰταλός** 'bull', lemma in Hesych. ι 1079 (V/VI AD), is suggested by Immisch (1885: 326) as from *vitulus* 'calf' or a similar word in another Italic language. *DÉLG*, LSJ. Cf. οὔϊτουλος.
non-existent	**ἴτεμ**, from *item* 'likewise': papyrus *Rom.Mil.Rec.* 35.2 etc. (III AD) is Latin in Greek script. Daris (1991a: 47).
foreign	*iter* 'right of way': Antec. 2.3.pr. *iter* (VI AD).
foreign	**ἰτερατίων** 'repetition', from *iterātiō* 'repetition': Just. *Nov.* in Latin script 78.pr. (VI AD). Zilliacus (1935a: 192–3), *LBG*.
rare	**ἰτινεράριον** 'journey', from *itinerārium* 'description of a journey' (*TLL s.v. itinerārius*): papyrus *P.Mich.* VIII.501.17 (II AD). Daris (1991a: 47), *LBG*.
not Latin	**ἰτράριος, ἐτράριος**, an occupational term, probably means 'cake-maker' and comes from ἴτρια 'cake' + -άριος, though it used to be defined 'glass-worker' and considered a variant of οὐετράριος (*q.v.*). Drew-Bear (1972: 78), Robert (1965: 342–3), *I.Tyr* p. 25, Hofmann (1989: 137), *DÉLG* (*s.v.* ἴτριον), LSJ suppl.

K

rare   **κάβαθα, γαβάθα, γάβαθον** (ἡ or τό) 'bowl' seems to be a borrowing of Latin *gabata* (a term for a dish) when it appears at Edict.Diocl. 15.51 (IV AD), but in other passages it is more likely to come directly from the Semitic source of the Latin. Both spelling and accentuation are uncertain. Lauffer (1971: 257), Hofmann (1989: 137), *DÉLG* (*s.v.* γάβαθον), Frisk (1954–72: 1.280–1 *s.v.* γάβαθον), Beekes (2010 *s.v.* γάβαθον), Meyer (1895: 19 *s.v.* γαβάθα), Andriotis (1967 *s.v.* γαβάθα), Kriaras (1968– *s.v.* γαβάθι), *TLL* (*s.v. gabata*, quoting κάβαθα and γάβαθαν), Walde and Hofmann (1938–54 *s.v. gabata*), LSJ (*s.vv.* κάβαθα, γαβαθόν), LSJ suppl. (*s.v.* γαβαθόν).

    καβαλ-: see καβαλλ-.

Deriv.? of loan
IV AD – Byz.   **καβαλ(λ)αρικός** (-ή, -όν) 'horse-drawn', 'of horses or cavalry', probably ultimately from Latin, but exact source disputed. Lauffer (1971: 257) suggests unattested **caballāricus*, Daris barely attested *caballāris* 'of horses' (*TLL*), Hofmann and Zervan (2019: 58) more convincingly *caballārius* via καβαλλάριος + -ικός.

Documents: *SB* 11075.9 (V AD); *P.Ness.* III.18.28 (VI AD).

Inscriptions: Edict.Diocl. 19.33 etc. (IV AD).

Post-antique: numerous. *LBG*, Kriaras (1968– *s.v.* καβαλαρικός).

Notes: Daris (1991a: 47), Hofmann (1989: 137 *s.v.* καβαλλάριος), *DÉLG* (*s.v.* καβάλλης), Frisk (1954–72: 1.749), Beekes (2010 *s.v.* καβάλλης), Lampe (1961), *TLL* (*s.v. caballāricus*), LSJ (*s.v.* καβάλλης), LSJ suppl. See §4.3.3, §4.6.1, §8.1.7, §10.2.2 K.

Direct loan?
IV AD – modern   **καβαλ(λ)άριος, καβελλάριος** (-ου, ὁ) 'rider', 'driver', 'cavalryman', probably from *caballārius* 'horseman' (*TLL*), or perhaps from καβάλλης + -άριος.

Documents: *P.Münch.* I.11.8, I.12.2 etc. (both VI AD); *Stud.Pal.* VIII.1136.3, X.160.1 etc. (both VI AD).

Inscriptions: *SEG* XXXVIII.1766 (IV AD); *I.Estremo Oriente* 54.3 etc. (VI AD).

Literature: Teucer, Boll 1903: 42.17 (I AD?); Evagr.Schol. *HE* p. 235.21 etc. (VI AD). Unverified example (VI AD) in Zilliacus (1937: 322, 329).

Post-antique: common, forming derivatives καβαλλαρία 'cavalry', καβαλλαρίκιον 'riding school', etc. Daris (1991a: 48), *LBG* (*s.vv.* καβαλλάριος, καβαλλάρης), Zervan (2019: 57–8), Kriaras (1968– *s.vv.* καβαλάρης, καβαλάριος), Triandaphyllidis (1909: 129, 132). Modern καβαλ(λ)άρης, καβαλλάρις 'rider': Babiniotis (2002), Andriotis (1967), Kahane and Kahane (1972–6: 531), Meyer (1895: 22).

Notes: *caballarius* is late and poorly attested, so a Greek formation cannot be ruled out. Daris (1991a: 48), Hofmann (1989: 137–8), Zilliacus (1935a: 218–19, 1937: 329), Meinersmann (1927: 19), *DÉLG* (*s.v.* καβάλλης), Frisk (1954–72: 1.749), Beekes (2010 *s.v.* καβάλλης), *TLL* (*s.v. caballārius*), Lampe (1961 *s.vv.* καβαλλάρης, καβαλλάριος), LSJ suppl. See §4.2.4.1 n. 50, §4.6.1, §8.2.3 n. 51, §10.2.1, §10.2.2 K.

not ancient   **καβαλλάτιον**, plant name attested in an interpolation in Dsc. 4.127 RV, seems to come from probably unattested **caballātium*. For another possible attestation see *TLL* (*s.v. caballion* 3.36). Hofmann (1989: 138 καβαλλάτον), *DÉLG* (*s.v.* καβάλλης), Frisk (1954–72: 1.749), Beekes (2010 *s.v.* καβάλλης), LSJ (*s.v.* καβάλλης).

not Latin?	**καβάλ(λ)ης, καβάλ(λ)ις** 'nag', 'horse' (with derivative καβάλ(λ)(ε)ιον 'working horse') is probably not from *caballus* 'horse'. *DÉLG*, Frisk (1954–72: I.749–50, III.114), Beekes (2010), LSJ, LSJ suppl.
not Latin?	**καβαλ(λ)ικεύω** 'ride a horse' may be from *caballicō* 'ride horseback' (*TLL*) + -εύω, but that is rare and late: Greek derivation from καβάλλης is also possible. Coleman (2007: 796), Hofmann (1989: 138), Zilliacus (1935a: 218–19), Zervan (2019: 58), Kriaras (1968– *s.v.* καβαλικεύγω), Meyer (1895: 22 ἀποκαβαλκεύω and καλικεύω *s.v.* καβάλλος), Andriotis (1967), Lampe (1961).
	καβάλλιον, καβάλ(λ)ις: see καβάλλης.
rare	**καβάτωρ** 'gem-cutter', from *cavātor* 'one who hollows out': papyri *Stud.Pal.* XX.202.2 (VI AD) and VIII.813.2 (VI AD?). Daris (1991a: 48), Hofmann (1989: 138), Meinersmann (1927: 19), LSJ suppl., and for Byzantine survival *LBG*, Kriaras (1968–).
	καβελλάριος: see καβαλλάριος.
not Latin?	**καβιδάριος, καβιδάρης**, perhaps with variant **καβιδιάριος**, 'gem-engraver', may be from doubtfully extant *cavidārius* 'gem-engraver' (*TLL*) or a word from another language + -άριος (cf. *TLL s.v.* 647.27–8). Ihm (1907), Diethart (1993: 225–6, 1999: 179), Hofmann (1989: 138–9), *LBG*, *TLL* (*s.v. cavidārius* 647.32–6), Lampe (1961), LSJ, LSJ suppl.
	καβιδειν: see κάπιτον.
not ancient	**καβιδερή** 'henhouse', perhaps from *cavea* 'coop' via unattested **cavidium*: no ancient examples. Meyer (1895: 22).
not ancient?	**καβικλάριος** 'gaoler', apparently from unattested **cāvīclārius*, variant of *clāvīculārius* 'turnkey': inscriptions *I.Ephesos* 1347.2; *MAMA* III.648. Perhaps connected to the καβικουλάριοι that appears as a variant reading for κλαβικουλάριοι in Lyd. *Mag.* p. 142.2 (VI AD). Hofmann (1989: 139), LSJ suppl. Cf. κλαβικουλάριος.
not ancient?	**καβιόθυρον** 'trapdoor', apparently related to *cavea* 'enclosure': probably no ancient examples. Hofmann (1989: 139), *LBG*.
not Latin	**καβουρᾶς** 'crab-fisher', suggested by Meyer (1895: 22–3) as a borrowing of *cammarus* 'lobster' (itself from κάμμαρος 'lobster'), is probably a Greek formation. Beekes (2010 *s.v.* κάβουρος), Andriotis (1967), LSJ suppl.
	καγγελ-: see καγκελ-.
	καγκελα-, καγκελι-: see καγκελλα-, καγκελλι-.
Direct loan V AD – modern	**καγκελ(λ)άριος 1, κανκελλάριος, καγγελλάριος** (-ου, ὁ), an official title, from *cancellārius*, an official (*TLL*). Documents: e.g. *Stud.Pal.* III.166.2 (VI AD); *P.Oxy.* 2046.41 etc. (VI AD); *P.Cair.Masp.* 67005.19 (VI AD). Inscriptions: *I.Chr.Asie Mineure* I.13.2 (V AD); *IGLS* II.687.2 (V AD); *IGLS* II.530.5 (VI AD); *SEG* IX.356.63 (VI AD); *SEG* IX.414.6 (VI AD); *IGR* III.256.3; *SEG* XX.371; perhaps *I.Didyma* 604.2.

Literature: Nil. 1.59.1 etc. (v AD); Just. *Nov.* 161.1 (vi AD); Dioscorus frag. 7.1 etc., Heitsch 1963: 137 (vi AD); Lyd. *Mag.* p. 8.12 etc. (vi AD).

Post-antique: numerous, forming derivative καγκελάριον (a tax). *LBG* (*s.v.* καγγελάριος), Zervan (2019: 59), Kriaras (1968–), Triandaphyllidis (1909: 103, 126), Daris (1991a: 48). Modern καγκελάριος 'chancellor': Babiniotis (2002), Andriotis (1967), Kahane and Kahane (1972–6: 531).

Notes: a *cancellarius* was originally the usher standing at the *cancellus* of a courtroom (*OED s.v. chancellor*). Benaissa (2009: 59–61), Avotins (1992), Daris (1991a: 48), Mason (1974: 58), Hofmann (1989: 139), Zilliacus (1935a: 176–7, 218–19, 1937: 329), Meinersmann (1927: 19–20), *DÉLG* (*s.v.* κάγκελ(λ)οι), Frisk (1954–72: 1.751), Beekes (2010 *s.v.* κάγκελ(λ)οι), *TLL* (*s.v. cancellārius* 226.28–32), Lampe (1961), LSJ suppl. (replacing LSJ *s.v.* κάγκελος). See §4.2.4.1 n. 50, §8.2.3 n. 51, §10.2.1, §10.2.2 D; cf. πρωτοκαγκελλάριος.

non-existent   **καγκελλάριος 2** 'sieved' (i.e. passed through a lattice), cited by Hofmann (1989: 140 *s.v.* κάγκελλος) as derivative of κάγκελλος and thus of *cancellus* 'latticed barrier': all attestations have been reinterpreted as forms of κάγκελλος. Harrauer and Sijpesteijn (1988: 114).

Deriv. of loan   **καγκέλ(λ)ιον, κανκέλ(λ)ιον, κακέλιον** (-ου, τό) 'lattice', 'railing', 'gate', 'function
v AD – modern   of the *cancellarius*', from *cancellus* 'latticed barrier' via κάγκελλος + -ιον.
Documents: *Stud.Pal.* XX.151.18 (vi AD); Benaissa 2009 p. 58.5 (vi AD).
Inscriptions: *SEG* XVIII.466.5.
Literature: Anton.Hag. *V.Sym.Styl.* 16 (v AD).
Post-antique: survives. *LBG.* Modern dialectal καγκέλι: Meyer (1895: 23).
Notes: meaning 'function of the *cancellarius*' only once (Benaissa 2009: 61). Daris (1991a: 48, with derivation from medieval *cancellum*, *DMLBS*), Hofmann (1989: 140 *s.v.* κάγκελλος), Meinersmann (1927: 20), LSJ suppl. See §4.3.2, §4.6.1 n. 83, §10.2.2 J.

not ancient   **καγκελ(λ)οειδῶς** 'in the form of a lattice', from *cancellus* 'latticed barrier' via κάγκελλος + -ειδής (cf. εἶδος 'form') + -ως: no ancient examples. Hofmann (1989: 140 *s.v.* κάγκελλος), LSJ suppl. (replacing LSJ). See §8.2.2, §10.3.1 n. 31.

non-existent   **κάγκελλον** does not exist: LSJ suppl. (replacing LSJ).

Direct loan   **κάγκελ(λ)ος, κάνκελλος, κάνγελος, κάγγελ(λ)ος, κάκελλος, γάγκελ(λ)ος** (-ου, ὁ)
I AD – modern   'latticed barrier or balustrade', 'railing', 'gate' (also a measure), from *cancellus* 'latticed barrier'.
Documents: common (esp. vi AD), e.g. *SB* 12169.13 (I AD); perhaps *P.Ryl.* II.233.4 (II AD); *P.Oxy.* 2146.12 (III AD); *P.Oxy.* 3400.15 (IV AD); *P.Sorb.* 1.60.14 (v AD); *P.Oxy.* 1997.3 (vi AD).
Inscriptions: e.g. *SEG* XXII.167.7 (I AD); *I.Thespies* 319.8 (I/II AD); *SEG* XVII.596.8 (III AD).
Literature: e.g. Athan. *Ep.Encycl.* 4.2 (IV AD); Philogelos 163 (IV AD); *ACO* II.I.I p. 64.37 (v AD); Hesych. as gloss δ 2445, κ 2615 (v/vi AD); Cyr.S. *Vit.Sab.* 185.6 (vi AD); as gloss in old scholia to Ar. *Eq.* 641a, 675b.

Post-antique: numerous, forming derivatives καγγελίζω 'wriggle', καγκελοειδῶς 'in the form of a lattice', etc. Often in post-antique papyri (though that is not visible from Daris 1991a). *LBG*, Kriaras (1968– *s.v.* κάγκελον), Triandaphyllidis (1909: 120). Modern κάγκελο 'fence', 'rail' and derivatives: Babiniotis (2002), Andriotis (1967), Meyer (1895: 23).

Notes: forms derivatives καγκέλλιον, καγκελλωτός, σκαμνοκάγκελος. Daris (1991a: 48), Hofmann (1989: 139–40), Meinersmann (1927: 19, 20), Immisch (1885: 369), *DÉLG* (*s.v.* κάγκελ(λ)οι), Frisk (1954–72: I.751), Beekes (2010 *s.v.* κάγκελ(λ)οι), Lampe (1961 *s.vv.* κάγκελλον, κάγκελλος), LSJ suppl. (*s.v.* κάγκελλος, replacing LSJ *s.vv.* κάγκελλον, κάγκελος). See §4.1.1, §4.2.4.1 n. 51, §4.3.2, §4.6.1, §5.2.1, §5.2.2 n. 10, §8.2.2, §8.2.3 n. 51, §10.2.1, §10.2.2 J.

Deriv. of loan
I AD – modern

καγκελ(λ)ωτός, καγγελλωτός, κανκερλοτός (-ή, -όν) 'latticed', from *cancellus* 'latticed barrier' via κάγκελλος + -ωτός.
Documents: *Chrest.Wilck.* 443.12 (I AD); *P.Ryl.* II.233.3 etc. (II AD).
Inscriptions: *SEG* XVII.545.8.
Literature: Pollux 8.124, marked (II AD); John Chrysostom, *PG* LXIV.1037.5 (IV/V AD); Hesych. as gloss δ 1838, κ 2606 (V/VI AD); scholion to Ar. *V.* 124c.
Post-antique: survives. *LBG*. Modern καγκελωτός 'made of bars': Babiniotis (2002).
Notes: for -ωτός forming adjectives without parallel verb in -όω, see Chantraine (1933: 305–6). Latin *cancellō* with pf. part. *cancellātus* 'having a lattice pattern' may be relevant in meaning but not in form. Daris (1991a: 48, with derivation from *cancellātus*), Hofmann (1989: 140 *s.v.* κάγκελλος), Meinersmann (1927: 20), Immisch (1885: 369), *DÉLG* (*s.v.* κάγκελ(λ)οι), Frisk (1954–72: I.751), Beekes (2010 *s.v.* κάγκελ(λ)οι), Lampe (1961), LSJ suppl. (*s.v.* καγκελλωτός, replacing LSJ *s.v.* καγκελωτή). See §4.6.1, §10.2.2 J.

καγκελοειδῶς: see καγκελλοειδῶς.

not ancient

καγκελοθυρίς 'latticed gate', from *cancellus* 'latticed barrier' via κάγκελλος + θυρίς 'window': no ancient examples. Hofmann (1989: 140 *s.v.* κάγκελλος), Kriaras (1968–), LSJ.

κάγκελος: see κάγκελλος.

καγκελωτός: see καγκελλωτός.

foreign

κάγκρους transliterating acc. pl. of *cancer* 'lattice' (*OLD cancer²*): Lyd. *Mag.* p. 190.7 (VI AD). *TLL* (*s.v.* 1. *cancer*).

foreign

καδουκεύομαι 'become caducary', from *cadūcus* 'caducary' (via κάδουκος?): Thüngen 2016: A6 etc. in Latin script (V AD); later in Greek script. *LBG*.

rare

κάδουκος 'caducary', from *cadūcus* 'caducary': Thüngen 2016: A11 etc. in Latin script (V AD); Just. Const. Δέδωκεν 6b (VI AD). LSJ suppl.

καδρουπλικατίων: see *quadruplicātiō*.

καινόκουφον: see κοῦπα.

Direct loan
I AD – modern

Καῖσαρ, Καῖσσαρ (-αρος, ὁ) 'Caesar', 'emperor', 'emperor-designate', from *Caesar*.
Documents: common, e.g. *SB* 16704.5 (II AD); *P.Oxy.* 4747.26 (III AD); *P.Oxy.* 4357.6 (IV AD); *P.Eirene* II.28.4 (VI AD).

Inscriptions: common, e.g. *IG* II/III².II.1996.1 (I AD); *I.Anazarbos* 57
(I/II AD); *I.Stratonikeia* 255.3 (II AD); *IG* XII.V.I.292.3 (III AD); *IG*
V.I.1420.8 (IV AD).

Coins: ΚΑΙΣΑΡΙ ΝΙΚΗ in Egypt, Head 1911: 862 (II AD).

Literature: common, e.g. NT Luke 2:1 (I AD); Jos. *AJ* 8.157 (I AD); *V.Secundi*
70.16 (II/III AD); Dio Cassius 66.1.1 (II/III AD); Eus. *VC* 1.1.3 (IV AD);
Soz. 1.2.1 (V AD); Lyd. *Mag.* p. 12.19 (VI AD).

Post-antique: common, with derivatives καισάρισσα 'empress', καισαρέκγονος
'descended from an emperor', etc. *LBG*, Zervan (2019: 60–1), Kriaras
(1968–), Triandaphyllidis (1909: 126). Modern καῖσαρ 'emperor' and
derivatives: Babiniotis (2002).

Notes: Zervan (2019: 60, 263, citing Diodorus Siculus 1.4.7) sees Καῖσαρ
as borrowed into Greek in I BC, but at that stage it was a personal name
and thus outside the scope of this study. Forms derivatives φιλόκαισαρ,
Καισαρογερμανίκεια (using Καῖσαρ as a name), ἀποκαισαρόομαι, Καισαρεύω,
and πολυκαισαρίη (using Καῖσαρ 'emperor'). Leclercq (1997: 294), García
Domingo (1979: 487), Mason (1974: 58), Hofmann (1989: 140), Zilliacus
(1937: 329), Meinersmann (1927: 20), *TLL* (*s.v. Caesar e.g.* 37.41–7), LSJ.
See §4.2.5, §4.6.1, §4.6.2, §8.2.3 n. 51, §9.1 n. 4, §9.3 nn. 21 and 23 and 25,
§10.2.1, §10.2.2 A, §12.2.2.

foreign **καισάραι** and acc. **καισάριεν** transliterating *caesariēs* 'long hair': Hesych. as lemma
κ 275 (V/VI AD); Lyd. *Mens.* 4.102.30 (VI AD). Immisch (1885: 336), LSJ.

Καισάρεια: see Καισάρειος.

Καισαρειανός: see Καισαριανός.

Direct? loan with **Καισάρ(ε)ιος, Καισάρηος, Καισάρεος, Κησάριος, Κεσάρ(ε)ιος** (-ον) 'of Caesar'; as
influence masc. subst. a month, an official title, a member of Caesar's party during
I BC – Byz. the civil wars; as neut. sing. subst. 'temple or shrine of Caesar', 'temple
dedicated to the emperor', 'complex of buildings in honour of the
emperor'; as neut. pl. subst. 'games in honour of Caesar': from *Caesareus* 'of
Caesar' with influence from -ειος, or perhaps *Caesar* via Καῖσαρ + -(ε)ῖος.

Documents, month: very common, e.g. *P.Oxy.* 271.2 (I AD); *P.Ryl.* II.174.13
(II AD); *P.Oxy.* 1725.10 (III AD).   Official title: *SB* 13232.23 (I AD);
P.Graux II.9.6 (I AD); *O.Bodl.* II.609.3, 963.5 (both I AD); perhaps *P.Oxy.*
3463.3 (I AD); *P.Oxy.* 477.5 (II AD); *P.Bingen* 68.2 (II AD); *PSI* XII.1225.2,
XIII.1325.4 (both II AD); *P.Tebt.* II.317.3 (II AD).   Temple etc.: e.g.
P.Mich. VIII.476.23 (II AD); *Chrest.Wilck.* 41.ii.10 etc. (III AD); *P.Oxy.*
1683.19 (IV AD); *P.Mert.* I.41.12 (V AD).

Inscriptions, adj.: *I.Selge* 15.15 (III AD).   Month: *I.Portes du désert* 65.6,
perhaps 69.9 (both I AD); *IGR* I.1319.A4 (I AD); *SB* 13315.3 (I AD);
probably *I.Pergamon* II.278.B2 (II AD); perhaps *SB* 6121.5.   Official
title: *IG* XII.Suppl.124.7 (I AD).   Temple etc.: e.g. *I.Olympia* 56.48 (I
BC/AD); Bean and Mitford 1970: 60 no. 32.2, 97 no. 74.1 (both I AD);
SEG LI.808.13 (II AD).   Games: e.g. *I.Cos Segre* EV203.6 etc. (I BC); *IG*
IX.I.90.2 (I BC/AD); *SEG* XVII.581.1 (I AD); *Corinth* VIII.I.80.2, 81.2
(both II AD); *SEG* XLIX.817.8 (III AD).

Literature, adj.: not at Jos. *BJ* 1.402 = 1.21.1 as alleged.   Member of Caesar's
   party: Dio Cassius 41.39.4, 76.14.2, etc. (II/III AD); probably also others.
   Temple etc.: Strabo 17.1.9 (I BC/AD); perhaps Hdn. *Pros.Cath.* III.1.375.14
   (II AD); Athan. *H.Ar.* 56.3, 74.2 (IV AD).

Post-antique: survives. *LBG* (*s.v.* καισαρεία 'imperial rank').

Notes: apparently returned to Latin as *Caesarēus*, with neut. sing. subst.
   becoming *Caesarēum* 'shrine of Caesar' (cf. *TLL Onomasticon s.v. Caesar* 40.8–
   39). *TLL* (40.17–21) implies a month name *Caesarēus* but cites only Greek
   examples: this usage is not directly attested in Latin. On the month also
   Scott (1931: 253–4), Bagnall (2009: 181). Chantraine (1933: 61, for -εῖον),
   Mason (1974: 6, 58), Hofmann (1989: 140 *s.v.* Καῖσαρ, 171 *s.v.* Κεσάριον),
   LSJ, LSJ suppl. See §4.4, §4.6.1, §8.1.5, §10.2.1, §10.2.2 D, §10.3.1 n. 26,
   §12.2.1, §12.2.2.

rare	**Καισαρεύω** 'play the Caesar', from *Caesar* via Καῖσαρ + -εύω: Dio Cassius 66.8.6 (II/III AD). Mason (1974: 6, 59), Hofmann (1989: 140 *s.v.* Καῖσαρ), LSJ.
rare	**Καισαρεών, Κεσαρεών**, month name from *Caesareus* 'of Caesar' + -ών: inscriptions *I.Kaunos* 34.18 (II AD); *I.Ephesos* 1601.m13 etc. (II AD); Reinach 1906: 268 no. 163.9; Cormack 1964: 17 no. 4.4. Forms derivative Νεοκαισαρεών. Scott (1931: 265), *TLL* (*Onomasticon s.v. Caesar* 40.20), LSJ (*s.v.* Καῖσαρ).
rare	**Καισαρήσιος** 'from Caesarea' (designating a garment), from *Caesariēnsis* 'of Caesarea': papyrus *P.Cair.Masp.* 67006v.85 (VI AD). LSJ suppl.
Direct loan **II AD – Byz.**	**Καισαριανός, Καισαρειανός, Κεσαριανός, Κεσαρανός** (-οῦ, ὁ) 'member of the Caesarian party', or used for the officials more often called καισάρειος (see above), from *Caesariānus* 'supporter of Caesar', 'supporter of the Roman emperor'.

Documents: numerous (esp. II AD), e.g. *O.Claud.* IV.714.ii.14 (I/II AD); *BGU*
   V.1210.241 (II AD); *O.Did.* 84.13 (III AD).

Inscriptions: *SEG* VII.561.3 (II AD); *MAMA* X.114.31 (III AD);
   IG II/III².V.13249.25 etc. (IV AD); *IG* XII.VIII.581.12; *TAM* V.II.1407.2;
   I.Kyzikos 210.4; perhaps *I.Ephesos* 4117.d5; perhaps *TAM* V.I.334.

Literature: Epict. *Diss.* 1.19.19, 3.24.117 (I/II AD); App. *BC* 3.13.91
   (I/II AD).

Post-antique: numerous. *LBG*.

Notes: Mason (1974: 59), Hofmann (1989: 140), *TLL* (*Onomasticon s.v. Caesar*
   39.23–40), LSJ (*s.v.* Καισαριανοί). See §4.2.4.1 n. 51, §10.2.1, §10.2.2 D,
   §10.4.2.

not ancient?	**Καισαριασταί** 'worshippers of Caesar', from *Caesar* via Καῖσαρ + -ιαστής: inscription *IGR* IV.1348.1 etc. Hofmann (1989: 140 *s.v.* Καισαριανοί), LSJ (*s.v.* Καισαρεύω).
	καισάριεν: see καισάραι.
not ancient?	**Καισαρικός** 'of the emperor', from *Caesar* via Καῖσαρ + -ικός: unverified example (IV AD) in Zilliacus (1937: 329); Byzantine and modern texts. Zervan (2019: 60), *LBG*, Babiniotis (2002), Andriotis (1967).

rare   **Καισαρογερμανίκεια** 'games in honour of Germanicus', from the names *Caesar*
(via Καῖσαρ) and *Germānicus*: inscription *SEG* XXIII.638.7 (I AD). Drew-
Bear (1972: 200), LSJ suppl.

     Καῖσσαρ: see Καῖσαρ.

foreign   **καίτρεαι**, a kind of Spanish shield, probably from *caetra* 'small, light shield':
Hesych. as lemma κ 283 (V/VI AD). Immisch (1885: 342), Hofmann (1989:
141), LSJ.

     κακέλιον: see καγκέλλιον.

     κάκελλος: see κάγκελλος.

     Καλάδαι, Καλαδες: see Καλάνδαι.

not Latin?   **καλαμάριον** 'pen-case', 'container for writing implements', 'inkwell' is clearly
related to *calamārius* 'for holding pens' (itself ultimately from κάλαμος), but
the direction of influence is uncertain. Kahane and Kahane (1978: 214–15),
Hofmann (1989: 141), *DÉLG* (*s.v.* κάλαμος), Frisk (1954–72: 1.760), Beekes
(2010 *s.v.* κάλαμος), Lampe (1961), LSJ, and for Byzantine texts (where it
is common) *LBG* and Triandaphyllidis (1909: 91, 94, 121, 168, claiming a
Latin borrowing); cf. Andriotis (1967). See §6.3.

Direct loan   **Καλάνδαι, Καλένδαι, Καλάνται, Καλάντε, Καλάδαι, Καλαδες** (-ων, αἱ) 'first day of
II BC – modern   the month', 'month', from *Kalendae* 'first day of the month'.
     Documents: common, e.g. *SB* 17164.13 (I/II AD); *P.Wisc.* II.72.16 (II AD);
     P.Dura 30r.2 (III AD); *SB* 15799.3 (IV AD); *P.Petra* III.23.2 (VI AD).
     Inscriptions: common, e.g. *CID* IV.119D.2 (II BC); *SEG* XLII.837.8 (I BC);
     IG V.I.1359.A3 (I AD); *Corinth* VIII.III.306.16 (II AD); *SEG* XLIX.817.11
     (III AD); *I.Cret.* IV.285.31 (IV AD); *I.Lipára* 790.4 (V AD); Bulić and Egger
     1926: no. 252.6 (VI AD).
     Literature: common, e.g. DH *AR* 6.49.2 (I BC); Jos. *AJ* 14.228 (I AD); Galen
     XII.430.18 Kühn (II AD); Hippolytus, *Commentarium in Danielem* 4.23.3 (III
     AD); Julian, *Epistulae* 112 Bidez (IV AD); Lib. *Or.* 9.1 (IV AD); Soz. 7.18.12
     (V AD); Antec. 2.14.9 (VI AD); Lyd. *Mens.* 3.10.21 with false etymology: καὶ
     νέα ἡ πρώτη τοῦ μηνὸς παρὰ Ἀττικοῖς, ἕνη δὲ ἡ τελευταία. Καλάνδας δὲ αὐτὰς
     οἱ παλαιοὶ προσηγόρευσαν ἐξ ἑλληνικῆς σημασίας, ἀπὸ τοῦ καλεῖν τὸν ἀρχιερέα
     τὴν βουλὴν ἐν τῇ λεγομένῃ Καλαβρᾷ βασιλικῇ, καὶ σημαίνειν, εἴτε χρὴ κατὰ τὴν
     πεμπταῖαν, εἴτε κατὰ τὴν διχότομον τῆς σελήνης ἐπιτελέσαι τὴν τῶν Νωνῶν
     ἑορτήν, ἐξ ἧς τὴν μεσομηνίαν ἐπετήρουν (VI AD).
     Post-antique: common. *LBG* (*s.vv.* καλάνδη and κάλανδα), Zervan (2019: 61),
     Kriaras (1968–), Triandaphyllidis (1909: 120). Modern κάλαντα 'Christmas
     and New Year carols': Babiniotis (2002), Andriotis (1967), Kahane and
     Kahane (1972–6: 533), Meyer (1895: 23).
     Notes: occasionally in singular, e.g. Antiochus, Boll 1908: 126.2 (I BC/AD).
     Forms derivative καλανδικά, perhaps καλανδαρικά. Solin (2008), Binder
     (2000: 217–18), Avotins (1992), García Domingo (1979: 487–8), Strobach
     (1997: 195), Hofmann (1989: 141–2), Viscidi (1944: 32), Zilliacus (1935a:
     176–7, 1937: 329), Meinersmann (1927: 21), Lampe (1961), LSJ. See
     §4.1.1, §4.2.1, §4.2.2 n. 32, §4.3.2 n. 75, §4.6.1, **§8.1.4**, §8.2.3 n. 51,
     §10.2.1, §10.2.2 E.

Direct? loan with suffix IV–VI AD	**καλανδαρικά, καλανταρικά** (-ων, τά) 'new year's allowances', from *kalendāris* 'of first day of month' (*TLL*), or *kalendārius* 'of first day of month' (*TLL s.v. kalendārium* 760.35–42), or perhaps *Kalendae* 'first day of month' via Κάλανδαι, in any case + -ικός, neut. pl. subst. Documents: *P.Ross.Georg.* v.61v.C17 (IV AD); *P.Jena* II.21.2 (V/VI AD); *P.Thomas* 27.2 (V/VI AD); perhaps *PSI* VIII.891.1 (V/VI AD). Inscriptions: *SEG* IX.356.69, 414.7 (both VI AD). Notes: Daris (1991a: 48), Hofmann (1989: 142 *s.v.* καλανδαρικός), LSJ suppl. See §4.3.2, §10.2.1, §10.2.2 G.
rare	**καλανδάριον, καλενδάριον** 'account book', from *kalendārium* 'account book' (esp. one recording monthly interest on money lent by its owner): inscriptions *ILS* 9470.4 (II AD); *SEG* XLIV.553.2 (II/III AD). Mason (1974: 59), Hofmann (1989: 142), *TLL* (*s.v. kalendārium* 760.20), LSJ suppl. (*s.v.* καλενδάριον), and for later survival *LBG* and modern καλαντάρι 'calendar' (Babiniotis 2002; Andriotis 1967).
Deriv. of loan VI AD – Byz.	**καλανδικά, καλαντικά** (-ων, τά) 'new year's allowances', from *Kalendae* 'first day of the month' via Κάλανδαι + -ικός, neut. pl. subst. Documents: *P.Cair.Masp.* 67058.iii.18 (VI AD); *P.Oxy.* 2480.41 (VI AD); *PSI* XIV.1428.13 (VI AD); *P.Oxy.* 1869.2 (VI AD?). Literature: Just. *Edict* 13.3 = p. 781.26 (VI AD). Post-antique: survives. *LBG*, Daris (1991a: 48). Notes: Avotins (1992), Daris (1991a: 48), Hofmann (1989: 141–2 *s.v.* κάλανδαι), Meinersmann (1927: 21), LSJ (*s.v.* κάλανδαι). See §4.6.1, §10.2.2 G.
	καλανίσκος: see κανάλιον.
	καλαντ-: see καλανδ-.
	calāre, *calātis*: see *calō*.
not Latin?	**καλαφάτης** 'caulker' at *P.Oxy.* 2480.33 (VI AD) and *P.Lond.* v.1852.00 (VI AD) may come from Latin (e.g. *LBG*, citing *cal(e)facio* 'heat up'; Kahane and Kahane (1978: 214), citing unattested **calefa(c)tor*) or from Arabic. Derivative καλαφατίζω 'caulk' at *P.Oxy.* 3804.258, 262 (VI AD) must have same source. Zervan (2019: 61–2), Kriaras (1968–), Babiniotis (2002).
	καλδάριον: see καρδάρι.
	καλείκειν: see καλίγιον.
	καλενδ-: see καλανδ-.
	καληγ-, καληκ-: see καλιγ-.
rare	**καλιγαρικός, καλικαρικός** 'of boots', from *caligāris* 'of boots' + -ικός: Edict.Diocl. 9.1 (IV AD). In the Byzantine period reappears or is re-created with the meaning 'of a cobbler'. Hofmann (1989: 143–4), *LBG*, LSJ suppl. (replacing LSJ *s.v.* κάλικα).

non-existent?   **καλιγάριον** is cited by LSJ suppl. as a noun meaning 'boot', based on the idea
that καλιγαρίων μέλαν in a scholion to Luc. *Cat.* 15 must mean 'bootblack'.
On this basis Hofmann (1989: 143 *s.v.* καλίγη) claims that καλιγάριον comes
not from *caligārius* 'of boots' but from *caliga* 'boot', probably via κάλιξ. The
same scholion has also been taken as an attestation of καλιγάριος 'boot-
maker', based on the idea that καλιγαρίων μέλαν means 'boot-makers' black':
see Hofmann (1989: 143 *s.v.* καλιγάριος). As this scholion provides the only
evidence for the existence of καλιγάριον 'boot', the latter interpretation
would eliminate the word entirely.

Direct loan   **καλιγάριος, καλλιγάριος, καλ(λ)ικάριος, καληγάρηος, γαλικάριος, καλκάριος** (-ου,
IV AD – Byz.   ὁ) 'boot-maker', from *caligārius* 'boot-maker'.
Documents: *P.Genova* I.24.2.16 (IV AD); *SB* 12838.5 (V AD); *P.Ant.* II.103r.4
etc. (VI AD); *P.Naqlun* I.7.13 (VI AD).
Inscriptions: numerous Christian-era inscriptions from Cilicia, e.g. *MAMA*
III.235, 237; from other areas *SEG* VIII.45.2 (IV/V AD); *IG* II/
III².v.13595.2 (V/VI AD).
Literature: Nil. 2.203.1 (V AD); Hesych. as gloss σ 1196 (V/VI AD); with
caligarius in glossaries, e.g. Gloss. *Herm.Mp.* 308.20; perhaps a scholion to
Lucian (see above *s.v.* καλιγάριον).
Post-antique: survives. Daris (1991a: 48).
Notes: Daris (1991a: 48), Hofmann (1989: 142–3), Immisch (1885: 369), Lampe
(1961 *s.v.* καλλιγάριος), LSJ suppl. See §4.2.4.1 n. 50, §10.2.1, §10.2.2 H.

foreign   **καλιγᾶτος** transliterating *caligātus* 'booted', whence 'common soldier': Dio Cassius
48.12.3 διέσκωπτον γοῦν σφας, ἄλλα τε καὶ βουλὴν καλιγᾶταν ἀπὸ τῆς τῶν
στρατιωτικῶν ὑποδημάτων χρήσεως ἀποκαλοῦντες (II/III AD); Just. *Nov.*
74.4.3 (VI AD); Ath.Schol. in Latin script 11.3.5 (VI AD). Freyburger-Galland
(1997: 219, 1998: 138), Avotins (1992), Hofmann (1989: 143), Zilliacus
(1935a: 176–7), Lampe (1961), and for Byzantine use *LBG* (*s.v.* κολλιγᾶτος).

καλίγη: see κάλιξ.

Direct? loan with   **καλίγιον, καλλίγιον, καλήγιον, καλείκειν, καλ(λ)ίκιον** (and **καλήκιον**?) (-ου, τό)
suffix   'boot', from *caliga* 'boot' (via κάλιξ?) + -ιον.
III AD – modern   Documents: e.g. perhaps *P.Warr.* 18.12 (III AD); *P.Oxy.* 2599.31 (III/IV AD);
P.Gen. I(2).80.9 (IV AD); *SB* 9158.19 (V AD); *P.Jena* I.4.6 (V/VI AD); *Stud.
Pal.* VIII.810.2 (VI AD).
Inscriptions: *SEG* VII.423.1, 427.ii.1 (both III AD); variant at Edict.Diocl. 9.5
(apparatus of Lauffer 1971) (IV AD).
Literature: perhaps Diodorus Siculus 31.15.2 (I BC); perhaps Plut. *Mor.* 141a,
but κάλτιον is more likely (I/II AD); *Coll.Herm.* ME 2a (I–IV AD); perhaps
Stobaeus 4.23.45 (V AD); Aëtius 6.80.28, 7.101.93 (VI AD); as gloss in
scholia to Luc. *Rh.Pr.* 15 and Ar. *Pl.* 847; with *caliga* in Gloss. *Herm.L.* 24.23.
Post-antique: numerous. *LBG*, Zervan (2019: 62), Kriaras (1968–),
Triandaphyllidis (1909: 69, 121). Modern καλίκι 'shoe' and derivatives:
Andriotis (1967, 1974: 291), Meyer (1895: 23–4), Kahane and Kahane
(1972–6: 535, 1982: 136), cf. Babiniotis (2002 *s.v.* καλιγώνω).
Notes: Sijpesteijn (1988: 71), Daris (1991a: 48), Hofmann (1989: 143 *s.v.*
καλίγη), Cavenaile (1952: 195), *DÉLG*, LSJ, LSJ suppl. See §4.3.2 n. 69,
§10.2.1, §10.2.2 H.

κάλιγος (gen.): see κάλιξ.

καλικαρ-: see καλιγαρ-.

rare **καλίκιος** 'shoe', from *calceus* 'shoe': probably Polybius 30.18.3 (II BC). Dubuisson (1985: 33), LSJ (*s.vv.* καλίκιοι, κάλτιος). See §8.1.3 n. 17.

rare **καλικοφασκία** 'leggings worn with *caligae*', from *caliga* 'boot' (via κάλιξ?) + *fascia* 'strip' (via φασκία): unpublished ostracon O.Dios inv. 454.5 (II AD).

Direct loan
III AD – Byz.?
κάλιξ, καλ(λ)ίγη (-ιγος/-ικος or -ης, ἡ) 'boot', from *caliga* 'boot' (not *calix* 'cup').
  Documents: perhaps *P.Ryl.* IV.627.190 (IV AD).
  Inscriptions: Edict.Diocl. 9.5 etc. (IV AD).
  Literature: Aelian, frag. 24 Hercher (II/III AD); Dio Cassius, fragments
    p. 765.2 Boissevain (II/III AD?); Modestinus in Just. *Dig.* 27.1.10.1
    (III AD); EphraemSyr. 1 p. 126.12 (V/VI AD); with *caliga* in glossaries,
    e.g. Gloss. Ps.-Cyril. 337.27.
  Post-antique: numerous, forming derivative καλιγᾶς 'cobbler', 'blacksmith'.
    LBG (*s.v.* καλίγα), Zilliacus (1937: 329 *s.v.* κάλιγα). Perhaps modern
    καλιγώνω 'shoe a horse' and other derivatives, but these may come from
    καλ(λ)ίγιον: Meyer (1895: 23–4), Andriotis (1967 *s.v.* καλιγώνω), Babiniotis
    (2002 *s.v.* καλιγώνω).
  Notes: perhaps forms derivative καλίγιον. Sijpesteijn (1988: 71), Hofmann
    (1989: 143 *s.v.* καλίγη), *TLL* (*s.v. caliga* 154.83–4), Lampe (1961 *s.v.*
    καλίγη), LSJ suppl. (replacing LSJ *s.v.* κάλικα). See §4.2.3.1, §4.2.5, §9.5.6
    nn. 55 and 58, §10.2.1, §10.2.2 H.

καλκάριος: see καλιγάριος.

not ancient **καλκατούρα** 'treading', from *calcātūra* 'treading' (*TLL*): no ancient examples.
  Binder (2000: 226–7, wrongly claiming that the Latin is unattested),
  Zilliacus (1935a: 218–19), *LBG*.

κάλκιος: see κάλτιος.

rare **καλκουλάτωρ, καλκογλάτωρ, καυκουλάτωρ** 'accountant', 'teacher of
  mathematics', from *calculātor* 'teacher of mathematics': Modestinus in Just.
  Dig. 27.1.15.5 (III AD); Edict.Diocl. 7.67 (IV AD). Binder (2000: 227),
  Mason (1974: 12), Hofmann (1989: 164), LSJ suppl. (*s.vv.* καλκουλάτωρ,
  καυκουλάτωρ). See §9.5.6 nn. 55 and 58.

καλλιγ-, καλλικ-: see καλιγ-.

rare **καλλίκλιον** 'inkwell', from *caliculus* 'small vessel', 'inkwell' (*TLL s.v.* 1. *caliculus*)
  + -ιον: Lyd. *Mag.* p. 106.2, with an etymology from κάλυξ 'cup' (VI AD).
  Binder (2000: 161), Hofmann (1989: 144), *TLL* (*s.v.* 1. *caliculus* 150.59–
  61), LSJ, and for later survival *LBG*.

rare **καλλωσόν** 'pork-rind', from *callōsus* 'hard-skinned': Orib. *Col.* 3.5.2 etc. (IV
  AD); *Hippiatr.Par.* (Pel.) 541 (V AD?). Hofmann (1989: 144), Wackernagel
  (1916: 197), *LBG*, *TLL* (*s.v. callōsus* 175.66), LSJ.

foreign ***calō*** 'call': Antec. 2.10.1 *calare* and *calatis comitiis* (the latter being a type of will:
  TLL s.v. 1. *calo* 177.76–8) (VI AD).

rare   **καλουμνία** 'false accusation', from *calumnia* 'false accusation': Just. *Nov.* 49.3.1
(VI AD); Antec. in Latin script 4.16.1 *calumnian* etc. (VI AD); Byzantine
texts. Avotins (1992), Zilliacus (1935a: 176–7), *LBG.* See §9.5.6 n. 68.

non-existent   **καλτάριος** 'cobbler', from *calceārius* 'cobbler': superseded reading for καλιγάριος
in inscription *MAMA* III.616. Hofmann (1989: 144), LSJ suppl.

Direct loan
II AD – Byz.

κάλτιος, κάλκιος (-ου, ὁ) 'shoe', from *calceus* 'shoe'.
Documents: probably not *P.Gen.* 1.80.9 (IV AD).
Inscriptions: Edict.Diocl. 9.7 etc. (IV AD).
Literature: Plut. *Aem.* 5.3 (marked), *Pomp.* 24.7, *Mor.* 141a, 465a, 813e (I/II
AD); Pollux 7.90 (II AD, quoting Rhinthon (III BC) frag. 5 Kaibel).
Post-antique: survives, forming derivative καλτίκιον 'shoe'. Note κάλτιος in
scholia recentiora to Ar. *Pl.* 511, 758, *Nub.* 1452. *LBG* (*s.v.* κάλτιον), Kahane
and Kahane (1982: 151). Modern κάλτσα 'sock' is from Italian: Babiniotis
(2002), Andriotis (1967).
Notes: the Rhinthon quotation and the τ indicate early transmission via Sicily
(LSJ *s.v.* κάλτιος), probably from a different Italic language. Probably it then
died out and was later reborrowed from Latin, perhaps with influence from
the earlier form. Sijpesteijn (1988: 71), Binder (2000: 233), Hofmann (1989:
144–5), Meinersmann (1927: 20), *DÉLG*, Frisk (1954–72: 1.768), Beekes
(2010), LSJ (*s.vv.* κάλτιος, κάλκιος). See §4.2.4.1 n. 51, §10.2.1, §10.2.2 H.

foreign   **κάλτοι**, a variant of κάλτιος 'shoe' and therefore from *calceus* 'shoe': Hesych.
as lemma κ 523 (V/VI AD); perhaps Byzantine κάλτον, for which see
LBG. Hofmann (1989: 144 *s.v.* κάλτιος), Immisch (1885: 311), *DÉLG* (*s.v.*
κάλτιος), Beekes (2010 *s.v.* κάλτιος), LSJ (*s.v.* κάλτιος).

καμαλάριος: see καμαράριος.

καμαλαύκιον: see καμελαύκιον.

rare   **καμάρα** 'vault' is originally Greek and the source of *camera*, but it may have been
influenced by *camera* in three ways. (1) Hofmann (1989: 145) sees Latin
influence when the Greek word is spelled καμέρα. That spelling is rare in
antiquity, perhaps occurring only on inscription *IGR* III.1057.6 (II AD);
the papyrus where Hofmann claimed to find it, *P.Gen.* 1.12.16 (IV AD),
probably has καμάρα. (2) Biville (1990–5: 1.38), Andriotis (1967), and
Hatzidakis (1892: 436) claim that the changed accentuation of modern
κάμαρα is due to Latin influence; this could well be right, but the accent shift
is undated and need not be ancient. (3) Biville (1992: 235) and Döttling
(1920: 14–15) think the meaning 'room' that καμάρα acquired in the post-
Classical period arose under the influence of *camera* 'room' (*TLL*). That
would be semantic extension rather than borrowing, and not necessarily
due to Latin. In antiquity *camera* normally meant 'vault'; 'room' appeared
late in IV AD and was rare even after that (*TLL s.v.* 204.24–9). By contrast
καμάρα means 'vaulted (store-)room' in much earlier papyri (Husson 1983:
122–8; Meinersmann 1927: 21). (4) Some scholars combine points 2 and
3 and distinguish two Byzantine or modern words, κάμαρα 'room', 'cabin'
and καμάρα 'vault' (*DÉLG*, *LBG*, Kriaras 1968–, Babiniotis 2002). Cameron
(1931: 235), Frisk (1954–72: 1.770–1), Beekes (2010), Meyer (1895: 24),
LSJ, LSJ suppl.

not Latin?   **καμαράριος, καμεράριος, καμαλάριος** 'servant' is usually derived from *camerārius* (cf. LSJ suppl., Hofmann 1989: 145, Horrocks 2010: 128), but *camerārius* is attested only as an adj. meaning 'of the vault/chamber' until VI AD, when it acquires the meaning 'chamberlain' that has continued into the Romance languages; there is no direct evidence for the Latin ever having the meaning 'servant' found in the Greek (*TLL*, cf. Meyer 1895: 24 *s.v.* κάμαρα). On papyrus *P.Oxy.* 1300.7 (V AD) it probably comes from καμάρα + -άριος. Common in Byzantine texts but meaning 'chamberlain' and likely to be a reborrowing of the developed Latin meaning; Zervan dates the Byzantine borrowing to XII AD (2019: 62–3, 266). Meinersmann (1927: 21), *LBG*.

       καμάσ(ι)ον: see καμίσιον.

foreign   **κάμελα**, from the context clearly a kind of hat, is stated to be an 'Italian' (παρ' Ἰταλοῖς) word by Lyd. *Mens.* frag. incert. 12 (VI AD); at that date 'Italian' must mean Latin. *TLL* has with some hesitation created an entry for unattested **camela*, while *LBG* (*s.v.* καμέλλα) believes that Lydus was thinking of *camella* 'bowl', 'cup'. *Camella* is a diminutive of *camera* 'vault', and it is not difficult to imagine that a diminutive of 'vault' with the meaning 'bowl' could also have referred to a kind of hat; moreover *camella* is rare and tends to occur in subliterary texts, so it may have had more uses than are preserved in extant literature (*TLL*). See §8.1.7; cf. κάμηλα.

not Latin?   **καμελαύκιον, καμηλαύκιον, καμαλαύκιον, καμιλαύκιον** 'cap' is said by Lyd. *Mens.* frag. incert. 12 (VI AD) to be derived from a Latin word that must be either **camela* or *camella* (see *s.v.* κάμελα), but this etymology is disputed (see notes to *P.Berl.Sarisch.* 21.38). *LBG*, Zervan (2019: 62), Kriaras (1968– *s.v.* καμηλαύκι), Andriotis (1967 *s.v.* modern καμηλαύκι), Babiniotis (2002 *s.v.* modern καμιλαύκι), *TLL* (*s.v. camela*), Lampe (1961), LSJ suppl. See §8.1.7.

       καμέρα: see κάμαρα.

       καμεράριος: see καμαράριος.

rare   **κάμηλα, καμέλλα** 'bowl', 'cup', from *camella* 'bowl', 'cup': Edict.Diocl. 15.51 (IV AD); perhaps Pollux 10.110 (II AD), where some manuscripts have τὴν παρὰ Ῥωμαίοις καμέλλαν and others τὴν παρὰ Ῥωμαίοις ματέλλαν; superseded reading of papyrus *P.Oxy.* 1165.5 (VI AD). Lauffer (1971: 257), Hofmann (1989: 145), *LBG* (*s.v.* καμέλλα), *TLL* (*s.v. camella* 201.24), LSJ.

not Latin?   **καμηλάριος, καμιλάριος** 'camel-driver' may be from *camēlārius* 'camel-driver' (*TLL*), but a Greek formation from κάμηλος 'camel' + -άριος is more likely; the Greek, first attested on inscription *I.Anazarbos* 99 (III AD), seems to be earlier than the Latin. Hofmann (1989: 145–6), Cavenaile (1952: 202), *DÉLG* (*s.v.* κάμηλος), Beekes (2010 *s.v.* κάμηλος), Lampe (1961), LSJ, LSJ suppl. See §6.1.

       καμηλαύκιον, καμιλαύκιον: see καμελαύκιον.

foreign   **κάμιλ(λ)ος** transliterating *camillus* 'boy attendant of the priest of Jupiter': DH *AR* 2.22.3 (I BC); Plut. *Numa* 7.5 (I/II AD); Ps.-Gregorius Nyssenus, *In annuntiationem* 32 = Montagna 1962: 537. Hofmann (1989: 146).

rare   **καμισαγοραστής, καμισογοραστής** 'shirt-seller', from *camīsia* 'shirt' (*TLL*)
via καμίσιον + ἀγοραστής 'purchaser': inscription *Corinth* VIII.III.522.4
(IV AD); the meaning is not what would be expected for ἀγοραστής. LSJ
suppl.

Direct loan?   **καμίσιον, κάμισον, κάμασον, καμάσιον** (-ου, τό) 'shirt', probably from *camīsia*
III AD – modern   'shirt' (*TLL*).

> Documents: e.g. probably *SB* 15922.31 (II/III AD); *P.Gen.* 1.80.1 (IV AD);
> *P.PalauRib.* 39.11 (V AD); *P.Berl.Sarisch.* 21.2 (V/VI AD); *P.Rain.Cent.* 157.1
> etc. (VI AD).
>
> Literature: Hippolytus, *Narratio de virgine Corinthiaca* p. 277.6 Achelis (III
> AD?); Gregorius Nazianzenus, *Testamentum*, Pitra 1868: 158.7 etc. (IV AD);
> Pall. *H.Laus.* 65.4.3 (IV/V AD); EphraemSyr. I p. 213.9 (V/VI AD); Gloss.
> Ps.-Cyril. 338.1.
>
> Post-antique: numerous, forming derivatives καμίσινον 'shirt', καμισιομαφόριον
> 'shirt with hood'. Daris (1991a: 49), *LBG* (*s.vv.* καμάσιν, κάμασον),
> Sophocles (1887 *s.v.* καμίσιον), Zervan (2019: 63), Triandaphyllidis (1909:
> 121, 170). Modern dialectal καμίσιν 'shirt' (Shipp 1979: 548; Andriotis
> 1974: 293), καμίσj 'under-jacket' (Meyer 1895: 24–5).
>
> Notes: etymology is disputed because of καμασ- forms and gender of *camisia*
> (normally fem.), though the gender change is well paralleled (§4.2.3.1).
> Cavenaile (1952: 197) suggests that *camisia* was reinterpreted as neut. pl.;
> *TLL* (*s.v.* camisia 207.13–16) suggests that *camisia* sometimes was neut. pl.;
> Zervan (2019: 63) doubts that Latin is the source; Kramer (1994, 2011:
> 195–205) argues that both *camis(i)a* and κάμασον/καμάσιον were originally
> borrowed from an ancient Balkan language but that from V AD καμίσιον
> replaced κάμασον/καμάσιον under Latin influence – but *SB* 15922.31 (II/
> III AD) has καμί(σια). Forms derivatives καμισαγοραστής, ὑποκαμίσιον.
> Mossakowska-Gaubert (2017: 325–7), Cromwell (2020: 142), Daris (1991a:
> 48–9), Hofmann (1989: 146), Viscidi (1944: 39), Meinersmann (1927: 21),
> *DÉLG*, Lampe (1961), LSJ and LSJ suppl. (*s.vv.* καμίσιον, καμάσιον). See
> §4.2.3.1, §10.2.1, §10.2.2 H.

rare   **κάμον**, a kind of beer, from *camum*, a kind of beer: Jul.Afric. *Cest.* 1.19.20 (II/
III AD); Edict.Diocl. 2.11 (IV AD); Priscus, *Fragmenta* 8.314 Bornmann,
marked (V AD). Hofmann (1989: 146).

Direct loan with   **καμπάγιον** (-ου, τό), a kind of boot, from *campagus*, a kind of boot (*TLL*) + -ιον.
suffix   Documents: *P.Münch.* III.1.142.14 etc. (VI AD).
VI AD – Byz.   Literature: Malal. 13.8.25 (VI AD); Lyd. *Mag.* p. 4.25 (VI AD).
> Post-antique: common. *LBG*, Triandaphyllidis (1909: 121).
> Notes: Daris (1991a: 49), *TLL* (*s.v.* campagus 208.6, 17), Lampe (1961), LSJ
> suppl. (*s.v.* καμπάγια). See §4.3.2, §10.2.1, §10.2.2 H.

foreign   **κάμπαγος** transliterating *campagus*, a kind of boot (*TLL*): Lyd. *Mag.* pp. 32.2,
32.5 (VI AD). *LBG*, *TLL* (*s.v.* campagus 208.7).

rare   **καμπαγών**, a kind of boot, from *campagus*, a kind of boot (*TLL*): Edict.Diocl.
9.11 (IV AD). Hofmann (1989: 146), *TLL* (*s.v.* campagus 208.12), LSJ, LSJ
suppl.

rare	**καμπανίζω** 'weigh', from *campāna* 'steelyard' (*TLL s.v. 2. campānus* 208.59–65) via κάμπανος + -ίζω: papyrus *P.Lond.* v.1708.130 (VI AD). Forms derivative καμπανιστής. Modern καμπανίζω: Andriotis (1967), Meyer (1895: 24). Daris (1991a: 49), Hofmann (1989: 147 *s.v.* καμπανος), *DÉLG* (*s.v.* κάμπανος), Lampe (1961), LSJ, and for later survival *LBG* (with derivative καμπανισμός 'weighing'), Zervan (2019: 64), Kriaras (1968–).
rare	**καμπανιστής**, perhaps 'user of false weights', from *campāna* 'steelyard' (*TLL s.v. 2. campānus* 208.59–65) via καμπανίζω + -της: Joannes Jejunator, *PG* LXXXVIII.1924b (VI AD). Hofmann (1989: 147 *s.v.* καμπανος), *LBG*, Lampe (1961).
name	**Καμπανός** 'Campanian', from *Campānus* 'Campanian'. Triantaphyllides (1892: 262).
Direct loan **V AD – modern**	**κάμπανος, γάμπανος** (-ου, ὁ) 'steelyard' (a weighing device), from *campāna* 'steelyard' (*TLL s.v. 2. campānus* 208.59–65). Documents: *P.Herm.* 27.8 (V AD); *P.Cair.Masp.* 67325.ivr.37 (VI AD); *SB* 14227.4, 14240.11, 16857.2 (all VI AD). Literature: with *stater* in Gloss. Ps.-Cyril. 338.8. Post-antique: common. *LBG* (*s.vv.* καμπανός, καμπανόν), Kriaras (1968–), Triandaphyllidis (1909: 122), Daris (1991a: 49). Modern dialectal κάμπανο and derivatives: Meyer (1895: 24). Notes: Meyer and Zervan (2019: 63–4, 266) merge it with καμπάνα 'bell', which is also from *campāna* (*TLL s.v. campānus* 208.55–9) but not attested in antiquity; Zervan puts the borrowing in XII AD. Actually *campāna* must have been borrowed twice, first as κάμπανος 'steelyard' and later as καμπάνα 'bell'. Forms derivative καμπανίζω. Schirru (2013: 316), Gignac (1981: 9), Daris (1991a: 49), Hofmann (1989: 147), Meinersmann (1927: 21), *DÉLG*, Beekes (2010), *TLL* (*s.v. campānus* 208.63–5), Lampe (1961), LSJ. See §4.2.3.1, §9.2, §10.2.1, §10.2.2 G.
	κάμπεστρον: see κάμπιστρον.
Direct loan **IV AD – Byz.**	**καμπιδούκτωρ, καμπιδίκτωρ, καμπιδήκτωρ, κανπιδούκτωρ** (-ορος, ὁ) 'drill-master', 'leader', from *campidoctor/campiductor*, perhaps with similar meaning (*TLL*). Documents: *P.Münch.* I.15.17 (V AD); *P.Lond.* I.113.5a.4 (V AD). Inscriptions: *MAMA* I.168.4 (IV AD), *SEG* LXV.1408.A56 etc. (V/VI AD). Literature: John Chrysostom, *PG* LII.534.3 (IV/V AD); Pall. *V.Chrys.* 13.28 (IV/V AD). Post-antique: numerous, forming derivatives καμπηδηκτόρια 'insignia of the *campiductor*' (*LBG*), καμπιδουκτώριον 'flag of the *campiductor*' (Sophocles 1887). *LBG*, Zervan (2019: 64–5), Triandaphyllidis (1909: 129). Notes: Daris (1991a: 49), Hofmann (1989: 147), Zilliacus (1935a: 218–19), Meinersmann (1927: 22), *TLL* (*s.v. campidoctor* 211.51), Lampe (1961), LSJ suppl. See §4.2.5, §4.5, §10.2.1, §10.2.2 C.
Direct loan **I BC – IV AD?**	**κάμπιστρον, κάμπεστρον** (-ου, τό) 'loincloth', from *campestre* 'loincloth'. Documents: *SB* 11946.19 (I BC); *P.Münch.* III.I.138.2 (IV AD); *P.Gascou* 63.5 (IV AD); *P.Ryl.* IV.627.19 etc. (IV AD); perhaps *P.Lond.* v.1657.9 (IV/V AD). Inscriptions: Reinach 1906: 104 no. 17.5 (II/III AD). Notes: Daris (1991a: 49), Hofmann (1989: 147), LSJ suppl. See §4.2.5, §4.3.2 n. 75, §8.1.5, §10.2.1, §10.2.2 H.

Direct loan
I AD – modern

κάμπος (-ου, ὁ) 'field', 'camping place', 'Campus Martius', from *campus* 'field'.

Documents: *P.Oxy.* 247.22 (I AD); *P.Mich.* III.171.16, 179.13 (both I AD); *Rom.Mil.Rec.* 76.xix.9, xx.24 (II AD); *SB* 6222.16 (IV AD).

Literature: e.g. perhaps Diodorus Siculus 37.29.1 (I BC); Strabo 5.1.11 etc., always as a place name (I BC/AD); Plut. *Brutus* 38.4, marked and place name (I/II AD); Hdn. *Pros.Cath.* III.1.187.15 (II AD); Athan. *Pet.Ar.* 1.18 (IV AD); Hesych. as lemma κ 614 (V/VI AD); Malal. 7.3 (VI AD); Antec. 2.20.4, 4.3.4 (VI AD).

Post-antique: numerous, forming derivative καμπικός 'on or for a field'. *LBG*, Zervan (2019: 65), Kriaras (1968–), Triandaphyllidis (1909: 32–3, 119). Modern κάμπος 'plain': Babiniotis (2002), Andriotis (1967), Meyer (1895: 25).

Notes: Hesychius calls it Sicilian (Σικελοί) and glosses with ἱππόδρομος; Willi (2008: 29) takes that reference as distinct from, and probably earlier than, the main borrowing, and suggests a connection with Greek κάμπτω 'turn'. In early documents it could be considered a place name, but the place referred to (on the outskirts of Oxyrhynchus) also had a more commonly used Greek name. Daris (1991a: 49), Hofmann (1989: 147–8), Zilliacus (1935a: 218–19), Meinersmann (1927: 22), Immisch (1885: 331–2), *DÉLG*, Lampe (1961), LSJ (*s.v.* κάμπος II). See §4.2.4.1 n. 51, §5.3.2 passage 13, §8.2.3, §10.2.1, §10.2.2 C.

not Latin?

κά(μ)ψα 'basket', 'case' is usually considered to come from *capsa* 'case' (thus *DÉLG s.v.* κάψα, Diethart 1988: 56–7, Hofmann 1989: 148, Meyer 1895: 29), but Beekes (2010 *s.v.* κάψα) argues that since the Latin word has no etymology, it is more likely to come from the Greek than *vice versa*; he sees the -μ- as evidence of derivation from a pre-Greek word. In my view the real difficulty with the Latin etymology is that κά(μ)ψα seems to be the source of κα(μ)ψάκης (thus e.g. *DÉLG*, Beekes) and κα(μ)ψάκης is securely attested in III BC: *P.Cair.Zen.* 1.59012.85 etc., *P.Iand.Zen.* 53.ii.15 etc., *P.Lond.* VII.1930.152 etc., *SB* 16505.7. A Latinism of this type would be most unexpected in those papyri, and therefore it is probable that this whole group of words (apart from the κα(μ)ψάρ- set, *q.v.*) does not come from Latin; Daris (1991a) must also have held this view, as he does not include these words. One could, however, argue for a Latin derivation by positing that the original word was not κά(μ)ψα but rather κα(μ)ψάκης, which would have to be borrowed into Latin as *capsa* and then back into Greek as κά(μ)ψα. Derivatives that would be Latinate if κάμψα were include κα(μ)ψάκης 'flask', κα(μ)ψάκιον 'little flask', κάμψιον 'basket', 'case', καψικός 'like a case'. LSJ, LSJ suppl.

rare

καμψαρικόν 'loincloth worn by a *capsarius*', probably from *capsārius* 'slave who carries schoolbooks or watches clothes at the baths' via καμψάριος + -ικός in neuter: Dan.Sket. *M.* 10 = *Vita Danieli*, Clugnet 1900: 60.9 (VI AD); Byzantine texts. Hofmann (1989: 165 *s.v.* καψαριος), *LBG*, Lampe (1961).

rare

κα(μ)ψάριον 'cupboard for clothes', probably from *capsārium* 'cupboard for clothes' (*TLL s.v. capsārius* 363.1–3): papyri *P.Giss.* 50.3 etc. (III AD); *SB* 9921.10 (III AD). Hofmann (1989: 164–5), Cavenaile (1952: 196, with derivation from κά(μ)ψα + -άριον), LSJ suppl. (*s.v.* καψαριον).

Direct loan?
II AD – Byz.

κα(μ)ψάριος (-ου, ὁ) 'slave in charge of clothes', 'slave who carries schoolbooks', 'paramedic soldier', probably from *capsārius* 'slave who carries schoolbooks or watches clothes at the baths'.

Documents: e.g. *P.Stras.* IV.260.2 (II AD); *P.Flor.* 1.63.4 (III AD); *PSI* III.217.2 (IV AD); *SB* 13053.1 (V AD); *P.Gascou* 43.4 (V/VI AD); *P.Prag.* II.180.4 (VI AD).

Inscriptions: *IG* II/III².II.2276.3 (I/II AD?); *SEG* XII.120.151 (II AD); *IG* II/III².II.2193.150 (II/III AD); *IG* II/III².II.2221.end (III AD); *IG* II/III².II.2245.41 (III AD); Edict.Diocl. 7.75 (IV AD); *I.Tyr* 151 bis.

Literature: Epiph. *Pan.* II.313.2 (IV AD).

Post-antique: survives. *LBG*.

Notes: Greek formation from κά(μ)ψα + -άριος is possible (*DÉLG s.v.* κάψα, Beekes 2010 *s.v.* κάψα), but Latin is probably attested first. For form *campsarius* see *TLL* (*s.v. capsārius* 362.58–60). Meaning 'paramedic soldier' occurs only once, on papyrus of III AD: Benaissa (2010: 179). Forms derivative καμψαρικόν. Hofmann (1989: 165), *TLL* (*s.v. capsārius* 362.61–2), Lampe (1961), LSJ and LSJ suppl. (*s.vv.* καμψάριος, καψάριος). See §4.2.4.1 n. 50, §8.2.2, §10.2.1, §10.2.2 N.

κάμψιον: see κάμψα.

not Latin?

κανακεύω 'wheedle', perhaps from *canis* 'dog' via unattested *canicāre*: no ancient examples. Meyer (1895: 25), Andriotis (1967), Kriaras (1968–).

rare

καναλικλάριος, a title apparently from *canāliclārius*, an army official (defined as 'culvert-maker' by *TLL*, but Gilliam (1976: 51) presents good evidence of a reasonably high rank): inscription *IGUR* IV.1672.2. Probably the same word as the title κανανικλάριος: papyri *P.Oxy.* 2925.1, 3366.28 etc. (both III AD). Gilliam (1976), commentary on *P.Oxy.* 3366, Daris (1991a: 49 *s.v.* κανανικλάριος), LSJ suppl. (*s.v.* κανανικλάριος).

Direct loan
III AD – modern

κανάλιον (-ου, τό) 'culvert', 'road', from *canālis* 'culvert', itself from κάννα 'reed' via *canna*.

Documents: *P.Dura* 26.16 (III AD).

Literature: Athan. *Apol.Sec.* 50.1 (IV AD); Jo.Scholast. 3 p. 57.17 (VI AD). Κανᾶλις occurs with *cloaca* and καλανίσκος (sic) with *cloax* in Gloss. Ps.-Cyril. 338.21, 22 and *Idiomata Codicis Harleiani, CGL* II.492.55.

Post-antique: numerous, with κανάλης 'drain', κάναλος 'drain', καναλοπλύτης 'drain-cleaner', etc. *LBG*, Kriaras (1968–), Triandaphyllidis (1909: 124, 168). Modern κανάλι 'channel': Babiniotis (2002), Andriotis (1967), Meyer (1895: 25).

Notes: Daris (1991a: 49), Hofmann (1989: 148), Lampe (1961), LSJ suppl. See §4.2.5, §8.2.3 n. 51, §10.2.1, §10.2.2 J.

κανανικλάριος: see καναλικλάριος.

κανγελ-: see καγκελ-.

κανδελ-: see κανδηλ-.

κανδῆλα: see κανδήλη.

rare   **κανδηλάπτης** 'candle-lighter', from *candēla* 'candle' via κανδήλη + -άπτης (cf. ἅπτω 'set on fire'): Teucer, Boll 1903: 42.3 (I AD?); often in Byzantine texts. Hofmann (1989: 149 *s.v.* κανδῆλα), *LBG*, Kriaras (1968–), Andriotis (1974: 294), LSJ suppl.

non-existent?   **κανδηλάριον**, meaning uncertain, cited by Viscidi (1944: 41) and Hofmann (1989: 149 *s.v.* κανδῆλα) as from *candēla* 'candle' via κανδήλη: I can find no examples. *LBG* (*s.v.* κανδηλάριος).

not ancient?   **κανδηλαῦρον, κανδέλαβρον** 'candelabra', from *candēlābrum* 'candelabra': inscription *CIG* 9528.1; perhaps same word as Byzantine κανδηλάβρα. Hofmann (1989: 149), *LBG* (*s.vv.* κανδέλαβρον, κανδηλάβρα), on the accent Bartoli (1912: 989).

Direct loan
III AD – modern   **κανδήλη, κανδῆλα, κανδίλη** (-ης, ἡ) 'candle', 'torch', from *candēla* 'candle'.
         Documents: *O.Trim.* II.531.14 (IV AD); tachygraphy in Menci 2000: 283 (V AD).
         Inscriptions: Edict.Diocl. 36.33 (IV AD); *I.Ephesos* 557.4 (V AD?).
         Literature: e.g. Athenaeus 15.701b (II/III AD); *Coll.Herm.* ME 11s (II–IV AD); Epiph. *Pan.* III.147.24 (IV AD); Callin. *V.Hypat.* 9.6 (V AD); Orion, *Etymologicum* p. 178.16 Sturz, as lemma with a Greek etymology (V AD); Malal. 12.3.23 (VI AD); Cyr.S. *Vit.Eu.* 76.21 (VI AD).
         Post-antique: numerous. *LBG* (*s.v.* κανδέλα), Zervan (2019: 65–6), Kriaras (1968– *s.v.* κανδήλα), Triandaphyllidis (1909: 120). Modern καντήλα 'votive lamp' and derivatives: Babiniotis (2002), Andriotis (1967), Coleman (2007: 795), Meyer (1895: 26).
         Notes: forms derivatives κανδηλάπτης, κουκουμοκανδήλη, πολυκάνδηλος. Menci (2000: 283), Hofmann (1989: 148–9), Viscidi (1944: 40–1), Lampe (1961), LSJ, LSJ suppl. See §8.2.3 n. 51, §10.2.1, §10.2.2 M.

not ancient?   **κανδηλοσβέστης, κανδηλοσβεστρία** (ὁ, ἡ) 'moth', from *candēla* 'candle' via κανδήλη + -σβέστης (cf. σβέννυμι 'quench'): scholia to Nic. *Ther.* 763a and Opp. *H.* 1.404; Byzantine texts. Hofmann (1989: 149 *s.v.* κανδῆλα), *LBG*, Andriotis (1974: 294), LSJ.

rare   **κανδιδάριος** 'baker of white bread', from *candidārius* 'baker of white bread': inscriptions *SEG* XXXIX.649.11 (II/III AD); *MAMA* V.254.2. Hofmann (1989: 149), LSJ suppl.

Direct loan
II AD – Byz.   **κανδιδᾶτος** (-ου, ὁ) 'candidate for office', later an official title, from *candidātus* 'candidate'.
         Inscriptions: e.g. *IG* IV.588.9 (II AD); *I.Ephesos* 677.3 (II/III AD); *I.Ephesos* 3085.10 etc. (III AD); *SEG* XXX.1556 (IV–VI AD).
         Literature: Nil. 1.207.1 etc. (V AD); Malal. 13.19 (VI AD); Lyd. *Mag.* p. 44.10 etc. (VI AD); *V.Luc.Styl.* 29 (VI AD); Procop. *Bell.* 7.38.5, marked (VI AD).
         Post-antique: survives, forming derivatives κανδιδάτισσα 'wife of a *candidatus*', κανδιδατίκιον 'chain of office of a *candidatus*', etc. Sophocles (1887), *LBG* (*s.v.* κανδιδάτης), Triandaphyllidis (1909: 129).
         Notes: Mason (1974: 5, 7, 59), Hofmann (1989: 149–50), Zilliacus (1935a: 218–19), Lampe (1961), LSJ suppl. See §4.2.4.1 n. 51, §6.6 n. 40, §10.2.1, §10.2.2 D.

rare	**κάνδιδος** 'shining' (a kind of silver and a game), from *candidus* 'bright': Galen XIV.49.3 Kühn (II AD); inscription *TAM* III.1.536.4 (as a name?); Byzantine texts. Durling (1979: 220), Hofmann (1989: 150), Zilliacus (1937: 329, citing a further undated example), *LBG*.
	κανδίλη: see κανδήλη.
non-existent?	**κανδίλιον**, presumably 'little candle', from *candēla* 'candle' via κανδήλη: perhaps inscription *I.Mylasa* 629.10.
not ancient	**κανίνος** transliterating *canīnus* 'canine': interpolations in Dsc. 4.75 RV, 80 RV. Sophocles (1887 *s.v.* κανῖνους).
not Latin?	**κάνιστρον** 'basket', from *canistrum* 'basket' (Hofmann 1989: 150–1) or a variant of Greek κανάστρον (LSJ): Theognis historicus, *FHG* IV frag. 1.15 (III AD); papyrus *P.Lond.* v.1657.9, apparently as fem. sing. (IV/V AD). The spelling variant κάνιτρον, cited by LSJ, may not exist: Hesych. κ 653 and Photius, *Lexicon* κ 158 should probably both read κανήτιον.
	κανκελ-: see καγκελ-.
semantic extension	**κάννα** 'reed' is purely Greek, but its meaning 'pen' may be taken from *canna* 'pen' (*TLL s.v.* 1. *canna* 262.25–9), itself from κάννα 'reed'. Hofmann (1989: 151), Frisk (1954–72: I.779), Meyer (1895: 25).
not Latin?	**κανναβάριος** 'worker in hemp', suggested as a borrowing of unattested **cannabārius* 'worker in hemp' and/or of *canabārius* 'inhabitant of the trading settlement surrounding a Roman camp', is probably a Greek formation from κάνναβις 'hemp' + -άριος. Robert (1963: 142–4), Drew-Bear (1972: 79), Wahrmann (1933: 43), Hofmann (1989: 151), *DÉLG* (*s.v.* κάνναβις), Beekes (2010 *s.v.* κάνναβις), *LBG*, LSJ suppl. (replacing LSJ).
Direct loan with suffix **VI AD – modern**	**καννίον** (-ου, τό), a container, from *canna*, a container (*TLL s.v.* 2. *canna*) + -ιον. Documents: *SB* 15300.8 (VI AD). Literature: Hesych. as gloss α 2724 (V/VI AD). Post-antique: numerous. *LBG*, Kriaras (1968–). Modern καννί 'thurible' (Meyer 1895: 25–6, though Babiniotis 2002 derives that from κάννα 'reed'). Notes: Diethart (1995a: 84, 1999: 179), *LBG*, Lampe (1961). See §4.3.2, §10.2.1, §10.2.2 M.
Direct loan **VI AD – Byz.**	**κανονικάριος, κανωνικάριος** (-ου, ὁ) 'tax collector', from *canonicārius* 'tax collector' (*TLL*). Documents: *P.Cair.Masp.* 67057.2.5 (VI AD). Literature: Just. *Codex* 10.19.9.0, *Nov.* 30.7.1, etc. (VI AD); Ath.Schol. 20.1.6 (VI AD). Post-antique: survives in legal texts. Notes: κανανικλάριος, once considered a misspelling of this word, is now considered a variant of καναλικλάριος (*q.v.*). Hofmann (1989: 151–2), Cavenaile (1952: 202), Zilliacus (1935a: 176–7), LSJ, LSJ suppl. See §4.2.4.1 n. 50, §8.2.2, §10.2.1, §10.2.2 D.
	κανστρήσιος: see καστρήσιος.
not ancient	**καντάτωρ** 'herald', from *cantātor* 'singer': no ancient examples. Zilliacus (1935a: 218–19), *LBG*.

καπειδειν, κάπειτον: see κάπιτον.

Καπειτώλια: see Καπετώλια.

foreign   **κάπερε** transliterating inf. of *capiō* 'take': Lyd. *Mag.* p. 68.22 οὕτω δὲ τοὺς ἀπὸ ῥάβδων κοφίνους ἐκάλεσαν ἀπὸ τοῦ κάπερε, οἷον εἰ χωρεῖν (VI AD). Sophocles (1887). See §9.5.5 n. 47.

not Latin   **καπετάνος, καπιτάνος** 'captain' (esp. in the military sense), perhaps from unattested (in antiquity) *capitānus, variant of *capitāneus* 'leading' (*TLL*): no certainly ancient examples (*I.Ephesos* 925a.8 is probably a name; *I.Chr.Asie Mineure* 1.235.3 is heavily restored). By the Byzantine period Italian *capitano* is a more plausible source than Latin; Zervan (2019: 68, 266) dates the borrowing to XIV AD. Hofmann (1989: 153), *LBG* (*s.v.* καπετάνος), Kriaras (1968– *s.v.* καπετάνιος).

Καπετολει-, Καπετωλει-: see Καπετωλι-.

Deriv. of loan   **Καπετώλια, Καπιτώλια, Καπιτώλεια, Καπετώλεια, Καπετόλεια, Καπειτώλια,**
I–III AD   **Καπητώλια, Καπιτώνεια** (-ων, τά) 'Capitoline games', from *Capitōlius* 'Capitoline' (in neut. pl. 'Capitoline games') via Καπετώλιος.
      Documents: *Pap.Agon.* 1.20 etc. (III AD); *Pap.Agon.* 8.6 (III AD).
      Inscriptions: e.g. *I.Iasos* 107.5 (I AD); *I.Sinope* 105.3 (I/II AD); *F.Delphes* III. VI.143.9 (II AD); *I.Ephesos* 1615.7 (II/III AD); *I.Didyma* 278.5 (II/III AD); *IG* II/III².III.3169/70.13 etc. (III AD).
      Coins: ΚΑΠΕΤΩΛΙΑ at Aphrodisias, Head 1911: 610.
      Literature: Dio Cassius 79.10.3 (II/III AD).
      Notes: forms derivatives ἰσοκαπετώλιος, Καπετωλιονίκης, Καπετωλιακός. The games were discontinued in IV AD. Meinersmann (1927: 22), LSJ (*s.v.* καπετώλιον), LSJ suppl. See §4.6.2, §9.1 n. 4, §9.2, §10.2.2 F.

Deriv. of loan   **Καπετωλιακός, Καπιτωλιακός** (-ή, -όν) 'Capitoline' (of games), from *Capitōlius*
III–IV AD   'Capitoline' via Καπετώλια + -ιακός.
      Documents: *P.Oxy.* 3135.7 (III AD); *Pap.Agon.* 8.10, 10.12 (both III AD); *P.Harr.* 1.97v.11 (IV AD); *P.Oxy.* 4357.7, perhaps 4079.13 (both IV AD).
      Notes: the games were discontinued in IV AD. All examples come from Oxyrhynchus. Cavenaile (1951: 397, 1952: 197), *LBG* (*s.v.* καπιτωλιακός). See §4.6.1, §8.2.1, §9.2, §10.2.2 F.

rare   **Καπετωλιάς**, gen. Καπετωλιάδος 'celebration of the Capitoline games', 'victory in the Capitoline games', from *Capitōlius* 'Capitoline' via Καπετώλια + -άς: inscription *SEG* XXXVII.712 ep.4 (II AD). LSJ suppl.

Καπετωλίδος (gen.): see Καπετωλίς.

rare   **Καπετωλῖνος, Καπετωλεῖνος, Καπιτωλ(ε)ῖνος** 'Capitoline', from *Capitōlīnus* 'Capitoline': often as the name of the Capitoline Hill in Rome, e.g. DH *AR* 3.69.4 (I BC). Occasionally in other senses: as an epithet of Zeus/Jupiter, perhaps on inscription *IG* XII.VI.1.7.39 (I BC?); in the compound genitive Ζευκαπιτωλίνου in *Coll.Herm.* Mp 6a (III AD?); in the feminine as the name of a tribe on inscription *IGBulg.* II.690.4; with *Capitolinus* in a list of divine names in Gloss. *Herm.Mp.* 289.66. Binder (2000: 133), Hofmann (1989: 154), Sophocles (1887 *s.v.* καπιτωλῖνος), *TLL* (*Onomasticon s.v. Capitōlium* 165.36, 66).

Direct loan
II BC – VI AD

Καπετώλιον, Καπιτώλιον (-ου, τό) 'Capitol', 'citadel (in any town)', from *Capitōlium* 'Capitol'.

Documents: *P.Oxy.* 2128.4 (II AD); *P.Oxy.* 2109.8 etc. (III AD); *P.Oxy.* 4541.2 (III AD); tachygraphy in Menci 2000: 283 (III AD); *P.Oxy.* 3757.3, 3758.78, etc. (both IV AD); *SB* 9883.6 (IV AD).

Inscriptions: e.g. *IG* IV².1.63.8 (II BC); *IG* VII.2225.33 etc. (II BC); *SEG* XXXV.823.42 (II BC); Sherk 1969: no. 22.25 (I BC); *MAMA* IV.143.B22 (I AD); *IG* II/III².III.3299.6 (II AD); *SEG* XXIX.807.8 (V AD).

Literature: common, e.g. Polybius 1.6.3 (II BC); DH *AR* 1.32.2 (I BC); Musonius Rufus frag. 44.8 Lutz (I AD); App. *BC* 3.5.34 (I/II AD); Dio Cassius 3.13.2a (II/III AD); Eus. *PE* 4.2.8 (IV AD); Soz. 9.6.3 (V AD); Lyd. *Mag.* p. 78.21 (VI AD).

Post-antique: modern Καπιτώλιο 'Capitol' (Babiniotis 2002) is probably revival not survival.

Notes: probably forms derivative Καπετωλίς. Binder (2000: 133–4), Menci (2000: 283), García Domingo (1979: 489), Hofmann (1989: 154), Meinersmann (1927: 22), *TLL* (*Onomasticon s.v. Capitōlium* 159.76–80), Lampe (1961), LSJ, LSJ suppl. See §2.2.3 with passage 2, §4.2.4.1 n. 54, §4.3.2 n. 75, §4.6.1, §8.1.3, **§8.1.4**, §8.2.3, §10.2.1, §10.2.2 O.

Deriv. of loan
II–III AD

Καπετωλιονίκης, Καπιτωλιονίκης, Καπετωλιονείκης, Καπιτωλιονείκης (-ου, ὁ) 'victor in the Capitoline games', from *Capitōlius* 'Capitoline' via Καπετώλια (or *Capitōlium* 'Capitol' via Καπετώλιον) + -νίκης (cf. νικάω 'win').

Documents: *Pap.Agon.* 1.17 etc., 3.19 etc., 10.5 (all III AD); *PSI* XII.1251.6 (III AD).

Inscriptions: *I.Ephesos* 22.7 (II AD); perhaps *SEG* LII.999.7 (II AD); *I.Milet* II.939.3 (II/III AD); *CIG* 6829.22 (II/III AD); *I.Cos Segre* EV53.5 (III AD); *I.Didyma* 370.9 etc.; *SB* 5725.2.

Notes: Meinersmann (1927: 22), LSJ (*s.v.* Καπετώλιον). See §4.6.2, §9.2, §10.2.2 F.

Direct loan
II BC – VI AD

Καπετώλιος, Καπιτώλιος, Καπετώριος (-α, -ον or -ου, ὁ) 'Capitoline' (usually epithet of Zeus, equivalent to *Capitōlīnus*), from *Capitōlius* 'Capitoline'.

Documents: *BGU* II.362.3.5 etc. (III AD); *P.Mil.Vogl.* IV.233.7 (III AD).

Inscriptions: e.g. *SEG* XXXIII.637.3 (II BC); *Syll.³* 781.4 (I BC); *I.Assos* 26.32 (I AD); *Syll.³* 810.17 (I AD); *I.Cos Segre* EV135.2 (I AD); *I.Stratonikeia* 209.1 (II AD); *I.Stratonikeia* 16.9 (II/III AD).

Coins: ΖΕΥΣ ΚΑΠΕΤΩΛΙΟΣ at Antiocheia ad Maeandrum, Head 1911: 608 (I–III AD).

Literature: e.g. Polybius 3.26.1 (II BC); DH *AR* 8.39.1 (I BC); Jos. *AJ* 14.36 (I AD); Pausanias 2.4.5 (II AD); Philostratus, *Vita Apollonii* 5.30 Kayser (II/III AD); Malal. 10.10 (VI AD); Procop. *Bell.* 3.5.4 (VI AD).

Notes: source of Καπετώλια. Hofmann (1989: 154–5), *TLL* (*Onomasticon s.v. Capitōlium* 165.25–37), Lampe (1961 *s.v.* Καπιτώλιος), LSJ (*s.v.* Καπετώλιον). See §4.2.2, §4.6.1, §8.1.3, **§8.1.4**, §9.1 n. 4, §10.2.1, §10.2.2 O, §12.2.2.

Deriv. of loan
VI AD

Καπετωλίς, Καπιτωλίς (fem. adj., gen. Καπιτωλίδος) 'Capitoline', probably from *Capitōlius* 'Capitoline' via Καπετώλιος or *Capitōlium* 'Capitol' via Καπετώλιον.

Literature: Lyd. *Mag.* p. 178.17 (VI AD); Paulus Silentiarius, *Descriptio Sanctae Sophiae* 152 (VI AD); *Anthologia Graeca* 9.656.11 (VI AD).

Notes: Hofmann (1989: 154 *s.v.* καπιτώλιον), *LBG*, *TLL* (*Onomasticon s.v. Capitōlium* 165.37), Lampe (1961). See §4.6.1, §10.2.2 O.

καπητόν: see κάπιτον-.

Καπητώλια: see Καπετώλια.

Direct loan
V AD – Byz.

καπικλάριος (-ου, ὁ) 'prison guard', apparently from *capiclārius*, meaning uncertain, perhaps variant of *capitulārius* 'exactor of tribute and of recruits' (*TLL*).

Inscriptions: *I.Cret.* IV.507.2 (V AD); perhaps *I.Chr.Macédoine* 48 (V/VI AD).

Literature: Hesychius of Jerusalem, *Homilia* 20.10 Aubineau (V AD?); others of doubtful date. Unverified examples (III and IV AD) in Zilliacus (1937: 323, 329).

Post-antique: numerous. Kriaras (1968–), *LBG* (*s.v.* κλαβικουλάριος).

Notes: Byzantine lexica (*LBG*, Kriaras 1968–) derive this from *clāvīculārius* 'turnkey' and consider it a variant of κλαβικουλάριος (*q.v.*); although καπικλάριος and κλαβικουλάριος were effectively equivalent, the fact that each matches a different Latin word suggests two separate borrowings. Binder (2000: 180–1), Hofmann (1989: 152), Zilliacus (1937: 329), *TLL* (*s.v.* capitulārius 349.64), Lampe (1961). See §4.2.4.1 n. 50, §10.2.1, §10.2.2 D.

rare

καπίλα 'hair', from *capillus* 'hair': Callin. *V.Hypat.* 28.21 (V AD). Hofmann (1989: 152), Lampe (1961).

not ancient

καπιλλάρεμ transliterating acc. of *capillāris*, a plant: interpolation in Dsc. 4.135 RV. *TLL* (*s.v.* capillāris 312.77).

non-existent?

καπιλλάριος 'barber', supposedly from *capillāris*, but as that word refers to plants and has no meaning approaching 'barber', unattested **capillārius* 'barber' or a Greek formation from *capillus* 'hair' (via καπίλα?) + -άριος is also possible: perhaps papyrus *P.Ant.* II.109.10 (VI AD). Medieval *capillārius* 'buckle-maker' (*DMLBS*) is probably irrelevant. Daris (1991a: 49), Hofmann (1989: 152), *LBG*.

non-existent?

καπιλλᾶτος 'hairy', from *capillātus* 'long-haired', 'hairy': perhaps Epict. *Diss.* 4.7.37 (I/II AD); perhaps Hesych. κ 2042 (V/VI AD). Latte (1952: 34), Hofmann (1989: 152), *LBG*.

non-existent?

καπιστέλλον 'rein', from *capistellum* 'rein' (*TLL*): perhaps Edict.Diocl. 10.6 (IV AD). Hofmann (1989: 152).

Direct? loan with
suffix
VI AD – modern

καπίστριον (-ου, τό) 'halter', from *capistrum* 'halter' (via κάπιστρον?) + -ιον.

Documents: *SB* 15961.3 (V/VI AD).

Literature: Hesych. as gloss ε 2141, ι 865, φ 749, 752, as lemma κ 715 (V/VI AD).

Post-antique: numerous. *LBG*, Kriaras (1968–). Modern καπίστρι 'bridle': Babiniotis (2002), Andriotis (1967), Meyer (1895: 26).

Notes: Hofmann (1989: 152–3), Walde and Hofmann (1938–54 *s.v.* capistrum), LSJ. See §4.3.2 n. 69, §9.5.4 n. 42, §10.2.1, §10.2.2 K.

rare

κάπιστρον 'halter', from *capistrum* 'halter': *Hippiatr.Par.* (Apsyrtus) 21 (III/IV AD?); Edict.Diocl. 10.4 etc. in *SEG* XXXVII.335.iii (IV AD); perhaps papyrus *P.Lond.* V.1657.9 κάνιστρα (IV/V AD). Hofmann (1989: 152–3), *LBG*, LSJ suppl.

κάπιτα: see καπιτόν.

rare	**καπιτᾶλις**, from *capitālis* 'capital' (esp. of punishment): inscription *I.Ephesos* 3035.11, as part of title τριούμβουρα καπιτᾶλιν, acc. of *triumvir capitālis* (II AD). Mason (1974: 6, 59), Hofmann (1989: 447 *s.v.* τριούμβουρ).
	καπιτάνος: see καπετάνος.
rare	**καπιτατίων** 'allowance of fodder', 'rations', 'poll tax', from *capitātiō* 'tax or tribute per head' (*TLL*): Just. *Nov.* 8.2 etc. (VI AD); Byzantine texts. Avotins (1992), Hofmann (1989: 153), Viscidi (1944: 20), Zilliacus (1935a: 176–7), *LBG*, Triantaphyllides (1892: 262), *TLL* (*s.v. capitātio* 347.30), Lampe (1961), LSJ suppl.
foreign	**κάπιτις**, from gen. of *caput* 'head', as part of the phrase κάπιτις δεμινουτίων (*capitis dēminūtiō*) 'loss of status': *Schol.Sinai.* in Latin script 46 *kapitis deminutiona* (V/VI AD); *Antec.* in Latin script 1.16.pr. *capitis deminution* etc. (VI AD); later in Greek script. Zilliacus (1935a: 176–7). See §7.1.3 n. 16, §9.5.6; cf. κάπιτον, though κάπιτις does not function as a genitive of κάπιτον.
foreign	**καπιτίων** apparently transliterating an unknown Latin word (**capitiō* is unattested): a passage found both in Her.Mech. *Mens.* 60.4 and in Epiph. *Mens.4* 83.4: δύο δὲ δίδραγμα, ἃ καλεῖται ἐπικεφάλαια, κατὰ δὲ Ῥωμαικὴν διάλεκτον καπιτίων· καπούδ γὰρ τὴν κεφαλὴν καλοῦσιν (IV AD).
Direct loan III AD – Byz.	**κάπιτον, κάπειτον, καπητόν, καβιδειν, καπειδειν** (-ου, τό) 'ration allowance', 'daily ration of fodder', 'poll tax', from *caput* 'head' (via plural *capita* and/or oblique stem *capit-*). Documents: common, e.g. *P.Oxy.* 43r.4.9 (III AD); *O.Waqfa* 31.4 (IV AD); *O.Douch.* III.184.2 etc. (IV/V AD); *O.Oasis Bahria* 14.3 (IV/V AD); *P.Herm.* 78.3 (V AD); *BGU* III.836.2 (VI AD). Literature: Hesych. as lemma κ 693 (V/VI AD); Just. *Edict* 13.3 = p. 781.25 (VI AD); Lyd. *Mag.* p. 68.21 with false etymology, etc. (VI AD). Also meaning 'head', DH *AR* 4.61.2, marked (I BC). Also in Latin script as part of *in capita* 'by individuals' (as opposed to *in stirpes* 'by families', of inheritance division), e.g. Just. *Nov.* 22.46.2 (VI AD); Ath.Schol. 9.10.4 (VI AD); *Antec.* 3.1.6 *in capita* (VI AD). Post-antique: some survival, esp. in papyri. Notes: borrowed back into Latin as *capītum* 'fodder': *TLL* (*s.v. capītum*). Forms derivative ἀννωνοκάπιτον. Avotins (1992) suggests Greek derivation from poetic κάπη 'manger'. Cervenka-Ehrenstrasser (1996: 84), Hofmann (1989: 153–4), Viscidi (1944: 20), Zilliacus (1935a: 176–7, 218–19), Meinersmann (1927: 22), *TLL* (*s.v. capītum*), Lampe (1961 *s.v.* κάπιτα), LSJ suppl. (replacing LSJ *s.v.* καπητόν). See §4.2.5, §10.2.1, §10.2.2 D.
non-existent?	**καπιτουλάριος** 'of recruitment of soldiers', from *capitulārius* 'of recruitment of soldiers or payment of tribute' (*TLL*): papyri perhaps *P.Sakaon* 47.7, spelled καπτονάριος (IV AD); perhaps *P.Ant.* II.109.12, spelled καπιταυλ (VI AD). Daris (1991a: 49), Hofmann (1989: 154).
foreign	**καπίτουλον** transliterating *capitulum* 'little head': Lyd. *Mag.* p. 68.23 (VI AD); Byzantine texts. Binder (2000: 180), *LBG*, Kriaras (1968– *s.v.* καπίτολον), Triandaphyllidis (1909: 132).

καπιτωλ-: see καπετωλ-.

Καπιτώνεια: see Καπετώλια.

| not ancient | καπίων 'acquisition', from *capiō* 'take': no ancient examples. Zilliacus (1935a: 176–7), *LBG*. |

not ancient   κάπλα 'rump (of a horse)', perhaps from *scapula* 'shoulder blade': no ancient examples. Binder (2000: 185–6), Meyer (1985: 26).

foreign   κάπουτ, κάπουδ transliterating *caput* 'head': Epiph. *Mens.4* 83.4 (IV AD); Hesych. as lemma κ 726, 2042 (V/VI AD); Her.Mech. *Mens.* 60.4. Immisch (1885: 332–3).

not ancient?   κάππα 'coat', perhaps from *cappa* 'cape' (*TLL s.v.* 2. *cappa* 354.32–5): probably no ancient examples. Meyer (1895: 26–7), *LBG*.

foreign   κάπρα 'nanny goat', from *capra* 'nanny goat': Plut. *Rom.* 29.3, *Publ.* 11.7, *Cam.* 33.10, all marked (I/II AD); Ps.-Alexander Aphrodisiensis, *Problemata* 4.141 Usener, marked (II/III AD?); Hesych. as lemma α 8767, κ 736 (V/VI AD). Hofmann (1989: 155), Immisch (1885: 320–1), LSJ.

name   Καπράριος, a personal name, from *caprārius* 'goatherd'. Sophocles (1887).

rare   Καπρατῖναι, Καπρατεῖναι, the name of a Roman festival, from (*nōnae*) *Caprōtīnae/Caprātīnae*, a festival: Plut. (often marked) *Rom.* 29.2, 29.9, *Numa* 2.1, *Cam.* 33.8, 33.10, *Mor.* 320c (I/II AD); inscription *SEG* LXVI.526.5 (III AD). Strobach (1997: 195), Hofmann (1989: 155–6).

foreign   καπρίφικος transliterating *caprifīcus* 'wild fig tree': Plut. *Rom.* 29.9, *Cam.* 33.9 (I/II AD). Hofmann (1989: 156), Sophocles (1887).

rare   κάπων 'capon' (a castrated cockerel), from *cāpō* 'capon': Ps.-Hippocrates, Delatte 1939: 483.12; with *gallus castratus* in Gloss. Ps.-Cyril. 338.49; Byzantine texts. Hofmann (1989: 156), *LBG*, LSJ.

not ancient   καραγός 'barricade made of wagons', from *carrāgō* 'barricade made of wagons' (*TLL*): no ancient examples. Zilliacus (1935a: 218–19), *LBG*.

Direct loan with suffix III AD – modern   καρακάλλιον (-ου, τό) 'hood', from *caracalla* 'long cloak with hood' (*TLL*) + -ιον.
Documents: e.g. *P.Oxf.* 15.12 (III AD); *P.Münch.* III.1.138.8 (IV AD); *P.Princ.* II.82.37 (V AD); *P.Cair.Masp.* 67006v.64 (VI AD).
Literature: Pall. *H.Laus.* 46.3 (IV/V AD); with *cuculla* in Gloss. Ps.-Cyril. 338.52.
Post-antique: survives. Daris (1991a: 49), Kahane and Kahane (1982: 135), Triandaphyllidis (1909: 121). Modern καρκάλι 'cock's comb' (Andriotis 1967), dialectal καρακάλλιν 'shirt-like garment' (Kahane and Kahane 1972–6: 535, 1982: 135–6).
Notes: probably not borrowed via καράκαλλον, as καρακάλλιον is earlier and better attested. Forms derivative στιχαροκαρακάλλιον. Kramer (2002, 2011: 207–17), Daris (1991a: 49), Hofmann (1989: 156 *s.v.* καράκαλλον), Meinersmann (1927: 22), Frisk (1954–72: 1.786), Beekes (2010 *s.v.* καράκαλλον), *TLL* (*s.v. caracalla* 428.10, 12–16), Lampe (1961), LSJ (*s.v.* καράκαλλον), LSJ suppl. See §4.3.2, §10.2.1, §10.2.2 H.

Direct? loan
IV AD – modern

κᾰράκαλλον, κᾰράκαλλος (-ου, τό or ὁ) 'hood', 'cloak with hood', from *caracalla* 'long cloak with hood' (*TLL*), perhaps via back-formation from καρακάλλιον.

Documents: *P.Oxy.* 4001.18 (IV AD).

Inscriptions: Edict.Diocl. 7.44 etc. (IV AD).

Literature: *Anthologia Graeca* 11.345.3.

Post-antique: survives. *LBG* (*s.v.* καράκαλλος). Modern dialectal καράκαλλος of a bird: Andriotis (1974: 297).

Notes: gender is ambiguous in most attestations, and most scholars prefer neuter, but Kramer (2011: 213) prefers masc., since modern word is masc. and papyrus has masc. article τόν. But papyrus is badly spelled and has -ν incorrectly added in αὐτήν for αὐτή, line 13. Kramer (2002, 2011: 207–17), *DÉLG*, Frisk (1954–72: 1.786), Beekes (2010), Hofmann (1989: 156), *TLL* (*s.v. caracalla* 428.11–13), LSJ. See §4.2.3.1, §4.3.2 n. 74, §8.2.2, §10.2.1, §10.2.2 H.

not Latin?

κᾰραρύες, a type of wagon, perhaps from *carrus* 'wagon' (via κάρρον?): Hesych. as lemma κ 773 (V/VI AD). Hofmann (1989: 159 *s.v.* κάρρον), LSJ.

καρβόνιον: see καρβώνιον.

not ancient?

καρβούνη 'coal', presumably from *carbō* 'piece of charcoal' via κάρβων: unverified examples in Zilliacus (1937: 322–3, 329). Lampe (1961).

καρβούνιον: see καρβώνιον.

Direct loan
VI AD – modern

κάρβων (-ωνος, ὁ) 'coal', from *carbō* 'piece of charcoal'.

Documents: *P.Cair.Masp.* 67058.8.14 (VI AD); *P.Flor.* III.297.368 etc. (VI AD).

Literature: Aëtius 1.135.15, 12.59.11 (VI AD); Dor.Gaz. *Doct.Div.* 8.91.10 (VI AD); Thdr.Pet. p. 30.11 etc. (VI AD). Hesychius Sinaiticus, *De temperantia et virtute* 16.4 Waegeman is probably not ancient.

Post-antique: survives as Byzantine κάρβωνον (*LBG*) or κάρβουνο (Kriaras 1968–), cf. Triandaphyllidis (1909: 91, 121). Modern κάρβουνο 'charcoal' and derivatives: Babiniotis (2002), Andriotis (1967), Meyer (1895: 27).

Notes: Binder (2000: 223), Daris (1991a: 50), Hofmann (1989: 156), *DÉLG*, Lampe (1961), LSJ. See §4.2.5, §8.2.3, §10.2.1, §10.2.2 M.

not ancient?

καρβώνιον, καρβούνιον, καρβόνιον 'coal', from *carbō* 'piece of charcoal' via κάρβων + -ιον: perhaps Hdn. Κλισ.Ὀνομ. III.11.678.37 (II AD); Byzantine texts. Zervan (2019: 69–70) dates the loan to VIII AD. Modern dialectal καρβώνιν, καρβούνι, etc.: Andriotis (1974: 297), Meyer (1895: 27). Binder (2000: 223), Daris (1991a: 50), *LBG*, Kriaras (1968–), Lampe (1961).

not ancient

καρδάρι 'milk-pail', from *cal(i)dārius* 'used for hot water': no ancient examples. Binder (2000: 202–3), Meyer (1895: 27), *LBG* (*s.v.* καλδάριον), Kriaras (1968–), Andriotis (1967), Babiniotis (2002).

foreign

καρῆρε transliterating inf. of *careō* 'lack': Plut. *Rom.* 21.3 (I/II AD). Sophocles (1887).

name

Καρῖνα, from *carīna* 'keel', is a place name in Dio Cassius 48.38.2 (II/III AD). Meyer (1895: 27), Sophocles (1887), Andriotis (1967).

name

καρκαρέα, meaning uncertain, perhaps from *carcer* 'prison' via κάρκαρον: inscription *I.Hierapolis Judeich* 76.2, where it is probably a name. Hofmann (1989: 157 *s.v.* κάρκαρος).

Direct loan
II AD – modern
κάρκαρον, κάρκαρος (-ου, τό or ὁ) 'prison', 'stable', from *carcer* 'prison' (masc.).
Literature: Sophron frag. 145 Kassel–Austin (V BC); perhaps Rhinthon frag.
17 Kassel–Austin (III BC); Diodorus Siculus 31.9.1, 2, marked (I BC); Vet.
Val. *Anth.* 2.15.15 (II AD); Hesych. as lemma κ 831 (V/VI AD); Rhetor.
Cap. 140.5 (VI AD).
Post-antique: survives. *LBG* (*s.vv.* κάρκαρον, κάρκαρος). Modern dialectal
κάρκαρον 'prison' (Meyer 1895: 27), κάρκαρος 'hard' (Andriotis 1974: 297).
Notes: the Sophron 'example' is just a note in Photius' *Lexicon* κ 194 (IX AD)
that Sophron used the word, without any context; this must be treated
with caution. But in Vettius Valens and Rhetorius it is used as if readers
were expected to know it. Willi (2008: 30) takes Sophron, Rhinthon, and
Hesychius as evidence of an early Sicilian borrowing from an Italic language
other than Latin, separate from the later borrowing from Latin. Binder
(2000: 217), Bellocchi (2016: 327), Shipp (1979: 304–5), Hofmann (1989:
157), Immisch (1885: 311–12), *DÉLG* (*s.vv.* κάρκαρον, κάρκαροι), Frisk
(1954–72: 1.789), Beekes (2010), LSJ, LSJ suppl. See §4.2.5, §8.1.3 n. 20,
§8.2.2, §10.2.1, §10.2.2 D, §12.2.1.

foreign
κάρκερε transliterating abl. of *carcer* 'prison': Plut. *Aem.* 37.2 (I/II AD). Sophocles
(1887). See §7.2.1.

foreign
κάρμενα, κάρμινα transliterating pl. of *carmen* 'song', 'poem': DH *AR* 1.31 (I BC);
Plut. *Rom.* 21.2, *Mor.* 278c (I/II AD); Lyd. *Mens.* frag. incert. 9 (VI AD).
Binder (2000: 134), Hofmann (1989: 157), Sophocles (1887 *s.v.* κάρμινα).

rare
Καρμεντάλια, festival name from *Carmentālia* 'festival of the goddess Carmentis':
Plut. *Rom.* 21.1 (I/II AD). Hofmann (1989: 157).

rare
καρμεντία 'prophecy', from *Carmentis/Carmenta*, a Roman goddess, + -ία: Lyd.
Mens. frag. incert. 9 (VI AD). *TLL* (*Onomasticon s.v. Carmentis* 198.50), *LBG*.

κάρμινα: see κάρμενα.

not Latin?
καρνάριος, an occupational term in papyri of III AD, could mean 'butcher', in
which case it probably comes from *carnārius* 'dealer in meat', or 'carter',
in which case it could come from *carrārius* 'wagon-maker' or be a Greek
formation from κάρνον 'cart' + -άριος. Used with κάρνον in *SB* 9471.5,
making the Greek derivation likely. Daris (1991a: 50), Hofmann (1989:
157), Cavenaile (1952: 201), LSJ (*s.v.* κάρνον), LSJ suppl.

rare
καρνάρις 'in the flesh', 'butcher', 'man of blood', from *carnālis* 'in the flesh' (*TLL*)
or *carnārius* 'dealer in meat': Gryllus, fragment in *P.Oxy.* 2331.12 (III AD).

κάρον: see κάρρον.

Direct loan
III AD – Byz.
καροῦχα, καροῦχον (-ης?, ἡ or -ου, τό) 'carriage', from *carrūca* 'travelling-carriage'.
Inscriptions: Edict.Diocl. 15.37 (IV AD).
Literature: perhaps Hdn. Ὀρθογρ. III.II.577.11 (II AD); Symmachus,
Isaiah 66:20 = Field 1875: II.565 (II/III AD); *Martyrium Polycarpi* 8.2 etc.
in Musurillo 1972 (III AD?); Eusebius, *Commentarius in Isaiam* 2.58.94
Ziegler (IV AD); Anton.Hag. *V.Sym.Styl.* 31 (V AD); Priscus, *Fragmenta* 3a
Bornmann (V AD); Hesych. as gloss α 7297, ρ 248 (V/VI AD); Malal. 14.16
(VI AD); Antec. 2.1.48 (VI AD); as glosses in scholia to Aes. *Th.* 151d, Eur.
Ph. 847, *Od.* 4.42b.

Post-antique: survives. Kriaras (1968–), Sophocles (1887), Triandaphyllidis (1909: 124).

Notes: probably forms derivative καρούχιον. Hofmann (1989: 157–8), Zilliacus (1937: 329), Immisch (1885: 369), *TLL* (*s.v. carrūca* 498.18), Lampe (1961), LSJ. See §4.2.3.1, §10.2.1, §10.2.2 K, §12.2.1.

rare   **καρουχαρεῖον** 'carriage-house', 'stable', from *carrūcārium* 'stable', neuter of *carrūcārius* 'of carriages' (*TLL*) with influence from -εῖον, and/or from *carrūca* 'travelling-carriage': Malal. 13.38 (VI AD). Hofmann (1989: 158), *TLL* (*s.v. carrūca* 499.1–2, *s.v. carrūcārius* 499.11–12), Lampe (1961).

rare   **καρουχάριος, χαρουχᾶς** 'carriage-driver' or 'carriage-maker', from *carrūcārius/car(r)ūchārius* 'carriage-driver' (*TLL*): inscription *I.Tyr* 205 (VI AD); Gloss. Ps.-Cyril. 338.61. Hofmann (1989: 158), *I.Tyr* (pp. 112, 155), *TLL* (*s.v. carrūcārius* 499.10), LSJ (*s.v.* καρούχα), LSJ suppl.

rare   **καρούχιον** '(little) carriage', from *carrūca* 'travelling-carriage' via καρούχα + -ιον: papyrus *SB* 9365.8 (III AD); with *raeda* in Gloss. Ps.-Cyril. 338.62; Byzantine texts. Hofmann (1989: 157 *s.v.* καρουχα), Kriaras (1968–), *LBG* (with definition 'carriage', 'covered wagon'), *TLL* (*s.v. carrūca* 498.20, 499.1), LSJ (*s.v.* καρούχα).

καρούχον: see καρούχα.

rare   **κάρπεντον**, a vehicle, from *carpentum* 'two-wheeled carriage': Dio Cassius 60.22.2, 60.33.2.1 (II/III AD). Sophocles (1887).

rare   **καρραρικός** 'of a wagon', apparently from unattested **carrāricus*: Edict.Diocl. 15.30 (IV AD). Hofmann (1989: 158), *TLL* (*s.v. carrāricus*), LSJ suppl. See §8.1.7.

rare   **καρρικός** 'enough to fill a wagon', from *carrus* 'wagon' via κάρρον + -ικός: inscription *OGIS* 629.16 (II AD). Hofmann (1989: 159 *s.v.* κάρρον), *DÉLG* (*s.v.* κάρρον), Frisk (1954–72: 1.793), Beekes (2010 *s.v.* κάρρον), LSJ.

rare   **καρρίον**, a vehicle, presumably from *carrus* via κάρρον + -ιον: with *covinus* in Gloss. Ps.-Philox. 117.27. Beekes (2010 *s.v.* κάρρον).

Direct loan   **κάρ(ρ)ον, κάρρος** (-ου, τό or ὁ) 'cart', from *carrus* 'wagon'.
I AD – modern   Documents: *P.Cair.Goodsp.* 30.29.21 (II AD).

Inscriptions: *SEG* XXVI.1392.31 etc. (I AD); Edict.Diocl. 15.38 etc. (IV AD).

Literature: variant reading in Septuagint 1 Esdras 5:53 (interpolation, since there is no word for 'carts' in the Hebrew, but found in a manuscript of V AD and therefore added between I BC and V AD); with *raeda* in Gloss. Ps.-Cyril. 339.16.

Post-antique: modern κάρο 'cart': Babiniotis (2002), Andriotis (1967), Meyer (1895: 28).

Notes: forms derivatives καρρικός, καρρίον, καρροπηγός. Hofmann (1989: 158–9), *DÉLG*, Frisk (1954–72: 1.793), Beekes (2010), LSJ. See §4.2.4.1 n. 58, §8.2.2, §8.2.3, §10.2.1, §10.2.2 K, §12.2.1.

rare   **καρροπηγός** 'wagon-maker', from *carrus* 'wagon' via κάρρον + πηγός (cf. πήγνυμι 'build'): with *carrocarpentarius* in Gloss. Herm.Mp. 308.25. Hofmann (1989: 159 *s.v.* κάρρον), *DÉLG* (*s.v.* κάρρον), Frisk (1954–72: 1.793), Beekes (2010 *s.v.* κάρρον).

not ancient? | **καρροποιός** 'wagon-maker', from *carrus* 'wagon' via κάρρον + ποιός (cf. ποιέω 'make'): with *carrocarpentarius* in Gloss. *Herm. V.* 525.50. Hofmann (1989: 159 *s.v.* κάρρον), *DÉLG* (*s.v.* κάρρον), Frisk (1954–72: 1.793), Beekes (2010 *s.v.* κάρρον).

not Latin? | **καρσανάριος**, an occupational term, is probably not from unattested **casanārius*. Cameron (1931: 240), LSJ suppl.

καρτουλάριος: see χαρτουλάριος.

rare | **κάρφινος**, a kind of wood, from *carpīnus* 'hornbeam' (a kind of wood): Apollodorus, *Poliorcetica* p. 176.5 Wescher (I/II AD). Hofmann (1989: 159), LSJ.

not ancient | **καρῶτα** transliterating *carōta* 'carrot' (*TLL*): interpolation in Dsc. 3.52 RV. Καρωτόν is not Latinate. *DÉLG* (*s.v.* καρωτόν), Frisk (1954–72: 1.796), Sophocles (1887).

foreign | **κάσα** 'hut', from *casa* 'hut': Hesych. as lemma κ 956 (V/VI AD); perhaps ostracon *O.Bodl.* II.2330.3 (II AD); perhaps Ath.Mech. 25.7 (I BC?); Byzantine texts. Hofmann (1989: 159), Viscidi (1944: 45), Immisch (1885: 342), *LBG* (where note also κάσος), LSJ.

κασανάριος: see καρσανάριος.

κάση: see κασσίς.

κασίδα: see κασσίς.

Direct loan with suffix III AD – Byz. | **κασίδιον, κασσίδιον** (-ου, τό) 'helmet', from *cassis* 'helmet' + -ίδιον or from *cassid-* (oblique stem of *cassis*) + -ιον.
Documents: *P.Mich.* III.214.25, 216.11, perhaps 217.17 (all III AD).
Literature: as gloss in old scholia to Aes. *Th.* 385d, 459j.
Post-antique: numerous. *LBG* (*s.v.* κασσίδιον, with definition 'helmet'), Zervan (2019: 71–2), Kriaras (1968– *s.v.* κασσίδιον), Daris (1991a: 50).
Notes: Sijpesteijn (1987c, on a papyrus of VII AD), Daris (1991a: 50), Hofmann (1989: 160 *s.v.* κασσίς), Cavenaile (1951: 397, 1952: 196), LSJ. See §4.3.2, §10.2.1, §10.2.2 C; cf. κασσίς.

κασίς: see κασσίς.

Direct loan VI AD – Byz. | **κᾶσος, κάσσος** (-ου, ὁ) 'occasion', 'occurrence', 'portion', from *cāsus, -ūs* 'event'.
Documents: *CPR* I.30.2.23 (VI AD?); *P.Cair.Masp.* 67312.100 (VI AD).
Literature: Just. *Nov.* 53.5.1 etc., but in Latin script 22.45.1 (VI AD); Antec. 4.8.6, but in Latin script 3.19.2 *cason* etc. (VI AD).
Post-antique: numerous. *LBG*, Kriaras (1968– *s.vv.* κάσσον I, κάσσος I), Triandaphyllidis (1909: 120).
Notes: Binder (2000: 242–3), Avotins (1992 *s.v.* κάσσος, explaining legal meanings), Daris (1991a: 50), Zilliacus (1935a: 176–7), Meinersmann (1927: 22), LSJ suppl. (*s.v.* κάσσος B). See §4.2.4.2, §10.2.1, §10.2.2 O.

not ancient | **κασουάλιος** 'dependent on chance', from *cāsuālis* 'dependent on chance': no ancient examples. Zilliacus (1935a: 176–7), *LBG*.

κασοῦλα: see κασσοῦλα.

non-existent?	**κάσσης** transliterating *cassis* 'hunting-net': variant in Lyd. *Mag.* p. 190.7 (VI AD). Sophocles (1887).
	κασσίδα: see κασσίς.
	κασσίδιον: see κασίδιον.
Direct loan **IV? AD –** **modern**	**κασ(σ)ίς, κασ(σ)ίδα, κάση** (-ίδος or -ας?, ἡ) 'helmet', from *cassis* (gen. *cassidis*) 'helmet'. Documents: *SB* 13353.5 (I/II AD); perhaps *P.Lond.* III.1177.299 (II AD). Literature: Pausanias Damascenus Historicus, *FHG* IV frag. 4.100 (IV AD); Cyril of Alexandria, *De exitu animi*, *PG* LXXVII.1084a (IV/V AD); Ps.-John Chrysostom, *PG* LIX.569.67 (IV/V AD?); Hesych. as gloss π 1729, κ 3596 (V/VI AD); Malal. 8.16 (VI AD); Just. *Nov.* 85.4 (VI AD); Romanus Melodus, *Cantica dubia* 55.15.3 Maas and Trypanis (VI AD?). Post-antique: numerous. *LBG*, Kriaras (1968– *s.vv.* κασίδα, κάσσις), Triandaphyllidis (1909: 129), Katsanis (2007: 804). Modern κασ(σ)ίδα 'disease causing hair loss': Babiniotis (2002), Andriotis (1967, 1974: 299), cf. Meyer (1895: 28). Notes: spelled κάση only on *SB* 13353, a Mons Claudianus ostracon, which may be a separate borrowing from the other examples. Avotins (1992), Daris (1991a: 50), Hofmann (1989: 160), Zilliacus (1935a: 220–1), Lampe (1961). See §4.2.5, §4.3.2, §9.2, §10.2.1, §10.2.2 C; cf. κασίδιον.
	κάσσος: see κᾶσος.
foreign	**κασ(σ)οῦλα** transliterating *casula* or *casul(u)la*, a garment (*TLL s.vv.* 572.82–573.16): Procop. *Bell.* 4.26.26 (VI AD). Cf. modern κατσούλα 'cap': Andriotis (1967), Meyer (1895: 29) – but Babiniotis (2002) favours another etymology. Hofmann (1989: 159–60), Viscidi (1944: 39). Cf. κουσούλιον.
rare	**καστεία** 'ascetic practice', from *castus* 'pure' + -εία: Marinus, *Vita Procli* 469 Masullo (V AD). Hofmann (1989: 160), LSJ.
	καστελ-: see καστελλ-.
not ancient	**καστελλᾶτος** 'fortified', from *castellātus*, pf. part. of medieval *castellō* 'fortify' (*DMLBS s.v.* 1. *castellare*): no ancient examples. Daris (1991a: 50), Meinersmann (1927: 23), *LBG*, Kriaras (1968–), Lampe (1961).
Deriv. of loan **V AD – modern**	**καστέλ(λ)ιον** (-ου, τό) 'fort', from *castellum* 'fort' via κάστελλος + -ιον. Inscriptions: *I.Chr.Bulgarien* 89.4 (VI AD); *I.Ephesos* 458.2. Literature: Callin. *V.Hypat.* 3.10 etc. (V AD); Thdr.Anag. *HE* 3.420 etc. (V/VI AD); Malal. 15.12 etc. (VI AD); *ACO* III p. 87.10 (VI AD); Cyr.S. *Vit.Sab.* 111.19 etc. (VI AD). Post-antique: survives, forming derivative καστελλίτζιν 'little fortress'. *LBG* (*s.v.* καστέλλιν), Zervan (2019: 73), Kriaras (1968–). Modern καστέλ(λ)ι 'fortress': Babiniotis (2002), Kahane and Kahane (1972–6: 532). Notes: Zervan (2019: 73) conflates it with κάστελλος and therefore dates borrowing to II AD. Hofmann (1989: 160–1 *s.v.* κάστελλον), Viscidi (1944: 14), Zilliacus (1935a: 220–1), Lampe (1961). See §4.3.2, §4.6.1, §10.2.2 C.

rare   **καστελ(λ)ίτης** 'reservoir-overseer', from *castellum* 'water reservoir' via κάστελλος + -ίτης, perhaps on the model of *castellārius* 'keeper of a reservoir' or *castellānus* 'keeper of a fortress' (*TLL*): papyrus *P.Lond.* v.1652.6 (IV AD). Daris (1991a: 50, with derivation from *castellānus*), Hofmann (1989: 161 *s.v.* κάστελλον), Cavenaile (1952: 193), LSJ suppl.

Direct loan   **κάστελ(λ)ος, κάστελ(λ)ον** (-ου, τό or ὁ) 'fort', 'water reservoir', from *castellum/*
II AD – modern   *castellus* 'fort', 'water reservoir'.
     Documents: *P.Lond.* III.1177.8 etc. (II AD); *P.Narm.* 2006.132.1 etc. (II/III AD); *SB* 12497.40 (III AD); perhaps *SB* 16525.4 (III/IV AD); *Stud. Pal.* x.205.8 (VI AD).
     Inscriptions: perhaps *SEG* XL.1315.4 (I AD); *SEG* XX.324.12 (III AD); *IGLS* XXI.V.1.92.3, 128.4, 130.4 (all V AD).
     Literature: e.g. Epiph. *Pan.* III.33.8–10 (IV AD); John Chrysostom, *Epistulae ad Olympiadem* 9.3 Malingrey (IV/V AD); *ACO* II.I.II p. 6.19 (V AD); Procop. *Aed.* 2.5.9, marked (VI AD).
     Post-antique: survives in both senses, forming derivatives καστελλοειδῶς 'like a fortress', καστελλοῦτζον 'little fortress'. *LBG*, Triandaphyllidis (1909: 130). Kriaras (1968–) and Andriotis (1967) derive Byzantine and modern καστέλλο from Italian *castello*, implausibly given the ancient evidence; Babiniotis (2002 *s.v.* καστέλι) links modern καστέλο and κάστελος 'fortress' with Latin.
     Notes: forms derivatives καστέλλιον, καστελλίτης, καστελλοφύλαξ, πυργοκάστελλος. Binder (2000: 247), Daris (1991a: 50), Hofmann (1989: 160–1), Viscidi (1944: 14), Meinersmann (1927: 23), Immisch (1885: 354), Lampe (1961), LSJ suppl. See §4.2.4.1 n. 51, §4.3.2, §4.6.1, §10.2.1, §10.2.2 C, §12.2.1.

rare   **καστελλοφύλαξ** 'guardian of the fort' (a Persian court official), from *castellum* 'fort' via κάστελλος + φύλαξ 'guard': multilingual inscription *Res gestae divi Saporis* = *SEG* XX.324.63 (III AD). Hofmann (1989: 161 *s.v.* κάστελλον), LSJ suppl.

     κάστρα: see κάστρον.

foreign   **καστρᾶτος** 'eunuch by castration', from *castrātus* 'eunuch by castration': Antec. 1.11.9, marked (VI AD). Zilliacus (1935a: 176–7), *LBG*, Kriaras (1968–), Babiniotis (2002 *s.v.* καστράτο). See §7.1.1 passage 21.

     καστρε(ν)σ-: see καστρησ-.

not ancient   **καστρεύω** 'fortify', from *castrum* 'fort' via κάστρον + -εύω: no ancient examples. Hofmann (1989: 161 *s.v.* κάστρα), *LBG*.

     καστρήνσιος: see καστρήσιος.

Direct loan   **καστρησιανός, καστρεσιανός** (-ου, ὁ) 'soldier of the frontier guard', also a court
IV AD – Byz.?   official, from *castrēnsiānus* 'of the (army) camp or imperial court' (*TLL*).
     Documents: *O.Trim.* II.518.2 (IV AD); *P.Cair.Masp.* 67054.2.7, 67126.9 etc. (both VI AD); *P.Oxy.* 3805.73 (VI AD).
     Inscriptions: *SEG* IX.356.46 etc., perhaps 414.9 (both VI AD); perhaps *LBW* 1406.
     Literature: Malal. 18.10 (VI AD).

Post-antique: survival perhaps indicated by Triandaphyllidis (1909: 129).

Notes: probably a patronymic at *P.Cair.Masp.* 67146.5 (VI AD) and *SB*
14671.26 (VI AD). Commentary on *O.Trim.* 11.518, Daris (1991a: 50),
Hofmann (1989: 161–2), Zilliacus (1935a: 220–1), Meinersmann (1927:
23), *TLL* (*s.v. castrēnsiānus* 544.29), Lampe (1961), LSJ suppl. See §4.2.4.1
n. 51, §6.4, §6.7 n. 46, §10.2.1, §10.2.2 C.

Direct loan
I AD – Byz.   **καστρήσιος, καστρίσιος, καστρήνσιος, γαστρήσιος, γαστρίσιος, -ένσιος** (-α, -ον)
originally 'of the camp', later 'of the imperial court' (including of the *modius
castrēnsis*, a unit of measurement), also in masc. subst. the title of an official,
from *castrēnsis* 'of the (army) camp', 'of the imperial court' (*TLL*).

Documents: *P.Oxy.* 1471.5 etc. (I AD); *P.Stras.* v.340.14 (II AD); perhaps *SB*
9228.24 (II AD); *P.Cair.Isid.* 11.50 (IV AD); *O.Douch.* I.13.7, 21.12 (both
IV/V AD); perhaps *P.Cair.Masp.* 67166.7 etc. (VI AD).

Inscriptions: *I.Ephesos* 852.16 (II AD); Ramsay 1895–7: 704 no. 641.8 (II AD);
Edict.Diocl. 1.1a etc., abbreviated (IV AD); perhaps *CIG* 9222.3.

Literature: *Hippiatr.Berl.* (Apsyrtus) 130.134 (III/IV AD?); Athan. *H.Ar.* 15.3,
Apol.Sec. 36.2 (IV AD); Marc.Diac. 37, 40 (V AD); *V.Dan.Styl.* A. 25.15 etc.
(V AD); Nil. 2.281.1 (V AD); Just. *Nov.* in Latin script 22.34 *castrensiων* etc.
(VI AD); Antec. in Latin script 2.12.pr. *canstrension* etc. (VI AD); Her.Mech.
Mens. 17.1.

Post-antique: common, sometimes with the spelling κανστρ- seen in Antec. *LBG*.

Notes: Daris (1991a: 50), Mason (1974: 4, 59), Hofmann (1989: 162),
Zilliacus (1935a: 176–7, 220–1), Meinersmann (1927: 23), Triantaphyllides
(1892: 263), LSJ (*s.v.* γαστρήσιος), LSJ suppl. See §4.2.2, §6.7, §10.2.1,
§10.2.2 C.

non-existent?   **κάστρις** is probably an abbreviation for καστρήσιος (*q.v.*) on papyrus *P.Cair.Masp.*
67166.7, 11 (VI AD). Commentary *ad loc.*, Hofmann (1989: 162).

καστρίσιος: see καστρήσιος.

not ancient   **καστροκτισία** 'fort-building' and **καστροκτιστής** 'fort-builder', from *castrum*
'fort' via κάστρον + κτίζω 'found' + -ία/-τής: no ancient examples. Hofmann
(1989: 161 *s.v.* κάστρα), *LBG s.vv.*

Direct loan
I AD – modern   **κάστρον, κάστρα** (-ου, τό or -ων, τά) 'army camp', 'fort' (in papyri and
inscriptions usually plural up to IV AD, usually singular from V AD), from
castrum 'fort' (in Latin usually plural, *castra* 'camp').

Documents: common, e.g. *SB* 16996.6 (I AD); *P.Panop.Beatty* 1.39 etc.
(III AD); *P.Oxy.* 4089.4 (IV AD); *P.Vind.Tand.* 19.6 etc. (V AD); *P.Oxy.*
1883.2 (VI AD).

Inscriptions: common in the title μήτηρ κάστρων = *māter castrōrum* 'mother of
the camp' (*TLL s.v. castrum* 562.38–54), e.g. *IG* II/III².11.3415.6 (II AD);
IGBulg. II.732.2 (III AD); *IG* VII.2503.3 (IV AD). Other uses: e.g. perhaps
Studia Pontica III.66.4 (I BC); *I.Syringes* 1733.1 (I AD); perhaps *IGR* I.1275.9
(II AD); *IGBulg.* v.5637.5 (III AD); perhaps *I.Side* 41.5 (III AD); *I.Philae*
217.1 (V/VI AD); *IGLS* IV.1682.10, 1859.3 (both VI AD); perhaps *SEG*
XXXII.1554.A29 (VI AD); *SEG* XXXV.1494 is probably not ancient.

Literature: common, e.g. *Testmentum Salomonis* rec. C 80.11 (III AD?); Magnus,
FHG IV frag. 1 (IV AD); Agath. *Arm.* 54.18 (V AD); Hesych. as gloss ο 2059,
π 819 (V/VI AD); Just. *Nov.* 128.20 (VI AD); Antec. 2.11.pr (VI AD).

Post-antique: common, forming derivatives καστρομαχία 'siege', καστροπολεμέω 'besiege', etc. Sophocles (1887), Zervan (2019: 73–4), Kriaras (1968–), Triandaphyllidis (1909: 130), Daris (1991a: 51). Modern κάστρο 'castle' and derivatives: Babiniotis (2002), Andriotis (1967), Meyer (1895: 28).

Notes: Viscidi (1944: 14–15) and Cameron (1931: 240–1) consider κάστρα 'army camp' and κάστρον 'fort' two separate borrowings; Cameron treats μήτηρ κάστρων as a third borrowing. Editor of *Studia Pontica* III p. 80, Binder (2000: 245, 251), Avotins (1992 *s.v.* κάστρα), Ghiretti (1996: 290), Daris (1991a: 50–1), Mason (1974: 5, 59, 138), Hofmann (1989: 161, 162–3), Zilliacus (1935a: 220–1, 1937: 329), Meinersmann (1927: 22–3), Lampe (1961), LSJ suppl. (*s.v.* κάστρα). See §4.2.4.1 n. 55, §6.7, §7.1.1 passage 16, §8.2.3 n. 51, §10.2.1, §10.2.2 C.

not ancient? **καστροφύλαξ** 'commander of the fort', from *castrum* 'fort' via κάστρον + φύλαξ 'guard': probably no ancient examples. Hofmann (1989: 163 *s.v.* κάστρον), *LBG*, Kriaras (1968–), Lampe (1961).

rare **καταλέκτια** 'bedclothes', apparently from κατά 'down' + *lectus* 'bed' + -ιον: EphraemSyr. VI pp. 210–12.26 (V/VI AD); Byzantine texts. Sophocles (1887), Lampe (1961).

Direct loan **καταφρακτάριος** (-ον) 'armoured', from *catafractārius* 'armoured'.
IV AD Documents: *P.Panop.Beatty* 2.28 (III/IV AD); *SB* 13852.28 (IV AD); *BGU* 1.316.6 (IV AD).

Notes: not attested in feminine; LSJ suppl. infers from form that it would be two-termination. Palme (2004), Hofmann (1989: 163), Zilliacus (1935a: 220–1). See §4.2.2, §10.2.1, §10.2.2 C.

Direct loan **κατήνα, κατίνα** (-ας, ἡ) 'chain', from *catēna* 'chain'.
II AD – modern Documents: *O.Krok.* 1.100.6 (I/II AD); *O.Trim.* II.531.15 (IV AD); *PSI* VIII.959.29 (IV AD).

Inscriptions: Edict.Diocl. 15.15 (IV AD).

Literature: Thdt. *HE* p. 104.17 (V AD); Isidore of Pelusium, *PG* LXXVIII.448a (V AD); *ACO* III p. 175.22 etc. (VI AD); with *catella* in Gloss. Ps.-Cyril. 346.9. Unverified example (III AD) in Zilliacus (1937: 323, 329).

Post-antique: survives, forming derivatives κατηναρᾶς 'chain-maker', κατήνιον 'chain', κατήνωμα 'fixing in position'. *LBG*, Kriaras (1968–), Triandaphyllidis (1909: 120). Modern κατήνα, κατίνα 'door bolt' and derivatives: Meyer (1895: 28–9), Dieterich (1901: 589), but Italian etymology in Andriotis (1967).

Notes: Daris (1991a: 51), Hofmann (1989: 163), Cavenaile (1951: 397), Zilliacus (1937: 329), Lampe (1961). See §4.2.3.1, §10.2.1, §10.2.2 M.

not Latin? **κατηνάριον** probably designates a kind of boat and is a Greek formation; although several ways of connecting it to Latin have been proposed, none is convincing. Olsson (1935), commentary on *P.Hamb.* III.229.5, Meinersmann (1927: 23), *LBG*.

non-existent **κατηνᾶτος**, from *catēnātus* 'chained': superseded reading of papyrus *P.Princ.* II.57.3 (II AD). Daris (1991a: 51).

foreign	**κάτιλλος ὀρνᾶτος**, a food, from *catīllus* 'bowl' and *ornātus*, pf. part. of *ornō* 'decorate': Athenaeus 14.647e, marked (II/III AD). Hofmann (1989: 163), Sophocles (1887).

κατίνα: see κατήνα.

not Latin	**κάτινον** 'bowl', perhaps from an Italic word related to *catinus* 'bowl', is not directly attested in Greek but mentioned by Varro (*De lingua Latina* 5.120), who describes it as Sicilian and suggests that it could be the ancestor of *catinus*. Willi (2008: 30), Hofmann (1989: 163–4), Hahn (1906: 9 unnumbered note).

foreign	**κάτος** transliterating *catus* 'clever': Plut. *Cat.Ma.* 1.3 (I/II AD). Hofmann (1989: 164).

κατσούλα: see κασσούλα.

not Latin?	**κάττα**, **κάττος**, **κάττης** 'cat' may be from *cattus* 'cat' (*TLL*): Viscidi (1944: 38), Meyer (1895: 29), Andriotis (1967 *s.vv.* κάτα, κάτος), Triandaphyllidis (1909: 33, 119, 170), Kriaras (1968– *s.v.* κάτος). Without suggestion of Latin: *DÉLG*, Beekes (2010), LSJ.

not Latin?	**καυκίον** 'cup' is probably not from Latin: *DÉLG* (*s.v.* καῦκος), Frisk (1954–72: 1.802), Beekes (2010: *s.v.* καῦκος), Kriaras (1968–). Zilliacus (1937: 329), Lampe (1961), LSJ (*s.v.* καῦκος), LSJ suppl.

καυκουλάτωρ: see καλκουλάτωρ.

rare	**καύνη** 'settlement of camp-followers', from *canabae* 'settlement of camp-followers': papyrus Rostovtzeff *et al.* 1936: 434.2 (III AD). Hofmann (1989: 164), LSJ suppl.

foreign	**καῦσα** 'cause', from *causa* 'cause': Just. *Nov.* as part of μόρτις καῦσα (*q.v.*) 22.22. pr. etc. (VI AD); Antec. in Latin script 4.17.3 *causan* etc. (VI AD); Byzantine texts. Zilliacus (1935a: 176–7), *LBG*. See §9.5.6 n. 68.

Direct loan **II AD – Byz.**	**καυσάριος** (-α, -ον) 'dismissed because of illness', 'being grounds for dismissal', or as masc. subst. 'invalid', from *causārius* 'diseased', 'on grounds of health'.
	Documents: *O.Claud.* II.212.15, IV.854.5 (both II AD); *SB* 9230.15 (III AD); probably not *P.Stras.* VII.618.19 (IV AD).
	Literature: Modestinus in Just. *Dig.* 27.1.8.5 (III AD); Antec. 2.11.2 in Latin script as part of *causaria missione* 'discharge on grounds of ill health' (VI AD).
	Post-antique: survives. *LBG*.
	Notes: refers to broken stone in *O.Claud.* IV.854. Daris (1991a: 51), Mason (1974: 12), Hofmann (1989: 164), Zilliacus (1935a: 176–7). See §4.2.2, §6.1 n. 11, §9.5.6 n. 55, §10.2.1, §10.2.2 B, §10.3.2.

foreign	**καυτίων** 'security', from *cautiō* 'guarantee': Antec. in Latin script 2.4.2 *cautionos* etc. (VI AD); later in Greek script. Zilliacus (1935a: 176–7), *LBG*. See §9.5.6 n. 68.

καψα-: see καμψα-.

καψικός: see κάμψα.

κειβαρ-: see κιβαρ-.

κειρκείτορ: see κιρκίτωρ.

κελαρ-: see κελλαρ-.

κέλεβρον: see κέρεβρον.

foreign   **κέλερ, κελέριος** transliterating *celer* 'swift' (in pl. a group of fighters): DH *AR* 2.13.2, 2.64.3 (I BC); Plut. *Numa* 7.4, *Rom.* 10.3, 26.2 (I/II AD); Lyd. *Mag.* pp. 20.15, 106.11 (VI AD). *TLL* (*s.v. celer* 750.50–70), Hofmann (1989: 165–6, two entries), Mason (1974: 60), *LBG* (*s.v.* κελέριος).

κελίον: see κελλίον.

Direct loan   **κέλλα, κέλλη** (-ης/-ας, ἡ) 'room', 'chamber', from *cella* 'room'.
II AD – modern   Documents: common, e.g. *O.Claud.* IV.715.13 etc. (I/II AD); *Chrest.Mitt.* 118.28 (II AD); *P.Mich.* XI.620.12 etc. (III AD); *BGU* II.606.5 (IV AD); *PSI* VI.708.10 (V AD); *CPR* X.28.5 (VI AD).
          Inscriptions: probably *I.Ephesos* 462.3.
          Literature: common, e.g. Callin. *V.Hypat.* 3.6 (V AD); Hesych. as gloss τ 236 (V/VI AD); Cyr.S. *Vit.Sab.* 166.16 (VI AD).
          Post-antique: survives with numerous derivatives. Kriaras (1968–), Zervan (2019: 76), Triandaphyllidis (1909: 120), Sophocles (1887), Daris (1991a: 51). Modern κέλ(λ)α 'cell': Andriotis (1967), Kahane and Kahane (1972–6: 534), Meyer (1895: 30).
          Notes: forms derivatives κελλίον, συγκελλάριος, σύγκελλος. Husson (1983: 136–42), Shipp (1979: 311–12), Gignac (1981: 7–8), Daris (1991a: 51), Hofmann (1989: 167), Viscidi (1944: 8), Zilliacus (1935a: 176–7, 1937: 329), Meinersmann (1927: 24), *DÉLG*, Lampe (1961), LSJ. See §4.2.3.1, §4.6.1 n. 83, §4.6.2, §6.1, §6.13, §10.1, §10.2.1, §10.2.2 J.

κελλαράριος: see κελλαρικάριος.

κελλαρει-: see κελλαρι-.

rare   **κελλαρεύω, κελλαρεύγω** 'be a cellarer', from *cellārius* 'cellarer' (*OLD cellārius²*) via κελλάριος + -εύω: inscriptions Cook 1973: 401 no. 17.2 (V/VI AD); *SEG* XXIX.1227.5 (VI AD); Byzantine texts. *LBG*, LSJ suppl.

κελλαρηκάριος: see κελλαρικάριος.

rare   **κελλαρία** 'female cellarer', from *cellāria*, feminine of *cellārius* 'cellarer' (*TLL s.v. cellārius* 762.60–2), or from *cellārius* 'cellarer' (*OLD cellārius²*) via κελλάριος with a Greek feminine ending: Hesych. as gloss τ 103 (V/VI AD). May survive in Byzantine κελλαρέα: *LBG*. Hofmann (1989: 166), LSJ suppl. (*s.v.* κελλάριος). See §6.2 n. 13.

rare   **κελ(λ)αρίδιον** 'little cupboard', probably from *cellārium* 'storeroom' via κελλάριον + -ίδιον: papyrus *P.Brookl.* 84.11 (II/III AD). Daris (1991a: 51), Hofmann (1989: 166 *s.v.* κελλάριον), Cavenaile (1952: 196, with derivation from *cella*), LSJ.

κελ(λ)αρικά: see κελλαρικός.

Deriv. of loan
v–vi AD

κελλαρικάριος, κελλαρηκάριος (-ου, ὁ) 'cellarer', from the Latin source of κελλαρικός (via κελλαρικός, probably neut. pl. subst.) + -άριος.

Documents: *Stud.Pal.* VIII.1000.1 (V AD); perhaps *P.Prag.* II.149.2 (V AD?); perhaps *CPR* XIX.18.2 (V AD); *P.Herm.* 29.6 etc. (VI AD); *PSI* VIII.955.13 with reading of Sijpesteijn 1992 (VI AD).

Notes: Daris (1991a: 52), considering this κελλαράριος extended with -ικ-, equates it with Byzantine κελλαράριος 'cellarer' (*LBG s.vv.* κελλαράριος and κελλαράρης, Triandaphyllidis 1909: 125) and derives it from *cellārārius* 'cellarer' (*TLL*). But Cavenaile's (1952: 202) derivation from κελλαρικός is better because -ικ- occurs in every single ancient example. Cavenaile (1951: 397), LSJ suppl. See §6.1, §10.2.2 I.

Deriv.? of loan
III AD – Byz.

κελ(λ)αρικός (-ή, -όν) 'of a cellar or storeroom', 'concerning food' (neut. pl. subst. 'provisions', 'wine delivered to a landlord's cellar'; neut. sing. subst. 'storeroom'), from *cellārium* 'storeroom' via κελλάριον, and/or *cellārius* 'of a storeroom' (*OLD cellārius¹*), + -ικός.

Documents, adj.: *P.Panop.Beatty* 1.219 etc. (III AD); *Stud.Pal.* XX.75.2.1 etc. (IV AD); *Stud.Pal.* VIII.990.2 (V AD); *CPR* XXV.14.3 (VI AD).   Neut. pl. subst.: *P.Ryl.* IV.627.65 etc. (IV AD); *P.Fouad* 83.3 etc. (IV AD); *P.Oxy.* 2732.4 (VI AD); *PSI* VIII.953.73, perhaps 956.17 (both VI AD); perhaps *SB* 14212.1 (VI AD).   Neut. sing. subst.: *Stud.Pal.* XX.75.2.9 etc. (IV AD) and see below.

Literature: Pall. *H.Laus.* 13.1, neut. pl. subst. (IV/V AD); Geront. *V.Mel.* 2.19.58, ἄρτου τε καὶ κελλαρικοῦ (V AD); bilingual glossaries, e.g. Gloss. Ps.-Cyril. 347.33.

Post-antique: numerous. Sophocles (1887), *LBG* (*s.v.* κελλαρικόν).

Notes: many scholars take one or both of the substantivized neuters to be separate words, but they are not amenable to a clear-cut separation; note in particular Gerontius, where neut. sing. subst. is used of a beverage. In *SB* 14339.25 (III/IV AD) neut. sing. subst. κελλαρικοῦ may mean 'groceries' (Maspero 1912: 154), but it is an emendation of κελλαρίου in γράψατε οὖν μοι τί θέλεται κελλαρίου, which without emendation could mean 'write to me what you want from the storeroom'. Forms derivative κελλαρικάριος. Husson (1983: 147), Diethart (1990a: 103–4), Daris (1991a: 51, 52), Hofmann (1989: 166 *s.v.* κελλάριον), Cavenaile (1952: 197), Zilliacus (1935a: 176–7), Meinersmann (1927: 24), *DÉLG* (*s.v.* κέλλα), *TLL* (*s.v. cellārius* 762.75–6), Lampe (1961 *s.v.* κελλαρικά), LSJ (*s.v.* κελλαρικά), LSJ suppl. (*s.v.* κελλαρικός). See §4.3.3, §4.6.1, §6.1, §10.2.2 I.

Direct loan
II AD – modern

κελλάριον, κελλάρειον (-ου, τό) 'cupboard', 'storeroom', 'vessel', from *cellārium* 'storeroom'.

Documents: e.g. *P.Oxy.* 741.12 (II AD); *P.Turner* 39.A8 (III AD); *P.Cair.Isid.* 56.3 (IV AD); *CPR* V.26.455 (V AD); *P.Oxy.* 2058.9 (VI AD).

Inscriptions: *I.Sardis* I.192 (III/IV AD).

Literature: Hdn. Διχρ. III.II.13.25, repeated by Lentz as *Pros.Cath.* III.1 365.12 (II AD); Ps.-Basil Caesariensis, *PG* XXXI.1313a (IV AD?); Dor.Gaz. *Ep.* 3.1, *Vit.Dos.* 6.6, 26 (VI AD); Cyr.S. *Vit.Eu.* 27.14 (VI AD); scholion to *Od.* 1.140 as gloss; with *penus* in glossaries, e.g. Gloss. Ps.-Cyril. 347.32.

Post-antique: numerous. *LBG* (*s.v.* κελλάριν), Kriaras (1968– *s.v.* κελάρι), Zilliacus (1937: 329). Modern κελλάρι 'cellar': Babiniotis (2002), Andriotis (1967), Kahane and Kahane (1972–6: 534).

Notes: Cavenaile (1952: 196) prefers derivation from *cella* 'room' + -άριον. For meaning 'vessel' see Diethart (1998: 173). Forms derivatives κελλαρίδιον, ἑπτακελλάριον, πολυκελλάριον; perhaps κελλαρικός, κελλαρίτης. Husson (1983: 147), Daris (1991a: 52), Hofmann (1989: 166), *DÉLG* (*s.v.* κέλλα), *TLL* (*s.v. cellārius* 762.74–5), Lampe (1961), LSJ. See §4.2.4.1 n. 54, §4.6.1, **6.3 n. 17**, §8.2.3 n. 51, §10.2.1, §10.2.2 J.

Direct loan
I AD – modern

κελλάριος, κελλάρειος (-ου, ὁ) 'cellarer', from *cellārius* 'cellarer' (*OLD cellārius*²).

Documents: *P.Ryl.* 11.228.24 (I AD); *P.Oxy.* 1727.16 etc. (II/III AD); perhaps *P.Ryl.* IV.692.14 (III AD); perhaps *P.Ryl.* IV.639.195 (IV AD); perhaps *CPR* XIX.18.2 (V AD); *P.Oxy.* 2049.9 (VI AD). Unverified example (II AD) in Wessely (1902: 131); probably not in *P.Laur.* 1.17.15 (III AD): *BL* VIII.163.

Literature: common, e.g. Basil Caesariensis, *PG* XXXI.1064d (IV AD); Callin. *V.Hypat.* 48.39 (V AD); Barsanuph.Jo. 11.1 ep. 360.4 (VI AD).

Post-antique: numerous. *LBG* (*s.v.* κελλάρης), Kriaras (1968– *s.v.* κελάρης), Triandaphyllidis (1909: 126), Sophocles (1887 *s.v.* κελλάριος 2a). Modern κελλάρης 'cellarer': Babiniotis (2002), Kahane and Kahane (1972–6: 533–4, 1982: 135).

Notes: forms derivative κελλαρεύω, perhaps κελλαρίτης. Daris (1991a: 52), Hofmann (1989: 166–7), Zilliacus (1935a: 176–7), Meinersmann (1927: 23–4), *DÉLG* (*s.v.* κέλλα), Lampe (1961), LSJ, LSJ suppl. See §4.2.4.1 n. 50, §6.1, §10.2.1, §10.2.2 I.

Deriv. of loan
IV AD – Byz.

κελλαρίτης (-ου, ὁ) 'cellarer', probably from *cellārium* 'storeroom' via κελλάριον or *cellārius* 'cellarer' via κελλάριος + -ίτης.

Documents: perhaps *O.Trim.* 1.46.3 (III/IV AD); *Stud.Pal.* XX.85v.ii.18 (IV AD); *Stud.Pal.* XX.107.4 (IV AD); perhaps *CPR* X.43.4 (V AD); perhaps *CPR* XIX.18.2 (V AD); perhaps *SB* 11340.1 (VI AD).

Literature: e.g. Dor.Gaz. *Doct.Div.* 4.58.3 (VI AD); *V.Luc.Styl.* 8 (VI AD).

Post-antique: numerous. Kriaras (1968– *s.v.* κελαρίτης), Sophocles (1887), Daris (1991a: 52), *LBG* (*s.v.* κελλαρῖτις 'female steward').

Notes: often said to be from *cellārītēs* 'cellarer' (first decl. masc.: *TLL*), which is probably a later reborrowing of κελλαρίτης: Biville (1990–5: 1.39, 1992: 236). Daris (1991a: 52), Hofmann (1989: 166–7 *s.v.* κελλάριος), Cavenaile (1952: 193), Meinersmann (1927: 24), *DÉLG* (*s.v.* κέλλα), *TLL* (*s.v. cellārītēs*), Lampe (1961), LSJ. See §4.6.1 n. 86, §10.2.2 I.

κελλεκτάριος: see κολλεκτάριος.

κέλλη: see κέλλα.

rare

κελλία 'small room', 'cell', from *cella* 'room' (via κέλλα or κελλίον?): papyrus *CPR* VII.44.3 etc. (V/VI AD); Byzantine texts. Daris (1991a: 52), *LBG*, LSJ suppl.

non-existent **κελλικάριος**, cited in LSJ, Daris (1991a: 52 *s.v.* κελλαρ(ικ)άριος), *DÉLG* (*s.v.* κέλλα), Hofmann (1989: 166 *s.v.* κελλάριος): superseded reading of papyrus *PSI* VIII.955.13 (VI AD). Sijpesteijn (1992), LSJ suppl.

Deriv. of loan **κελ(λ)ίον** (-ου, τό) 'room', 'small room', 'garret', '(monk's) cell', from *cella* 'room'
II AD – modern via κέλλα + -ιον.

Documents: e.g. *O.Claud.* 1.152.4 (II AD); *P.Münch.* 1.15.5 etc. (V AD); *P.Amh.* II.152.14 etc. (V/VI AD); *BGU* 1.305r.13 etc. (VI AD).

Inscriptions: *IGLS* V.2072.1, 2075.1 (both VI AD).

Literature: common, e.g. *Acta Joannis* 5r = Bonnet 1898: 153.27 (II AD?); *Test.Sal.* p. 117*.32 (III AD?); Athan. *Apol.Sec.* 37.9 (IV AD); *Historia monachorum in Aegypto* 2.67 (V AD); Hesych. as gloss δ 2718 (V/VI AD); Barsanuph.Jo. 1 ep. 36.13 (VI AD).

Post-antique: common, forming derivatives κελλίτζι(ν) 'little (monk's) cell', κελλικός 'private'. *LBG* (*s.v.* κελλίν), Zervan (2019: 76), Kriaras (1968– *s.v.* κελίν). Modern κελ(λ)ί 'cell': Babiniotis (2002), Andriotis (1967), Meyer (1895: 30); 'hut': Shipp (1979: 311–12); cf. Kahane and Kahane (1972–6: 534).

Notes: forms derivative κελλιώτης. Avotins (1992), Husson (1983: 142–6), Daris (1991a: 52), Hofmann (1989: 167 *s.v.* κέλλη), Cavenaile (1952: 196), Viscidi (1944: 8), Zilliacus (1935a: 176–7, 1937: 329), Meinersmann (1927: 24), *DÉLG* (*s.v.* κέλλα), Lampe (1961), LSJ. See §4.6.1 n. 83, §8.2.3 n. 51, §10.2.2 J.

rare **κελλιώτης** 'cell-dweller', from *cella* 'room' via κελλίον + -ώτης: Dor.Gaz. *Ep.* 1.1 (VI AD); Cyr.S. *Vit.Sab.* 113.10, 138.9 (VI AD). Lampe (1961), Hofmann (1989: 167 *s.v.* κέλλη). Apparently only with other meanings in Byzantine texts: *LBG*, Zervan (2019: 76), Kriaras (1968–), but note κελλιωτικός 'established from individual monks' cells' (*LBG*). Modern κελλιώτης 'monk who lives in a cell' (Babiniotis 2002): survival or revival? See §8.2.3.

rare **κέλοξ, κέλωξ** (gen. -οκος/-ωκος), a kind of boat, from *celōx* 'light, fast boat': Lyd. *Mag.* p. 106.10, marked (VI AD); scholion to Thuc. 8.38.1 as gloss. Hofmann (1989: 167), Sophocles (1887 *s.v.* κήλοξ), LSJ suppl.

κενδηνάριον: see κεντηνάριον.

κενσ-: see κηνσ-.

not ancient? **κένταρχος** 'centurion', from *centum* 'hundred' + -αρχος: no certainly ancient examples. Zilliacus (1935a: 220–1, 1937: 322, 329), *LBG*.

foreign **κέντε** transliterating *centum* 'hundred': Orion, *Etymologicum* κ p. 90.34 Sturz (V AD).

κεντενάριον: see κεντηνάριον.

κεντεριωνία, κεντερυωνέα: see κεντουρία.

rare **κεντηναρία** 'position of *centenarius*', from *centēnārius* 'having or containing a hundred' (via κεντηνάριος?) + -ία: inscription *IGUR* II.424.2 (II/III AD). LSJ (*s.v.* κεντηνάριος), Hofmann (1989: 168 *s.v.* κεντηνάριος).

**Direct loan
III AD? –
modern**

κεντηνάριον, κεντινάριον, κεντενάριον, κενδηνάριον (-ου, τό), a weight (of 100 pounds) and an amount of money, from *centēnārium* '100 pounds weight'.

Documents: common, e.g. *P.Panop.Beatty* 1.121 etc. (III AD); *P.Cair.Isid.* 61.4.40 (IV AD); *P.Oxy.* 4388.8 (V AD); *P.Oxy.* 1920.5 etc. (VI AD).

Inscriptions: Edict.Diocl. 18.5 etc. (IV AD).

Literature: e.g. perhaps Philoxenus frag. 324* Theodoridis (I BC); Jul.Afric. *Cest.* 4.1.63, marked (II/III AD); Epiph. *Mens.4* 83.2 (IV AD); Marc.Diac. 53 (V AD); Malal. 10.53 (VI AD); Cyr.S. *Vit.Sab.* 177.3 (VI AD).

Post-antique: numerous. *LBG* (*s.vv.* κεντηνάριν, κεντενάριον), Zervan (2019: 76–7), Kriaras (1968–), Triandaphyllidis (1909: 125), Zilliacus (1937: 329). Modern dialectal κεντηνάρι 'hundred': Andriotis (1974: 310), Meyer (1895: 30).

Notes: Daris (1991a: 52–3), Hofmann (1989: 167), Viscidi (1944: 30), Meinersmann (1927: 24), Lampe (1961), LSJ (*s.v.* κεντηνάριος). See §4.2.4.1 n. 54, §10.2.1, §10.2.2 E.

**Direct loan
IV AD – Byz.**

κεντηνάριος (-ου, ὁ), an official drawing a salary of 100,000 sesterces or a freedman with an estate worth at least 100,000 sesterces, from *centēnārius* 'having or containing a hundred'.

Documents: e.g. *P.Oxy.* 1253.8 (IV AD); *BGU* XII.2141.5 (V AD); *P.Warr.* 3.4 (VI AD).

Inscriptions: perhaps *IGUR* I.59.8 (II AD); *IGBulg.* V.5129.8 (IV AD); *I.Perinthos* 284.3 (IV/V AD).

Literature: Athan. *Apol.Sec.* 76.1 (IV AD); Lyd. *Mag.* p. 140.18 etc. (VI AD); Cyr.S. *Vit.Sab.* 177.20 etc. (VI AD); Antec. in Latin script 3.7.3 *centenariu* etc. (VI AD).

Post-antique: survives. *LBG* (*s.v.* κεντενάριος).

Notes: variant κεντινάριος (Cameron 1931: 241) is not ancient. Daris (1991a: 53), Mason (1974: 4, 60), Hofmann (1989: 168), Cavenaile (1951: 397), Zilliacus (1935a: 176–7, 220–1), Meinersmann (1927: 24), Lampe (1961), LSJ, LSJ suppl. See §4.2.4.1 n. 50, §10.2.1, §10.2.2 G.

κεντηριον, κεντηρίων: see κεντουρίων.

κεντινάριον: see κεντηνάριον.

κεντοιρίων: see κεντουρίων.

foreign

κέντον transliterating *centum* 'hundred': Procop. *Bell.* 1.22.5 (VI AD); Just. *Nov.* in Latin script 28.4.1 (VI AD). Sophocles (1887).

κεντόνιον: see κεντώνιον.

κεντορ-: see κεντουρ-.

rare

κέντουκλον 'piece of cloth', 'garment made of rough cloth', 'blanket', from *centunculus* 'patchwork' (*TLL*): Edict.Diocl. 7.52 etc. (IV AD); Byzantine texts. Mihăescu (1993: 347–8), Binder (2000: 161–2, 174, 251), Daris (1991a: 53), Hofmann (1989: 168), Zilliacus (1935a: 220–1), Meinersmann (1927: 24), *LBG*, Zervan (2019: 77), Kriaras (1968– *s.vv.* κεντούκλα, κέντουκλο), Triandaphyllidis (1909: 121), Andriotis (1974: 311), LSJ suppl.

not ancient

κεντουκουλάρις is stated to be a Latin plant name in an interpolation in Dsc. 3.117 RV; *TLL* accordingly lists unattested *centunculāris* but also considers this among the pieces of evidence for the plant name *centunculus* (830.5–7). Hofmann (1989: 439 *s.v.* τουκουλαρίς). See §8.1.7.

foreign	**κέντουμ** transliterating *centum* 'hundred': Epiph. *Mens.4* 83.2 (IV AD); same passage in Her.Mech. *Mens.* 60.2.

Direct loan
I BC – VI AD

κεντ(ο)υρία, κεντορία, κεντεριωνία, κεντερυωνέα, κυντυρεία (-ας, ἡ) 'century' (a military unit, also a unit of taxation), from *centuria* 'century'.

Documents: e.g. *SB* 9223.3 etc. (I BC); *P.Mich.* XII.637.8 etc. (I AD); *P.Lond.* II.142.4 etc. (I AD); *BGU* II.455.11 (II AD); *Rom.Mil.Rec.* 78 no. 65.1 (II/III AD).

Inscriptions: e.g. *I.Callatis* 30.7 (I BC/AD); *IGR* I.1347.5 (I AD); *CIRB* 691.7 (II AD).

Literature: Procop. *Bell.* 4.13.2 (VI AD); Just. *Nov.* 128.1 etc. (VI AD).

Notes: spelled κυντυρεία on unpublished ostracon O.Max. inv. 118.19 (II/III AD). Ghiretti (1996: 286–7), Avotins (1992), Daris (1991a: 53), Mason (1974: 60, 163), Hofmann (1989: 168), Zilliacus (1935a: 220–1), Meinersmann (1927: 24), LSJ suppl. See §4.2.3.1, §4.3.2 n. 75, §8.1.5, §10.2.1, §10.2.2 C, §12.2.1.

Direct loan
I BC – VI AD?

κεντ(ο)υρίων, κεντορίων, κεντηρίων, κεντοιρίων, κεντηριον, κυντυρίων (-ωνος/ -ονος, ὁ) 'centurion', from *centuriō* 'centurion'.

Documents: e.g. perhaps *P.Oslo* II.26.23 (I BC); *O.Did.* 353.9 (I AD); *O.Amst.* 19.7 (II AD); perhaps *P.Dura* 43.25 (III AD); *O.Bodl.* II.2116.4 (IV/V AD); *SB* 13321.1 (V/VI AD); *P.Lond.* V.1727.68 (VI AD).

Inscriptions: e.g. *I.Philae* 63.9 (I BC); *IGR* I.1057.10 (I AD); *CIRB* 666.2 (II AD); *I.Chr.Macédoine* 246.4 (IV/V AD).

Literature: common, e.g. Polybius 6.24.6, marked (II BC); NT Mark 15:39 (I AD); *Acta Pauli* frag. 11.12 Schmidt and Schubart (II AD); Philogelos 138 (IV AD); John Chrysostom, *PG* LVIII.776.35 (IV/V AD); Hesych. as lemma κ 2235 (V/VI AD).

Post-antique: little evidence of survival outside references to the biblical passages containing it, but note Kriaras (1968– *s.v.* κεντυρίων).

Notes: Ghiretti (1996: 280) thinks this was replaced by ἑκατόνταρχος in early I AD. Dubuisson (1985: 33–4), Bartalucci (1995: 109), Daris (1991a: 53), Mason (1974: 5, 60, 163), Hofmann (1989: 168–9), Zilliacus (1935a: 220–1, 1937: 329), Meinersmann (1927: 24), Immisch (1885: 366), Lampe (1961 *s.v.* κεντυρίων), LSJ (*s.v.* κεντορίων). See §4.2.5, §5.1, §5.2.1, §5.2.3, §8.1.3 n. 17, §8.1.5, §9.3 n. 21, §10.2.1, §10.2.2 C.

Direct loan with influence
II BC – Byz.

κέντ(ρ)ων (-ωνος, ὁ) 'rag', 'patchwork', 'garment', 'cento', perhaps 'pen-wiper', probably from *centō* 'patchwork', with influence from κέντρον 'goad' when spelled with ρ.

Literature: Biton 55.4 = Marsden 1971: 72.1 (III/II BC); Galen XIII.1044.10 Kühn (II AD); *Coll.Herm.* S 10a (I–IV AD); Gregorius Nyssenus, *Contra Eunomium* 2.1.128 Jaeger (IV AD); Aëtius 12.55.34 (VI AD); scholion to Ar. *Nu.* 450.

Post-antique: survives. *LBG* (*s.v.* κέντων), Sophocles (1887 *s.v.* κεντών).

Notes: forms derivative κεντρωνοράφος; perhaps κεντώνιον, κεντρωνάριον. Belardi (1958), Hofmann (1989: 169–70), *DÉLG* (*s.v.* κεντέω), Frisk (1954–72: I.821, III.124), Beekes (2010 *s.v.* κέντρων 2), Lampe (1961), LSJ (*s.v.* κέντρων II). See §4.2.5, §4.3.2 n. 75, §4.4, §4.6.1 n. 83, §8.1.3, §10.2.1, §10.2.2 H.

rare   **κεντρωνάριον 1, κεντρωνόριον** 'case for κέντρωνες', from unattested *centrōnārium* or from *centō* 'patchwork' via κέντρων + -άριον: papyrus *SB* 10241v.5 (I AD). Hofmann (1989: 168), Palmer (1945: 84), Beekes (2010 *s.v.* κέντρων 2), LSJ, LSJ suppl. See §6.3 n. 21.

           κεντρωνάριον 2: see κεντωνάριον.

rare   **κεντρωνορ(ρ)άφος** 'maker of patchworks', from *centō* 'patchwork' via κέντρων + -ραφος (cf. ῥάπτω 'sew'): with *centronarius* in glossaries, e.g. Gloss. *Herm.Mp.* 308.24. Hofmann (1989: 169 *s.v.* κεντων), *TLL* (*s.v. centōnārius* 821.61), LSJ.

           κεντυρ-: see κεντουρ-.

           κέντων: see κέντρων.

rare   **κεντωνάριον, κεντονάριον, κεντρωνάριον** 'patched garment', from *centō* 'patchwork' via κέντρων + -άριον: *Apophth.Patr.* 8.23.5, 14.12.6 (V AD); Byzantine texts. *LBG* (*s.vv.* κεντωνάριον, κεντρωνάριον, with implausible derivation from *centōnārius* 'fireman'). See §6.3 n. 21.

Deriv.? of loan   **κεντώνιον, κεντόνιον** (-ου, τό) 'rag', from *centō* 'patchwork' (via κέντρων?) + -ιον.
V–VI AD   Literature: Nil. 3.137.12 (V AD); Dor.Gaz. *Doct.Div.* 3.45.15 (VI AD); Cyr.S. *Vit.Sab.* 119.2 etc. (VI AD); Dan.Sket. *AP* 51 (VI AD).
           Notes: Hofmann (1989: 169 *s.v.* κεντων), Lampe (1961, also listing κεντώνη 'patched cloak', whose existence I cannot verify). See §4.3.2 n. 69, §4.6.1 n. 83, §10.2.2 H.

non-existent   **κέπα**: superseded reading of interpolation in Dsc. 2.180 RV. Sophocles (1887).

rare   **κερβήσιος, κερβησία** 'beer', from *cervēsia* 'beer': Jul.Afric. *Cest.* 1.19.20 (II/ III AD); Edict.Diocl. 2.11 (IV AD). Hofmann (1989: 170), LSJ suppl.

Direct loan with   **κερβικάριον, κερβρικάριον, κερπικάριον, κερουικάριον** (-ου, τό) 'pillow', from
influence?   *cervīcal* 'pillow' with influence from -άριον, or rare *cervīcārium* 'pillow' (*TLL*).
II–VI AD   Documents: e.g. *P.Leid.Inst.* 31.14 (I/II AD); *O.Did.* 436.9 (II AD); *BGU* III.814.11 (III AD); *P.Ant.* II.93.32 (IV AD); *P.Heid.* VII.406.10 (IV/V AD); *P.Pintaudi* 18.5 (V/VI AD); *CPR* VIII.65.8 (VI AD).
           Literature: Hermas, *Pastor* 9.4 Whittaker (II AD); Geront. *V.Mel.* 2.69 (V AD); Dor. Gaz. *Doct.Div.* 3.45.12 (VI AD); Ps.-Herodian, Περὶ σολοικισμοῦ καὶ βαρβαρισμοῦ p. 312.2 Nauck (λέγομεν δὲ βαρβαρίζειν καὶ τὸν ἀλλοφύλῳ λέξει χρώμενον, ὡς εἴ τις τὸ μὲν ὑπαυχένιον κερβικάριον λέγει, τὸ δὲ χειρόμακτρον μάππαν).
           Notes: spelled κερουικάριον in unpublished ostracon O.Dios inv. 944.7 (II AD). Commentary on *P.Heid.* VII.406, Diethart (2002: 153), Palmer (1945: 84), Daris (1991a: 53–4), Hofmann (1989: 170), Zilliacus (1937: 329), Meinersmann (1927: 24–5), *TLL* (*s.v. cervīcārium*), Lampe (1961), LSJ suppl. See §4.2.4.1 n. 54, §4.4 n. 79, §10.2.1, §10.2.2 H.

rare   **Κερβούκολος**, a festival, from *cervulus*, a type of games (*TLL*) with influence from βουκόλος 'cowherd': Nil. 3.252.20 (V AD). Hofmann (1989: 170–1), Lampe (1961).

rare   **κερεάλιος** 'of grain', from *cereālis* 'of Ceres', 'of grain': inscription *SEG* VI.555.8 (II AD); frequent as a personal name. Mason (1974: 6, 60), Hofmann (1989: 9 *s.v.* αιδιλις κερεαλις), LSJ suppl.

non-existent?	**κέρεβρον** 'brain', from *cerebrum* 'brain': emendation for manuscripts' κέλεβρον in Galen III.629.7, 8 Kühn (II AD). Κελεβρά, Hesych. as lemma κ 2147 (V/VI AD), may be related. Hofmann (1989: 165), LSJ.
	κερκείδωρ, **κερκείτωρ**: see κιρκίτωρ.
	κερκήσιον, **κερκέσιον**: see κιρκήσιος.
	κερκήτωρ, **κερκίτωρ**, etc.: see κιρκίτωρ.
	κερκιτεύω: see κιρκητεύω.
name	**Κερμαλόν**, a place name, from *Cermalus*, a hill in Rome. Hofmann (1989: 171).
	κερπικάριον: see κερβικάριον.
rare	**κέρτος** 'certain', from *certus* 'fixed': Just. *Codex* 6.48.1.31 (VI AD); Antec. in Latin script 3.15.pr. *certon* etc. (VI AD); Byzantine texts. Avotins (1989), Zilliacus (1935a: 176–7), *LBG*. See §9.5.6 n. 68.
	κεσαρ-: see καισαρ-.
foreign	*cessicios* = *cessicius* 'appointed by *cessio*': *Schol.Sinai.* 51 (V/VI AD). See §7.1.2, §9.5.6 nn. 56 and 57.
foreign	**κεσσιωνάριος** occurs on inscription *I.Tralleis* 189.3 (III AD) as part of the Latinate title τούτωρ κεσσιωνάριος, and *TLL* accordingly includes an entry for *cessiōnārius* (related to *cessiō* 'concession'), though the Latin is unattested until the medieval period (*DMLBS*). Hofmann (1989: 440 *s.v.* τούτωρ), Cameron (1931: 261). See §8.1.7.
not Latin?	**κεσσωνάριος**, **κεσσωπάριος**, meaning uncertain, perhaps from *quaestiōnārius*, a military title: papyrus *SB* 2253.5 (III/IV AD). LSJ suppl. (*s.v.* κεσσωνάριοι). Cf. κυαιστιωνάριος.
foreign	**κηλάρι** transliterating pres. pass. inf. of *cēlō* 'conceal': Plut. *Mor.* 269d (I/II AD). Sophocles (1887 *s.v.* κηλᾶρε).
foreign	**κῆνα** transliterating *cēna* 'dinner': Plut. *Mor.* 726e (I/II AD). Strobach (1997: 196), Hofmann (1989: 182–3, reading κοῖνα).
	κηνσείτωρ, **κηνσήτωρ**: see κηνσίτωρ.
not ancient	**κήνσευσις** 'taxation', from *cēnseō* 'appraise' via κηνσεύω + -σις: no ancient examples. Hofmann (1989: 172 *s.v.* κῆνσος), *LBG*.
not ancient	**κηνσεύω** 'appraise', from *cēnseō* 'appraise' + -εύω: no ancient examples. Hofmann (1989: 172 *s.v.* κῆνσος), Zilliacus (1935a: 176–7), *LBG*, Zervan (2019: 78, 265, dating the borrowing to IX AD).
not ancient	**κηνσιστικός**, **κενσιστικός** 'tax list', from *cēnsus, -ūs* 'census' via κῆνσος: no ancient examples. Daris (1991a: 54), *LBG*.
rare	**κηνσιτορεύω** 'serve as *censitor*', from *cēnsitor* 'registrar or taxation officer in a Roman province' via κηνσίτωρ + -εύω: papyri *P.Col.* VII.181.8 (IV AD); *SB* 12692.49 (IV AD); perhaps *BGU* IV.1049.5 (IV AD). Daris (1991a: 54), LSJ suppl.

rare   **κηνσιτορία** 'office of *censitor*', from *cēnsitor* 'registrar or taxation officer in a
Roman province' via κηνσίτωρ + -ία: Isidore of Pelusium, *PG* LXXVIII.345a
(V AD). Hofmann (1989: 171 *s.v.* κηνσιτωρ), Lampe (1961).

Direct loan   **κηνσίτωρ, κηνσείτωρ, κηνσήτωρ, κενσίτωρ, κενσήτωρ, κινσίτωρ** (-ορος/-ωρος, ὁ),
III–VI AD   an official, from *cēnsitor* 'registrar or taxation officer in a Roman province'.
       Documents: e.g. *P.Cair.Isid.* 4.3 (III AD); *BGU* III.917.6 (IV AD); *P.Herm.* 32.11
       (VI AD).
       Inscriptions: e.g. *SEG* XX.335.10 (III AD); *SEG* VII.1055.3 (III/IV AD).
       Literature: e.g. Gregorius Nyssenus, *Epistulae* 2.1 Pasquali (IV AD); Basil
       Caesariensis, *Epistulae* 83.1 Courtonne (IV AD); Hesych. as lemma κ 2518
       (V/VI AD).
       Notes: forms derivatives κηνσιτορεύω, κηνσιτορία. Daris (1991a: 54), Hofmann
       (1989: 171), Zilliacus (1935a: 176–7), Meinersmann (1927: 25), Immisch
       (1885: 354), Lampe (1961), LSJ (*s.v.* κηνσίτωρ), LSJ suppl. (*s.v.* κενσίτωρ).
       See §4.2.5, §6.7 n. 46, §10.2.1, §10.2.2 D.

Direct loan   **κῆνσος, κῖνσος** (-ου, ὁ) 'assessment for taxes', 'tribute', from *cēnsus, -ūs* 'census'.
I AD – Byz.   Documents: e.g. *CPR* V.4r.14 (III AD); *P.Panop.Beatty* 2.147 (III/IV AD);
       P.Col. VII.174.2 etc. (IV AD); *SB* 11039.5 (IV/V AD).
       Inscriptions: e.g. *I.Ephesos* 3048.7 (II AD); *IGR* I.1107.4 (II/III AD);
       Knackfuss 1924: 338 no. 266.2 (III AD); *I.Cos Segre* ED90.17 (IV AD).
       Literature: e.g. NT Matthew 22:17 (I AD); Origen, *Commentarium in evangelium
       Matthaei* 17.26 Klostermann (II/III AD); Eus. *VC* Pin 4.2 (IV AD); many
       commentators on biblical examples; Hesych. as gloss υ 792, as lemma κ 2742
       (V/VI AD); Just. *Nov.* 168 (VI AD); Antec. 1.5.3 (VI AD) twice in Greek script
       and once in Latin script, the Latin being a term for a kind of manumission: τὸ
       δὲ CENSU προέβαινε τοῦτον τὸν τρόπον. κῆνσος ἦν σανὶς ἤτοι χάρτης, ἔνθα Ῥωμαῖοι
       ἀπεγράφοντο τὰς οἰκείας περιουσίας ἐπὶ τῷ ἐν καιρῷ πολέμου κατὰ τὸ μέτρον τῆς
       ἰδίας ὑποστάσεως ἕκαστον εἰσφέρειν. ἐν τούτῳ οὖν τῷ κήνσῳ εἴποτε οἰκέτης κατὰ
       κέλευσιν δεσπότου ἑαυτὸν ἐλεύθερον ἐνέγραψεν, ἀπηλλάττετο τῆς δουλείας.
       Post-antique: survives, forming derivatives κηνσεύω 'tax', κήνσευσις 'taxation'.
       Zervan (2019: 77–8).
       Notes: forms derivatives κηνσοφύλαξ, μαγιστρόκηνσος, ὁμόκηνσος. Binder (2000:
       244), Daris (1991a: 54), Mason (1974: 5, 61), Hofmann (1989: 171–2),
       Zilliacus (1935a: 176–7), Meinersmann (1927: 25), Immisch (1885: 367),
       Lampe (1961), LSJ, LSJ suppl. See §4.2.4.2, §6.7 n. 46, §9.2, §9.3 n. 21,
       §9.5.4 n. 42, §10.2.1, §10.2.2 D.

rare   **κηνσουάλιον** 'poll tax', from *cēnsuālis* 'of the census' (neut. subst.): Lyd. *Mag.*
       p. 242.18 (VI AD). *LBG*.

Direct loan   **κηνσουάλιος, κηνσουάλης, κινσουάλιος, κενσουάλιος, κλησουάλιος** (-ου, ὁ), a tax
V AD – Byz.   official, from *cēnsuālis* 'of the census'.
       Inscriptions: *MAMA* III.29, 206.
       Literature: Nil. 1.156.1 (V AD); Just. *Nov.* 17.8.pr. etc. (VI AD); Ath.Schol.
       4.P.22.3 (VI AD); Lyd. *Mag.* p. 128.24 (VI AD).
       Post-antique: numerous. *LBG*.
       Notes: Caimi (1981: 325–6), Hofmann (1989: 172), Zilliacus (1935a: 176–7),
       Lampe (1961 *s.vv.* κηνσουάλιος, κλησουάλιος), LSJ suppl. See §4.2.5, §6.7
       n. 46, §10.2.1, §10.2.2 D.

rare	**κηνσοῦρα** 'office of censor', from *cēnsūra* 'office of censor': Lyd. *Mag.* pp. 6.5, 60.18 (VI AD). *LBG*.
rare	**κηνσοφύλαξ** 'keeper of the census', from *cēnsus, -ūs* 'census' via κῆνσος + φύλαξ 'guard': Nil. 2.146.1 (V AD); Ath.Schol. 20.1.4 (VI AD). Hofmann (1989: 172 *s.v.* κῆνσος), Lampe (1961).
non-existent?	**κηνσόω** 'punish', said to be a Greek verb derived from *cēnsus, -ūs* 'census' via κῆνσος: I can find no examples, and the work traditionally cited (Krauss 1899: 554–5) discusses only a Hebrew verb and derives it not from a Greek verb but from κῆνσος. Hofmann (1989: 172 *s.v.* κῆνσος), Hahn (1906: 266).
Direct loan **IV AD – modern**	**κήνσωρ, κίνσωρ, κένσωρ** (-ορος/-ωρος, ὁ) 'censor', from *cēnsor* 'censor'. Literature: Athan. *Apol.Sec.* 65.1 etc. (IV AD); Eutropius 2.9 (IV AD); Socr. 1.27.97–106 (IV/V AD); Lyd. *Mag.* p. 60.25 etc. (VI AD). Post-antique: numerous. *LBG*. Modern κήνσορας 'censor': Babiniotis (2002). Notes: influences ἀντικήνσωρ. Hofmann (1989: 172–3), Lampe (1961). See §4.2.5, §4.4, §6.7 n. 46, §10.2.1, §10.2.2 D.
rare	**κήρα** 'wax tablet', from *cēra* 'wax', 'wax tablet': papyrus *P.Oxy.* 2110.4 etc. (IV AD); occasional Byzantine texts. Hofmann (1989: 173), *LBG*, LSJ.
rare	**κηριολάριον** 'candelabrum', from *cēriolāre* 'candlestick' or its variant *cēriolārium* (*OLD* and *TLL s.v. cēriolāre*): with *cerilarium* in Gloss. Ps.-Cyril. 349.8. Hofmann (1989: 173), LSJ.
Direct loan **II AD – Byz.**	**κηρίολος** (-ου, ὁ) 'wax taper or figure'?, apparently from *cēreolus* 'candelabrum' (*TLL*). Inscriptions: *I.Ephesos* 3216.5 (II AD); *I.Ephesos* 2227.2.4 (III AD?). Literature: Ps.-Herodian, *Philetaerus* 215 Dain κηρίνην, θρυαλλίδα· Ἄρχιππος ὁ κωμικός· ὃ οἱ νῦν κηρίολον (II–IV AD?); *ACO* I.1.11 p. 66.8 (V AD). Post-antique: survives with meaning 'candelabrum'. *LBG*. Notes: the Byzantine meaning is possible for some ancient examples; if it is not ancient, it could have arisen from further contact with Latin, or the word could have died out and been reborrowed. Hofmann (1989: 173), Frisk (1954–72: 1.844), Lampe (1961), LSJ, LSJ suppl. See §4.2.4.1 n. 51, §10.2.1, §10.2.2 M.
rare	**κηρίων** 'wax taper', 'candle', from *cēriō*, variant of *cērium* (*TLL s.v. cērium*; the Latin is normally a kind of cyst, but *TLL* 863.45–7 suggests that the Greek is evidence for a similar meaning in Latin): Plut. *Mor.* 263f, marked (I/II AD); Galen XVIIB.267.3 Kühn, marked (II AD); Athan. *Ep.Encycl.* 4.2 (IV AD); with *candela* in Gloss. Ps.-Philox. 97.15; perhaps Agath. *Arm.* 149.4 (V AD); perhaps papyrus *P.Prag.* II.178.i.13 (V/VI AD). Hofmann (1989: 173), Lampe (1961), LSJ.
rare	**κηρουλ(λ)άριος** 'candlemaker', 'candle-seller', from *cēriolārius* 'maker or seller of candles', or medieval *cērulārius* 'candle-seller' (Du Cange 1883–7), or *cērula* 'small piece of wax' (*TLL*) via κηρούλλιον + -άριος: Philogelos 135 (IV AD); unverified example (IV AD) in Zilliacus (1937: 322, 336); often in Byzantine texts (with derivative κηρουλαρικός 'of a candlemaker'). Hofmann (1989: 173), Lampe (1961).

not ancient? **κηρούλ(λ)ιον** 'wax taper', 'candle', from *cērula* 'small piece of wax' (*TLL*) + -ιον: unverified example (IV AD) in Zilliacus (1937: 322, 336). Hofmann (1989: 174), *LBG*, Sophocles (1887 *s.v.* κηρούλιον), Lampe (1961).

rare **κηρύσση** 'white lead', from *cērussa* 'white lead': *Hippiatr.Berl.* (Apsyrtus) 130.65 (III/IV AD).

κησαρ-: see καισαρ-.

Deriv.? of loan II–III AD
κιβαριάτωρ, κειβαριάτωρ (-ορος, ὁ) or more frequently **κ(ε)ιβαριάτης** (-ου, ὁ), an army official issuing food and wine to the troops, must be Latin, but the exact source word is debated.
Documents: common, e.g. *O.Claud.* IV.709.17 (I/II AD); *O.Florida* 16.6 (II AD); *SB* 16235.4 (II/III AD); *SB* 9230.3 (III AD).
Notes: often derived from unattested *cibār(i)ātor* with same meaning (*TLL*), but more likely from *cibāria* 'food rations' (via κιβάριον?) + -τωρ/-της: discussion in *O.Claud.* III pp. 58–9, Cavenaile (1952: 201). Daris (1991a: 54), Hofmann (1989: 174), Meinersmann (1927: 25), LSJ suppl. See §4.2.5, §4.3.2, §6.8, §6.9, §8.1.7, §9.2, §10.2.2 C.

Direct loan I AD – modern
κιβάριον, κειβάρ(ε)ιον (-ου, τό) 'rations', 'provisions', from *cibāria, -ōrum* 'rations', 'provisions'.
Documents: e.g. *O.Did.* 343.9 (I AD); *O.Claud.* III.417.3 (II AD); *O.Did.* 84.6 (III AD); *P.Ryl.* IV.630/637.17 (IV AD); *SB* 15302.190 etc. (V AD).
Inscriptions: *IG* IV².1.92.10 (III/IV AD); Peek 1969: 34 no. 40.11 (III/IV AD); *SEG* VII.434.2.
Literature: Modestinus in Just. *Dig.* 34.1.4.pr. (III AD); with *cibarium* in Gloss. *Herm.L.* 14.28.
Post-antique: survives. *LBG*, Kriaras (1968– *s.v.* κιβαρόν). Modern dialectal κιβαρό, τσίβαρα, etc. 'bran': Andriotis (1974: 315).
Notes: also read (unconvincingly) in *SB* XXIV.16132.10 (I BC) by Capponi (2016: 1710). Cuvigny (2010b: 40–4), Daris (1991a: 54), Hofmann (1989: 174), Meinersmann (1927: 25), LSJ suppl. See §4.2.4.1 n. 54, §6.3 n. 22, §6.9, §9.5.6 nn. 55 and 58, §10.2.1, §10.2.2 I.

Direct loan II–IV AD?
κιβάριος (-α, -ον) 'of the household', 'made of coarse meal' (of bread), from *cibārius* 'concerning food'.
Documents: *P.Petaus* 45.1 (II AD); *P.Lond.* III.1159.8 (II AD); *P.Ryl.* IV.627.71 etc., 629.35 etc., 630/637.65 etc., 639.67 etc. (all IV AD).
Inscriptions: variant at Edict.Diocl. 3.3 (IV AD); *I.Ephesos* 910.3, 3010.11.
Literature: with *cibarius* in Gloss. *Herm.A.* 87.19.
Post-antique: may survive in Byzantine adjs κιβαρός, κιβαρίτης (*LBG*).
Notes: Daris (1991a: 54–5), Hofmann (1989: 174), LSJ suppl. See §4.2.2, §10.2.1, §10.2.2 I, §10.3.2.

not ancient **κίγκλα** 'saddle girth', from *cingula* 'saddle girth': no ancient examples. Binder (2000: 196), Meyer (1895: 30), Kriaras (1968– *s.v.* κίγγλα).

foreign **κίκερ** transliterating *cicer* 'chickpea': Plut. *Cicero* 1.4 (I/II AD); interpolations in Dsc. 2.104 RV etc. Strobach (1997: 196), Sophocles (1887).

not ancient   **κικοῦτα** transliterating *cicūta* 'hemlock': interpolation in Dsc. 4.78 RV. Sophocles (1887).

κινδεκέμουιρ: see κυινδεκέμβηρ.

κινσίτωρ: see κηνσίτωρ.

κῖνσος: see κῆνσος.

κινσουάλιος: see κηνσουάλιος.

κινστέρνα: see κιστέρνα.

κίνσωρ: see κῆνσωρ.

κιντηνάρι: see κεντηνάριον.

Direct loan   **κιρκήσιος** (-α, -ον) 'of the circus', esp. in neut. subst. **κιρκήσιον, κιρκίσιον,**
II AD – Byz.   **κερκήσιον, κερκέσιον** 'circus show' (often in plural), from *circēnsis* 'of the circus'.
            Inscriptions: *IGLS* III.1.965.4 (II AD?); *SEG* XLIX.1333.
            Literature: Epict. *Diss.* 4.10.21 (I/II AD); Ps.-Macar. *Serm.* 4.6.2 (V AD?);
                Malal. 7.4 (VI AD).
            Post-antique: numerous. *LBG* (*s.vv.* κιρκίσιον, κερκήσιος).
            Notes: Hofmann (1989: 174), LSJ (*s.v.* κιρκήσια). See §4.2.2, §6.7, §10.2.1,
                §10.2.2 F.

rare   **κιρκητεύω, κερκιτεύω** 'patrol', from *circitō* 'go around': unpublished ostracon
                O.Dios inv. 157.16 (II/III AD); unverified example (II AD) in Zilliacus
                (1937: 323, 329). Probably the same word as Byzantine κερκετεύω: *LBG*,
                Triandaphyllidis (1909: 130).

not ancient   **κιρκιλλίζω** 'knock on a door', from *circellus* 'little circle' (*TLL*): no ancient
                examples. Meyer (1895: 30).

non-existent   **κίρκινος** 'pair of compasses', from *circinus* 'pair of compasses': does not exist.
                Hofmann (1989: 174–5), Sophocles (1887), LSJ suppl.

Direct loan   **κιρκίτωρ, κερκήτωρ, κερκίτωρ, κερκείτωρ, κειρκείτορ, κειρκείδωρ** (-ορος, ὁ)
II AD – Byz.   'inspector of frontier posts', from *circitor* 'person who goes around'.
            Documents: unpublished O.Dios inv. 1303.ii.2 (II AD); *P.Neph.* 33.22 (IV AD);
                P.Gascou 79.4 etc. (IV AD); *CPR* XXIV.15.20 etc. (V/VI AD); *P.Lond.*
                v.1889v.4 (VI AD); perhaps *P.Worp* 33.3 (VI AD).
            Inscriptions: *SEG* IX.356.35 (VI AD); perhaps *SEG* XXXII.1554.A38 (VI AD);
                IGBulg. II.530.2; *CIL* III.14184⁹.6.
            Literature: Lyd. *Mag.* p. 74.10, marked (VI AD).
            Post-antique: survives. *LBG* (*s.v.* κιρκίτωρ).
            Notes: Binder (2000: 124), Daris (1991a: 54), Hofmann (1989: 175), Zilliacus
                (1935a: 220–1), Meinersmann (1927: 25), LSJ suppl. See §4.1.1, §4.2.5,
                §10.2.1, §10.2.2 C.

foreign   **κίρκλος λιξόλας**, a cake name that must be partially from *circulus* 'ring': Athenaeus
                14.647d, marked (II/III AD). Binder (2000: 160), Hofmann (1989: 175).

Direct loan
II–VI AD?

κίρκος (-ου, ὁ) 'circus', from *circus* 'place where games are held', itself perhaps from κίρκος 'circle'.

Documents: Audollent 1904: no. 241.32 (II/III AD); Audollent 1904: no. 242.49 (III AD); *P.Oxy.* 145.2 (VI AD).

Literature: perhaps Polybius 30.22.2 (II BC); Plut. *Aem.* 32.2, marked (I/II AD); Epict. *Diss.* 3.16.14 (I/II AD); Athenaeus 14.615b, quoting Polybius (II/III AD); Nil. 2.205.7, 2.290.15 (V AD); Lyd. *Mens.* 1.12.10 αὕτη γοῦν ἡ Κίρκη διὰ κάλλους ὑπερβολὴν τοῦ Ἡλίου θυγάτηρ εἶναι ἐκόμπαζε καὶ εἰς τιμὴν τοῦ οἰκείου δῆθεν πατρὸς ἱππικὸν ἀγῶνα πρώτη ἐν Ἰταλίᾳ ἐτέλεσεν, ὃς δὴ καὶ ἐξ αὐτῆς ὠνομάσθη κίρκος (VI AD); perhaps others.

Notes: owing to difficulty of distinguishing this from κίρκος in other senses, there may be significantly more examples than cited here. Dubuisson (1985: 34), Daris (1991a: 55), Hofmann (1989: 176), Meinersmann (1927: 25), *DÉLG* (*s.v.* κρίκος), Frisk (1954–72: II.20), LSJ (*s.v.* κίρκος IV). See §4.2.4.1 n. 51, §6.7, §8.1.3 n. 17, §10.2.1, §10.2.2 F.

non-existent?

κιρκουλᾶς and **κιρκουλάτωρ**, from *circulātor* 'itinerant performer': superseded reading of *P.Athen.* 34.7. Cavenaile (1951: 397).

Direct loan
VI AD – modern

κιστέρνα, κινστέρνα (-ης/-ας, ἡ) 'cistern', from *cisterna* 'cistern'.

Documents: *SB* 8073.2, 8075.3 (both VI AD).

Literature: *Hippiatr.Par.* (Pel.) 1069 (V AD?); Hesych. as lemma κ 2796 (V/VI AD); Malal. 16.10 etc. (VI AD); Just. *Nov.* 159.pr. (VI AD); *ACO* III p. 35.35 etc. (VI AD); Philoponus, *In libros de generatione animalium commentaria* p. 109.28 Hayduck, marked (VI AD); Pelagonius 531 = Fischer 1980: 91.12 (post IV AD); Her.Mech. *Mens.* 20.1 *passim*.

Post-antique: numerous, forming derivative κινστερνοειδής 'like a cistern'. *LBG* (*s.v.* κινστέρνα), Zervan (2019: 78–9), Triandaphyllidis (1909: 124). Modern κιστέρνα, κινστέρνα, στέρνα 'cistern': Babiniotis (2002), Andriotis (1967, 1974: 316), Meyer (1895: 30), Kahane and Kahane (1972–6: 534).

Notes: Daris (1991a: 55), Hofmann (1989: 176), Zilliacus (1935a: 220–1), Lampe (1961), LSJ suppl. See §10.2.1, §10.2.2 J.

rare

κίστιβερ, a title from (*quīnquevir*) *cis Tiberim* '(member of the board of five) on the near side of the Tiber': inscription *IGUR* III.1157.2 (II/III AD). Hofmann (1989: 176), LSJ.

rare

κιτάτωρ 'summoner', apparently from medieval *citātor* 'inciter' (*DMLBS*): papyrus *Rom.Mil.Rec.* 76.xx.24 (II AD). Daris (1991a: 55), Hofmann (1989: 176), Meinersmann (1927: 25), LSJ suppl.

Deriv. of loan
VI AD – Byz.

κιτρᾶτον (-ου, τό), a citron drink, probably from *citrum* via κίτρον + -ᾶτον; **citrātum* is unattested, and adj. *citrātus* comes from *citra* 'on this side' (*TLL*).

Documents: Andorlini 2001: no. 15.7 (VI AD).

Literature: Aëtius 16.161.1 (VI AD); Alex.Trall. II.341.17 (VI AD).

Post-antique: occasional survival. *LBG*.

Notes: Maravela-Solbakk (2010: 261–2), Andorlini (2001: 170), Hofmann (1989: 176–7), *DÉLG* (*s.v.* κίτριον), Frisk (1954–72: I.861), Beekes (2010 *s.v.* κίτριον), LSJ. See §4.6.1, §6.5, §10.2.2 I.

not ancient	**κιτρέα** 'citrus tree', from *citrea* 'citrus tree': no ancient examples. Hofmann (1989: 178 *s.v.* κίτριον), *DÉLG* (*s.v.* κίτριον), Frisk (1954–72: 1.861), Beekes (2010 *s.v.* κίτριον), Kriaras (1968–), LSJ.
non-existent	**κιτρειαβολή**, name of a Jewish ritual, Greek formation derived ultimately from *citrum* 'wood or fruit of the citrus tree' (*TLL*) or *citrium* 'citron' (*TLL*): probably not in papyrus *SB* 9843.9 (II AD). Commentary in *P.Yadin* II p. 357, LSJ suppl.
rare	**κίτρεος** 'yellow', from *citreus* 'of a citrus tree': papyrus *Stud.Pal.* XX.245.5 etc. (VI AD). Daris (1991a: 55), Hofmann (1989: 177), *DÉLG* (*s.v.* κίτριον), Frisk (1954–72: 1.861), Beekes (2010 *s.v.* κίτριον), LSJ.
not ancient?	**κιτρινοειδής** 'of a citron colour', immediately from κίτρινος and ultimately from that word's Latin source + -ειδής (cf. εἶδος 'form'): old scholia to Theocritus 5.94/95c, twice. Hofmann (1989: 177 *s.v.* κίτρινος), LSJ.
Deriv. of loan **II AD – modern**	**κίτρινος** (-η, -ον) 'yellow', 'of a citrus tree', as neut. subst. 'yellow salve', probably from *citrum* 'wood or fruit of the citrus tree' (*TLL*) or *citrium* 'citron', 'of a citrus tree' (*TLL*), via κίτρον or κίτριον, + -ινος. Documents: perhaps *P.Heid.* VII.406.24 (IV/V AD); *P.Cair.Masp.* 67006v.83 (VI AD); perhaps *CPR* X.139.2 (VI AD). Literature: Archigenes p. 9.22 Brescia (I/II AD); Vet.Val. *Anth.* 1.1.9 (II AD); Dio Cassius 61.10.3 (II/III AD); *Test.Sal.* p. 105*.6 (III AD?); Rhetor. *Plan.* 219.16 (VI AD). Post-antique: numerous, forming derivatives κιτρινάερος 'yellow and blue', κιτρινίζω 'be yellow', etc. *LBG*, Kriaras (1968–). Modern κίτρινος 'yellow': Babiniotis (2002), Meyer (1895: 31). Notes: Hofmann prefers derivation from medieval *citrīnus* 'yellow' (*DMLBS*). Forms derivative ὁλοκίτρινος. Cervenka-Ehrenstrasser (1996: 96), Daris (1991a: 55, with derivation from *citreus*), Hofmann (1989: 177), *DÉLG* (*s.v.* κίτριον), Frisk (1954–72: 1.861), Beekes (2010 *s.v.* κίτριον), LSJ. See §4.6.1, §8.2.3, §10.2.2 O.
rare	**κιτριοειδής** 'citron-like', immediately from κίτριον and ultimately from that word's Latin source + -ειδής (cf. εἶδος 'form'): Ps.-Galen XIV.392.12 Kühn. Hofmann (1989: 178 *s.v.* κίτριον), *DÉLG* (*s.v.* κίτριον), Frisk (1954–72: 1.860–1), Beekes (2010 *s.v.* κίτριον), LSJ.
Direct loan with suffix? **I AD – Byz.**	**κίτριον** (-ου, τό) 'citron', 'citrus tree', from *citrum* 'wood or fruit of the citrus tree' (*TLL*) + -ιον, or perhaps *citrium* 'citron', 'of a citrus tree' (*TLL*). Documents: *SB* 9017 no. 13.10 (I/II AD); *P.Warr.* 15.15 (II AD); *SB* 9843.7 (II AD); *P.Mich.* XI.619.3 etc. (II AD); *P.Wisc.* II.60.7 etc. (III AD); *P.Oxy.* 1631.24, 1764.19 (both III AD). Inscriptions: *IG* IV².1.126.9 (II/III AD?). Literature: common, e.g. perhaps Phaenias, frag. 47a–b Wehrli (IV BC); perhaps Juba, *FHG* III frag. 24.4 (I BC/AD); Dsc. 1.115.5, marked τὰ δὲ Μηδικὰ λεγόμενα ἢ Περσικὰ ἢ κεδρόμηλα, Ῥωμαιστὶ δὲ κίτρια, πᾶσι γνώριμα (I AD); Jos. *AJ* 13.372 (I AD); Galen VI.617.13 Kühn (II AD); Athenaeus 3.84c τὸ νῦν κιτρίον λεγόμενον (II/III AD); *Hippiatr.Camb.* (Julius Africanus) 71.15 (III AD?); Methodius Olympius, *Symposium* 9.3.16 Debidour and Musurillo (III/IV AD); Orib. *Ecl.* 127.1 (IV AD); Hesych. as lemma κ 2800 (V/VI AD); Aëtius 3.94.5 (VI AD).

Post-antique: survives. Kriaras (1968–), LSJ, Daris (1991a: 55), Meyer (1895: 31).

Notes: derivation from *citrium* unlikely because that is rare, first attested considerably later than the Greek, and perhaps a reborrowing of κίτριον. Daris (1991a: 55), Hofmann (1989: 177–8), *DÉLG*, Frisk (1954–72: 1.860–1), Beekes (2010), LSJ. See §4.2.4.1 n. 54, §4.3.2 n. 69, §4.6.1, §8.1.3 n. 20, **§9.5.3**, §10.1, §10.2.1, §10.2.2 I.

rare   **κίτρις** 'citrus fruit', from the Latin source of κίτριον via κίτριον or from *citreus* 'of a citrus tree': ostracon *O.Heid.* 396.20 (III AD); undated marginal gloss in some manuscripts of Septuagint Leviticus 23:40. LSJ suppl.

rare   **κιτρόμηλον** 'citron', from *citrum* 'wood or fruit of the citrus tree' (*TLL*) via κίτρον + μῆλον 'fruit from a tree': Dsc. 3.104.1 (I AD). *TLL* (*s.v. citromēlon*, citing only a Latin version of Dsc.), Hofmann (1989: 178 *s.v.* κίτρον), *DÉLG* (*s.v.* κίτριον), Frisk (1954–72: 1.861), Beekes (2010 *s.v.* κίτριον), LSJ; for Byzantine survival *LBG* (*s.v.* κιτριόμηλον), Kriaras (1968– *s.v.* κιτρομηλέα); for modern dialectal survival Andriotis (1974: 316).

Direct loan
II AD – modern   **κίτρον** (-ου, τό) 'citron' (a fruit), from *citrum* 'wood or fruit of the citrus tree' (*TLL*).

Documents: none. *SB* 4483.12, cited by *TLL s.v. citrum* 1208.15, is post-antique.

Literature: e.g. Galen, *De victu attenuante* 83.6 Kalbfleisch (II AD); Aelius Promotus, Περὶ τῶν ἰοβόλων θηρίων 50.14 Ihm (II AD); Athenaeus 3.85c, marked (II/III AD); Hieroph. *Nut.* 1.7 (IV–VI AD?); Palladius Medicus, Dietz 1834: 149.4 (VI AD); Alex.Trall. 1.473.17 (VI AD).

Post-antique: survives, forming derivatives κιτρόφυτον 'citron-tree', κιτρόχρους 'citron-coloured' (LSJ). Kriaras (1968–), Daris (1991a: 55). Modern κίτρο 'citron': Babiniotis (2002), Andriotis (1967), Meyer (1895: 31).

Notes: forms derivatives κιτράτον, κιτρόμηλον, κιτρόφυλλον. Daris (1991a: 55), Hofmann (1989: 178), Meinersmann (1927: 25), *DÉLG* (*s.v.* κίτριον), Frisk (1954–72: 1.861), Beekes (2010 *s.v.* κίτριον), *TLL* (*s.v. citrum* 1207.76), LSJ. See §4.2.4.1 n. 55, §4.6.1, §6.5, **§9.5.3** passages 67–8, §10.2.1, §10.2.2 L.

non-existent   **κίτρος** 'citrus tree', from *citrus* 'citrus tree': not in papyri *SB* 4483 or 4485.4 (both VII AD). Kovarik (2007), Hofmann (1989: 178).

rare   **κιτρόφυλλον** 'leaf of a citrus tree', from *citrum* 'wood or fruit of the citrus tree' (*TLL*) via κίτρον + φύλλον 'leaf': Aëtius 1.129.14 (VI AD); Byzantine texts. Hofmann (1989: 178 *s.v.* κίτρον), *LBG*, LSJ.

not ancient   **κλαβαρίζω** and **γλαβαρίζω** 'put a border on (a garment)', perhaps from *clāvus* 'purple stripe on tunic': no ancient examples. Meyer (1895: 31).

Direct loan
VI AD – Byz.   **κλαβικουλάριος, κλαουϊκουλάριος, κλαβικάριος** (-ου, ὁ) 'prison guard', from *clāvīculārius* 'turnkey'.

Documents: *O.Ashm.Shelt.* 51.4 (VI AD); *P.Oxy.* 2050.3 etc. (VI AD); *PSI* VIII.957.5 (VI AD); *SB* 15723.1 (VI AD).

Literature: Lyd. *Mag.* p. 142.2 etc. (VI AD).

Post-antique: numerous. *LBG*.

Notes: Byzantine lexica (*LBG*, Kriaras 1968– *s.v.* καπικλάριος) consider it a variant of καπικλάριος (*q.v.*); although καπικλάριος and κλαβικουλάριος were effectively equivalent, the fact that each matches a different Latin word suggests two separate borrowings. Daris (1991a: 55), Hofmann (1989: 179), Cavenaile (1951: 397), Zilliacus (1935a: 178–9), LSJ suppl. (*s.v.* κλαουικουλάριοι). See §4.2.4.1 n. 50, §10.2.1, §10.2.2 D.

rare   **κλάβιον** 'bracelet', from *clāvus* 'fastening' + -ιον: Malal. 18.56.20 (VI AD); occasional Byzantine texts. Sophocles (1887), Triandaphyllidis (1909: 122), *TLL* (*s.v.* clāvus 1328.28), Lampe (1961).

foreign   **κλάβος** transliterating *clāvus* 'tiller', 'helm': Lyd. *Mens.* 1.31 (VI AD). *LBG*.

foreign   **κλαβουλάριος** probably transliterating *clāvulārius* 'of a transport wagon' (*TLL*): Lyd. *Mens.* 1.31 (VI AD). *LBG*, *TLL* (*s.v.* clāvulārius 1328.3–4).

foreign   **κλάμ** transliterating *clam* 'secretly': Plut. *Mor.* 269d (I/II AD). Sophocles (1887).

κλαουϊκουλάριος: see κλαβικουλάριος.

not ancient   **κλάρος**, from *clārus* 'bright', 'clear': probably no ancient examples. Hofmann (1989: 179), *LBG*.

κλασ-: see κλασσ-.

Direct loan
I–IV AD   **κλάσ(σ)α** (-ης, ἡ) 'fleet', from *classis* 'fleet'.
Documents: e.g. *Chrest.Wilck.* 458.2 (II AD); *O.Claud.* III.540.2 (II AD); *CPR* V.10.7 (IV AD).
Inscriptions: *I.Perinthos* 44.7 (I AD); perhaps *I.Kios* 88.2 (II AD); *IG* II/III². III.8358a.2 (II/III AD); *I.Tomis* 106.13 (III AD); *I.Ephesos* 737.9 (III AD); *IGR* I.1370.9; *I.Kyzikos* 243.7; *IG* XIV.698.4 (Latinate).
Notes: on nomenclature of fleets in papyri see Benaissa (2014: 212). Binder (2000: 260–1) wrongly claims that the nominative ends in -η: the nominative is unattested, and the accusative ends in -αν. Gignac (1981: 7), Daris (1991a: 55), Mason (1974: 5, 61), Hofmann (1989: 179), Meinersmann (1927: 25), LSJ suppl. See §4.2.3.1, §4.2.5, §4.6.1, §10.2.1, §10.2.2 C.

Direct? loan
II–V AD   **κλασσικός, κλασεικός** (-ή, -όν) 'naval', as masc. subst. a naval official, from *classicus* 'naval' or *classis* 'fleet' via κλάσσα + -ικός.
Documents: *SB* 17079.4 (II AD); perhaps *P.FuadUniv.* 10.7 (III AD).
Inscriptions: *SEG* XXXIV.1243.25 etc. (V AD).
Literature: Lyd. *Mag.* p. 44.2, marked (VI AD).
Post-antique: probably no survival. Modern κλασικός 'classical' is also from Latin but probably a separate borrowing: Babiniotis (2002), Andriotis (1967), Meyer (1895: 31).
Notes: Daris (1991a: 55), Hofmann (1989: 179–80), *LBG*, Lampe (1961), LSJ suppl. See §4.2.2, §4.6.1, §10.2.1, §10.2.2 C.

foreign   **κλάσ(σ)ις** transliterating *classis* 'class' (of citizens): DH *AR* 4.18.2, 4.18.3 (I BC). Mason (1974: 6, 61), Hofmann (1989: 179 *s.v.* κλασση), Meyer (1895: 31), Babiniotis (2002 *s.v.* κλάση²), Coleman (2007: 795 *s.v.* κλάση, though Andriotis 1967 gives a Greek derivation for modern κλάση 'class'). Cf. κλῆσις.

rare   **Κλαυδιανός** 'Claudian', from *Claudiānus* 'Claudian': a wide range of things associated with various people named 'Claudius', most falling outside the terms of this study. Relevant to us: a kind of granite, Edict.Diocl. 33.6 (IV AD); an alloy of copper and lead, undated alchemical works. The latter survives in modern dialectal κλαυδιανόν, an alloy (Andriotis 1974: 317). Lauffer (1971: 281), LSJ suppl.

name   **Κλαύδιος** 'Claudian', from the name *Claudius*. LSJ suppl. Cf. φιλοκλαύδιος.

foreign   **κλαυσουλία, κλαύσουλα** '(legal) clause', from *clausula* '(legal) clause': Antec. in Latin script 3.15.7 *clausula* (VI AD); later in Greek script. Zilliacus (1935a: 178–9), *LBG*.

Direct loan with influence
V AD – modern

κλεισούρα (-ας, ἡ) 'narrow pass', from *clausūra* 'closure' (*TLL*) with influence from κλείω 'close'.

Literature: Agath. *Arm.* 10 (V AD); Procop. *Bell.* 2.29.25 etc. (VI AD). Example in Marcus Eremita is probably post-antique.

Post-antique: common, with numerous derivatives. *LBG*, Zervan (2019: 79), Kriaras (1968–), Triandaphyllidis (1909: 107, 119). Modern κλεισούρα 'pass', 'defile': Babiniotis (2002), Andriotis (1967), Meyer (1895: 31).

Notes: Coleman (2007: 797), Hofmann (1989: 180), Zilliacus (1935a: 178–9), Viscidi (1944: 8), Sophocles (1887), *TLL* (*s.v. clausūra* 1327.51–3), Lampe (1961), LSJ, LSJ suppl. See §4.2.3.1, §4.4, §6.11, §10.2.1, §10.2.2 O.

semantic extension

κλῆσις 'class of citizens', Hellenized form of *classis* (*cīvium*) 'class of citizens': DH *AR* 4.18.2, 7.59.8 (I BC). Mason (1974: 15, 61), LSJ (*s.v.* κλῆσις IV), LSJ suppl. Cf. κλάσσις.

κλησουάλιος: see κηνσουάλιος.

Direct loan
V–VI AD

κλιβανάριος, κριβανάριος (-ου, ὁ) 'armoured cavalryman', 'baker', probably from *clībanārius* 'armoured', 'using a clay oven' (*TLL*).

Documents: e.g. *P.Würzb.* 17.7 (V AD); *P.Leid.Inst.* 67.3 etc. (V AD); *P.Lund* II.5.7 (V/VI AD); *PSI* XIV.1426.8 (V/VI AD); *P.Oxy.* 1882.11 (VI AD); *P.PalauRib.* 41.1 (VI AD).

Inscriptions: *SEG* XX.332.2 (V AD).

Literature: Lyd. *Mag.* p. 74.4, marked (VI AD).

Notes: all examples use spelling κλιβ-; κριβ- is modern invention to match κρίβανος 'clay oven'. The two meanings make an odd combination; Meinersmann (1927: 25–6) suggests origin in a joke that the armour resembled an oven. But Rundgren (1957: 31–52, esp. 49) more convincingly derives *clībanārius* from merger of (1) *clībanus* 'clay oven' (from κρίβανος) + -*ārius* and (2) Middle Persian *grīvbānar* 'wearer of a coat of mail' (or perhaps *grīvbān* 'coat of mail'), borrowed via unattested **crībānārius* with -*r*- changed by dissimilation. Often as part of name of military unit Λεοντοκλιβανάριοι or Λέονες κλιβανάριοι, which may be intended even when κλιβανάριος appears on its own (Palme 2004: 323–4). Hofmann (1989: 180), Zilliacus (1935a: 220–1), *DÉLG* (*s.v.* κρίβανος), Frisk (1954–72: 1.873), Beekes (2010 *s.v.* κλίβανος), *TLL* (*s.v. clībanārius* 1342.1, 12), LSJ and LSJ suppl. (*s.v.* κριβανάριος, with some confusion). See §2.1, §4.2.4.1 n. 50, §10.2.1, §10.2.2 C, §12.2.1.

foreign	**κλιέντης** transliterating pl. of *cliēns* 'client': Plut. *Rom.* 13.7, *Mor.* 323b (I/II AD); Lyd. *Mag.* p. 34.3 (VI AD). Mason (1974: 6, 61), Hofmann (1989: 180).
rare	**κλιπεᾶτος** '(soldier) with a large shield', from *clipeātus* 'armed with a round bronze shield': Lyd. *Mag.* p. 20.12 (VI AD). *LBG*.
rare	**κλίπεος, κλίπεον** 'large shield', from *clipeus/clipeum* 'round bronze shield': Lyd. *Mag.* pp. 4.16, 20.20, 22.2 (VI AD). Hofmann (1989: 180), *LBG* (*s.v.* κλίπεον).
not ancient?	**κλόκιον, κοκλί,** and **κουκλί** 'chamber pot', perhaps from *cloāca* 'sewer': no certainly ancient examples. Meyer (1895: 31), LSJ, LSJ suppl.
foreign	**κλοπία** transliterating *clupea*, a fish: Lyd. *Mens.* 3.11.40 (VI AD); occasionally later. *LBG*, Sophocles (1887).
not ancient	**κλόστρα** 'colostrum', from *colostra* 'colostrum': no ancient examples. Binder (2000: 203), Meyer (1895: 31).
foreign	**Κλούσιος** transliterating *Clūsius*, epithet of Janus: Lyd. *Mens.* 4.1.12 (VI AD). Sophocles (1887).
foreign	**κλοῦστρον**, a cake name from *clustrum* (variant of *crustulum* 'small cake'): Athenaeus 14.647c–d, marked (II/III AD). Hofmann (1989: 181), *TLL* (*s.v. crustulum* 1254.53–4), LSJ. See §9.4 passage 61.
foreign	**κλουστροπλακοῦς**, a cake name from *clustrum* (variant of *crustulum* 'small cake') (via κλοῦστρον?) + πλακοῦς 'flat cake': Athenaeus 14.647d, marked (II/III AD). *TLL* (*s.v. crustulum* 1254.53–4).
rare	**κλῶστρον**, from *claustrum* 'gate', 'prison': unpublished ostracon O.Claud. inv. 5745.1 (II AD).
	κοαίστωρ: see κουαίστωρ.
	κοάκτωρ: see κομάκτωρ.
rare	**κογγιάριον, κονγιάριον**, a unit of measurement from *congiārium* 'vessel with the capacity of one congius': ostracon *O.Florida* 6.5 (II AD); Epiph. *Mens.* 606, 819 (IV AD); Byzantine texts. Daris (1991a: 55), Hofmann (1989: 181), Sophocles (1887), Lampe (1961).
rare	**κογνᾶτα** 'kinswoman', perhaps 'sister-in-law', from *cognāta* 'kinswoman': *I.Albanie méridionale* 156.2. Editor *ad loc.*
rare	**κογνατικός** 'of relationship on mother's side', from *cognātus* 'blood relative' (via κογνᾶτος?) + -ικός (*cognaticus* is not attested): Just. *Nov.* 84.pr.pr. etc., but in Latin script 118.5 (VI AD); Ath.Schol. 3.P.9 in Latin script (VI AD); Antec. in Latin script 3.2.3a *cognaticēn* etc. (VI AD); occasional Byzantine legal texts. Avotins (1992), Hofmann (1989: 181 *s.v.* κογνᾶτος), Zilliacus (1935a: 178–9), Lampe (1961), LSJ suppl.
foreign	**κογνατίων** 'relationship on mother's side', from *cognātiō* 'blood relationship': Antec. in Latin script 1.10.2 *cognation* etc. (VI AD); later in Greek script. Zilliacus (1935a: 178–9), *LBG*.

rare   **κογνᾶτος** 'blood relative', 'relative on mother's side', from *cognātus* 'blood
relative': Just. *Nov.* 115.3.14, but in Latin script 118.4 etc. (VI AD); Ath.
Schol. in Latin script 9.10.9 etc. (VI AD); Antec. in Latin script 1.10.1
cognatoi etc. (VI AD); often in Byzantine legal texts. Inscription *Agora*
XVII.1052.8 (II AD) is Latin in Greek script. Forms derivative κογνατικός.
Avotins (1992), Hofmann (1989: 181), Zilliacus (1935a: 178–9), Lampe
(1961), LSJ suppl. See §9.5.6 n. 68.

Direct loan   **κο(γ)νιτίων** (-ωνος/-ονος, ἡ), a type of judicial investigation, from *cognitiō*
IV–V AD   'inquiry'.
     Documents: *P.Oxy.* 4361.4 (III/IV AD); *Chrest.Mitt.* 55.17 (IV AD).
     Literature: *ACO* II.I.I p. 149.20 etc. (V AD).
     Notes: Daris (1991a: 55), Hofmann (1989: 181), Zilliacus (1935a: 178–9),
     Meinersmann (1927: 26), Lampe (1961). See §4.2.5, §10.2.1, §10.2.2 B.

foreign   *cognōmen* 'surname': Antec. 2.20.29 *cognomen* (VI AD).

     κόγχος: see κόκχος.

     κοδικιλλ-: see κωδικιλλ-.

     κόδιξ: see κῶδιξ.

Direct loan   **κοδράντης, κουαδράντης** (-ου, ὁ), a coin, from *quadrāns* 'quarter', 'coin worth a
I BC – IV AD?   quarter of an *as*'.
     Inscriptions: *I.Cret.* II.XI.3.39 (I BC); perhaps *SEG* LV.821.A6.
     Literature: e.g. NT Matthew 5:26, Mark 12:42 (I AD); Plut. *Cicero* 29.5,
     marked (I/II AD); Hippolytus, *Refutatio omnium haeresium* 6.25.3 (III AD);
     Gregorius Nyssenus, *De beneficentia* IX p. 98.20 Van Heck (IV AD); Hesych.
     as lemma α 7646, κ 3201, 3207 (V/VI AD).
     Post-antique: survives mainly in discussions of the biblical passage.
     Notes: Binder (2000: 264), Hofmann (1989: 181–2), Immisch (1885: 366),
     Lampe (1961), LSJ. See §4.2.3.2, §4.2.5, §4.3.2 n. 75, §8.1.5, §9.3 n. 21,
     §10.2.1, §10.2.2 G.

     κοδρᾶτος: see κουαδρᾶτος.

rare   **κόδριν** 'quadrangular moneybox', from *quadrum* 'square' + -ι(ο)ν: Cyr.S. *Vit.Eu.*
69.19, 28, *Vita Theodosii* 238.9 (VI AD). Hofmann (1989: 182), Lampe (1961).

     κοιαισίτωρ: see κυαισίτωρ.

     κοιαιστωρ-: see κουαιστωρ-.

     Κοιγκτίλιος: see Κοιντίλιος.

     κοῖνα: see κῆνα.

     Κοϊνκτ(ε)ίλιος: see Κοιντίλιος.

     κοινταν-: see κουινταν-.

Direct loan   **Κοιντίλιος, Κοιντίλλιος, Κυντίλ(λ)ιος, Κυιντίλ(λ)ιος, Κοϊνκτ(ε)ίλιος, Κοιγκτίλιος**
II–I BC   (-α, -ον) 'July', from *Quintīlis* 'July'.
     Inscriptions: *IG* IX.II.89.a10 (II BC); *I.Cret.* III.IV.10.76 (II BC); Sherk 1969:
     no. 4.13 (II BC); *SEG* IV.48.ii.12 (I BC).

Literature: DH *AR* 6.13.4 etc., marked (I BC); Plut. *Cam.* 33.7 etc., marked (I/II AD); App. *BC* 2.16.106 etc., marked (I/II AD); Lyd. *Mens.* 3.10 etc., marked (VI AD).

Notes: disappeared in late I BC, when month name changed to *Iulius*; later occurrences marked as obsolete. García Domingo (1979: 504), Hofmann (1989: 183), Lampe (1961 *s.v.* Κυντίλιος). See §4.2.2, **§8.1.4**, §8.2.1, §10.2.1, §10.2.2 E, §10.3.1 n. 26.

κοκκοβάγη: see κουκούβη.

κοκκόμανα, κόκκομας, κόκκουμα: see κούκκουμα.

κοκκούλ(λ)ιον: see κουκούλλιον.

κοκκούμιον: see κουκκούμιον.

κοκλί: see κλόκιον.

κόκομα, κοκόμανος, κόκουμα: see κούκκουμα.

κόκουλλος: see κουκκοῦλλος.

κοκούμιον: see κουκκούμιον.

not Latin? | **κόκχος, κόγχος** 'cookpot' in papyrus *P.Hamb.* 1.10.36 (II AD) is cited by Hofmann (1989: 183), *DÉLG*, Beekes (2010), LSJ as a borrowing of *coculum* 'bronze cooking vessel'. Sijpesteijn (1987a) considers it a misspelling of Greek κόγχος 'thing [in this case a jar] shaped like a mussel-shell', and Daris (1991a: 55) suggests derivation from *concha* 'sea-shell'.

κολάριον: see κολλάριον.

not ancient? | **κολεγεᾶτος** 'colleague', apparently from *collēgiātus* 'fellow member of a *collēgium*': no certainly ancient examples. Hofmann (1989: 183).

κολεκτάριος: see κολλεκτάριος.

κολήγας: see κολλήγας.

foreign | ***collactāneus*** 'foster brother': Antec. 1.6.5 *collactaneos* (VI AD).

Direct loan II AD – Byz. | **κολ(λ)άριον** (-ου, τό) 'collar', from *collāre* 'collar'.
Documents: *Pap.Choix* 10.18 (II AD).
Literature: Hesych. as gloss κ 3025 (V/VI AD); scholia to Ar. *V.* 897b as gloss; with *collarium* in Gloss. Ps.-Cyril. 352.18.
Post-antique: survives. *LBG*. Modern κολάρο 'collar' probably from Italian *collaro*: Babiniotis (2002), Andriotis (1967).
Notes: Daris (1991a: 56), Hofmann (1989: 183), Cavenaile (1951: 397), LSJ, LSJ suppl. See §4.2.5, §10.2.1, §10.2.2 H.

κολλέγας: see κολλήγας.

rare | **κολλεγιάτης** 'member of a *collegium*', from *collēgiātus* 'fellow member of a *collegium*': *Collectio tripartita*, Van der Wal and Stolte 1994: 23.22 (VI AD); Lyd. *Mag.* p. 80.20 in Latin script (VI AD). *LBG*. See §9.5.5 passage 78.

κολλέγιον: see κολλήγιον.

Direct loan
V AD – Byz.

κολ(λ)εκτάριος, κελλεκτάριος (-ου, ὁ) 'banker', 'money-changer', from *collēctārius* 'banker', 'money-changer' (*TLL*).

Documents: *P.Stras.* 1.35.11 (IV/V AD); *P.Mich.* XV.742.2 etc. (VI AD); *P.Oxy.* 3867.7 etc. (VI AD); *Stud.Pal.* III.385.2, perhaps XX.145.11 (both VI AD).

Post-antique: survives, forming derivative κολλεκτάριον 'exchange office'; appears as gloss in lexica. *LBG*, Daris (1991a: 56).

Notes: Bogaert (1985), Daris (1991a: 56), Hofmann (1989: 183–4), Zilliacus (1935a: 178–9), Meinersmann (1927: 26), *TLL* (*s.v. collēctārius* 1582.70–3), LSJ suppl. See §4.2.4.1 n. 50, §8.2.2, §10.2.1, §10.2.2 G.

Direct loan
II AD – modern

κολ(λ)ήγα(ς), κολλέγας (-α, ὁ) 'colleague', from *collēga* 'colleague'.

Documents: e.g. *O.Florida* 3.2 (II AD); *P.Mich.* III.220.25 (III AD); *P.Oxy.* 3819.13 (IV AD).

Inscriptions: *IGBulg.* IV.2250.8; *IGBulg.* III.I.1519.2; *IGBulg.* IV.2039.3; probably a name in *IGUR* I.37.8 (III AD).

Literature: Eus. *HE* 10.5.18 etc. (IV AD).

Post-antique: survives. Zervan (2019: 81). Modern κολ(λ)ήγας 'share-cropper': Babiniotis (2002), Andriotis (1967), Meyer (1895: 31).

Notes: forms derivative συγκολλήγας. Daris (1991a: 56), Mason (1974: 61), Hofmann (1989: 184), Viscidi (1944: 23), Zilliacus (1935a: 178–9), Meinersmann (1927: 26), Lampe (1961), LSJ. See §4.2.3.2, §10.2.1, §10.2.2 N.

non-existent?

κολληγατάριος, from *collēgātārius* 'joint legatee': cited as an ancient loan by Zilliacus (1935a: 178–9), but I can find no examples.

κολλήγειον: see κολλήγιον.

non-existent

κολληγιᾶς, from *collēgiātus* 'fellow member of a *collegium*': κολληγιᾶτες is superseded reading for Κολλητίαν on papyrus *P.Athen.* 67.9 (III/IV AD). Daris (1991a: 56), Cavenaile (1951: 397).

Direct loan
I AD – Byz.

κολλήγιον, κολλέγιον, κολλήγειον (-ου, τό) 'council', 'band', 'guild', 'shared enterprise', from *collēgium* 'board', 'guild'.

Documents: *SB* 9066.1.7 (II AD); *P.Gen.* I.73.15 (III AD); *SB* 15970.4 (V AD); perhaps *P.Gen.* IV.195.1 (VI AD). Probably not *SB* 9527.9 (IV/V AD): *BL* XIII.202.

Inscriptions: e.g. *SEG* XXVII.962bis.2 (I AD); *TAM* V.I.71.1 (II AD); *SEG* XLVII.954.4 etc. (III AD).

Literature: Dio Cassius 38.13.2, marked (II/III AD); *Coll.Herm.* H 21e (II–IV AD); Pall. *H.Laus.* 19.3 (IV/V AD); *ACO* I.I.III p. 7.22 (V AD); *Apophth.Patr.* 17.15.2 etc. (V AD); Lyd. *Mag.* p. 80.14, marked (VI AD).

Post-antique: survives. *LBG* (*s.v.* κολλέγιον), Kriaras (1968– *s.v.* κολλέγιον), Meyer (1895: 31). Modern κολλέγιο 'college' at least partly a later borrowing: Andriotis (1967).

Notes: Lee (2015: 32), Daris (1991a: 56), Mason (1974: 6, 61), Hofmann (1989: 184), Zilliacus (1935a: 178–9), Meinersmann (1927: 26), Lampe (1961), LSJ. See §4.2.4.1 n. 54, §10.2.1, §10.2.2 O.

non-existent

κολλήγιος is cited by Mason (1974: 62) as a borrowing of *collēga* 'colleague' on the basis of κολληγίῳ in papyrus *SB* 9207.7 (II/III AD), now read κολληγίω(νι).

non-existent? **κολληγίων** 'colleague', from *collēga* 'colleague' + -*ίων*?: papyri perhaps *P.Flor.*
I.91.27 (II AD); perhaps *SB* 9207.7 (II/III AD). Cavenaile (1951:
397, with further references) thinks the reading should be κολλητίων;
Meinersmann (1927: 26) considers κολληγίων a Greek derivation from
κολλήγας (*q.v.*). Daris (1991a: 56), Hofmann (1989: 184 *s.v.* κολλήγας), LSJ
suppl. (*s.v.* κολλητίων).

Direct loan **κολλητίων** (-ωνος/-ονος, ὁ) 'filing clerk' from Latin, but exact word uncertain.
II AD – Byz. Documents: e.g. *P.Laur.* III.64.6 etc. (II AD); *P.Oxy.* 1100.19 (III AD); *SB*
12949.26 (III AD).
Inscriptions: *TAM* v.1.611.21, perhaps 419.11 (III AD), perhaps 154.5.
Post-antique: survives in papyri. Daris (1991a: 56).
Notes: Cervenka-Ehrenstrasser (1996: 53) favours derivation from *glūtinātor*
'papyrus-gluer', Daris (1991a: 56) from *collēctiō* 'gathering', Cavenaile
(1952: 194) from diminutive of *collēctārius* 'banker' (*TLL*) + -ών. Robert
(1943: 114–19), Drew-Bear (1972: 204), Mason (1974: 4, 62), Hofmann
(1989: 184), Cavenaile (1951: 397), LSJ (*s.v.* κολλητίωνες, with definition
'military police-agents'), LSJ suppl. See §4.2.5, §8.2.2, §10.2.1, §10.2.2 N.

κολλικλάριος: see κορνικουλάριος.

not Latin **κολλούριον** 'eye-salve' is sometimes taken as a borrowing of *collūrium*, variant
of *collȳrium* 'eye-salve', itself a borrowing of κολλύριον 'eye-salve' (*TLL s.v.*
collȳrium 1668.1). But κολλύριον is a diminutive of κολλύρα, which can
also appear as κολλούρα, so the ου vowel is not necessarily a sign of Latin
influence: Beekes (2010 *s.v.* κολλύρα), *DÉLG* (*s.v.* κολλύρα). The idea of
Latin influence comes from an early version of Blass *et al.* (1979: §42.4),
which in more recent editions no longer supports it. Hofmann (1989: 184),
Hahn (1906: 263 n. 9).

κολοβιομαφόριον: see μαφόρτης.

κολον(ε)ία: see κολωνία.

not Latin? **Κολονίσιος**, the name of a statue in Antioch, perhaps from *colōnus* 'colonist' (no
*colonisius is attested): Malal. 16.6.43 (VI AD). Hofmann (1989: 185).

κολονός: see κόλων.

Direct loan **κόλων** (-ωνος, ὁ), **κολωνός, κολονός** (-οῦ, ὁ) 'colonist', 'tenant farmer', from
II AD – Byz. *colōnus* 'colonist', 'tenant farmer'.
Documents (all κόλων): *Pap.Agon.* 3.32 etc. (III AD); *P.Herm.Landl.* 2.322
(IV AD).
Inscriptions (usually κόλων): e.g. *SEG* XIV.832.3 (II AD); *SEG* 11.824.2 (III
AD); *I.Ephesos* 1548.16 (III AD); *IGR* III.399.1.
Literature (all κολωνός): Charax, *FHG* III frag. 22.6 (II AD?); Just. *Nov.* 123.35
etc. (VI AD); Antec. 4.15.3 etc., but in Latin script 4.6.7 *colonos* etc. (VI AD).
Arrian, *Acies contra Alanos* 1 (I/II AD, cited by Mason 1974: 109) is proper
name and disputed reading (see version in Jacoby IIB 156 frag. 12.6).
Post-antique (all κολωνός): numerous in legal texts. *LBG* (*s.v.* κολωνός).
Notes: κολωνός may be Classicizing, influenced by κολωνός 'hill'. Millar (2006b:
167), Daris (1991a: 56), Mason (1974: 6, 62, 109), Hofmann (1989: 185),
Zilliacus (1935a: 178–9), LSJ, LSJ suppl. See §4.2.5, §10.2.1, §10.2.2 N, §12.2.1.

rare   **κολωνάριος** 'colonist': with *colōnārius* 'of colonists' (*TLL*) in *Tractatus de manumissionibus*, *CGL* III.51.8 (II AD). *LBG*.

        κολωνείτης: see κολωνίτης.

Direct loan   **κολωνία, κολωνεία, κολον(ε)ία** (-ας, ἡ) 'colony', 'province', 'land allocation', from
I BC – Byz.   *colōnia* 'colony'.

         Documents: e.g. *BGU* II.587.7 etc. (II AD); *SB* 16169.15 (III AD); *BGU*
           I.316.2 (IV AD); *P.Petra* III.23.3 (VI AD).

         Inscriptions: e.g. *SEG* XXXI.952.17 (I BC); *IG* XII.VI.1.186.67 (I AD); *IG*
           XIV.830.40 (II AD); *SEG* XXXVII.1176.2 (II/III AD); *IG* X.II.1.164.6 (III
           AD); *SEG* LII.1367.2 (IV AD).

         Coins: ΑΝΤ. ΚΟΛΩΝΙΑ ΤΥΑΝΩΝ and ΑΥΡ. ΚΟΛΩΝΙΑΣ ΤΥΑΝΩΝ at Tyana, Head 1911:
           753 (II–III AD); ΕΜΙΣΩΝ ΚΟΛΩΝΙΑΣ at Emissa, Head 1911: 780 (III AD);
           ΦΙΛΙΠΠΟΠΟΛΙΤΩΝ ΚΟΛΩΝΙΑΣ S. C. at Philippopolis, Head 1911: 812 (III AD);
           Head 1911: 814, 815.

         Literature: e.g. NT Acts 16:12 (I AD); Jos. *AJ* 19.291 (I AD); perhaps Hdn.
           Pros.Cath. III.1.339.25 (II AD); Ptol. *Geog. passim* (II AD); Dio Cassius
           72.15.2 (II/III AD); Eus. *HE* 5.19.3 (IV AD).

         Post-antique: survives despite absence from lexica.

         Notes: forms derivative μητροκολωνεία. Freyburger-Galland (1997: 37), Daris
           (1991a: 56), Mason (1974: 5, 6, 11, 62, 109–10), Hofmann (1989: 185–6),
           Meinersmann (1927: 26), Lampe (1961), LSJ (*s.vv.* κολωνεία, κολωνία). See
           §4.2.3.1, §4.3.2 n. 75, §4.6.2, §7.3 passage 31, §8.1.5, §9.1 n. 4, §9.3 nn. 21
           and 25, §10.2.1, §10.2.2 D.

rare   **κολωνίτης, κολωνείτης** 'colonist', from *colōnus* 'colonist' + -ίτης: inscription *I.Syria
        PAES* 797¹.2 (I AD). Mason (1974: 6, 62).

Deriv. of loan   **κομακτορία, κομακτορεία, κωμακτορεία** (-ας, ἡ) 'bank', from *coāctor* 'collector of
II–III AD   money' via κομάκτωρ + -ία.

         Documents: *P.Köln* II.83.12 (II AD); perhaps *P.IFAO* I.3.2.5 (II AD); *P.Stras.*
           III.135.12 (II/III AD); *P.Oxy.* 1523.4 (III AD); *CPR* VII.9.220 etc. (III AD).

         Notes: Daris (1991a: 57), Hofmann (1989: 186 *s.v.* κομάκτωρ), LSJ suppl. See
           §4.6.1, §10.2.2 G.

Direct loan   **κομάκτωρ, κοάκτωρ** (-ορος, ὁ), probably 'collector of money', from *coāctor*
I BC? – ?   'collector of money'.

         Documents: *P.Stras.* I.79.3 etc. (I BC).

         Inscriptions: *I.Magnesia* 217.2 (I BC?).

         Literature: Hesych. as lemma κ 3423 (V/VI AD), citing Rhinthon (III BC);
           with *argentarius* and *coactor* in Gloss. Ps.-Philox. 19.22, 102.23.

         Notes: forms derivative κομακτορία. Daris (1991a: 57), Hofmann (1989: 181
           s.v. κοάκτωρ, 186), Meinersmann (1927: 26), *DÉLG*, Frisk (1954–72: 1.907),
           Beekes (2010), *TLL* (*s.v.* 1. *coāctor* 1369.57), LSJ (*s.vv.* κοάκτωρ, κομάκτωρ),
           LSJ suppl. See §4.2.5, §4.6.1, §6.8, §8.1.5, §10.2.1, §10.2.2 G.

foreign   **κομᾶτος** transliterating *comātus* 'long-haired': Dio Cassius, 46.55.5 (II/III AD).
        Freyburger-Galland (1997: 218–19, 1998: 138), Sophocles (1887).

rare   **κομβέντιον**, probably 'gathering', from *conventiō* 'assembly', 'agreement': Malal.
        7.10 (VI AD); cf. Byzantine κονβεντίων 'contract' (*LBG*). Hofmann (1989:
        187), Viscidi (1944: 23), Lampe (1961).

κόμβεντος: see κόνβεντος.

foreign   **κομβίκιον, κονβίκιον** transliterating *convīcium* 'uproar', 'insult': unpublished ostracon O.Dios inv. 1460.13 (II AD); meaning 'assault in public', Antec. in Latin script 4.4.1 *convicion* etc. (VI AD); in latter use also later in Greek script. Zilliacus (1935a: 180–1), *LBG*.

rare   **κομβίνευμα** 'yoking together of horses for racing', from *combīnō* 'combine' (*TLL*) via κομβινεύω + -μα: Ps.-John Chrysostom, *PG* LIX.569.46 (V AD?). Hofmann (1989: 185 *s.v.* κομβινεύειν), Lampe (1961).

rare   **κομβινεύω** 'drive a racing chariot', from *combīnō* 'combine' (*TLL*) + -εύω: Ps.-John Chrysostom, *PG* LIX.569.47 (V AD?). Hofmann (1989: 185), *LBG* (*s.v.* κομπινεύω), Lampe (1961). Cf. κομβίνευμα.

κομεατ-: see κομιατ-.

κομεντ-: see κομμεντ-.

κομερκ-: see κομμερκ-.

κόμες: see κόμης.

κομετᾶτον: see κομιτᾶτον.

Direct loan
II BC – III AD   **κομέτιον, κομίτιον** (-ου, τό) 'assembly', 'place of assembly', 'meeting', from *comitium* 'assembly'.
       Inscriptions: e.g. *IG* VII.2225.2 (II BC); *I.Ephesos* 204.1 (II/I BC); *IGUR* I.1.b4 (I BC).
       Literature: Jos. *AJ* 13.260 (I AD); Plut. *Rom.* 11.2 etc., often marked (I/II AD); Dio Cassius 1.5.7 etc. (II/III AD); Antec. in Latin script 2.10.1 *comitiis* (VI AD).
       Post-antique: occasional examples.
       Notes: Binder (2000: 125), García Domingo (1979: 506), Strobach (1997: 196), Mason (1974: 62), Hofmann (1989: 191–2), LSJ. See §4.2.4.1 n. 54, §4.3.2 n. 75, **§8.1.4**, §8.2.1, §10.2.1, §10.2.2 D.

Direct loan
III AD – modern   **κόμης, κόμες** (-ητος/-ιτος/-ετος, ὁ) 'count', from *comes* 'count' (*TLL s.v.* 1. *comes* 1776.67–1779.70).
       Documents: common, e.g. *P.Oxy.* 43r.ii.17 etc. (III AD); *P.Oxy.* 2267.29 (IV AD); *P.Oxy.* 4394.3 (V AD); *SB* 9616v.30 (VI AD).
       Inscriptions: common, e.g. *IGUR* II.904.6 (III AD); *SEG* XXXV.1537 (IV AD); *MAMA* III.73.4 (IV/V AD); *IG* VII.26.1 (V AD); Bulić and Egger 1926: no. 273.3 (VI AD).
       Literature: common, e.g. Eus. *VC* 3.53.2 (IV AD); Pall. *H.Laus.* 41.3 (IV/V AD); *V.Dan.Styl.* A. 49.11 (V AD); Malal. 7.9.46 (VI AD); Just. *Nov.* 8.5 (VI AD). Unverified example (III AD) in Zilliacus (1937: 322, 330).
       Post-antique: common, forming derivatives κομητόπουλος 'son of a count', etc. *LBG*, Zervan (2019: 81–2), Kriaras (1968– *s.vv.* κόμης, κόμις), Triandaphyllidis (1909: 126), Daris (1991a: 58). Cf. Zilliacus (1937: 338). Modern κόμης 'count' and derivatives: Babiniotis (2002), Andriotis (1967), Meyer (1895: 31).

Notes: forms derivatives κομήτισσα, ἀποκόμης. Binder (2000: 128–9), Avotins (1989, 1992), Daris (1991a: 57–8), Mason (1974: 3, 6, 11, 62), Hofmann (1989: 188–90), Viscidi (1944: 23–4), Zilliacus (1935a: 220–1, 1937: 330), Meinersmann (1927: 27), Immisch (1885: 358–9), *TLL* (*s.v.* 1. *comes*, esp. 1777–9), Lampe (1961), LSJ, LSJ suppl. See §4.2.5, §4.6.1, §8.2.3 n. 51, §10.2.1, §10.2.2 D.

κομητατ-: see κομιτατ-.

κομητ(ε)ιανός: see κομιτιανός.

not ancient?　**κομητικός** 'of a count', from *comes* 'count' via κόμης + -ικός: perhaps only in papyrus *P.Lond.* 1.113.6c.23 (VII AD); doubtful examples include papyrus *P.Leipz.* 13r.6 (III AD); Hesych. κ 3875 (V/VI AD). Hofmann (1989: 189 *s.v.* κόμης), Lampe (1961), LSJ (*s.v.* κόμης).

Deriv. of loan　**κομήτισσα, κομίτισσα** (-ης, ἡ) 'countess', from *comes* 'count' via κόμης + -ισσα.
V AD – Byz.　　Inscriptions: probably only as a name (*IGLS* XXI.II.97.4, 100.a6, both VI AD).
　　Literature: Nil. 2.213.1 etc. (V AD); *V.S.Aux.* 12.2 etc. (VI AD).
　　Post-antique: survives. *LBG.* Modern κόμισσα 'countess' probably separately derived from κόμης: Babiniotis (2002).
　　Notes: derived by *LBG* from medieval *comitissa/cometissa* 'countess' (*DMLBS*), but Cavenaile (1952: 195) must be right that -ισσα was borrowed from Greek into medieval Latin (thence into English and Romance languages). Hofmann (1989: 189 *s.v.* κόμης), Lampe (1961 *s.vv.* κομήτισσα, κομίτισσα). See §4.6.1, §10.2.2 D.

not ancient?　**κομιατάλιον, κομ(μ)εατάλιον** 'vacation money', from neut. subst. of *commeātālis* 'on leave' (*TLL*): papyrus *SB* 9613.1 etc. (VI/VII AD). Daris (1991a: 58), *LBG* (*s.v.* κομιατάλια).

Direct loan　**κομιᾶτον, κομιᾶτος, κομ(μ)εᾶτον, κομ(μ)εᾶτος** (-ου, τό or ὁ) 'leave of absence',
I AD – Byz.　　'supplies', 'reprieve', from *commeātus, -ūs* 'supplies', 'leave of absence'.
　　Documents: common, e.g. *P.Turner* 18.10 (I AD); *P.Mich.* VIII.466.39 (II AD); *P.Oxy.* 1666.14 (III AD); *P.Mich.* X.593.2.10 etc. (IV AD).
　　Literature: Origen, *In Jeremiam* 17.6.27 Nautin (II/III AD); Pall. *H.Laus.* 38.9 (IV/V AD); Hesych. as lemma κ 3449 (V/VI AD).
　　Post-antique: numerous. *LBG* (*s.v.* κομεᾶτον).
　　Notes: Diethart (2006: 15), Daris (1991a: 58), Hofmann (1989: 190), Zilliacus (1935a: 222–3), Meinersmann (1927: 26–7), Immisch (1885: 360), Lampe (1961 *s.v.* κομίατος), LSJ (*s.v.* κομίατον), LSJ suppl. (*s.v.* κομεᾶτος). See §4.2.4.2, §10.2.1, §10.2.2 C.

foreign　**κομῖρε** transliterating inf. of *coeō* 'come together': Plut. *Rom.* 19.10 (I/II AD). Sophocles (1887).

κομίσατον: see κωμισσᾶτον.

non-existent?　**κομισσάριος** is cited as a borrowing of unattested **cōmissārius* by Hofmann (1989: 190) on the basis of a variant in Just. *Nov.* 113.1.1 (VI AD), but the reading κομπρομισσαρίων is better.

Direct loan
IV AD – Byz.

κομιτατήσιος, κομητατήσιος (-α, -ον), 'belonging to the imperial court', as masc. subst. an official, from *comitātēnsis*, an official and a type of soldier (*TLL*).

Documents: *P.Oxy.* 4084.6 (IV AD).

Literature: Thdt. *HE* 252.20 (V AD); Agath. *Arm.* 135.10, 16 (V AD); Lyd. *Mag.* p. 242.24 (VI AD). Unverified example (IV AD) in Zilliacus (1937: 322, 330).

Post-antique: survives. Zervan (2019: 82), *LBG*.

Notes: Hofmann (1989: 190–1), Zilliacus (1937: 330), *TLL* (*s.v. comitātēnsis* 1793.21), Lampe (1961 *s.v.* κομητατήσιος). See §4.2.2, §6.7, §10.2.1, §10.2.2 A.

Direct loan
III AD – Byz.

κομιτᾶτον, κομετᾶτον, κομητᾶτον, κωμιτᾶτον, κομιδᾶτον (-ου, τό) 'staff', 'retinue' (esp. of the emperor), 'imperial court', from *comitātus, -ūs* 'escort', 'attendants', 'court'.

Documents: e.g. *P.Oxy.* 3366.25 (III AD); *ChLA* XLI.1198.8 (III AD); *P.Abinn.* 45.5, 58.7 (both IV AD); *P.Ammon* 1.3.3.26 (IV AD).

Inscriptions: perhaps Heberdey and Kalinka 1897: 2 no. 6.4.

Literature: e.g. Epiph. *Pan.* III.145.18 Koll (IV AD); Pall. *V.Chrys.* 49.14 (IV/V AD); Gel.Cyz. 3.13.15 (V AD); Malal. 13.4 (VI AD); Lyd. *Mag.* p. 94.11 οἱ μὲν γὰρ λεγόμενοι στρατηλάται τὴν τῶν κομίτων ἔχουσιν ἐκ τῆς ἀρχαιότητος καὶ μόνην τιμήν (ταύτῃ καὶ κομιτιανοὺς τοὺς δευτεροστρατηλατιανοὺς ἡ παλαιότης οἶδεν· κόμιτας δὲ τοὺς φίλους καὶ συνεκδήμους Ἰταλοὶ λέγουσι καὶ κομιτᾶτον ἁπλῶς τὴν βασιλέως συνοδίαν) (VI AD).

Post-antique: survives. Sophocles (1887 *s.v.* κομιτᾶτος), Triandaphyllidis (1909: 127), *LBG* (*s.v.* κομητᾶτον 'county'). Modern κομιτᾶτο 'committee' is from Italian: Babiniotis (2002), Andriotis (1967).

Notes: usually (e.g. LSJ suppl.) given as masculine κομιτᾶτος, but many examples are unambiguously neuter and none unambiguously masculine. Binder (2000: 132, 242, with superseded reading of Pall.), Diethart (2006: 13), Daris (1991a: 58), Hofmann (1989: 191), Zilliacus (1935a: 222–3), Meinersmann (1927: 27), Lampe (1961). See §4.2.4.2, §6.7, §10.2.1, §10.2.2 A.

Direct loan
V AD – Byz.

κομιτιανός, κομητ(ε)ιανός (-ή, -όν) 'of a count', as masc. subst. an official, from *comitiānus* 'of a count' (*TLL*).

Documents: *P.Ant.* II.92.20 (IV/V AD).

Inscriptions: perhaps *I.Chr.Macédoine* 240.2 (IV/V AD).

Literature: Thdt. *Ep.Sirm.* 42.45, 50 (V AD); *ACO* II.I.III p. 17.4 etc. (V AD); Lyd. *Mag.* p. 94.9 (VI AD); Just. *Nov.* 8.2 etc. (VI AD).

Post-antique: survives. *LBG*.

Notes: Avotins (1992 *s.v.* κομητιανός), Daris (1991a: 58, with derivation from *comes*), Hofmann (1989: 191), Viscidi (1944: 24, with derivation from κόμης), Zilliacus (1935a: 178–9), *TLL* (*s.v. comitiānus* 1799.65–8, 82), Lampe (1961 *s.v.* κομητιανός). See §4.2.2, §10.2.1, §10.2.2 D.

κομίτιον: see κομέτιον.

κομίτισσα: see κομήτισσα.

not ancient? κομιτοτριβοῦνος, from *comes tribūnus*, a title: no certainly ancient examples.
Filos (2010: 250), Daris (1991a: 58), Hofmann (1989: 446 *s.v.* τριβοῦνος),
Zilliacus (1935a: 222–3), Meinersmann (1927: 28).

κομμεατ-: see κομιατ-.

κομμέντα: see κομμέντον.

Direct loan
III AD – Byz.

κομ(μ)ενταρήσιος, κομ(μ)ενταρίσιος, κομενταρήνσιος, κομμετ- (-ου, ὁ) 'secretary',
'accountant', 'registrar', from *commentāriēnsis* 'secretary'.
Documents: e.g. *SB* 12949.27 (III AD); *P.Herm.Landl.* 1.540 etc. (IV AD);
BGU XII.2162.2 ἀπὸ κομμενταρησίων (V AD); *PSI* VIII.891.9 (V/VI AD);
P.Cair.Masp. 67090.1 (VI AD).
Inscriptions: perhaps *I.Ephesos* 3054.9 (III AD); *SEG* XXXII.1554.A18
(VI AD); perhaps *I.Ephesos* 1989A; Calder 1912a: 88 no. 7; Sterrett 1888b:
172 no. 280.1 ἀπὸ κομενταρηνσίων.
Literature: e.g. Athan. *Apol.Sec.* 8.3 (IV AD); Basil Caesariensis, *Epistulae* 286.1
Courtonne (IV AD); Marc.Diac. 99 (V AD); EphraemSyr. VII p. 196.9
(V/VI AD); Hesych. as lemma κ 3441 (V/VI AD); Just. *Nov.* 13.1.2 (VI AD);
Lyd. *Mag.* p. 136.26 (VI AD). Unverified examples (III AD) in Zilliacus
(1937: 322–3, 330).
Post-antique: survives. *LBG*.
Notes: seems to combine *commentariensis* with *a commentariis* 'secretary'.
Bartalucci (1995: 116), Avotins (1992), Daris (1991a: 58), Mason (1974:
62, 142), Hofmann (1989: 192–3), Zilliacus (1935a: 178–9, 1937: 330),
Meinersmann (1927: 27), Immisch (1885: 358), Lampe (1961 *s.v.*
κομενταρήσιος), LSJ suppl. See §4.2.5, §4.4, §6.7 n. 45, §10.2.1, §10.2.2 N;
cf. ἀκομενταρήσιος.

Direct loan
II AD – Byz.

κομ(μ)εντάριον (-ου, τό) 'shorthand', 'magistrate's court', from *commentārium*
'notes' (*OLD s.v. commentārius* 4).
Documents: *P.Oxy.* 724.8 (II AD); tachygraphy in Menci 2000: 283 (III/IV AD).
Inscriptions: perhaps *I.Ephesos* 3054.9 (III AD); perhaps *I.Ephesos* 1989A;
perhaps *SEG* XXXIII.896.6.
Literature: Athan. *Apol.Const.* 29.3, marked (IV AD).
Post-antique: survives. *LBG* (*s.v.* κομμεντάριος).
Notes: sometimes cited as κομμεντάριος, but clearly neut. in antiquity. Menci
(2000: 283–4), Daris (1991a: 58), Hofmann (1989: 187–8), Zilliacus
(1935a: 178–9), Meinersmann (1927: 27), Lampe (1961 *s.v.* κομεντάριον),
LSJ suppl. See §4.2.4.1 n. 54, §10.2.1, §10.2.2 O; cf. ἀκομενταρήσιος.

Direct loan
IV AD – Byz.

κομ(μ)έντον (-ου, τό) 'records', from *commentum* 'comment' (*TLL*).
Documents: *P.Bagnall* 27.4 (IV AD); *PSI* VIII.951.2 (IV AD); *CPR* XIV.39.19
(V AD); *P.Oxy.* 1877.2 etc. (V AD); *P.Wisc.* II.63.2 (V AD); *P.Oxy.* 1837.12
(VI AD); perhaps *PSI* I.97r.6 (VI AD).
Literature: Basil Medicus, *PG* XXX.733c, marked (IV AD); Lyd. *Mag.* p. 160.15 etc.,
marked (VI AD). Unverified example (III AD) in Zilliacus (1937: 323, 330).
Post-antique: survives. Sophocles (1887).
Notes: in papyri usually part of title βοηθὸς τῶν κομμέντων = *adiutor e
commentariis*. Daris (1991a: 59), Hofmann (1989: 193–4), Viscidi (1944:
20, 23), Zilliacus (1935a: 178–9, 1937: 330), Meinersmann (1927: 27), LSJ
suppl. (*s.v.* κομμέντα). See §4.2.4.1 n. 55, §10.2.1, §10.2.2 O.

**Direct loan
VI AD – Byz.**

κομ(μ)ερκιάριος (-ου, ὁ) 'merchant', 'tax collector', 'official silk-trader' from *commerciārius* 'merchant' (*TLL*).

Inscriptions: perhaps *IGLS* XIII.1.9046.12 (V/VI AD); *SEG* XXXII.1554.A5 (VI AD); perhaps *SEG* XX.390.2 (VI AD); perhaps *IGLS* IV.1473.2 (VI AD).

Literature: Malal. 16.6 (VI AD); Just. *App.* 5 = p. 798.15 etc. (VI AD).

Post-antique: survives. *LBG*, Kriaras (1968– *s.v.* κομμερκιάρης), Triandaphyllidis (1909: 124), Zilliacus (1937: 330).

Notes: Oikonomidès (1986), Avotins (1992), Hofmann (1989: 194), Zilliacus (1935a: 178–9), *TLL* (*s.v. commerciārius* 1871.62–70), Lampe (1961), LSJ suppl. See §4.2.4.1 n. 50, §10.2.1, §10.2.2 G.

foreign

κομ(μ)έρκιον 'right to acquire something', from *commercium* 'trade': Antec. in Latin script 2.20.4 *commercion* etc. (VI AD). Triantaphyllides (1892: 264), Triandaphyllidis (1909: 124, 127). Probably independently, κομ(μ)έρκιον 'trade', from *commercium* 'trade': cited by Daris (1991a: 59), Zilliacus (1935a: 178–9), LSJ suppl. on the basis of a superseded reading (*BL* X.224) of papyrus *SB* 13930.1 (VI/VII AD); also on inscription Dumont and Homolle 1892: 404 no.76[23]. Numerous Byzantine examples (Lampe 1961, *LBG*, Zervan 2019: 82–3, Kriaras 1968–) and modern dialectal κουμ(μ)έρκι (Andriotis 1974: 325; Meyer 1895: 34) mean 'toll' or 'tax'.

κομμεταρή(ν)σιος: see κομμενταρήσιος.

not ancient

κομμισσόριος, κομμισσώριος 'containing a forfeiture clause', from *commissōrius* 'containing a forfeiture clause': no ancient examples. Zilliacus (1935a: 178–9), *LBG*.

foreign

κομμιτεύω, κομμιττεύω 'come into effect', from *committō* 'begin' + -εύω: Antec. in Latin script 3.17.2 *committeuetai* 'an action lies' (VI AD); perhaps *Schol. Sinai.* in Latin script 24 *committere* or *committeuθῆναι* (V/VI AD); later in Greek script. Zilliacus (1935a: 178–9), *LBG*. See §7.1.2, §9.5.6 nn. 56 and 68.

foreign

κομμοδᾶτος 'lent', from *commodātus* (pf. part. of *commodō* 'lend'): Antec. in Latin script 3.14.2 *commodaton* 'loan for use' etc. (VI AD); later in Greek script. Zilliacus (1935a: 178–9), *LBG*. See §7.2.2 with passage 28, §9.5.6 n. 68.

κομμόδιον: see κομόδιον.

**Direct loan
V AD – Byz.**

κομ(μ)ονιτώριον, κομ(μ)ωνιτώριον, κομονιδώριον, κομμουνιτώριον, κομονητούριον (-ου, τό) 'letter of instruction' (esp. from the emperor), from *commonitōrium* 'emperor's orders' (*TLL s.v. commonitorius* 1934.17, 1934.81–1935.12).

Documents: *P.Mert.* 1.45r.1 (V/VI AD); *SB* 14674.11 (V/VI AD); *P.Oxy.* 1106.1 etc. (VI AD); *P.Lond.* V.1680.22 (VI AD); *P.Cair.Masp.* 67058.3.12, 67282.1 etc., 67330.2.15 (all VI AD).

Inscriptions: Marek 1993: 191, Appendix 6 no. 10.5 (VI AD); *I.Ephesos* 1333.10.

Literature: *ACO* II.1.1 p. 96.32, II.1.3 p. 20.9 (V AD); *Carth.* 201.4 (V AD); Just. *Codex* 1.4.26.5 etc., *Nov.* 128.17 etc., but in Latin script 31.2 etc. (VI AD); Evagr.Schol. *HE* 71.23 (VI AD).

Post-antique: limited survival. Sophocles (1887).

Notes: Avotins (1989, 1992), Daris (1991a: 59), Hofmann (1989: 194–5), Zilliacus (1935a: 178–9), Meinersmann (1927: 27), *TLL* (*s.v. commonitorius* 1934.17–20, 1935.8–12), Lampe (1961), LSJ suppl. See §4.2.4.1 n. 54, §10.2.1, §10.2.2 A.

κομμουλᾶτος: see κουμουλᾶτος.

foreign	**κομ(μ)οῦνις** 'both praetorial and judicial' (of legal stipulations), from *commūnis* 'common', 'shared': Antec. in Latin script 3.18.pr. *communes* etc. (VI AD). Zilliacus (1935a: 178–9).

κομμουνιτώριον, κομμωνιτώριον: see κομμονιτώριον.

rare	**κομοδάριον**, from *commodum* 'reward' via κομόδιον + -άριον: unpublished ostracon O.Dios inv. 25.9 (II AD).
Direct loan with suffix **III AD – Byz.**	**κομόδιον, κομμόδιον, κωμόδιον** (-ου, τό) 'gratuity', from *commodum* 'reward' + -ιον. Documents: *P.Bodl.* 166.19 etc. (III AD); perhaps *O.Mich.* III.976.5 (III/IV AD); *P.Oxy.* 3874.32 etc. (IV AD); *BGU* I.21r.2.15 etc. (IV AD); *P.Oxy.* 3358v.4, 3424.3 (both IV AD); *Stud.Pal.* XX.96.11 (IV AD); *PSI* XIII.1366.7 (IV/V AD); *P.Oxy.* 3864.12 (V AD). Post-antique: survives with meaning 'bribe'. *LBG* (*s.v.* κομμόδιον). Notes: Daris (1991a: 59), Meinersmann (1927: 28, 31), LSJ suppl. See §4.3.2, §8.2.2, §9.2, §10.2.1, §10.2.2 G.

κομονητούριον, κομονιδώριον, κομονιτώριον: see κομμονιτώριον.

rare	**κομονοπλάρις** 'fellow soldier', from *commanipulāris* 'fellow soldier': ostracon O.Did. 325.8 etc. (I AD). Commentary *ad loc.* Cf. μανιπλάριος.

κομοῦνις: see κομμοῦνις.

foreign	**κομπενσατεύω, κομπεσ(σ)ατεύω** 'offset one debt against another', from *compēnsātus* (pf. part. of *compēnsō* 'balance') + -εύω: *Schol.Sinai.* in Latin script 18 *compensateúetai* (V/VI AD); Antec. in Latin script 4.6.30 *compensateusas* (VI AD); later in Greek script. Zilliacus (1935a: 178–9), *LBG* (*s.v.* κομπεσατεύω). See §7.1.2, §7.1.3, §9.5.6 n. 56.
foreign	**κομπενσατίων, κομπεσ(σ)ατίων** 'offsetting one debt against another', from *compēnsātiō* 'balancing': Antec. in Latin script 4.6.30 *compensationa* etc. (VI AD); later in Greek script. Zilliacus (1935a: 178–9), *LBG* (*s.v.* κομπεσσατίων).

κομπινεύω: see κομβινεύω.

foreign	**Κομπιτάλια** transliterating *Compitālia*, a festival: DH *AR* 4.14.4 (I BC). Hofmann (1989: 195).
foreign	**κόμπιτος** (in acc. pl. κομπίτους) transliterating *compitum* 'crossroads': DH *AR* 4.14.4 (I BC). Hofmann (1989: 195).
not ancient	**κομπλατεύω** 'authenticate', from *complētus, -ūs* 'completion' (*TLL s.v.* 1. *complētus*) + -εύω: no ancient examples. Zilliacus (1935a: 180–1 *s.v.* κομπλετεύειν), *LBG*.

rare	**κομπλατίων, κομπλητίων** 'formality', 'ratification', 'authentication', from *complētiō* 'completion' (*TLL*): Lyd. *Mag.* p. 142.22 (VI AD); Antec. in Latin script 3.23.pr. *complationes* (VI AD); Byzantine texts. Zilliacus (1935a: 180–1 *s.v.* κομπλετίων), *LBG*, Lampe (1961).
rare	**κομπλεύσιμος** 'concerning writing out (legal documents)', as masc. subst. 'one who writes out (legal documents)', as neut. subst. 'writing out (of a legal document)': probably from *compleō* 'fill' (via κομπλεύω?) + -(ευ)σιμος. Neut. subst.: inscription *SEG* LIII.1841.iii.7 (V AD); masc. subst.: Lyd. *Mag.* p. 170.25 (VI AD). Di Segni *et al.* (2003: 290), Hofmann (1989: 195 *s.v.* κομπλεύειν), LSJ suppl.
non-existent	**κομπλευτήρ** 'one who writes out (legal documents)': superseded interpretation of κόμπλευτρον, *q.v.*
rare	**κόμπλευτρον** 'writing out (of legal documents)', apparently from *compleō* 'fill' (via κομπλεύω?) + -(ευ)τρον: inscription *SEG* LIII.1841.i.15 (V AD). *SEG ad loc.*, Feissel (2004: 684), Di Segni *et al.* (2003: 285–6, with superseded interpretation κομπλευτήρ).
rare	**κομπλεύω** 'fill out', 'complete' (of documents), probably from *compleō* 'fill' + -εύω: papyrus *P.Giss.Univ.* III.33.2 (VI AD). Daris (1991a: 59), Hofmann (1989: 195), LSJ suppl. Cf. κομπλεύσιμος.
	κομπλητίων: see κομπλατίων.
rare	**κομπρομισ(σ)άριος** '(judge) of an arbitrated compromise', from *comprōmissārius* '(judge) accepted as arbitrator by both parties': Just. *Nov.* 113.1.1, but in Latin script 82.11.1 (VI AD); Byzantine texts. Avotins (1992), Hofmann (1989: 195), Zilliacus (1935a: 180–1), *LBG*, LSJ suppl. See §9.5.6 n. 68.
Direct loan V AD – Byz.	**κομπρόμισσον** (-ου, τό) 'arbitrated compromise', from *comprōmissum* 'joint promise to abide by the decision of an arbitrator'. Documents: *P.Genova* I.23.7 (IV/V AD); *P.Lond.* III.992.3 etc., V.1707.2 (both VI AD); *SB* 4673.2 (VI AD); *CPR* VI.8.4 (VI AD). *P.Erl.* 74.6 is VII AD (Kovarik 2019: 251). Literature: Just. *Nov.* 113.1.1 (VI AD). Post-antique: numerous in legal texts despite absence from lexica. Notes: Avotins (1992), Daris (1991a: 59), Hofmann (1989: 195), Zilliacus (1935a: 180–1), Meinersmann (1927: 28), LSJ suppl. See §4.2.4.1 n. 55, §10.2.1, §10.2.2 B.
rare	**κόμτον, κόμπτον** 'piece of jewellery', from *cōmptus* 'adorned': papyrus *P.Oxy.* 995 (V AD?). Daris (1991a: 59), *LBG*.
rare	**κομφέκτωρ** 'killer', from *cōnfector* 'destroyer': *Martyrium Polycarpi* 16.1 in Musurillo 1972 (III AD?); Eus. *HE* 4.15.39 (IV AD); Byzantine texts. Unverified example (II AD) in Zilliacus (1937: 322, 330). Hofmann (1989: 196), *LBG*, Lampe (1961).

foreign κομφεσ(σ)όριος, κονφεσσώριος 'relating to a confession' is a Byzantine borrowing (*LBG*); *comfessorios* 'positive' (of legal actions), Antec. in Latin script 4.6.2 *comfessorios* (VI AD), may be its earliest appearance or a separate borrowing from *cōnfessōrius*, which could mean both 'based on a confession' and 'claiming a right', 'positive' (cf. *OLD*). Zilliacus (1935a: 180–1), Triantaphyllides (1892: 264). See §10.3.1 n. 30.

Direct loan with suffix
VI AD – Byz. κομφιρματεύω, κονφιρματεύω 'confirm', from *cōnfirmātus* (pf. part. of *cōnfirmō* 'strengthen') + -εύω.
Documents: *P.Cair.Masp.* 67312.33 (VI AD); *P.Cair.Masp.* 67151.65 in Latin script, *comfirmateumenous* (VI AD).
Literature: Just. *Nov.* 89.14 in Latin script (VI AD); Antec. in Latin script 2.25.1 '*econfirmateusen* etc. (VI AD).
Post-antique: numerous in legal texts. *LBG*.
Notes: Fournet (2019: 81–2), Mandilaras (1973: 67), Daris (1991a: 59), Hofmann (1989: 196), Zilliacus (1935a: 180–1), Meinersmann (1927: 28). See §4.3.1, §8.2.2, §9.5.6 n. 68, §10.2.1, §10.2.2 B, §10.3.1.

foreign κομφιρματίων, κονφιρματίων 'confirmation', from *cōnfirmātiō* 'confirmation': Antec. in Latin script 2.25.1 *comfirmationos* (VI AD); later in Greek script. Zilliacus (1935a: 180–1), *LBG*. See §9.5.6 n. 68.

foreign κομφουσίων, κονφουσίων 'merger', from *cōnfūsiō* 'mixing': Antec. in Latin script 2.20.32 *confusion* (VI AD); later in Greek script. Zilliacus (1935a: 180–1), *LBG*. See §9.5.6 n. 68.

κομωνιτώριον: see κομμονιτώριον.

rare κοναμέντον, κοναπμέντον 'garden fork', from *cōnāmentum*, a garden implement: papyrus *SB* 14205.1 (VI AD). Diethart (1990a: 91, 1991b: 121), *LBG*.

rare κονβενταρχέω 'run an assembly', from *conventus* 'assembly' via κόνβεντος + -αρχέω 'be in charge of' (cf. -άρχης): inscription *I.Hierapolis Judeich* 32.15 (III AD or earlier). Mason (1974: 6, 62), Hofmann (1989: 196 *s.v.* κόνβεντος), LSJ.

foreign κονβεντιονάλιος 'concerning a contract', from *conventiōnālis* 'based upon an agreement': Antec. in Latin script 3.18.3 *conventionaliae* etc. (VI AD); later in Greek script. Hofmann (1989: 196), Zilliacus (1935a: 180–1), *LBG* (with derivation from *conventiō* 'agreement' via κονβεντίων, *q.v.*). See §7.2.1.

foreign κονβεντίων 'contract', from *conventiō* 'agreement': Thüngen 2016: B7 in Latin script (V AD); Byzantine texts. Zilliacus (1935a: 180–1), *LBG*.

Direct loan
V AD – Byz. κόνβεντος, κόμβεντος (-ου, ὁ) 'assembly', 'Roman community in a non-Roman town', from *conventus, -ūs* 'assembly', 'Roman community in a non-Roman town'.
Inscriptions: *TAM* V.II.1002.7.
Literature: *V.Dan.Styl.* A. 55.7 (V AD); Malal. 5.7.29 etc. (VI AD); Lyd. *Mens.* 1.30.3, marked (VI AD); Antec. in Latin script 1.6.4 *conventos* 'fixed time appointed for the settlement of lawsuits' etc. (VI AD).
Post-antique: survives. *LBG* (*s.vv.* κονβέντος, κονβέντον), Zervan (2019: 83–4), Triandaphyllidis (1909: 127).

Notes: Binder (2000: 244–5), Diethart (2006: 15), Mason (1974: 6, 62),
Hofmann (1989: 187, 196), Viscidi (1944: 23), Zilliacus (1935a: 180–1),
Lampe (1961 *s.v.* κόμβεντος), LSJ suppl. See §4.2.4.2, §10.2.1, §10.2.2 O; cf.
κομβέντιον, κουβέντα.

κονβίκιον: see κομβίκιον.

κονγιάριον: see κογγιάριον.

κονδειτ-: see κονδιτ-.

foreign **κονδεμνατίων** 'condemnation', from *condemnātiō* 'condemnation': Antec. in Latin
script 4.10.2 *condemnationa* (VI AD); later in Greek script. Zilliacus (1935a:
180–1), *LBG*. See §9.5.6 n. 68.

foreign **κόνδερε** transliterating inf. of *condō* 'hide': Lyd. *Mag.* p. 46.10 (VI AD).

κονδηταρία: see κονδιταρία.

foreign *condīcō* 'give notice': Antec. 4.6.15 *condicere* (VI AD).

not ancient **κονδικτικεύω** 'reclaim', from *condīcō* 'claim redress' and/or *condictīcius* 'relating
to the reclaiming of property' via κονδικτίκιος + -εύω: no ancient examples.
Zilliacus (1935a: 180–1), *LBG*.

foreign **κονδικτίκιος**, a legal action (*condictiō*, a claim for restitution), from *condictīcius*
'relating to the reclaiming of property': in Latin script in legal texts, e.g.
Antec. 4.6.15 *condicticioi* (VI AD); Just. *Codex* 1.3.45.6, *Nov.* 162.1.2 (VI
AD); later in Greek script. Avotins (1989, 1992), Zilliacus (1935a: 180–1),
LBG, LSJ suppl. See §9.5.6 n. 68.

rare **κονδιταρία, κονδηταρία, κονδειταρία** 'female maker/seller of spiced wine',
'proprietress of a spiced-wine bar', from *condītārius* 'dealer in preserved
foods' via κονδιτάριος: inscription Orsi 1893: 309 no. 129 (V AD);
post-antique papyrus. Kramer (1997: 554), Daris (1957: 100, 1962:
137–8, 1991a: 59, with derivation from *condītāria*), *LBG*, LSJ suppl. (*s.v.*
κονδιτάριος). See §6.2 n. 13.

Direct loan **κονδιτάριος** (-ου, ὁ) 'maker/seller of spiced wine', 'proprietor of a spiced-wine
V–VI AD bar', from *condītārius* 'dealer in preserved foods'.
Documents: *CPR* x.39.7 etc. (V AD); *P.Mich.* xv.740.14 etc. (VI AD); *P.Mil.*
II.71.1 (VI AD).
Notes: forms derivative κονδιταρία. Kramer (1997: 553–4), Daris (1957: 100–1,
1991a: 59), Hofmann (1989: 196), LSJ suppl. See §4.2.4.1 n. 50, §10.2.1,
§10.2.2 I.

Direct loan **κονδῖτον, κονδεῖτον** (-ου, τό) 'spiced wine', from *condītum*, neuter (to agree with
IV AD – Byz. *vīnum*: cf. *TLL s.v. condio* 143.13–23) of *condītus* 'seasoned'.
Documents: *P.Ryl.* IV.629.367 (IV AD); *Stud.Pal.* xx.107.r4 (IV AD); *SB*
14226.17 (IV/V AD); Maravela-Solbakk 2009: 129.7 (V/VI AD); *P.Ant.*
II.64.4 (VI AD); Andorlini 2001: no. 15.3 (VI AD).
Inscriptions: Edict.Diocl. 2.17 (IV AD).
Literature: common, e.g. Cyran. 2.24.36 (II AD?); Orib. *Col.* 5.33.8 (IV AD);
Geront. *V.Mel.* 2.22.10 (V AD); Aëtius 3.112.3 (VI AD); Simplicius,
Commentarius in Epicteti enchiridion p. 4.15 Hadot (VI AD); Ps.-Galen
XIV.383.8 Kühn.

Post-antique: numerous. Kriaras (1968–), Sophocles (1887).

Notes: in Greek terms not substantivization of κονδῖτος 1 but a separate, earlier borrowing. Kramer (1997: 549–51 = 2011: 232–3) demonstrates that *Stud. Pal.* xx.107 is this rather than κονδῖτος 1 and argues that Ps.-Macar. *Hom. Spir.* 16.140 (v ad?) is not this but κονδῖτος 2. Maravela-Solbakk (2009: 132, 2010: 255–6), Kramer (1997 = 2011: 229–39), Andorlini (2001: 167–8), Daris (1991a: 59), Hofmann (1989: 196), *TLL* (*s.v. condio* 143.13), Lampe (1961 *s.v.* κονδῖτος), LSJ suppl. See §4.2.4.1, §6.5, §10.2.1, §10.2.2 I, §12.2.1.

rare	**κονδῖτος 1**, **κονδεῖτος** 'spiced', from *condītus* 'seasoned': Ps.-Athanasius, *PG* xxviii.1157b (iv ad?); Aëtius 11.13.18 (vi ad); perhaps papyrus *Stud. Pal.* viii.967.4 (vi ad). Kramer (1997: 549–50, 552–3 = 2011: 232, 235–6), Daris (1991a: 59), Hofmann (1989: 197, but including examples of κονδῖτον), Meinersmann (1927: 28), Lampe (1961). See §12.2.1; cf. σαλακονδεῖτον.
not ancient?	**κονδῖτος 2** 'spice', from *condītus* 'seasoned': perhaps papyrus *Stud.Pal.* viii.967.4 (vi ad); perhaps Ps.-Macar. *Hom.Spir.* 16.140 (v ad?); Byzantine texts. Kramer (1997: 549–50, 552–3 = 2011: 232–3, 235–6), Kriaras (1968–).
non-existent	**κονδίτωρ** 'baker of spiced baked goods', from *condītor* 'one who seasons': superseded reading of papyrus *Stud.Pal.* viii.967.4 (vi ad). Hofmann (1989: 197), Meinersmann (1927: 28).
	κονδοβράκιν: see κοντοβράκιον.
	κονδόκτωρ: see κονδούκτωρ.
foreign	**κονδοῦκτι** 'of hiring', from *conductī*, gen. of *conductum* 'lease': Antec. in Latin script 3.24.pr. *conducti* etc. (vi ad); later in Greek script. *LBG* (*s.v.* κονδοῦκτος).
not ancient	**κονδουκτίων** 'lease contract', from *conductiō* 'renting': no ancient examples. Zilliacus (1935a: 180–1), *LBG*.
rare	**κονδουκτορία** 'office of contractors', from *conductor* 'contractor' via κονδούκτωρ + -ία: papyri *P.Oxy.* 900.6 etc., 2110.4 (both iv ad). Daris (1991a: 59, with derivation from *conductoria*), Hofmann (1989: 197 *s.v.* κονδούκτωρ), Meinersmann (1927: 28), LSJ suppl.
rare	**κονδουκτορικόν**, **κουνδουκτορικόν**, a tax, probably from *conductor* 'contractor' via κονδούκτωρ + -ικός, neut. subst.: ostracon *O.Bodl.* ii.2066.5 (iv ad). Daris (1991a: 60, with derivation from *conductoria*), *LBG*.
Deriv. of loan III–IV AD	**κονδουκτόριον** (-ου, τό) 'board of contractors', probably from *conductor* 'contractor' via κονδούκτωρ + -ιον. Documents: *SB* 15603.10 (iii ad); *P.Oxy.* 2115.3 (iv ad); *SB* 14507.45 (iv ad). Notes: both the provenanced examples are from the region of Oxyrhynchus. Implausibly derived by Cavenaile (1952: 197, followed by Daris 1991a: 60) from medieval fem. *conductoria* 'contractor's district' (Du Cange 1883–7) reinterpreted as plural. Hofmann (1989: 197, with derivation from unattested *conductorium), Cavenaile (1951: 397), LSJ suppl. See §4.6.1, §9.2, §10.2.2 O.

rare   **κονδούκτρια** 'contractor (fem.)', probably meaning a keeper of prostitutes, from *conductor* 'contractor' via κονδούκτωρ: ostracon *O.Did.* 401.7 (II AD). Editor *ad loc.* connects it to ἡ κονδούκτριξ and τὴν κονδούκτοραν on unpublished ostraca from Krokodilo: three ways of forming a feminine of κονδούκτωρ.

Direct loan   **κονδ(ο)ύκτωρ, κονδόκτωρ, κονδούκτορ, κοντούκτωρ, κωντούκτωρ** (-ορος/-ωρος,
I–VI AD   ὁ) 'contractor', from *conductor* 'contractor'.
         Documents: e.g. *O.Did.* 54.1 (I AD); *O.Krok.* II.184.11 (I/II AD); *P.Bagnall* 12.10 (II AD); *P.Panop.Beatty* 1.60 etc. (III AD); *P.Oxy.* 2115.6 (IV AD); *P.Mich.* XI.624.24 (VI AD).
         Literature: Hesych. as lemma κ 3498 (V/VI AD).
         Notes: forms derivatives κονδουκτόριον, κονδουκτορία, κονδουκτορικόν, κονδούκτρια. Schubert (1988: 174), commentary on *P.Bagnall* 12, Daris (1991a: 60), Hofmann (1989: 197), Cavenaile (1951: 397), Immisch (1885: 354–5), LSJ suppl. See §4.2.5, §4.6.1, §6.8, §10.2.1, §10.2.2 N.

         κονδυβέρνιον: κοντουβέρνιον.

not ancient?   **κονδωμῆνος, κονδῶμος**, meaning uncertain, perhaps from *conduma/condoma* 'household (?)' (*TLL*), medieval *condominus* 'joint lord' (*DMLBS*), or unattested **condominum*: inscription *MAMA* III.486.3, 486.6. Editor *ad loc.*, Cameron (1931: 243), Lampe (1961 *s.vv.* κονδωμῆνος, κονδῶμος), Hofmann (1989: 198).

         κόνικλος: see κουνίκολος.

foreign   **κονιοῦγκτιμ** 'jointly', 'all together' (e.g. of conditions that must all be fulfilled for a clause to take effect), from *coniunctim* 'jointly': Antec. in Latin script 2.14.11 *coniunctim* etc. (VI AD); later in Greek script. *LBG* (*s.v.* κονιοῦγκτος).

non-existent?   **κονκορδιε**, or κονκορδι corrected to κονκορδε, perhaps for *concordē* 'amicably': *O.Claud.* II.312.8 (II AD), where editor originally read Κονκορδία but now (personal communication) sees -ε.

non-existent   **κονκουράτωρ** 'joint guardian', from *concūrātor* 'joint guardian': superseded reading of Antec. 1.24.1 (VI AD), now συγκουράτωρ (*q.v.*). Zilliacus (1935a: 180–1).

rare   **κοννολῆνγος**, apparently used for *cunnilingus* on graffito *SEG* LXII.148.3 (II AD?): see *SEG ad loc.*

         κονρήκτωρ: see κορρήκτωρ.

         κονσανγυίνεος: see κωνσανγυίναιος.

         κονσεκρατίων: see κωνσεκρατίων.

foreign   **κονσένσο(υ)** 'by agreement', from *cōnsēnsū*, abl. of *cōnsēnsus, -ūs* 'agreement': Antec. in Latin script 3.22.1 *consensu* etc. (VI AD); later in Greek script. Zilliacus (1935a: 180–1 *s.v.* κονσένσος), *LBG* (*s.v.* κονσένσος). See **§7.2.2** with passage 29.

         κονσίλια: see κωνσίλιον, Κωνσουάλια.

not ancient   **κονσιλιάριος** 'adviser', from *cōnsiliārius* 'adviser': inscription *IG* XIV.2263.2, now
         dated after AD 600 (*SEG* L.1045). Hofmann (1989: 198), *LBG*, Lampe
         (1961).

         κονσίλιον: see κωνσίλιον.

rare   **κονσιστοριανός** 'of the imperial assembly', from *cōnsistōriānus* 'of the emperor's
         council' (*TLL*): Procopius of Gaza, *Epistulae* 45.11 Garzya and Loenertz
         (VI AD); Just. *Nov.* in Latin script 13.3 (VI AD); Byzantine texts. Hofmann
         (1989: 198), Zilliacus (1935a: 180–1), *LBG*, Lampe (1961).

Direct loan   **κονσιστώριον, κονσιστόριον, κωνσιστώριον** (-ου, τό) 'imperial assembly', from
IV AD – Byz.   *cōnsistōrium* 'place of assembly', 'emperor's council' (*TLL*).
         Documents: e.g. *SB* 16262.3 (IV AD); *P.Oxy.* 4696.4 (V AD); *P.Rain.Cent.*
         123.5 (V AD); *P.Ross.Georg.* III.37.4 (VI AD); *PSI* VIII.933.3 (VI AD).
         Inscriptions: *I.Philae* 194.3 (V AD).
         Literature: *ACO* I.I.III p. 37.18 etc. (V AD); *ACO* II.I.I p. 65.16 (V AD); Marc.
         Diac. 51 (V AD); Procopius of Gaza, *Epistulae* 45.6 Garzya and Loenertz
         (V/VI AD); Hesych. as lemma κ 3537 (V/VI AD); Cyr.S. *Vit.Sab.* 142.15
         (VI AD).
         Post-antique: common. Sophocles (1887 *s.v.* κωνσιστώριον), Triandaphyllidis
         (1909: 127).
         Notes: Daris (1991a: 60), Hofmann (1989: 198), Zilliacus (1935a: 180–1),
         Meinersmann (1927: 28), Immisch (1885: 359), Lampe (1961), LSJ suppl.
         See §4.2.4.1 n. 54, §10.2.1, §10.2.2 A.

foreign   **κονσοβρῖνα** 'cousin', from *cōnsobrīna* 'daughter of one's maternal aunt': Antec. in
         Latin script 3.6.4 *consobrina* etc. (VI AD). Sophocles (1887).

foreign   **κονσοβρῖνος, κονσωβρῖνος** 'cousin', from *cōnsobrīnus* 'son of one's maternal aunt':
         Antec. in Latin script 3.6.4 *consobrinos* etc. (VI AD); later in Greek script.
         Zilliacus (1935a: 180–1), *LBG*.

foreign   **κονσολιδατίων** 'merger', from *cōnsolidātiō* 'merger of usufruct in property':
         Antec. in Latin script 2.4.3 *consolidation* (VI AD); later in Greek script. *LBG*.

foreign   ***cōnsorōrīnus***, variant of *cōnsobrīnus*, a type of cousin: Antec. 3.6.4 *consororinos* etc.
         (VI AD).

         κόνσουλ: see κῶνσουλ.

Direct loan   **κονσουλάριος** (-α, -ον) 'consular', as masc. subst. 'provincial governor', from
V AD – Byz.   *cōnsulāris* 'of a consul', 'ex-consul'.
         Documents: *P.Rain.Unterricht* 96.6 etc. (V AD).
         Inscriptions: perhaps *I.Caesarea Maritima* 84 (V/VI AD).
         Literature: John Chrysostom, *PG* LII.642.25 etc. (IV/V AD); *ACO* II.I.I
         p. 29.5 etc. (V AD); Hesych. as lemma κ 3538 (V/VI AD); Just. *Nov.* 8.1 etc.
         (VI AD).
         Post-antique: survives. Sophocles (1887).
         Notes: Avotins (1992), Daris (1991a: 60), Hofmann (1989: 198), Zilliacus
         (1935a: 180–1), Immisch (1885: 359), *TLL* (*s.v.* *cōnsulāris* 570.44–5),
         Lampe (1961), LSJ suppl. See §4.2.2, §10.2.1, §10.2.2 D.

foreign	***cōnsulō*** 'provide for', 'consult': Antec. 1.2.5 *consulere* etc. (VI AD). See §7.2.1 passage 27.
rare	**κονσ(ο)υλτατίων** 'advice', from *cōnsultātiō* 'consultation': Just. *Nov.* 28.8 etc., but in Latin script 30.10 etc., *Codex* in Latin script 8.10.12.7b (VI AD); Ath. Schol. in Latin script 7.P.10 (VI AD); Byzantine texts. Avotins (1989, 1992), Hofmann (1989: 199), Zilliacus (1935a: 180–1), *LBG*, Lampe (1961, with wrong reference).
foreign	**κονστιτουτίων** 'law' (esp. one made by the emperor), from *cōnstitūtiō* 'decree (esp. from the emperor)': Antec. in Latin script 1.2.6 *constitution* etc. (VI AD); later in Greek script. Zilliacus (1935a: 180–1), *LBG*.
	κονσυλτατίων: see κονσουλτατίων.
	κονσωβρῖνος: see κονσοβρῖνος.
foreign	**κοντινουατεύω** 'continue', from *continuātus* (pf. part. of *continuō* 'make continuous') + -εύω: Antec. in Latin script 2.6.12 *continuateuesthai* etc. (VI AD); later in Greek script. Zilliacus (1935a: 180–1), *LBG*.
foreign	**κοντίνουος** 'continuous', from *continuus* 'uninterrupted': Antec. in Latin script 3.9.11 *continuos* (VI AD); later in Greek script. Zilliacus (1935a: 180–1), *LBG*. See §9.5.6 n. 68.
	κοντοβερνάλιος, κοντοβερνάριος: see κοντουβερνάλιος.
rare	**κοντοβράκιον, κονδοβράκιν** 'short trousers', from κοντός 'short' + *brācae* 'trousers' via βράκιον: papyrus *P.Münch.* III.142.14 (VI AD). Filos (2010: 244, 250), Daris (1991a: 60).
not Latin	**κοντός** 'pole', accented thus, is etymologically Greek; *TLL* (*s.v. contus* 809.23) quotes a glossary entry accented κόντος, and as that would be a Latinate accentuation Hofmann (1989: 199) claims κόντος as a borrowing of *contus* 'pole'. But the accent is modern, from *CGL* VI.272 *s.v. contus*; it does not appear in Gloss. *Herm.M.* 205.33.
Direct loan **IV AD – modern**	**κοντο(υ)βερνάλιος, κοντο(υ)βερνάριος, κοντουβελάνιος** (-ου, ὁ) 'comrade', 'aide', from *contubernālis* 'comrade', 'aide'. Documents: perhaps *P.Mich.* VIII.466.43 (II AD); *P.Abinn.* 42.2 etc. (IV AD); *O.Douch.* II.61.3, II.83.3, perhaps I.5.4 (all IV/V AD); *P.Lips.* I.40.ii.22 (IV AD); *P.Vars.* 47 (V AD); *P.Bon.* 46.12 (V AD); *P.Oxy.* 2046.43–54 (VI AD); *SB* 9455.4 (VI AD). Inscriptions: graffito in Rostovtzeff 1934: 39.2. Literature: Hesych. as lemma κ 3542 (V/VI AD). Post-antique: common despite claim of Coleman (2007: 795) that it 'disappeared after Roman rule'. *LBG*. Modern dialectal κουντουβερνάλις 'hired field worker in relation to owner of fields, and owner in relation to hired worker': Meyer (1895: 35). Notes: Binder (2000: 150), Daris (1991a: 60), Hofmann (1989: 199, twice), Zilliacus (1935a: 222–3), Meinersmann (1927: 28), Immisch (1885: 360), LSJ suppl. (*s.v.* κοντοβερνάλιος). See §4.2.5, §4.4 n. 79, §10.2.1, §10.2.2 N, §12.2.1.

rare	**κοντ(ο)υβέρνιον, κονδυβέρνιον** 'room', 'group of comrades', 'military unit', 'military camp', from *contubernium* 'comradeship', 'shared lodging': ostraca *SB* 17086.4 (I/II AD); *O.Krok.* II.275.6 etc. (II AD); probably Polyaenus, *Excerpta* 7.1.4 (II AD); commonly in Byzantine texts. Daris (1991a: 60), Hofmann (1989: 199), Zilliacus (1935a: 145–6, 222–3), *LBG*.
	κοντούκτωρ: see κονδούκτωρ.
not ancient	**κοντουμακία** 'disobedience', from *contumācia* 'disobedience': no ancient examples. Zilliacus (1935a: 180–1), *LBG*.
foreign	**κοντούμαξ** 'one who repeatedly defies a judicial summons', from *contumāx* 'wilfully disobedient': Ath.Schol. in Latin script 7.P.3.2 (VI AD); later in Greek script. Hofmann (1989: 199), Zilliacus (1935a: 180–1), *LBG*, Lampe (1961, with wrong reference).
foreign	**κοντράκτον** 'contract', from *contractus, -ūs* 'contract': Antec. in Latin script 4.1.pr. *contractu* etc. (VI AD); later in Greek script. Zilliacus (1935a: 180–1).
foreign	**κοντράριος** 'opposite', from *contrārius* 'opposite': Antec. in Latin script 2.21.pr. *contrariois* etc. (VI AD); later in Greek script. Kriaras (1968–) derives the Byzantine term from Italian. Zilliacus (1935a: 180–1), Sophocles (1887). See §7.1.1 passage 19, §9.5.6 n. 68.
foreign	**κόντρα ταβούλλας** 'against the provisions of a will', from *contrā tabulās* 'against (the provisions of a) will': Antec. in Latin script 2.13.7 *contra tabulas* etc. (VI AD); later in Greek script. *LBG* (*s.v.* κοντραταβούλιος).
not ancient	**κοντροβερσία** 'argument', from *contrōversia* 'argument': no ancient examples. Zilliacus (1935a: 180–1), *LBG*.
	κοντυβέρνιον: see κοντουβέρνιον.
	κονφ-: see κομφ-.
rare	**κόξα** 'back', 'hip', from *coxa* 'hip': *V.S.Aux.* 19.2, 16 (VI AD); with *clunis* in Gloss. Ps.-Philox. 102.18; Byzantine texts. Meaning 'corner of a fort' in unpublished ostraca O.Max. inv. 730.1–4, 783.9 (II AD). Meyer (1895: 31–2), *LBG*, Triandaphyllidis (1909: 120), Kriaras (1968–), Lampe (1961).
rare	**κοξάλιον** 'loincloth', from *coxāle* 'loincloth' (*TLL*): Edict.Diocl. 27.2 etc. (IV AD). Hofmann (1989: 199), LSJ suppl. (*s.v.* κοξάλια).
rare	**κο(ο)ρταλῖνος**, an official, from *cohortālīnus/cōrtālīnus*, an official (*TLL*): *ACO* II.I.III p. 123.20 (V AD); Just. *Codex* 1.5.12.6, 1.5.12.15 (VI AD). Byzantine examples may have a different meaning: *LBG* (*s.v.* κορταλῖνος). Avotins (1989), Hofmann (1989: 202), *TLL* (*s.v.* cohortālīnus 1560.9–11), Lampe (1961 *s.v.* κορτάλινος), LSJ suppl.
rare	**κοορτάλιος** 'belonging to a cohort', from *cohortālis* 'of a cohort': Lyd. *Mag.* p. 136.10 (VI AD). Hofmann (1989: 200), *LBG*. Cf. χωρτάριος.
Direct loan I AD – modern?	**κοόρτη, χώρτη, κώρτη, χόρτη, κόρτη** (-ης, ἡ) 'cohort', from *cohors/chōrs/cōrs* 'cohort', 'farmyard'. Documents: e.g. *BGU* XV.2492.13 etc. (II AD); *P.Oxy.* 3365.13 (III AD); *SB* 16214.4 (III/IV AD); perhaps *O.Stras.* I.171.3 (IV AD).

Inscriptions: common, e.g. *IGR* I.1243.3 (I AD); *IGBulg.* II.591.3 (II AD); *I.Ephesos* 737.5 (III AD); *IG* XIV.2433.6 (III AD).

Literature: Lyd. *Mag.* p. 70.1, marked (VI AD); Gloss. Ps.-Philox. 156.23, 27.

Post-antique: common but with new meanings and standardization of spelling to κ- (most ancient papyri and inscriptions use χ-), perhaps indicating reborrowing; *LBG* (s.v. κόρτη 'emperor's headquarters', 'court'), Zervan (2019: 87), Kahane and Kahane (1972–6: 510, 1982: 131), Triandaphyllidis (1909: 127), Kriaras (1968– s.vv. κόρτε and κούρτη, with non-Latin etymologies). Modern dialectal κοῦρτα 'farmyard', κούρτη 'royal court': Meyer (1895: 36).

Notes: Ghiretti (1996: 282–3), Gignac (1981: 8), Binder (2000: 261), Daris (1991a: 60, 117), Mason (1974: 5, 7, 62, 163), Hofmann (1989: 484–5), Viscidi (1944: 15), Zilliacus (1935a: 142–3, 220–1), Meinersmann (1927: 65), Lampe (1961 s.v. κόρτη), LSJ suppl. (s.vv. κοόρτη, χώρτη). See §4.2.3.1, §4.2.5, §8.1.3 n. 17, §10.2.1, §10.2.2 C.

foreign	**κοόρτις** transliterating *cohors* 'cohort': Polybius 11.23.2, 11.33.1 (II BC). Dubuisson (1985: 34–5), Langslow (2012: 100), Hofmann (1989: 485 s.v. χώρτη), Viscidi (1944: 15), LSJ. See §8.1.3 n. 17.
rare	**κοπενδάριον** 'shortcut', from *compendiārium* 'shortcut': Dor.Gaz. *Doct.Div.* 1.20.8, 9 (VI AD). Hofmann (1989: 200), Lampe (1961).
rare	**κόπλα, κῶπλα** 'tether', from *cōpula* 'leash': papyrus *P.Aberd.* 70.3 (II AD). Binder (2000: 185), Daris (1991a: 64), *LBG*.
not Latin	**κοπτούρα, κοπτόρα** 'mortar for flour-making' is probably from κόπτω 'strike' + -ούρα, but Hofmann (1989: 200) derives it from unattested **coptūra*. Palmer (1945: 66), LSJ. See §6.11.
	κοράτωρ: see κουράτωρ.
foreign	**κόρβος, κόρουος** transliterating *corvus* 'raven': DH *AR* 15.1.4 (I BC). Hofmann (1989: 201).
not ancient	**κόρδα, κορδέλλα** 'gut string', from *corda* 'tripe', 'string' (itself from χορδή 'gut'): no ancient examples. *LBG*, Zervan (2019: 86–7), Kriaras (1968–), Meyer (1895: 32), Andriotis (1967), Triandaphyllidis (1909: 122, 168), Lampe (1961).
not ancient	**κορέλι** 'crest', **κουρέλι** 'rags', 'scraps', perhaps from *corium* 'hide' via unattested **corellum* and **coriellum*: no ancient examples. Meyer (1895: 32), Andriotis (1967 s.v. κουρέλι).
foreign	**κορνίκινες** transliterating pl. of *cornicen* 'trumpeter': Lyd. *Mag.* p. 70.17 (VI AD). *LBG*.
Direct loan **I–VI AD**	**κορνικουλάριος, κορνικλάριος, κορνικολάριος, κορνου(κ)λάριος, κορνοκλάριος, κολλικλάριος** (-ου, ὁ) 'assistant', from *corniculārius* 'adjutant'. Documents: e.g. *Chrest.Wilck.* 174.11 (II AD); *O.Theb.* 143.6 (III AD); *P.Oxy.* 1253.12 (IV AD); *P.Oxy.* 2004.1 etc. (V AD). Inscriptions: e.g. Bosch 1967: 93 no. 97.7 (I AD); *IG* XII.VI.II.571.4 (I/II AD); *IGLS* II.448.5 (II AD); *SEG* XXVII.846.15 (III AD); *I.Syringes* 1828.1 (III/IV AD).

Literature: Lyd. *Mag.* p. 134.21 etc. (VI AD). Unverified example (IV AD) in Zilliacus (1937: 323, 330).

Notes: Binder (2000: 166, 174–5), Daris (1991a: 60), Mason (1974: 4, 62, 170), Hofmann (1989: 200), Zilliacus (1935a: 222–3, 1937: 330), Meinersmann (1927: 26), Lampe (1961), LSJ, LSJ suppl. See §4.2.4.1 n. 50, §6.1, §10.2.1, §10.2.2 C.

rare   **κόρνιξ** 'horn' (the musical instrument), from *cornicen* 'trumpeter' (Daris 1991a: 60) or a conflation of *cornū* 'horn' and *cornix* 'crow' (*LBG*): papyri *SB* 16234.1 (II/III AD); *Rom.Mil.Rec.* 78 no. 40.1 (II/III AD); occasional Byzantine texts. Also (independently) transliterating *cornicen*, inscription *SEG* LXV.1408.A47 etc. (V/VI AD).

κορνο(υ)(κ)λάριος: see κορνικουλάριος.

foreign   **κορνο(υ)κόπιον**, apparently transliterating *cornū cōpiae* 'horn of plenty' (*OLD s.v. cornū* 3): said to be a kind of brooch, Lyd. *Mag.* p. 88.12 (VI AD). Binder (2000: 151), *LBG*. See §9.5.5 passage 71.

not ancient?   **κορνοῦτος, κουρνοῦτος** transliterating *cornūtus* 'horned', a military unit: Philostorgius, *Historia ecclesiastica* frag. ap. Photium 7.7 Winkelmann. Hofmann (1989: 200), Sophocles (1887), Lampe (1961).

non-existent?   **κορόλλιον**, meaning uncertain, perhaps from *corōna* 'wreath', 'crown': alleged by Wessely (1902: 134) to occur in a papyrus that no-one can trace. Daris (1991a: 60), Meinersmann (1927: 28), Meyer (1895: 32 *s.v.* κορέλι).

rare   **κορορἀτωρ** 'dyer', from *colōrātor* 'colourer': Edict.Diocl. 7.54 (IV AD). Hofmann (1989: 200–1), LSJ suppl.

κορούλης: see κουρούλλιος.

κόρουος: see κόρβος.

foreign   **κορρεκτόριος** apparently transliterating rare *corrēctōrius* 'of the *corrector*' (*TLL s.v. corrēctīvus, DMLBS*): Just. *Nov.* 8.1 (VI AD). Avotins (1992), Hofmann (1989: 201), Zilliacus (1935a: 182–3), Sophocles (1887 *s.v.* κορρηκτόριος), Lampe (1961).

Direct loan IV AD – Byz.   **κορρήκτωρ, κορρέκτωρ, κορρίκτωρ, κονρήκτωρ** (-ορος/-ῶρος, ὁ), an official, from *corrēctor* 'special commissioner supervising the finances of a city'.

Documents: *P.Oxy.* 4385.9 (IV AD); P.Vindob. G 21595.6 = Benaissa 2011: 241 (VI AD).

Literature: Eus. *HE* 10.5.23 (IV AD); Isidore of Pelusium, *Epistulae* 1498.1 Évieux etc. (V AD); *Acta Eupli* 1.1 in Musurillo 1972.

Post-antique: survives, forming derivative κουρικτοριανός 'assistant to the *corrector*'. *LBG*.

Notes: dat. sing. accented κορρηκτῶρι on P.Vindob. G 21595. Bartalucci (1995: 115–16), Hofmann (1989: 201–2), Lampe (1961 *s.v.* κονρήκτωρ). See §4.2.5, **§5.3.1**, §10.2.1, §10.2.2 D.

Direct loan IV–VI AD   **κορριγία** (-ας, ἡ) 'thong', from *corrigia* 'thong'.

Inscriptions: Edict.Diocl. 10.19 (IV AD).

Literature: Hesych. as part of gloss ι 609 (V/VI AD).

Notes: Hofmann (1989: 202), *LBG*, LSJ suppl. See §4.2.3.1, §10.2.1, §10.2.2 M.

κορρίκτωρ: see κορρήκτωρ.

not ancient   **κορροῦδα** 'wild asparagus', from *corrūda* 'wild asparagus': no ancient examples. Meyer (1895: 32).

κορταλῖνος: see κοορταλῖνος.

κόρτη: see κοόρτη.

rare   **κορτιανός** 'member of a cohort', from *cortālis* (variant of *cohortālis* 'of a cohort': *TLL s.v. cohortālis* 1560.13) + -ιανός or from *cohors* via κοόρτη + -ιανός: papyrus *P.Oxy.* 1253.4 (IV AD). Daris (1991a: 61), Hofmann (1989: 202 with derivation from unattested **c(h)ortiānus*), Meinersmann (1927: 29), LSJ suppl. See §6.4.

Direct loan
IV AD – modern
    κορτίνα, κορτίνη (-ης, ἡ) 'arch', 'vault', 'curtain', from *cortīna* 'arch', 'vault'.
    Documents: *P.Cair.Masp.* 67006v.48 (VI AD); *SB* 15249.3 (VI AD).
    Inscriptions: *IGLS* XIII.1.9136.3, perhaps 9135.2 (both VI AD).
    Literature: Philogelos 162 (IV AD); Anton.Hag. *V.Sym.Styl.* 29 (V AD); Agath. *Greg.* 165 (V AD); Hesych. as gloss κ 860 (V/VI AD); Cyr.S. *Vit.Sab.* 186.5 (VI AD); Cos.Indic. 5.26 etc. (VI AD); scholion to *Od.* 2.130.
    Post-antique: common. *LBG*, Kriaras (1968–), Triandaphyllidis (1909: 98, 120, 130). Modern κουρτίνα 'curtain': Babiniotis (2002), Andriotis (1967), Meyer (1895: 36), Kahane and Kahane (1972–6: 535).
    Notes: Binder (2000: 219–20), Daris (1991a: 61), Hofmann (1989: 202), Cavenaile (1951: 397–8), Lampe (1961 *s.v.* κορτίνη), LSJ suppl. See §8.2.3 n. 51, §10.2.1, §10.2.2 J.

κόρτος: see κουάρτος.

non-existent?   **κορύπτωρ**, meaning uncertain, from *corruptor* 'one who ruins': perhaps tachygraphy in Menci 2000: 284 (IV/V AD), *q.v.*

not Latin?   **κορωλλικός** on inscription *I.Stratonikeia* 289.11 (II AD), probably a misspelling of κοραλλικός 'of coral', might be from an unattested *corollicus related to *corallium* 'coral'. Hofmann (1989: 202), LSJ.

semantic extension   **κορώνη** 'crow', 'curved thing', etymologically Greek, sometimes acquired a meaning 'crown' under the influence of *corōna* 'wreath', 'crown': the last definition (καὶ εἶδος στεφάνου) in Hesych. κ 3739 (V/VI AD); κορῶνα transliterating *corōna*, Plut. *Mor.* 726f (I/II AD); in pl. for part of a horse, *Hippiatr.Par.* (Apsyrtus) 356 (III/IV AD?); often in Byzantine texts. The χορωνός mentioned by Athenaeus 15.680d may be the same word. Strobach (1997: 196), Hofmann (1989: 202–3), Immisch (1885: 298), *LBG* (*s.v.* κορόνα), Kriaras (1968– *s.v.* κορόνα), Triandaphyllidis (1909: 127, 168), Meyer (1895: 32), Andriotis (1967 *s.v.* modern κορόνα), Babiniotis (2002 *s.v.* modern κορόνα), LSJ (*s.vv.* κορώνη, χορωνός), LSJ suppl.

κοστοδία, κοστωδ(ε)ία: see κουστωδία.

rare   **κοτ(τ)ιδιανός** 'daily', from *cottīdiānus* 'daily': papyrus *P.Oxy.* 2408.10 (IV AD); Lyd. *Mag.* p. 164.5 etc. (VI AD). Daris (1991a: 61), Hofmann (1989: 203), LSJ suppl.

foreign   *quadrāns* 'quarter of an inheritance': Antec. 2.14.5 (VI AD). See §7.1.1 passage 18.

κουαδράντης: see κοδράντης.

Direct loan
IV AD

κουαδράριος (-ου, ὁ), perhaps 'stonemason', from *quadrātārius* 'relating to stonemasonry'.

Documents: *P.Col.* VII.141.32 etc. (IV AD); *P.Stras.* III.129.5, 149.5 (both with same text, IV AD); *BGU* I.21.i.5 (IV AD); *CPR* XVIIA.31.10 (IV AD); *P.Cair. Goodsp.* 12.1.6 (IV AD); *P.Cair.Isid.* 73.2 (IV AD); *P.Cair.Isid.* 131.2 (IV AD); perhaps *P.Cair.Isid.* 71.8 (IV AD).

Notes: Daris (1991a: 61), Hofmann (1989: 203), Meinersmann (1927: 29), LSJ suppl. See §4.1.1 n. 17, §4.2.4.1 n. 50, §9.2, §10.2.1, §10.2.2 J.

foreign

κουαδρᾶτος and **κοδρᾶτος** transliterating *quadrātus* 'rectangular': Plut. *Rom.* 9.4 (I/II AD); Athenaeus 3.114e (II/III AD).

foreign

quadruplicātiō 'making fourfold' (L&S): Antec. 4.14.3 *quadruplication* 'response to the *triplication*' (VI AD); *LBG*'s κουαδρεπλικατίων occurs only as a variant at Antec. 4.14.2 (spelled κουατρουπλατίων in the manuscript, according to the apparatus of Lokin *et al.* 2010). Zilliacus (1935a: 204–5), Triantaphyllides (1892: 262 *s.v.* καδρουπλικατίων).

κουαεστίων: see κυαιστίων.

κουαέστωρ: see κουαίστωρ.

rare

κουαιστορεία, κυαιστορεία 'quaestorship', from *quaestor* 'quaestor' via κουαίστωρ + -(ε)ία: inscription *IGLS* XIII.1.9112.1 (IV AD). LSJ suppl.

Direct loan
II AD – Byz.

κουαίστωρ, κο(ι)αίστωρ, κυαίστωρ, κυέστωρ, κουαέστωρ (-ορος/-ωρος, ὁ), a title, from *quaestor* 'quaestor'.

Documents: *ChLA* XLI.1196.1 (VI AD); *P.Flor.* III.292.1, 293r.1 (both VI AD).

Inscriptions: e.g. *SEG* VI.555.5 (II AD); *I.Ephesos* 677.3 (II/III AD); *IG* II/ III².II.2243.50 etc. (III AD); *SEG* XVI.813.4 (III AD).

Literature: common, e.g. Julian, *Epistulae* 96 Bidez (IV AD); Pall. *V.Chrys.* 19.19 (IV/V AD); Marc.Diac. 50 (V AD); Nil. 2.305.1 (V AD); Cyr.S. *Vit. Sab.* 178.10 (VI AD); Antec. 2.23.12 etc., but in Latin script 1.5.3 *quaestoros* etc. (VI AD).

Post-antique: common, forming derivatives κοιαιστωρικός 'of a quaestor', κυαιστώριον 'office of the quaestor', etc. *LBG* (*s.v.* κυαίστωρ), Zervan (2019: 98), Kriaras (1968– *s.v.* κυαίστωρ), Triandaphyllidis (1909: 126).

Notes: forms derivative κουαιστορεία. Famerie (1998: 58, 1999), Freyburger-Galland (1997: 161–2), Avotins (1989 *s.v.* κυαίστωρ, 1992 *s.v.* κοιαίστωρ), Daris (1991a: 63), Mason (1974: 3, 6, 63), Hofmann (1989: 203–4, two entries), Viscidi (1944: 11, 21, 27), Zilliacus (1935a: 204–5, 1937: 330), Meinersmann (1927: 31), Lampe (1961 *s.v.* κυαίστωρ), LSJ suppl. See §4.2.5, §10.2.1, §10.2.2 D.

Direct loan
II AD – Byz.

κουαιστώριος, κοιαιστώριος, κυαιστώριος (-α, -ον) 'of a quaestor'; as masc. subst. 'ex-quaestor'; as neut. subst. 'office of quaestor', 'residence of the quaestor', from *quaestōrius* 'of a quaestor', 'ex-quaestor'.

Inscriptions: Ramsay 1883: 275 no. 17.10 (II AD); *I.Ephesos* 1540.11.

Literature: Malal. 14.38 (VI AD); Evagr.Schol. *HE* 240.34 (VI AD).

Post-antique: survives. *LBG* (*s.v.* κυαιστώριος), Triandaphyllidis (1909: 126).

Notes: Drew-Bear (1972: 206), Mason (1974: 63), Hofmann (1989: 219), Zilliacus (1935a: 204–5), Lampe (1961 *s.v.* κυαιστώριον), LSJ suppl. See §4.2.2, §10.2.1, §10.2.2 D.

foreign   **κουάρτος, κόρτος** transliterating *quārtus* 'fourth': ostracon *SB* 14180.67 etc.
(II AD); cf. J. N. Adams (2003: 395–6), Daris (1991a: 61). Also in Latin
script: Just. *Nov.* 12.3.pr. (VI AD); Antec. 2.15.1 *quartos* etc. (VI AD); cf.
Zilliacus (1935a: 204–5), *LBG* (*s.v.* κουάρτα 'quarter'), Triandaphyllidis
(1909: 125 *s.v.* κάρτη). See §5.2.1.

foreign   **κουάσι** 'as if', from *quasi* 'as if': in Latin script as part of phrases such as *quasi
castrēnsis* 'as if belonging to a military camp', e.g. Just. *Nov.* 22.34 (VI AD),
Antec. 2.11.6 *quasi canstrensia* (VI AD). Hofmann (1989: 204).

rare   **κουαττόρουιρ** 'member of a board of four', from *quattuorvir* 'member of a board
of four': inscriptions *SEG* XVII.571.3, Latinate (I/II AD); *IG* XII.II.235.4
(II AD). Mason (1974: 6, 7, 63), Hofmann (1989: 204), Cameron (1931:
255), LSJ suppl.

not ancient   **κουβέντα** 'talk', from *conventum* 'agreement': no ancient examples. Coleman
(2007: 795, suggesting borrowing via a Balkan Latin dialect), Meyer (1895:
33), Andriotis (1967), Kriaras (1968–).

κουβηκουλάρις: see κουβικουλάριος.

κουβικλ(ε)ῖον, κουβίκλον: see κουβουκλ(ε)ῖον.

Direct? loan   **κουβικουλαρία, κουβικουλαρέα** (-ας, ἡ) 'chamberlain (fem.)', 'chambermaid',
V AD – Byz.   from *cubiculāria* 'chambermaid' (*TLL s.v. cubiculārius* 1266.20–5) or
cubiculārius 'of the bedchamber' via κουβικουλάριος.
Inscriptions: *SEG* XXXIV.1262.10 (V AD); *I.Chr.Bulgarien* 250.a3 etc. (V AD);
SEG VIII.175.4 (VI AD).
Literature: Callin. *V.Hypat.* 44.1 (V AD); Aëtius 6.65.29 (VI AD); *V.S.Aux.* 61.2
(VI AD).
Post-antique: numerous. *LBG* (*s.v.* κουβικουλαρέα), Kriaras (1968–).
Notes: Hofmann (1989: 205 *s.v.* κουβικουλάριος), Lampe (1961), LSJ suppl.
See §4.2.3.1, §4.6.1, §6.2 n. 13, §10.2.1, §10.2.2 N.

Direct loan   **κουβικουλάριος, κουβηκουλάρις, κουβουκουλάριος, κουβουκλάριος,**
III AD – Byz.   **κουβουλ(λ)άριος** (-ου, ὁ) 'servant connected with the bedroom',
'chamberlain', from *cubiculārius* 'of the bedchamber'.
Inscriptions: *SEG* IV.416.1 (II/III AD); *I.Mylasa* 612.6 (V AD); Asdracha
1997: 381 no. 195 (V/VI AD); tile stamps *I.Perinthos* 250, 251, 252, 253 (all
VI AD); *TAM* V.I.563.2.
Literature: common, e.g. Eutychianus, *FHG* IV frag. 1.17 (IV AD); *ACO* I.I.
v p. 135.22 (V AD); Callin. *V.Hypat.* 12.4 (V AD); Marc.Diac. 26 (V AD);
Nil. 1.37.1 (V AD); *V.Dan.Styl. A.* 48 (V AD); Malal. 5.3 (VI AD); Cyr.S. *Vit.
Sab.* 142.14 (VI AD).
Post-antique: common. *LBG* (*s.v.* κουβουκλάριος), Zervan (2019: 88),
Triandaphyllidis (1909: 126).
Notes: Binder (2000: 170, 175–6), Avotins (1992), Hofmann (1989: 205),
Zilliacus (1935a: 182–3, 1937: 330), Lampe (1961), LSJ suppl. See §4.2.4.1
n. 50, §10.2.1, §10.2.2 A.

not ancient?   **κούβιτος** 'bed', 'camp', from *cubitus, -ūs* 'bed': papyrus *P.Lond.* v.1905 may be
VII AD. Daris (1991a: 61), *LBG*.

κουβουκλάριος: see κουβικουλάριος.

Direct loan with suffix
II AD – modern

κουβουκλ(ε)ῖον, κουβικλ(ε)ῖον, κουβοῦκλιν, κουβίκλον (-ου, τό) 'bedroom', 'tomb', 'emperor's bedchamber', from *cubiculum* 'bedroom' + -εῖον.

Documents: *P.Oxy.* 4087.11 (IV AD).

Inscriptions: *IGUR* II.391.3 (II AD).

Literature: common, e.g. Clemens Alexandrinus frag. 74 Früchtel (II/III AD); *Act.Xanth.Polyx.* 11 (III AD); Marc.Diac. 45 (V AD); Agathangelus, *Vita acephala* 76 Garitte (V AD); EphraemSyr. II p. 23.6 (V/VI AD); Just. *Nov.* 8.Ed.not.1 (VI AD).

Post-antique: common. *LBG* (s.v. κουβούκλιον), Kriaras (1968– s.v. κουβούκλιον), Triandaphyllidis (1909: 120). Modern κουβούκλιο, κουβούκλι 'canopy', 'cubicle': Babiniotis (2002), Andriotis (1967), Meyer (1895: 33).

Notes: Viscidi (1944: 7, 33–4) considers the phonetic changes evidence of integration. Probably forms derivative κουβουκλείσιος. Niehoff-Panagiotidis (2019: 465–6), Binder (2000: 169–70, 175–6), Avotins (1992), Hofmann (1989: 204, 205–6), Viscidi (1944: 7, 33), Zilliacus (1935a: 182–3, 1937: 330), Lampe (1961), LSJ suppl. See §4.3.2, §6.7 n. 44, §10.2.1, §10.2.2 J.

rare

κουβουκλείσιος 'chamberlain of the patriarch', from *cubiculum* 'bedroom' (via κουβουκλεῖον?) + a variant of -ήσιος: *V.Luc.Styl.* 27 (VI AD); Byzantine texts. Forms Byzantine derivative κουβουκλεισιάτον 'office of the patriarch's chamberlain'. Zervan (2019: 88–9, 265) dates the borrowing to VIII AD. *LBG*, Triandaphyllidis (1909: 125), Lampe (1961). See §6.7 n. 44.

κουβοῦκλιν, κουβουκλίον: see κουβουκλεῖον.

κουβουκουλάριος, κουβουλ(λ)άριος: see κουβικουλάριος.

κοῦγλιν: see κουκούλλιον.

not ancient?

κουδισάμιος, perhaps 'tool-grinder': inscription *MAMA* III.724.2. Editor *ad loc.*, Hofmann (1989: 206), Cameron (1931: 243, with derivation from unattested *cudisamārius*), LSJ suppl. (with derivation from *cudis* 'anvil' (*TLL*) and *samiārius* 'weapon polisher' (Forcellini *et al.* 1864–1926)).

not ancient

κουδούμεντον 'parsley', from *condīmentum* 'seasoning': no ancient examples. Meyer (1895: 33), *LBG* (s.v. κονδιμέντον 'spice'), Kriaras (1968– s.v. κοδιμέντον).

rare

κουδριγάριος 'for a team of four', from *quadrīgārius* 'of chariot-racing': *Hippiatr. Berl.* 130.98 etc., sometimes marked. Hofmann (1989: 206), *LBG*, LSJ (s.v. κουδριγάριον).

foreign

κουηεμπτίων apparently transliterating *coēmptiō*, marriage by mock sale: papyrus *BGU* V.1210.93 (II AD). Daris (1991a: 61), Mason (1974: 63), Meinersmann (1927: 29).

foreign

quīncūnx 'five twelfths of an inheritance': Antec. 2.14.5 (VI AD). See §7.1.1 passage 18.

Direct loan
I–II AD

κο(υ)ιντάνα, κυι(ν)τάνα, κουτάνα (-ας, ἡ), a tax, apparently from *quīntāna* 'street in a Roman camp where markets were held'.

Documents: e.g. *O.Berenike* II.138.3 (I AD); *SB* 17096.6 (I/II AD); *O.Krok.* II.180.7 (II AD); O.Dios. inv. 1246.12 = Cuvigny (2013: 434) (II AD).

Notes: Cuvigny (2010a: 163–6), editors of *O.Berenike* II pp. 5–6, 51–2. See §4.1.1, §4.2.3.1, §9.2, §10.2.1, §10.2.2 D; cf. κουιντανήσιος, κυντανός.

Direct loan
I AD

κο(υ)ιντανήσιος, κυ(ι)ντανήσιος, κουτανίσιος (-ου, ὁ), soldier in charge of a
market, from *quīntānēnsis*, a kind of soldier.
Documents: common, e.g. *O.Berenike* I.53.1, I.55.1, II.139.1, II.185.2, II.187.3
(all I AD).
Notes: found only at Berenike. Editors of *O.Berenike* I p. 12, II pp. 6–7, 51–2.
See §4.2.5, §6.7 n. 45, §9.2, §10.2.1, §10.2.2 C; cf. κουιντάνα, κυντανός.

foreign

κουίντος 'fifth', from *quīntus* 'fifth': Antec. in Latin script 2.14.6 *quintos* (VI AD).
Zilliacus (1935a: 204–5).

non-existent

κουιουράτωρ 'joint sworn witness', from *co-* 'joint' (*TLL s.v. cum* 1340.76) +
iūrātor 'sworn witness': superseded reading of papyrus *P.Thead.* 54 = *P.Sakaon*
2.21 (III AD). Cavenaile (1951: 398).

Κουϊρῖται: see Κυιρῖται.

κουκκόλ(λ)ος: see κουκκοῦλλος.

κούκκομα: see κούκκουμα.

κουκκούλ(λ)ιον: see κουκούλλιον.

rare

κουκ(κ)ο(ῦ)λ(λ)ος, κόκουλλος 'hood', from *cucullus* 'hood': documents *P.Oxy.*
3060.5 (II AD); unpublished *O.Claud.* inv. 1759.4 (II AD); perhaps *P.Jena*
II.38.8 (VI AD). Perhaps source of κουκουλάριος. Daris (1991a: 61), LSJ
suppl. (*s.v.* κουκκούλλος). See §5.2.3; cf. κουκούλλιον.

Direct loan
II AD – modern

κούκκο(υ)μα, κόκ(κ)ο(υ)μα, κόκκομας, κούκ(κ)ουμος, κοκκόμανα (pl.), κοκόμανος
(-ης?, ἡ and -ου?, ὁ) 'jar', 'kettle', from *cucuma* 'kettle' (also spelled *cuccuma*:
TLL).
Documents: *P.Sarap.* 55.30 (II AD); *P.Hamb.* I.10.36 (II AD); *Stud.Pal.*
XX.67r.16 (II/III AD); unpublished *O.Max.* inv. 87.7 (II/III AD); *P.Oxy.*
4340.27 (III AD); perhaps *P.Ross.Georg.* V.5.10 (III AD); *P.Oxy.* 1160.23
(III/IV AD); *SB* 13593.28 (III/IV AD); *P.Cair.Isid.* 137.4 (III/IV AD);
P.Giss.Univ. III.25.8 (IV AD); *P.Oxy.* 3998.36 (IV AD); perhaps *P.Wash.Univ.*
1.58.18 (V AD).
Literature: with *cucuma* in glossaries, e.g. Gloss. *Herm.L.* 23.7.
Post-antique: survives, forming derivative κουκουμάριον 'pot'. *LBG* (*s.v.*
κούκουμον), Triandaphyllidis (1909: 121). Modern dialectal κούκκουμα
'vessel for boiling coffee', κουκουμάρι 'little vessel', etc.: Shipp (1979: 336),
Meyer (1895: 34).
Notes: probably forms derivatives κουκκούμιον, κουκουμοκανδήλη. Binder (2000:
145–6), commentary on *P.Oxy.* 3998.36, Gignac (1981: 9), Daris (1991a:
61), Hofmann (1989: 206), Meinersmann (1927: 29), *DÉLG*, Lampe (1961
s.v. κούκουμος), LSJ. See §4.2.3.1, §4.6.1 n. 83, §10.2.1, §10.2.2 I, §12.2.1.

Deriv.? of loan
II AD – modern

κουκ(κ)ούμιον, κοκ(κ)ούμιον (-ου, τό) 'jar', 'kettle', from *cucuma* 'kettle' (via
κούκκουμα?) + -ιον.
Documents: *P.Brookl.* 17.8 (III AD); *P.Oxy.* 1658.9 (IV AD); *P.Stras.*
VIII.736.11 (IV AD); *P.Kellis* IV.96.1770 (IV AD); *P.Ryl.* IV.639.71 etc.
(IV AD); *P.Oxy.* 1290.3 (V AD); tachygraphy in Menci 2000: 284 (V AD);
perhaps *P.Wash.Univ.* 1.58.18 (V AD); *P.Berl.Sarisch.* 21.16 (V/VI AD);
Chrest.Wilck. 135.23 (V/VI AD).

Literature: Epict. *Diss.* 3.22.71 (I/II AD); Cyr.S. *Vita Theodosii* 237.12 (VI AD); with *cucuma* in Gloss. Serv. 521.58.

Post-antique: numerous, forming derivative κουκουμίκιον 'little pot'. *LBG* (*s.v.* κουκούμιν), Kriaras (1968– *s.v.* κουκούμιν). Modern κουκούμι 'large metal jug': Andriotis (1967), Meyer (1895: 34), Kahane and Kahane (1972–6: 535).

Notes: Menci (2000: 284–5), commentary on *P.Oxy.* 3998.36, Daris (1991a: 61), Hofmann (1989: 206 *s.v.* κουκκουμα), Cavenaile (1952: 196), Viscidi (1944: 41), Lampe (1961 *s.v.* κουκούμιον), LSJ (*s.v.* κούκκουμα). See §4.3.2 n. 69, §4.6.1 n. 83, §10.2.2 I.

κούκκουμος: see κούκκουμα.

κουκλί: see κλόκιον.

κούκλιν: see κουκούλλιον.

κουκόλ(λ)ος: see κουκκοῦλλος.

not ancient?	**κουκούβη, κουκουβαία** 'owl', apparently from *cuccubiō* 'hoot': as gloss in scholia to *Od.* 3.372 and Opp. *H.* 1.170; Hesychius' lemma κοκκοβάγη at κ 3285 (V/VI AD) may be the same word. *LBG* (*s.v.* κουκουβάια), LSJ suppl.
rare	**κουκουλάριος** 'maker of hoods', from *cucullus* 'hood' (via κουκοῦλλος?) + -άριος: inscription *SEG* XXXIX.649.6 (II/III AD). Binder (2000: 199), LSJ suppl.
Direct loan with suffix **II AD – modern?**	**κουκούλ(λ)ιον, κο(υ)κκούλ(λ)ιον, κούκλιν, κοῦγλιν** (-ου, τό) 'hood', from *cucullus* 'hood' + -ιον.

Documents: *P.Mich.* VIII.482.4 (II AD); *SB* 14178.26 (II AD); perhaps *P.Sijp.* 60a.11 (IV AD); *P.Heid.* VII.406.7 etc. (IV/V AD); *P.Oxy.* 1300.9 (V AD); perhaps *P.Jena* II.38.8 (VI AD).

Literature: e.g. Evagrius Ponticus, *Practicus* prol. 8 Guillaumont (IV AD); Ps.-Athanasius, *PG* XXVIII.857d (IV AD?); Pall. *H.Laus.* 32.3 (IV/V AD); Geront. *V.Mel.* 2.31 (V AD); EphraemSyr. I p. 236.5 (V/VI AD); Barsanuph. Jo. I ep. 1.25 (VI AD).

Post-antique: survives. Sophocles (1887). Probably connected to Byzantine κουκούλλα 'hood' (*LBG*, Triandaphyllidis 1909: 121) and modern κουκούλ(λ)α 'hood', κουκούλι 'cocoon', κούκλα 'doll' (Babiniotis 2002; Andriotis 1967; Kahane and Kahane 1972–6: 535; Meyer 1895: 33–4). But the feminine forms may not descend directly from the ancient neuter: there is no evidence that the Greek word was ever feminine during antiquity, though a Latin feminine *cuculla* is attested from IV AD (*TLL s.v.* 2. *cucullus* 1281.23–40). Kriaras (1968–) accordingly suggests an Italian source for κουκούλα; he then derives κουκούλι from κουκούλα, but that might be directly descended from the ancient borrowing even if κουκούλα is not.

Notes: Binder (2000: 150, 199–200), Daris (1991a: 61), Hofmann (1989: 207), Cavenaile (1952: 196), Viscidi (1944: 36), Zilliacus (1937: 330), Meinersmann (1927: 29), Lampe (1961), LSJ suppl. See §4.3.2 n. 69, §8.2.3 n. 51, §10.2.1, §10.2.2 H, §12.2.1.

κουκοῦλ(λ)ος: see κουκκοῦλλος.

κουκούμιον: see κουκκούμιον.

rare   **κουκουμοκανδήλη**, a device for producing gentle and even heat, probably from *cucuma* 'kettle' and *candēla* 'candle' (probably via κούκκουμα and κανδήλη): Zosimus alch., Berthelot and Ruelle 1888: 141.13 (III/IV AD).

         κούκουμος: see κούκκουμα.

not ancient   **κούκουρον** 'quiver', perhaps from medieval *cucurum* 'quiver' (Du Cange 1883–7): no ancient examples. Hofmann (1989: 207), Viscidi (1944: 13), *LBG*, Meyer (1895: 34), Kriaras (1968– s.v. κούκκουρον).

foreign   **κοῦλπα** 'fault', from *culpa* 'fault': *Schol.Sinai.* in Latin script 31 *cu[l]pa[m]* (V/VI AD), Antec. in Latin script 3.25.9 *culpas* etc. (VI AD); later in Greek script. Zilliacus (1935a: 182–3), *LBG*. See §7.1.2, §9.5.6 nn. 56 and 68.

         κούλσωρ: see κούρσωρ.

foreign   *cum* 'with': Antec. as part of phrases, e.g. 1.6.1 *cum libertate* (VI AD).

         κούμαλον, κούμελον, κούμηλον, κούμολον: see κούμουλον.

         κουμέρκι: see κομμέρκιον.

Direct loan III AD – Byz.   **κουμουλᾶτος, κομμουλᾶτος** (-η, -ον) 'heaping' (of measurements, esp. with μόδιος), from *cumulātus* 'piled up'.
Documents: *P.Lond.* v.1718.14 etc. (VI AD).
Literature: Origen, *Homiliae in Job*, PG XVII.89d: τινὲς δέ φασιν, ὅτι "γάβις" λέγεται τὸ ὑπερέχον τοῦ χείλους τοῦ μεδίμνου, ὃ καλεῖται "κομμουλᾶτον" (II/III AD); Epiph. *Mens.4* 84.7 etc. (IV AD); Her.Mech. *Mens.* 61.7.
Post-antique: survives. *LBG*, Triandaphyllidis (1909: 131).
Notes: Binder (2000: 149), Daris (1991a: 61), Hofmann (1989: 195), Meinersmann (1927: 29), Lampe (1961 s.v. κομμουλᾶτον). See §4.2.2, §5.2.3, §6.6, §10.2.1, §10.2.2 E.

Direct loan IV AD – modern   **κούμουλον, κούμολον, κούμαλον, κούμελον, κούμηλον** (-ου, τό), a measure and a tax or levy, from *cumulus* 'heap', 'accumulation', 'increase'.
Documents: e.g. *P.Oxy.* 4346.8 (IV AD); *P.Stras.* VII.654.19 (V AD); *SB* 11480.5 etc. (V/VI AD); *P.Lond.* v.1718.8 etc. (VI AD).
Literature: perhaps Cleopatra alch., *De ponderibus et mensuris* frag. 80.7 = Hultsch 1864: 257.17 (I AD); perhaps Hdn. in Ps.-Arcadius, Roussou 2018: 185.17, omitted by Lentz at Hdn. *Pros.Cath.* III.1.165.22 (II AD).
Post-antique: survives. *LBG* (s.vv. κούμουλος, κουμούλιος), Kriaras (1968– s.v. κουμούλι). Modern κουμούλα 'heap', κούμουλος 'full', etc.: Babiniotis (2002), Andriotis (1974: 331–2), Meyer (1895: 34), Kahane and Kahane (1972–6: 533).
Notes: Herodian has masc. κούμουλος. Roussou (2018: 449–50), Binder (2000: 149), Daris (1991a: 61), Hofmann (1989: 208, with derivation from *cumulātus modius*), Viscidi (1944: 30), Meinersmann (1927: 29), *TLL* (s.v. *cumulus* 1388.36–8), LSJ suppl. See §4.2.4.1 n. 58, §5.3.2 passage 11, §6.6, §10.2.1, §10.2.2 E.

not ancient   **κοῦνα** 'wedge', from *cuneus* 'wedge': no ancient examples. Zilliacus (1935a: 222–3), *LBG*.

κουνδουκτορικόν: see κονδουκτορικόν.

foreign **κούνεος** transliterating *cuneus* 'wedge': Strabo 3.1.4 (I BC/AD). Sophocles (1887).

foreign **κ(ο)υνίκ(ο)λος, κόνικλος** (ὁ) 'rabbit', from *cunīculus* 'rabbit' (the Latin variant *cunīclus* is first attested long after the Greek, *TLL s.v. cunīculus* 1407.23–4): Polybius 12.3.9 etc., marked (II BC); Erot. *Voc.Hipp.* 93.15, marked (I AD); Galen VI.666.11 Kühn, marked (II AD); Athenaeus 9.400f etc., marked, quoting earlier writers (II/III AD); Aelian, *De natura animalium* 13.15, marked (II/III AD); variant at Edict.Diocl. 4.33 (IV AD). Binder (2000: 148, 164–5), Dubuisson (1985: 35), Langslow (2012: 99–100), Hofmann (1989: 220–1), Meyer (1895: 35), LSJ (*s.v.* κύνικλος), LSJ suppl. See §8.1.3 n. 17.

rare **κούνιον** 'cradle', from *cūnae* 'cradle' + -ιον: as gloss in a scholion to Callimachus, *Hymn 1* sch. 48; with *cuneum* in Gloss. Ps.-Cyril. 354.20 (cf. *CGL* VI.295 *s.v. cuneum*); in Byzantine texts. Hofmann (1989: 208), Zilliacus (1935a: 222–3), *LBG*, Zervan (2019: 91), Kriaras (1968–), Triandaphyllidis (1909: 122), Lampe (1961), LSJ suppl., and note modern κούνια 'cradle' (Babiniotis 2002; Andriotis 1967) and κουνί (Meyer 1895: 35).

not ancient **κουνοῦκλα**, a plant name perhaps from *colus* 'distaff' via unattested *conucula: interpolation in Dsc. 3.93 RV. Binder (2000: 161), Meyer (1895: 35).

κουντουβερνάλις: see κοντουβερνάλιος.

foreign **κουοδιούσω, κ(ο)υοδιοῦσο**, a legal term from *quod iussū* 'legal action concerning contracts made with another person's slave': Antec. in Latin script 4.7.1 *quod iussu* etc. (VI AD); later in Greek script.

Direct loan **κοῦπα** (-ης/-ας?, ἡ) 'grave', from *cūpa* 'cask', 'tub', 'barrel', 'niche for holding the
V AD – ? ashes of the dead'.

Inscriptions: Libertini 1931: 369 no. 1.3 (III AD or later); *I.Jud.Western Europe* 1.149.7 (IV/V AD); *IGUR* II.300.3; perhaps κοίπας in *IG* XIV.566.1.

Post-antique: does not survive in meaning 'grave', but often argued to survive in Byzantine κοῦπα 'cup', 'cask' (*LBG*). Modern κούπα 'cup' is normally derived from *cūpa*: Babiniotis (2002), Andriotis (1967), Meyer (1895: 35).

Notes: all examples come from Sicily and Italy. There may be ancient evidence for the Byzantine meaning: κοῦπα 'cup' in Her.Mech. *Stereom.* 1.51.1 etc. (date uncertain); κοῦφα used for a container (esp. for wine) in some Roman-period papyri (this could be a variant of κοῦπα or a Greek creation from κοῦφος 'light' via κοῦφον (κεράμιον), resulting in a meaning '(empty) jar'; derivatives include καινόκουφον (Cavenaile 1952: 199, LSJ, LSJ suppl.)). LSJ (*s.v.* κοῦφος I.6, with references to papyri), Hofmann (1989: 208, with arguments for κοῦφα = κοῦπα, references to more papyri), Meinersmann (1927: 30, with references to compounds), Sophocles (1887 *s.v.* κοῦφος, tentatively supporting the connection), Zervan (2019: 91, 263, dating borrowing to I AD via unreliable date for Heron's works), Kriaras (1968–), Triandaphyllidis (1909: 121), LSJ suppl. See §9.2, §10.2.1, §10.2.2 O.

foreign	**κοῦρα** 'care', from *cūra* 'care': in marked contexts, e.g. as part of κοῦρα ἐπιστουλάρουμ (*cūra epistulārum*) in Lyd. *Mag.* p. 166.16 (VI AD); Antec. in Latin script 1.2.7 *cura* (VI AD). Cited by Daris (1991a: 62) on the basis of κοῦρα περσωνάρουμ in papyrus *P.Wash.Univ.* 1.6.3 etc. (VI AD), which is more often read κουρά(τωρ) περσωνάρουμ or as a variant of κουροπερσονάριος. Worp (1982: 564–5), Zilliacus (1935a: 182–3). May survive in Byzantine texts: see *LBG*, but Kriaras (1968–) derives it from Italian. For a possible occurrence in Dio Cassius see Freyburger-Galland (1997: 91). Cf. κουροπαλάτης, κουροπερσονάριος.
foreign	**κουρανδάρουμ** transliterating *cūrandārum* in title κουαττόρουιρ οὐιάρουμ κουρανδάρουμ 'member of a board of four men responsible for roads': inscription *SEG* XVII.571.5 (I/II AD). Drew-Bear (1972: 206).
	κουραπαλάτης: see κουροπαλάτης.
rare	**κουρατίων** 'office or position of curator', from *cūrātiō* 'position of curator': perhaps Modestinus in Just. *Dig.* 27.1.2.9 (III AD); Antec. 1.25.13, but in Latin script 1.25.pr. *curationa* etc. (VI AD); Byzantine texts. Zilliacus (1935a: 182–3), *LBG*. See §9.5.6 n. 55.
	κουράτορ: see κουράτωρ.
rare	**κουρατορατίων**, meaning uncertain, ultimately from *cūrātor* 'curator' (*cūrātōrātiō* is unattested), probably via κουράτωρ + -ατίων: papyrus *ChLA* XLIII.1247.7 (V AD). See §6.10.
	κουρατορεία: see κουρατορία.
Deriv. of loan II AD – Byz.	**κουρατορεύω, κουρατωρεύω** 'act as curator', in pass. 'be under the authority of a curator', from *cūrātor* 'curator' via κουράτωρ + -εύω. Documents: *P.Harr.* 11.228.14 etc. (III AD); *P.Cair.Masp.* 67151.230 (VI AD). Inscriptions: e.g. *IGR* IV.1531.8 (I/II AD); *SEG* XXXIV.1124.7 (II AD); *I.Leukopetra* 113.6 (III AD). Literature: Modestinus in Just. *Dig.* 27.1.15.3 etc. (III AD); Just. *Codex* 3.10.1.1 (VI AD); Antec. 1.23.pr. etc., but in Latin script 1.23.5 *curatoreuontai* etc. (VI AD). Post-antique: common despite absence from lexica. Notes: Avotins (1989), Mandilaras (1973: 67), Daris (1991a: 62), Mason (1974: 6, 63), Hofmann (1989: 209 *s.v.* κουράτωρ), Zilliacus (1935a: 182–3), *TLL* (*s.v. cūrātor* 1479.45–6), Lampe (1961), LSJ (*s.v.* κουράτωρ), LSJ suppl. See §2.4, §4.6.1 n. 91, §9.5.6 n. 55, §10.2.2 B, §10.3.2.
Deriv. of loan III AD – Byz.	**κουρατορία, κουρατορεία, κουρατωρ(ε)ία** (-ας, ἡ) 'office or position of curator', 'wardship', from *cūrātor* 'curator' via κουράτωρ + -ία. Documents: *P.Giss.* 104.3 (IV AD); *SB* 6257.4, 6258.2 (both VI AD); *P.Flor.* III.294.17 etc. (VI AD). Literature: Modestinus in Just. *Dig.* 27.1.2.2 etc. (III AD); Just. *Codex* 3.10.1.2, *Nov.* 123.5 (VI AD); Antec. 1.25.5 (VI AD). Post-antique: common. *LBG*, Lampe (1961). Notes: Avotins (1989, 1992), Daris (1991a: 62, with derivation from *cūrātōria*), Mason (1974: 6, 63), Hofmann (1989: 209 *s.v.* κουράτωρ), Zilliacus (1935a: 182–3), Triantaphyllides (1892: 266), *TLL* (*s.v. cūrātor* 1479.45), LSJ (*s.v.* κουράτωρ), LSJ suppl. See §4.6.1, §9.5.6 n. 55, §10.2.2 B, §10.3.2.

rare   **κουρατορικός, κουρατωρικός** 'concerning a curator', from *cūrātor* 'curator' via
κουράτωρ + -ικός: Just. *Nov.* 131.15.1 (VI AD); occasionally later. *LBG*,
Kriaras (1968–). See §9.5.6 n. 68.

Direct loan   **κουράτωρ, κουράτορ, κοράτωρ, γουράτωρ** (-ορος/-ωρος, ὁ) 'curator' (a public
I AD – modern   office, a military position, an office in a *collēgium*, and a type of guardian for
a minor), from *cūrātor* 'curator'.
     Documents: common, e.g. *SB* 13303.11 (I AD); *Pap.Choix* 6.5 (II AD); *P.Oxy.*
1120.13 (III AD); *P.Oxy.* 3756.4 (IV AD); *P.Münch.* III.102.11 (V AD);
P.Lond. V.1787.23 (VI AD).
     Inscriptions: common, e.g. *I.Pan du désert* 51.20 (I AD); *I.Syringes* 901.2 (II
AD); *I.Leukopetra* 65.17 (III AD); *I.Mylasa* 613.2 (V AD); *IGLS* IV.1905.6
(VI AD); *SEG* XX.390.2 (VI AD).
     Literature: common, e.g. Hadrian in Just. *Dig.* 5.1.48 (II AD); Modestinus in
Just. *Dig.* 19.2.49 (III AD); Thdt. *Ep.Pat.* 46.1 (V AD); Nil. 2.179.1 (V AD);
Malal. 18.23 (VI AD); Just. *Nov.* 117.1.1 (VI AD); Antec. 1.21.3 etc., but in
Latin script 1.24.3 *curatores* etc. (VI AD).
     Post-antique: survives. Zervan (2019: 91), Kriaras (1968–), Sophocles (1887),
Triandaphyllidis (1909: 126), Zilliacus (1937: 330). Modern dialectal
κοράτορα 'chief shepherd': Andriotis (1974: 332).
     Notes: forms derivatives κουρατορεύω, κουρατορία, ἀντικουράτωρ,
κουρατορατίων, κουρατορικός, συγκουράτωρ. Cuvigny (2010b), Avotins
(1989, 1992), Daris (1991a: 62), Mason (1974: 5, 6, 12, 63, 151), Hofmann
(1989: 208–9), Viscidi (1944: 10, 20–1), Zilliacus (1935a: 182–3),
Meinersmann (1927: 29–30), Lampe (1961), LSJ, LSJ suppl. See §2.4,
§4.2.5, §4.6.1, §6.8, §6.10, §7.1.1, §9.5.6 n. 55, §10.2.1, §10.2.2 B, §10.3.2.

     κουρατωρεία: see κουρατορία.

     κουρατωρεύω: see κουρατορεύω.

     κουρατωρία: see κουρατορία.

     κουρατωρικός: see κουρατορικός.

     κουρέλι: see κορέλι.

rare   **κουρεπιστουλάριος**, an official, from *cūra epistulārum* 'official in charge of
correspondence' (*TLL* s.v. *cūra* 1466.53–4, 1469.58): papyrus *P.Mich.*
XVIII.794.1 (VI AD). Hagedorn and Mitthof (1997).

rare   **κουρία** 'senate building', from *cūria* 'senate building': inscription *IG* XII.II.35.
b39 = Sherk 1969: no. 26.b39 (I BC). Transliterating *cūria* 'subdivision of
a tribe': DH *AR* 2.7.2 etc. (I BC); App. *BC* 3.13.94 (I/II AD); Lyd. *Mag.*
p. 30.2 (VI AD); occasionally later. Famerie (1998: 136–9), Freyburger-
Galland (1997: 91–2), García Domingo (1979: 507), Mason (1974: 6, 63),
Hofmann (1989: 209), *LBG*, LSJ suppl.

foreign   **κουριάτ(ι)ος** transliterating *cūriātus* 'of the thirty groups into which the Roman
people could be divided' (e.g. in *comitia curiata*): DH *AR* 9.41.2, 9.46.4
(I BC); App. *BC* 3.13.94 (I/II AD); inscriptions *I.Ephesos* 1544.11, 1545.6
(both I/II AD). Famerie (1998: 136–9), Freyburger-Galland (1997:
94), Mason (1974: 5, 63), Hofmann (1989: 210), Sophocles (1887 *s.v.*
κουριᾶτις), LSJ suppl.

not Latin **κουρικός** 'for cutting hair', as subst. 'barber's chair', is a purely Greek term attested mainly in papyri (e.g. *P.Oxy.* 646, II AD) but also in Epiph. *Pan.* III.476.16: τινὲς γὰρ γυναῖκες κουρικόν τινα κοσμοῦσαι ἤτοι δίφρον τετράγωνον (IV AD). Scholars unaware of the papyri sometimes argue that in Epiphanius it refers to a vehicle and comes from *curriculum* 'chariot'. Hofmann (1989: 210), Sophocles (1887 *s.v.* κούρικος), Lampe (1961), LSJ, LSJ suppl.

κουριόσ(σ)ος, κουριοῦσος: see κουριῶσος.

foreign **κουρίων** transliterating *cūriō* 'president of the curia': DH *AR* 2.7.4, 2.64.1 (I BC); perhaps inscription *SEG* XXX.158.3 (II AD); probably not Lyd. *Mag.* p. 20.3 (reading now δεκουρίωνας). Mason (1974: 6, 63), Hofmann (1989: 210), Sophocles (1887).

Direct loan **κουριῶσος, κουριόσ(σ)ος, κουριοῦσος** (-ου, ὁ) 'inquiry agent' (an official),
III AD – Byz. 'informer', from *cūriōsus* 'inquiring', which can also designate an official (*TLL s.v.* 1494.23–43).
Documents: *P.Coll.Youtie* II.74.4 (III AD); *P.Harrauer* 53.4 (V AD); *P.Oxy.* 4387.3 (V AD); *P.Vind.Sijp.* 22v.2 etc. (V AD?); *SB* 12252.5 etc. (V AD).
Inscriptions: *I.Chr.Macédoine* 150.4 (V/VI AD); *SEG* XXXV.1523.9 (VI AD).
Literature: DH *AR* 2.64.1 (3rd decl. dat. pl. κουρίωσιν, slightly marked) (I BC); Athan. *Apol.Sec.* 73.4, 76.1, *H.Ar.* 81.5 (IV AD); John Chrysostom, *PG* LII.532.18 (IV/V AD); Pall. *V.Chrys.* 11.4 (IV/V AD); Geront. *V.Mel.* 2.52 (V AD); Lyd. *Mag.* p. 100.4 etc. (VI AD). Unverified examples (III AD) in Zilliacus (1937: 322–3, 330).
Post-antique: survives. *LBG* (*s.v.* κουριοσσός).
Notes: Paschoud (1983: 236–8), Triantaphyllopoulos (1966), Daris (1991a: 62), Hofmann (1989: 211), Zilliacus (1935a: 182–3, 1937: 330), Lampe (1961), LSJ suppl. See §4.2.4.1 n. 51, §10.2.1, §10.2.2 D.

Direct loan **κούρκουμον, κούρκωμον** (-ου, τό) 'halter', from *curcuma* 'basket' (*TLL*).
VI AD – Byz. Literature: Hesych. as gloss ε 3157 (V/VI AD); Malal. 16.5 (VI AD).
Post-antique: survives. *LBG*, Kriaras (1968–), Triandaphyllidis (1909: 119).
Notes: Hofmann (1989: 211), *TLL* (*s.v. curcuma* 1480.19–20), LSJ. See §4.2.3.1, §10.2.1, §10.2.2 K.

κουρνοῦτος: see κορνοῦτος.

Loan compound **κουροπαλάτης, κουραπαλάτης** (-ου, ὁ) 'palace supervisor', from *cūra* 'care' +
VI AD – modern *palātium* 'imperial residence', probably in the form *cūra palātiī* 'person in charge of the imperial residence' (*TLL s.v. cūra* 1469.60–4) + -(τ)ης.
Inscriptions: *SEG* XLIV.584.6 (VI AD).
Literature: Malal. 18.135 etc. (VI AD); Evagr.Schol. *HE* 195.9 (VI AD).
Post-antique: survives, forming derivatives κουροπαλάτισσα 'wife of palace supervisor', κουροπαλατίκιον 'position of palace supervisor', etc. *LBG*, Zervan (2019: 92), Kriaras (1968–). Modern dialectal surname: Andriotis (1974: 332).
Notes: Cameron (1931: 244) suggests implausible derivation from unattested *cūropalātēs*. Triandaphyllidis (1909: 107), Hofmann (1989: 212), Viscidi (1944: 34), Lampe (1961). See §4.2.3.2, §4.5, §9.2, §10.2.1, §10.2.2 A; cf. κοῦρα, παλάτιον.

Loan compound
V–VI AD

κουροπερσονάριος, κουροπερσωνάριος, κουρωπερσωνάριος (-ου, ὁ), a job title, from *cūra* 'care' + *persōnālis* 'personal' (or perhaps *persōnārum* 'of persons'?).
Documents: *P.Laur.* 1.10.2 etc. (V AD); *P.Oxy.* 2050.5 (VI AD); *O.Ashm.Shelt.* 51.5 (VI AD).
Notes: both provenanced examples are from Oxyrhynchus. Κουρα περσωνάρουμ on *P.Wash.Univ.* 1.6.3 etc. (VI AD) may be the same word. Worp (1982: 564–5), Filos (2010: 250), Daris (1991a: 62, with derivation from *cūra* + *persōna*), Hofmann (1989: 212), LSJ suppl. (*s.v.* κουροπερσονάριοι). See §4.2.5, **§4.5**, §9.2, §10.2.1, §10.2.2 N; cf. κοῦρα, περσονάλιος.

foreign

κουρούλ(λ)ιος, κο(υ)ρούλης transliterating *curūlis* 'curule': inscriptions *SEG* XVIII.744.11 (II AD); *IG* IV.588.13 (II AD); *IG* V.I.533.18 (II AD); *I.North Galatia* 414.7 (III AD); Dio Cassius 39.32.2 etc. (II/III AD); Antec. in Latin script 1.2.7 *aediles curules* (VI AD). Freyburger-Galland (1997: 164, 1998: 142), Mason (1974: 6, 63), Hofmann (1989: 212), LSJ, LSJ suppl.

rare

κουρσεύω 'seize', 'ravage', from *cursus, -ūs* 'charge' (via κοῦρσον?) + -εύω: *Test.Sal.* p. 119*.13, 21 (III AD?); anonymous commentary on Aristotle, Rabe 1896: 204.34; often in Byzantine texts. Survives into modern Greek (Meyer 1895: 35; Andriotis 1967). Zilliacus (1935a: 222–3), Zervan (2019: 94), Kriaras (1968–), Sophocles (1887), LSJ.

not ancient?

κοῦρσον 'attack', 'band of attackers', from *cursus, -ūs* 'charge' (probably not *cursor* 'runner'; κούρσωρ was already established in a different sense): no securely ancient examples. Common in Byzantine texts; Zervan (2019: 93–4, 265) dates borrowing to VII AD. Modern κούρσα 'race', κουρσάρος 'corsair', κούρσος 'piracy', etc.: Babiniotis (2002), Andriotis (1967), Meyer (1895: 35). Binder (2000: 244), Daris (1991a: 62–3), Hofmann (1989: 212), Zilliacus (1935a: 222–3), Meinersmann (1927: 30), Kahane and Kahane (1972–6: 589, 1982: 151), *LBG* (*s.vv.* κοῦρσον and κοῦρσος, τό), Kriaras (1968–), Triandaphyllidis (1909: 131), Lampe (1961).

κούρσορ: see κούρσωρ.

rare

κουρσόριος, κουρσώριος 'for running', from *cursōrius* 'for running' (*TLL*): Edict. Diocl. 9.14 (IV AD). Hofmann (1989: 213), *TLL* (*s.v. cursōrius* 1528.75–7), LSJ suppl. (superseding LSJ *s.v.* κούρσωρ).

Direct loan
III AD – Byz.

κούρσωρ, κούρσορ, κούρσουρ, κούλσορ (-ορος/-ωρος, ὁ) 'courier' (a title), from *cursor* 'runner'.
Documents: e.g. *PSICongr.XXI* 12.8.13 (III AD); *P.Oxy.* 1958.6 etc. (V AD); *P.Ness.* III.35.10 (VI AD).
Inscriptions: *I.Aphrodisias Late Ant.* 150.5 (III/IV AD); *IG* X.II.1.792.2 (IV AD); variant at Edict.Diocl. 9.14 (IV AD); *I.Aphrodisias Late Ant.* 116.3 (V AD); *IG* II/III².V.13331.2 (V/VI AD); *I.Chr.Macédoine* 152.2 (V/VI AD); *IGLS* VI.2939.A2.
Literature: Severianus, *In Job, PG* LVI.572.31, marked (IV AD); Nil. 1.118.1 etc. (V AD); Lyd. *Mag.* p. 140.24 (VI AD); Ps.-Caesarius 106.31 Riedinger (VI AD); Ps.-Dioscorides, *De lapidibus* 31 in Ruelle 1898: 182; Philostorgius, *Historia ecclesiastica* frag. e vita Constantini 2.4a.35 etc.; with *exercipes* in Gloss. Ps.-Philox. 63.52. Unverified examples (III and IV AD) in Zilliacus (1937: 322–3, 330).

Post-antique: survives with the sense 'attacker'. *LBG*, Zervan (2019: 94–5), Kriaras (1968–), Triandaphyllidis (1909: 126), perhaps Meyer (1895: 35).

Notes: forms derivative πρωτοκούρσωρ. Daris (1991a: 63), Hofmann (1989: 213), Zilliacus (1935a: 222–3, 1937: 330), Meinersmann (1927: 30), Lampe (1961), LSJ suppl. (superseding LSJ). See §4.2.5, §10.2.1, §10.2.2 D.

κουρσώριος: see κουρσόριος.

κοῦρτα: see κοόρτη.

κουρτίνα: see κορτίνα.

name   **Κούρτιος λάκκος**, a place name, from *Curtius lacus*. Hofmann (1989: 213), LSJ (*s.v.* λάκκος 4), LSJ suppl. (*s.v.* λάκκος A.b). Cf. λάκκος.

κουρωπερσωνάριος: see κουροπερσονάριος.

Direct loan with suffix
V AD – Byz.   **κουσούλιον, κουσσούλιον** (-ου, τό), a garment (probably a hooded cloak), seems to come from *casula* or *casul(u)la*, a garment (*TLL s.vv.* 572.82–573.16) + -ιον.
Documents: *P.Heid.* IV.333.7 etc. (V AD); *P.Princ.* II.82.36 (V AD); *P.Berl. Sarisch.* 21.10 (V/VI AD).
Literature: *Apophth.Patr.* 6.9.2 (V AD).
Post-antique: survives in form κουσ(σ)ούλ(λ)ιον.
Notes: Daris (1991a: 63), Hofmann (1989: 159–60 *s.v.* κασοῦλα), *LBG* (*s.v.* κουσούλιν), LSJ, LSJ suppl. See §4.3.2 n. 69, §10.2.1, §10.2.2 H; cf. κασσοῦλα.

foreign   **κουσπάτωρ** 'prison guard', from *cuspus* 'wooden shoe' (*TLL*) via κοῦσπος + -άτωρ: Lyd. *Mag.* p. 72.5, marked (VI AD). *LBG*. See §6.9, §9.5.5 passage 76.

rare   **κοῦσπος** 'wooden foot-fetter': Lyd. *Mag.* p. 72.5, marked (VI AD); Malal. 2.17, as long-established soldiers' slang (VI AD). For later survival see *LBG*, Kriaras (1968–), Triandaphyllidis (1909: 122). Probably from *cuspus* 'wooden shoe' (*TLL*), which has a Romance descendant but for which the only direct evidence is Gloss. Ps.-Philox. 119.30, where *cuspus* is glossed with ξύλινον σανδάλιον. *TLL* takes that entry at face value, but Goetz (*CGL* VI.299 *s.v. cuspus*) and Heraeus (*CGL* VII.564 *s.v.* κοῦσπος) suggest that Ps.-Philoxenus' *cuspus* represents Greek κοῦσπος; that interpretation would provide an additional example of κοῦσπος but eliminate the only direct evidence for *cuspus*. Andriotis (1974: 332) derives κοῦσπος from *cuspis* 'sharp point' and cites two Byzantine descendants, κουσπίον 'throwing-spear' and κοῦσπος 'foot-fetter', both surviving into modern dialects; cf. Binder (2000: 262–3) and Meyer (1895: 36), who argues for an original meaning 'axe', with 'fetter' a Byzantine development. But the meanings that could come from *cuspis* are much later attested than 'fetter'; probably ancient κοῦσπος 'fetter', from *cuspus*, underwent semantic extension in the Byzantine period under the influence of *cuspis*. Lampe (1961). See §9.5.5 passages 76–7.

foreign   **κουστώδης πέδουμ** transliterating *custōdēs pedum* 'guardians of the feet' (from *custōs* 'guardian'): Lyd. *Mag.* p. 72.6 (VI AD). Chantraine (1937: 91), Sophocles (1887 *s.v.* κούστως). See §9.5.5 passage 76.

Direct loan
I AD – modern

κουστωδία, κοστωδ(ε)ία, κο(υ)στοδία, κωστωδία (-ας, ἡ) 'guard', 'prison', 'custody', from *custōdia* 'custody'.

Documents: *O.Did.* 357.3 (I AD); *P.Oxy.* 294.20 (I AD); *P.Ryl.* II.189.2 (II AD); *O.Bankes* 34.4 (II AD); *O.Claud.* II.360.5 (II AD); *O.Krok.* 1.65.5 (II AD); *P.Aberd.* 78.4 (II AD); *O.Heid.* 430.13 (III/IV AD).

Inscriptions (in form κουστωδιῶν, apparently from a different noun or a verb): *IGLS* XIII.I.9088.4 (III AD); *IGLS* XXI.v.1.63.1.

Literature: NT Matthew 27:65 etc. (I AD); *Acta Alexandrinorum* 9a.2.8 Musurillo (II/III AD); Pall. *H.Laus.* 38.4, marked (IV/V AD); Hesych. as lemma κ 3867, 3868, τ 821 (V/VI AD); Antec. 3.23.3a *custodiam* in Latin script (VI AD); common in biblical commentators. Unverified early examples in Zilliacus (1937: 322, 330).

Post-antique: numerous, forming derivatives κουστωδιακός 'of arrest', κουστωδιώτης 'protector'. *LBG*, Zervan (2019: 95), Kriaras (1968–). Modern κουστωδία 'police escort': Babiniotis (2002: 36), Andriotis (1967), Coleman (2007: 795), Meyer (1895).

Notes: Daris (1991a: 63), Hofmann (1989: 214), Zilliacus (1935a: 182–3, 222–3, 1937: 330), Meinersmann (1927: 31), Immisch (1885: 367), Lampe (1961), LSJ, LSJ suppl. See §4.1.1, §4.2.3.1, §7.2.1, §9.3 n. 21, §10.2.1, §10.2.2 D; cf. συγκουστουδιάζω.

κούστωρ: see ἀρμικούστωρ.

κούστως: see κουστώδης πέδουμ.

not Latin?

κουτάλι 'spoon', κουταλίζω 'hackle flax', etc. may be from *scutella* 'shallow dish' (thus Meyer 1895: 61 *s.v.* σκουτέλλα; Triandaphyllidis 1909: 121), but Shipp (1979: 349), *LBG* (*s.v.* κουτάλη), and Kriaras (1968–) suggest non-Latin etymology; cf. Andriotis (1967, *s.v.* κουτάλα suggesting a different Latin etymology and *s.v.* κουτάλι suggesting a non-Latin etymology). The only example that could be ancient is κουτάλη 'ladle': scholion to Ar. *Eq.* 984e as gloss.

κουτάνα: see κουιντάνα.

κουτανίσιος: see κουιντανήσιος.

κοῦφα: see κοῦπα.

Direct loan
I BC – modern

κοχλιάριον, κοχληάρηον (-ου, τό) 'spoon', 'spoonful', from *cochlear* 'spoon' (originally one for eating snails), 'spoonful', itself from κοχλίας 'snail'.

Documents: *P.Eleph.Wagner* I.325.3 (V/VI AD); *SB* 14531.2 (V/VI AD); *CPR* VIII.66.7 etc. (VI AD); *P.Lond.* III.1007a.9 etc. (VI AD); *P.Oxy.* 1901.6.68 etc., 2419.10 (both VI AD); *Stud.Pal.* XX.151.5 etc. (VI AD).

Literature: common, e.g. Philoxenus frag. 527 Theodoridis (I BC); Dsc. 4.170.4 (I AD); Galen XII.357.10 Kühn (II AD); Pollux 6.87 (II AD); Phrynichus, *Eclogae* 292 (II AD); *Coll.Herm.* LS 11g (III/IV AD); Orib. *Ecl.* 33.1 (IV AD); Hesych. as gloss β 593 (V/VI AD), Aëtius 2.175.22 (VI AD); numerous scholia glosses.

Post-antique: common. *LBG* (*s.vv.* κοχλιαρέα, κοχλιάρια), Kriaras (1968–), Triandaphyllidis (1909: 67, 69, 121 *s.v.* χουλιάρι). Modern κοχλιάριο 'spoon' (Babiniotis 2002), χουλιάριν (Meyer 1895: 72, but Andriotis 1967 *s.v.* χουλιάρι has a non-Latin etymology).

Notes: the Atticists' comparison with λίστρ(ι)ον 'tool for smoothing stone' suggests that κοχλιάριον may also have had that meaning. Hofmann (1989: 215–16), Meinersmann (1927: 30–1), *DÉLG* (*s.v.* κόχλος), Frisk (1954–72: 1.937), LSJ. See §2.1, §4.2.5, §4.3.2 n. 75, §6.3, §8.1.5, §9.2, **§9.4** passage 51, **§9.5.3** passages 64–5, §10.2.1, §10.2.2 I, §12.2.1.

κραβακτήρ(ι)ος: see κραβατάριος.

κραβάκτιον, κράβακτον, κράβακτος: see κράββαττος.

not ancient?	**κραβατάλιον**, something like 'bed', probably ultimately from *grabātārius* 'of a bed' (*TLL*): papyrus *BGU* III.950.3 (IV–VII AD).
rare	**κραβαταρία, κραβαταρέα** 'bier', from *grabātārius* 'of a bed' (*TLL*): Malal. 16.6, 18.18 (VI AD); occasionally later. Lampe (1961), Sophocles (1887).
rare	**κραβατάριος, κρεβ(β)αττάριος, κραβάτριος, κραβακτήρ(ι)ος, κραββατηρός** 'of a bed', as masc. subst. perhaps 'chamberlain' and/or 'bed-seller', probably comes from *grabātārius* 'of a bed' (*TLL*) when it has the -άριος suffix; the forms in -τήριος and -τριος are probably not Latinate unless the root is itself from Latin (see below on κράββαττος). With the -άριος suffix: inscriptions *CIRB* 711.1 (II AD); Edict.Diocl. 19.5 (IV AD); perhaps papyrus *SB* 15301.2.13 (V/VI AD), but the editor restores κραββ[ατηρόν]. With other suffixes: inscription *CIRB* 709.2 (II AD); papyrus *P.Cair.Masp.* 67006v.46 (VI AD). Hofmann (1989: 216), LSJ (κραβακτήριος *s.v.* κράββατος – but note that the papyrus cited there, *P.Cair.Masp.* 67006v, actually has κραβάκτηρος), LSJ suppl. (*s.vv.* κραβάτριος (replacing LSJ *s.v.* κραβάτριος) and κρεβαττάριος).

κραβάτη, κραβάτ(τ)ιον, κραβατοπόδιον: see κράββαττος.

κραββατηρός: see κραβατάριος.

κραββάτ(τ)ιον: see κράββαττος.

not Latin?	**κράβ(β)ατ(τ)ος, κράβακτος, κρέβατος** 'couch', 'bed', 'bier' (with variants and derivatives γράβακτον, κράβακτον, κραβάτη 'bed'; κραβάτιον, κραβ(β)άτ(τ)ιον, κρεβ(β)άτιον, κραβάκτιον 'little bed'; κραβατοπόδιον 'leg of a bed') may be from *grabātus/grabattus* 'camp bed', but the loan could go in the other direction, or both come independently from a third language. Kramer (1995a, 2011: 241–51), Shipp (1979: 106–7), Hofmann (1989: 216–17), *DÉLG*, *DÉLG Suppl.*, Frisk (1954–72: II.1), Beekes (2010), *LBG* (*s.v.* κράβαττον), Lampe (1961), LSJ, LSJ suppl.

κραπιδάριος: see κρηπιδάριος.

foreign	**κρᾶς** transliterating *crās* 'tomorrow': Soz. 4.10.6 (V AD); Thdr.Anag. *Tripart.* 2.98.5 (V/VI AD); *Apophthegmata patrum (collectio alphabetica)*, *PG* LXV.164.1–5. Sophocles (1887).
foreign	**Κρασσιανόν**, a cake name from *Crassiānus* 'of Crassus' (not attested of cakes): Athenaeus 14.647c, marked (II/III AD). Hauri-Karrer (1972: 120). See §9.4 passage 61.
foreign	**κράσσος** transliterating *crassus* 'fat': Lyd. *Mag.* p. 38.2 (VI AD). Sophocles (1887).

rare	**κρατίκλη**, a torture device apparently from *crātīcula* 'gridiron': John Chrysostom, *PG* LXII.412.36 (IV/V AD). Binder (2000: 160), Hofmann (1989: 217), Lampe (1961). Cf. ῥατίκλα.
	κρέβατος: see κράββαττος.
	κρεβ(β)άτιον: see κράββαττος.
	κρεβ(β)αττάριος: see κραβατάριος.
foreign	**κρεδίτωρ** 'creditor', from *crēditor* 'creditor': Antec. in Latin script 3.12.pr. *creditorsi* etc. (VI AD); later in Greek script. Zilliacus (1935a: 182–3), *LBG*. See §9.5.6 n. 68.
not ancient	**κρηνέλλα** 'gutter', from *crēna* 'notch', 'serration': no ancient examples. Meyer (1895: 36).
rare	**κρηπιδάριος, κραπιδάριος, κριπιδάριος** 'boot-maker', from *crĕpĭdārius* 'boot-maker' (itself from κρηπῖδα, acc. of κρηπίς 'boot') with influence from κρηπίς: papyrus *BGU* I.344.5 (II/III AD); inscription Sotiriou 1929: 157 no. 19.4. Diethart (1988: 58), Zingerle (1930: 76), Daris (1991a: 63), Hofmann (1989: 217–18), Meinersmann (1927: 31), *TLL* (1167.26), LSJ suppl.
foreign	**κρηπιδᾶτος** transliterating *crepidātus* 'wearing boots' (a kind of drama): Lyd. *Mag.* pp. 60.29, 62.1 (VI AD). *TLL* (*s.v. crepidātus* 1167.35–6), Sophocles (1887).
rare	**κρητάριον 1, κριτάριον** 'piece of chalk', from *crēta* 'chalk' via κρήτη + -άριον: *Anonymus Bobiensis* as gloss p. 34.6 De Nonno (V AD?); Aëtius 2.10.1 (VI AD); *Hippiatr.* e.g. *Hippiatr.Berl.* 103.18. Hofmann (1989: 218 *s.v.* κρητη), LSJ. See §6.3 n. 21.
rare	**κρητάριον 2**, a kind of pottery vessel, from (*ars*) *crētāria* 'way of making pottery vessels' (*TLL s.v. crētārius* 1187.34): papyrus *P.Bodl.* 48v.6 (II/III AD). Kramer (1998a: 40), *LBG*.
rare	**κρήτη** 'chalk', from *crēta* 'chalk' with influence from Κρήτη 'Crete': *Pap.Graec. Mag.* 7.858 (III/IV AD). Apparently forms derivative κρητάριον 1. Hofmann (1989: 218), LSJ.
rare	**κρητηρία** 'piece of chalk', probably from *crētārius* 'of chalk' (*TLL*): *Pap.Graec. Mag.* 7.170 (III/IV AD). Hofmann (1989: 218), LSJ (*s.v.* κρήτη).
	κριβανάριος: see κλιβανάριος.
rare	**κρικέλ(λ)ιον** 'hoop', 'ring', from *circellus* 'little circle' (*TLL*) + -ιον: Alex.Trall. II.377.19 (VI AD); Byzantine texts. Hofmann (1989: 218 *s.v.* κρίκελλος), *LBG*, Meyer (1895: 30), Babiniotis (2002 *s.v.* κρικέλλι), Andriotis (1967 *s.v.* κρικέλι, with non-Latin derivation), LSJ suppl. (replacing LSJ).
rare	**κρίκελλος** 'ring', from *circellus* 'little circle' (*TLL*): with *circulus* in Gloss. Ps.-Cyril. 355.19; with *circellus* in Gloss. *Herm.L.* 23.12; occasional Byzantine texts. Hofmann (1989: 218), *LBG*, Meyer (1895: 30), *TLL* (*s.v. circellus* 1095.78), LSJ.
foreign	**κρινῖτος** transliterating *crīnītus* 'long-haired': Lyd. *Mens.* 4.23 (VI AD). Sophocles (1887).

κριπιδάριος: see κρηπιδάριος.

rare | **κρισσοκάβων** 'suffering from varicocele', apparently a compound of κιρσός/ κρισσός 'enlarged vein' and *cabō* 'horse' (*TLL*): *Hippiatr.Berl.* (Apsyrtus) 14.1 (III/IV AD?). LSJ.

not ancient | **κρίστα** transliterating *crista* 'crest': interpolation in Dsc. 4.59 RV. Meyer (1895: 36–7).

κριτάριον: see κρητάριον 1.

rare | **κροκᾶτον** 'yellow parchment', from *crocātus* 'saffron-coloured' (itself from κρόκος 'saffron'): Edict.Diocl. 7.38 (IV AD). Hofmann (1989: 218), *DÉLG* (*s.v.* κρόκος), Frisk (1954–72: II.23), LSJ, LSJ suppl.

non-existent | **κρουστᾶτα**, from *crustāta* 'crustaceans': superseded reading of *P.Oxy.* 1978.2 (VI AD). Hofmann (1989: 218).

rare | **κρούστη** apparently from *crusta* 'crust', 'thin leaf of stone': inscription *IG* X.II.1.357.2 (II AD). LSJ *s.v.* χρούστη cites superseded reading of same inscription (*AE* 1905 no. 172.2), followed by Hofmann (1989: 484).

not Latin? | **κροῦστος** on papyrus *P.Oxy.* 1978.2 (VI AD) may mean 'woven' and come from an uncertainly attested *crustus* 'woven' (not in lexica) or from *crusta* 'crust', 'thin leaf of stone' (Diethart and Kislinger 1987: 8–9). Editors of *CPR* XXX.14.4 (VII AD) *ad loc.*, Daris (1991a: 63); LSJ's κρουστός is a different word and not from Latin. Meyer (1895: 37, cf. Babiniotis 2002, Andriotis 1967) relates modern κροῦστα and κροῦστον 'crust' to Latin. Cf. κρούστη.

foreign | **κυαισίτωρ, κοιαισίτωρ** transliterating *quaesītor* 'investigator': Procop. *Arc.* 20.10, 11 (VI AD); Lyd. *Mag.* p. 40.30 etc. (VI AD); Just. *Nov.* 80.t (bilingual) has in the Greek *quaesitoros* in Latin script and in the Latin *quaestore* (VI AD). Hofmann (1989: 218–19), *LBG*.

foreign | **κυαιστίων, κουαιστίων, κουαεστίων** transliterating *quaestiō* 'inquiry', 'examination (often by torture)': Lyd. *Mag.* p. 40.21, stating that the Latin means 'punishment' (VI AD). Zilliacus (1935a: 204–5), *LBG*. See §9.5.5 n. 47.

Direct loan III AD – Byz. | **κυαιστιωνάριος, κυαιστεωνάριος, κυεστωνάριος, κυεσσ(ι)ωνάριος** (-ου, ὁ) 'torturer', 'interrogator', from *quaestiōnārius* 'torturer' (L&S).
Documents: *P.Sijp.* 33r.7 (III AD); *P.Bagnall* 27.2 etc. (IV AD); *P.Herm.Landl.* 1.147, 2.366 (both IV AD); *P.Oxy.* 3986.10 (V AD); *P.Oxy.* 2050.2 (VI AD).
Literature: Hesych. as lemma κ 4337 (V/VI AD); Lyd. *Mag.* p. 40.21, marked (VI AD); *V.S.Mam.* 17. Unverified examples (II, III, and IV AD) in Zilliacus (1937: 323, 329).
Post-antique: numerous. *LBG*.
Notes: Editor of *P.Sijp.* 33 *ad loc.*, Binder (2000: 232), Daris (1991a: 63), Hofmann (1989: 219–20), Zilliacus (1937: 329), Immisch (1885: 355), LSJ suppl. (*s.v.* κυεσσωνάριοι). See §4.1.1 n. 17, §4.2.4.1 n. 50, §10.2.1, §10.2.2 D.

κυαιστορεία: see κουαιστορεία.

foreign | **κυαίστους** transliterating *quaestus, -ūs* 'acquisition of income': Lyd. *Mag.* p. 42.2 (VI AD). Sophocles (1887).

κυαιστωρ-: see κουαιστωρ-.

not Latin   κύβιτον 'elbow' and κυβιτίζω 'nudge with the elbow' are probably not from *cubitum* 'elbow' but an early Sicilian borrowing from an Italic language. Willi (2008: 30), Hofmann (1989: 219), Immisch (1885: 312), *DÉLG*, Frisk (1954–72: 11.39), Beekes (2010), LSJ.

not Latin?   κύδνος 'swan', perhaps from *cycnus/cygnus* 'swan': Hesych. as lemma κ 4420 (V/VI AD). Hofmann (1989: 219), LSJ suppl.

foreign   κυερῆλα transliterating *querēla* 'complaint': Lyd. *Mag.* p. 42.7 (VI AD). Sophocles (1887).

foreign   κυεριμωνία transliterating *querimōnia* 'complaint': Lyd. *Mag.* p. 42.7 (VI AD). Sophocles (1887).

κυεστωνάριος, κυεσσ(ι)ωνάριος: see κυαιστιωνάριος.

κυέστωρ: see κουαίστωρ.

rare   κυθραπαλαρία, apparently an item of kitchen equipment from κύθρα (a variant of χύτρα 'clay pot') + *epulāris* 'of feasts' via ἀπαλαρέα: papyrus *SB* 15301.2.7 (V/VI AD). Diethart (1995a: 90–1).

foreign   κυινδεκέμβηρ, κυινδεκίμβερος, κινδεκέμουιρ, and κυινδεκέμουιρος transliterating *quīndecimvir* 'member of a board of fifteen': inscriptions *SEG* XXXIII.342.3 (II AD); perhaps *SEG* XXIX.741.4 (II AD); *TAM* II.278.13 (III AD); perhaps *IGR* IV.372.3. Mason (1974: 6, 64, 116), Hofmann (1989: 220), Cameron (1931: 256).

not ancient?   κυινκ(ο)εννάλις, κυινκυεννάλις transliterating *quīnquennālis* 'every five years', 'holding office for five years': inscriptions perhaps *I.Cret.* IV.443.2; perhaps *IGR* I.1462.4; occasional Byzantine texts. Mason (1974: 64), Sophocles (1887 *s.v.* κυινκεννάλια), Lampe (1961 *s.v.* κυϊνκεννάλια).

κυι(ν)τάνα: see κουιντάνα.

κυιντανήσιος: see κουιντανήσιος.

κυιντανός: see κυντανός.

Κυιντίλ(λ)ιος: see Κοιντίλιος.

Direct loan   Κυιρῖται, Κυρῖται, Κουϊρῖται (-ῶν, οἱ), from *Quirītēs* 'Roman citizens'.
I BC – VI AD   Literature: DH *AR* 2.46.2 etc. (I BC); Strabo 5.3.1 etc. (I BC/AD); Plut. *Rom.* 19.9 etc. (I/II AD); Dio Cassius 36.25.1 etc. (II/III AD); Hesych. as part of gloss λ 328 (V/VI AD); Antec. 1.2.2, but in Latin script 1.5.3 *Quirites* (VI AD).
     Notes: sometimes marked, often unmarked. Freyburger-Galland (1997: 217, 1998: 142–3), Strobach (1997: 196), Mason (1974: 12, 64), Zilliacus (1935a: 204–5), *LBG* (*s.v.* κουιρίται). See §4.2.3.2, §8.1.5, §10.2.1, §10.2.2 N.

not Latin?   κυμινᾶτον 'preparation of cummin' may be from *cumīnātum*, neut. subst. of *cumīnātus* 'with cummin' (*TLL*), or a Greek formation from κύμινον 'cummin' + -ᾶτον. Diethart (1988: 55), LSJ. See **§6.5**.

κυνίκ(ο)λος: see κουνίκολος.

κυντανήσιος: see κουιντανήσιος.

rare   **κυ(ν)τανός** and **κυιντανός**, apparently from *quīntānus* 'of the fifth': documents *ChLA* III.200.30, Latinate (II AD); *C.Epist.Lat.* 234.12 (IV/V AD); *P.Ross. Georg.* III.10.3 etc. (IV/V AD); perhaps *P.Mert.* I.43v.17 (V AD). Daris (1991a: 63), Mason (1974: 4, 64), Zilliacus (1935a: 232–3), Lampe (1961 *s.v.* κυϊντανός). Cf. κουιντάνα, κουιντανήσιος.

Κυντίλ(λ)ιος: see Κοιντίλιος.

κυοδιοῦσο: see κουοδιούσω.

name   **Κυρίνα** 'Quirinal', from *Quirīnālis* 'of Quirinus' or *Quirīnus* 'Quirinus', the name of a hill in Rome. Hofmann (1989: 221, with derivation from *Quirīna*, the name of a tribe).

rare   **Κυρινάλιος** 'Quirinal', from *Quirīnālis* 'of Quirinus', is usually a name (particularly, but not exclusively, of a hill in Rome), but neut. pl. subst. Κυρινάλια is a festival: Plut. *Mor.* 285d (I/II AD). Hofmann (1989: 221), Sophocles (1887 *s.v.* Κυρινάλια).

name   **Κυρίνιος** 'Quirinal' from *Quirīnālis* 'of Quirinus', the name of a hill in Rome. Sophocles (1887).

name   **Κυρῖνος** from *Quirīnus*, the name of the deified Romulus: Lyd. *Mag.* 14.17 with etymology from κύριος (VI AD). Strobach (1997: 196), Hofmann (1989: 221), Sophocles (1887).

foreign   **κύρις** transliterating *curis* 'spear': DH *AR* 2.48.4 (I BC); Plut. *Rom.* 29.1, *Mor.* 285c (I/II AD). Hofmann (1989: 221–2).

Κυρῖται: see Κυιρῖται.

κυτανός: see κυντανός.

κωδηκέλ(λ)ος: see κωδικίλλος.

κώδηξ: see κῶδιξ.

non-existent?   **κωδικάριος** 'secretary', from *caudex/cōdex* via κῶδιξ + -άριος with influence from *ā cōdicillīs* 'secretary' (*TLL s.v. ā, ab* 23.20; *cōdicārius* 'sailor' (*TLL*) has the wrong meaning for the context): perhaps inscription *SEG* VI.541.10. Mason (1974: 8, 65, 142).

not ancient   **κωδικεία**, meaning uncertain, from *caudex/cōdex* 'book' via κῶδιξ + -εία (or a mistake for κωδίκιον?): no ancient examples. Daris (1991a: 64).

κωδικέλ(λ)ος: see κωδικίλλος.

non-existent?   **κωδικεύω**, from *caudex/cōdex* 'book' via κῶδιξ + -εύω: cited as an ancient loan by Zilliacus (1935a: 178–9), but I can find no examples.

rare   **κωδικίλλιον** 'codicil', 'writing', from *cōdicillus* 'codicil of a will' via κωδικίλλος + -ιον: Malal. 15.9 (VI AD); often later. Hofmann (1989: 222 *s.v.* κωδίκιλλος), *LBG*, Lampe (1961).

Direct loan
II AD – modern

κωδικίλλος, κοδικίλλος, κωδικέλ(λ)ος, κωδηκέλ(λ)ος (-ου, ὁ) 'official imperial letter', 'codicil to a will', from *cōdicillus* 'codicil to a will', 'rescript of the emperor'.

Documents: *P.Oxy.* 2857.22 (II AD); *Chrest.Mitt.* 316.ii.15 etc. (II AD); *SB* 12581.3 (IV AD); *P.Cair.Masp.* 67151.53 etc., 67312.24 etc. (both VI AD); perhaps *P.Köln* X.421.30 (VI AD).

Inscriptions: e.g. *SEG* XXIX.127.ii.36 (II AD); *I.Cret.* IV.300.B3 (II AD); Bosch 1967: 197 no. 156.11 (II AD).

Literature: e.g. Epict. *Diss.* 3.7.30 (I/II AD); Modestinus in Just. *Dig.* 26.3.1.1 (III AD); Gregorius Nazianzenus, *Testamentum*, Pitra 1868: 158.14 (IV AD); Hesych. as lemma κ 4778 κωδίκιλλα n. pl. (V/VI AD); Antec. 2.21.pr. etc., but in Latin script 2.25.pr. *codicillon* etc. (VI AD).

Post-antique: common. *LBG* (s.v. κωδίκιλλον), Kriaras (1968– s.v. κωδίκελλος), Sophocles (1887 s.vv. κωδίκελλος, κωδίκιλλος). Modern κωδίκελλος 'codicil': Babiniotis (2002), Andriotis (1967).

Notes: forms derivatives κωδικίλλιον, κωδικιλλόω. Avotins (1989, 1992), Drew-Bear (1972: 82), Bartalucci (1995: 121–2), Daris (1991a: 64), Mason (1974: 4, 12, 65, 141), Hofmann (1989: 222), Zilliacus (1935a: 178–9, 1937: 330), Meinersmann (1927: 31), Immisch (1885: 355 s.v. κωδίκιλλα), *TLL* (s.v. *cōdicillus*), Lampe (1961 s.v. κωδίκελλος), LSJ suppl. See §4.2.4.1 n. 51, §7.1.1 passages 19–20, §9.5.6 n. 55, §10.2.1, §10.2.2 B.

non-existent

κωδικίλλουν, κοδικίλλουν: cited by Daris (1991a: 64) and Hofmann (1989: 222 s.v. κωδίκιλλος) as a noun formed from *cōdicillus* 'codicil to a will' on the basis of papyrus *P.Oxy.* 2283.11 (VI AD), but the editors rightly take it as a form of κωδικιλλόω.

rare

κωδικιλλόω, κοδικιλλόω 'add as a codicil', from *cōdicillus* 'codicil to a will' via κωδικίλλος + -όω: papyrus *P.Oxy.* 2283.11 (VI AD). LSJ suppl.

not ancient

κωδίκιον, apparently 'codicil', from *caudex/cōdex* 'book' via κῶδιξ + -ιον, with influence from *cōdicillus* 'codicil to a will' (itself a diminutive of *cōdex*): headings (not original) to pronouncements of Justinian, Amelotti and Migliardi Zingale 1977: 38.1, 58.1 (VI AD); frequently later. Zervan (2019: 99), Sophocles (1887), Lampe (1961).

not ancient

κώδικον 'tax book', from *caudex/cōdex* 'book' via κῶδιξ: no ancient examples. Daris (1991a: 64), *LBG*.

Direct loan
V AD – modern

κῶδιξ, κώδηξ, κόδιξ (-ικος, ὁ) 'book', 'law book', from *caudex/cōdex* 'book' (in the modern form, not a bookroll).

Documents: *ChLA* XLI.1194.11 (VI AD); *P.Cair.Masp.* 67097r.41 (VI AD); *P.Mich.* XIII.667.10 (VI AD); *P.Herm.* 32.10 (VI AD); *P.Michael.* 40.25, 41.23, 42a.19 (all VI AD); *P.Petra* III.19.4 (VI AD); *P.Gascou* 30.12 (VI AD); perhaps *SB* 14670.2 (VI AD).

Literature: perhaps Hdn. *Pros.Cath.* III.1.44.1 (II AD); Ps.-Athanasius, *PG* XXVIII.945b (IV AD?); John Chrysostom, *PG* XLIX.353.7 (IV/V AD); Isidore of Pelusium, *Epistulae* 1697.36 Évieux (V AD); Hesych. as lemma κ 4780 (V/VI AD); Malal. 16.20 (VI AD); Just. *Nov.* 19.pr. etc. (VI AD); Lyd. *Mens.* 1.28 (VI AD); Evagr.Schol. *HE* 20.21 (VI AD); Ath.Schol. 2.1.1 etc. (VI AD); Antec. 2.10.10 etc. (VI AD).

Post-antique: common, forming derivatives κωδικεύτης 'one of compilers of *Codex* of Justinian', κώδικον 'tax book', etc. *LBG*, Zervan (2019: 98–9), Kriaras (1968–), Triandaphyllidis (1909: 128), Daris (1991a: 64). Modern κώδικας 'code' and derivatives: Babiniotis (2002), Andriotis (1967), Meyer (1895: 37).

Notes: in legal works means the overall text, while βιβλίον means part of the text: *Schol.Sinai.* 2 ἐν τῷ γ´ βιβλίῳ τοῦ Θεοδοσιανοῦ κώδικος τίτλῳ ιε´ (v/vι AD). Binder (2000: 263), Avotins (1992), Daris (1991a: 64), Hofmann (1989: 222–3), Viscidi (1944: 24), Zilliacus (1935a: 178–9, 1937: 330), Meinersmann (1927: 31), Immisch (1885: 355), Lampe (1961 *s.v.* κώδηξ). See §4.2.5, §7.1.2, §7.1.3, §8.2.3 n. 51, §9.5.6 n. 56, §10.2.1, §10.2.2 B.

foreign **κωετη** transliterating *quietē* 'peacefully': unpublished ostracon O.Max. inv. 743 (ιι AD).

rare **κώλικ(λ)ος**, a plant name from *cauliculus/cōliculus* 'little cabbage': *Hippiatr.Par.* (Apsyrtus) 356, 572 (ιιι/ιν AD?).

κωμακτορεία: see κομακτορία.

foreign **κωμισσᾶτον** 'revelry', apparently from *cōmissātum*, pf. part. of *cōmissor* 'revel': Plut. *Mor.* 726f, marked (ι/ιι AD). Strobach (1997: 196), Hofmann (1989: 190, κομίσατον), Sophocles (1887, κωμεσσᾶτον).

κωμιτᾶτον: see κομιτᾶτον.

κωμόδιον: see κομόδιον.

Κωνσάλια: see Κωνσουάλια.

rare **κωνσανγυίναιος, κονσανγυίνεος** 'related by blood', from *cōnsanguineus* 'related by blood': papyrus *P.Thomas* 20.2.4 (ιιι AD); Antec. in Latin script 3.2.1 *consanguineoi* (νι AD). Zilliacus (1935a: 180–1).

foreign **κωνσεκρατίων, κονσεκρατίων** transliterating *cōnsecrātiō* 'consecration': Lyd. *Mag.* p. 128.11 (νι AD). *LBG*.

foreign **κωνσίλιον, κονσίλιον** transliterating *cōnsilium* 'advice', 'meeting': DH *AR* 4.76.2 (ι BC); Plut. *Rom.* 14.3 (ι/ιι AD); Antec. in Latin script 1.6.4 *consilion* etc. (νι AD); Lyd. *Mag.* p. 46.9 (νι AD); Byzantine texts. Mason (1974: 6, 65), Hofmann (1989: 223), Zilliacus (1935a: 180–1), *LBG* (*s.v.* κονσίλιον), Kriaras (1968– *s.v.* κονσίλιον).

κωνσιστώριον: see κονσιστώριον.

foreign **κωνσκρίπτος** transliterating *cōnscrīptus* as part of πάτρης κωνσκρίπτους (*patrēs cōnscrīptōs*) 'senators': Lyd. *Mag.* p. 4.23, in Latin script p. 30.1 *patres conscripti*, 28.26 *conscriptos* (νι AD). *LBG*.

foreign **Κωνσουάλια, Κωνσάλια, Κονσίλια** transliterating *Cōnsuālia*, a festival: DH *AR* 1.33.2, 2.31.2 (ι BC); Plut. *Rom.* 15.7, *Mor.* 276c (ι/ιι AD); Malal. 7.9.47, 53 (νι AD); Lyd. *Mag.* p. 46.12 (νι AD). Hofmann (1989: 223).

foreign   **κώνσουλ, κόνσουλ** transliterating *cōnsul* 'consul': DH *AR* 4.76.2 (I BC); Plut. *Rom.* 14.3 (I/II AD); Lyd. *Mag.* pp. 46.5, 46.11 (VI AD); perhaps inscription *I.Caesarea Maritima* 84 (V/VI AD). Binder (2000: 222), Mason (1974: 6, 65); for later occurrences *LBG* (*s.v.* κόνσουλος), Hofmann (1989: 224), Zervan (2019: 85), Kriaras (1968– *s.v.* κόνσουλος). Modern κόνσολος comes from Venetian *consolo*: Andriotis (1967).

name   **Κωνσταντιακός** 'Constantinian', from *Cōnstantiānus* 'Constantinian' (*TLL s.v. Cōnstantius* 579.60–82). Hofmann (1989: 224), Cavenaile (1952: 197).

rare   **Κωνσταντιανός** 'Constantinian' from *Cōnstantiānus* 'Constantinian' (*TLL s.v. Cōnstantius* 579.60–82), in fem. pl. subst. as the name of baths in Constantinople: Socr. 4.8.8, 6.18.50 (IV/V AD); Pall. *V.Chrys.* 56.20 (IV/V AD). *LBG.*

non-existent   **κωντοναίτωρ**, meaning uncertain, from *centōnārius* 'fireman' or *contiōnātor* 'demagogue': superseded reading of papyrus *P.Dubl.* 33 = *SB* 5175.21 (VI AD). Schubert (1988), Cavenaile (1951: 398).

         κωντούκτωρ: see κονδούκτωρ.

         κῶπλα: see κόπλα.

         κῶρος: see χῶρος.

         κώρτη: see κοόρτη.

         κωστωδία: see κουστωδία.

Λ

rare   **λάβαρον, λάβωρον**, a kind of military standard, from *labarum*, a kind of military standard (*TLL*): Soz. 1.4.1, 9.4.6, both marked (V AD); EphraemSyr. VII p. 137.15 (V/VI AD); Byzantine texts. Zervan (2019: 99) is unsure of the etymology. Niehoff-Panagiotidis (2019: 468–70), *LBG* (*s.v.* λάβωρον), Kriaras (1968–), Sophocles (1887), Triandaphyllidis (1909: 130), *TLL* (*s.v. labarum*), Lampe (1961).

rare   **λαβέλλιον** 'small basin, bowl', from *lābellum* 'basin' + -ιον: papyrus *CPR* VIII.65.18 (VI AD). Daris (1991a: 64), LSJ suppl.

rare   **λάβελλος** 'water bowl', from *lābellum* 'basin': papyrus *P.Bodl.* 48v.4 (II/III AD). Kramer (1998a: 40), *LBG.*

foreign   **λάβρα** transliterating pl. of *labrum* 'lip': Plut. *Mor.* 727a (I/II AD). Strobach (1997: 196), Hofmann (1989: 225).

         λαγγιάριος: see λαγκιάριος.

non-existent?   **λαγηνάριος** 'maker of flagons', perhaps from *lagēnārius* 'maker of flagons' (Bartal 1901 *s.v.*, cf. *TLL s.v. lagoenārius* 'of flagon-selling'): perhaps inscription *IGR* III.837.4. May be variant of Greek λαγυνάριος (from λάγυνα + -άριος, on inscription *MAMA* III.236.4). Hofmann (1989: 225), Cameron (1931: 247), *DÉLG* (*s.v.* λάγυνος), Frisk (1954–72: II.69), Beekes (2010 *s.v.* λάγυνος), LSJ, LSJ suppl. (*s.v.* λαγυνάριος).

not Latin | **λαγήναρχος** 'person having power over wine' is cited by LSJ on the basis of Hesych. λ 55 lemma (v/vi ad); this is spelled λαγύναρχος by editors and with that spelling is not Latinate, but the manuscript has λαγιν-, so LSJ reconstructs λαγήναρχος from *lagēna* (see *s.vv.* λάγηνος, λάγυνος 2). The manuscript is from xv ad, when ι, η, and υ had completely merged in pronunciation, so it is not evidence of Latin influence.

Direct loan with suffix
II AD – modern?

λαγήνιον (-ου, τό) 'little flagon', from *lagēna* 'flagon' + -ιον.
Documents: *SB* 11903v.16 (ii ad); *P.Stras.* v.394.5 (v/vi ad); *P.Berl.Zill.* 7r.25 (vi ad).
Post-antique: common. *LBG* (combining λαγήνιον with λαγίνιον, which could represent either λαγήνιον or Greek λαγύνιον: see on λαγήναρχος). Modern λαγήνι 'water jug' may be a descendant despite non-Latin etymology of Babiniotis (2002).
Notes: Latin derivation depends heavily on first example, from time when Greek speakers unlikely to confuse υ and η; both later ones have been taken as misspellings of λαγύνιον. Gignac (1976: 265), Hofmann (1989: 225 *s.v.* λάγηνος), Meinersmann (1927: 31). See §4.3.2, §9.2, §10.2.1, §10.2.2 I.

rare | **λάγηνος** 'flagon' (also used as a unit of measurement), from or at least influenced by *lagēna*, variant of *lagōna/lagoena/lagūna* 'flagon' (itself from Greek λάγυνος), perhaps as a back-formation via λαγήνιον: probably Galen xi.663.13 Kühn (ii ad); Hippolytus, *Refutatio omnium haeresium* 4.37.3 (iii ad); old scholia to Theocritus 10.13. Byzantine λαγήνα may be a separate, later borrowing of the same Latin: Zervan (2019: 100, 266), *LBG*, Kriaras (1968–). Hofmann (1989: 225), Meinersmann (1927: 31), *DÉLG* (*s.v.* λάγυνος), Frisk (1954–72: ii.69), Beekes (2010 *s.v.* λάγυνος), LSJ (*s.v.* λάγυνος 2).

λαγκεάριος: see λαγκιάριος.

not ancient | **λαγκεύω** 'throw lances', from *lanceō* 'strike with a lance' (*TLL*) + -εύω: no ancient examples. Zilliacus (1935a: 226–7), *LBG*.

not ancient? | **λάγκη** (written *lance*): with *lanx* 'dish' in the transliterated Gloss. Serv. 507.43, on which basis Hofmann (1989: 229) has an entry for *lance* 'dish'. LSJ.

foreign | **λαγκία** transliterating *lancea* 'lance': Diodorus Siculus 5.30.4 (i bc); Plut. *Marc.* 29.15 (i/ii ad). Byzantine use probably unrelated: Zilliacus (1935a: 226–7), *LBG*, Kriaras (1968–), Triandaphyllidis (1909: 130). Hofmann (1989: 226), LSJ.

Direct loan
III AD – Byz.

λαγκιάριος, λανκιάριος, λαγγιάριος, λαγχιάριος, λαχηαήριος, λαγκεάριος (-ου, ὁ) 'lancer', from *lanceārius* 'lancer' (*TLL*).
Documents: *P.Panop.Beatty* 2.260 etc. (iii/iv ad).
Inscriptions: probably *I.Anazarbos* 72.3 (ii/iii ad); *IGLS* ii.654.7 (iv ad); perhaps *SEG* xxxi.1116.6 (iv ad); *MAMA* i.167.7 (iv/v ad); *MAMA* i.169.2, 306.5; *CIG* 4004.1; *IG* xiv.157.3; Cronin 1902: 353 no. 97.2.
Literature: Magnus, *FHG* iv frag. 1.34 (iv ad); Malal. 13.21, copying Magnus (vi ad); Lyd. *Mag.* p. 70.22, marked (vi ad).
Post-antique: survives. *LBG*, Triandaphyllidis (1909: 129).
Notes: Schirru (2013: 316), Daris (1991a: 64), Hofmann (1989: 226), Zilliacus (1935a: 226–7), LSJ (*s.v.* λαγκία). See §4.2.4.1 n. 50, §10.2.1, §10.2.2 C.

rare   **λαγκίδιον** 'short lance', from *lancea* 'lance' + -ίδιον: Malal. 18.56 (VI AD); occasionally later. Hofmann (1989: 226 *s.v.* λαγκία), Zilliacus (1935a: 226–7), *LBG*, Lampe (1961).

not ancient   **λαγκίολα**, a plant name transliterating *lanciola* 'little lance' (not attested as a plant name): interpolation in Dsc. 3.144 RV. Hofmann (1989: 226), *TLL* (*s.v. lanceola*), LSJ.

rare   **λαγκιολᾶτος** 'with lancet-shaped pattern', from *lanceolātus* 'decorated with lancets' (*TLL*): Lyd. *Mag.* p. 88.24 (VI AD). *LBG*.

rare   **λάγκλα, λάνκλα** 'dish', from *lancla*, variant of *lancula/langula* 'little plate' (cf. *TLL s.v. lancula*): papyrus *BGU* III.781.v.18 etc. (I/II AD). Forms derivative λάγκλιον. Binder (2000: 157), Daris (1991a: 64), Hofmann (1989: 229), Meinersmann (1927: 32), LSJ.

rare   **λάγκλιον, λάγκλειον** 'little dish', from *lancla*, variant of *lancula/langula* 'little plate' (cf. *TLL s.v. lancula*) via λάγκλα + -ιον: papyrus *BGU* III.781.iv.1 (I/II AD); with *lanx* in Gloss. *Idiom.* 545.53. Daris (1991a: 64, with derivation from *lanx*), Hofmann (1989: 229 *s.v.* λανκλα), Cavenaile (1952: 195), LSJ (*s.v.* λάγκλα).

     λαγυνάριος: see λαγηνάριος.

     λαγχιάριος: see λαγκιάριος.

Direct loan?   **Λαδικηνός, Λαοδικηνός, Λαυδικηνός** (-ή, -όν) 'Laodicean', 'from Laodicea' (of
I AD – Byz.   garments, wine, jars, and people), as neut. subst. 'jar for Laodicean wine', probably from *Lāodicēnus/Lāudicēnus* 'of Laodicea', itself ultimately from Λαοδίκεια 'Laodicea' and formed perhaps by analogy with e.g. *Pergamēnus*.
     Documents, adj.: e.g. *O.Berenike* II.147.4 (I AD); *O.Did.* 412.9 (II AD); *P.Oxy.* 3169.143 (III AD); *P.Sijp.* 55.b7 (III/IV AD); *P.Oxy.* 3776.41 (IV AD). Neut. subst.: numerous in *O.Berenike*, e.g. 1.39.5, 1.94.4 (all I AD); *O.Petr.* 289.5, 290.4 (both I AD); *O.Stras.* 1.788.3 (II AD).
     Inscriptions, adj., of garments: Edict.Diocl. 19.37 etc. (IV AD); probably Baur *et al.* 1933: 153 no. 300.16.
     Literature, adj.: *Periplus Maris Erythraei* 6.55 etc. Casson, of wine (I/II AD); Ptol. *Geog.* 5.15.20, of cities; Malal. 9.5.16 etc., of roads (VI AD); Alex.Trall. II.483.31, of wine (VI AD).
     Post-antique: some survival. *LBG*.
     Notes: could have Greek etymology, but examples are concentrated in Latin-influenced areas, in contrast to more common Λαοδικεύς. Tomber (1998, of jars), editors of *O.Berenike* I (pp. 16–18, of wine and jars), Hofmann (1989: 226, of garments), LSJ suppl. (*s.v.* λαυδικηνόν, of garments). See §4.2.2, §10.2.1, §10.2.2 I.

     λάεινος: see λάϊνος.

foreign   **λαῖνα** transliterating *laena* 'woollen double cloak': Strabo 4.4.3 (I BC/AD); Plut. *Numa* 7.5 (I/II AD). Strobach (1997: 196), Hofmann (1989: 226–7), LSJ. Cf. ληίνη.

rare   **λάϊνος, λάεινος** 'made of wool', probably from *lāna* 'wool' + -ινος: *P.Oxy.* 1741.11 (IV AD). Cervenka-Ehrenstrasser (2000: 146).

not ancient	**λακέρδα, λακέρτα** 'salted tuna', from *lacerta* 'Spanish mackerel': no ancient examples. Meyer (1895: 37), Kriaras (1968–), Triandaphyllidis (1909: 119), Andriotis (1967).
rare	**λακέρνιον** 'cloak', from *lacerna* 'cloak fastened at the shoulder' + -ιον: papyrus *BGU* XVI.2669.41 (I BC/AD); inscription *SEG* VII.373.ii.3 (II AD). Hofmann (1989: 227), LSJ. **λακέρτα**: see λακέρδα.
foreign	**λακιναρίδιον** is said by Hesych. λ 203 (V/VI AD) to be a Roman word for 'shoe', on which basis *TLL* includes unattested **lacinaridium*. But Immisch (1885: 344) and *LBG* derive it from *lacinia* 'fringe'. Hofmann (1989: 227). See §8.1.7.
not ancient	**λακινιά** 'herd', from *lacinia* 'small group': no ancient examples. Meyer (1895: 37), *LBG*, Andriotis (1967), Kriaras (1968–).
not ancient	**λακίνιον** 'fragment', from *lacinia* 'fringe', 'rag': post-antique papyrus *Stud.Pal.* XX.244.18. Hofmann (1989: 227 *s.v.* λακινια), LSJ suppl.
semantic extension	**λάκκος** 'pond', though etymologically Greek (LSJ, *DÉLG s.v.* 1 λάκκος, Beekes 2010 *s.v.* λάκκος 1), sometimes stands for *lacus, -ūs* 'lake' as part of Roman place names (e.g. Plut. *Rom.* 18.6). Its meaning 'cistern' in Eastern Desert ostraca (e.g. Cuvigny 2019: 290 no. 7.12, II AD) may also be Latinate. Hofmann (1989: 213, 227), Meinersmann (1927: 31–2), Sophocles (1887), LSJ suppl. See §2.3 n. 58; cf. Κούρτιος λάκκος.
rare	**λακτέντον** 'suckling pig', from *lactēns* (gen. *lactentis*) 'suckling': Hieroph. *Nut.* 9.2, 10.2, 11.1, Πῶς 465.15 (IV–VI AD); Byzantine texts. Λακέντιον at *Apophth. Patr.* 4.72.3 (V AD), evidently some kind of food (cf. *LBG*), is probably a variant or corruption of this. Hofmann (1989: 228), Viscidi (1944: 38), Meinersmann (1927: 32), Wessely (1902: 136, with reference to a papyrus that I cannot trace), *LBG* (with derivatives λακτεντόπουλον 'suckling pig', λακτεντοχοιροκριοβουτραγοσφάγος 'butcher for piglets, pigs, rams, cattle, and goats'), Kriaras (1968– *s.v.* λακτένδον), Meyer (1895: 38 *s.v.* λαχτέντο).
rare	**λακωνάριος** 'panelled', from *lacūnāria*, plural of *lacūnar* 'panel' (*lacūnārius* exists but not in a relevant sense: *TLL s.v.*): quotation from Constantine recorded by Eus. *VC* 3.32.1–2 (IV AD) and by several other writers (e.g. Socr. 1.9.392–9). Hofmann (1989: 228), Lampe (1961).
Direct loan **IV AD – modern**	**λᾶμνα** (-ης?, ἡ) 'metal plate', from *lāmina/lāmna* 'thin sheet of metal'. Documents: *Pap.Graec.Mag. passim*, e.g. no. 7.459 (III/IV AD), 4.2154 etc. (IV AD), 9.8 (IV/V AD), 10.26 (IV/V AD). Inscriptions: Edict.Diocl. 30.5 (IV AD). Literature: Zosimus alch., Berthelot and Ruelle 1888: 139.22 (III/IV AD); *Hippiatr.Par.* (Apsyrtus) 351, 1026 (III/IV AD?); Hesych. as part of gloss λ 578 (V/VI AD); as gloss in scholia to Luc. *Cal.* 12, *Tim.* 20; with *lamella* in Gloss. Ps.-Cyril. 358.25. Post-antique: numerous. *LBG*. Modern λάμνα with altered meanings: Meyer (1895: 37), Andriotis (1967). Notes: may form derivative λαμνίον. Binder (2000: 207), Daris (1991a: 64), Hofmann (1989: 228), Meinersmann (1927: 32), LSJ suppl. (replacing LSJ). See §4.6.1 n. 84, §10.2.1, §10.2.2 M.

Deriv.? of loan
III AD –
modern?

λαμνίον (-ου, τό) 'little metal plate', from *lāmina/lāmna* 'thin sheet of metal' (via λᾶμνα?) + -ιον.
    Documents: *Pap.Graec.Mag.* 4.3014 (IV AD); *Suppl.Mag.* 94.37 (VI AD).
    Inscriptions: none; Binder's reference (2000: 207) is confused (cf. Cavenaile 1952: 195).
    Literature: Iamblichus alch., Berthelot and Ruelle 1888: 287.10, 12 (II/III AD).
    Post-antique: occasional survival. *LBG* (*s.v.* λαμνίν). Perhaps modern λαμνί with altered meanings: Meyer (1895: 37), Andriotis (1967).
    Notes: Daris (1991a: 64), Hofmann (1989: 228 *s.v.* λᾶμνα), Cavenaile (1952: 195), Meinersmann (1927: 32), LSJ suppl. See §4.3.2 n. 69, §4.6.1 n. 84, §10.2.2 M.

rare

λαμπαδάριος 'torch-bearer', from *lampadārius* 'torch-bearer' (itself ultimately from λαμπάς 'torch'): Teucer, Boll 1903: 42.4 (I AD?); Byzantine texts. Hofmann (1989: 228), Lampe (1961), *LBG*, Kriaras (1968–), LSJ suppl.

Direct loan
II AD – modern

λανάριος (-ου, ὁ) 'wool-worker', from *lānārius* 'wool-worker'.
    Documents: *P.Oxy.* 3403.9 (IV AD); *BGU* III.941r.5 etc. (IV AD); *P.Genova* 1.24.10 (IV AD); *P.Lond.* I.125r.22 (IV AD); perhaps *P.Stras.* V.309r.5 (IV AD); perhaps *P.Mert.* 1.34r.2 (IV AD); *P.Prag.* 1.34r.A10 (VI AD); perhaps *P.Herm.* 41.2 (VI AD).
    Inscriptions: e.g. *I.Ephesos* 727.7 (II AD); *TAM* V.I.85.5 (II AD); *TAM* V.II.1019.11 (III AD); Edict.Diocl. 21.1 etc. (IV AD).
    Literature: old scholion to Apollonius Rhodius, p. 270.19: λήνεσσιν· τοῖς ἐρίοις, ὅθεν καὶ λανάριοι καλοῦνται οἱ κτενισταί.
    Post-antique: numerous papyri (though not in Daris 1991a); literature has Byzantine derivatives λανάρι 'carding-comb' (*LBG*, Kriaras 1968–), ληνάριος (λῆνος + λανάριος: *LBG*). Modern λαναράς 'wool-worker', λανάρι 'carding-comb', etc.: Babiniotis (2002), Andriotis (1967), Meyer (1895: 38).
    Notes: Daris (1991a: 64), Hofmann (1989: 229), LSJ suppl. See §4.2.4.1 n. 50, §10.2.1, §10.2.2 H.

Deriv. of loan
VI AD

λανάτιον (-ου, τό) 'wool garment', from *lānātus* 'woollen' via λανᾶτον + -ιον.
    Documents: *P.Berl.Sarisch.* 21.5 (V/VI AD); *SB* 12249.13 (V/VI AD); *SB* 12251.5 etc. (VI AD); *P.Cair.Masp.* 67143.v10 (VI AD).
    Notes: Daris (1991a: 65), Hofmann (1989: 229 *s.v.* λανᾶτον). See §4.6.1 n. 83, §9.2, §10.2.2 H.

Direct loan
V AD – modern

λανᾶτον (-ου, τό) 'wool garment', from neut. of adj. *lānātus* 'woollen' or unattested neut. subst. **lānātum* 'wool garment'.
    Documents: *SB* 15191.5 etc. (V AD); *P.Cair.Masp.* 67006v.87 (VI AD); *P.Rain. Cent.* 156.3 (VI AD).
    Literature: Barsanuph.Jo. II.1 ep. 326.19 (VI AD); Dor.Gaz. *Doct.Div.* 3.45.15 (VI AD).
    Post-antique: survives. *LBG*, Kriaras (1968–), Kahane and Kahane (1972–6: 535). Modern dialectal λανάτα 'sheepskin': Andriotis (1974: 349).
    Notes: forms derivatives λανάτιον, λανατουργός. Daris (1991a: 65), Hofmann (1989: 229), Meinersmann (1927: 32), *TLL* (*s.v.* *lānātus* 916.78–80), Lampe (1961 *s.v.* λανᾶτος). See §4.2.4.1 n. 55, §4.6.1 n. 83, §9.2, §10.2.1, §10.2.2 H.

rare	**λανατουργός** 'wool-worker', from *lānātus* 'woollen' via λανᾶτον + -ουργός (cf. ἔρδω 'do'): papyrus *P.Mert.* 1.42.6 (v ad). Filos (2010: 250), Daris (1991a: 65, with derivation from *lāna*), Cavenaile (1952: 199).
non-existent?	**λανιάριος**: cited by Daris (1991a: 65) as from *laniō* 'tear', 'cut up' on the basis of papyrus *P.Stras.* v.309r.5 (iv ad), where it could be a misspelling of λανάριος.
	lance: see λάγκη.
	λανκιάριος: see λαγκιάριος.
	λάνκλα: see λάγκλα.
foreign	**λαξαμέντον** 'respite', from *laxāmentum* 'respite': Just. *Nov.* in Latin script 72.6 (vi ad); later in Greek script. Zilliacus (1935a: 192–3), *LBG*.
	Λαοδικηνός: see Λαδικηνός.
	λαργετίων, λαργητίων: see λαργιτίων.
	λαργιλιατ: see λαργιτιωναλικός.
non-existent?	**λαργιτιονάλια** 'money tax on landed property', from *largītionālia*, neut. pl. of *largītionālis* 'of the imperial treasury' (*TLL*): probably not papyrus *SB* 14674.19 etc. (v/vi ad). Gascou and Worp (1988), LSJ suppl.
	λαργιτιοναλικός: see λαργιτιωναλικός.
Direct loan v ad – Byz.	**λαργιτίων, λαργητίων, λαργετίων** (-ωνος,/-ονος, ἡ) 'distribution of gifts' (with technical sense in imperial administration), from *largītiō* 'distribution of gifts' (with same technical sense). Documents: perhaps *SB* 17260.2 (v ad); *SB* 16575.3, perhaps 14674.23 (both v/vi ad); *SB* 4707.9 (vi ad?). Inscriptions: *I.Perinthos* 284.2 (iv/v ad); *I.Mylasa* 612.1 (v ad); *I.Ephesos* 38.11 (v ad?); *IGLS* iii.ii.1142.2 (vi ad); two weights in Delmaire 1989: 520 (vi ad); perhaps *IGLS* iii.ii.1242³.2 (vi ad); perhaps *SEG* xxxv.1523.5 (vi ad); perhaps *SEG* xxxvi.1281.6 (vi ad); probably not *IGLS* ii.528.8 (vi ad). Literature: e.g. Thdt. *HE* 252.20 (v ad); *ACO* i.i.iii p. 51.1 (v ad); Malal. 16.7 (vi ad); Just. *Nov.* 44.2 etc., but in Latin script *Edict* 13.20 = p. 790.16 (vi ad). Post-antique: survives. *LBG* (*s.v.* λαργετζίων), Zervan (2019: 100–1), Triandaphyllidis (1909: 127). Notes: Avotins (1989, 1992), Daris (1991a: 65), Hofmann (1989: 230), Zilliacus (1935a: 192–3), Lampe (1961), LSJ suppl. See §4.2.5, §10.2.1, §10.2.2 D.
Direct loan with suffix v–vi ad	**λαργιτιωναλικός, λαργιτιοναλικός, λαργιλιατ** (-ή, -όν) 'related to distribution of gifts' (with technical sense in imperial administration), from *largītionālis* 'of the imperial treasury' (*TLL*) + -ικός. Documents: *Stud.Pal.* xx.143.9 (v ad); perhaps *SB* 14674.19 etc. (v/vi ad); *P.Flor.* iii.377.15 (vi ad); *P.Cair.Masp.* 67057.1.18 (vi ad). Literature: Just. *Edict* in Latin script 13.11 = p. 785.31 etc. (vi ad). Notes: Daris (1991a: 65), Hofmann (1989: 230), Cavenaile (1952: 197), Meinersmann (1927: 32), *TLL* (*s.v. largītionālis*), LSJ suppl. See §4.3.3, §10.2.1, §10.2.2 D.

rare   **λαρδηγός** 'purveyor of salted meat', from *lāridum/lārdum* 'bacon' via λάρδος + -ηγός (cf. ἄγω): inscription *SEG* XXXIV.1243.26 (V AD). Hofmann (1989: 230 *s.v.* λάρδος), *DÉLG* (*s.v.* λάρδος), Frisk (1954–72: II.85), Beekes (2010 *s.v.* λάρδος), LSJ.

Direct loan   **λάρδος** (-ου, ὁ) 'salted meat', from *lāridum/lārdum* 'bacon'.
I AD – modern
           Documents: probably none. P.Lond. ined. 2147 (IV AD) has long been cited, but by now the lack of publication raises suspicions.
           Literature: Severus Iatrosophista p. 41.26 Dietz (I AD); *Coll.Herm.* C 52b (II–IV AD); Lyd. *Mens.* 4.92 (VI AD); Her.Mech. *Stereom.* 2.54.3; with *laridus* in Gloss. Ps.-Cyril. 358.48.
           Post-antique: survives, forming derivatives λαρδίον 'bacon' (cf. Zervan 2019: 101; Lampe 1961), λαρδόομαι 'become fat', etc. *LBG*, Kriaras (1968–), Triandaphyllidis (1909: 121). Modern λαρδί 'lard': Babiniotis (2002), Andriotis (1967), Meyer (1895: 38).
           Notes: forms derivative λαρδηγός. Binder (2000: 208), Hofmann (1989: 230–1), *DÉLG*, Frisk (1954–72: II.85), Beekes (2010), LSJ, LSJ suppl. (*s.v.* λᾶρδος, accent technically correct but not otherwise used). See §4.2.4.1 n. 58, §9.2, §10.2.1, §10.2.2 I.

foreign   **Λαρενταλία** transliterating *Lārentālia*, a festival: Plut. *Rom.* 4.5 (I/II AD). Hofmann (1989: 231).

foreign   **Λάρητες** transliterating *Larēs*, pl. of *Lar* 'household god': Plut. *Mor.* 276f, 277a (I/II AD). Hofmann (1989: 231 *s.v.* Λαρητοί).

not Latin?   **λάσαρον, λάσαρ** 'silphium juice' is suggested by Biville (1992: 235) as from *lāser/lāsar* 'silphium juice' but is normally considered not to be from Latin. *DÉLG*, Frisk (1954–72: II.87), Beekes (2010), LSJ.

           Λατεῖνος: see Λατῖνος.

rare   **λατερκουλίσιος, λατερκουλήσιος** 'employee of the registry', from *laterculēnsis*, an official at the registry (*TLL*): Just. *Nov.* 25.ep. etc., but in Latin script 24.6 (VI AD). Avotins (1992), Zilliacus (1935a: 192–3), LSJ suppl.

rare   **λατέρκουλον 1** 'registry of public offices', from *laterculum* 'register of offices and dignities' (*TLL s.v.* 1. *laterculus* 1001.83–1002.35): Just. *Nov.* 8.Ed.not.1 etc. (VI AD). Avotins (1992), Hofmann (1989: 231), Zilliacus (1935a: 192–3), Lampe (1961), LSJ suppl., and for later survival *LBG*.

rare   **λατέρκουλον 2** 'brick', from *laterculus* 'small brick': Lyd. *Mens.* 1.28 (VI AD); occasionally later. Hofmann (1989: 231), *LBG*.

rare   **Λατιάριος** 'of Latium', from *Latiāris* 'of Latium' (an epithet of Jupiter), is usually outside the parameters of this study, except neut. pl. Λατιάρια for *Latiāria*, a festival in honour of Jupiter Latiaris: Dio Cassius 47.40.6 (II/III AD). LSJ.

foreign   **λατικλάβιος, λατοκλάος** 'having a broad purple stripe', from *lāticlāvius* 'having a broad purple stripe': Lyd. *Mag.* p. 30.14, marked (VI AD); inscription *SEG* LVII.1407.8, Latinate. *LBG*, Meyer (1895: 31 *s.v.* κλαβαρίζω).

           Λατίνη: see Λατῖνος.

name   **Λατίνιον** 'Latium', from *Latium* 'Latium'; cf. DH *AR* 1.72.3 (I BC).

Deriv. of loan **V AD – Byz.**	**Λατινίς** (fem. adj., gen. Λατινίδος) 'Latin', from *Latīnus* 'Latin' via Λατῖνος + -ίς. Literature: Nonnus, *Dionysiaca* 41.160, *Paraphrasis sancti evangelii Joannei* 19.102 (V AD); *Anthologia Graeca* 2.1.303 (V/VI AD); *Oracula Sibyllina* 3.356 etc. Geffcken. Post-antique: numerous. *LBG.* Notes: Lampe (1961), LSJ suppl. See §4.6.1, §10.2.2 O.
Direct loan **III BC – modern**	**Λατῖνος, Λατεῖνος** (-η, -ον) 'Latin', 'Roman', as masc. subst. 'Romans' or 'Latin peoples' (sometimes in opposition to Romans), as fem. subst. 'Latium' (a region), as adverb Λατίνως 'in Latin': from *Latīnus* 'Latin'. Documents: e.g. *BGU* V.1210.66 (II AD); *P.Louvre* I.67.5 (III AD); *P.Sakaon* 71.7 (IV AD); *BGU* XIII.2328.9 (V AD). Inscriptions (two copies of a Roman law): *SEG* III.378.B6 (II/I BC); *I.Knidos* 31.ii.8 etc. (II/I BC). Literature: very common, e.g. Theophrastus, *Historia plantarum* 5.8.1 (IV/III BC); Lycophron, *Alexandra* 1254 (II BC?); Polybius 1.6.4 (II BC); DH *AR* 1.29.2 (I BC); Strabo 3.1.4 (I BC/AD); Plut. *Rom.* 4.2 (I/II AD); Dionysius Periegetes, *Orbis descriptio* 350 Brodersen (II AD); Porphyry, *De abstinentia* 4.16.28 (III AD); Epiph. *Mens.* 274 καὶ τοῖς ἐν τῇ Ἑλλάδι Ῥωμαίοις οὔπω Ῥωμαίοις καλουμένοις ἀκμὴν ἀλλὰ Λατίνοις (IV AD); Orion, *Etymologicum* σ p. 150.29 Sturz as part of gloss (V AD); Hesych. as lemma λ 392 (V/VI AD); *Schol.Sinai.* 45, but in Latin script 54 *Latino* (V/VI AD); Lyd. *Mens.* 3.5.9 (VI AD). Post-antique: very common, forming derivatives Λατινίζω 'learn Latin', Λατινισμός 'Latinism', etc. *LBG*, Kriaras (1968–). Modern Λατῖνος 'Roman', Λατινικός 'Latin', etc.: Babiniotis (2002), Andriotis (1967), Meyer (1895: 38). Notes: appears earlier as a name. Kramer (1993), editor of *P.Louvre* I.67.5 *ad loc.*, Mason (1974: 65), Hofmann (1989: 231–2), Meinersmann (1927: 32), Immisch (1885: 327), LSJ (*s.vv.* Λατίνη, Λατῖνος), LSJ suppl. See §4.1.1, §4.2.2, §4.6.1, §5.3.2 passage 12, §7.1.2, §7.3 passage 31, **§8.1.2**, §8.1.3, **§8.1.4**, §8.2.3 n. 51, §9.5.4, §9.5.6 n. 56, §10.2.1, §10.2.2 O, §10.3.1, §12.2.2.
foreign	**Λατινότης** 'Latin rights' (a legal term), from *Latīnitās* 'Latin rights' + -ότης: Just. *Nov.* in Latin script 78.pr. (VI AD); later in Greek script. Zilliacus (1935a: 192–3), *LBG.* See §9.5.6 n. 68.
rare	**Λάτιον** 'Latin rights', from *Latiī iūs* 'Latin rights': Strabo 4.1.12, 4.2.2 (I BC/AD); App. *BC* 2.4.26 (I/II AD). Mason (1974: 65), LSJ.
	λατοκλάος: see λατικλάβιος.
	Λαυδικηνός: see Λαδικηνός.
rare	**λαυρᾶτον, λαυρεᾶτον** 'image of the emperor crowned with a laurel wreath', from *laureātus* 'wearing laurel': *ACO* II.I.II p. 24.8 (V AD); Romanus Melodus, *Cantica dubia* 81.26.2 Maas and Trypanis (VI AD?); Byzantine texts. Hofmann (1989: 232), *LBG* (*s.v.* λαυρεᾶτον), Lampe (1961).
name	**Λαυρῆτον**, a place name, from *Laurētum.* Hofmann (1989: 232), Sophocles (1887).
foreign	**λαῦρος** 'laurel', from *laurus* 'laurel': Hesych. as lemma λ 424 (V/VI AD). Sophocles (1887).

foreign **λαύτια, λαύτεια** transliterating *lautia* 'entertainment provided for foreign guests of the state at Rome': Plut. *Mor.* 275c τὸ γὰρ παλαιὸν ὡς ἔοικεν οἱ ταμίαι ξένια τοῖς πρεσβεύουσιν ἔπεμπον (ἐκαλεῖτο δὲ "λαύτια" τὰ πεμπόμενα) καὶ νοσούντων ἐπεμέλοντο καὶ τελευτήσαντας ἔθαπτον ἐκ δημοσίου (ι/ιι AD). Hofmann (1989: 232), Sophocles (1887).

λαχηαήριος: see λαγκιάριος.

λαχτέντο: see λακτέντον.

not Latin? **λεβητωνάριον, λεβητονάριον, λεβιτωνάριον, λεβιτονάριον, λευϊτωνάριον** 'hair shirt', 'monk's garment' is derived from *lebitonārium* 'sleeveless linen garment used by Egyptian monks' (*TLL*) by Hofmann (1989: 237), but from λεβήτων 'monk's garment' (*LBG*) + -άριον by Zilliacus (1937: 335).

non-existent? **λέβιρος** 'brother-in-law', from *lēvir* 'brother-in-law': cited as an ancient loan by Zilliacus (1935a: 192–3), but I can find no examples.

λεβιτονάριον, λεβιτωνάριον: see λεβητωνάριον.

λεγατ-: see ληγατ-.

foreign **λέγερε** transliterating inf. of *legō* 'read': Eutropius 2.6, meaning 'speak' (IV AD).

foreign **λέγες** 'laws', from *lēgēs*, plural of *lēx* 'law': Byzantine legal texts. Various forms of *lex* used by Antec. in Latin script: 1.2.4 *lex*, 1.2.5 *legem*, etc. (VI AD). Zilliacus (1935a: 192–3). See §7.2.1.

λεγετάριος: see ληγατάριος.

Direct loan **λεγεών, λεγιών, ληγιών, λεγυών, λογίων, λογήων** (-ῶνος/-όνος, ἡ) 'legion', from
ι BC – modern *legiō* 'legion'.
Documents: common, e.g. *BGU* XVI.2644.5 etc. (ι BC); *P.Mich.* IX.571.2 etc. (ι AD); *P.Oxy.* 4434.2 (ιι AD); *P.Oxy.* 3111.5 (ιιι AD); *P.Grenf.* II.74.2 (ιV AD); *SB* 15801.6; *P.Münch.* I.8.41 etc. (VI AD).
Inscriptions: common, e.g. *I.Ephesos* 705a.3 (ι BC); *I.Cos Segre* EV233.5 (ι AD); *IG* II/III².III.13212.4 (ιι AD); *I.Histria* 292.2 (ιιι AD); *IGBulg.* V.5129.4 (ιV AD); *I.Philae* 225.4 (VI AD).
Literature: common, e.g. perhaps Diodorus Siculus 26.5.1 (ι BC); NT Matthew 26:53 (ι AD); *Act.Andr.* 30.11 (ιι AD); *Test.Sal.* p. 40*.4 (ιιι AD?); Eus. *HE* 5.5.1 (ιV AD); Basil Seleuciensis, *PG* LXXXV.472a (V AD); *V.S.Aux.* 19.5 (VI AD).
Post-antique: common. Zervan (2019: 102), Triandaphyllidis (1909: 130). Modern λεγεώνα 'legion': Babiniotis (2002), Andriotis (1967), Coleman (2007: 795).
Notes: for λογίων (e.g. *P.Oslo* II.33v.7, ι AD) as folk etymology from λόγος 'word' see Cavenaile (1951: 403). For spelling with ε vs ι, Gignac (1976: 253). Kittel *et al.* (1932–79 *s.v.* λεγιών), Ghiretti (1996: 286), Freyburger-Galland (1997: 185–6, 1998: 139–40), Strobach (1997: 196), Daris (1991a: 65), Mason (1974: 5, 6, 7, 8, 65, 138, 163), Hofmann (1989: 232–3), Zilliacus (1935a: 143, 226–7, 1937: 330), Meinersmann (1927: 32), Immisch (1885: 360), Lampe (1961), LSJ, LSJ suppl. See §4.2.5, §4.3.2 n. 75, §5.2.3, §6.1, §8.1.5, §9.3 nn. 21 and 23, §10.2.1, §10.2.2 C.

Direct loan
I–IV AD

λεγεωνάριος, λεγεωνάρειος, λεγιωνάριος, λεγιονάριος, ληγιωνάριος, ληγιονάριος, λογιωνᾶρις (-ου, ὁ) 'legionary', from *legiōnārius* 'legionary'.
Documents: e.g. *SB* 8247.2 etc. (I AD); *P.Cair.Goodsp.* 30.31.15 (II AD); *P.Oxy.* 1419.7, 2794.1 (both III AD); *P.Col.* VII.179.3 (III/IV AD); *P.Lond.* III.1254.5 etc. (IV AD).
Inscriptions: e.g. *IG* X.II.II.124.3 (II AD); *SEG* VII.372.10 (II AD); *I.Fayoum* II.124.4 (II AD); *IG* X.II.I.546.1 (III AD).
Literature: Modestinus in Just. *Dig.* 27.1.8.6 (III AD); *Acta Phileae* 1.8 in Musurillo 1972 (IV AD?).
Post-antique: modern λεγεωνάριος 'legionary' (Babiniotis 2002) is probably revival not survival.
Notes: Daris (1991a: 65–6), Mason (1974: 7, 65), Hofmann (1989: 232), Cavenaile (1951: 403), Meinersmann (1927: 32), LSJ suppl. (replacing LSJ *s.v.* λεγεών). See §4.2.4.1 n. 50, **§4.4**, §6.1, §8.2.3, §9.5.6 nn. 55 and 58, §10.2.1, §10.2.2 C.

Direct loan
VI AD – Byz.

λεγίτιμος (-α, -ον) 'based on law', 'statutory', from *lēgitimus* 'of the law'.
Literature: *Schol.Sinai.* in Latin script 51 *legitimon* etc. (V/VI AD); Just. *Nov.* 22.47.2 etc., but in Latin script 81.2 etc. (VI AD); Antec. 2.19.7, but in Latin script 1.19.pr. *legitimoi* etc. (VI AD).
Post-antique: numerous. *LBG.*
Notes: Avotins (1992), Zilliacus (1935a: 192–3), LSJ suppl. See §4.2.2, §7.1.2, §7.1.3, §9.5.6 nn. 56 and 68 and passage 79, §10.2.1, §10.2.2 B.

λεγιών: see λεγεών.

λεγιωνάριος: see λεγεωνάριος.

non-existent

λεγιώνη 'legion', from *legiō* 'legion': superseded reading of inscription *Syll.*[3] 830.5 = *F.Delphes* III.IV.98.5 (II AD). LSJ. Cf. λεγεών.

rare

λεγουμενᾱλε 'of a sieve', from *legūmināle*, neuter of *legūminālis* 'for separating vegetables' (*TLL*): Edict.Diocl. 15.60 (IV AD). Binder (2000: 128), Hofmann (1989: 233), LSJ suppl.

λεγυών: see λεγεών.

λειβέρτα: see λιβέρτα.

λειβράριος: see λιβράριος.

Direct loan
I AD – Byz.

λεκτ(ε)ίκα, λεκτίκη, λεττείκα (-ης?, ἡ) 'litter' (the conveyance), from *lectīca* 'litter'.
Documents: *P.Berl.Moeller* 11.3 (I AD); *O.Did.* 372.5 (I AD); but *P.Oxy.* 5163.i.10 is Latin in Greek script (I/II AD).
Inscriptions: *SEG* XXIX.1206.1.6 (IV AD).
Literature: Cyr.S. *Vit.Sab.* 182.11 (VI AD).
Post-antique: limited survival. *LBG* (*s.v.* λεκτίκη).
Notes: forms derivatives λεκτίκιον, λεκτίς. Daris (1991a: 66), Hofmann (1989: 234), Lampe (1961 *s.v.* λεκτίκη), LSJ suppl. See §4.6.1, §10.2.1, §10.2.2 K.

Direct loan
III–VI AD

λεκτικάριος, λεκτεικάριος (-ου, ὁ) 'pall-bearer', 'officer', 'stone-carter', from *lectīcārius* 'litter-bearer'.

Documents: *P.Iand.* VIII.154.9 (VI AD).

Inscriptions: *IG* X.II.1.475.3 (II/III AD); Waelkens 1986: 196 no. 486.3 (III AD); *MAMA* IV.32 (III AD); *SEG* XXVII.996.7; Rey-Coquais 2006 no. 156.

Literature: Thdt. *Ep.Sirm.* 110.19 (V AD); *Vita Alexandri*, De Stoop 1911: 689.15 (V AD); Just. *Nov.* 43.pr. etc. (VI AD).

Notes: Avotins (1992), Daris (1991a: 66), Hofmann (1989: 233–4), Cavenaile (1951: 398), Zilliacus (1935a: 192–3), (Cameron 1931: 248), LSJ suppl. See §4.2.4.1 n. 50, §10.2.1, §10.2.2 N.

λεκτίκη: see λεκτεῖκα.

Deriv. of loan
V AD – Byz.

λεκτίκιον (-ου, τό) 'litter' (the conveyance), from *lectīca* 'litter' via λεκτεῖκα + -ιον.

Literature: e.g. Pall. *H.Laus.* 55.2.10 (IV/V AD); Geront. *V.Mel.* 2.55 (V AD); EphraemSyr. VII p. 189.14 (V/VI AD); Alex.Trall. II.457.15 (VI AD).

Post-antique: survives. Zervan (2019: 103), Sophocles (1887), Triandaphyllidis (1909: 122).

Notes: Hofmann (1989: 234 *s.v.* λεκτίκη), Zilliacus (1937: 330–1), *TLL* (*s.v. lectīca* 1080.25), Lampe (1961), LSJ. See §4.6.1, §10.2.2 K.

non-existent?

λεκτίνιον 'litter', from *lectīna* 'bedroom' (*TLL*) + -ιον: cited by Hofmann (1989: 234) on the basis of an anonymous life of John Chrysostom, Savile 1612: 358.9, 16 (V AD?). As this work has never received a modern edition the attestations could be illusory. Lampe (1961).

rare

λεκτίς 'litter', 'tomb', from *lectīca* 'litter' via λεκτεῖκα: in the 'litter' sense Symmachus (II/III AD) quoted in Eusebius, *Commentarius in Isaiam* 2.58.94 Ziegler (IV AD); in the 'tomb' sense inscriptions *SEG* XXVI.1314, 1320 (both IV–VI AD). Hofmann (1989: 234 *s.v.* λεκτίκη), LSJ, LSJ suppl.

not ancient

λένς (in acc. λέντεμ) transliterating *lēns* 'lentil': interpolation in Dsc. 2.107 RV. Sophocles (1887).

not ancient?

λεντιαρία 'female linen-dealer', from *linteāria* 'seller or weaver of linen' (*OLD s.v. linteārius*) or from *linteārius* 'seller or weaver of linen' via λεντιάριος: inscription *SEG* XVII.531.2. Hofmann (1989: 234), LSJ suppl.

rare

λεντιάριον 'linen closet', from *linteārius* 'of linen' (also spelled *lentiarius*: *TLL s.v. linteārius*): inscriptions *I.Cos Segre* EV356.3 (II AD); *I.Tomis* 389.2 (III AD). *TLL* (*s.v. linteārius* 1463.70–3), LSJ suppl.

Direct loan
II AD – Byz.

λεντιάριος (-ου, ὁ) 'linen-dealer', 'cloakroom attendant', from *linteārius* 'seller or weaver of linen' (also spelled *lentiarius*: *TLL s.v. linteārius*).

Documents: perhaps *CPR* VI.62.3 (IV AD).

Inscriptions: e.g. *IG* II/III².II.2130.221 (II AD); *SEG* LI.1898–9.A5 etc. (II/III AD); *SEG* XXXIII.158.54 (III AD); *IG* II/III².II.2243.40 (III AD).

Post-antique: survives. *LBG.*

Notes: Daris (1991a: 66), Hofmann (1989: 234), LSJ suppl. (replacing LSJ *s.v.* λέντιον). See §4.2.4.1 n. 50, §8.2.2, §10.2.1, §10.2.2 H.

non-existent?	**λεντίκιον** 'cloth', 'napkin', 'towel', from *linteum* via λέντιον: probably superseded reading of papyrus *P.Oxy.* 1741.10–12 (IV AD). Diethart (1995b: 240), Daris (1991a: 66), LSJ.
not ancient	**λεντίκουλα, λεντίκλα** transliterating *lenticula* 'lentil': interpolation in Dsc. 2.107 RV. Binder (2000: 163), Sophocles (1887).
Direct loan I AD – modern	**λέντιον** (-ου, τό) 'linen cloth', 'napkin', 'towel', from *linteum* 'linen cloth', 'towel or napkin' (also spelled *lentium*: *TLL s.v. linteum*). Documents: *SB* 12314.24 (II AD); *P.Oxy.* 929v.10 (II/III AD); *P.Oxy.* 3978.10 (III AD); *SB* 12694.3 etc. (III/IV AD); *PSI* VIII.971.18 (III/IV AD); perhaps *SB* 9746.16 (IV AD); *O.Wilck.* 1611.1 etc. (I–IV AD). Inscriptions: *I.Magnesia* 116.34 (II AD); Woodward 1926: 228.12 (II AD). Literature: e.g. NT John 13:4 (I AD); *Acta Joannis* 6 = Bonnet 1898: 155.1 (II AD); *Apocalypsis Baruchi* 3.5.6 Picard (III AD?); *Coll.Herm.* Mp 13f (III AD?); Gregorius Nazianzenus, *PG* XXXVI.328b (IV AD); *Historia monachorum in Aegypto* 8.44 (V AD); Hesych. as gloss ε 5583, as lemma λ 644 (V/VI AD). Post-antique: common. *LBG*, Kriaras (1968–), Zervan (2019: 103), Triandaphyllidis (1909: 122). Modern dialectal λεντίον 'apron': Andriotis (1974: 352). Notes: forms derivative λεντιυφαντής. Binder (2000: 122–3), Daris (1991a: 66), Hofmann (1989: 235), Zilliacus (1937: 331), Meinersmann (1927: 32), Immisch (1885: 367), Lampe (1961), LSJ, LSJ suppl. See §4.2.4.1 n. 54, §9.3 n. 21, §9.5.4 n. 42, §10.2.1, §10.2.2 H.
rare	**λέντιος** 'made of linen', from *linteus* 'made of linen' (also spelled *lentius*: *TLL s.v. linteum*): papyrus *P.Oxy.* 3060.7 (II AD). Daris (1991a: 66), LSJ suppl.
rare	**λεντιυφαντής** 'towel-weaver', from *linteum* 'linen towel' via λέντιον + -υφαντής from ὑφαίνω 'weave': inscription *I.Ephesos* 454e (II/III AD). Hofmann (1989: 235 *s.v.* λέντιον), LSJ.
not Latin?	**λεόπαρδος** 'leopard' might be from or influenced by *leopardus* 'leopard'. *DÉLG*, Frisk (1954–72: II.104), Beekes (2010), Lampe (1961), LSJ.
name?	**λέπιδος** transliterating *lepidus* 'charming': probably a name in inscription *IG* XIV.40.2. Wilhelm (1928b: 227), Drew-Bear (1972: 206), Hofmann (1989: 235), LSJ suppl.
non-existent?	**λέπορις** 'hare' is not directly attested in Greek but mentioned by Varro (*De lingua Latina* 5.101, *Res rusticae* 3.12.6) as Sicilian and related to *lepus* (gen. *leporis*) 'hare'. Willi (2008: 31) suggests a pre-Italic source. Campanile (1969: 313–14), Hofmann (1989: 236), LSJ.
rare	**λεπταμικτόριον** 'fine wrap', from λεπτός 'fine' + *amictōrium* 'shawl', 'scarf' via ἀμικτώριον: papyrus *SB* 9238.18 (III AD). Filos (2010: 250), Daris (1991a: 66), Hofmann (1989: 20 *s.v.* αμικτωριον), LSJ suppl.
	λεττεῖκα: see λεκτεῖκα.
not Latin?	**λεύγη**, defined by Hesych. λ 712 (V/VI AD) as 'measure of milk', may be from *leuga*, a measure of distance (*TLL*). Hofmann (1989: 236), Hahn (1906: 253), Immisch (1885: 341), LSJ.
	λευϊτωνάριον: see λεβητωνάριον.

Direct loan
III AD – Byz.

ληγατάριος, λεγατάριος, λιγατάριος, λεγετάριος (-ου, ὁ) 'legatee', from *lēgātārius* 'recipient of a legacy'.
Documents: perhaps *BGU* 11.600v.4 (II AD); *P.NYU* 11.39.18 (IV AD).
Literature: e.g. Modestinus in Just. *Dig.* 26.6.2.3 (III AD); Just. *Nov.* 1.1.1 (VI AD); Antec. 2.20.4 etc., but in Latin script 3.27.7 *legatariu* etc. (VI AD); with *legator* in Gloss. *Herm.S.* 454.21.
Post-antique: common both in ancient meaning and for official with policing duties. Sophocles (1887), *LBG* (*s.v.* λεγατάριος), Kriaras (1968– *s.v.* λεγατάριος), Triandaphyllidis (1909: 126).
Notes: forms derivative συλληγατάριος. Avotins (1989, 1992), Daris (1991a: 66), Mason (1974: 12), Hofmann (1989: 237), Zilliacus (1935a: 192–3), Lampe (1961), LSJ suppl. See §4.2.4.1 n. 50, §9.5.6 n. 55, §10.2.1, §10.2.2 B.

Deriv.? of loan
V AD – Byz.

ληγατεύω, λεγατεύω 'bequeath', from *lēgātum* 'legacy' via ληγᾶτον, or directly from *lēgātus* (pf. part. of *lēgō* 'bequeath'), + -εύω.
Literature: e.g. Marc.Diac. 54 (V AD); Just. *Codex* 1.5.15.12 (VI AD); Antec. 2.20.6 etc., but in Latin script 3.27.7 *legateuomenon* etc. (VI AD); with *lego* in Gloss. Ps.-Cyril. 360.9.
Post-antique: common, forming derivatives λεγατευτικός 'of legacies', λεγάτευμα 'legacy'. *LBG* (*s.v.* λεγατεύω), Kriaras (1968– *s.v.* λεγατεύω).
Notes: Avotins (1989), Hofmann (1989: 237), Zilliacus (1935a: 192–3), Lampe (1961), LSJ suppl. See §4.3.1 n. 68, §4.6.1 n. 91, §10.2.2 B.

rare

ληγατίων 'alms', from *lēgātiō* 'alms' (*TLL s.v.* 1. *lēgātio* 1103.54–81): Marc.Diac. 54 (V AD); probably not on papyrus *P.Oxy.* 2561.19 (IV AD). Hofmann (1989: 237), Lampe (1961).

Direct loan
II AD – Byz.

ληγᾶτον, λεγᾶτον (-ου, τό) 'legacy', from *lēgātum* 'legacy'.
Documents: e.g. *PSI* VII.738.12 etc. (I/II AD); *P.Col.* VIII.221.7 etc. (II AD); *SB* 10537.31 (III AD); *SB* 15957.3 etc. (VI AD).
Inscriptions: *SEG* XXXV.1167.9 (III AD); *IGR* III.828.6; *IGLS* XIII.1.9424.2.
Literature: e.g. Scaevola in Just. *Dig.* 33.8.23.2 (II AD); Philogelos 139 (IV AD); Malal. 18.23 (VI AD); Dan.Sket. *AA* 82 (VI AD); Antec. 2.20.pr. etc., but in Latin script 3.27.7 *legatois* etc. (VI AD); Just. *Nov.* 129.pr., but in Latin script 107.1 (VI AD).
Post-antique: common. Kriaras (1968– *s.v.* λεγᾶτον), Sophocles (1887 *s.v.* ληγᾶτος 2), Triandaphyllidis (1909: 128), Meyer (1895: 38).
Notes: may form derivative ληγατεύω. Avotins (1989, 1992), Daris (1991a: 66), Mason (1974: 5, 65–6), Hofmann (1989: 237–8), Zilliacus (1935a: 192–3), Meinersmann (1927: 33), Lampe (1961), LSJ suppl. See §4.2.4.1 n. 55, §4.3.1 n. 68, §10.2.1, §10.2.2 B.

Direct loan
III AD – modern

ληγᾶτος 1, λεγᾶτος (-ου, ὁ) 'deputy', 'envoy', from *lēgātus* 'envoy'.
Inscriptions: *I.Perge* 289.4 (III AD); *I.Ephesos* 710b.17 (III AD).
Literature: e.g. Eutropius 2.9.22 (IV AD); *ACO* I.I.III p. 14.1 (V AD); Lyd. *Mag.* p. 58.27, marked (VI AD); Antec. 1.26.1 (VI AD).
Post-antique: numerous. *LBG* (*s.v.* λεγᾶτος), Zervan (2019: 102), Kriaras (1968– *s.v.* λεγᾶτος), Triandaphyllidis (1909: 126). Modern dialectal ληγᾶτος 'papal legate': Meyer (1895: 38).
Notes: Binder (2000: 97, 270), Zilliacus (1935a: 192–3), Sophocles (1887), Lampe (1961). See §4.2.4.1 n. 51, §5.2.3, §10.2.1, §10.2.2 D.

rare	**ληγᾶτος 2** 'bequeathed', from *lēgātus*, pf. part. of *lēgō* 'bequeath': inscription *SEG* xxxiv.1213.3 (ii ad). LSJ suppl.
	ληγιονάριος: see λεγεωνάριος.
	ληγιών: see λεγεών.
	ληγιωνάριος: see λεγεωνάριος.
rare	**ληίνη** 'cloak' from *laena* 'woollen double cloak': papyrus *P.Giss.Apoll.* 28.5 (ii ad). Daris (1991a: 66), Hofmann (1989: 238), LSJ. Cf. λαῖνα.
	λιβελ(λ)άριος: see λιβράριος.
rare	**λιβελ(λ)ήσιος**, an official title from *libellēnsis*, an officer in charge of petitions (*TLL*): Just. *Nov.* 20.7 (vi ad); Byzantine texts. Avotins (1992), Hofmann (1989: 238), Zilliacus (1935a: 192–3), Sophocles (1887), Triandaphyllidis (1909: 126), Lampe (1961), LSJ suppl.
non-existent?	**λιβελλίκιος**, cited as an ancient loan by Zilliacus (1935a: 192–3): I can find no examples.
rare	**λιβέλλιον** 'little writing', from *libellus* 'document' via λιβέλλος + -ιον (Cavenaile 1952: 196): papyri *BGU* iii.874.7 (vi ad); probably not *P.Oxy.* 66.17 (iv ad); probably not *SB* 12814v.1 (iv ad). Daris (1991a: 66), Zilliacus (1935a: 192–3), Meinersmann (1927: 33).
Direct loan **I AD – modern**	**λιβέλ(λ)ος, λιβέλ(λ)ον** (-ου, ὁ or τό) 'petition', 'writing', 'document', from *libellus* 'document'. Documents: common, e.g. *O.Edfou* iii.467.8 (i ad); *P.Wisc.* ii.48.5 (ii ad); *SB* 15496.23 (iii ad); *P.Herm.* 20.11 etc. (iv ad); *P.Oxy.* 2268.6 (v ad); *P.Oxy.* 1883.7 (vi ad). Inscriptions: *I.Salamine* 29.4 (iii ad); *I.Delta* 2.1 p. 526 (iii/iv ad); Edict. Diocl. 7.41 (iv ad). Literature: common, e.g. Epiph. *Pan.* iii.259.5 (iv ad); *ACO* i.i.i p. 5.12 (v ad); Just. *Nov.* 25.1 (vi ad). Post-antique: common, forming derivative λιβελλικός 'documented' (*LBG*). Zervan (2019: 103–4), Kriaras (1968–), Sophocles (1887), Triandaphyllidis (1909: 128). Modern λίβελλος 'libel': Babiniotis (2002), Andriotis (1967), Meyer (1895: 38). Notes: Daris (1991a: 66–7), Mason (1974: 6, 66), Hofmann (1989: 238–9), Zilliacus (1935a: 192–3), Lampe (1961), LSJ, LSJ suppl. See §4.2.4.1 n. 51, §5.2.1, §10.2.1, §10.2.2 D.
foreign	**λίβερ** transliterating *liber* 'book' and *līber* 'free': Lyd. *Mens.* 1.28, 4.51 (vi ad); occasionally later. Sophocles (1887).
name	**Λίβερ**, the name of a god identified with Bacchus, from *Līber*: acc. Λίβερουμ πάτρεμ in Plut. *Mor.* 288f (i/ii ad). Strobach (1997: 196), Sophocles (1887).
foreign	**λιβερατίων** 'discharge of debt', from *līberātiō* 'freeing': Antec. in Latin script 2.20.13 *liberationa* (vi ad); later in Greek script. Zilliacus (1935a: 194–5), *LBG*. See §9.5.6 n. 68.

Deriv.? of loan
IV–VI AD

λιβερνάριος, λιβυρνάριος, λοιβερνάριος (-ου, ὁ) 'sailor on a *liburna* ship', from unattested *liburnārius*, or from *liburna* 'fast warship' via λίβερνος + -άριος.
Documents: *P.Vind.Bosw.* 13.i.4 (IV AD); perhaps *BGU* XIX.2776.A.ii.35 (IV AD); *Stud.Pal.* XX.123v.33 (V AD); *P.Rain.Cent.* 137.1 (VI AD); *P.Oxy.* 1902.4 (VI AD).
Notes: commentary on *P.Vind.Bosw.*, Daris (1991a: 67), Cavenaile (1951: 398), Zilliacus (1935a: 226–7), LSJ (*s.v.* Λιβυρνοί), LSJ suppl. See §4.2.4.1 n. 50, §6.1, §9.2, §10.2.2 C.

rare

λιβέρνιος 'Liburnian', probably from *Liburnus* 'Liburnian' with influence from λίβερνος: papyrus *P.Oxy.* 2032.52 etc. (VI AD). Daris (1991a: 67 *s.v.* λιβύρνιος), LSJ suppl.

Direct loan
I AD – Byz.

λίβερνος, λίβερνον, λίβυρνος, λίβυρνον, λύβερνος (-ου, ὁ or τό), a type of ship, probably from *liburna* 'light, fast-sailing warship'.
Documents: *O.Petr.* 279.1 (I AD); *BGU* II.455.9, III.741.7, III.709.2 etc. (all II AD); Benaissa 2014 p. 211.3 (II AD); *P.Oxy.* 2042.11 etc. (V AD); *Stud.Pal.* VIII.1094.2, 1126.6 (both VI AD).
Inscriptions: probably *SEG* III.565.11 (III AD).
Literature: *Historia Alexandri Magni* rec. α 1.26.3 etc. Kroll (III/IV AD); Eunapius, L. Dindorf 1870: 264.24 etc., marked (IV/V AD); Zosimus, *Historia nova* 5.20.3 Paschoud, marked (V AD); Hesych. as lemma λ 948 (V/VI AD); Malal. 9.10 etc. (VI AD); with *liburnum* in Gloss. Ps.-Cyril. 360.47.
Post-antique: numerous. *LBG* (*s.vv.* λίβυρνον, λίβυρνος), Kriaras (1968– *s.v.* λίβερνο), Triandaphyllidis (1909: 131).
Notes: may form derivative λιβερνάριος. Daris (1991a: 67), Hofmann (1989: 240), Zilliacus (1935a: 226–7), Meinersmann (1927: 33), LSJ (*s.vv.* λίβερνος, Λιβυρνοί). See §4.2.3.1, §6.1, §10.2.1, §10.2.2 C; cf. λιβύρνα.

foreign

λίβεροι 'offspring', from *līberī* 'children': Antec. in Latin script 1.12.pr. *liberi* etc. (VI AD); later in Greek script. Zilliacus (1935a: 194–5), *LBG*.

rare

λιβέρτα, λειβέρτα 'freedwoman', from *līberta* 'freedwoman': lead tablets *SEG* XXIX.929 and XXXV.1011 (both I BC?); inscription *IG* X.II.II.121.1 (I/II AD). Probably direct from Latin, not via λιβέρτος, because -α not -η. LSJ suppl. (*s.v.* λιβέρτος).

foreign

λιβέρτας 'freedom', a Byzantine legal term from *lībertās* 'freedom', is prefigured by the use in Latin script of forms of *libertas* in certain phrases by Antec., e.g. 1.14.1 *sine libertate* (VI AD).

foreign

λιβερτῖνος 'freedman', from *lībertīnus* 'member of the class of freedmen': NT Acts 6:9, marked (I AD); later explanations of that passage, e.g. John Chrysostom, *PG* LX.120.34 (IV/V AD). Inscription *IG* XIV.1781 = *IGUR* II.718 is Latin in Greek script. Kittel *et al.* (1932–79 *s.v.*), Danker *et al.* (2000), Bruce (1990: 187), Leclercq (1997: 296), Hofmann (1989: 239), Zilliacus (1935a: 194–5), LSJ. See §9.3.

foreign

λιβέρτος transliterating *lībertus* 'freedman': perhaps Polybius 30.18.4 (II BC); App. *Mithridatica* 5 (I/II AD); Byzantine texts. Famerie (1998: 139–41), Dubuisson (1985: 36), Mason (1974: 6, 66), Hofmann (1989: 240), *LBG*, LSJ (λίβερτος *s.v.* λιβερτῖνος), LSJ suppl. See §8.1.3 n. 17.

name   **Λιβιτίνη, Λιβίτινα**, from *Libitīna*, name of the goddess of funerals. Sophocles (1887).

         λιβλάριος: see λιβράριος.

foreign   **λίβος**, a cake name from *lībum/lībus*, a cake: Athenaeus 3.126a, 14.647d, marked (II/III AD). Hofmann (1989: 240), LSJ. See §9.4 passage 60.

foreign   **λίβρα** transliterating *lībra* 'pound': Hesych. λ 1151 (V/VI AD); Her.Mech. *Mens.* 60.20.

Direct loan?   **λιβράριος, λιβλάριος, λειβράριος, λιβελ(λ)άριος** (-ου, ὁ), a kind of scribe, from
II–V AD   *librārius* 'scribe', 'bookseller' or rare *libellārius* 'of rent-books' (*TLL*) or
         libellus 'petition' via λιβέλλος + -άριος.
         Documents: e.g. *P.Col.* VIII.221.12 (II AD); *SB* 16170.33 (III AD); *P.Herm. Landl.* 2.605 etc. (IV AD).
         Inscriptions: e.g. Ramsay 1883: 275 no. 17.11 (II AD); *I.Tomis* 106.18 (III AD); Edict.Diocl. 7.69 (IV AD); *I.Zoora* 197.3 (V AD).
         Literature: Modestinus in Just. *Dig.* 27.1.15.5 (III AD).
         Post-antique: not attested. Byzantine λιβελλάριον 'bookroll' (*LBG*) is probably independent.
         Notes: uncertain how many words this is and how many Latin sources it/ they have; there are no obvious distinctions in meaning between different spellings, but many passages are unclear. There are no certain attestations of λιβελ(λ)άριος, *pace* Daris (1991a: 66); possible occurrences are *O.Bodl.* II.2358.7 (I–IV AD); *O.Kell.* 69.6 (III AD); *P.Mich.* XV.726.9 (IV/V AD). Λιβλάριος is frequent; its derivation from *libellārius* is supported by *TLL s.v. libellārius*, Bowersock (1991: 339), etc., but *libellārius* is an adjective with the wrong meaning. Both *libellārius* and *librārius* are unproblematic phonetically as sources of λιβλάριος (§4.1.1 nn. 8, 15), but a Greek formation in -άριος is also possible, as is merger of multiple sources. Editor of *I.Zoora ad loc.*, Gignac (1976: 103–4), Daris (1991a: 66, 67), Mason (1974: 4, 66), Hofmann (1989: 240), Meinersmann (1927: 33), LSJ (*s.v.* λιβλάριος), LSJ suppl. See §4.2.4.1 n. 50, §9.5.6 nn. 55 and 58, §10.2.1, §10.2.2 N.

foreign   **λιβύρνα** transliterating *liburna* 'light, fast-sailing warship': Lyd. *Mag.* p. 200.14 (VI AD); Byzantine texts. Zervan (2019: 104). Cf. λίβερνος.

         λιβυρνάριος: see λιβερνάριος.

         λίβυρνον, λίβυρνος: see λίβερνος.

foreign   **λιγᾶρε** transliterating inf. of *ligō* 'bind': Plut. *Rom.* 26.3, *Mor.* 280a (I/II AD). Sophocles (1887).

         λιγατάριος: see ληγατάριος.

not ancient   **λίγγουα** transliterating *lingua* 'tongue': interpolations in Dsc. 4.127 RV, 185 RV. Sophocles (1887).

Direct loan   **λίγλα, λίγγλα, λίνγλα** (-ης?, ἡ) 'spoon', 'spoonful', from *ligula/lingula*, a kind of spoon.
II AD – ?   Documents: *BGU* III.781.vi.3 etc. (I/II AD).
         Literature: Pollux 6.87 (II AD).
         Post-antique: perhaps papyrus *P.Apoll.* 88.8 (VII AD). *LBG* (*s.v.* λίγγλα).
         Notes: Binder (2000: 195), Daris (1991a: 67), Hofmann (1989: 241), Meinersmann (1927: 33), LSJ suppl. See §8.1.1 passage 38, §10.1, §10.2.1, §10.2.2 I.

rare   **λιγνατίων**, from *lignātiō* 'collection of firewood': unpublished ostracon O.Dios inv. 687.8 (II AD).

foreign   **λίκτωρ** transliterating *līctor* 'official attendant on a magistrate': Plut. *Rom.* 26.3, 26.4, *Mor.* 280a (I/II AD); in acc. λείκτορα on inscriptions *I.Ephesos* 1544.11, 1545.5 (both I/II AD). Strobach (1997: 196), Mason (1974: 6, 66), Hofmann (1989: 241).

foreign   **λιμβός**, a garment, from *limbus* 'band or girdle': Lyd. *Mag.* p. 88.13, marked (VI AD). Hofmann (1989: 241), LSJ.

foreign   *līmen* 'threshold': Antec. 1.12.5 *limen* (VI AD).

λιμητ-: see λιμιτ-.

Direct loan V AD – Byz.   **λιμιτάνεος, λιμητάνεος, λιμιτάναῖος** (-ου, ὁ) 'frontier troops', as adj. 'of the frontier', from *līmitāneus* 'of the frontier' (*TLL*).
Documents: perhaps *O.Bodl.* II.2152.7 (IV AD).
Inscriptions: *SEG* XXXII.1554.A53 etc. (VI AD).
Literature: *ACO* II.I.III p. 123.20 (V AD); Malal. 12.40 etc. (VI AD); Just. *Nov.* 103.3.1 (VI AD); Procop. *Arc.* 24.13, marked (VI AD).
Post-antique: survives. *LBG* (s.v. λιμιτανᾶιοι), Triandaphyllidis (1909: 129).
Notes: Binder (2000: 130), Avotins (1992), Daris (1991a: 67), Hofmann (1989: 241), Zilliacus (1935a: 226–7), Lampe (1961), LSJ suppl. (s.vv. λιμιτάνεος, λιμιτανᾶιος). See §4.2.4.1 n. 51, §10.2.1, §10.2.2 C.

Direct loan IV AD – Byz.   **λιμιτόν, λιμητόν** (-ου, τό) 'frontier', from *līmes* (gen. *līmitis*, masc.) 'boundary'.
Documents: e.g. *P.Oxy.* 4367.3 (IV AD); *SB* 9598.3 (V AD); *P.Cair.Masp.* 67076.13 (VI AD).
Inscriptions: e.g. *I.Philae* 194.5 (V AD); *SEG* VIII.296.1 (V/VI AD); *SEG* XXXII.1554.B6 etc. (VI AD).
Literature: e.g. *Vita Alexandri*, De Stoop 1911: 684.3 (V AD); Malal. 2.7.18 (VI AD); Just. *Edict* 13.11.2 = p. 785.27 (VI AD); with *limes* in Gloss. Ps.-Cyril. 361.9. Unverified example (III AD) in Zilliacus (1937: 323, 331).
Post-antique: numerous. Sophocles (1887), Triandaphyllidis (1909: 119), *LBG* (s.v. λιμητόν).
Notes: for meaning see Mayerson (1989). Viscidi (1944: 7) considers change in gender evidence of integration (but his example of λίμης has now been reread as λιμιτόν). Binder (2000: 129, 263), Diethart (2006: 16), Avotins (1992), Daris (1991a: 67), Hofmann (1989: 241–2), Zilliacus (1935a: 226–7, 1937: 331), Meinersmann (1927: 33), Lampe (1961), LSJ suppl. See §4.2.5, **§4.2.6**, §10.2.1, §10.2.2 D.

not ancient?   **λιμιτοτρόφος, λιμητοτρόφος** 'furnishing subsistence to troops stationed on the frontier', from *līmes* 'frontier' via λιμιτόν + τροφός 'feeder': probably no ancient examples in Greek texts, but Latin *līmitotrophus* 'furnishing subsistence to frontier troops' (*TLL*) is attested in antiquity and looks like a borrowing into Latin. Hofmann (1989: 242 s.v. λίμιτον), *LBG* (s.v. λιμητοτρόφος), *TLL*, LSJ suppl.

λίνγλα: see λίγλα.

Deriv. of loan
with influence
V–VI AD

λινόπηξος, λινόπιξος (-ον) 'of combed linen', from λίνον 'linen' + *pexus*, pf. part.
of *pectō* 'brush' via πεξός with influence from πῆξις 'fixing'.
Documents: *SB* 9570.8 (IV/V AD); *P.Wash.Univ.* 11.97.12 etc. (V AD); *P.Mich.*
XIV.684.8 (V/VI AD); *BGU* XVII.2725.12 (VI AD).
Notes: not attested in feminine; LSJ suppl. infers from form that it would be
two-termination. Commentary on *BGU* XVII.2725, Bataille (1956: 87). See
§4.6.2, §9.2, §10.2.2 H; cf. πεξός.

λίτερα: see λίττερα.

rare

λιτιγάτωρ 'litigant', from *lītigātor* 'litigant': Lyd. *Mag.* p. 148.26, marked
(VI AD); Just. *Nov.* 93.t, but in Latin script 115.2 etc. (VI AD); Ath.Schol.
in Latin script 4.15.3 etc. (VI AD); Antec. in Latin script 4.16.1 *litigatora*
(VI AD); often in Byzantine legal texts. Avotins (1992), Hofmann (1989:
242–3), Zilliacus (1935a: 194–5), *LBG*, Lampe (1961).

foreign

λιτιγίοσος, λιτιγιῶσος 'litigious', 'contested', from *lītigiōsus* 'litigious': Just.
Nov. in Latin script 112.1 etc. (VI AD); Ath.Schol. in Latin script 5.2 etc.
(VI AD); later in Greek script. Hofmann (1989: 243), Zilliacus (1935a:
194–5), *LBG*, Lampe (1961).

λίτουον, λίτουους: see λίτυον.

not Latin?

λίτρα 1 'pound' (with derivatives ἡμίλιτρον 'half-pound', λιτραῖος 'of a pound',
etc.) is a borrowing from an Italic language; not from the Latin we know,
where the equivalent is *lĭbra*, but conceivably from Latin of an earlier
period, when the Italic languages had *lītrā* (cf. Sihler 1995: 139; Lejeune
1993: 10–11; the Greek is attested from VI BC, LSJ suppl.). But since at
that period Greek speakers were in contact with several Italic languages,
there is no particular reason to believe that Latin *per se* was the source of the
loan. Like its counterpart οὐγγία, λίτρα was often seen as Roman by later
Greeks (e.g. Polybius 21.43.19; Galen XII.389.16 Kühn), but it is treated
differently here for four reasons: (1) modern scholars (e.g. LSJ) very often
consider οὐγγία to be a Latin loan and λίτρα not; (2) the two are parallel
only in their meanings 'pound' and 'ounce'; both also have other meanings,
and in those οὐγγία shows much more connection to Latin than λίτρα; (3)
the appearance of these words in the Athenian agora is not at all parallel,
suggesting a different borrowing pattern: οὐγγία is attested on both weights
and pots from III BC, while λίτρα does not appear on (datable) weights or
pots until the Roman period; (4) the phonetic differences between λίτρα and
libra are significant and probably contributed to Greek speakers handling
this pair differently from οὐγγία and *uncia*. Simkin (2012: 170–6), Cassio
(2012: 254–6), Willi (2008: 31), Lejeune (1993), Bellocchi (2016: 327),
Avotins (1989), Dubuisson (1985: 36), Blass *et al.* (1979: §5.1), Hofmann
(1989: 123, 243–4), Meinersmann (1927: 34), Immisch (1885: 312–13),
DÉLG, Frisk (1954–72: II.131), Beekes (2010), Meyer (1895: 38), *TLL* (*s.v.*
libra 1342.25–6), LSJ (*s.vv.* λίτρα, ἡμιλιτριαῖος, etc.), LSJ suppl. (*s.vv.* λίτρα,
ἡμιλίτριον, etc.), and for post-antique survival *LBG* (*s.vv.* λίτρα¹, ἡμίλιτρον,
etc.), Andriotis (1974: 357), Babiniotis (2002: *s.v.* λίτρο). See §8.1.2 n. 15.

λίτρα 2 'writing': see λίττερα.

λιτραῖος, λιτριαῖος, λιτρασμός: see λίτρα 1.

foreign   λίτ(τ)ερα, λίτρα 'writing', from *littera* 'writing': Antec. in Latin script 3.13.2 *litteris* etc. (VI AD); later in Greek script. *LBG* (*s.v.* λίτρα²). See §7.2.2 with passage 29.

foreign   λίτυον, λίτουον, and λίτουους transliterating *lituus* 'augur's staff': Plut. *Rom.* 22.1, *Cam.* 32.7 (I/II AD); Hesych. as lemma λ 1102 (V/VI AD); Lyd. *Mens.* 4.73 (VI AD). Vaahtera (2001: 127 n. 138), Hofmann (1989: 244), LSJ.

λογίων: see λεγεών.

λογιωνᾶρις: see λεγεωνάριος.

λοδίκιον: see λωδίκιον.

λόδιξ: see λῶδιξ.

λοιβερνάριος: see λιβερνάριος.

λοκάνικον: see λουκάνικον.

foreign   λοκᾶτος 'renting out', from *locātus*, pf. part. of *locō* 'hire out': Antec. in Latin script 3.24.pr. *locati* etc. (VI AD); later in Greek script. Zilliacus (1935a: 194–5).

not ancient   λοκάτωρ 'landlord', from *locātor* 'landlord': no ancient examples. Zilliacus (1935a: 194–5), *LBG*.

λοροτόμος: see λωροτόμος 1.

λοσώριον: see λουσώριον.

not ancient?   λουδάριος 'staff member at a gladiatorial school', from *lūdārius* (defined by *TLL* as '*ludens vel ludificans*', i.e. 'playing', but this may misinterpret the evidence): inscription *I.Smyrna* 416.8; *Martyrium Tarachi*, Ruinart 1689: 490; Byzantine texts. Robert (1971: 285–6 n. 2), Hofmann (1989: 244–5), Zilliacus (1937: 323, 331, with unverified example from III AD), *LBG*, *TLL* (*s.v.* 1. *lūdārius*), Lampe (1961), LSJ suppl. (*s.v.* λουδάριοι).

rare   λουδεμπιστής 'person in charge of putting on games', presumably from *lūdus* 'games' via λοῦδος + *emō* 'buy' + -ιστης (no **lūdēmptor* is attested): *Constitutiones Apostolorum* 8.32.27 Metzger (IV AD); Byzantine texts. Hofmann (1989: 245 *s.v.* λοῦδος), *LBG*, Lampe (1961).

Direct loan II AD – Byz.   λοῦδος (-ου, ὁ) 'gladiatorial school', 'games', from *lūdus* 'games', '(gladiatorial) school'.
Documents: *P.Lips.* 1.57r.11 (III AD).
Inscriptions: e.g. *I.Ephesos* 852.22 (II AD); *IG* X.II.1.486.8 (III AD); *I.Pergamon Asklepieion* 99.2.
Literature: *Constitutiones Apostolorum* 5.1.3 Metzger (IV AD); Hesych. λ 1354, marked but not lemma (V/VI AD).
Post-antique: survives. *LBG*.
Notes: forms derivatives λουδεμπιστής, λουδοτρόφος. Papanikolaou (2019), Daris (1991a: 67), Mason (1974: 9, 66), Hofmann (1989: 245), Meinersmann (1927: 34), *TLL* (*s.v. lūdus* 1793.41–52), Lampe (1961), LSJ suppl. See §4.2.4.1 n. 51, **§4.2.6**, §8.2.2, §9.5.4 n. 42, §10.2.1, §10.2.2 F.

rare	**λουδοτρόφος** 'trainer of gladiators', presumably from *lūdus* '(gladiatorial) school' via λοῦδος + τροφός 'nurse': with *lanista* in Gloss. Ps.-Philox. 120.51, 53 and Gloss. Ps.-Cyril. 362.46. LSJ.
Direct loan **III AD – modern**	**λουκάνικον, λοκάνικον, λυκανική** (usually -ου, τό) 'sausage', from *lūcānica*, a kind of sausage. Documents: *P.Euphrates* III.17.24 (III AD); *P.Lond.* III.1259r.30 (IV AD); *P.Ryl.* IV.627.208, 629.27 etc. (both IV AD); *SB* 15302.49 etc. (V AD). Inscriptions: Edict.Diocl. 4.15 etc. (IV AD). Literature: Philogelos 237 (IV AD); as gloss in scholia to Luc. *Gall.* 14. Post-antique: survives. *LBG*, Kriaras (1968–), Triandaphyllidis (1909: 121). Modern λουκάνικο 'sausage': Babiniotis (2002), Andriotis (1967), Meyer (1895: 39). Notes: Wackernagel (1916: 197), Hofmann (1989: 246), LSJ suppl. See §4.2.3.1, §8.2.3, §10.2.1, §10.2.2 I.
foreign	**λοῦκαρ** transliterating *lūcar* 'sum of money allocated for public entertainments': Plut. *Mor.* 285d (I/II AD). Strobach (1997: 196), Hofmann (1989: 246).
name	**Λουκῖνα**, from *Lūcīna*, name of goddess of childbirth and epithet of Juno. Strobach (1997: 196), Sophocles (1887).
not ancient?	**λούκιος**, a fish, from *lūcius*, a fish (*TLL*): probably no ancient examples. Meyer (1895: 39).
foreign	**λοῦκος** transliterating *lūcus* 'grove': Plut. *Rom.* 20.2, *Mor.* 285d (I/II AD); Lyd. *Mens.* 1.7 (VI AD). Hofmann (1989: 246).
foreign	**λούκουντλος**, a cake, from *lucuntulus* 'fritter made with cheese and honey': Athenaeus 14.647d, marked (II/III AD). Binder (2000: 179), Hofmann (1989: 246), LSJ. See §5.2.1.
foreign	**λουκρατίβος** 'profitable', from *lucrātīvus* 'profitable': Just. *Nov.* in Latin script 131.5 (VI AD); later in Greek script. Zilliacus (1935a: 194–5), *LBG*.
rare	**λοῦμβοι** 'loins', from *lumbus* 'loin': *Hippiatr.Par.* (Apsyrtus) 1046 (III/IV AD?). *LBG*.
	λουμενάριον: see νουμενάρια.
foreign	**λούπα** transliterating *lupa* 'she-wolf': DH *AR* 1.84.4 (I BC); Plut. *Rom.* 4.4 (I/II AD); Suetonius, Περὶ βλασφημιῶν 32 (I/II AD). Hofmann (1989: 246–7), Immisch (1885: 313), LSJ suppl., and for Byzantine survival *LBG*.
not Latin	**λουπάρισμα** 'phallus', said to be a Greek word of Italic (not specifically Latin) origin. Hofmann (1989: 247), Hahn (1906: 9).
rare	**Λουπερκάλια**, a festival, from *Lupercālia*, a festival: Plut. *Caesar* 61.1 etc. (I/II AD); App. *BC* 2.16.109 (I/II AD). Strobach (1997: 197), Hofmann (1989: 247), Sophocles (1887).
name	**Λουπερκάλιον**, a place name, from *Lupercal*. Hofmann (1989: 247), Sophocles (1887).
rare	**Λούπερκος**, a kind of priest, from *Lupercus*, a kind of priest: Plut. *Mor.* 280b (marked), *Rom.* 21.5, etc. (I/II AD); Lyd. *Mens.* 4.25.6 (VI AD); *Oracula Sibyllina* P 41 Geffcken, marked. Sophocles (1887).

not Latin?	**λούπης**, a bird, perhaps from *lupus* 'wolf'. Meyer (1895: 39 *s.v.* λούπις), *LBG*, Triandaphyllidis (1909: 92, 119), LSJ.
rare	**λ(ο)υπινάριον** 'lupin', from *lupīnārius* 'of lupins': as gloss for θέρμος 'lupin' in Philoponus, *De vocabulis quae diversum significatum exhibent secundum differentiam accentus* p. 163.5 Daly (VI AD); often in Byzantine texts. *LBG*, Kriaras (1968–).
not ancient	**λούπινον, λουππίνουμ** transliterating *lupīnum* 'lupin': interpolations in Dsc. 2.109 RV etc. Sophocles (1887), Lampe (1961); for Byzantine and modern survival *LBG* (*s.vv.* λούπινον, λουπίνος), Meyer (1895: 39), Andriotis (1967 *s.v.* λούπινο), Babiniotis (2002 *s.v.* λούπινο).
foreign	**λοῦπος** transliterating *lupus* 'wolf': Plut. *Mor.* 280c (I/II AD); perhaps (in gen. λούποδος, implying a nominative λούπους?) *Hippiatr.Camb.* (Apsyrtus) 30.1 (III/IV AD?). Hofmann (1989: 247), *LBG*, Kriaras (1968–).
	λουρ-: see λωρ-.
	λουσόριον, λουσόριος: see λουσώριον.
foreign	**λοῦστρον** transliterating *lūstrum* 'purification of offerings', 'period of five years': DH *AR* 4.22.2 (I BC); Lyd. *Mens.* 3.22.35 (VI AD). Hofmann (1989: 247), Sophocles (1887).
rare	**λουσωρία**, a kind of ship, from *lūsōria* (*nāvis*) 'pleasure ship' (*OLD s.v. lūsōrius*): papyrus *P.Oxy.* 1048.2 etc. (IV AD). Daris (1991a: 68), Hofmann (1989: 247–8 *s.v.* λουσώριον), Meinersmann (1927: 34).
Direct loan II AD – Byz.	**λουσώριον, λουσόριον, λοσώριον** (-ου, τό) 'place for games', 'pleasure ship', from *lūsōrius* 'used for amusement', neut. subst. Documents: *SB* 9563.i.15 etc., perhaps 16813.23 (both IV AD); *P.Harr.* 1.150.2 (V AD). Inscriptions: Paris and Holleaux 1886: 228 no. 8.18 (III AD); Pugliese Carratelli 1993: 267.12 (III AD). Literature: *Martyrium S. Eleutherii* 10 = De Cavalieri 1901: 159.7 (II AD); Epiph. *Anc.* 106.9 (IV AD). Post-antique: survives. *LBG*. Notes: Lampe (1961 *s.v.* λουσόριος) and Sophocles (1887 *s.v.* λουσώριος) take it as adj. because of Epiph.'s ἐν λουσορίῳ πλοίῳ, but other examples look like nouns. Daris (1991a: 68), Hofmann (1989: 247–8), Zilliacus (1937: 331), LSJ suppl. See §4.2.4.1 n. 54, §10.2.1, §10.2.2 F.
	λουσώριος: see λουσώριον.
	λύβερνος: see λίβερνος.
not Latin?	**λυγγούριον** 'amber' is suggested by Whatmough (1962: 243) as folk etymology of a Latin loan, but the regular form of the Latin is *lyncūrium* 'amber' (a borrowing from Greek: *TLL*), and the variant preferred by Whatmough, *ligūrium*, is rare (*TLL*). Whatmough's theory is accepted by Frisk (1954–72: III.147) and Hofmann (1989: 248–9), but not *DÉLG* (*s.v.* 2 λύγξ) or Beekes (2010). LSJ, LSJ suppl. See §2.3 n. 58.

foreign	**λυδίων** transliterating *lūdiō* 'dancer': DH *AR* 2.71.4 (I BC). Hofmann (1989: 249), LSJ.
foreign	**λυδός**, apparently 'Etruscan procession', perhaps connected to *lūdius* 'stage performer': App. *Libyca* 295 (I/II AD). Famerie (1998: 141–2).
	λυκανική: see λουκάνικον.
not Latin?	**λυκάριος**, meaning and etymology uncertain: no ancient examples. Harrauer and Sijpesteijn (1988: 111–12), Hofmann (1989: 249).
rare	**λωδικάριος** 'blanket-maker', from *lōdīx* 'blanket' via λῶδιξ + -άριος: Teucer, Boll 1903: 45.10 (I AD?). LSJ suppl.
Deriv. of loan II AD – Byz.	**λωδίκιον, λωτίκιον, λοδίκιον, λωτίκην, λωδίκειν, λώδικον, λώδικος, λώζικον, λωδικίων** (-ου, τό) 'blanket', from *lōdīx* 'blanket' (via λῶδιξ) + -ιον. Documents: common, e.g. *SB* 7572.5 (II AD); *P.Michael.* 18.B6 etc. (III AD); *P.Ryl.* IV.627.31 (IV AD); *P.Princ.* II.82.38 (V AD); *P.Cair.Masp.* 67006v.88 (VI AD). Inscriptions: *SEG* VII.423.3 (III AD). Literature: Epiph. *Pan.* III.143.4 as gloss (IV AD). Post-antique: survives. Daris (1991a: 68). Notes: probably not from rare *lōdīcula* 'little blanket' (*TLL*). O'Callaghan (1987), Daris (1991a: 68), Hofmann (1989: 249 s.v. λῶδιξ), Cavenaile (1952: 196), Meinersmann (1927: 34), *DÉLG* (s.v. λώδιξ), Beekes (2010 s.v. λώδιξ), *TLL* (s.v. *lōdīx* 1609.71–2), Lampe (1961), LSJ (s.vv. λῶδιξ, λωτίκιον). See §4.6.1 n. 83, §10.2.2 H.
Direct loan I–IV AD	**λῶδιξ, λῶζιξ, λόδιξ** (-ικος, ἡ) 'blanket', from *lōdīx* 'blanket'. Documents: e.g. *P.Oxy.* 1153.20 (I AD); *BGU* VII.1564.8 etc. (II AD); *P.Oxy. Hels.* 40.8 etc. (III AD); *SB* 9834.b14 (III/IV AD). Literature: *Periplus Maris Erythraei* 24.6, 24.214 Casson (I/II AD). Notes: forms derivatives λωδικάριος, perhaps λωδίκιον. O'Callaghan (1987), Schirru (2013: 305), Biville (1992: 235), Daris (1991a: 68), Hofmann (1989: 249), Cavenaile (1951: 398), *DÉLG*, Beekes (2010), *TLL* (s.v. *lōdīx* 1609.71), LSJ. See §4.2.5, §4.6.1 n. 83, §10.2.1, §10.2.2 H.
	λώζικον: see λωδίκιον.
	λῶζιξ: see λῶδιξ.
rare	**λωραμέντα** 'harness', from *lōrāmenta*, plural of *lōrāmentum* 'strap': Edict.Diocl. 8.8 etc. (IV AD); Byzantine texts. Hofmann (1989: 249), *LBG* (s.v. λοριμέντον), LSJ suppl.
rare	**λωρ(ε)ικάτης**, probably from *lōrīcātus* 'wearing a corselet': inscriptions *I.Ephesos* 736.6 (I/II AD), 3046.7 (II AD), perhaps 2061.i.9 (II AD), always with (acc.?) ending -ης. The paradigm is uncertain: Mason gives the nominative as λωρεικᾶτα (1974: 67), λωρεικάτης (1974: 68 s.v. μονήτη), and λωρικᾶτος (1974: 4). Byzantine λωρικᾶτος (Zilliacus 1935a: 228–9, *LBG*, Kriaras 1968–, Triandaphyllidis 1909: 129, Lampe 1961) may be unconnected.
	λώρεικος: see λωρῖκος.

Direct loan I BC – III AD?	**λωρῖκα, λουρίκη** (-ης/-ας?, ἡ) 'corselet', from *lōrīca* 'corselet'. Documents: *P.Oxy.* 812.7 (I BC); *P.Panop.Beatty* 1.343 (III AD). Literature: scholia to Ar. *Pl.* 450. Post-antique: occasional examples. Kriaras (1968– *s.v.* λώριξ). Notes: forms derivatives λωρίκιον, perhaps λωρῖκος. Gignac (1981: 8), Daris (1991a: 68), Hofmann (1989: 250), LSJ suppl. See §4.3.2 n. 75, §4.6.1, §8.1.5, §10.2.1, §10.2.2 C.
non-existent?	**λωρικάριος**, presumably from *lōrīcārius* 'of corselets', 'corselet-maker' (*TLL*): perhaps papyrus *P.Oxy.* 812.5 (I BC). Daris (1991a: 68), *TLL* (*s.v. lōrīcārius* 1678.45–7).
	λωρικάτης: see λωρεικάτης.
Deriv. of loan III AD – modern	**λωρίκιον, λουρίκιον** (-ου, τό) 'corselet', from *lōrīca* 'corselet' via λωρῖκα + -ιον. Documents: *P.Mich.* III.217.18 (III AD). Literature: Hesych. as gloss θ 1014, μ 230 (V/VI AD); Just. *Nov.* 85.4 (VI AD); scholion to Ar. *Pl.* 450. Post-antique: common. *LBG*, Zervan (2019: 105–6), Kriaras (1968–), Triandaphyllidis (1909: 130). Modern λουρίκι: Andriotis (1967). Notes: Avotins (1992), Daris (1991a: 68), Hofmann (1989: 250 *s.v.* λωρίκα), Cavenaile (1951: 398, 1952: 195), Zilliacus (1935a: 228–9), Lampe (1961), LSJ, LSJ suppl. See §4.6.1, §10.2.2 C.
rare	**λωρῖκος, λώρεικος** 'armoured', probably from *lōrīca* 'corselet' (via λωρῖκα?): papyrus *P.Lond.* II.191.14 (II AD). Gignac (1981: 8, considering it a variant of λωρῖκα), Daris (1991a: 68), Hofmann (1989: 250 *s.v.* λωρίκα), Meinersmann (1927: 34).
Deriv. of loan II AD – modern	**λωρίον, λουρίον** (-ου, τό) 'thong', 'strap', 'rein', 'thin strip', from *lōrum/lōrus* 'leather strap' via λῶρος + -ιον. Literature: Cephalion, *FHG* III frag. 7 (II AD) = Malal. 4.19.18 (VI AD); *Coll. Herm.* Mp 16d, probably meaning 'Gallic sandals' (III AD?); Geront. *V.Mel.* 2.61 (V AD). Post-antique: common. *LBG*, Kriaras (1968–), Triandaphyllidis (1909: 122). Modern λουρί 'strap': Babiniotis (2002), Andriotis (1967, cf. ὑπολώριον 1974: 572). Notes: Binder (2000: 223), Zilliacus (1937: 331), Lampe (1961), LSJ. See §4.6.1 n. 83, §8.2.3 n. 51, §9.2, §10.2.2 M.
foreign	**λωρόν** 'bitter', from *lōra* 'drink made from watered grapeskins': Hesych. as lemma λ 1514 (V/VI AD). Hofmann (1989: 250), LSJ.
Direct loan II AD – modern	**λῶρος, λῶρον** (-ου, ὁ or τό) 'thong', 'strap', 'rein' (also other meanings), from *lōrum/lōrus* 'leather strap'. Literature: common, e.g. Apollonius Sophista, *Lexicon Homericum* p. 119.2 as gloss (I/II AD); Pollux 5.55 (II AD); Ps.-Macar. *Serm.* 2.3.19 etc. (V AD?); Hesych. as gloss η 594, ε 2769, ι 612, etc. (V/VI AD); Palladius Medicus, Irmer 1977: 50.5 (VI AD); scholion to Ar. *Ach.* 724.

Post-antique: common, forming derivatives λωροπεδέω 'tie up with straps', λωροτύπτω 'beat with straps', etc. *LBG* (*s.vv.* λῶρον, λῶρος), Zervan (2019: 106), Kriaras (1968– *s.vv.* λώρον, λῶρος). Modern λουρίδα 'strip' (Babiniotis 2002), λοῦρον 'yoke-strap' (Meyer 1895: 39–40), λῶρος (Andriotis 1967) and derivatives.

Notes: forms derivatives λωρίον, λωροτόμος 1. Binder (2000: 223), Shipp (1979: 372), Hofmann (1989: 250–1), Zilliacus (1935a: 228–9), Immisch (1885: 369–70), LSJ, LSJ suppl. See §2.4, §4.2.4.1 n. 58, §4.6.1 n. 83, §4.6.2, §8.2.3 n. 51, §9.2, §10.2.1, §10.2.2 M.

not ancient   **λωρόσοκον** 'leather lasso', from *lōrum/lōrus* 'leather strap' via λῶρος + σόκκος 'lasso': no ancient examples. Zilliacus (1935a: 228–9), *LBG* (*s.v.* λωρόσοκκον).

not ancient   **λωροτομέω** 'cut into thongs', from *lōrum/lōrus* 'leather strap' via λωροτόμος 1: no securely ancient examples (the scholion to Ar. *Eq.* 768b, cited by LSJ, is Triclinian). Hofmann (1989: 250 *s.v.* λῶρος), *LBG*, Lampe (1961).

**Deriv. of loan
II AD – Byz.**   **λωροτόμος 1, λοροτόμος** (-ου, ὁ) 'strap-cutter', from *lōrum/lōrus* 'leather strap' via λῶρος + -τόμος (from τέμνω 'cut').

Literature: Aelius Dionysius σ 29 Erbse as gloss (II AD); EphraemSyr. III p. 48.37 (V/VI AD); Hesych. as gloss σ 1203 (V/VI AD); Rhetor. *Cap.* 216.5 (VI AD); scholia to Plato, *Gorgias* 517e as gloss.

Post-antique: survives. *LBG*.

Notes: Filos (2010: 244, 250), Daris (1991a: 68), Hofmann (1989: 250 *s.v.* λῶρος), LSJ (*s.v.* adj. λωροτόμος), LSJ suppl. See §2.4, §4.6.2, §9.2, §10.2.2 N.

non-existent   **λωροτόμος 2** 'cutting thongs': cited by LSJ as adj., but all examples are λωροτόμος 1.

λωτίκην, λωτίκιον: see λωδίκιον.

M

μάγγιψ: see μάγκιψ.

μαγίσστωρ, μάγιστερ: see μάγιστρος.

μαγιστέριον: see μαγιστήριον.

μαγίστερ(ος), μάγιστηρ: see μάγιστρος.

rare   **μαγιστήριον, μαγιστέριον**, an office, from *magisterium* 'office of superintendant': papyrus *P.Ryl.* IV.630/637.501 (IV AD); Lyd. *Mag.* p. 98.25 etc., marked (VI AD). Daris (1991a: 69), Hofmann (1989: 251), and for Byzantine survival *LBG* (*s.v.* μαγιστέριος).

μαγίστορος: see μάγιστρος.

μαγιστρανός: see μαγιστριανός.

rare   **μαγιστράτη** 'magistracy', probably from *magistrātus, -ūs* 'magistracy': inscription
I.Histria 363.10 (III AD). Mason (1974: 10, 67), Hofmann (1989: 251 *s.v.*
μαγιστρατος), LSJ suppl.

Direct loan
II AD – Byz.

μαγίστρατος (-ου, ὁ) 'magistrate', from *magistrātus, -ūs* 'magistrate'.
Inscriptions: *I.Histria* 378.c22 (II AD); Robert and Robert 1970: 414 no. 398
(III AD); *IGR* I.596.2.
Literature: Antec. in Latin script 1.2.7 *magistratus populi Romani* (VI AD).
Post-antique: some survival. *LBG* (*s.v.* μαγιστράτος).
Notes: Diethart (2006: 15), Mason (1974: 10, 67), Hofmann (1989: 251), LSJ
suppl. See §4.2.4.2, §10.2.1, §10.2.2 D.

Direct loan
IV AD – Byz.

μαγιστριανός, μαγιστρανός (-οῦ, ὁ), an official, from *magistriānus*, an official
(*TLL*).
Documents: common, e.g. *Stud.Pal.* XX.122.11 etc. (V AD); *P.Oxy.* 1960.4
(VI AD).
Inscriptions: e.g. *IGPorto* 75.5 (IV/V AD); *I.Sardis* I.18.8 (V AD); Bean and
Mitford 1970: 55 no. 31.B31 etc. (V AD); *I.Gerasa* 278.2 (VI AD).
Literature: common, e.g. Athan. *Decr.* 40.43 (IV AD); *ACO* I.I.I p. 6.12 (V
AD); Cyr.S. *Vit.Sab.* 149.5 (VI AD); with *agens in rebus* in Gloss. Ps.-Philox.
11.20, 12.7. Unverified example (II AD) in Zilliacus (1937: 322, 331).
Post-antique: numerous. Sophocles (1887).
Notes: Avotins (1989, 1992), Paschoud (1983: 234–5), Daris (1991a:
69), Hofmann (1989: 251–2), Zilliacus (1935a: 194–5, 1937: 331),
Meinersmann (1927: 34), Lampe (1961), LSJ suppl. See §4.2.4.1 n. 51,
§8.2.1, §10.2.1, §10.2.2 D.

rare   **μαγιστρόκηνσος** 'registrar of Constantinople', from *magister cēnsūs* 'master of
the census' via μάγιστρος and κῆνσος: Just. *Codex* 1.2.17.2 etc. (VI AD);
Byzantine texts. Avotins (1989), Hofmann (1989: 252), *LBG*, LSJ suppl.

Direct loan
III AD – modern

μάγιστρος, μαγίστερος, μαγίστορος, μαγόστορος, μαγίστηρ, μάγιστερ, μαγίστωρ,
μαΐστωρ, μαγίσστωρ (-ου/-ερος/-ορος/-ωρος, ὁ) 'master' (a title), from
magister 'master'.
Documents: common, e.g. *P.Oxy.* 2423.iii.15 (II/III AD); *P.Panop.Beatty* 1.140
etc. (III AD); *SB* 14726.Av.3 (IV AD); *SB* 8262.2 (V AD); *CPR* IX.79.10 (V
AD); *P.Lond.* v.1790.10 (V/VI AD); *P.Lond.* v.1678.1 (VI AD).
Inscriptions: common, e.g. *SEG* XXXIV.1095.4 (III AD); *I.Syringes* 1293.4 (IV
AD); Bean and Mitford 1970: 57 no. 31.C18 (V AD); *SEG* XXXVII.1474.B1
(VI AD).
Literature: common, e.g. Athan. *Apol.Const.* 3.6 (IV AD); Nil. 2.167.5 (V AD);
Hesych. as gloss κ 3505, as lemma μ 19 (V/VI AD); Evagr.Schol. *HE* 125.28
(VI AD). Antec. 4.7.2 etc., but in Latin script (in unusual meaning) 3.12.pr.
magistros (VI AD).
Post-antique: common, forming derivatives μαγίστρισσα 'wife of the *magister*',
πρωτομάγιστρος 'first *magister*', etc. *LBG* (*s.vv.* μαγίστερ, μαγίστωρ, μαΐστερος,
μαΐστηρ), Zervan (2019: 106–7), Kriaras (1968– *s.vv.* μάγιστρος, μαγίστρος,
μαγίστωρ, μαΐστορος), Triandaphyllidis (1909: 126). Modern μάστορας,
μάστορης 'craftsman', μαΐστωρ 'director', μάγιστρος 'Roman or Byzantine
official': Babiniotis (2002), Andriotis (1967), Meyer (1895: 43), Coleman
(2007: 795).

Notes: forms derivatives μαγιστρότης, μαγιστρόκηνσος. Binder (2000: 255–6, arguing that ending -ρος shows vulgar *magistrus*), Hasenohr (2008: 58–9), Avotins (1989, 1992 *s.vv.* μάγιστερ, μαγίστρος), Chantraine (1937: 91), Daris (1991a: 69 *s.vv.* μάγιστερ, μάγιστρος, μαγίστωρ), Mason (1974: 67 *s.vv.* μαγίστερ, μάγιστρος), Hofmann (1989: 252–4), Cavenaile (1952: 200–1), Viscidi (1944: 16), Zilliacus (1935a: 194–5, 1937: 331), Meinersmann (1927: 34–5), Immisch (1885: 364–5), *TLL* (*s.v.* *magister* 77.37–48), Lampe (1961), LSJ suppl. (*s.vv.* μάγιστερ, μάγιστρος, μαγίστωρ). See §4.2.4.1, §4.6.1, §8.2.3 n. 51, §9.5.4 n. 42, §10.2.1, §10.2.2 D.

Deriv. of loan
IV–VI AD

μαγιστρότης, μαγιστρώτης (-τητος, ἡ) 'office of the *magister*', from *magister* 'master' via μάγιστρος + -ότης.
Documents: *P.Oxy.* 3416.A7 (IV AD); *P.Lond.* III.1105 (IV AD); *P.Amh.* II.138.11 (IV AD); *CPR* XXIV.22.2 (VI AD).
Literature: Eus. *HE* 8.11.2 (IV AD).
Notes: Gignac (1981: 50), Palmer (1945: 116), Daris (1991a: 69, with derivation from *magistrātus*), Hofmann (1989: 251 *s.v.* μαγιστρατος), Meinersmann (1927: 34), Lampe (1961), LSJ suppl. See §4.6.1, §10.2.2 D.

μαγίστωρ: see μάγιστρος.

μαγκήπιον: see μαγκίπιον 1.

rare

μαγκιπατίων 'emancipation', from *mancipātiō* 'formal conveyance of property' and *ēmancipātiō* 'emancipation': Just. *Codex* 3.12.8.3 (VI AD); Antec. in Latin script 1.12.6 *mancipationon* etc. (VI AD). *LBG*. Cf. ἐμαγκιπατίων.

Deriv.? of loan
VI AD – Byz.

μαγκίπιον 1, μαγκιπεῖον, μαγκίππιον, μανκίπ(π)ιον, μαγκήπιον, μαγκύπειον (-ου, τό) 'bakery', 'mill', probably from *manceps* 'contractor', 'overseer' (*TLL*, esp. 252.68–75) via μάγκιψ + -ιον; or perhaps from *mancipium* 'sale', 'ownership'.
Literature: Thdr.Anag. *Tripart.* 4.278 (V/VI AD); Malal. 18.131 (VI AD); Cyr.S. *Vit.Eu.* 24.19, *Vit.Sab.* 117.7 (VI AD); with *pistrinum* in glossaries, e.g. Gloss. *Herm.Mp.* 306.52.
Post-antique: common, μαγκυπεῖον glosses ἀρτοπωλεῖον in *Suda* (α 4050). *LBG* (*s.v.* μαγκίπιον 1), Kriaras (1968–). Zilliacus (1937: 331).
Notes: Hofmann (1989: 260), Lampe (1961), LSJ. See §4.2.4.1 n. 54, §4.6.1, §10.2.2 I.

rare

μαγκίπιον 2, a technical term for a particular emancipation process, apparently from a combination of *mancipium* 'slave' and *ēmancipātiō* 'emancipation': Antec. 3.9.3 (VI AD). Cf. ἐμαγκιπατίων, μαγκιπατίων.

foreign

μαγκίπιον 3 'slave', from *mancipium* 'slave': Antec. in Latin script 1.3.3 *mancipia* (VI AD); later in Greek script. *LBG* (*s.v.* μαγκίπιον 2).

not ancient?

μαγκίπισσα 'female baker', from *manceps* 'contractor' via μάγκιψ + -ισσα: scholion to Septuagint 1 Kings 8:13; Byzantine texts. Hofmann (1989: 254 *s.v.* μάγκιψ), *LBG*, Kriaras (1968–), LSJ suppl.

μαγκίππιον: see μαγκίπιον 1.

Direct loan
V AD – modern

μάγκιψ, μάνκιψ, μάγγιψ, μάκηψ (-ιπος/-ηπος, ὁ) 'contractor', 'baker', from *manceps* 'contractor', 'overseer' (*TLL*, esp. 252.68–75).

Documents: *CPR* XIX.55.2 (VI AD); *P.Flor.* I.93.9 (VI AD); *P.Lond.* V.1713.11 (VI AD).

Inscriptions: *IG* XIV.2491.4; *MAMA* III.242a, 292, 409, 415, 756.4.

Literature: Socr. 5.18.8 etc., marked (IV/V AD); Eusebius of Alexandria, *PG* LXXXVI.I.444c, meaning 'servants', 'waiters' (V AD); Lyd. *Mag.* p. 140.5 etc. (VI AD); Cyr.S. *Vit.Sab.* 89.21 (VI AD); *V.S.Aux.* 51.14 (VI AD).

Post-antique: numerous, forming derivatives μαγκιπικός 'of a bakery', μαγκιπίδιον 'baker's boy', etc. *LBG*, Zervan (2019: 108), Kriaras (1968–), Triandaphyllidis (1909: 124). Modern dialectal μάγκιπας 'baker' and derivatives: Andriotis (1974: 362), Meyer (1895: 40), Kahane and Kahane (1972–6: 533, 1982: 135).

Notes: probably originally meant 'contractor', used for large bakeries with military contract, then extended to mean 'baker' (Meyer 1895: 40; Meinersmann 1927: 35). Probably forms derivative μαγκίπιον 1. Daris (1991a: 69), Hofmann (1989: 254), *TLL* (*s.v. manceps* 251.35–8), Lampe (1961), LSJ suppl. See §4.2.5, §4.6.1, §10.2.1, §10.2.2 I.

not ancient

μαγκλάβι 'torture' and derivatives, from *manus, -ūs* 'hand' and *clāvus* 'nail' perhaps via unattested **man(u)clavium*: no ancient examples. Binder (2000: 200), *LBG* (*s.v.* μαγλάβιον 'whip'), Zervan (2019: 108), Kriaras (1968–), Viscidi (1944: 27), Triandaphyllidis (1909: 124), Meyer (1895: 40), Andriotis (1974: 362).

μαγκύπειον: see μαγκίπιον 1.

μαγνιφέρ: see ἰμαγίνιφερ.

name

Μάγνος, cited by Sophocles (1887) as a borrowing of *magnus* 'great': only as name, e.g. Plut. *Pomp.* 22.6, *Crassus* 7.1.

μαγόστορος: see μάγιστρος.

not ancient?

μάγουλον 'cheek', apparently from *magulus* (*TLL*; poorly attested, meaning uncertain): allegedly Melampus, Franz 1780: 503.4 (III BC); Byzantine and modern texts. Binder (2000: 197–8), *LBG*, Zervan (2019: 108–9), Kriaras (1968–), Triandaphyllidis (1909: 89, 120), Meyer (1895: 40–41), Andriotis (1967), Babiniotis (2002), *TLL* (*s.v. magulus*), Lampe (1961), LSJ suppl.

μαῖορ: see μαίωρ.

Direct loan
II BC – modern

Μάϊος (-α, -ον or -ου, ὁ) 'May', from *Māius* 'May'.

Documents: common, e.g. *P.Hever* 61.6 (II AD); *SB* 16169.16 (III AD); *P.Cair. Isid.* 87.8 (IV AD); *P.Berl.Sarisch.* 14.5 (VI AD).

Inscriptions: common, e.g. *F.Delphes* III.IV.353.C = Sherk 1969: no. 1.C1 (II BC); Sherk 1969: no. 22.3 (I BC); *IGUR* IV.1645.5 (I/II AD); *IGBulg.* IV.1917.b3 (II AD); *SEG* LIII.1104.2 (II/III AD); perhaps *IGBulg.* I².70bis.7 (III AD); *SEG* XXXII.1057.3 (IV AD); *I.Sardis* I.18.4 (V AD); *IG* II/III².V.13527.4 (VI AD).

Literature: e.g. DH *AR* 10.59.1 (I BC); Plut. *Rom.* 12.1 (I/II AD); Theophilus
of Antioch, *Ad Autolycum* 3.27.6 Grant (II AD); Dio Cassius 78.31.4
(II/III AD); Cyril of Alexandria in *Carth.* 424.5 (V AD); *ACO* II.I.I
p. 177.2 (V AD); *ACO* III p. 154.12 (VI AD).
Post-antique: common. Kriaras (1968–). Modern Μάιος, Μάης, Μάϊς: Babiniotis
(2002), Andriotis (1967), Kahane and Kahane (1972–6: 533), Meyer
(1895: 41).
Notes: Solin (2008), Sijpesteijn (1979), García Domingo (1979: 521),
Strobach (1997: 197), Hofmann (1989: 254), LSJ. See **§4.2.1**, §4.2.2,
§8.1.4, §8.1.7, §8.2.3 n. 51, §10.2.1, §10.2.2 E.

rare   **Μαιουμάρχης** 'one who presides over the *Maioumas*', from the Latin source of
Μαιουμᾶς via Μαιουμᾶς + -άρχης: inscription *I.Aphrodisias Late Ant.* 40.1 (V
AD). LSJ suppl.

Direct? loan
III AD – Byz.   **Μαιουμᾶς, Μαειουμᾶς** (-ᾶ, ὁ) 'May day' (a festival), perhaps from *maiūma*, a
festival (*TLL*); but the festival is only attested in the East and the Latin
appears to be later than the Greek, so perhaps derivative from *Māius* 'May'
via Μάϊος, with an unknown suffix.
Inscriptions: *I.Mus.Iznik* 63.5 (III AD), *I.Gerasa* 279.4 (VI AD).
Literature: Julian, *Misopogon* 362d (IV AD); Malal. 14.17.4, but marked at
12.3.21 (VI AD); Lyd. *Mens.* 4.80 (VI AD); Procop. *Epistulae* 77 (VI AD).
Post-antique: survives. *LBG*.
Notes: if not the source, *maiuma* is a reborrowing of this. Robert (1936b:
9–14), *TLL* (*s.v. maiūma*), Lampe (1961), LSJ suppl. See §4.2.3.2, §10.2.1,
§10.2.2 F.

rare   **Μαιουμίζω** 'celebrate May day', from the Latin source of Μαιουμᾶς via Μαιουμᾶς
+ -ίζω: Lyd. *Mens.* 4.80 (VI AD); inscription *I.Tyr.* 151.1. *LBG*, *TLL* (*s.v.*
maiūma), LSJ suppl.

non-existent   **μαιοῦρος, μαηοῦρος**, a title, from *maiōrius*, a military title: superseded reading of
inscription *I.Syringes* 1293.4 = *IGR* I.1220.4 (IV AD). Daris (1991a: 69).

μαΐστωρ: see μάγιστρος.

foreign   **μαίωρ, μαῖορ** 'larger', from *maior* 'larger': as qualification of proper names on
Latinate ostraca *O.Claud.* II.404.1; probably also *O.Claud.* II.390.8, 392.5,
394.6, 407.3 (all II AD); μαϊώρεις transliterating *maiōrēs* 'elders', Plut. *Numa*
19.3 (I/II AD). For the Latin influence on the ostraca see *O.Claud.* II
pp. 229–30. Hofmann (1989: 255).

μακελάρειως, μακελ(λ)άρη(ο)ς: see μακελλάριος.

μακελλάριον: see μάκελλος.

Direct loan
IV AD – modern   **μακελ(λ)άριος, μακελ(λ)άρη(ο)ς, μακελάρειως** (-ου, ὁ) 'provision-dealer', from
macellārius 'provision-dealer'.
Inscriptions: e.g. Gibson 1975: 151 (IV AD); *IG* II/III².V.13468.3 (V/VI AD);
I.Chr.România 8.1 (VI AD).
Literature: Rhetor. *Plan.* 225.25 (VI AD); Aesop, *Fabulae* 99.1.7 Hausrath and
Hunger; with *laniator* and *lanio* in Gloss. Ps.-Cyril. 364.5.

Post-antique: numerous, forming derivative μακελλαρικός 'of a butcher'. *LBG* (*s.v.* μακελλάρης), Zervan (2019: 110), Kriaras (1968– *s.vv.* μακελλάρης, μακελλάριος), Triandaphyllidis (1909: 124). Modern μακελλάρης, μακελλάρις 'butcher': Babiniotis (2002), Andriotis (1967), Meyer (1895: 41).

Notes: De Meyer (1962: 149), Daris (1991a: 70), Hofmann (1989: 255), Frisk (1954–72: 11.164), Beekes (2010 *s.v.* μάκελλον), LSJ (*s.v.* μάκελλον), LSJ suppl. (*s.vv.* μακελλάριος, μάκελλον). See §4.2.4.1 n. 50, §10.2.1, §10.2.2 I.

μακελλεῖον, μακέλλιον: see μάκελλος.

μακελλίτης: see μάκελλος.

semantic extension	**μάκελλος, μάκελλον** 'market' (with relatives **μακελλίτης** 'butcher', **μακελλεῖον** 'butcher's stall', and **μακελλάριον** 'provision market'): often said to be a loanword, but probably semantic extension. Although there is some dispute about the etymology, most likely μάκελλον in its early meaning 'enclosure' is a Semitic loan in Greek, *macellum* 'provision market' is a Greek or Semitic loan in Latin, and later μάκελλος/μάκελλον 'market' is semantic extension of μάκελλον 'enclosure' under influence of Latin. De Meyer (1962), Pisani (1951: 293–6), Wackernagel (1916: 197), Strobach (1997: 197), Daris (1991a: 69–70), Hofmann (1989: 255–6), Viscidi (1944: 41), Cameron (1931: 249–50), Meinersmann (1927: 35), Hahn (1906: 249), *DÉLG*, Frisk (1954–72: 111.149, cf. 11.164), Beekes (2010 *s.v.* μάκελλον), Kahane and Kahane (1972–6: 535), Palmer (1945: 84), *LBG* (*s.vv.* μακελλίτης, μακέλλιον, μακελλάριον), Kriaras (1968– *s.v.* μακελλεῖον), Andriotis (1967 *s.v.* modern μακελλειό), Lampe (1961 *s.vv.* μάκελλος, μακελλεῖον), LSJ (*s.vv.* μάκελλος, μακελλίτης, μακελλεῖον, μακελλάριον). See §5.2.1.
not Latin?	**μακκοάω** 'be stupid' and **ἀπομακκόω** 'strike dumb' are from *Maccus* or the Oscan source of *Maccus*; the latter is more likely since μακκοάω is attested very early. García Domingo (1983: 252), Hofmann (1989: 256), *DÉLG*, Frisk (1954–72: 11.164), Beekes (2010), LSJ, LSJ suppl. (*s.v.* ἀπομακκόω).
rare	**μάλημπτος** 'bought as a bad bargain', from *male ēmptus* 'badly bought': inscribed tile *SEG* XXXIX.1062B (I BC/AD). LSJ suppl.
foreign	***malus*** 'bad', part of *malā fidē* 'not in good faith': Antec. 2.1.30 *mala fide* etc. (VI AD). See §7.3 passage 33.
not Latin	**Μάμερτος** 'Mars', probably from Oscan. Hofmann (1989: 256), *OLD s.v. Māmers*, LSJ.
	μαμπ-: see μαππ-.
not Latin?	**μαμυλίων** 'breastplate', perhaps related to *mamillāre* 'breastband': papyrus *P.Oxy.* 2598.b4 etc. (III/IV AD). Editor *ad loc.*, Daris (1991a: 70, with derivation from *mamilla*), *LBG*.
not ancient	**μανδατάριος** 'official representative', from *mandātārius* 'agent' (*TLL*): several papyri now thought to be post-antique (*Stud.Pal.* III².1.72.A2, X.251.B8, perhaps X.79.2.3). Daris (1991a: 70, with derivation from *mandātor*), Hofmann (1989: 256), Meinersmann (1927: 35), *LBG*, *TLL* (*s.v. mandātārius*).

Direct loan **V AD – modern**	**μανδᾶτον, μαντᾶτον** (-ου, τό) 'consensual contract', 'order', 'message', from *mandātum* 'order', 'consensual contract'. Documents: tachygraphy in Menci 2000: 285 (V/VI AD); *P.Oxy.* 2416.8 etc. (VI AD). Literature: e.g. *V.Dan.Styl. A.* 84 (V AD); *Schol.Sinai.* in Latin script 29 *mandaton* (V/VI AD); Malal. 5.11.28 (VI AD); Just. *Nov.* 112.3.1 (VI AD); Antec. 3.26.6 etc., but in Latin script 3.26.pr. *mandaton* etc. (VI AD). Post-antique: common, forming derivative μανδατοφόρος 'messenger'. *LBG*, Zervan (2019: 111), Kriaras (1968– *s.v.* μαντάτον), Triandaphyllidis (1909: 123). Modern μαντάτο 'news' and derivatives: Babiniotis (2002), Andriotis (1967), Meyer (1895: 42). Notes: Rodríguez Martín (2019: 421–2), Menci (2000: 285), Avotins (1992), Daris (1991a: 70), Hofmann (1989: 256–7), Zilliacus (1935a: 194–5, 228–9), Lampe (1961), LSJ suppl. See §4.2.4.1 n. 55, §7.1.1, §7.1.2, §7.1.3, §9.5.6 n. 56, §10.2.1, §10.2.2 B.
	μανδατορεύω: see μανδατωρεύω.
Direct loan **V AD – Byz.**	**μανδάτωρ** (-ωρος/-ορος, ὁ) 'guarantor', 'messenger', from *mandātor* 'guarantor', 'one who issues an order'. Documents: *P.Bagnall* 33.4 (V AD); *P.Flor.* III.384.16 etc. (V AD); *P.Oxy.* 4394.26 etc., 4395.19 etc. (both V AD); perhaps *P.Stras.* VIII.717.7 (V AD). Inscriptions: perhaps *I.Aphrodisias Performers* 46.A. Literature: Just. *Nov.* 4.1 etc. (VI AD); Ath.Schol. 4.3.21 etc. (VI AD); Antec. in Latin script 3.29.pr. *mandatores* (VI AD). Post-antique: common, forming derivatives μανδατόρισσα 'wife of a *mandator*', πρωτομανδάτωρ 'first *mandator*', etc. *LBG*, Zervan (2019: 111), Kriaras (1968–). Notes: forms derivatives ἀλληλομανδάτορες, μανδατωρεύω. Avotins (1992), Daris (1991a: 70), Hofmann (1989: 257), Zilliacus (1935a: 194–5, 228–9), Lampe (1961), LSJ suppl. See §4.2.5, §10.2.1, §10.2.2 B.
rare	**μανδατωρεύω, μανδατορεύω** 'mandate', from *mandātor* 'guarantor', 'one who issues an order' via μανδάτωρ + -εύω: Just. *Nov.* 4.1 (VI AD); Byzantine texts. Avotins (1992), Zilliacus (1935a: 194–5), *LBG*, LSJ suppl. See §9.5.6 n. 68.
Direct loan **II AD – modern**	**μανδήλη, μανδῆλα, μαντήλη** (-ης, ἡ) 'towel', from *mantēle* 'hand towel'. Documents: *P.Princ.* II.82.42 (V AD); *SB* 15249.5 etc. (VI AD); *P.Rain.Cent.* 156.5 (VI AD). Literature: Pollux 7.74 (II AD). Post-antique: survives. *LBG* (*s.vv.* μανδήλη, μαντήλα), Kriaras (1968– *s.v.* μαντήλα). Modern μαντήλα, μαντίλα 'kerchief': Babiniotis (2002), Meyer (1895: 42). Notes: forms derivatives μανδήλιον, μαντηλαρία, μαντηλάριος. Daris (1991a: 70), Hofmann (1989: 257), *TLL* (*s.v. mantēlium* 332.30–4), LSJ, LSJ suppl. See §4.2.3.1, §4.2.5, §4.6.1 n. 84, **§8.1.1** passage 39, §8.2.2, §10.2.1, §10.2.2 H.
Deriv.? of loan **VI AD – modern**	**μανδήλιον, μαντήλιον, μανδίλιον, μανδύλιον** (-ου, τό) 'little towel', from *mantēle* 'hand towel' via μανδήλη + -ιον, or from *mantēlium* 'hand towel'. Documents: perhaps *P.Oxy.* 3860.47 etc. (IV AD); *P.Berl.Sarisch.* 21.39 (V/VI AD).

Literature: Hesych. as gloss χ 299 (V/VI AD); Lyd. *Mens.* 1.12.56 (VI AD); with *mantele* in Gloss. Serv. 523.20.

Post-antique: common. *LBG*, Kriaras (1968– *s.v.* μαντήλι I), Triandaphyllidis (1909: 122). Modern μαντήλι, μαντίλι 'handkerchief': Babiniotis (2002), Andriotis (1967), Meyer (1895: 42).

Notes: Daris (1991a: 70), Hofmann (1989: 257 *s.v.* μανδήλη), Meinersmann (1927: 35), Immisch (1885: 370), *TLL* (*s.v.* *mantēlium* 332.30–4), LSJ (*s.v.* μανδήλη). See §4.2.4.1 n. 54, §4.6.1 n. 84, §8.2.3, §10.2.2 H.

rare   **μάνδιξ** 'wallet', from *mantica* 'travelling-bag': *V.Aesopi* G 4, 6, 8 (II AD?). Hofmann (1989: 257), LSJ suppl.

μανδίον: see μαντίον.

foreign   **mandō** 'consign', 'commit': Antec. in Latin script 2.24.3 *mando* (VI AD).

μανδύλιον: see μανδήλιον.

μανδύον: see μαντίον.

foreign   **μάνης** transliterating *mānēs* 'spirits of the dead': Zosimus, *Historia nova* 2.3.2 Paschoud (V AD?).

not Latin   **μανιάκης, μανιάκη** 'necklace', 'torc', is Indo-Iranian or Celtic in origin, though a case has been made for derivation via the Latin cognate *monīle*. Hofmann (1989: 258), *DÉLG*, Frisk (1954–72: II.171), Beekes (2010), *OLD s.v. monīle*, LSJ, LSJ suppl.

μανίγιν: see μανίκιον.

rare   **μάνικα, μᾶνιξ** 'sleeve', from *manicae* 'cuffs', 'sleeves': papyrus *BGU* I.40.3 (II/III AD); Lyd. *Mag.* p. 30.17, marked (VI AD). Hofmann (1989: 259), Zilliacus (1935a: 228–9), Meinersmann (1927: 35), *LBG* (*s.vv.* μάνικα, μᾶνιξ), Kriaras (1968–), Meyer (1895: 41), Babiniotis (2002). Cf. χειρομανίκιον, χειρομάνικον.

not ancient?   **μανικέλ(λ)ιον**, meaning uncertain, perhaps from *manicillium*, which could mean 'glove' or 'sleeve' (*TLL*): no securely ancient examples. Heraeus (1937: 29 n. 1), Hofmann (1989: 258), Zilliacus (1935a: 228–9), *LBG*, Kriaras (1968– *s.v.* μανικέλι).

rare   **μανίκιον, μανίγιν** 'cuff', 'sleeve', from *manicium* (*TLL*), diminutive of *manicae* 'cuffs', 'sleeves', or from *manicae* + -ιον: unpublished ostracon O.Dios inv. 706.6 (II AD); Byzantine texts. Source of χειρομανίκιον. Hofmann (1989: 258), Zilliacus (1935a: 228–9, 1937: 331, citing unverified example from III AD), *LBG*, Zervan (2019: 111–12), Kriaras (1968–), Meyer (1895: 41), Triandaphyllidis (1909: 122), Andriotis (1967 *s.v.* μανίκι), Babiniotis (2002 *s.v.* μανίκι), Lampe (1961 *s.v.* μανίκια), LSJ (*s.v.* μανίκια).

μᾶνιξ: see μάνικα.

foreign   **μανιπλάριος** transliterating *manipulāris/maniplāris* 'common soldier': Plut. *Rom.* 8.7 (I/II AD). Strobach (1997: 197), Hofmann (1989: 259), Sophocles (1887). Cf. κομονοπλάρις.

foreign	**μανίπλον** transliterating *maniplum*, variant of *manipulus* 'handful' (*TLL s.v. manipulus* 316.45): Plut. *Rom.* 8.7 (I/II AD). Hofmann (1989: 259), Sophocles (1887 *s.v.* μανίπλα).
foreign	**μάνιπλος** is said by Lyd. *Mag.* p. 20.9 (VI AD) to be Latin for 'standard-bearer', perhaps based on *manipulus/maniplus* 'maniple' (a unit of infantry) and/or *manipulāris/maniplāris* 'common soldier'. Binder (2000: 184–5), *LBG*.
foreign	**μανίφεστος** 'manifest': Antec. in Latin script 4.1.3 *manifeston* etc. (VI AD); later in Greek script. Zilliacus (1935a: 194–5), *LBG*.
	μανκίπ(π)ιον: see μαγκίπιον 1.
	μάνκιψ: see μάγκιψ.
rare	**μανουάλιον, μανοάλλειν**, meaning uncertain, probably from *manuālis* 'held in the hand' (neut. subst.): papyrus *P.Oxy.* 2599.33, with editor's commentary (III/IV AD). No certainly ancient examples of meaning 'large candlestick', common in Byzantine texts. Daris (1991a: 70), Hofmann (1989: 260), Meinersmann (1927: 35), *LBG*, Zervan (2019: 112), Kriaras (1968–), Triandaphyllidis (1909: 125), Meyer (1895: 41–2), Lampe (1961).
rare	**μανούβριον** 'handle', from *manubrium* 'handle': documents *BGU* 11.544.22 (II AD); *O.Claud.* IV.757.6 (II AD); tachygraphy in Menci 2000: 285 (IV AD); Byzantine texts. Menci (2000: 285–6), Daris (1991a: 70), Hofmann (1989: 260), Meinersmann (1927: 35–6), *LBG*, Lampe (1961), LSJ suppl.
foreign	*manūmissiō* 'manumission': Antec. 1.5.pr. *manumissio* (VI AD).
foreign	**μανουμίσ(σ)ωρ** 'manumitter', from *manūmissor* 'one who manumits': Antec. in Latin script 3.9.3 *manumissoros* etc. (VI AD); later in Greek script. Zilliacus (1935a: 194–5), *LBG*.
	μαντᾶτον: see μανδᾶτον.
rare	**μαντηλαρία** 'slave who brings towels or napkins to a banquet', from *mantēle* 'napkin' via μαντηλάριος or via μανδήλη + -άριος in the feminine: inscription *I.Ephesos* 1078.14 (III AD). LSJ suppl. See §6.2 n. 13.
rare	**μαντηλάριος** 'slave who brings towels or napkins to a banquet', from *mantēle* 'napkin' via μανδήλη + -άριος: inscriptions *I.Ephesos* 1060.14; *SEG* XXXIV.1126.3 (both III AD). Hofmann (1989: 260), LSJ suppl.
	μαντήλη: see μανδήλη.
	μαντήλιον: see μανδήλιον.
Direct loan with suffix **V AD – modern**	**μαντίον, μανδίον, μανδύον** (-ου, τό), an outer garment, from *mantus, -ūs* 'short cloak' (*TLL*) + -ιον; some spellings influenced by μανδύα/μανδύας 'cloak', borrowed from Persian. Literature: Thdt. *PG* LXXX.569a: τί ἐστι μανδύας; εἶδος ἐστιν ἐφεστρίδος. οἶμαι δὲ ἢ ἀρκαδίκιν εἶναι, ἢ τὸ παρὰ πολλῶν μαντίον ὀνομαζόμενον (V AD); Malal. 17.16.115 (VI AD); Cyr.S. *Vit.Eu.* 73.20 (VI AD); Lyd. *Mag.* p. 102.27 ὁ δὲ μανδύης χλαμύδος εἶδός ἐστι τὸ παρὰ τῷ πλήθει μαντίον λεγόμενον (VI AD); with *paludamentum* in Gloss. Ps.-Philox. 141.16. Μανδύον in Septuagint 1 Kings 17:39 (II BC) may have a different source.

Post-antique: common. *LBG* (*s.vv.* μαντί, μανδύον), Kriaras (1968– *s.v.* μαντί), Triandaphyllidis (1909: 122). Modern μαντί: Andriotis (1967).

Notes: some scholars prefer a single etymology, but Triandaphyllidis (1909: 71, 103) makes a good case for the double one. All three spellings would have been pronounced identically in late Greek. Hofmann (1989: 261 *s.v.* μαντος), Frisk (1954–72: II.170), *TLL* (*s.v. mantus* 334.43–4), Lampe (*s.vv.* μανδύας, μαντίον), LSJ, LSJ suppl. See §4.3.2, **§4.4**, §10.2.1, §10.2.2 H.

rare | **μάντος** 'short cloak', from *mantus, -ūs* 'short cloak' (*TLL*): Edict.Diocl. 19.71 (IV AD). Hofmann (1989: 261), *TLL* (*s.v. mantus* 334.43), LSJ suppl.

rare | **μαξίλα** 'jaw', from *maxilla* 'jaw': *Hippiatr.Par.* (Pel.) 120 (V AD?). *LBG* (*s.v.* μαξίλλα).

not ancient | **μαξιλλάρι** 'pillow', from *maxilla* 'jaw' or *maxillāris* 'of jaws': no ancient examples. Meyer (1895: 42), *LBG* (*s.v.* μαξιλλάριον), Kriaras (1968– *s.v.* μαξιλάρι), Andriotis (1967).

not Latin? | **μαξιλλάριος**, perhaps an occupational term, perhaps from *maxillāris* 'of jaws' (thus Buck and Petersen 1945: 96), or variant of otherwise unattested ἀμαξιλλάριος 'wagon-driver' from ἄμαξα 'wagon' + -άριος (thus editor *ad loc.*, tentatively): papyrus *P.Kellis* I.53.5 (IV AD); Byzantine texts (perhaps without continuity). Daris (1997: 141–2), *LBG*.

not ancient | **μαξίλλας** 'slap in the face', from *maxilla* 'jaw': no ancient examples. Meyer (1895: 42), *LBG* (*s.v.* μαξίλλα).

non-existent | **μαξιλλοπλουμάκιος** 'feather pillow', said to be from *maxilla* 'jaw' and *plūmācium* 'pillow' (*TLL*) (via πλουμάκιον): variant reading for name Μαξιλλοπλουμβάκιος, Lyd. *Mag.* p. 222.27 (VI AD). Sophocles (1887), *TLL* (*s.v.* μαξιλλοπλουμάκιον). See §8.1.7 n. 34.

foreign | **μάξιμος** 'greatest', from *maximus* 'greatest': Antec. in Latin script 1.16.pr. *maxima* etc. (VI AD); later in Greek script. Used earlier as a name, sometimes with explanation of the Latin meaning: e.g. Polybius 3.87.6; Plut. *Fab.* 1.3. Sophocles (1887). See §8.1.3 passage 41.

| **μαπίον**: see μαππίον.

not Latin? | **μάπουλον**, apparently 'wallet', perhaps from *mappa* 'napkin': Philogelos 213 (IV AD). *LBG*.

Direct loan
VI AD – modern | **μάππα** (-ης?, ἡ) 'napkin', 'signal-cloth', from *mappa* 'napkin', 'signal-cloth'.
Documents: *P.Berl.Sarisch.* 21.15 (V/VI AD).
Literature: *V.Aesopi* G 44 (II AD?); Malal. 17.8 (VI AD); Just. *Nov.* 105.1 etc., marked (VI AD); Lyd. *Mag.* p. 48.19, *Mens.* 1.12.55, both marked (VI AD); Ath.Schol. 22.1.4 etc. (VI AD); condemned as foreign in Ps.-Herodian, Περὶ σολοικισμοῦ καὶ βαρβαρισμοῦ p. 312.2 Nauck.
Post-antique: survives. *LBG*, Zervan (2019: 112–13), Kriaras (1968–), Triandaphyllidis (1909: 122). Modern μάπ(π)α 'face': Babiniotis (2002), Andriotis (1967).
Notes: forms derivatives μαππάριον, μαππάριος. Avotins (1992), Hofmann (1989: 261), Lampe (1961), LSJ suppl. See §4.3.2, §8.2.3 n. 51, §10.2.1, §10.2.2 H.

rare	**μαππάριον, μαμπάριον** 'napkin', 'tablecloth', from *mappa* 'napkin' via μάππα + -άριον: papyrus *Chrest.Wilck.* 135.12 etc. (V/VI AD). Daris (1991a: 70), Hofmann (1989: 261 *s.v.* μάππα), Meinersmann (1927: 35). LSJ suppl. *s.v.* μαππάριος properly belongs here. See §6.3 n. 21.
rare	**μαππάριος, μαμπάριος** 'signaller' (at the start of a race), probably from *mappa* 'signal-cloth' via μάππα + -άριος: Ps.-John Chrysostom, *PG* LIX.570.5, 8 (IV/V AD?); Lyd. *Mens.* 1.12.50, 57, marked (VI AD); with *vexillarius* in Gloss. *Herm.M.* 174.14. Hofmann (1989: 262, with derivation from unattested **mappārius*), Lampe (1961), LSJ, and for Byzantine survival *LBG*, Triandaphyllidis (1909: 126).
Direct loan with suffix **III–VI AD**	**μαπ(π)ίον, μαμπίον** (-ου, τό) 'napkin', 'cloth', 'tablecloth', 'altar cloth', from *mappa* 'napkin' + -ιον. Documents: *P.Wisc.* I.30.8 (III AD); *P.Mil.* II.72.3 (III AD); *P.Oxy.* 1051.17 etc. (III AD); *P.Ryl.* IV.627.20 (IV AD); *P.Oxy.* 1741.17 (IV AD); *P.Sijp.* 60a.13 (IV AD); *P.Heid.* VII.406v.3.22 (IV/V AD); *P.Prag.* II.178.1.9 (V/VI AD). Literature: *Anonymus Bobiensis* p. 34.10 De Nonno as gloss (V AD?); with *mappa* and *mantele* in Gloss. Serv. 523.26, 545.62. Notes: probably not borrowed via μάππα, given the chronology. Forms derivative χειρομάππιον. Daris (1991a: 70), Hofmann (1989: 261 *s.v.* μάππα), LSJ suppl. (replacing LSJ). See §4.3.2, §10.2.1, §10.2.2 H.
not ancient	**μαρῖνος** transliterating *marīnus* 'marine': interpolations in Dsc. 3.122 RV etc. Hofmann (1989: 262 *s.v.* μαρίνα).
not ancient?	**μαρίτα, μαρίτη** 'wife', from *marīta* 'wife': inscription *IGR* III.12.4 (bilingual). Hofmann (1989: 262).
non-existent	**μαρῖτος** 'husband', from *marītus* 'husband': superseded reading of inscription *SEG* XXXVII.1343.9 (II AD). Hofmann (1989: 262), Cameron (1931: 250).
Direct loan with influence **IV–VI AD?**	**μαρμαράριος, μαρμάριος** (-ου, ὁ) 'marble-mason', from *marmorārius* 'marble-mason' with influence from μάρμαρος 'marble'. Inscriptions: e.g. *IGUR* IV.1567.12 (III AD?); *IG* IV.437.3 (IV AD?); Edict.Diocl. 7.5 (IV AD); *I.Olympia* 657.4 (V AD); perhaps *SEG* VIII.240.2 (VI AD). Literature: Teucer, Boll 1903: 44.6 (I AD?); with *marmorarius* in Gloss. Ps.-Cyril. 364.61. Notes: Robert (1960b: 28–30), Hofmann (1989: 262), *DÉLG* (*s.v.* μάρμαρος), Frisk (1954–72: II.177), Beekes (2010 *s.v.* μάρμαρος), Lampe (1961), LSJ, LSJ suppl. (*s.vv.* μαρμαράριος, μαρμάριος B). See §4.2.4.1 n. 50, §4.4, §10.2.1, §10.2.2 J.
rare	**μαρμαρωσσός** 'with sores on the feet', from *marmorōsus* 'having a hard tumour' or unattested **marmarōsus* (presumably itself derived from μάρμαρον 'sore on the feet of asses'): *Hippiatr.Berl.* (Apsyrtus) 53.1, cf. 130.10 (III/IV AD?). J. N. Adams (1995: 261), Hofmann (1989: 262), *DÉLG* (*s.v.* μάρμαρος), Beekes (2010 *s.v.* μάρμαρος), *TLL* (*s.v.* marmorōsus), LSJ.
Direct loan with suffix **IV AD – modern**	**μαρούλιον, μαρούλλ(ι)ον** (-ου, τό) 'lettuce', from *amārus* 'bitter' perhaps via unattested **amārulla (lactuca)* + -ιον. Literature: Philogelos 16 (IV AD); Hesych. as gloss θ 751 (V/VI AD); Alex. Trall. II.61.6 etc. (VI AD); Ps.-Hippocrates, Delatte 1939: 489.13; Ps.-Galen, Delatte 1939: 392.16; Hieroph. *Πῶς* 460.19 etc.

Post-antique: common. *LBG*, Kriaras (1968–), Triandaphyllidis (1909: 119). Modern μαρούλι 'lettuce': Babiniotis (2002), Andriotis (1967), Meyer (1895: 43).

Notes: Babiniotis and Andriotis prefer derivation via **amārulla*. *DÉLG*, LSJ. See §4.3.2 n. 69, §8.2.3, §9.2, §10.2.1, §10.2.2 I; cf. ἀμᾶρον.

not Latin?   **μάρρον**, a word for an iron tool in Hesych. as lemma μ 317 (V/VI AD), probably has a Semitic origin, but derivation from Latin *marra* 'mattock' is suggested by Immisch (1885: 362), Sophocles (1887). LSJ.

not ancient?   **Μαρτήσιοι, Μαρτίσιοι**, name of an organization, apparently from *Martēnsēs*, probably sellers of a particular kind of food (*TLL s.v. martēnsis* 416.8–12): inscription *CIG* 9449.5. Hofmann (1989: 263).

name   **Μαρτιάλιος**, a man's name, from *Mārtiālis* 'of Mars'. Hofmann (1989: 263).

Direct loan   **Μάρτιος** (-α, -ον or -ου, ὁ) 'March', from *Mārtius* 'March'.
I BC – modern   Documents: e.g. *Chrest.Mitt.* 316.ii.11 (II AD); *SB* 13775.17 (III AD); *CPR* XVIIA.15.16 (IV AD); *SB* 16521.5 as lemma (IV/V AD); *P.Oxy.* 1942.6 (VI AD).

Inscriptions: common, e.g. *SEG* XXXIX.1290.33 (I BC); *IGR* IV.661.31 (I AD); *I.Ephesos* 27.448 (II AD); *IOSPE* I².4.42 (III AD); *SEG* LI.1438.3 (IV AD); *I.Lipára* 790.4 (V AD); *SEG* VIII.42.3 (VI AD).

Literature: e.g. DH *AR* 2.70.2, marked (I BC); Plut. *Publ.* 9.8 (I/II AD); Jul. Afric. *Chron.* frag. 49.93 (II/III AD); Eusebius, *De martyribus Palaestinae* (rec. brevior) 11.30 Bardy (IV AD); *ACO* II.I.I.II p. 61.28 (V AD); Lyd. *Mens.* 3.7 (VI AD).

Post-antique: common. Kriaras (1968–). Modern Μάρτιος, Μάρτης: Babiniotis (2002), Andriotis (1967), Meyer (1895: 43).

Notes: Solin (2008), Sijpesteijn (1979), García Domingo (1979: 522), Strobach (1997: 197), Hofmann (1989: 263), Meinersmann (1927: 36), LSJ. See **§2.2.3** with passage 2, §4.1.1, **§4.2.1**, §4.2.2, §8.2.3 n. 51, §10.2.1, §10.2.2 E.

Μαρτίσιοι: see Μαρτήσιοι.

not Latin?   **μαρυπτόν**, a cake mentioned by Athenaeus 14.647c (II/III AD), has been suggested as a Latinism, but there is no good Latin equivalent. Hofmann (1989: 263). See §9.4 passage 61.

not ancient?   **μάσσα** 'mass', 'plot of ground', from *massa* 'parcel of land' (itself from μᾶζα 'mass'): *Acta Petri et Pauli* 80 = Lipsius 1891: 214.8; Her.Mech. *Stereom.* 1.90.1. Hofmann (1989: 263), *LBG*, Kriaras (1968–, with derivation from Venetian), Lampe (1961).

not Latin?   **μαστιχᾶτον** 'drink flavoured with mastic' may be from *mastichātum*, neuter of *mastichātus* 'flavoured with mastic' (*TLL*), itself from μαστίχη 'mastic'; a Greek formation from μαστίχη + -ᾶτον is also possible. Aëtius 16.160.1 (VI AD); Alex.Trall. II.341.17 (VI AD); as adj., papyrus *P.Ant.* II.64.19: σκευασία χυλοῦ μαστιχᾶτου (VI AD). Maravela-Solbakk (2010: 260), Hofmann (1989: 263–4), LSJ. See **§6.5**.

rare   **ματερία** 'dough', from *māteria* 'material': Athenaeus 3.113c (II/III AD). Probably unrelated to Byzantine ματέριον 'wooden beam' (*LBG*, Kriaras 1968– *s.v.* ματέρια). Hofmann (1989: 264), LSJ suppl.

foreign	**ματερτέρα** 'aunt', from *mātertera* 'mother's sister': Antec. in Latin script 1.10.5 *materteran* etc. (VI AD); later in Greek script. Daris (1991a: 70), Cavenaile (1951: 398), Zilliacus (1935a: 194–5), *LBG*. See §7.1.1.
not ancient?	**μάτλα** 'chamber pot', from *matula* 'chamber pot': ostracon *SB* 1160.6. Diethart (1998: 173), Binder (2000: 179), Daris (1991a: 71), Hofmann (1989: 264), Meinersmann (1927: 36), LSJ suppl.
rare	**ματουτ(ε)ῖνος**, from *mātūtīnus* 'of the early morning': as part of λούδου ματουτείνου, a gladiatorial establishment, inscriptions *I.Ephesos* 852.22 (II AD); *IGUR* II.1060.5 (II/III AD); perhaps *IGUR* II.282.7. Hofmann (1989: 264).
rare	**ματρικάριος**, 'woodworker' or an official, apparently from confusion of *māteriārius* 'timber-merchant' and *mātrīcārius*, a kind of soldier (*TLL*): Just. *Nov.* 13.5 (VI AD); Lyd. *Mens.* 1.28, marked (VI AD); Byzantine texts. Avotins (1992), Hofmann (1989: 264), Zilliacus (1935a: 194–5), *LBG*, *TLL* (*s.v. mātrīcārius* esp. 474.24–7), LSJ suppl.
	μάτρικες: see μάτριξ.
Deriv. of loan V AD – Byz.	**ματρίκιον** (-ου, τό) 'register', 'wooden board', from *mātrīx* 'list' via μάτριξ + -ιον. Literature: *Carth.* 331.18, 394.17 (V AD); Barsanuph.Jo. II.II ep. 495.31 (VI AD); Lyd. *Mens.* 1.28, marked (VI AD). Post-antique: survives. *LBG*. Notes: *LBG* has unlikely derivation from *mātrīcula* 'register' (*TLL*). Hofmann (1989: 265 *s.v.* ματριξ), *TLL* (*s.v.* ματρίκιον), Lampe (1961). See §4.6.1 n. 84, §8.1.7 n. 34, §10.2.2 O.
rare	**ματρικουλάριος** 'archivist', from *mātrīculārius* 'of registers' (*TLL*): Lyd. *Mag.* pp. 236.15 (marked), 238.12 (VI AD); Byzantine texts. Hofmann (1989: 264), *LBG*.
foreign	*mātrimōnium* 'marriage': Antec. 1.9.1 *matrimonium* etc. (VI AD).
Direct loan II–VI AD	**μάτριξ** (-ικος, ἡ) 'list', 'roster', 'master register of a military unit', 'mother church', from *mātrīx* 'list', 'female parent'. Documents: *ChLA* XI.466.17 (II AD); *P.Panop.Beatty* 1.31 etc. (III AD); *P.Erl. Diosp.* 1.28 (IV AD); *P.Münch.* 1.2.8 (VI AD); *P.Pommersf.* 1.182 etc. (VI AD); *P.Gascou* 21.4 etc. (VI AD). Inscriptions: *IGLS* XIII.1.9046.27 etc. (V/VI AD); *SEG* LXV.1408.A30 etc. (V/VI AD); *SEG* IX.356.6 etc. (VI AD); *SEG* XXXII.1554.A8 etc. (VI AD). Literature: *Carth.* 248.19, 390.1 (V AD); Lyd. *Mag.* p. 186.29 etc. (VI AD). Notes: forms derivative ματρίκιον. Daris (1991a: 71), Hofmann (1989: 265), Zilliacus (1935a: 228–9), Meinersmann (1927: 36), Lampe (1961), LSJ suppl. See §4.2.5, §4.6.1 n. 84, §10.2.1, §10.2.2 O.
	ματρονικ-: see ματρωνικ-.
Direct loan II–IV AD?	**ματρῶνα** (-ης/-ας, ἡ) 'noblewoman', from *mātrōna* 'matron'. Documents: e.g. *P.Oxy.* 2712.3 (III AD); *P.Flor.* 1.16.2 (III AD); *P.Stras.* 1.8.11 (III AD). Inscriptions: e.g. *I.Cilicie* 31.10 (II AD); *I.Ephesos* 3072.8 (III AD); *MAMA* X.358.1 (III/IV AD).

Literature: e.g. *Acta Pauli* frag. 4.2 Schmidt and Schubart (II AD); *Acta Alexandrinorum* 4b.1.3 Musurillo (II/III AD); *Passio Perpetuae* 18.5 Robinson (IV AD?); Lyd. *Mens.* 3.22, marked (VI AD); *V.S.Mam.* 4; *Anthologiae Graecae Appendix* 714.5.

Post-antique: some survival or revival. Kriaras (1968–), Sophocles (1887). Modern ματρώνα 'madam' (Babiniotis 2002) may be revival or reborrowing.

Notes: often part of ματρῶνα στολᾶτα, for which see στολᾶτος. Often accented ματρώνα, e.g. LSJ suppl. *s.v.* ματρώνα, but ματρῶνα in LSJ suppl. *s.v.* στολᾶτα. Forms derivatives ματρωνίκιον, ματρωνίκιος. Daris (1991a: 71), Mason (1974: 5, 67), Hofmann (1989: 265), Zilliacus (1937: 331), Meinersmann (1927: 36), Lampe (1961). See §4.2.3.1, §8.2.3, §10.2.1, §10.2.2 D.

foreign

Ματρωνάλια transliterating *Mātrōnālia*, a festival (*TLL s.v. mātrōnālis* 490.16–25): Plut. *Rom.* 21.1 (I/II AD). Hofmann (1989: 266).

rare

ματρωνίκιον, ματρονίκιον 'women's area of the baths', in meaning perhaps from *mātrōnālis* 'of matrons' but in form from *mātrōna* 'matron' via ματρώνα + -ικός + -ιον: papyrus *P.Flor.* III.384.7 etc. (V AD); Lyd. *Mens.* 4.29: αἱ δὲ σώφρονες γυναῖκες – ματρώνας δὲ αὐτὰς οἱ Ῥωμαῖοι καλοῦσιν, οἱ δὲ Ἕλληνες οἰκοδεσποίνας – τοσοῦτον τῆς αἰδοῦς ἐφρόντιζον, ὡς μηδὲ ταῖς πολλαῖς τῶν γυναικῶν ὁμιλεῖν, ἀλλὰ καὶ τόπους τινὰς ἡσυχίους ἐν τοῖς βαλανείοις ἔξω τοῦ πλήθους ἑαυταῖς ἀφορίζειν, οὓς ἔτι καὶ νῦν ματρωνίκια καλοῦσιν (VI AD). Daris (1991a: 71), *LBG*, *TLL* (*s.v.* ματρωνίκιος 490.39–46), LSJ suppl. See §8.1.7 n. 34.

rare

ματρωνίκ(ι)ος, ματρονίκιος, neut. subst. **ματρωνικόν**, designating the qualification of medicines known in Latin as *mātrōnāle* (*TLL s.v. mātrōnālis* 490.1–7), from *mātrōna* 'matron' via ματρώνα + -ικ(ι)ος: Aelius Promotus, Δυναμερόν 54.5 Crismani (II AD?); *Hippiatr.Par.* (Pel.) 334 (V AD?); Aëtius 15.15.721 (p. 100) (VI AD). *LBG* (*s.v.* ματρονίκιον), *TLL* (*s.v.* ματρωνίκιος). See §8.1.7 n. 34.

rare

ματτιάριος 'javelin-carrier', from *mattiārius* 'auxiliary soldier armed with a lead spear' (*TLL s.v.* 1. *mattiārius*): Zosimus, *Historia nova* 3.22.2 Paschoud (V AD); Malal. 13.21 (VI AD). Hofmann (1989: 266), *LBG*, Triandaphyllidis (1909: 129), Lampe (1961).

not Latin?

μαῦρος 'black' (with derivative ἀχαόμαυρος perhaps 'dark red') has been suggested as a borrowing of *Maurus* 'Moorish' (e.g. Meyer 1895: 43–4), but a Greek derivation from ἀμαυρός 'dark' is given in Ps.-Arcadius' epitome of Herodian: Τὰ εἰς ΡΟΣ δισύλλαβα τῇ ΑΥ διφθόγγῳ παραληγόμενα ἐπὶ ἐμψύχων τιθέμενα βαρύνεται· φλαῦρος, σαῦρος, καῦρος (ὁ κακός). σημείωσαι τὸ σταυρός ἄψυχον· καὶ τὸ μαῦρος ἀπὸ τοῦ ἀμαυρός γέγονε (Roussou 2018: 202.6–9). Lentz at Hdn. *Pros.Cath.* III.I.193.4–11 emended this by importing material from Stephanus of Byzantium to read Μαῦρος ἔθνος μέγα Λιβύης, ὃ καὶ Μαυρούσιοι. ... καὶ τὸ μαυρός ἀπὸ τοῦ ἀμαυρός γέγονεν. Babiniotis (2002) combines the two etymologies by deriving *Maurus* from ἀμαυρός and μαῦρος from *Maurus*. LSJ and many other works accent μαυρός. Filos (2010: 249), Cervenka-Ehrenstrasser (1996: 125), Shipp (1979: 384), *DÉLG* (*s.v.* ἀμαυρός), Frisk (1954–72: I.88), Beekes (2010 *s.v.* ἀμαυρός), Andriotis (1967), Lampe (1961), LSJ, LSJ suppl. See §2.1 n. 9.

not Latin?	**μαφόρτης, μαφόριον, μαφόρτιον** 'short cloak with a hood' (with derivatives κολοβιομαφόριον and στιχαρομαφόριον 'tunic and veil'), perhaps from *maforte* and *mafortium*, a type of mantle (*TLL s.v. mafor(t)ium*), or perhaps directly from the Semitic source of the Latin. From Latin: Daris (1991a: 56, 71), Hofmann (1989: 266), Cavenaile (1952: 196), Meinersmann (1927: 36), Wessely (1902: 138), Babiniotis (2002 *s.v.* μαφόριο). Directly from Semitic: Cervenka-Ehrenstrasser (2000: 221 with n. 547, 228–9), *DÉLG*, Frisk (1954–72: II.186), Beekes (2010). Lampe (1961), LSJ, LSJ suppl.
rare	**Μεγαλήσια**, a festival, from *Megalēnsia*, a festival: Dio Cassius 37.8.1 etc. (II/III AD). Sophocles (1887).
not ancient?	**μεδιανόν, μεδειανόν** 'central hall', 'middle part', from *mediānum* 'middle': inscription *I.Smyrna* 192.6. Editor *ad loc.*, Hofmann (1989: 266), LSJ suppl.
foreign	**μεδιούμ** transliterating *medium* 'middle': Epiph. *Mens.* 621 etc. (IV AD); Her. Mech. *Mens.* 61.5. Sophocles (1887 *s.v.* μέδιους).
foreign	***medius*** 'middle': Antec. 1.16.pr. *median* (VI AD).
	μειλι-: see μιλι-.
non-existent	**μεῖμος** 'mime', from *mīmus* 'mime': superseded reading of inscription *IGR* III.1479.3. Robert (1936a: 243), Hofmann (1989: 267).
rare	**μελίνη**, the name of an animal (badger?), perhaps from *mēlēs* 'badger' and *mēlīnus* 'of a badger' (*TLL s.v. 3. mēlīnus*): Edict.Diocl. 8.29 (IV AD). Sophocles (1887), LSJ, LSJ suppl.
rare	**μέλκα, μέλκη**, a medicinal food, from *melca* 'sour milk': Galen II.811.12, X.468.2 Kühn, both marked (II AD); Orib. *Eun.* 1.5.2 (IV AD); Alex.Trall. II.261.20, marked (VI AD). Hofmann (1989: 267), *DÉLG*, Frisk (1954–72: II.202), Beekes (2010), LSJ.
	μεμβραίνα: see μεμβράνα.
not ancient	**μεμβραϊνάριος** 'parchment-worker', from *membrānārius* 'parchment-worker' (*TLL*): probably papyrus *Stud.Pal.* XX.194.1 (VI/VII AD). Cervenka-Ehrenstrasser (2000: 146 n. 75), Daris (1991a: 71), Hofmann (1989: 267), Cavenaile (1952: 202, citing a papyrus that does not contain this word), Meinersmann (1927: 36), LSJ (*s.v.* μεμβράνα).
Deriv.? of loan VI AD – modern	**μεμβράϊνος, βεβράϊνος, βέβρινος, βέ(μ)βρανος** (-η, -ον) 'made of parchment', probably from *membrāna* 'parchment' via shortened forms of μεμβράνα + -ινος, though usually said to be from *membrāneus* 'made of parchment' (or **membrānus*, which is now thought never to have existed: *TLL s.v. membrānum*). Documents: *P.Prag.* II.178.1.5 (V/VI AD); *P.Cair.Masp.* 67144.6 (VI AD). Literature: Hesych. as part of gloss φ 53 (V/VI AD). Post-antique: numerous. *LBG* (*s.vv.* μεμβράϊνος, μέμβρανος, μέμβρινος, βεβράϊνος, βέβρινος, βεμβραΐνης, βέμβρανος), Zervan (2019: 25), Kriaras (1968– *s.vv.* μεμβράϊνος, μέμβρινος). Modern dialectal βεβράϊνος, μένμπρινος, πράϊνος: Meyer (1895: 44).

Notes: for etymology see Cervenka-Ehrenstrasser (2000: 145–6). Zervan (2019: 25) includes Lydus' neuter μέμβρανον here rather than as variant of μεμβράνα. Diethart (1998: 169), Daris (1991a: 71), Hofmann (1989: 268 *s.v.* μεμβράνα), LSJ (*s.v.* μεμβράνα). See §4.6.1, §10.2.2 O.

Direct loan
I AD – modern

μεμβράνα, μεμβραίνα, μεμβράνη, μενβρά(ε)ινα, μέμβρανον (-ης, ἡ or -ου, τό) 'parchment', from *membrāna* 'parchment'.
Documents, all fem.: *P.Petaus* 30.4 (II AD); *P.Oxy.* 2156.9 (IV/V AD); *SB* 11372.4 etc. (V/VI AD).
Literature, mainly fem.: e.g. NT 2 Timothy 4:13 (I AD); Charax, *FHG* III frag. 14.2 (II AD?); *Vita Alexandri*, De Stoop 1911: 686.15 (V AD); EphraemSyr. VII p. 340.2 (V/VI AD); Ps.-Caesarius 8.7 Riedinger (VI AD); also biblical quotations.   Neuter occasionally, e.g. Lyd. *Mens.* 1.28.27, 29 (VI AD).
Post-antique: numerous, forming derivatives μεμβραναρική 'parchment manufacture', μεμβρανάριος 'parchment-maker', etc. Used as gloss in *Suda* π 1034. *LBG* (*s.vv.* βεμβράνα, μεμβράνη), Zervan (2019: 24–5), Kriaras (1968– *s.v.* μέμβρανον), Sophocles (1887 *s.v.* μέμβρανον). Modern μεμβράνη, μεμβράνα, βεμβράνα 'membrane': Babiniotis (2002), Andriotis (1967), Meyer (1895: 44).
Notes: Zervan (2019: 25) considers neuter to be substantivization of the adj. rather than variant of the feminine. Probably forms derivative μεμβράϊνος. Daris (1991a: 72), Hofmann (1989: 267–8), Viscidi (1944: 41), Lampe (1961), LSJ. See §4.2.3.1, §4.6.1, §8.2.3 n. 51, §9.3 n. 21, §10.1, §10.2.1, §10.2.2 M.

μεμοράδιος, μεμοράλιος: see μεμοράριος.

rare

μεμοράριος, an official, occurs in a small group of papyri of IV AD from Panopolis, all referring to the same individual (*P.Ammon* II.28.1, 29.4, 30.3, 31.3, 38.29). Before their discovery its only attestation was the μεμοραρίοις to which some editors emended μεμοραδίοις in Epiph. *Pan.* III.250.26 (IV AD); its existence was therefore disputed, though *TLL* has an entry for unattested **memorārius* on the basis of Epiphanius. *LBG* sees μεμοράριος and μεμοράδιος as variant spellings of μεμοράλιος, a Byzantine official not otherwise attested in antiquity; μεμοράλιος is said to be derived from *memorālius*, an official (*TLL*). These may all be the same word as μεμοριάλιος (*q.v.*). Discussion in *P.Ammon* II p. 22 n. 14, *LBG* (*s.v.* μεμοράλιος), *TLL* (*s.vv.* memorārius, memorālius), Lampe (1961 *s.v.* μεμοράδιος). See §8.1.7.

μεμορία: see οὐέτερεμ μεμορίαμ.

Direct loan
V AD – Byz.

μεμοριάλιος (-ου, ὁ), a class of clerk in the civil service, from *memoriālis*, an official (*TLL s.v.* memoriālis 685.9–12).
Literature: Thdt. *Ep.Pat.* 33.25 (V AD); Nil. 1.86.1 etc. (V AD); Lyd. *Mag.* p. 172.16 etc. (VI AD); Just. *Codex* 4.59.1.2 (VI AD).
Post-antique: numerous. *LBG.*
Notes: could be same word as μεμοράριος (*q.v.*). Avotins (1989), Hofmann (1989: 268), Zilliacus (1935a: 194–5), Lampe (1961), LSJ suppl. See §4.2.5, §10.2.1, §10.2.2 D.

Direct loan
II–VI AD

μεμόριον, μημόριον, μνημόριον, μιμόριον, μημώριον, μνημώριων, μημούρηων
(-ου, τό) 'grave monument', from *memoria* 'memorial', with some spellings
influenced by μνημεῖον 'memorial'.
Documents: *P.Aberd.* 195.6 (III AD).
Inscriptions: common, e.g. *SEG* xxv.806.6 (I/II AD); Ramsay 1895–7: 736
no. 672.5 (III AD); *SEG* xLIX.688 (IV AD); *I.Chr.Macédoine* 159.1 (V AD?);
I.Ano Maked. 203.1 (VI AD).
Literature: *ACO* II.I.II p. 115.3–4 etc. (V AD).
Notes: forms derivatives μεμορίτης, μεμοροφύλαξ. Daris (1991a: 72), Hofmann
(1989: 268–9), *DÉLG*, Frisk (1954–72: II.207), Beekes (2010), Dieterich
(1898: 18, claiming modern survival), Lampe (1961), LSJ (*s.v.* μνημόριον),
LSJ suppl. (*s.vv.* μεμόριον, μνημόριον). See §4.2.3.1, **§4.4**, §10.2.1, §10.2.2 O.

rare

μεμορίτης 'custodian of a martyr-sanctuary', from *memoria* 'memorial' via μεμόριον
+ -ίτης: *ACO* II.I.II pp. 114.34, 115.2 (V AD). Hofmann (1989: 268 *s.v.*
μεμόριον), Lampe (1961).

rare

μεμοροφύλαξ 'custodian of a martyr-sanctuary', from *memoria* 'memorial' via
μεμόριον + φύλαξ 'guard': *ACO* II.I.II p. 114.32 (V AD). Hofmann (1989:
268 *s.v.* μεμόριον), Lampe (1961).

μέναυλον: see βήναβλον.

μενβρά(ε)ινα: see μεμβράνα.

μενεπικιάριος: see βενεφικιάριος.

μένσα: see μῆνσα.

rare

με(ν)σάδιον 'for the table', apparently from *mēnsa* 'table' + -άδιον: spelled μεσατιν,
papyrus *P.Cair.Masp.* 67167.10 (VI AD). Editor *ad loc.* (μεσάδιον), Daris
(1991a: 72, μενσάδιον), Cavenaile (1952: 196), Meinersmann (1927: 36).

foreign

μενσούρα, from abl. *mēnsūrā* 'by measure': Antec. in Latin script 2.8.2 *mensura*
etc. (VI AD); later in Greek script. *LBG*. See §9.5.6 n. 68.

non-existent?

μενστροῦος 'monthly', from *mēnstruus* 'monthly': cited as an ancient loan by
Zilliacus (1935a: 194–5), but I can find no examples.

non-existent

μένσυλα, from *mēnsula* 'little table': misreading for μήσυλα (*q.v.*) on papyrus *BGU*
III.781.iv.10 etc. (I/II AD). Daris (1991a: 72).

μένσωρ: see μήνσωρ.

μενσώριον: see μηνσώριον.

not ancient

μέντα transliterating *menta* 'mint': interpolations in Dsc. 3.34.2 RV, 3.35.6 RV.
Hofmann (1989: 269), *LBG*.

rare

μεντάγρα, a skin disease, from *mentagra*, a disease of the chin: Galen XII.839.15–
842.17 Kühn (II AD), largely repeated in Aëtius 8.16.118 etc. (VI AD).
Hofmann (1989: 269), LSJ.

foreign

μέντις, μέντεμ transliterating gen. and acc. of *mēns* 'mind': Plut. *Rom.* 21.3, *Mor.*
322c (I/II AD). See §7.2.1.

not ancient   **μεντούλα, μεντιλιά**, and **μέντλαρος**, derogatory terms for poor people, perhaps from *mentula* 'penis': no ancient examples. Binder (2000: 183–4), Meyer (1895: 44).

foreign   **Μερκηδόνιος** and **Μερκηδῖνος** transliterating *Mercēdonius*, an intercalary month: Plut. *Numa* 18.2, *Caesar* 59.4 (I/II AD); Lyd. *Mens.* 4.144 (VI AD). Hofmann (1989: 269), *LBG* (*s.v.* Μερκηδῖνος), *TLL* (*s.v. Mercēdōnius*).

Direct loan   **μερμίλλων, μορμίλλων, μουρμίλλων, μυρμύλλων, μορβίλλων** (-ωνος/-ονος, ὁ), a
I–III AD   type of gladiator, from *murmillō/myrmillō*, a type of gladiator.
        Inscriptions: e.g. *I.Thrake Aeg.* 484.1 (I AD); *I.Byzantion* 182.2 (II AD); *SEG* L.583.B1 (III AD).
        Literature: Monodia *Mirmillionis amatrix* 1 in Heitsch 1963: 45 (II AD).
        Notes: Binder (2000: 148), Hofmann (1989: 277), Cameron (1931: 251), Meinersmann (1927: 38), LSJ, LSJ suppl. See §4.2.5, §10.2.1, §10.2.2 F.

        μεσάδιον, μεσατιν: see μενσάδιον.

        μεσατώριον: see μητατώριον.

        μεσκελλάνειν: see μισκελλάνιον.

        μεσοῦρι: see μηνσώριον.

        μεσσατώριον: see μητατώριον.

        μεσσίκιος: see μισσίκιος.

        μεσώριον: see μηνσώριον.

semantic   **μέταλλον** 'mine', 'metal', a Greek word but influenced by *metallum* 'mosaic work'
extension   (*TLL s.v.* 874.60–7) into meaning 'marble paving-slab' on inscription Bruneau 1988: 30.1. LSJ suppl. See §2.3.

rare   **μεταξαβλάττη** 'purple-dyed raw silk', from μέταξα 'raw silk' + *blatta* 'purple' (*TLL s.v.* 2. *blatta*) via βλάττα: Edict.Diocl. 24.13 etc. (IV AD). Steigerwald (1990: 223–4), Bogensperger (2017: 244), Hofmann (1989: 63 *s.v.* βλαττα), LSJ, LSJ suppl.

        μετᾶτον: see μητᾶτον.

        μετάτωρ: see μητάτωρ.

foreign   **μέτους καῦσα** 'because of intimidation', from *metūs causā*: Antec. in Latin script 4.6.25 *metus causa* etc. (VI AD); later in Greek script.

not ancient   **μετριόκρουστος**, from μέτριος 'moderate' + *crusta* 'crust', 'thin leaf of stone': no ancient examples. Diethart and Kislinger (1987: 8–9), Filos (2010: 250), Daris (1991a: 72).

rare   **μηλοδωράκινον**, a fruit, from μῆλον 'apple' + *dūracinum* (a kind of peach, *TLL s.v. dūracinus*), neut. subst. of *dūracinus* 'having a hard berry', via δωράκινον: with *duracinum* in glossaries, e.g. Gloss. *Herm.Mp.* 316.21. Hofmann (1989: 103 *s.v.* δωράκινον), *LBG*, LSJ.

semantic extension	**μηλωτή** 'sheepskin' is purely Greek, the source of Latin *mēlōta* 'sheepskin' (*TLL s.v.* 1. *mēlōta*). But in Christian texts μηλωτή refers to a monastic garment (e.g. Pall. *H.Laus.* 22.11), probably influenced by a similar use of *mēlōta* (*TLL s.v.* 627.45–58). Hofmann (1989: 269) accents the word for the garment μηλώτη, arguing that this accent shows a loanword, but I cannot find his evidence for that accent: μηλωτή is usual. Lampe (1961), LSJ. See §2.3 n. 58.
	μημόριον, μημούρηων, μημώριον: see μεμόριον.
foreign	**μῆνσα** transliterating *mensa* 'table': Plut. *Mor.* 726f (I/II AD); Antec. in Latin script 1.5.3 *per mensam* (VI AD). Strobach (1997: 197), Hofmann (1989: 269), Sophocles (1887 *s.v.* μένσα), Triandaphyllidis (1909: 125), Meyer (1895: 44).
foreign	**μήνσωρ**, transliterating *mensor* 'measurer' (military official responsible for soldiers' accommodation): inscription *SEG* LXV.1408.C18 (V/VI AD); Lyd. *Mag.* p. 70.14 (VI AD); Byzantine texts. Hofmann (1989: 269), Zilliacus (1935a: 228–9), *LBG* (*s.v.* μένσωρ).
Direct loan **V AD – modern**	**μηνσώριον, μηνσώρριον, μινσώρ(ρ)ιον, μισσώρ(ρ)ιον, μυσσώριον, μενσώριον, μεσώριον** (-ου, τό) 'basket', 'dish', from *missōrium/mēnsōrium* 'dish' (*TLL s.v.* 1. *missōrium et mēnsōrium*). Documents: *SB* 15284.3 (V AD); *P.Amst.* I.87.7 (V/VI AD); *Stud.Pal.* XX.151.3 etc. (VI AD); *CPR* VIII.66.14 (VI AD); P.Vindob. G. 29.938 (VI AD; unpublished but reading reported in Diethart and Hasitzka 2001: 34). Literature: Antec. 2.1.44 (VI AD). *Anthologia Graeca* headings to 9.585 and 9.822 are often cited but may be Byzantine. Post-antique: numerous. *LBG* (*s.v.* μισσώριον), Kriaras (1968– *s.v.* μισσούριον). Modern dialectal μοσσόρα, μισούρα, μεσούρι 'dish': Andriotis (1974: 379), Meyer (1895: 44), Kahane and Kahane (1972–6: 535). Notes: Diethart (1988: 60), Daris (1991a: 72 *s.v.* μενσώριον, 73 *s.v.* μισσώριον), Hofmann (1989: 270), Zilliacus (1935a: 194–5), Meinersmann (1927: 36), *TLL* (VIII.1141.82–1142.2), LSJ suppl. (*s.vv.* μηνσώριον, μισσώριον). See §4.2.4.1 n. 54, §6.7 n. 46, §10.2.1, §10.2.2 M.
non-existent	**μηνσωρων** is sometimes cited as Greek gen. pl. of *mensis* 'month' on the basis of Latin inscriptions in Greek script, where it is variously spelled but never μηνσωρων. *TLL s.v. mensis* 746.56, J. N. Adams (2003: 492–3), Hofmann (1989: 270).
rare	**μήσυλα**, a vessel, apparently from *mensula* 'little table': papyrus *BGU* III.781.iv.10 etc. (I/II AD). Kramer (1983: 118–19, 2011: 33–4), Daris (1991a: 72 *s.v.* μένσυλα), Hofmann (1989: 271), Meinersmann (1927: 37).
Direct? loan with **suffix** **V AD – Byz.**	**μητατεύω, μιτατεύω, μητεύω** 'commandeer', 'quarter', from *mētor* 'measure' (when spelled with -τατ-, from pf. part. *mētātum* or via μητᾶτον) + -εύω. Literature, spelled with -τατ-: Marc.Diac. 63 (V AD); Ath.Schol. index p. 12.3 (VI AD?). Spelled without -τατ-: Just. *App.* 4 = p. 797.31, 35 (VI AD); Ath. Schol. 20.5.1 etc. (VI AD). Post-antique: survives. *LBG* (*s.v.* μιτατεύω).

Notes: Lampe (1961) treats μητεύω as a variant of μητατεύω, but Hofmann
(1989: 272 *s.v.* μητάτον, 273) sees two words, μητατεύω and μητεύω; Avotins
(1992) and LSJ suppl. have only μητεύω. See §4.3.1, §4.6.1 n. 91, §10.2.1,
§10.2.2 C, §10.3.1.

Direct loan
III AD – modern

μητᾶτον, μετᾶτον, μιτᾶτον (-ου, τό) '(military) quarters', 'housing', from
mētātum, pf. part. of *mētor* 'measure', 'lay out (esp. camps)'.
Documents: *P.PalauRib.* 42.5 (VI AD); *SB* 15008.12 (VI AD).
Inscriptions: perhaps *IGLS* IV.1952 (V AD); *SEG* IX.356.40 etc. (VI AD); *IGLS*
IV.1397.
Literature: *V.Secundi* 68.8 (II/III AD); Malal. 13.42 (VI AD); *ACO* III
p. 159.24 (VI AD); Just. *Nov.* 130.9 etc. (VI AD); Ath.Schol. 20t (VI AD).
Post-antique: common, forming derivative μητατάριος 'guest'. *LBG*, Zervan
(2019: 115), Kriaras (1968–), Triandaphyllidis (1909: 123), Daris (1991a:
72). Modern μιτάτο, μητάτο 'sheepfold', 'shepherd's hut': Babiniotis
(2002), Andriotis (1967), Meyer (1895: 45).
Notes: Kramer (1983: 119, 2011: 34–7), Avotins (1989, 1992), Daris (1991a:
72), Hofmann (1989: 272), Zilliacus (1935a: 194–5), Meinersmann (1927:
37), Lampe (1961 *s.v.* μιτᾶτον), LSJ suppl. See §4.2.4.1 n. 55, §10.2.1,
§10.2.2 C.

rare

μητατορικός, μητατωρικός, a tax, from *mētātōrius* 'like a measurer' (*TLL*) + -ικός:
Lyd. *Mag.* p. 242.21 (VI AD). Caimi (1981: 346–7), Hofmann (1989: 272–3
s.v. μητατώριον), LSJ suppl., and for later survival *LBG* (*s.v.* μητατωρικός),
Triandaphyllidis (1909: 131).

Direct loan
IV AD – Byz.

μητάτωρ, μιτάτωρ, μετάτωρ (-ορος/-ωρος, ὁ) 'measurer' (a position in the
Roman army), from *mētātor* 'one who measures or marks out (a camp,
etc.)'.
Documents: *SB* 2253.7 (III/IV AD); *P.Erl.Diosp.* 1.182 etc. (IV AD); *P.Oxy.*
4628.10 etc. (IV AD).
Inscriptions: *I.Thèbes Syène* 166.2.
Literature: Lyd. *Mag.* p. 70.19, marked (VI AD); *Passion of Paphnutios* 365 =
Delehaye 1923a: 198.8 (VI AD).
Post-antique: survives. *LBG*.
Notes: Daris (1991a: 72), Hofmann (1989: 272), Zilliacus (1935a: 228–9),
Meinersmann (1927: 37). See §4.2.5, §10.2.1, §10.2.2 C; cf. προμητάτωρ.

rare

μητατώριον, μιτατώριον, μεσ(σ)ατώριον 'sacristy', probably from *mētātōrius* 'like
a measurer' (*TLL*): Thdr.Anag. *HE* 4.453 (V/VI AD). Hofmann (1989:
272–3), *TLL* (*s.v. mētātōrius* 879.60–1), Lampe (1961 *s.v.* μιτατώριον); for
Byzantine use in a different sense *LBG*, Triandaphyllidis (1909: 125).

μητεύω: see μητατεύω.

μήτηρ κάστρων: see κάστρον.

Deriv. of loan
III AD

μητροκολων(ε)ία (-ας, ἡ) 'mother-colony' (i.e. colonial metropolis), from μήτηρ
'mother' + *colōnia* 'colony' via κολωνία.
Inscriptions: *IGLS* XXI.IV.48.3 (II/III AD); perhaps *Agora de Palmyre* V.17.1,
p. 171 (II/III AD); perhaps *IGLS* XXI.IV.78 (II/III AD); *Agora de Palmyre*
Annexe 40.11 etc., p. 254 (III AD); perhaps *IGLS* XXI.IV.24.5 (III AD).

Coins: ΑΝΤΙΟΧΕΩΝ ΜΗΤΡΟ. ΚΟΛΩΝ. at Antiocheia ad Orontem, Head 1911: 780 (III
AD); ΜΗΤΡΟ. ΚΟΛ. ΕΜΙΣΩΝ at Emissa, Head 1911: 780 (III AD).

Notes: Hofmann (1989: 186 *s.v.* κολωνία), *TLL* (*s.v.* μητ⟨ροκολω⟩νείας), LSJ. See
§4.6.2, §8.1.7 n. 34, §9.1 n. 4, §9.2, §10.2.2 D.

not Latin **μηχανάριος** 'engineer', 'mechanic' is probably a Greek formation from μηχανή
'machine' + -άριος, though Hofmann (1989: 273) suggests a borrowing of
unattested **mēchanārius*. Palmer (1945: 7 n. 1), Cavenaile (1952: 201),
DÉLG (*s.v.* μηχανή), Beekes (2010 *s.v.* μηχανή), LSJ, LSJ suppl. See §6.1.

rare **μιλιάζω** 'measure by miles', 'mark with milestones', from *mīlle* 'thousand' via
μίλιον + -άζω: Strabo 6.3.10 (I BC/AD, perhaps following Polybius 34.11.8,
II BC). Forms derivative μιλιασμός; perhaps survives in Byzantine μιλίζω
(*LBG*). Hofmann (1989: 274 *s.v.* μίλιον), *TLL* (*s.v.* μιλιασμῷ), LSJ. See §8.1.3
n. 17, §8.1.7 n. 34.

Direct loan **μιλιαρήσιον, μιλιαρίσιον, μειλιαρίσιον** (-ου, τό), a coin, from *mīliārēnse* 'silver
IV AD – Byz. coin worth a thousandth part of a pound of gold', neuter of *mīliārēnsis*
'containing a thousand' (*TLL*).

Inscriptions: *I.Estremo Oriente* 55.36 (VI AD).

Literature: Eusebius, *De mensuris* 5.21 = Hultsch 1864: 278.18 (IV AD); Epiph.
Mens. 801 etc., marked (IV AD); Marc.Diac. 100 (V AD); Olympiodorus
alch., Berthelot and Ruelle 1888: 76.6 (V/VI AD); Malal. 18.14.16 (VI AD);
Aëtius 3.101.5 (VI AD); Lyd. *Mens.* 4.9 *passim* (VI AD); Evagr.Schol. *HE*
237.13 etc. (VI AD); Cos.Indic. 11.18 etc. (VI AD); Her.Mech. *Mens.* 60.16.

Post-antique: common. *LBG* (*s.vv.* μιλιαρίσιν, μιλιαρήσιον), Zervan (2019:
115–16), Triandaphyllidis (1909: 125).

Notes: apparently with different meaning, marked, in Just. *Nov.* 105.2.1 etc.
(VI AD); *LBG* suggests that the meaning there is 'vessel' and arises from
conflation with μιλιάριον. Avotins (1992), Daris (1991a: 72 *s.v.* μιλιαρίσιον),
Hofmann (1989: 273), Zilliacus (1935a: 194–5, 1937: 331 with a further
undated example), Meinersmann (1927: 37), Triantaphyllides (1892: 267),
TLL (*s.v.* mīliārēnsis), Lampe (1961), LSJ. See §4.2.5, §6.7 n. 45, §10.2.1,
§10.2.2 G.

Direct loan **μιλιάριον, μειλιάριον** (-ου, τό), a copper vessel, a unit for measuring volume,
III AD – Byz. 'mile', or perhaps 'milestone'; from *mīliārium*, with largely the same
meanings.

Inscriptions: *SEG* XVI.754.6 (III AD) meaning 'mile' or perhaps 'milestone';
perhaps also on milestones from Ionia, e.g. *I.Smyrna* 815.b8, 817.8 (both III
AD), but there always abbreviated to μι, so the intended word could be μίλια.

Literature: Athenaeus 3.98c, marked as Latin but with implication that it is
usual (II/III AD); Ps.-Herodian, *Philetaerus* 216 Dain as gloss (II–IV AD?);
Ps.-Galen XIV.550.9 etc. Kühn; Her.Mech. *Pneum.* 2.34, 35; *Anthologia Graeca*
11.244.1; scholia to Luc. *Lex.* 8 as gloss; with *miliarium* in Gloss. Ps.-Cyril.
371.51; with *authepsa* in Gloss. Serv. 521.16. These all refer to the vessel or
the unit of measurement; LSJ cites meaning 'milestone' from Lyd. *Mens.*
4.49 (VI AD), where editors now prefer μίλια.

Post-antique: survives, forming derivative μιλιαράς. Kriaras (1968–).

Notes: Daris (1991a: 72), Hofmann (1989: 273), Meinersmann (1927: 37),
LBG, LSJ, LSJ suppl. See §4.2.4.1 n. 54, **§9.4** passage 59, §10.2.1, §10.2.2 E.

Direct loan
II AD

μιλιάριος, μειλιάριος (-α, -ον) 'of a thousand', 'of milestones', from *mīliārius* 'of a thousand'.
Documents: *P.Yadin* I.11.2 etc. (II AD).
Inscriptions: *SEG* LIV.601.9 (II AD); *IGR* IV.1565.5.
Notes: Daris (1991a: 72), Mason (1974: 5, 68), Hofmann (1989: 267, 273). See §4.2.2, §10.2.1, §10.2.2 E.

μιλιαρίσιον: see μιλιαρήσιον.

rare

μιλιασμός 'measuring by miles', 'marking with milestones', from *mīlle* 'thousand' via μιλιάζω + -μός: Strabo 6.2.1 (I BC/AD). LSJ, *TLL* (*s.v.* μιλιασμῷ), for possible survival *LBG*. See §8.1.7 n. 34.

non-existent?

μιλινάριος 'commander of a thousand', from *mīllēnārius* 'commander of a thousand' (*TLL*): suggested by Bees (1941: 88) as the interpretation of μυλιναρίου on inscription *IG* II/III².V.13479.5 (V/VI AD). But the word could really be μυλινάριος (*q.v.*). Hofmann (1989: 274).

Direct loan
I BC – modern

μίλιον, μείλιον (-ου, τό) 'mile', 'milestone', from *mīlle* 'thousand' via *mīlia passuum* 'thousands of paces' (*TLL s.v. mīlle* 972.79).
Documents: *O.Did.* 400.7 etc. (II AD); perhaps *O.Krok.* 1.6.7 (II AD); *SB* 9584.1 etc. (III AD); *P.Stras.* 1.57r.6 (III AD); *P.Ryl.* IV.627.224 etc., 638.9 etc. (both IV AD); *SB* 14507.46 (IV AD).
Inscriptions: e.g. *I.Didyma* 391.Aii.10 (I BC); *I.Tralleis* 172.6, bilingual (I AD); *I.Caesarea Maritima* 99.9 (II AD); Mitford 1939: 193 no. 5.10 (II AD); *I.Anazarbos* 17.7 (III AD); *IGBulg.* IV.2021.17 (III AD); *I.Kaunos* 145.6 (IV AD); Edict.Diocl. 17.1a–5 (IV AD); *I.Erythrai Klazomenai* 520.B12 (V AD).
Literature: common, e.g. perhaps Polybius 34.12 (II BC); Strabo 5.1.11 (I BC/AD); NT Matthew 5:41 (I AD); *Acta Joannis* 18 = Bonnet 1898: 161.3 (II AD); *Acta Thomae* 30 = Bonnet 1903: 147.3 (III AD); Eusebius, *Onomasticon* p. 28.26 Klostermann (IV AD); Marc.Diac. 79 (V AD); Cyr.S. *Vit.Eu.* 82.7 (VI AD); Antec. 1.25.16 (VI AD).
Post-antique: common. *LBG*, Kriaras (1968–), Triandaphyllidis (1909: 125). Modern μίλι 'mile': Babiniotis (2002), Andriotis (1967), Meyer (1895: 44).
Notes: forms derivative μιλιάζω. Dubuisson (1985: 36), García Domingo (1979: 96, 534), Daris (1991a: 72), Mason (1974: 12), Hofmann (1989: 274), Viscidi (1944: 30), Zilliacus (1935a: 194–5, 1937: 331), Immisch (1885: 341), *TLL* (*s.v. mīlle* 972.79, 980.8–31), Lampe (1961), LSJ (*s.vv.* μίλιον, μείλιον), LSJ suppl. See §4.2.5, §4.3.2 n. 75, §8.1.3 n. 17, §8.1.5, §8.2.3 n. 51, §9.3 n. 21, §10.2.1, §10.2.2 E.

foreign

mīlitāria 'public road' (i.e. *via mīlitāris; mīlitārius* 'military' is rare and pre-Classical, so probably not the source here): Antec. 4.3.5 *militaria* (VI AD).

foreign

μίλιτες transliterating pl. of *mīles* 'soldier': Lyd. *Mens.* 4.72.8–9 (VI AD). *LBG*.

foreign

μιλιτία transliterating *mīlitia* 'military service': Lyd. *Mens.* 4.9.11 (VI AD); Her. Mech. *Mens.* 60.16. *LBG*.

μιμόριον: see μεμόριον.

foreign

minimus 'least': Antec. 1.16.pr. *minima* (VI AD).

rare

μίνιον 'red lead', from *minium* 'bright red pigment': Dsc. 5.94.1 (I AD), repeated in Orib. *Col.* 13.κ.5 (IV AD). Hofmann (1989: 274), *LBG*, LSJ.

μίνσα: see μίσσα.

μινσώρ(ρ)ιον: see μηνσώριον.

foreign   μίνωρ 'lesser', from *minor* 'lesser': as a qualification of Roman names, probably ostraca *O.Claud.* II.392.3 etc., 400.2 etc., 402.9 (all II AD). These are all Latinate (*O.Claud.* II pp. 229–30). Μίνωρ also occurs as part of names (e.g. *P.Diog.* 2.1, II AD); Antec. in Latin script 1.16.pr. *minor* (VI AD).

foreign   μίξτος 'mixed' (a legal action), from *mixtus* 'mixed': Antec. in Latin script 4.6.19 *mixta* (VI AD); later in Greek script.

rare   μισκελλάνιον, μισκιλλάνειν, μεσκελλάνειν 'mixture', from *miscellāneum*, neut. subst. of *miscellāneus* 'mixed': ostracon *O.Krok.* II.235.4 etc. (I/II AD). Commentary *ad loc.*

foreign   μισκέλ(λ)ας transliterating a form of *miscellus* 'miscellaneous': Just. *Nov.* 22.43 in Latin script. Avotins (1992).

foreign   μίσκελλος, a wine, from *miscellus*, an inferior grape and wine: Hesych. as lemma μ 1461 (V/VI AD). Hofmann (1989: 274), LSJ.

foreign   μισκῆρε transliterating inf. of *misceō* 'mix': Plut. *Mor.* 726f (I/II AD). Strobach (1997: 197).

μισκιλλάνειν: see μισκελλάνιον.

rare   μισορ(ρ)ώμαιος 'Roman-hater', from μισο- 'hating' + *Rōma* 'Rome' via Ῥωμαῖος: Plut. *Ant.* 54.6 (I/II AD); Agathias, Keydell 1967: 93.21 (VI AD); Byzantine texts. *LBG*, LSJ.

μίσος: see μίσσος.

μισούρα: see μηνσώριον.

not ancient   μίσσα, μίνσα 'dismissal', from *missa* 'dismissal' (*TLL*): no ancient examples. Zilliacus (1935a: 228–9), *LBG*, Meyer (1895: 45 *s.v.* μισσεύω), *TLL* (*s.v.* 2. *missa* 1135.80–2), Lampe (1961).

rare   μισσιβίλια 'throwing-spears', from *missibilia* 'missiles' (*TLL s.v. missibilis*): Just. *Nov.* 85.4 (VI AD). Avotins (1992), LSJ suppl.

Direct loan   μισσίκιος, μεσσίκιος (-ου, ὁ) 'discharged soldier', from *missīcius* 'discharged'.
I–II AD   Documents: *O.Did.* 353.7 (I AD); *P.Fouad* 21.10 (I AD); *SB* 9668.3 (I AD); *BGU* V.1210.138 etc. (II AD); *SB* 9636.8 etc. (II AD).
        Notes: Binder (2000: 126), Daris (1991a: 73, 1991b: 53–4), Mason (1974: 5, 68), Hofmann (1989: 275), Meinersmann (1927: 37), LSJ suppl. See §4.2.4.1 n. 51, §10.2.1, §10.2.2 C.

rare   μίσσος 'chariot race', from *missus, -ūs* 'race': papyrus *P.Oxy.* 2707.3 etc. (VI AD); Byzantine texts. Zervan (2019: 117) sees it as the ancestor of Byzantine μίσος 'course (at a meal)' (cf. *LBG*, Kriaras 1968–). Daris (1991a: 73), Sophocles (1887), Triandaphyllidis (1909: 121), LSJ suppl.

μισσώρ(ρ)ιον: see μηνσώριον.

μιτατ-: see μητατ-.

foreign   **μίτλος** transliterating *mītulus*, a kind of mussel: Athenaeus 3.85e (II/III AD).
           Binder (2000: 179), Hofmann (1989: 275), *LBG*.

not ancient   **μιττενδάριος** 'emissary', from *mittendārius*, a title (*TLL*): no ancient examples.
           Zilliacus (1935a: 194–5), *LBG* (*s.v.* μιττεντάριος).

not Latin?   **μίτυλος, μύτιλος** 'hornless' may be from *mutilus* 'mutilated', 'hornless'. Hofmann
           (1989: 275), *DÉLG*, Frisk (1954–72: II.246), Beekes (2010), LSJ, LSJ suppl.

                   μνημόριον, μνημώριων: see μεμόριον.

                   μοδάριος: see μοδιάριος.

rare   **μοδεράτωρ** (-ορος/-ωρος, ὁ) 'provincial governor', from *moderātor* 'ruler': Just. *Nov.*
           20.pr. etc. (VI AD); Byzantine texts. Avotins (1992), Hofmann (1989: 275),
           Zilliacus (1935a: 194–5), *LBG*, Lampe (1961), LSJ suppl. See §9.5.6 n. 68.

rare   **μοδ(ι)άριος**, an official responsible for grain, probably from *modius* 'peck' via μόδιος
           + -άριος (derivation from unattested **mod(i)ārius* has also been suggested):
           ACO III p. 87.16 (VI AD). Hofmann (1989: 276), Lampe (1961).

rare   **μοδίολος** 'nave of a wheel', from *modiolus* 'nave of a wheel': Edict.Diocl. 15.3
           (IV AD). Byzantine μοδίολος 'head-covering' (*LBG*) is probably unrelated.
           Hofmann (1989: 276), LSJ.

Direct loan   **μόδιος, μόδιον** (-ου, ὁ or τό), a measure and a vessel of that size, from *modius*
I BC – modern   'peck', a measure of 8.75 litres.
           Documents: common, e.g. *P.Ryl.* IV.692.7 (III AD); *P.Sakaon* 15.5 (IV AD);
           P.Oxy. 2004.4 (V AD); *P.Cair.Masp.* 67006v.102 (VI AD).
           Inscriptions: common (though often abbreviated), e.g. *Syll.*³ 741.10
           (I BC); Bosch 1967: 35 no. 51.37 (I AD); *I.Tralleis* 80.6 (II AD);
           SEG XXXIX.1279.15 (III AD); Edict.Diocl. 15.49 etc. (IV AD); *SEG*
           XXXIV.1243.30 (V AD); *Agora* XXI.Ha.44, dipinto on amphora (V/VI AD).
           Literature: very common, e.g. perhaps Polybius 21.43.19 (II BC); DH *AR*
           12.1.2 (I BC); NT Mark 4:21 (I AD); Epict. *Diss.* 1.17.9 (I/II AD); Galen
           XIII.1045.11 Kühn (II AD); Porphyry, *In Aristotelis Categorias expositio*
           p. 102.17 (III AD); Epiph. *Mens.* 607 (IV AD); Soz. 5.16.10 (V AD); Antec.
           2.4.2 (VI AD).
           Post-antique: common. *LBG* (*s.vv.* μόδιον, μόδιος), Zervan (2019: 117), Kriaras
           (1968– *s.vv.* μόδιον, μόδιος), Triandaphyllidis (1909: 125), Daris (1991a: 73).
           Modern μόδι 'grain-measure': Babiniotis (2002), Andriotis (1967), Meyer
           (1895: 45), Kahane and Kahane (1972–6: 533).
           Notes: often claimed to occur in Dinarchus (IV BC) and hence to be oldest
           direct Latin borrowing made in mainland Greece (e.g. Immisch 1885: 277;
           Viscidi 1944: 45; García Domingo 1983: 252 with reference '*Din.* 1,34'), but
           I can find no trace of it even in old editions. Forms derivatives: see §4.6.2
           Figure 1, and perhaps μοδιάριος. Dubuisson (1985: 36–7), Daris (1991a:
           73), Hofmann (1989: 276), Viscidi (1944: 30), Zilliacus (1937: 331),
           Meinersmann (1927: 37), Lampe (1961 *s.vv.* μόδιον, μόδιος), LSJ, LSJ suppl.
           See §4.2.4.1 nn. 51 and 58, §4.3.2 n. 75, §8.1.3 n. 17, §8.1.5, §9.2, §9.3
           nn. 21 and 23, §9.5.1, §9.5.3, §10.2.1, §10.2.2 E.

not ancient?	**μοδισμός** 'measurement', 'measuring by *modii*', from *modius* 'peck' via μόδιος + -σμός: no certainly ancient examples, though common in Her.Mech. (lived I AD, but the words are probably not his), *Geom.* 4.13a.22 etc. *LBG*, Kriaras (1968–), LSJ.

Μοθωνήσιος: see Μουτουνήσιος.

not Latin?	**μοῖτος, μοῖτον** 'gratitude', related to *mūtuus* 'on loan', is probably an early Sicilian borrowing from an Italic language. Willi (2008: 32), Hofmann (1989: 276–7), Immisch (1885: 317–18), Frisk (1954–72: II.249), Beekes (2010), LSJ.

not ancient	**μομεντάριος** 'temporary', from *mōmentārius* 'temporary': no ancient examples. Zilliacus (1935a: 194–5), *LBG*.

Direct loan **II AD – Byz.**	**μονῆτα, μονήτη, μονίτη, μόνιτα** (-ης, ἡ) 'mint', 'coinage', from *monēta* 'mint'. Documents: *P.Oxy.* 3618.15 (IV AD). Inscriptions: *I.Ephesos* 3046.8, perhaps 2061.i.11, perhaps 736.7 (all II AD); *I.Perinthos* 185.3 (IV/V AD). Coins: in Roman Egypt, Head 1911: 863. Literature: Thdr.Anag. *Tripart.* 1.26 (V/VI AD); Malal. 12.38.30–1 (VI AD); Cos.Indic. 11.18 (VI AD); with *cusio* in Gloss. *Herm.S.* 444.77 and *Glossae Stephani*, *CGL* III.478.59. Unverified example (VI AD) in Zilliacus (1937: 322, 331). Post-antique: common. *LBG*, Triandaphyllidis (1909: 125). Notes: Daris (1991a: 73), Mason (1974: 68), Hofmann (1989: 277), Zilliacus (1935a: 194–5, 1937: 331), *TLL* (*s.v. monēta* 1413.61–3, 1414.21), Lampe (1961), LSJ suppl. (*s.v.* gen. μονήτης). See §9.1 n. 4, §10.2.1, §10.2.2 D.

non-existent?	**μονητᾶλις** 'mint-overseer', from *monētālis* 'overseer of the mint': inscriptions perhaps *IG* VII.89.4 (II AD); perhaps *I.Callatis* 114.1 (II AD); perhaps Keil and Premerstein 1914: 93 no. 129.2 (III AD). Mason (1974: 6, 68), Hofmann (1989: 277).

Direct loan **V AD – Byz.**	**μονητάριος, μονιτάριος** (-ου, ὁ) 'coin-maker', from *monētārius* 'one who makes coins'. Inscriptions: *I.Perinthos* 181.1 (IV/V AD); *SEG* XL.1310. Literature: Hesych. as lemma μ 1608 (V/VI AD); Malal. 12.30.29 (VI AD). Post-antique: some survival. *LBG*, Triandaphyllidis (1909: 126). Notes: Zilliacus (1935a: 194–5), Immisch (1885: 356). See §4.2.4.1 n. 50, §10.2.1, §10.2.2 D.

μονήτη: see μονῆτα.

μονιτάριος: see μονητάριος.

μονίτη: see μονῆτα.

μονόβανδον: see βάνδον.

rare	**μονοκέλλιον** 'single cell', from μονο- + *cella* 'room' via κελλίον: *Apophth.Patr.* 5.42.2 (V AD); Byzantine texts. *LBG*.

non-existent?   **μονόμισσα, μουνούμισσα**, perhaps 'midday rest', in Lyd. *Mag.* p. 156.11 is suggested by *TLL* (*s.v.* μονόμισσα) as perhaps from μόνος 'alone' + *missa*, pf. part. fem. of *mittō* 'release'; the reading is uncertain. LSJ. See §8.1.7 n. 34.

rare   **μονορεκαῦτον, μονορεγκαῦτον** 'separate receipt', 'receipt signed by one person', from μόνος 'alone' + *recautum* 'receipt' (*TLL s.v. recaveo*): papyrus *SB* 9455.7 etc. (VI AD). Filos (2010: 250), Daris (1991a: 73), Cavenaile (1952: 199), Zilliacus (1935a: 196–7), Meinersmann (1927: 37), *LBG, TLL* (*s.v.* μονορεγκαυτον). See §8.1.7 n. 34; cf. ῥέκαυτον.

foreign   **Μοντιανόν**, a cake name apparently from unattested **Montiānum*: Athenaeus 14.647c, marked (II/III AD). Hauri-Karrer (1972: 120). See §9.4 passage 61.

foreign   **μόρα** 'delay', from *mora* 'delay': *Schol.Sinai.* in Latin script 23 *moras* (V/VI AD); Just. *Codex* in Latin script 1.3.45.4 (VI AD); later in Greek script. Avotins (1989), Zilliacus (1935a: 194–5), *LBG*. See §7.1.2, §9.5.6 nn. 56 and 68.

    μορβίλλων: see μερμίλλων.

not ancient   **μόρβος** 'illness', from *morbus* 'illness': no ancient examples. Zilliacus (1935a: 194–5), *LBG*.

    μορμίλλων: see μερμίλλων.

not Latin?   **μόρρια, μουρρίνη**, perhaps 'agate', perhaps from *murrinus* 'made of agate'. Hofmann (1989: 279 *s.v.* μούρρινος), *LBG* (*s.v.* μουρρίνη), LSJ.

rare   **μόρτις καῦσα** 'because of death', from *mortis causā*: Just. *Nov.* 22.22.pr. etc., but in Latin script 1.1.4 etc. (VI AD); Antec. in Latin script 2.7.pr. *mortis causa* etc. (VI AD); Byzantine legal texts. Various other forms of *mors* (though not the nom. sing.) also in Latin script in phrases in Antec. Triantaphyllides (1892: 267). See §9.5.6 n. 68.

not Latin?   **μοσμονάριος**, designating either an animal or an animal-keeper: *P.Rain. UnterrichtKopt.* 256.74 (VI AD). Bell and Crum (1925: 187.74), with commentary; cf. Wahrmann in Kretschmer and Wahrmann (1929: 221). Hofmann (1989: 277–8, cf. 279 *s.v.* μούσμων) derives it from an unattested **musmonārius* related to *mus(i)mō*, a kind of sheep or small horse (*TLL*). But LSJ suppl. defines it as 'keeper of μοσμένια' (μοσμένια occurs only in the same text, where it designates an animal, and must be related to *mus(i)mō* but not necessarily by direct derivation); on this interpretation μοσμονάριος could be a Greek formation in -άριος. Cf. μούσμων.

    Μοτονήσιος, Μοτυνήσειος, Μουθο(υ)νήσιος: see Μουτουνήσιος.

not ancient   **μούκουρα** 'heap of seaweed', perhaps from *mūcus* 'mucus' via unattested **mūculus*: no ancient examples. Meyer (1895: 45).

Direct loan
II AD – modern   **μοῦλα, μούλη** (-ης, ἡ) 'female mule', from *mūla* 'mule'.
      Documents: *P.Sijp.* 29.33 etc. (II AD); *Pap.Graec.Mag.* 36.332 (IV AD); *P.Lips.* 1.97.xxi.20 (IV AD); *P.Oxy.* 3741v.47 (IV AD).
      Literature: Cyran. 2.15.4 etc. (II AD?); Anton.Hag. *V.Sym.Styl.* 31 (V AD); Thdr.Anag. *HE* 4.460 (V/VI AD); Hesych. as gloss on ἡμίονος η 511 (V/VI AD); Alex.Trall. 1.571.14 (VI AD); Antec. 4.3.10 (VI AD); *Hippiatr.Berl.* 26.30.

Post-antique: survives. *LBG*, Zervan (2019: 118), Kriaras (1968–), Triandaphyllidis (1909: 119). Modern μούλα 'mule' etc.: Babiniotis (2002), Andriotis (1967), Meyer (1895: 45).

Notes: may form derivatives μουλάριον, μουλικός. Diethart (1992: 238–9), Daris (1991a: 74), Hofmann (1989: 278), Zilliacus (1935a: 194–5), Meinersmann (1927: 38), *DÉLG* (*s.v.* μούλη), LSJ, LSJ suppl. See §4.6.1, §10.2.1, **§10.2.2 K**; cf. ἄμβλα μοῦλα.

not ancient   **μούλα** 'stomach', perhaps from an unknown Latin word: no ancient examples. Meyer (1895: 45).

not ancient?   **μουλαγόρας**, perhaps 'mule-seller', from *mūla* and/or *mūlus* 'mule' via μούλα and/or μοῦλος + ἀγόρας (cf. ἀγοράζω 'occupy the marketplace'): inscription *MAMA* III.86. Hofmann (1989: 278 *s.v.* μούλος), *DÉLG* (*s.v.* μούλη), LSJ suppl.

Deriv. of loan   **μουλάριον** (-ου, τό) '(little) mule', from *mūla* and/or *mūlus* 'mule' via μούλα and/or μοῦλος + -άριον.
VI AD – modern

Documents: perhaps *SB* 15587r.8 (V AD); *SB* 9920.ii.10.2 etc. (VI AD); *P.Oxy.* 3805.82 (VI AD); *SB* 16746.3 (VI AD).

Literature: with *muscella* in Gloss. Ps.-Cyril. 373.29.

Post-antique: numerous. *LBG*, Zervan (2019: 118), Kriaras (1968–). Modern μουλάρι 'mule': Babiniotis (2002), Andriotis (1967), Meyer (1895: 45).

Notes: Daris (1991a: 73), Hofmann (1989: 278 *s.v.* μούλη), *DÉLG* (*s.v.* μούλη), LSJ. See §4.6.1, §6.3, §8.2.3, §10.2.2 K.

μούλη: see μούλα.

non-existent?   **μουλιατρός** 'mule-doctor', from *mūla* and/or *mūlus* 'mule' via μούλα and/or μοῦλος + ἰατρός 'doctor', on the model of *mūlomedicus* 'veterinarian' (*TLL*): dubious supplement instead of [ἱππ]ιατρῷ on Edict.Diocl. 7.20 (IV AD). LSJ suppl.

rare   **μουλικός** 'for mules', from *mūla* and/or *mūlus* 'mule' via μούλα and/or μοῦλος + -ικός: Edict.Diocl. 10.6, variant at 10.7 (IV AD). Lauffer (1971) reads μουλιωνικός in both, but see *SEG* XXXVII.335.iii.12, 14. Perhaps also ostracon *O.Brux.* 20.7 (II AD); Daris (1991a: 74) puts this under μουλίων, but the ostracon has μουλικηω[; cf. LSJ suppl. Byzantine μουλικός 'like a mule' (Lampe 1961, *LBG*) may be independent.

Direct loan   **μουλίων, μουλλίων** (-ωνος, ὁ) 'muleteer', from *mūliō* 'muleteer'.
II AD – Byz.

Documents: *SB* 12764.iii.13 (I/II AD); *P.Mich.* IV.1.224.1792 etc. (II AD); *O.Leid.* 312.11 (III AD); *P.Panop.Beatty* 2.303 (III/IV AD); *P.Ryl.* IV.640.13 etc. (IV AD); *Stud.Pal.* XX.85r.ii.13 (IV AD).

Inscriptions: *SEG* XLIII.392.2 (III AD); *TAM* IV.1.39.4 (III AD); *IG* X.II. II.400.2 (III/IV AD); probably Edict.Diocl. 7.19 (IV AD); *SEG* LII.639 (IV–VI AD); *SEG* II.405.2.

Literature: Basil Caesariensis, *Epistulae* 231.1.26 Courtonne (IV AD); Antec. 4.3.8 (VI AD).

Post-antique: some survival. Triandaphyllidis (1909: 124).

Notes: Drew-Bear (1972: 210), Robert (1955: 50), Daris (1991a: 74), Hofmann (1989: 278), Zilliacus (1935a: 196–7), Meinersmann (1927: 38), *DÉLG* (*s.v.* μούλη), Lampe (1961), LSJ, LSJ suppl. See §4.2.5, §10.2.1, §10.2.2 K.

rare   **μουλιωνικός** 'for muleteers', from *mūliōnicus* 'for muleteers' (*TLL*): Edict.Diocl.
9.5a etc. (IV AD). Hofmann (1989: 278 and *s.v.* μουλίων), LSJ (*s.v.* μουλίων,
incorrectly implying a spelling μουλωνικός).

Direct loan   **μοῦλος** 1 (-ου, ὁ) 'male mule', from *mūlus* 'mule'.
II AD – modern?   Documents: e.g. *P.Sijp.* 29.35 (II AD); *P.Mich.* XI.620v.284 etc. (III AD);
P.Corn. 39.3 (III/IV AD); *SB* 16511.2 (VI AD).
Literature: perhaps with *burdo* in Gloss. *Herm.M.* 189.7 (cf. *CGL* VI.157 *s.v.*
burdo).
Post-antique: some survival. Modern μούλος, μούλα 'bastard': Dieterich (1901:
590), Meyer (1895: 45, with derivation from μοῦλα), Babiniotis (2002, with
derivation from Italian *mulo*). Modern dialectal μουλαδέρφι 'half-brother':
Meyer (1895: 45).
Notes: may form derivatives μουλάριον, μουλικός. Daris (1991a: 74), Hofmann
(1989: 278), LSJ suppl. See §4.2.4.1 n. 51, §4.6.1, §10.2.1, **§10.2.2 K**.

     μοῦλος 2 'breakwater': see μῶλος.

foreign   **μοῦνδος** transliterating *mundus* 'world': Plut. *Rom.* 11.2 (I/II AD); Procop. *Bell.*
5.7.8 (VI AD). Hofmann (1989: 278), Sophocles (1887).

foreign   **μουνεράριος** transliterating *mūnerārius* 'giver of entertainments': Lyd. *Mag.*
p. 72.2 (VI AD). Sophocles (1887).

Direct loan   **μουνικίπιον** (-ου, τό) 'self-governing community', from *mūnicipium* 'self-
I–II AD   governing community'.
Inscriptions: *I.Ephesos* 3048.13 (II AD); *I.Mus.Palermo* 44.1 (II AD); *IG*
XIV.367.1; perhaps *IG* XIV.954.6.
Literature: Jos. *AJ* 19.291 (I AD).
Notes: Mason (1974: 6, 11, 68–9, 109), Hofmann (1989: 278–9), *LBG*, LSJ
suppl. See §4.2.4.1 n. 54, §10.2.1, §10.2.2 D.

rare   **μουνίφεξ**, a type of soldier, from *mūnifex* 'soldier who does not have exemption
from duties': papyrus *P.Panop.Beatty* 2.28 (III/IV AD); inscription *SEG*
LXV.1408.C28, transliterating the Latin (V/VI AD). Daris (1991a: 74), LSJ
suppl.

not ancient   **μουρδάρις, μουρδούλης** 'dirty' and derivatives, perhaps from *merda* 'dung': no
ancient examples. Meyer (1895: 46).

not ancient   **μοῦρκα** 'sediment', from *amurca* 'watery fluid contained in the olive in addition to
the oil': no ancient examples. Meyer (1895: 46).

     μουρμίλλων: see μερμίλλων.

not Latin   **μουρμουρίζω** 'murmur', perhaps from *murmurō* 'murmur' but more likely from
μορμυρίζω, a variant of μορμύρω 'roar': no ancient examples. Meyer (1895:
46), Andriotis (1967), Kriaras (1968–).

     μουρρίνη: see μόρρια.

rare   **μουσιάριος** 'mosaic-worker', from *musārius/musa(e)iārius* 'mosaic-worker':
probably Edict.Diocl. 7.6 (IV AD). LSJ.

not ancient	**μούσκλα** 'gloomy face', perhaps from *mūsculus* 'muscle': no ancient examples. Meyer (1895: 46).
not ancient	**μούσκουλο** 'moss', from *muscus* 'moss' via unattested **musculus* 'moss': no ancient examples. Binder (2000: 171), Meyer (1895: 46), Andriotis (1967 *s.v.* μούσκλι).
rare	**μούσμων** 'mule', from *mus(i)mō*, a kind of sheep or small horse (*TLL*): Hesych. as gloss η 511 (V/VI AD). Also Strabo 5.2.7, marked, meaning 'sheep' (I BC/AD). Binder (2000: 146, 208), Hofmann (1989: 279–80), *DÉLG*, *LBG*, LSJ, LSJ suppl. Cf. μοσμονάριος.
rare	**μουστάκιον** 'cake made with must', from *mustāceus/mustāceum/mustācium* 'cake made with must': Athenaeus 14.647d, marked (II/III AD); Aëtius 16.164.1 (VI AD). Hofmann (1989: 280), *DÉLG* (*s.v.* μοῦστος), *LBG*, LSJ. See §9.4 passage 61.
rare	**μουστάριον**, meaning uncertain, from *mustum* 'must' via μοῦστος + -άριον and/or *mustārius* 'of must' (*TLL s.v.* 1. *mustārius*): papyri *P.Flor.* 1.65.18 (VI AD); perhaps *CPR* VIII.63.2 (VI AD), but that could be a form of μουστάριος (*q.v.*); several Byzantine papyri. Variously interpreted as 'jar of must' and as a unit of measurement for wine (translation and commentary on *P.Oxy.* 4132.33, Sijpesteijn 1985: 78). Means 'must' in Byzantine literature (*LBG*). Palmer (1945: 84), Daris (1991a: 74, with derivation from *mustārium*), Hofmann (1989: 280), Meinersmann (1927: 38), *DÉLG* (*s.v.* μοῦστος), LSJ. See §6.3 n. 21.
non-existent?	**μουστάριος** 'of must', from *mustārius* 'of must' (*TLL s.v.* 1. *mustārius*): perhaps papyrus *CPR* VIII.63.2 (VI AD). Editor *ad loc.*, Daris (1991a: 74 *s.v.* μουστάριον), LSJ suppl.
not ancient?	**μουστόπιττα** 'cake made with must', from *mustum* 'must' via μοῦστος: several undated texts that could be ancient. Hofmann (1989: 280 *s.v.* μουστος), *LBG*, Kriaras (1968–), LSJ.
Direct loan V AD – modern	**μοῦστος** (-ου, ὁ) 'new wine', from *mustum* 'must' (i.e. unfermented or partially fermented grape juice). Documents: e.g. *CPR* XIX.31.7 (V AD); *P.Erl.* 111.11 (V/VI AD); *P.Lond.* III.1001.11 (VI AD). Literature: Aëtius 16.164.3 (VI AD); Lyd. *Mens.* 1.4 (VI AD); scholion to Nic. *Alex.* 493a: γλεῦκος, ὃ λέγεται ἐν συνηθείᾳ μοῦστον. Post-antique: numerous. *LBG*, Kriaras (1968–), Daris (1991a: 74). Modern μούστος 'must': Babiniotis (2002), Andriotis (1967), Meyer (1895: 46). Notes: may form derivative μουστάριον. Binder (2000: 246), Daris (1991a: 74, taking it as an adjective), Hofmann (1989: 280), Meinersmann (1927: 38), *DÉLG*, *TLL* (*s.v.* 1. *mustus* 1712.49–53), LSJ. See §4.2.4.1, §5.2.3, §10.2.1, §10.2.2 I.
non-existent?	**μουτᾶτος**, meaning uncertain, from *mūtātus*, pf. part. of *mūtō* 'exchange': perhaps tachygraphy in Menci 2000: 286 (V/VI AD), *q.v.*

Direct loan III–V AD	**Μο(υ)τουνήσιος, Μουθο(υ)νήσιος, Μοτυνήσ(ε)ιος, Μο(υ)τονήσιος, Μοθωνήσιος, Μωτωνήσιος, Μωθωνήσιος** (-α, -ον), 'of Mutina (in Italy)', used for a type of sheep, a type of wool, and clothing made from that wool; from *Mutinēnsis* 'of Mutina'. Documents: *P.Louvre* I.67.6 (III AD); *P.Sakaon* 71.7 etc. (IV AD); *P.Jena* II.2.10 (IV AD); *P.Oxy.* 1741.12 (IV AD); *SB* 11075.8 (V AD); *P.Oxy.* 1026.19 (V AD). Inscriptions: Edict.Diocl. 20.4 etc. (IV AD). Notes: the use in papyri for a type of sheep suggests that the breed was exported from Italy to Egypt. Bingen (1966: 377–8), commentary on *P.Jena* II.2, Lauffer (1971: 263–4, 268), Hofmann (1989: 280). See §4.2.2, §6.7 n. 45, §10.2.1, §10.2.2 H.
foreign	**μούτουον**, a type of contract, from *mūtuum* 'loan': Antec. in Latin script 3.14.pr. *mutuum* (VI AD); later in Greek script. *LBG*.
non-existent?	**μυλινάριος** 'miller', perhaps a conflation of *molīnārius* 'miller' (*TLL*) and μύλος/μύλη 'mill': perhaps inscriptions *IG* IV.411.3 (V/VI AD) and/or *IG* II/III².V.13479.5 (V/VI AD), but cf. s.v. μιλινάριος. Bees (1941: 87–8), Hofmann (1989: 281), Lampe (1961), LSJ suppl.
not Latin?	**μύρκος** 'dumb', a Syracusan (Συρακούσιοι) lemma in Hesych. μ 1901 (V/VI AD), is related to *murcus* 'coward who cuts off his thumb to escape military service' (*TLL*) but probably borrowed from an early Italic language. Hofmann (1989: 281), *DÉLG*, LSJ, LSJ suppl.
	μυρμύλλων: see μερμίλλων.
Direct loan IV AD – Byz.	**μυρσινᾶτος** (-η, -ον) 'with myrtle' (as neut. subst. oil flavoured with myrtle, plaster with myrtle oil, or myrtle wine), from *myrsinātus* 'made with myrtle oil' (*TLL*). Documents: Maravela-Solbakk 2009: 129.3 (V/VI AD); Andorlini 2001: no. 15.1 (VI AD). Literature: Orib. *Syn.* 3.9–10 *passim* (IV AD); Aëtius 1.121.1 etc. (VI AD); Alex.Trall. II.327.29 (VI AD). Post-antique: survives. *LBG*. Notes: Maravela-Solbakk (2009: 131, 2010: 259–60), Andorlini (2001: 166–7), Hofmann (1989: 282), *TLL* (s.v. *myrsinātus*), LSJ (s.v. μυρσινᾶτον). See §4.2.2, **§6.5**, §6.6, §10.2.1, §10.2.2 L.
	μυσσώριον: see μηνσώριον.
	μύτιλος: see μίτυλος.
not Latin?	**μῶδα** 'grains of corn', perhaps from *mola* 'millstone': Hesych. as lemma μ 2021 (V/VI AD). Hofmann (1989: 282), Immisch (1885: 346), LSJ.
	Μωθωνήσιος: see Μουτουνήσιος.
Direct loan VI AD – **modern?**	**μῶλος, μοῦλος** (-ου, ὁ) 'breakwater', from *mōlēs* (gen. *mōlis*) 'large mass'. Literature: Procop. *Aed.* 4.10.7 etc. (VI AD); Just. *Codex* 10.30.4.pr. (VI AD); with *moles* in Gloss. Ps.-Cyril. 374.42. Post-antique: numerous. *LBG* (s.vv. μῶλος, μοῦλος), Triandaphyllidis (1909: 124). Probably modern μόλος 'breakwater', though Babiniotis (2002) and Andriotis (1967) derive that from Italian *molo*. Notes: Avotins (1989), Lampe (1961), LSJ suppl. See §4.2.5, §8.2.3 n. 51, §10.2.1, §10.2.2 J.

not Latin?	μῶμαρ 'ridicule', perhaps from *mōmar* 'foolish person' or *vice versa*. Hofmann (1989: 282), Immisch (1885: 275), *TLL* (*s.v. mōmar*), LSJ.
rare	μώρανς 'delaying' (in dat. μωραντι), from *morāns*, pres. part. of *moror* 'delay': papyrus *BGU* IV.1141.6 (I BC). Daris (1991a: 74), Meinersmann (1927: 38). See §8.1.5.

Μωτωνήσιος: see Μουτουνήσιος.

N

ναβιτατίων: see ἀβιτατίων.

not Latin?	νάρα 'understand', perhaps from *nārus*, variant of *gnārus* 'knowing': Hesych. as lemma ν 95 (V/VI AD). Immisch (1885: 314).
rare	ναστούρκιον, a plant, from *nasturcium* 'cress': *Hippiatr.Berl.* 129.15. *LBG*.
not Latin?	νάτιβος, a type of stone, perhaps from *nātīvus* 'native': Epiph. *Gem.* 1.7 (IV AD). Hofmann (1989: 283), Lampe (1961).
non-existent?	νατλεια, perhaps on inscription *CIL* III.14184⁹.8, could be from *nātālis* 'birthday' (perhaps with gender from γενέθλια 'birthday feast'). Hofmann (1989: 283), *LBG* (*s.v.* νατάλιον 'birthday').
foreign	νατουράλιος 'natural' (i.e. subject to the *ius gentium*), from *nātūrālis* 'natural': Antec. in Latin script 2.2.pr. *naturalia* (VI AD); probably later in Greek script, though Kriaras (1968– *s.v.* νατουράλες) gives Italian etymology. *LBG*.
Direct loan IV AD – Byz.	**Ναυατιανός, Νουατιανός, Νοουατιανός, Νοβατιανός** (-ή, -όν) 'Novatianist' (member of a Christian sect), usually masc. pl. subst., from *Novātiānī* 'followers of Novatius' (L&S). Literature: common, e.g. Eus. *VC* 3.64.1 (IV AD); Soz. 1.22.1 (V AD); *V.S.Aux.* 2.16 (VI AD). Post-antique: common. *LBG* (*s.v.* Νοβατιανοί). Notes: Sophocles (1887), Lampe (1961). See §4.2.2, §10.2.1, §10.2.2 N, §12.2.2.
not ancient	ναυκέλιον 'boat', from *nāvicella* 'boat' (*TLL*): no ancient examples. Zilliacus (1935a: 228–9), *LBG*, *TLL* (*s.v. nāvicella* 220.67).
not ancient	ναῦκλα 'boat', from *nāvicula* 'boat': no ancient examples. Binder (2000: 169, 204), Zilliacus (1935a: 228–9), *LBG*, Andriotis (1974: 389), Meyer (1895: 47), Lampe (1961).
rare	ναυτοτίρων 'naval recruit', from ναύτης 'sailor' + *tīrō* 'recruit' via τίρων: papyrus *PSI* VII.781.9 (IV AD). Sijpesteijn (1991a: 48), Hofmann (1989: 436 *s.v.* τίρων), LSJ suppl.
rare	ναυφραγέω 'suffer a shipwreck', from *naufragō* 'suffer shipwreck' (or perhaps *naufragus* 'shipwrecked'): Didymus Caecus, *Commentarii in Ecclesiasten 3–4.12* p. 106.11 Gronewald (IV AD). *LBG*.
rare	ναυφράγιον 'shipwreck', from *naufragium* 'shipwreck': Volusius Maecianus in Just. *Dig.* 14.2.9 (II AD); Ps.-Clemens Romanus, *Homiliae* 12.10.1 etc. Irmscher. Hofmann (1989: 284), Lampe (1961), LSJ suppl.

foreign νεγατόριος, νεγατώριος 'negating', 'negative', from *negātōrius* 'restraining': Antec. in Latin script 4.6.2 *negatorios* etc. (VI AD); later in Greek script. Hofmann (1989: 284), Zilliacus (1935a: 196–7), *LBG*. See §9.5.6 n. 68, §10.3.1 n. 30.

foreign νεκ 'not', from *nec* 'and not': Antec. in Latin script as part of phrases, e.g. 4.1.3 *nec manifeston* (VI AD); later in Greek script in the same phrases.

foreign νεκεσσάριος 'compulsory', from *necessārius* 'necessary': *Schol.Sinai.* in Latin script 16 *necessaria* etc. (V/VI AD); Antec. in Latin script 2.19.pr. *necessarioi* etc. (VI AD); later in Greek script. Hofmann (1989: 284), Zilliacus (1935a: 196–7), *LBG*. See §7.1.2 with passage 23, §9.5.6 nn. 56 and 68.

rare Νεοκαισαρεών, a month name from νέος 'new' + *Caesareus* 'of Caesar' via Καισαρεών: inscriptions *I.Ephesos* 614b.7 (I AD); *IGR* IV.1665.3; perhaps *I.Ephesos* 1601.d11 (II AD). Scott (1931: 266), LSJ, LSJ suppl.

not ancient νεόκαστρον 'new fort', from νεός 'new' + *castrum* 'fort' via κάστρον: no ancient examples. Hofmann (1989: 161 *s.v.* κάστρα), *LBG*.

not Latin? νεόλεκτος, νεολέκτης 'newly enlisted', 'recruit', perhaps from νεός 'new' + *lectus* 'picked' (thus Cavenaile 1952: 199), or from λέγομαι 'choose' (λέγω B.I.2). *LBG* (*s.v.* νεολέκτης), Lampe (1961), LSJ.

foreign νέπετος, νεπέτα, νέπιτα transliterating *nepeta* 'catnip': Dsc. 3.35.1 (I AD); Galen XIV.43.4, 44.7 Kühn (II AD); Orib. *Col.* 11.κ.1 (IV AD); Hesych. as lemma ν 373 (V/VI AD); Lyd. *Mag.* p. 64.22 (VI AD). Hofmann (1989: 285), *LBG* (*s.v.* νεπέτα), LSJ.

foreign νέπως, νεπός 'offspring', apparently from *nepōs* 'grandson': Philoxenus frag. 328 Theodoridis, marked (I BC); perhaps as νεποτας on papyrus *P.Lond.* III.653.6 (IV AD); Lyd. *Mag.* pp. 6.8, 64.4–23, marked (VI AD); probably inscription Gardner 1885: 357 no. 121.5, but the stone has νεκος. Hofmann (1989: 285), *LBG*. See §5.3.2 passage 15.

rare νέρβος 'stocks', from *nervus* 'apparatus for securing the feet or necks of prisoners' (*OLD s.v.* 4): *Passio Perpetuae* 8 Robinson (IV AD?); John Chrysostom, *PG* LX.255.39 (IV/V AD). Hofmann (1989: 285), Lampe (1961).

νερεδιτάριος: see ἑρεδιτάριος.

not Latin νερίνη, cited as Sabine term for 'bravery' by Lyd. *Mens.* 4.60 (VI AD). Hofmann (1989: 285).

Direct loan (with suffix?)
I AD Νερών(ε)ιος, Νερόνιος (-α, -ον?) 'of Nero' (an Egyptian month), also part of Νερώνειος Σεβαστός (a month), from *Nerōnēus* 'of Nero' or the name *Nerō* + -ειος.
Documents: e.g. *P.Oxy.* 3780.6 (I AD); *SB* 15702.3 (I AD).
Notes: Νερώνειος and Νερώνειος Σεβαστός were different months and belonged to different calendars. Scott (1931: 255–8), Bagnall (2009: 181), LSJ suppl. See §4.3.3, §4.4 n. 79, §9.2, §10.2.1, §10.2.2 E.

not Latin νέρωνες, cited as Sabine term for 'brave men' by Lyd. *Mens.* 4.60 (VI AD). Hofmann (1989: 285–6).

rare	**Νερωνιανός**, a gemstone, from *Nerōniānus* 'of Nero': Damigeron, Mesk 1898: 319.5 (II AD); Epiph. *Gem.* 1.3 (IV AD). In *O.Claud.* IV.776.16, 777.2 (I–II AD) is the name of a stone-quarry. *LBG*, LSJ suppl.
rare	**νεφάριος** 'immoral', from *nefārius* 'wicked': Just. *Codex* 1.3.44.3, but in Latin script *Nov.* 12.1 etc. (VI AD); Byzantine texts. Modern νεφάριος 'nefarious': Babiniotis (2002). Avotins (1989), Zilliacus (1935a: 196–7), *LBG*, LSJ suppl.
foreign	**νηνία** transliterating *nēnia* 'funeral song' (L&S): Lyd. *Mag.* p. 50.16 (VI AD). LSJ.
not ancient	**νίγλα** 'saddle girth' and derivatives, perhaps from *ligula* 'tongue-shaped projection': no ancient examples. Meyer (1895: 47–8).
name	**Νίγρος**, personal name, from *niger* 'black'. Strobach (1997: 197), Sophocles (1887).
foreign	**νοβατεύω** 'renew a loan', from *novātus* (pf. part. of *novō* 'renew') + -εύω: Thüngen 2016: B9 in Latin script (V AD); Antec. in Latin script 3.29.2 *enovateuen, enovateuse* (VI AD); later in Greek script. Zilliacus (1935a: 196–7), *LBG*. See §9.5.6 n. 68.
	Νοβατιανός: see Ναυατιανός.
foreign	**νοβατίων** 'renewal', 'transformation', from *novātiō* 'substituting a new obligation for an old one': Antec. in Latin script 3.29.3 *novation* etc. (VI AD); later in Greek script. Zilliacus (1935a: 196–7), *LBG*. See §9.5.6 n. 68.
	νοβελ(λ)ήσιμος, νοβελ(λ)ίσ(σ)ιμος: see νωβελλίσσιμος.
	Νοβέμβριος: see Νοέμβριος.
foreign	**νόβος** transliterating *novus* 'new': Lyd. *Mag.* p. 108.1 (VI AD). Sophocles (1887).
Direct loan **I BC – modern**	**Νοέμβριος, Νοένβριος, Νοβέμβριος, Νοουέμβριος** (-α, -ον or -ον or -ου, ὁ) 'November', from *November* 'November'. Documents: e.g. *Chrest.Mitt.* 316.ii.6 (II AD); *SB* 16167.5 (III AD); *SB* 13856.10 etc. (IV AD). Inscriptions: common, e.g. Sherk 1969: no. 23.60 (I BC); *IG* X.II.II.300.16 (I AD); Dumont and Homolle 1892: 441 no. 110b.12 (II AD); *I.Laodikeia Lykos* 85.8 (III AD); *SEG* IV.127.8 (IV AD); *SEG* XXXVII.1078.7 (V/VI AD); *SEG* LI.920.4 (VI AD). Literature: common, e.g. Plut. *Marc.* 3.7 (I/II AD); *Act.Andr.* 19.2 (II AD); Dio Cassius 57.18.2 (II/III AD); Epiph. *Pan.* II.299.8 (IV AD); *ACO* II.I.I p. 100.4 (V AD); Aëtius 3.164.45 (VI AD). Post-antique: common. *LBG* (*s.vv.* Νοέβριος, Νοέμβρης), Kriaras (1968–). Modern Νοέμβριος, Νοέμβρης, Νοέβρις: Babiniotis (2002), Andriotis (1967), Meyer (1895: 48), Kahane and Kahane (1972–6: 533). Notes: Kramer (1983: 120, 2011: 37) argues for derivation from medieval *Novembrius* (*DMLBS*). Solin (2008), Sijpesteijn (1979), García Domingo (1979: 542), Hofmann (1989: 286), Meinersmann (1927: 38), Lampe (1961), LSJ suppl. See **§4.2.1**, §4.2.2, §8.2.3 n. 51, §10.2.1, §10.2.2 E.
rare	**νοκτοῦρνος** 'valet', from *nocturnus* 'nocturnal': Lyd. *Mag.* p. 24.27 (VI AD); Malal. 12.3 (VI AD) is Latin in Greek script. Hofmann (1989: 286), *LBG*.
	νομεγκλάτωρ, νομενκλάτωρ: see νομενκλάτωρ.

νόμερος: see νούμερος.

rare   **νομιν-** 'name', from *nōmen* 'name': gen. pl. νομίνων, papyrus *Stud.Pal.* I (p. 7).1.30 (V AD); *nomen* in Latin script, Antec. 2.20.29 etc. (VI AD); νόμινε often in Byzantine legal texts. Also as part of ἀδνούμιον, ἐνεραδνούμιον, ἀλιενονόμινε, *q.v.*

foreign   **νομινάτιμ** 'by name', from *nōminātim* 'by name': Antec. in Latin script 2.13.pr. *nominatim* etc. (VI AD); later in Greek script. Hofmann (1989: 286–7).

νόμιον: see νούμμιον.

non-existent?   **νομμοκλάριος** 'money-changer', from *nummulārius* 'money-changer': perhaps inscription *MAMA* III.302.3. Editor *ad loc.*, Hofmann (1989: 287), LSJ suppl.

νομοκλάτωρ: see νωμενκλάτωρ.

νόμος: see νοῦμμος.

foreign   **νόν** 'not', from *nōn* 'not': Antec. in Latin script 2.21.pr. *non* etc. (VI AD); later in Greek script. See §7.1.1 passage 19.

not ancient?   **νόνα** 'aunt', perhaps from *nonna* 'nun' (cf. L&S *s.v. nonnus*): inscription *I.Chr.Asie Mineure* I.16.2. Hofmann (1989: 287), Sophocles (1887 *s.v.* νόννος), Meyer (1895: 48, citing modern νουννά 'godmother'), Andriotis (1967 *s.v.* modern νόνα 'grandmother'), Lampe (1961). Babiniotis (2002) derives modern νόνα 'grandmother' from Italian *nonna* and νοννά or νουννά 'godmother' from Latin *nonnus*.

Νόν(ν)αι: see Νῶναι.

not Latin?   **νόννος, νόνος** 'father' may be from *nonnus* 'monk', 'tutor' (L&S). Hofmann (1989: 287), Kriaras (1968–), Sophocles (1887 *s.v.* νόννος), Babiniotis (2002 *s.v.* νοννός), entries for modern νουν(ν)ός 'godfather' in Meyer (1895: 48) and Andriotis (1967), Lampe (1961), LSJ.

νονοράριος: see ὀνοράριος.

foreign   **νόξα** 'person or thing that causes damage', 'injury' from *noxa* 'injurious behaviour': Antec. in Latin script 4.6.31 *noxan* etc. (VI AD); later in Greek script. Zilliacus (1935a: 196–7), *LBG*. See §9.5.6 n. 68.

foreign   **νοξάλιος** 'concerning damage', from *noxālis* 'concerning injury': Antec. in Latin script 4.8.pr. *noxalia* etc. (VI AD); often later in Greek script. Zilliacus (1935a: 196–7), *LBG*, Kriaras (1968–). See §9.5.6 n. 68.

foreign   **νοξία** 'damage', 'injury', from *noxia* 'injury': probably Antec. in Latin script 4.8.1 *noxia* (VI AD). Zilliacus (1935a: 196–7).

Νοουατιανός: see Ναυατιανός.

Νοουέμβριος: see Νοέμβριος.

rare   **νοουίκιος** 'of recent standing', from *novīcius* 'recently arrived': inscription *SEG* XXXIX.1180.117, Latinate (I AD). Brixhe (2007: 908), LSJ suppl.

rare	**νότα** (τά) 'notes', from *nota* (fem. sing.) 'mark': papyrus *P.Giss.* 105.6 (v AD); Orion excerpt 152 = Micciarelli Collesi 1970: 535, marked (v AD). Daris (1991a: 75); for Byzantine νότα (fem. sing.) *LBG*, Kriaras (1968–), Kahane and Kahane (1972–6: 589, 590); for modern νότα '(musical) note' Babiniotis (2002), Andriotis (1967). See §8.2.3 n. 51.
Direct loan **I AD – modern**	**νοτάριος, νωτάριος** (-ου, ὁ) 'notary', 'secretary', from *notārius* 'shorthand writer'.

Documents: common, e.g. *P.Oxy.* 3197.8 etc. (II AD); *P.Harrauer* 35.24 (III AD); *P.Abinn.* 17.4 (IV AD); *P.Harr.* 1.100.10 (V AD); *P.Mich.* XIII.660.1 (VI AD).

Inscriptions: e.g. *I.Sestos* 58.13 (I AD); Edict.Diocl. 7.68 (IV AD); *I.Chr. Macédoine* 247.3 (V AD?); *I.Cilicie* 91.5 (VI AD).

Literature: common, e.g. Julian, *Epistulae* 107.13 Bidez (IV AD); Eunapius, L. Dindorf 1870: 235.5 (IV/V AD); Callin. *V.Hypat.* 41.14 (V AD); *ACO* III p. 166.12 (VI AD).

Post-antique: common, forming derivatives νοταρικός 'of a notary', νοταρεύω 'be a notary', etc. Kriaras (1968– *s.vv.* νοτάρης, νοτάριος), Sophocles (1887), Zilliacus (1937: 331), Zervan (2019: 121–2), Triandaphyllidis (1909: 124), Daris (1991a: 75). Modern νοτάριος 'notary': Babiniotis (2002), Andriotis (1967), Kahane and Kahane (1972–6: 531).

Notes: Avotins (1992), Daris (1991a: 74–5), Mason (1974: 4, 69–70), Hofmann (1989: 287–8), Zilliacus (1935a: 196–7, 228–9), Meinersmann (1927: 38), Lampe (1961), LSJ suppl. See §4.1.1, §4.2.4.1 n. 50, §6.1, §10.2.1, §10.2.2 N.

not ancient?	**νοτωρία** 'indictment', from *nōtōria* 'written statement notifying the authorities of a crime': *Martyrium Agapae etc.* 3.1 in Musurillo 1972 (IV AD?). Bartalucci (1995: 117–18), Hofmann (1989: 288), Lampe (1961).

Νουατιανός: see Ναυατιανός.

νουβελίσσιμος: see νωβελλίσσιμος.

rare	**νουμενάρια** (τά) 'windows', apparently from *lūmināria*, plural of *lūmināre* 'window' (*TLL*): papyrus *P.Got.* 7.5 (III AD). Gignac (1976: 109), Daris (1991a: 68 *s.v.* λουμενάριον), Hofmann (1989: 288–9), Cavenaile (1951: 398), *TLL* (*s.v. lūmināre* 1824.9), LSJ (*s.v.* λουμενάριον), LSJ suppl.

νουμενάρχος: see νουμέραρχος.

Direct loan **IV AD – Byz.**	**νουμεράριος** (-ου, ὁ) 'keeper of accounts', from *numerārius* 'accountant' (L&S).

Documents: e.g. *P.Haun.* III.58.20 (V AD); *CPR* XXIV.12.1 (V AD); *P.Mich.* XI.624.26 (VI AD); *P.Lond.* v.1788.7 (VI AD).

Inscriptions: e.g. *I.Chr.Bulgarien* 91.6, 240.10 (both V/VI AD); *IG* X.II.1.674.3 (VI AD); *SEG* IX.356.17 etc., 414.7 (both VI AD).

Literature: Basil Caesariensis, *Epistulae* 142.1 Courtonne etc. (IV AD); Nil. 1.130.1 (V AD); Just. *Codex* 1.42.2.2 etc. (VI AD).

Post-antique: numerous. Triandaphyllidis (1909: 129).

Notes: Avotins (1989), Daris (1991a: 75), Hofmann (1989: 289), Zilliacus (1935a: 196–7, 228–9), Meinersmann (1927: 39), Lampe (1961), LSJ suppl. See §4.2.4.1 n. 50, §10.2.1, §10.2.2 G.

rare

νουμέραρχος 'leader of a corps', from *numerus* 'corps' via νούμερος + ἄρχω 'rule': Agath. *Arm.* 15.8, 19.16 (V AD); the νουμενάρχος that Zilliacus (1937: 322, 331) found in an allegedly IV AD source may be the same word. Hofmann (1989: 289 *s.v.* νούμερος), Lampe (1961).

Direct loan
II AD – Byz.

νούμερος, νόμερος (-ου, ὁ), a military unit, from *numerus* 'corps'.
Documents: common (esp. in *O.Claud.*), e.g. *O.Claud.* III.555.2 etc. (II AD); *BGU* I.316.8 (IV AD); *P.Berl.Zill.* 5.15 (V AD); perhaps *BGU* III.836.6 (VI AD).
Inscriptions: e.g. *I.Anazarbos* 72.2 (II/III AD); *TAM* IV.1.39.3 (III AD); *IG* II/III².V.13529.4 (III/IV AD); *MAMA* I.167.7 (IV/V AD); *SEG* XXXVII.1287.4 (V AD); *I.Chr.Macédoine* 26.2 (V/VI AD).
Literature: e.g. Ast.Soph. 22.6 (IV AD); John Chrysostom, *PG* LX.171.34 as gloss (IV/V AD); Callin. *V.Hypat.* 3.2 (V AD); Hesych. as gloss ε 1679 (V/VI AD); Cyr.S. *Vit.Sab.* 87.11 (VI AD). Unverified examples (II and III AD) in Zilliacus (1937: 322–3, 331).
Post-antique: numerous but with change of gender. *LBG* (*s.v.* νούμερον, cf. νούμερος 'commander of the palace guard'), Kriaras (1968– *s.v.* νούμερον), Triandaphyllidis (1909: 130). Modern νούμερο 'number' probably from Italian: Babiniotis (2002), Andriotis (1967).
Notes: forms derivative νουμέραρχος. Daris (1991a: 75), Mason (1974: 11, 70), Hofmann (1989: 289), Zilliacus (1935a: 143–4, 228–9, 1937: 331), Meinersmann (1927: 38), Immisch (1885: 370), Lampe (1961), LSJ suppl. See §4.2.4.1 n. 51, §10.2.1, §10.2.2 C; cf. ἀννούμερος.

Deriv. of loan
IV AD – Byz.

νούμ(μ)ιον, νόμιον (-ου, τό) 'coin', from *nummus* 'coin' via νοῦμμος + -ιον.
Documents: e.g. *O.Douch.* IV.403.11 etc. (IV/V AD); *Stud.Pal.* XX.164.3 (V AD); *CPR* VIII.62.30 (VI AD); *P.Oxy.* 1165.6 (VI AD).
Literature: e.g. Epiph. *Mens.* 799 τὸ δὲ νουμίον τετύπωται ἀπὸ Νουμᾶ τινὸς βασιλεύσαντος τῶν Ῥωμαίων (IV AD); *Apophth.Patr.* 12.10.19 (V AD); Hesych. as gloss α 7646, κ 3201, ο 21, χ 107 (V/VI AD); Dan.Sket. *M.* 16 (VI AD); with *assarium* in Gloss. Ps.-Philox. 24.7.
Post-antique: numerous. *LBG*, Kriaras (1968–), Zilliacus (1937: 331).
Notes: Daris (1991a: 75), Hofmann (1989: 290 *s.v.* νοῦμμος), Cavenaile (1952: 195), Zilliacus (1935a: 196–7), Lampe (1961), LSJ suppl. See §4.6.1 n. 83, §10.2.2 G.

Direct loan
II? BC – Byz.

νοῦμ(μ)ος, νόμος (-ου, ὁ) 'coin', from *nummus* 'coin' (originally a particular currency unit, later a generic term).
Documents: e.g. *Chrest.Mitt.* 316.ii.4 etc. (II AD); *P.Bagnall* 5v.8 (III AD); *C.Pap.Gr.* 1.40.7 etc. (IV AD).
Inscriptions: Sherk 1969: no. 10A.10, 10.B13 (both II BC); *I.Délos* 407.21 (II BC); *MAMA* III.81.3.
Literature: e.g. Epicharmus frag. 134 Kassel–Austin (V BC); perhaps Sophron frag. 161 Kassel–Austin (V BC); Plut. *Sulla* 1.4 (I/II AD); Pollux 9.79–80: ὁ δὲ νοῦμμος, δοκεῖ μὲν εἶναι Ῥωμαίων τοὔνομα τοῦ νομίσματος, ἔστι δὲ καὶ Ἑλληνικὸν τῶν ἐν Ἰταλίᾳ καὶ Σικελίᾳ Δωριέων … καὶ Ἀριστοτέλης ἐν τῇ Ταραντίνων πολιτείᾳ φησὶ καλεῖσθαι νόμισμα παρ' αὐτοῖς νοῦμμον (II AD); Epiph. *Mens.4* 83.15 (IV AD); Antec. primarily in Greek script but also in Latin script, e.g. 2.8.2 *nummoi*, νούμμων, νοῦμμοι (VI AD); bilingual glossaries, e.g. Gloss. Ps.-Cyril. 285.20.

Post-antique: numerous, forming derivative νουμμοδότης 'alms-giver'. *LBG*,
Zervan (2019: 122).

Notes: in south Italy and Sicily seems already to have been current (in form
νόμος) in v BC. At that period the source was probably not Latin but a south
Italian language, which was probably also the source of Latin *nummus*, since
until 190 BC *nummus* meant a particular south Italian coin, not Roman
coins (*OLD s.v.* 1a). By II BC at the latest both Greek and Latin speakers
apparently considered νόμος and *nummus* equivalent. By II AD νόμος had
spread over a wider geographical area and changed spelling to νοῦμ(μ)ος
to reflect the equation with *nummus* (cf. Pollux, quoted above). Later it
formed derivative νούμμιον. García Domingo (1979: 544), Daris (1991a: 76),
Hofmann (1989: 289–90), Zilliacus (1935a: 196–7), Meinersmann (1927:
39), LSJ (*s.vv.* νοῦμμος, νόμος III), LSJ suppl. See §4.2.4.1 n. 51, §4.3.2 n. 75,
§4.6.1 n. 83, §8.1.2 n. 16, **§8.1.4**, §10.2.1, §10.2.2 G.

foreign **νούνδιναι, νουνδῖναε** (acc. νουνδίνας) transliterating *nūndinae* 'market day': Plut.
Cor. 19.1, *Mor.* 275b (I/II AD). Strobach (1997: 197), Mason (1974: 6, 70),
Hofmann (1989: 290), *LBG*.

νουννά: see νόνα.

νουν(ν)ός: see νόννος.

foreign *nuptiae* 'marriage': Antec. 1.9.1 *nuptiae* (VI AD).

non-existent **νύνδιον**, from *nūndinum* 'period of eight days': superseded reading of papyrus
P.Cair.Isid. 90.8 (IV AD). Daris (1991a: 76).

rare **νωβελ(λ)ίσ(σ)ιμος, νοβελ(λ)ίσ(σ)ιμος, νοβελ(λ)ήσιμος** (-η, -ον) 'very noble',
from *nōbilissimus* 'very noble': Zosimus, *Historia nova* 2.39.2 Paschoud
(v AD?); Philostorgius, *Historia ecclesiastica*, frag. e passione Artemii
2.16a.14 Winkelmann; common in Byzantine texts. Lampe (1961) and
Sophocles (1887) cite additional examples that might be ancient, but I am
suspicious even of the two listed here. Binder (2000: 131), Daris (1991a:
74), Hofmann (1989: 290), Viscidi (1944: 35), Meinersmann (1927: 38),
LBG (*s.v.* νουβελίσσιμος), Zervan (2019: 123), Triandaphyllidis (1909: 126),
Sophocles (1887).

Direct loan **νωμενκλάτωρ, νομενκλάτωρ, νομεγκλάτωρ, νομοκλάτωρ, νωμενκουλάτωρ**
II–III AD (-ορος/-ωρος, ὁ) 'name-reminder', 'name-announcer', from *nōmenclātor/*
nōmenculātor 'name-reminder'.
Documents: *P.Oxy.* 1244v (II AD); *P.Oxy.* 2794.2 (III AD).
Inscriptions: *I.Ephesos* 1665.
Literature: Theophilus of Antioch, *Ad Autolycum* 3.27.19 Grant (II AD); Lyd.
Mag. p. 142.8–10 etc. (VI AD).
Notes: Binder (2000: 166–7), Daris (1991a: 74), Mason (1974: 69),
Hofmann (1989: 286, 291), Meinersmann (1927: 39), Lampe (1961 *s.v.*
νομεγκλάτωρ), LSJ suppl. See §4.2.5, §10.2.1, §10.2.2 N.

Direct loan **Νῶναι, Νόν(ν)αι** (-ων, αἱ) 'Nones', from *Nōnae* 'Nones', a monthly festival used
II BC – Byz. for dating.
Documents: e.g. *P.Yadin* 1.16.9 etc. (II AD); *P.Dura* 29.2 (III AD); *SB*
13856.11 (IV AD).

Inscriptions: e.g. *F.Delphes* III.IV.279.B18 (II BC); Hassall, Crawford, and Reynolds 1974: 202.iii.5 (II/I BC); *SEG* XXXIX.1290.33 (I BC); *IGR* IV.661.31 (I AD); *I.Cret.* IV.300.B7 (II AD); *I.Smyrna* 725.7 (III AD); *IG* X.II.1.779.2 (IV AD); *I.Chr.Macédoine* 130.A2 (V AD).

Literature: common, e.g. DH *AR* 8.55.5, marked (I BC); Juba, *FHG* III frag. 10.6 (I BC/AD); Plut. *Cam.* 33.7 (I/II AD); Eusebius, *De martyribus Palestinae* (rec. brev.) 4.15 Bardy (IV AD); *ACO* II.I.III p. 122.12 (V AD); *ACO* III p. 126.1 (VI AD).

Post-antique: numerous. Triandaphyllidis (1909: 120).

Notes: Solin (2008), García Domingo (1979: 545–6), Strobach (1997: 197), Hofmann (1989: 291), Meinersmann (1927: 38), Lampe (1961), LSJ suppl. See §4.2.1, §4.2.2 n. 32, §4.3.2 n. 75, **§8.1.4**, §10.2.1, §10.2.2 E.

νωτάριος: see νοτάριος.

Ξ

ξάγι: see ἐξάγιον.

non-existent ξεστασία, from *sextārius* 'pint measure': superseded reading of ostracon *SB* 1160. ctr.10. Daris (1991a: 76), LSJ.

Direct loan with influence
I AD – modern
ξέστης (-ου, ὁ) 'pint', 'cup', from *sextārius* 'pint measure', apparently via unattested *ξεστάριον with removal of what looked like the suffix -άριον and interchange of σ and ξ.

Documents: common, e.g. *BGU* XVI.2669.14 etc. (I BC/AD); *P.FuadUniv.* 8.15 (II AD); *P.Meyer* 20.43 (III AD); *P.Oxy.* 3818.3 (IV AD); *P.Oxy.* 3639.15 (V AD); *P.Prag.* II.154.2 etc. (VI AD).

Inscriptions: common (though almost always abbreviated), e.g. *IG* X.II. II.325.I.10 (I AD); *I.Didyma* 279.b8 (II AD); Edict.Diocl. 1.35 etc. (IV AD); *SEG* XXXIV.1243.25 (V AD).

Literature: very common, e.g. Philoxenus frag. 317 Theodoridis, marked (I BC); NT Mark 7:4 (I AD); Jos. *AJ* 8.57 (I AD); Epict. *Diss.* 2.16.22 (II AD); Galen *passim* (II AD); *Coll.Herm.* LS 11p (III/IV AD); Orib. *Col.* 5.18.1 (IV AD); Soz. 5.16.10 (V AD); Hesych. as gloss β 33, π 4055, 4099 (V/VI AD); Aëtius 1.104.4 (VI AD); D scholion to *Iliad* 24.304: πρόχοον· τὸν παρ' ἡμῖν καλούμενον ξέστην.

Post-antique: common, forming derivative τρίξεστον (*LBG*). Kriaras (1968–), Daris (1991a: 76–7). Modern dialectal survival: Andriotis (1974: 397), Kahane and Kahane (1972–6: 533), Meyer (1895: 49 *s.v.* ξεστή).

Notes: forms derivatives ξεστίον, ξεστισμός, ξέστος, perhaps ξεστιαῖος, χερνιβόξεστον, and see §4.6.2 Figure 1. Kramer (1998a: 39), Daris (1991a: 76–7), Hofmann (1989: 291–2), Meinersmann (1927: 39), *DÉLG*, Frisk (1954–72: II.335), Beekes (2010), Schwyzer (1939: 269), LSJ. See **§2.2.3** with passage 3, §4.4, §4.6.1, §4.6.2, §4.6.3, §9.3 n. 21, §9.5.1, §9.5.3, §10.2.1, §10.2.2 E; cf. σεξτάριος.

Deriv. of loan
II AD, VI AD?
ξεστιαῖος (-α, -ον) 'of a pint', from *sextārius* 'pint measure' via ξεστίον + -αῖος, or perhaps via ξέστης + -ιαῖος.

Documents: perhaps *P.Princ.* II.106.2 (VI AD).

Literature: Galen XIII.435.6 Kühn (II AD); Simplicius, *In Aristotelis Physicorum libros commentaria* vol. x p. 803.12 Diels (VI AD); Philoponus, *In Aristotelis Categorias commentarium* p. 153.28 Busse etc. (VI AD).

Notes: the early example may be unrelated to the later ones, since any Greek speaker could have formed ξεστιαῖος from ξεστίον. Forms derivatives τετραξεστιαῖος, πενταξεστιαῖος, ἑξαξεστιαῖος, ὀκταξεστιαῖος, δεκαξεστιαῖος. *DÉLG* (*s.v.* ξέστης), Beekes (2010 *s.v.* ξέστης), LSJ. See §4.6.1, §4.6.3, §8.2.1, §10.2.2 E.

Deriv. of loan
II AD – modern

ξεστίον, ξηστίν (-ου, τό) 'pint', 'cup', from *sextārius* 'pint measure' via ξέστης + -ιον.

Documents: *O.Petr.* 357.5 (II AD); perhaps *P.Lond.* II.191.8 (II AD); *SB* 9834.b.r.27 (III/IV AD); *P.Eirene* II.16.2 (V/VI AD); *P.Iand.* VI.103.15 (VI AD); *SB* 9778.11 (VI AD); *Stud.Pal.* VIII.1100.2 etc., 1279.4 (both VI AD).

Inscriptions: *SEG* LI.1392.3 (VI AD); *SEG* I.549.1; *IGLS* V.2033.1.

Literature: Orib. *Col.* 5.33.8 etc. (IV AD); Syn.Cyr. *Ep.* 134 (IV/V AD); John Chrysostom, *PG* LXIV.1037a (IV/V AD); Aëtius 1.135.5 etc. (VI AD); with *urceolus* in Gloss. Ps.-Philox. 211.45.

Post-antique: survives and is used as gloss in Byzantine scholia to Ar. *Nu.* 272b. *LBG* (*s.vv.* ξεστίν, ξηστίον), Kriaras (1968–), Triandaphyllidis (1909: 125 *s.v.* ξιστί), Daris (1991a: 77). Modern dialectal ξεστί: Andriotis (1974: 397), Meyer (1895: 49), Kahane and Kahane (1972–6: 533).

Notes: probably forms derivative ξεστιαῖος. Daris (1991a: 77), Hofmann (1989: 292 *s.v.* ξέστης), *DÉLG* (*s.v.* ξέστης), Frisk (1954–72: II.335), Beekes (2010 *s.v.* ξέστης), LSJ. See §4.6.1, §4.6.3, §8.2.1, §10.2.2 E.

rare

ξεστι(σ)μός 'quota of pints', from *sextārius* 'pint measure' via ξέστης + -(σ)μός: papyri *P.Panop.Beatty* 2.151 (III/IV AD); *P.Oxy.* 2114.13 (IV AD). LSJ suppl.

rare

ξέστος 'of a pint', adj. from *sextārius* 'pint measure' via ξέστης: Aëtius 1.122.2 (VI AD). Daris (1991a: 77).

ξεφτέρι: see ξιφτέρι.

ξηστίν: see ξεστίον.

not Latin?

ξιφτέρι, ξεφτέρι, a bird, perhaps from *accipiter* 'hawk' via unattested **accipitārius*: no ancient examples. Meyer (1895: 49), Kriaras (1968– *s.v.* ξεφτέρι, with a Greek etymology).

ξόμπλι: see ἔξεμπλον.

non-existent?

ξυλοκαβαλλάριος 'rider armed with wooden lance', from ξύλον 'wood' + καβαλλάριος (*q.v.*): perhaps inscription *SEG* XXXV.1360.7 (VI AD). LSJ suppl.

not ancient

ξυλόκαστρον 'wooden tower', from ξύλον 'wood' + *castrum* 'fort' via κάστρον: no ancient examples. Hofmann (1989: 161), Zervan (2019: 74), *LBG*, Kriaras (1968–).

O

όατρανός: see ούετερανός.

foreign   **ὄβα** apparently transliterating *ovīs*, acc. pl. of *ovis* 'sheep': Plut. *Marc.* 22.8
(I/II AD). Binder (2000: 259), Strobach (1997: 197), Sophocles (1887).

ὄβαν: see ὄουαν.

foreign   **ὀβατίων** transliterating *ovātiō* 'ovation' (a minor triumph): Lyd. *Mens.* 4.3
(VI AD). Hofmann (1989: 292–3), *LBG*.

rare   **ὀβιφέρι** in δέρμα ὀβιφέρι at Edict.Diocl. 8.25 (IV AD) is genitive of 'wild sheep',
from not *ovis fera* (gen. *ovis ferae*) but *ovifer* (gen. *oviferī*), which occurs
in the Latin of Edict.Diocl. 8.25 (spelled *obiferi*). Lauffer (1971: 244),
Hofmann (1989: 86–7 *s.v.* δερμα οβιφερι), *TLL* (*s.v. ovifer(us)*), LSJ suppl.
See §9.5.1; cf. φέρι.

foreign   **ὀβλᾶτος**, a kind of theft, from *oblātus* '(theft) in which the stolen goods are
maliciously transferred to a third party': Antec. in Latin script 4.1.3 *oblaton*
etc. (VI AD); later in Greek script. *LBG*.

οβο-, ὀβουεντίων: see οὐνδίκιος.

not Latin   **ὄβρυζος** 'pure' and **ὄβρυζα** 'assaying of gold' are probably not from Latin.
Meinersmann (1927: 39–40), Wessely (1902: 139), *DÉLG* (*s.v.* ὄβρυζα), Frisk
(1954–72: II.346), Beekes (2010 *s.v.* ὄβρυζα), LSJ, LSJ suppl.

ὀγκία: see οὐγγία.

ὀγκιαρήσιον: see οὐγκιαρήσιον.

rare   **ὀγκινάρα**, perhaps 'poker', probably from *uncīnus* 'hook' via ὄγκινος: papyrus *SB*
15301.ii.12 (V/VI AD). Diethart (1998: 174).

Direct loan   **ὄγκινος** (-ου, ὁ) 'hook', from *uncīnus* 'hook'.
IV AD – modern   Literature: perhaps Hdn. Ὀρθογρ. III.II.569.13 as gloss (II AD); perhaps
Pollux 1.137 (II AD); *Acta Philippi* 23 = Bonnet 1903: 12.23 etc. (IV AD);
EphraemSyr. III *De recta vivendi ratione* ch. 31.5 (V/VI AD); Hesych. as
gloss α 563, 7389 (V/VI AD); *Mart.Euph.* 13a (VI AD?); Ps.-Caesarius 158.2
Riedinger (VI AD); Gloss. Ps.-Cyril. 373.39, 378.53; note also ὀγκινοειδῆ in
old scholia to Ar. *Nu.* 178a.
Post-antique: numerous, forming derivatives ὀγκινόλογχος 'barbed lance',
ὀγκινίσκος 'little hook', etc. *LBG*. Modern dialectal ὄντζινα etc. 'hook':
Andriotis (1974: 400).
Notes: Binder (2000: 149), Hofmann (1989: 293), *DÉLG* (*s.v.* 1 ὄγκος), Frisk
(1954–72: II.347), Beekes (2010 *s.v.* ὄγκος 1), Lampe (1961), LSJ. See
§4.2.4.1 n. 51, §9.2, §10.2.1, §10.2.2 M.

not Latin   **ὄδερος**, a medical term in Hesych. as lemma ο 74 (V/VI AD), may be related to
uterus 'womb' but is probably from another Italic language. Hofmann (1989:
293), Immisch (1885: 332).

ὀδωνάριον: see οὐδωνάριον.

ὀεντικᾶτος: see οὐινδικᾶτος.

non-existent?	**ὀθονεμπλουμάριος**, probably 'tapestry-weaver in linen', from ὀθόνη 'fine linen' + ἐν 'in' + *plūmārius* 'tapestry-weaver' via πλουμάριος: perhaps papyrus *SB* 11077.26 (IV/V AD). Wild and Dross-Krüpe (2017), Filos (2010: 250), Daris (1991a: 77), LSJ suppl.
foreign	**ὄκ ἄγε** transliterating *hoc age* 'do this': Plut. *Numa* 14.2, *Cor.* 25.4 (I/II AD). Sophocles (1887 *s.v.* ἄγω 2). See §7.3.
rare	**ὄκρεα** 'shin-guard', from *ocrea* 'shin-guard': ostracon *O.Claud.* IV.824.6 (I/II AD). Commentary *ad loc.*
foreign	**ὀκρεᾶτος**, a type of soldier, from *ocreātus* 'wearing shin-guards': Lyd. *Mag.* p. 72.9, marked (VI AD). Hofmann (1989: 293–4), *LBG*.
not ancient	**ὀκρίδιον** 'legging', from *ocrea* 'shin-guard' + -ίδιον: no ancient examples. Zilliacus (1935a: 228–9), *LBG*.
not ancient?	**ὀκτᾶβα**, a tax, from *octāva* 'tax of 12.5% on the produce of land' (*OLD s.v. octāvus*): no certainly ancient examples. Hofmann (1989: 294), Lampe (1961).
not ancient?	**ὀκταβάριος**, a kind of tax collector, from *octāvārius* 'collector of the *octāva* tax' (*TLL*): no certainly ancient examples, since *I.Chr.Asie Mineure* I.10.2 (IV/V AD) probably reads Ὀκταθερήου not ὀκταβερήο. Hofmann (1989: 294), Lampe (1961), LSJ suppl.
rare	**ὀκταξεστιαῖος, ὀκτοξεστιαῖος, ὀκτωξεστιαῖος** 'of eight pints', from ὀκτώ 'eight' + *sextārius* 'pint measure' via ξεστιαῖος: papyrus *P.Mich.* XV.734.16 (VI AD). Filos (2010: 250), Daris (1991a: 77), LSJ suppl. See §4.6.2.
rare	**ὀκτάξεστος** 'holding eight pints', from ὀκτώ 'eight' + *sextārius* 'pint measure' via ξέστης: papyri *P.Oxy.* 1896.19 etc., 5069.14 etc. (both VI AD). Daris (1991a: 77 *s.v.* ὀκτάξεστον), LSJ; for a later example *LBG* (*s.v.* ὀκτώξεστος). See §4.6.2.
rare	**ὀκταούγκιον, ὀκταούγγιον** 'eight twelfths', from ὀκτώ 'eight' + *uncia* 'one twelfth' via οὐγγία: Just. *Codex* 6.4.4.16c, *Nov.* 18.1 (VI AD); with *bes* in Gloss. Ps.-Cyril. 381.41; Byzantine legal texts. Avotins (1989, 1992), *LBG*, LSJ, LSJ suppl. See §4.6.2.
rare	**ὀκτασσαριαῖος**, an interest rate, from ὀκτώ 'eight' + *assārius* 'of one as' (via ἀσσάριον or perhaps ἀσσαριαῖος) + -αῖος: inscription Reinach 1906: 247 no. 142.30. LSJ suppl. See §4.6.2.
	Ὀκτόβριος: see Ὀκτώβριος.
	ὀκτοξεστιαῖος: see ὀκταξεστιαῖος.
Direct loan **II BC – modern**	**Ὀκτώβριος, Ὀκτώμβριος, Ὀκτόβριος, Ὠκτόβριος, Ὀκτόμβριος** (-α, -ον or -ου, ὁ), from *Octōber* 'October'.

Documents: e.g. *P.Yadin* I.14.17 (II AD); *P.Dura* 30.2 (III AD); *C.Pap.Gr.* I.40.8 etc. (IV AD); *P.Cair.Masp.* 67321.A9 etc. (VI AD).

Inscriptions: common, e.g. *IG* VII.2225.3 etc. (II BC); Sherk 1969: no. 23.6 (I BC); *IGNapoli* I.84.i.4 (I AD); *I.Cret.* IV.300.B11 (II AD); *SEG* XLIX.817.11 (III AD); *SEG* XXX.585 (IV AD); *I.Cret.* IV.498.3 (V AD); *SEG* XLIV.584.7 (VI AD).

Literature: common, e.g. Jos. *AJ* 14.228 (I AD); Vet.Val. *App.* 9.7 (II AD);
Epiph. *Pan.* III.298.5 (IV AD); Socr. 2.40 (IV/V AD); Malal. 11.3 (VI AD);
Cyr.S. *Vit.Eu.* 54.10 (VI AD).

Post-antique: common. Kriaras (1968–). Modern Οκτώβριος, Ὀκτώβρης,
Ὀχτώβρης, Ὀχτώβρις: Babiniotis (2002), Andriotis (1967), Meyer
(1895: 50).

Notes: Kramer (1983: 120, 2011: 37) argues for derivation from rare *Octo(m)-brius*. Solin (2008), Sijpesteijn (1979), García Domingo (1979: 553),
Avotins (1992), Hofmann (1989: 294), Meinersmann (1927: 40), *TLL* (*s.v.
octōbrius*), Lampe (1961 *s.vv.* Ὀκτώβριος, Ὀκτώμβριος), LSJ suppl. See §4.2.1,
§4.2.2, **§8.1.4**, §8.2.3 n. 51, §10.2.1, §10.2.2 E.

ὀκτωξεστιαῖος: see ὀκταξεστιαῖος.

rare | **ὀλεάριος** 'bath attendant', apparently from *oleārius* 'maker or seller of oil': Epiph.
Pan. I.356.17 (IV AD). Hofmann (1989: 294–5), Lampe (1961).

foreign | **ὀλῆρε** transliterating inf. of *oleō* 'smell': Stephanus of Byzantium δ 81 (VI AD).

rare | **ὀλοκίτρινος** 'entirely citron-yellow', from ὅλος 'whole' + κίτρινος (*q.v.*): Cyran.
6.2.2 (II AD?); Damigeron, Mesk 1898: 321.29 (II AD); repeated by
Socrates and Dionysius 39.8 = Halleux and Schamp 1985: 172. *LBG*, LSJ
suppl.

rare | **ὀλοκοτίνιν** '*solidus* coin', from the Latin source of ὀλοκόττινος via ὀλοκόττινος +
-ιον: *Apophth.Patr.* 6.8.16 (V AD); Byzantine texts. *LBG*.

rare | **ὀλοκοττινοπερίπατος** 'whose picture goes around on the coins', from *coctum* via
ὀλοκόττινος + περίπατος 'walking about': papyrus *P.Cair.Masp.* 67097v.F17
(VI AD). Hofmann (1989: 295 *s.v.* ὀλοκόττινος), Meinersman (1927: 40).

**Loan compound
III AD – Byz.** | **ὀλοκότ(τ)ινος, ὀλοκότ(τ)ι(ν)ον** (-ου, ὁ or τό), the name of a gold coin known in
Latin as a *solidus*, from ὅλος 'whole' + *coctum* (*aurum*) 'smelted gold' + -ινος.
Documents: common, e.g. *P.Mich.* III.218.9 (III AD); *P.Oxy.* 3860.18 (IV AD);
P.Rain.Cent. 161.22 (V AD); *P.Princ.* III.170.7 etc. (VI AD).
Inscriptions: Edict.Diocl. 30.1a (IV AD); *IG* XIV.142.6 (V AD); *I.Chr.Macédoine*
198.2 (V/VI AD).
Literature: *Apophth.Patr.* 6.26.9 etc. (V AD); Ps.-Macar. *Serm.* 34.14.1 (V AD?);
possibly ancient texts cited in Lampe (1961).
Post-antique: numerous. Kriaras (1968– *s.v.* ολοκότινον).
Notes: etymology above is supported by Kretschmer (1912: 313–14), *DÉLG*,
Frisk (1954–72: II.379), Beekes (2010). Kriaras (1968–) has less convincing
derivation from *quātinus*, variant of *quātenus* 'how far?'. Meinersmann
(1927: 40) prefers Greek etymology. Forms derivative ὀλοκοττινοπερίπατος.
Lauffer (1971: 279), Hofmann (1989: 295), LSJ suppl. (*s.vv.* ὀλοκότιον,
ὀλοκόττινος). See §2.4, §4.5, §10.2.1, §10.2.2 G.

ὀλοσηρικός, ὀλοσειρικός: see σηρικός.

not ancient? | **Ὁμηροκέντρων** 'poem made of a patchwork of Homeric phrases', from Homer's
name + *centō* 'patchwork' via κέντ(ρ)ων: *Anthologia Graeca* 1.119 title; old
scholia to Ar. *Nu.* 450b; Byzantine texts. Hofmann (1989: 169 *s.v.* κεντων),
LBG (*s.v.* Ὁμηρόκεντρον), LSJ.

rare	**ὁμόκηνσος** 'jointly liable for taxes', from ὁμός 'joint' + *cēnsus, -ūs* 'census' via κῆνσος, a translation of *contribūtārius* 'jointly liable for taxes' (*TLL*): Just. *Nov.* 128.8 etc. (VI AD); Lyd. *Mag.* p. 242.19 (VI AD); Byzantine legal texts (*LBG*). Caimi (1981: 327), Avotins (1992), Hofmann (1989: 172 *s.v.* κῆνσος), *TLL* (*s.v. contribūtārius*), LSJ.
rare	**ὁμόπαγος** 'from the same district', from ὁμός 'same' + *pāgus* 'country district' (via πᾱγος?): DH *AR* 4.15.4 (I BC). LSJ.
	ὀνκία: see οὐγγία.
rare	**ὀνομάγγων, ὀνομάνγων** 'donkey-seller', from ὄνος 'donkey' + *mangō* 'dealer': papyri *P.Oxy.* 3192.10 = 4491.10, 3728.4 (all IV AD). Filos (2010: 250), Daris (1991a: 77), LSJ suppl.
Direct loan **VI AD – Byz.**	**ὀνοράριος, νονοράριος** (-α, -ον) 'honorary', from *honōrārius* 'voluntary', 'complimentary'. Literature: Just. *Nov.* 70.pr. (VI AD); Ath.Schol. index = p. 7.27, but in Latin script 8.3 etc. (VI AD); Antec. in Latin script 3.13.1 *honorariae* etc. (VI AD). Post-antique: numerous in legal texts. *LBG*. Notes: Avotins (1992), Hofmann (1989: 295), Zilliacus (1935a: 190–1), Lampe (1961). See §4.1.1 n. 23, §4.2.2, §9.5.6 n. 68, §10.2.1, §10.2.2 B.
foreign	**ὀνῶρεμ, ὀνῶρις**, and **ὀνώρει** transliterating forms of *honor/honōs* 'honour': Plut. *Mor.* 266f, 318e (I/II AD). Sophocles (1887 *s.v.* ὄνωρ). See §7.2.1 with n. 23.
Direct loan **I BC – modern**	**ὀξύγγιον, ἀξούγγιον, ἀξύγγιον, ὀξύγγειον, ἀξουγγία** (-ου, τό or -ας, ἡ) 'tallow', 'grease', 'lard', from *axungia* 'axle-grease'. Documents: *SB* 15917.21 (II AD); *P.Oxy.* 4001.24 etc. (IV AD). Inscriptions: only supplement at Edict.Diocl. 4.11 (IV AD). Literature: e.g. Crateuas frag. 9 in Wellmann 1906–14: III (I BC); Dsc. 1.125.3 (I AD); Galen XII.346.6 Kühn (II AD); Jul.Afric. *Cest.* 1.12.9 (II/III AD); Orib. *Col.* 45.29.73 (IV AD); Aëtius 7.87.28 (VI AD); *Hippiatr. passim*; bilingual glossaries, e.g. Gloss. Ps.-Cyril. 384.47. Post-antique: survives, forming derivatives ἀξουγγιασμός 'treatment with ἀξούγγιον' (LSJ), ἀξουγγώδης 'like fat'. *LBG* (*s.v.* ἀξούγγιον), Kriaras (1968– *s.v.* ἀξούγγιον), Triandaphyllidis (1909: 119). Modern ξίγγι 'fat': Babiniotis (2002), Andriotis (1967), Meyer (1895: 10–11). Notes: Triandaphyllidis (1909: 107) attributes spelling with ο- to influence of ὀξύς. Hofmann (1989: 295), *DÉLG*, Beekes (2010), *DGE* (*s.v.* ἀξούγγιον), LSJ (*s.vv.* ἀξουγγία, ὀξύγγιον), LSJ suppl. (*s.v.* ἀξουγγία). See §4.2.3.1, §4.3.2 n. 75, §8.1.5, **§9.5.3** passage 66, §10.2.1, §10.2.2 I.
not ancient?	**ὀξυγγοσάπουνον** 'lard soap', from *axungia* 'axle-grease' via ὀξύγγιον + *sāpō* 'soap' (L&S) (via σάπων?): alchemist, Berthelot and Ruelle 1888: 380.18. Hofmann (1989: 295 *s.v.* ὀξύγγιον), LSJ suppl.
foreign	**ὄουαν** (acc. sing.), **ὄουας, ὄβαν** apparently transliterating forms of *ovātiō* 'ovation' (a minor triumph): Plut. *Marc.* 22.1, 9, *Crassus* 11.11 (I/II AD); in form ὠάν, perhaps DH *AR* 8.67.10 (I BC). Mason (1974: 8, 71), Hofmann (1989: 292–3 *s.v.* ὀβατίων), Sophocles (1887 *s.v.* ὤας), LSJ suppl. Cf. οὐαστής.
	ὀουινδίκιος: see οὐνδίκιος.

rare	ὀουῶν as a spelling of ᾠῶν 'of sheepskins' on papyrus *BGU* XIII.2358.4 etc. (IV AD) probably reveals confusion with Latin *ovis* 'sheep'.
	ὀπεινάτωρ: see ὀπινάτωρ.
	ὀπεινίω: see ὀπινίω.
foreign	ὄπεμ transliterating acc. of *ops* (here meaning 'abundance'): Plut. *Rom.* 16.6 (I/II AD). Sophocles (1887 *s.v.* ὄψ). See §7.2.1.
foreign	ὄπερα 'service', from *opera* 'effort': Antec. in Latin script 4.5.1 *operas* etc. (VI AD); later in Greek script. Zilliacus (1935a: 196–7), *LBG*, Triandaphyllidis (1909: 124). See §9.5.6 n. 68.
rare	ὀπεράριος 'workman', from *operārius* 'one who works for hire': inscription *I.Cilicie* 46.4 (I/II AD). LSJ suppl.
	ὀπίκιον: see ὀφφίκιον.
foreign	ὀπίμ(ι)ος transliterating *opīmus* as part of *spolia opīma*, a special type of trophy: Plut. *Rom.* 16.6 etc. (I/II AD); Dio Cassius 44.4.3, 51.24.4 (II/III AD). Freyburger-Galland (1997: 206–7), Mason (1974: 6, 71), Hofmann (1989: 295).
Direct loan **III–IV AD**	ὀπινάτωρ, ὀπιννάτωρ, ὀπινιάτωρ, ὀπεινάτωρ, ὀπεινειάτωρ (-ορος, ὁ), a military official, from *opīnātor* 'collector of the *annona* tax' (*TLL s.v.* 713.49–78). Documents: *P.Oxy.* 1419.5a, perhaps 3029.4 (both III AD); *P.Panop.Beatty* 2.41 etc. (III/IV AD); *SB* 13852.16 etc. (IV AD); *P.Oxy.* 2114.10 (IV AD); *P.Erl. Diosp.* 1.102 etc. (IV AD). Notes: Mitthof (2001: 160–5, 361 n. 347), Daris (1964: 48, 1991a: 77), Hofmann (1989: 296), Cavenaile (1951: 398), *LBG*, LSJ suppl. See §4.2.5, §9.2, §10.2.1, §10.2.2 C.
Direct loan **III AD**	ὀπινίω, ὀπεινίω, ὀπινίων (-ωνος, ἡ) 'legal opinion', perhaps also 'valuation of tribute', from *opīniō* 'opinion'. Documents: *PSI* IX.1076.14 (III AD); *P.Oxy.* 2130.1 etc. (III AD); *P.Laur.* IV.157.4 (III AD); *P.Flor.* II.278r.5.4 etc. (III AD). Literature: Antec. in Latin script 1.2.8 *opinion, opiniona, opiniones* (VI AD). Notes: Daris (1964: 48, 1991a: 77), Hofmann (1989: 296), Cavenaile (1951: 398), Zilliacus (1935a: 196–7), *LBG*, LSJ suppl. See **§4.2.5**, §7.2.1 passage 27, §10.2.1, §10.2.2 B.
	ὀπιννάτωρ: see ὀπινάτωρ.
not ancient	ὀπισθελίνα 'crupper', partly from *postilēna* 'crupper': no ancient examples. Zilliacus (1935a: 230–1), *LBG*.
foreign	ὄπους transliterating *opus* 'work': Plut. *Rom.* 16.6 (I/II AD).
not ancient?	ὀπτιμᾶτος, ὀπτημᾶτος, claimed to be from *optimās* (gen. *optimātis*) 'optimate' (Hofmann 1989: 296; Zilliacus 1935a: 230–1): I can find no ancient examples. Numerous Byzantine occurrences, which *LBG* derives from medieval *optimātus* 'noble' (a variant of *optimās*: *DMLBS s.v. optimas*). Triandaphyllidis (1909: 129), Lampe (1961 *s.v.* ὀπτιμᾶτοι).

foreign	**ὄπτιμος** transliterating *optimus* 'best': Dio Cassius 68.23.1–2 (II/III AD). Sophocles (1887).
rare	**ὀπτιοπρίγκεψ** 'assistant to the chief centurion', from unattested **optioprīnceps* (thus *TLL s.v.* *optioprinceps) or a Greek univerbation of *optiō* + *prīnceps*, which together formed a title (thus Filos 2006: 44, 2010: 252): papyri *P.Ness.* III.19.6, 36.13 (both VI AD). Daris (1991a: 77), *LBG*. See §8.1.7.
Direct loan **I AD – Byz.**	**ὀπτίων, ὤπτι, ὤπτίων** (-ωνος/-ονος, ὁ) 'assistant', 'adjutant', from *optiō* 'centurion's assistant'. Documents: common, e.g. *O.Did.* 349.7 (I AD); *BGU* II.600.14 (II AD); *P.Oxy.* 3366.25 (III AD); *P.Mil.* II.84.7 (IV AD); *CPR* XXIV.4.27 (V AD); *P.Berl. Sarisch.* 14.4 etc. (VI AD). Inscriptions: e.g. *I.Byzantion* 294.4 (III AD); *SEG* XVI.754.16 (III AD); *SEG* XXXI.1116.6 etc. (IV AD). Literature: e.g. Plut. *Galba* 24.1, marked (I/II AD); Just. *Nov.* 130.1. (VI AD); Ath.Schol. 4.P.23.2 (VI AD); *V.S.Aux.* 2.10 (VI AD); Antec. in Latin script meaning 'option, choice', 2.20.23 *option* (VI AD). Post-antique: numerous. *LBG*, Triandaphyllidis (1909: 129). Notes: forms derivative ὑποπτίων. Bartalucci (1995: 110–12), Avotins (1992), Daris (1991a: 78), Mason (1974: 5, 71), Hofmann (1989: 296–7), Zilliacus (1935a: 230–1), Meinersmann (1927: 40), LSJ. See §4.2.5, §10.2.1, §10.2.2 C. **ὀπφικάλις**: see ὀφφικιάλιος.
Direct loan **III AD – modern**	**ὀράριον, ὠράριον** (-ου, τό) 'kerchief', 'scarf', 'deacon's stole', from *ōrārium* 'kerchief' (*TLL*). Documents: e.g. perhaps *SB* 12291.5 (III AD); *P.Sijp.* 60a.12 (IV AD); *P.Princ.* II.82.42 (V AD); *P.Münch.* III.1.142.17 (VI AD). Inscriptions: Edict.Diocl. 27.8 etc. (IV AD). Literature: e.g. *V.Aesopi* G 21 (II AD?); Cyran. 2.14.12 (II AD?); *Ev.Barth.* 4.70 (III AD); Dor.Poet. *Visio* 332 (III/IV AD); Hesych. as gloss σ 663 (V/VI AD); Jo.Scholast. 2 p. 19.2 (VI AD). Post-antique: common. Kriaras (1968–), Sophocles (1887 *s.v.* ὠράριον). Modern ὀράριο, an ecclesiastical vestment: Babiniotis (2002). Notes: Editor of *P.Münch.* III.1.142 *ad loc.*, O'Callaghan (1973), Daris (1991a: 117), Hofmann (1989: 485–6), Meinersmann (1927: 41), *TLL* (*s.v. ōrārium* 875.69–72), Lampe (1961 *s.v.* ὠράριον), LSJ, LSJ suppl. See §4.2.4.1 n. 54, **§4.2.6**, §10.2.1, §10.2.2 H, §12.2.1.
rare	**ὀρατίων, ὠρατίων** (ἡ) 'emperor's legislative proposal', from *ōrātiō* 'speech': Modestinus in Just. *Dig.* 27.1.1.4 (III AD); Lyd. *Mens.* 4.28.1, marked (VI AD); Byzantine legal texts. Unverified form ὠραιῶν, III AD, in Zilliacus (1937: 332). Zilliacus (1935a: 196–7), *LBG*, LSJ suppl. See §9.5.6 nn. 55 and 58. **ὀρβανός**: see οὐρβανός.
non-existent	**ὀρβήλας**, superseded reading for ἀρβήλας in Artemidorus, *Onirocriticon* 2.32.28 (II AD). Hofmann (1989: 297).

rare   ὀρβικουλᾶτος (-ον), ὀρβικλᾶτον (-ου, τό), a kind of fruit (with μῆλον expressed or understood), from (*mālum*) *orbiculātum* (*OLD s.v.* orbiculātus 'round'; for the variant with -*cl*- see *TLL s.v.* orbiculātus): Dsc. 1.115.4, marked (I AD); Galen XIII.289.14 Kühn (II AD); Athenaeus 3.80f, marked, and 3.81a (II/III AD); Jul.Afric. *Cest.* 1.19.110, marked (II/III AD). Binder (2000: 163–4), Durling (1979: 220), Hofmann (1989: 297), Viscidi (1944: 39), LSJ suppl. (replacing LSJ *s.v.* ὀρβικλᾶτον).

rare   ὀργανάριος 'piper', from *organārius*, a type of musician (*TLL*): papyrus *P.Wash. Univ.* 11.95.16 (V/VI AD); Byzantine texts. Editor *ad loc.*, *LBG*, LSJ, LSJ suppl.

Direct loan
IV AD – Byz.
      ὀρδινάριος 1, ὀρτινάριος, ὀρτηνάριος, ὠρδινάριος, ὀρδε(ι)νάριος, ὠρδενάριος (-ου, ὁ), an officer, from *ōrdinārius* 'regular'.
        Documents: e.g. perhaps *O.Douch.* V.556.3 (IV/V AD); perhaps *P.Münch.* 1.16.49 (V AD); *P.Oxy.* 5123.4 (VI AD); *P.Princ.* III.138.1 (VI AD).
        Inscriptions: *MAMA* I.168.5 (IV AD); perhaps *I.Chr.Égypte* 70.6 (IV AD); Bean and Mitford 1970: 54 no. 31.A6 (V AD); *MAMA* I.306.4; perhaps *IGBulg.* V.5794.1.
        Literature: Syn.Cyr. *Ep.* 144 (IV/V AD); Lyd. *Mag.* p. 70.10 as lemma (VI AD); of a kind of slave, Antec. in Latin script 2.20.17 *ordinarion* etc. (VI AD).
        Post-antique: survives in papyri with original sense and in legal texts with Antec.'s meaning. Daris (1991a: 78).
        Notes: the usage in Antec. is a second, independent borrowing; Antec. puts it in Latin script and ὀρδινάριος 2 in Greek script. Binder (2000: 127–8), Daris (1991a: 78), Mason (1974: 3, 4, 100, 168, merging with next), Hofmann (1989: 486–7, merging with next), Zilliacus (1935a: 196–7), Meinersmann (1927: 41), Lampe (1961), LSJ suppl. (merging with next). See §4.2.4.1 n. 50, §10.2.1, §10.2.2 C.

Direct loan
III AD – Byz.
      ὀρδινάριος 2, ὠρδινάριος (-α, -ον) 'regular', from *ōrdinārius* 'regular'.
        Documents: e.g. *P.Lond.* III.775.5 (VI AD); *P.Oxy.* 133.4 (VI AD); *P.Princ.* 11.96.54 (VI AD).
        Inscriptions: e.g. *I.Ephesos* 710b.28 (III AD); *TAM* 11.572.5 (III AD); *MAMA* III.197A.1.22 (VI AD).
        Literature: Malal. 13.37.19 (VI AD); Just. *Nov.* 20.3 etc. (VI AD); Ath.Schol. 8.1.1 (VI AD); Antec. 3.9.7 etc. (VI AD). Unverified example in Zilliacus (1937: 331).
        Post-antique: numerous, forming derivative ὀρδιναρίως. *LBG*, Kriaras (1968–), Triandaphyllidis (1909: 126).
        Notes: Coleman's spelling ἀορδινάριος (2007: 796) is probably typographical error. Avotins (1992), Daris (1991a: 78), Mason (1974: 3, 4, 100, 168, merging with preceding), Hofmann (1989: 486–7, merging with preceding), Zilliacus (1935a: 230–1), LSJ suppl. (merging with preceding). See §4.2.2, §6.1 n. 11, §6.10, §10.2.1, §10.2.2 D, §10.3.2.

not ancient   ὀρδινατεύω 'arrange', from *ōrdinātus* (pf. part. of *ōrdinō* 'arrange') + -εύω: no ancient examples. Zilliacus (1935a: 196–7), *LBG*.

Direct loan
II AD – Byz.

ὀρδινατίων (-ονος, ἡ) 'order' (e.g. of a list), from *ōrdinātiō* 'arrangement'.
Inscriptions: *IGLS* XIII.1.9046.27 (V/VI AD); *SEG* XXXII.1554.A8 (VI AD).
Literature: Epict. *Diss.* 3.24.117 (I/II AD).
Post-antique: survives. *LBG*.
Notes: Mason (1974: 8, 72), Hofmann (1989: 297–8), Zilliacus (1935a: 230–1). See §4.2.5, §6.10, §10.2.1, §10.2.2 O.

Direct loan
III–IV AD?

ὀρδινᾶτος, ὀρτινᾶτος, ὠρδινᾶτος (-ου, ὁ) 'appointed' (an official title), from *ōrdinātus*, pf. part. of *ōrdinō* 'appoint'.
Documents: *P.Flor.* II.278r.2.26 etc. (III AD); *O.Did.* 29.1 (III AD); *P.Panop. Beatty* 2.60 etc. (III/IV AD); *SB* 12663.2, perhaps 11975.4 (both IV AD).
Inscriptions: *IG* X.II.1.546.3 (III AD); *SEG* XXXI.1116.7 (IV AD); *IGBulg.* III.I.1127.2; *IGBulg.* III.II.1712.1; *TAM* V.1.564.2; *IGBulg.* III.I.983.1; perhaps *IGBulg.* III.I.1126.8; perhaps *IGBulg.* V.5794.1.
Notes: Rea (1980), Daris (1991a: 78), Mason (1974: 100), Hofmann (1989: 298), Meinersmann (1927: 41), *LBG*, LSJ suppl. See §4.2.4.1 n. 51, §6.10, §10.2.1, §10.2.2 D.

rare

ὀρδινεύω 'arrange', 'bring about', 'ordain', from *ōrdinō* 'arrange' or *ōrdō* 'order' via ὄρδινος + -εύω: EphraemSyr. VII p. 326.14 (V/VI AD); *Acta Petri et Pauli* 7, 16 = Lipsius 1891: 182.4, 186.9; Byzantine texts. Hofmann (1989: 298), Meyer (1895: 50), Zilliacus (1935a: 230–1), *LBG*, Zervan (2019: 124), Lampe (1961).

Direct loan
V AD – modern

ὄρδινος (-ου, ὁ) 'order', from *ōrdō* (gen. *ōrdinis*) 'order'.
Literature: Ps.-Basil Caesariensis, *PG* XXXI.1309a etc. (IV AD?); Horapollo, *Hieroglyphica* 2.94.3 Sbordone (IV/V AD); Hesych. as gloss σ 1878 (V/VI AD); *V.S.Aux.* 2.19 (VI AD).
Post-antique: common. *LBG* (s.vv. ὄρδινον, ὄρδινος), Kriaras (1968–), Zilliacus (1937: 331). Modern dialectal ὄρδινον and derivatives: Meyer (1895: 50), Dieterich (1901: 591).
Notes: may form derivative ὀρδινεύω. Hofmann (1989: 298), Zilliacus (1935a: 230–1), Lampe (1961). See §4.2.5, §6.10, §10.2.1, §10.2.2 O.

not ancient

ὀρδίνως 'in line', apparently from *ōrdine* 'in a row' (abl. of *ōrdō* 'order') + adverbial -ως (§10.3.1): no ancient examples, since the version of the *Physiologus* reported by Karnejev (1894: 44) is not original. Hofmann (1989: 298), *LBG*, Kriaras (1968–), Lampe (1961).

rare

ὄρδο, ὄρδω 'order', from *ōrdō* 'order': inscription *SEG* XX.409. Mason (1974: 72). Cf. s.v. ἔξτρα.

rare

ὀρθόπλουμος, probably 'tapestry woven with a vertical design', from ὀρθός 'upright' + *plūma* 'feather': Edict.Diocl. 29.12 etc. (IV AD); papyrus *P.Princ.* II.82.39 (V AD); occasional Byzantine texts. Wild and Dross-Krüpe (2017), Filos (2010: 250), Daris (1991a: 78), Hofmann (1989: 333 s.v. πλοῦμο-), *LBG*, LSJ, LSJ suppl. Cf. πλουμίον, ἔμπλουμος, ἐμπλούμιος, εὔπλουμος, πλοῦμος.

ὀριάριος: see ὀρριάριος.

rare

ὀριεντάλιος 'eastern', from *orientālis* 'eastern': papyrus *P.Panop.Beatty* 2.187 etc. (III/IV AD). LSJ suppl.

ὄριον: see ὄρριον.

rare	ὀρκίνος, a type of freedman, from *orcīnus* 'appointed under the terms of a will': Just. *Codex* 6.4.4.233 (VI AD); Antec. in Latin script 3.11.1 *orcinoi* etc. (VI AD). Avotins (1989), Zilliacus (1935a: 196–7), *LBG*.
rare	ὀρκίολος, ὀρκίωλος, ὀρκίολον 'little water-jar', from *urceolus* 'little jug': inscriptions *IG* XII.Suppl.413.5 (II AD); *TAM* IV.1.6.14. Unverified ὀρκιόλιον (IV AD) in Zilliacus (1937: 323, 336). Hofmann (1989: 298), LSJ suppl., and for possible later survival *LBG* (*s.v.* ὀρκιόλιον), Kriaras (1968– *s.v.* ὀρκιόλιον), Triandaphyllidis (1909: 120 *s.v.* ἰρκιόλι).
foreign	ὀρναμέντον 'decoration', from *ōrnāmentum* 'ornament': inscription *SEG* LXV.1408.A58, B59 transliterating the Latin (V/VI AD); Just. *Codex* in Latin script 10.30.4.35 (VI AD); perhaps later in Greek script. Daris (1991a: 78), Zilliacus (1935a: 196–7), Triantaphyllides (1892: 268), *LBG*.

ὀρνᾶτος: see κάτιλλος ὀρνᾶτος.

rare	ὀρνεύω 'arm', 'outfit', from *ōrnō* 'prepare' + -εύω: Ps.-John Chrysostom, *Visio Danielis* p. 36.30 Vassiliev (V AD?). Hofmann (1989: 298–9), *LBG* (*s.v.* ὀρνεύομαι), Triandaphyllidis (1909: 122), Lampe (1961).
rare	ὀρνιθοπούλ(λ)(ι)ον 'young fowl', from ὄρνις 'bird', 'chicken' + *pullus* 'young bird' via πουλλίον: Hieroph. *Nut.* 4.3 (IV–VI AD); Byzantine texts. Filos (2010: 244, 250), Diethart (1999: 181), Daris (1991a: 78), Cavenaile (1952: 199), *LBG*, Kriaras (1968–), LSJ suppl.
not Latin?	ὀροβάγχη, ὀροβάκχη, a plant, perhaps from *bāca/bacca* 'fruit of a tree or shrub', but attested very early for Latin: e.g. Theophrastus, *Historia plantarum* 8.8.4 (IV/III BC). Hofmann (1989: 299), *LBG*, LSJ.
not Latin	ὀρούα, ὀρύα 'sausage', 'political club', probably from an Italic language. Willi (2008: 32), García Domingo (1983: 253), Hofmann (1989: 299), Immisch (1885: 314), LSJ (*s.v.* ὀρύα). ·

ὄρρεον: see ὄρριον.

rare	ὀρρεοπραιποσιτία 'office of the granary supervisor', from *horreum* 'granary' (via ὄρριον?) + *praepositus* 'person in charge' via πραιπόσιτος + -ία: inscription *IG* VII.24.7 (V AD). Hofmann (1989: 300 *s.v.* ὄρρεον), *TLL* (*s.v.* ὀρρεοπραιποσιτία), LSJ. See §8.1.7 n. 34.
non-existent	ὀρριάνος, supposedly from unattested *horriānus: I can find no examples. Hofmann (1989: 300), Viscidi (1944: 21).
Direct? loan **III AD – ?**	ὀρ(ρ)ιάριος (-ου, ὁ) 'granary supervisor', from *horreārius* 'one who manages a warehouse' (or its variant (*h*)*orriārius*, *TLL s.v. horreārius* 2975.46–7), or *horreum* via ὄρριον + -άριος. Documents: *P.Coll.Youtie* II.74.6 (III AD). Inscriptions: *AE* 2016 no. 1394.b5 (III AD); Ormerod and Robinson 1914: 28 no. 37.2. Post-antique: some survival. *LBG* (*s.v.* ὀριάριος), Kriaras (1968–). Notes: Daris (1991a: 78), Hofmann (1989: 300), LSJ (*s.v.* ὀριάριος). See §4.2.4.1 n. 50, §10.2.1, §10.2.2 N.

Direct loan
II AD – modern

ὄρ(ρ)ιον, ὠρεῖον, ὤρριον, ὄρρεον (-ου, τό) 'granary', from *horreum* 'granary'.
Documents: e.g. O.Dios. inv. 480.4 = Cuvigny 2010b: 38 (II AD); *P.Coll. Youtie* II.74.7 (III AD); *P.Oxy.* 2408.9 (IV AD); *SB* 12252.3 (V AD); *BGU* III.838.26 (VI AD).
Inscriptions: e.g. *SEG* IV.106.4 (II AD); *IGLS* II.306.3 (IV AD); *IG* VII.24.11 (V AD); *IGLS* V.2081.3 (VI AD).
Literature: e.g. *Martyrium Pauli* 1 = Lipsius 1891: 104.4 (II AD); Socr. 7.39 (IV/V AD); Hesych. as gloss π 761, as lemma ο 1089 (V/VI AD); Malal. 3.8 (VI AD); Antec. 2.1.45 (VI AD).
Post-antique: numerous. Daris (1991a: 79), *LBG* (*s.v.* ὄριον 2), Triandaphyllidis (1909: 124). Modern dialectal ὀρρειός 'cellar', ρεῖον 'granary' etc.: Andriotis (1974: 418, 614), Kahane and Kahane (1972–6: 534, 1982: 135).
Notes: Meinersmann (1927: 41) sees confusion with ὅριον 'border' in the spelling with one ρ. May form derivatives ὀρριάριος, ὀρρεοπραιποσιτία. Daris (1991a: 79), Hofmann (1989: 299–300), Zilliacus (1935a: 190–1), Immisch (1885: 316), Lampe (1961 *s.v.* ὄριον), LSJ (*s.vv.* ὄρριον, ὠρεῖον). See §4.2.4.1 n. 54, §9.5.4 n. 42, §10.2.1, §10.2.2 J.

foreign

ὀρτάρι transliterating inf. of *hortor* 'urge': Plut. *Mor.* 275f (I/II AD). Sophocles (1887).

ὀρτηνάριος, ὀρτινάριος: see ὀρδινάριος 1.

ὀρτινᾶτος: see ὀρδινᾶτος.

ὀρύα: see ὀρούα.

not Latin?

ὀρχηστοπαλάριος, ὀρχιστοπαλάριος 'skilled in a combination of dancing and wrestling' on late antique inscription *I.Ephesos* 2949.2.2 may be from *orchēstopalārius* 'skilled in a combination of dancing and wrestling' (*TLL*), or *vice versa*. Hofmann (1989: 300), *TLL* (*s.vv.* orchēstopala, orchēstopalārius), LSJ, LSJ suppl.

ὀσπήτιον: see ὀσπίτιον.

rare

ὄσπις 'lodger', from *hospes* 'guest': papyri *P.Abinn.* 22.9 etc. (IV AD); *P.Oxy.* 3860.10 etc. (IV AD); Byzantine legal texts. Menci (2000: 286), Daris (1991a: 79), *LBG*, LSJ suppl.

Direct loan
IV AD – modern

ὀσπίτιον, ὀσπήτιον (-ου, τό) 'house', 'poorhouse', 'lodging', from *hospitium* 'house' (*OLD s.v.* 3c).
Documents: *P.Lips.* I.40.iii.18 (IV AD); *P.Daris* 22.19 (VI AD).
Inscriptions: *IG* II/III².V.13352.1 (V AD).
Literature: e.g. Pall. *H.Laus.* 6.8 (IV/V AD); *ACO* II.I.I p. 176.3 (V AD); Malal. 13.38 (VI AD); as gloss in scholia to *Od.* 2.59d, 4.744c, etc.
Post-antique: common, forming derivatives ὀσπητικός 'of the house', ὀσπιτοτόπιον 'land attached to house', etc. *LBG*, Zervan (2019: 124–5), Kriaras (1968–), Triandaphyllidis (1909: 123 *s.v.* σπίτι). Lampe (1961 *s.v.* σπίτι). Modern σπίτι 'house' and derivatives: Babiniotis (2002), Andriotis (1967), Meyer (1895: 63).
Notes: Carnoy (1950), Husson (1983: 217–18), Daris (1991a: 79, commentary to *P.Daris* 22.19), Hofmann (1989: 300–1), Meinersmann (1927: 41), Sophocles (1887), Lampe (1961), LSJ suppl. See §4.2.4.1 n. 54, §8.2.3, §10.1, §10.2.1, §10.2.2 J.

foreign
: ὀσσίφραγος transliterating *ossifragus*, a bird of prey: Dsc. 2.53.1 etc. (I AD). Sophocles (1887).

rare
: ὀστιάριον 'vestibule', 'porter's lodge', from the neuter of *ōstiārius* 'of doors' (*TLL*; probably not from *ōstiārium* 'tax on doors'): Ps.-Basil Caesariensis, *PG* XXXI.1312c (IV AD?). Sophocles (1887), Lampe (1961 *s.v.* ὀστιάριος).

Direct loan
IV AD – Byz.
: ὀστιάριος, ὠστιάριος (-ου, ὁ) 'door-keeper', from *ōstiārius* 'door-keeper'.
  Documents: *Stud.Pal.* XX.85.v.ii.24 (IV AD); *P.Lond.* V.1711.69 etc. (VI AD); *P.Oxy.* 2046.41 etc. (VI AD); *PSI* VIII.956.37 (VI AD); *BGU* II.672.7 etc. (VI AD). On *P.Flor.* I.71.518 (= *P.Herm.Landl.* 2.518) the word is probably ἀστιάριος, and on *BGU* II.672 the word begins with ο-, so ἀστιάριος is probably not attested as a variant spelling of this term, *pace* LSJ suppl.
  Inscriptions: probably *I.Lipára* 789.3 (V AD); *SEG* IX.356.32 (VI AD).
  Literature: *Coll.Herm.* ME 6e (II–IV AD); Dor.Poet. *Visio* 131 (III/IV AD); Callin. *V.Hypat.* 42.5 etc. (V AD); *ACO* III p. 176.8 (VI AD); Dan.Sket. *Eu.* 156 (VI AD); scholion to Ar. *Pl.* 330, marked.
  Post-antique: numerous. *LBG* (*s.v.* ὠστιάριος), Kriaras (1968–), Triandaphyllidis (1909: 126), Sophocles (1887 *s.v.* ὀστιάριος), Zilliacus (1935a: 230–1, 1937: 331), Zervan (2019: 146–7 *s.v.* πρωτοοστιάριος).
  Notes: Daris (1991a: 79), Hofmann (1989: 301), Meinersmann (1927: 41), Lampe (1961), LSJ suppl. See §4.2.4.1 n. 50, §10.2.1, §10.2.2 N.

not Latin
: ὀστρῖνος 'purple' has been argued by Wessely (1902: 140), Meinersmann (1927: 41), and Hofmann (1989: 301) to be from *ostrīnus* 'purple' when it occurs on Roman-period papyri: *P.Oxy.* 109.5 (III/IV AD); *SB* 12594.17 (III AD); perhaps *SB* 14178.1.16 (II AD). But it also occurs on *BGU* VI.1300.16 (III/II BC), where a Latin loan is less likely, so it probably has an internal Greek derivation: LSJ (*s.v.* ὀστρέϊνος II).

Direct loan
I AD – modern
: οὐά, οὐᾶ, an exclamation, from *vāh*, an exclamation.
  Literature: NT Mark 15:29 (I AD); Epict. *Diss.* 3.23.24 etc. (I/II AD); Irenaeus, *Adversus haereses* 1.13.2 Harvey (II AD); *V.Aesopi* G 8 etc. (II AD?); Dio Cassius 63.20.5 (II/III AD); Epiph. *Pan.* II.34.15 etc. (IV AD); John Chrysostom, *PG* XLVIII.1035.36 (IV/V AD); with *vah* in Gloss. Ps.-Cyril. 388.50; also numerous biblical quotations.
  Post-antique: survives chiefly as a marked term, esp. in discussions of the biblical passage. Kriaras (1968–). Modern dialectal βουά: Andriotis (1974: 421).
  Notes: Hofmann (1989: 301), LSJ. See §9.3 n. 21, §10.2.1, §10.2.2 O, §10.3.1.

name
: οὐάδα, βάδα transliterating pl. of *vadum* 'shallow water': part of a place name, Strabo 4.6.1 (I BC/AD). Zilliacus (1935: 238–9), Sophocles (1887).

not Latin
: οὐαί 'woe!', sometimes used to represent *vae* 'alas!': not etymologically Latin. Lowe (1967), Hilhorst (1976: 179–82), *DÉLG*, Beekes (2010), Blass *et al.* (1979: §5 n. 7), LSJ.

Direct loan
II AD – Byz.
: Οὐαλεντινιανοί, Οὐαλεντῖνοι, Οὐαλεντιανοί, Βαλεντινιανοί (-ῶν, οἱ) 'Valentinians' (a Christian sect), from *Valentīniānī* 'Valentinians' (L&S).
  Literature: e.g. Justin Martyr, *Dialogus cum Tryphone* 35.6 Goodspeed (II AD); Clemens Alexandrinus, *Excerpta ex Theodoto* 1.24.1 Sagnard (II/III AD); Eus. *HE* 4.22.5 (IV AD); Nil. 1.234.1 (V AD); Leontius of Jerusalem, *Testmonia sanctorum* p. 54.24 Gray (VI AD).

Post-antique: survives. *LBG*.

Notes: gen. pl. Βαλεντινιανηνσιουμ on inscription *IGChr.Occidentis* 130.3 may also be relevant. Sophocles (1887 *s.vv.* Οὐαλεντινιανοί, Οὐαλεντῖνος). See §4.2.4.1 n. 51, §6.4, §10.2.1, §10.2.2 N, §12.2.2.

οὐαλῆρε: see βαλῆρε.

non-existent?	**οὐαλλάριος** 'of a rampart', from (*corōna*) *vallāris* 'garland awarded to the first soldier to cross the wall surrounding an enemy camp': perhaps inscription *TAM* II.563.12 (I AD). Hofmann (1989: 301), Cameron (1931: 261, with derivation from unattested *vallārius).
rare	**οὐάρα**, an implement usable with a stone column, from *vāra* 'forked pole': *O.Claud.* IV.873.2 (II AD). Cuvigny (2021).
non-existent?	**οὐαστής** transliterating *ovātiō* 'ovation' (a minor triumph): perhaps DH *AR* 5.47.2, 5.47.3, 8.67.10 (I BC), but it is an emendation for the manuscripts' εὐάστης. Mason (1974: 8, 72), Hofmann (1989: 292–3 *s.v.* ὀβατίων), LSJ (*s.vv.* οὐαστὴς θρίαμβος, εὐάστης II). Cf. ὄουαν.
foreign	**οὐᾶτις** (in pl. οὐάτεις) transliterating *vātēs* 'prophet': Strabo 4.4.4 (I BC/AD). Sophocles (1887).
Direct loan **III BC – modern**	**οὐγγία, οὐγκία, οὐνκία, ὀγκία, ὀνκία, γουγκία, ὠνκία, ὠκία** (-ας, ἡ) 'ounce', 'one twelfth' (esp. of an inheritance, since in Roman law a complete inheritance was an *as* and shares in it were measured in twelfths), from *uncia* 'ounce', 'one twelfth'.

Documents: common, e.g. *P.Oxy.* 2679.8 (II AD); *P.Oxy.* 1449.49 (III AD); *P.Lond.* V.1823.7 (IV AD); *P.Gen.* IV.186.29 (V AD); *P.Oxy.* 3204.23 (VI AD).

Inscriptions: common, e.g. *SEG* XLV.1423, two bronze weights from Sicily (V/IV BC); *Agora* XXI.Hb.3, graffito on amphora (III BC); probably *Agora* X.LW.70, lead weight (III BC); *Agora* XXI.He.7, dipinto on amphora (I AD); *SEG* IX.176.15 etc. (II AD); *I.Arykanda* 122.9 (III AD); *Agora* XXI.Hb.22, dipinto on amphora (IV AD); *IGPannonia* p. 66 (V AD); *SEG* LI.1392.4 (VI AD).

Literature: very common, e.g. Epicharmus frag. 138 Kassel–Austin (V BC); Sophron frag. 148 Kassel–Austin (V BC); Aristotle frag. 510 Rose, marked as Sicilian (IV BC); Dsc. 1.10.2 (I AD); Phrynichus, *Praeparatio sophistica* frag. 327* de Borries (II AD); Galen VI.451.2 Kühn (II AD); Jul.Afric. *Cest.* 4.1.90 (II/III AD); Zosimus alch., Berthelot and Ruelle 1888: 181.1 (III/IV AD); Orib. *Col.* 5.25.36 (IV AD); Soz. 6.29.5 (V AD); Hesych. often as part of glosses, e.g. δ 1486, 2352 (V/VI AD); Cyr.S. *Vit.Sab.* 107.25 (VI AD); Antec. 2.14.5 etc., but in Latin script 2.14.5 *uncia* (VI AD).

Post-antique: common. *LBG* (*s.v.* ὀγγία), Zervan (2019: 125–6), Kriaras (1968–), Triandaphyllidis (1909: 125). Modern οὐγκιά, οὐγγιά 'ounce' etc.: Babiniotis (2002), Andriotis (1967, 1974: 400), Meyer (1895: 50).

Notes: entered Greek very early, via Sicily, but was probably not Latinate until III BC (§8.1.2); for comparison with λίτρα see *s.v.* λίτρα 1. Forms derivatives οὐγκιασμός, οὐγκιαρήσιον, and see §4.6.2 Figure 1. Willi (2008: 32),

Simkin (2012: 174), Cassio (2012: 255–6), Lejeune (1993: 2–3), Bellocchi (2016: 327), Drew-Bear (1972: 228), Avotins (1992 *s.v.* οὐγκία), Daris (1991a: 79), Hofmann (1989: 301–2), Zilliacus (1935a: 212–13, 1937: 331), Meinersmann (1927: 41–2), Triantaphyllides (1892: 268), Immisch (1885: 344), *DÉLG*, Frisk (1954–72: III.159), Beekes (2010), Lampe (1961 *s.v.* ὀγκία), LSJ, LSJ suppl. See §4.2.3.1, §4.3.2 n. 75, §4.6.1, **§7.1.1** passage 18, §8.1.1 n. 3, **§8.1.2**, §8.2.1, §8.2.3 n. 51, §10.2.1, §10.2.2 E.

οὐγγιασμός: see οὐγκιασμός.

οὐγκία: see οὐγγία.

non-existent | **οὐγκιαῖος** 'of one twelfth', from *ūncia* 'one twelfth' via οὐγγία or from *unciālis* 'of one twelfth': superseded reading for χοινικιαῖος on inscription *IG* II/ III².1.1366.23 (I AD). Hofmann (1989: 302 twice, independently and *s.v.* οὐγκία), *DÉLG* (*s.v.* οὐγγία), LSJ (*s.v.* οὐγγία).

rare | **οὐγκιαρήσιον, ὀγκιαρήσιον**, perhaps the name of a coin, from *ūncia* 'one twelfth' via οὐγγία + an -αρήσιον suffix resegmented from μιλιαρήσιον (*q.v.*): papyrus *P.Iand.* VI.103.14 (VI AD). Daris (1991a: 79), LSJ suppl. (*s.v.* ὀγκιαρήσιον).

Deriv. of loan IV AD – Byz. | **οὐγκιασμός, οὐγγιασμός** (-οῦ, ὁ) 'measurement in twelfths', 'assignment of shares in an inheritance', from *ūncia* 'one twelfth' via οὐγγία + -σμός.
Literature: Zosimus alch., Berthelot and Ruelle 1888: 164.2 etc. (III/IV AD); Just. *Nov.* 107.1 (VI AD); Barsanuph.Jo. I ep. 166.6n (VI AD); Ath.Schol. 9.8.1 (VI AD); Antec. 2.14.6 etc. (VI AD); Her.Mech. *Mens.* 23.1 etc.
Post-antique: survives. Kriaras (1968–).
Notes: Avotins (1992), Hofmann (1989: 302 *s.v.* οὐγκία), Zilliacus (1935a: 212–13), *DÉLG* (*s.v.* οὐγγία), LSJ (*s.v.* οὐγγία), LSJ suppl. See §4.6.1, §10.2.2 E.

not ancient? | **οὐγκινᾶτος** 'hooked', from *uncīnātus* 'furnished with hooks': probably no ancient examples. Daris (1991a: 79), *LBG*.

non-existent | **οὐγκίον** is cited by Hofmann (1989: 302 *s.v.* οὐγκία) as from *ūncia* 'one twelfth' via οὐγγία on the basis of papyrus *P.Lond.* I.113(1).83 (VI AD), where it is probably a misspelling of gen. pl. οὐγκίων. Cavenaile's claim (1952: 197) that diminutive οὔγκιον occurs in *P.Harr.* I.94.3 etc. is wrong: all those occurrences are abbreviated.

rare | **οὐδών** 'felt shoe', from or otherwise related to *ūdō* 'felt slipper': Pollux 10.50 (II AD). Hofmann (1989: 302–3), *DÉLG*, Beekes (2010, deriving the Latin from the Greek), LSJ, LSJ suppl. See §4.6.1.

Deriv.? of loan IV–VI AD | **οὐδωνάριον, ὀδωνάριον** (-ου, τό) 'sock', 'felt shoe', from *ūdō* 'felt slipper' (via οὐδών?) + -άριον.
Documents: *P.Ryl.* IV.627.35 (IV AD); *P.Münch.* III.1.142.15 (VI AD).
Literature: *Anonymus Bobiensis* as gloss p. 33.11 De Nonno (V AD?); with *udo* in Gloss. Ps.-Cyril. 389.24.
Notes: Daris (1991a: 77), Hofmann (1989: 302 *s.v.* οὐδών), *DÉLG* (*s.v.* οὐδών), Beekes (2010 *s.v.* οὐδών, with non-Latin etymology), *LBG* (*s.v.* ὀδωνάριον), LSJ (*s.v.* οὐδών). See §4.3.2, §4.6.1, §6.3, §10.2.2 H.

rare	**οὐδώνιον** 'felt shoe', probably from *ūdō* 'felt slipper' (via οὐδών?) + -ιον: Edict. Diocl. 7.47 (IV AD). Hofmann (1989: 302 *s.v.* οὐδών), *DÉLG* (*s.v.* οὐδών), Beekes (2010 *s.v.* οὐδών, with non-Latin etymology), LSJ (*s.v.* οὐδών), LSJ suppl.
	οὐεικάριος: see βικάριος.
	οὐεΐκουλον: see βεΐκουλον.
rare	**οὐεῖλλος**, from *vīlis* 'cheap': inscription *SEG* VII.428 (III AD); perhaps οὐειλις in *P.Warr.* 15.29 (II AD). Hofmann (1989: 303), LSJ suppl.
name	**Οὐέλια**, a personal name. Hofmann (1989: 303).
	οὐένδ(): see οὐνδίκιος.
	οὐενετιανός: see βενετιανός.
rare	**οὐενέτιος** 'blue' (in the sense of the blue circus faction), from *venetus* 'blue' + -ιος: Dio Cassius 61.6.3, 65.5.1, 77.10.2 (II/III AD), distinguishing it from Οὐένετος 'Venetian'. Hofmann (1989: 304 *s.v.* οὐένετος), LSJ (*s.v.* οὐένετος).
	οὐένετος: see βένετος.
	οὐεξιλ(λ)ατίων: see βηξιλλατίων.
	οὐερεδάριος, οὐεριδάριος: see βερεδάριος.
	οὐέρνακλος: see βέρνακλος.
	οὐέρνα(ς): see βέρνας.
rare	**οὐέρτραγος** 'greyhound', from *vertragus* 'greyhound' (originally Celtic): Arrian, *Cynegetica* 3.6 (I/II AD). Hofmann (1989: 304), LSJ suppl.
	οὐεσσιγατ-: see οὐεστιγατ-.
	οὐεστάριον: see βεστάριον.
rare	**οὐεστιγατίων, οὐεσσιγατείων** 'hunting trip', from *vestīgātiō* 'tracking down': ostraca *O.Krok.* I.76.3 (II AD); probably *O.Amst.* 8.63 = *SB* 14180.63 (II AD). Cuvigny (2006: 330), Rea (1990), Daris (1991a: 80).
rare	**οὐεστιγάτου, οὐεσσιγάτου** 'on patrol', apparently from *vestīgātu(s)*, pf. part. of *vestīgō* 'search out': ostraca *O.Krok.* I.74.6, perhaps 75.2 (both II AD). See commentary *ad loc.*
rare	**οὐεστιγάτωρ, οὐεστικάτωρ**, perhaps **οὐεσσιγάτωρ** 'tracker', from *vestīgātor* 'tracker': documents *SB* 9272.7 (I/II AD); perhaps *O.Krok.* I.75.2 (II AD); *SB* 15516 (III AD). Rea (1990: 126), Daris (1991a: 80), *LBG*.
Direct loan I AD – modern	**οὐετ(ε)ρανός, βετ(ε)ρανός, οὐιτρανός, ὀατρανός, οὐτρανός, βατρανός, ἐτρανός, μετρανός** (-ή, -όν) 'veteran', masc. subst. 'a veteran', from *veterānus* 'veteran'. Documents, masc. subst.: common, e.g. *P.Lond.* II.175a.17 (I AD?); *BGU* I.4.3 (II AD); *P.Hamb.* I.41.7 (III AD); *P.Abinn.* 75.35 (IV AD); *P.Rain.Cent.* 91.12 (V AD); *P.Flor.* III.297.99 (VI AD). Adj.: e.g. *P.Gen.* II.1.135.2 (II AD); *P.Grenf.* II.51.5 (II AD); *P.Mich.* VI.428.3 etc. (II AD); *Rom.Mil.Rec.* 76.i.1 etc. (II AD).

Inscriptions, masc. subst.: common, e.g. *IG* x.ii.ii.251.1 (I AD); *I.Ano Maked.*
11.2 (II AD); *IGUR* ii.410.3 (III AD); *IGLS* ii.523.1 (IV AD); *SEG* li.806.4
(IV/V AD).   Adj.: probably Marek 1993: 168, Appendix 5 no. 40.A4;
perhaps others.

Literature, masc. subst. only: Epiph. *Pan.* iii.13.21 (IV AD); Athanasius, *PG*
xxvi.1265a (IV AD); Thdt. *Er.* 102.18 (V AD); Lyd. *Mag.* p. 70.24 etc.
(VI AD); Antec. in Latin script 2.10.9 *veteranon* etc. (VI AD).

Post-antique: common as subst. *LBG* (*s.v.* βετερανός). Modern βετεράνος
'veteran': Babiniotis (2002), Andriotis (1967).

Notes: in papyri of all periods the spelling in οὐ- is normal, with βετ- only in
SB 6304.7 (II AD, Latin in Greek script) and βατ- only in *BGU* ii.380.5
(III AD); in inscriptions βετ- is common, and there are many different
spelling variants (including υετρανός with Latin first letter, *Studia Pontica*
iii.169.4). Forms derivatives οὐετρανικός, συνουετρανός. Binder (2000: 200–
2), Freyburger-Galland (1997: 191), Daris (1991a: 80–1), Mason (1974: 5,
6, 8, 9, 72), Hofmann (1989: 304–5), Viscidi (1944: 16), Zilliacus (1935a:
214–15, 238–9), Meinersmann (1927: 42), Lampe (1961 *s.vv.* βετερᾶνος,
οὐέτρανος), LSJ, LSJ suppl. See §4.1.1, §4.2.2, §4.6.2, §5.2.2, §7.1.1 passage
22, §10.2.1, §10.2.2 C, §12.2.1.

foreign   **οὐέτερεμ μεμορίαμ** transliterating acc. of *vetus memoria* 'ancient memory': Plut.
Numa 13.7 (I/II AD). Sophocles (1887 *s.v.* οὐέτους). See §7.3; cf. βέτερες.

non-existent   **οὐετρανίζω** 'retire from duty', from *veterānus* 'veteran' via οὐετερανός + -ίζω:
superseded reading of Epiphanius. Lampe (1961).

rare   **οὐετρανικός, οὐιτρανικός** 'man of veteran status', from *veterānus* 'veteran' via
οὐετερανός + -ικός: inscriptions *I.Syria PAES* 765¹³.5 etc. (III AD); *LBW* 2227.
Mason (1974: 6, 72), LSJ suppl.

οὐετρανός: see οὐετερανός.

not ancient?   **οὐετράριος, οὐιτράριος** 'glass-worker', from *vitrārius*, a variant of *vitreārius* 'glass-
worker': inscription *I.Tyr* 117; perhaps three others that read ἰτράριος
(*MAMA* iii.549b.2, 598.2; *I.Tyr* 33.B2), but that is probably a different word
(see *s.v.*). *I.Tyr* p. 155, LSJ suppl.

οὐηλάριον: see βηλάριον.

rare   **οὐηλάριος**, probably from *vēlārius* 'curtain-maker': documents *P.Erl.* 54.11
(IV AD); perhaps *O.Did.* 146.2, perhaps 147.2 (both I AD). Daris (1991a:
81), Hofmann (1989: 305).

foreign   **οὐηλᾶτος** transliterating *vēlātus* 'reserve soldier': inscriptions *I.Ephesos* 1544.10,
1545.4 (both I/II AD). Hofmann (1989: 305).

οὐηλόθυρον: see βηλόθυρον.

οὐῆλον: see βῆλον.

οὐηνάτωρ: see βηνάτωρ.

οὐηξιλλάριος: see βηξιλλάριος.

οὐηξιλ(λ)ατίων: see βηξιλλατίων.

non-existent?	**οὐηξίλλιφερ, οὐηξίλλιφαρ** 'standard-bearer', from *vexillifer* 'standard-bearing' (L&S): perhaps inscription *SEG* XXXVIII.1861a; perhaps ostracon *O.Bodl.* II.1665.2 (II AD). Daris (1991a: 81).
	οὐήξιλλον: see βήξιλλον.
foreign	**οὐιάρουμ** transliterating gen. pl. of *via* 'road': as part of title κουαττόρουιρ οὐιάρουμ κουρανδάρουμ, inscription *SEG* XVII.571.4 (I/II AD). Drew-Bear (1972: 212), Mason (1974: 7, 63 *s.v.* κουαττόρουιρ). Cf. βία.
	οὐιατικόν: see βιατικόν.
	οὐιάτωρ: see βιάτωρ.
	οὐίγλης: see βίγλης.
rare	**οὐιγλίδιον, οὐιγκλίδιον** on ostracon *O.Amst.* 31.7 (II AD) is suggested by the editor as from *vigil* 'watchman'; Cervenka-Ehrenstrasser and Diethart (1997, cf. Diethart 1998: 174) more convincingly suggest *vinculum/vinclum* 'chain' + -ίδιον, meaning 'a little string'.
Direct loan **II–III AD**	**οὐίγουλ, βίγουλ, οὐίγουλος, βιγλός** (-?, ὁ) 'watchman', from *vigil* 'watchman'. Documents: *P.Stras.* V.459.3 (III AD); *P.Oxy.* 2231.15, 3365.13 (both III AD); *P.Mich.* XI.620.2 etc. (III AD). Inscriptions: *I.Ephesos* 651.13 (II AD); *IGBulg.* III.II.1570.5 (III AD); *IGR* I.142.3 (III AD). Notes: Daris (1991a: 81), Mason (1974: 5, 9, 72), Hofmann (1989: 306), LSJ suppl. See §4.2.5, §10.2.1, §10.2.2 N; cf. βίγλα, βιγλεύω, βίγλης, βιγλίον.
	οὐιδίκτα: see βινδίκτα.
	οὐικάριος: see βικάριος.
	οὐικεννάλια: see βικεννάλια.
	οὐικήσιμον: see βικήσιμον.
	οὐῖκος: see βῖκος.
	οὐῖλον: see βῆλον.
rare	**οὐινδικᾶτος, οὐινδικτᾶτος, ὀεντικᾶτος** 'freedman emancipated by *vindicta*', from *vindicātus*, pf. part. of *vindicō* 'assert as free': papyri *SB* 14710.3.6 (III AD); perhaps *BGU* I.344.15 (II/III AD); perhaps *P.Oxy.* 2937.2.14 (III AD). Οὐίνδικτος in *Suda* ο 836 as lemma. Olsson (1926: 112), Daris (1991a: 82), Hofmann (1989: 293), Meinersmann (1927: 40, 43), *LBG* (*s.v.* οὐίνδικτος).
	οὐινδίκτα: see βινδίκτα.
rare	**οὐινδικτάριος** 'freedman emancipated by *vindicta*', apparently from unattested **vindictārius*: inscriptions Lanckoroński 1890: 176 no. 59.17, 177 no. 60.25, perhaps 177 no. 61.5. Mason (1974: 73), Hofmann (1989: 307), LSJ suppl.
	οὐιξιλλάριος: see βηξιλλάριος.
	οὐιξιλ(λ)ατίων: see βηξιλλατίων.
	οὐιξίλλον: see βήξιλλον.

ουἱόκουρος: see βιόκουρος.

foreign　ουἱρτοῦτις transliterating gen. sing. of *virtūs* 'excellence': Plut. *Mor.* 322c (I/II AD). Sophocles (1887). See §7.2.1.

foreign　ουἱτίκλη transliterating *vīticula* 'little vine': Dsc. *Eup.* 2.65.1 (I AD). Binder (2000: 157).

not Latin　Οὐιτουλία 'Italy' is said by DH *AR* 1.35.3 (I BC, but perhaps following Hellanicus, no. 4 frag. 111 Jacoby, V BC) to be derived from οὐΐτουλος from *vitulus* 'calf'; the word and Hellanicus' theory are mentioned by LSJ (*s.v.* οὐΐτουλος) in the form Οὐιταλία, on which basis Hofmann (1989: 307) considered Οὐιταλία a Latin loan, suggesting derivation from unattested *Vitalia*. The etymology is probably fanciful. Poccetti (2012: 90–1).

foreign　οὐΐτουλος, βίτουλος transliterating *vitulus* 'calf': DH *AR* 1.35.2 (I BC, but perhaps following Hellanicus, no. 4 frag. 111 Jacoby, V BC); occasional Byzantine texts. Willi (2008: 34) takes this as evidence of a Sicilian term οὐΐτουλος 'calf', but DH specifies that the users of this term were not Greek speakers. Hofmann (1989: 307), Meyer (1895: 14 *s.v.* βετοῦλι), LSJ.

ουἱτρανικός: see οὐετρανικός.

ουἱτρανός: see οὐετερανός.

ουἱτράριος: see οὐετράριος.

not ancient　οὔλτιμος 'last', from *ultimus* 'last': cited as ancient by Zilliacus (1935a: 238–9), but all examples are Byzantine. *LBG*.

foreign　οὖνδε 'whence', from *unde* 'whence': Antec. in Latin script as part of phrases, e.g. 3.9.3 *unde* (VI AD); later in Greek script.

rare　οὐνδίκιος, ἀουνδίκιος, and/or ὁ(ο)υινδίκιος, meaning uncertain, apparently related to *vindicō* 'claim': papyri, each with a different spelling: ἀουνδικίων *P.Oxy.* 3205.14 etc. (III/IV AD); ὀουινδικίων *P.Oslo* III.113.11 (IV AD); οὐεντι[*SB* 9883.4 (IV AD); ὀουενδι() *P.Ryl.* IV.655v.4 (IV AD); ὀβενδικ() *P.Ryl.* IV.655v.13 (IV AD); οὐένδ() or ὀουένδ() *P.Oxy.* 1660r.8 (IV AD); οβο() *P.Freer* 1+2.300 etc. (VI AD). The abbreviated forms are often restored as other words: ὀουενδι(κάτης) *P.Ryl.* IV.655v.4, ὀβενδικ(άτης) *P.Ryl.* IV.655v.13, οὐένδ(ιτον) *P.Oxy.* 1660r.8, ὀβο(υεντίονος) *P.Freer* 1+2.300 etc. Daris (1991a: 77) takes the base form to be ὀουινδίκιος, while Cervenka-Ehrenstrasser (1996: 87) prefers οὐνδίκιος and Binder (2000: 126) οὐινδίκτος; LSJ suppl. includes only ἀουνδίκιος. Since many contexts are fragmentary, these examples need not all be of the same word, though Daris groups them all together: see editors *ad locc.* Note in particular MacCoull (1994) arguing for a form of *obventio* in *P.Freer*, and *P.Oxy.* 1660r, where the editor tentatively restores οὐένδ(ιτον) and thinks that 'some form of the passive of *vendo* is meant'; cf. Meinersmann (1927: 42).

foreign　*ūniversitās* 'corporate body': Antec. 2.1.6 *universitatis* etc. (VI AD).

οὐνκία: see οὐγγία.

rare	οὐρβανικιανός 'of the city', 'garrison', from *urbāniciānus* 'garrisoned in the city of Rome' (L&S): inscription *I.Apameia Pylai* 8.8 (III AD); perhaps *IGBulg.* III. II.1570.6 (III AD). Hofmann (1989: 307), LSJ suppl.
rare	οὐρβανός, ὀρβανός 'of the city' (usually as part of titles and other phrases), from *urbānus* 'of the city': inscriptions Bosch 1967: 205 no. 158.16 (II AD); *I.Byzantion* S.31.2 (II AD); *SEG* XXXIX.597. Literature: Lyd. *Mag.* p. 60.4 etc., marked (VI AD); Stephanus of Byzantium α 200, marked (VI AD); Antec. 1.20.pr., marked, and in Latin script 1.2.7 *urbano* etc. (VI AD); Byzantine texts. Binder (2000: 149), Mason (1974: 73), Hofmann (1989: 297, 307), Zilliacus (1935a: 212–13), *LBG*, LSJ, LSJ suppl.
foreign	οὖρβς 'city', from *urbs* 'city': Antec. in Latin script 1.2.7 *urbs* (VI AD); later in Greek script.
rare	οὔρνα, a weight, from *urna* 'urn': Jul.Afric. *Cest.* 4.1.54 (II/III AD); Ps.-Galen, *De ponderibus* frag. 64.10 = Hultsch 1864: 240.17 etc.; Her.Mech. *Geom.* 23.63; Byzantine texts. Binder (2000: 142), Hofmann (1989: 307), *LBG*.
rare	οὖρος 'wild ox', from *ūrus* 'wild ox': *Anthologia Graeca* 6.332.3 (II AD); Ps.-Epiph. *PG* XLIII.520c. Hofmann (1989: 307), Lampe (1961), LSJ (*s.v.* οὖρος D).
foreign	οὖσος 'use', from *ūsus, -ūs* 'use': Antec. in Latin script 2.5.1 *uson* etc. (VI AD); later in Greek script. Hofmann (1989: 448 *s.v. usos*), Zilliacus (1935a: 214–15), *LBG*. See §9.5.6 n. 68.
foreign	οὐσουάριος 'person with rights of use', from *ūsuārius* 'one who has the right to use something owned by another': Antec. in Latin script 2.5.1 *usuario* (VI AD); later in Greek script. Zilliacus (1935a: 212–13), *LBG*. See §9.5.6 n. 68.
foreign	οὐσουκαπιτεύω 'acquire ownership by virtue of uninterrupted possession' is formed from *ūsūcapiō* 'acquire ownership by virtue of uninterrupted possession' by adding -εύω not to pf. part. *ūsūcaptus* or pres. stem *ūsūcapi-*, but to a *ūsūcapit* that could be either the pres. indicative active third person singular or the stem of an imaginary pf. part. **ūsūcapitus* (perhaps created on the analogy of *trāditus* from *trādō*, which became τραδιτεύω in Greek). *Schol.Sinai.* in Latin script 44, abbreviated to *u.c.* (V/VI AD); Antec. in Latin script 2.6.pr. *usucapiteuesθai* etc. (VI AD); later in Greek script. Zilliacus (1935a: 212–13), *LBG*. See §7.1.2, §7.1.3, §9.5.6 nn. 56 and 68.
foreign	οὐσουκαπίων 'ownership arising from uninterrupted possession', from *ūsūcapiō* 'acquisition of ownership by virtue of uninterrupted possession': Antec. in Latin script 2.6.1 *usucapiona* etc. (VI AD); later in Greek script. Zilliacus (1935a: 212–13), *LBG*. See §9.5.6 n. 68.
Direct loan (with univerbation?) **VI AD – Byz.**	οὐσούφρουκτος, οὐσόφροκτος (-ου, ὁ) 'usufruct' (the right to use and derive profit from property belonging to another person), from *ūsus frūctus* 'usufruct' (perhaps univerbated already in late Latin: *DMLBS s.v. usufructus*, *OED s.v.* 'usufruct'). Documents: *P.Lond.* III.1044.13 etc. (VI AD); *P.Cair.Masp.* 67151.72 in Latin script, *ousufructu* (VI AD). But *P.Ital.* 1.16.38 (VI AD?) is Latin in Greek script.

Literature: Just. *Nov.* 7.pr. etc., but in Latin script 117.pr. (VI AD); Ath.Schol. in Latin script 2.1.7 (VI AD); Antec. in Latin script 2.1.9 *usufructu* etc. (VI AD). Post-antique: common. *LBG.*

Notes: Fournet (2019: 83), Avotins (1992), Daris (1991a: 82), Hofmann (1989: 308), Zilliacus (1935a: 212–13), Meinersmann (1927: 43), Lampe (1961), LSJ suppl. See §4.2.4.2, §4.5, §7.1.1, §10.2.1, §10.2.2 B.

foreign   **οὐσουφρουκτουάριος** 'person with rights of use and profit but not ownership', from *ūsūfrūctuārius* 'person with right of usufruct': Antec. in Latin script 2.4.3 *usufructuariu* etc. (VI AD); later in Greek script. Zilliacus (1935a: 212–13), *LBG.* See §9.5.6 n. 68.

foreign   ***ut*** and ***utī***: Antec. as part of phrases 4.15.7 *uti possidetis* etc. (VI AD).

foreign   **οὐτίλιος** 'useful', from *ūtilis* 'useful': Antec. in Latin script 2.23.6 *utilios* etc. (VI AD); later in Greek script. Hofmann (1989: 308), Zilliacus (1935a: 214–15), *LBG.* See §9.5.6 n. 68, §10.3.1 n. 30.

        οὐτρανός: see οὐετερανός.

foreign   **οὔτρουβι** 'where (of two possibilities)', from *utrubī* 'in which of two places': Antec. in Latin script 4.15.4 *utrubi* etc. (VI AD); later in Greek script.

rare   **ὀφέλλιον, ὠφέλ(λ)ιον** 'morsel', from *ofella* 'small piece of meat' + -ιον: with *ofella* in Gloss. Ps.-Cyril. 390.47; *P.Bodl.* 153.3 is probably post-antique. Daris (1991a: 117), Hofmann (1989: 308), *LBG* (s.vv. ὀφέλλιον, ὠφέλιν), Meyer (1895: 69 s.v. φελλί), LSJ.

        ὀφήκιον, ὀφίκιον: see ὀφφίκιον.

        ὀφικιάλιος: see ὀφφικιάλιος.

not ancient?   **ὀφλάριον** 'morsel', from *ofella* 'small piece of meat' + -άριον: no datable examples (the one in Gloss. *Herm.L.* 14.42 may be a later addition). Binder (2000: 198–9), Hofmann (1989: 308), LSJ.

Direct loan
II AD – modern   **ὀφ(φ)ικιάλιος, ὀφφικιᾶλις, ὀπφικάλις** (-ου, ὁ), a title, from *officiālis* 'official attending on a magistrate'.

Documents: common, e.g. *P.Tebt.* II.335.13 (II AD); *P.Lips.* I.57r.2 (III AD); *P.Abinn.* 29.8 (IV AD); *P.Köln* II.123.6 (V AD); *P.Oxy.* 3600.24 (VI AD).

Inscriptions: e.g. *IGLS* XIII.1.9088.8 (III AD); perhaps *I.Zoora* 4.3 (IV AD); *SEG* XXXII.1554.A8 (VI AD).

Literature: Eus. *HE* 9.10.8 (IV AD); Basil Caesariensis, *Epistulae* 198.1 Courtonne (IV AD); Ps.-Macar. *Serm.* 4.29.11 etc. (V AD?); Hesych. as lemma o 1963 (V/VI AD).

Post-antique: numerous, forming derivative ὀφφικιαλαία 'wife of an *officialios*'. *LBG*, Zervan (2019: 126), Kriaras (1968– s.vv. οφφικιάλης, οφφικιάλιος), Triandaphyllidis (1909: 103, 126). Modern ὀφ(φ)ικιάλιος, a title: Babiniotis (2002), Kahane and Kahane (1972–6: 531, 1982: 135), cf. Andriotis (1967 s.v. ὀφιτσιάλος).

Notes: editor of *I.Zoora ad loc.*, Daris (1991a: 82), Mason (1974: 4, 9, 73), Hofmann (1989: 308–9), Zilliacus (1935a: 196–7, 228–9), Meinersmann (1927: 43), Immisch (1885: 356), Lampe (1961), LSJ suppl. (s.v. ὀφικιάλιος). See §4.2.5, §10.2.1, §10.2.2 D.

Direct loan
II AD – modern

ὀφ(φ)ίκιον, ὀφήκιον, ὀπίκιον (-ου, τό) 'official appointment', 'duty', from *officium* 'duty'.

Documents: e.g. *P.Oxy.* 3312.13 (II AD); *P.Lips.* 1.57r.22 (III AD); *P.Abinn.* 35.16 (IV AD); *CPR* VI.6.3 (V AD); *P.Cair.Masp.* 67126.58 (VI AD).

Inscriptions: *IGR* III.130.4 (II AD); *I.Tomis* 373.7, Latinate (III AD); *I.Ephesos* 2222B.4 (III AD); Ramsay 1895–7: 529 no. 373.9 (IV AD); Bean and Mitford 1970: 54 no. 31.A5 etc. (V AD).

Literature: e.g. Marc.Diac. 41 (V AD); Just. *Nov.* 2.t (VI AD); Antec. in Latin script 2.1.28 *officion* etc. (VI AD); Gloss. Ps.-Philox. 74.3. Unverified example (II AD) in Zilliacus (1937: 322, 331).

Post-antique: numerous. Kriaras (1968–), Sophocles (1887), Zervan (2019: 127), Triandaphyllidis (1909: 127). Modern ὀφ(φ)ίκιο 'rank': Babiniotis (2002), Andriotis (1967), Meyer (1895: 50).

Notes: Daris (1991a: 82–3), Mason (1974: 3, 5, 73), Hofmann (1989: 309), Zilliacus (1935a: 196–7, 1937: 331), Meinersmann (1927: 43), Lampe (1961), LSJ suppl. (*s.v.* ὀφίκιον). See §4.2.4.1 n. 54, §10.2.1, §10.2.2 D.

ὄψ: see ὄπεμ.

foreign

ὀψεκουέντις transliterating gen. of *obsequēns* 'obedient', 'docile': Plut. *Mor.* 322f (I/II AD). On this basis Strobach (1997: 198) gives ὀψεκουηνς and Sophocles (1887) ὀψεκουέντα as borrowings of *obsequēns*. See §7.2.1.

Deriv.? of loan
IV AD – modern

ὀψικεύω 'accompany', from *obsequor* 'comply with' or *obsequium* 'compliance' via ὀψίκιον + -εύω.

Literature: *Test.Abr.* A 10.11, 20.34 (I AD?); Philogelos 154 (IV AD); Thdr. Anag. *HE* 2.387 (V/VI AD).

Post-antique: numerous including glosses in lexica. *LBG*, Kriaras (1968–), Zilliacus (1937: 331). Modern dialectal 'ψικεύγω 'conduct to the grave': Andriotis (1974: 425).

Notes: Hofmann (1989: 309), Lampe (1961). See §4.3.1 n. 68, §4.6.1 n. 91, §10.2.2 O.

Direct loan
IV AD – modern

ὀψίκιον (-ου, τό) 'followers', 'escort', from *obsequium* 'compliance'.

Literature: *Acta Philippi* 66 = Bonnet 1903: 27.14 (IV AD); Dan.Sket. *Eu.* 137, 201 (VI AD); Just. *Nov.* in Latin script 78.2.pr. (VI AD).

Post-antique: numerous including glosses in lexica. *LBG* (*s.v.* ὀψίκιν), Kriaras (1968–), Triandaphyllidis (1909: 123, 127). Modern ψίκι 'wedding procession' and related words: Andriotis (1967), Meyer (1895: 72–3).

Notes: Avotins (1992), Hofmann (1989: 309–10), Viscidi (1944: 34), Zilliacus (1935a: 196–7, 1937: 331), Lampe (1961). See §4.2.4.1 n. 54, §4.3.1 n. 68, §10.2.1, §10.2.2 N.

Direct loan
III AD – Byz.

ὀψωνάτωρ, ὀψωνιάτωρ, ὀψονάτωρ (-ορος/-ωρος, ὁ) 'caterer', from *obsōnātor* 'caterer' (itself ultimately from ὄψον 'prepared food').

Documents: *Stud.Pal.* VIII.976.1 (VI AD).

Literature: Athenaeus 4.171a (II/III AD); Ast.Soph. 13.24 (IV AD); with *stipendiarius* in Gloss. Ps.-Cyril. 391.39.

Post-antique: survives. *LBG* (*s.v.* ὀψωνιάτωρ).

Notes: Athenaeus offers compelling evidence of more widespread use than has survived. Daris (1991a: 83), Hofmann (1989: 310), Cavenaile (1952: 200, implausibly suggesting Greek formation in -τωρ), *DÉLG* (*s.v.* ὄψον), Frisk (1954–72: 11.459), Beekes (2010 *s.v.* ὄψον), Lampe (1961), LSJ, LSJ suppl. (*s.v.* ὀψωνιάτωρ). See §2.1, **§2.2.1**, §4.2.5, §6.9, §10.2.1, §10.2.2 I.

Π

foreign

Παγανάλια transliterating *Pāgānālia*, a festival: DH *AR* 4.15.3 (I BC). Hofmann (1989: 310), Sophocles (1887).

rare

παγανεύω 'live as a civilian', from *pāgānus* 'civilian' via παγανός + -εύω: EphraemSyr. VII p. 427.2 (V/VI AD); *Martyrium Tarachi*, Ruinart 1689: 459. Lampe (1961, with wrong reference).

Direct? loan
II AD, V AD –
Byz.?

παγανικός (-ή, -όν) 'civilian', 'unofficial', 'lay', from *pāgānicus* 'civilian' or *pāgānus* 'civilian' via παγανός + -ικός.
Documents: e.g. perhaps *O.Claud.* IV.641.2 (I/II AD); *O.Claud.* II.362.10 (II AD); *BGU* III.936.10 (V AD); *P.Cair.Masp.* 67002.2.23 (VI AD).
Literature: Antec. 2.12.pr. etc. (VI AD).
Post-antique: numerous. *LBG*, Kriaras (1968–).
Notes: early examples, found only at Mons Claudianus, may be a separate borrowing from the more widespread later loan. Daris (1991a: 83), Hofmann (1989: 310), Zilliacus (1935a: 196–7, 230–1), Meinersmann (1927: 44), Lampe (1961), LSJ. See §4.2.2, §4.6.1, §8.2.1, §9.2, §10.2.1, §10.2.2 N.

Direct loan
II AD – modern

παγανός, πακανός (-ου, ὁ) 'civilian', 'private person', 'gladiator', from *pāgānus* 'civilian'.
Documents: e.g. *O.Claud.* IV.649.7 (I/II AD); *O.Florida* 2.8 (II AD); *BGU* IV.1043.25 (III AD); *P.Oxy.* 3758.9 etc. (IV AD); *O.Douch.* IV.434.3 (IV/V AD); *P.Lond.* V.1711.32 (VI AD).
Inscriptions: Robert 1971: 85 no. 20.1 (II/III AD); perhaps Rey-Coquais 2002 nos 7, 8 (V/VI AD?); *TAM* IV.I.109.2.
Literature: e.g. *Apocryphon Ezechiel* frag. a.9 in Denis 1970 (I/II AD); Epiph. *Pan.* II.516.26 (IV AD); Hesych. as lemma π 5 (V/VI AD); Dor.Gaz. *Doct. Div.* 2.34 (VI AD); Antec. 2.11.4 (VI AD).
Post-antique: common, forming derivative παγανόω 'dismiss from office'. *LBG*, Kriaras (1968–). Modern παγανός, παγανά 'goblin(s)': Babiniotis (2002), Andriotis (1967), Meyer (1895: 50–1).
Notes: forms derivatives παγανεύω, perhaps παγανικός. Feissel (2003), Daris (1991a: 83), Hofmann (1989: 310), Zilliacus (1935a: 230–1), Meinersmann (1927: 43), Immisch (1885: 365), Lampe (1961), LSJ, LSJ suppl. See §4.2.4.1 n. 51, §4.6.1, §8.2.1, §9.5.4, §10.2.1, §10.2.2 N.

Deriv. of loan
IV AD – Byz.

παγαρχέω 'hold the office of pagarch' (pass. 'be under a pagarch'), from *pāgus* 'country district' via παγάρχης.
Documents: *P.Oxy.* 133.8, 3204.12, 4785.11, 4787.9 (all VI AD); *P.Lond.* III.776.6 (VI AD).
Inscriptions: *CIG* 3989.12.

Literature: *Codex Theodosianus* 8.15.1 (IV AD); Just. *Edict* 13.25 = p. 793.16 (VI AD).

Post-antique: survives in papyri. Daris (1991a: 83).

Notes: according to Pedone (2020a: 15–17), in IV AD referred not to pagarch but to *praepositus pagi*. Daris (1991a: 83), Hofmann (1989: 311 *s.v.* πᾶγος), Meinersmann (1927: 43), LSJ. See §4.6.1, §4.6.3, §8.2.2, §10.2.2 D.

Deriv. of loan IV AD – Byz.

παγάρχης, πάγαρχος (-ου, ὁ) 'pagarch' (a local governor), from *pāgus* 'country district' via πᾶγος + -άρχης/-αρχος (cf. ἄρχω 'rule').

Documents, first declension: e.g. *P.Oxy.* 4371.9 (IV AD); *P.Lond.* v.1677.11 (VI AD). Second declension: e.g. *P.Oxy.* 3865.63 (V AD); *P.Münch.* III.I.152.4 (VI AD).

Inscriptions: perhaps Rey-Coquais 2002 nos 7, 8 (V/VI AD?).

Literature, declension uncertain: Basil Caesariensis, *Epistulae* 3.2.15 Courtonne (IV AD). First declension: Just. *Edict* 13.pr. = p. 780.14 etc. (VI AD). Second declension: Dioscorus frag. 17t, Heitsch 1963: 144 (VI AD).

Post-antique: numerous in papyri in both declensions. Daris (1991a: 83, 84).

Notes: forms derivatives παγαρχία, παγαρχέω, παγαρχικός. According to Pedone (2020a: 15–17), in IV AD referred not to pagarch but to *praepositus pagi*. Feissel (2003), Filos (2010: 244, 250), Daris (1991a: 83, 84), Hofmann (1989: 311 *s.v.* πᾶγος), Cavenaile (1952: 199), Meinersmann (1927: 43), Lampe (1961 *s.v.* πάγαρχος), LSJ (*s.vv.* παγάρχης, πάγαρχος). See §4.6.1, §4.6.2, §4.6.3, §10.2.2 D.

Deriv. of loan IV AD – Byz.

παγαρχία (-ας, ἡ) 'district under a pagarch', 'office of pagarch', from *pāgus* 'country district' via παγάρχης + -ία.

Documents: e.g. *P.Oxy.* 2110.4 (IV AD); *ChLA* XLIII.1259.8 (V AD); *P.Oxy.* 1829.3 (VI AD).

Literature: Just. *Edict* 13.12.1 = p. 786.25 (VI AD).

Post-antique: numerous in papyri. Daris (1991a: 83).

Notes: according to Pedone (2020a: 15–17), in IV AD referred not to pagarch but to *praepositus pagi*. Filos (2010: 244, 250), Daris (1991a: 83), Hofmann (1989: 311 *s.v.* πᾶγος), LSJ, LSJ suppl. See §4.6.1, §4.6.3, §10.2.2 D.

rare

παγαρχικός 'of a pagarch', from *pāgus* 'country district' via παγάρχης + -ικός: papyri *P.Cair.Masp.* 67019.4, 67354.2.2 (both VI AD). Hofmann (1989: 311 *s.v.* πᾶγος), Filos (2010: 250), Daris (1991a: 84), LSJ.

not ancient?

παγαρχίτης, a title from *pāgus* 'country district' via παγάρχης + -ίτης: probably no ancient examples. Filos (2010: 250), Daris (1991a: 84).

πάγαρχος: see παγάρχης.

Direct loan IV–VI AD

πᾶγος (-ου, ὁ) 'district', from *pāgus* 'country district'.

Documents: common (esp. IV AD), e.g. *P.Oxy.* 4129.10 (IV AD); *P.Select.* 13.3 (V AD); *SB* 14505.17 (VI AD).

Literature: DH *AR* 2.55.5 etc., marked (I BC); Plut. *Numa* 16.4, marked (I/II AD); Eus. *HE* 9.1.6 (IV AD); perhaps also others.

Notes: forms derivatives παγάρχης, probably ὁμόπαγος. Daris (1991a: 84), Hofmann (1989: 311), Zilliacus (1935a: 196–7), Meinersmann (1927: 43), LSJ. See §4.2.4.1 n. 51, §4.6.2, §4.6.3, §10.2.1, §10.2.2 D.

παιδατοῦρα: see πεδατοῦρα.

παίνουλα: see φαινόλη.

foreign   **πάκ-** transliterating forms of *pax* 'peace': πάκις = *pacis*, *O.Krok.* 1.125.2, 128.2
(I/II AD); πάκε = *pace*, *O.Claud.* 11.328.13 (II AD); πάκης = *pacis*, *Carth.*
249.15 (V AD). Lampe (1961: *s.v.* πάκης).

πακανός: see παγανός.

πακιάλιον: see φακιάλιον.

rare   **πακτάριος** 'contractor', from *pactum* 'agreement' via πάκτον + -άριος: papyri
P.Oxy. 2024.11, 2032.55 (both VI AD); occasionally later. Daris (1991a: 85),
Zilliacus (1935a: 196–7), Meinersmann (1927: 44), LSJ suppl.

rare   **πακτ(ε)ίκια** 'agreed payments', from *pactīcia*, neut. pl. of *pactīcius* 'arranged',
'negotiated': inscription *SEG* XL.1133.10 (III AD), where the title ἐπίτροπος
πακτεικιῶν = *a pacticiis*. Christol and Demougin (1990: 183), Mason (1974:
4, 73), Hofmann (1989: 312), LSJ suppl.

Deriv. of loan   **πακτεύω** 'make an agreement', from *pactum* 'agreement' via πάκτον + -εύω.
V AD – Byz.   Literature: Thüngen 2016: A12 etc. (V AD); *Schol.Sinai.* partially in Latin script
13 *ἐρactευσεν* (V/VI AD); Petrus Patricius, L. Dindorf 1870: 431.9 (VI AD);
Antec. 3.25.2 etc., but in Latin script 4.6.7 *pacteusas* (VI AD).
Post-antique: common, forming derivative πάκτευσις 'leasing'. *LBG*, Kriaras
(1968–).
Notes: Hofmann (1989: 312 *s.v.* πακτον), Zilliacus (1935a: 196–7), Lampe
(1961), LSJ. See §4.6.1 n. 91, §7.1.2, §7.1.3, §9.5.6 n. 56, §10.2.2 B.

πακτίκια: see πακτείκια.

Direct loan   **πάκτον** (-ου, τό) 'agreement', 'lease', 'agreed sum', from *pactum* 'agreement'.
V AD – modern   Documents: e.g. *SB* 16682.4 (V AD); *P.Ross.Georg.* III.43.3 (VI AD).
Literature: e.g. Agath. *Greg.* 174.5 (V AD); Hesych. as lemma π 118
(V/VI AD); *Schol.Sinai.* in Latin script 13 *pacton*, 21 *pactov*, 27 *pactu*
(V/VI AD); Malal. 11.3.23 (VI AD); Just. *Nov.* 120.11 (VI AD); Antec.
3.25.1 etc., but in Latin script 2.3.4 *pactois* (VI AD).
Post-antique: common, forming derivative πακτώνω 'lease'. *LBG*, Zervan
(2019: 129), Kriaras (1968–), Triandaphyllidis (1909: 130). Modern
πακτώνω, παχτώνω 'lease' (Babiniotis 2002; Andriotis 1967, 1974: 427;
Meyer 1895: 52), dialectal πάχτος/πάκτο 'rent', πάχτωμα 'renting'
(Andriotis 1974: 427; Kahane and Kahane 1972–6: 532, 1982: 135).
Notes: forms derivatives πακτεύω, πακτάριος. Avotins (1992), Daris (1991a:
85), Hofmann (1989: 312), Viscidi (1944: 24), Zilliacus (1935a: 196–7),
Lampe (1961), LSJ, LSJ suppl. See §4.2.4.1 n. 55, §7.1.2, §7.1.3, §9.5.6
n. 56, §10.2.1, §10.2.2 B.

not ancient?   **πακτονάριον** 'rent', apparently from *pactum* 'agreement' via πάκτον + -άριον:
papyrus *SB* 4323.14 (IV–VII AD). Unconnected to πακτονάριον 'small boat'
(a Greek formation from πάκτων 'light wicker boat' + -άριον, for which see
LSJ suppl.). Hofmann (1989: 312), Zilliacus (1935a: 196), Meinersmann
(1927: 44).

not ancient?	**πακτονάριος, πακτωνάρης**, an occupational term from *pactum* via πάκτον that occurs in Byzantine texts (*LBG*, Kriaras 1968–): perhaps papyrus *P.Thead.* 23.7 (IV AD). Buck and Petersen (1945: 97).
non-existent?	**πακτόω** 'lease', from *pactum* 'agreement' via πάκτον (and therefore a different word from πακτόω 'close', for which see LSJ): perhaps papyrus *SB* 12279.3 (VI AD?). Hagedorn (1986: 90–1), Daris (1991a: 85), Meinersmann (1927: 44), *LBG*.
	πακτωνάρης: see πακτονάριος.
rare	**πᾶλα** 'spade', from *pāla* 'spade': Edict.Diocl. 15.45 (IV AD). Hofmann (1989: 312), LSJ suppl.
not ancient?	**παλαιόκαστρον** 'ancient fort', from παλαιός 'ancient' + *castrum* 'fort' via κάστρον: probably no ancient examples. Hofmann (1989: 161 *s.v.* κάστρα), *LBG*, Kriaras (1968–).
rare	**παλάριος** 'with a stake', from *pālāris* 'of stakes': papyrus *BGU* 1.40.5 (II/III AD); occasional Byzantine texts. Hofmann (1989: 312–13), *LBG*, LSJ suppl.
Direct loan **IV AD – Byz.**	**παλατῖνος 1** (-ου, ὁ), the title of a palace official, from *Palātīnus* 'imperial'. Documents: e.g. *P.Oxy.* 4370.9 (IV AD); *P.Oxy.* 4918.6 (V AD); *SB* 9548.6 (VI AD). Inscriptions: e.g. *SEG* XLII.639.7 (IV/V AD); *IG* X.II.1.781.2 (V/VI AD). Literature: common, e.g. DH *AR* 2.70.1, marked (I BC), Athan. *Apol.Sec.* 59.6 (IV AD); Nil. 2.149.1 (V AD); Just. *Nov.* 30.6.2 (VI AD). Post-antique: numerous. *LBG*, Zervan (2019: 129), Kriaras (1968–). Notes: Avotins (1989, 1992), Daris (1991a: 85), Hofmann (1989: 313), Zilliacus (1935a: 196–7), Lampe (1961), LSJ suppl. (replacing LSJ *s.v.* παλάτιον). See §4.2.4.1 n. 51, §10.2.1, §10.2.2 A.
foreign	**παλατῖνος 2** 'of the Palatine', 'belonging to the palace', from *Palātīnus* 'Palatine': DH *AR* 2.70.1, 4.14.1, both marked (I BC); Malal. 13.9, marked (VI AD). Hofmann (1989: 313), Lampe (1961), LSJ suppl. (replacing LSJ *s.v.* παλάτιον).
Direct loan **I BC – modern**	**παλάτιον** (-ου, τό) 'Palatine Hill', 'palace or court of the Roman emperor', 'palace', from *palātium* 'Palatine Hill', 'imperial residence'. Documents: e.g. *P.Panop.Beatty* 1.260 (III AD); *Stud.Pal.* XX.230.4 (IV AD); *P.Oxy.* 4394.14 etc. (V AD); *P.Lond.* v.1679.4 (VI AD). Inscriptions: e.g. *I.Aphrodisias and Rome* 8.3 (I BC); *MAMA* IV.143.B19 (I AD); *I.Smyrna* 598.2 (II AD); *IG* II/III².III.13218.4 (II/III AD); *I.Perinthos* 188.4 (III/IV AD); *I.Syringes* 1293.2 (IV AD); Heberdey and Wilhelm 1896: 89 no. 168.1 (V AD); Marek 1993: 191, Appendix 6 no. 10.2 (VI AD). Literature: very common, e.g. Diodorus Siculus 4.21.2 (I BC); Jos. *AJ* 19.75 (I AD); Epict. *Diss.* 4.1.73 (I/II AD); Galen XIII.362.5 Kühn (II AD); *Acta Thomae* 17 = Bonnet 1903: 125.7 (III AD); Athan. *H.Ar.* 15.5 (IV AD); Callin. *V.Hypat.* 37.3 (V AD); Cyr.S. *Vit.Sab.* 142.4 (VI AD). Post-antique: common, forming derivatives παλατιανός 'belonging to the palace', παλατοφύλαξ 'palace guard', etc. *LBG*, Zervan (2019: 129–30), Kriaras (1968–), Triandaphyllidis (1909: 123, 126), Lampe (1961). Modern παλάτι 'palace': Babiniotis (2002), Andriotis (1967), Meyer (1895: 51).

Notes: considered Greek by Procopius, *Bell.* 3.21.4 (Freeman 1883: 384).
Avotins (1989, 1992), García Domingo (1979: 573), Daris (1991a: 85),
Mason (1974: 74 *s.v.* ἐκ Παλατίου), Hofmann (1989: 313), Zilliacus (1935a:
198–9, 1937: 332), Meinersmann (1927: 44), Lampe (1961), LSJ suppl.
(superseding LSJ). See §4.2.4.1 n. 54, §4.3.2 n. 75, §8.1.5, §8.2.3 n. 51,
§10.2.1, §10.2.2 A ; cf. κουροπαλάτης.

πάληον, πάλιον: see πάλλιον.

foreign | **Παλλία**, a contest, probably from *Palīlia*, variant of *Parīlia* 'festival of Pales':
Hesych. as lemma π 37, 243 (v/vi AD). LSJ. Cf. Παρίλια.

foreign | **παλλιᾶτα** transliterating (*fābula*) *palliāta* 'Greek comedy': Lyd. *Mag.* p. 62.3–4
(VI AD). *LBG.*

Direct loan with suffix
I–VI AD | **παλλιόλιον, παλλιώλιον** (-ου, τό) 'small cloak', from *palliolum* 'little mantle' + -ιον.
Documents: e.g. *P.Eirene* III.2v.9 (I AD); *P.Athen.* 63.17 (II AD); *P.Tebt.*
II.405.3 (III AD); *SB* 9834b.8 etc. (III/IV AD); *SB* 13749.3 (VI AD).
Notes: all provenanced examples come from Arsinoite nome. Probably not
derived via παλλίολον, which is later and less frequent. Daris (1991a: 85),
Hofmann (1989: 313 *s.v.* παλλίολον), Cavenaile (1952: 196), *LBG*, LSJ
suppl. See §4.3.2, §9.2, §10.2.1, §10.2.2 H.

Direct loan
II–III AD | **παλλίολον, παλλίωλον, παρίωλον** (-ου, τό) 'small cloak', from *palliolum* 'little mantle'.
Documents: *BGU* III.781.vi.6 (I/II AD); *O.Krok.* II.221.18 (I/II AD); *Stud.
Pal.* XX.15.9 (II AD); *P.Ryl.* II.189.5 (II AD); perhaps *P.Oxy.* 1449.32 etc.
(III AD); probably not *P.Lips.* I.57r.28 (III AD): *BL* XII.98.
Notes: Daris (1991a: 85), Hofmann (1989: 313), Meinersmann (1927: 44),
LSJ suppl. See §4.2.4.1 n. 55, §4.3.2, §9.2, §10.2.1, §10.2.2 H.

Direct loan
I AD – Byz. | **πάλ(λ)ιον, πάληον** (-ου, τό) 'mantle', from *pallium* 'mantle'.
Documents: common, e.g. *P.Mich.* V.343.6 (I AD); *P.Oxy.* 3491.7 (II AD);
P.Michael. 21.9 (III AD); *P.Oslo* III.119.11 (IV AD); *P.Stras.* VII.695.7
(V AD); *P.Prag.* I.93.3 (VI AD).
Inscriptions: perhaps *SEG* XXXIII.196.4 (II AD); *SEG* VII.420.2 (III AD).
Literature: e.g. *Acta Joannis* 5r = Bonnet 1898: 154.21 (II AD?); *Coll.Herm.* C 8
(I–IV AD); Epiph. *Pan.* III.143.4 as gloss (IV AD); Hesychius of Jerusalem
as gloss, *Commentarius brevis* psalm 108.29 in Jagić 1917 (V AD); Hesych. as
gloss τ 1357 (V/VI AD); Cyr.S. *Vit.Eu.* 64.1 (VI AD).
Post-antique: numerous. *LBG*, Kriaras (1968–), Triandaphyllidis (1909: 122),
Zilliacus (1937: 332).
Notes: forms derivative σουβρικοπάλλιον. Dross-Krüpe (2017: 297), Daris
(1991a: 85–6), Hofmann (1989: 314), Zilliacus (1935a: 230–1),
Meinersmann (1927: 44), Immisch (1885: 344–5), Lampe (1961), LSJ
suppl. See §4.1.1, §4.2.4.1 n. 54, §4.6.2, §10.2.1, §10.2.2 H.

παλλιωλ-: see παλλιολ-.

rare | **πάλμη 1** 'date', 'hand', from *palma* 'date', 'palm of the hand': papyri *P.Oxy.*
519.18, meaning 'date' (II AD); *P.Rain.UnterrichtKopt.* 256.277 etc.,
meaning 'hand' (VI AD). Daris (1991a: 86), Hofmann (1989: 314,
confusing this with πᾶλος), Meinersmann (1927: 44), *LBG*, LSJ.

πάλμη 2 'shield': see πάρμη.

rare	**παλμουλάριος**, a type of gladiator, from *parmulārius* 'gladiator armed with a small round shield': Marc.Aurel. 1.5.1 (II AD). Hofmann (1989: 314 *s.v.* παλμουράριος), LSJ.
Direct loan **II AD – modern**	**πᾶλος** (-ου, ὁ) 'stake', 'pike', 'squad of gladiators', from *pālus* 'stake'. Documents, meaning 'stake': *P.Lond.* II.191.12 (II AD). Inscriptions, meaning 'stake': Edict.Diocl. 14.1 etc. (IV AD). Meaning 'squad of gladiatiors': e.g. Bosch 1967: 191 no. 150.7 (II AD); *I.Beroia* 388.2 (II/III AD); Robert 1971: 182 no. 179.3. Literature, meaning 'stake': Agath. *Arm.* 88.2 etc. (V AD); Zosimus, *Historia nova* 2.35.2 Paschoud (V AD?); EphraemSyr. VII p. 191.7 (V/VI AD); Aesop, *Fabulae* 296 Hausrath and Hunger; scholion to Ar. *Pl.* 301 as gloss; with *palus* in Gloss. Ps.-Cyril. 393.9. Post-antique: survives only in meaning 'stake'. Zervan (2019: 130–1), Kriaras (1968–), Sophocles (1887), Triandaphyllidis (1909: 124), Daris (1991a: 86). Modern dialectal πάλος 'stake' and derivatives: Andriotis (1974: 428), Meyer (1895: 51), Dieterich (1901: 591). Notes: in meaning 'squad of gladiators' usually combined with πρῶτος or δεύτερος designating the specific squad (Robert 1971: 28–31). Sidro and Maravela (forthcoming), Daris (1991a: 86), Hofmann (1989: 314–15, with some examples under πάλμη), Zilliacus (1935a: 230–1), Meinersmann (1927: 45), *DÉLG*, Beekes (2010), Lampe (1961), LSJ. See §4.2.4.1 n. 51, §10.2.1, §10.2.2 F; cf. πρωτόπαλος.
foreign	**παλουδαμέντον**, a garment, from *palūdāmentum* 'military cloak fastened with a brooch at the shoulder': Lyd. *Mag.* p. 88.9, marked (VI AD). *LBG*.
not ancient	**παλούδιον** 'swamp', from *palūs* 'swamp' + -ιον: no ancient examples. Zilliacus (1935a: 230–1), *LBG*.
Direct loan **I–IV AD**	**πανάριον, πανάρειν** (-ου, τό) 'breadbox', 'medicine chest', 'box', from *pānārium* 'breadbox'. Documents: *P.Oxy.* 300.4 (I AD); *P.Oxy.* 1272.8 (II AD); *P.Oxy.* 1294.6 etc. (II/III AD); *SB* 16645.30 (II/III AD); *SB* 9834.b.r.23 (III/IV AD). Literature: Sextus Empiricus, *Adversus mathematicos* 1.234 (II/III AD); Epiph. *Pan.* 1.155.15 (IV AD). Notes: Diethart (1992: 237–8, 1998: 174), Daris (1991a: 86), Hofmann (1989: 315), Meinersmann (1927: 45), Lampe (1961), LSJ suppl. (superseding LSJ). See §4.2.4.1 n. 54, §6.3 n. 22, **§9.4** passage 56, §10.2.1, §10.2.2 I.
not Latin	**πανία** 'fullness' (fem. sing.) and **πάνια** 'fodder' (neut. pl.) are cited by Willi (2008: 33) and Hofmann (1989: 315–16) as having Italic roots on the basis of Athenaeus 3.111c (quoted *s.v.* πᾶνις); LSJ.
Direct loan **V AD – modern**	**πανίκουλα, πανοῦκλα** (-ας, ἡ) 'tumour', from *pānicula*, a kind of wart (with variants *pānucula, pānucla*: *TLL s.v.* 1. *pānicula*). Literature: Aelius Promotus, Δυναμερόν 21.6 Crismani (II AD?); Anton. Hag. *V.Sym.Styl.* 17 (V AD); Alex.Trall. II.113.7 (VI AD); with *panicula* in glossaries, e.g. Gloss. Ps.-Cyril. 393.32. Post-antique: numerous. *LBG* (*s.v.* πανούκλα), Zervan (2019: 131), Kriaras (1968– *s.v.* πανούκλα), Triandaphyllidis (1909: 119). Modern πανούκλα 'plague': Babiniotis (2002), Andriotis (1967).

Notes: Zervan (2019: 131) thinks this is the source of πανουκλίζω and therefore older than attestations suggest. Binder (2000: 167, 175), *LBG* (*s.v.* πανίκουλα), Meyer (1895: 51–2), *TLL* (*s.v.* 1. *pānicula* 75–6). See §4.2.3.1, §9.5.3 n. 38, §10.2.1, §10.2.2 L.

not ancient   **πανικουλάριος**, a type of clothing, from *panniculārius* 'ragged' (*TLL*): no ancient examples. Zilliacus (1935a: 198–9), *LBG* (*s.v.* πανικουλάρια), *TLL* (*s.v.* *panniculārius* 230.9).

not ancient   **πανίκουλο** 'Turkish wheat', from *pānicula* 'feathery head of certain grasses': no ancient examples. Meyer (1895: 51).

                πανίον: see παννίον.

foreign   **πᾶνις** (in acc. πᾶνιν) transliterating *pānis* 'bread': Plut. *Mor.* 726f (I/II AD). Also acc. πᾶνα, Athenaeus 3.111c: ἄρτος ὁ προσαγορευόμενος λεκιθίτας, ὥς φησιν Εὐκράτης. πανὸς ἄρτος· Μεσσάπιοι. καὶ τὴν πλησμονὴν πανίαν καὶ πάνια τὰ πλήσμια· Βλαῖσος ἐν Μεσοτρίβᾳ καὶ Δεινόλοχος ἐν Τηλέφῳ Ῥίνθων τε ἐν Ἀμφιτρύωνι. καὶ Ῥωμαῖοι δὲ πᾶνα τὸν ἄρτον καλοῦσι (II/III AD). Strobach (1997: 198), Hofmann (1989: 316).

not ancient?   **παν(ν)ίον** 'cloth', from *pannus* 'piece of cloth': probably not paraliterary papyrus Kramer 2001a: no. 4.12 (III/IV AD), see Fressura (2021: 151); glossary mentioned in *CGL* II p. xxxvii; common in Byzantine texts. Hofmann (1989: 316 *s.v.* πάννος), *LBG*, Zervan (2019: 131), Kriaras (1968– *s.v.* πανίον), Triandaphyllidis (1909: 122), Meyer (1895: 51 *s.v.* παννί), Andriotis (1967 *s.v.* πανὶ), Lampe (1961).

foreign   **πάννος** 'cloth', from *pannus* 'piece of cloth': Dio Cassius 49.36.5, marked (II/III AD). Hofmann (1989: 316), LSJ.

not Latin   **πανός**, Messapian word for 'bread' according to Athenaeus (3.111c, quoted *s.v.* πᾶνις). Hofmann (1989: 316), *DÉLG*, LSJ.

                πανοῦκλα: see πανίκουλα.

rare   **πανουκλίζω**, apparently 'unwind from a reel', probably from *pānicula*, a kind of wart (via πανίκουλα?) + -ίζω: Orib. *Ecl.* 141.2: πηνιζούσης, ὃ δὴ λέγομεν πανουκλιζούσης (IV AD). Zervan (2019: 131), LSJ.

rare   **παόνιος** 'of a peacock', from *pāvō* 'peacock' + -ιος: Edict.Diocl. 18.9 (IV AD). Byzantine παώνιον 'peacock' may be related. Hofmann (1989: 324 *s.v.* πάων), *LBG*, LSJ suppl. Cf. παός, πάων.

rare   **παός** 'peacock', from *pāvō* 'peacock: with *pavo* in glossaries, e.g. Gloss. *Herm.Mp.* 318.70. *LBG*. Cf. πάων, παόνιος.

semantic extension   **πάπας** 'pope' is a Greek word (cf. πάπ(π)ας 'papa') with meaning influenced by *pāpa* 'pope' (*TLL*), itself originally from πάπ(π)ας. Zervan (2019: 131–2).

not ancient   **παπίλλα**, an illness, from *papilla* 'pustule' (*TLL s.v.* 255.83–256.14): no ancient examples. Meyer (1895: 52).

not ancient   **πάπουλα** 'slag', perhaps from *papula* 'pimple': no ancient examples. Meyer (1895: 52), Kriaras (1968– *s.v.* πάπουλον).

παπυλαιών, παπυλεών: see παπυλιών.

rare	**παπυλιονάριος** 'tent-maker', perhaps from medieval *pāpiliōnārius* 'tent-maker' (*DMLBS*), or *pāpiliō* 'tent' (*TLL*) via παπυλιών + -άριος: inscriptions perhaps *SEG* LXV.1417.3 (V/VI AD); *SEG* XLIV.588.6 (VI AD). Byzantine παπυλεωνάριος 'tent-dweller' (*LBG*) may be unconnected. *TLL* (corrigenda, X.1.2782.24–6).
Direct loan **II AD – Byz.**	**παπυλιών, παπυλεών, παπυλαιών** (-ῶνος, ὁ) 'tent', from *pāpiliō* 'tent' (*TLL*). Documents: *P.Col.* VIII.221.5 (II AD); *SB* 1.3 etc. (III AD); *P.Mich.* III.214.26, 216.13 (both III AD). Inscriptions: Edict.Diocl. 19.4 (IV AD); perhaps *I.Heraclea Pontica* 69.16. Literature: Ast.Soph. 26.7, marked (IV AD); Magnus, *FHG* IV frag. 1.92 (IV AD); Eutychianus, *FHG* IV frag. 1.22 etc. (IV AD); Malal. 5.7 etc. (VI AD); Procop. *Bell.* 2.21.3, marked (VI AD); Cos.Indic. 5.40, marked (VI AD). Post-antique: survives. *LBG* (*s.vv.* παπιλέων, παπύλαιον), Triandaphyllidis (1909: 131). Notes: may form derivative παπυλιονάριος. Niehoff-Panagiotidis (2019: 465–6), Daris (1991a: 86), Hofmann (1989: 316–17), Cavenaile (1951: 399), *TLL* (*s.v. pāpilio* 253.7), Lampe (1961), LSJ, LSJ suppl. See §4.2.5, §10.2.1, §10.2.2 H.
not ancient	**παραβέρεδος, παραβέρηδος**, a type of post-horse, from *paraverēdus* 'horse used on minor streets' (*TLL*): no ancient examples. Zilliacus (1935a: 198–9), *LBG*, *TLL* (*s.v. paraverēdus* 323.77). Cf. βέρεδος.
not Latin	**παραγαύδης, βαρυγαύδης, παραγαύδιον, παραγαύδιος, παραγαύδωτος, παρακαυτωδόν**, and **παρακαυδωτός** 'garment with a purple border' etc. are not from Latin. Cervenka-Ehrenstrasser (2000: 272–3), Brust (2005: 502–6), Daris (1991a: 86), Cavenaile (1951: 399), Palmer (1945: 45), *DÉLG*, Frisk (1954–72: III.166–7), Beekes (2010), LSJ, LSJ suppl. (*s.vv.* βαρυγαύτης, παραγαύδιον).
not ancient?	**παρακέλλιον** 'adjoining cell', from παρά 'beside' + *cella* 'room' via κελλίον: scholion to Eur. *Or.* 1450; perhaps papyrus *BGU* II.459.11 (II AD). For later use see *LBG* and modern dialectal παρακέλλι 'small compartment' (Meyer 1895: 30). Husson (1983: 143 n. 1), Filos (2010: 244, 250), Daris (1991a: 86).
rare	**παραπαλάριος**, a type of entertainer, probably from παρά 'beside' + *pālāria*, a military and gladiatorial exercise (*TLL s.v. pālāris*): Teucer, Boll 1903: 44.10 (I AD?). Hofmann (1989: 317), Zilliacus (1935a: 198–9), LSJ suppl.
Deriv. of loan **VI AD – modern**	**παράτιτλον, παράτιτλος** (-ου, τό or ὁ) 'marginal scholion', 'note', from παρά 'beside' + *titulus* 'section of a book' via τίτλος. Literature: Ath.Schol. 1.P.t etc. (VI AD). At Just. *Codex* 1.17.2.21 (VI AD) appears as Greek word in a Latin context, so there was no direct Latin equivalent. Post-antique: numerous. *LBG*. Modern παράτιτλος 'subtitle' is probably survival, *pace* Babiniotis (2002). Notes: LSJ suppl. (superseding LSJ). See §4.6.2, §9.5.6 n. 68, §10.2.2 B.

Direct loan III AD – Byz.

παρατοῦρα, περατοῦρα (-ας, ἡ) 'distinctive dress', 'full dress', 'equipment', from *parātūra* 'preparation' (*TLL*).

Documents: *P.Louvre* 1.67.4 (III AD); perhaps *P.Amh.* 11.142.16 (IV AD).

Literature: Lyd. *Mag.* pp. 18.5, 104.24, marked (VI AD); Gloss. Ps.-Cyril. 397.2 (cf. *CGL* VI.276).

Post-antique: survives in papyri. *LBG*.

Notes: forms derivative παρατουρᾶτος. Worp (2005: 148–9 with n. 10), Daris (1991a: 86), Hofmann (1989: 317), Meinersmann (1927: 45), Sophocles (1887), *TLL* (*s.v. paratura* 321.8–13, 78–80). See §4.2.3.1, §6.6, §6.11, §8.2.2, §10.2.1, §10.2.2 H.

not ancient?

παρατουρᾶς 'maker or seller of curtains/tapestries/hangings', from *parātūra* 'preparation' (*TLL*) via παρατοῦρα + -ᾶς: inscription *I.Tyr* 133. *I.Tyr* (pp. 74, 156), LSJ suppl.

rare

παρατουρᾶτος 'decorated', from *parātūra* 'preparation' (*TLL*) via παρατοῦρα + -ᾶτος: papyrus *P.Münch.* III.1.142.4 (VI AD). Daris (1991a: 86), *LBG*. See §6.6.

foreign

παρατούριον, perhaps 'border', apparently from *parātūra* 'preparation' (*TLL*) via παρατοῦρα + -ιον: Hesych. as lemma π 707 (VI AD). Hofmann (1989: 317 *s.v.* παρατοῦρα), Immisch (1885: 361–2), LSJ, LSJ suppl.

rare

παραφοσσεύω 'encamp by', 'circumvallate', from παρά 'beside' + *fossa* 'ditch' via φοσσεύω: Malal. 18.66 (VI AD). Hofmann (1989: 476 *s.v.* φοσσεύειν), Lampe (1961).

not Latin?

πάρδος 'male panther', perhaps from *pardus* 'panther', or *vice versa*. *DÉLG* (*s.v.* πάρδαλις), Frisk (1954–72: II.473), Beekes (2010 *s.v.* πάρδαλις), Hofmann (1989: 317–18), LSJ, and for later survival *LBG*.

not Latin?

πάρεα 'dowry', perhaps from *pallium* 'mantle': no ancient examples. Meyer (1895: 52).

foreign

πάρενς (in pl. παρέντης) transliterating both *părēns* 'parent' and *pārēns*, pres. part. of *pāreō* 'obey': Lyd. *Mag.* p. 42.21 (VI AD). Also in Latin script: Antec. 1.12. pr. *parentes* (VI AD). Sophocles (1887), Triantaphyllides (1892: 269). See §9.5.5 n. 47.

not ancient?

Παρεντάλια, a festival, from *Parentālia*, a festival: inscription *SEG* 11.415.3; manuscript reading in DH *AR* 1.88.3 (for Παρίλια). Hofmann (1989: 318).

παρέντης: see πάρενς.

foreign

Παρίλια, a festival, from *Parīlia*, a festival: normally marked as foreign or obsolete, e.g. DH *AR* 1.88.3 (I BC); Plut. *Rom.* 12.2 (I/II AD); Athenaeus 8.361f (II/III AD); Dio Cassius 43.42.3 (II/III AD). Hofmann (1989: 318), Sophocles (1887). Cf. Παλλία.

παρίωλον: see παλλίολον.

rare

πάρμη, πάλμη 'light shield', from *parma* 'round shield': DH *AR* 2.71.4 (I BC); elsewhere always marked, e.g. Polybius 6.22.2 (II BC); Clemens Alexandrinus, *Stromata* 1.16.75.6 Früchtel (II/III AD); Hesych. as lemma π 251, 949 (V/VI AD); Lyd. *Mag.* p. 4.16 (VI AD). Dubuisson (1985: 38), Hofmann (1989: 318–19), Immisch (1885: 346), *LBG* (*s.v.* πάρμα), LSJ (*s.vv.* πάλμη, πάρμη). See §8.1.3 n. 17.

not ancient? **πάρος**, a small bird, perhaps from *parvus* 'small': probably no ancient examples. Meyer (1895: 52).

foreign **παρρικίδας** transliterating acc. pl. of *parricīda* 'parricide': Lyd. *Mag.* p. 42.19 (VI AD); Antec. in Latin script 4.18.6 *parricidae* (VI AD). Sophocles (1887).

foreign **παρρικίδιον** transliterating *parricīdium* 'parricide': Lyd. *Mag.* p. 42.18 (VI AD). *LBG.*

foreign *pars* 'part': Antec. as part of phrases, e.g. 2.23.5 *partis et pro parte* (VI AD).

rare **παρτικουλάριον, παρτικλάριον** 'share (of inheritance)', from *particulāris* 'particular' (neut. subst.), 'specific' (*TLL*): papyrus *Stud.Pal.* XXII.61.3 (II/III AD). Binder (2000: 158), Daris (1991a: 86, with derivation from *particula*), Meinersmann (1927: 45), *TLL* (*s.v. particulāris* 512.66–9).

foreign **παρτιτιάριος** 'of sharing', probably from *partiārius* 'of sharing' (there is no **partītiārius*): Antec. in Latin script 2.23.5 *partitiariu* (VI AD). Zilliacus (1935a: 198–9), *TLL* (*s.v. partiārius* 492.73–5).

foreign **παρτιτίων** 'sharing', from *partītiō* 'sharing': Antec. in Latin script 2.23.5 *partition* (VI AD). Zilliacus (1935a: 198–9).

πασίολος: see φασίολος.

πασκαύλιον: see βασκαύλιον.

not ancient **πασσαρίνα** apparently transliterating *passarīnus*, a plant (variant of *passerīnus* 'of sparrows', *TLL*): interpolation in Dsc. 3.123 RV. Hofmann (1989: 319), *TLL* (*s.v. passerīnus* 608.11–13).

non-existent? **πασσίον** 'raisin wine', from *passum* 'raisin wine': perhaps papyrus *P.IFAO* III.14.5 (III AD), cf. *BL* VIII.153, Ihnken (1982: 236).

not ancient? **πάσσον 1** 'step', 'pace' (as a unit of measurement), from *passus, -ūs* 'step', 'pace': Her.Mech. *Def.* 130.1 etc. (lived I AD, but the words are probably not his). Binder (2000: 242), *LBG*, Sophocles (1887).

rare **πάσσον 2** 'raisin wine', from *passum* 'raisin wine': *Agora* XXI.Hd.9 (II AD), Hd.12 (II/III AD), amphorae with πάσσον painted on them to indicate the contents. Also Polybius 6.11a.4, marked (II BC), quoted in Athenaeus 10.440e (II/III AD); that passage is probably the basis of Eustathius' explanation (*Commentarii ad Iliadem*, Van der Valk 1971–87: IV.306.13–17) μεταφορικῶς δὲ καὶ παστὸς ὁ νυμφικός, ὁ ἔχων πέπλους οἷς ἐμπάσσονται τρόπον τινὰ τὰ ἐπιπολῆς δαίδαλα ποικίλματα, κατὰ τὸ "πολέας δ' ἐνέπασσεν ἀέθλους". εἰ δὲ ἐκ τοῦ τοιούτου πάσσειν καὶ ὁ πάσσος, ἐθνικὴ αὕτη λέξις, γίνεται, τίς ἂν εἰδείη; ἔστι δέ, φασί, πάσσος οἶνος ἐξ ἀσταφίδων παρὰ Ῥωμαίοις, οὗ πίνειν γυναῖκας ἀπείρητο. χρῆσις δὲ πάσσου παρὰ Πολυβίῳ. Dubuisson (1985: 38–9), Binder (2000: 246), Hofmann (1989: 319), LSJ suppl. (*s.v.* adjectival πάσσος 'from raisins', apparently following Eustathius; replacing LSJ *s.v.* πάσσον). See §8.1.3 n. 17.

πάστελ-: see πάστιλ-.

παστιλλᾶδες: see παστιλλᾶς.

not ancient? **παστιλλάρ(ι)ος** 'confectioner', from *pāstillārius* 'maker of pastilles' (*TLL*): undated inscriptions *MAMA* III.495, 636, 754; perhaps *SEG* XXXVI.970. B26 (III AD); Byzantine texts. Hofmann (1989: 319), Zilliacus (1937: 332), *DÉLG* (s.v. πάστιλλος), *LBG*, *TLL* (s.v. *pastillārius*), LSJ.

Deriv. of loan
IV AD – Byz.
 παστιλλᾶς, βαστιλᾶς (-ᾶ, ὁ) 'confectioner', from *pāstillus* 'pastille' via πάστιλλος + -ᾶς.

Documents: *P.Oxy.* 3390.3 (IV AD); *P.Oxy.* 1891.4 etc. (V AD); *SB* 15599.4 (V/VI AD); *P.Iand.* III.42.2 etc. (VI AD).

Inscriptions: *I.Hierapolis Judeich* 222.2.

Post-antique: some survival. Daris (1991a: 86).

Notes: declension usually first, occasionally third (παστιλλᾶδες in *SB* 15599, Gignac 1981: 16–21). Olsson (1925: 249), Daris (1991a: 86), Hofmann (1989: 319 s.v. παστιλλάριος), *DÉLG* (s.v. πάστιλλος), LSJ, LSJ suppl. See §4.6.1, §8.2.2, §10.2.2 I.

rare **παστίλλιον** 'pastille', from *pāstillus* 'pastille' via πάστιλλος + -ιον: papyri *BGU* I.34.5.19 (IV AD); perhaps *BGU* XIII.2358.17 (IV AD); Byzantine texts. Daris (1991a: 87, with derivation from *pāstillum*), Hofmann (1989: 320 s.v. πάστιλλος), Cavenaile (1952: 195), Meinersmann (1927: 45), Andriotis (1967 s.v. modern παστέλι), Lampe (1961 s.v. πάστιλλος), LSJ (s.v. πάστιλλος), *LBG*.

Direct loan
IV AD – Byz.
 πάστιλ(λ)ος, πάστελλος (-ου, ὁ) 'pastille', from *pāstillus* 'pastille'.

Documents: perhaps *BGU* XIII.2358.17 (IV AD).

Literature: *Hippiatr.* e.g. *Hippiatr.Par.* (Eumelus) 30 (III AD?); Orib. *Col.* 8.47.13 etc. (IV AD); Ps.-Macar. *PG* XXXIV.245b (V AD?); Pall. *V.Chrys.* 45.9 (IV/V AD); Ps.-Martyrius 76 in Wallraff 2007 (V AD); Aëtius 3.100.1 etc. (VI AD); Alex.Trall. 1.549.6 etc. (VI AD).

Post-antique: numerous, mainly in the sense 'sesame honeycake', forming derivative παστελλοπούλης 'seller of sesame honeycakes'. *LBG* (s.vv. πάστελλος, πάστιλλος). Modern παστέλι 'sweet of honey and sesame' probably from Italian *pastello*: Babiniotis (2002), Andriotis (1967).

Notes: forms derivatives παστιλλᾶς, παστιλλόω, παστίλλιον, παστιλλᾶδες, παστιλλώδης. Hofmann (1989: 319–20), *DÉLG*, Lampe (1961), LSJ (s.vv. πάστιλλος, παστιλώδης, with reference to Latin medical writer Celsus 5.17.2). See §4.2.4.1 n. 51, §4.6.1, §10.2.1, §10.2.2 L.

Deriv. of loan
IV AD – Byz.
 παστιλλόω, παστελ(λ)όω 'make into a paste', from *pāstillus* 'pastille' via πάστιλλος + -όω.

Literature: Orib. *Ecl.* 101.3 (IV AD); Aëtius 8.74.38 etc. (VI AD); Alex.Trall. II.177.16 (VI AD).

Post-antique: survives in medical texts. *LBG* (s.v. παστελλόω).

Notes: Hofmann (1989: 320 s.v. πάστιλλος), *DÉLG* (s.v. πάστιλλος), LSJ. See §4.6.1, §8.2.2, §10.2.2 L.

rare **παστιλ(λ)ώδης** 'like a pastille', from *pāstillus* 'pastille' via πάστιλλος + -ώδης (cf. εἶδος 'form'): Severus Iatrosophista p. 40.15 Dietz (I AD?). Hofmann (1989: 320 s.v. πάστιλλος), *DÉLG* (s.v. πάστιλλος), LSJ.

rare	**πάστωρ** 'herdsman', from *pāstor* 'herdsman': usually a name, but perhaps common noun on tablet *SB* 801.2 (II/III AD). Daris (1991a: 87), Hofmann (1989: 320), Meinersmann (1927: 45), LSJ suppl.

πασχίδιον: see φασκίδιον.

not Latin	**πατάνη** 'dish' and related **πάτανον, πατάνιον, βατάνη, βατάνιον, πατάνα, πατάνια, βατάνια** are not from Latin but may be Italic. Willi (2008: 33), Campanile (1969: 310–11), Hofmann (1989: 320–1), Immisch (1885: 314–15), *DÉLG*, Frisk (1954–72: I.226, II.480, III.167), Beekes (2010), LSJ. For the Latinate versions of these words see πατέλλα, πατελλίκιον, etc.

πατελήκιον: see πατελλίκιον.

not Latin?	**πατελίς** 'limpet', perhaps from *patella* 'little dish': scholia to Ar. *Pl.* 1096 and Opp. *H.* 1.138. *LBG* (*s.v.* πατέλιν), LSJ.

Direct loan **II AD – modern?**	**πάτελλα, βάτελλα** (-ης, ἡ) 'dish', 'plate', from *patella* 'little dish'. Documents: *SB* 9042.2 (II AD); *P.Oxy.* 741.17 (II AD); *P.Oxy.* 2423.iv.15 (II/III AD); *P.Ryl.* IV.630/637.387 (IV AD). Inscriptions: Ramsay 1906: 319.2.4 (III AD); probably *SEG* XXXVI.970.A1 (III AD). Literature: Pollux 6.85 (II AD); *Coll.Herm.* Mp 20e (III AD?); Orib. *Syn.* 4.35.5 (IV AD); Alex.Trall. II.161.30 (VI AD); with *patina* in Gloss. Ps.-Cyril. 399.41. Post-antique: survives. *LBG*. Modern πάτελ(λ)α: Meyer (1895: 52), but Andriotis (1967) derives that from Italian *patella*. Notes: forms derivatives πατελλίκιον and perhaps πατέλλιον. Gignac (1981: 9) considers πάτελλον variant spelling of this. Cervenka-Ehrenstrasser (2000: 143 *s.v.* βάτελλα), Schirru (2013: 315), Daris (1991a: 33), Hofmann (1989: 321), Meinersmann (1927: 10), *DÉLG*, Beekes (2010), LSJ (*s.vv.* βάτελλα, πάτελλα). See §4.6.1, §6.13, **§8.1.1** passage 37, §10.2.1, §10.2.2 I.

πατελλίδιον: see πατελλίκιον.

Deriv. of loan **V AD – Byz.**	**πατελλίκιον, πατελήκιον, βατελλίκιον, βατελλήκηον** (-ου, τό) 'little dish', 'little plate', from *patella* 'little dish' via πάτελλα + -ικός + -ιον. Documents: *SB* 9158.5 (V AD); *PSI* XIV.1447.4 (V AD); *P.Eleph.Wagner* 1.325.1 (V/VI AD); *CPR* VIII.66.10 (VI AD); *P.Oxy.* 1901.34 etc., 2419.9 etc. (both VI AD). Literature: with *scutella* in Gloss. *Herm.M.* 203.27 (transliterated *patillicion* and misinterpreted as unattested *πατελλίδιον in *CGL* VII.247 *s.v.* *scutella*). Post-antique: survives. *LBG*. Notes: probably unattested intermediate form *πατελλικός between this and πάτελλα. Cervenka-Ehrenstrasser (2000: 144 *s.v.* βατελλίκιον), Daris (1991a: 33, 87), LSJ suppl. (superseding LSJ πατελλίδιον *s.v.* πάτελλα). See §4.6.1, §10.2.2 I.

Deriv.? of loan
II–VI AD

πατέλλιον, βατέλλιον (-ου, τό) 'little dish', from *patella* 'little dish' (via πάτελλα?) + -ιον.

Documents: *P.Oxy.* 1657.5 (III AD); *O.Wilck.* 1218.3 (I–IV AD); *P.Kellis* I.71.26 etc. (IV AD); *SB* 15284.4 etc. (V AD).

Literature: Pollux 6.91 εἴη δ' ἂν ἡ πατάνη λοπάδιον ἐκπέταλον, ὃ νῦν ἴσως ἀπὸ τούτου καλοῦσι πατέλλιον, 10.107 καὶ πατάνη δὲ καὶ πατάνιον τὸ ἐκπέταλον λοπάδιον, ὅ τινες καλοῦσι, πατέλλιον (II AD); Zosimus alch., Berthelot and Ruelle 1888: 142.1 (III/IV AD); Christianus alch., Berthelot and Ruelle 1888: 404.8 etc. (VI AD); *Hippiatr.Berl.* 26.36; with *patella* in Gloss. *Herm.Mp.* 326.39.

Notes: Hofmann (1989: 321 *s.v.* πατελλα) considers the πατάλλια mentioned by Pollux (10.108) a variant of this: Ἄλεξις δὲ ἐν Ἀσκληπιοκλείδῃ πατάνια εἴρηκεν· ἐν δὲ ταῖς Ἱππάρχου Παννυχίσιν εὑρῆσθαί φασι κατὰ τὴν τῶν ἰδιωτῶν συνήθειαν εἰρημένον βατάνιον. οἷς μέντοι τὰς κριθὰς φρύγοντες μετέβαλλον ἢ καὶ τοὺς κυάμους, πατάλλια ταῦτα ἐκαλεῖτο. Cervenka-Ehrenstrasser (2000: 144–5 *s.v.* βατέλλιον), Daris (1991a: 33 *s.v.* βατέλλιον), *DÉLG* (*s.v.* πάτελλα), LSJ (*s.vv.* βάτελλα, πάτελλα). See §4.3.2 n. 69, §4.6.1 n. 84, §10.2.2 I.

rare

πάτελλον 'dish', from *patella* 'little dish': papyrus *BGU* III.781.vi.2 (I/II AD); cf. name Πατελλοχάρων, Alciphron, *Epistulae* 3.18.1 (II/III AD). Daris (1991a: 87), Hofmann (1989: 321 *s.v.* πατελλα), Meinersmann (1927: 45), *DÉLG* (*s.v.* πάτελλα), Gignac (1981: 9, considering this a variant of πάτελλα), LSJ (*s.v.* πάτελλα).

foreign

πάτερ transliterating *pater* 'father': in πάτερ πατρᾶτος for *pater patrātus*, a title, Plut. *Mor.* 279b (I/II AD); in σίνε πάτρις apparently for *sine patre* 'fatherless', Plut. *Mor.* 288f (I/II AD). Sophocles (1887). See §7.3.

rare

πατερεύω 'be a *pater civitatis*', from *pater* 'father' + -εύω: inscription Knackfuss 1924: 303 no. 206.9 (VI AD); perhaps papyrus *CPR* X.127.6 (VI AD). Lampe (1961), LSJ, LSJ suppl.

name

Πατέρνος, evidently from *paternus* 'paternal': cited by Hdn. *Pros.Cath.* III.1.175.25 (II AD) as Italian (Ἰταλιωτικόν); elsewhere it occurs only as a personal name, so Herodian (who often used names as examples) was probably thinking of the name here. Roussou (2018: 193.12, 457).

not Latin?

πατικουρᾶς, meaning uncertain, perhaps from *pāstus* 'pasturing' + *cūrō* 'care for' + -ᾶς: papyrus *BGU* II.594.3 (I AD). Filos (2010: 251), Daris (1991a: 87), Meinersmann (1927: 45), *TLL* (*s.v.* πατικουρας), LSJ. See §8.1.7 n. 34.

foreign

πατρᾶτος transliterating (*pater*) *patrātus*, a title: Plut. *Mor.* 279b (I/II AD). Strobach (1997: 198), Mason (1974: 74 *s.v.* πατήρ 3), Hofmann (1989: 321–2).

πάτρης κωνσκρίπτους: see κωνσκρίπτος.

Deriv. of loan
V AD – Byz.

πατρικία (-ας, ἡ) 'wife of a patrician' (in the late-imperial sense of 'patrician'), from *patricius* 'patrician' via πατρίκιος.

Documents: e.g. *P.Oxy.* 4754.4 (VI AD); *P.Erl.* 67.5 (VI AD); *Stud.Pal.* VIII.1094.1 (VI AD).

Inscriptions: *SEG* XLI.1408.2 (V AD).

Literature: e.g. *V.Dan.Styl.* A. 82 (V AD); Cyr.S. *Vit.Sab.* 145.7 (VI AD).

Post-antique: survives. *LBG*.

Notes: Daris (1991a: 87), Hofmann (1989: 322), LSJ (*s.v.* πατρίκιος). See §4.6.1, §10.2.2 D.

rare   **πατρικιᾶτος** 'patrician' (a type of shoe), perhaps from unattested **patriciātus*: Edict.Diocl. 9.7 (IV AD). Hofmann (1989: 322), *TLL* (*s.v.* 2. *patriciātus*), LSJ suppl. See §8.1.7.

Direct loan
II BC – modern   **πατρίκιος** (-ου, ὁ) 'patrician man' (designation that became a title in the late Empire), from *patricius* 'patrician'.

Documents: common, e.g. *P.Tebt.* 11.567.12 (I AD); *P.Oxy.* 3770.18 (IV AD); *P.Oxy.* 1134.2 (V AD); *P.Oxy.* 4785.4 (VI AD).

Inscriptions: e.g. *I.Ephesos* 701.11 (I AD); *I.Side* 60.4 (II AD); *I.Tralleis* 56.i.2 (IV/V AD); *SEG* XXXVII.605.5 (V/VI AD); *SEG* XXXV.849, seal (VI AD).

Literature: very common, e.g. Polybius 10.4.2 (II BC); Diodorus Siculus 12.25.2 (I BC); Augustus, *Res gestae* 8.1 Volkmann (I AD); Plut. *Cor.* 1.1 (I/II AD); Athan. *Apol.* 76.5 (IV AD); *V.Dan.Styl. A.* 55.9 (V AD); Cyr.S. *Vit. Sab.* 145.8 (VI AD); Antec. 1.2.4 (VI AD).

Post-antique: numerous. Zervan (2019: 133–4), Triandaphyllidis (1909: 126), Daris (1991a: 87). Modern πατρίκιος 'patrician': Babiniotis (2002), Andriotis (1967).

Notes: forms derivatives πατρικία, πατρικιότης, πρωτοπατρίκιος. Famerie (1998: 150–1), Freyburger-Galland (1997: 76–8), Strobach (1997: 198), Avotins (1992), Dubuisson (1985: 39), Daris (1991a: 87), Mason (1974: 5, 74), Hofmann (1989: 322), Zilliacus (1935a: 198–9, 1937: 332), Meinersmann (1927: 45–6), LSJ. See §4.2.4.1 n. 51, §4.6.1, §4.6.2, §8.1.3, §8.1.4, §10.2.1, §10.2.2 D.

Deriv. of loan
V AD – Byz.   **πατρικιότης** (-τητος, ἡ) 'patriciate', 'patrician dignity', from *patricius* 'patrician' via πατρίκιος + -ότης.

Literature: Priscus, *Fragmenta* 31.31 etc. Bornmann (V AD); Just. *Nov.* 38.pr.3 (VI AD); Ath.Schol. 18.P.4 etc. (VI AD); Antec. 1.12.4 (VI AD).

Post-antique: numerous. *LBG*.

Notes: Hofmann (1989: 322 *s.v.* πατρίκιος), Zilliacus (1935a: 198–9), LSJ. See §4.6.1, §10.2.2 D.

πατριμον-, πατριμουν-: see πατριμων-.

Direct loan
IV AD – Byz.   **πατριμωνάλιος, πατριμο(υ)νάλιος** (-α, -ον) 'belonging to the imperial property', from *patrimōniālis* 'belonging to the imperial property' (*TLL*).

Documents: e.g. *P.Oxy.* 900.5 (IV AD); *P.Col.* X.286.7 (IV AD); perhaps *P.Petra* III.25.10 (VI AD).

Post-antique: numerous, forming derivative πατριμωναλικός. *LBG* (*s.vv.* πατριμονάλιος, πατριμονιάλιος).

Notes: Daris (1991a: 87), Hofmann (1989: 323), Cavenaile (1951: 399), Zilliacus (1935a: 198–9), *TLL* (*s.v. patrimōniālis* 750.32–4). See §4.2.2, §10.2.1, §10.2.2 A.

non-existent?   **πατριμωνιανός** 'patrimonial', from *patrimōnium* '(imperial) property': emendation in papyrus *P.Ryl.* IV.655v.11 (IV AD). Daris (1991a: 87).

Direct loan
II AD – Byz.

πατριμώνιον, πατριμόνιον, πατριμούνιον, πατρεμούνιον, βατριμούνιον (-ου, τό) 'property', 'estate' (esp. of the emperor), from *patrimōnium* '(imperial) property'.

Documents: e.g. perhaps *P.Amst.* 1.28.4 (I BC); *P.Harrauer* 39v.8 (IV AD); *P.Petra* I.5.5 (VI AD).

Inscriptions: *I.Ephesos* 627.11 (II AD).

Literature: e.g. Just. *Nov.* 69.4.1 (VI AD); Ath.Schol. 4.13.3 (VI AD); Procop. *Bell.* 5.4.1: καὶ οὐχ ἥκιστά γε τὴν βασίλειον οἰκίαν αὐτήν, ἣν δὴ πατριμώνιον Ῥωμαῖοι καλεῖν νενομίκασι (VI AD); bilingual glossaries, e.g. Gloss. *Herm.Mp.* 297.74.

Post-antique: numerous. *LBG* (*s.v.* πατριμόνιον), Triandaphyllidis (1909: 128).

Notes: Binder (2000: 128, 222), Hagedorn (1980: 85), Avotins (1992 *s.v.* πατριμόνιον), Daris (1991a: 87–8), Mason (1974: 5, 74–5), Hofmann (1989: 322–3), Zilliacus (1935a: 198–9), Meinersmann (1927: 46), Lampe (1961 *s.v.* πατριμόνιον), LSJ suppl. See §4.2.4.1 n. 54, §8.1.5, §10.2.1, §10.2.2 A.

rare

πατριμώνιος 'administrator of the imperial property', from *patrimōnium* 'imperial property' via πατριμώνιον: Lyd. *Mag.* p. 124.15 (VI AD). *LBG.*

πατρον-: see πατρων-.

foreign

πατρούελες, πατρούελος 'of a paternal uncle', from *patruēlēs*, plural of *patruēlis* 'of a paternal uncle': Antec. in Latin script as part of phrases, e.g. 3.6.4 *fratres patrueles, sorores patrueles* (VI AD). Zilliacus (1935a: 198–9).

foreign

patruus 'paternal uncle': Antec. 3.6.3 *patruus* (VI AD). See §7.1.1, §7.2.1.

Direct loan
II BC – modern

πάτρων, πάτρον (-ωνος/-ονος, ὁ), πατρώνης (-ου, ὁ) 'patron', from *patrōnus* 'patron'.

Documents: common, e.g. *BGU* IV.1155.13 (I BC); *P.Oxy.* 2349.10 (I AD); *Pap.Choix* 10.9 (II AD); *BGU* I.96.9 (III AD); *P.Oxy.* 3420.1 (IV AD); *P.Princ.* II.104.3 (V AD); *SB* 14506.10 (VI AD).

Inscriptions: common, e.g. *SEG* XXXIX.1244.iii.11 (II BC); *I.Thrake Aeg.* 5.23 (II BC); *I.Délos* 1802.4 (II/I BC); *IGNapoli* II.133.7 (I AD); *SEG* XXXII.1231.5 (II AD); *TAM* V.II.840.a7 (III AD); *Corinth* VIII.III.502.4 (IV AD); *I.Jud.Western Europe* I.114.2 (IV/V AD).

Coins: ΝΕΡΩΝΙ ΔΗΜΟΣΙΩ ΠΑΤΡΩΝΙ ΕΛΛΑΔΟΣ at Apollonia, Head 1911: 314 (I AD).

Literature: e.g. perhaps Diodorus Siculus 29.27.1 (I BC); Epict. *Diss.* 3.9.18 (I/II AD); Artemidorus, *Onirocriticon* 4.81 (II AD); Modestinus in Just. *Dig.* 26.3.1 (III AD); Themistius, Ἐρωτικός 168a Downey and Schenkl (IV AD); Hesych. as lemma π 1141 (V/VI AD); Malal. 14.19 (VI AD); Just. *Nov.* 155.1 (VI AD); Antec. 3.7.pr. (VI AD); with *patronus* in glossaries, e.g. Gloss. Ps.-Philox. 143.27.

Post-antique: common. Zervan (2019: 134), Triandaphyllidis (1909: 128). Modern πάτρωνας 'patron': Babiniotis (2002), Andriotis (1967).

Notes: variant πατρώνης occurs only on inscriptions. Forms derivatives πατρωνεία, πατρωνεύω, πατρώνισσα, πατρωνικός. Daris (1991a: 88), Mason (1974: 75 and *passim*), Hofmann (1989: 323–4), Zilliacus (1935a: 198–9), Meinersmann (1927: 46), Immisch (1885: 338–9), Avotins (1989), Lampe (1961), LSJ (*s.vv.* πάτρων, πατρώνης), LSJ suppl. See §4.2.5, §4.6.1, §7.1.1, §7.1.2, §7.3 passage 30, **§8.1.4**, §8.1.5, §9.1 n. 4, §9.5.4, §9.5.6 nn. 55 and 56, §10.2.1, §10.2.2 N, §10.3.2, §12.2.1.

non-existent?

πατρώνα 'patroness', from *patrōna* 'patroness': perhaps inscription *SGDI* 11.2282.3 (I BC). Hofmann (1989: 324), LSJ (*s.v.* πάτρων).

Deriv. of loan II BC – modern

πατρων(ε)ία, πατρωνήα (-ας, ἡ) 'patronage', from *patrōnus* 'patron' via πάτρων + -ία.
  Inscriptions: *SEG* XXXIX.1243.ii.30 (II BC); *SEG* XXXII.825.19 (II BC); *I.Aphrodisias and Rome* 3.51 (I BC).
  Literature: DH *AR* 2.10.1 etc. (I BC); Plut. *Rom.* 13.3, marked (I/II AD); Paulus Alexandrinus, *Elementa apotelesmatica* p. 55.8 Boer (IV AD); Heliodorus Astrologus, *Commentarium in Paulum Alexandrinum* p. 64.23 Boer (IV AD); Rhetor. *Cap.* 170.20 (VI AD); with *patrocinium* in Gloss. *Idiom.* 548.4.
  Post-antique: Byzantine survival despite absence from lexica. Modern πατρωνία 'patronage': Babiniotis (2002).
  Notes: Mason (1974: 6, 75), Hofmann (1989: 323–4 *s.v.* πάτρων), LSJ. See §4.3.2 n. 75, §4.6.1, **§8.1.4**, §10.2.2 O, §10.3.2.

πατρώνεισα: see πατρώνισσα.

Deriv. of loan I BC – Byz.

πατρωνεύω, πατρονεύω 'be patron', from *patrōnus* 'patron' via πάτρων + -εύω.
  Documents: *P.Cair.Masp.* 67151.229 (VI AD).
  Inscriptions: *IGBulg.* I².314.a8 (I BC); *I.Ephesos* 630b.1 (I BC); *SGDI* 11.2688.7 (I BC); *I.Mus.Iznik* 1201.14.
  Literature: perhaps Diodorus Siculus 40.5.1 (I BC); *Acta Philippi* 1.15 = Bovon *et al.* 1999: 35.6 (IV AD); EphraemSyr. V p. 26.13 (V/VI AD); with *patrocinor* in Gloss. Ps.-Cyril. 399.56.
  Post-antique: survives despite absence from lexica.
  Notes: Mandilaras (1973: 67), Daris (1991a: 88), Mason (1974: 6, 75), Hofmann (1989: 323 *s.v.* πάτρων), Lampe (1961), LSJ, LSJ suppl. See §4.6.1, §8.1.5, §10.2.2 O, §10.3.2.

πατρωνήα: see πατρωνεία.

πατρώνης: see πάτρων.

πατρωνία: see πατρωνεία.

rare

πατρωνίκιον, πατρωνικίων 'rights of a patron', clearly Latinate but of uncertain source (in form it resembles *patrōnicius* 'of a patron' (*TLL*), but in meaning the more common *patrōcinium* 'patronage'): papyrus *P.Cair.Masp.* 67029.5 (VI AD). Daris (1991a: 88, with derivation from *patrōnātus*), Hofmann (1989: 324 *s.v.* πάτρων), Zilliacus (1935a: 198–9), Meinersmann (1927: 46), LSJ; for possible Byzantine survival *LBG*.

Deriv. of loan III AD – Byz.

πατρωνικός, πατρονικός (-ή, -όν) 'of or for a patron', from *patrōnus* 'patron' via πάτρων + -ικός.
  Documents: *SB* 12533.6 (II/III AD); *P.Oxy.* 1205.6 (III AD); *PSI* IX.1040.17 (III AD); perhaps *BGU* I.96.14 (III AD).
  Literature: Just. *Nov.* 1.4.1 etc. (VI AD); Ath.Schol. 9.1.6 etc. (VI AD); Antec. 3.7.2 etc. (VI AD).
  Post-antique: numerous despite absence from lexica.

Notes: direct derivations from *patrōnicius* 'of a patron' (*TLL*) and/or *patrōnālis* 'of a patron' are sometimes suggested but much less likely. Avotins (1989), Daris (1991a: 88), Mason (1974: 6, 75), Hofmann (1989: 324 *s.v.* πάτρων), Cavenaile (1952: 197), Zilliacus (1935a: 198–9), LSJ, LSJ suppl. See §4.6.1, §10.2.2 O, §10.3.2.

Deriv. of loan II AD – Byz.
πατρώνισ(σ)α, πατρόνισσα, πατρώνεισα (-ης, ἡ) 'patroness', from *patrōnus* 'patron' via πάτρων + -ισσα.

Documents: *P.Oxy.* 478.27 (II AD); *P.Diog.* 6.17 (II AD); *P.Matr.* 2.18 (II AD); *P.Lips.* II.151.10 (III AD).

Inscriptions: e.g. *I.Perge* 123.4 (II AD); *I.Ephesos* 1562.13 (II/III AD); *IG* X.II.1.187.13 (III AD).

Literature: Just. *Codex* 6.4.4.14c (VI AD); Antec. 3.7.3 (VI AD); with *patrona* in glossaries, e.g. Gloss. Ps.-Cyril. 399.58.

Post-antique: common in legal texts despite absence from lexica.

Notes: *patrōna* 'patroness' probably not relevant. Avotins (1989), Daris (1991a: 88), Hofmann (1989: 324 *s.v.* πάτρων), LSJ, LSJ suppl. See §4.6.1, §10.2.2 N, §10.3.2 n. 33.

rare
παῦγλα 'rammer', from *pavīcula* 'rammer': Edict.Diocl. 15.43 (IV AD). Binder (2000: 158, 204), Hofmann (1989: 324), LSJ suppl.

foreign
Παυλινιανόν, a cake, apparently from the rare name *Paulīniānus* (not in lexica but attested) or more common *Paulīnus* + *-iānus*: Athenaeus 14.647d, marked (II/III AD). Hauri-Karrer (1972: 120). See §9.4 passage 61.

foreign
pauperiēs 'poverty': Antec. 4.9.pr. *pauperiem* (VI AD).

παχτώνω: see πάκτον.

rare
πάων 'peacock', from *pāvō* 'peacock': variants at Edict.Diocl. 4.39 etc. (IV AD). Byzantine παώνιον 'peacock' may be related: Zervan (2019: 134), *LBG*. Hofmann (1989: 324), LSJ. Cf. παός, παόνιος.

rare
πεδάνεος, a type of judge, from (*iūdex*) *pedāneus* 'subordinate judge': Lyd. *Mag.* p. 142.17 (VI AD). *LBG*, Sophocles (1887).

Direct loan V AD – Byz.
πεδατοῦρα, παιδατοῦρα (-ας, ἡ) '(watchman's) allotted area', 'watch', from *pedātūra* 'measured area'.

Documents: perhaps (Worp 2005: 148–9 n. 10) *P.Amh.* II.142.16 (IV AD); *P.Flor.* III.384.118 (V AD); *P.Oxy.* 4394.192 etc. (V AD); Daris also cites unpublished Papiri Milanesi inv. 7401.5 (V/VI AD).

Inscriptions: *I.Chr.România* 8.2, perhaps 9.1 (both VI AD).

Literature: Malal. 14.2 (VI AD).

Post-antique: numerous. *LBG*, Triandaphyllidis (1909: 130).

Notes: Daris (1991a: 88), Hofmann (1989: 324–5), Zilliacus (1935a: 230–1), Lampe (1961). See §4.2.3.1, §6.11, §10.2.1, §10.2.2 O.

not ancient
πέδικλον 'shackle', from *pediculum* 'snare' (*TLL s.v.* 3. *pediculus*): no ancient examples. Binder (2000: 162, 175), Zilliacus (1935a: 230–1), *LBG*, Andriotis (1967 *s.v.* πέδικλο). See §5.2.2 n. 10; cf. πεδουκλώνω.

not ancient	**πεδίτης** 'foot soldiers' (collective singular), from *pedes* 'foot soldier': the alleged ancient example, *P.Cair.Masp.* 67147.2 (VI AD), is probably a form of πέδιτον (*q.v.*). Zilliacus (1935a: 230–1).
rare	**πέδιτον** 'expedition', from *expedītiō* 'expedition': papyrus *P.Cair.Masp.* 67147.2 (VI AD). Diethart (2006: 16 n. 37) offers a plausible derivation via ἐξπέδιτον. Byzantine πέδιτον 'infantry', from *peditātus, -ūs* 'infantry', is probably a different word. Daris (1991a: 88), Hofmann (1989: 325 *s.v.* πεδιτου), Meinersmann (1927: 46), Triandaphyllidis (1909: 130), *LBG*.
not ancient	**πεδουκλώνω** 'shackle the feet', from *pediculum* 'snare' (*TLL s.v.* 3. *pediculus*): no ancient examples. Binder (2000: 162, 175), Meyer (1895: 53), Andriotis (1967). Cf. πέδικλον.
not ancient	**πέδουλο** 'shoelace', from *pedūlis* 'of the feet': no ancient examples. Meyer (1895: 53).
	πεῖλα: see πίλα 2.
	πειλάριον: see πιλάριον.
not ancient	**πεκουλᾶτος, πεκουλᾶτον** 'embezzlement', from *pecūlātus, -ūs* 'embezzlement': no ancient examples. Zilliacus (1935a: 198–9), *LBG*.
not ancient	**πεκουλεύω**, meaning uncertain, perhaps from *pecūliō* 'provide with personal property' + -εύω: no ancient examples. Zilliacus (1935a: 198–9), *LBG* (*s.v.* πεκουλεύομαι).
rare	**πεκουλ(ι)άριον** 'personal property', from neut. subst. of *pecūliāris* 'personal' or *pecūliārius* 'personal': inscription *I.Ano Maked.* 22.7 (II/III AD). Byzantine πεκουλιάριος 'of personal property' (*LBG*), used in Latin script by Antec. 4.7.3 *peculiaria* etc. (VI AD), may be a different word. Zilliacus (1935a: 198–9), Triantaphyllides (1892: 269), LSJ suppl.
Direct loan **II AD – modern**	**πεκούλιον** (-ου, τό) 'personal property', from *pecūlium* 'personal property of a slave etc.'.

Documents: e.g. *SB* 10893.9 (II AD); *PSI* IX.1040.18 (III AD); *P.Kellis* I.48.6 (IV AD); *P.Cair.Masp.* 67314.1.33 (VI AD).

Inscriptions: *I.Ephesos* 25.36 (II AD); *I.North Galatia* 218.4 (I–IV AD); *SEG* XXXV.1267.7; *MAMA* VIII.379.

Literature: e.g. Plut. *Publ.* 11.6, marked (I/II AD); Gregorius Nazianzenus, *Testamentum*, Pitra 1868: 156.9 (IV AD); Asterius Amasenus, *Homiliae* 2.6.2 Datema (IV/V AD); Hesych. as lemma π 1271 (V/VI AD); Just. *Nov.* 128.8 etc., but in Latin script 81.1.1 (VI AD); Antec. 2.20.17 etc., but in Latin script 2.20.20 *peculiu* etc. (VI AD).

Post-antique: numerous. *LBG* (*s.v.* πεκούλιν). Modern dialectal πεκούλ' 'private property' etc.: Andriotis (1974: 443), Kahane and Kahane (1972–6: 532, 1982: 135).

Notes: Avotins (1992), Strobach (1997: 198), Daris (1991a: 88–9), Mason (1974: 5, 75), Hofmann (1989: 325), Zilliacus (1935a: 198–9), Cameron (1931: 253), Meinersmann (1927: 46), Immisch (1885: 357), Lampe (1961), LSJ, LSJ suppl. See §4.2.4.1 n. 54, §7.1.1, §10.2.1, §10.2.2 B.

foreign   **πεκουνία** transliterating *pecūnia* 'money': Lyd. *Mag.* p. 34.30 (VI AD); Antec. in Latin script as part of phrases, e.g. 4.6.8 *pecuniae constitutae* (VI AD). *LBG.*

foreign   **πέκους** 'livestock', from *pecus, pecudis* 'livestock': Antec. in Latin script 4.3.pr. *pecus* etc. (VI AD). Zilliacus (1935a: 198–9). See §7.2.1 n. 24.

rare   **πεκτοράλιον, πεκτοράριν** 'breastplate', from *pectorāle* 'breastplate': papyri *SB* 12574.7 (VI AD); perhaps *P.Mich.* XV.742.5 (VI AD). Diethart (1998: 175), Daris (1991a: 89), Triandaphyllidis (1909: 122), LSJ suppl. (*s.v.* gen. pl. πεκτοραλίων); for later survival *LBG.*

non-existent   **πελαγικός**, from *pelagicus* 'of the sea': superseded reading for πελάγιος in Plut. *Mor.* 685e (I/II AD). Sophocles (1887), LSJ.

πελεγρῖνος: see περεγρῖνος.

rare   **πελλοράφος** 'sewing skins together', from *pellis* 'skin' + ῥάπτω 'sew': Gloss. Ps.-Philox. 144.46. Hofmann (1989: 325), *DÉLG*, Beekes (2010), LSJ.

non-existent   **πελλούκιδος**, from *pellūcidus* 'transparent': superseded reading for περλούκιδον (*q.v.*) in Athenaeus 14.647c (II/III AD). Sophocles (1887).

foreign   **πενᾶτες** transliterating *penātēs* 'household gods': DH *AR* 1.67.3, 1.68.1 (I BC); Procop. *Bell.* 5.25.19 (VI AD). Hofmann (1989: 325).

πένουλα: see φαινόλη.

rare   **πενταμοδιαῖος** 'holding five pecks', from πεντα- 'five' + *modius* 'peck' via μόδιος: Edict.Diocl. 15.48 (IV AD). LSJ. See §4.6.2.

rare   **πενταμόδιον** 'vessel holding five pecks', from πεντα- 'five' + *modius* 'peck' via μόδιος: Malal. 11.14 (VI AD). Lampe (1961). See §4.6.2.

Deriv. of loan VI AD   **πενταξεστιαῖος** (-ον) 'holding five pints', from πέντε 'five' + *sextārius* 'pint measure' via ξεστιαῖος.
Documents: e.g. *CPR* VIII.63.2 (VI AD); *PSI* VIII.881.5 (VI AD); *SB* 15725.6 (VI AD).
Notes: not attested in feminine; LSJ suppl. (superseding LSJ *s.v.* πενταξεστιαῖον) infers from form that it would be two-termination. Filos (2010: 251), Daris (1991a: 89). See §4.6.2, §4.6.3, §9.2, §10.2.2 E.

rare   **πενταούγκιον, πεντόγκιον** 'five ounces', 'five twelfths of an inheritance', from πέντε 'five' + *ūncia* 'one twelfth' via οὐγγία: Epicharmus frag. 9, 10 Kassel–Austin (V BC) (both quoted in Pollux 9.82); perhaps inscribed weight *SEG* L.1008.B1 (II AD); with *quincunx* in Gloss. Ps.-Cyril. 401.17; Byzantine texts. Hofmann (1989: 302 *s.v.* οὐγκία), *LBG* (*s.v.* πενταούγγιον), LSJ, LSJ suppl. (*s.v.* πεντόγκιον). See §4.6.2.

rare   **πενταρρόστουλον**, perhaps 'five-beaked vase' or 'five-beaked lamp', from πέντε 'five' + *rōstrum* 'beak' (via unattested **rostulum?*): papyrus *P.Cair.Masp.* 67167.11 (VI AD). Filos (2010: 251), Daris (1991a: 89), Cavenaile (1952: 199), Meinersmann (1927: 46). Cf. ῥῶστρον.

πεντόγκιον: see πενταούγκιον.

Direct loan **IV–VI AD?**	**πεξός** (-ή, -όν) 'brushed', from *pexus*, pf. part. of *pectō* 'brush'. Documents: *P.Dubl.* 20.25 (IV AD); *PSI* XIV.1427.20 (VI AD). Inscriptions: Edict.Diocl. 20.12 etc. (IV AD). Literature: πεξονειματιον with *prosa pexa tunica*, Gloss. Ps.-Philox. 162.43. Post-antique: perhaps *P.Wash.Univ.* II.104.18 (VI/VII AD). Notes: Commentary on *P.Dubl.* 20, Lauffer (1971: 269), Hofmann (1989: 326), LSJ suppl. (superseding LSJ *s.v.* πεξόν). See §4.2.2, §4.6.2, §10.2.1, §10.2.2 H; cf. λινόπηξος.
non-existent	**πεξουτός**, from *pexātus* 'wearing a garment that still has a nap on it (i.e. a new one)': superseded reading of Edict.Diocl. 20.12 (IV AD). Sophocles (1887).
rare	**πεπερᾶτον** 'wine flavoured with pepper' or 'pepper dressing', from neut. subst. of *piperātus* 'flavoured with pepper': inscription *I.Cret.* I.XVII.17.10 (I BC); *Coll.Herm.* ME 11h (II–IV AD). Buck and Peterson (1945: 475), *LBG*, LSJ (*s.v.* πεπερᾶτος). See §6.5 n. 31.
	περατοῦρα: see παρατοῦρα.
rare	**περγαμηνός** 'parchment', from *pergamēnus* 'parchment' (L&S): Edict.Diocl. 7.38 (IV AD); Lyd. *Mens.* 1.28: ἀντευδοκιμεῖται δὲ ὅμως παρὰ τοῦ Περγαμηνοῦ Ἀττάλου, Κράτητος τοῦ γραμματικοῦ ἡγησαμένου τῆς σπουδῆς πρὸς ἔριν Ἀριστάρχου τοῦ ἀντιτέχνου αὐτοῦ· δέρματα γὰρ τὰ ἐκ προβάτων ἀποξέσας εἰς λεπτὸν ἔστειλε τοῖς Ῥωμαίοις τὰ λεγόμενα παρ' αὐτοῖς μέμβρανα· εἰς μνήμην δὲ τοῦ ἀποστείλαντος ἔτι καὶ νῦν Ῥωμαῖοι τὰ μέμβρανα Περγαμηνὰ καλοῦσιν (VI AD). Hofmann (1989: 326), LSJ (*s.v.* Πέργαμος), LSJ suppl.
not ancient	**πέργουλο** 'trellis for grapevines', from *pergula* 'trellis': no ancient examples. *LBG* (*s.v.* περγουλέα), Zervan (2019: 136, 143), Meyer (1895: 53), Andriotis (1967 *s.v.* modern πέργουλα).
foreign	**περδουελλίων** transliterating *perduelliō* 'treason': Dio Cassius 37.27.2 (II/III AD). Freyburger-Galland (1997: 216–17, 1998: 139), Mason (1974: 6, 12, 75), *LBG*.
Direct loan **III AD – Byz.**	**περεγρῖνος, περεγρῆνος, περεγρεῖνος** (-η, -ον) 'foreign', 'for foreigners', from *peregrīnus* 'foreign'. Documents: *P.Oxy.* 2951.27 (III AD). Inscriptions: *I.Perge* 289.4 (III AD); *MAMA* VI.181 (III AD). Literature: Lyd. *Mag.* p. 60.5, marked (VI AD); Antec. 1.12.1, but in Latin script 1.2.7 *peregrinois* etc. (VI AD); Just. *Nov.* in Latin script 78.5 etc. (VI AD). Post-antique: numerous. *LBG*, Zervan (2019: 135–6). Byzantine meaning 'pilgrim' and alternative spelling πελεγρῖνος come from medieval meaning/form of *peregrīnus*, owing to contact during Crusades (Kahane and Kahane 1982: 151). Notes: more common as a name. Diethart (1988: 62, 1999: 181), Daris (1991a: 89), Mason (1974: 6, 75), Zilliacus (1935a: 198–9). See §4.2.2, §8.2.2, §10.2.1, §10.2.2 B, §12.2.2.

rare περεμπτόριος 'decisive', from *perēmptōrius* 'decisive': papyrus *P.Cair.Masp.* 67097v. D87 (VI AD); Antec. in Latin script 4.13.8 *peremptoriae* etc. (VI AD); often later. Daris (1991a: 89), Cavenaile (1951: 399), Zilliacus (1935a: 198–9), *LBG*.

not Latin? περεσίκα 'pocket', perhaps from *byrsa* 'hide' (*TLL*): probably no ancient examples. Meyer (1895: 53).

περιπρέσσα: see περπρέσσα.

rare περισκουτλόω 'surround with *opus sectile*', from περί 'around' + *scutula* 'diamond shape' via σκουτλόω: inscription *TAM* III.1.713.5 (II AD). LSJ.

Loan compound V AD – Byz. περιστερόπουλ(λ)ος, περιστερόπουλ(λ)ον (-ου, ὁ or τό) 'small dove', from περιστερά 'pigeon' + *pullus* 'young bird'.
Documents: *CPR* VII.42.ii.1 (V AD).
Literature: Hieroph. *Nut.* 1.2 etc. (IV–VI AD); Ps.-Hippocrates, Delatte 1939: 484.1.
Post-antique: survives. *LBG* (*s.v.* περιστερόπουλον).
Notes: Diethart (1988: 62–3, 1999: 181), editor of *P.Oxy.* 3869.10 *ad loc.*, Filos (2010: 244, 251), Daris (1991a: 89), LSJ suppl. See §4.5, §10.2.1, §10.2.2 I; cf. πουλλίον.

foreign περλούκιδον, a cake, from *perlūcidus* 'transparent': Athenaeus 14.647c, marked (II/III AD). Hauri-Karrer (1972: 82), Hofmann (1989: 326), *LBG* (*s.v.* περλούκιδος). See §9.4 passage 61.

foreign περμουτατίων 'exchange', from *permūtātiō* 'exchange': Antec. in Latin script 2.1.35 *permutationos* etc. (VI AD); later in Greek script. Zilliacus (1935a: 198–9), *LBG*, Sophocles (1887). See §9.5.6 n. 68.

Direct loan I BC – Byz. πέρνα, πέρνη, πτέρνη (-ης, ἡ) 'ham', from *perna* 'ham'.
Documents: *PSI* VI.683.33 (II AD); perhaps *O.Claud.* II.415.iv.2 (II AD).
Inscriptions: Edict.Diocl. 4.8 (IV AD); *SEG* VII.435.1.
Literature: *Batrachomyomachia* 37 (II/I BC); Strabo 3.4.11 (I BC/AD); Hdn. Μον.Λεξ. III.II.939.8, perhaps *Pros.Cath.* III.1 327.13 (II AD); Pollux 2.193, 6.53 (II AD); Athenaeus 14.657e (II/III AD); Orib. *Syn.* 7.34.4 (IV AD); Aëtius 12.65.17 etc. (VI AD); Gloss. Ps.-Philox. 198.24.
Post-antique: numerous despite absence from *LBG*.
Notes: In *O.Claud.* II.415 may refer to a shellfish, one called *perna* in Latin (editors *ad loc.*). Wackernagel (1916: 195–8), Daris (1991a: 89), Hofmann (1989: 326), *DÉLG*, Frisk (1954–72: II.516), Beekes (2010), LSJ (*s.vv.* πέρνα, πτέρνη III), LSJ suppl. (*s.v.* πτέρνη). See **§4.2.6**, §4.3.2 n. 75, §4.4, §8.1.5, §10.2.1, §10.2.2 I.

not ancient περπέρι 'newly emerged butterfly', perhaps from *pāpiliō* 'butterfly': no ancient examples. Meyer (1895: 53–4).

not Latin πέρπερος 'boastful' and relatives περπερ(ε)ία 'vanity', περπερότης 'vanity', περπερεύομαι 'boast', ἐμπερπερεύομαι 'boast', ῥωποπερπερήθρα 'empty braggart talk': often said to come from *perperam* 'wrongly' or rarer *perperus* 'wrong', but probably Greek formations from πρέπω 'be fitting' with metathesis + -ερος. Blanc (1996, 1997), Hofmann (1989: 326), *DÉLG*, *DÉLG Suppl.*, Frisk (1954–72: II.517), Beekes (2010), LSJ.

non-existent	**περπετεύω** 'continue', from *perpetuō* 'continue': superseded reading of Antec. 2.1 (VI AD). Zilliacus (1935a: 198–9).
foreign	**περπετοῦος** 'perpetual', from *perpetuus* 'perpetual': Antec. in Latin script 4.12.pr. *perpetuos* etc. (VI AD); later in Greek script. Zilliacus (1935a: 198–9), *LBG*. See §9.5.6 n. 68.
not ancient	**περπρέσσα, περιπρέσσα** transliterating *perpressa*, a plant: interpolation in Dsc. 1.10 RV. Sophocles (1887 *s.v.* περιπρέσσα).
rare	**περσεκουτίων** 'prosecution', from *persecūtiō* 'persecution', 'prosecution' (*TLL*): Just. *Nov.* 135.pr. (VI AD); Antec. in Latin script 4.6.17 *persecutiona* etc. (VI AD); Byzantine texts. Avotins (1992), Zilliacus (1935a: 198–9), *LBG*. See §9.5.6 n. 68.
foreign	**πέρ ση** transliterating *per sē* 'through himself': Lyd. *Mag.* p. 96.23 (VI AD). Sophocles (1887).
Direct loan **VI AD – Byz.**	**περσονάλιος** (-α, -ον) 'personal', from *persōnālis* 'personal'. Literature: Just. *Nov.* 4.2 etc. (VI AD); Lyd. *Mag.* p. 164.20 etc. (VI AD); Ath. Schol. 15.1.2 (VI AD); Antec. in Latin script 1.2.6 *personaliai* etc. (VI AD). Post-antique: numerous. *LBG*. Notes: Avotins (1992), Hofmann (1989: 327), Zilliacus (1935a: 198–9), Lampe (1961), LSJ suppl. See §4.2.2, §9.5.6 n. 68, §10.2.1, §10.2.2 B; cf. κουροπερσονάριος.
foreign	**περσῶνα** transliterating *persōna* 'person': as part of κουράτωρ (or κοῦρα) περσωνάρουμ, *P.Wash.Univ.* 1.6.3 etc. (VI AD); as plant name, Aëtius 11.10.22 (VI AD); Antec. in Latin script as part of *unde decem personae*, 3.9.3 etc. (VI AD); as plant name, interpolation in Dsc. 4.106 RV. Worp (1982: 564–5), Daris (1991a: 89).
	περτρακτάτωρ: see πρετακτάτωρ.
foreign	**πέρφεκτος** from *perfectus* 'complete': Antec. in Latin script 3.19.18 *perfecton* (VI AD); later in Greek script. Zilliacus (1935a: 198–9), *LBG*.
	πετεῖτορ: see πετίτωρ.
foreign	**πετιτεύω** 'petition', from *petītus*, pf. part. of *petō* 'seek' (or perhaps *petītiō* 'petition') + -εύω: Antec. in Latin script as part of phrases, e.g. 4.6.33b *plus petiteuei* (VI AD); later in Greek script. Zilliacus (1935a: 198–9), *LBG*. See §9.5.6 n. 68.
rare	**πετιτίων** 'petition', 'seeking', from *petītiō* 'petition': papyrus *P.Oxy.* 2561.9 etc. (III/IV AD); Antec. in Latin script as part of phrases, e.g. 4.6.33a *plus petition* (VI AD); common in Byzantine texts. Daris (1991a: 89), Zilliacus (1935a: 198–9), *LBG*.
rare	**πετίτωρ, πετεῖτορ** 'applicant', a title, from *petītor* 'applicant': inscriptions Rostovtzeff *et al.* 1939: 87.6 (II/III AD); *IGR* III.1202.5; Byzantine texts. Mason (1974: 5, 76), Zilliacus (1935a: 198–9), *LBG*, LSJ suppl.
	πημεντάριος: see πιμεντάριος.

rare	**πιᾶκλον** 'expiatory offering', from *piāculum* 'expiatory offering': inscription *SEG* VII.351.1 (III AD). Binder (2000: 158), Hofmann (1989: 327), LSJ suppl.
	πιβρᾶτος: see πριβᾶτος.
not Latin?	**πιγκέρνης, πινκέρνης, πινκίρνας** (-ου, ὁ) 'bar-keeper', 'cup-bearer', perhaps from *pincerna* 'cup-bearer' (*TLL*), but probably *vice versa*. Daris (1991a: 89), Hofmann (1989: 327), Meinersmann (1927: 46), *TLL* (*s.v. pincerna* 2152.37–41), LSJ, LSJ suppl.
	πιγμεντάριος: see πιμεντάριος.
	πιγμέντις: see ἀ πιγμέντις.
foreign	**πιγνερατίκιος** 'concerning giving as a pledge', from *pignerātīcius* 'concerning a pledge or mortgage': Antec. in Latin script 4.1.14 *pigneratician* etc. (VI AD); later in Greek script. Zilliacus (1935a: 198–9), *LBG*. See §9.5.6 n. 68.
foreign	**πιετατις** transliterating *pietātis*, gen. of *pietās*: *O.Claud.* II.329.13 (II AD).
foreign	**πικέλα** 'pitch', from *picula* 'liquid pitch' (*TLL*): Hesych. as lemma π 2275 (V/VI AD). Immisch (1885: 342).
foreign	**πῖκος** transliterating *pīcus* 'woodpecker': DH *AR* 1.14.5 (I BC); Strabo 5.4.2 (I BC/AD). Hofmann (1989: 327).
rare	**πίλα 1** 'mortar' (i.e. receptacle for pounding things in), from *pīla* 'mortar' (*OLD pila¹*): papyri *P.Mert.* 1.39.10 (IV/V AD); *P.Oxy.* 1890.12 (VI AD). If it is source of πιλάριον it must be earlier. Daris (1991a: 89), Hofmann (1989: 327), Cavenaile (1951: 399), *DÉLG*, Beekes (2010), LSJ. See §4.6.1.
Direct loan II AD – Byz.	**πίλα 2, πεῖλα** (-ας, ἡ) 'pier', 'mole', 'jetty', from *pīla* 'pillar', 'pier' (*OLD pila²*). Inscriptions: *IG* V.I.233.4 (II AD); *I.Ephesos* 23.17 (II AD). Literature: DH *AR* 3.22.9, marked, meaning 'pillar' (I BC); Hesych. as gloss ε 4732, but entry is corrupt (V/VI AD); Malal. 11.14 (VI AD). Post-antique: survives. *LBG* (*s.v.* πίλα 1). Notes: from a Greek perspective may have been same word as πίλα 'mortar'. Hofmann (1989: 327), Lampe (1961), LSJ suppl. (*s.v.* πεῖλα). See §2.2.1, §4.2.3.1, §10.2.1, §10.2.2 J.
Deriv.? of loan II–VI AD	**πιλάριον, πειλάριον** (-ου, τό), an eye-salve, a lead plaster, and a cap, probably from *pīla* 'mortar' (via πίλα 1?) or *pīlum* 'pestle' + -άριον. Documents: *PSI* XV.1541.2 (II AD); *SB* 11964.11 etc. (V/VI AD); *SB* 14402.3 etc. (V/VI AD). Literature: Orib. *Ecl.* 89.23 (IV AD); Aëtius 6.1.45 etc. (VI AD). Notes: must have different etymology in meaning 'cap'. Daris (1991a: 89), *DÉLG* (*s.v.* πίλα), Beekes (2010 *s.v.* πίλα), LSJ. See §4.3.2, §4.6.1, §6.3, §10.2.2 L.
foreign	**πιλάριος** 'javelin-fighter', from *pīlāris* 'of javelins' (*TLL*): Lyd. *Mag.* p. 72.20, marked (VI AD). *TLL* (*s.v.* 1. *pīlāris*), *LBG* (with implausible derivation from *pilārius* 'juggler').
	πίλεον: see πιλίον.

non-existent?	**πίλεος** 'cap' is cited by LSJ as a borrowing of *pilleus/pīleus* 'felt cap indicating freedman status' on the basis of a variant reading in Polybius 30.18.3 (II BC); the form there is accusative, so even if the variant is accepted there is no evidence for a masculine (i.e. a borrowing) as opposed to a Latin-influenced spelling of πιλίον. Cf. πιλίον.
semantic extension	**πιλίον, πίλεον** 'cap' is a Greek diminutive of πῖλος 'felt cap', but when spelled with ε and/or referring specifically to a freedman's cap it may be influenced by *pilleus/pīleus* 'felt cap indicating freedman status'. Dubuisson (1985: 39–40), Hofmann (1989: 327–8 *s.v.* πίλεον), LSJ (*s.vv.* πίλεος, πιλίον), LSJ suppl. (*s.v.* πιλίον). See §2.3 n. 58, cf. πίλεος.
rare	**πιλλᾶτος** 'freedman', from *pilleātus* 'wearing a freedman's cap': Epict. *Diss.* 4.7.37 (I/II AD). Mason (1974: 8, 76), Hofmann (1989: 328), LSJ.
semantic extension	**πῖλος 1** 'felt cap', a Greek word, may occasionally mean 'freedman's cap' under influence from Latin *pilleus/pīleus* 'felt cap indicating freedman status'. Hofmann (1989: 328 *s.v.* πίλεον), *DÉLG*, Beekes (2010), LSJ. See §2.3 n. 58.
foreign	**πῖλος 2**, used with πρῶτος 'first' as calque of *prīmus pīlus* 'senior centurion' (*OLD pilus²*): Dio Cassius 48.42.3 (II/III AD). Freyburger-Galland (1997: 196), Mason (1974: 76), Hofmann (1989: 328–9), LSJ (*s.v.* πῖλος IV). Cf. πριμίπιλος.
semantic extension	**πῖλος 3** 'hair' on Edict.Diocl. 11.1a etc. (IV AD) is probably Greek πῖλος 'felt' with meaning influenced by *pilus* 'hair' (*OLD pilus¹*). Hofmann (1989: 328).
Direct loan III AD – Byz.	**πιμεντάριος, πιγμεντάριος, ποιμεντάριος, πημεντάριος** (-ου, ὁ) 'spicer', 'apothecary', from *pigmentārius* 'dealer in paints or cosmetics'.
	Documents: tachygraphy in Menci 2000: 287 (V AD).
	Inscriptions: *MAMA* VIII.574.9 (II/III AD).
	Literature: EphraemSyr. III *Sermones paraenetici ad monachos Aegypti* or. 2.54 (V/VI AD); Hesych. as lemma π 2296 (V/VI AD); Olympiodorus Philosophus, *In Platonis Gorgiam commentaria* 1.13.49 etc. Westerink (VI AD); Asclepius, *In Aristotelis Metaphysicorum libros A–Z commentaria* p. 154.19 Hayduck (VI AD).
	Post-antique: numerous. *LBG*.
	Notes: Immisch (1885: 349) claims that the Hesychius is interpolated. Menci (2000: 287), Hofmann (1989: 329), Lampe (1961 *s.v.* πημεντάριος), LSJ, LSJ suppl. See §4.2.4.1 n. 50, §10.2.1, §10.2.2 I.
	πινκέρνης: see πιγκέρνης.
foreign	**πίος** 'dutiful', from *pius* 'dutiful': part of name of military unit λεγιῶνος κβ′ Πρειμιγενίας Πίας Φιδήλεως in inscriptions, e.g. *I.Ephesos* 28.15 (II AD); Hesych. as lemma π 2331 (V/VI AD). Hofmann (1989: 329), Immisch (1885: 337), *LBG*.
	πιρμίπιλον: see πριμίπιλον.
rare	**πισκάριον** 'fish market', from (*forum*) *piscārium* 'fish market': inscription *SEG* XIX.115.23 (II/III AD). Hofmann (1989: 239), LSJ suppl.

rare   πισκ(ε)ῖνα, πισκίνη, φισκῖνα, πυσκίννα 'basin', 'grave', from *piscīna* 'pond', 'tank': papyrus *Stud.Pal.* xx.211.7 (v/vi ad); inscriptions *I.Hadrianoi Hadrianeia* 47.7 (i/ii ad); *CIL* iii.14894.9; Hippolytus, *Refutatio omnium haeresium* 9.12.1, marked (iii ad). Diethart (1998: 175), Daris (1991a: 90), Hofmann (1989: 329), Meinersmann (1927: 51), Lampe (1961 *s.vv.* πισκινή, φισκίνα), LSJ suppl.; for Byzantine survival *LBG* (*s.vv.* πισκίνα, φισκίνα), Triandaphyllidis (1909: 124); for modern dialectal survival Kahane and Kahane (1972–6: 534).

not Latin?   πιστίκιον, πισσίκιον, a cereal, perhaps related to *pistor* 'miller', 'baker'. Lauffer (1971: 214 on 1.7), Cavenaile (1951: 399), LSJ suppl.

non-existent?   πιστρίνη 'bakery', from *pistrīna* 'bakery': perhaps ostracon *O.Douch.* 1.39.7 (iv/v ad). Daris (1991a: 90), LSJ suppl.

rare   πιστρῖνον 'mill', from *pistrīnum* 'mill': Hippolytus, *Refutatio omnium haeresium* 9.12.4 (iii ad). Hofmann (1989: 330).

rare   πλαγιαρία 'kidnapping', apparently from *plagiārius* 'kidnapper' (via πλαγιάριος?) + -ία: papyrus *SB* 10929.5 (ii ad).

rare   πλαγιάριος 'kidnapper', from *plagiārius* 'kidnapper': Teucer, Boll 1903: 50.33 (i ad?); Gloss. Ps.-Cyril. 408.29; Byzantine texts. Probably source of πλαγιαρία. Hofmann (1989: 330), *LBG*, LSJ suppl.

not Latin   πλακουντάριος 'cake-maker', cited by Zilliacus (1937: 332) as a Latin loan, comes from πλακοῦς 'flat cake' + -άριος. LSJ, LSJ suppl. See §6.1.

not ancient?   πλάνη 'plane' (the carpentry tool), from *plāna*, fem. of *plānus* 'even': probably no ancient examples. Meyer (1895: 54), Andriotis (1967 *s.v.* πλάνη II).

foreign   πλανιπεδαρία transliterating (*fābula*) *plānipēs*, a kind of drama: Lyd. *Mag.* p. 62.4, 8 (vi ad). *LBG*, Sophocles (1887).

not ancient   πλάντρα, part of a mill, perhaps from *planta* 'sole of the foot': no ancient examples. Meyer (1895: 54).

foreign   πλεβίσκιτον 'decree of the people', from *plēbiscītum* 'decree of the people': Antec. in Latin script 1.2.4 *plebiscitu* etc. (vi ad); later in Greek script. Zilliacus (1935a: 198–9), *LBG*, Sophocles (1887).

     πλετώριον: see πραιτώριον.

rare   πλήβ(ε)ιος 'plebeian', from *plēbēius* 'plebeian': inscription *I.Perge* 289.3 (iii ad); DH *AR* 2.8.1, 5.18.1, both marked (i bc). Mason (1974: 6, 76), Hofmann (1989: 330).

foreign   πλῆβις transliterating gen. of *plēbs* 'common people' in τριβούνους πλῆβις: Eutropius 1.13 (iv ad).

Direct loan with influence   πληγᾶτος (-η?, -ον) 'wounded', from *plāgātus*, pf. part. of *plāgō* 'wound' (*TLL*), with influence from πληγή 'blow'.
v ad – Byz.   Literature: Callin. *V.Hypat.* 6.2 (v ad); Malal. 12.36, 18.26 (vi ad). Post-antique: numerous. *LBG*.

Notes: taken by Zilliacus (1937: 335) as Greek combination of πληγή + -*ātus*, and by Gusmani (1981–3: I.121) as remodelling of *vulneratus*. Hofmann (1989: 330), *TLL* (*s.v. plāgo* 2304.43), Lampe (1961). See §4.2.2, §4.4, §6.6, §10.2.1, §10.2.2 C.

Direct loan with influence VI AD – Byz.

πληναρία (-ας, ἡ) 'completeness', probably fem. subst. of *plēnārius* 'complete' (*TLL*) with influence from -ία.

Documents: *P.Lond.* v.1674.41 (VI AD); *P.Petra* III.35.15 (VI AD); *P.Wash. Univ.* I.8.5 (VI AD).

Literature: Just. *Edict* 13.6 = p. 782.31 etc. (VI AD).

Post-antique: survives despite absence from lexica.

Notes: Daris (1991a: 90), Hofmann (1989: 330), Palmer (1945: 76–7), Meinersmann (1927: 46–7), LSJ. See §4.4, §6.2, §10.2.1, §10.2.2 O.

rare

πληνάριος 'comprehensive', 'full', from *plēnārius* 'complete' (*TLL*): perhaps curse tablet Audollent 1910: 546.8 (III AD); decree recorded in inscriptions *SEG* XLIV.909.8 and *I.Keramos* 65.8 (both V AD); Just. *Nov.* 128.3 (VI AD); Byzantine texts. Avotins (1992), Hofmann (1989: 331), Zilliacus (1935a: 198–9), Cameron (1931: 253), *LBG*, LSJ suppl.

foreign

πηνιλούνιον transliterating *plēnilūnium* 'full moon': Lyd. *Mens.* 3.10.74 (VI AD). *LBG*, Sophocles (1887).

not Latin

πλίκιον, a cake mentioned in Athenaeus 14.647c (II/III AD), has been unconvincingly derived from some unspecified, unattested Latin word containing -*plic*- weakened from the *plec*- root found in *plectō* 'beat'. Hauri-Karrer (1972: 130), Hofmann (1989: 331), Beekes (2010), LSJ. See §9.4 passage 61.

non-existent

πλινθάριος, from unattested **plinthārius* 'brickmaker': superseded reading for πλινθάρια 'bricks', Dor.Gaz. *Doct.Div.* 13.145.13 (VI AD). Hofmann (1989: 331), Sophocles (1887), Lampe (1961).

not ancient

πλουβιάτικος transliterating *pluviāticus* 'of rain' (*TLL*), part of a plant name: interpolation in Dsc. 4.125 RV. Sophocles (1887 *s.v.* πλουβιάτικους), *TLL* (*s.v. pluviāticus*).

Direct loan IV AD – modern

πλουμάκιον, φλουμάκειον (-ου, τό) 'pillow', from *plūmācium* 'feather pillow' (*TLL*).

Documents: *P.Berl.Sarisch.* 20.6 (IV AD); *SB* 15961.6 (V/VI AD); perhaps *P.Lond.* v.1885 (V/VI AD); *P.Ness.* III.18.31 etc. (VI AD); *Stud.Pal.* XX.172.2 (VI AD).

Literature: Barsanuph.Jo. I ep. 191.18: εὑρίσκω κοιμηθῆναι ἐπάνω πλουμακίων (VI AD); with *plumacium* in Gloss. Ps.-Cyril. 410.18.

Post-antique: Byzantine examples exist despite absence from lexica. Modern dialectal survival: Kahane and Kahane (1972–6: 536), Meyer (1895: 54).

Notes: LSJ has definition 'embroidery'; *LBG* has definition 'feather pillow'; in Barsanuph.Jo. 'pillow' is certain, and in several papyri it must refer to a concrete object. Ensslin (1926: 445) and Hofmann (1989: 331) suggest that προμάξιον and προμάξιμον (*q.v.*) may be mistakes for this. Daris (1991a: 90). See §4.2.4.1 n. 54, §10.2.1, §10.2.2 H.

rare	**πλουμαρία**, probably 'female tapestry-weaver', from *plūmārius*, probably 'tapestry-weaver', via πλουμάριος: papyrus *P.Oxy.* 4001.20 (IV AD). Wild and Dross-Krüpe (2017), *LBG*. See §6.2 n. 13.
Deriv. of loan **IV AD – Byz.**	**πλουμαρικός, φλουμαρικός, προυμαρικός** (-ή, -όν), probably 'tapestry woven', from *plūmārius*, probably 'tapestry-weaver', via πλουμάριος + -ικός. Documents: e.g. *P.Dubl.* 20.3 (IV AD); *SB* 11075.11 (V AD); *P.Mich.* XIV.684.12 (V/VI AD). Literature: Thdt. *PG* LXXX.633a: τὸν δὲ χιτῶνα τὸν ἀστραγαλωτόν, ὁ μὲν Ἀκύλας "καρπωτόν" ἡρμήνευσεν, ἀντὶ τοῦ καρποὺς ἐνυφασμένους ἔχοντα· οἱ νῦν δὲ αὐτὸν καλοῦσι "πλουμαρικόν" (V AD); scholia to Lycophron, *Alexandra* 864. Post-antique: some survival. Daris (1991a: 90). Notes: for meaning see Wild and Dross-Krüpe (2017). Editor of *P.Dubl.* 20 *ad loc.*, Daris (1991a: 90), Hofmann (1989: 331–2 *s.v.* πλουμαριος), Cavenaile (1952: 197), Lampe (1961), LSJ (*s.vv.* πλουμαρικός, φλουμαρικός), LSJ suppl. See §4.6.1, §10.2.2 H.
not ancient	**πλουμάριον**, probably 'tapestry weaving', from some derivative of *plūma* 'feather': no ancient examples. Wild and Dross-Krüpe (2017), Daris (1991a: 90, with derivation from *plūmārium*), *LBG*.
Direct loan **IV AD – Byz.**	**πλουμάριος, πλουμμάριος, φλουμάρης** (-ου, ὁ), probably 'tapestry-weaver', from *plūmārius*, probably 'tapestry-weaver'. Documents: e.g. *P.Oslo* III.161.14 (III/IV AD); *P.Eleph.Wagner* I.324.2 etc. (IV/V AD); *P.Aberd.* 59.3.2 (V/VI AD); *SB* 10935.21 (VI AD). Inscriptions: e.g. Edict.Diocl. 20.1 (IV AD); *I.Cilicie* 38.3 (V/VI AD); *MAMA* III.496. Literature: Rhetor. *Cap.* 213.26 (VI AD); as gloss in old scholion to Aeschines 1.97 line 21; with *plumarius* in Gloss. *Herm.Mp.* 309.22. Post-antique: numerous despite absence from lexica, forming derivative πλουμαρίζω (*LBG*). Daris (1991a: 90). Notes: for meaning see Wild and Dross-Krüpe (2017). Forms derivatives πλουμαρικός, πλουμαρία, πλουμάρισις, πλουμάρισσα. Pruneti (1998), Daris (1991a: 90), Hofmann (1989: 331–2), Meinersmann (1927: 47), LSJ, LSJ suppl. See §4.2.4.1 n. 50, §4.6.1, §10.2.1, §10.2.2 H.
rare	**πλουμαρίσιμος**, perhaps 'tapestry woven', probably from *plūmārius*, probably 'tapestry-weaver' (via πλουμάρισις or πλουμάρισσα?) + -ιμος: papyrus *SB* 16204.9 (IV/V AD). Cavenaile (1952: 199) considers it a hybrid compound of *plūma*, but could -αρίσιμος be the second element of a compound? Wild and Dross-Krüpe (2017), Daris (1991a: 90, with derivation from *plūma*), Hofmann (1989: 332 *s.v.* πλουμαριος), LSJ suppl.
rare	**πλουμάρισις**, probably 'tapestry weaving', from *plūmārius*, probably 'tapestry-weaver', via πλουμάριος + -σις: Edict.Diocl. 19.6 etc. (IV AD); perhaps papyrus *P.Lond.* V.1885 (V/VI AD). Perhaps source of πλουμαρίσιμος. Wild and Dross-Krüpe (2017), Hofmann (1989: 332 *s.v.* πλουμαριος), LSJ.
rare	**πλουμάρισσα**, probably 'female tapestry-weaver', from *plūmārius*, probably 'tapestry-weaver', via πλουμάριος + -ισσα: papyrus *P.Aberd.* 59.i.7 (V/VI AD). Perhaps source of πλουμαρίσιμος. Wild and Dross-Krüpe (2017), Daris (1991a: 90), Hofmann (1989: 332 *s.v.* πλουμαριος), Cavenaile (1952: 195), LSJ suppl.

non-existent	**πλουμᾶτος**, probably 'tapestry woven', from *plūmātus*, pf. part. of *plūmō* probably 'tapestry weave': probably not (*BL* XI.152) papyrus *P.Oxy.* 1741.16 (IV AD). Wild and Dross-Krüpe (2017), Daris (1991a: 90, with derivation from *plūma*), Hofmann (1989: 332), Meinersmann (1927: 47), LSJ.
not ancient?	**πλουμβατίζω** 'beat using a whip fitted with lead balls', from *plumbāta* 'whip fitted with lead balls' (*TLL s.v. plumbo* 2454.20–9) + -ίζω: Hesychius of Jerusalem, *Homilia* 20.8 Aubineau (V AD?). *LBG*.
not ancient?	**πλουμβᾶτος** 'leaded', probably from *plumbātus*, pf. part. of *plumbō* 'lead': no certainly ancient examples. Zilliacus (1937: 332).
non-existent?	**πλουμίκιον**, meaning uncertain, presumably from *plūma* 'feather': perhaps papyrus *P.Harr.* 1.158.4 (V/VI AD). Daris (1991a: 90).
Direct loan with suffix? **V AD – modern**	**πλουμίον, πλουμμίον** (-ου, τό), probably 'tapestry weaving', from *plūma* 'feather' + -ιον, or neuter of *plūmeus* 'feathery'.

Documents: *PSI* III.225.6 (VI AD); perhaps *Stud.Pal.* XX.245.6 etc. (VI AD).
Literature: Geront. *V.Mel.* 2.31 (V AD); Malal. 17.9.20 (VI AD); Procop. *Aed.* 3.1.23: χιτὼν ἐκ μετάξης ἐγκαλλωπίσμασι χρυσοῖς πανταχόθεν ὡραϊσμένος, ἃ δὴ νενομίκασι πλούμια καλεῖν (VI AD); with *pluma* in Gloss. Ps.-Philox. 152.17, cf. Gloss. Ps.-Cyril. 410.19.
Post-antique: numerous. *LBG*, Triandaphyllidis (1909: 122). Modern πλουμί 'ornamentation' and derivatives: Babiniotis (2002), Andriotis (1967), Kahane and Kahane (1972–6: 535), Meyer (1895: 54).
Notes: for meaning see Wild and Dross-Krüpe (2017). Daris (1991a: 90), Hofmann (1989: 332), Meinersmann (1927: 47), Lampe (1961), LSJ. See §4.2.4.1 n. 54, §4.3.2 n. 69, §4.6.2, §10.2.1, §10.2.2 H; cf. ἔμπλουμος, ἐμπλούμιος, εὔπλουμος, ὀρθόπλουμος, πλοῦμος.

πλουμμάριος: see πλουμάριος.

πλουμμίον: see πλουμίον.

rare	**πλοῦμος, πλοῦμον** 'down', from *plūma* 'feather', 'down': Edict.Diocl. 18.1–4 (IV AD). Hofmann (1989: 332–3), LSJ suppl. Cf. πλουμίον, ἔμπλουμος, ἐμπλούμιος, εὔπλουμος, ὀρθόπλουμος.
not ancient	**ποδηλον**, meaning uncertain, is cited as an ancient borrowing of *podiolum* 'stool' (*TLL*) by Cameron (1931: 253) and Hofmann (1989: 333) on the basis of an inscription that probably dates to the late Byzantine period: Keil and Premerstein 1914: 91–2 no. 125, with commentary.

ποεν-: see ποιν-.

ποιμεντάριος: see πιμεντάριος.

foreign	**ποῖνα, ποένα** 'penalty' seems to be a borrowing of *poena* 'penalty' in Byzantine Greek (*LBG*), and an early stage of that borrowing may be seen in the use in Latin script of *poenas* and *poenan* in *Schol.Sinai.* 2, 6, 7 (V/VI AD) and *poenην* in Antec. 3.19.19 (VI AD). Antec. frequently uses Greek ποινή 'penalty' (e.g. 3.19.19), apparently without a distinction. Cavenaile (1951: 399), Zilliacus (1935a: 200–1). See §2.3 n. 57, §7.1.2, §7.1.3, §9.5.6 nn. 56 and 68.

foreign   **ποινάλιος, ποενάλιος** 'demanding punishment beyond bare recompense for the damage done', from *poenālis* 'concerned with punishment': Antec. in Latin script 4.3.9 *poenalian* etc. (VI AD); later in Greek script. Hofmann (1989: 333), Zilliacus (1935a: 200–1), *LBG*. See §9.5.6 n. 68.

rare   **πολιτικοπραιτώριος** 'in accordance with civil and praetorian law', from πολιτικός 'civic' or *polīticus* 'concerned with civil government' + *praetōrius* 'praetorian' via πραιτώριος: papyrus *P.Cair.Masp.* 67151.44 (VI AD). Filos (2010: 251), Daris (1991a: 90), Hofmann (1989: 345 *s.v.* πραιτώριος), Cavenaile (1952: 199), Meinersmann (1927: 47), LSJ.

not Latin   **πολλαχρός** 'beautiful', a lemma in Hesych. π 2801 (V/VI AD), is cited by Immisch (1885: 315) and Hofmann (1989: 333) as a derivative of an unattested word from an Italic language (probably not Latin), related to Latin *pulcher* 'beautiful'.

rare   **πόλλινος**, apparently gen. of *pollen* 'finely ground flour': *Hippiatr.Par.* (Apsyrtus) 452 (III/IV AD?).

rare   **πολταρίδιον, πουλταρίδιον, βουλταρίδιον** 'little pot', from *pultārius* 'cooking pot' via πολτάριος + -ίδιον: alchemist in *P.Holm.*, frag. 10.5 Halleux (IV AD); Ps.-Galen XIV.422.6, 469.17 Kühn (after II AD). Hofmann (1989: 333 *s.v.* πολτάριος), *DÉLG* (*s.v.* πόλτος), Frisk (1954–72: II.577), *LBG*, LSJ (βουλταρίδιον *s.v.* πολτάριος).

    πολτάριον: see πόλτος.

rare   **πολτάριος** 'pot', from *pultārius* 'cooking pot' (itself ultimately from πόλτος 'porridge'): Galen XII.432.16, XIII.280.11 Kühn (II AD); Ps.-Galen XIV.438.6, 480.17; with *pultarium* in Gloss. *Herm.Mp.* 326.42. Forms derivative πολταρίδιον. Hofmann (1989: 333), *DÉLG* (*s.v.* πόλτος), Frisk (1954–72: II.577), LSJ.

not Latin   **πόλτος** 'porridge' (with diminutive πολτάριον 'bad porridge'), is given by García Domingo (1983: 251), Hofmann (1989: 333–4, cf. Hahn 1906: 2, 8), and Immisch (1885: 315) as a borrowing of an Italic word related to Latin *puls* 'porridge', but *DÉLG*, Frisk (1954–72: II.577), Beekes (2010), Biville (1992: 234), and Campanile (1969: 302–3) reject this view. The source is in any case not Latin, though Bellocchi (2016: 327) implies that it might be. LSJ.

rare   **πολυκαισαρίη** 'excess of Caesars', from πολύς + *Caesar* via Καῖσαρ + -ία (in an Ionic form): Plut. *Ant.* 81.5 (I/II AD). Hofmann (1989: 140 *s.v.* Καῖσαρ), LSJ.

rare   **πολυκάνδηλος, πολυκάνδηλον** 'chandelier', 'candelabra', from πολύς 'many' + *candēla* 'candle' via κανδήλη: papyrus *SB* 15526.6 (V AD); perhaps inscription Feissel and Philippidis-Braat 1985: 366 no. 74; Byzantine texts. *LBG*, Lampe (1961), LSJ suppl.

not ancient?   **πολυκανδίλιον**, probably 'chandelier' or 'candelabra', from *candēla* 'candle' (via πολυκάνδηλος + -ιον?): on a candelabrum, Içten and Engelmann 1992: 286 no. 5.

rare   **πολυκελλάριον**, a container, from πολύς 'many' + *cellārium* 'storeroom' via κελλάριον: papyrus Maravela-Solbakk 2009: 139.7 (V/VI AD). Maravela-Solbakk (2009: 143).

not Latin · **πόλυντρα** 'barley groats', a lemma in Hesych. π 2895 (v/vi AD), is sometimes said to be connected to *polenta* 'barley groats' but is probably Aeolic Greek. Hofmann (1989: 334), Immisch (1885: 332), LSJ, LSJ suppl.

πομαρι-: see πωμαρι-.

foreign · **πόνδερε** 'by weight', from *pondere*, abl. of *pondus* 'weight': Antec. in Latin script 2.8.2 *pondere* etc. (vi AD); later in Greek script.

foreign · **πόντεμ, πόντης,** and **πόντην,** transliterations of forms of *pōns, pontis* 'bridge': Plut. *Numa* 9.2 (i/ii AD); Lyd. *Mens.* 4.15 (vi AD); Procop. *Aed.* 4.6.16 (vi AD). Luc. *Hist.Conscr.* 15 (ii AD) may indicate that it was sometimes used as Greek. Hofmann (1989: 334 *s.v.* πόντην), Hahn (1907: 708 n. 114, on Lucian), *LBG* (*s.v.* πόντης), Sophocles (1887 *s.v.* πόνς). See §7.2.1, §9.4 passage 53.

rare · **ποντίλιον:** transliterating *pontīle* 'bridge-shaped structure' (*TLL*): Lyd. *Mens.* 4.15 (vi AD); with *pons* in Gloss. Ps.-Cyril. 413.33. Hofmann (1989: 334), *LBG*, Meyer (1895: 54), *TLL* (*s.v. pontīle*), LSJ.

rare · **πόντιλον** 'floorboard', from *pontīle* 'bridge-shaped structure' (*TLL*): *Hippiatr. Camb.* (Pel.) 56.5 (v AD?). Zilliacus (1935a: 230–1), *LBG*.

not ancient? · **ποντιλόω** 'cover with floorboards', from *pontīle* 'bridge-shaped structure' (*TLL*): no ancient examples (but see ποντίλωμα). Zilliacus (1935a: 230–1), *LBG*.

rare · **ποντίλωμα** 'floor beam', from *pontīle* 'bridge-shaped structure' (*TLL*) + ωμα: *V.Luc.Styl.* 23.21 (vi AD). Nouns in -ωμα normally come from verbs in -όω (Buck and Petersen 1945: 222), so ποντίλωμα may come from ποντιλόω, which in that case would be older than it looks. *LBG*.

**Direct loan
II AD – modern** · **ποντίφεξ, ποντίφιξ** (-ικος/-εκος, ὁ), a priestly title, from *pontifex* 'one of the college of priests having supreme control in matters of public religion'.
Inscriptions: e.g. *IG* ii/iii².iii.4072.4 (ii AD); *SEG* xxxiv.678.iii.2 (iii AD).
Literature: common in authors dealing with Roman matters, e.g. DH *AR* 1.38.3, marked (i BC); Plut. *Numa* 9.1, marked (i/ii AD); Dio Cassius 7.25.5 (ii/iii AD); Eus. *PE* 4.16.18, marked (iv AD); Zosimus, *Historia nova* 4.36.1 Paschoud, marked (v AD?); Lyd. *Mag.* p. 52.23 (vi AD).
Post-antique: survives. *LBG*. Modern ποντίφικας, ποντίφηκας 'pontiff': Babiniotis (2002), Andriotis (1967).
Notes: despite its wide distribution the term is often marked as foreign in literature; evidently it was a technical term for Roman culture. Vaahtera (2001: 56–64), Freyburger-Galland (1997: 219, 1998: 139), Strobach (1997: 198), Mason (1974: 4, 77, 115), Hofmann (1989: 334–5), LSJ. See §4.2.5, §10.2.1, §10.2.2 D.

foreign · **ποντιφικάλιος** transliterating *pontificālis* 'of a pontifex': Lyd. *Mens.* 4.25.11 (vi AD). *LBG*.

ποντίφιξ: see ποντίφεξ.

ποπῖνα: see προπῖνα.

not ancient	**ποπουλάριος** 'of the people', from *populāris* 'of the people': no ancient examples. Zilliacus (1935a: 200–1), *LBG*.
foreign	**ποπούλους** transliterating *populus* 'people': Plut. *Rom.* 13.2 (I/II AD). *LBG* (*s.v.* πόπουλος), Sophocles (1887 *s.v.* πόπουλους).
not Latin?	**πορθμάριος, προθμάριος** 'ferryman', perhaps from unattested **porthmārius* but probably a Greek combination of πορθμός 'ferry' + -άριος. Hofmann (1989: 335), Cavenaile (1952: 202), LSJ suppl. See §6.1.
non-existent	**πόρκινος**, from *porcīnus* 'of a pig': superseded reading of Plut. *Publ.* 11.7 (I/II AD). Sophocles (1887).
foreign	**πόρκος** transliterating *porcus* 'pig': Plut. *Publ.* 11.7 (I/II AD). Hofmann (1989: 335), LSJ (*s.v.* πόρκος II).
Direct loan **V AD – modern**	**πόρτα** (-ης/-ας, ἡ) '(city) gate', from *porta* 'gate'. Documents: Ricci 1903: 570 no. 149.1. Inscriptions: Knackfuss 1924: 303 no. 206.5 (VI AD); *SEG* XXXV.1475.8.3 (VI AD); *MAMA* VII.310.2; *I.Chr.Égypte* 685.1. Literature: common, e.g. Ps.-Athanasius, *PG* XXVIII.33d (IV AD?); Pausanias Damascenus Historicus, *FHG* IV frag. 4.105, marked (IV AD); *Apophth.Patr.* 20.24.33 (V AD); Malal. 5.6 (VI AD); *Vita S. Marinae* 4.122 Clugnet (VI AD). Unverified example (II AD) in Zilliacus (1937: 322, 332). Post-antique: common. Zervan (2019: 137–8), Triandaphyllidis (1909: 95, 99, 120), Daris (1991a: 91), Sophocles (1887). Modern πόρτα 'door', 'gate': Babiniotis (2002), Andriotis (1967), Meyer (1895: 54). Notes: Daris (1991a: 91), Hofmann (1989: 335), Zilliacus (1937: 332), Meinersmann (1927: 47), Immisch (1885: 342), Lampe (1961). See §8.2.3, §10.1, §10.2.1, §10.2.2 J.
not Latin?	**πόρτακος** 'shoulder', a lemma in Hesych. π 3073 (V/VI AD), could come ultimately from *portō* 'carry'. Hofmann (1989: 336), Hahn (1906: 10–11), Immisch (1885: 316), LSJ.
	πορταρῆνσις: see πορταρῆσις.
	πορτάρης: see πορτάριος.
Direct loan **V AD?**	**πορταρῆσις, πορταρήσιος, πορταρῆνσις** (declension uncertain, ὁ) 'gate-keeper', apparently from unattested **portārēnsis*. Documents: *O.Douch.* 1.41.1 etc., probably also 1.31.1, v.548v.5, v.573.2 (all IV/V AD). Inscriptions: *I.Chr.Égypte* 475 (perhaps name Πορδαρησις, but see commentary on *O.Douch.* 1.31). Notes: inscription and ostraca were found not far apart. Daris (1991a: 91, with derivation from *portārius*), *TLL* (*s.v.* πορταρήσιος), LSJ suppl. See §4.2.5, §6.7 n. 45, §8.1.7 n. 34, §9.2, §10.2.1, §10.2.2 N.
rare	**πορτάριος, πορτάρης** 'gate-keeper', from *portārius* 'door-keeper' (*TLL*): Malal. 16.16 (VI AD); Byzantine and modern Greek (*LBG s.v.* πορτάρης; Byzantine πορταΐτισ(σ)α 'female gate-keeper'; Andriotis 1967 *s.v.* πορτάρης). Hofmann (1989: 336), Triandaphyllidis (1909: 124), *TLL* (*s.v. portārius* 10.2), Lampe (1961).

not Latin?	**πορτᾶς**, an occupational term probably on papyrus *P.Oxy.* 1519.7 (III AD), may mean 'dealer in calves' and have a Greek etymology, or mean 'gate-keeper' and be from *porta* 'gate' via πόρτα + -ᾶς. Hofmann (1989: 335 *s.v.* πόρτα), LSJ, LSJ suppl.
foreign	**πόρτικος** 'colonnade', from *porticus, -ūs* 'colonnade': Hesych. as lemma π 3074 (V/VI AD); numerous Byzantine examples. Hofmann (1989: 336), Immisch (1885: 342), Triandaphyllidis (1909: 120 *s.v.* πόρτιξ), Sophocles (1887), Lampe (1961).
name	**Πόρτος**, a place name, from *Portus, -ūs* (Forcellini *et al.* 1864–1926: Onomasticon): no secure ancient examples of a generic sense (i.e. one derived from *portus, -ūs* 'harbour'). Daris (1991a: 91, citing place name in *P.Mich.* VIII.490.10 etc.), Hofmann (1989: 336, citing place name in Ps.-Clemens Romanus, *Homiliae* 12.10.1 Irmscher), Zilliacus (1937: 332, citing unverified example), Cavenaile (1951: 399), Lampe (1961, citing superseded reading for πόρων in Ath.Schol. 4.3.3); for later survival *LBG.* See §12.2.2.
foreign	**ποσσεσσίων** 'possession', from *possessiō* 'possession': Antec. in Latin script as part of *bonorum possessio* 2.9.6 (VI AD); occasionally later in Greek script. Zilliacus (1935a: 200–1).
foreign	**ποσσέσσωρ** 'owner', from *possessor* 'owner': Antec. in Latin script as part of phrases, e.g. 2.6.12 *bonorum possessor* (VI AD); later in Greek script. Zilliacus (1935a: 200–1), *LBG.* See §9.5.6 n. 68.
foreign	**ποστλιμίνιον** 'right to restoration of one's former privileges', from *postlīminium* 'resumption of civic rights': Antec. in Latin script 1.12.5 *postliminion* etc. (VI AD); later in Greek script. Zilliacus (1935a: 200–1), *LBG*, Sophocles (1887). See §9.5.6 n. 68.
rare	**πόστουμος** 'born after his father's death', from *postumus* 'born after his father's death': Plut. *Sulla* 37.4, marked (I/II AD); *Schol.Sinai.* in Latin script 40 *postumois* (V/VI AD); Just. *Codex* 6.48.1.1 (VI AD); Antec. in Latin script 1.13.4 *postumois* etc. (VI AD); common in Byzantine legal texts. Strobach (1997: 198), Avotins (1989), Zilliacus (1935a: 200–1), *LBG*, Sophocles (1887). See §7.1.2, §9.5.6 n. 56.
	πότενς: see πότηνς.
foreign	**ποτέστας** 'power', from *potestās* 'power': Antec. in Latin script 1.8.1 *potestas* etc. (VI AD); later in Greek script. Zilliacus (1935a: 200–1), *LBG* (*s.v.* ποτεστάτης), Zervan (2019: 138). Cf. ἰνποτέστατος.
foreign	**πότηνς** transliterating *potēns* 'powerful': Plut. *Numa* 9.2 (I/II AD). Sophocles (1887 *s.v.* πότενς). See §7.2.1.
rare	**πότιον 1** 'drink', from *pōtiō* 'drink': *Hippiatr.Berl.* 129.31. *LBG* (*s.v.* πότιον A).
foreign	**πότιον 2**, transliterating *puteus/puteum* 'well': Stephanus of Byzantium δ 81 (VI AD). *LBG* (*s.v.* πότιον B).
foreign	*potior* (in acc. pl. *potioras*) 'having a better claim': *Schol.Sinai.* 53 (V/VI AD). See §7.1.2, §9.5.6 nn. 56 and 57.

πουβλικάριος: see πουλικάριος.

not ancient | πουβλικίζω 'make public', from *pūblicō* 'make public' (or *pūblicus* 'public' via πούβλικος?) + -ίζω: no ancient examples. Zilliacus (1935a: 232–3), *LBG*.

Direct loan
II AD – Byz.

πούβλικος, πουπλικός (-η, -ον) 'public' (in neut. pl. a type of payment), from *pūblicus* 'public'.

Documents: *O.Krok.* 1.70.4 (I/II AD); O.Dios inv. 480.5 etc., 972.4 = Cuvigny 2010b: 38, 45 (both II AD); perhaps *O.Did.* 97.3 (III AD).

Literature: Hippolytus, *Refutatio omnium haeresium* 9.12.1 (III AD); *Carth.* 261.9 (V AD); Lyd. *Mens.* 4.10, marked (VI AD); Antec. in Latin script 1.26.3 *publican* etc. (VI AD).

Post-antique: common, forming derivatives πουβλικίζω 'publicize', etc. *LBG*.

Notes: Cuvigny (2010b: 44–50), Hofmann (1989: 336–7), Zilliacus (1935a: 202–3), Lampe (1961). See §4.2.2, §10.2.1, §10.2.2 O.

not Latin? | πουγγίον, πούγγα 'bag' may come from *punga* 'little bag' (*TLL*) or directly from the Germanic source of the Latin. Common in Byzantine texts and yields modern πουγκί, πουγγί, etc. 'purse' (Babiniotis 2002; Andriotis 1967, 1974: 462), but no certainly ancient examples. Kramer (2011: 269–77), Hofmann (1989: 337), Viscidi (1944: 13), *LBG*, Sophocles (1887), Meyer (1895: 55), Triandaphyllidis (1909: 122), *TLL* (s.v. *punga*).

πουγίων: see φουγίων.

not ancient | ποῦκτον, meaning uncertain, from *punctum* 'point': no ancient examples. Zilliacus (1935a: 202–3).

πουλβεῖνον, πουλβεῖνος: see πουλβῖνον.

rare | πουλβινάριον, φλουβινάριον 'little cushion', from *pulvīnus* 'cushion' via πουλβῖνον + -άριον: papyrus *P.Berl.Sarisch.* 21.1.7 (V/VI AD); perhaps with *pulvinus* in Gloss. Serv. 516.23. Hofmann (1989: 337 s.v. πούλβινον), *LBG* (s.v. φλουβινάριον), LSJ (s.v. πουλβῖνον). See §6.3 n. 21.

Direct loan
I–V AD

πουλβῖνον, πουλβεῖνον, φουλβῖνον, φολβεῖνον, φουλβίν, φουλβῖνα(ν), πούλβιον, πουλβ(ε)ῖνος (-ου, τό or ὁ) 'cushion', 'pillow', from *pulvīnus* 'cushion', 'pillow'.

Documents: *SB* 1.10 (III AD); *P.Berl.Sarisch.* 20.7 (IV AD); *P.Gen.* 1.80.13 (IV AD); *P.Oxy.* 1290.7 (V AD). Perhaps also πουιῶν in *P.Warr.* 18.12 (III AD).

Inscriptions: Edict.Diocl. 28.56 (IV AD).

Literature: Erot. *Voc.Hipp.* 118.11 as gloss (I AD); Epict. *Diss.* 3.23.35 (I/II AD).

Notes: masc. only in Edict.Diocl.; πούλβιον only in Erotian. LSJ suppl.'s definition for πουλβῖνος, 'bed-tick', means 'mattress'. Forms derivative πουλβινάριον. Daris (1991a: 91), Hofmann (1989: 337, 477), Cavenaile (1951: 399 s.v. πουιῶνα), Meinersmann (1927: 47), *LBG* (s.vv. φολβῖνον, πούλβιον), LSJ (s.vv. πουλβῖνον, φουλβῖνον, φουλβίν), LSJ suppl. (s.vv. πουλβῖνον, φουλβῖνον, πουλβῖνος, πουιῶν). See §4.2.4.1 n. 58, §9.2, §9.5.1, §10.2.1, §10.2.2 H.

rare	**πουλικάριος, πουβλικάριος**, a description of a blanket, from *pūlicāre*, a word for 'covering' etymologically meaning 'thing for fleas' (*TLL s.v. pūlicāris* 2580.11–15): Edict.Diocl. 8.43 (IV AD). Hofmann (1989: 337), *TLL loc. cit.*, LSJ suppl.
	πουλίον: see πουλλίον.
not ancient	**πουλλικρούρα**, a plant, perhaps from unattested **pullīcrūs* 'chicken leg' (*TLL*): interpolation in Dsc. 3.123 RV. Hofmann (1989: 337–8), *TLL* (*s.v. pullicrus*). See §8.1.7.
Direct loan with suffix IV AD – **modern**	**πουλ(λ)ίον** (-ου, τό) 'chicken', 'cockerel', 'bird', from *pullus* 'young bird' + -ιον. Documents: *SB* 15243.1 etc. (IV AD); *SB* 15302.315 (V AD); probably *P.Oxy.* 1913.26 (VI AD). Literature: *Physiologus* 16 Sbordone (II–IV AD); Ps.-Hippocrates, Delatte 1939: 483.9. The standardly cited example in the Infancy Gospel of Thomas is a late corruption (Burke 2010: 343.11). Post-antique: common. *LBG*, Triandaphyllidis (1909: 119). Modern πουλί 'bird': Babiniotis (2002), Andriotis (1967). Notes: forms derivative ὀρνιθοπούλλιον. Daris (1991a: 91), Hofmann (1989: 338, with derivation from unattested **pullium*), Cavenaile (1952: 195), Meinersmann (1927: 47), LSJ suppl. See §4.3.2, §8.2.3, §10.2.1, §10.2.2 I; cf. περιστερόπουλλος.
not ancient?	**ποῦλλος** 'chicken', from *pullus* 'young bird': no securely ancient examples: papyrus *P.Oxy.* 1913.26 (VI AD) probably reads πουλλίον (*BL* XI.155); Dsc. 2.139 RV (πέδεμ πούλλι transliterating *pedem pulli*) is an interpolation. Daris (1991a: 91), Diethart (1999: 181), Kahane and Kahane (1972–6: 534), Sophocles (1887: 37 and *s.v.*), Babiniotis (2002 *s.vv.* -πουλο, πούλος), Andriotis (1967 *s.vv.* -πουλος, -πουλο), LSJ suppl.
rare	**πούλπιτον** 'platform', from *pulpitum* 'platform': Gloss. Ps.-Cyril. 414.57; superseded reading of Malal. 15.7 (cf. L. Dindorf 1831: 387.13). Binder (2000: 142), Hofmann (1989: 338), Zilliacus (1935a: 232–3, 1937: 332), *LBG*, Lampe (1961).
not ancient	**πουλπιτόω** 'put boards over', from *pulpitō* 'put boards over': no ancient examples. Zilliacus (1935a: 232–3), *LBG*, *TLL* (*s.v. pulpito*).
name?	**πουλσάτωρ**, apparently from *pulsātor* 'one who strikes' (*TLL*), could be either a name or a description of a gladiator: inscription *IGBulg.* III.I.1453 (II/III AD). Hofmann (1989: 338).
	πουλταρίδιον: see πολταρίδιον.
name	**Πούλχερ**, a personal name, from *pulcher* 'beautiful'. Sophocles (1887).
	ποῦνδα: see φοῦνδα.
foreign	**πουπιλλάριος** 'concerning a minor', 'concerning a ward', from *pūpillāris* 'concerning a minor', 'concerning a ward': Antec. in Latin script 2.16.pr. *pupillarian* etc. (VI AD); later in Greek script. Zilliacus (1935a: 202–3), *LBG*. See §9.5.6 n. 68, §10.3.1 n. 30.

foreign	**πούπιλ(λ)ος** 'minor', 'ward', from *pūpillus* 'minor', 'ward': Thüngen 2016: A12 in Latin script (v AD); Antec. in Latin script 1.23.5 *pupilloi* etc. (vi AD); later in Greek script. Zilliacus (1935a: 202–3), *LBG*. See §7.1.1, §7.3 passage 33, §9.5.6 n. 68.
	πουπλικός: see πούβλικος.
not ancient	**πουράτα** 'pus', from *pūs* 'pus' via unattested **pūrātum*: no ancient examples. Binder (2000: 252), Meyer (1895: 55).
not Latin?	**πούριον**, a cake mentioned in Athenaeus 14.647d (II/III AD), may be related to *pūrus* 'pure'. Hofmann (1989: 339), LSJ. See §9.4 passage 61.
foreign	**ποῦρος** 'absolute', 'unconditional', from *pūrus* 'pure': Antec. in Latin script 2.14.9 *puros* (adverb), 3.29.3 *puran*, etc. (vi AD); later in Greek script. Zilliacus (1935a: 202–3), Triantaphyllides (1892: 270), *LBG* (*s.vv.* ποῦρος, πούρως). See §9.5.6 n. 68, §10.3.1.
not ancient	**πουτιαλογονθρια** (corrupt), transliterating a plant name: interpolation in Dsc. 3.94 RV. *TLL* (*s.v.* πουτιαλογονθρια). See §8.1.7 n. 34.
not Latin?	**ποῦτριν** 'rotten', a gloss in Hesych. π 3177 (v/vi AD), might come from *putris* 'rotten' or πύθω 'cause to rot'. Hofmann (1989: 339), Immisch (1885: 348), LSJ, LSJ suppl.
not ancient	**πραεβαρικατεύω, πραιβαρικατεύω** 'collude', from *praevāricātus* (pf. part. of *praevāricor* 'collude') + -εύω: no ancient examples. Zilliacus (1935a: 200–1), *LBG*.
not ancient	**πραεβαρικατίων, πραιβαρικατίων** 'collusion', from *praevāricātiō* 'collusion': no ancient examples. Zilliacus (1935a: 200–1), *LBG*.
not ancient	**πραεβαρικάτωρ, πραιβαρικάτωρ** 'colluder', from *praevāricātor* 'colluder': no ancient examples. Zilliacus (1935a: 200–1), *LBG*.
non-existent?	**πραεδικατίων** 'announcement', from *praedicātiō* 'announcement', cited as an ancient loan by Zilliacus (1935a: 200–1): I can find no examples.
not ancient	**πραέδιον** 'landed property', from *praedium* 'landed property': no ancient examples. Zilliacus (1935a: 200–1), *LBG*.
foreign	**πραεϊουδικ(ι)άλιος, πραιϊουδικιάλιος** 'concerning preliminary issues', from *praeiūdiciālis* 'concerning a preliminary enquiry': Antec. in Latin script 4.6.13 *praeiudicaliae* etc. (vi AD); later in Greek script. Zilliacus (1935a: 200–1), *LBG*.
foreign	**πραεϊουδίκιον, πραιϊουδίκιον** 'preliminary enquiry', from *praeiūdicium* 'preliminary enquiry': Antec. in Latin script 4.6.13 *praeiudicion* etc. (vi AD); later in Greek script. Zilliacus (1935a: 200–1), *LBG*.
foreign	**πραεκάριος, πρεκάριος, πραικάριος** 'at request', 'liable to revocation', from *precārius* 'depending on the will of others': Antec. in Latin script 1.14.1 *precaria* (vi AD); later in Greek script. Zilliacus (1935a: 200–1), Triantaphyllides (1892: 271), *LBG*, Sophocles (1887 *s.v.* πρεκάριος). See §9.5.6 n. 68.

foreign	**πραεποστέρα, πραιπόστερος** 'inverted stipulation', from *praeposterus* 'inverted': Antec. in Latin script 3.19.14 *praeposteran* (VI AD); later in Greek script. Zilliacus (1935a: 200–1), *LBG* (*s.v.* πραεπόστερος).
non-existent?	**πραεσκριπτίων** 'precept', from *praescrīptiō* 'precept', cited as an ancient loan by Zilliacus (1935a: 200–1): I can find no examples.
not ancient	**πραεσκρίπτος** 'prescribed', from *praescrīptus*, pf. part. of *praescrībō* 'prescribe': no ancient examples. Zilliacus (1935a: 200–1).
not ancient	**πραεστατίων** 'obligatory service', from *praestātiō* 'obligatory service or payment' (*TLL*): no ancient examples. Zilliacus (1935a: 200–1), *LBG*.
	πραετακτάτωρ: see πρετακτάτωρ.
foreign	***praetexta*** 'toga worn by youths': Antec. 4.4.1 *praetexta* (VI AD).
foreign	**πραετεριτεύω, πραιτεριτεύω** 'pass over' (i.e. not mention in one's will), from *praeteritus* (pf. part. of *praetereō* 'omit') + -εύω: Antec. in Latin script 2.18.pr. *praeteriteuθηnai* etc. (VI AD); later in Greek script. Zilliacus (1935a: 200–1), *LBG*. See §9.5.6 n. 68.
foreign	**πραετεριτίων, πραιτεριτίων** 'passing over' (i.e. failing to mention a person in one's will), from *praeteritiō* 'omission' (*TLL*): Just. *Nov.* in Latin script 115.4.9 etc. (VI AD); Ath.Schol. in Latin script 3.8 (VI AD); Antec. in Latin script 2.13.pr. *praeteritionos* etc. (VI AD); later in Greek script. Hofmann (1989: 343), Zilliacus (1935a: 200–1), *LBG*, *TLL* (*s.v. praeteritio* 1028.59), Lampe (1961). See §9.5.6 n. 68.
foreign	**πραετέριτος** 'passed over' (i.e. not mentioned in a will), from *praeteritus*, pf. part. of *praetereō* 'pass over': Just. *Nov.* in Latin script 115.3.pr. etc. (VI AD); Antec. in Latin script 2.13.7 *praeteritoi* etc. (VI AD); common in Greek script in Byzantine legal texts. Zilliacus (1935a: 200–1, spelled πραιτέριτος), *LBG*. Distinct from πραιτέριτος (*q.v.*). See §9.5.6 n. 68.
	πραετωρ-: see πραιτωρ-.
rare	**πραεφεκτώριος, πραιφεκτώριος** 'of the prefect', from *praefectōrius* 'having the rank of a prefect': Just. *Nov.* 38.pr.3 (VI AD); occasionally later. Avotins (1992), Zilliacus (1935a: 230–1), *LBG*.
	πραιβαρικατ-: see πραεβαρικατ-.
Direct loan II AD – modern	**πραῖδα, πρέδα** (-ας, ἡ) 'loot', from *praeda* 'loot'. Documents: *P.Abinn.* 28.15 (IV AD). Literature: Apollonius Sophista, *Lexicon Homericum* p. 108.8 as gloss (I/II AD); Athan. *Ep.Encycl.* 4.1 (IV AD); John Chrysostom, *PG* XLIX.161.30 (IV/V AD); Hesych. as gloss δ 1571, λ 924, σ 1162 (V/VI AD); Malal. 5.12 etc. (VI AD). Post-antique: common. Zervan (2019: 140), Sophocles (1887), Triandaphyllidis (1909: 130). Modern πραίδα 'loot' etc.: Andriotis (1967), Kahane and Kahane (1972–6: 532). Notes: may form derivative πραιδεύω. Daris (1991a: 91), Hofmann (1989: 340), Zilliacus (1935a: 230–1), Meinersmann (1927: 48), Immisch (1885: 371), Lampe (1961). See §4.2.3.1, §4.3.1 n. 68, §10.2.1, §10.2.2 C.

πραῖδες: see πραῖς.

Deriv.? of loan
II AD – modern

πραιδεύω, πραιτεύω 'plunder', from *praeda* 'loot' via πραῖδα + -εύω, or perhaps from *praedor* 'plunder' + -εύω.

Documents: *P.Cair.Masp.* 67002.2.24, 67002.3.13, 67004.10, 67021v.9 (all VI AD); *P.Lond.* v.1674.91 (VI AD); *SB* 7436.2 (VI AD).

Literature: common, e.g. Arrian, Jacoby IIB 156 frag. 49a.5 (I/II AD); *Seniores Alexandrini* 10 = Pitra 1884: 344.7 (II AD); Callin. *V.Hypat.* 3.11 (V AD); Hesych. as gloss δ 937, κ 1066 (V/VI AD); Cyr.S. *Vit.Sab.* 175.11 (VI AD); old scholion to Eur. *Ph.* 202.

Post-antique: numerous, forming derivatives πραίδευσις 'plundering', καταπραιδεύω 'plunder', etc. Zervan (2019: 140), Sophocles (1887), Triandaphyllidis (1909: 130), Zilliacus (1937: 332). Modern πραιδεύω in various senses: Andriotis (1967), Shipp (1979: 471–2), Kahane and Kahane (1972–6: 532).

Notes: Daris (1991a: 91), Hofmann (1989: 340), and Zilliacus (1935a: 230–1) derive this from *praedor*; Cavenaile (1952: 198) from *praeda*; and Mandilaras (1973: 67) implausibly from *praetor*. Meinersmann (1927: 48), Immisch (1885: 371), Lampe (1961), LSJ, LSJ suppl. See §4.3.1 n. 68, §4.6.1 n. 91, §9.2, §10.2.2 C.

foreign

πραιέναι 'come', apparently from *prae* 'before' + εἶμι 'go': Hesych. as lemma π 3186 (V/VI AD).

πραιϊουδικ-: see πραεϊουδικ-.

πραικάριος: see πραεκάριος.

foreign

πραικεπτίων 'taking beforehand', from *praeceptiō* 'receiving in advance': Antec. in Latin script 2.20.2 *praeception* etc. (VI AD). Zilliacus (1935a: 200–1), Triandaphyllidis (1909: 128).

foreign

πραικίπουος (in fem. acc. πραικίπουαν) transliterating *praecipuus* 'special': inscription *I.Perge* 331.i.9 (III AD).

Direct loan
II AD – modern

πραικόκ(κ)ιον, πρεκόκ(κ)ιον (-ου, τό) 'little apricot', from *praecocia/praecoqu(i)a*, neut. pl. of *praecox* 'apricot' (*TLL* s.v. 513.69–514.3).

Literature: Galen VI.466.5 Kühn etc. (II AD); Orib. *Col.* 1.48t etc. (IV AD); Aëtius 1.279.1 etc. (VI AD).

Post-antique: occasional survival in medical texts. Modern dialectal πραικόπι: Andriotis (1974: 462).

Notes: spellings βερικόκκιον, βερεκόκκιον, βερόκκιον probably not from Latin but diminutives of Greek βερίκοκκον (related to *praecox* but not a borrowing). Dsc. 1.115.5 (I AD) quotes the Roman word as βρεκόκ(κ)ιον, apparently blending Greek and Latin forms. Hofmann (1989: 347–8), *DÉLG* (s.v. βερίκοκκον), Beekes (2010 s.v. βερίκοκκον), Kriaras (1968– s.vv. βερίκοκιον, βερίκοκον), Sophocles (1887 s.v. πραικόκιον), Meyer (1895: 14), LSJ (s.v. βερίκοκκον), LSJ suppl. See §4.2.5, §10.2.1, §10.2.2 L.

Direct loan II AD – Byz.	**πραίκων, πρέκων, πρέκωρ, βρέκων, βρέχων** (-ωνος/-ονος, ὁ) 'herald', from *praecō* 'herald'. Documents: e.g. *Stud.Pal.* xx.85v.2.12 (IV AD); *P.Oxy.* 1901.80 (VI AD). Inscriptions: *I.Beroia* 383.10 (II AD); Lemerle 1935: 157 no. 53.2 (III/IV AD); *SEG* LXV.1408.C22 (V/VI AD); *I.Kyzikos* 400.3; *I.Smyrna* 414.1. Literature: Hesych. as lemma π 3187 (V/VI AD); Lyd. *Mag.* p. 142.25 (VI AD); *Acta Pilati* A.1.2 = Tischendorf 1876: 217. Post-antique: survives. *LBG* (*s.v.* πρέκων). Notes: Daris (1991a: 91), Hofmann (1989: 340–1), Zilliacus (1935a: 230–1), Meinersmann (1927: 47, 48), Lampe (1961), LSJ, LSJ suppl. See §4.2.5, §10.2.1, §10.2.2 N.
rare	**πραιλῆκτος** 'chosen man' (?), apparently from *praelēctus*, pf. part. of *praelegō* 'select': papyrus *P.Abinn.* 59.12 (IV AD). Daris (1991a: 91), Zilliacus (1935a: 232–3), Meinersmann (1927: 48).
rare	**πραιποσιτεύω, πρεποσιτεύω** 'be *praepositus*', from *praepositus* 'person in charge' via πραιπόσιτος + -εύω: papyri *P.Sakaon* 35.15 (IV AD); *P.Amh.* II.140.1 (IV AD). Daris (1991a: 91), Hofmann (1989: 341–2 *s.v.* πραιπόσιτος), Meinersmann (1927: 48), LSJ (πραιποσιτεύομαι, *s.v.* πραιπόσιτος – but the active is attested).
non-existent	**πραιπόσιτιος** in some transcriptions of *P.Oxy.* 2731.17 (IV/V AD) is a typographical error for the πραιπόσιτος on the papyrus.
Direct loan III AD – Byz.	**πραιπόσιτος, πρεπόσιτος, πρεπόσειτος** (-ου, ὁ), a title, from *praepositus* 'person in charge'. Documents: common (esp. IV AD), e.g. *SB* 15498.1 (III AD); *P.Oxy.* 4359.5 (IV AD); *P.Oxy.* 4677.3 (V AD); *P.Gron.* 10.26 etc. (VI AD). Inscriptions: e.g. *SEG* XXXIX.1698.4 (III AD); *I.Portes du désert* 91.5 (IV AD); *SEG* XLVI.845bis (V AD); *I.Thèbes Syène* 237.4 (VI AD). Literature: common, e.g. Dor.Poet. *Visio* 17 (III/IV AD); Eus. *HE* 9.1.6 (IV AD); Geront. *V.Mel.* 2.13 (V AD); Cyr.S. *Vita Theodosii* 240.19 (VI AD). Post-antique: common. *LBG* (*s.v.* πρεπόσιτος), Zervan (2019: 141), Triandaphyllidis (1909: 126). Notes: forms derivatives πραιποσιτεύω, ὀρρεοπραιποσιτία. Editor of *I.Zoora* 254.2 *ad loc.*, Binder (2000: 202), Avotins (1992), Daris (1991a: 91–2), Mason (1974: 5, 77–8), Hofmann (1989: 341–2), Zilliacus (1935a: 232–3, 1937: 332), Meinersmann (1927: 48), Lampe (1961), LSJ, LSJ suppl. See §4.2.4.1 n. 51, §10.2.1, §10.2.2 D.
rare	**πραιποσιτούρα** 'office of the *praepositus*', from *praepositūra* 'position of overseer' (*TLL*): papyrus *P.Lips.* I.111.16 (IV AD). Daris (1991a: 92), Hofmann (1989: 342), Meinersmann (1927: 48), LSJ (*s.v.* πραιπόσιτος).
	πραιπόστερος: see πραεποστέρα.
rare	**πραῖς** 'surety', from *praes* (gen. *praedis*) 'surety': inscription *SEG* XXXIX.1180.102, dat. pl. πραισί (I BC). Brixhe (2007: 908), LSJ suppl.
	πραισείδιον: see πραισίδιον.

rare   **πραισεντάλιος** 'serving in the imperial palace', from *praesentālis* 'present', 'serving in the emperor's escort' (*TLL*): Just. *Edict* 13.2 = p. 781.9 (VI AD). Avotins (1992), Zilliacus (1935a: 200–1), *TLL* (*s.v. praesentālis* 851.43–5), LSJ suppl.; for (limited) Byzantine survival *LBG*, Triandaphyllidis (1909: 127).

foreign   **πραισεντεύω** is said to be a Latin word meaning 'remain' by Malal. 7.5: πραισεντεύειν γὰρ λέγεται τὸ παραμένειν (VI AD). It is unclear exactly which Latin word is intended: *praesentō* means 'exhibit', so perhaps adj. *praesēns* (gen. *praesentis*) 'present' + -εύω. Hofmann (1989: 342), *LBG*, Sophocles (1887), Lampe (1961).

Direct loan   **πραίσεντον** (-ου, τό) 'troops serving in the imperial palace', from *praesēns* (gen.
VI AD – Byz.   *praesentis*) 'present'.
           Literature: e.g. Malal. 14.46 (VI AD); Just. *Nov.* 22.48.ep. (VI AD).
           Post-antique: some survival. Zervan (2019: 141), Sophocles (1887), Triandaphyllidis (1909: 130).
           Notes: Avotins (1992), Hofmann (1989: 342), Zilliacus (1935a: 200–1), Lampe (1961), LSJ suppl. See §4.2.5, §9.2, §10.2.1, §10.2.2 A.

rare   **πραίσεντος** 'member of the palace guard', from *praesēns* (gen. *praesentis*) 'present': Malal. 18.10 (VI AD); Evagr.Schol. *HE* 154.14, marked (VI AD). Hofmann (1989: 342) and for Byzantine survival Sophocles (1887).

rare   **πραισιδιάριος** 'soldier of the garrison in a *praesidium*', from *praesidium* 'garrison' via πραισίδιον + -άριος: unpublished ostracon O.Claud. inv. 6615 (II AD).

Direct loan   **πραισίδιον, πραισίδια, πραισείδιον, πρεσίδιον, πρασίδιον** (-ου, τό) 'garrison', from
I–III AD   *praesidium* 'garrison'.
           Documents: common, e.g. *P.Wisc.* II.53.7 (I AD); *P.Mich.* III.203.15 (II AD); *O.Did.* 462.11 (III AD).
           Inscriptions: *IGR* I.1337.2 (I AD).
           Notes: all examples come from Egypt. Forms derivative πραισιδιάριος. Daris (1991a: 92), Mason (1974: 5, 78), Hofmann (1989: 342–3), Meinersmann (1927: 49), LSJ (*s.v.* πραισίδια). See §4.2.4.1 n. 54, §9.2, §10.2.1, §10.2.2 C.

           πραισόριον: see πρισόριον.

foreign   **πραιστίτεις** transliterating *praestitēs*, pl. of *praestes* 'protector' (*TLL*): Plut. *Mor.* 276f (I/II AD). Hofmann (1989: 343), Sophocles (1887).

rare   **πραιτεντούρα, πρετεντούρη**, apparently from *praetentūra* 'military guard on the boundaries of a province': papyri *SB* 15498.2, 15499.2 (both III AD). Feissel and Gascou (1995: 102–4).

rare   **πραιτεξτᾶτος, πρετεξτᾶτος** 'wearing the *toga praetexta*': inscription *Mélanges de l'Université Saint-Joseph* 38.1 (1962) 18.3; Antec. in Latin script 4.4.1 *praetextata* etc. (VI AD); transliterating (*fābula*) *praetexta* (a literary genre), Lyd. *Mag.* p. 62.1, 2 (VI AD); Byzantine texts. Binder (2000: 227), Zilliacus (1935a: 200–1), *LBG*.

           πραιτεριτεύω: see πραετεριτεύω.

           πραιτεριτίων: see πραετεριτίων.

Direct loan
II–IV AD

πραιτέριτος, πρετέριτος, προτεριτός (-η?, -ον or -ου, ὁ) 'in arrears', 'delayed', (as masc. subst.) 'former comrade', from *praeteritus* 'former', 'past'.

Documents: *SB* 16941.5 (II AD); *CPR* VI.76.6 (III AD); perhaps *O.Did.* 30.11 (III AD); *P.Panop.Beatty* 2.112 etc. (III/IV AD); *P.Michael.* 29.5 etc. (IV AD); *Chrest.Wilck.* 424.i.10 (IV AD).

Notes: distinct from πραετέριτος (*q.v.*). Cuvigny (2002: 246–8), Daris (1991a: 92), Hofmann (1989: 343), Meinersmann (1927: 49), LSJ suppl. See §4.2.2, §10.2.1, §10.2.2 O, §10.3.2.

πραιτεύω: see πραιδεύω.

πραιτοριανός: see πραιτωριανός.

rare

πραιτούρα 'office of praetor', from *praetūra* 'office of praetor': Thdt. *Ep.Pat.* 33.8, 52.8 (V AD); Just. *Nov.* 13.4.pr. (VI AD); Byzantine texts. Avotins (1992), LSJ suppl., *LBG*.

Direct loan
II AD – modern

πραίτωρ, πραέτωρ (-ορος/-ωρος, ὁ), an official title, from *praetor* 'praetor'.

Documents: *P.Rain.Unterricht* 63.45 (V AD); *Stud.Pal.* XX.127.3 (V AD); *P.Rain.Unterricht* 96.1 etc. (V AD).

Inscriptions: e.g. *IG* VII.1866.4 (II AD); *I.Ephesos* 3085.11 (III AD).

Literature: e.g. Porphyry, *Vita Plotini* 7.35 (III AD); Eutropius 5.3 (IV AD); Socr. 5.8 (IV/V AD); Zosimus, *Historia nova* 2.38.3 Paschoud (V AD); *Schol. Sinai.* in Latin script 39 *praetor* (V/VI AD); Just. *Nov.* 13.1.1 (VI AD); Antec. 1.13.5 etc., but in Latin script 1.2.7 *praetor* etc. (VI AD).

Post-antique: common, forming derivatives πραιτωρικός 'of the praetor', πραιτωράτον 'office of the praetor', etc. Avotins (1992), Lampe (1961), *LBG* (*s.v.* πραέτωρ), Zervan (2019: 141–2), Triandaphyllidis (1909: 126). Modern πραίτορας 'praetor': Babiniotis (2002), Coleman (2007: 795).

Notes: Daris (1991a: 92), Mason (1974: 3, 6, 7, 78), Hofmann (1989: 343–4), Zilliacus (1935a: 200–1, 232–3), LSJ suppl. See §4.2.5, §7.1.1, §7.1.2, §9.5.6 n. 56, §10.2.1, §10.2.2 D.

Direct loan
I AD – modern

πραιτωριανός, πραιτοριανός, πρετωριανός, πραιτωρεανός (-ή, -όν) 'praetorian', as masc. subst. 'soldier of the praetorian guard', from *praetōriānus* 'praetorian'.

Documents, adj.: *ChLA* XLI.1193.1 (VI AD); *P.Lond.* V.1679r.4 (VI AD); perhaps *P.Erl.* 55.1 (VI AD).

Inscriptions, adj.: e.g. *SEG* XXXV.649 (I AD); *I.Leukopetra* 41.3 (II AD); *IGBulg.* III.I.1075.6 etc. (III AD). Masc. subst.: e.g. *IGBulg.* V.5409.6 (III AD); *I.Perge* 316.15 (III AD); perhaps *CIG* 4350.12 (IV AD).

Literature, adj.: e.g. *Acta Alexandrinorum* 9a.r.1.9 Musurillo (II/III AD); Socr. 1.2 (IV/V AD); *ACO* II.I.1 p. 72.13 (V AD); Just. *Nov.* 24.1 (VI AD). Masc. subst.: e.g. Hdn.Hist. 5.4.8, marked (II/III AD); Eutropius 10.2 (IV AD); Lyd. *Mag.* p. 70.21, marked (VI AD).

Post-antique: both adj. and subst. survive. *LBG*. Modern πραιτωριανός 'praetorian': Babiniotis (2002).

Notes: Avotins (1992), Daris (1991a: 93), Mason (1974: 5, 78), Hofmann (1989: 344), Zilliacus (1935a: 200–1, 232–3), LSJ (*s.v.* πραιτωριανοί), LSJ suppl. See §4.2.2, §6.4, §10.2.1, §10.2.2 C, §10.3.2.

rare   **πραιτωρίδιον** 'small house', from *praetōrium* 'headquarters' via πραιτώριον + -ίδιον: Epict. *Diss.* 3.22.47 (I/II AD). Hofmann (1989: 344 *s.v.* πραιτώριον, 345 *s.v.* πραιτώριος), LSJ.

rare   **πραιτωριοκτυπέω** 'knock at the door of the praetorium', from *praetōrium* 'headquarters' via πραιτώριον + κτυπέω 'knock': Pall. *V.Chrys.* 29.21 (IV/V AD). Hofmann (1989: 344 *s.v.* πραιτώριον, 345 *s.v.* πραιτώριος), Lampe (1961).

Direct loan
I AD – modern   **πραιτώριον, πραετώριον, πρετώριον, πλετώριον** (-ου, τό) 'official residence of the governor', 'residence', 'praetorian guard', 'imperial household', from *praetōrium* 'headquarters', 'praetorian guard'.

Documents: common, e.g. *P.Oxy.* 3917.3 (II AD); *P.Laur.* 1.19.28 (III AD); *P.Oxy.* 3984.2 (IV AD); *P.Berl.Zill.* 5.3 (V AD); *P.Oxy.* 3150.14 (VI AD).

Inscriptions: common, e.g. *IG* X.II.II.251.2 (I AD); *IG* X.II.I.705.4 (II AD); *IGBulg.* IV.2023.4 (III AD); *I.Cret.* IV.284a.7 (IV AD); *I.Cos Segre* EV63.4 (IV/V AD); Asdracha 1995: 287 no. 117.1 (VI AD).

Literature: common, e.g. NT Matthew 27:27 (I AD); *Act.Andr.* 1.6 (II AD); *Acta Thomae* 18 = Bonnet 1903: 126.1 (III AD); Athan. *Apol.Sec.* 76.1 (IV AD); *ACO* I.I.V p. 8.36 (V AD); Barsanuph.Jo. II.I ep. 226.61 (VI AD).

Post-antique: common. *LBG*, Zervan (2019: 142), Triandaphyllidis (1909: 127). Modern πραιτώριο 'Roman praetorium': Babiniotis (2002).

Notes: forms derivatives πραιτωρίδιον, πραιτωριοκτυπέω. Menci (2000: 287–8), Avotins (1992), Daris (1991a: 93), Mason (1974: 5, 78), Hofmann (1989: 344), Zilliacus (1935a: 200–1, 1937: 332–3), Meinersmann (1927: 48), Immisch (1885: 360), Lampe (1961), LSJ, LSJ suppl. See §4.2.4.1 n. 54, §9.3 nn. 21 and 25, §10.2.1, §10.2.2 D, §12.2.1.

Direct loan
II AD – Byz.   **πραιτώριος, πραετώριος, πρετώριος** (-α, -ον) 'praetorian', as masc. subst. 'member of the praetorian guard', from *praetōrius* 'praetorian'.

Documents, adj.: e.g. *Chrest.Mitt.* 316.ii.16 (II AD); *BGU* I.327.3 (II AD); *SB* 9228.22 (II AD). Masc. subst.: e.g. perhaps *P.Rain.Cent.* 92.4 (V AD); *P.Cair.Masp.* 67305.5 (VI AD); *P.Oxy.* 1974.3 (VI AD).

Inscriptions, adj.: e.g. *IGR* I.1046.1 (II AD); *IGBulg.* III.II.1570.4 etc. (III AD); *I.Ephesos* 737.6 etc. (III AD). Masc. subst.: e.g. *I.Side* 52.12 (IV AD); *I.Mylasa* 613.1 (V AD).

Literature, adj.: e.g. Eutropius 3.10 (IV AD); Malal. 13.30 (VI AD); Lyd. *Mag.* p. 152.21 (VI AD); Antec. in both scripts e.g. 1.21.3 *praetorios*, πραιτώριος (VI AD). Masc. subst.: e.g. Eutropius 6.20 (IV AD); *ACO* I.I.I p. 7.20 (V AD); Cyr.S. *Vit.Sab.* 146.1 (VI AD).

Post-antique: common, forming adverb πραιτωρίως. *LBG* (*s.v.* πραετώριος), Zervan (2019: 142).

Notes: subst. more common than adj., but both well attested. Forms derivative πολιτικοπραιτώριος. Daris (1991a: 93), Mason (1974: 5, 78), Hofmann (1989: 345–6), Zilliacus (1935a: 200–1, 232–3), Lampe (1961), LSJ suppl. See §4.2.2, §10.2.1, §10.2.2 C, §12.2.1.

πραιφεκτορία: see πρεφεκτορία.

Direct loan
II AD – Byz.

πραίφεκτος, πρίφεκτος, πρόφεκτος (-ου, ὁ) 'prefect', from *praefectus* 'prefect'.
  Documents: e.g. probably *P.Abinn.* 3.2 (IV AD); *P.Petra* III.23.3 (VI AD);
    P.Cair.Masp. 67008.2 (VI AD).
  Inscriptions: perhaps *IG* XIV.680.2 (II AD?); *IG* XIV.2433.7–10 (III AD); *SEG*
    IX.356.51, 414.1 (both VI AD); *CIL* III.7051.4; perhaps *MAMA* III.43.4.
  Literature: e.g. Polybius 6.26.5, marked (II BC); *Martyrium Pauli* 3 = Lipsius
    1891: 112.4 (II AD); *Acta Philippi* 6.21 = Bovon *et al.* 1999: 219.8 (IV AD);
    Lyd. *Mag.* p. 92.8 (VI AD).
  Post-antique: survives. *LBG* (*s.v.* προφέκτος).
  Notes: Dubuisson (1985: 40), Daris (1991a: 93), Mason (1974: 6, 8, 78),
    Hofmann (1989: 346), Zilliacus (1935a: 230–1), Meinersmann (1927: 48),
    Lampe (1961), LSJ suppl. See §4.2.4.1 n. 51, §8.1.3 n. 17, §9.2, §10.2.1,
    §10.2.2 D.

πραιφεκτώριος: see πραεφεκτώριος.

foreign

πράνδιον transliterating *prandium* 'lunch': Plut. *Mor.* 726e (I/II AD). Unverified
    πράνδεον in Zilliacus (1937: 322, 333). Strobach (1997: 198), Hofmann
    (1989: 347), *LBG*, Triandaphyllidis (1909: 122).

πραπιναρέα: see προπιναρία.

not Latin?

Πραράτιος, Πραράτριος, an Argive month, has been cited as a Latinism
    (Hofmann 1989: 26 *s.v.* ἀρᾶν) but probably is not. Schwyzer (1922: 1–2),
    DÉLG, Frisk (1954–72: II.589), LSJ.

rare

πρασιανός 'member of the green circus faction', from *prasiniānus* 'supporter
    of the charioteers whose colour was green' (itself from πράσινος 'green'):
    Marc.Aurel. 1.5.1 (II AD). Cameron (1976), Hofmann (1989: 347), *TLL*
    (*s.v. prasiniānus* 1128.46), LSJ.

πρασίδιον: see πραισίδιον.

πρατακτάτωρ: see πρετακτάτωρ.

πρεβᾶτος: see πριβᾶτος.

πρέδα: see πραῖδα.

πρειβᾶτος: see πριβᾶτος.

πρειμ(ε)ιπειλ-, πρειμοπ(ε)ιλ-: see πριμιπιλ-.

πρεῖμος: see πρῖμος.

πρεινκείππεια: see πριγκίπια.

πρειουᾶτος: see πριβᾶτος.

πρεκάριος: see πραεκάριος.

πρεκόκ(κ)ιον: see πραικόκκιον.

πρέκων, πρέκωρ: see πραίκων.

πρεποσ-: see πραιποσ-.

πρεσίδιον: see πραισίδιον.

rare   **πρετακτάτωρ, πρα(ε)τακτάτωρ, περτρακτάτωρ** 'agent', from *pertractātor* 'agent'
(*TLL*): papyrus *P.Cair.Isid.* 13.1 (IV AD). Daris (1991a: 93), Cavenaile
(1951: 400), *TLL* (*s.v. pertractātor*).

                πρετεντούρη: see πραιτεντούρα.

                πρετεξτᾶτος: see πραιτεξτᾶτος.

                πρετέριτος: see πραιτέριτος.

                πρετωρ-: see πραιτωρ-.

foreign   **πρεφεκτορία, πραιφεκτορία** 'position of authority', from *praefectūra* 'position of
authority' + -ία: Ath.Schol. in Latin script 8.1.1 etc. (VI AD). Hofmann
(1989: 346), Lampe (1961).

                πρημηκιρις, πρημικύριος: see πριμικήριος.

                πρημηπηλάριος: see πριμιπιλάριος.

                πρησώριον: see πρισόριον.

rare   **πριβατάριος, πριβάριος** 'keeper of a private bath', from *prīvātārius* 'of a
private bath' (*TLL*) or *prīvātus* 'private' (via πριβᾶτος in the neut. sing.
subst. πριβᾶτον) + -άριος: papyrus *P.Oslo* III.119.11 (IV AD); undated
inscriptions *MAMA* III.26, 259, 332, 557, 585a, 585b. Daris (1991a:
93), Hofmann (1989: 348), Cavenaile (1951: 400), *TLL* (*s.v. prīvātārius*
1383.55–6), LSJ.

                πριβάτη: see πριβᾶτος.

not ancient   **πριβατιανός**, an official title, from *prīvātiānus*, a title (*TLL*): no ancient
examples. Zilliacus (1935a: 202–3), *LBG*.

rare   **πριβάτιος** 'private', from *prīvātus* 'private' via πριβᾶτος + -ιος: papyri *P.Cair.Masp.*
67009v.23 (VI AD); *Stud.Pal.* VIII.1033.2 etc. (VI AD). Daris (1991a: 95
s.v. πριουᾶτος), Hofmann (1989: 349 *s.v.* πριβατος), LSJ suppl.

Direct loan   **πριβᾶτος, πρ(ε)ιουᾶτος, πρειβᾶτος, πρεβᾶτος, προυᾶτος, πιβρᾶτος** (-η, -ον)
III AD – Byz.   'private', fem. subst. 'emperor's private property', neut. (usually pl.) subst.
'emperor's private property', neut. sing. subst. 'private bath': from *prīvātus*
'private', with meaning of fem. subst. and perhaps neut. pl. subst. influenced
by *rēs prīvāta*, and neut. sing. subst. by (*balneum*) *prīvātum*.
Documents, adj.: *P.Flor.* III.320.3 (IV AD); *SB* 11345.3 (IV AD); *P.Flor.*
III.384.6 (V AD).   Fem. subst.: e.g. *P.Panop.Beatty* 1.193 etc. (III AD);
P.Vind.Sijp. 1.1.17 etc. (IV AD).   Neut. sing. subst.: *P.Flor.* III.384.11
etc. (V AD).   Zervan (2019: 143) and Meinersmann (1927: 48) find an
example from II AD in πρεβέτοις at *BGU* III.781.vi.8b, which is probably for
πρεσβυτέροις.
Inscriptions, adj.: *SEG* XXXII.1279.3 (II/III AD); *I.Ephesos* 2078.5 (III AD).
Fem. subst.: probably Knackfuss 1924: 338 no. 266.4 (III AD); *I.Ephesos*
3054.4 (III AD); *IG* XIV.911.b3 (III AD); *IG* XIV.2433.11 (III AD).
Neut. pl. subst.: *I.Mylasa* 613.2 (V AD); *I.Keramos* 65.2 etc. (V AD); *I.Ephesos*
1323.6 (VI AD?).   Neut. sing. subst.: Edict.Diocl. 7.76 (IV AD); *IGLS* III.
II.998.C4 (V AD); *SEG* XXXV.1582.5 (VI AD).

Literature, adj.: Antec. in Latin script 4.3.11 *privaton* etc. (VI AD).   Neut. pl. subst.: e.g. Julian, *Epistulae* 115.14 Bidez (IV AD); *ACO* II.I.I p. 55.16, II.I.II p. 69.17 (V AD); Just. *Nov.* 22.48.ep. (VI AD); Lyd. *Mag.* p. 124.10 (VI AD); bilingual glossaries, e.g. Gloss. *Herm.Mp.* 298.1.   Πριούατον 'workplace', Hesych. as lemma π 3293 (V/VI AD).

Post-antique: numerous, forming derivative πριβατιανός 'official subordinate to the *comes rerum privatarum*'. *LBG*, Zervan (2019: 143), Triandaphyllidis (1909: 127, 131), Sophocles (1887 *s.v.* πριουᾶτος).

Notes: spelling with -ou- is common even in late Empire. Variant πιβρᾶτος is just a stonecarver's error on one copy of Edict.Diocl. 7.76, taken too seriously by LSJ and LSJ suppl. (cf. already Sophocles 1887). Forms derivatives πριβάτιος, perhaps πριβατούρα. Binder (2000: 128), Avotins (1989, 1992), Daris (1991a: 95 *s.v.* πριουᾶτος), Mason (1974: 4, 79), Hofmann (1989: 347, 349), Zilliacus (1935a: 202–3), Meinersmann (1927: 50), Immisch (1885: 357), *LBG*, Lampe (1961), LSJ suppl. (*s.vv.* πριβᾶτον, πιβρᾶτος). See §4.2.2, §10.2.1, §10.2.2 A, §10.3.2, §12.2.1.

rare | **πριβατούρα**, meaning uncertain, probably from *probātōria* 'letter of commendation from the emperor' (*TLL s.v. probātōrius* 1456.58–61) via προβατωρία (cf. the use of πριβατωρία as a variant of προβατωρία), or perhaps from *prīvātus* 'private' via πριβᾶτος: papyrus *P.Lips.* I.97.xii.23 (IV AD). Daris (1991a: 93), Hofmann (1989: 349), Meinersmann (1927: 49), *TLL* (*s.v.* πριβατούρα).

πριβατωρία: see προβατωρία.

not ancient | **πριβιλεγιάριος** 'privileged person', from *prīvilēgiārius* 'privileged person': no ancient examples. Zilliacus (1935a: 202–3), *LBG*, *TLL* (*s.v. prīvilēgiārius*).

Direct loan V AD – Byz. | **πριβιλέγιον, πριβιλήγιον, πριβιλίγιον, πριμιλίγιον** (-ου, τό) 'privilege', from *prīvilēgium* 'privilege'.

Literature: *ACO* II.I.III p. 61.24 (V AD); *Carth.* 430.8 (V AD); Hesych. as lemma π 3285 (V/VI AD); Lyd. *Mens.* 1.23, marked (VI AD).

Post-antique: common. *LBG*.

Notes: Hofmann (1989: 350), Zilliacus (1935a: 202–3, 232–3), Immisch (1885: 357), Lampe (1961 *s.v.* πριμιλίγιον). See §4.2.4.1 n. 54, §10.2.1, §10.2.2 O.

Direct loan II AD – modern | **πρίγκεψ, πρίγκιψ, πρίνκεψ, πρίνκιψ, πρίγκιπος** (usually -ιπος, ὁ), a military and civil rank, from *prīnceps* 'first'.

Documents: common, e.g. O.Claud. inv. 7309.4 = Cuvigny 2019: 277 (II AD); *O.Theb.* 143.8 (III AD); *SB* 11592.20 etc. (IV AD); *PSI* X.1114.2 (V AD); *P.Flor.* III.377.26 (VI AD).

Inscriptions: e.g. *CIRB* 666.3 (II AD); *IGBulg.* III.II.1570.7 (III AD); Dunant 1971: 43 no. 31.3 (IV AD); *I.Thèbes Syène* 235.4 (VI AD).

Literature: e.g. Polybius 6.21.7, implicitly marked (II BC); DH *AR* 20.11.2, marked (I BC); *Martyrium Pionii* 15.5 in Musurillo 1972 (IV AD?); Pall. *V.Chrys.* 43.20 (IV/V AD); Nil. 3.41.1 (V AD); Lyd. *Mag.* p. 170.8 (VI AD). Unverified examples (II and III AD) in Zilliacus (1937: 323, 333).

Post-antique: common, forming derivatives πριγκιπικός 'of a *princeps*', πριγκίπισσα 'wife of a *princeps*'. *LBG*, Zervan (2019: 143–4), Triandaphyllidis (1909: 127). Modern πρίγκιπας 'prince' and derivatives: Babiniotis (2002), Andriotis (1967), Meyer (1895: 55). The Greek term apparently evolved with influence from cognates in other languages, but there is no real discontinuity suggesting reborrowing.

Notes: the πρίγκιπος variant, which occurs only once (in Nilus), is considered by Sophocles (1887) to be a separate word. Cuvigny (2019: 279), introduction to *O.Claud.* IV.862, Freyburger-Galland (1997: 147), Dubuisson (1985: 41), Bartalucci (1995: 112), Binder (2000: 129), Daris (1991a: 94 *s.v.* πρίγκιψ), Mason (1974: 5, 6, 79, 144, 149), Hofmann (1989: 353–4), Zilliacus (1935a: 202–3, 232–3, 1937: 333), Cameron (1931: 255), Meinersmann (1927: 49), Lampe (1961 *s.v.* πρίγκιψ), LSJ suppl. (replacing LSJ *s.v.* πρίγκιπες). See §4.2.5, §8.1.3 n. 17, §8.2.3 n. 51, §10.2.1, §10.2.2 C; cf. ὀπτιοπρίγκεψ.

Direct loan
II AD – Byz.?

πριγκιπάλι(ο)ς, πριγκιπάρι(ο)ς, πρινκιπάλι(ο)ς, πρινκιπάρι(ο)ς (-ου, ὁ) 'officer', from *prīncipālis* 'principal'.

Documents: e.g. *P.Worp* 52.9 etc. (II AD); *P.Flor.* II.278r.iii.8 etc. (III AD); *BGU* III.931.1 (III/IV AD); *CPR* VII.39.13 (V AD); probably *ChLA* X.407.14 etc. (V/VI AD).

Inscriptions: probably Naour 1980: no. 9.5.

Literature: as adj. meaning 'principal', Antec. in Latin script 2.16.5 *principalian* etc. (VI AD).

Post-antique: numerous as adj. meaning 'principal'. *LBG*.

Notes: adj. in Antec. and Byzantine writers could be unrelated to original borrowing. Cuvigny (2019: 293–4), Daris (1991a: 94), Mason (1974: 5, 79), Hofmann (1989: 350), Zilliacus (1935a: 202–3), Meinersmann (1927: 49), LSJ suppl. (*s.vv.* πριγκιπάλιος, πριγκιπᾶρις). See §4.2.5, §4.4 n. 79, §10.2.1, §10.2.2 C.

Direct loan
I–III AD?

πριγκίπια, πρινκίπια, πρεινκείππεια (-ων, τά) 'headquarters', from *prīncipia, -ōrum* 'headquarters' (*OLD s.v. principium*[1] 10).

Documents: *SB* 8247.10 (I AD); *P.Col.* VIII.221.4 etc. (II AD); *BGU* I.140.9 (II AD); perhaps *PSICom.* XI.8.a5 (II AD); *O.Did.* 31.6 (II/III AD); perhaps *Chrest.Wilck.* 41.iii.10 (III AD).

Literature: Plut. *Galba* 12.2, marked (I/II AD).

Post-antique: occasional examples. *LBG*.

Notes: Daris (1991a: 94), Mason (1974: 4, 79), Hofmann (1989: 350), Meinersmann (1927: 49), LSJ suppl. See §4.2.4.1 n. 54, §10.2.1, §10.2.2 C.

πρίγκιπος, πρίγκιψ: see πρίγκεψ.

foreign

πρίδιε 'on the day before', from *prīdiē* 'on the day before': as part of Roman dating formulae on papyri *BGU* I.140.8 (II AD); *P.Cair.Isid.* 9.285 (IV AD); Antec. in Latin script 3.19.13 *pridie* (VI AD). See Solin (2008: 267–9) and Sijpesteijn (1979: 233–5) for reasons it is not more common. Daris (1991a: 94), Hofmann (1989: 351), Meinersmann (1927: 49).

πριμάκηρος: see πριμικήριος.

foreign   **πριμάριος** transliterating *prīmārius* 'of the first rank': papyrus *BGU* III.958d.2
(IV/V AD). Daris (1991a: 94), Hofmann (1989: 351), Meinersmann (1927:
49), LSJ suppl.

πριμειπ-: see πριμιπ-.

foreign   **πριμιγένεια** transliterating *prīmigenia* 'firstborn', epithet of Fortuna: Plut. *Mor.*
289b, 322f (I/II AD). Sophocles (1887).

πριμικήρ: see πριμικήριος.

rare   **πριμικηρᾶτον**, an office, from *prīmicēr(i)ātus, -ūs* 'office of a chief' (*TLL*):
Malal. 18.71 (VI AD); occasional Byzantine texts. The ancient example is
ambiguous as to gender, making the masculine an attractive match for the
Latin, but there are unambiguously neuter Byzantine examples. Diethart
(2006: 19), Hofmann (1989: 351 *s.v.* πριμικηρατος), Zilliacus (1935a:
232–3 *s.v.* πριμικηρᾶτος), *LBG* (*s.v.* πριμ(μ)ικηρᾶτον), Lampe (1961 *s.v.*
πριμικηρᾶτος).

Direct loan
IV AD – modern   **πριμικήριος, πρημηκιρις, πριμικίριος, πριμικύριος, πρημικύριος, πριμάκηρος,**
πριμμικήριος, πριμικήρ (usually -ου, ὁ), a title, from *prīmicērius* 'official
whose name comes first' (*TLL*).
      Documents: e.g. *P.Oxy.* 1513.17 (III/IV AD); *SB* 15168.10 (IV AD); *P.Oxy.*
3986.9 (V AD); *P.Oxy.* 5069.9 (VI AD).
      Inscriptions: e.g. *SEG* VII.1194.3 (IV AD); *IGLS* XXI.V.I.128.6 (V AD);
I.Thrake Aeg. 356.4 (V/VI AD); *I.Chr.Bulgarien* 241.4 (VI AD).
      Literature: common, e.g. *ACO* I.I.II p. 7.34 (V AD); *ACO* II.I.I p. 84.29
(V AD); *V.Dan.Styl.* A. 49.18 (V AD); Hesych. as lemma π 3284 (V/VI AD);
Just. *Nov.* 8.Ed.not.1 (VI AD). Unverified examples (II and III AD) in
Zilliacus (1937: 323, 333).
      Post-antique: common, forming derivative πριμικήρισσα 'empress's chief lady-
in-waiting'. *LBG* (*s.v.* πριμμικήριος), Zervan (2019: 144–5), Triandaphyllidis
(1909: 127). Modern πριμικήριος: Andriotis (1967).
      Notes: LSJ suppl. treats as a separate word the variant πριμικήρ (only at *P.Abinn.*
42.12 (IV AD); Dor.Poet. *Visio* 49, 126 (III/IV AD)). But as there is no
discernible difference in meaning, and πριμικήριος admitted an enormous
variety of spellings (even more than are given here), they are probably all
to be considered one word. Editor of *I.Zoora* 231.4 *ad loc.*, Avotins (1992),
Daris (1991a: 94), Hofmann (1989: 351), Zilliacus (1935a: 200–1, 232–3,
1937: 333), Meinersmann (1927: 49), Immisch (1885: 359), *TLL* (*s.v.*
prīmicērius 1244.34), Lampe (1961), LSJ suppl. See §4.2.4.1 n. 51, §10.2.1,
§10.2.2 D.

πριμιλίγιον: see πριβιλέγιον.

πριμιπειλ-: see πριμιπιλ-

Direct loan
II AD – Byz.   **πριμιπιλάριος, πριμιπιλλάριος, πριμοπ(ε)ιλάριος, πρειμοπειλάριος,**
πρημηπηλάριος, πρ(ε)ιμιπειλάριος, πρινπιλάριος (-ου, ὁ), a military and
civilian rank, from *prīmipīlāris/prīmipīlārius/prīmopīlāris* 'senior centurion'
(*TLL*).
      Documents: e.g. *SB* 15940.12 (III AD); *P.Mich.* XX.808.5 (IV AD); *P.Oxy.*
1133r.5 (IV AD).

Inscriptions: e.g. *SEG* XXX.1255.2 (I AD?); *SEG* XXXIII.1194.12 (I/II AD); *I.Gerasa* 102.3 (II AD); *F.Delphes* III.IV.473.4 (III AD); *IG* X.II.II.192.4 (III AD); *I.Aphrodisias Late Ant.* 10.2 (IV AD).

Literature: Phlegon, *De longaevis* 3.111 Stramaglia (II AD); Galen XIII.1031.8 Kühn (II AD); *V.Aesopi* G 87 (II AD?); Modestinus in Just. *Dig.* 27.1.8.12 etc. (III AD).

Post-antique: survives. *LBG.*

Notes: Carrié (1979) suggests that papyrus examples have a meaning different from Latin. Widespread abbreviation makes it difficult to distinguish examples of πριμιπιλάριος from πριμίπιλον and πριμίπιλος. Daris (1991a: 94), Mason (1974: 4, 8, 9, 79), Hofmann (1989: 352), Cavenaile (1951: 403), LSJ suppl. See §4.2.5, **§4.4**, §9.5.6 nn. 55 and 58, §10.2.1, §10.2.2 C.

Direct loan
II AD – Byz.

πριμίπιλον, πρ(ε)ιμ(ε)ίπειλον, πριμίπιλλον, πιρμίπιλον, πρ(ε)ιμόπ(ε)ιλον (-ου, τό) 'senior centurion tax', 'office of the senior centurion', from *prīmum pīlum/prīmipīlum* 'office of senior centurion' (*TLL s.v. prior* 1362.66).

Documents: e.g. *BGU* IX.1894.73 (II AD); *P.Neph.* 44.2.24 etc. (IV AD); perhaps *CPR* XXIV.4.36 (V AD).

Literature: Modestinus in Just. *Dig.* 27.1.8.12 etc. (III AD).

Post-antique: survives. *LBG.*

Notes: Carrié (1979), Daris (1991a: 95), Hofmann (1989: 352), Meinersmann (1927: 49–50), *TLL* (*s.v. prior* 1363.18–27), LSJ suppl. (mis-accented πριμιπίλον). See §4.2.4.1 n. 55, §9.5.6 nn. 55 and 58, §10.2.1, §10.2.2 C.

Direct loan
III–VI AD?

πριμίπιλος, πρ(ε)ιμοπῖλος, πρειμιπεῖλος (-ου, ὁ), a military rank, from *prīmipīlus/prīmus pīlus* 'senior centurion'.

Documents: *O.Did.* 84.9 (III AD); *SB* 16170.15 (III AD); perhaps *P.Dura* 43.29 (III AD); *SB* 16318.28 (IV AD); *P.Cair.Masp.* 67057.i.23 etc. (VI AD).

Inscriptions: perhaps *IGBulg.* III.II.1570.7 (III AD); perhaps *IGLS* II.504 (IV AD); Heberdey and Kalinka 1897: 39 no. 53.14.

Literature: DH *AR* 9.10.2, marked (I BC).

Post-antique: for possible survival see Zilliacus (1935a: 232–3).

Notes: this is difficult to distinguish from πριμιπιλάριος because of widespread abbreviation, but Carrié's (1979: 163) suggestion that it never existed is disproved by texts discovered since. Freyburger-Galland (1997: 196), Daris (1991a: 95), Mason (1974: 79), Hofmann (1989: 352), Meinersmann (1927: 49). See §4.2.4.1 n. 51, §10.2.1, §10.2.2 C; cf. πῖλος 2.

Direct loan
V AD – Byz.

πριμισκρίνιος, προμοσκρίνιος (-ου, ὁ) 'chief secretary', from *prīmiscrīnius* 'chief secretary' (*TLL*).

Inscriptions: perhaps *IGLS* XIII.1.9046.96 (V/VI AD); *IGLS* IV.1729 (VI AD); *SEG* XXXII.1554.A19 etc., marked (VI AD); *SEG* IX.356.17 etc. (VI AD).

Literature: Nil. 1.239.1 etc. (V AD); Lyd. *Mag.* p. 136.25 etc. (VI AD). Unverified example (II AD) in Zilliacus (1937: 323, 333).

Post-antique: some survival. *LBG*, Triandaphyllidis (1909: 127).

Notes: Hofmann (1989: 353), Zilliacus (1935a: 232–3, 1937: 333), Lampe (1961), LSJ suppl. See §4.2.4.1 n. 51, §10.2.1, §10.2.2 D.

non-existent?

πριμιτῖβος 'early', from *prīmitīvus* 'early': cited as an ancient loan by Zilliacus (1935a: 202–3), but I can find no examples.

non-existent?	**πριμογένιτος** 'firstborn', from *prīmogenitus* 'firstborn' (*TLL*): cited as an ancient loan by Zilliacus (1935a: 200–1), but I can find no examples.
	πριμοπ(ε)ιλάριος: see πριμιπιλάριος.
Direct loan **II AD – Byz.?**	**πρῖμος, πρεῖμος** (-η/-α, -ον) 'first', from *prīmus* 'first'. Documents: *SB* 14180.64 etc. (II AD); *Chrest.Wilck.* 480.28 (II AD); *P.Col.* VII.183.8 (IV AD). Inscriptions: *I.Hatshepsout* 126.2 (I/II AD); perhaps *SEG* LIII.713.B3 (II/III AD); *IGLS* VI.2829.2; as part of πρειμοπαρθικός 'first Parthian (legion)' in Naour 1980: no. 8.4 (III AD). Literature: Ps.-Marcus Aurelius, *Epistula ad senatum*, Otto 1876: 248.10 (after II AD); Malal. 7.3 etc., marked (VI AD); Lyd. *Mag.* p. 72.10, marked (VI AD); Antec. in Latin script 2.14.6 *primon* etc. (VI AD). Post-antique: survives. *LBG.* Modern πρίμος 'first' may be survival (thus Babiniotis 2002), but Andriotis (1967) sees that as later borrowing from Italian *primo*. Notes: normally a technical military term designating units of the Roman army, but in Malalas is old name for month of March. Strobach (1997: 198), Daris (1991a: 95), Hofmann (1989: 353), Zilliacus (1935a: 202–3, 232–3), Meinersmann (1927: 48, 49), Lampe (1961). See §4.2.2, §10.2.1, §10.2.2 C.
foreign	**πριμοσαγιττάριος** 'first archer', ostensibly transliterating unattested **prīmosagittārius*: Lyd. *Mag.* p. 74.3 (VI AD). *TLL* (*s.v.* πριμοσαγιττάριοι) suggests that real source is *prīmus sagittārius* 'first archer'. *LBG.* See §8.1.7.
foreign	**πριμοσκουτάριος** 'first shield-bearer', ostensibly transliterating unattested **prīmoscutārius*: Lyd. *Mag.* p. 74.1 (VI AD). *TLL* (*s.v.* πριμοσκουτάριοι) suggests that real source is *prīmus scutārius* 'first shield-bearer' or its better-attested plural *prīmī scūtāriī*. Hofmann (1989: 353), *LBG*, Sophocles (1887). See §8.1.7.
	πρινκ-: see πριγκ-.
	πρινπιλάριος: see πριμιπιλάριος.
	πρίορ: see πρίωρ.
	πριουᾶτος: see πριβᾶτος.
foreign	**πρίσκος** 'elder', from *prīscus* 'ancient': DH *AR* 1.45.2, marked (I BC). Sophocles (1887).
rare	**πρισόριον, πρησώριον, πραισόριον** 'press', 'press-house', from *pressōrium* 'press' (*TLL s.v. pressōrius* 1196.5): Callin. *V.Hypat.* 38.7 (V AD); papyrus *P.Mich.* XIV.684.3 (V/VI AD). The editor of the papyrus takes it as a name, but see Diethart (1991a: 233). Hofmann (1989: 343), *TLL* (*s.v. pressōrius* 1196.7–8), Lampe (1961: *s.v.* πραισόριον), LSJ suppl.
non-existent?	**πριστινάριος**, meaning uncertain, is cited by *LSJ* as from *pistrīnārius* 'miller' on the basis of inscription *MAMA* III.667. That actually has abbreviated πριστιν, which could instead be expanded to πριστίνου, also otherwise unattested and also probably a Latinism. Editor *ad loc.*, Hofmann (1989: 354 *s.v.* πριστιν).

πρίφεκτος: see πραίφεκτος.

Direct loan
VI AD – Byz.

πρίωρ, πρίορ (-ορος, ὁ), a title, from *prior* 'in front'.

Documents: e.g. *P.Münch.* 1.2.18 (VI AD); *P.Ness.* III.36.12 (VI AD); *P.Petra* IV.43.156 etc. (VI AD).

Inscriptions: *SEG* XXXI.1453.4 (VI AD).

Literature: Just. *Nov.* 117.11 (VI AD).

Post-antique: numerous. *LBG*, Lampe (1961 *s.v.* πρίορες).

Notes: Avotins (1992 *s.v.* πρίορες), Daris (1991a: 95), Hofmann (1989: 355 *s.v.* πριωροι, but most forms are third declension), Zilliacus (1935a: 232–3), Meinersmann (1927: 50), LSJ suppl. (*s.v.* πριόρες, but singular occurs). See §4.2.5, §10.2.1, §10.2.2 D.

foreign

prō 'for', 'as': Antec. as part of phrases, e.g. 4.15.3 *pro possessore* (VI AD). Hofmann (1989: 355). Cf. προνερεδεγεριτεύω.

rare

πρόβα 'test', 'verification', from *proba* 'examination' (*TLL*): inscription *SEG* XXXIV.1243.28 etc. (V AD); Byzantine texts. Hofmann (1989: 355), *LBG*, Triandaphyllidis (1909: 126), *TLL* (*s.v.* proba), LSJ suppl.

foreign

προβᾶρε transliterating inf. of *probō* 'approve': Lyd. *Mag.* p. 134.8 (VI AD). Sophocles (1887).

non-existent?

προβατίων 'approval', from *probātiō* 'approval': cited as an ancient loan by Zilliacus (1935a: 202–3), but I can find no examples apart from Byzantine compound δεπροβατιονιβους (*dē probātiōnibus*).

Direct loan
VI AD – Byz.

προβατωρία, προβατο(υ)ρία (-ας, ἡ) 'imperial letter of commendation', from *probātōria* 'letter of commendation from the emperor' (*TLL s.v. probātōrius* 1456.58–61).

Documents: *P.Münch.* 1.2.3 etc. (VI AD).

Inscriptions: *SEG* IX.356.78, marked (VI AD).

Literature: Just. *Codex* 11.8.16, *Nov.* 24.1 etc. (VI AD); Lyd. *Mag.* p. 134.5 etc. (VI AD); Ath.Schol. 4.4.1 (VI AD).

Post-antique: numerous. *LBG*, Triandaphyllidis (1909: 127).

Notes: Lydus says πριβατωρία used by folk etymology for προβατωρία; cf. *TLL* (*s.v.* 2. *prīvātōrius*), *LBG* (*s.v.* προβατωρία). Avotins (1989), Daris (1991a: 95), Hofmann (1989: 356), Zilliacus (1935a: 202–3, 232–3), Meinersmann (1927: 50), *TLL* (*s.v. probātōrius* 1456.61), Lampe (1961 *s.v.* προβατουρία), LSJ suppl. See §4.2.3.1, §4.4, **§9.5.5** passage 74, §10.2.1, §10.2.2 A; cf. πριβατούρα.

rare

προβιγκάλιος 'provincial', from *prōvinciālis* 'provincial': Pall. *V.Chrys.* 128.20 (IV/V AD); Byzantine texts. *LBG* (*s.vv.* προβιγκάλιος, προβιντζιάλιος, προβιντζιάλης).

Direct loan
II–III AD

προβοκάτωρ, πρωβοκάτωρ (-ορος, ὁ), a type of gladiator, from *prōvocātor* 'challenger'.

Inscriptions: e.g. *I.Kyzikos* 206.1 (II AD); *I.Tomis* 288.1 (II/III AD); *I.Thrake Aeg.* 330.2 (III AD).

Literature: Artemidorus, *Onirocriticon* 2.32.27 (II AD).

Notes: Hofmann (1989: 359), *LBG*, LSJ suppl. See §4.2.5, §4.4, §10.2.1, §10.2.2 F.

foreign	**προδερέλικτος** 'ownerless', from *prō dērelictō* (*habeō*) '(consider) as abandoned': Just. *Nov.* in Latin script 22.12 (VI AD); Antec. in Latin script 2.1.47 *proderelicto* (VI AD); Byzantine texts. Hofmann (1989: 356), Zilliacus (1935a: 202–3), Lampe (1961), *LBG*, *TLL* (s.v. προδερέλικτον). See §8.1.7 n. 34.
Direct? loan with influence VI AD	**προδηληγᾶτον** (-ου, τό) 'advance instructions about taxes' seems to be from *praedēlēgātiō* 'advance instructions about taxes' (*TLL*) with substitution of προ- for *prae* and change of suffix; or from πρό + *dēlēgātum*, neuter of *dēlēgātus*, pf. part. of *dēlēgō* 'assign'. Documents: *ChLA* XLI.1193.1.4 etc. (VI AD); *P.Cair.Masp.* 67321.B5 (VI AD); *P.Erl.* 55.13 (VI AD); *P.Lond.* v.1663.23 (VI AD). Notes: the papyri are all from Antinoöpolis and nearby Antaiopolis. Diethart (2006: 21), editor of *P.Lond. ad loc.*, Filos (2010: 251), Daris (1991a: 95), Hofmann (1989: 356), Cavenaile (1952: 199), Zilliacus (1935a: 200–1), Meinersmann (1927: 50), *LBG*, *TLL* (s.v. *praedēlēgātio*). See §4.2.5, §4.4, §9.2, §10.2.1, §10.2.2 D.
rare	**προδισπόσιτος** 'previously dispatched for post carrying' (?), from unattested **prodispōnō* or dubiously attested *praedispōnō* 'arrange before' (*TLL*, cf. Livy 40.56.11), in the latter case with substitution of προ- for *prae*-: O.Dios. inv. 145.5 = Cuvigny 2013: 430 (II AD). Editor *ad loc.*
	προερεδεγεριτεύω: see προνερεδεγεριτεύω.
	προθμάριος: see πορθμάριος.
foreign	**προϊβιτόριος**, **προνιβιτόριος** 'forbidding', from *prohibitōrius* 'prohibiting': Antec. in Latin script 4.15.1 *prohibitorion* etc. (VI AD); later in Greek script. Zilliacus (1935a: 202–3), *LBG*. See §4.1.1 n. 23.
Direct loan V AD – Byz.	**πρόκεσσον**, **πρόκενσον**, **πρόκεσσος**, **πρόκενσος** (-ου, τό?) 'procession', 'departure of the emperor from the palace at Constantinople', from *prōcessus, -ūs* 'progress'. Literature: e.g. *V.Dan.Styl. A.* 55.24 (V AD); Malal. 11.33 (VI AD); Romanus Melodus, *Cantica* 5.6.6 Grosdidier de Matons (VI AD). Post-antique: common. *LBG*, Sophocles (1887), Triandaphyllidis (1909: 127). Notes: ancient examples are all ambiguous in gender, making Lampe's masculine an attractive match for the Latin, but some Byzantine examples are unambiguously neuter; I can find no unambiguously masculine ones at any period. Diethart (2006: 15), Binder (2000: 243), Hofmann (1989: 357), Zilliacus (1937: 333), Lampe (1961 s.v. πρόκενσος). See §4.2.4.2, §9.2, §10.2.1, §10.2.2 A.
foreign	***prōcīnctus***, *-ūs* 'readiness for battle': Antec. 2.10.1 *procinctu* (VI AD).
not ancient	**προκουρατίων**, from *prōcūrātiō* 'office of procurator': no ancient examples. Zilliacus (1935a: 202–3).
	προκουρατόριος: see προκουρατώριος.
Direct loan IV AD – Byz.	**προκουράτωρ**, **προκοράτωρ**, **προυκωράτωρ** (-ορος/-ωρος, ὁ), 'administrator', 'financial agent', from *prōcūrātor* 'administrator'. Documents: e.g. perhaps *BGU* III.815.5 (II AD); *SB* 9683.13 (IV AD); *PSI* v.477.2 (V AD); *P.Ross.Georg.* III.45.1 (VI AD).

Literature: *Carth.* 230.10 (V AD); *Schol.Sinai.* in Latin script 29 *procuratopα* etc. (V/VI AD); Just. *Nov.* 161.1.1 (VI AD); Antec. in both scripts e.g. 4.11.4 προκουράτωρα, *procurator* (VI AD).

Post-antique: common, forming derivatives προκουρατορεύω 'have authority', προκουρατορεία 'administration', etc. *LBG* (s.v. προκοράτωρ), Triandaphyllidis (1909: 126).

Notes: Avotins (1992), Daris (1991a: 95), Mason (1974: 80), Hofmann (1989: 357–8), Zilliacus (1935a: 202–3), Meinersmann (1927: 50), Lampe (1961, citing inscription of VII AD), LSJ suppl. See §4.1.1, §4.2.5, §7.1.2, §7.1.3, §9.5.6 n. 56, §10.2.1, §10.2.2 B.

foreign **προκουρατώριος, προκουρατόριος** 'on someone else's behalf', from *prōcūrātor* 'administrator' via προκουράτωρ + -ιος: Antec. in Latin script 4.13.11 *procuratoriae* etc. (VI AD); later in Greek script. Zilliacus (1935a: 202–3), *LBG*. See §10.3.1 n. 30.

not ancient **προκ(ο)υρσάριος**, apparently from *praecursor* 'one who runs on ahead' + -άριος, with substitution of Greek πρό for *prae*: no ancient examples. Daris (1991a: 96), Zilliacus (1935a: 230–1), Meinersmann (1927: 50), *LBG* (s.v. προκουρσάριος 'corsair').

rare **προμάγιστρος** 'acting leader', from *prōmagister* 'deputy head': probably inscription *IGUR* II.904.4. Hofmann (1989: 358).

Loan compound **προμάξιμον, προμάξιον** (-ου, τό), a garment, apparently from πρό 'before' + **V–VI AD** *maximum* 'greatest'.
Documents: *P.Princ.* II.82.42 (V AD); *SB* 12249.5 (V/VI AD); perhaps *P.Oxy.* 1837.16 (VI AD).
Literature: EphraemSyr. VII p. 93.6 (V/VI AD).
Notes: sometimes argued to be a misspelling of πλουμάκιον: Ensslin (1926: 445), Hofmann (1989: 331 *s.v.* πλουμακιον). Filos (2010: 251), Daris (1991a: 96), Lampe (1961), LSJ. See §2.4, §4.5, §10.2.1, §10.2.2 H.

rare **προμητάτωρ, προμετάτωρ** 'surveyor sent on ahead', perhaps from unattested **praemētātor* 'person who measures in advance', with substitution of Greek πρό for *prae*; or a Greek combination of πρό + *mētātor* 'one who measures or marks out (a camp, etc.)' via μητάτωρ: Just. *Nov.* 130.6 (VI AD). Apparently borrowed back into Latin as *promētātor* 'person who measures in advance', attested only rarely and in Greek-influenced contexts. Avotins (1992), Zilliacus (1935a: 202–3), Sophocles (1887 *s.v.* προμετάτωρ), *TLL* (*s.v. promētātor*), LSJ suppl.

rare **προμίττενς** 'promising' is cited by Daris (1991a: 96) as borrowing of *prōmittēns*, pres. part. of *prōmittō* 'promise', on the basis of papyrus *P.Hamb.* I.23.7 (VI AD), where ῥέον προμιττέντων is apparently intended as gen. pl. of *reī prōmittentēs* 'joint sharers of an obligation'; cf. commentary *ad loc.*, Hofmann (1989: 366 *s.v.* ῥέοι προμιττέντες). Antec. (VI AD) uses *reoi promittendoi* 'joint promisers' (3.16.pr., in Latin script), which appears from its meaning to be from *prōmittentēs* rather than *prōmittendī*, and which later appears in Byzantine legal texts as ῥέοι προμιτ(τ)ένδοι. Chantraine (1937: 91, claiming implausibly that the Latin source of ῥέων προμιττεντων is *reōrum prōmittendī*), Zilliacus (1935a: 202–3 *s.v. promittendus*/προμιττένδος), Meinersmann (1927: 50), *LBG* (*s.v.* προμιτένδος). See §9.5.6 n. 68.

προμοσκρίνιος: see πριμισκρίνιος.

προμοτίων: see προμωτίων.

προμώτης: see προμῶτος.

rare   **προμωτίων, προμοτίων, προμουτίων, πρωμοτίων** 'promotion', from *prōmōtiō*
'promotion': papyrus *P.Abinn.* 59.13 (IV AD); inscription *SEG* LXV.1408.
B13 (V/VI AD). Daris (1991a: 96), Meinersmann (1927: 50); for Byzantine
survival *LBG*.

Direct loan   **προμῶτος, προμώτης** (-ου, ὁ) 'promoted', from *prōmōtus*, pf. part. of *prōmoveō*
IV AD – Byz.   'cause to move forward'.

        Documents: e.g. *P.Panop.Beatty* 2.198 etc. (III/IV AD); *Chrest.Mitt.* 196.7
(IV AD); *P.Charite* 7.3 (IV AD); *SB* 11916.3 (IV AD).

        Literature: Lyd. *Mag.* p. 76.23 etc. (VI AD).

        Post-antique: survives. *LBG*.

        Notes: most examples ambiguous between first and second declensions, but
both occasionally used unambiguously: προμώτης *SB* 11916.3, προμῶτος
P.Abinn. 33.6, προμώτοις *P.Panop.Beatty* 2.204. Daris (1991a: 96), Hofmann
(1989: 358), Meinersmann (1927: 50). See §4.2.4.1 n. 51, §10.2.1,
§10.2.2 D, §12.2.1.

foreign   **προνερεδεγεριτεύω, προερεδεγεριτεύω** 'act as an heir', from *prō hērēde gerō* 'act as
heir' by adding -εύω not to the pf. part. of *gerō* 'act' (*gestus*) or pres. stem
(*ger-*), but to a *gerit* that could be either the pres. indicative active third
person singular or the stem of an imaginary pf. part. *geritus* (perhaps
created on the analogy of *trāditus* from *trādō*, which became τραδιτεύω in
Greek): Antec. in Latin script 2.19.7 *pro herede geriteuein* etc. (VI AD); later
in Greek script. Binder (2000: 16), Hofmann (1989: 79, 357), Zilliacus
(1935a: 202–3), *TLL* (*s.v. gero* 1929.10–12), *LBG*. See §4.1.1 n. 23, **§9.5.6**
passage 81.

        προνιβιτόριος: see προϊβιτόριος.

not ancient   **προνουντιατεύω** 'announce', from *prōnūntiātus* (pf. part. of *prōnūntiō*
'announce') + -εύω: no ancient examples. Zilliacus (1935a: 202–3), *LBG*.

not ancient   **προνουντιατίων** 'announcement', from *prōnūntiātiō* 'announcement': no ancient
examples. Zilliacus (1935a: 202–3), *LBG*.

Direct loan   **πρόξιμος, πρώξιμος** (-ου, ὁ) 'adjutant', 'deputy', 'first secretary', from *proximus*
IV AD – Byz.   'nearest'.

        Documents: e.g. *P.Lips.* 1.40.iii.17 (IV AD); *CPR* XIV.39.7 etc. (V AD); *P.Oxy.*
2419.4 (VI AD).

        Inscriptions: *I.Delta* 2.1 p. 526 (III/IV AD).

        Literature: *ACO* II.I.I p. 149.19 etc. (V AD). Meaning 'nearest', Antec. in
Latin script 3.2.5 *proximon* etc. (VI AD).

        Post-antique: numerous. *LBG* (*s.v.* πρώξιμος), Triandaphyllidis (1909: 127),
Daris (1991a: 96).

        Notes: in Antec. probably a separate borrowing. Sijpesteijn (1987b), Daris
(1991a: 96 *s.v.* πρώξιμος), Hofmann (1989: 358), Zilliacus (1935a:
202–3), Meinersmann (1927: 51), Lampe (1961). See §4.1.1, §4.2.4.1
n. 51, §10.2.1, §10.2.2 N.

semantic extension?	**προοίμιον** 'preface' is etymologically Greek, but when acting as a legal term it may be influenced by *prooemium* 'preface'. Zilliacus (1935a: 202–3), Frisk (1954–72: 11.363). See §2.3 n. 58.
	προπεινάριον: see προπινάριον.
rare	**προπῖνα, ποπῖνα** 'tavern', from *popīna* 'cook-shop' (with influence from προπινάριος and/or προπίνω 'drink to'; cf. also προπῖν 'drink or snack taken before a meal'): Just. *Nov.* 117.15.pr. (VI AD); Ath.Schol. 10.9.16 (VI AD); with *popina* in Gloss. *Herm.Mp.* 306.61 (as a later addition to the manuscript); occasionally later. Avotins (1992), Hofmann (1989: 358), *LBG*, LSJ, LSJ suppl.
rare	**προπιναρία, πραπιναρέα** 'female keeper of a cook-shop' or 'wife of a keeper of a cook-shop', from *popīnāria* 'woman who keeps a cook-shop' with influence from προπινάριος, or from *popīnārius* 'keeper of a cook-shop' (*TLL*) via προπινάριος: inscription *I.Pessinous* 187.5 (IV/V AD). LSJ suppl. See §6.2 n. 13.
rare	**προπινάριον, προπεινάριον** (ου, τό) 'jug', from *popīna* 'cook-shop' + -άριον (with influence from προπινάριος and/or προπίνω 'drink to'), or from *popīnārius* 'keeper of a cook-shop' (*TLL*) via προπινάριος: documents *SB* 13593.24 (III/IV AD); *O.Trim.* 11.531.4 (IV AD); perhaps *P.Oxy.* 1297.8 (IV AD). It may have been local to the Dakhla oasis. Commentary on *O.Trim.* 11.531, Daris (1991a: 96), LSJ. See §6.3 n. 21, §9.2 n. 19.
Direct loan with influence **V–VI AD**	**προπινάριος, πρωπινάριος** (-ου, ὁ) 'keeper of a cook-shop', from *popīnārius* 'keeper of a cook-shop' (*TLL*), with influence from προπίνω 'drink to'. Inscriptions: *MAMA* III.168 (IV–VI AD); *SEG* XXXIX.1577.8 (V AD). Literature: Cyr.S. *Vit.Sab.* 160.3 (VI AD). Notes: consistent spelling with ρ indicates diffusion of a single borrowing. If it is the source of προπινάριον and προπιναρία, it is older than it looks. Hofmann (1989: 359), Cameron (1931: 253), Lampe (1961), LSJ, LSJ suppl. See §4.2.4.1 n. 50, §4.4, §10.2.1, §10.2.2 I.
non-existent?	***propior*** 'closer' perhaps Antec. 3.6.5 *propior sobrino* καὶ *propior sobrina* (VI AD), but the word might instead be πρόπριος (*q.v.*).
Direct loan with suffix **VI AD – Byz.**	**προπριεταρία, προπριαιταρία** (-ας, ἡ) 'ownership', from *proprietārius* 'owner' + -ία. Documents: *P.Cair.Masp.* 67120r.1, 67151.150 (both VI AD). Literature: Antec. in Latin script 2.4.1 *proprietarian* etc. (VI AD). Post-antique: numerous in legal texts. Notes: Daris (1991a: 96, with derivation from *proprietāria*), Meinersmann (1927: 50), *LBG* (*s.v.* προπριετάριος). See §4.3.2, §6.2, §10.2.1, §10.2.2 B.
foreign	**προπριετάριος** 'owner', from *proprietārius* 'owner': Antec. in Latin script 2.1.9 *proprietariu* etc. (VI AD); later in Greek script. Zilliacus (1935a: 202–3), *LBG*. See §9.5.6 n. 68.
not ancient?	**πρόπριος** 'one's own', from *proprius* 'one's own': perhaps Antec. in Latin script 3.6.5 (VI AD), but the word could be *propior* (*q.v.*); later in Greek script. Zilliacus (1935a: 202–3), *LBG*.
rare	**προσεκουτωρία** 'covering note', 'letter of authorization', from *prōsecūtōria* 'letter of authorization' (*TLL*): papyrus *SB* 14674.17 etc. (V/VI AD). Diethart (1988: 63), Daris (1991a: 96), *TLL* (*s.v. prōsecūtōria* 2183.57), LSJ suppl.

rare   **προσκουλκάτωρ** 'advanced scout', probably from *prōculcātor/proscultātor* 'scout' (*TLL*): Malal. 13.21.24 (VI AD); occasionally later. Lampe (1961) suggests that the occurence in Malalas is a mistake for προσπεκουλάτωρ, but that is unlikely in view of the later attestations and Byzantine προσκουλκεύω 'scout' (*LBG*): this was a real word, not a scribal error. Hofmann (1989: 359), *TLL* (*s.v. prōculcātor* 1565.30–2).

non-existent?   **πρόσφουγος** 'fugitive', from *profugus* 'fugitive': cited as an ancient loan by Zilliacus (1935a: 232–3), but I can find no examples. Πρόσφυγος 'fleeing for refuge' and related words are not from Latin (LSJ, *LBG*).

   προτέκτωρ: see προτήκτωρ.

   προτεριτός: see πραιτέριτος.

rare   **προτεσσαράριος**, **προτεσσελάριος**, an army title apparently from πρό + *tesserārius* 'soldier who circulates the *tessera* with the password' via τεσσαράριος: ostraca QAB146 and QAB129 in Cuvigny 2006: 343 (II AD?).

Direct loan
III AD – Byz.   **προτήκτωρ**, **πρωτήκτωρ**, **προτέκτωρ**, **πρωτέκτωρ**, **προτίκτωρ**, **πρωτίκτωρ** (-ορος/-ωρος, ὁ), a title, from *prōtector* 'guardian'.

     Documents: e.g. *P.Oxy.* 43r.2.7 etc. (III AD); *P.Oxy.* 1253.4 etc. (IV AD); *P.Oxy.* 4905.3 (V AD); *SB* 14124.9 (VI AD). Superseded in *SB* 9118.4 (II AD).

     Inscriptions: e.g. *IGBulg.* III.II.1570.4 etc. (III AD); *SEG* XXXIX.1609.5 (IV AD); *I.Chr.Bulgarien* 224.12 (V/VI AD); *SEG* XLVIII.776.1 (VI AD).

     Literature: e.g. Nil. 1.233.1 (V AD); *Historia monachorum in Aegypto* 19.41 (V AD); Malal. 18.129 (VI AD); Just. *Edict* 8.1.pr. = p. 769.5 (VI AD); *Martyrium Ignatii* 1.2 in Diekamp and Funk 1913. Unverified examples (II and III AD) in Zilliacus (1937: 322–3, 333).

     Post-antique: numerous, forming derivative πρωτικτόρισσα 'wife of a *protector*'. *LBG* (*s.v.* προτίκτωρ), Triandaphyllidis (1909: 129).

     Notes: forms derivative ἀποπροτήκτωρ. Avotins (1992 *s.v.* πρωτήκτωρ), Daris (1991a: 96 *s.v.* πρωτήκτωρ), Mason (1974: 4, 11, 82), Hofmann (1989: 359–60), Zilliacus (1935a: 202–3, 232–3, 1937: 333), Meinersmann (1927: 51), LSJ suppl. See §4.2.5, §4.4, §10.2.1, §10.2.2 D.

   προτο-: see πρωτο-.

   προυᾶτος: see πριβᾶτος.

   προυκωράτωρ: see προκουράτωρ.

   προυμαρικός: see πλουμαρικός.

not ancient   **προφεκτίκιος** 'from the father of the bride', from *profectīcius* 'from the father of the bride': no ancient examples. Zilliacus (1935a: 202–3), *LBG*.

   πρόφεκτος: see πραίφεκτος.

Direct loan
II AD?   **προφεσσίων**, **προφεστίων** (-ωνος/-ονος, ἡ) 'declaration (of birth)', from *professiō* 'formal declaration'.

     Documents: e.g. *P.Diog.* 7.22 etc. (II AD); *P.Col.* VIII.225r.13 (II AD); *Chrest. Wilck.* 460.16 (II AD).

     Notes: Daris (1991a: 96), Mason (1974: 5, 82), Cavenaile (1951: 400), Meinersmann (1927: 51), *LBG*. See §4.2.5, §4.4, §9.2, §10.2.1, §10.2.2 D.

πρωβοκάτωρ: see προβοκάτωρ.

πρωμοτίων: see προμωτίων.

πρώξιμος: see πρόξιμος.

πρωπινάριος: see προπινάριος.

not ancient? πρωτασηκρήτης/-ις, πρωτοασηκρήτης/-ις 'first secretary', from πρῶτος
'first' + ἀσηκρῆτις (*q.v.*): probably no ancient examples. Lampe (1961 *s.v.*
πρωτοασηκρήτης), Hofmann (1989: 35 *s.v.* ἀ σηκρήτις), *LBG*.

rare πρωταυράριος 'first goldsmith', from πρῶτος 'first' + *aurārius* 'goldsmith' (*TLL
s.v.* 1. *aurārius* 1481.40), probably via αὐράριος: papyrus *BGU* XVII.2691.4
(VI AD); undated inscriptions *TAM* II.457.2; *MAMA* I.281.2; *MAMA*
III.335, 351. Hofmann (1989: 43 *s.v.* αυραριος), *LBG*, LSJ.

πρωτέκτωρ, πρωτήκτωρ: see προτήκτωρ.

rare πρώτηλα (τά) 'pair of oxen', from *prōtēlum* 'tandem team of draught animals':
probably inscription *SEG* XVI.754.4 (III AD). Hofmann (1989: 360), LSJ
suppl.

πρωτίκτωρ: see προτήκτωρ.

πρωτοασηκρήτης: see πρωτασηκρήτης.

not ancient? πρωτοβεστιάριος 'first clothes-person', from πρῶτος 'first' + *vestiārius* 'clothes-
person' via βεστιάριος: probably no ancient examples. Hofmann (1989: 52,
πρωτοβεσθάριοι *s.v.* βεστιάριος), *LBG*.

not ancient? πρωτοδρακωνάριος 'first *draconarius*', from πρῶτος 'first' + *dracōnārius* 'standard-
bearer' (*TLL*) via δρακονάριος: inscription *I.Tyr* 33.C3 with p. 26. LSJ suppl.

not ancient? πρωτοκαγκελλάριος , a title, from πρῶτος 'first' + *cancellārius*, an official (*TLL*)
via καγκελλάριος: perhaps inscription *I.Didyma* 604.2; Byzantine texts. *LBG*.

non-existent πρωτοκόμης 'first count' (a title), from πρῶτος 'first' + *comes* 'count' (*TLL s.v.*
1. *comes* 1776.67–1779.70) via κόμης: superseded reading of Palladius.
Hofmann (1989: 189 *s.v.* κόμης), Sophocles (1887).

rare πρωτοκούρσωρ 'first courier' (a title), from πρῶτος 'first' + *cursor* 'runner' via
κούρσωρ: Malal. 14.2 (VI AD); occasionally later. Hofmann (1989: 213 *s.v.*
κοῦρσορ), *LBG*, Triandaphyllidis (1909: 126), Lampe (1961).

not ancient? πρωτομαΐστωρ, προτομαΐστωρ 'first master' (a title), from πρῶτος 'first' + *magister*
'master' via μάγιστρος: *Test.Sal.* p. 7*.1 (III AD?); Byzantine texts. Hofmann
(1989: 253 *s.v.* μάγιστρος), *LBG* (*s.vv.* πρωτομάγιστρος, πρωτομαΐστορος,
πρωτομαΐστωρ, πρωτομάστωρ), Lampe (1961 *s.v.* πρωτομαΐστωρ).

not ancient? πρωτονοτάριος 'first shorthand writer', from πρῶτος + *notārius* 'shorthand
writer' via νοτάριος: probably no ancient examples. Hofmann (1989: 288 *s.v.*
νοτάριος), *LBG*, Sophocles (1887), Babiniotis (2002), Lampe (1961).

rare πρωτόπαλος 'member of the first gladiatorial squad', from πρῶτος 'first' + *pālus*
'gladiator's wooden sword' via πᾶλος: inscription *SEG* XXXII.605.1 (II AD) and
perhaps XXV.473.1 (II/III AD); Dio Cassius 72.22.3 (II/III AD). Effectively
the same word as πρῶτος πᾶλος, for which see *s.v.* πᾶλος. LSJ, LSJ suppl.

Deriv. of loan **VI AD – Byz.**	**πρωτοπατρίκιος** (-ου, ὁ) 'first patrician', from πρῶτος 'first' + *patricius* 'patrician' via πατρίκιος. Documents: e.g. *P.Oxy.* 4794.5 (VI AD); *SB* 12484.3 (VI AD). Literature: Malchus frag. 1.42 Cresci (V/VI AD). Post-antique: numerous. Sophocles (1887). Notes: the papyri (all from Oxyrhynchus) are all the same formula. Filos (2010: 244, 251), Daris (1991a: 96), Hofmann (1989: 322 *s.v.* πατρίκιος), Cavenaile (1952: 199), Meinersmann (1927: 46), Lampe (1961), LSJ. See §4.6.2, §9.2 n. 19, §10.2.2 D.
	πρωτοσπαθάριος: see σπαθάριος. **πτέρνη**: see πέρνα.
rare	**πυργοκάστελλος** 'siege tower', from πύργος 'tower' + *castellum* 'fort' via κάστελλος: Procop. *Aed.* 2.5.8 (VI AD); occasionally later. Hofmann (1989: 161 κάστελλος), *LBG*, Lampe (1961), LSJ (*s.v.* πυργοκάστελλον, but later examples are clearly masculine).
	πυσκίννα: see πισκεῖνα. **πυτιναῖος, πυτίνη, πυτινοπλόκος**: see βυτίνη.
not ancient	**πωμαρικός** 'concerning fruit-growing', from *pōmārium* 'orchard' via πωμάριον + -ικός: no ancient examples. Daris (1991a: 97), LSJ suppl.
Direct loan **I BC – Byz.**	**πωμάριον, πομάριον** (-ου, τό) 'orchard', from *pōmārium* 'orchard'. Documents: common, e.g. *SB* 12569.20 (I BC); *P.Oxy.* 707.19 etc. (II AD); *P.Oxy.* 1631.25 etc. (III AD); *P.Charite* 4.4 etc. (IV AD); *PSI* VII.774.6 etc. (V AD); *P.Hamb.* 1.68.6 etc. (VI AD). Inscriptions: *I.Ephesos* 1625B.1. Post-antique: numerous in papyri. Notes: forms derivative πωμαρίτης. Daris (1991a: 97), Hofmann (1989: 361), Meinersmann (1927: 51), Wessely (1902: 145 with n. 1), *DÉLG*, Beekes (2010), LSJ, LSJ suppl. See §2.4, §4.1.1, §4.2.4.1 n. 54, §4.3.2 n. 75, §4.6.1 n. 86, §6.3 n. 22, **§8.1.5**, §10.2.1, §10.2.2 I.
rare	**πωμάριος** 'fruit-seller', 'fruit-grower', from *pōmārius* 'fruit-seller': *P.Oxy.* 43v.5.8 (III AD); Byzantine texts. Hofmann (1989: 361), Meinersmann (1927: 51 *s.v.* πωμαριτης), Wessely (1902: 145 *s.v.* πωμαρίου), *LBG*.
Deriv. of loan **II AD – Byz.**	**πωμαρίτης, πομαρίτης** (-ου, ὁ) 'fruiterer', from *pōmārium* 'orchard' via πωμάριον + -ίτης. Documents: e.g. *P.Oxy.* 2781.5 (II AD); *P.Oxy.* 3923.3 (III AD); *P.Oxy.* 1133.3 (IV AD); *P.Princ.* II.104.4 (V AD); *P.Oxy.* 4789r.12 etc. (VI AD). Post-antique: numerous in papyri. Daris (1991a: 97). Notes: forms derivatives πωμαριτικός, πωμαρίτισσα. Daris (1991a: 97), Cavenaile (1952: 193), Meinersmann (1927: 51), *DÉLG* (*s.v.* πωμάριον), Beekes (2010 *s.v.* πωμάριον), LSJ. See §2.4, §4.6.1 n. 86, §8.2.2, §9.2, §10.2.2 I.
rare	**πωμαριτικός** 'concerning fruit-selling', from *pōmārium* 'orchard' via πωμαρίτης + -ικός: papyrus *BGU* III.900.24 (VI AD). Daris (1991a: 97), Cavenaile (1952: 197), Meinersmann (1927: 52), *LBG*.

rare   **πωμαρίτισσα** 'female fruiterer', from *pōmārium* 'orchard' via πωμαρίτης + -ισσα: papyrus *Stud.Pal.* VIII.809.1 (VI AD). Daris (1991a: 97), Cavenaile (1952: 195), Meinersmann (1927: 51–2), *DÉLG* (*s.v.* πωμάριον), Beekes (2010 *s.v.* πωμάριον), LSJ (*s.v.* πωμαρίτης).

rare   **πωμήριον** 'city boundary', from *pōmērium* 'city boundary': Plut. *Rom.* 11.4, marked (I/II AD); Dio Cassius 39.39.7 etc. (II/III AD). Strobach (1997: 198), Mason (1974: 5, 7, 82), Hofmann (1989: 361), *LBG*.

Ρ

rare   **ῥάδις** 'spoke (of a wheel)', from *radius* 'spoke': Edict.Diocl. 15.5 (IV AD). Hofmann (1989: 362), LSJ.

Direct loan
I–IV AD?   **ῥαῖδα, ῥῆδα, ῥέδα** (-ης?, ἡ) 'carriage', from *raeda* 'carriage'.
Inscriptions: Edict.Diocl. 15.33 etc. (IV AD).
Literature: NT Revelation 18:13 (I AD); quotation of that in Hippolytus, *De antichristo* 41.20 Achelis (III AD); Lyd. *Mens.* 1.32 (VI AD); Oecumenius, *Commentarius in Apocalypsin* p. 197.7–17 Hoslier: "καὶ ἵπποι" φησὶ "καὶ ῥέδων καὶ σωμάτων". τὸ ῥέδον Ῥωμαϊκὴ μὲν λέξις ἐστίν· Ῥωμαίων γὰρ κρατούντων, οὐδὲν ἀπεικὸς τὸν θεσπέσιον εὐαγγελιστὴν Ῥωμαίᾳ λέξει συγχρήσασθαι· ἐξελλήνισε δὲ αὐτὴν ἡ γραφή. ῥεδιούμ γάρ ἐστι παρὰ Ῥωμαίοις τὸ ὄχημα, γενικὴν δὲ πληθυντικὴν τέθεικε πτῶσιν· καὶ δέον κατὰ Ῥωμαίους ῥεδιορούμ εἰπεῖν, ὡς ἐξελληνίσας αὐτὴν Ἑλληνικὴν γέγραφε κατάληξιν, ῥέδων εἰπών, ἵνα ᾖ τὸ εἰρημένον τοιοῦτον. "καὶ ἵπποι" φησὶ "ῥέδων καὶ σωμάτων", οἷον καὶ ὀχημάτων ἵπποι οἱ εἰς ὀχήματα ἐπιτήδειοι, καὶ σωμάτων, τουτέστι, κέλητες καὶ εἰς ἀναβάτας πεποιημένοι (VI AD).
Post-antique: survives chiefly in commentary on the biblical use, but see *LBG*, Triandaphyllidis (1909: 130 *s.v.* ῥέντα). Cf. Byzantine ῥαῖδος (Lampe 1961, *LBG*).
Notes: probably forms derivative ῥαίδιον. Hofmann (1989: 362), Blass *et al.* (1979: §5 n. 6), LSJ, LSJ suppl. See §4.6.1 n. 83, §9.3 n. 21, §10.2.1, §10.2.2 K.

Deriv.? of loan
III AD – Byz.   **ῥαίδιον, ῥήδιον, ῥέδιον** (-ου, τό) 'carriage', from *raeda* 'carriage', probably via ῥαῖδα, + -ιον.
Literature: perhaps Hdn. Ὀρθογρ. III.II.577.11: ῥηδίων καρούχων ῥαιδίων. – ῥεδίων ἁρμάτων (II AD); Clemens Alexandrinus, *Paedagogus* 3.3.24.3 Harl (II/III AD); Pall. *V.Chrys.* 30.6 (IV/V AD); *Historia monachorum in Aegypto* 23.11 (V AD); Hesych. as lemma ρ 177 etc. (V/VI AD); with *raeda* in Gloss. Ps.-Cyril. 427.21. Unverified example (IV AD) in Zilliacus (1937: 322, 333).
Post-antique: survives. *LBG*.
Notes: Hofmann (1989: 362 *s.v.* ῥαιδα), Zilliacus (1937: 333), Immisch (1885: 371), LSJ (*s.vv.* ῥαίδιον, ῥηδίων). See §4.3.2 n. 69, §4.6.1 n. 83, §9.2, §10.2.2 K.

     ῥαιφερενδάριος: see ῥεφερενδάριος.

not ancient   **ῥαμπτάρια** perhaps transliterating unattested **rāmitārius*: interpolation in Dsc. 3.12 RV. *TLL s.v.* See §8.1.7.

foreign   **ῥᾶνα** transliterating *rāna* 'frog': Hesych. ρ 111 (V/VI AD). Immisch (1885: 333), LSJ.

not ancient   **ῥάπα** transliterating *rāpa* 'turnip': interpolation in Dsc. 2.110 RV. *LBG*, Sophocles (1887).

rare   **ῥᾶσον**, a garment and a kind of cloth, apparently from *rāsum*, neuter of *rāsus* 'shorn of its pile', 'thin': *Acta Pilati* B.10.3 = Tischendorf 1876: 305 (IV AD?); *Evangelium Nicodemi* 10.1.3a rec. m1 Gounelle (V AD?); occasional Byzantine texts. Later there seems to be an adj. ῥάσος of which this could be neut. subst. Modern ράσο 'priest's garment': Babiniotis (2002), Andriotis (1967), Meyer (1895: 55). Hofmann (1989: 363 *s.v.* ῥᾶσος), Viscidi (1944: 36), Zilliacus (1935a: 232–3, 1937: 333), Triandaphyllidis (1909: 122, 125), Zervan (2019: 147–8), *LBG* (*s.v.* ῥάσος), Sophocles (1887), Lampe (1961 *s.v.* ῥάσος). See §8.2.3 n. 51.

not ancient?   **ῥατίκλα** 'gridiron', from *crātīcula* 'gridiron': undated saint's life that could be from IV AD. Zilliacus (1937: 333), *LBG*. Cf. κρατίκλη.

ῥατιονάλιος: see ῥατιωνάλιος.

rare   **ῥατίων** 'calculation', from *ratiō* 'calculation': ostracon *O.Did.* 392.3 (III AD); Lyd. *Mag.* p. 140.9, marked (VI AD). Zilliacus (1935a: 204–5), *LBG*, Sophocles (1887).

foreign   **ῥατιωνάλιος, ῥατιονάλιος** transliterating *ratiōnālis*, a title: Lyd. *Mag.* p. 140.8 (VI AD); Byzantine texts. Zilliacus (1935a: 204–5), *LBG*, Sophocles (1887).

not ancient?   **ῥατοναβιτεύω** 'endorse', from *ratum habeō* 'endorse' via *habitus* (pf. part. of *habeō* 'have') + -εύω: probably no ancient examples. Hofmann (1989: 363), Zilliacus (1935a: 204–5), *LBG*.

foreign   **ῥέ** 'matter', from *rē* (abl. of *rēs*) and treated as indeclinable: Antec. in Latin script 3.14.pr. *re* etc. (VI AD); later in Greek script. See §7.2.2 with passage 29, §9.5.6 n. 68; cf. ῥέμ.

foreign   **ῥεβερεντία** 'reverence', from *reverentia* 'reverence': Just. *Nov.* in Latin script 78.2.pr. etc. (VI AD); later as ῥεβεντία. Hofmann (1989: 367), Zilliacus (1935a: 206–7), *LBG* (*s.v.* ῥεβεντία).

foreign   **ῥεβοκατορία, ῥεβοκατωρία, ῥεουοκατορία** 'letter of recall', from *revocātōria* 'letter of recall' (L&S *s.v. revocātōrius*): in Latin script in legal texts of VI AD, e.g. Just. *Nov.* 8.13; Ath.Schol. 20.1.24. Hofmann (1989: 366), Zilliacus (1935a: 206–7), Lampe (1961).

rare   **ῥεγενδάριος, ῥεγερεντάριος**, a title probably from *regerendārius*, a title (*TLL*): tablet in Harrauer and Pintaudi 2003: 143.9 (VI AD); Lyd. Mag. pp. 136.27, 166.12, marked (VI AD). Hofmann (1989: 363), *LBG*, Sophocles (1887), *TLL* (*s.vv. regendārius, regerendārius*).

ῥεγεονάριος: see ῥεγεωνάριος.

rare   **ῥέγεστα, ῥήγεστα** (τά) 'register', from *regesta, -ōrum* 'register' (*TLL s.v. regero* 731.10–37): Lyd. *Mag.* p. 164.5 etc. (VI AD); Byzantine texts (where it often appears as ῥέγεστρα and singular ῥέγεστρον). Hofmann (1989: 364, 368), *LBG* (*s.vv.* ῥέγεστα, ῥέγεστρον), Sophocles (1887 *s.v.* ῥέγιστρον). See §9.5.5 passage 70.

Direct loan
III AD – Byz.

ῥεγεών, ῥεγιών (-ωνος, ἡ) 'district (within a city or its suburbs)', from *regiō* 'region'.

Documents: *SB* 14606.2.3, misspelled λεγ- (V AD).

Inscriptions: *I.Leukopetra* 65.6 (III AD); Cousin 1900: 337(2).2; *OGIS* 526.2.

Literature: *ACO* II.I.III p. 59.11 etc. (V AD); Ps.-Clementina, *Epitome de gestis Petri* 163.2, 175.3 Dressel.

Post-antique: numerous. Sophocles (1887 *s.vv.* ῥεγεών, ῥεγιών), *LBG* (*s.v.* ῥεγιών), Triandaphyllidis (1909: 123).

Notes: forms derivative ῥεγεωνάρχης, perhaps ῥεγεωνάριος. Mason (1974: 6, 83, 135), Hofmann (1989: 364), Zilliacus (1935a: 204–5), Lampe (1961), LSJ (*s.vv.* ῥεγεών, ῥεγιών). See §4.2.5, §10.2.1, §10.2.2 D.

rare

ῥεγεωνάριος, ῥεγεωνάριος 'police officer of a city ward', from *regiōnārius* 'of a region' (*TLL*) or from *regiō* 'region' via ῥεγεών + -άριος: probably inscription Sterrett 1888a: 121 no. 92/3.A5 (III AD); Hesych. as lemma ρ 170 (V/VI AD); Byzantine texts. Hofmann (1989: 364), Immisch (1885: 359), *LBG* (*s.v.* ῥεγεονάριος), Sophocles (1887), *TLL* (*s.v. regiōnārius* 758.3–4), Lampe (1961), LSJ suppl.

rare

ῥεγεωνάρχης 'president of a district', from *regiō* 'region' via ῥεγεών + ἄρχω 'rule': Lyd. *Mens.* 4.138 (VI AD); occasionally later. Hofmann (1989: 364 *s.v.* ῥεγιών), *LBG*, LSJ.

ῥέγιος: see ῥήγιος.

ῥεγιών: see ῥεγεών.

regula: see ῥῆγλα.

ῥέδα: see ῥαῖδα.

not Latin?

ῥέδεγενς (in abbreviated form ρεδεγεντ), meaning uncertain, perhaps from *redigēns*, pres. part. of *redigō* 'return': papyrus *P.Lond.* v.1716.18 (VI AD). Binder (2000: 133), Daris (1991a: 97), Zilliacus (1935a: 204–5), Meinersmann (1927: 52).

not ancient

ῥεδιβιτόριος 'concerning returns', from *redhibitōrius* 'relating to the return of defective purchases': no ancient examples. Zilliacus (1935a: 204–5), *LBG*.

ῥέδιον: see ῥαίδιον.

not ancient

ῥεδνιβιτεύω 'refund' from *redhibitus* (pf. part. of *redhibeō* 'return', 'take back') + -εύω: no ancient examples. Zilliacus (1935a: 204–5), *LBG*.

not ancient?

ῥεϊκουρένδος, ῥεκουϊρένδος 'sought', from *requīrendus*, gerundive of *requīrō* 'seek': probably no ancient examples. Zilliacus (1935a: 204–5), *LBG*.

foreign

ῥέκαυτον 'receipt' (used in plural), from *recautum* 'receipt' (*TLL s.v. recaveo*): Just. *Nov.* in Latin script 130.3 etc. (VI AD); Ath.Schol. in Latin script 20.2.3 etc. (VI AD); sometimes later in Greek script. Hofmann (1989: 364–5), *LBG*, *TLL* (*s.v. recaveo* 268.6), Lampe (1961). Cf. μονορεκαῦτον.

foreign

ῥεκεπτίκιος 'concerning payment from a pledge', from *receptīcius* '(property) retained by the wife and not included in the dowry': Antec. in Latin script 4.6.8 *receptician* etc. (VI AD); later in Greek script. Pedone (2020b), Zilliacus (1935a: 204–5), *LBG*.

foreign	ῥέκηνσον 'authenticated copy', from *recēnsus, -ūs* 'review': Lyd. *Mag.* p. 148.21, marked (VI AD); occasional Byzantine texts. *LBG.* Cf. ῥέκινον, ῥεκιτᾶτον.
non-existent	ῥέκινον 'written counterpart' is cited by Sophocles (1887) and Hofmann (1989: 365) from Lyd. *Mag.* p. 148.21 (VI AD), where ῥέκηνσον is now read.
foreign	***reciperandus*** 'recovery of possession', gerundive of *reciperō* 'recover': Antec. in Latin script 4.15.2 *reciperandae* etc. (VI AD).
non-existent	ῥεκιτᾶτον: superseded reading for ῥέκηνσον in Lyd. *Mag.* p. 148.21 (VI AD). Hofmann (1989: 365).
non-existent?	ῥεκολλᾶτα, ῥεκολλοκᾶτα, ῥελοκᾶτα, a tax, perhaps from unspecified Latin word: perhaps Lyd. *Mag.* p. 242.20 (VI AD). Caimi (1981: 334–42), *LBG.*
	ῥεκουϊρένδος: see ῥεϊκουρένδος.
foreign	ῥεκτός, a garment, probably from *rēctus* 'straight': Hesych. as lemma ρ 204, 205 (V/VI AD). Immisch (1885: 334–5).
not ancient	ῥέκτωρ, a title, perhaps from *rēctor* 'governor': no ancient examples. Zilliacus (1935a: 204–5), *LBG* (*s.v.* ῥέκτωρ B).
rare	ῥελατωρία, ῥελατορία 'receipt brought back after delivery', from *relātōria* 'receipt' (L&S) or *relātor* 'one who registers' + -ία: papyri *P.Oxy.* 3125.6 (IV AD); *SB* 10931.4 etc. (IV AD); tachygraphy in Menci 2000: 288 (IV AD). *Relātōria* occurs only in *Codex Theodosianus* 13.5.8, where *DÉLG* thinks it is a transliteration of the Greek. Commentary on *P.Oxy.* 3125, Menci (2000: 288), Daris (1991a: 97), Beekes (2010), *LBG* (*s.v.* ῥελατορία 'report'), LSJ suppl.
rare	ῥελέβατος 'with tax reduction', from *relevātus*, pf. part. of *relevō* 'lighten': Hesychius Illustrius, frag. 6.12 in *FHG* IV (VI AD); perhaps Lyd. *Mag.* p. 242.20 (VI AD). Caimi (1981: 334–42), *LBG.*
foreign	ῥελεγατεύω, ῥεληγατεύω 'banish', from *relēgātus* (pf. part. of *relēgō* 'banish') + -εύω: Antec. in Latin script 1.12.2 *relegateuthosin* (VI AD); later in Greek script. Zilliacus (1935a: 204–5), *LBG.* See §7.1.3, §9.5.6 n. 68.
not ancient	ῥελεγατίων 'banishment', from *relēgātiō* 'banishment': superseded reading for *revocationos* in Ath.Schol. 4.1.16 (VI AD); Byzantine texts. Hofmann (1989: 365), Zilliacus (1935a: 204–5), *LBG*, Lampe (1961).
foreign	ῥελεγᾶτος, ῥελήγατος 'banished', from *relēgātus*, pf. part. of *relēgō* 'banish': Antec. in Latin script 1.12.2 *relegatos* etc. (VI AD); perhaps Lyd. *Mag.* p. 242.20 (VI AD); later in Greek script. Caimi (1981: 334–41), Zilliacus (1935a: 204–5), *LBG.*
foreign	ῥελεγίοσος, ῥελιγίοσος 'religious', from *religiōsus* 'religious': Antec. in Latin script 2.1.9 *religioson* etc. (VI AD); later in Greek script. Zilliacus (1935a: 204–5), *LBG* (*s.v.* ῥελιγίοσος). See §9.5.6 n. 68.
rare	ῥελεγίων 'religion', from *religiō* 'religion': Lyd. *Ost.* 16.2 (VI AD). *LBG* (*s.v.* ῥελεγιῶνες).
	ῥεληγατ-: see ῥελεγατ-.

ῥελιγίοσος: see ῥελεγίοσος.

ῥελοκᾶτα: see ῥεκολλᾶτα.

foreign   ῥέμ, from *rem*, acc. of *rēs* 'thing': Antec. in Latin script as part of phrases, e.g. 4.6.1 *in rem* (VI AD); later often in Greek script as part of phrases. See §7.3 passage 33; cf. ῥέ.

not ancient   ῥεμισ(σ)ίων, ῥεμεσ(σ)ίων 'remission', from *remissiō* 'remission': no ancient examples. Zilliacus (1935a: 204–5), *LBG*.

not ancient   ῥενοβατεύω 'renew', from *renovātus* (pf. part. of *renovō* 'renew') + -εύω: no ancient examples. Zilliacus (1935a: 204–5), *LBG*.

Direct loan   ῥέος (-ου, ὁ) 'defendant', 'accused person', from *reus* 'defendant'.
VI AD – Byz.   Documents: *P.Hamb.* 1.23.7 (VI AD).
    Literature: Ath.Schol. 5.2, but in Latin script 5.4.3 etc. (VI AD); Antec. in Latin script 4.6.30 *reon* etc. (VI AD).
    Post-antique: numerous. *LBG*.
    Notes: often part of *reoi promittendoi* 'joint promisers' or *reoi stipulandoi* 'joint stipulators', e.g. Antec. 3.16.pr.; cf. ῥέον προμιττέντων (for ῥέων προμιττέντων) on *P.Hamb.* Daris (1991a: 97), Hofmann (1989: 366 *s.vv.* ῥέοι προμιττέντες, ῥέος), Zilliacus (1935a: 206–7), Meinersmann (1927: 52), Triandaphyllidis (1909: 128), Lampe (1961). See §4.2.4.1 n. 51, §9.5.6 n. 68, §10.2.1, §10.2.2 B; cf. προμίττενς, στιπουλάνδος.

foreign   ῥεουξορία 'legal action for the recovery of the dowry', from (*āctiō*) *reī uxōriae*: *Schol.Sinai.* in Latin script abbreviated *r.u.*, 22 etc. (V/VI AD); Antec. in Latin script 4.6.29 *reuxoria* (VI AD); later in Greek script. *LBG*. See §7.1.2 with passage 23, **§9.5.6**.

ῥεουοκατορία: see ῥεβοκατορία.

rare   ῥεπαρατίων 'renewal', from *reparātiō* 'renewal' (L&S): papyrus *Stud.Pal.* XX.123v.33 (V AD); Just. *Nov.* in Latin script 126.2 (VI AD); Byzantine texts. Daris (1991a: 97), Hofmann (1989: 366), Zilliacus (1935a: 204–5, 232–3), Meinersmann (1927: 52), *LBG*, LSJ suppl.

foreign   ῥεπετιτεύω 'claim back', from *repetītus* (pf. part. of *repetō* 'claim back') + -εύω: Antec. in Latin script 2.7.1 *repetiteuein* etc. (VI AD); Ath.Schol. in Latin script 9.1.5 (VI AD); later often in Greek script. Hofmann (1989: 367), Zilliacus (1935a: 204–5), *LBG*, Lampe (1961). See §9.5.6 n. 68.

foreign   ῥεπετιτίων 'act of claiming back', from *repetītiō* 'act of claiming back': Antec. in Latin script 3.20.1 *repetitiona* etc. (VI AD); later in Greek script. Zilliacus (1935a: 204–5), *LBG*. See §9.5.6 n. 68.

foreign   ῥεπλικατίων 'reply' (a legal action), from *replicātiō* 'objection made by the plaintiff to the *exceptio* of a defendant': Antec. in Latin script 4.14.pr. *replication* etc. (VI AD); later in Greek script. Zilliacus (1935a: 204–5), *LBG*. See §9.5.6 n. 68.

rare   ῥεποστώριον 'stand for serving food at a meal', from *repositōrium* 'portable stand for serving courses at meals': papyrus *P.Select.* 6.9 (I AD). Binder (2000: 202), Daris (1991a: 98), LSJ suppl.

foreign	**ῥεπουδιατεύω** 'divorce' or 'reject an inheritance', from *repudiātus* (pf. part. of *repudiō* 'reject', 'divorce') + -εύω: Antec. in Latin script 2.17.2 *'erepudiateusen* etc. (VI AD); Ath.Schol. in Latin script 2.P.8 (VI AD); later in Greek script. Hofmann (1989: 367), Zilliacus (1935a: 204–5), *LBG*, Lampe (1961). See **§9.5.6** passage 79.
foreign	**ῥεπουδιατίων** 'rejection of an inheritance', from *repudiātiō* 'refusal': Antec. in Latin script 2.19.5 *repudiation* etc. (VI AD); later in Greek script. Zilliacus (1935a: 204–5), *LBG*.
Direct loan IV AD – Byz.	**ῥεπούδιον, ῥιπούδιον** (-ου, τό) 'divorce letter', from *repudium* 'divorce'. Documents: e.g. *P.Lips.* I.39.10 (IV AD); *P.Oxy.* 3581.15 (IV/V AD); *P.Oxy.* 129.1 etc. (VI AD). Literature: e.g. Justin Martyr, *Apologia secunda* 2.6 Minns and Parvis, marked (II AD); Thdr.Heracl. 34 (IV AD); Thdt. *Is.* 16.10: βιβλίον δὲ ἀποστασίου, ὃ καλεῖν εἰώθασιν οἱ πολλοὶ ῥεπούδιον, ὀνομάζει (V AD); Nil. 2.181.13, marked (V AD); *Schol.Sinai.* in Latin script 6 *repudio* etc. (V/VI AD); Just. *Nov.* 19.pr., but in Latin script 22.15.pr. etc. (VI AD). Post-antique: common in Byzantine legal texts. Zervan (2019: 148), Sophocles (1887). Notes: Avotins (1989, 1992), Daris (1991a: 98), Hofmann (1989: 367), Zilliacus (1935a: 204–5), Meinersmann (1927: 52), *LBG* (*s.v.* ῥιπούδιον), Lampe (1961), LSJ suppl. See §4.1.1, §4.2.4.1 n. 54, §7.1.2, §9.5.6 n. 56, §10.2.1, §10.2.2 B.
non-existent?	**ῥεσιδοῦος** 'left over', from *residuus* 'left over': cited as an ancient loan by Zilliacus (1935a: 206–7), but I can find no examples.
not ancient	**ῥεσκισ(σ)όριος, ῥεσκισσώριος** 'concerned with annulling', from *rescissōrius* 'concerned with annulling': no ancient examples. Zilliacus (1935a: 206–7), *LBG*.
Direct loan V AD – Byz.	**ῥέσκριπτον** (-ου, τό) 'rescript', from *rescrīptum* 'emperor's written decision, having the force of law'. Documents: *SB* 9763.33 (V AD); *P.Mich.Aphrod.* 1.65 (VI AD). Literature: Antec. in Latin script 3.11.2 *rescripton* (VI AD). Post-antique: survives in legal texts. *LBG*. Notes: the masculine gender given by LSJ suppl. *s.v.* ῥέσκριπτος is not attested. Daris (1991a: 98), Zilliacus (1935a: 206–7), Meinersmann (1927: 52). See §4.2.4.1 n. 55, §8.2.2, §10.2.1, §10.2.2 A.
foreign	**ῥέσπονσον** 'jurist's pronouncement', from *respōnsum* 'response': *Schol.Sinai.* in Latin script 4 *responson* etc. (V/VI AD); Antec. in Latin script 1.2.8 *responson* etc. (VI AD); later in Greek script. Zilliacus (1935a: 206–7), *LBG*. See §7.1.2, §7.2.1 passage 27, §9.5.6 nn. 56 and 68.
non-existent?	**ῥεστιπουλατίων** 'demand for a counter-guarantee', from *restipulātiō* 'demand for a counter-guarantee': cited as an ancient loan by Zilliacus (1935a: 206–7), but I can find no examples.
foreign	**ῥεστιτουτόριος** 'restitutory', from *restitūtōrius* 'concerned with restoring a person's position in a case to what it was before proceedings began': Antec. in Latin script 4.15.1 *restitutoria* etc. (VI AD); later in Greek script. *LBG*.

not ancient   ῥέτενο 'rein', from reconstructed *retina 'rein' (Meyer-Lübke 1935): no ancient examples. Meyer (1895: 55), *LBG* (*s.v.* ῥέτινον).

rare   ῥετεντίων 'retention', from *retentiō* 'retention': papyrus *P.Cair.Masp.* 67295.2.9 (VI AD); *Schol.Sinai.* in Latin script 18 *retention*, 21 *retentiona* (V/VI AD); Antec. in Latin script 4.6.37 *retentiona* (VI AD); occasionally later. Daris (1991a: 98), Zilliacus (1935a: 206–7), Meinersmann (1927: 52), *LBG*. See §7.1.2, §9.5.6 n. 56.

foreign   *retinendus* 'retention of possession', gerundive of *retineō* 'hold fast': Antec. 4.15.2 *retinendae* etc. (VI AD).

Direct loan
V AD – Byz.   ῥεφερενδάριος, ῥαιφερενδάριος, ῥηφερενδάριος (-ου, ὁ), an official, from *referendārius*, an official (*TLL*).
Documents: *P.Cair.Masp.* 67002.2.1 etc. (VI AD).
Inscriptions: *I.Cos Segre* EV63.2 (IV/V AD); probably *I.Sardis* 1.19.4 (VI AD).
Literature: e.g. *V.Dan.Styl.* A. 76.2 (V AD); Malal. 13.20 (VI AD); *ACO* III p. 29.24 (VI AD); Just. *Nov.* 10.t (VI AD).
Post-antique: common. *LBG* (*s.v.* ῥαιφερενδάριος), Zervan (2019: 147), Triandaphyllidis (1909: 127).
Notes: Avotins (1989, 1992), Daris (1991a: 98), Hofmann (1989: 368), Zilliacus (1935a: 204–5, 1937: 333), Meinersmann (1927: 52), *TLL* (*s.v. referendārius* 601.29–35), Lampe (1961), LSJ suppl. See §4.2.4.1 n. 50, §10.2.1, §10.2.2 D.

foreign   ῥεφούγια, meaning uncertain, probably from *refugia*, plural of *refugium* 'refuge': Hesych. as lemma ρ 230 (V/VI AD). Immisch (1885: 357).

ῥέφουγος: see ῥίφουγος.

rare   ῥεφοῦσα (τά), a tax, from *refūsum*, pf. part. of *refundō* 'restore': Lyd. *Mag.* p. 242.20 (VI AD). Caimi (1981: 334–42), *LBG*.

ῥήγας: see ῥήξ.

ῥήγεστα: see ῥέγεστα.

rare   Ῥηγία, a place in Constantinople, from *rēgia* 'palace': Malal. 13.8 etc. (VI AD); Byzantine texts. Designating a place in Rome: Plut. *Rom.* 18.9 etc., marked (I/II AD). Hofmann (1989: 368), Sophocles (1887 *s.v.* ῥήγιον).

foreign   ῥήγιος, ῥέγιος transliterating *rēgius* 'royal': Lyd. *Mag.* p. 10.30 etc. (VI AD); Antec. in Latin script 1.2.6 *regiu* (VI AD); later in Greek script. More widely used in the place name Ῥήγιον. Zilliacus (1935a: 204–5), *LBG*. See §12.2.2.

rare   ῥήγισσα 'queen', from *rēx* 'king' via ῥήξ + -ισσα: Malal. 18.13 *passim* (VI AD); occasional Byzantine texts. Hofmann (1989: 369 *s.v.* ῥήξ), *LBG*, Sophocles (1887), Lampe (1961).

rare   ῥῆγλα, from *rēgula* 'rule', 'bar': Edict.Diocl. 15.13 (IV AD), designating part of a wagon; Hesych. as lemma ρ 238 (V/VI AD); *Schol.Sinai.* in Latin script 35 *reg.* (V/VI AD); Byzantine texts (with more meanings). Binder (2000: 198), Hofmann (1989: 369), Immisch (1885: 362), *LBG*, Triandaphyllidis (1909: 124), Meyer (1895: 56), Babiniotis (2002, *s.v.* ῥέγουλα), Andriotis (1967 *s.v.* modern ῥήγλα 'ruler'), LSJ suppl. See §7.1.2, §9.5.6 nn. 56 and 57.

rare	**ῥηγλίον** 'bar of gold', probably from *rēgula* 'bar' (L&S *s.v.* 1.B.1) + -ιον: Edict. Diocl. 30.1a (IV AD); Byzantine texts (in other meanings). Hofmann (1989: 369 *s.v.* ρηγλα), *LBG*, LSJ suppl.
not ancient?	**ῥηγλοχύτης, ῥιγλοχύτης, ῥυγλοχύτης** 'ingot mould', probably from *rēgula* 'bar' (L&S *s.v.* 1.B.1) + χύτης 'caster' from χέω 'pour': alchemists, Berthelot and Ruelle 1888: 322.24, 325.10. LSJ suppl.

ῥῆδα: see ῥαῖδα.

ῥήδιον: see ῥαίδιον.

Direct loan **IV AD – modern**	**ῥήξ** (ῥηγός, ὁ) '(western) king', also a military unit, from *rēx* 'king'. Literature: common, e.g. Plut. *Mor.* 279c, marked, as part of ῥῆγι σακρώρουμ (I/II AD); Ast.Soph. 13.20 (IV AD); *V.Dan.Styl. A.* 56.2 (V AD); Malal. 7.11 (VI AD); Lyd. *Mag.* p. 38.23 (VI AD). Unverified example (III AD) in Zilliacus (1937: 322–3, 333). Post-antique: common. Zervan (2019: 149–50), Sophocles (1887), Triandaphyllidis (1909: 127). Modern ῥήγας 'king': Babiniotis (2002), Andriotis (1967), Meyer (1895: 55–6). Notes: forms derivative ῥήγισσα. Hofmann (1989: 369), Mason (1974: 6, 83), Zilliacus (1937: 333), Lampe (1961), LSJ suppl. See §4.2.5, §8.2.3 n. 51, §10.2.1, §10.2.2 D.
foreign	**ῥῆς γέστας** transliterating acc. of *rēs gestae* '(record of) things done': Lyd. *Mag.* p. 164.7 (VI AD). See §9.5.5 passage 70; cf. ῥέγεστα.
Direct loan **I–IV AD**	**ῥητιάριος, ῥητιάρειος, ῥιτιάρις** (-ου, ὁ), a type of gladiator, from *rētiārius* 'gladiator with a net'. Inscriptions: e.g. *I.Prusa* 171.2 (I AD); *SEG* XXXIX.1339.14 etc. (II AD?); *I.Thrake Aeg.* 167.3 (III AD); perhaps *I.Cret.* IV.452e (III/IV AD). Literature: Artemidorus, *Onirocriticon* 2.32.22 (II AD). Notes: Mason (1974: 3), Hofmann (1989: 369), LSJ. See §4.2.4.1 n. 50, §6.1, §10.2.1, §10.2.2 F.

ῥηφερενδάριος: see ῥεφερενδάριος.

ῥιγλοχύτης: see ῥηγλοχύτης.

rare	**ῥῖπα** 'riverbank fortifications', from *rīpa* 'bank' (probably also with the fortification meaning): ostracon O.Claud. inv. 7309.14 = Cuvigny 2019: 277 (II AD); see Cuvigny 2019: 280–3. Separately, ῥῖπα transliterating *rīpa* 'bank': Procop. *Aed.* 4.5.12 (VI AD); cf. *LBG*.
rare	**ῥιπαρεύω** 'serve as water-watchman', from *rīpārius* 'of riverbanks' via ῥιπάριος + -εύω: papyrus *P.Cair.Masp.* 67281.3 (VI AD). Daris (1991a: 98), Meinersmann (1927: 52), *LBG*.
Deriv. of loan **VI AD – Byz.**	**ῥιπαρία** (-ας, ἡ) 'office of water-watchman', from *rīpārius* 'of riverbanks' via ῥιπάριος + -ία. Documents: *BGU* XIX.2772.2 (V/VI AD); *CPR* XIV.48.3 (VI AD); *P.Cair.Masp.* 67287.4.30 (VI AD); *P.Oxy.* 2032.50 (VI AD). Post-antique: one papyrus. Notes: probably restricted to Egypt; see on ῥιπάριος. Daris (1991a: 98), Hofmann (1989: 370 *s.v.* ριπαριος), Meinersmann (1927: 52), LSJ suppl. See §4.6.1, §6.2, §9.2, §10.2.2 D.

Direct loan
III AD – Byz.

ῥιπάριος (-ου, ὁ) 'water-watchman', from *rīpārius* 'of riverbanks'.
    Documents: common, e.g. perhaps *P.FuadUniv.* 8.30 (II AD); *SB* 16250.2
    (II/III AD); *P.Oxy.* 4090.5 (IV AD); *P.Oxy.* 2268.7 (V AD); *P.Mich.*
    XVIII.794.3 (VI AD).
    Inscriptions: perhaps Marek 1993: 191, Appendix 6 no. 10.13 (VI AD).
    Post-antique: numerous in papyri. Daris (1991a: 98).
    Notes: probably originated in Egypt, perhaps spread to Asia Minor (Sänger
    2010: 120–1 with n. 43). Consistency of spelling is striking. Forms
    derivatives ῥιπαρία, ῥιπαρεύω. Commentary to *P.Harr.* II.218.2, commentary
    to *P.Cair.Masp.* 67091.2, Daris (1991a: 98), Hofmann (1989: 370), Zilliacus
    (1935a: 206–7), Meinersmann (1927: 52–3), LSJ. See §4.2.4.1 n. 50, §4.6.1,
    §6.2, §8.2.2, §9.2, §10.2.1, §10.2.2 D.

ῥιπούδιον: see ῥεπούδιον.

ῥιτιάρις: see ῥητιάριος.

not ancient

ῥίφουγος, ῥέφουγος 'fugitive', from *refuga* 'fugitive': no ancient examples.
    Zilliacus (1935a: 232–3), *LBG*.

not ancient?

ῥόβα on inscription *MAMA* III.581 (in gen. pl. ῥόβον) seems to be from medieval
    roba 'garment' (*DMLBS*). Cameron (1931: 256), LSJ.

Direct loan
V AD – modern

ῥόγα, ῥῶγα, ῥῶγας (-ας, ἡ) 'distribution of wages', 'allowance', 'rations',
    probably from from *roga* 'largess' (Souter 1949) not *ērogātiō* 'expenditure',
    'distribution'.
    Documents: e.g. *P.Berl.Zill.* 13.8 (VI AD); *P.Oxy.* 1913.60 (VI AD).
    Inscriptions: *SEG* XXXII.1554.A53 (VI AD).
    Literature: Nil. 4.1.47 (V AD); Thdr.Anag. *HE* 4.503.4 (V/VI AD).
    Post-antique: numerous. Zervan (2019: 150), Sophocles (1887), *LBG* (s.v.
    ῥῶγα B). Modern ῥόγα 'wages' and derivatives: Babiniotis (2002), Andriotis
    (1967), Meyer (1895: 56), Kahane and Kahane (1972–6: 532). Also survives
    in Albanian (Baldwin 1991).
    Notes: Kramer (1992 = 2011: 279–85, 1983: 121–2), commentary on *CPR*
    XXIV.31.11, Mayerson (1994), Daris (1991a: 99), Hofmann (1989: 370),
    Viscidi (1944: 24–5), Zilliacus (1935a: 224–5, 232–3), Meinersmann (1927:
    53), Lampe (1961), LSJ suppl. See §4.2.3.1, §10.2.1, §10.2.2 G.

rare

ῥογᾱτον, apparently 'request', probably from neut. of *rogātus*, pf. part. of *rogō*
    'ask': papyrus *P.Abinn.* 10.15 (IV AD). Daris (1991a: 99), Meinersmann
    (1927: 53).

rare

ῥογᾱτος, ῥωγᾱτος 'summoned', from *rogātus*, pf. part. of *rogō* 'ask': papyri *P.Cair.*
    Masp. 67312.16 (VI AD); Ath.Schol. in Latin script 5.5.3 (VI AD). But
    P.Ital. II.30.93 (VI AD) is Latin in Greek script. Daris (1991a: 99), Hofmann
    (1989: 370), Zilliacus (1935a: 206–7), *LBG*, Lampe (1961).

Direct loan
V AD – Byz.

ῥογάτωρ, ῥωγάτωρ, ἠρογάτωρ (-ορος, ὁ), an official, also 'mercenary', from
    ērogātor 'distributor' (*TLL*).
    Documents: *P.Lond.* v.1889.14 (VI AD); *P.Lond.Herm.* 1.27.v.22 (VI AD).
    Inscriptions: *SEG* XXXII.1554.A48 etc. (VI AD).
    Literature: Nil. 2.314.1 (V AD).
    Post-antique: numerous. Zervan (2019: 150–1), Daris (1991a: 99), *LBG*.

Notes: spelling ἠρογάτωρ (only on inscription) confirms Sophocles' (1887) derivation from ērogātor; Daris (1991a: 99) and Zilliacus (1935a: 206–7) suggest rogātor 'requester', which has wrong meaning. For the word group into which this fits see Kramer (1992 = 2011: 279–85). Hofmann (1989: 370), TLL (s.v. ērogātor 799.18–20), LSJ suppl. (s.v. ἠρογάτωρ). See §4.2.5, §6.9, §10.2.1, §10.2.2 D.

non-existent?   **ῥογάω** 'hire', from ērogō 'pay out': perhaps papyrus P.Oxy. 1929.2 etc. (IV/V AD). Parássoglou (1978: 68–9), Kramer (1992: 185 n. 4 = 2011: 279 n. 4), Daris (1991a: 99), LBG.

Direct loan with suffix
V AD – modern   **ῥογεύω, ῥωγεύω** 'pay in kind', later 'distribute money', from ērogō 'pay out' + -εύω.

Documents: e.g. O.Douch. 11.61.2 (IV/V AD); P.Cair.Masp. 67076.8, 11 (VI AD).

Literature: e.g. Callin. V.Hypat. 20.1 (V AD); EphraemSyr. 1 p. 204.9 (V/VI AD); V.S.Aux. 12.9 (VI AD). Unverified example (III AD) in Zilliacus (1937: 322–3, 333).

Post-antique: numerous. Zervan (2019: 151), Daris (1991a: 99), LBG. Modern dialectal ῥογεύ(γ)ω etc. 'pay wages': Andriotis (1974: 481), Kahane and Kahane (1972–6: 532).

Notes: Kramer (1992 = 2011: 279–85), commentary on CPR XXIV.31.11, Baldwin (1991), Mandilaras (1973: 67), Avotins (1992), Daris (1991a: 99), Hofmann (1989: 370–1), Zilliacus (1935a: 206–7, 224–5, 1937: 333), Meinersmann (1927: 53), Triantaphyllides (1892: 272), Lampe (1961), LSJ suppl. See §4.3.1, §6.9, §10.2.1, §10.2.2 G, §10.3.1.

not Latin?   **ῥογός** 'granary', 'barn' may come from rogus 'pyre' or (more likely) from a related Sicilian word. Bellocchi (2016: 327), Willi (2008: 33), Shipp (1979: 484), Hofmann (1989: 371 with a discussion of different views on the etymology), Immisch (1885: 316), DÉLG, Beekes (2010), LBG, LSJ.

rare   **ῥοδακινέα** 'peach tree', from dūracinus 'having a hard berry' via δωράκινον: Alex. Trall. 11.595.25 (VI AD); Byzantine texts. LSJ (s.v. ῥοδάκινον) suggests that it refers to a fruit, fitting the passage in Aexander but not Byzantine usage. Hofmann (1989: 103 s.v. δωράκινον), LBG.

ῥοδάκινον: see δωράκινον.

Ῥομαῖος: see Ῥωμαῖος.

foreign   **ῥόμιξα**, a kind of javelin, from rumex, a kind of javelin: Hesych. as lemma ρ 431 (V/VI AD). Hofmann (1989: 371), LSJ.

not ancient   **ῥόσα** transliterating rosa 'rose': interpolations in Dsc. 1.99 RV etc. Sophocles (1887).

Direct loan
IV AD – Byz.   **ῥοσᾶτον, ῥοσσᾶτον, ῥωσᾶτον** (-ου, τό) 'rose-flavoured wine', from rosātum 'rose wine' (L&S).

Documents: SB 14625.19 (V/VI AD); perhaps Maravela-Solbakk 2009: 129.2 (V/VI AD).

Inscriptions: Edict.Diocl. 2.19 (IV AD).

Literature: medical writers, e.g. Ps.-Galen XIV.563.12 Kühn (after II AD); Orib. *Col.* 5.33.1 (IV AD); Hieroph. *Nut.* 8.6 (IV–VI AD); Aëtius 3.73.1 (VI AD); Alex.Trall. 1.585.9 (VI AD).

Post-antique: survives in medical texts.

Notes: forms derivative ὑδροροςᾱτον. Maravela-Solbakk (2009: 130–1, 2010: 258–9), Daris (1991a: 99), Hofmann (1989: 371–2), *LBG* (s.v. ῥοσᾱτος), LSJ. See §4.2.4.1 n. 55, §4.6.2, **§6.5**, §8.2.2, §9.5.1, §10.2.1, §10.2.2 I.

not Latin? **ῥοσικόν**, a commodity mentioned on papyrus *BGU* XIII.2357.2.16 (III AD), may be related to ῥούσιος 'reddish' and therefore to *russeus* 'red-coloured'. LSJ suppl.

ῥοσσᾱτον: see ῥοσᾱτον.

not ancient **ῥούβια** transliterating *rubia* 'madder': interpolation in Dsc. 3.143 RV. Sophocles (1887).

not ancient **ῥούβους** transliterating *rubus* 'bramble', 'blackberry': interpolation in Dsc. 4.37 RV. Sophocles (1887).

rare **ῥουβρίκα** 'red ochre', from *rubrīca* 'red ochre': *Hippiatr.Par.* (Apsyrtus) 244 (III/IV AD?). *LBG*.

not ancient **ῥοῦγα** 'fold', 'wrinkle', from *rūga* 'crease': no ancient examples. Meyer (1895: 56–7), Andriotis (1967), *LBG* (s.v. ῥοῦγα 'street').

ῥούδης: see σεκουνδαρούδης, σουμμαρούδης.

foreign **ῥοῦμα** (in acc. ῥοῦμαν) transliterating *rūma*, variant of *rūmis* 'teat': Plut. *Rom.* 4.1, *Mor.* 278c (I/II AD). Hofmann (1989: 372), Sophocles (1887).

foreign **Ῥουμινᾱλις, Ῥωμινᾱλις** transliterating *Rūminālis*, a tree in Rome: Plut. *Rom.* 4.1, *Mor.* 320c, etc. (I/II AD). Strobach (1997: 199), Hofmann (1989: 372), Sophocles (1887).

not ancient **ῥουπτεύω** 'overturn' (in the legal sense), from *rumpō* 'cancel', 'rescind' (*OLD* s.v. 12) + -εύω: no ancient examples. Zilliacus (1935a: 206–7), *LBG*.

foreign **ῥοῦπτος** 'nullified', 'avoided', from *ruptus*, pf. part. of *rumpō* 'break': Antec. in Latin script 2.13.1 *ruptan* etc. (VI AD); later in Greek script. Zilliacus (1935a: 206–7), *LBG*. See §7.2.1 passage 26, §9.5.6 n. 68.

ῥουσαῖος, ῥούσεος: see ῥούσιος.

rare **ῥουσίζω, ῥουσσίζω** 'be reddish', from *russeus* 'red-coloured' via ῥούσιος + -ίζω: Alex.Trall. III.154.3 (VI AD); occasionally later. Hofmann (1989: 373 s.v. ῥούσιος), *DÉLG* (s.v. ῥούσσεος), Frisk (1954–72: II.663), Beekes (2010 s.v. ῥούσσεος), *LBG*, Sophocles (1887 s.v. ῥουσσίζω), LSJ.

Direct loan III AD – modern **ῥούσιος, ῥούσσιος, ῥο(ύ)σ(σ)εος, ῥουσαῖος** (-α, -ον) 'reddish', 'red circus faction', from *russeus* 'red-coloured'.
Documents: e.g. Audollent 1904: no. 237.4 etc. (II/III AD); Audollent 1904: no. 242.53 (III AD); *O.Trim.* 1.350.3 (IV AD); *SEG* LII.988.25, Latinate (IV AD?); Audollent 1904: no. 160.80 (IV/V AD); *P.Cair.Masp.* 67006v.62 etc. (VI AD); *P.Münch.* III.1.142.3 (VI AD).

Literature: Malal. 2.8.27 etc. (VI AD); Lyd. *Mens.* 1.12.75 etc. (VI AD); Ps.-Nonnus 4.38.2 in Nimmo Smith 1992 (VI AD); *Anthologia Graeca* 16.386.3, 387.1; as gloss in scholia to Opp. *H.* 1.97; Gloss. Ps.-Cyril. 428.48.

Post-antique: numerous, forming derivatives ῥουσιαίνω 'become red', ῥουσιοδάκτυλος 'red-fingered', etc. Daris (1991a: 99), *LBG*, Triandaphyllidis (1909: 131). Modern ῥούσ(σ)ος 'blond', 'red': Babiniotis (2002), Andriotis (1967), Meyer (1895: 57).

Notes: forms derivative ῥουσίζω. Binder (2000: 145), Daris (1991a: 99), Hofmann (1989: 372–3), *DÉLG* (s.v. ῥούσσεος), Frisk (1954–72: 11.663), Beekes (2010 s.v. ῥούσσεος), Lampe (1961 s.v. ῥουσαῖος), LSJ, LSJ suppl. See §4.2.2, §10.2.1, §10.2.2 F, §10.3.2.

not ancient?	**ῥουσιώδης** 'of a reddish colour', from *russeus* 'red-coloured' via ῥούσιος + -ώδης (cf. εἶδος 'form'): as gloss in old scholion to *Od.* 9.125. *DÉLG* (s.v. ῥούσσεος), Hofmann (1989: 373 s.v. ῥούσιος), *LBG*, LSJ.
foreign	**ῥουσμαρίνα** transliterating *rusmarīna*, a plant (Forcellini *et al.* 1864–1926): Dsc. 4.1.1 (I AD). Hofmann (1989: 373).
foreign	**ῥουσμαρῖνον, ῥωσμαρῖνον** transliterating *rōs marīnum* 'rosemary': Dsc. 3.75.1 etc. (I AD); Galen XII.61.5 Kühn (II AD); Orib. *Col.* 11.λ.9 (IV AD). Hofmann (1989: 373), *LBG* (s.v. ῥωσμαρῖνος).
foreign	**ῥουσσᾶτοι** 'red circus faction', from *russātī*, pl. of *russātus* 'dressed in red': Lyd. *Mens.* 4.30.18, 20, marked (VI AD). Hofmann (1989: 373), *DÉLG* (s.v. ῥούσσεος), Frisk (1954–72: 11.663), Beekes (2010 s.v. ῥούσσεος), *LBG* (s.v. ῥουσσάτος), LSJ.
	ῥούσσεος: see ῥούσιος.
	ῥουσσίζω: see ῥουσίζω.
	ῥούσσιος: see ῥούσιος.
not ancient	**ῥουστικός** transliterating *rūsticus* 'wild': interpolations in Dsc. 1.10 RV etc. Sophocles (1887); for possible Byzantine use Daris (1991a: 99), Meinersmann (1927: 53), Wessely (1902: 146).
	ῥυγλοχύτης: see ῥηγλοχύτης.
not Latin	**ῥυτή** 'rue' (the plant) is sometimes said to come from *rūta* 'rue', but see *DÉLG*, LSJ.
	ῥωγ-: see ῥογ-.
	Ῥῶμα: see Ῥώμη.
Deriv. of loan II BC – III AD	**Ῥωμαῖα** (-ων, τά), a set of games (*lūdī Rōmānī*), from *Rōma* 'Rome' via Ῥωμαῖος. Inscriptions: e.g. *SEG* LIV.516.2 (II BC); *IG* IV².1.629.6 etc. (II/I BC); *SEG* XXXVIII.179.26 etc. (I BC); *Syll.*³ 1065.5 (I AD); *IGNapoli* 1.52.3 (II AD). Literature: Dio Cassius 37.8.1 (II/III AD); Athenaeus 8.361f: ἔτυχεν δὲ οὖσα ἑορτὴ τὰ Παρίλια μὲν πάλαι καλουμένη, νῦν δὲ Ῥωμαῖα (II/III AD). Notes: Drew-Bear (1972: 218), LSJ (s.v. Ῥωμαῖος), LSJ suppl. (s.v. Ῥωμαῖος). See §4.3.2 n. 75, **§8.1.4**, §10.2.2 F, §10.3.2, §12.2.2.

**Deriv. of loan
I AD – Byz.** Ῥωμαΐζω 'speak Latin', 'speak Greek' (§10.4.1), 'hold with Rome', from *Rōma* 'Rome' via Ῥωμαῖος + -ίζω.

> Literature: Jos. *BJ* 2.562 (I AD); App. *Libyca* 304 etc. (I/II AD); Dio Cassius 50.6.4 etc. (II/III AD); Philostratus, *Vita Apollonii* 5.36.51 Kayser (II/III AD); Leontius of Constantinople, *Homiliae* 11.176, 11.353 Allen and Datema (VI AD); *De scientia politica dialogus* 209 = Mazzucchi 1982: 52.22 (VI AD); with *latino* in Gloss. Ps.-Cyril. 429.10.

> Post-antique: numerous. *LBG*.

> Notes: may form derivative Ῥωμαϊστής. LSJ. See §4.6.1, §4.6.3, §10.2.2 O, §10.3.2, §10.4.1.

Ῥωμαιιστής: see Ῥωμαϊστής.

rare Ῥωμαϊκόν, a garment, from *Rōma* 'Rome' via Ῥωμαϊκός: papyrus *P.Ryl.* IV.627.18 (IV AD). LSJ suppl., Daris (1991a: 99 *s.v.* Ῥωμαικός).

**Deriv. of loan
II BC – modern** Ῥωμαϊκός (-ή, -όν) 'Roman', 'Latin', 'Greek' (§10.4.1), as neut. pl. subst. 'Latin words', 'Roman interests', as adverb (Ῥωμαϊκῶς) 'in the Roman way', 'in Latin', 'in Greek', from *Rōma* 'Rome' via Ῥωμαῖος + -ικός.

> Documents: e.g. *BGU* IV.1113.5 (I BC); *SB* 13219.3 (I AD); *P.Harr.* 1.67.2.11 (II AD); *BGU* V.1210.35 (II AD); *P.Oxy.* 43r.2.10 etc. (III AD); *Chrest.Mitt.* 55.9 etc. (IV AD); *P.Ness.* III.18.20 (VI AD).

> Inscriptions: e.g. *SEG* XXXV.665.A38 etc. (II BC); *I.Délos* 442.B139 (II BC); *I.Pessinous* 7.9 (II BC); Sherk 1969: no. 65.D53 (I BC); *I.Kibyra* 42A.11 (I AD); Bean and Mitford 1970: 75 no. 49.2 (II AD); *I.Ephesos* 813.8 (III AD); Edict.Diocl. 7.70 (IV AD).

> Literature: very common, e.g. Polybius 1.16.2 (II BC); DH *AR* 1.6.1 (I BC); Jos. *AJ* 14.68 (I AD); Plut. *Aem.* 13.7 (I/II AD); Luc. *Alex.* 30 (II AD); Dio Cassius 48.30.2 (II/III AD); Porphyry, *De abstinentia* 3.5 (III AD); Eus. *PE* 2.7.9 (IV AD); *ACO* I.1.1 p. 78.10 (V AD); Hesych. as part of gloss σ 1598 (V/VI AD); Procop. *Bell.* 1.18.54 (VI AD).

> Post-antique: common. *LBG*. Modern ρωμαίικος etc. 'of modern Greece', but ρωμαϊκός 'Roman': Babiniotis (2002), Andriotis (1967).

> Notes: forms derivative Ῥωμαϊκόν. Kramer (1993: 236), Leclercq (1997: 299), Avotins (1992), Shipp (1979: 238), Daris (1991a: 99, with derivation from *Rōmānus*), Lampe (1961), LSJ, LSJ suppl. See §4.6.1, §8.1.3 passage 40, **§8.1.4**, §8.1.5, §8.2.3 n. 51, **§9.4** passage 49, §10.2.2 O, §10.3.1, §10.3.2, §10.4.1.

rare Ῥωμαῖον 'temple of Roma', from *Rōma* 'Rome' via Ῥωμαῖος: inscription Knackfuss 1924: 293 no. 203.A22 (II BC); Dio Cassius 71.31.1 (II/III AD). Sophocles (1887 *s.v.* ῥωμαῖος), LSJ suppl. See §8.1.4 n. 22.

**Deriv. of loan
IV BC – modern** Ῥωμαῖος, Ῥωμέος, Ῥομαῖος, (-α, -ον) 'Roman', 'Latin', later 'Greek' (§10.4.1), often masc. or fem. subst. meaning 'Roman person', 'Roman citizen', from *Rōma* 'Rome' via Ῥώμη + -αῖος, perhaps with influence from *Rōmānus* 'Roman'.

> Documents: common, e.g. *P.Lond.* VII.1986.12 (III BC); *P.Tebt.* 1.33.3 (II BC); *BGU* XIV.2430.26 etc. (I BC); *P.Oxy.Hels.* 10.20 (I AD); *P.Oxy.* 1451.7 etc. (II AD); *P.Freib.* II.8.3 etc. (II AD); *P.Col.* X.274.1 (III AD); *P.Oxy.* 1714.3 (III/IV AD); perhaps *P.Sakaon* 59.5 (IV AD); *SB* 10728.4 (IV AD); *Stud. Pal.* XX.114.3 (V AD); *SB* 8028.9 etc. (VI AD).

Inscriptions: very common, e.g. *IG* XI.II.115.25 (III BC); *I.Kos Bosnakis* 14.2 (III/II BC); *SEG* XXXVIII.114.v.116 etc. (II BC); *SEG* XXXIV.153.33 etc. (I BC); *IGNapoli* I.6.8 (I AD); *I.Stratonikeia* 186.6 (II AD); *I.Aphrodisias and Rome* 25.9 (III AD); *SEG* XXXV.1055.18 (IV AD); *I.Estremo Oriente* 54.17 (VI AD).

Coins: ΡΩΜΑΙΩΝ at Rome, Crawford 1974: 131 no. 1 (IV BC); later often in Greek-speaking areas, e.g. Head 1911: 704, 710, 808, 814, 863 (I–III AD).

Literature: very common, e.g. perhaps Hellanicus, no. 4 frag. 31 Jacoby (V BC); Theophrastus, *Historia plantarum* 5.8.2 (IV/III BC); Polybius 1.2.7 (II BC); Diodorus Siculus 1.83.8 (I BC); NT Acts 16:37 (I AD); Luc. *Demon.* 18.1 (II AD); Diogenes Laertius 2.104 (III AD); Lib. *Or.* 24.20 (IV AD); *V.Dan.Styl. Tert.* 27 (V AD); Procop. *Bell.* 1.9.24 (VI AD).

Post-antique: very common, forming derivatives ῥωμαιοκράτωρ 'ruler of Romans', ῥωμαιοκτόνος 'Roman-killer', etc. *LBG.* Modern Ρωμιός '(modern) Greek', Ρωμαῖος 'Roman': Babiniotis (2002), Andriotis (1967).

Notes: feminine Ῥωμαία is common despite existence of Ῥωμαΐς. For Ῥωμαῖοι and Ἰταλικοί in early inscriptions from Delos, see J. N. Adams (2003: 642–63). Forms derivatives Ῥωμαία, Ῥωμαϊκός, φιλορώμαιος, Ῥωμαΐζω, Ῥωμαΐς, Ῥωμαϊστί, Ῥωμαῖον, Ῥωμαιότης, μισορρώμαιος. Kramer (1993), Freyburger-Galland (1997: 31), Leclercq (1997: 300), LSJ, LSJ suppl. See **§2.2.3** with passage 2, §2.4, §4.6.1, §4.6.2, §4.6.3, §5.3.2 n. 25, **§8.1.2**, §8.1.3 passage 40, **§8.1.4**, §8.1.5, §8.2.3 n. 51, §9.1 n. 4, §9.3 nn. 21 and 25, **§9.4**, §9.5.4, §10.2.2 N, §10.3.1, §10.3.2, **§10.4.1**, §10.5, §12.2.2.

rare | **Ῥωμαιότης** 'Roman citizenship', from *Rōma* 'Rome' via Ῥωμαῖος + -ότης: inscription De Visscher 1940: 18 no. 1.39 (I BC). Mason (1974: 14, 83), García Domingo (1979: 627), LSJ, *LBG.*

Deriv. of loan I AD – Byz. | **Ῥωμαΐς** (fem. adj. or subst., gen. Ῥωμαΐδος) 'Roman', 'Latin', later 'Greek' (§10.4.1), from *Rōma* 'Rome' via Ῥωμαῖος.
Documents: *BGU* XVI.2577r.333 (I BC/AD); *SB* 14576.113 (I AD).
Inscriptions: e.g. *MAMA* VIII.413.A6 (II AD).
Literature: e.g. perhaps Diodorus Siculus 25.19.1 (I BC), perhaps Hdn. *Pros. Cath.* III.1.84.6 (II AD); Damascius, *Vita Isidori* frag. 158.3 Zintzen (V/VI AD); Stephanus of Byzantium ρ 62 (VI AD).
Post-antique: common. *LBG.*
Notes: treated as noun by LSJ but often acts as adj., fem. of ῥωμαῖος. Lampe (1961), LSJ. See §4.6.1, §10.2.2 O, §10.3.2, §10.4.1.

Deriv.? of loan II–I BC | **Ῥωμαϊστής, Ῥωμαιιστής** (-οῦ?, ὁ), a kind of athlete or 'actor of Latin comedies', from *Rōma* 'Rome' (via Ῥωμαΐζω?) + -της.
Inscriptions: *IG* XI.II.133.81 (II BC); perhaps *IG* XI.II.132.14 (II BC); *I.Délos* 2618.d8 (I BC); *I.Thèbes Syène* 326.1 (I BC); Le Rider 1966: 258.3.4.
Literature: undated bilingual glossary (Ferri 2008).
Notes: derivation via Ῥωμαΐζω is chronologically difficult. Ferri (2008), Robert and Robert (1983: 182–4), LSJ, LSJ suppl. See §4.6.1 n. 86, **§8.1.4**, §10.2.2 F, §10.3.2.

Deriv. of loan I AD – modern | **Ῥωμαϊστί** 'in Latin', later 'in Greek' (§10.4.1), from *Rōma* 'Rome' via Ῥωμαῖος + -στί.
Literature: common, e.g. NT John 19:20 (I AD); Epict. *Diss.* 1.17.17 (I/II AD); Galen XII.453.16 Kühn (II AD); Sextus Empiricus, *Adversus mathematicos* 1.218 (II/III AD); Athan. *H.Ar.* 26.2 (IV AD); Geront. *V.Mel.* 2.26 (V AD); Ath.Schol. 16.2 (VI AD).

Post-antique: numerous. *LBG.* Modern ρωμαϊστί 'in Latin': Babiniotis (2002).
Notes: Kramer (1993: 236), Leclercq (1997: 299), LSJ. See §4.6.1, §4.6.3, §9.3
n. 21, §10.2.2 O, §10.3.1, §10.3.2, §10.4.1.

Direct loan
IV AD – modern

Ῥωμανήσιος, Ῥωμανίσιος (-α, -ον), an architectural construction, from
Rōmānēnsis 'belonging to a locality having the epithet *Romanus*'.
Literature: Athan. *Pet.Ar.* 1.2 (IV AD); Pausanius Damascenus Historicus, *FHG*
IV frag. 4.105 (IV AD); John Chrysostom, *PG* L.441.19 (IV/V AD); Pall.
V.Chrys. 30.5 (IV/V AD); Malal. 8.16 (VI AD); Just. *Codex* 8.10.12.5
(VI AD).
Post-antique: survives, mainly meaning 'door bolt'. *LBG*, Triandaphyllidis
(1909: 120). Modern dialectal ρωμανίσιν 'door bolt', either direct survival or
via Byzantine derivative ῥωμανίζω 'bolt a door' (*LBG*), which also survives in
modern dialect: Andriotis (1974: 484).
Notes: Avotins (1989, suggesting meaning 'balcony' or 'terrace'), Drew-Bear
(1972: 218), Hofmann (1989: 374), Lampe (1961), LSJ suppl. See §4.2.2,
§6.7 n. 45, §10.2.1, §10.2.2 J, §10.3.2.

Direct loan with
suffix?
IV AD – modern

Ῥωμανία (-ας, ἡ) 'Roman empire', from *Rōmānus* 'Roman' + -ία or *Rōmānia*
'Roman empire' (Souter 1949, *DMLBS*).
Inscriptions: *I.Estremo Oriente* 54.3 (VI AD); *IGPannonia* 138.4 (VI AD);
Paribeni and Romanelli 1914: 140 no. 105.
Literature: e.g. Epiph. *Pan.* III.17.8 (IV AD); Agath. *Arm.* 16.8 (V AD); Evagr.
Schol. *HE* 235.21 (VI AD).
Post-antique: common. Sophocles (1887). Modern Ῥωμανία 'Roman/Byzantine
empire': Babiniotis (2002), Andriotis (1974: 484).
Notes: *Romania* is first attested in V AD (Souter 1949) and used especially for
the Eastern empire (*DMLBS*): could it come from Greek? Sophocles (1887),
Lampe (1961). See §4.3.2, §10.2.1, §10.2.2 D, §10.3.2.

Ῥωμανίσιος: see Ῥωμανήσιος.

Ῥωμέος: see Ῥωμαῖος.

Direct loan
II BC – modern

Ῥώμη (-ης, ἡ) 'Rome', 'Constantinople' (§10.4.1), occasionally of other cities,
also the deified personification of Rome, from *Rōma* 'Rome'.
Documents: e.g. *P.IFAO* II.28.3 (I AD); *P.Oxy.* 3798.8 (II AD); *P.Oxy.* 1407.16
(III AD); *P.Ammon* II.41.24 (IV AD); *P.Cair.Masp.* 67032.6 (VI AD).
Inscriptions: common, e.g. *SEG* XXXIV.558.27 etc. (II BC); *SEG*
XXXIX.1290.3 (I BC); *IG* VII.2711.42 (I AD); *I.Eleusis* 483.17 (II AD);
IG VII.49.21 (III AD); *I.Cret.* IV.320.5 (IV AD); *SEG* XVIII.748.1
(VI AD).
Coins: often in imperial period, e.g. Head 1911: 536, 661, 863.
Literature: very common, e.g. Aristotle (?), *De plantis* 821b7 ἐν ὀλίγοις δὲ τόποις
γίνεται ἡ τοιαύτη φυτεία, καὶ οὐδέποτε γίνεται εἰ μὴ ἀραιῶς ἐν τῇ Ῥώμῃ κατὰ
τήνδε τὴν ὥραν (IV BC?); Polybius 1.6.2 (II BC); Diodorus Siculus 1.4.2
(I BC); NT Acts 18:2 (I AD); Luc. *Alex.* 27 (II AD); Porphyry, *Vita Plotini*
3.24 (III AD); Lib. *Ep.* 1063.2 (IV AD); Callin. *V.Hypat.* 8.4 (V AD); Just.
Nov. 70.1 (VI AD).
Post-antique: very common. Sophocles (1887). Modern Ῥώμη 'Rome':
Babiniotis (2002).

Notes: probably borrowed long before first secure attestation, for derivative Ῥωμαῖος appears in IV BC. Freyburger-Galland (1997: 31–2), Leclercq (1997: 299), Strobach (1997: 199), Mason (1974: 83, 139), Immisch (1885: 335 *s.v.* Ῥῶμα), LSJ, LSJ suppl. See §2.4, §4.1.1, §4.2.3.1, §4.3.2 n. 75, §4.6.3, **§8.1.2**, **§8.1.4**, §8.2.3 n. 51, §9.1 n. 4, §9.3 nn. 21 and 25, §10.2.1, §10.2.2 O, §10.3.2, **§10.4.1**, §12.2.2.

Ῥωμινᾶλις: see Ῥουμινᾶλις.

ῥωποπερπερήθρα: see πέρπερος.

ῥωσᾶτον: see ῥοσᾶτον.

not Latin?   **ῥωσιτάριον**, meaning uncertain, is suggested by Hofmann (1989: 374) as related to *rosa* 'rose'. LSJ suppl.

ῥωσμαρῖνον: see ῥουσμαρῖνον.

rare   **ῥῶστρον** 'ship's beak', in plural a speaking-platform in Rome, from *rōstrum*, with the same meanings: in singular Hesych. as lemma ρ 594 (V/VI AD); in plural Eutropius 2.7, 2.20 (IV AD). Hofmann (1989: 374), Immisch (1885: 339), *LBG* (*s.v.* ῥῶστρα), LSJ. Cf. πενταρρόστουλον.

Σ

σαβάνιον: see σάβανον.

σαβάνις: see ἀ σαβάνις.

not Latin?   **σάβανον** 'linen cloth', 'towel' (with diminutive σαβάνιον) is cited by Wessely (1902: 146) and Hofmann (1989: 374) as a borrowing of *sabanum* 'linen cloth', but most scholars think the loan (originally from Semitic) went in the other direction. Lauffer (1971: 276 on 28.57), Meinersmann (1927: 53), *DÉLG*, Frisk (1954–72: II.669), Beekes (2010), Ernout and Meillet (1979 *s.v. sabanum*), Walde and Hofmann (1938–54 *s.v. sabanum*), LSJ, LSJ suppl.; rejected by Daris (1991a).

rare   **σαβανοφακιάριον** 'facecloth', from σάβανον 'linen cloth' + *faciāle* 'facecloth' (*TLL*) via φακιάλιον: papyri *P.Oxy.* 921v.11 etc. (III AD); *P.Ryl.* IV.627.16 (IV AD). Filos (2010: 251), Daris (1991a: 99), Hofmann (1989: 452 *s.v.* φακιαλιον), *LBG*, LSJ. See §6.3 n. 21.

Direct loan
IV AD – Byz.   **Σαβελ(λ)ιανός** (-ή, -όν) 'Sabellian' (a Christian sect), from *Sabelliānī* 'Sabellians' (L&S).
Literature: e.g. Epiph. *Pan.* II.389.6 (IV AD); Socr. 2.19.109 (IV/V AD); Gennadius, *Laudatio Leonis epistulae* 8 = Diekamp 1938: 77.20 (V AD); Leontius of Jerusalem, *Testimonia sanctorum* p. 54.24 Gray (VI AD).
Post-antique: numerous. *LBG*.
Notes: Lampe (1961). See §4.2.2, §10.2.1, §10.2.2 N, §12.2.2.

Direct loan with
suffix
IV AD – Byz.   **Σαβελλίζω** 'hold Sabellian views', from name *Sabellius* (L&S) + -ίζω.
Literature: e.g. Eusebius, *De ecclesiastica theologia* 1.15.2 Hansen and Klostermann (IV AD); Athan. *Decr.* 25.3.3 (IV AD); Socr. 1.23.14 (IV/V AD).
Post-antique: numerous.
Notes: Lampe (1961). See §4.3.1, §10.2.1, §10.2.2 O, §10.3.1.

Direct loan
II AD – modern

σαβούρα (-ας, ἡ) 'ballast', from *saburra* 'ballast'.
Literature: Aelius Dionysius α 133 Erbse as part of gloss (II AD); Nil. 4.60.24 (V AD); Hesych. as gloss α 4949 (V/VI AD).
Post-antique: survives. Zervan (2019: 153), *LBG*, Triandaphyllidis (1909: 131). Modern σαβούρα 'ballast' and derivatives: Babiniotis (2002), Andriotis (1967), Meyer (1895: 57 *s.v.* σαβούρρα).
Notes: first example apparently indeclinable. Lampe (1961). See §4.2.3.1, §6.11, §8.2.3 n. 51, §9.2, §10.2.1, §10.2.2 K.

rare

σαβουρᾶτος 'filled with ballast', from *saburrātus*, pf. part. of *saburrō* 'fill with ballast': papyrus *P.Mert.* 1.46.10 (V/VI AD); occasional Byzantine texts. Daris (1991a: 99), Hofmann (1989: 374–5), Cavenaile (1951: 400), *LBG*, LSJ suppl.

not ancient?

σάβουρος 'in ballast', 'empty', from *saburra* 'ballast': no certainly ancient examples (LSJ's '*AB*401' is the Συναγωγὴ λέξεων χρησίμων, α 1358 Cunningham). Hofmann (1989: 375), Zilliacus (1937: 333), Lampe (1961), LSJ, LSJ suppl.

σαβούρρα: see σαβούρα.

not ancient

σαγγουινᾶλις transliterating *sanguinālis*, a plant: interpolation in Dsc. 3.154 RV. Sophocles (1887).

rare

σαγηφορέω 'wear a cloak', from *sagum* 'military cloak' via σάγος + φορέω 'wear': Strabo 4.4.3 (I BC/AD). LSJ.

Deriv. of loan
III AD – modern

σαγίον (-ου, τό) 'blanket', 'saddle cloth', or a garment, from *sagum* 'military cloak' via σάγος + -ιον.
Documents: e.g. *P.Flor.* 1.76.32 (III AD); *PSI* V.481.10 (V/VI AD).
Literature: Philogelos 211 (IV AD); Socr. 7.22.49 (IV/V AD); EphraemSyr. VII p. 359.8 (V/VI AD); with *lodix* in Gloss. Ps.-Cyril. 429.26. Unverified example (VI AD) in Zilliacus (1937: 322–3, 333).
Post-antique: numerous, forming derivatives σαγίζω 'saddle', σάγισμα 'saddle cloth', etc. (*LBG*). Sophocles (1887), Triandaphyllidis (1909: 122). Modern dialectal σαγί(ν) etc., a garment: Andriotis (1974: 485), Meyer (1895: 57).
Notes: Daris (1991a: 99), Hofmann (1989: 375 *s.v.* σάγος), Cavenaile (1952: 195), Viscidi (1944: 40), Zilliacus (1937: 333), Meinersmann (1927: 53), *DÉLG* (*s.v.* σάγος), Lampe (1961), LSJ, LSJ suppl. See §4.6.1 n. 83, §10.2.2 H.

σαγιτ-: see σαγιττ-.

Direct loan
V AD – modern

σαγίτ(τ)α (-ης, ἡ) 'arrow', from *sagitta* 'arrow'.
Inscriptions: perhaps *I.Smyrna* 546.1 (II/III AD).
Literature: Anton.Hag. *V.Sym.Styl.* 27 (V AD); Malal. 2.17.43 etc. (VI AD); Lyd. *Ost.* 8.14, marked (VI AD); scholion to Opp. *H.* 2.482 as part of gloss; scholion to Eur. *Hec.* 363: ὄργανά τινα δι' ὧν συνέχονται τὰ ὑφαινόμενα, ἃ αἱ γυναῖκες ἰδιωτικῶς σαγίτας καλοῦσι.

σαβούρα – σάγος

Post-antique: numerous, forming derivatives σαγιττόβολον 'bowshot', σαγιττοποιός 'arrow-maker', etc. (*LBG*). Zervan (2019: 153), Sophocles (1887), Triandaphyllidis (1909: 130), Zilliacus (1935a: 232–3 *s.vv.* σαγίττα, σαγιττόβολον). Modern σαΐτ(τ)α 'arrow': Babiniotis (2002), Andriotis (1967), Meyer (1895: 57–8).

Notes: Hofmann (1989: 375), Viscidi (1944: 17), Lampe (1961). See §10.2.1, §10.2.2 C.

Direct loan **IV–VI AD?**	**σαγιττάριος** (-ου, ὁ) 'archer', from *sagittārius* 'archer'. Documents: perhaps *P.Flor.* II.278r.5.5 (III AD); *P.Panop.Beatty* 2.162 (III/IV AD); *Stud.Pal.* XX.230.13 (IV AD). Inscriptions: e.g. *SEG* XXXIV.1598.6 (IV AD); *I.Beroia* 443.6 (VI AD). Literature: Lyd. *Mag.* p. 70.20, marked (VI AD). Notes: Daris (1991a: 100), Hofmann (1989: 375), Zilliacus (1935a: 234–5), Meinersmann (1927: 53), Lampe (1961), LSJ suppl. See §4.2.4.1 n. 50, §10.2.1, §10.2.2 C.
not ancient?	**σαγιττάτωρ** 'archer', from *sagittātor* 'archer' (Souter 1949): probably no ancient examples. Zilliacus (1935a: 234–5), *LBG*. Cf. ἀντισαγιττάτωρ, ἀρχισαγιττάτωρ.
not ancient?	**σαγιτ(τ)εύω** 'shoot', from *sagitta* 'arrow' via σαγίττα + -εύω: no certainly ancient examples. Hofmann (1989: 375), *LBG*, Lampe (1961 *s.v.* σαγιτεύω).
foreign	**σαγκτίων** 'sanction', from *sānctiō* 'sanction': Antec. in Latin script 2.1.10 *sanctionas* (VI AD); later in Greek script. Zilliacus (1935a: 206–7).
foreign	**σάγκτος** 'holy', 'inviolable', from *sānctus* 'holy': always marked, e.g. Plut. *Mor.* 271e (I/II AD); Antec. in Latin script 2.1.10 *sancton* etc. (VI AD); Byzantine legal texts. Zervan (2019: 153–4), Zilliacus (1935a: 206–7), *LBG*.
rare	**σαγόβυρος** 'mantle with hood', from *sagum* 'military cloak' via σάγος + *birrus* 'hooded cloak' (*TLL*) via βίρρος: papyrus *P.Bon.* 38.7 (IV AD). Commentary *ad loc.*, Filos (2010: 251), Daris (1991a: 100), *LBG*.
Direct loan **II BC – modern**	**σάγος** (-ου, ὁ) 'blanket', 'cloak', from *sagum* 'military cloak'. Documents: *P.Oxy.* 1051.20 (III AD); *P.Heid.* VII.406.8 etc. (IV/V AD); *SB* 15302.366 (V AD); *P.Prag.* II.178.2.4 etc. (V/VI AD); *SB* 13967.2, 15301.2.1 (both V/VI AD). Inscriptions: Edict.Diocl. 7.60 etc. (IV AD). Literature: e.g. Polybius 2.30.2 (II BC); Diodorus Siculus 5.30.1 (I BC); Strabo 3.3.6 (I BC/AD); App. *Iberica* 173 (I/II AD); *Hippiatr.Berl.* (Apsyrtus) 99.6 (III/IV AD?); Philogelos 211 (IV AD); Hesych. as lemma σ 33 (V/VI AD); bilingual glossaries, e.g. Gloss. Ps.-Cyril. 429.29. Post-antique: numerous despite absence from lexica, forming derivatives σαγμάντιον 'cape', σαγοπῶλος 'coat-seller', etc. (*LBG*). Modern dialectal σάγο 'shepherd's cloak' and derivatives: Andriotis (1974: 486). Notes: forms derivatives σαγίον, σαγηφορέω, σαγόβυρος. Dubuisson (1985: 42), Daris (1991a: 100), Hofmann (1989: 375), Hahn (1907: 707), *DÉLG*, Frisk (1954–72: II.670), Beekes (2010), LSJ. See §4.1.1, §4.2.4.1 n. 58, §4.3.2 n. 75, §4.6.1 n. 83, **§8.1.3** passage 40, §8.1.4, §10.2.1, §10.2.2 C.

foreign	**σαικλᾶρις, σαικουλάριος** transliterating (*lūdī*) *saeculārēs* 'century games': e.g. Augustus, *Res gestae* 22.10 Volkmann (I AD); Dio Cassius 54.18.2 (II/III AD). Binder (2000: 165), García Domingo (1979: 629), Mason (1974: 83), Hofmann (1989: 375–6).
foreign	**σαίκουλουμ** transliterating *saeculum* 'age': Hesych. σ 49 (V/VI AD). Binder (2000: 165), Immisch (1885: 345), Sophocles (1887 *s.v.* σαίκουλον).
	σάκελα: see σάκελλα.
not ancient?	**σακελίζω, σακ(κ)ελ(λ)ίζω** 'strain', 'filter', apparently from *sacellus* 'purse' + -ίζω: several texts that might be ancient: Ps.-Galen XIV.512.15 Kühn etc.; Ps.-Theodosius, περὶ γραμματικῆς p. 72.26 Göttling; scholion to Ar. *Pl.* 1087. *DÉLG* (*s.v.* σάκκος), *LBG* (*s.v.* σακελλίζω), Andriotis (1974: 486), Lampe (1961 *s.v.* σακκελίζω), LSJ.
rare	**σάκελ(λ)α** 'purse', 'treasury' from *sacellus* 'purse': Hesych. as lemma σ 69 (V/VI AD); inscription Marek 1993: 191, Appendix 6 no. 10.13 (VI AD); Byzantine texts. Gignac (1981: 7, with erroneous derivation from *sacellum* 'shrine'), Daris (1991a: 100), Hofmann (1989: 376), Zilliacus (1935a: 206–7, 1937: 333), Meinersmann (1927: 53), *DÉLG* (*s.v.* σάκκος), *LBG*, Triandaphyllidis (1909: 127), Lampe (1961).
not ancient	**σακελλάριος, σακκελλάριος** 'finance minister', from *sacellus* 'purse' or *saccellārius* 'keeper of the purse' (Souter 1949): no ancient examples. Daris (1991a: 100), Zilliacus (1937: 333), *DÉLG* (*s.v.* σάκκος), *LBG*, Zervan (2019: 154–5), Lampe (1961).
	σακελλίζω: see σακελίζω.
rare	**σακέλλιον, σακκέλλιον** 'purse', from *sacellus* 'purse' perhaps via σάκελλα or σάκελλος + -ιον: Gregorius Nazianzenus, *PG* XXXV.661a, 705b (IV AD); Hesych. as lemma σ 70 (V/VI AD); perhaps Pausanias Grammaticus, Ἀττικῶν ὀνομάτων συναγωγή μ 6 Erbse as gloss (II AD). Hofmann (1989: 376 *s.v.* σακέλα), Viscidi (1944: 22), Immisch (1885: 362), *DÉLG* (*s.v.* σάκκος), Lampe (1961), LSJ; for Byzantine use (often in the sense 'treasury') *LBG*, Zervan (2019: 155).
rare	**σάκελλος** 'purse', from *sacellus* 'purse': Aëtius 8.76.12 (VI AD). LSJ.
rare	**σακερδώτιον** 'priesthood', from *sacerdōtium* 'priesthood': inscription *SEG* XLVII.1656.8 (III AD). *LBG* interprets it as σακερδώτιος 'priest', but see Millar (1999: 95).
name	**Σακέρδωτις** 'priestess' is suggested by Lampe (1961) as a borrowing of *sacerdōs* 'priest', but the only example is probably a name, feminine of the well-attested name Σακερδώς: Gregorius Nazianzenus, *Epistulae* 210.3 Gallay (IV AD). See §12.2.2.
	σακκελ-: see σακελ-.
not ancient?	**σακκουλάριος** 'counterfeiter', suggested by Hofmann (1989: 376) as a borrowing of *sacculārius* 'pickpocket', 'cutpurse': no securely ancient examples. *LBG*.

Direct loan IV AD – Byz.	**σάκρος** (-α, -ον) 'sacred', esp. of the imperial household; fem. subst. of the imperial correspondence, from *sacer* 'sacred'. Documents: *PSI* v.481.13 (v/vi AD); *P.Petra* III.29.155 (vi AD). Inscriptions: *SEG* XXIX.741.5, Latinate (II AD). Literature: e.g. Plut. *Mor.* 279c, σακρώρουμ transliterating *sacrōrum* (I/II AD); Ast.Soph. 22.4 (IV AD); *ACO* I.I.I p. 4.2 (V AD); Just. *Nov.* in Greek script, conspicuously next to another loan in Latin script 41.1 (VI AD); Antec. in Latin script meaning 'sacred' 2.1.8 *sacron* etc. (VI AD). Post-antique: numerous. *LBG*, Triandaphyllidis (1909: 127). Notes: originally rare and used only to transliterate *sacer*, but spreads once it develops meaning 'imperial correspondence'. Antec.'s revival of meaning 'sacred' perhaps a separate borrowing. Avotins (1992), Daris (1991a: 100 *s.v.* σάκραι), Hofmann (1989: 376–7 *s.v.* σάκρα), Zilliacus (1935a: 206–7), Meinersmann (1927: 53), Lampe (1961 *s.v.* σάκρα), LSJ suppl. (superseding LSJ *s.v.* σάκρα). See §4.2.2, §10.2.1, **§10.2.2 A**.
rare	**σαλακονδεῖτον** 'spiced salt', from *sāl condītum* 'spiced salt': *Coll.Herm.* Mp 18e (III AD?); Edict.Diocl. 3.9 (IV AD). LSJ suppl. Cf. κονδῖτος 1.
non-existent?	**σαλαρίζω**, from *salārium* 'salary': perhaps concealed in σολλαρίσης on papyrus *SB* 9616v.35 (VI AD). *SB* editor *ad loc.*, Daris (1991a: 100).
Direct loan I AD – Byz.	**σαλάριον** (-ου, τό) 'salary', from *salārium* 'salary'. Documents: e.g. *BGU* III.981.ii.12 (I AD); *P.Mich.* XI.603.24 (II AD); *P.Oxy.* 4597.15 etc. (III AD); *P.Oxy.* 2859.11 etc. (IV AD); *P.Prag.* III.229.3 (VI AD). Inscriptions: *I.Magnesia* 116.55 (II AD); *I.Ephesos* 627.13, 3056.6 (both II AD). Literature: Modestinus in Just. *Dig.* 27.1.6.11 (III AD); Eus. *HE* 5.18.2 etc. (IV AD); Just. *Nov.* 128.16 (VI AD). Post-antique: numerous. Zervan (2019: 155–6), Sophocles (1887), *LBG* (*s.v.* σαλάριος). Notes: forms derivative σαλάριος. Avotins (1992), Daris (1991a: 100), Mason (1974: 8, 83), Hofmann (1989: 377), Zilliacus (1935a: 206–7), Meinersmann (1927: 53–4), Lampe (1961), LSJ, LSJ suppl. See §4.2.4.1 n. 54, §9.5.6 n. 55, §10.2.1, §10.2.2 G.
rare	**σαλάριος, σαλλάριος** 'of salaries', from *salārium* 'salary' via σαλάριον: papyri *P.Cair. Masp.* 67100.20, 67243.13 (both VI AD). Daris (1991a: 100), Hofmann (1989: 377 *s.v.* σαλάριον), LSJ (*s.v.* σαλάριον).
foreign	**σάλβια** transliterating *salvia* 'sage', a plant: Galen XIII.1037.11 Kühn (II AD); interpolations in Dsc. 3.33 RV etc. *LBG*.
rare	**σαλγαμαρικός, σαλκαμαρικός** 'of a pickle-seller', from *salgamārius* 'pickle-maker' via σαλγαμάριος + -ικός: papyrus *P.Ross.Georg.* III.38.11 (VI AD). Daris (1991a: 100, with derivation from *salgamum*), LSJ suppl. (citing the same papyrus twice).
Direct loan V AD – Byz.	**σαλγαμάριος** (-ου, ὁ) 'seller of pickled foods', from *salgamārius* 'pickle-maker'. Inscriptions: perhaps *SEG* XXXVIII.451 (V/VI AD); *Corinth* VIII.III.540.2, 551.2 (both V/VI AD). Literature: *ACO* II.I.III p. 52.30 (V AD).

Post-antique: numerous. Sophocles (1887), Triandaphyllidis (1909: 124).
Notes: forms derivative σαλγαμαρικός. Hofmann (1989: 377), Lampe (1961),
LSJ suppl. See §4.2.4.1 n. 50, §10.2.1, §10.2.2 I.

Direct loan
III–IV AD?

σάλγαμον, σάργαμον (-ου, τό) 'pickling material', from *salgama, -ōrum* 'vegetables
for pickling'.
Documents: *P.Col.* VII.136.6 (III AD); *P.Panop.Beatty* 2.246 etc. (III/IV AD);
P.Oxy. 2561.17 (IV AD).
Post-antique: perhaps modern dialectal σαλγάμι 'turnip': Meyer (1895: 58).
Notes: Daris (1991a: 100), Hofmann (1989: 377), LSJ suppl. See §4.2.4.1
n. 55, §8.2.3, §9.2, §10.2.1, §10.2.2 I.

Direct loan
VI AD – modern

σαλιβάριον (-ου, τό) 'bridle', 'bit', from *salīvārium* '(horse's) bit' (Souter 1949).
Inscriptions: perhaps Edict.Diocl. 10.5 (IV AD).
Literature: Romanus Melodus, *Cantica* 39.22.5 Grosdidier de Matons (VI AD);
Alexander, *Inventio crucis, PG* LXXXVII.III.4064b (VI AD?); with *lupa* in
Gloss. Ps.-Cyril. 429.39.
Post-antique: numerous. *LBG*, Triandaphyllidis (1909: 119). Modern dialectal
σαλιβάρι 'rein': Meyer (1895: 58).
Notes: Hofmann (1989: 378, with additional unverified example), Lampe
(1961). See §4.2.4.1 n. 54, §10.2.1, §10.2.2 K.

foreign

σάλιξ transliterating *salix* 'willow': Hesych. as lemma σ 113 (V/VI AD);
interpolations in Dsc. 1.103 RV etc. Hofmann (1989: 378), Immisch (1885:
341), *LBG*.

Direct loan
I–III AD

σάλιος (-ου, ὁ), a type of priest, from *Salius* 'Salic priest'.
Inscriptions: *IG* XII.VI.1.381.6 (II AD); *AE* 2016 no. 1525.3 (II AD).
Literature: Polybius 21.13.10, marked (II BC); DH *AR* 2.70.1 etc., marked
(I BC); Augustus, *Res gestae* 10.2 Volkmann (I AD); Plut. *Numa* 12.3 etc.
(I/II AD); Luc. *Salt.* 20, marked (II AD); Dio Cassius 2.7.5 (II/III AD);
Lyd. *Mens.* 4.2, 4.55, marked (VI AD).
Post-antique: minimal survival.
Notes: Strobach (1997: 199), Dubuisson (1985: 42–3), García Domingo
(1979: 629), Mason (1974: 4, 83, 117), Hofmann (1989: 378), LSJ suppl.
See §4.2.4.1 n. 51, §8.1.3 n. 17, §10.2.1, §10.2.2 D.

foreign

σαλιούγκα transliterating *saliunca*, a plant: Dsc. 1.8.1 (I AD). Hofmann (1989:
378), LSJ.

foreign

σαλῖρε transliterating inf. of *saliō* 'leap': DH *AR* 2.70.4 (I BC). Sophocles (1887).

non-existent

σαλίτωρ 'dancer', from *saltātor* 'dancer': superseded reading for σαλτάτωρ (*q.v.*)
in DH *AR* 2.70.5 (I BC). Sophocles (1887).

σαλκαμαρικός: see σαλγαμαρικός.

σαλλάριος: see σαλάριος.

foreign

σαλοῦτις transliterating gen. of *salūs* 'health': *O.Krok.* 1.122.2 (I/II AD).

not Latin?

σαλσίκιον, a food: cited by Hofmann (1989: 378) as a borrowing of *salsāmentum*
'salted fish', but the connection is uncertain; no ancient examples. Diethart
(1988: 64), *LBG*, Lampe (1961).

**Direct? loan
III–VI AD?** σαλτάριος, σαλτουάριος (-ου, ὁ) 'forester', 'steward', from *saltuārius* 'person
employed in looking after an estate' and/or *saltus, -ūs* 'woodland' via
σάλτον + -άριος.
Inscriptions: e.g. *IGBulg.* IV.2319.2 (III AD); *IG* XII.VI.II.1266.3 (V/VI AD);
MAMA VI.303.1.
Notes: the spelling σαλτουάριος is rare, suggesting derivation via σάλτον, but
chronology is against that. Mason (1974: 4, 83), Hofmann (1989: 379), LSJ,
LSJ suppl. See §4.2.4.1 n. 50, §6.1, §10.2.1, §10.2.2 N.

foreign σαλτάτωρ transliterating *saltātor* 'dancer': DH *AR* 2.70.5 (I BC). Hofmann
(1989: 379).

**Direct loan
IV AD – Byz.** σάλτον, σάλτος (-ου, τό or ὁ) 'forest', 'imperial estate', from *saltus, -ūs* 'woodland'.
Inscriptions: *SEG* XLIX.2105.6 (IV AD); *SEG* LIV.1643.4.4 (VI AD).
Literature: Thdt. *PG* LXXX.828a (V AD); *ACO* I.I.II p. 29.14 etc. (V AD);
Procopius of Gaza, *PG* LXXXVII.I.1212c (VI AD); as part of place names,
Hierocles, *Synecdemus* 701.6 etc. in Honigmann 1939 (VI AD).
Post-antique: survives. *LBG* (*s.vv.* σάλτον, σάλτος).
Notes: Latin probably also has meaning 'imperial estate' despite absence from
lexica. Binder (2000: 242), Hofmann (1989: 379), *LBG*, Sophocles (1887),
Lampe (1961). See §4.2.4.2, §6.1, §10.2.1, §10.2.2 A.

σαλτουάριος: see σαλτάριος.

foreign σαμιάριος transliterating *samiārius* 'armour-polisher' (Forcellini *et al.* 1864–
1926): Lyd. *Mag.* p. 72.17 (VI AD). Zilliacus (1935a: 234–5), *LBG*.

not ancient σαμιάτωρ 'weapon-polisher', from *samiātor* 'polisher' (L&S): no ancient
examples. Zilliacus (1935a: 234–5), *LBG*.

non-existent? σαμίτωρ 'weapon-polisher', from *samiātor* 'polisher' (L&S): cited as an ancient
loan by Zilliacus (1935a: 234–5), but I can find no examples.

rare σαννίων 'buffoon', from *sanniō* 'buffoon': Epict. *Diss.* 3.22.83 (I/II AD).
Sophocles (1887), LSJ.

rare σαντονικόν, plant name from *santonicum*, a kind of wormwood (*OLD s.v.
Santonicus*): medical writers, usually marked as foreign: Dsc. 3.23.6 etc.
(I AD); Galen XI.804.8 Kühn: ὁ θαυμασιώτατος Πάμφιλος … ὅμως ἔσφαλται
μέγιστα, νομίζων ὑπὸ Ῥωμαίων σαντόνικον ὀνομάζεσθαι τὴν βοτάνην. διαφέρει
γὰρ ἀβρότονον σαντονίκου … etc. (II AD); Orib. *Col.* 12.σ.6 etc. (IV AD).
Beekes (2010) claims a Greek etymology. Hofmann (1989: 379), Hahn
(1906: 253 n. 6), LSJ.

**Direct loan
II AD – Byz.** σαξίφραγον, σαξίφραγγον, σαφίφραγος, σαξίφραγ(γ)α, σαρξιφάγον, σαρξιφαγές
(usually -ου, τό or ὁ or ἡ), plant name, from *saxifragum* 'maiden-hair fern'
(*OLD s.v. saxifragus*).
Literature: Galen VI.339.2 Kühn etc. (II AD); *Hippiatr.Par.* (Apsyrtus) 63
(III/IV AD?); Orib. *Col.* 5.33.8 etc. (IV AD); Aëtius 3.152.8 etc.
(VI AD); Alex.Trall. II.469.18 (VI AD); interpolation in Dsc. 4.16 RV,
where distinguished from fem. σαξίφραγα transliterating the Latin.
Post-antique: numerous. *LBG* (*s.vv.* σαρξίφαγος, σαρξιφαγές).
Notes: Hofmann (1989: 379–80), LSJ (*s.vv.* σαξίφραγον, σαρξιφαγές). See
§4.2.4.1 n. 55, §10.2.1, §10.2.2 L.

foreign	**σαπίηνς** transliterating *sapiēns* 'wise': Plut. *Gracchi* 8.5 (I/II AD). Strobach (1997: 199), Sophocles (1887 *s.v.* σάπιενς).
	σαπονᾶς: see σαπουνᾶς.
not ancient?	**σαπουλανᾶς**, perhaps 'wool-cleaner', apparently from *sāpō* 'soap' (L&S) (via σάπων?) + *lāna* 'wool' + -ᾶς: inscription *MAMA* III.224. Hofmann (1989: 380), Cameron (1931: 256), LSJ.
	σάπουν: see σάπων.
	σαπουναρικός: see σαπωναρικός.
rare	**σαπουνᾶς, σαπονᾶς** 'soap-merchant', from *sāpō* 'soap' (L&S) via σάπων + -ᾶς: inscription *I.Chr.Bulgarien* 105.5 (VI AD). Byzantine σαπωνᾶς 'soap' (*LBG*) may be a different word. Drew-Bear (1972: 218), Hofmann (1989: 380 *s.v.* σάπων), LSJ suppl.
	σαπουνίζω: see σαπωνίζω.
	σαπούνιον: see σαπώνιον.
not Latin?	**σαπρομωπάριος** on inscription *MAMA* III.760.7 is claimed by the editor (followed by Cameron 1931: 253 and Hofmann 1989: 361 *s.v.* πωμάριος) to be a mistake for σαπροπωμάριος (otherwise unattested) and therefore to come from *pōmārius* 'fruit-seller' via πωμάριος.
Direct loan **II AD – modern**	**σάπων, σήπων, σάπουν** (-ωνος, ὁ) 'soap', probably from *sāpō* 'soap' (L&S). Documents: none. Probably not in *BGU* IV.1058.35. Inscriptions: Edict.Diocl. 36.44 (IV AD). Literature: e.g. Galen x.569.13 Kühn (II AD); *Coll.Herm.* LS 2c (II–IV AD); Orib. *Syn.* 3.164.1 (IV AD); Hieroph. Πῶς 461.1 (IV–VI AD); *Hippiatr.Berl.* (Pel.) 26.28 (V AD?); Aëtius 3.160.25 (VI AD); scholion to Luc. *Lex.* 2 as gloss; with *sapo* in glossaries, e.g. Gloss. Ps.-Cyril. 429.49. Post-antique: numerous, forming derivatives σαπωνοπράτης 'soap-maker', σαπωνάριον 'soap dish', etc. (*LBG*). Sophocles (1887). Modern σάπων 'soap' and derivatives: Babiniotis (2002). Notes: normally considered Germanic word borrowed into Latin and thence into Greek (Kramer 1996a: 125, 2011: 51–2; *DÉLG*; Frisk 1954–72: II.677; Walde and Hofmann 1938–54 *s.v. sapo*), but argued by André (1956) to have come not via Latin but via a Celtic language of Asia Minor. Forms derivatives σαπώνιον, σαπουνᾶς, σαφωνίτης. Diethart (1988: 64–5 *s.v.* σαφωνιστής), Binder (2000: 223), Beekes (2010), Daris (1991a: 100), Hofmann (1989: 380–1), LSJ (*s.vv.* σάπων, σήπων). See §2.1, §4.1.1, §4.2.5, §4.6.1, §8.2.3 n. 51, **§9.5.3**, §10.2.1, §10.2.2 M.
rare	**σαπωναρικός, σαπουναρικός** 'soapy', 'concerning soap', from *sāpōnārius* 'concerned with soap-making' (Souter 1949) + -ικός: Zosimus alch., Berthelot and Ruelle 1888: 142.3, 226.15 etc. (III/IV AD); Olympiodorus alch., Berthelot and Ruelle 1888: 104.19 (V/VI AD); Byzantine texts. Hofmann (1989: 381), *LBG* (*s.v.* σαπουναρικός), Sophocles (1887), LSJ.
not ancient?	**σαπωνίζω, σαπουνίζω** 'wash with soap', from *sāpō* 'soap' (L&S) via σάπων + -ίζω: no certainly ancient examples. *LBG*, LSJ suppl.

Deriv. of loan **IV AD – modern**	**σαπώνιον, σαφώνιον, σαπούνιον** (-ου, τό) 'soap', from *sāpō* 'soap' (L&S) via σάπων + -ιον. Documents: e.g. *P.Ryl.* IV.629.106 etc. (IV AD); *SB* 11621.4 (V AD); *P.Oxy.* 1924.3 (V/VI AD); *P.Vind.Worp* 11.8 (VI AD). Literature: Cyran. 2.33.5, 4.28.26 (II AD?); Zosimus alch., Berthelot and Ruelle 1888: 143.7 (III/IV AD); Hieroph. *Nut.* 4.9 (IV–VI AD); Hesych. as gloss ν 585, 590 (V/VI AD); Ps.-Galen XIV.536.14 Kühn. Post-antique: numerous. Lampe (1961 *s.v.* σαπούνιον), *LBG*, Triandaphyllidis (1909: 122). Modern σαπούνι 'soap': Babiniotis (2002), Andriotis (1967). Notes: Kramer (1996a: 124–5, 2011: 52) argues that the σαφώνιον variant (usual in papyri) comes directly from Germanic, not via σάπων. But Schirru (2013: 316) derives it from σάπων with φ from Coptic interference. In any case σαπώνιον, the variant that prevailed in the long run, must be from σάπων. Diethart (1988: 64–5 *s.v.* σαφωνιστής), Binder (2000: 223), Daris (1991a: 101 *s.v.* σαφώνιον), Hofmann (1989: 380 *s.v.* σάπων), Cavenaile (1952: 195), Meinersmann (1927: 54), LSJ (*s.vv.* σαπώνιον, σαφώνιον), LSJ suppl. (*s.v.* σαφώνιον). See §4.6.1, §8.2.3, §10.2.2 M.
	σαπωνιστής: see σαφωνίτης.
not Latin?	**σαράγαρον**, a kind of wagon, perhaps from unattested **sarragārum*. Hofmann (1989: 381), LSJ.
	σάργαμον: see σάλγαμον.
Direct loan **II–IV AD**	**σάρδα** (-ης, ἡ) 'sardine', from *sarda* 'sardine'. Inscriptions: Edict.Diocl. 5.12 (IV AD). Literature: Galen VI.729.3 Kühn etc. (II AD); Athenaeus 3.120f (II/III AD); Orib. *Col.* 4.1.40: ἄριστα δ' ἐστὶ τῶν εἰς ἐμὴν πεῖραν ἐλθόντων τά τε Γαδειρικὰ ταρίχη (σάρδας δ' αὐτὰς καλοῦσιν οἱ νῦν) οἵ τε ἐκ τοῦ Πόντου κομιζόμενοι μύλλοι, etc. (IV AD); with *sarda* in Gloss. *Herm.A.* 89.42. Notes: Hofmann (1989: 381 *s.v.* σάρδης), Frisk (1954–72: II.677–8), LSJ. See §9.5.3, §10.2.1, §10.2.2 I.
rare	**σάρδης 1**, a kind of fuller's earth, probably from (*crēta*) *sarda*, a kind of fuller's earth (*OLD s.v. Sardus*): Galen XIII.734.1 Kühn (II AD). Hofmann (1989: 381), LSJ (*s.v.* Σαρδώ I end).
not Latin?	**σάρδης 2** 'sardonyx': cited by Hofmann (1989: 381) as from *sarda*, a type of carnelian (*OLD s.v. sarda²*), but probably from Greek σαρδώ. LSJ (*s.v.* Σαρδώ II), *LBG*.
foreign	**σάρκινα** transliterating *sarcina* 'baggage': Lyd. *Mag.* p. 106.12 (VI AD). Sophocles (1887).
foreign	**σαρκινάριος** transliterating *sarcinārius* 'for baggage': Lyd. *Mag.* p. 106.12 (VI AD). *LBG* (*s.v.* σαρκιναρία).
	σαρξιφάγον, σαρξιφαγές: see σαξίφραγον.
foreign	**σατισδατίων** 'giving of security', from *satisdatiō* 'giving of security': Antec. in Latin script 4.11.pr. *satisdationon* etc. (VI AD); later in Greek script. Zilliacus (1935a: 206–7), *LBG*.
not ancient?	**σατισφακτίων** 'satisfaction', from *satisfactiō* 'satisfaction': probably no ancient examples. Zilliacus (1935a: 206–7).

not ancient   **σατισφάκτον** 'satisfaction', from *satisfactus*, pf. part. of *satisfaciō* 'give satisfaction':
        no ancient examples. Zilliacus (1935a: 206–7), *LBG*.

Direct loan   **Σατορνάλια, Σατουρνάλια** (-ων, τά), a festival, from *Sāturnālia, -ium* 'festival of
II–IV AD   Saturn'.
      Documents: *P.Fay.* 119.28 (II AD).
      Literature: e.g. Epict. *Diss.* 1.29.31 (I/II AD); Athenaeus 14.639e (II/III
      AD); Epiph. *Pan.* 11.284.12, marked (IV AD); old scholia to Ar. *Nu.* 398a:
      ἔστι δὲ Κρόνια παρὰ τοῖς Ἕλλησιν ἑορτή, τὰ παρὰ τοῖς Ῥωμαίοις καλούμενα
      Σατουρνάλια, ἢ Ἀπατούρια.
      Post-antique: no real evidence of Byzantine survival; modern Σατουρνάλια
      'Saturnalia' (Babiniotis 2002) is probably a revival.
      Notes: seems to have been an integrated loanword during the time when
      the festival was celebrated. Daris (1991a: 101), Hofmann (1989: 381),
      Meinersmann (1927: 54), Lampe (1961 *s.v.* Σατουρνάλια), LSJ. See §4.2.5,
      §8.2.3, §10.2.1, §10.2.2 F, §12.2.2.

rare   **Σατορνιλιανός, Σατορνινιανός** 'Saturninian' (a Christian sect), from *Sāturniānī/*
      Sāturnīliānī/Sāturnīniānī (Du Cange 1883–7): too rare to be included here
      (see §12.2.2). Hofmann (1989: 381–2), Lampe (1961). See §6.4.

foreign   **Σατόρνιος, Σατούρνιος** transliterating *Sāturnius* 'of Saturn': e.g. DH *AR* 1.18.3
      (I BC); Stephanus of Byzantium α 10.10 (VI AD). Hofmann (1989: 382),
      Sophocles (1887 *s.v.* Σατο(υ)ρνία 'Italy').

foreign   **σατούρα** 'bread-basket', from *satura* 'dish of mixed ingredients': Lyd. *Mens.* 1.29,
      marked (VI AD). *LBG*. See **§9.5.5** passage 73.

      Σατουρνάλια: see Σατορνάλια.

name   **Σατοῦρνος** 'Saturn', from *Sāturnus* 'Saturn'. Sophocles (1887).

not ancient?   **σαῦλα** 'dandruff', from *sabulum* 'sand': probably no ancient examples. Binder
      (2000: 252), Meyer (1895: 58).

      σαφίφραγος: see σαξίφραγον.

      σαφώνιον: see σαπώνιον.

rare   **σαφωνίτης** 'soap-maker', 'soap-seller', from *sāpō* 'soap' (L&S) via σάπων + -ίτης:
      papyrus *P.Ross.Georg.* v.6ov.7 (IV AD); perhaps continued by Byzantine
      σαπωνιστής. Diethart (1988: 64–5 *s.v.* σαφωνιστής), Schirru (2013: 316),
      Daris (1991a: 101), *LBG* (*s.v.* σαπωνιστής).

      σγάλη: see σκάλα.

      Σεβήρεια: see Σευήρεια.

      Σεβηριανός: see Σευηριανός.

rare   **σέγεστρον** 'blanket', from *segestre* 'covering', 'wrap': Edict.Diocl. 8.42–3 (IV AD).
      Conflated with Greek στέγαστρον. Lauffer (1971: 245), Hofmann (1989:
      382), LSJ, LSJ suppl. (*s.vv.* σέγεστρον, στέγαστρον).

foreign   **σέδας** transliterating acc. pl. of *sēdēs* 'seat': Hesych. σ 323 (V/VI AD). Binder
      (2000: 259), Immisch (1885: 345), Sophocles (1887 *s.v.* σέδα), LSJ.

rare	**σέδετον** 'standing place', 'station', apparently from *sēdēs* 'seat', perhaps via unattested **seditum* or barely attested *sedetum* (Du Cange 1883–7): Just. *Codex* 1.4.18 (VI AD); Antec. in Latin script 2.11.pr. *sedetois* (VI AD); perhaps Macarius of Magnesia, *Apocriticus* 3.77.15 Goulet (IV/V AD); Byzantine texts. Binder (2000: 132, 263), Hofmann (1989: 382), Zilliacus (1935a: 208–9, 234–5), Triantaphyllides (1892: 272), *LBG*, Lampe (1961), LSJ. See §7.1.1 passage 16, §7.1.3, §7.2.1.

σειρικάριος: see σηρικάριος.

σεκόνδος: see σεκοῦνδος.

not ancient	**σεκουέστωρ** 'holder of a deposit', from *sequester* 'intermediary': no ancient examples. Zilliacus (1935a: 208–9), *LBG*.
Direct loan with univerbation II–III AD?	**σεκουνδαρούδης** (-ου, ὁ), a position in a gladiatorial establishment, from *secunda rudis* 'deputy to the chief instructor of a gladiatorial school' (*OLD s.v. rudis*[2] 3). Inscriptions: *I.Beroia* 383.4 (II AD); *IG* X.II.1.550.1 (III AD); *SEG* XLVII.954.2 (III AD); Ramsay 1941: 250 no. 246.2; *I.Hierapolis Judeich* 336.2; *TAM* II.117. Notes: Robert (1971: 27), Hofmann (1989: 382), LSJ, LSJ suppl. See §4.2.3.2, §4.5, §10.2.1, §10.2.2 F; cf. σουμμαρούδης.
Direct loan VI AD – Byz.	**σεκουνδοκήριος, σεκουνδοκέριος, σεκουνδικήριος** (-ου, ὁ), a title, from *secundicērius* 'functionary of the second rank' (L&S). Literature: Just. *Codex* 4.59.1.1 etc. (VI AD); *ACO* III p. 52.10 etc. (VI AD). Unverified example (III AD) in Zilliacus (1937: 323, 333). Post-antique: survives. *LBG* (*s.v.* σεκουνδικήριος), Triandaphyllidis (1909: 127). Notes: Hofmann (1989: 383), Zilliacus (1935a: 208–9, 234–5, 1937: 333), Lampe (1961), LSJ (*s.v.* σεκουνδοκέριος). See §4.2.4.1 n. 51, §4.5, §10.2.1, §10.2.2 D.
foreign	**σεκοῦνδος, σεκόνδος, σεκοῦντος** transliterating *secundus* 'second', 'fortunate': papyri *SB* 14180.65 etc. (II AD); *P.Grenf.* II.74.2 (IV AD); Lyd. *Mens.* 3.10.97 (VI AD); Procop. *Aed.* 4.1.30 (VI AD); Antec. in Latin script 2.14.6 *secundon* etc. (VI AD). Menci (2000: 288), Daris (1991a: 101), Hofmann (1989: 383), Zilliacus (1935a: 208–9, 234–5), Meinersmann (1927: 54), and for Byzantine use *LBG*. See §5.2.1.
rare	**σεκούριον** 'axe', from *secūris* 'axe': Edict.Diocl. 7.35 (IV AD); with *securis* in Gloss. *Herm.S.* 368.63. Byzantine σικούριον/τζικούριον may be a separate, later borrowing. Hofmann (1989: 383), *LBG* (*s.v.* τζικούριον), Zervan (2019: 187), Sophocles (1887 *s.v.* σικούριον), Triandaphyllidis (1909: 124 *s.v.* τσεκούριον), Meyer (1895: 67 *s.v.* τσεκούρι), Andriotis (1967 *s.v.* τσεκούρι), LSJ.

σεκούσωρ: see σουκκέσσωρ.

Direct loan II–IV AD	**σεκούτωρ** (-ορος/-ωρος, ὁ), a kind of gladiator and a military aide, from *secūtor* 'follower' (a type of gladiator). Documents: *P.Brookl.* 124.5 (II AD); *P.Mich.* VIII.485.4 (II AD); *SB* 11390.15 (II AD); *P.Aberd.* 196.7 (II AD); Cuvigny 2006: 343 (II AD?). Inscriptions: *SEG* XXXII.605.2 (II AD); Robert 1971: 79 no. 12.4 (II AD); *SEG* XXXIX.1339.4 etc. (II AD?); *SEG* XLVI.901.2 (II/III AD); Knibbe *et al.* 1993: 143 no. 60.1; probably *TAM* V.I.139.2; *TAM* II.355.2 etc.

Literature: Artemidorus, *Onirocriticon* 2.32.19 (II AD); Dio Cassius 72.22.3 etc.
(II/III AD); Philogelos 87 (IV AD).

Notes: notes to *P.Mich.* VIII.485.4, Daris (1991a: 101), Hofmann (1989: 383),
LBG, LSJ suppl. See §4.2.5, §10.2.1, §10.2.2 F.

σεκρετ-, σεκρητ-: see σηκρητ-.

rare   **σελάριον, σελλάριον** 'privy', apparently from *sellārium* 'privy': Esaias Abbas, *Or.* 5.3
= Esaias 1911: 36 (V AD); Hesych. as gloss α 8586 (V/VI AD). Hofmann
(1989: 383–4), Lampe (1961).

σελαριώτης: see σελλαριώτης.

σελεντ-: see σιλεντ-.

not ancient?   **σελία** 'seat', apparently from *sella* 'seat' via σέλλα: inscription Swoboda *et al.* 1935:
53 no. 110.2. LSJ suppl.

σελιγν-: see σιλιγν-.

Direct loan   **σέλλα** (-ης, ἡ) 'seat', 'saddle', from *sella* 'seat'.
II AD – modern   Documents: *P.Oxy.* 1146.6 (IV AD); *P.Berl.Sarisch.* 21.26 (V/VI AD); *P.Mich.*
XV.740.11 (VI AD); *P.Ross.Georg.* III.16.31 (VI AD).

Literature: *Act.Andr.* 13.17 (II AD); *Hippiatr.* e.g. *Hippiatr.Camb.* (Hierocles?)
17.2 (IV/V AD?); Hesych. as gloss α 8586, κ 3021 (V/VI AD); Lyd. *Mag.*
pp. 50.3 (marked), 56.4 (VI AD); Antec. in Latin script 1.2.7 *sellη*, with
reference to the *sella curulis* (VI AD); as gloss in scholia to Luc. *Hist.Conscr.*
45, Luc. *Nav.* 30, Ar. *V.* 1142b: σάγος δέ φασι τὴν κοινῶς σέλλαν λεγομένην, ἣν
ἐπιτιθέασι τοῖς ἵπποις; with *sella* in Gloss. Ps.-Cyril. 430.32. Unverified
example (VI AD) in Zilliacus (1937: 322, 333).

Post-antique: numerous, forming derivatives σελλοχάλινον 'saddle and bridle',
σελλοποιός 'saddle-maker', etc. *LBG*, Zervan (2019: 159), Triandaphyllidis
(1909: 119, 120). Modern σέλ(λ)α 'saddle' and related words: Babiniotis
(2002), Andriotis (1967), Kahane and Kahane (1972–6: 534), Meyer (1895:
58–9).

Notes: forms derivatives σελλίον, σελλοφόρος, τρίσελλος; perhaps ἐπισέλλιον,
ἐκσελλίζω. Daris (1991a: 101), Hofmann (1989: 384), Viscidi (1944: 41–2),
Zilliacus (1935a: 208–9, 234–5, 1937: 333), Meinersmann (1927: 54), LSJ.
See §4.6.1 n. 84, §6.13, §7.1.3, §8.2.3 n. 51, §10.2.1, §10.2.2 K.

σελλάριον: see σελάριον.

not ancient?   **σελλάριος,** from *sellārius* 'member of a chariot-racing establishment', is variously
understood by different scholars. LSJ suppl. considers it a masculine noun
meaning 'horse', on the basis of a Geneva scholion to *Iliad* 15.679 (κελητίζειν
εὖ εἰδώς· ἵππον κέλητα ἐλαύνειν ἐπιστάμενος. κέλης ὁ μονάμπυξ, ὁ νῦν λεγόμενος
σελλάριος, ἐπεὶ τὸ παλαιὸν ὡς ἐπὶ πᾶν τοῖς ἅρμασιν ἐχρῶντο); cf. Cavenaile
(1951: 400). Lampe (1961) considers it a masculine noun meaning a kind
of horse or a kind of Persian cavalry officer. Daris (1991a: 101), *LBG*, and
Sophocles (1887) consider it an adj. and cite Byzantine examples in which
it clearly is one; cf. Zilliacus (1935a: 234–5). There are no certain ancient
examples; in *P.Sakaon* 54.16 = *P.Abinn.* 80v.14 (IV AD) the reading is
superseded, and inscription *I.Smyrna* 403.3 (cited by Hofmann 1989: 384) is
now read with ἐσσεδάριος.

rare	**σελ(λ)αριώτης** 'horse-racer', from *sellārius* 'member of a chariot-racing establishment' (via σελλάριος?) + -της: Nil. 3.252.1 (V AD). Daris (1991a: 101), Hofmann (1989: 384 *s.v.* σέλλα), Cavenaile (1951: 400).
not ancient?	**σελλάστρωσις**, suggested by Hofmann (1989: 384) as a borrowing/adaptation of *sellisternia*, plural of *sellisternium* 'religious banquet offered to female deities': no certainly ancient examples. The occurrence in Gloss. Ps.-Cyril. 430.33 may be a later addition. LSJ.

Deriv. of loan
IV AD – modern
	σελλίον (-ου, τό) 'little seat', 'little saddle', from *sella* 'seat' via σέλλα + -ιον.
	    Documents: *Stud.Pal.* XX.107.6 (IV AD); *SB* 14625.9 (V/VI AD); *CPR* XIV.51.4 (VI AD); *P.Cair.Masp.* 67006v.88, 67143.19 (both VI AD).
	    Literature: Lyd. *Mag.* p. 18.9 (VI AD); old scholion to Ar. *Ec.* 734 as part of gloss.
	    Post-antique: numerous. *LBG*, Zervan (2019: 159), Zilliacus (1937: 333). Modern σελ(λ)ί and derivatives: Andriotis (1967), Meyer (1895: 58), Kahane and Kahane (1972–6: 534).
	    Notes: Daris (1991a: 101), Hofmann (1989: 384 *s.v.* σέλλα), Cavenaile (1952: 196), Meinersmann (1927: 54), Lampe (1961), LSJ. See §4.6.1 n. 84, §10.2.2 M.

not ancient?	**σελλίς** 'chair', 'bench', perhaps ultimately from *sella* 'seat': no certainly ancient examples. Hofmann (1989: 384 *s.v.* σέλλα), *LBG*, LSJ suppl.
not ancient	**σελλοξύλινον** 'wooden saddle', from *sella* 'seat' via σέλλα + ξύλινος 'wooden': no ancient examples. LSJ suppl.
not ancient	**σελλοποιός** 'saddle-maker', from *sella* 'seat' via σέλλα + ποιός from ποιέω 'make': no ancient examples. Filos (2010: 244, 251), Daris (1991a: 101), Cavenaile (1952: 199), *LBG*, LSJ suppl.
not ancient	**σελλοπούγγιον** 'saddlebag', from *sella* 'seat' via σέλλα + πουγγίον 'bag' (which may also be Latinate: see *s.v.*): no ancient examples. Hofmann (1989: 384 *s.v.* σέλλα), Zilliacus (1935a: 236–7), *LBG*.
rare	**σελλοφόρος** 'litter-bearer', from *sella* 'seat', 'litter' via σέλλα + -φορος (cf. φέρω 'bear'): inscription *I.Aphrodisias Late Ant.* 80.5 (V/VI AD). LSJ suppl.
not Latin?	**σέλπον**, a plant, claimed as Latinism without a convincing source word: Hesych. as lemma σ 399 (V/VI AD). Hofmann (1989: 384), LSJ.
foreign	**σεμεντίλιος** transliterating a Latin word in Lyd. *Mens.* 4.135, 4.152 (VI AD), causes Sophocles (1887 *s.v.* σημεντίλιος) to reconstruct unattested *sēmentilius 'of sowing seed'.
foreign	*sēmis* 'half (an inheritance)': Antec. 2.14.5 (VI AD). See §7.1.1 passage 18.
	σεμσέλιον, σεμψέλ(λ)ιον: see συμψέλλιον.
foreign	**σενᾶτος, σενᾶτον, σηνᾶτος** transliterating *senātus, -ūs* 'senate': Plut. *Rom.* 13.3 (I/II AD); Malal. 13.8, 13.30 (VI AD); Hesychius Illustrius, *Patria Constantinopoleos* 41 in Preger 1901 (VI AD); Lyd. *Mag.* pp. 96.8, 244.21 (VI AD); Antec. in Latin script as part of phrase 1.2.5 *senatus consultois* etc. (VI AD); Byzantine texts. Binder (2000: 219, 242), Mason (1974: 84), Hofmann (1989: 384–5), Zilliacus (1935a: 208–9), Triantaphyllides (1892: 272–3), *LBG* (*s.vv.* σενᾶτον, σενᾶτος), Zervan (2019: 159), Triandaphyllidis (1909: 127), Sophocles (1887 *s.vv.* σενᾶτος, σενατουσκονσούλτον), Lampe (1961 *s.v.* σενᾶτον).

Direct loan
IV AD – Byz.

σενάτωρ, σηνάτωρ, σινάτωρ (-ορος/-ωρος, ὁ) 'senator' (a military rank), from *senātor* 'senator'.
    Documents: *BGU* I.316.8 (IV AD).
    Inscriptions: e.g. *SEG* XXXVII.1081.2 (IV AD); *ILS* 8883.1.
    Literature: Eutropius 1.2.4, 1.2.22 (IV AD); Procop. *Aed.* 1.3.14 (VI AD).
    Unverified example (IV AD) in Zilliacus (1937: 323, 333).
    Post-antique: numerous. *LBG*, Triandaphyllidis (1909: 129).
    Notes: Drew-Bear (1972: 219–20), Binder (2000: 219), Diethart (1998: 175), Daris (1991a: 103 *s.v.* σινάτωρ), Hofmann (1989: 385), Zilliacus (1935a: 208–9, 1937: 333), Meinersmann (1927: 54), LSJ suppl. (*s.v.* σινάτωρ). See §4.2.5, §10.2.1, §10.2.2 C.

foreign

σενίωρ, σενέωρ transliterating *senior* 'elder' as part of a title: inscription Grégoire 1909: 34 no. 12.6 (IV AD); Eusebius, *PG* XIX.305b (IV AD); probably not in *P.Abinn.* 59 = *SB* 9634.26. Daris (1991a: 101), Hofmann (1989: 385), Lampe (1961).

σενσέλιον: see συμψέλλιον.

foreign

σεντεντία 'judicial pronouncement', from *sententia* 'judicial pronouncement': Antec. in Latin script 1.2.8 *sententiam* etc. (VI AD); later in Greek script. Zilliacus (1935a: 208–9), *LBG*. See §7.2.1 passage 27.

not Latin

σεντίνα 'lower hold on a ship', perhaps from *sentīna* 'bilge water' but probably from Italian: no ancient examples. Meyer (1895: 59).

rare

σεξαγηνάριος 'of 60,000 sesterces', from *sexāgēnārius* 'of 60,000 sesterces': inscription *IGUR* II.424.4 (II/III AD). Mason (1974: 4, 84).

foreign

σεξβερᾶτι apparently transliterating *sexvirātū* (abl. of *sēvirātus, -ūs* 'office of *sevir*'): inscription *AE* 1976 no. 686.11 (II AD). Millar (2006b: 166).

foreign

sextāns 'one sixth (of an inheritance)': Antec. 2.14.5 (VI AD). See §7.1.1 passage 18; cf. ἑξᾶς, which is effectively the same word but not borrowed directly from Latin.

rare

σεξτάριος 'pint measure', from *sextārius* 'pint measure', seems to occur in abbreviated form at Edict.Diocl. 6.52–6 (IV AD), but this is an anomaly: the usual Greek version of *sextārius* is ξέστης (*q.v.*). See §9.5.1.

rare

Σεξτίλιος 'August', from *Sextīlis* (the name used for the sixth month of the Roman year until it was renamed after the emperor Augustus): DH *AR* 9.25.1 (I BC); Plut. usually marked, *Rom.* 15.7: ἐτολμήθη μὲν οὖν ἡ ἁρπαγὴ περὶ τὴν ὀκτωκαιδεκάτην ἡμέραν τοῦ τότε Σεξτιλίου μηνός, Αὐγούστου δὲ νῦν, ἐν ᾗ τὴν τῶν Κωνσαλίων ἑορτὴν ἄγουσιν, etc. (I/II AD); Dio Cassius 55.6.6, marked (II/III AD); Lyd. *Mens.* 4.111 etc., usually marked (VI AD); Byzantine texts as archaism. Hofmann (1989: 386), LSJ. See §4.2.2 n. 32, §8.1.5.

name

σεξτοδαλμάτης, name of a military unit, probably containing *sextus* 'sixth': papyrus *P.Cair.Masp.* 67126.66 (VI AD). Hofmann (1989: 386), Meinersmann (1927: 54).

foreign

sēparātim 'separately': Antec. 2.14.11 *separatim* (VI AD).

foreign	**Σέπτα** transliterating *saepta* 'enclosure' (*OLD s.v. saeptum* 2), a building in Rome: Dio Cassius 53.23.1 etc. (II/III AD). Sophocles (1887).
	Σεπτέβριος: see Σεπτέμβριος.
foreign	**σέπτεμ** transliterating *septem* 'seven': Philo Judaeus, *De opificio mundi* 127 (I BC/ AD); Lyd. *Mens.* 4.121.5 (VI AD). Sophocles (1887).
Direct loan **I BC – modern**	**Σεπτέ(μ)βριος** (-α, -ον or -ου, ὁ) 'September', from *September* 'September'. Documents: e.g. *P.Yadin* I.21.3 (II AD); *P.Oxy.* 1204.12 (III AD); *P.Oxy.* 2561.16 (IV AD); *P.Ness.* III.30.2 (VI AD). Inscriptions: e.g. Sherk 1969: no. 27.4 (I BC); *IG* VII.2711.42 (I AD); *I.Cret.* IV.300.B6 (II AD); *I.Aphrodisias Late Ant.* 1.b6 (III AD); *SEG* XXX.585 (IV AD); *I.Lipára* 789.7 (V AD); *IG* X.II.II.149.C (VI AD). Literature: e.g. DH *AR* 9.67.3 (I BC); Plut. *Publ.* 14.6 (I/II AD); Dio Cassius 51.1.1 (II/III AD); Julian, *Epistulae* 108 Bidez (IV AD); Marc.Diac. 34 (V AD); *ACO* III p. 85.14 (VI AD); old scholia to *Od.* 1.22, Hes. *Op.* 448a, Demosthenes 37.2, Aratus 443, etc. Post-antique: common. *LBG* (s.v. Σεπτέβριος). Modern Σεπτέμβριος, Σεπτέμβρης: Babiniotis (2002), Andriotis (1967). Meyer (1895: 59) distinguishes between learned Σεπτέμβριος from Latin and vernacular Σετέβρις from Italian *settembre*. Notes: Kramer (1983: 120, 2011: 37) argues for derivation from rare *Septembrius* (Souter 1949). Sijpesteijn (1979: 238) reports spelling ἑπτέμβριος, which I cannot verify. Solin (2008), Avotins (1992), García Domingo (1979: 630), Hofmann (1989: 386), Meinersmann (1927: 54), LSJ. See §4.2.1, §4.2.2, §8.2.3 n. 51, §10.2.1, §10.2.2 E.
foreign	**σεπτέμουιρ, σεπτίμβερ**: often in inscriptions as part of formulaic (and always accusative) title σεπτεμουίρουμ (or σεπτέμουιρα) ἐπουλώνουμ, transliterating *septemvirum epulōnum* 'member of the seven-man board responsible for sacred feasts'. E.g. *SEG* XVII.569.5 (I/II AD); *I.Pergamon* II.440.4 (II AD); *IGR* IV.383.9 (II AD); *I.Cret.* IV.296.5 (II AD). Drew-Bear (1972: 220), Mason (1974: 7, 84, 116), Hofmann (1989: 386). See §7.3 passage 32.
foreign	**Σεπτομούντιον** transliterating *Septimontium*, a festival and a place: Plut. *Mor.* 280c, 280d (I/II AD). Strobach (1997: 199), Hofmann (1989: 386).
name	**Σέπτον**, part of a place name in Procop. *Bell.* 3.1.6 etc. (VI AD), from *septem* 'seven'. Hofmann (1989: 386–7).
foreign	*septūnx* 'seven twelfths of an inheritance': Antec. 2.14.5 (VI AD). See §7.1.1 passage 18.
foreign	**σέρβος** transliterating *servus* 'slave': Lyd. *Mag.* p. 22.15 (VI AD); Antec. in Latin script 1.3.3 *servi* etc. (VI AD); occasional Byzantine texts. Zilliacus (1935a: 208–9), *LBG*.
not ancient	**σερήνικο** 'dew', perhaps from *serēnus* 'clear': no ancient examples. Meyer (1895: 59).
foreign	**σέρουιος**, normally transliterating the name *Servius*: explained as meaning 'servile' in DH *AR* 4.1.3 (I BC), on which basis Sophocles (1887) cites it as a borrowing of *servius* 'servile' (attested only as a name, though transparently from *servus* 'slave' + *-ius*).

σεσκουπλικάριος: see σησκουπλικάριος.

rare   σεσσιών 'seat' (in a carriage), from *sessiō* 'seat': Edict.Diocl. 15.7 (IV AD).
       Hofmann (1989: 387), LSJ.

σεστέρτιος: see σηστέρτιος.

Direct loan with suffix **II–III AD**   Σευήρεια, Σεβήρεια (-ων, τά) 'Severan games', from imperial name *Severus* + -ειος.
       Inscriptions: e.g. *F.Delphes* III.1.555.18 (II AD); *IG* II/III².III.3169/70.21 etc.
       (III AD); *IG* II/III².II.2193.22 (III AD); *TAM* V.III.1507.14.
       Notes: Drew-Bear (1972: 220–1), LSJ, LSJ suppl. (*s.v.* Σεβήρεια). See §4.3.2,
       §10.2.1, §10.2.2 F.

Direct loan **IV AD – Byz.**   Σευηριανός, Σεβηριανός (-ή, -όν) 'Severian' (a Christian sect), from *Sevēriānī*
       'Severians' (Gaffiot 1934).
       Literature: e.g. Epiph. *Pan.* I.158.14 (IV AD); Eus. *HE* 4.29.4 (IV AD); Thdt.
       PG LXXXIII.372b (V AD).
       Post-antique: survives. Sophocles (1887).
       Notes: Lampe (1961). See §4.2.2, §10.2.1, §10.2.2 N.

σηγμέντον: see σημέντον.

rare   σήκαλις, σίκαλις 'rye', from *secale* 'rye' (vowel quantities are uncertain): Aëtius
       15.11.26 (VI AD); Ps.-Galen, Delatte 1939: 391.6; perhaps Gloss. *Herm.V.*
       429.64 (cf. *CGL* VII.238 *s.v. scandula*); Byzantine texts. Modern σίκαλη 'rye':
       Babiniotis (2002), Andriotis (1967), Meyer (1895: 59). Georgacas (1958:
       181), Hofmann (1989: 393), *LBG* (*s.v.* σίκαλις), Zervan (2019: 161), LSJ
       (*s.v.* acc. σήκαλιν). See §8.2.3 n. 51.

not ancient?   σηκρητάριον, σικριτάριον 'courtroom', from *sēcrētārium* 'council chamber' (L&S):
       Acta Eupli 1.1 in Musurillo 1972. Hofmann (1989: 394), Lampe (1961 *s.v.*
       σικριτάριον); for Byzantine use *LBG* with definition 'sacristy'.

Direct loan **V AD – modern**   σηκρητάριος, σεκρετάριος, σικριτάριος (-ου, ὁ) 'secretary', from *sēcrētārius*
       'secretary' (Souter 1949).
       Inscriptions: probably *I.Beroia* 421.4 (V/VI AD).
       Literature: *ACO* II.1.1 p. 65.16 etc. (V AD); *ACO* III p. 52.31 etc. (VI AD);
       Lyd. *Mag.* p. 148.24 etc. (VI AD); Evagr.Schol. *HE* 86.17 (VI AD).
       Post-antique: numerous. *LBG* (*s.v.* σεκρετάριος), Zervan (2019: 158–9),
       Zilliacus (1937: 333). Modern σεκρετάριος: Andriotis (1967).
       Notes: Bartalucci (1995: 119–20), Hofmann (1989: 387), Lampe (1961). See
       §4.2.4.1 n. 50, §10.2.1, §10.2.2 N.

σηκρήτις: see ἀσηκρῆτις.

Direct loan **III AD – Byz.**   σήκρητον, σέκρετον, σέκρητον, σίκριτον (-ου, τό) 'court', 'secret', 'cabinet', from
       sēcrētum 'secret'.
       Documents: *P.Oxy.* 1204.12 (III AD).
       Inscriptions: *I.Ephesos* 495.2 (VI AD).
       Literature: e.g. Eus. *HE* 7.30.9 (IV AD); *V.Dan.Styl.* A. 81 (V AD); Hesych. as
       lemma σ 363 (V/VI AD); *ACO* III p. 29.24 (VI AD). Unverified example
       (III AD) in Zilliacus (1937: 322, 333).
       Post-antique: common, forming derivative σεκρετικός 'of court'. *LBG* (*s.v.*
       σήκρητος), Zervan (2019: 161–2), Triandaphyllidis (1909: 120).

Notes: forms derivative ἐπισήκρητος, perhaps ἐπισηκρητεύω. Daris (1991a: 101, with derivation from *secret(ari)um*), Hofmann (1989: 388), Zilliacus (1937: 333, also citing an unverified example of σεκρήτιον), Meinersmann (1927: 54), Immisch (1885: 359), Lampe (1961), LSJ suppl. See §4.2.4.1 n. 55, §9.5.5 passage 75, §10.2.1, §10.2.2 B.

foreign   **σήλεκτος**, a kind of judge, from *sēlectus* 'judge appointed by the praetor': Hesych. as lemma σ 490 (v/vi AD). Immisch (1885: 357), *LBG*.

     σηληγνάριος: see σιλιγνάριος.

foreign   **σήλια** 'little jars', from *sēria* 'large clay storage vessel': Hesych. as lemma σ 491 (v/vi AD). Hofmann (1989: 388), LSJ.

     σηλίξ: see σίλιξ.

foreign   **σημαντῖβος** transliterating *sēmentīvus* 'of sowing': Lyd. *Mens.* 3.9 (vi AD). *LBG*.

     σημεντίλιος: see σεμεντίλιος.

rare   **σημέντον, σηγμέντον** 'gold stripe on the border of a garment', from *segmentum* 'decorative piece': Lyd. *Mag.* p. 88.22 etc. (vi AD); Byzantine texts. *LBG* (*s.vv.* σεμέντον, σηγμέντον), Sophocles (1887 *s.v.* σηγμέντον), Triandaphyllidis (1909: 122). See §9.5.5 passage 72.

rare   **σημικίνθιον, σιμικίνθιον** 'belt', 'apron', 'kerchief', from *sēmicīnctium* 'narrow girdle': NT Acts 19:12 (I AD); later references to that passage, e.g. (to pick the ones that are least obviously quotations) Basil Seleuciensis, *Homilia in pentecosten* p. 102.6 Marx (v AD); EphraemSyr. VII p. 114.8 (v/vi AD); Hesych. as lemma σ 663 (v/vi AD); *V.Luc.Styl.* 18.15 (vi AD). Strelan (2003), Danker *et al.* (2000 *s.v.* σιμικίνθιον), Binder (2000: 227, 231–2), Barrett (1998: 907), Leary (1990), Hofmann (1989: 389), Immisch (1885: 367), Lampe (1961 *s.v.* σιμικίνθιον), LSJ. See §9.3.

     σημισσάλιος: see σιμισάλιος.

     σημίσσιον: see σιμίσιον.

rare   **σημοδιαῖος** 'holding half a peck', from *sēmodiālis* 'holding half a peck' with influence from -αῖος: Edict.Diocl. 15.51 (IV AD). Lauffer (1971: 257), LSJ. See §9.5.1.

rare   **σημούνκιον**, from *sēmuncia* 'one twenty-fourth': unpublished ostracon O.Dios inv. 454.6 (II AD).

     σηνάτωρ: see σενάτωρ.

rare   **σήουιρ**, a title, from *sēvir* 'member of a board of six': inscription *IGUR* 1.172.5 (III AD). Mason (1974: 84).

     σήπων: see σάπων.

Direct loan   **σηρικάριος, σειρικάριος, σιρικάριος, σηφικάριος** (-ου, ὁ) 'silk-worker', from
IV AD – Byz.   *sēricārius* 'dealing in silk'.
     Inscriptions: *IG* II/III².v.13445.2 (IV AD); Edict.Diocl. 20.1 etc. (IV AD); Renan 1864: 348.3.

Literature: EphraemSyr. III p. 48.41 (V/VI AD).
Post-antique: numerous. *LBG*.
Notes: Hofmann (1989: 389–90, 391), Lampe (1961 *s.v.* σηφικάριος), LSJ. See §4.2.4.1 n. 50, §10.2.1, §10.2.2 H.

not Latin?   **σηρικός** 'silken' (with derivative ὁλοσηρικός, ὁλοσειρικός 'of pure silk'), perhaps from *sēricus* 'silken', or *vice versa*. Hofmann (1989: 390 *s.v.* σηρικόν), Lampe (1961), LSJ.

rare   **σησαμᾶτος** 'with sesame' (of cake), apparently from unattested **sēsamātus*: Athenaeus 14.647d (II/III AD). Hofmann (1989: 390); for later use as a noun meaning 'sesame cake' *LBG* (*s.v.* σησαμάτον). See §8.1.7 n. 34, §9.4 passage 61.

Direct loan   **σησκουπλικάριος, σησκουπλικιάριος, σεσκουπλικάριος** (-ου, ὁ) 'soldier receiving
II–III AD?   1.5 times the normal rations', from *sēsquiplicārius* 'soldier who receives 1.5 times the normal pay'.
Documents: e.g. *O.Krok.* 1.87.ii.109 (II AD); *BGU* II.614.11 (III AD).
Inscriptions: *IGBulg.* II.520.2; *MAMA* VIII.300.2; *IGLS* V.2503.3; perhaps Bollini 1975: no. 2.
Notes: σησκούπλικα in *O.Claud.* 1.126.5 (II AD) may be acc. of otherwise unattested variant σησκοῦπλιξ or σησκουπλικᾶς; see commentary *ad loc.* Daris (1991a: 101), Mason (1974: 4, 84), Hofmann (1989: 390–1), Meinersmann (1927: 55), LSJ suppl. See §4.2.4.1 n. 50, §10.2.1, §10.2.2 C.

rare   **σηστέρτιον, σεστέρτιον**, probably from neut. pl. *sēstertia* 'thousand sesterces' (*OLD s.v. sestertius* 3b), though it is not certain that the genders had the same meanings in Greek as in Latin: papyri *BGU* V.1210.91 and perhaps other lines (II AD); *P.Oxy.* 3364.42 (III AD); perhaps inscription *SEG* XXXIX.1037 no. 27. Daris (1991a: 102), LSJ (*s.v.* σηστέρτιος).

Direct loan   **σηστέρτιος, σεστέρτιος** (νοῦμμος/νόμος) (-ου, ὁ) 'sesterce', from *sēstertius*
II BC – III AD   (*nummus*), a sesterce coin.
Documents: *BGU* VII.1655.48 (II AD); *Chrest.Mitt.* 316.ii.4 etc. (II AD); *P.Hamb.* 1.73.14 (II AD); perhaps *BGU* V.1210.84 etc. (II AD); *P.Oxy.* 2857.28 (II AD); *P.Bagnall* 5v.8 (III AD); *P.Oxy.* 2348.42 (III AD).
Inscriptions: Sherk 1969: no. 10A.10, 10B.13 (both II BC); *F.Delphes* III.IV.37. C21 (II BC); *IG* IX.II.89.b34 (II BC); perhaps *IGLS* III.1.718.66 (I BC); *Studia Pontica* III.263.12.
Literature: Plut. *Fab.* 4.6 (I/II AD); Antec. in Latin script 3.7.2 *sestertion* etc. (VI AD).
Notes: García Domingo (1979: 631), Daris (1991a: 102), Hofmann (1989: 391), Meinersmann (1927: 55), LSJ. See §4.2.4.1 n. 51, §4.3.2 n. 75, **§8.1.4**, §8.2.1, §10.2.1, §10.2.2 G.

σήστουπλουμ: see ζήστουπλομ.

σηφικάριος: see σηρικάριος.

rare   **σιγγιλίων, σιγιλλίων, σινγιλίων**, a kind of shirt or tunic, from *singiliō* 'short garment' (L&S): Edict.Diocl. 19.59–62 (IV AD); Gregorius Nazianzenus, *Testamentum*, Pitra 1868: 158.11 (IV AD). Hofmann (1989: 391), Lampe (1961 *s.v.* σιγιλλιών), LSJ suppl. (*s.v.* σινγιλίων).

Direct loan **II AD – Byz.**	**σιγγλάριος, σινγλάρ(ε)ιος, σιγγουλάριος, σινγ(ου)λάριος** (-ου, ὁ), originally a type of soldier, later a type of messenger, from *singulāris* 'officer's aide' (*OLD s.v. singulāris* 6). Documents: common, e.g. *P.Freib.* 4.66.3 (II AD); *P.Oxy.* 3810.14 (II/III AD); *P.Ross.Georg.* III.1.6 (III AD); *P.Ant.* 1.33v.20 (IV AD); *P.Eirene* 11.12.4 etc. (V AD); *P.Cair.Masp.* 67284.5 etc. (VI AD). Inscriptions: e.g. Robert and Robert 1954: 181 no. 78.14 (II AD); *IG* X.II.1.495.2 (III AD); Edict.Diocl. 29.9 (IV AD); perhaps *SEG* LIII.1841. ii.5 (V AD); *I.Philae* 216.9 (VI AD). Literature: Lyd. *Mag.* p. 138.27 etc. (VI AD); *Martyrium Cononis* 1.3 in Musurillo 1972. Unverified example (III AD) in Zilliacus (1937: 322, 333). Post-antique: survives in papyri. Daris (1991a: 102). Notes: commentary to *P.Oxy.* 3810.14, Binder (2000: 197), Daris (1991a: 102), Mason (1974: 5, 84), Hofmann (1989: 395), Zilliacus (1935a: 236–7, 1937: 333), Meinersmann (1927: 55–6), Lampe (1961 *s.v.* σιγγουλάριοι), LSJ, LSJ suppl. See §4.2.5, §10.2.1, §10.2.2 C.
not ancient	**σιγελλᾶτος** 'authenticated', from *sigillātus*, pf. part. of *sigillō* 'mark', 'seal' (Souter 1949): no ancient examples. Diethart and Kislinger (1987: 7), Daris (1991a: 102), *LBG*, LSJ suppl.
rare	**σιγιλλάρια** 'puppets', from *sigillāria, -ōrum* 'small clay objects stamped with figures': Marc.Aurel. 7.3.1 (II AD). Byzantine σιγιλλάρια 'documents with seals' (*LBG*) is probably a separate borrowing. Hofmann (1989: 391), Zilliacus (1935a: 208–9), LSJ.
not ancient	**σιγίλλιον** 'document with seal', 'treaty', from *sigillum* 'seal': no ancient examples. Daris (1991a: 102), Cavenaile (1952: 196), Zilliacus (1935a: 208–9), Meinersmann (1927: 55), Babiniotis (2002 *s.v.* modern σιγίλιο), Lampe (1961), *LBG*. **σιγιλλίων**: see σιγγιλίων.
not Latin	**σίγλα 1** 'earring' (with derivative σιγλοφόρος 'wearing earrings') has been implausibly claimed to come from medieval *sigla* 'earring' (*DMLBS*). Daris (1991a: 102), Meinersmann (1927: 55), *DÉLG* (*s.v.* σίγλος), Frisk (1954–72: II.702), Beekes (2010 *s.v.* σίγλος), LSJ.
foreign	**σίγλα 2** 'abbreviation', 'ligature', from *sigla, -ōrum* 'abbreviations' (L&S): Just. *Const.* Δέδωκεν 22, marked (VI AD); Byzantine texts. Binder (2000: 208–9), *LBG*, Sophocles (1887), LSJ suppl.
not Latin	**σίγλος, σίγλον, σίκλος**, a unit of weight and value, is sometimes said to be from Latin but probably comes from a Semitic word related to Hebrew *shekel*. Hofmann (1989: 391), *DÉLG*, Frisk (1954–72: II.702), Beekes (2010), LSJ, LSJ suppl. **σιγλοφόρος**: see σίγλα 1. **σίγνα**: see σίγνον.

Direct loan
III–VI AD

σίγνιφερ, σιγνίφηρ, σιγνιφέρης, σιγνίφερος, σιγνήφορος (-ος/-ου, ὁ) 'standard-bearer', from *signifer* (gen. *signiferī*) 'standard-bearer'.
Documents: e.g. *P.Panop.Beatty* 2.190 etc. (III/IV AD); *PSI* VIII.886.10 (IV AD); *O.Douch.* III.203.1 (IV/V AD).
Inscriptions: *IGBulg.* V.5786.4 (III AD); *MAMA* I.169b.7 (IV AD).
Literature: Lyd. *Mag.* p. 70.11 as lemma (VI AD).
Notes: Daris (1991a: 102 *s.vv.* σίγνιφερ, σιγνίφερος), Hofmann (1989: 392), Cavenaile (1951: 400), Zilliacus (1935a: 236–7), *LBG*. See §4.2.4.1, §10.2.1, §10.2.2 C.

Direct loan
I AD – modern

σίγνον, σίκνον (-ου, τό) 'statue', 'place in camp', 'watchword', 'second name', 'sign of the cross', 'standard', from *signum* 'sign'.
Documents: e.g. *O.Krok.* 1.124.2 (I/II AD); O.Claud. inv. 7537.7 = Cuvigny 2019: 290 (II AD); *P.Oxy.* 3616.5 (III AD); *P.Lond.* VI.1914.19 (IV AD); *CPR* XIV.39.5 (V AD); *P.Cair.Masp.* 67004.17 (VI AD).
Inscriptions: e.g. Legrand and Chamonard 1893: 266 no. 52.6 (I AD); *I.Perinthos* 216.6 (II AD); *IGUR* I.119.2 (III AD); *IG* II/III².III.8395.8 (III/IV AD); *SEG* XX.417.6 (VI AD).
Literature: e.g. *Martyrium Apollonii* 45 in Musurillo 1972 (II–IV AD); Athanasius, *PG* XXVII.333b (IV AD); Gel.Cyz. 1.6t (V AD); Hesych. as gloss π 107, σ 493 (V/VI AD).
Post-antique: numerous, forming derivatives σιγνοπροτάσσω 'put the sign in front', σιγνογραφέω 'write the sign on', etc. *LBG*, Zervan (2019: 162–3), Sophocles (1887), Triandaphyllidis (1909: 130). Modern dialectal σίγνα, σίχνα 'spot': Andriotis (1974: 492), Meyer (1895: 59).
Notes: σίγνος in *I.Perinthos* 216.6. Forms derivative σιγνοφόρος. Cuvigny (2019: 291), Binder (2000: 248–9), Daris (1991a: 103), Hofmann (1989: 392–3), Zilliacus (1935a: 236–7), Meinersmann (1927: 55), Lampe (1961), LSJ, LSJ suppl. See §4.2.4.1 n. 55, §10.2.1, §10.2.2 C.

rare

σιγνοφόρος 'standard-bearer', 'image-bearer', calque of *signifer* 'carrying images' from *signum* 'sign' via σίγνον + -φορος (cf. φέρω 'bear'): *Acta Pilati* A.1.5 (= Tischendorf 1876: 220); with *manipularius* in Gloss. Ps.-Cyril. 431.20; Byzantine texts. *LBG*, Triandaphyllidis (1909: 129, merging this with σίγνιφερ), Lampe (1961, merging this with σίγνιφερ), LSJ.

not ancient

σιγνοφύλαξ 'guard over the standard', from *signum* 'sign' via σίγνον + φύλαξ 'guard': no ancient examples. Filos (2010: 251), Daris (1991a: 103), *LBG*, Lampe (1961).

σίδλιν: see σιτλίον.

σῖκα: see σίκη.

σίκαλις: see σήκαλις.

Direct loan with
suffix
II–III AD

σικάριον (-ου, τό) 'dagger', from *sīca* 'dagger' + -άριον.
Documents: *O.Krok.* II.304.6 (I/II AD); *P.Oxy.* 1294.8 (II/III AD); *P.Wisc.* 1.30.iii.3 (III AD).
Post-antique: occasional attestation, usually marked. *LBG*.
Notes: Kramer (2011: 287–93), Daris (1991a: 103), Hofmann (1989: 393 *s.v.* σῖκα), Meinersmann (1927: 55), LSJ suppl. See §4.3.2, §6.3, §10.2.1, §10.2.2 C.

Direct loan
I–III AD

σικάριος (-ου, ὁ) 'bandit' (esp. of certain marauders in I AD Judaea), from *sīcārius* 'assassin' (L&S).

Literature: NT Acts 21:38 (I AD); Jos. *AJ* 20.186.1 etc., once marked (I AD); Origen, *Contra Celsum* 2.13 Borret (II/III AD); Hippolytus, *Refutatio omnium haeresium* 9.26.2 (III AD); *ACO* III p. 78.3 (VI AD); Lyd. *Mag.* p. 98.1, marked, meaning 'butcher' (VI AD); Antec. in Latin script 4.18.5 *sicarii* (VI AD); also references to the biblical passage.

Post-antique: survives in discussions of the biblical passage; Zervan (2019: 163, 261) considers it an integrated loan in late Byzantine Greek.

Notes: Kramer (2011: 287–93), Smith (1971), Bruce (1990: 453), Kittel *et al.* (1932–79 s.v.), Danker *et al.* (2000), Hofmann (1989: 393), Zilliacus (1935a: 208–9), *LBG*, Lampe (1961), LSJ. See §4.2.4.1 n. 50, §6.1, **§9.3**, §10.2.1, §10.2.2 N, §10.4.2 n. 43.

foreign

σικᾶτα 'meat cut into small pieces': said by Lyd. *Mag.* p. 98.2 (VI AD) to be a Latin word derived from *sīca* 'dagger'. *LBG*.

foreign

σίκη, σῖκα transliterating *sīca* 'dagger': Jos. *AJ* 20.186 (I AD); Lyd. *Mag.* p. 98.1 (VI AD). Hofmann (1989: 393), LSJ; for later use *LBG* (s.v. σῖκα).

σικιάριος: see ἰσικιάριος.

σίκλα: see σίτλα.

rare

σικλάριον, which may mean 'little dagger' and come from *sīcula* 'little dagger', or 'little bucket' and come from *situla* 'bucket' (via σίτλα?), or 'little earring' and come from σίγλα 1 'earring', in any case + -άριον or -ιον: papyrus *CPR* VIII.65.10 (VI AD). Diethart (1988: 65–6, 1999: 181), Daris (1991a: 103), *LBG*, LSJ suppl. See §6.3 n. 21.

σίκλος: see σίγλος.

σίκνον: see σίγνον.

σικούριον: see σεκούριον.

σικριτ-: see σηκρητ-.

rare

σιλεντιαρίκιον 'place of the silentiaries', from *silentiārius* 'privy councillor' (L&S) via σιλεντιάριος + -ικός + -ιον: Cyr.S. *Vit.Sab.* 142.4 (VI AD). Hofmann (1989: 394 s.v. σιλεντιάριος), Sophocles (1887), Lampe (1961).

Direct loan
V AD – Byz.

σιλεντιάριος, σελεντιάριος (-ου, ὁ) 'silentiary', an official, from *silentiārius* 'privy councillor' (L&S).

Documents: perhaps *CPR* VI.62.3 (IV AD); *P.Berl.Cohen* 19.9 (VI AD).

Inscriptions: *SEG* XXVI.436.3 (V/VI AD); *SEG* VIII.171.1 (VI AD).

Literature: e.g. *ACO* II.I.I p. 94.35 (V AD); Nil. 2.12.1 (V AD); *V.Dan.Styl.* A. 76.2 (V AD); Cyr.S. *Vit.Sab.* 142.5 (VI AD). Unverified example (III AD) in Zilliacus (1937: 333).

Post-antique: numerous, forming derivative σιλεντιάρισσα 'wife of a *silentiarius*'. Zervan (2019: 163), Sophocles (1887), Triandaphyllidis (1909: 127).

Notes: forms derivative σιλεντιαρίκιον. Binder (2000: 131–2), Hofmann (1989: 394), Zilliacus (1935a: 208–9, 1937: 333), LSJ, LSJ suppl. See §4.2.4.1 n. 50, §10.2.1, §10.2.2 D.

Direct loan
VI AD – Byz.

σιλέντιον, σελέντιον (-ου, τό) 'imperial audience', from *silentium* 'silence'.
  Literature: e.g. Malal. 18.30 (VI AD); Lyd. *Mag.* p. 110.10, marked (VI AD);
    Ps.-Caesarius 198.47 Riedinger (VI AD).
  Post-antique: survives. *LBG*, Zervan (2019: 164), Triandaphyllidis (1909: 127).
  Notes: Binder (2000: 131–2), Hofmann (1989: 394), Lampe (1961). See
    §4.2.4.1 n. 54, §9.2, §10.2.1, §10.2.2 A.

Direct loan with
influence
VI AD – Byz.

σιλιγνάριος, σιλιγινάριος, σιλιγνιάριος, σηληγνάριος (-ου, ὁ) 'seller of siligo
  bread', from *silīginārius* 'seller of siligo' (a type of wheat), with influence
  from σιλίγνιον.
  Documents: e.g. *Stud.Pal.* VIII.1226.1 (V/VI AD); *Stud.Pal.* XX.145.9a (VI
    AD).
  Inscriptions: *MAMA* III.700.3, 727.3.
  Post-antique: numerous in papyri, occasionally in literature. Daris (1991a:
    103), LSJ, *LBG*.
  Notes: Daris (1991a: 103), Hofmann (1989: 394), Meinersmann (1927: 55),
    DÉLG (s.v. σίλιγνον), Frisk (1954–72: II.705–6), Beekes (2010 s.v. σίλιγνον),
    LSJ. See §4.2.4.1 n. 50, §4.4, §8.2.2, §10.2.1, §10.2.2 I.

σιλιγνείτης: see σιλιγνίτης.

rare

σιλιγνιαρία 'female seller of siligo bread', probably not from *silīginārius* 'seller of
  siligo' but from *silīgineus* 'made from siligo' via σιλίγνιον + feminine of -άριος:
  papyrus *SB* XVI.12281.1 (VI AD); perhaps *P.Amst.* I.57.1 (VI AD). Daris
  (1991a: 103, with derivation from unattested *silīgināria*), *LBG*. See §6.2.

σιλιγνιάριος: see σιλιγνάριος.

σιλιγνίας: see σιλιγνίτης.

Direct loan
II AD – modern

σιλίγνιον, σελίγνιον (-ου, τό) 'loaf of siligo', probably from neut. of *silīgineus*
  'made from siligo', or possibly *silīgō* (gen. *silīginis*) 'soft wheat' + -ιον. Latin
  normally has third syllable -gin- (*silīgnus*, L&S s.v. *silīgineus*, is rare and
  late), but that -i- never appears in any Greek words on this stem until VI
  AD. Therefore Greek probably made a single original borrowing, probably
  σιλίγνιον, and formed related words from that.
  Documents: e.g. *P.Stras.* IV.299v.4 (II AD); *P.Michael.* 125.2 etc. (III AD); *CPR*
    VII.42.i.1 etc. (V AD); *P.Oxy.* 2046.5 etc. (VI AD).
  Literature: Athenaeus 14.647e (II/III AD); Pall. *H.Laus.* 13.2 (IV/V AD);
    Apophth.Patr. 6.3.2 (V AD); *Hippiatr.Par.* (Pel.) 417 (V AD?); Dor.Gaz. *Doct.*
    Div. 7.82.21 (VI AD); bilingual glossaries, e.g. Gloss. *Herm.L.* 14.26.
  Post-antique: numerous, forming derivative σιλιγνιοπράτης 'seller of siligo
    bread'. Daris (1991a: 103), *LBG*, Zilliacus (1937: 333). Modern dialectal
    σιλίγνιν etc.: Andriotis (1974: 492), Kahane and Kahane (1972–6: 533).
  Notes: LSJ cites a variant σίλιγνον in *P.Lond.* II.266.112 (I/II AD?), and
    Hofmann (1989: 394–5) takes that as original borrowing and σιλίγνιον as its
    diminutive. But the form in *P.Lond.* is abbreviated and probably not σίλιγνον
    at all. Σιλίγνιον does not mean 'small loaf of siligo', for papyri specify both
    σελιγνίων μεγάλων (*SB* 10785.8) and σελίγνια μικρά (*SB* 10561.3). Earlier
    papyri tend to have spelling σελ- and later ones σιλ-. Σιλίγνιον was probably
    a lower-register equivalent of σιλιγνίτης. Forms derivative σιλιγνιαρία and
    probably σίλιγνις, σιλιγνίτης. Niehoff-Panagiotidis (2019: 470–3), Binder

(2000: 131), Daris (1991a: 103 *s.vv.* σιλίγνιον, σίλιγνον), Cavenaile (1952: 195), Cameron (1931: 258), Meinersmann (1927: 55), *DÉLG* (*s.v.* σίλιγνον), Frisk (1954–72: II.705–6), Beekes (2010 *s.v.* σίλιγνον), Lampe (1961), LSJ, LSJ suppl. See §4.2.4.1 n. 54, §4.3.2 n. 69, §4.4, §4.6.1, §10.2.1, §10.2.2 I.

Deriv.? of loan
II AD – Byz.

σίλιγνις, σέλιγνις (-εως, ἡ) 'flour from siligo', probably from *silīgineus* 'made from siligo' via σιλίγνιον, or perhaps *silīgō* 'soft wheat' with influence from σιλίγνιον, in any case + -ις.
Literature: Galen VI.483.16, XIII.12.1 Kühn, marked (II AD); Athenaeus 14.647e (II/III AD); Orib. *Col.* 8.46.16 (IV AD).
Post-antique: some survival. Andriotis (1974: 493) lists numerous descendants in modern dialects, but these could come from σιλίγνιον.
Notes: Niehoff-Panagiotidis (2019: 470–3), *DÉLG* (*s.v.* σίλιγνον), Frisk (1954–72: II.706), Beekes (2010 *s.v.* σίλιγνον), Hofmann (1989: 394 *s.v.* σιλίγνον), LSJ. See §4.3.2, §4.4, §4.6.1, **§9.4** passage 55, §10.2.2 I.

Deriv.? of loan
II AD – Byz.

σιλιγνίτης, σιλιγνείτης, σιλιγνίας (ἄρτος) (-ου, ὁ) '(bread) from siligo', probably from *silīgineus* 'made from siligo' via σιλίγνιον, or perhaps *silīgō* 'soft wheat' with influence from σιλίγνιον, in any case + -ίτης.
Inscriptions: *I.Ephesos* 938.11 (I/II AD).
Literature: Galen VI.483.15 Kühn etc. (II AD); *Coll.Herm.* Mp 17c (III AD?); Orib. *Col.* 3.13.5 etc. (IV AD); Aëtius 8.55.53 etc. (VI AD); Alex.Trall. 1.449.5 (VI AD); Ps.-Galen XIV.310.5 Kühn etc.; bilingual glossaries, e.g. Gloss. *Herm.A.* 87.17.
Post-antique: numerous. *LBG.*
Notes: was probably a higher-register equivalent of σιλίγνιον. May form derivative σιλιγνοπώλιον. Hofmann (1989: 394 *s.v.* σιλίγνον), *DÉLG* (*s.v.* σίλιγνον), Frisk (1954–72: II.706), Beekes (2010 *s.v.* σίλιγνον), LSJ. See §4.3.2, §4.4, §4.6.1 n. 86, §10.2.2 I.

σίλιγνον: see σιλίγνιον.

σιλιγνοπάλιον: see σιλιγνοπώλιον.

rare

σιλιγνοπώλιον 'shop selling siligo bread': Zosimus alch., Berthelot and Ruelle 1888: 221.15 (III/IV AD). LSJ (followed by *DÉLG s.v.* σίλιγνον and Hofmann 1989: 394 *s.v.* σιλίγνον) suggests that this may be a mistake for an otherwise unattested σιλιγνοπάλιον 'flour from siligo' compounded from *silīgō* 'soft wheat' + πάλη 'very fine meal'. Derivation via σιλιγνίτης is more likely than direct borrowing.

not ancient?

σίλιξ 'flint-stone', from *silex* 'hard stone': *Acta Petri et Pauli* 77 = Lipsius 1891: 211.11; occasional Byzantine texts. Hofmann (1989: 395), *LBG* (*s.v.* σηλίξ), Lampe (1961).

σιμικίνθιον: see σημικίνθιον.

rare

σιμισάλιος, σημισσάλιος, perhaps 'paid half a *solidus*', from *sēmissālis* 'of half an *as*': papyri *P.Prag.* II.164.7 (V AD); probably (*BL* XIII.5) *P.Amh.* II.148.3 (V AD); inscription *SEG* LXV.1408.C25 etc. (V/VI AD); Lyd. *Mag.* p. 72.11, marked (VI AD). Bandy (1983: 281–2), Daris (1991a: 103), Hofmann (1989: 395), Meinersmann (1927: 55), *LBG.*

Direct loan
IV–VI AD

σιμίσιον, σημίσσιον (-ου, τό), a coin name, from *sēmis* (gen. *sēmissis*) 'half an *as*'.
　Documents: *P.Rain.Cent.* 136.3 (VI AD).
　Inscriptions: *I.Cret.* I.XXII.65.A6 etc. (IV AD).
　Literature: Cyr.S. *Vit.Sab.* 116.13–14 (VI AD).
　Notes: Hofmann (1989: 389), *LBG*, Triandaphyllidis (1909: 125), LSJ suppl.
　　See §4.2.4.1 n. 57, §4.2.5, §10.2.1, §10.2.2 G.

rare

σιμπλάριος, σινπλάριος 'simple amount paid', adj. attested only in fem., from
　simplārius 'simple': inscription *Syll.*³ 901.14 (IV AD). Hofmann (1989: 396
　s.v. σινπλαρία), LSJ suppl. (replacing LSJ *s.v.* σινπλαρία, but misdating the
　inscription).

σινάτωρ: see σενάτωρ.

σινγ-: see σιγγ-.

foreign

σίνε transliterating *sine* 'without': Plut. (e.g. *Mor.* 282d); Antec. in Latin script
　in phrases, e.g. 2.14.6 *sine parte* (VI AD); Byzantine legal texts. Sophocles
　(1887). See §7.3.

foreign

σίνερε transliterating inf. of *sinō* 'let go': Plut. *Mor.* 282d (I/II AD); occasional
　Byzantine legal texts. Sophocles (1887).

foreign

σίνιστρος, σινιστέριος transliterating *sinister* 'left': Plut. *Mor.* 282d (I/II AD).
　Strobach (1997: 199), Hofmann (1989: 395), Sophocles (1887).

foreign

σίνος transliterating *sinus, -ūs* 'bay': Strabo 5.3.6 (I BC/AD). Sophocles (1887).

σινπλαρία: see σιμπλάριος.

σιρικάριος: see σηρικάριος.

Direct loan
V AD – modern

σίτλα (-ας, ἡ) 'bucket', 'pail', from *situla* 'bucket'.
　Documents: *P.Wash.Univ.* 1.58.17 etc. (V AD); *SB* 14211.8 (V AD); *SB*
　　15301.2.4 (V/VI AD); *CPR* VIII.65.19 (VI AD); *SB* 13749.5 etc., 15250.3
　　(both VI AD).
　Literature: Anton.Hag. *V.Sym.Styl.* 5 (V AD); *Apophth.Patr.* 9.16.9 (V AD);
　　Hieroph. Πῶς 457.24 (IV–VI AD); Alex.Trall. 1.447.23 etc. (VI AD); old
　　scholion to Demosthenes 21.471a as gloss.
　Post-antique: numerous, forming derivatives σιτλοεπιχυτάριον 'pail and jug',
　　σιτλολέκανον 'pail and basin'. *LBG*, Triandaphyllidis (1909: 54, 121), Sophocles
　　(1887). Modern σίκλα 'metal scoop', σοῦκλα 'wine measure', σικλί 'scoop', etc.:
　　Meyer (1895: 59–60), Andriotis (1967 *s.v.* σίκλα), Katsanis (2007: 801).
　Notes: forms derivative σιτλίον. Binder (2000: 175, 179–80), Diethart
　　(1986: 90), Daris (1991a: 103), Hofmann (1989: 396), *DÉLG*, Beekes
　　(2010), Lampe (1961), LSJ, LSJ suppl. See §4.2.3.1, §4.6.1 n. 84, §10.2.1,
　　§10.2.2 M.

Deriv. of loan
V AD – Byz.

σιτλίον, σίδλιν (-ου, τό) 'little bucket', from *situla* 'bucket' via σίτλα + -ιον.
　Documents: *P.Oxy.* 1290.9 (V AD); *SB* 7635.14 (V/VI AD).
　Literature: Hesych. as gloss κ 4006 (V/VI AD).
　Post-antique: some survival. *LBG*.
　Notes: Daris (1991a: 104), Hofmann (1989: 396 *s.v.* σίτλα), Cavenaile (1952:
　　196), Meinersmann (1927: 56), *DÉLG* (*s.v.* σίτλα), LSJ (*s.v.* σίτλα), LSJ
　　suppl. See §2.2.1, §4.6.1 n. 84, §8.2.2, §10.2.2 M.

Direct loan
II AD – modern

σκάλα, σκάλη, perhaps σγάλη (-ης/-ας, ἡ) 'stairs', 'ladder', 'gangway', 'landing place', from *scālae* 'ladder', 'stairs'.
Documents: *P.Col.* x.291.6 (v/vi AD); *P.Vat.Aphrod.* 1.12 (vi AD).
Inscriptions: perhaps Edict.Diocl. 14.6 (iv AD), spelled σγάλη: see Lauffer (1971: 253), LSJ (*s.v.* σγάλη).
Literature: Plut. *Rom.* 20.5 as part of place name (i/ii AD); Pollux 1.93 (ii AD); Philogelos 194 (iv AD); Anton.Hag. *V.Sym.Styl.* 27 (v AD); *V.Dan. Styl. A.* 28 etc. (v AD); Hesych. as lemma σ 806 (v/vi AD); Malal. 13.35, 18.61 (vi AD); Just. *Nov.* 159.pr. = p. 738.7 (vi AD); Philoponus, *In Nicomachi arithmeticam introductionem* 2.134.11 Giardina (vi AD); Procop. *Bell.* 4.17.3, marked, part of place name (vi AD).
Post-antique: common, forming derivatives σκαλία 'steps', σκαλόω 'land', etc. *LBG*, Zervan (2019: 165–6), Triandaphyllidis (1909: 95–6, 99, 119–20, 131). Modern σκάλα 'stairs' and derivatives: Babiniotis (2002), Andriotis (1967), Meyer (1895: 60).
Notes: forms derivatives σκάλωσις, σκαλοβάτης. Kramer (1995b, 2011: 295– 9), Avotins (1992), Daris (1991a: 104), Hofmann (1989: 396), Zilliacus (1935a: 234–5, 1937: 333), Immisch (1885: 342), Lampe (1961), LSJ. See §4.6.1, §8.1.1 passage 36, **§8.2.3**, §9.5.4, §10.2.1, §10.2.2 J.

rare

σκαλοβατέω, σκαλαβατέω, σκαλαβατάω 'climb a ladder', from *scālae* 'ladder' via σκαλοβάτης: Anton.Hag. *V.Sym.Styl.* 14 (v AD); Hesych. as lemma σ 820 (v/vi AD). Hofmann (1989: 396 *s.v.* σκάλα), *LBG* (*s.v.* σκαλαβατάω), LSJ (*s.v.* σκαλοβάτης).

rare

σκαλοβάτης 'one who climbs a ladder', from *scālae* 'ladder' via σκάλα + -βάτης 'goer' (cf. βαίνω 'go'): perhaps inscription *SEG* xxvii.266.3 (ii AD); with *funambulus* in Gloss. Ps.-Cyril. 432.31. Probably source of σκαλοβατέω and σκαλοβατικός. Hofmann (1989: 396 *s.v.* σκάλα), *LBG*, LSJ.

rare

σκαλοβατικός 'of climbing a ladder', from *scālae* 'ladder' via σκαλοβάτης + -ικος: Sopater, Walz 1833: 22.25, 32 (iv AD). *LBG* (*s.v.* σκαλοβατική), LSJ suppl.

Deriv. of loan
V AD – Byz.

σκάλωσις (-εως, ἡ) 'scaffolding', from *scālae* 'ladder' via σκάλα + -σις.
Literature: *V.Dan.Styl. A.* 99 etc. (v AD); Cyr.S. *Vit.Sab.* 169.19 (vi AD).
Post-antique: survives. *LBG*. Modern σκαλωσιά probably not survival but from σκάλα via σκαλώνω: Babiniotis (2002), Andriotis (1967).
Notes: sparse attestation is probably because scaffolding is rarely discussed in surviving texts. *LBG*, Lampe (1961). See §4.6.1, §8.2.2, §10.2.2 J.

rare

σκαμνάλιον 'cloth spread over a seat', from *scamnum* 'bench' via σκάμνος: *ACO* iii p. 94.39 etc. (vi AD). Lampe (1961), *LBG*, Triandaphyllidis (1909: 120).

Deriv. of loan
IV AD – modern

σκαμνίον (-ου, τό) 'seat', 'couch', from *scamnum* 'bench' via σκάμνος + -ιον.
Literature: Sopater, W. Dindorf 1829: 741.6 etc. (iv AD); Dan.Sket. *M.* 16 (vi AD); scholion to *Od.* 1.145d as gloss.
Post-antique: numerous, forming derivative ἀρκλοσκάμνιν 'chest–seat combination'. *LBG*, Zervan (2019: 166), Triandaphyllidis (1909: 120). Modern σκαμνί 'stool': Babiniotis (2002), Andriotis (1967).
Notes: Zilliacus (1937: 333), Sophocles (1887), Lampe (1961). See §4.6.1 n. 84, §8.2.3, §9.2, §10.2.2 M.

rare   **σκαμνοκάγκελος, σκαμνοκάνκελος** 'railing separating benches', from *scamnum* 'bench' via σκάμνος + *cancellus* 'barrier' via κάγκελλος: inscription *I.Smyrna* 844.a5 (IV/V AD). Editor *ad loc.*, Hofmann (1989: 140 *s.v.* κάγκελλος), LSJ suppl.

Direct loan
III AD – modern   **σκάμνος, σκάμνον** (-ου, ὁ or τό) 'bench', 'couch', from *scamnum* 'bench'.
Documents: *P.Dura* 33.12 (III AD).
Literature: Ps.-John Chrysostom, *PG* LIX.523.30 etc. (IV/V AD?); Callin. *V.Hypat.* 40.13 (V AD); David, *Prolegomena philosophiae* p. 16.20 etc. Busse (VI AD); S. *Alypii Stylitae vita prior* 10 = Delehaye 1923b: 155.23 (VI AD); scholion to *Od.* 4.51a as gloss. Scholion to Ar. *Nu.* 633 is probably not ancient.
Post-antique: numerous. *LBG* (*s.vv.* σκάμνον, σκάμνος), Zervan (2019: 166). Modern dialectal σκάμνος 'pew' etc.: Andriotis (1974: 496), Meyer (1895: 60).
Notes: forms derivatives σκαμνίον, σκαμνάλιον, σκαμνοκάγκελος. Binder (2000: 248), Shipp (1979: 500–1), Hofmann (1989: 396–7), LSJ, LSJ suppl. See §4.2.4.1 n. 58, §4.6.1 n. 84, §10.2.1, §10.2.2 M.

rare   **σκανδαλάριος, σκανδουλάριος** 'roof-shingler', from *scandulārius* 'roof-shingler': Rhetor. *Cap.* 215.15 (VI AD); inscription *IGR* IV.1646.3. Hofmann (1989: 397), Cameron (1931: 256), LSJ.

rare   **σκαπλάριον**, a garment, probably from *scapulāre*, a garment (Souter 1949): papyrus *P.Ryl.* IV.713.v.2 (IV AD). Binder (2000: 186), Daris (1991a: 104, with derivation from medieval *scapulārium*, *DMLBS*), Hofmann (1989: 397), LSJ suppl.

name   **Σκαῦρος** 'bent or twisted outwards' (of feet), probably from *scaurus* 'having a deformity of the feet': all ancient examples are names. Hofmann (1989: 397), LSJ, LSJ suppl.

rare   **σκεπτούριον** 'filtering and distributing reservoir or cistern', from *exceptōrium* 'water tank': Cyr.S. *Vit.Sab.* 187.7–14 (VI AD). Binder (2000: 225–6), Hofmann (1989: 398, proposing as intermediary unattested **sceptūrium* or **sceptōrium*), Lampe (1961).

rare   **σκευᾶς** 'left-handed gladiator', from *scaeva* 'left-handed person' probably with influence from the root of σκεῦος 'implement': inscriptions *IG* X.II.1.1035.1 (II/III AD); *SEG* XXXIX.531; perhaps *I.Iasos* 414.C2. Common as a name. Hofmann (1989: 398), LSJ suppl.

rare   **σκηπίων** 'ritual staff', from *scīpiō* 'ceremonial rod': Malal. 15.9.19 (VI AD). Hofmann (1989: 399), *LBG*, Triandaphyllidis (1909: 103, 127), Lampe (1961).

not ancient   **σκιεντία** 'knowledge', from *scientia* 'knowledge': no ancient examples. Zilliacus (1935a: 206–7), *LBG*.

σκληνίολον: see σκρινίολον.

σκόδισκος: see σκορδίσκος.

not Latin?   **σκολύπτω** 'strip', perhaps from *glūbō* 'peel': Hesych. as lemma σ 1078 (V/VI AD). *DÉLG* (*s.v.* σκολύπτειν), *LBG*, Sophocles (1887), LSJ.

not Latin	**σκοπελάριος** 'watchtower guard' is a Greek formation from σκόπελος 'lookout place' + -άριος. Hofmann (1989: 399), LSJ suppl. See §6.1.
rare	**σκο(ρ)δίσκος** 'leather saddle-blanket', from *scordiscus*, traditionally thought to mean 'leather riding-saddle' (e.g. Souter 1949) but probably meaning 'leather saddle-blanket' (editor of *O.Did. ad loc.*): Edict.Diocl. 10.2 (IV AD); probably documents *O.Did.* 448.5 (II AD) and *P.Lond.* II.191.14 (II AD). Sidro and Maravela (forthcoming), Hofmann (1989: 400 *s.v.* σκορδισκον), LSJ suppl. (*s.vv.* σκοδίσκος, σκορδίσκος).
rare	**σκόρτια** (ἡ) 'leather item', 'leather coat', from *scortea* 'leather coat' (*OLD s.v. scorteus*): Edict.Diocl. 10.16 etc. (IV AD). Lauffer (1971: 249), Hofmann (1989: 400 *s.v.* σκόρτιο-), LSJ suppl.
	σκότουλα: see σκούτουλα.
	σκοτουλᾶτος: see σκουτουλᾶτος.
not ancient?	**σκοῦλκα** 'watch', 'sentry', 'outpost', from *sculta* '(military) forces' (Souter 1949): probably no ancient examples. Binder (2000: 226, with derivation from non-existent **exculca*), Zilliacus (1935a: 234–5), *LBG*, Lampe (1961).
not ancient?	**σκουλκάτωρ** 'scout', from *exculcātor*, a kind of light-armed soldier (*TLL*) or *scultātor* 'guard', 'scout' (Souter 1949): probably no ancient examples. Binder (2000: 226), Zilliacus (1935a: 234–5), *LBG*, Triandaphyllidis (1909: 124).
not ancient?	**σκουλκεύω** 'scout out', from *scultor* 'search out' (Souter 1949) or a related word: probably no ancient examples. Zilliacus (1935a: 234–5, 1937: 333), *LBG*.
not ancient?	**σκοῦπα** 'broom' and derivatives, from *scōpae* 'broom': probably no ancient examples. Binder (2000: 223), *LBG*, Meyer (1895: 60–1), Andriotis (1967).
foreign	*scurra* 'fashionable city idler' is said by Cicero, *De natura deorum* 1.93 (I BC) to have been used by the Epicurean Zeno of Sidon (II–I BC) as a derogatory term for Socrates, evidently as a code-switch: *Zeno quidem non eos solum qui tum erant, Apollodorum, Sillim, ceteros, figebat maledictis, sed etiam Socraten ipsum, parentem philosphiae, Latino verbo utens scurram Atticum fuisse dicebat, Chrysippum numquam nisi Chrysippam vocabat.* J. N. Adams (2003: 331 n. 67), Pease (1955: 455).
not ancient?	**σκοῦτα** 'shield', from *scūtum* 'large shield': Her.Mech. *Mens.* 14.1 (lived I AD, but the words are probably not his). Binder (2000: 250), Hofmann (1989: 400), LSJ. Cf. σκοῦτον.
Direct loan with suffix? **VI AD – modern**	**σκουτάριον** (-ου, τό) 'shield', from *scūtum* 'large shield' + -άριον or *scūtārius* 'of shields' (L&S). Documents: *P.Oxy.* 1839.4, 2480.99 (both VI AD). Literature: Ps.-Macar. *Serm.* 32.3.2 (V AD?); Hesych. as gloss α 7771, 7777, 7780, θ 940 (V/VI AD); Malal. 10.51.26 etc. (VI AD); Just. *Nov.* 85.4 (VI AD); Nonnosus, *FHG* IV frag. 1.33 (VI AD); as gloss in scholia to Opp. *H.* 1.735, Luc. *D.Mort.* 12.2 and *Macr.* 2, Ar. *Pl.* 450, Aes. *Th.* 43 etc; with *caetra* in Gloss. Ps.-Cyril. 434.7.

Post-antique: common, forming derivative σκουταρᾶτος 'soldier with a shield'.
LBG, Zervan (2019: 168), Triandaphyllidis (1909: 130). Modern σκουτάρι
'shield': Babiniotis (2002), Andriotis (1967), Meyer (1895: 61).

Notes: Daris (1991a: 104), Hofmann (1989: 400 *s.v.* σκοῦτα), Zilliacus (1935a:
234–5), Meinersmann (1927: 56), LSJ (*s.v.* σκοῦτα). See §4.2.4.1 n. 54,
§4.3.2, §6.3, §10.2.1, §10.2.2 C.

Direct loan
II AD – Byz.

σκ(ο)υτάριος (-ου, ὁ) 'shield-bearer' (a type of guard), from *scūtārius* 'guard
armed with a large shield' (L&S).

Documents: e.g. *P.Oxy.* 4088.28 etc. (IV AD); *BGU* XII.2139.4 (V AD); *Stud.
Pal.* VIII.1050.3 (VI AD).

Inscriptions: *SEG* XXXVII.1081.1 (IV AD); *SEG* XXXVIII.1736.2 (IV AD);
SEG XX.332.2 (V AD); *I.Prusias* 95.5.

Literature: Marc.Aurel. 1.5.1 (II AD); *ACO* I.I.VII p. 68.32 (V AD); Zosimus,
Historia nova 3.29.3 Paschoud (V AD?).

Post-antique: numerous. *LBG*, Sophocles (1887 *s.vv.* σκουτάριος, σκουτέριος),
Triandaphyllidis (1909: 129).

Notes: Daris (1991a: 104), Hofmann (1989: 401), Zilliacus (1935a: 234–5),
LSJ, LSJ suppl. See §4.2.4.1 n. 50, §9.2, §10.2.1, §10.2.2 C.

foreign

σκουτᾶτος 'heavily armed soldier', from *scūtātus* 'equipped with a large shield':
Lyd. *Mag.* p. 20.10, 12, marked (VI AD); Byzantine texts. Zilliacus (1935a:
234–5), *LBG*.

Direct loan with
suffix
V AD – modern

σκουτέλλιον (-ου, τό) 'dish', 'plate', from *scutella* 'shallow dish' + -ιον.

Documents: *SB* 15284.7 (V AD); *Stud.Pal.* XX.151.4 etc. (VI AD); *CPR*
VIII.66.16 (VI AD).

Literature: scholion to Ar. *Pl.* 813 as gloss; probably with *scutella* in Gloss. Ps.-
Cyril. 434.9 (see below *s.v.* σκουτελλον).

Post-antique: numerous, forming derivatives σκουτελλίκι 'little dish', σκουτελλίτσιν
'little dish'. *LBG*, Zervan (2019: 168), Triandaphyllidis (1909: 43, 121).
Modern σκουτέλλα 'soup plate', σκουτέλλι 'small bowl', etc.: Babiniotis (2002),
Andriotis (1967), Meyer (1895: 61), Kahane and Kahane (1972–6: 535).

Notes: Daris (1991a: 104, merging with σκούτλιον), Hofmann (1989: 401 *s.v.*
σκουτελλον), Cavenaile (1952: 196), LSJ (merging with σκούτλιον). See
§4.3.2, §10.2.1, §10.2.2 I.

non-existent?

σκουτελλον occurs with *scutella* in Gloss. Ps.-Cyril. 434.9; Hofmann (1989: 401)
takes this to be the original borrowing of *scutella* 'shallow dish' and the
source of σκουτέλλιον, but Goetz (*CGL* VII.247 *s.v. scutella*) takes it as a
misspelling of σκουτέλλιον.

not ancient?

σκουτεύω 'protect with a shield', from *scūtum* 'large shield' + -εύω: probably no
ancient examples. Zilliacus (1935a: 234–5), *LBG*.

rare

σκούτλα 'lozenge', 'chequerwork', from *scutula* 'diamond shape': inscription
I.Ephesos 3065.11 (I AD); Her.Mech. *Stereom.* 2.18.1 etc.; Gloss. Ps.-Cyril.
434.8. Εἰσκότλα on inscription *SEG* VII.371.i.7 (II AD) is probably a
different σκούτλα meaning 'shallow dish', from *scutella* 'shallow dish'. May
form derivative σκουτλόω and if so was probably more widespread than now
appears. Binder (2000: 147, 181, 225), Hofmann (1989: 401–2), Cameron
(1931: 257), LSJ. See §4.3.1, §4.6.1.

rare	**σκουτλάριος** 'maker of *scutula* mosaic tiles', probably from *scutula* 'diamond shape' + -άριος (*scutellārius/scutulārius* is medieval and has very different meanings: *DMLBS*): inscriptions *I.Pergamon* 11.341.5 (I AD?); *IGBulg.* v.5584. Hofmann (1989: 402), Cameron (1931: 257), LSJ, LSJ suppl.
	σκουτλᾶτος: see σκουτουλᾶτος.
Direct loan with suffix II–III AD	**σκούτλιον** (-ου, τό) 'dish', 'plate', from *scutula* 'dish' + -ιον. Documents: *P.Oxy.* 4483.4 (II AD); *P.Lond.* 11.191.10 (II AD); *P.Oxy.* 741.18 (II AD); perhaps *P.Alex.Giss.* 46.11 (II AD); *P.Mich.* IX.576.6 (III AD); *P.Oxy.* 1657.3 (III AD). Notes: considered by LSJ a variant of σκουτέλλιον, but there is a sharp chronological divide. Considered by Hofmann (1989: 401 *s.v.* σκουτλα) a diminutive of σκούτλα, which has the wrong meaning. Therefore probably a separate, short-lived borrowing. For *scutula* as source see commentary on *P.Oxy.* 4483, Hofmann (1989: 402); *scutella* 'shallow dish' also suggested but less plausible. Daris (1991a: 104 *s.v.* σκουτέλλιον), Cavenaile (1952: 195), Meinersmann (1927: 56), *LBG*, LSJ (*s.v.* σκουτέλλιον). See §4.3.2 n. 69, §9.2, §10.2.1, §10.2.2 I.
Deriv.? of loan I–III AD	**σκουτλόω** 'decorate with *opus sectile*' probably from *scutula* 'diamond shape' (via σκούτλα?) + -όω. Inscriptions: e.g. *I.Ephesos* 3005.16 (I AD); *I.Iasos* 248.2 etc. (II AD); *I.Stratonikeia* 684.10 (II AD); *SEG* XLVI.1304.10 (III AD). Notes: forms derivatives σκούτλωσις, ἀποσκουτλόω, περισκουτλόω. Binder (2000: 181), Hofmann (1989: 401 *s.v.* σκουτλα), Cameron (1931: 257), LSJ, LSJ suppl. See §4.3.1, §4.6.1, §10.2.2 J.
Deriv. of loan II–VI AD	**σκούτλωσις** (-εως, ἡ) 'chequered work', 'decoration with *opus sectile*', from *scutula* 'diamond shape' via σκουτλόω + -σις. Inscriptions: e.g. *IOSPE* I².174.7 (II AD); *I.Ephesos* 430.25 (II AD); *I.Sardis* I.63.16 (III AD); *SEG* XXXVI.1099.11 (V/VI AD). Literature: Her.Mech. *Geom.* 23.3. Notes: Hofmann (1989: 401 *s.v.* σκουτλα), Cameron (1931: 257), LSJ, LSJ suppl. See §4.6.1, §10.2.2 J.
foreign	**σκοῦτον** transliterating *scūtum* 'large shield': Lyd. *Mag.* p. 20.20 etc. (VI AD); Byzantine texts. Binder (2000: 250), Zilliacus (1935a: 234–5), *LBG*, Triandaphyllidis (1909: 130). Cf. σκοῦτα.
rare	**σκουτοποιός** 'shield-maker', from *scūtum* 'large shield' + -ποιός from ποιέω 'make': papyrus *P.Oxy.* 2480.100 (VI AD). *LBG*.
foreign	**σκούτουλα, σκότουλα** apparently transliterating *scutula* 'dish': papyrus *BGU* III.781.iv.8 (I/II AD). Binder (2000: 147, 181), Daris (1991a: 104), Hofmann (1989: 401 *s.v.* σκουτλα).
Direct loan II–VI AD	**σκουτουλᾶτος, σκοτουλᾶτος, σκουτλᾶτος** (-ον) 'with a checked pattern', from *scutulātus* 'with a checked pattern'. Documents: *Stud.Pal.* XX.41v.5 (II AD). Inscriptions: Edict.Diocl. 20.11 (IV AD).

Literature: *Periplus Maris Erythraei* 24.5 Casson (I/II AD); Lyd. *Mag.* p. 20.24 (VI AD).

Notes: not attested in feminine, but LSJ infers that it would be two-termination. Wild (1964), Binder (2000: 181), Daris (1991a: 104), Hofmann (1989: 402), Cameron (1931: 257), Meinersmann (1927: 56), LSJ suppl. See §4.2.2, §10.2.1, §10.2.2 O.

σκρείβα(ς): see σκρίβας.

σκρεινειάριος, σκρηνιάριος: see σκρινιάριος.

σκρείνιον, σκρήνιον: see σκρίνιον.

Direct loan
II AD – Byz.

σκρίβα(ς), σκρείβα(ς) (-α/-ου, ὁ) 'scribe', from *scrība* 'scribe'.

Documents: e.g. *P.Oxy.* 1191.7 (III AD); *P.Oxy.* 2110.40 (IV AD); *O.Douch.* v.599.5 (IV/V AD); perhaps *Stud.Pal.* I (p. 8).3.3 etc. (V AD); *P.Cair.Masp.* 67353r.25 (VI AD).

Inscriptions: Ramsay 1883: 275 no. 17.10 (II AD); *I.Ephesos* 1540.10, 2283.2.

Literature: perhaps paraliterary papyrus P.Berol. inv. 21860.38 = Dickey 2012–15: II.282 (IV AD); Just. *Nov.* 94.2.ep. (VI AD); Lyd. *Mag.* p. 128.24 etc., marked (VI AD); Ath.Schol. 13.2.2 (VI AD).

Post-antique: survives. *LBG*, Zervan (2019: 169–70), Triandaphyllidis (1909: 127).

Notes: forms derivative ἀντισκρίβας. Avotins (1992), Daris (1991a: 104), Mason (1974: 4, 7, 10, 85), Hofmann (1989: 403), Zilliacus (1935a: 206–7), Meinersmann (1927: 56–7), Lampe (1961), LSJ suppl. (*s.v.* σκρείβας). See §4.2.3.2, §10.2.1, §10.2.2 N.

rare

σκριβηνδάριος 'secretary' on inscription *SEG* XXXVI.1335.4 (VI AD) may come from unattested *scrībendārius 'secretary' but is probably a back-formation from *subscrībendārius* 'under-secretary' (L&S), perhaps via σουβσκριβενδάριος; in any case it must come ultimately from the root of *scrībō* 'write'. LSJ suppl.

foreign

σκριβλίτης, a kind of pastry, from *scrib(i)līta* 'kind of cheese tart' (perhaps itself originally Greek): Athenaeus 14.647d, marked (II/III AD). Hofmann (1989: 403), *DÉLG*, Frisk (1954–72: II.740), Beekes (2010), LSJ. See §9.4 passage 61.

Direct loan
V AD – Byz.

σκρίβων (-ωνος, ὁ), an officer of the imperial bodyguard, from *scrībō*, an officer of the imperial bodyguard (Souter 1949).

Documents: *SB* 16222.2 (VI AD).

Inscriptions: Marek 1993: 191, Appendix 6 no. 10.2 (VI AD); seal *SEG* XXXIV.927.2 in Latin script (VI AD); perhaps εἰσκρίβωνος on Sarre 1896: 33 no. 15.

Literature: Nil. 2.204.1 (V AD); Agathias, Keydell 1967: 102.33, marked (VI AD).

Post-antique: numerous, forming derivatives σκιβώνισσα 'wife of a *scribon*', σκριβωνιακός 'subordinate to a *scribon*'. *LBG*, Triandaphyllidis (1909: 127).

Notes: Hofmann (1989: 403), Zilliacus (1935a: 234–5), Lampe (1961), LSJ suppl. See §4.2.5, §10.2.1, §10.2.2 A.

σκρίνειον: see σκρίνιον.

Direct loan
IV AD – Byz.

σκρινιάριος, σκρινάριος, σκρηνιάριος, ἰσκρηνάριος, σκρεινειάριος (-ου, ὁ) 'secretary', 'archivist', from *scrīniārius* 'secretary'.

Documents: e.g. *P.Oxy.* 2408.13 (IV AD); *P.Oxy.* 4902.5 (V AD); *P.Lond.* v.1714.13 (VI AD).

Inscriptions: e.g. *SEG* XLI.1277.2 (V AD); *MAMA* IV.34 (V/VI AD); *IGLS* XIII.I.9046.24 (V/VI AD); *SEG* XXXII.1554.A20 (VI AD).

Literature: e.g. Paulus Alexandrinus, *Elementa apotelesmatica* p. 67.11 Boer (IV AD); Nil. 1.82.1 (V AD); Just. *Nov.* 30.7.1 (VI AD).

Post-antique: numerous. Zervan (2019: 170), Sophocles (1887), *LBG*, Triandaphyllidis (1909: 127).

Notes: Avotins (1992), Daris (1991a: 104–5), Mason (1974: 3), Hofmann (1989: 403–4), Zilliacus (1935a: 206–7, 234–5), Meinersmann (1927: 57), Lampe (1961), LSJ, LSJ suppl. See §4.2.4.1 n. 50, §10.2.1, §10.2.2 N.

rare

σκρινίολον, σκληνίολον 'little case', from *scrīniolum* 'little case' (L&S): papyrus *P.Köln* IX.369.8 (II/III AD). Editor *ad loc.*, *LBG*.

Direct loan
II AD – modern

σκρίνιον, σκρήνιον, σκρείνιον, σκρίνειον (-ου, τό) 'dossier', 'box', from *scrīnium* 'writing-case'.

Documents: e.g. *Chrest.Mitt.* 91.ii.24 etc. (II AD); *P.Mil.Vogl.* III.203.3 (II AD); *BGU* I.40.10 (II/III AD); *ChLA* XLI.1197.14 etc. (VI AD); *P.Cair.Masp.* 67340v.78 (VI AD).

Inscriptions: *SEG* XXXII.1554.A19 etc. (VI AD); Calder 1912b: 260 no. 21.14 (VI AD); *TAM* III.I.657.11.

Literature: e.g. Dositheus, *Ars grammatica* VII.391.10 Keil (IV AD); Cyril of Alexandria in *Carth.* 423.9 (V AD); *ACO* II.I.I p. 149.19 (V AD); Callin. *V.Hypat.* 40.35 (V AD); Just. *Nov.* 8.Ed.not.1 (VI AD). Unverified example (III AD) in Zilliacus (1937: 322, 333–4).

Post-antique: numerous. *LBG*, Triandaphyllidis (1909: 123), Sophocles (1887). Modern σκρίνιο 'glass-fronted cabinet', σκρινί 'chest': Babiniotis (2002), Andriotis (1967), Kahane and Kahane (1972–6: 534), Meyer (1895: 61).

Notes: gap in papyrus attestation is probably real: in early papyri means 'box' and in late ones 'dossier'. Menci (2000: 289), Avotins (1992), Daris (1991a: 105), Hofmann (1989: 404), Zilliacus (1935a: 206–7, 1937: 333–4), Meinersmann (1927: 57), Lampe (1961), LSJ. See §4.1.1, §4.2.4.1 n. 54, §10.2.1, §10.2.2 M.

foreign

σκρίπτος 'appointed' (of an heir appointed in a will), from *scrīptus*, pf. part. of *scrībō* 'write': Antec. in Latin script 2.10.10 *scripton* etc. (VI AD); later in Greek script. Zilliacus (1935a: 206–7), *LBG*. See §9.5.6 n. 68.

σκύτα: see σκύτη.

σκυτάριος: see σκουτάριος.

not Latin?

σκύτη, σκύτα 'head', 'throat' is claimed by Immisch (1885: 316–17) to be from *scutula* (whether *OLD scutula¹* 'dish', 'lozenge' or *scutula²* 'wooden cylinder' is uncertain). *DÉLG*, Frisk (1954–72: II.744), LSJ.

foreign

σοβρίνη 'female cousin', from *sobrīna* 'female second cousin': Antec. in Latin script 3.6.6 *sobrina* (VI AD); later in Greek script. *LBG* (s.v. σοβρίνα). See §9.5.6 n. 68.

foreign	**σοβρῖνος** 'male cousin', from *sobrīnus* 'male second cousin': Antec. in Latin script 3.6.6 *sobrinos* (VI AD); later in Greek script. Zilliacus (1935a: 208–9), *LBG*. See §9.5.6 n. 68.
foreign	**σοδᾶλις, σωδᾶλις**, only as part of Latinate multi-word titles, from *sodālis* 'member', 'comrade': inscriptions e.g. *IG* V.I.533.5 (II AD); *SEG* XXIX.741.5 (II AD). Mason (1974: 4, 85, 117), Hofmann (1989: 428), *LBG*.
non-existent	**σόκιος** 'ally', from *socius* 'ally', cited as an ancient loan by Zilliacus (1935a: 208–9): no examples.
rare	**σόκκος, σῶκος** 'slipper', from *soccus* 'slipper': unpublished ostracon O.Dios inv. 1124.7 (II AD); Edict.Diocl. 9.20a–23 (IV AD); Gloss. *Herm.Mp.* 326.61. Hofmann (1989: 404), LSJ suppl.
	σολαία: see σολέα.
	σολάρ(ι)ον: see σωλάριον.
not ancient?	**σόλδιον**, name of a coin, from *solidus* 'gold coin worth 12–25 denarii' (L&S *s.v.* 1.B.2) + -ιον: no securely ancient examples. Zervan (2019: 170, dating the borrowing to XIII AD), *LBG* (*s.v.* σόλιδος), LSJ suppl.
not ancient	**σολέα, σολεία** 'raised floor in front of inner sanctuary of a church', from *solea* 'sill' (L&S): no ancient examples. Hofmann (1989: 404), Viscidi (1944: 37), Zervan (2019: 177), *LBG* (*s.v.* σωλέα), Triandaphyllidis (1909: 125), Lampe (1961 *s.v.* σολαία).
rare	**σολέμνιος, σολλέμνιος** 'customary', 'annual', in neut. pl. 'customary services or expenditures', from *sollemnis* 'traditional': Just. *Nov.* 128.16 etc. (VI AD); Byzantine texts. Avotins (1992), Hofmann (1989: 405), Zilliacus (1935a: 208–9), *LBG*, LSJ suppl.
foreign	**σόλιδος** transliterating *solidus* 'solid': Lyd. *Mag.* p. 18.10 (VI AD). Zilliacus (1935a: 208–9), *LBG*.
	σολῖνον, σολῖνος: see σόλιον 1.
rare	**σολιοθήκη** 'container for slippers', from *solea* 'sandal' via σόλιον 1 + θήκη 'container': papyrus *P.Bodl.* 48v.7 (II/III AD). Editor *ad loc.*, Kramer (1998a: 40–1), *LBG*.
Direct loan with suffix **II–IV AD**	**σόλιον 1, σολῖνος, σολῖνον** (-ου, usually τό) 'slipper', 'sandal', from *solea* 'sandal' + -ιον. Documents: e.g. *P.Oxy.* 741.8 (II AD); *PSI* IX.1054.8 (III AD); *P.Ryl.* IV.629.309 (IV AD); *P.Oxy.* 4127.33 (IV AD). Inscriptions: Edict.Diocl. 9.24 (IV AD). Literature: Gloss. Ps.-Cyril. 434.57. Post-antique: modern σολέα, part of an Orthodox church, is not a survival but may also come from *solea*: Babiniotis (2002), Andriotis (1967). Notes: although often considered same word as σόλιον 2, is distinct in both meaning and etymology. Forms derivatives σολιοθήκη, σολίτης. Matthews (2006: 194), Daris (1991a: 105), Hofmann (1989: 405 *s.v.* ᾽σόλιον), Cavenaile (1952: 196), Meinersmann (1927: 57), *DÉLG*, Beekes (2010), LSJ (*s.vv.* σόλιον, σολῖνος), LSJ suppl. See §4.3.2, §10.2.1, §10.2.2 H, §12.2.1.

Direct loan III–VI AD	**σόλιον 2** (-ου, τό) 'seat', 'stool', from *solium* 'chair'. Documents: *SB* 1.10 (III AD); perhaps *P.Oxy.* 1158.18 (III AD); *P.Cair.Masp.* 67006v.47 (VI AD). Literature: Lyd. *Mag.* p. 4.4 etc., marked (VI AD). Notes: Daris (1991a: 105), Hofmann (1989: 405–6 *s.v.* ²σόλιον), Meinersmann (1927: 57), *DÉLG*, Beekes (2010), *LBG*, LSJ. See §4.2.4.1 n. 54, §10.2.1, §10.2.2 M, §12.2.1.
rare	**σολίτης** 'sandal-maker', 'sandal-seller', from *solea* 'sandal' via σόλιον 1 + -ίτης: probably inscription *Corinth* VIII.III.522.3 (IV AD). LSJ suppl.
foreign	**σόλος** 'by himself', from *sōlus* 'alone': Antec. in Latin script 1.6.1 *solos* (VI AD). Zilliacus (1935a: 208–9).
foreign	**σολουτίων** 'dissolving', from *solūtiō* 'dissolving': Antec. in Latin script 3.29.1 *solutionos* etc. (VI AD); later in Greek script. Zilliacus (1935a: 208–9), *LBG*. See §7.2.2 passage 29.
non-existent?	**σομμα** is cited by Hofmann (1989: 406) as from *summa* 'sum of money' on the basis of σομμακολ on inscription *SEG* 11.824 (III AD), but both reading and interpretation are doubtful.
foreign	**σόρδιδον** transliterating *sordidus* 'dirty': Hesych. as lemma σ 1339 (V/VI AD). Immisch (1885: 345).
not Latin?	**σορδισμός** 'impure Greek', a lemma in Hesych. σ 1338 (V/VI AD), is cited by Hofmann (1989: 406) as from *sordidus* 'dirty', but LSJ prefers a connection with Greek σαρδισμός 'mixture of dialects'.
foreign	**σόριξ** (in acc. σόρικα) transliterating *sōrex* 'shrew-mouse': Plut. *Marc.* 5.6 (I/II AD). Hofmann (1989: 406), *LBG*.
Direct loan V AD – Byz.	**σουβαδιούβας** (-α, ὁ) 'under-assistant', from *subadiuva* 'assistant' (L&S). Documents: perhaps *CPR* XIV.39.10 (V AD); *P.Bodl.* 26.3 (VI AD); *P.Oxy.* 1042.14 (VI AD); *PSI* VIII.953.10 (VI AD). Inscriptions: perhaps *I.Chr.Macédoine* 148.2 (V/VI AD). Literature: Syn.Cyr. *Ep.* 145, marked (IV/V AD); *ACO* II.I.II p. 21.37 (V AD); Marc.Diac. 26.23 (V AD); Lyd. *Mag.* p. 108.26 etc. (VI AD). Post-antique: survives. *LBG*, Triandaphyllidis (1909: 127). Notes: Daris (1991a: 105, with derivation from *sub* + *adiuvō*), Hofmann (1989: 406), Zilliacus (1935a: 236–7), Meinersmann (1927: 59), Lampe (1961 *s.v.* σουβαδιουβᾶ), LSJ suppl. See §4.2.3.2, §10.2.1, §10.2.2 N.
Direct loan II AD	**σουβαλάριον** (-ου, τό), a container for water (a water-bag?) and a kind of belt, from *subālāre* 'under-girdle' (L&S). Documents (meaning 'water-bag'): *SB* 17086.2 (I/II AD); *O.Claud.* II.276.5 (II AD); unpublished ostraca cited by editor of *O.Claud.* II.276. Inscriptions (meaning 'belt'): Edict.Diocl. 10.10 in *SEG* XXXVII.335.iii.21 (IV AD). Notes: all documents from Eastern Desert of Egypt. Commentary on *O.Claud.* II.276, LSJ suppl. See §4.2.5, §9.2, §10.2.1, §10.2.2 M.
non-existent?	**σουβδρομεδάριος**, from *sub* 'under' + *dromadārius* 'soldier mounted on a dromedary' via δρομεδάριος: perhaps papyrus *CPR* VIII.53.10 (V AD). Daris (1991a: 105).

foreign	**σουβίτυλλος**, a cake, from *sāvillum*, a cheesecake: Athenaeus 14.647d, marked (II/III AD). LSJ. See §9.4 passage 61.
not ancient?	**σοῦβλα** 'skewer', from *sūbula* 'awl': *Acta Pilati* B.1.4 (= Tischendorf 1876: 290 n. 4) (IV AD?); *Evangelium Nicodemi* rec. M3, 1.4m Gounelle (V AD?); old scholion to Xenophon, *Anabasis* 7.3.21; Byzantine and modern texts. Binder (2000: 187–8), Hofmann (1989: 406–7), Zervan (2019: 170–1), Sophocles (1887), Andriotis (1967), Meyer (1895: 61–2), Lampe (1961).
not ancient?	**σουβλίζω** 'skewer', from *sūbula* 'awl' via σουβλίον + -ίζω: no certainly ancient examples. LSJ, *LBG*.
Direct loan with suffix **VI AD – modern**	**σουβλίον** (-ου, τό) 'skewer', 'awl', from *sūbula* 'awl' + -ιον. Documents: *SB* 15300.9 (VI AD). Literature: as gloss in scholia to *Od.* 3.463c, *Od.* 3.460d2, *Ar. Av.* 359c, etc.; with *subula* in glossaries, e.g. Gloss. Ps.-Cyril. 434.62. Post-antique: numerous. *LBG*, Lampe (1961). Modern σουβλί 'little skewer' and derivatives: Babiniotis (2002), Andriotis (1967), Meyer (1895: 61–2). Notes: Diethart (1998: 176), Hofmann (1989: 406 *s.v.* σούβλα), LSJ. See §4.3.2 n. 69, §8.2.3 n. 51, §10.1, §10.2.1, §10.2.2 M.
rare	**σουβρίκιον** 'hood', from *subricula*, meaning uncertain (Du Cange 1883–7) or *sublica*, a garment (normally a stake or pile, but see Forcellini *et al.* 1864–1926 *s.v.* 3) + -ιον: papyri *P.Mich.* III.201.8 (I AD); *P.Athen.* 67.10 (III/IV AD); perhaps *O.Bodl.* II.1948.2 συβρικινθοιν (III AD); with *subricula* in Gloss. Ps.-Cyril. 434.63. Youtie (1976: 53–4), Sijpesteijn (1988: 75–6, arguing that it can be adj. meaning 'upper'), Daris (1991a: 105), Hofmann (1989: 407), Cavenaile (1951: 400, 1952: 196), LSJ, LSJ suppl. See §4.6.2.
rare	**σουβρικομαφόρτης**, **σωβρικομαφόρτης** 'outer veil' on papyrus *P.Stras.* IV.222.14 (II AD) probably has the same etymology as σουβρικομαφόρτιον (*q.v.*). Filos (2010: 251), Daris (1991a: 105), *LBG*.
rare	**σουβρικομαφόρτιον** 'outer veil' on payrus *P.Oxy.* 905.7 (II AD) is claimed by *DÉLG* (*s.v.* μαφόρτης), Frisk (1954–72: II.186), and Beekes (2010 *s.v.* μαφόρτης) to be a borrowing of a hybrid compound formed in Latin, but I can find no evidence of it in Latin, and it has the Greek linking vowel -o- rather than Latin -*i*- (§4.5). Probably formed in Greek from the Latin source of σουβρίκιον (via σουβρίκιον or σουβρικός?) + μαφόρτιον (see *s.v.* μαφόρτης). Filos (2010: 251), Daris (1991a: 105), Hofmann (1989: 407), LSJ.
Deriv. of loan(s) **II–IV AD**	**σου(β)ρικοπάλλιον** (-ου, τό) 'outer cloak', from the Latin source of σουβρίκιον (via σουβρίκιον or σουβρικός?) + *pallium* 'mantle' via πάλλιον. Documents: e.g. *PSI* IX.1033.11 (II AD); *Stud.Pal.* XX.41v.2 etc. (II AD); *P.Oxy.* 921v.4 (III AD); *P.Ryl.* II.244.12 (III AD); *P.Jena* II.2.9 (IV AD). Notes: suggested to mean 'Syrian cloak' by Dross-Krüpe (2017: 297), taking σουρι- as main form and σουβρι- as variant; but σουρι- in only two examples, both III AD. Apparently borrowed back into Latin: see line 4 of papyrus in Bernini (2020). Filos (2010: 251), Daris (1991a: 105), Hofmann (1989: 407), Meinersmann (1927: 59), *LBG*, LSJ. See §4.5, **§4.6.2**, §9.2, §10.2.2 H.

rare	**σουβρικός**, meaning uncertain, from the Latin source of σουβρίκιον, perhaps via σουβρίκιον by back-formation (thus Hofmann): papyrus *SB* 11585.5 (I AD); *Anonymus Bobiensis* as gloss (itself then glossed) p. 33.27 De Nonno (V AD?); with *superaria* in Gloss. *Idiom.* 541.46. Youtie (1976: 53–4), Daris (1991a: 105, with derivation from *sublica*), Hofmann (1989: 407 *s.vv.* σουβρίκιον, σουβρικός), LSJ, LSJ suppl. See §4.6.2.
not ancient	**σουβσιγνᾶτον** 'signature', from *subsignātum*, pf. part. neut. of *subsignō* 'write below as a signature': no ancient examples. Zilliacus (1935a: 210–11).
foreign	**σουβσιδιάριος** 'in reserve', from *subsidiārius* 'in reserve': Antec in Latin script. 1.24.2 *subsidiaria* etc. (VI AD); later in Greek script. Zilliacus (1935a: 210–11), *LBG*.
rare	**σουβσκριβενδάριος, σουπσκριβενδάριος** 'under-secretary', from *subscrībendārius* 'under-secretary' (L&S): inscriptions *SEG* XXXII.1554.A13 etc. (VI AD); perhaps *SEG* IX.356.65 (VI AD); perhaps *SEG* IX.414.6 (VI AD). Zilliacus (1935a: 236–7), LSJ suppl. Cf. σκριβηνδάριος.
rare	**σουβσταντία** 'substance', from *substantia* 'substance': Athan. *Syn.* 28.6, marked (IV AD); Socr. 2.30.122 (IV/V AD); Soz. 4.6.9 (V AD). Zervan (2019: 171), *LBG*.
not ancient	**σουβστιτοῦτος** 'substitute', from *substitūtus*, pf. part. of *substituō* 'substitute': no ancient examples. Zilliacus (1935a: 210–11), *LBG*.
	σουβφρουμεντάριος: see σουφρουμεντάριος.
foreign	**σουγγερεύω** 'suggest', from *suggerō* 'suggest' + -εύω: Antec. in Latin script 1.5.3 *suggereuontos* (VI AD). Zilliacus (1935a: 210–11).
rare	**σ(ο)υγγεστίων** 'suggestion', 'supplying an answer to one's own question', from *suggestiō* 'supplying an answer to one's own question': inscription *I.Mylasa* 611.b.2, bilingual (V AD); Just. *Codex* 4.59.1.1 (VI AD); Antec. in Latin script 1.5.3 *suggestiona* etc. (VI AD); meaning 'elucidation', Lyd. *Mag.* p. 174.17, 24, both marked (VI AD). Avotins (1989), Hofmann (1989: 407), Zilliacus (1935a: 210–11), LSJ suppl.; for (rare) Byzantine use *LBG*.
	σουγχῖνος: see σούκινος.
not ancient	**σοῦδα** 'furrow', suggested as a borrowing of *sudis* 'stake' or medieval *suda* 'ditch', 'wall' (Du Cange 1883–7): no ancient examples. Binder (2000: 260), *DÉLG*, *LBG*, Zervan (2019: 171–2), Andriotis (1967), Viscidi (1944: 17), Meyer (1895: 62), Lampe (1961).
Direct loan **I AD – modern**	**σουδάριον, σωδάριον, σουδέριον, σουδάρειον** (-ου, τό) 'towel', 'napkin', 'neckcloth', 'headcloth of shroud', from *sūdārium* 'handkerchief', 'napkin'. Documents: perhaps *BGU* VII.1668.13 (I–IV AD); perhaps *Stud.Pal.* XX.15.7 (II AD); perhaps *SB* 14178.23 (II AD); *SB* 9568.5 (II/III AD); *Stud.Pal.* XX.31.2.19 (III AD); *Pap.Graec.Mag.* 36.268 (IV AD). Inscriptions: *SEG* VII.417.5 etc. (III AD).

Literature: common, e.g. NT John 11:44 (I AD); Hdn. Διχρ. III.II.13.25, repeated by Lentz as *Pros.Cath.* III.1.365.12 (II AD); Pollux 7.71 as gloss (II AD); Moeris σ 20 (III AD); *Acta Philippi* 14.4 = Bovon *et al.* 1999: 323.3 (IV AD); Nonnus, *Paraphrasis sancti evangelii Joannei* 11.173 (V AD); Romanus Melodus, *Cantica* 27.11.2 Grosdidier de Matons (VI AD); as gloss in scholia to Luc. *D.Deor.* 6.2, Ar. *Pl.* 729; often in biblical commentary.

Post-antique: numerous. Zervan (2019: 172), Sophocles (1887), *LBG*. Modern σουδάριο, σουδάριν: Andriotis (1967), Meyer (1895: 62).

Notes: if one takes seriously the attribution to Hermippus (§9.4 passage 52), the first attestation is in V BC. Strelan (2003), O'Callaghan (1973), Barrett (1998: 907), Daris (1991a: 106), Hofmann (1989: 408), Zilliacus (1937: 334), Meinersmann (1927: 59), Lampe (1961), LSJ. See §4.2.4.1 n. 54, **§6.3 n. 17** and n. 22, §9.3 with nn. 21 and 23 and 25, **§9.4** passage 52, §10.2.1, §10.2.2 H.

σουκεσσ-: see σουκκεσσ-.

σούκινον: see σούχινον.

rare — **σούκινος, σουγχῖνος, σούχινος** 'made of amber', from *sūcinus* 'made of amber' or *sūcinum* 'amber' via σούχινον: Artemidorus, *Onirocriticon* 2.5 (II AD); Edict. Diocl. 13.10 (IV AD). Hofmann (1989: 409), *DÉLG* (s.v. σούχινον), Beekes (2010 s.v. σούχινον), Sophocles (1887), LSJ (s.vv. σούκινος, σουγχῖνος). Cf. σούχινον 'amber'.

foreign — **σουκ(κ)εσσίων** 'succession' (a way of transferring an inheritance), from *successiō* 'succession': Antec. in Latin script 3.2.7 *successiona* etc. (VI AD); later in Greek script. Zilliacus (1935a: 210–11), *LBG* (s.v. σουκεσσίων).

Direct loan I–II AD — **σουκ(κ)έσσωρ, σουπκέσωρ, σεκούσωρ, σουκέστωρ, συπκέστορ** (-ορος/-ωρος, ὁ) 'relief' (i.e. the next person due to take over a military post), from *successor* 'successor'.
Documents: *O.Did.* 339.8, 341.8 (both I AD); *O.Krok.* 1.96.9 (I/II AD); unpublished ostraca O.Dios inv. 59.14, 721.6 (both II AD).
Post-antique: probably unrelated to Byzantine σουκέσσωρ 'successor' (*LBG*).
Notes: all examples from Eastern Desert. Commentary on *O.Did.* See §4.2.5, §9.2, §10.2.1, §10.2.2 C.

σοῦκλα: see σίτλα.

not ancient — **σουλιτάρι** 'bellwether', from *sōlitārius* 'solitary': no ancient examples. Meyer (1895: 62).

rare — **σουμάριον** 'summary', from *summārium* 'summary': Iamblichus alch., Berthelot and Ruelle 1888: 289.9 (II/III AD). Hofmann (1989: 409), LSJ suppl.

rare — **σουμ(μ)άριος**, an official title, from *summārius* 'accountant' (*DMLBS*): Just. *Nov.* 30.1.1 etc., but in Latin script 64.1 (VI AD); Ath.Schol. 21.1 (VI AD). Avotins (1992), Hofmann (1989: 409), Zilliacus (1935a: 210–11), Lampe (1961), LSJ suppl.; for (rare) later use *LBG*.

rare — **σουμμάρος**, probably variant of σουμμαρούδης (*q.v.*): inscription *Studia Pontica* III.7.4 (I AD). Editor suggests derivation from unattested **summārius* 'gladiator hired for a fixed fee' (with reference to Daremberg and Saglio 1877–1919 s.v. *Gladiator* p. 1576, where this word is not mentioned). Cameron (1931: 259–60).

Direct loan with univerbation II AD?	**σουμμαρούδης** (-ου, ὁ) 'chief instructor at a gladiatorial school', from *summa rudis* 'chief instructor at a gladiatorial school' (*OLD s.v. rudis²* 3).
	Inscriptions: *I.Beroia* 383.1 etc. (II AD); Bosch 1967: 188 no. 149.A5 etc. (II AD); *I.Mylasa* 533.3; Lane 1971: no. 290.2.
	Notes: if σουμμάρος is a variant, existed already in I AD. Robert (1971: 27), Hofmann (1989: 409), LSJ, LSJ suppl. See §4.2.3.2, §4.5, §10.2.1, §10.2.2 F; cf. σεκουνδαρούδης.
Direct loan II–IV AD, VI AD – modern?	**σοῦμμος** (-η, -ον) 'highest in rank', as masc. subst. position in a board game, from *summus* 'highest'.
	Documents: e.g. *Rom.Mil.Rec.* 76.i.11 etc. (II AD); *P.Panop.Beatty* 1.393 etc. (III AD); *CPR* VII.21.9 etc. (IV AD).
	Inscriptions: *IGBulg.* III.II.1774.3; *IGLS* VII.4037.3; *I.Syringes* 1484.3.
	Literature: *Anthologia Graeca* 9.482.9, 11 (VI AD).
	Post-antique: survives with new meanings. Sophocles (1887), *LBG* (s.v. σοῦμμα). Modern σούμα 'sum': Babiniotis (2002), Andriotis (1967).
	Notes: board game meaning only in *Anthologia Graeca* and probably linked to Byzantine sense 'highest cast of the dice'. Probably died out and was reborrowed. Binder (2000: 145, citing a dubious inscriptional attestation), Daris (1991a: 106), Mason (1974: 4, 85), Hofmann (1989: 410), Meinersmann (1927: 57), LSJ suppl. See §4.2.2, §8.2.1, §10.2.1, §10.2.2 D.
rare	**σοῦος** 'his/her/their own', from *suus* 'his/her/their own': Just. *Nov.* 107.pr. (VI AD); Antec. in Latin script 2.13.pr. *suoi* etc. (VI AD); later legal texts. Avotins (1992), Hofmann (1989: 410), Zilliacus (1935a: 210–11), Triantaphyllides (1892: 273, taking neut. subst. σοῦον separately as a rendering of medieval *suitas* 'being one's own' (Du Cange 1883–7)), *LBG*. See §9.5.6 n. 68.
foreign	**σούπερβος** transliterating *superbus* 'proud': historians explaining the name of Tarquinius Superbus, e.g. DH *AR* 4.41.4 (I BC); Theophilus of Antioch, *Ad Autolycum* 3.27.12 Grant (II AD). Sophocles (1887); for later use *LBG*.
rare	**σουπερνουμεράριος** 'supernumerary', from *supernumerārius* 'supernumerary': *P.Panop.Beatty* 2.183 etc. (III/IV AD). Daris (1991a: 106), Hofmann (1989: 410), LSJ suppl.
not ancient	**σουπερνούμερος** 'supernumerary', from *supernumerārius* 'supernumerary' (thus *LBG*) or *super numerum* 'supernumerary' (thus Zilliacus): no ancient examples. Zilliacus (1935a: 210–11), *LBG*, Triandaphyllidis (1909: 131).
non-existent?	**σουπερστράτωρ**, a title, from *super* 'above' + *strātor* 'groom' (via στράτωρ?) or unattested **superstrātor*: perhaps papyrus *P.Stras.* VIII.717.4 etc. (V AD). Daris (1991a: 106), *LBG*.
not ancient	**σουπερφίκιον, σουπερφιτζίων, σουπερφίτζιον**, a kind of building, from *superficium* 'building' (L&S s.v. *superficies* II.A): no ancient examples. Zilliacus (1935a: 210–11), *LBG*.
	σουπκέσωρ: see σουκκέσσωρ.

foreign   **σουπλημέντα** transliterating pl. of *supplēmentum* 'reinforcements': inscription *SEG* XXXVIII.1244.7 (II AD).

          σουπσκριβενδάριος: see σουβσκριβενδάριος.

foreign   **σούρα** transliterating *sūra* 'lower leg': Plut. *Cicero* 17.4 (I/II AD). *LBG*.

not ancient?   **σοῦρβα** 'service tree', **σουρβιά** 'service tree', and **σοῦρβον** 'serviceberry', from *sorbum* 'serviceberry': probably no ancient examples. *LBG* (*s.vv.* σουρβία, σοῦρβον), Meyer (1895: 62).

not Latin?   **σουρελιανός**, a word of unknown meaning at Edict.Diocl. 15.62 (IV AD), is suggested as a Latinism by Hofmann (1989: 410) following Doyle (1976: 95), who cites *syrellianus*, adj. from an otherwise unknown place name. Lauffer (1971: 258).

not ancient   **σουρικάρα** 'mousetrap', perhaps from *sōrex* 'shrew-mouse' via unattested **sōricāria*: no ancient examples. Meyer (1895: 62).

          σουρικοπάλλιον: see σουβρικοπάλλιον.

foreign   **σούσπεκτος** 'under suspicion', from *suspectus* 'under suspicion': Antec. in Latin script 1.26.2 *suspectoi* etc. (VI AD); later in Greek script. Zilliacus (1935a: 210–11), *LBG*. See §9.5.6 n. 68.

not Latin?   **σοῦφρα** 'fold', 'wrinkle' and **σουφρώνω** 'fold', perhaps from *supplicō* 'supplicate' (cf. *plicō* 'fold') via unattested **sup(p)la*: no ancient examples. *LBG* (with different etymology), Andriotis (1967), Meyer (1895: 62).

rare   **σουφράγιον**, **σουφφράγιον** 'payment for protection', 'suffrage', from *suffrāgium* 'suffrage', 'help': Lyd. *Mag.* p. 242.24 (VI AD); Just. *Nov.* 29.2, marked, and in Latin script 8.pr.1. etc. (VI AD); Byzantine texts. Avotins (1992), Hofmann (1989: 410), Zilliacus (1935a: 210–11), *LBG*.

rare   **σουφρουμεντάριος**, **σοφρομηντάριος**, **σουβφρουμεντάριος** 'corn-supply assistant', from unattested **suffrūmentārius* or from *sub* 'under' + *frūmentārius* 'concerned with the corn supply' via φρουμεντάριος: papyrus *P.Oxy.* 1903.7 (VI AD); occasionally later. Daris (1991a: 106), Hofmann (1989: 410), Zilliacus (1935a: 236–7), Cavenaile (1951: 400), LSJ suppl.

          σουφρώνω: see σοῦφρα.

          σουφφράγιον: see σουφράγιον.

rare   **σούχινον**, **σούκινον**, **σούχειον** 'amber', probably from *sūcinum* 'amber': Clemens Alexandrinus, *Stromata* 2.6.26.2 Früchtel (II/III AD); Aëtius 2.35.1 etc. (VI AD); Ps.-Dioscorides, *De lapidibus* 10 in Ruelle 1898: 180. Hofmann (1989: 411), *DÉLG*, Beekes (2010), *LBG* (*s.vv.* σούγχινον, σούκινον, σούχινον), Sophocles (1887 *s.v.* σούκινον), Lampe (1961: *s.v.* σούχειον), LSJ. Cf. σούκινος 'made of amber'.

          σούχινος: see σούκινος.

          σουψειρικός: see συψειρικός.

          σοφρομηντάριος: see σουφρουμεντάριος.

not Latin?	**σπαθάριος** 'member of ceremonial bodyguard' (with derivatives σπαθαρικός 'for a *spatharius*', πρωτοσπαθάριος 'first *spatharius*') may well come from *spatārius* 'man armed with a broad-bladed sword' (*OLD s.v. spatārius¹* and *spatha* 1b), especially as the Latin word seems to go back to early I AD (*CIL* 6.9043) and the Greek is not attested until IV AD (Eutychianus, *FHG* IV frag. 1.17; examples in papyri and inscriptions are all from VI AD or later); cf. Cameron (1931: 259), Hofmann (1989: 411). But *DÉLG* (*s.v.* σπάθη), Frisk (1954–72: II.755), Beekes (2010 *s.v.* σπάθη), and Zilliacus (1937: 335, though he endorsed the derivation from *spatharius* in 1935a: 236–7) all prefer a Greek formation from σπάθη 'broad blade' + -*ārius*. Lampe (1961), *LBG*, LSJ. See §6.1.
not ancient	**σπανάκι** 'spinach', perhaps from *spīna* 'thorn' via unattested *spīnāceum: no ancient examples. *LBG*, Meyer (1895: 62), Andriotis (1967).
	σπάρτουλα: see σπόρτουλον.
rare	**σπάτιον** 'circuit' (in a race), from *spatium* 'circuit': Malal. 7.4.52 (VI AD); Lyd. *Mens.* 1.12.58, marked (VI AD); Byzantine texts. Hofmann (1989: 412), *LBG*, Zervan (2019: 174), Sophocles (1887), Triandaphyllidis (1909: 123), Lampe (1961).
foreign	**σπεκιάλιος** 'particular', from *speciālis* 'particular': Antec. in Latin script 4.17.2 *specialias* (VI AD); later in Greek script. Zilliacus (1935a: 208–9), *LBG*. See §9.5.6 n. 68.
Direct loan **III AD – Byz.**	**σπεκλάριον, σφεκλάριον** (-ου, τό) 'transparent stone', 'window pane made of such stone', from (*lapis*) *speculāris* 'transparent stone'. Documents: *O.Bodl.* II.1997.4 (II/III AD); *O.Stras.* I.789.3 (II/III AD). Literature: Galen XIII.663.10 Kühn, marked (II AD); Cyran. 1.10.12 (II AD?); Zosimus alch., Berthelot and Ruelle 1888: 139.2 (III/IV AD); Orib. *Ecl.* 77.2 etc. (IV AD); Aëtius 2.53.1 etc. (VI AD); alchemist in *P.Holm.*, frag. 18.2 Halleux; *Hippiatr.Berl.* 82.4. Post-antique: survives. *LBG*. Notes: the mineral concerned was probably selenite or perhaps mica, not talc (*pace* LSJ). In medical texts this is a technical term and sometimes marked as Latin, used along with or instead of the Greek apparently because it aided comprehension. Forms derivative σφεκλαρᾶς. Fischer (2019), Husson (1972), Binder (2000: 159–60), Hofmann (1989: 412), LSJ, LSJ suppl. See §4.2.5, §10.2.1, §10.2.2 J.
	σπεκλάτωρ: see σπεκουλάτωρ.
Direct loan **III AD – Byz.**	**σπέκλον, σφέκλον** (-ου, τό) 'mirror', 'window pane', from *speculum* 'mirror'. Documents: *P.Wisc.* II.66.1 etc. (VI AD). Literature: Alexander Aphrodisiensis, *In librum de sensu commentarium* p. 29.7 Wendland (II/III AD); Basil Caesariensis, *Homiliae in hexaemeron* 3.4.48 Giet (IV AD); Dor.Gaz. *Doct.Div.* 3.40.23 (VI AD); Philoponus, *In Aristotelis libros de anima commentaria* p. 335.14 Hayduck, etc. (VI AD); Olympiodorus Philosophus, *In Platonis Gorgiam commentaria* 48.3.11 Westerink (VI AD); perhaps *Hippiatr.Berl.* 70.2, 130.150.

Post-antique: numerous. *LBG*.

Notes: Fischer (2019: 112–13) argues that the *Hippiatrica* examples do not come from this but from φαίκλα (*q.v.*) and that therefore LSJ's second definition (the mineral *lapis specularis*) is wrong. Forms derivative σπεκλοποιός. Husson (1972: 279–81), Binder (2000: 158–60), Daris (1991a: 106), Hofmann (1989: 412), Lampe (1961), LSJ (*s.vv.* σπέκλον, σφέκλον), LSJ suppl. (*s.vv.* σπέκλον, σφέκλον). See §4.2.4.1 n. 55, §10.2.1, §10.2.2 M.

rare **σπεκλοποιός** 'mirror-maker', from *speculum* 'mirror' via σπέκλον + -ποιός from ποιέω 'make': with *specularius* in Gloss. Ps.-Cyril. 435.37. LSJ.

Direct loan
I AD – Byz. **σπεκουλάτωρ, σπεκλάτωρ** (-ορος/-ωρος, ὁ), a military functionary whose duties changed over the course of the Empire ('executioner', 'officer in the immediate service of the general', 'member of the imperial bodyguard'), from *speculātor* 'scout'.

Documents: e.g. *P.Mich.* VIII.469.24 (II AD); *P.Bodl.* 166.11 etc. (III AD); *P.Oxy.* 3414.2 (IV AD); *P.Oxy.* 4910.3 (V AD); perhaps *P.Eirene* III.24.8 (VI AD).

Inscriptions: *I.Tomis* 327.2 (II/III AD); *I.Klaudiupolis* 19.10; *IGLS* VI.2980.2.

Literature: e.g. NT Mark 6:27 (I AD); *Martyrium Pauli* 5 = Lipsius 1891: 115.17 (II AD); *V.Secundi* 72.15 (II/III AD); Athan. *Apol.Sec.* 8.3 (IV AD); Chrysippus of Jerusalem, *Encomium in Joannem Baptistam* p. 45.23 Sigalas (V AD). Unverified examples (III AD) in Zilliacus (1937: 322–3, 334).

Post-antique: numerous. Zervan (2019: 175).

Notes: editor of *P.Bodl.* 166 *ad loc.*, Bartalucci (1995: 113–14), Binder (2000: 165), Daris (1991a: 106), Mason (1974: 4, 85), Hofmann (1989: 412–13), Zilliacus (1935a: 236–7, 1937: 334), Meinersmann (1927: 57), Lampe (1961), LSJ, LSJ suppl. See §4.2.5, §6.8, §9.3 n. 21, §10.2.1, §10.2.2 C.

non-existent? **σπεκούλιον** 'small mirror', from *speculum* 'mirror' + -ιον: perhaps papyrus *P.Cair. Goodsp.* 30.7.31 (II AD). Husson (1972: 281–2), Hofmann (1989: 412 *s.v.* σπέκλον), Meinersmann (1927: 57), LSJ.

rare **σπεκταβίλιος**, a rank, from *spectābilis* 'worthy of consideration': Just. *Nov.* 20.pr. etc., but in Latin script 20.pr. etc. (VI AD); Ath.Schol. in Latin script 4.4.1 etc. (VI AD); Byzantine texts. Koch (1903: 22), Avotins (1992), Hofmann (1989: 413), Zilliacus (1935a: 208–9), *LBG*, Lampe (1961), LSJ suppl.

foreign **σπεκτᾶτος** 'respected', 'worthy', from *spectātus* 'distinguished': inscription *CIL* III.7126.9, Latinate. Hofmann (1989: 413).

Direct loan
IV AD – Byz. **σπικᾶτον** (-ου, τό) 'embrocation of spikenard', apparently from neut. of *spīcātus* 'in a spike shape', eventually 'prepared with spikenard' (*DMLBS*).

Literature: Galen VI.427.4 Kühn etc., always marked (II AD); *Hippiatr.Par.* (Apsyrtus) 453 (III/IV AD?); Aëtius 6.56.26 etc. (VI AD); *Hippiatr.Camb.* 69.4.

Post-antique: survives in medical texts. *LBG* (*s.v.* σπικᾶτος).

Notes: Hofmann (1989: 413–14), LSJ (*s.v.* σπικᾶτα). See §4.2.4.1 n. 55, **§6.5**, §8.2.2, §10.2.1, §10.2.2 L.

not ancient **σπίνα** transliterating *spīna* 'thorn': interpolations in Dsc. 3.16 RV etc. Sophocles (1887).

foreign	**σπῖρα**, cake name from *spīra* 'coil': Athenaeus 14.647d, marked (II/III AD). Hofmann (1989: 414), LSJ (*s.v.* σπεῖρα 7, with Greek etymology).
	σπίτι: see ὁσπίτιον.
foreign	**σπόλιον** transliterating *spolium* 'spoils': Plut. *Marc.* 8.9 (I/II AD). Strobach (1997: 199), Hofmann (1989: 414), Sophocles (1887).
not ancient	**σπονσάλια** 'betrothal', from *spōnsālia* 'betrothal': no ancient examples. Zilliacus (1935a: 208–9).
not ancient	**σπόνσωρ** 'guarantor', from *spōnsor* 'guarantor': no ancient examples. Zilliacus (1935a: 208–9), *LBG*.
	σπόρδουλον: see σπόρτουλον.
not Latin	**σπόριον** is stated by Plut. *Mor.* 288f (I/II AD) to be a Sabine word for female genitalia. Strobach (1997: 200), Hofmann (1989: 415), LSJ.
	σπόριος: see σπούριος.
foreign	**σπόρτα** 'little basket', from *sporta* 'basket': Lyd. *Mens.* 12, marked (VI AD); later perhaps a real borrowing (*LBG*, Meyer 1895: 63). Σπορτία, perhaps 'for picnics', lemma in Hesych. σ 1559 (V/VI AD) with gloss ἑορτὴ ἀγομένη, may be a derivative.
not Latin?	**σπορτηληνοί**, probably an ethnic, perhaps from Latin: undated inscriptions *IGBulg.* IV.2232.2, 2233.3, 2234.3. Hofmann (1989: 415), LSJ.
	σπορτία: see σπόρτα.
Direct loan **IV AD – Byz.**	**σπόρτουλον, σπόρδουλον, σπάρτουλα, σπόρτυλλον** (mostly -ου, τό), a type of payment, from *sportula, -ae* 'dole given by patrons to their clients'. Documents: e.g. *P.Abinn.* 26.32 (IV AD); *P.Lond.* V.1703.2 (VI AD); *ChLA* XLI.1196.6 etc. (VI AD). Inscriptions: *SEG* LIII.1841.i.4 (V AD). Literature: John Chrysostom, *PG* LII.731.23 (IV/V AD); *ACO* II.I.III p. 26.14 (V AD); Geront. *V.Mel.* 2.52.26 (V AD); Hesych. as lemma σ 1560 (V/VI AD); Malal. 18.67 (VI AD); Just. *Nov.* 53.3.2 etc. (VI AD); Lyd. *Mag.* p. 226.11, marked (VI AD); Ath.Schol. 1.2.47 etc. (VI AD); Antec. in Latin script 4.6.24 *sportulon* etc. (VI AD); with *concussio* in glossaries, e.g. Gloss. *Herm.S.* 443.9. Post-antique: numerous. *LBG*, Triandaphyllidis (1909: 123). Notes: the inscriptional example is usually thought to be a separate word, σπορτοῦλα 'fee' (see *LBG* s.v. σπορτοῦλα and editors' accentuation of the gen. pl. σπορτουλῶν, which implies a feminine noun), but separation may not be justified: Feissel (2004: 683) accents the gen. pl. σπορτούλων, implying derivation from neuter σπόρτουλον. Di Segni *et al.* (2003: 281), Avotins (1992), Gignac (1981: 9), Daris (1991a: 106), Hofmann (1989: 411, 416), Zilliacus (1935a: 208–9, 1937: 334), Meinersmann (1927: 57), Immisch (1885: 357), LSJ. See §4.2.3.1, §10.2.1, §10.2.2 G.

Direct loan
II AD – Byz.

σπο(ύ)ριος (-α, -ον) 'bastard', 'false', from *spurius* 'son of an unknown father'.
Documents: *SB* 15704.65 (II AD); perhaps *P.Petaus* 71.20 (II AD); *P.Flor.*
1.5.16 (III AD); *P.Oxy.* 3347.2 (III AD); *SB* 14584.35 (III AD); *P.Cair.Masp.*
67097v.D46 (VI AD).
Literature: Plut. *Mor.* 288e, marked (I/II AD); Pall. *V.Chrys.* 96.15 (IV/V AD);
Antec. in Latin script 1.10.12 *spurius* (VI AD); old scholion to *Od.* 10.441.
Post-antique: numerous. *LBG.*
Notes: Binder (2000: 146–7), Daris (1991a: 106), Hofmann (1989: 415),
Zilliacus (1935a: 208–9), Meinersmann (1927: 57), Lampe (1961), LSJ. See
§4.2.2, §10.2.1, §10.2.2 N.

non-existent?

σταβλάριον 'little stable', from *stabulum* 'stable' via στάβλον: probably not papyrus
P.Oxy. 1676.38 (IV AD), which probably has a form of ταβλάριος. Rea
(1992), Daris (1991a: 107), Meinersmann (1927: 58), LSJ, LSJ suppl.

rare

σταβλησιανός, a type of soldier, perhaps from rare *stablēsiānī* (Forcellini *et al.*
1864–1926): inscription *SEG* VI.187.4 (IV AD); Byzantine texts. Hofmann
(1989: 416, citing one inscription twice), *LBG*, LSJ (*s.v.* Σταβλησιανοί).

Deriv. of loan
IV AD – modern

σταβλίτης, σταυλίτης (-ου, ὁ) 'stableman', from *stabulum* 'stable' via στάβλον +
-ίτης.
Documents: e.g. *O.Waqfa* 63.5 (IV AD); perhaps *P.Eirene* III.20.7 (V AD); *P.Erl.*
67.8 etc. (VI AD); *P.Oxy.* 140.7 etc. (VI AD).
Literature: perhaps Callin. *V.Hypat.* 38.10, spelled σταβλιστής (V AD); old
scholion to Ar. *Th.* 491 as gloss.
Post-antique: numerous. *LBG.* Modern σταβλίτης 'stable worker': Babiniotis
(2002).
Notes: forms derivative ἀρχισταβλίτης. Daris (1991a: 107), Hofmann (1989:
417 *s.v.* στάβλος), Cavenaile (1952: 193), Zilliacus (1935a: 236–7),
Meinersmann (1927: 58), Lampe (1961 *s.v.* σταβλιστής), LSJ, LSJ suppl. See
§4.6.1 n. 86, §4.6.2, §4.6.3, §10.2.2 K.

Direct loan
II AD – modern

στάβλον, στάβλος, σταῦλον, σταῦλος (-ου, τό or ὁ) 'stable', 'posting-station', from
stabulum 'stable'.
Documents: e.g. *O.Claud.* inv. 1538+2921.10 = Cuvigny 2005: 312 (II AD);
O.Did. 91.3 (II/III AD); *P.Eirene* III.18.4 (III AD); *P.Oxy.* 4441.4.10
(IV AD); *P.Gen.* IV.186.12 (V AD); *P.Oxy.* 3804.225 etc. (VI AD).
Inscriptions: Bean 1971: 18 no. 36.10 (I/II AD); *SEG* XXXIV.1437.5
(V/VI AD).
Literature: e.g. Philogelos 10 (IV AD); John Chrysostom, *PG* LXIV.1004a
(IV/V AD); Callin. *V.Hypat.* 38.10 (V AD); Hesych. as gloss κ 844
(V/VI AD); Malal. 16.6 (VI AD); scholion to Eur. *Or.* 1449 as gloss.
Post-antique: numerous, forming derivatives σταβλίζω 'stable', σταβλοκόμης
'marshall', etc. *LBG* (*s.vv.* στάβλον, στάβλος). Modern στάβλος 'stable' and
derivatives: Babiniotis (2002), Andriotis (1967), Meyer (1895: 63).
Notes: forms derivatives σταβλίτης, ἔκσταβλα. Husson (1983: 254–6), Binder
(2000: 188–9, 248), Menci (2000: 289), Daris (1991a: 107), Hofmann
(1989: 417), Zilliacus (1937: 334), Meinersmann (1927: 58), Lampe (1961
s.vv. στάβλος, σταῦλος, σταῦλον), LSJ, LSJ suppl. See §4.1.1 n. 10, §4.2.4.1
n. 55, §4.6.3, §8.2.3 n. 51, §10.1, §10.2.1, §10.2.2 K.

not ancient   **σταβουλάριος** 'stable-keeper', from *stabulārius* 'stable-keeper': no ancient examples. Hofmann (1989: 417), Viscidi (1944: 42), *LBG*.

not ancient   **στάπλον**, cited as a borrowing of medieval *stapulum* 'post', 'bar' (*DMLBS s.v. stapellus*) by Zilliacus (1935a: 208–9): no ancient examples.

rare   **στατάριον 1** 'candlestick' on papyrus *SB* 15301.2.6 (v/vi AD) is related to ἀστατάρια and Byzantine σταταραία; the whole word group probably comes from *statārius* 'stationary'. Diethart (1995a: 88–90), *LBG*.

not Latin?   **στατάριον 2** 'slave market' may come from *statārium* 'slave market' (attested, but not in lexica) but could have been created within Greek, perhaps from Latin elements. Inscriptions *MAMA* VI.260.4 (I BC); *I.Magnesia* 240 (I BC); *TAM* V.II.932.1; Robert and Robert (1977: 399 no. 422). Poccetti (1985, with discussion of the Latin), Coarelli (1982: 134–6), Diethart (1995a: 89–90), Cervenka-Ehrenstrasser (1996: 113–14), Hofmann (1989: 418), Cameron (1931: 259), LSJ.

στατιονάριος: see στατιωνάριος.

Direct loan   **στατίων** (-ωνος/-ονος, ἡ) 'station', 'military guardpost', 'meeting place',
II AD – Byz.   'association (esp. of foreigners)', 'office (of notaries)', 'period of fasting', from *statiō* 'station', 'military guardpost'.
Documents: e.g. *P.Aberd.* 78.4 (II AD); *O.Wilck.* 273.4 (III AD); *P.NYU* I.11a.69 (IV AD); *P.Stras.* VIII.719.14 (v/vi AD); *CPR* XXIII.33.11 etc. (VI AD).
Inscriptions: e.g. *IG* XIV.830.5 etc. (II AD); *I.Milet* III.1139.4 (II/III AD); *IGUR* I.84.4 (III AD); *IGUR* I.246.b23 (IV AD).
Literature: Hermas, *Pastor* 54.1, 2 Whittaker (II AD); Hesych. as gloss σ 2463 (v/vi AD); Just. *Nov.* 44.1.1 etc. (VI AD); bilingual glossaries, e.g. Gloss. Ps.-Philox. 138.12.
Post-antique: numerous. Sophocles (1887).
Notes: forms derivative στατιωνίζω. Hilhorst (1976: 168–79), Mohrmann (1979: 307–30), Drew-Bear (1972: 93), Avotins (1992), Daris (1991a: 107), Mason (1974: 85, 141), Hofmann (1989: 418–19), Zilliacus (1935a: 208–9, 236–7), Meinersmann (1927: 58), *DÉLG*, Beekes (2010), Lampe (1961), LSJ (*s.v.* στατιών), LSJ suppl. See §4.2.5, §10.2.1, §10.2.2 C.

Direct loan   **στατιωνάριος, στατιονάριος, ἰστατιώναρις** (-ου, ὁ) 'member of foreigners'
II AD – Byz.   association', 'constable', 'supervisor of road traffic', from *statiōnārius* 'member of a military detachment'.
Documents: common, e.g. *O.Claud.* I.69.2 (I/II AD); *O.Claud.* I.50.2 (II AD); *P.Ant.* II.87.8 (III AD); *P.Oxy.* 4371.5 (IV AD); *P.Oxy.* 4689.4 (V AD); *P.Mil.* II.71.2 (VI AD).
Inscriptions: e.g. *I.Beroia* 260.2 (II AD); *IG* XIV.830.22 etc. (II AD); *SEG* XVI.754.32 etc. (III AD).
Literature: *Martyrium Agapae etc.* 3.1 in Musurillo 1972 (IV AD?).
Post-antique: minimal survival. *LBG*.
Notes: *O.Claud.* I pp. 59–60, Bartalucci (1995: 114–15), Binder (2000: 225), Robert (1943: 113), Menci (2000: 289), Daris (1957: 101–3, 1991a: 107), Mason (1974: 4, 85), Hofmann (1989: 419), Zilliacus (1935a: 236–7), Meinersmann (1927: 58), *DÉLG* (*s.v.* στατιών), Beekes (2010 *s.v.* στατιών), Lampe (1961), LSJ (*s.v.* στατιών), LSJ suppl. See §4.2.4.1 n. 50, §10.2.1, §10.2.2 N.

rare	**στατιωνίζω, στατιωνείζω** 'be on duty', from *statiō* 'station' via στατίων + -ίζω: papyrus *P.Amh.* 11.80.12 (III AD); *Martyrium Agapae etc.* 4.3 in Musurillo 1972 (IV AD?). Classical στατίζω sometimes takes on the meaning of στατιωνίζω: *LBG*, LSJ (*s.v.* στατίζω). Daris (1991a: 107), Hofmann (1989: 419 *s.v.* στατιών), Meinersmann (1927: 58), *DÉLG* (*s.v.* στατίων), Lampe (1961), LSJ (*s.v.* στατιών).
Direct loan **VI AD – Byz.**	**στατοῦτος** (-η, -ον) 'fixed', 'determined', or as neut. subst. 'fixed amount', 'complement', 'statute', from *statūtus* 'appointed', 'fixed'. Literature: Just. *Nov.* 3.2.1 etc. (VI AD); Ath.Schol. 1.10 etc. (VI AD). Post-antique: numerous. *LBG*. Notes: Avotins (1992), Hofmann (1989: 419–20), Zilliacus (1935a: 210–11), Lampe (1961), LSJ suppl. See §4.2.2, §9.5.6 n. 68, §10.2.1, §10.2.2 B.
Direct loan **I BC – III AD**	**στάτωρ** (-ορος, ὁ), a position in the Roman army, from *stator* 'official messenger' (*OLD stator¹*). Documents: *BGU* XVI.2618.11 (I BC); *BGU* XVI.2671.21 (I BC/AD); *P.Oxy.* 3917.1 (II AD); *Rom.Mil.Rec.* 76.xvii.1 (II AD). Inscriptions: e.g. *OGIS* 665.23 (I AD); *SEG* VII.554.3 (II AD); *IGUR* I.131.6 (III AD); perhaps *IGBulg.* IV.1990.2 (see *SEG* XLV.880). Notes: forms derivative ἀρχιστάτωρ. Daris (1991a: 108), Mason (1974: 4, 6, 85), Hofmann (1989: 420), Meinersmann (1927: 58), LSJ. See §4.2.5, §6.8, §8.1.5, §10.2.1, §10.2.2 C.
foreign	**Στάτωρ** transliterating *Stator*, epithet of Jupiter (*OLD stator²*): Plut. *Rom.* 18.9, *Cicero* 16.3 (I/II AD). Sophocles (1887).
	σταυλ-: see σταβλ-.
not Latin	**σταφυλινάριον** on papyrus *P.Ryl.* IV.629.214 (IV AD) has been taken as a form of σταφυλινάριος, from unattested **staphylīnārius* 'carrot-seller', but is probably a diminutive in -άριον of σταφυλῖνος 'carrot'. Editor *ad loc.*, Hofmann (1989: 420), LSJ suppl.
	στέγαστρον: see σέγεστρον.
non-existent	**στειβάριος**, from unattested **stibārius* 'seller of antimony': superseded reading of inscription *MAMA* III.557.3. Hofmann (1989: 420), Lampe (1961).
	στελιον-: see στελλιον-.
not Latin?	**στελλάριον**, perhaps 'star-shaped object', perhaps from *stella* 'star' or a related word: papyrus *CPR* VIII.66.12 etc. (VI AD). Daris (1991a: 108, with tentative derivation from *stellāre*, neuter of *stellāris*, L&S), LSJ suppl.
not ancient	**στελ(λ)ιονᾶτον, στελ(λ)ιονάτους** 'deceit', from *stelliōnātus, -ūs* 'deceitful dealing': no ancient examples. Zilliacus (1935a: 210–11), *LBG*.
foreign	**στιπενδιάριος** 'tributary', from *stīpendiārius* 'paying tribute': Antec. in Latin script 2.1.40 *stipendariai* etc. (VI AD). Zilliacus (1935a: 210–11).
Direct loan **II AD – Byz.**	**στιπένδιον, στο(υ)πένδιον, ἱστοπένδιον** (-ου, τό) 'wages', 'year's service', from *stīpendium* 'wages', 'year of military service'. Documents: *P.Panop.Beatty* 2.55 etc. (III/IV AD); *CPR* VII.21.15 (IV AD); *P.Mich.* X.593.ii.1 etc. (IV AD); *P.Oxy.* 1047.2, 2561.16 (both IV AD).

Inscriptions: Bosch 1967: 136 no. 113.6 etc., 138 no. 115.4 (both I/II AD);
IGBulg. III.II.1741bis.ii.5, Latinate (III AD); *IGR* I.1089.3 (IV AD); *IGBulg.*
v.5129.7 (IV AD); Breccia 1911: 179 no. 364.3. But *Agora* XVII.1052.7
(II AD) is Latin in Greek script.

Post-antique: survives in legal texts. *LBG.*

Notes: Binder (2000: 225), Daris (1991a: 108), Mason (1974: 4, 85),
Hofmann (1989: 421), Meinersmann (1927: 58), LSJ suppl. See §4.2.4.1
n. 54, §8.2.2, §10.2.1, §10.2.2 C.

foreign   **στιπουλάνδος** 'stipulator', from (participle of?) *stipulor* 'exact a solemn promise':
Antec. in Latin script as part of *reoi stipulandoi* 'joint stipulators', e.g. 3.16.pr.
reon stipulandon (VI AD); later in Greek script. Triantaphyllides (1892: 273),
LBG. See §9.5.6 n. 68; cf. ῥέος.

rare   **στιπουλατίων** 'verbal agreement', from *stipulātiō* 'verbal guarantee': Thüngen
2016: A4 etc. (V AD); *Schol.Sinai.* in Latin script 4 *stipulatio[n]* (V/VI AD);
Antec. in Latin script 3.15.pr. *stipulation* (VI AD); Byzantine texts. Zilliacus
(1935a: 210–11), *LBG.* See §7.1.2, §9.5.6 n. 56.

foreign   **στιπουλᾶτον** 'verbal agreement', from *stipulātus, -ūs* 'stipulation': Antec. in Latin
script 3.15.3 *ex stipulatu* etc. (VI AD); Just. *Nov.* in Latin script 162.1.2 etc. (VI
AD); later in Greek script. Zilliacus (1935a: 210–11), *LBG.* See §9.5.6 passage
80 and n. 68.

rare   **στιχαροκαρακάλλιον** 'tunic with a hood', from στιχάριον 'tunic' + *caracalla* 'long
cloak with a hood' (*TLL*) via καρακάλλιον: papyrus *SB* 16649.4 (VI AD);
occasionally later. Mossakowska-Gaubert (2017: 338), *LBG.*

   στιχαρομαφόριον: see μαφόρτης.

   στιχαροφελώνιον, στιχαροφελόνιον, στιχαροφαιλόνιον: see φαινόλη.

non-existent   **στιχομαφόριον** is cited by Cavenaile (1952: 199) on the basis of *P.Princ.* II.82.39,
which actually has στιχαρομαφόριον (for which see μαφόρτης).

Direct loan   **στολᾶτος** (-α, -ον) (always with ματρῶνα 'matron') 'wearing a *stola*', i.e. matron
III–IV AD   with particular honour, from *stolāta* (*mātrōna*) 'matron granted particular
honours' (cf. *OLD s.v. stolātus* b).

Documents: e.g. *P.Oxy.* 907.4 (III AD); *P.Ryl.* II.165.9 (III AD).

Inscriptions: e.g. *SEG* VIII.703.4 (II/III AD); *I.Ephesos* 3072.9 (III AD); *TAM*
V.I.758.6 (III AD); *MAMA* X.358.2 (III/IV AD).

Notes: Cameron (1931: 250) treats *matrona stolata* as a unit, but in Greek it
probably was not: the order may vary (*P.Flor.* 1.16.1–2 has στολάτα ματρώνα),
and ματρῶνα also appears separately. Daris (1991a: 108), Hofmann (1989:
421), Meinersmann (1927: 59), LSJ suppl. (*s.v.* στολᾶτα). See §4.2.2,
§10.2.1, §10.2.2 D.

rare   **στομαχέω** is used for *stomachor* 'be angry' in *O.Krok.* I.99.9 (I/II AD); material
dubiously attributed to Dositheus, VII.432.14 Keil (IV AD?); some Byzantine
texts. Note also Hesych. δ 1681: διεστομαχίζετο· ἐλοιδόρησε, κακῶς εἶπεν (V/
VI AD). From IV AD it also occurs in the sense 'have a weak stomach' (not in
LSJ, but see Lampe 1961); this meaning is purely Greek but apparently later
than the Latinate sense. Commentary on *O.Krok.* I.99, Benveniste (1965: 7–8),
Gourevitch (1977), Hofmann (1989: 421), Frisk (1954–72: II.801–2), *LBG*, LSJ.

semantic extension

στόμαχος 'throat', 'stomach', a Greek word, sometimes means 'anger' under influence from *stomachus* 'bad temper': e.g. papyrus *P.Oxy.* 533.14 (II/III AD); Vet.Val. *Anth.* 5.4.61 (II AD). Its derivative στομαχώδης 'irascible' (*V.Aesopi* G 28 (II AD?)) has only the Latinate meaning. Benveniste (1965: 7–8), Gourevitch (1977), Hofmann (1989: 421), Frisk (1954–72: II.801–2), LSJ, LSJ suppl. (*s.v.* στομαχώδης).

στο(υ)πένδιον: see στιπένδιον.

not ancient

στουππί 'stopper' and **στουππώνω** 'stop up', from *stuppa* 'hemp' (itself from στύππη): no ancient examples. *LBG* (*s.vv.* στοῦππα, στουππίον, στουπόω), Meyer (1895: 63).

rare

στοῦπρον 'illicit sex', from *stuprum* 'illicit sex': Just. *Codex* 5.4.29.8 (VI AD); Ath.Schol. in Latin script 9.3.4 (VI AD); later legal texts. Avotins (1989), Hofmann (1989: 421), Zilliacus (1935a: 210–11), *LBG*, Lampe (1961), LSJ suppl.

non-existent?

στράγλον 'coverlet', from *strāgulum* 'coverlet': cited as an ancient loan by Zilliacus (1935a: 210–11), but I can find no examples. Στραγλίον is Byzantine: *LBG*, Binder (2000: 195).

Direct loan
II AD – modern

στρᾶτα (-ας, ἡ) '(paved) street', from (*via*) *strāta* 'paved road', pf. part. of *sternō* 'spread'.

Documents: *P.Theon.* 7.3 (II AD); *CPR* XVIIA.18.2 (IV AD).

Inscriptions: *SEG* XXXVII.496.4 (IV/V AD); perhaps others.

Literature: *Test.Sal.* p. 113.14 (III AD?); Ps.-Macar. *Serm.* 3.2.1 (V AD?); Orion, *Etymologicum* σ p. 150.29 Sturz, marked (V AD, but this entry probably comes from Philoxenus, I BC); Callin. *V.Hypat.* 20.1 (V AD); *Apophth.Patr.* 2.33.1 (V AD); Hesych. as gloss γ 467 (V/VI AD); Barsanuph.Jo. II.II ep. 570c.66 (VI AD); Procop. *Bell.* 2.1.7, marked (VI AD); Ps.-Basil Caesariensis, *Homilia de virginitate* 3.51 Amand and Moons; scholion to Eur. *Hec.* 281 as gloss.

Post-antique: common. Zervan (2019: 176), Sophocles (1887), Triandaphyllidis (1909: 123). Modern στράτα, στρατί 'street' and derivatives: Babiniotis (2002), Andriotis (1967), Meyer (1895: 63–4, 14 *s.v.* βία).

Notes: Daris (1991a: 108), Hofmann (1989: 422), Meinersmann (1927: 59), Lampe (1961), LSJ suppl. See §4.2.3.1, §10.2.1, §10.2.2 J.

Direct loan
I AD – Byz.

στράτωρ (-ορος, ὁ), groom on staff of Roman officer and an imperial dignitary, from *strātor* 'groom'.

Documents: perhaps O.Claud. inv. 1538+2921.7 = Cuvigny 2005: 312, 336–7 (II AD); *O.Did.* 84.8 (III AD); *CPR* X.57.8, 64.5 (both VI AD).

Inscriptions: *OGIS* 628.1 (I AD); *SEG* XVI.810.5 (III AD); Grégoire 1909: 66 no. 45.2 (III AD?); *IGBulg.* III.II.1692.3; perhaps *SEG* XLV.880.2; Laminger-Pascher 1992: no. 143.2; perhaps *SEG* XXXVI.1269.

Literature: scholion to Thuc. 5.15.1.

Post-antique: numerous, forming derivative πρωτοστράτωρ 'chief *strator*'. *LBG*, Zervan (2019: 176–7).

Notes: forms derivative ἀρχιστράτωρ. Commentary on *OGIS* 628, Daris (1991a: 108, citing only a superseded reading), Mason (1974: 4, 6, 87), Hofmann (1989: 422), Zilliacus (1935a: 236–7), Lampe (1961), LSJ, LSJ suppl. See §4.2.5, §6.8, §10.2.1, §10.2.2 C.

rare	**στρήνα** 'new year's gift', from *strēna* 'new year's gift': papyrus *P.Iand.* VI.94.30 (II/III AD); Athenaeus 3.97d, marked (II/III AD); Lyd. *Mens.* 4.4, marked (VI AD). Daris (1991a: 108), Hofmann (1989: 422), Cavenaile (1951: 400), Sophocles (1887), Andriotis (1974: 516), Meyer (1895: 64), LSJ.
not Latin?	**στρίγλα** is argued by Meyer (1895: 64, cf. Andriotis 1967) to be two separate Latin loans. In the sense 'currycomb' (not attested in antiquity) it may come from *strigula* (L&S), diminutive of *strigilis* 'strigil'. In the sense 'monster' (old scholion to Aelius Aristides, Παναθηναϊκός 102.5.8: cf. LSJ suppl.) it may come from a different (and unattested) **strigula*, diminutive of *striga* 'evil spirit'. Binder (2000: 196, 260).
	στρίγξ: see στρίξ.
rare	**στρικτόν**, a kind of shoe, from *strictus* 'compact': as gloss in scholion to Luc. *Rh.Pr.* 15. LSJ, Hofmann (1989: 423 *s.v.* στρικτός), Triandaphyllidis (1909: 122).
rare	**στρικτόριον** 'top course of stonework on a wall', apparently from *strictōrium* 'string' (Souter 1949): Hesych. as gloss σ 2005 (V/VI AD). Hofmann (1989: 423), LSJ.
rare	**στρικτός** 'strict', 'literal', from *strictus* 'strict': Antec. in Latin script 4.6.30 *stricton* etc. (VI AD); with *strigōsus* 'lean' in Gloss. Ps.-Cyril. 438.60. Zilliacus (1935a: 210–11), LSJ; for Byzantine and modern use *LBG*, Andriotis (1974: 517).
rare	**στρικτωρία**, a garment, from *strictōria* 'shirt with long sleeves' (L&S): Edict.Diocl. 22.7 etc. (IV AD). Hofmann (1989: 423–4), LSJ suppl.
not Latin?	**στρίξ, στρίγξ** 'owl' may come from *strīx* 'owl', or *vice versa*. Hofmann (1989: 423), *DÉLG* (*s.v.* στρίγξ), Frisk (1954–72: II.810), Beekes (2010), *LBG*, LSJ.
rare	**στρούκτωρ, στρώκτωρ** 'waiter', from *strūctor* 'waiter': Athenaeus 4.170e, marked (II/III AD); Zosimus alch., Berthelot and Ruelle 1888: 138.7, marked (III/IV AD); Eusebius of Alexandria, *PG* LXXXVI.1.444c (V AD); papyrus *P.Oxy.* 2480.40 (VI AD). Daris (1991a: 108), Hofmann (1989: 424), *LBG* (*s.v.* στρώκτωρ), Lampe (1961), LSJ suppl.
rare	**στρουκτώριον** perhaps 'dining room' and if so related to *strūctor* 'waiter': inscription *CID* IV.148.4 (I AD). Editor *ad loc.*, Hofmann (1989: 425, with derivation from unattested **strūctōrium* related to *strūctōrius* 'of building', L&S), LSJ.
	στρουμέντον: see ἰνστρουμέντον.
	στρώκτωρ: see στρούκτωρ.
not Latin?	**στύβη**, apparently a coarse fibre, perhaps from *stuppa* 'coarse flax or hemp': Hesych. as gloss φ 661 (V/VI AD). Hofmann (1989: 425), *LBG*, LSJ.
	συγγεστίων: see σουγγεστίων.
Deriv. of loan **II–V AD**	**συγκελλάριος, συνκελλάριος** (-ου, ὁ) 'comrade', 'sharing a room', evidently the equivalent of *contubernālis* 'tent-mate', 'comrade', probably from σύν 'with' + *cella* 'room' via κέλλα + -άριος. Documents: *O.Claud.* 1.143.7 (II AD); *O.Did.* 447.8 (II AD).

Inscriptions: *IG* x.ii.i.443.3 (ii/iii AD); *I.Smyrna* 417.3 (iii–v AD); *TAM* ii.107.

Notes: derivation via σύγκελλος unlikely on chronological grounds. Derived by Hofmann (1989: 425) from unattested *concellārius*. Filos (2010: 251), LSJ. See §4.6.2, **§6.1**, §10.2.2 N.

not ancient	**συγκέλλιος** 'cellmate', from *cella* 'room' via σύγκελλος: no ancient examples. Daris (1991a: 108), *LBG*.
Deriv. of loan **V AD – modern**	**σύγκελλος, σύνκελλος** (-ου, ὁ), ecclesiastical title, from σύν 'with' + *cella* 'room' via κέλλα. Documents: *P.Berl.Zill.* 14.21 (VI AD). Inscriptions: perhaps *I.Chr.Asie Mineure* 1.47.b (VI AD). Literature: *ACO* i.i.v p. 9.24 etc. (V AD); *ACO* ii.i.ii p. 20.4 etc. (V AD); Cyr.S. *Vit.Sab.* 193.16, 195.9 (VI AD). Post-antique: common, forming derivative πρωτοσύγκελλος 'first *syncellus*'. Lampe (1961), Sophocles (1887). Modern σύγκελ(λ)ος, ecclesiastical title: Babiniotis (2002), Andriotis (1967). Notes: Filos (2010: 244, 251), Daris (1991a: 108), Hofmann (1989: 167 *s.v.* κέλλη). See §4.6.2, §10.2.2 N.
rare	**συγκολλήγας, συνκολλήγας** 'colleague', from σύν 'with' + *collēga* 'colleague' via κολλήγας: papyri perhaps *P.Oxy.* 3917.4 (II AD); perhaps *P.Princ.* iii.132.5 etc. (II AD); *SB* 14379.29 and *P.Col.* vii.188.26 etc., which are duplicates (both IV AD). Filos (2010: 251), Daris (1991a: 108), LSJ suppl.
rare	**συγκουρατορεύω, συγκουρατωρεύω** 'act as joint guardian', from *cūrātor* 'guardian' via συγκουράτωρ + -εύω (or, less probably, via σύν 'with' + κουρατορεύω): Antec. 1.24.1 (VI AD); Byzantine legal texts. *LBG*.
rare	**συγκουράτωρ** 'joint guardian', a calque of *concūrātor* 'joint guardian' made from σύν 'with' + *cūrātor* 'guardian' via κουράτωρ: Antec. 1.24.1 (VI AD); Byzantine legal texts. *LBG*.
	συγκουρατωρεύω: see συγκουρατορεύω.
not ancient?	**συγκουστουδιάζω** 'watch together', from *custōdiō* 'protect': Ps.-John Chrysostom, *PG* lx.684.49. Binder (2000: 222), Lampe (1961).
rare	**συλληγατάριος** 'joint legatee', a calque of *collēgātārius* 'joint legatee' formed from σύν 'with' + *lēgātārius* 'recipient of a legacy' via ληγατάριος: Antec. 2.20.23 etc. (VI AD); often in Byzantine legal texts. Hofmann (1989: 425), *LBG*. See §9.5.6 n. 68.
	συμβετέρανος: see συνουετρανός.
	συμσέλιον: see συμψέλλιον.
rare	**συμφιβλόω** 'pin together', from σύν 'with' + *fībula* 'pin' via φιβλόω: Hesych. as gloss σ 2329, but in a context suggesting that the prefix may have been added spontaneously and only the base verb was already known to readers: συμπεπερονημένους· συμπεφιβλωμένους, συρραφέντας περόνη (V/VI AD). *LBG*, LSJ (*s.v.* συμφιβλόομαι).
	συμψειρικός: see συψειρικός.

Direct loan with influence **I AD – Byz.**	**συμψέλ(λ)ιον, συψέλ(λ)ιον, συνψέλιον, συμσέλιον, συμψίλιον, σεμσέλιον, σεμψέλ(λ)ιον, σενσέλιον** (-ου, τό) 'bench', from *subsellium* 'low seat' with influence from συν-. Documents: e.g. *BGU* XVI.2669.1.17 (I BC/AD); *P.Petaus* 34.17 (II AD); *P.Michael.* 18.3.10 (III AD); *Chrest.Wilck.* 135r.37 (V/VI AD); *P.Cair.Masp.* 67006v.89 (VI AD). Inscriptions: *I.Ephesos* 3065.12 (I AD); perhaps *I.Ephesos* 4134.27 (VI AD); *TAM* V.II.1101.9; *TAM* II.210.A3; perhaps Petersen and Luschan 1889: 29 no. 39. Literature: Hermas, *Pastor* 9.4 Whittaker etc. (II AD); *Acta Thomae* 49 = Bonnet 1903: 165.19 (III AD); Epiph. *Pan.* II.358.23 (IV AD); Athan. *H.Ar.* 56.1 (IV AD); *Anthologiae Graecae Appendix* 31.2; with *scamnum* in *Glossarium Leidense, CGL* III.418.46. Post-antique: survives. *LBG* (*s.v.* σουβσέλιον), Sophocles (1887 *s.v.* συψέλλιον). Notes: Cameron (1931: 235) suggests influence from σελίς 'block of seats in a theatre' or ψαλίς 'vault'. Wilhelm (1928b: 231–2), Daris (1991a: 109), Hofmann (1989: 426), Cavenaile (1951: 403), Viscidi (1944: 8), Meinersmann (1927: 59), Lampe (1961), LSJ (*s.v.* συμψέλια). See §4.2.4.1 n. 54, §4.4, §8.2.2, §10.2.1, §10.2.2 M.
rare	**συνακουμβίζω** 'join in reclining', from σύν 'with' + *accumbō* 'recline' (via ἀκκουμβίζω?): Nil. 3.92.8 (V AD). Hofmann (1989: 13 *s.v.* ἀκουμβίζω), Lampe (1961). **συνβετ(ε)ρανός**: see συνουετρανός.
non-existent?	**συνδουπλικάριος** 'fellow *duplicarius*', from σύν 'with' + *duplicārius* 'soldier receiving double pay' via δουπλικάριος: perhaps ostracon *O.Claud.* 1.144.6 (II AD).
not Latin	**συνθηκάριος** 'schemer', suggested by Hofmann (1989: 426) as from unattested **synthēcārius*, is probably a Greek formation from συνθήκη 'agreement' + -άριος. *LBG*, Lampe (1961). **συνκ-**: see συγκ-.
Deriv. of loan **II–III AD**	**συνουετρανός, συμβετέρανος, συνβετ(ε)ρανός** (-οῦ, ὁ) 'fellow veteran', from σύν 'with' + *veterānus* 'veteran' via οὐετερανός. Documents: *BGU* I.327.4 (II AD). Inscriptions: perhaps Ruppel 1930: 3 no. 2.7 (I–III AD); *IGBulg.* III.II.1834.7. Literature: Modestinus in Just. *Dig.* 27.1.8.6 (III AD). Post-antique: some survival in legal works. *LBG* (*s.v.* συμβετράνος). Notes: Filos (2010: 251), Daris (1991a: 109), Mason (1974: 90), LSJ (*s.vv.* συνβετρανός, συνουετρανός), LSJ suppl. (*s.v.* συμβετέρανος). See §4.6.2, §9.5.6 nn. 55 and 58, §10.2.2 C. **συνψειρικός**: see συψειρικός. **συνψέλιον**: see συμψέλλιον.
not ancient?	**σύσκουτον** 'wall of shields', from σύν 'with' + *scūtum* 'large shield': probably no ancient examples. Zilliacus (1935a: 234–5), *LBG*.

not Latin?   **συφετώριον**, a piece of kitchen equipment on unpublished papyrus P.Vindob. G 29.938 (VI AD), is suggested as a Latin borrowing by Diethart and Grassien (2004: 95–6).

rare   **συψ(ε)ιρικός, σουψειρικός, συνψειρικός, συμψειρικός, συψηρικός** 'partly silk', from *subsēricus* 'half silken' (L&S): Edict.Diocl. 22.8 etc. (IV AD). Hofmann (1989: 411), *LBG* (s.v. συψηρικός), LSJ suppl. (replacing LSJ s.v. συψειρικόν).

    συψέλ(λ)ιον: see συμψέλλιον.

    συψηρικός: see συψειρικός.

    σφεκλαράριος: see σφεκλαρᾶς.

rare   **σφεκλαρᾶς** (formerly read as σφεκλαράριος) 'glazier' on inscription *SEG* VII.197.3 (V/VI AD) is probably from (*lapis*) *speculāris* 'transparent stone' via σπεκλάριον + -ᾶς, but it has also been derived from *speculum* 'mirror' via σπέκλον, from *speculārius/speculār(i)ārius* 'mirror-maker', and from unattested **speclarārius*. Robert (1965: 339–42), Drew-Bear (1972: 93–4), Hofmann (1989: 427), *DÉLG*, Beekes (2010), LSJ suppl. (replacing LSJ σφεκλαράριος s.v. σπεκλάριον).

    σφεκλάριον: see σπεκλάριον.

    σφέκλη: see φαίκλα.

    σφέκλον: see σπέκλον.

not ancient   **σφογγᾶτον** 'sponge cake' or 'omelet', perhaps from an unattested **sphongātum* related to *spongia* 'sponge': no ancient examples. Hofmann (1989: 427), *LBG*, Lampe (1961).

not Latin   **σχισματάριος** 'schismatic' in Pall. *V.Chrys.* 99.20 (IV/V AD) may come from unattested **schismatārius* but is probably a Greek combination of σχίσμα (gen. σχίσματος) 'division' + -άριος. Hofmann (1989: 427), *LBG*, Lampe (1961).

not ancient?   **σχολὰ ἀρματούρων** is cited by Hofmann (1989: 427) as a borrowing of *schola armātūrārum* 'college of arms' on the basis of σχολῆς ἀρματούρω⟨ν⟩ on inscription *ILS* 8883.2. Cf. ἀρματοῦρα.

Direct loan V AD – Byz.   **σχολάριος** (-ου, ὁ) 'one of the imperial guards', from *scholāres* 'imperial guards' (L&S).
      Inscriptions: perhaps *MAMA* I.280.6 (IV/V AD); *CIG* 8869.2; *MAMA* VIII.225; *CIG* 9227.4; *I.Prusias* 120.4; perhaps *I.Prusias* 126.5; perhaps *SEG* XXXVII.1076.3.
      Literature: e.g. Nil. 1.162.1 (V AD); *V.Dan.Styl.* A. 75.19 (V AD); Malal. 15.13.18 (VI AD); Just. *Nov.* 30.7.2 (VI AD); Cyr.S. *Vit.Sab.* 128.18 (VI AD).
      Post-antique: common. Sophocles (1887).
      Notes: Hofmann (1989: 428), Zilliacus (1937: 334), LSJ, LSJ suppl. See §4.2.5, §10.2.1, §10.2.2 A.

semantic extension?   **σχολεῖον** 'place for sitting or resting' is etymologically Greek but may be influenced by *schola* 'circular area with benches'. Drew-Bear (1972: 224), LSJ suppl. (replacing LSJ).

σχολή: see σχολὰ ἀρματούρων.

σωβρικομαφόρτης: see σουβρικομαφόρτης.

σωδᾶλις: see σοδᾶλις.

σωδάριον: see σουδάριον.

Direct loan
III AD – Byz.

σωλάριον, σολάρ(ι)ον (-ου, τό) 'sun terrace', from *sōlārium* 'sun terrace'.
   Inscriptions: e.g. *I.Ephesos* 2200B.iii.3 (III AD); *I.Ephesos* 2222.1 (III AD); *I.Smyrna* 212.3 etc.
   Literature: Just. *Codex* 8.10.12.5 (VI AD); Zilliacus (1937: 334) cites an undated example.
   Post-antique: survives. *LBG*.
   Notes: Drew-Bear (1972: 225), Hofmann (1989: 428), Zilliacus (1935a: 208–9, 1937: 334), *DÉLG*, LSJ suppl. (replacing LSJ). See §4.2.4.1 n. 54, §10.2.1, §10.2.2 J.

σωλέα: see σολέα.

non-existent?

σωλύτος perhaps on papyrus *P.Flor.* III.284.9 (VI AD) could come from *solitus* 'usual' or *solūtus* 'loose'. Sijpesteijn (1991b), Daris (1991a: 109), Zilliacus (1935a: 208–9), Meinersmann (1927: 59–60).

T

Direct loan
I–III AD

ταβέλλα (-ης, ἡ) 'writing tablet', 'note', from *tabella* 'tablet'.
   Documents: e.g. *P.Hamb.* I.29.23 (I AD); *Chrest.Mitt.* 91.i.11 etc. (II AD); *PSI* IV.293.31 (II/III AD); *P.Oxy.* 3108.1 (III AD).
   Notes: Daris (1991a: 109), Mason (1974: 91 *s.v.* ταβούλη), Hofmann (1989: 429), Meinersmann (1927: 60), *DÉLG*, Beekes (2010), LSJ. See §4.2.3.1, §6.13, §9.2, §10.2.1, §10.2.2 M; cf. ταβούλη.

Direct loan
II–III AD

ταβελλάριος (-ου, ὁ) 'secretary', 'financial administrator', 'courier', from *tabellārius* 'clerk', 'courier'.
   Documents: e.g. perhaps *O.Did.* 53.5 (I AD); *O.Claud.* IV.896.2 (II AD); *BGU* XIII.2355.3 (II/III AD).
   Inscriptions: e.g. Waelkens 1986: 236 no. 606.1 (II/III AD); *I.Ephesos* 2222B.4 (III AD?); *IG* V.II.525.3; *SEG* IV.594.3 etc.
   Notes: some papyrus examples may instead come from a neuter ταβελλάριον: Diethart (1999: 182 *s.v.* ταβλάριον). Daris (1991a: 109), Mason (1974: 4, 6, 90–1), Hofmann (1989: 429), Zilliacus (1935a: 210–11), Meinersmann (1927: 60), *DÉLG* (*s.v.* τάβελλα), Beekes (2010 *s.v.* τάβελλα), LSJ, LSJ suppl. See §4.2.4.1 n. 50, §10.2.1, §10.2.2 N; cf. ταβλάριος.

Direct loan
IV AD – Byz.

ταβελλίων (-ωνος/-ονος, ὁ) 'notary', from *tabelliō* 'one who draws up legal documents'.
   Documents: e.g. *P.Oxy.* 3758.136 etc. (IV AD); *P.Stras.* I.1.15 (V AD); *P.Cair. Masp.* 67150.5 (VI AD).
   Literature: Ath.Schol. 14.3.5, 14.P.1 (VI AD); Procop. *Arc.* 28.6, marked (VI AD); Antec. in Latin script 3.23.pr. *tabellionos* (VI AD).
   Post-antique: numerous. *LBG*, Zervan (2019: 177–8), Triandaphyllidis (1909: 127).

Notes: Daris (1991a: 109), Hofmann (1989: 429), Zilliacus (1935a: 210–11), Meinersmann (1927: 60), *DÉLG* (*s.v.* τάβελλα), Beekes (2010 *s.v.* τάβελλα), LSJ. See §4.2.5, §10.2.1, §10.2.2 B.

Direct loan
II AD – modern

ταβέρνα (-ης/-ας, ἡ) 'shop', 'stall', from *taberna* 'shop'.
Inscriptions: *SEG* xxxiii.1123.26 (iii AD).
Literature: as part of place name in NT Acts 28:15 (i AD); Scaevola in Just. *Dig.* 20.1.34.1 (ii AD); Hesych. as lemma derived from the biblical passage, τ 11b (v/vi AD); commentaries on the biblical passage.
Post-antique: numerous. Triandaphyllidis (1909: 123). Modern ταβέρνα 'tavern': Babiniotis (2002), Andriotis (1967).
Notes: forms derivatives ταβέρνιον, ταβερνοδύτης. Hemer (1989: 156), Danker *et al.* (2000), Leclercq (1997: 300), Mason (1974: 12), Immisch (1885: 365), *LBG*, Meyer (1895: 64), LSJ suppl. See §4.6.1 n. 84, §8.2.3 n. 51, **§9.3**, §10.2.1, §10.2.2 J.

foreign

ταβερναρία transliterating (*fābula*) *tabernāria*, a kind of Latin comedy (from *tabernārius* 'common', L&S): Lyd. *Mag.* p. 62.3, 6 (vi AD). *LBG*.

rare

ταβερνάριος 'shopkeeper', from *tabernārius* 'shopkeeper': inscription *MAMA* iii.311.4; perhaps *I.Aphrodisias Late Ant.* 147.b (iii AD?); tachygraphy in Menci 2000: 290 (v AD). Menci (2000: 290), Hofmann (1989: 429), Triandaphyllidis (1909: 124), Andriotis (1967 *s.v.* ταβερνάρης), Meyer (1895: 64, ταβερνάρις and ταβερναρᾶς *s.v.* ταβέρνα), LSJ suppl.

Deriv. of loan
IV AD – modern

ταβέρνιον (-ου, τό) 'small shop', 'stall', from *taberna* 'shop' via ταβέρνα + -ιον.
Documents: *P.Ryl.* iv.627.293, 630/637.293 etc. (both iv AD).
Inscriptions: *SEG* xxxvii.496.2 (iv/v AD); probably *IGLS* iv.1260.2.
Literature: Hesych. as lemma τ 11 (v/vi AD).
Post-antique: survives. *LBG* (*s.v.* ταβερνεῖον). Modern ταβερνεῖον: Andriotis (1967).
Notes: Daris (1991a: 109), Immisch (1885: 365), LSJ suppl. See §4.6.1 n. 84, §8.2.3 n. 51, §10.2.2 J.

rare

ταβερνοδύτης 'one who dives into taverns', from *taberna* 'shop' via ταβέρνα + δύτης 'diver': with *ganeo* in Gloss. *Herm.Mp.* 336.1–2. LSJ.

Direct loan
I AD – modern

τάβλα, τάβλη (-ης, ἡ) 'tablet', 'label', 'dice-board', 'mummy label', from *tabula* 'board' (with variant *tabla*: Forcellini *et al.* 1864–1926).
Documents: *BGU* iv.1079.29 (i AD); *O.Did.* 441.10 (ii AD); *Chrest.Wilck.* 499.5, 460.15 (both ii AD); *P.Oxy.* 2924.6 (iii AD); *SB* 4514 (iii AD); *P.Fam.Tebt.* 49.B.2.6 (iii AD).
Inscriptions: *SEG* xxxv.1157.6 (ii AD); *SEG* xx.375.15 (iv AD); Edict.Diocl. 7.41 (iv AD); *I.Ephesos* 556.1.
Literature: Eus. *HE* 5.18.11 (iv AD); Hesych. as gloss π 2071 (v/vi AD); Malal. 5.9.35 (vi AD); *Anthologia Graeca* 9.482.27 (vi AD); *Acta Andreae et Matthiae* 3 = Bonnet 1898: 68.6; with *tabula* in Gloss. Ps.-Cyril. 450.60.
Post-antique: numerous. *LBG*, Zervan (2019: 178), Sophocles (1887). Modern τάβλα 'board', 'low table': Babiniotis (2002), Andriotis (1967), Meyer (1895: 64–5).

Notes: Gignac (1981: 8) considers τάβλον a variant spelling of this. Forms
derivatives ταβλίον, ταβλίζω, ταβλοπάροχος, ταβλιόπη. Binder (2000: 191–
3), Biville (1992: 235), Daris (1991a: 109), Hofmann (1989: 430), Viscidi
(1944: 37–8), Meinersmann (1927: 60), *DÉLG*, Beekes (2010), Lampe
(1961), LSJ. See §4.6, §4.6.1, §8.2.3 n. 51, §10.2.1, §10.2.2 M; cf. ταβούλη.

ταβλάρηος: see ταβλάριος.

ταβλάριον: see ταβουλάριον.

Direct loan
II AD – Byz.

ταβλάριος, ταβουλ(λ)άριος, ταβλάρηος (-ου, ὁ) 'registrar', 'notary', 'archivist',
from *tabulārius* 'book-keeper' and/or *tabellārius* 'book-keeper'.

Documents, spelled ταβουλ(λ)άριος: e.g. *PSI* IV.281.39 (II AD); *P.Köln* III.163.11
etc. (III AD); *P.Oxy.* 3411.3 (IV AD); *P.Oxy.* 3148.2 (V AD); *P.Wash.Univ.* 1.6.1
etc. (VI AD).   Spelled ταβλάριος: *P.Turner* 23.20 (II AD); *SB* 11612.12
(II AD); *P.Diog.* 5.15 (II AD); *ChLA* XI.466.16 (II AD).

Inscriptions, spelled ταβουλ(λ)άριος: e.g. *SEG* XLIV.553.2 (II/III AD); Bosch
1967: 286 no. 222.10 (III AD); *MAMA* III.161 (IV–VI AD); *I.Ephesos*
1138.8.   Spelled ταβλάριος: e.g. perhaps *MAMA* IV.53.10, bilingual (I AD);
I.Ephesos 1564.7, bilingual (II AD); *I.Ephesos* 651.16, bilingual (II AD); *IG*
X.II.1.471.B3 (III AD); *I.Ephesos* 3054.9 (III AD).

Literature, always spelled ταβουλάριος: Eusebius, *De martyribus Palaestinae*
(rec. brev.) 9.2 Bardy (IV AD); Pall. *V.Chrys.* 19.19 (IV/V AD); *ACO* I.I.III
p. 19.19, 33 (V AD); Nil. 2.214.1 (V AD); Just. *Nov.* 1.2.1 etc. (VI AD);
Ath.Schol. 5.5.5 etc. (VI AD); Antec. 1.11.3 (VI AD); old scholion to
Demosthenes 24.330: τὸν δημόσιον· τὸν ἀπογραφόμενον τὰ δημόσια, ὥσπερ
νῦν λέγομεν ταβουλάριον; with *tabularius* in Gloss. Ps.-Cyril. 451.2.

Post-antique: numerous, forming derivative ταβουλαρικός 'of a notary'. *LBG*
(*s.v.* ταβουλλάριος), Triandaphyllidis (1909: 127), Sophocles (1887 *s.v.*
ταβουλάριος).

Notes: most scholars prefer derivation from *tabulārius*, but Beekes suggests
tabellārius at least for the spelling ταβλάριος. Forms derivative ἀρχιταβλάριος.
Avotins (1992 *s.v.* ταβουλάριος), Binder (2000: 193), Drew-Bear (1972: 94),
Daris (1991a: 110), Hofmann (1989: 430–1), Zilliacus (1935a: 210–11),
Meinersmann (1927: 60), *DÉLG* (*s.v.* τάβλα), Beekes (2010 *s.v.* τάβλα),
Lampe (1961 *s.v.* ταβουλάριος), LSJ, LSJ suppl. See §4.2.4.1 n. 50, §10.2.1,
§10.2.2 N; cf. ταβελλάριος.

τάβλη: see τάβλα.

Deriv. of loan
IV AD – Byz.

ταβλίζω, ταυλίζω 'play dice', from *tabula* 'board' via τάβλα + -ίζω.

Literature: Philogelos 190 (IV AD); EphraemSyr. IV p. 80.10 (V/VI AD);
Hesych. as gloss κ 4368, ε 4460, π 2074 (V/VI AD); Malal. 5.9.32 (VI AD);
Just. *Nov.* 123.10.1 (VI AD); Ps.-Nonnus 4.62.2 in Nimmo Smith 1992
(VI AD); Ath.Schol. 1.2.20 (VI AD); Gloss. Ps.-Cyril. 450.61.

Post-antique: numerous. *LBG*, Sophocles (1887).

Notes: said by Binder (2000: 191–2) to be borrowed back into Latin as *tablisso*
and therefore to be very early (ζ>ss only in Republican era), but Latin is
poorly attested (L&S). Forms derivatives ταβλιστήριον, ταβλιστής. Avotins
(1992), Hofmann (1989: 430 *s.v.* ταβλα), Zilliacus (1935a: 210–11), *DÉLG*
(*s.v.* τάβλα), Beekes (2010 *s.v.* τάβλα), Lampe (1961 *s.v.* ταυλίζω), LSJ. See
§4.6, §4.6.1, §9.2, §10.2.2 O.

Deriv. of loan
III AD – modern

ταβλίον, ταυλίον (-ου, τό) 'tray', 'shell', 'stripe sewn on border of garment', from *tabula* 'board' via τάβλα + -ιον.

Documents: perhaps *P.Lond.* 11.191.14 (II AD); *P.Lond.* 111.964.11 (II/III AD); *P.Oslo* 11.46v.19 (III AD); *P.Fay.* 104.4 (III AD); *P.Mich.* XIV.684.12 (V/VI AD).

Literature: Malal. 2.8.35 etc. (VI AD); Lyd. *Mag.* p. 104.2: ὁ δὲ μανδύης χλαμύδος εἶδός ἐστι τὸ παρὰ τῷ πλήθει μαντίον λεγόμενον, μὴ πλέον ἄχρι γονάτων ἐξ ὤμων ἠρτημένον, σηγμέντων οὐκ ἐπιβαλλομένων τῷ μανδύῃ, τῶν ⟨δ'⟩ ἐν ἡμῖν λεγομένων ταβλίων, ἀντὶ τοῦ πτυχίων (VI AD); scholion to *Od.* 1.107b as gloss; perhaps with *vannus* in Gloss. Serv. 517.7.

Post-antique: numerous, with additional meanings. *LBG*, Sophocles (1887). Modern τάβλι 'backgammon': Babiniotis (2002), Andriotis (1967), Meyer (1895: 64–5).

Notes: Binder (2000: 191–2), Daris (1991a: 109), Hofmann (1989: 430 *s.v.* ταβλα), Cavenaile (1952: 195), Meinersmann (1927: 60), *DÉLG* (*s.v.* τάβλα), Lampe (1961), LSJ. See §4.6.1 n. 84, §8.2.3 n. 51, §10.2.2 M.

rare

ταβλιόπη 'game of dice' in *Anthologia Graeca* 11.373.2 (IV AD) is a pun made by combining τάβλα (from *tabula* 'board') with Καλλιόπη. Hofmann (1989: 430 *s.v.* ταβλα), *DÉLG* (*s.v.* τάβλα), Beekes (2010 *s.v.* τάβλα), LSJ.

rare

ταβλιστήριον 'gaming house', from *tabula* 'board' via ταβλίζω + -τήριον: old scholion to Aeschines 1.53.9: κυβεῖον λέγεται ὁ τόπος ἔνθα συνέρχονται οἱ κυβεύοντες, ὃ νῦν καλοῦσί τινες ταβλιστήριον. Binder (2000: 192), Hofmann (1989: 430 *s.v.* ταβλα), *DÉLG* (*s.v.* τάβλα), *LBG*, LSJ.

rare

ταβλιστής, ταυλιστής 'dice-player', from *tabula* 'board' via ταβλίζω + -της: Hesych. as gloss ε 7368 (V/VI AD); Gloss. Ps.-Cyril. 450.62; Byzantine lexicographers repeating Hesychius' entry. Binder (2000: 191–2), *DÉLG* (*s.v.* τάβλα), *LBG*, LSJ.

not ancient

ταβλοδόχος 'person who allows dice-playing in his house', from *tabula* 'board' via τάβλα + δοχός 'containing': no ancient examples. Hofmann (1989: 430 *s.v.* ταβλα), Viscidi (1944: 38), *LBG*.

ταβλοειδής: see ταυλοειδῶς.

rare

τάβλον, perhaps 'tray', probably from *tabula* 'board': papyri *BGU* 1.338.8 (II/III AD); *SB* 14533.5 (VI AD); perhaps *P.Ness.* III.18.29 (VI AD); perhaps *SB* 4924.2 (IV–VII AD). Daris (1991a: 109), Gignac (1981: 8, considering this a variant spelling of τάβλα), Herrmann (1985: 254 n. 13, suggesting the first example could be τάβλα), Meinersmann (1927: 60), LSJ.

rare

ταβλοπαρόχιον 'room for dice-tables', from *tabula* 'board' probably via ταβλοπάροχος + -ιον: Malal. 13.38 (VI AD). Binder (2000: 192), Hofmann (1989: 430 *s.v.* ταβλα), Lampe (1961).

rare

ταβλοπάροχος, perhaps 'keeper of a gaming house' and if so from *tabula* 'board' via τάβλα + πάροχος 'provider': Gloss. Ps.-Cyril. 451.1. Probably source of ταβλοπαρόχιον. Binder (2000: 192), Hofmann (1989: 430 *s.v.* ταβλα), Sophocles (1887), LSJ.

ταβλοτόν: see ταβλωτός.

not ancient?	**τάβλωμα, ταύλωμα** 'balcony' (?), from *tabula* 'board' probably via τάβλα: as gloss in scholia to Ar. *Eq.* 675b, *V.* 386c. Binder (2000: 192), Hofmann (1989: 430 *s.v.* ταβλα), *LBG*, LSJ.
rare	**ταβλωτός, ταυλωτός** 'boarded', from *tabula* 'board' (via τάβλα?) + -ωτός: as gloss in scholion to Ar. *V.* 349b; Byzantine texts. Probably the same word as **ταβλοτόν** 'with a stripe' on papyrus *P.Heid.* VII.406.11 (IV/V AD). Commentary on *P.Heid. ad loc.*, Binder (2000: 192), Hofmann (1989: 430 *s.v.* ταβλα), *LBG*, LSJ.
rare	**ταβουλάριον, ταβλάριον** 'archives', from *tabulārium* 'registry': papyri *SB* 11043r.16 (II AD); *P.Oxy.* 2116.10 (III AD); perhaps *P.Oxy.* 1676.38 (IV AD); perhaps inscription *MAMA* VII.524.3 (but that could be a form of ταβουλάριος). Diethart (1999: 182), Rea (1992), Daris (1991a: 110), Hofmann (1989: 430), Cavenaile (1951: 400), *LBG* (*s.vv.* ταβλάριον, ταβουλαρία), LSJ suppl.
	ταβουλάριος: see ταβλάριος.
rare	**ταβούλη** 'account book' on inscription *IGUR* III.1294.5 (II AD) = *Anthologiae Graecae Appendix* 293.4 = 715.4 must come from either *tabula* 'board' (in which case it would be a variant of τάβλα) or *tabella* 'tablet' (in which case it would be a variant of ταβέλλα). Binder (2000: 193), Mason (1974: 91, preferring the latter etymology), *LBG* (*s.v.* ταβούλα).
	ταβουλλάριος: see ταβλάριος.
foreign	**τάκιτος** transliterating *tacitus* 'silent': Plut. *Numa* 8.6 (I/II AD). Strobach (1997: 200).
Direct loan **II–IV AD**	**ταλάριον** (-ου, τό) 'sandal fastened at the ankles', from *tālāria*, neut. pl. of *tālāris* 'of the ankles'. Documents: *P.Mich.* VIII.476.8 (II AD); *CPR* VIII.10.6 (II/III AD); *P.Dura* 33.6 (III AD); perhaps *PSI* IX.1082.19 (IV AD). Literature: *Coll.Herm.* C 55b (II–IV AD). Notes: distinct from ταλάριον 'small basket' (LSJ, *LBG*), which also occurs in papyri. Cf. Isidore, *Etymologiae* 19.34.7: *talares calcei socci sunt, qui inde nominati videntur quod ea figura sunt ut contingant talum*. Daris (1991a: 110). See §2.3, §4.2.5, §9.2, §10.2.1, §10.2.2 H.
non-existent	**ταξαμέντον:** cited as a loan by Triantaphyllides (1892: 274) on the basis of Just. *Nov.* 72.6, where λαξαμέντον (*q.v.*) is now read.
rare	**ταξατίων** 'sum fixed by a judge', from *taxātiō* 'assessment': Just. *Nov.* 53.2 (VI AD); Ath.Schol. in Latin script 5.4.1 (VI AD); with meaning 'garrison' in Byzantine texts. Avotins (1992), Hofmann (1989: 431), Zilliacus (1935a: 210–11), *LBG*, Sophocles (1887), Triandaphyllidis (1909: 130), Lampe (1961).
rare	**ταξᾶτος** from *taxātus*, pf. part. of *taxō* 'assess': basically a Byzantine term meaning 'regular soldier', but apparently also papyrus *P.Iand.* II.9.33 (II AD). Daris (1991a: 110), Hofmann (1989: 431), Meinersmann (1927: 60), *LBG*, Sophocles (1887), Triandaphyllidis (1909: 129), Lampe (1961), LSJ.

rare   τάξος (ἡ) 'yew tree', from *taxus* (fem.) 'yew tree': Dsc. 4.79, marked (I AD); Galen XII.127.1 Kühn (II AD); Orib. *Col.* 9.16.3 (IV AD); Hesych. as lemma τ 160 (V/VI AD). Hofmann (1989: 432), LSJ.

     ταυλίζω: see ταβλίζω.

     ταυλίον: see ταβλίον.

     ταυλιστής: see ταβλιστής.

not ancient?   ταυλοειδῶς 'in the form of a tablet', from *tabula* 'board' via τάβλα + -ειδής (cf. εἶδος 'form') + -ως: alchemist, Berthelot and Ruelle 1888: 325.7. LSJ suppl. (*s.v.* adj. ταβλοειδής, which is not directly attested). See §10.3.1.

     ταύλωμα: see τάβλωμα.

     ταυλωτός: see ταβλωτός.

     ταυρειν-: see ταυριν-.

     ταυρινάδαι: see ταυρινᾶς.

rare   ταυρινᾶς, ταυρεινᾶς (gen. -άδος) 'shoemaker', from *taurīnus* 'made of oxhide' via ταυρίνη + -ᾶς: inscriptions *I.Ephesos* 2080.6, 2081.1; *MAMA* VI.234.a2 (all III AD). Hofmann (1989: 433 *s.v.* ταυρίνη), *DÉLG* (*s.v.* ταῦρος), LSJ suppl. (replacing LSJ *s.v.* ταυρινάδαι), and for the -ᾶς nouns in papyri more generally Olsson (1925).

not Latin?   ταυρίνδα, a game, cited as a possible Latinism by Hofmann (1989: 433): Hesych. as lemma τ 249 (V/VI AD). LSJ.

rare   ταυρίνη, ταυρείνη, a kind of shoe, from *taurīna* 'ox-leather shoe' (Souter 1949) from *taurīnus* 'made of oxhide': Edict.Diocl. 9.15 etc. (IV AD). Probably source of ταυρινᾶς. Hofmann (1989: 433), *DÉLG* (*s.v.* ταῦρος), Frisk (1954–72: II.860), Beekes (2010 *s.v.* ταῦρος), LSJ.

     τείρων: see τίρων.

not ancient?   τειρωνολογέω 'recruit for the army', from *tīrō* 'recruit' via τίρων + λέγω 'gather': inscription *IGBulg.* II.517.ii.2. LSJ suppl.

     τέμβλον: τέμπλον.

not ancient?   τεμπεράτωρ 'moderator', from *temperātor* 'one who exercises a moderating control': probably no ancient examples. Zilliacus (1935a: 210–11).

rare   τέμπλον, τένπλον, τέμβλον, from *templum* 'temple'. Meaning 'temple': tachygraphy in Menci 2000: 290 (III AD); Romanus Melodus, *Cantica* 44.6.8 Grosdidier de Matons (VI AD); *Passio Bartholomaei* 1 = Bonnet 1898: 130.14. Meaning uncertain: inscription *I.Cilicie* 24.6 (V/VI AD); Hesych. τ 464 (V/VI AD); cf. Immisch (1885: 359). Meaning a church furnishing: Byzantine texts. Modern τέμπλο, τέμπλος: Babiniotis (2002), Andriotis (1967), Meyer (1895: 65). Different uses may be unrelated. Editor of *I.Cilicie ad loc.*, Binder (2000: 247), Menci (2000: 290), Hofmann (1989: 433), Viscidi (1944: 37), *LBG*, Lampe (1961), LSJ suppl.

foreign	**τεμποράλιος** 'temporary', from *temporālis* 'temporary': Lyd. *Mag.* p. 106.20, marked (VI AD); Antec. in Latin script 4.13.10 *temporaliu* etc. (VI AD); Byzantine texts. Zilliacus (1935a: 210–11), *LBG*.
	τένπλον: see τέμπλον.
not ancient	**τέντα** 'tent', from *tentus*, pf. part. of *tendō* 'stretch out': no ancient examples. Daris (1991a: 110), Viscidi (1944: 17), Zilliacus (1935a: 236–7), Meinersmann (1927: 60), *LBG*, Zervan (2019: 181, dating the borrowing to VII AD), Andriotis (1967), Meyer (1895: 65).
not ancient	**τέντριον**, cited by Daris (1991a: 110) as from *tentōrium* 'tent': no ancient examples.
foreign	**Τερεντῖνον**, cake name, probably from unattested cake name **Terentīnum* from place name *Tarentum* or personal name *Terentius*: Athenaeus 14.647c, marked (II/III AD). Hauri-Karrer (1972: 125). See §9.4 passage 61.
	τερματική: see δελματική.
foreign	**Τερμινάλια** transliterating *Terminālia*, a festival: DH *AR* 2.74.3 (I BC); Plut. *Mor.* 267c (I/II AD). Strobach (1997: 200), Hofmann (1989: 433).
foreign	**τέρμινας** transliterating acc. pl. of *termen* 'boundary': DH *AR* 2.74.3 (I BC). **Τέρμινον**, apparently transliterating acc. sing.: Plut. *Mor.* 267c (I/II AD). Sophocles (1887 *s.vv.* τέρμινες, τέρμινος), Hofmann (1989: 433–4 *s.v.* τέρμινες).
non-existent?	**τέρμου**, meaning uncertain, perhaps from *termen* 'boundary': perhaps papyrus *BGU* 11.473.10 (III AD), but see Wilcken (1924: 84 n. 2). Hofmann (1989: 434), Meinersmann (1927: 60), Wessely (1902: 148–9).
rare	**τερτιανός** 'third', of military units, from *tertiānus* 'of the third': inscription *I.Pan du désert* 51.4 (I AD). *LBG*.
rare	**τερτιοδέλματος** 'of the third regiment of Dalmatians', from *tertius* 'third' and *Dalmatae/Delmatae* 'Dalmatians': Just. *Edict* 4.2.pr. = p. 762.9 etc. (VI AD); perhaps inscription Sartre 1993: no. 50.8 (V AD). Avotins (1992), *LBG* (*s.v.* τερτιοδαλματεῖς).
rare	**τερτιοκήριος**, an official, from *tertiōcērius* 'functionary of the third rank' (L&S): Just. *Codex* 4.59.1.1 (VI AD); occasional Byzantine texts. Hofmann (1989: 434), Zilliacus (1935a: 236–7), *LBG*, Triantaphyllides (1892: 274), Triandaphyllidis (1909: 127), LSJ.
rare	**τέρτιος** 'third', of military units, from *tertius* 'third': ostracon *SB* 14180.66 etc. (II AD); Antec. in Latin script 2.14.6 *tertion* etc. (VI AD). Daris (1991a: 110), Zilliacus (1935a: 210–11), *LBG*.
Direct loan I AD – Byz.	**τεσ(σ)αράριος, τεσ(σ)εράριος, τεσ(σ)αλάριος, θεσ(σ)αλάριος, τεσσαράλιος, θεσσάριος, θασσαλάριος**, etc. (-ου, ὁ), military officer who receives and distributes the watchword, also a civilian role, from *tesserārius* 'soldier who circulates the *tessera* with the password'. Documents: e.g. *O.Petr.Mus.* 142.1 (I AD); *O.Claud.* IV.708.3 (I/II AD); *O.Krok.* 1.94.3 (II AD); *P.Oxy.* 43r.2.21 etc. (III AD); *P.Oxy.* 4344.4 (IV AD); *SB* 15801.4 etc. (V AD); *CPR* XXIV.16.1 (V/VI AD).

Inscriptions: e.g. *SEG* XXVI.1853 (I AD); *I.Kibyra* 106.15, bilingual (II AD); perhaps Frye *et al.* 1955: 163 no. 61.3 (III AD).

Literature: Plut. *Galba* 24.1 (I/II AD); Lyd. *Mag.* p. 72.13, marked (VI AD).

Post-antique: minimal survival. *LBG* (*s.v.* τεσσεράριος), Triandaphyllidis (1909: 125 *s.v.* θεσσάριος).

Notes: probably a separate borrowing in phrase τεσσαράρια πλοῖα 'dispatch-boats' on Latinate inscription *IG* XII.V.II.941.5 (I BC). Triandaphyllidis (1909: 107) suggests that spelling θεσσάριος is influenced by θέσις. Forms derivative προτεσσαράριος. Daris (1991a: 110), Mason (1974: 5, 92), Hofmann (1989: 434), Viscidi (1944: 37), Meinersmann (1927: 60–1), Gignac (1976: 104), LSJ, LSJ suppl. See §4.2.4.1 n. 50, **§4.4**, §6.1, §10.2.1, §10.2.2 C.

non-existent **τεσσεδᾱρις**, from *tesserārius* via τεσσαράριος conflated with *essedārius* via ἐσσεδάριος: superseded reading of inscription *SEG* II.555 = *I.Mylasa* 532.2. Cameron (1931: 260), LSJ.

τεσσεράριος: see τεσσαράριος.

foreign **τεσταμεντάριος** 'appointed in a will', from *testāmentārius* 'of wills': *Schol.Sinai.* in Latin script 40 *testamentariōn*, 50 *testamentarian* (V/VI AD); Just. *Nov.* in Latin script 118.5 (VI AD); Antec. in Latin script 1.13.5 *testamentarion* etc. (VI AD); later in Greek script. Zilliacus (1935a: 210–11), *LBG*. See §7.1.2, §7.1.3, §9.5.6 nn. 56 and 68.

non-existent? **τεσταμεντάτωρ** 'maker of a will', from *testātor* 'maker of a will': cited as an ancient loan by Zilliacus (1935a: 212–13) and Viscidi (1944: 28) on the basis of Antec. in Latin script 1.24.pr. (VI AD), which is probably an error for *testatoros*, from τεστάτωρ (cf. Triantaphyllides 1892: 274).

foreign **τεσταμεντιφακτίων** 'right of being involved in a will' (as heir, testator, or witness), from *testāmentī factiō* 'making of a will': Antec. in Latin script 2.10.6 *testamentifactiona* etc. (VI AD); later in Greek script. *LBG*. See §9.5.6 n. 68.

foreign **τεσταμέντον** 'will', from *testāmentum*: Antec. in Latin script 1.5.3 *testamento* etc. (VI AD); later in Greek script. Hofmann (1989: 434), Zilliacus (1935a: 210–11), *LBG*. See §9.5.6 n. 68.

Direct loan VI AD – Byz. **τεστάτωρ** (-ορος, ὁ) 'maker of a will', from *testātor* 'maker of a will'.

Literature: Just. *Nov.* 18.t etc., but in Latin script 117.1.1 (VI AD); Ath.Schol. 9.1.2, but in Latin script 9.1.5 etc. (VI AD); Antec. in Latin script 1.15.pr. *testatoros* etc. (VI AD).

Post-antique: very common in legal texts.

Notes: Avotins (1992), Hofmann (1989: 435), Zilliacus (1935a: 212–13), Triantaphyllides (1892: 274), Lampe (1961), LSJ suppl. See §4.2.5, §7.1.1, §9.5.6 n. 68, §10.2.1, §10.2.2 B.

rare **τετραμόδιον** 'vessel holding four pecks', from τετρα- 'four' + *modius* 'peck' via μόδιος: Malal. 11.14 (VI AD); occasionally later. *LBG*, Lampe (1961). See §4.6.2.

non-existent **τετρᾱντα**, superseded reading of Hesych. lemma τ 630 (V/VI AD), is claimed by Immisch (1885: 317) to contain *as* 'penny'.

non-existent	**τετραντίας**, superseded reading of Hesych. lemma τ 629 (v/vi ad), is suggested by Immisch (1885: 317) to contain *as* 'penny'. LSJ.
Deriv. of loan VI AD – Byz.	**τετραξεστιαῖος** (-ον) 'holding four pints', from τετρα- 'four' + *sextārius* 'pint measure' via ξεστιαῖος. Documents: *P.Rein.* 11.102.5 (v/vi ad); *P.Cair.Masp.* 67314.1.13 (vi ad). Literature: Philoponus, *In Aristotelis Physicorum libros commentaria* vol. xvii p. 506.9 Vitelli (vi ad). Post-antique: some survival. Notes: not attested in feminine, but form suggests that it would be two-termination. Filos (2010: 244, 251), Daris (1991a: 110), *LBG*. See §4.6.2, §4.6.3, §10.2.2 E.
Deriv. of loan II AD, VI AD – Byz.	**τετραούγκιον, τετραούγγιον, τετρούγκιον** (-ου, τό) 'four ounces', 'four twelfths', 'one third of an inheritance', or a coin, from τετρα- 'four' + *uncia* 'one twelfth' via οὐγγία. Inscriptions: *SEG* xliv.760.3A (cf. xlix 1294), on a weight (ii ad); Cantacuzène 1932: 607, on a weight. Literature: Just. *Codex* 6.4.4.27 etc., *Nov.* 18.1 etc. (vi ad); Ath.Schol. 9.2 (vi ad); with *triens* in Gloss. Ps.-Cyril. 454.17. Post-antique: numerous. *LBG*. Notes: the vi ad examples have a different meaning and are probably a new formation. Avotins (1989, 1992), Hofmann (1989: 302 *s.v.* οὐγκία), LSJ (*s.vv.* τετραούγκιον, τετρούγκιον), LSJ suppl. See §4.6.2, §8.2.1, §10.2.2 G.
rare	**τετράσσαρον** 'fourpence', from τετρα- 'four' + *assārius* (*nummus*) 'penny' via ἀσσάριον: Epict. *Diss.* 4.5.17 (i/ii ad); Ps.-Galen, *De ponderibus* frag. 60.3 = Hultsch 1864: 234.9; Byzantine texts. Hofmann (1989: 37 *s.v.* ἀσσάριον), *LBG*, LSJ. See §4.6.2.
semantic extension	**τέτριξ**, a Greek term normally designating a bird: with *trīstis* 'unhappy' in *Glossae Bernenses* (*CGL* iii.504.53), probably by influence of *tetricus* 'severe'. Hofmann (1989: 435), LSJ. See §2.3 n. 58.
	τετρούγκιον: see τετραούγκιον.
not Latin	**τήβεννα, τήβεννος** 'toga' (with derivative τηβεννικός) does not resemble any Latin word; *DÉLG* suggests an Etruscan source. Famerie (1998: 183), Dubuisson (1985: 51), Mason (1974: 92), Hofmann (1989: 435), Immisch (1885: 339), Frisk (1954–72: 11.890), Beekes (2010), *LBG* (*s.vv.* τήβαινα, τηβαινομανία, τηβεννοφορέω, τηβεννοφόρος), LSJ.
	τήρων: see τίρων.
	τήτλος: see τίτλος.
name	**Τίβερις** 'Tiber', from *Tiberis* 'Tiber'. Hofmann (1989: 435).
foreign	**τίγνον** 'plank' (as the topic of a legal action), from *tignum* 'plank': Antec. in Latin script 2.1.29 *tignu* etc. (vi ad); occasionally later in Greek script. Zilliacus (1935a: 212–13), *LBG*.
	τίθλος: see τίτλος.
	τιλλάριον: see τιτλάριον.

foreign   **τίνα** transliterating *tīna*, a kind of wine jar: Alex.Trall. 1.327.18 (VI AD).
    Hofmann (1989: 436), LSJ.

    τιπλοκάριος: see δουπλικάριος.

Direct loan   **τίρων, τείρων, τήρων, τιρόνης, τιρώνης** (-ωνος/-ονος/-ου, ὁ) 'recruit', from *tīrō*
II AD – Byz.   'recruit'.
    Documents: e.g. *Rom.Mil.Rec.* 74.2.11 etc. (II AD); *P.Wisc.* I.29r.21 (III/IV AD);
     P.Oxy. 4373.2 (IV AD); *P.Oxy.* 2001.4 (V AD); *P.Oxy.* 2480.105 (VI AD).
    Inscriptions: e.g. *I.Ephesos* 43.30, bilingual (IV AD); *SEG* XXIV.1218.2
     (IV/V AD).
    Literature: Dor.Poet. *Visio* 43 (III/IV AD); Ps.-Macar. *Serm.* 14.13.1 etc.
     (V AD?); Lyd. *Mag.* p. 6.11 etc. (VI AD). Unverified examples (II and
     III AD) in Zilliacus (1937: 322–3, 334).
    Post-antique: survives. Sophocles (1887), Triandaphyllidis (1909: 129).
    Notes: forms derivative τιρωνικόν. Daris (1991a: 110 *s.v.* τιρόνης, 111 *s.v.*
     τίρων), Mason (1974: 4, 93), Hofmann (1989: 436), Zilliacus (1935a: 147,
     236–7, 1937: 334), Meinersmann (1927: 61), Lampe (1961), LSJ (*s.vv.*
     τίρων, τείρων), LSJ suppl. See §4.1.1, §4.2.5, §10.2.1, §10.2.2 C.

Direct loan   **τιρωνᾶτον, τιρωνᾶτος** (-ου, τό or ὁ) 'body of recruits', from *tīrōnātus, -ūs* 'state of
IV–V AD   a recruit' (L&S).
    Documents: *P.Oxy.* 3424.9 (IV AD); unpublished papyrus cited by LSJ (IV
     AD); *PSI* XIII.1366.7 (IV/V AD).
    Inscriptions: perhaps *SEG* XXXVIII.1706.4.
    Literature: *Carth.* 339.1 (V AD). Unverified example (II AD) in Zilliacus
     (1937: 322, 334).
    Notes: LSJ *s.v.* τιρωνᾶτος considers it masculine, but in *PSI* is neuter and in
     other examples ambiguous. Triandaphyllidis (1909: 130) may indicate
     attestation after V AD. Diethart (2006: 14), Daris (1991a: 111), Hofmann
     (1989: 436), Zilliacus (1937: 334), Lampe (1961 *s.v.* τιρωνᾶτος). See
     §4.2.4.2, §10.2.1, §10.2.2 C.

    τιρώνης: see τίρων.

rare   **τιρωνικόν** 'tax to provide recruits' pay', from *tīrō* 'recruit' via τίρων + -ικός in
     neut. subst.: Syn.Cyr. *Ep.* 79 (IV/V AD). Hofmann (1989: 436 *s.v.* τίρων),
     Sophocles (1887 *s.v.* τιρωνικός), Lampe (1961).

rare   **τιτλάριον, τιλλάριον**, a kind of writing tablet, from *titulus* 'inscription' via τίτλος +
     -άριον: Epict. *Diss.* 3.22.74 (I/II AD); inscription *SEG* XXXV.1475.8.7 etc.
     (VI AD). Hofmann (1989: 437 *s.v.* τίτλος), *LBG*, LSJ (*s.v.* τιτλάρια). See §6.3
     n. 21.

Direct loan   **τίτλος, τίθλος, τίτ(ο)υλος, τήτλος, τύτλος**, or **-ον** (-ου, ὁ or ἡ or τό) 'title',
I AD – modern   'inscription', 'notice', 'tattoo', 'mark', 'section', 'tax', from *titulus* 'title',
     'inscription', 'section'.
    Documents: e.g. perhaps *P.Stras.* VI.546.8 (II AD); *P.Lips.* I.62.ii.10 etc.
     (IV AD); *SB* 17260.6 etc. (V AD); *P.Oxy.* 1887.10 (VI AD).
    Inscriptions: common, e.g. Bosch 1967: 94 no. 98.ii.63 (II AD); *I.Histria*
     291.14 (III AD); *IG* II/III².I.1121.26 etc. (IV AD); *SEG* VI.291.8 (V AD);
     perhaps Marek 1993: 182, Appendix 5 no. 100.A18 (VI AD).

Literature: common, e.g. NT John 19:19 (I AD); Galen XVIIIB.599.4 Kühn (II AD); *Ev.Barth.frag.* 1.16–17 (III AD); Nil. 2.81.5 (V AD); Hesych. as lemma τ 990 (V/VI AD); Malal. 18.67 (VI AD); Just. *Nov.* 2.3 (VI AD); Antec. 1.19.pr. (VI AD); often in commentary/discussion on the biblical passage. Unverified example (IV AD) in Zilliacus (1937: 322, 334).

Post-antique: common, forming derivative τιτλοποιέω. *LBG* (*s.vv.* τίτλος, τίτουλος), Triandaphyllidis (1909: 123), Sophocles (1887). Modern τίτλος 'title' and derivatives: Babiniotis (2002), Andriotis (1967), Meyer (1895: 65).

Notes: separated by Lampe (1961) into two words, τίτλον 'mark' and τίτλος 'inscription', 'notice', 'tombstone', 'accord', 'letter', 'heading', 'section', 'title', 'variant'; LSJ suppl. sees one word. Forms derivatives παράτιτλον, τιτλάριον, τιτλόω, ὑπότιτλος. Binder (2000: 182–3), Avotins (1989, 1992), Daris (1991a: 111), Hofmann (1989: 437–8), Zilliacus (1935a: 212–13, 1937: 334), Meinersmann (1927: 61), Immisch (1885: 357), *DÉLG*, Beekes (2010), LSJ, LSJ suppl. See §4.2.4.1 n. 51, §4.6.2, §7.1.2, §8.2.3 n. 51, §9.3 n. 21, §9.5.6 n. 56, §10.2.1, §10.2.2 O, §12.2.1.

rare **τιτλόω**, from *titulus* 'title' via τίτλος + -όω: Malal. 10.20.19, meaning 'mark for confiscation' (VI AD); scholia to Hermogenes (Anonymi in Hermogenem, *Commentarium in librum* περὶ στάσεων VII.676.24), meaning 'tattoo (a slave)'; Byzantine example meaning 'title (a book)'. The variety of meanings suggests multiple independent derivations from τίτλος. Hofmann (1989: 437 *s.v.* τίτλος), *DÉLG* (*s.v.* τίτλος), *LBG*, Triandaphyllidis (1909: 128), Lampe (1961), LSJ.

τίτυλος: see τίτλος.

rare **τόγα** 'toga', from *toga* 'toga': DH *AR* 3.61.1, marked (I BC); inscription *I.Hadrianoi Hadrianeia* 1.8 (II AD); Eutropius 1.17, marked (IV AD); Proclus Constantinopolitanus, *Homilia in natalem diem domini* 49 Constas (V AD); Malal. 2.8.31 (marked), 18.45 (VI AD); Lyd. *Mag.* p. 4.13 etc., usually marked (VI AD); with *abolla* in Gloss. Ps.-Philox. 4.20. Byzantine τόγα 'tiara', 'turban' is probably a different word, from Persian (*LBG*, Sophocles 1887). Mason (1974: 93), Hofmann (1989: 438), Lampe (1961), LSJ suppl. See §2.2.3.

rare **τογατηφόρος** 'toga-wearing', from *toga* 'toga' or *togātus* 'toga-wearing' + -φορος (cf. φορέω 'wear'): Lyd. *Mag.* p. 52.7 (VI AD). *LBG*.

foreign **τογᾶτος** transliterating *togātus* 'toga-wearing', in fem. subst. a type of drama: Strabo 3.2.15 (I BC/AD); Ptol. *Geog.* 3.1.42 (II AD); Dio Cassius 46.55.5 etc. (II/III AD); Lyd. *Mag.* p. 62.3 etc. (VI AD). Freyburger-Galland (1997: 36, 218, 1998: 138), Mason (1974: 93), Hofmann (1989: 438), *LBG*.

τολάριον: see τοράλλιον.

τοορμάριος: see τουρμάριος.

rare **τοπιάριος** 'ornamental gardener', from *topiārius* 'ornamental gardener': inscriptions *TAM* v.1.524.5 (II AD); *TAM* v.1.53.1. Hofmann (1989: 438), LSJ suppl.

rare   **τοράλ(λ)ιον, τωράλ(λ)ιον, τολάριον** 'bedspread', from *toral/torāle* 'bedspread': inscriptions *SEG* VII.371.i.8 (II AD); perhaps *SEG* VII.417.10 (III AD); ostracon *O.Douch.* II.169.6 (IV/V AD). Daris (1991a: 113 *s.v.* τωράλιον), Hofmann (1989: 439), *DÉLG*, Beekes (2010), *LBG* (*s.v.* τωράλιον), LSJ (*s.vv.* τοράλλιον, τολάριον).

foreign   **τορκουᾶτος, τουρκουᾶτος** transliterating *torquātus* 'wearing a collar or necklace': e.g. inscription *SEG* LXV.1408.C25 (V/VI AD); Lyd. *Mag.* p. 70.25 (VI AD). More often a proper name. Strobach (1997: 200), *LBG*.

     τόρμα, τόρμη: see τοῦρμα.

not ancient?   **τοῦβα** 'trumpet', from *tuba* 'trumpet': probably no ancient examples. Zilliacus (1935a: 236–7), *LBG*.

not ancient?   **τουβάτωρ** 'trumpeter', from medieval *tubātor* 'trumpeter' (*DMLBS*): probably no ancient examples. Zilliacus (1935a: 236–7), *LBG*.

foreign   **τουβίκινες, τούβικες** transliterating pl. of *tubicen* 'trumpeter': inscription *SEG* LXV.1408.C19 etc. (V/VI AD); Lyd. *Mag.* p. 70.15 (VI AD). *LBG*.

not ancient   **τοῦβλον, τούβουλον** 'brick' and **τουβλώνω** 'cover with bricks', from *tubulus* 'small pipe': no ancient examples. Zervan (2019: 191, 267) dates borrowing to XIV AD. Binder (2000: 193–4), Meyer (1895: 65), *LBG*, Andriotis (1967 *s.v.* τοῦβλο).

rare   **τουβουλαμέντον** 'pleating', from *tubulātus* 'tubular' perhaps via unattested **tubulāmentum*: Lyd. *Mag.* p. 88.15 (VI AD). *LBG*.

     τούβουλον: see τοῦβλον.

     τουκουλαρίς: see κεντουκουλάρις.

not ancient   **τοῦμπα** 'hill', from *tumba* 'sepulchral mound' (L&S): no ancient examples. Meyer (1895: 65), Andriotis (1967), *LBG* (*s.v.* τούμβα).

     τούπαινα: see τούρπαινα.

     τουπλας: see δούπλα.

     τουρκουᾶτος: see τορκουᾶτος.

Direct loan I AD – modern   **τ(ο)ῦρμα, τόρμα, τ(ο)ύρμη, τόρμη**, (-ης, ἡ) 'troop', 'squadron', from *turma* 'squadron of cavalry'.

     Documents: e.g. *P.Lips.* II.133.5 (I AD); *Rom.Mil.Rec.* 76.i.9 etc. (II AD); *SB* 13030.3 (III AD); perhaps *P.Mich.* X.593.2.2 etc. (IV AD).

     Inscriptions: e.g. *IGR* I.1332.6 (I AD); *SB* 4596.4 (I AD); *I.Syringes* 901.2 (II AD); *IGR* I.1351.6 (II AD?); *SEG* XXXVIII.1668 (II/III AD).

     Literature: Lyd. *Mag.* p. 70.7 (VI AD).

     Post-antique: numerous, with some change of meaning and forming derivatives τουρμάρχης 'troop-leader', τουρμάρχισσα 'troop-leader's wife', etc. *LBG*. Modern τούρμα 'division of the Byzantine army': Babiniotis (2002).

     Notes: Binder (2000: 143–4), Hofmann (1989: 439), Mason (1974: 5, 93), Daris (1991a: 111), Zilliacus (1935a: 144, 238–9), Meinersmann (1927: 62), LSJ suppl. (*s.v.* τόρμα). See §4.2.3.1, §10.2.1, §10.2.2 C.

rare	**τουρμάλιος** 'of a cavalry squadron', from *turmālis* 'of a cavalry squadron': Lyd. *Mag.* p. 136.11 (VI AD). Hofmann (1989: 439), *LBG*.
rare	**τουρμάριος, τοορμάριος**, a legal official, apparently from *turmārius* 'recruiting officer of cavalry' (L&S *s.v. turmāriī*): Lyd. *Mag.* p. 142.20 (VI AD). Hofmann (1989: 438), *LBG*.
	τούρμη: see τοῦρμα.
rare	**τούρπαινα, τούπαινα**, a fish, from *torpēdō* 'electric ray' + -αινα: Cyran. 4.5.3 (II AD?); Alex.Trall. 11.575.20, 23 (VI AD). Hofmann (1989: 440), *DÉLG*, Beekes (2010), LSJ.
not Latin?	**τοῦρτα** may transliterate *torta* 'twisted loaf' (L&S *s.v. torqueo*) in Erot. *Voc.Hipp.* 56.5 (I AD), but Kahane and Kahane (1978: 207–8) prefer Egyptian etymology. Hofmann (1989: 440), *LBG*, LSJ suppl.
not Latin?	**τουρτίον**, a food mentioned in papyri, perhaps from *torta* 'twisted loaf' (L&S *s.v. torqueo*) + -ιον; but Kahane and Kahane (1978: 207–8) prefer Egyptian etymology. Daris (1991a: 111), Hofmann (1989: 440 *s.v.* τούρτα), LSJ suppl.
foreign	**τουτέλαε** (usually indeclinable) 'of guardianship' (a legal action), from gen. of *tūtēla* 'guardianship': Antec. in Latin script 1.20.7 *tutelae* etc. (VI AD); later in Greek script. Zilliacus (1935a: 212–13), *LBG* (*s.v.* τουτέλα).
rare	**τουτηλάριος**, an official, from *tūtēlārius* 'concerned with guardianship': Lyd. *Mag.* p. 128.20, in Latin script p. 78.5 acc. pl. *tutelarios* (VI AD). *LBG*. See §7.2.1 n. 27.
foreign	**Τουτιανόν**, a cake, apparently from unattested **Tutianum*: Athenaeus 14.647c, marked (II/III AD). Hauri-Karrer (1972: 120). See §9.4 passage 61.
rare	**τούτωρ**, a title from *tūtor* 'legal guardian': inscriptions *I.Tralleis* 189.3 (III AD); *I.Leukopetra* 51.2 (III AD); Antec. in Latin script 1.13.2 *tutores* (VI AD); Byzantine legal texts. Mason (1974: 6, 93), Hofmann (1989: 440), Cameron (1931: 261), *LBG*.
foreign	**τοῦφα** 'tuft', 'crest', 'mane', apparently from *tūfa* (meaning uncertain: L&S): Lyd. *Mag.* pp. 4.15, 18.23, marked (VI AD); Byzantine texts (with additional meanings). Modern τούφα 'tuft' and derivatives: Babiniotis (2002), Andriotis (1967), Meyer (1895: 65). Hofmann (1989: 441), Zilliacus (1935a: 236–7), Zervan (2019: 192), *LBG*, Lampe (1961).
not ancient?	**τουφίον** 'little tuft', from *tūfa*, meaning uncertain (L&S) + -ιον: probably no ancient examples. Zilliacus (1935a: 236–7), *LBG*.
not Latin	**τοφιών** 'burial ground', formerly derived from *tōfus* 'porous volcanic rock', is now considered etymologically Greek. Hofmann (1989: 441), LSJ suppl. (replacing LSJ).
not Latin	**τρά** 'string for stringing things' and related words are tentatively suggested by Meyer (1895: 66) as related to *trahō* 'pull'.

rare	**τραβέα, τραβαία** 'robe of state', from *trabea*, a garment: DH *AR* 2.70.2, 6.13.4, both marked (I BC); Eutropius 1.17, suggesting that it is more familiar than τόγα (IV AD); perhaps Dositheus, *Ars grammatica* VII.386.6 Keil (IV AD); Lyd. *Mag.* p. 4.13 etc., often marked (VI AD); occasionally later. Hofmann (1989: 441), *LBG*, LSJ. See §2.2.3 with passage 2.
not ancient	**τραγόλας**, transliterating *trāgula* 'spear with a throwing-strap': no ancient examples. LSJ, Hofmann (1989: 441).
	τραγτευτής: see τρακτευτής.
foreign	**τραδιτεύω** 'transmit', from *trāditus*, pf. part. of *trādō* 'hand over', + -εύω: Antec. in Latin script 2.9.5 *traditeuthentos* etc. (VI AD); Byzantine legal texts. Hofmann (1989: 442), Zilliacus (1935a: 212–13), *LBG*, Lampe (1961). See §7.1.3, §9.5.6 n. 68.
foreign	**τραδιτίων** 'handing over', from *trāditiō* 'handing over': Antec. in Latin script 2.1.40 *traditionos* etc. (VI AD); later in Greek script. Zilliacus (1935a: 212–13), *LBG*. See §9.5.6 n. 68.
foreign	**τραεκτίκιος, τραϊεκτίκιος** 'lent for the transportation of merchandise by ship', from *trāiectīcius* 'lent for the transportation of merchandise by ship': Just. *Nov.* in Latin script 106.pr. (VI AD); later in Greek script. Zilliacus (1935a: 212–13), *LBG*.
	τράκτα: see τρακτόν.
Direct loan with suffix **V AD – Byz.**	**τρακταΐζω** 'handle', 'manage', 'treat', 'discuss', from *tractō* 'deal with' + -ίζω. Literature: e.g. *ACO* II.I.II p. 126.1 (V AD); Malal. 12.36.18 (VI AD); Menander Protector, *De legationibus Romanorum* 3.180 De Boor (VI AD); Antec. 2.1.34 etc., but in Latin script 2.13.7 *tractaizetai* etc. (VI AD). Post-antique: common. *LBG*, Sophocles (1887). Additional post-antique meaning 'bleach or whiten like wax' may come separately via τρακτός 'bleached' (*q.v.*). Notes: forms derivative τρακταϊστής. Avotins (1992), Hofmann (1989: 442, merging it with τρακτεύω), Zilliacus (1935a: 212–13), *DÉLG* (*s.v.* τράκτα), Frisk (1954–72: II.917), Beekes (2010 *s.v.* τράκτα), Lampe (1961), LSJ, LSJ suppl. See §4.3.1, §10.2.1, §10.2.2 O, §10.3.1.
not ancient	**τρακταϊστέος** 'to be dealt with', the -τέος form of τρακταΐζω (i.e. the equivalent of *tractandus*, gerundive of *tractō* 'deal with'): superseded reading of *Carth.* 200.4 (V AD); Byzantine texts. Lampe (1961), *LBG*.
rare	**τρακταϊστής** 'one skilled in management of business', from *tractō* 'deal with' via τρακταΐζω + -της: Malal. 12.49 (VI AD); meaning 'commentator' in Byzantine texts. Hofmann (1989: 443 *s.v.* τρακτεύειν), *LBG*, Lampe (1961).
rare	**τρακτατίων** 'tax list', from *tractātiō* 'handling': papyrus *ChLA* XLI.1194.27 etc. (VI AD). Daris (1991a: 112), Hofmann (1989: 442), Zilliacus (1935a: 212–13), Meinersmann (1927: 61), LSJ suppl.
Direct loan **VI AD – Byz.**	**τρακτᾶτος** (-ου, ὁ) 'administration', 'treatment', 'device', 'procedure', from *tractātus, -ūs* 'management'. Literature: e.g. Malal. 18.65 (VI AD); *ACO* IV.I p. 236.17 (VI AD); Just. *Codex* 12.49.13.3 (VI AD); Gloss. Ps.-Philox. 199.60.

Post-antique: limited survival. *LBG*, Triandaphyllidis (1909: 123).

Notes: LSJ suppl. gives this as neuter τρακτᾶτον, but all the ancient examples are either masculine or ambiguous as to gender. Avotins (1989), Hofmann (1989: 442), Zilliacus (1935a: 212–13). See §4.2.4.2, §10.2.1, §10.2.2 O.

Deriv. of loan
IV AD – Byz.

τρακτευτής, τραγτευτής (-οῦ, ὁ), an imperial official, comes from *tractō* 'deal with' via τρακτεύω + -της, with influence in meaning from *tractātor*, an official.

Documents: e.g. *P.Flor.* III.303r.2 etc. (VI AD); *P.Oxy.* 3805.31 (VI AD).

Inscriptions: *IGLS* II.316.3, 318.3 (both VI AD).

Literature: Basil Caesariensis, *Epistulae* 144.1 Courtonne (IV AD); Malal. 16.12 (VI AD); Lyd. *Mag.* p. 166.18 etc. (VI AD); Cyr.S. *Vit.Sab.* 145.22 etc. (VI AD); Just. *Codex* 12.49.13.2, *Nov.* 28.pr. etc. (VI AD); Ath.Schol. 2.2.8 etc. (VI AD).

Post-antique: numerous. Sophocles (1887).

Notes: derivation via τρακτεύω supported by *DÉLG* (*s.v.* τράκτα), Frisk (1954–72: II.917), Beekes (2010 *s.v.* τράκτα), Cavenaile (1952: 198), and Hofmann (1989: 443 *s.v.* τρακτεύειν); but Daris (1991a: 112), Zilliacus (1935a: 212–13), and Palmer (1945: 7) suggest *tractātor*, the equivalent Latin title. Probably *tractātor* influenced meaning but not form. *Tracteuta* has equivalent meaning but was probably borrowed from Greek (Forcellini *et al.* 1864–1926). Forms derivative τρακτευτικός. Avotins (1992), Meinersmann (1927: 61), Lampe (1961), LSJ. See §4.6.1 n. 86, §9.2, §10.2.2 D.

rare

τρακτευτικός 'belonging to a *tracteutes*', from *tractō* 'deal with' via τρακτευτής + -ικός: Just. *Nov.* 30.3 (VI AD). Avotins (1992), Hofmann (1989: *s.v.* τρακτεύειν), *DÉLG* (*s.v.* τράκτα), Frisk (1954–72: II.917), Beekes (2010 *s.v.* τράκτα), LSJ (*s.v.* τρακτευτής).

Direct loan with
suffix
V AD – Byz.

τρακτεύω 'administer', 'investigate', from *tractō* 'deal with' + -εύω.

Documents: *P.Iand.* VI.102.14 (VI AD); *ChLA* XLI.1194.11 (VI AD).

Literature: Proclus Constantinopolitanus, *Laudatio de genitricis Mariae* 12.15 Leroy (V AD); *V.Dan.Styl.* A. 60.3, 62.2 (V AD); *Apophth.Patr.* 11.91.3 (V AD); Hesych. as lemma τ 1241a (V/VI AD); Malal. 7.9, 16.12 (VI AD); Just. *Nov.* 147.1 (VI AD); Lyd. *Mag.* p. 162.23 (VI AD); Evagr.Schol. *HE* 60.29 (VI AD); Romanus Melodus, *Cantica dubia* 78.8.1 Maas and Trypanis; Ps.-John Chrysostom, *PG* LXI.691.30 etc.

Post-antique: numerous. *LBG*, Zervan (2019: 193).

Notes: forms derivative τρακτευτής in IV AD and so is probably older than it looks. *DÉLG* (*s.v.* τράκτα), Frisk (1954–72: II.917), Beekes (2010 *s.v.* τράκτα), Avotins (1992), Daris (1991a: 112), Hofmann (1989: 442–3, combining this with τρακταΐζω), Zilliacus (1935a: 212–13), Meinersmann (1927: 61), Immisch (1885: 365), Lampe (1961), LSJ. See §4.3.1, §10.2.1, §10.2.2 O, §10.3.1.

rare

τρακτόν 'sheet of dough', from *tractum* 'thin sheet of pastry': Athenaeus 3.113d (II/III AD). Hofmann (1989: 443), *DÉLG* (*s.v.* τράκτα), Frisk (1954–72: II.917), Beekes (2010 *s.v.* τράκτα), LSJ (*s.v.* τρακτός).

Direct loan
IV AD – modern

τρακτός (-ή?, -όν?) 'bleached', as masc. subst. 'bleached wax', from *tractus*, pf. part. of *trahō* 'draw out', or from *tractō* 'handle'; the latter is favoured by most scholars but difficult because pf. part. of *tractō* is *tractātus*.
Literature: *Hippiatr.Par.* (Apsyrtus) 645 (III/IV AD?); Aëtius 8.6.50 etc. (VI AD).
Post-antique: numerous in Byzantine texts. *LBG*. Modern dialectal τραχτός 'raw' etc.: Andriotis (1974: 555).
Notes: forms derivative τράκτωμα. Hofmann (1989: 443–4), *DÉLG* (s.v. τράκτα), Frisk (1954–72: II.917), Beekes (2010 *s.v.* τράκτα), LSJ. See §4.2.2, §10.2.1, §10.2.2 L.

rare

τράκτωμα 'plaster of bleached wax', from the Latin source of τρακτός via τρακτός: *Hippiatr.Berl.* (Pel.) 26.23 (V AD?); Byzantine texts. *LBG*, LSJ.

rare

τρακτωρία 'letter authorising requisitions on a journey', from *tractōria* (L&S, same meaning): papyrus Pintaudi and Soldati 2021 line 2r (VI AD); Hesych. as lemma τ 1240b (V/VI AD). Zilliacus (1935a: 212–13 *s.v. tractorius*), for possible Byzantine continuation *LBG*.

τρακωνάριος: see δρακονάριος.

foreign

τράνς transliterating *trāns* 'across': Polybius 2.15.9 (II BC). Sophocles (1887). See §8.1.3 passage 42, §8.1.4.

foreign

τρανσλατεύω 'transfer', from *trānslātus* (pf. part. of *trānsferō* 'transfer') + -εύω: Antec. in Latin script 2.20.36 *translateuomenon* etc. (VI AD); later in Greek script. Zilliacus (1935a: 212–13), *LBG*.

foreign

τρανσλατίων 'transfer', from *trānslātiō* 'transfer': Antec. in Latin script 2.20.36 *translation* etc. (VI AD). Zilliacus (1935a: 212–13).

rare

τραουεσσάριν, an object, from *transversārium* 'crosspiece' (*OLD s.v. transversārius*): unpublished ostracon O.Dios inv. 442.8 (II AD).

τρειούνκιον: see τριούγκιον.

not ancient?

τρεκινάριος, a military rank, from *trecēnārius* 'centurion in command of the 300 *speculatores* in the praetorian guard': inscriptions Marek 1993: 159, Appendix 5 no. 5.B1, perhaps no. 112.3. Mason (1974: 4, 94), Hofmann (1989: 445), Cameron (1931: 260), LSJ suppl.

τρημίσειον: see τριμήσιον.

τριᾶντος: see τριᾶς.

rare

τριάριος, a type of soldier, from *triārius* 'soldier in the reserve line': Polybius 1.26.6 etc., marked (II BC); DH *AR* 5.15.4 etc. (I BC); (unrelatedly?) in nom. sing. τριάρες, inscription *SEG* XXXI.1116.6 (IV AD). Dubuisson (1985: 52), Mason (1974: 94), Hofmann (1989: 444), LSJ and LSJ suppl. (*s.v.* τριάριοι). See §8.1.3 n. 17, §8.1.4.

not Latin

τριᾶς, a Sicilian coin, is probably not from Latin. Bellocchi (2016: 327), Willi (2008: 35), Hofmann (1989: 444–5), Buck and Petersen (1945: 456), Immisch (1885: 317 *s.v.* τριᾶντος, arguing that it contains Latin *as*), LSJ.

semantic extension	**τρίβολος**, with many meanings, is influenced by *trĭbulum* 'threshing-sledge' when meaning 'threshing-sledge'. Hofmann 1989: 445), LSJ, LSJ suppl. See §2.3 n. 58.
foreign	**τρίβος**, normally a Greek word meaning 'track', sometimes transliterates *tribus, -ūs* 'tribe': e.g. Plut. *Rom.* 20.2 (I/II AD). Freyburger-Galland (1997: 90–1, 1998: 143), Strobach (1997: 200), Mason (1974: 6, 94 *s.v.* τρίβους), Hofmann (1989: 445), Cameron (1931: 260), LSJ, LSJ suppl. See §2.3 n. 58.
Direct loan VI AD – Byz.	**τριβουνάλιον** (-ου, τό) 'tribunal' (a place in Constantinople), from *tribūnal* 'judge's platform'. Documents: perhaps *P.Yadin* 1.14.13 (II AD). Literature: Oracula Tiburtina 10 in P. Alexander 1967 (VI AD); *ACO* III pp. 17.28, 229.37 (VI AD). Unverified examples (II and III AD) in Zilliacus (1937: 322, 334). Post-antique: numerous. Sophocles (1887), *LBG* (*s.v.* τριβουνάριον), Triandaphyllidis (1909: 127). Notes: Hofmann (1989: 445–6), Daris (1991a: 112), Zilliacus (1935a: 236–7, 1937: 334), Lampe (1961). See §4.2.5, §9.2, §10.2.1, §10.2.2 D.
not ancient?	**τριβουνᾶτον** transliterating *tribūnātus, -ūs* 'tribuneship': Romanus Melodus, *Cantica dubia* 66.6.3 Maas and Trypanis (VI AD?). Zilliacus (1937: 334), *LBG*, Lampe (1961 *s.v.* τριβουνᾶτος).
foreign	**τριβουνίκιος** transliterating *tribūnicius* 'former tribune': inscriptions *I.Ephesos* 1544.9, 1545.3 (both I/II AD). Mason (1974: 7, 94), Hofmann (1989: 446), *LBG*.
Direct loan II AD – Byz.	**τριβοῦνος** (-ου, ὁ) 'tribune', from *tribūnus* 'tribune'. Documents: common, e.g. perhaps *P.Mich.* XV.705.9 (II/III AD); *P.Panop. Beatty* 1.40 etc. (III AD); *P.Oxy.* 4088.33 (IV AD); *P.Oxy.* 4395.95 etc. (V AD); *P.Gron.* 10.31 (VI AD). Inscriptions: e.g. *IG* VII.1866.3 (II AD); *IG* X.II.1.151.4 (III AD); *I.Zoora* 30.3 (IV AD); *I.Chr.Macédoine* 247.3 (V AD?); *I.Ano Maked.* 203.4 (VI AD). Literature: common, e.g. DH *AR* 2.7.3, marked (I BC); Plut. *Rom.* 20.3, marked (I/II AD); *V.Secundi* 72.9, 11 (II/III AD); Julian, frag. 178 Bidez (IV AD); Callin. *V.Hypat.* 3.2 (V AD); Just. *Nov.* 8.Ed.not.1 (VI AD); Antec. 1.2.4 (VI AD). Unverified examples (III AD) in Zilliacus (1937: 323, 334). Post-antique: common, forming derivatives τριβούνισσα 'tribune's wife', τριβουνονοτάριος 'tribune's notary'. Zervan (2019: 193), Sophocles (1887), Triandaphyllidis (1909: 127). Notes: Freyburger-Galland (1997: 167–9), Strobach (1997: 200), editor of *I.Zoora ad loc.*, Avotins (1992), Daris (1991a: 112), Mason (1974: 6, 7, 9, 94), Hofmann (1989: 446–7), Zilliacus (1935a: 212–13, 236–7, 1937: 334), Meinersmann (1927: 61), Lampe (1961), LSJ suppl. See §4.2.4.1 n. 51, §10.2.1, §10.2.2 D.
foreign	**τριβοῦτον** 'tribute', from *tribūtum* 'tribute': Antec. in Latin script 2.1.40 *tributon* (VI AD); later in Greek script. Zilliacus (1935a: 212–13), *LBG*. See §9.5.6 n. 68.

foreign | **τριβουτόριος, τριβουτώριος** 'tributary', from *tribūtōrius,* a legal action: Antec. in Latin script 2.1.40 *tributoriai* etc. (VI AD); later in Greek script. Zilliacus (1935a: 212–13), *LBG.* See §9.5.6 n. 68.

foreign | ***triēns*** 'one third (of an inheritance)': Antec. 2.14.5 (VI AD). See §7.1.1 passage 18.

rare | **τρικέλλαρον,** an implement, probably from *cella* 'room' via κέλλα (or from a related word): papyrus *P.Oxy.* 1290.5 (V AD). LSJ suppl. (replacing LSJ).

rare | **τρικενναλικός** 'of a tricennial festival', from *trīcennālis* 'of thirty years' (L&S) or neut. pl. *trīcennālia* 'festival celebrated every thirty years' + -ικός: papyrus *SB* 10988.2 (IV AD). Daris (1991a: 112), LSJ suppl. (misdating the papyrus).

not Latin? | **τρικλίνιον** 'dining room', usually thought to be from *trǔlīnium* 'dining room', could be a Greek formation from τρίκλινον 'dining room' (the source of *trīclīnium*) + -ιον. An early example is unlikely to have anything to do with Latin (Theopompus frag. 65 Kassel–Austin, V/IV BC); otherwise it occurs only in bilingual glossaries (e.g. Gloss. *Herm.S.* 365.54) and as supplements in papyri whose editors probably intended to restore τρίκλινον. Wessely (1902: 149) took τρίκλινον itself as a Latinism, but that was rejected already by Meinersmann (1927: 62). Zilliacus (1935a: 212–13), *LBG,* LSJ.

non-existent? | **τριμένσις** 'growing in three months': suggested by Daris (1991a: 112) as from medieval *trimensis* 'growing in three months' (*DMLBS*), based on τρειμε̣ ιν on ostracon *O.Stras.* 1.795.5 (IV AD).

Direct loan VI AD – Byz. | **τριμήσιον, τρημίσειον, τριμίσ(σ)ιον** (-ου, τό), a coin, from *tremis* (gen. *trēmissis*) 'coin worth one third of an *aureus*' (L&S).
Documents: e.g. *P.Alex.* 40v.2 (V/VI AD); *P.Hamb.* 1.68.33 (VI AD). Probably not *PSI* IX.1073.4 (IV AD).
Inscriptions: probably a different word on *SEG* XXVIII.306.7.
Literature: Ps.-Basil Seleuciensis, *De vita et miraculis sanctae Theclae* 2.12.60 Dagron: ὃ καλεῖν ἔθος ἡμῖν τριμίσιον, ὡς ἂν καὶ τοῦ ὅλου στατῆρος τὸ τρίτον ὄν (V AD?); Thdr.Pet. p. 27.13 (VI AD); Cyr.S. *Vit.Sab.* 187.3 (VI AD); Dan. Sket. *De mendico caeco* 16 (VI AD). Unverified example (VI AD) in Zilliacus (1937: 323, 334).
Post-antique: numerous. *LBG* (s.v. τριμίσσιν), Triandaphyllidis (1909: 125).
Notes: Daris (1991a: 113), Hofmann (1989: 447), Zilliacus (1935a: 212–13 s.v. τριμίσιος, 1937: 334), Meinersmann (1927: 62), Lampe (1961), LSJ. See §4.2.4.1 n. 57, §4.2.5, §6.7, §10.2.1, §10.2.2 G.

Deriv. of loan V AD – modern | **τριμόδιον** (-ου, τό) 'vessel holding three pecks', from τρι- 'three' + *modius* 'peck' via μόδιος.
Literature: Polychronius, *Commentarii in Ezechielem* 2.45 Moutsoulas (V AD); Malal. 11.14 (VI AD).
Post-antique: survives. *LBG.* Modern dialectal τριμοδία 'mill hopper': Meyer (1895: 66).
Notes: derived by Hofmann (1989: 447) from *trimodium* (L&S), variant of *trimodia* (fem. sing.) 'three-peck measure', but given pattern of hybrid compounds for other measurements, the prefix is probably Greek. Lampe (1961). See §4.6.2, §10.2.2 E.

rare	**τριξαγίνη**, plant name from *trixāgō*, a plant name: *Hippiatr.Par.* (Apsyrtus) 697 (III/IV AD?). *LBG*.
rare	**τρίξεστον** 'three pints', from *sextārius* 'pint measure' via ξέστης: with *semicongium* in Gloss. Ps.-Cyril. 459.26; occasional Byzantine texts. *LBG*, LSJ. See §4.6.2.
rare	**τριομβυρατορία, τριουμβιρατορία, τριομβυρία** 'triumvirate', from *triumvirātus, -ūs* 'triumvirate' or *triumvir* 'triumvir': Malal. 9.2, 9.9 (VI AD). Hofmann (1989: 447 *s.v.* τριομβυράτωρ), Sophocles (1887 *s.v.* τριομβιρατορία), Lampe (1961).
rare	**τριομβυράτωρ, τριουμβιράτωρ** 'triumvir', from *triumvir* 'member of a group of three' + -άτωρ or perhaps an unattested variant **triumvirātor*: Malal. 9.2, 9.8, 9.11 (VI AD); Byzantine texts. Zervan (2019: 193–4), Hofmann (1989: 447), *LBG* (*s.v.* τριουμμοιράτωρ), Sophocles (1887 *s.v.* τριομβιράτωρ), Lampe (1961). See §6.9; cf. τριούμβουρα.
	τριομβυρία: see τριομβυρατορία.
Deriv. of loan VI AD – Byz.	**τριούγκιον, τριούνκιον, τρειούνκιον, τριούγγιον** (-ου, τό) 'three ounces', a coin, 'quarter of an inheritance', from τρι- 'three' + *ūncia* 'one twelfth' via οὐγγία.
	Inscriptions: *IG* XIV.2417.20.1 (on two weights: τριούγκιον Ἰταλικόν); Cantacuzène 1932: 607 (a weight, τριοῦνκιν Ἰταλικόν); *SEG* LV.821.A2 (mould for weights).
	Literature: Just. *Codex* 6.4.4.125 etc., *Nov.* 18.pr. etc. (VI AD); Ath.Schol. 8.1.2 etc. (VI AD); Antec. as gloss on *quadrans*, 2.14.5 (VI AD); with *quadrans* in Gloss. Ps.-Cyril. 459.30.
	Post-antique: survives. *LBG*.
	Notes: Avotins (1989, 1992), LSJ, LSJ suppl. See §4.6.2, §10.2.2 G.
	τριουμβιρατορία: see τριομβυρατορία.
	τριουμβιράτωρ: see τριομβυράτωρ.
rare	**τριούμβουρα**, evidently acc. of *triumvir* 'member of a group of three': inscription *I.Ephesos* 3035.10 as part of τριούμβουρα καπιτᾶλιν (acc.) (II AD). Mason (1974: 6, 94 *s.v.* τριούμουιρ/τριούμβουρ), Hofmann (1989: 447 *s.v.* τριούμβουρ καπιτᾶλις), Cameron (1931: 260), LSJ. Cf. τριομβυράτωρ.
foreign	**τριουμφάλιος**, from *triumphālis* 'triumphal': inscriptions *I.Ephesos* 3048.9, Latinate (II AD); perhaps *IGBulg.* III.1.884.5 (III AD); Lyd. *Mag.* p. 84.9, marked (VI AD). Mason (1974: 94), Hofmann (1989: 447), *LBG*.
	τριούνκιον: see τριούγκιον.
foreign	**τριπλικατίων**, a legal arrangement, from *triplicātiō*, a legal arrangement: Antec. in Latin script 4.14.2 *triplication* etc. (VI AD); later in Greek script. Zilliacus (1935a: 212–13), *LBG*.
rare	**τρισαυγούστιον** 'official sextarius measure with portraits of the three emperors', from τρίς 'thrice' + *Augustus* via Αὔγουστος or a related word: inscription *I.Chr.Asie Mineure* I.290.5, though that edition does not have this reading (IV AD). Rothenhöfer (2020), Cuvigny (2017: 104–6).
rare	**τρίσελλος** 'having three seats', from τρι- 'three' + *sella* 'seat' via σέλλα: papyrus *P.Fay.* 117.17 (II AD). Filos (2010: 251), Daris (1991a: 113), Hofmann (1989: 384 *s.v.* σέλλα), Meinersmann (1927: 62), LSJ suppl.

not ancient · **τριτικάριος**, an official, from *trīticārius* 'concerning wheat': no ancient examples. Zilliacus (1935a: 212–13), *LBG*.

not ancient · **τρίτικον**, from *trīticum* 'wheat': no ancient examples. Daris (1991a: 113).

rare · **τριφύλλινος, τριφολῖνος**, an Italian wine, from *Trifolīnus* 'from the district of Trifolium', with the τριφύλλινος spelling probably influenced by Greek τρίφυλλον 'clover' and φύλλινος 'made of leaves': Athenaeus 1.26e (II/III AD); Galen XIV.19.9 Kühn, marked (II AD). Hofmann (1989: 447), *DÉLG*, Beekes (2010), LSJ.

Direct loan
I AD – modern
τρ(ο)ῦλ(λ)α (-ας/-ης, ἡ) 'ladle', 'cup', 'dome', from *trulla* 'ladle'.
Documents: *O.Krok.* II.321.6 (I/II AD); *O.Krok.* 1.17.7 (II AD); *P.Sijp.* 54.5 etc. (II AD); *P.Alex.Giss.* 46.14 (II AD); *BGU* XIII.2360.3 (III/IV AD).
Inscriptions: *I.Salamine* 30.6 (I AD).
Literature: *Hippiatr.Berl.* (Hierocles) 90.20 (IV/V AD?); Asclepius, *In Aristotelis Metaphysicorum libros A–Z commentaria* p. 154.19 Hayduck (VI AD); with *trulla* in Gloss. Ps.-Cyril. 460.13.
Post-antique: numerous. *LBG*, Triandaphyllidis (1909: 124). Modern dialectal τρούλλη 'dome' (Andriotis 1974: 560), τροῦλλα 'top' and derivatives (Meyer 1895: 66–7).
Notes: Shipp (1979: 538), Kahane and Kahane (1978: 213–14), Daris (1991a: 113), Hofmann (1989: 447–8), Viscidi (1944: 9, 42), *DÉLG* (*s.v.* τρυηλίς), LSJ, LSJ suppl. See §4.6.1 n. 84, §10.2.1, §10.2.2 I.

Deriv.? of loan
III AD – Byz.
τρ(ο)ύλ(λ)ιον (-ου, τό), a dish, from *trulleus/trulleum/trūleum* 'basin' or its attested variant *trullium* (*OLD s.v. trulleus*), or from *trulla* 'ladle' via τροῦλλα + -ιον.
Documents: *Stud.Pal.* XX.67r.10 (II/III AD); *P.Wisc.* 1.30.2.8 (III AD); *BGU* III.814.10 (III AD); *BGU* XIII.2360.7 (III/IV AD); *P.Berl.Sarisch.* 21.25 (V/VI AD); *SB* 13966.3 (V/VI AD); *CPR* VIII.66.6 (VI AD).
Literature: *Hippiatr.Berl.* (Hierocles) 74.7 (IV/V AD?); Aëtius 3.177.16 etc. (VI AD); Dor.Gaz. *Doct.Div.* 11.118 (VI AD).
Post-antique: some survival. *LBG*, Meyer (1895: 66–7).
Notes: *DÉLG* (*s.v.* τρυηλίς) supports derivation via τροῦλλα; LSJ (*s.vv.* τροῦλλα, τρύλλιον) and Meinersmann (1927: 62) one from *trulleum*; Daris (1991a: 113) and Hofmann (1989: 448) one from *trullium*. Cavenaile (1952: 196). See §4.2.4.1 n. 54, §4.6.1 n. 84, §10.2.2 I.

Deriv.? of loan
IV AD – modern
τροῦλλος (-ου, ὁ), a vessel, also 'dome', from *trulleus* 'basin', or *trulla* 'ladle' via τροῦλλα, or τρούλλιον via back-formation.
Literature: Zosimus alch., Berthelot and Ruelle 1888: 164.12 etc. (III/IV AD); Malal. 18.128 etc. (VI AD); Her.Mech. *Pneum.* 1.8.12.
Post-antique: numerous, forming derivatives μεγάτρουλλος 'with a large dome', τρουλλωτός 'domed', etc. *LBG* (*s.v.* τροῦλλον), Sophocles (1887). Modern τρούλ(λ)ος 'dome' and derivatives: Babiniotis (2002), Andriotis (1967), Meyer (1895: 67).
Notes: Shipp (1979: 538), Hofmann (1989: 448 *s.v.* τροῦλλα), *DÉLG* (*s.v.* τρυηλίς), Lampe (1961), LSJ (*s.v.* τροῦλλος, but with Her.Mech. example considered form of τρούλλιον, *s.v.* τροῦλλα). See §8.2.3 n. 51, §10.2.2 M.

rare	**τρυηλίς** 'ladle', probably from *trulla/truella* 'ladle' via τρούλλα + -ίς: Luc. *Lex.* 7 (II AD); Hesych. as lemma τ 1555 (V/VI AD). *DÉLG*, Frisk (1954–72: II.936), Beekes (2010 *s.v.* τρυήλης), LSJ.
	τρυλ-: see τρουλ-.
	τύρμα, τύρμη: see τοῦρμα.
	τύτλος: see τίτλος.
rare	**τώμεντον** 'flock' (i.e. stuffing material), from *tōmentum* 'flock': Edict.Diocl. 18.7 (IV AD). Hofmann (1989: 448), LSJ suppl.
	τωράλ(λ)ιον: see τοράλλιον.

Υ

Deriv. of loan VI AD – Byz.	**ὑδροροσᾶτον** (-ου, τό) 'rose water', from ὕδωρ 'water' + *rosātum* 'rose wine' (L&S) via ῥοσᾶτον. Documents: Maravela-Solbakk 2009: 129.9 (V/VI AD). Literature: Ps.-Orib. *Col.* 5.33.3 (IV AD?); Aëtius 5.140.1 etc. (VI AD); Palladius Medicus, Dietz 1834: 97.31 (VI AD); Alex.Trall. 1.523.12 etc. (VI AD). Post-antique: survives in medical texts. *LBG* (*s.v.* ὑδροσάτον). Notes: contained no wine, despite ῥοσᾶτον meaning 'rose-flavoured wine'. Maravela-Solbakk (2009: 133–4, 2010: 262, 265), Sophocles (1887), LSJ. See §4.6.2, §6.5, §10.2.2 I.
	ὑεστιάριος: see βεστιάριος.
non-existent	**ὑπερινδικτίονος**, from ὑπέρ 'above' + *indictiō* 'indiction' (*TLL*) via ἰνδικτίων: superseded reading of papyrus *P.Lips.* I.84. Meinersmann (1927: 18), Hofmann (1989: 128 *s.v.* ἰνδικτίων).
rare	**ὑπερλιμιτανός** 'beyond the frontier', from *trānslīmitānus* 'from beyond the frontier' (L&S) with ὑπέρ 'beyond' substituted for *trāns* (probably not a calque using the pre-existing loan λιμιτάνεος, owing to the missing ε): inscription *IGR* III.70.4 (I/II AD). Hofmann (1989: 448), Cameron (1931: 260), Hahn (1906: 230, with derivation from unattested **trānslīmitāneus*).
rare	**ὑποβλάττα, ὑποβλάττη** 'light purple', 'purplish cloth', from ὑπό 'under' + *blatta* 'purple' (*TLL s.v.* 2. *blatta*) via βλάττα: Edict.Diocl. 19.9 etc. (IV AD). Bogensperger (2017: 244), Steigerwald (1990: 237–41), Hofmann (1989: 448, 63 *s.v.* βλαττα), LSJ.
rare	**ὑποκαμίσ(ι)ον** 'undershirt', from ὑπό 'under' + *camīsia* 'shirt' (*TLL*) via καμίσιον: papyrus *Stud.Pal.* XX.245.20 etc. (VI AD); Byzantine texts (with derivative ὑποκαμισοβράκιον 'shirt and trousers'). Modern πουκάμισο, ποκάμισο 'shirt': Babiniotis (2002), Andriotis (1967), Kahane and Kahane (1972–6: 535), Meyer (1895: 24 *s.v.* καμίσj). Kramer (1994, 2011: 195–205), Mossakowska-Gaubert (2017: 325–7), Filos (2010: 244, 251), Shipp (1979: 548), Daris (1991a: 113), Hofmann (1989: 146 *s.v.* καμίσιον), Meinersmann (1927: 62), *LBG*, Zervan (2019: 63), Sophocles (1887), Lampe (1961 *s.v.* ὑποκάμισον), LSJ. See §8.2.3 n. 51.

not ancient | ὑπονοτάριος, perhaps 'deputy shorthand writer', from ὑπό 'under' + *notārius* 'shorthand writer' via νοτάριος: no ancient examples. Daris (1991a: 113), Filos (2010: 251), *LBG*.

rare | ὑποπτίων 'sub-assistant', calque of *suboptiō* 'junior centurion's assistant' formed from ὑπό 'under' + *optiō* 'centurion's assistant' via ὀπτίων: Malal. 18.141.25, 36 (VI AD); occasional Byzantine texts. Sophocles (1887), Lampe (1961).

rare | ὑπότιτλος 'subtitle', 'subsection', from ὑπό 'under' + *titulus* 'title', 'section of a book' via τίτλος: Ath.Schol. 9.P.14 (VI AD); Byzantine texts (with derivative ὑποτιτλόω). Probably source of ὑποτίτλωσις. Modern υπότιτλος 'subtitle': Babiniotis (2002). *LBG*, Lampe (1961). See §8.2.3 n. 51.

rare | ὑποτίτλωσις 'entering in subsections', from *titulus* 'section of a book' via ὑπότιτλος + -σις: Jo.Scholast. 2 p. 9.3 (VI AD); Ath.Schol. heading p. 2.1 (VI AD); occasionally later. Modern υποτίτλωση 'giving a subtitle': Babiniotis (2002). Lampe (1961), *LBG*.

ὔσκα: see ἴσκα.

not Latin | ὑσσός 'javelin' has been implausibly derived from *hasta* 'spear', 'javelin'. Hofmann (1989: 448–9), *DÉLG*, Beekes (2010), *TLL* (s.v. ὑσσούς), LSJ.

not Latin | ὑστιακόν, ὑστιακκός, a kind of cup, is stated by Hesych. υ 853 (V/VI AD) to be an 'Italian' word (Ἰταλιῶται). Hofmann (1989: 449), *DÉLG*, LSJ.

Φ

Direct loan
III AD – modern | φάβα (-ατος, τό) 'beans', 'bean soup', from *faba, -ae* 'bean(s)'.
Documents: *BGU* XIII.2359.10 (III AD); *P.Oxy.* 3761.13, 3765.1 (both IV AD).
Inscriptions: Edict.Diocl. 1.9 etc. (IV AD).
Literature: perhaps Hdn. *Pros.Cath.* III.1.351.20 τὸ φάβα καὶ αὐτὸ βάρβαρον, εἰ καὶ κλίνοιτο (II AD); *Hippiatr.* e.g. *Hippiatr.Par.* (Apsyrtus) 22 (III/IV AD?); Philogelos 141 (IV AD); Orib. *Ecl.* 114.8.6 (IV AD); Hieroph. Πῶς 459.1 as gloss (IV–VI AD); Hesych. as gloss κ 4338 (V/VI AD); Ps.-Palchus, Cumont and Boll 1904: 182.3 (V/VI AD?); Aëtius 1.233.1 (VI AD); Lyd. *Mens.* 4.152.2, marked, meaning 'bean soup' (VI AD); Cyr.S. *Vit.Sab.* 130.31 (VI AD); as gloss in scholia to Ar. *Eq.* 1171b, *Ra.* 506: ἔτνους· Ὁ νῦν φάβα οἱ ἰδιῶται καὶ οἱ ἄγροικοι, τὸ διαλελυμένον ὑπὸ τῆς ἑψήσεως καὶ τῆς τορύνης; bilingual glossaries, e.g. Gloss. Ps.-Philox. 75.7–8.
Post-antique: numerous. *LBG* (s.v. φάβαν), Triandaphyllidis (1909: 121), Sophocles (1887). Modern φάβα 'fava bean': Babiniotis (2002), Andriotis (1967), Meyer (1895: 67). Probably also Byzantine φάβατον, surviving as modern dialectal φάβατο etc.: Andriotis (1974: 576), *LBG*.
Notes: forms derivative φαβάτινος. Shipp (1979: 548–9), Daris (1991a: 113), Hofmann (1989: 449), Immisch (1885: 341), *DÉLG* (s.v. 1 φάβα), LSJ, LSJ suppl. See §4.2.3.1, §4.2.5, §8.2.3 n. 51, §10.2.1, §10.2.2 I.

rare | φαβατάριον 'tureen for bean soup', from *fabātārium*, a vessel for beans (*TLL*): papyrus *P.Oxy.* 1657.6 (III AD). Daris (1991a: 113), Hofmann (1989: 449), Meinersmann (1927: 62), *DÉLG* (s.v. 1 φάβα), LSJ.

rare	**φαβάτινος** 'made of beans', from *faba* 'bean(s)' via φάβα + -ινος: Alex.Trall. 11.121.17, 373.24 (VI AD); Byzantine texts. Hofmann (1989: 449 *s.v.* φάβα), *DÉLG* (*s.v.* 1 φάβα), *LBG*, LSJ.
rare	**φαβᾶτον** 'bean flour' or 'cake', from *fabātus* 'made of beans': papyri *SB* 12993.7 (III/IV AD); *P.Ryl.* IV.630/637.406 (IV AD). Byzantine φάβατον 'broad bean' is not a survival; see *s.v.* φάβα. Daris (1991a: 113), Hofmann (1989: 449), *DÉLG* (*s.v.* 1 φάβα), LSJ suppl.
non-existent?	**φάβος**, from *favus* 'honeycomb': perhaps papyrus *BGU* IV.1097.13 (I AD). Daris (1991a: 113), Meinersmann (1927: 62).
	φαβρικά: see φαβρική.
rare	**φαβρικάρεις** 'armourer', from *fabricālis* 'of a smith' (*TLL*): inscription *I.Callatis* 194.6 (III/IV AD). Editor *ad loc.*
rare	**φαβρική, φαβρικά** 'making of arms', 'armoury', from *fabrica* 'metalworking': Malal. 12.38.26–9 (VI AD); Lyd. *Mag.* pp. 98.23, 194.23, both marked (VI AD); Byzantine texts. Hofmann (1989: 450), Zilliacus (1935a: 224–5), *LBG*, Triandaphyllidis (1909: 130), Lampe (1961 *s.v.* φαβρικόν). Cf. φάβριξ.
Direct loan **IV AD – Byz.**	**φαβρικήσιος, φαβρικίσιος, φαυρικίσιος** (-ου, ὁ) 'armourer', from *fabric(i)ēnsis* 'armourer'. Inscriptions: *SEG* XXIX.1206.1.4 (IV AD); *SEG* XXVI.1314, 1320 (both IV–VI AD); probably *SEG* XXXV.1486 (V/VI AD). Literature: Lyd. *Mens.* 4.28.3 (VI AD); Just. *Nov.* 85.3.pr. (VI AD); Ath.Schol. 20.4.1 in Latin script (VI AD). Post-antique: numerous. *LBG*, Triandaphyllidis (1909: 124). Notes: Avotins (1992), Hofmann (1989: 450), Zilliacus (1935a: 186–7), Lampe (1961), LSJ suppl. See §4.2.5, §6.7 n. 45, §10.2.1, §10.2.2 C.
	φαβρικόν: see φαβρική.
Direct loan **III–VI AD**	**φάβριξ** (-ικος, ἡ) 'workshop', from *fabrica* 'workshop'. Documents: *P.Panop.Beatty* 1.214 (III AD). Inscriptions: *SEG* XLV.816.1 (IV AD); *IGBulg.* V.5129.6 (IV AD). Literature: Athan. *H.Ar.* 18.2.4, marked (IV AD); Malal. 13.35 (VI AD); Just. *Nov.* 85.1 etc. (VI AD). Notes: probably merged with φαβρική in late period. Derived by Hofmann (1989: 450–1) from putative *fabrix* extrapolated from rare form *fabrece*, but *TLL* (*s.v. fabrica* 12.72) considers *fabrece* a form of *fabrica*. Avotins (1992), Daris (1991a: 113), Zilliacus (1935a: 186–7), Lampe (1961), LSJ suppl. See §4.2.3.1, §4.2.5, §10.2.1, §10.2.2 O.
foreign	**Φαβωνιανόν** (κλοῦστρον), a cake, from *Favōniānus* 'Favonian' (normally a pear; not attested of cake): Athenaeus 14.647d, marked (II/III AD). Hauri-Karrer (1972: 120). See §9.4 passage 61.
foreign	**Φαβώνιος** transliterating *Favōnius* 'west wind': Lyd. *Mens.* 4.152.5 (VI AD). Sophocles (1887).

Direct loan
II AD – Byz.

φαίκλα, φαίκλη, φάκλα, φέκλη, σφέκλη (-ης, ἡ) 'burned wine crust', from *faecula* 'dried lees of wine'.
  Documents: none. *P.Holm.* is literary.
  Literature: e.g. Isis, Berthelot and Ruelle 1888: 31.10 (I AD?); Galen XII.491.4 Kühn (II AD); Jul.Afric. *Cest.* 1.19.64, marked (II/III AD); Zosimus alch., Mertens 1995: 18.48 (III/IV AD); Orib. *Ecl.* 74.9.3 (IV AD); *Hippiatr.Berl.* (Pel.) 145 (V AD?); Alex.Trall. 11.543.25, marked (VI AD).
  Post-antique: numerous. *LBG* (*s.v.* φαίκλη).
  Notes: Binder (2000: 160), Hofmann (1989: 451), *LBG* (*s.vv.* σφέκλα, σφέκλης), LSJ (*s.vv.* φαίκλα, φέκλη, σφέκλη). See §9.5.3, §10.2.1, §10.2.2 L.

φαιλόνης, φαιλόνιον: see φαινόλη.

foreign

φαινέστρα transliterating *fenestra* 'window': Plut. *Mor.* 273b (I/II AD); **φενέστρα** occasionally in Byzantine texts. LSJ suppl. (*s.v.* φενέστρα) cites papyrus *P.Lond.* 11.481.28 (IV AD), which is Latin in Greek script. Hofmann (1989: 451), *LBG* (*s.v.* φενέστρα).

rare

φαινόλη, φαινόλης, φαινώλη(ς), φαίνο(υ)λα, φενόλη(ς), φαιλόνης, φελόνη, πένουλα, παίνουλα and diminutives **φαινόλιον, φαιλόνιον, φελόνιον, φελώνιον** 'cloak', eventually 'chasuble' (with derivative στιχαροφελώνιον, στιχαροφελόνιον, στιχαροφαιλόνιον 'tunic and cloak'), are normally Greek words derived from φαίνω (cf. Frisk 1954–72: 11.981–2). Latinate spellings φαίνουλα/πένουλα/παίνουλα, influenced by *paenula* 'hooded cloak' (itself from φαινόλης, *DÉLG s.v.* φαίνω A): Edict.Diocl. 19.63 etc. (IV AD); probably papyrus *P.Giss.Apoll.* 24.4.2 (II AD). The other spellings are much more frequent, so this word is rarely Latinate, and the diminutive is never Latinate, though Gignac (1976: 104, 154), Zervan (2019: 194), and Triandaphyllidis (1909: 107, 122) take this to be primarily a Latin borrowing. Mossakowska-Gaubert (2017: 338–9), Shipp (1979: 550), Hofmann (1989: 311–12), Meinersmann (1927: 62), Lampe (1961 *s.vv.* φαινόλιον, φελόνιον), LSJ (*s.vv.* φαιλόνη, φαιλόνης, φαινόλη), LSJ suppl. (*s.v.* στιχαροφελώνιον).

rare

φαινοῦκλον, φενοῦκλον, φενούκλουμ 'fennel', from *fenuclum*, variant of *faeniculum* 'fennel' (*TLL s.v. faeniculum* 164.13): Orib. *Col.* 11.1.5 (IV AD); interpolations in Dsc. 3.70.1 RV, 71.2 RV; Byzantine texts. Binder (2000: 157, 174), Hofmann (1989: 451), *TLL* (*s.v. faeniculum* 164.10–19), LSJ.

φαίνουλα, φαινώλη(ς): see φαινόλη.

Direct loan
III AD – modern

φακιάλιον, φακιάριον, φακιό(υ)λιον, φακιώλιον, φακιανον, πακιάλιον, etc. (-ου, τό) 'facecloth', 'turban', 'towel', from *faciāle* 'facecloth' (*TLL*).
  Documents: e.g. *P.Oxy.* 114.7 (II/III AD); *SB* 11575.13 (III AD); *P.Oxy.* 3776.28 (IV AD); *P.Oxy.* 1026.4 (V AD); *P.Cair.Masp.* 67006v.66 (VI AD).
  Inscriptions: *SEG* VII.417.22 (III AD); Edict.Diocl. 26.99 etc. (IV AD).
  Literature: e.g. Pall. *H.Laus.* 1.2 (IV/V AD); Hesych. as gloss σ 663 (V/VI AD); Malal. 18.56.21 (VI AD); Nonnosus, *FHG* IV frag. 1.26 (VI AD); as gloss in scholia to *Od.* 1.334n, *Od.* 4.623c, Ar. *Pl.* 729, etc.; scholion to Aes. *Pr.* 1045b: φάκελος δὲ ὁ δεσμός· ἀφ' οὗ καὶ "φακιόλιον".

Post-antique: numerous. *LBG* (*s.vv.* φακιάλιν, φακιάριον, φακιόλης, φακιόλιν, φακίολος), Zervan (2019: 194). Modern φακιόλι 'kerchief': Babiniotis (2002), Andriotis (1967), Kahane and Kahane (1972–6: 535), Meyer (1895: 68 *s.v.* φασκιά).

Notes: forms derivative σαβανοφακιάριον. Diethart (1990a: 87–8), Georgacas (1958: 187), O'Callaghan (1973), Koroli (2016: 195–6), Daris (1991a: 114), Hofmann (1989: 451–3), Meinersmann (1927: 62–3), Immisch (1885: 367), *DÉLG*, Frisk (1954–72: II.985), Beekes (2010), *TLL* (*s.v. faciāle*), Lampe (1961 *s.v.* φακιόλιον), LSJ (*s.vv.* φακιάλιον, πακιάλιον, φακιόλιον). See §4.2.5, §4.4 n. 79, §6.3 n. 21, §10.2.1, §10.2.2 H.

foreign	**φακίης** transliterating *faciēs* 'face': Lyd. *Mag.* p. 48.20 (VI AD). Sophocles (1887); for later use *LBG* (*s.v.* φακίη).

φακιό(υ)λιον, φακιώλιον: see φακιάλιον.

φάκλα: see φαίκλα and φακλεῖον.

not ancient	**φακλεῖον, φάκλα, φαγκλί**, from *facula* 'torch': no ancient examples. Binder (2000: 162–3), Daris (1991a: 114), Palmer (1945: 58), Meyer (1895: 67–8), Triandaphyllidis (1909: 123), *LBG* (*s.vv.* φακλίον 'torch', φακλαρέα 'torch-dance').
foreign	**φακτ(ι)ω** 'faction' (in the circus), from *factiō* 'faction': Latinate curse tablet *SEG* LII.988.1 etc. (IV AD?); Byzantine φακτίων. Zilliacus (1935a: 186–7 *s.v.* φακτίων), *LBG*, Triandaphyllidis (1909: 127).
Direct loan **IV AD – Byz.**	**φακτ(ι)ωνάριος, φακτιονάριος** (-ου, ὁ) 'leader of a (circus) faction', from *factiōnārius* 'member or head of a circus faction' (*TLL*). Documents: probably *P.Cair.Isid.* 58.13 (IV AD). Superseded reading on *SEG* 48.1297.25 (= 52.988.25); *SB* 12915 is not a document; *P.Lond.* V.1904.6 (V/VI AD) and *PSI* XVI.1644.5 (VI AD) are not this word (LSJ suppl. *s.vv.* πακτονάριον, φακτονάριον). Inscriptions: perhaps graffito *SEG* XXXIV.1562.1.2 (= *SB* 12915.2). Literature: Malal. 16.6 (VI AD). Post-antique: numerous. Sophocles (1887), *LBG*, Triandaphyllidis (1909: 126). Notes: Daris (1991a: 114), Hofmann (1989: 453), Zilliacus (1935a: 186–7), Meinersmann (1927: 63), *DÉLG*, Beekes (2010), Lampe (1961), LSJ suppl. See §4.2.4.1 n. 50, §10.2.1, §10.2.2 F.
Direct loan **V AD – Byz.**	**φάκτον** (-ου, τό) 'action', 'deed', from *factum* 'deed'. Literature: *ACO* II.I.II p. 46.32 (V AD); *Schol.Sinai.* in Latin script 4 *facto* (V/VI AD); Just. *Nov.* 68.t etc. (VI AD); Ath.Schol. 2.2.28 etc. (VI AD); Antec. 3.14.1 etc., but in Latin script 3.11.1 *facton* etc. (VI AD). Post-antique: numerous. *LBG*, Triandaphyllidis (1909: 128). Notes: Avotins (1992), Hofmann (1989: 453), Zilliacus (1935a: 188–9), *DÉLG* (*s.v.* 1 φάκτον), Beekes (2010 *s.v.* φάκτον 1), Lampe (1961). See §4.2.4.1 n. 55, §7.1.2, §9.5.6 n. 56, §10.2.1, §10.2.2 B.

φακτω-: see φακτιω-.

foreign	**φαλάρικα**, a kind of spear, from *falārica* 'heavy spear': Hesych. as lemma φ 95 (V/VI AD). Hofmann (1989: 453), Immisch (1885: 339–40).

Direct loan with influence I BC – Byz.	**Φαλερῖνος** (-ου, ὁ) 'Falernian wine', from *Falernus* 'Falernian', influenced by Greek -ῖνος. Inscriptions: Edict.Diocl. 2.7 (IV AD). Literature: common, e.g. DH *AR* 14.8.1 (I BC); Dsc. 5.6.6 (I AD); Plut. *Ant.* 59.8 (I/II AD); Galen, *De victu attenuante* 34.5 Kalbfleisch (II AD); Athenaeus 1.27c (II/III AD); Orib. *Col.* 3.4.1 (IV AD); Aëtius 2.252.24 (VI AD). Post-antique: minimal survival. *LBG* (*s.vv.* Φαλιήρινος, Φαλερικός). Notes: higher register than Φαλέρνος and restricted almost entirely to wine, while Φαλέρνος commonly used as personal and place name. Lauffer (1971: 218). See §4.2.4.1, §4.3.2 n. 75, **§4.4**, §8.1.5, §9.5.1, §10.2.1, §10.2.2 I.
rare	**Φαλερνίτης** 'Falernian wine', from *Falernus* 'Falernian' + -ίτης: Athenaeus 1.33a (II/III AD). Cf. Φαλερῖνος, Φαλέρνος.
Direct loan I–IV AD?	**Φαλέρνος** (-ου, ὁ) 'Falernian wine', from *Falernum* 'Falernian wine', neuter of *Falernus* 'Falernian'. Inscriptions: dipinto on amphora, *Agora* XXI.He.27 (III AD); variant in Edict. Diocl. 2.7 (IV AD). Literature: Strabo 5.4.3 (I BC/AD); Hdn. *Pros.Cath.* III.1.175.25 (II AD); Marc.Aurel. 6.13.1 (II AD); scholion to Luc. *Nav.* 23: οἶνος δὲ ἐξ Ἰταλίας· ὃν Φάλερνόν φασι. Post-antique: minimal survival. Notes: also many examples as personal and place name. LSJ suppl. (misaccented Φαλερνός). See §4.2.4.1, §4.4, **§5.3.2** passage 6, §10.2.1, §10.2.2 I, §12.2.2; cf. Φαλερῖνος, Φαλερνίτης.
not Latin?	**φάλκη**, which Hesych. (φ 112) says means 'bat', has been suggested as a borrowing of *falx* 'sickle' in *Oracula Sibyllina* 14.160 Geffcken and some Byzantine texts. Zervan (2019: 195), LSJ.
Direct loan VI AD – modern	**φαλκίδιον** (-ου, τό) 'minimum portion of an estate reserved by law for the heir(s)', from *Falcidia, -ae* 'quarter of an estate reserved for the heir(s) by the *Lex Falcidia*'. Documents: *P.Cair.Masp.* 67097v.D71, 67312.93, 67353v.A14 etc. (all VI AD). Literature: e.g. Just. *Nov.* 1.t (VI AD); Ath.Schol. 9.1 (VI AD). Sometimes in Latin script, e.g. Just. *Nov.* 1.2.1 (VI AD). Post-antique: common in legal texts, forming derivative φαλκιδιόω 'leave the legal minimum to'. *LBG* (*s.v.* Φαλκίδιος). Modern φαλκιδεύω 'restrict', 'undermine', φαλκίδευση: Babiniotis (2002), Andriotis (1967). Notes: Avotins (1992), Daris (1991a: 114, with derivation from *falcidium ius*), Hofmann (1989: 454), Zilliacus (1935a: 224–5), Meinersmann (1927: 63), LSJ. See §4.2.3.1, §10.2.1, §10.2.2 B, §12.2.2.
name	**Φαλκίδιος** 'Falcidian', from the name *Falcidius* (cf. *Lex Falcidia*): cf. Dio Cassius 48.33.5. Triantaphyllides (1892: 275).
not ancient	**φαλκόνι** 'falcon', from *falcō* 'falcon': no ancient examples. Meyer (1895: 68), Andriotis (1967).
rare	**φαλσόγραφος** 'forger', from *falsus* 'false' (via φάλσος?) + γράφω 'write': Leontius of Jerusalem, *Testimonia sanctorum* p. 104.22 Gray (VI AD); Byzantine texts. *LBG*, Lampe (1961).

rare	**φάλσος** 'forged', 'false', from *falsus* 'false': Adam. p. 8.23 etc. (IV AD); Byzantine texts (with derivatives φαλσεύω 'falsify', φάλσευμα 'falsification', etc.). Hofmann (1989: 455), *LBG*, Zervan (2019: 196), Lampe (1961). Cf. φαλσόγραφος.
	φαμειλ-, φαμελ-, φαμηλ-: see φαμιλ-.
foreign	**φάμης, φάμις** transliterating *famēs/famis* 'hunger', 'famine': Lyd. *Mag.* p. 22.18 (VI AD). Sophocles (1887 *s.v.* φάμις).
Direct loan II AD – modern	**φαμιλία, φαμελία, φαμηλία** (-ας, ἡ) 'family', 'household', 'group of gladiators', from *familia* 'household'. Documents: e.g. *O.Claud.* IV.673.5 (I/II AD); *O.Claud.* IV.871.3 (II AD); *P.Oxy.* 4088.24 etc. (IV AD); *P.Stras.* VIII.717.3 etc. (V AD); Harrauer and Pintaudi 2003: 138.16 (VI AD). Inscriptions: e.g. *IG* XII.Suppl.100.b (I BC?); *I.Aphrodisias Performers* 13.1 (I AD?); *I.Ephesos* 1620.1 (I/II AD); *I.Ephesos* 4346.1 (II AD); *I.Thrake Aeg.* 167.1 (III AD). Literature: Hesych. as lemma φ 133 (V/VI AD); Just. *Nov.* 119.11 (VI AD); Lyd. *Mens.* 1.18 etc. (VI AD); Romanus Melodus, *Cantica* 33.9.5 Grosdidier de Matons (VI AD); Ath.Schol. 9.11 (VI AD); Antec. in both scripts, e.g. 3.1.10 *familia* and φαμιλίαν (VI AD). Post-antique: common, forming derivative φαμιλικῶς 'with one's family'. *LBG* (*s.v.* φαμελία), Zervan (2019: 196–7), Triandaphyllidis (1909: 120). Modern φαμελιά, φαμιλιά, φαμίλια 'family': Babiniotis (2002), Andriotis (1967), Meyer (1895: 68). Triantaphyllides (1892: 220) derives φαμίλια from Italian but φαμελιά from Latin. Notes: Binder (2000: 125–6), Rodríguez Martín (2019: 421–3), Zuckerman (1988: 282), Avotins (1992), Daris (1991a: 114), Hofmann (1989: 455), Viscidi (1944: 37), Zilliacus (1935a: 188–9), Meinersmann (1927: 63), Immisch (1885: 343), Lampe (1961), LSJ. See §4.2.3.1, §10.2.1, §10.2.2 O.
foreign	*familiae ēmptor*, a legal term: Antec. 2.10.1 *familiemptor* etc. (VI AD).
Deriv. of loan II AD – Byz.	**φαμιλιαρικός, φαμελιαρικός, φαμηλιαρικός, φαμειλιαρεικός, φαμιλιαριχός** (-ή, -όν) 'of a servant', 'of a member of the household', probably from *familiāris* 'member of the household', 'servant' via φαμιλιάριος + -ικός. Documents: *O.Claud.* II.226.9, 257.3, perhaps 372.3 (all II AD); perhaps *O.Did.* 84.8 etc. (III AD). Inscriptions: Edict.Diocl. 26.10 etc. (IV AD); *I.Chr.Bulgarien* 215.1 (IV AD); *MAMA* III.100. Post-antique: survives. Sophocles (1887). Notes: derived by *TLL* (*s.v. familiāricus*, followed by Hofmann 1989: 456) from rare *familiāricus* 'of a servant', which works for Edict.Diocl., but in *O.Claud.* there is probably a closer relationship between φαμιλιάριος and φαμιλιαρικός. Binder (2000: 125–6), LSJ. See §4.6.1, §10.2.2 O.
Direct loan II AD – Byz.	**φαμιλιάριος, φαμελιάριος, φαμηλιάριος** (-ου, ὁ) 'member of the household', 'servant', from *familiāris* 'member of the household', 'servant'. Documents: *O.Claud.* II.264.3, 270.10, 274.8, 374.3, 375.7, 376.5, 382.6 (all II AD); *SB* 16941.20 (II AD); *O.Did.* 44.19 (III AD); *P.Lips.* I.102.2.5 (IV AD); perhaps *P.Turner* 47.5 etc. (IV/V AD); *P.Stras.* I.40.11 etc. (VI AD).

Inscriptions: Edict.Diocl. 26.96 etc. (IV AD).

Post-antique: some survival. *LBG*, Triandaphyllidis (1909: 120).

Notes: forms derivative φαμιλιαρικός. Daris (1991a: 114), Hofmann (1989: 456), Meinersmann (1927: 63), LSJ. See §4.2.5, §4.6.1, §10.2.1, §10.2.2 N.

non-existent?   **φαμιλιαρίς** (gen. -ίδος) 'female servant' (feminine of φαμιλιάριος), from *familiāris* 'servant': variant at Edict.Diocl. 28.43 etc. (IV AD). LSJ.

φάμις: see φάμης.

foreign   **φάμουλος** transliterating *famulus* 'servant': Lyd. *Mag.* p. 22.18 (VI AD). *LBG*.

foreign   **φάμωσον, φάμουσον** 'defamation', apparently from neut. of *fāmōsus* 'notorious' (i.e. *famosum carmen*): Lyd. *Mag.* p. 204.19, marked (VI AD); Byzantine texts. Binder (2000: 222–3), Zilliacus (1935a: 188–9, 1937: 334), *LBG* (*s.v.* φάμουσος), Zervan (2019: 197), Sophocles (1887), Lampe (1961 *s.v.* φάμουσον).

rare   **φάρ** (gen. φαρ(ρ)ός) 'emmer', from *far* 'emmer': DH *AR* 2.25.2–3, marked (I BC); Soranus, *Gynaecia* 2.29.2 Ilberg (I/II AD); Galen XIII.257.3 Kühn etc., marked (II AD); Aretaeus, *De curatione acutorum morborum* 2.2.20 Hude etc. (II AD); Aëtius 9.42.110 (p. 381) etc., sometimes marked (VI AD). For identification as emmer (rather than spelt, as suggested by LSJ and L&S) see Jasny (1944: 112). Hofmann (1989: 456–7), LSJ.

non-existent?   **φαρακράριος**, from *falcārius* 'scythe-maker': suggested on the basis of papyrus *BGU* I.344.13 (II/III AD), where abbreviated φαρακρ is used of a person. *BL* IV.4, Olsson (1926: 112), Hofmann (1989: 457), Meinersmann (1927: 63).

foreign   **φαρράχειος, φαρίχυλος** transliterating *farrāceus* 'of emmer': DH *AR* 2.25.2 (I BC); Alex.Trall. II.191.21 (VI AD). Hofmann (1989: 457), *LBG*, Sophocles (1887 *s.v.* φαρράκια), *TLL* (*s.v.* farrāceus 285.17–19).

not Latin?   **φάσηλος** 'kidney bean': perhaps from *phasēlus/faselus* 'bean', or *vice versa*. Hofmann (1989: 458), *DÉLG*, Beekes (2010), LSJ, LSJ suppl.

rare   **φασικλάριον**, from *fasciculāre* 'military forage' (*TLL*): unpublished ostracon O.Dios. inv. 849.2 (I/II AD).

Direct loan
II AD – modern   **φασίολος, φασήολος, πασίολος, φασ(ί)ωλος, φασίουλος, φασιούλυος** (-ου, ὁ) 'bean', probably from *phaseolus/phasiolus/passiolus* 'bean', itself perhaps from φάσηλος.

Inscriptions: Edict.Diocl. 1.21 etc. (IV AD).

Literature: Galen VI.542.3 Kühn etc. (II AD); Pollux 1.247 (II AD); Orib. *Col.* 1.26.1 etc. (IV AD); *Hippiatr.Berl.* (Pel.) 3.5 etc. (V AD?); Aëtius 1.93.2 etc. (VI AD); Alex.Trall. II.219.19 etc. (VI AD).

Post-antique: numerous. *LBG* (*s.vv.* φασίολον, φασιούλιον, φασίουλον, φασίουλος). Modern φασόλι, φασούλι, φασίολος 'haricot bean' are probably continuations: Babiniotis (2002), Andriotis (1967), Meyer (1895: 69).

Notes: Hofmann (1989: 319, 459), *DÉLG* (*s.v.* φάσηλος), Frisk (1954–72: II.996), Beekes (2010 *s.v.* φάσηλος), LSJ (*s.vv.* φασίολος, πασίολος), LSJ suppl. See §4.2.4.1 n. 51, §8.2.3 n. 51, §9.5.3, §10.2.1, §10.2.2 I.

φασκεία: see φασκία.

not Latin?	**φάσκελον**, a rude gesture, **φάσκελα** 'freckles', and related words, perhaps from *fascinum* 'evil spell': no ancient examples. Meyer (1895: 68–9), Andriotis (1967 *s.v.* φάσκελο).
foreign	**φάσκης** transliterating pl. of *fascis* 'bundle of rods': Plut. *Publ.* 12.5 (I/II AD). Mason (1974: 6, 97), Sophocles (1887). See §7.2.1.
Direct loan **II AD – modern**	**φασκία, φασκεία, φασκίνια** (-ας, ἡ or -ων, τά) 'bandage', 'strip', from *fascia* 'bandage', 'strip'.

Documents: *SB* 7575.5 (I/II AD); *BGU* III.814.9 (III AD); *P.Athen.* 67.11 (III/IV AD); *P.Oxy.* 109.26 (III/IV AD); *P.Prag.* II.176.6 (III/IV AD); *P.Ryl.* IV.627.41 (IV AD). LSJ suppl.'s ζεῦγος φασκιῶν in Sirat *et al.* 1986 line 17 (V AD) is written in Hebrew (no doubt transliterated from Greek: commentary p. 49).

Inscriptions: *SEG* VII.422.8 (III AD); Edict.Diocl. 28.37 (IV AD).

Literature: Soranus, *Gynaecia* 1.56.5 Ilberg (I/II AD); Pollux 2.166, marked (II AD); *Coll.Herm.* Mp 13d (III AD?); Basil Caesariensis, *Epistulae* 45.1.36 Courtonne (IV AD); Callin. *V.Hypat.* 22.13 (V AD); Hesych. as gloss π 2667, τ 392 (V/VI AD); Aëtius 16.37.81–2 (VI AD); Dan.Sket. *AP* 50 (VI AD); Ps.-Galen XIV.399.18 Kühn etc.; scholia to Thuc. 4.48 and 7.36, Luc. *Symp.* 47 as gloss, Ar. *Pl.* 586 as gloss; bilingual glossaries, e.g. Gloss. Ps.-Cyril. 453.20, 470.20.

Post-antique: numerous. *LBG* (*s.v.* φασκέα), Zervan (2019: 197), Sophocles (1887), Triandaphyllidis (1909: 122). Modern φασκιά 'swaddling-band' and derivatives: Babiniotis (2002), Andriotis (1967), Kahane and Kahane (1972–6: 535), Meyer (1895: 68).

Notes: forms derivatives φασκίδιον, φασκιόω, perhaps φασκιάριος. Daris (1991a: 114), Hofmann (1989: 459–60), *DÉLG*, Beekes (2010), Meinersmann (1927: 63), *TLL* (*s.v. fascia* 296.37–43, 78–80), LSJ, LSJ suppl. See §4.2.3.1, §4.6.1, §8.2.1, §10.2.1, §10.2.2 H.

non-existent?	**φασκιάρια** (τά) 'bundle', from *fascis* 'bundle' + -άριον: perhaps inscription *SEG* LVII.1427.43 (III AD). LSJ suppl.
rare	**φασκιάριος**, meaning uncertain ('bandage-maker'?), probably from *fascia* 'bandage', 'strip' via φασκία + -άριος (though unattested *fasciārius* has also been suggested): EphraemSyr. III p. 48.40 (V/VI AD). Hofmann (1989: 460), *LBG*.
	φασκίδες: see φασκίς.
Deriv. of loan **III–IV, VI AD?**	**φασκίδιον, φασχίδιον** (-ου, τό) 'bandage', 'belt', 'strap', from *fascia* 'bandage', 'strip' via φασκία + -ίδιον.

Documents (meaning 'bandage'): *P.Warr.* 18.16 (III AD); *P.Oxy.* 2598.a7 etc. (III/IV AD); *P.Stras.* IV.183.8 (IV AD).

Literature (meaning 'belt', 'strap'): *Vita Danieli*, Clugnet 1900: 52.25, 55.22 (VI AD).

Notes: change of meaning in VI AD may indicate that it died out after IV AD and was then (briefly) reborrowed. But perhaps **πασχίδιον** 'little girdle' on papyrus *P.Fouad* 77.10 (II AD) (commentary *ad loc.*) is the same word; if so there was probably one borrowing with several meanings. Daris (1991a: 114), Hofmann (1989: 460 *s.v.* φασκια), Cavenaile (1951: 400, 1952: 196), *DÉLG* (*s.v.* φασκία), *LBG*, Lampe (1961), LSJ suppl. See §4.6.1, §8.2.1, §10.2.2 H.

φασκίνια: see φασκία.

not ancient   **φασκιόλη**, from *fasciola* 'ribbon': no ancient examples. Hofmann (1989: 460), Immisch (1885: 367).

Deriv. of loan **φασκιόω** 'bandage up', from *fascia* 'bandage' via φασκία + -όω.
v AD – modern
                Literature: perhaps Dsc. *Eup.* 2.69.3, apparatus to Wellmann 1906–14:
                    III.280.8 (I AD); Cyran. 2.4.28 etc. (II AD?); Anton.Hag. *V.Sym.Styl.* 5
                    (V AD); Aëtius 16.132.14 (VI AD); Ps.-Galen XIV.561.7 Kühn etc.
                Post-antique: numerous. Sophocles (1887). Modern φασκιώνω 'swaddle':
                    Babiniotis (2002), Andriotis (1967).
                Notes: Hofmann (1989: 461), *DÉLG* (*s.v.* φασκία), Lampe (1961), LSJ (*s.v.*
                    φασκία). See §4.6.1, §10.2.2 L.

not Latin?   **φασκίς** (plural φασκίδες), meaning uncertain, perhaps from *fascis* 'bundle'. *DÉLG*, Beekes (2010), LSJ suppl.

rare   **φάσκος** 'bundle', from *fascis* 'bundle': Edict.Diocl. 14.7 etc. (IV AD). *DÉLG*, Beekes (2010), Hofmann (1989: 461), LSJ (*s.v.* φάσκον).

φασχίδιον: see φασκίδιον.

φατριάζω: see φρατριάζω.

φαυρικίσιος: see φαβρικήσιος.

foreign   **φαῦστος** transliterating *faustus* 'fortunate': Plut. *Sulla* 34.3 (I/II AD). Sophocles (1887).

foreign   **φέβερ** transliterating a Latin word for 'grief' (*februm* 'purification' or *feber* 'at the end'?): Lyd. *Mens.* 4.25.8 (VI AD). *TLL s.v.* 2. φέβερ. See §8.1.7 n. 34.

Direct loan **Φεβρουάριος, Φεβραῖος, Φεβροάριος, Φεβράριος** (-α, -ον or -ου, ὁ) 'February', from
II BC – modern   *Februārius* 'February'.
                Documents: e.g. *Chrest.Mitt.* 316.ii.18 (II AD); *P.Oxy.* 3054.11 (III AD);
                    P.Panop. 15.20 (IV AD); *SB* 16521.4 (IV/V AD); *P.Lond.* v.1663.20 (VI AD).
                Inscriptions: e.g. Sherk 1969: no. 10B.3 (II BC); Hassall, Crawford, and
                    Reynolds 1974: 202.iii.6 (II/I BC); Sherk 1969: no. 65.D74 (I BC); *IGUR*
                    IV.1645.2 (I/II AD); *IGR* IV.1156.b12 etc. (II AD); *SEG* XVII.528.24
                    (III AD); *I.Mus.Palermo* 111.5 (IV AD); *I.Cret.* IV.485.4 (V AD); *SEG*
                    XXXVII.1492C (VI AD).
                Literature: e.g. DH *AR* 1.32.5 (I BC); Jos. *AJ* 13.260 (I AD); Plut. *Mor.* 272c
                    (I/II AD); Vet.Val. *App.* 9.7.12 (II AD); Athenaeus 3.98a, marked (II/III
                    AD); Epiph. *Pan.* 11.295.16 (IV AD); *ACO* II.I.III p. 121.10 (V AD); *ACO*
                    III p. 56.20 (VI AD).
                Post-antique: common. Modern Φεβρουάριος, Φλεβάρης, Φλεβάρις: Babiniotis
                    (2002), Andriotis (1967), Meyer (1895: 69).
                Notes: Solin (2008), Binder (2000: 99–100), Sijpesteijn (1979), Dieterich
                    (1898: 73), García Domingo (1979: 684), Strobach (1997: 200), Hofmann
                    (1989: 461–2), Meinersmann (1927: 63), Lampe (1961), LSJ suppl. See
                    §4.2.1, §4.2.2, §6.1, **§8.1.4**, §8.2.3 n. 51, §10.2.1, §10.2.2 E.

φέκλη: see φαίκλα.

φελλί: see ὀφέλλιον.

rare	**φέλλουρα, φέρουλα** 'giant fennel', from *ferula* 'giant fennel': old scholia to Hes. *Op.* 52a, as gloss. André (1958: 60), *DÉLG* (*s.v.* φέλλουρα), Beekes (2010), *LBG* (*s.vv.* φέλλουρα, φέρουλλα).
	φελόνη, φελόνιον, φελώνιον: see φαινόλη.
Direct loan **II AD – Byz.**	**φεμινάλια, φημινάλια, φιμινάλια** (-ων, τά) 'trousers', from *feminālia, -ium* 'thigh-coverings'. Documents: *SB* 14178.16 etc. (II AD); *P.Münch.* III.I.142.8 etc. (VI AD). Literature: Hesych. as gloss α 4473, π 1865 (V/VI AD); with *vastrapes* in Gloss. Ps.-Philox. 204.52. Post-antique: numerous. *LBG* (*s.v.* φιμινάλια). Notes: Diethart (1986: 89, 1988: 68), Daris (1991a: 114 *s.v.* φημινάλιον), Hofmann (1989: 462), LSJ suppl. See §2.2.1, §4.2.5, §8.2.2, §10.2.1, §10.2.2 H.
	φενέστρα: see φαινέστρα.
rare	**φενίκουλα**, an object connected with vehicles, perhaps from unattested **fenicula* (distinct from, but perhaps related to, *faeniculum* 'fennel'): Edict.Diocl. 15.21 (IV AD). Lauffer (1971: 254), Hofmann (1989: 462), *TLL* (*s.v.* *fenicula*), LSJ suppl. See §8.1.7.
	φενόλη(ς): see φαινόλη.
	φενοῦκλον, φενούκλουμ: see φαινοῦκλον.
foreign	**φέρειν, φερῖρε**, and **φέρε** transliterating *ferīre* and *ferī*, inf. and imperative of *feriō* 'strike': Plut. *Marc.* 8.7–8, *Rom.* 16.6 (I/II AD). Sophocles (1887).
foreign	**φερεντάριοι**, a type of soldier, from *ferentārius* 'light-armed soldier': Hesych. as lemma φ 304 (V/VI AD); Lyd. *Mag.* p. 74.9, marked (VI AD); occasionally later. Hofmann (1989: 463), Immisch (1885: 340), *LBG*, LSJ suppl.
foreign	**Φερέτριος** transliterating *Feretrius*, epithet of Jupiter: e.g. DH *AR* 2.34.4 (I BC); Plut. *Rom.* 16.6 (I/II AD). Strobach (1997: 200), Hofmann (1989: 463), LSJ.
rare	**φέρετρον** 'bier', probably from *feretrum* 'bier': Polybius 8.29.4 (II BC). Biville (1987: 75, 1992: 229), LSJ. See §8.1.3 n. 17.
foreign	**φέρι** transliterating pl. of *ferus* 'wild': Hesych. φ 309 (V/VI AD). Immisch (1885: 358). Cf. ὀβιφέρι.
	φερῖρε: see φέρειν.
	φέρουλα: see φέλλουρα.
Direct loan **I–III AD**	**φετιάλιος, φητιᾶλις, φιτιᾶλις** (-ου/ος?, ὁ), a kind of priest, from *fētiālis* 'fetial priest'. Inscriptions: perhaps *IG* II/III².III.4212.2 (II AD); perhaps *I.Ephesos* 682.15 (II/III AD). Literature: DH *AR* 2.72.1 etc., all marked (I BC); Augustus, *Res gestae* 7.7 Volkmann (I AD); Plut. *Numa* 12.3 etc. (I/II AD); Dio Cassius 50.4.5 (II/III AD). Notes: Freyburger-Galland (1998: 141–2), Strobach (1997: 200), García Domingo (1979: 685), Mason (1974: 4, 97), Hofmann (1989: 464), LSJ (*s.v.* φετιάλιοι), LSJ suppl. (*s.v.* φετιάλιοι). See §4.2.5, §10.2.1, §10.2.2 D.

not ancient — **φηδεράτωρ** 'treaty-maker', from *foederātor* 'treaty-maker' (*TLL*): no ancient examples. Zilliacus (1935a: 188–9).

foreign — **φῆλιξ** transliterating *fēlix* 'lucky': Plut. *Sulla* 34.2, *Mor.* 318d (I/II AD). Strobach (1997: 200).

φημινάλια: see φεμινάλια.

φητιᾱλις: see φετιάλιος.

Direct loan
VI AD – Byz. — **φίβλα, φίβουλα** (-ης?, ἡ) 'brooch', from *fībula* 'pin', 'brooch' (also spelled *fibla*: *TLL s.v. fībula* 643.71–3).
Literature: Hesych. as gloss α 4986, π 3052, as lemma φ 435 (V/VI AD); Malal. 2.8.26 (VI AD); Lyd. *Mag.* pp. 88.11, 104.15 (VI AD); old scholion to Callimachus, *Hymns* 2.32 as gloss; Geneva scholion to *Iliad* 18.401 as gloss; with *fibula* in Gloss. Ps.-Cyril. 471.17.
Post-antique: numerous. Lampe (1961), *LBG*, Triandaphyllidis (1909: 122).
Notes: forms derivatives φιβλόω, φιβλίον. Binder (2000: 190–1), Hofmann (1989: 464), Viscidi (1944: 42), LSJ, LSJ suppl. See §4.1.1 n. 8, §4.6.1, §9.5.4 n. 42, **§9.5.5** passage 71, §10.2.1, §10.2.2 H.

Direct loan
III AD – Byz. — **φιβλατώριον, φιβουλατώριον** (-ου, τό), a garment, from *fībulātōrium*, a garment (one using pins) (*TLL*).
Documents: perhaps *P.Lond.* II.191.5 (II AD); *P.Oxy.* 1051.11 etc. (III AD).
Inscriptions: Edict.Diocl. 19.24 etc. (IV AD).
Literature: Philogelos 106 (IV AD). Unverified example (IV AD) in Zilliacus (1937: 322, 334).
Post-antique: numerous. *LBG*, Triandaphyllidis (1909: 122).
Notes: Sidro and Maravela (forthcoming), Binder (2000: 191), Daris (1991a: 115), Hofmann (1989: 465 *s.vv.* φιβλατωριν, φιβουλατωριον), Zilliacus (1937: 334), Meinersmann (1927: 63), LSJ suppl. See §4.2.4.1 n. 54, §10.2.1, §10.2.2 H; cf. ἰμφειβλατώριον.

rare — **φιβλίον** 'brooch', from *fībula* 'brooch' via φίβλα + -ιον: *Hippiatr.Par.* (Pel.) 54 (V AD?); with *fibula* in Gloss. Ps.-Philox. 71.49; Byzantine texts. Binder (2000: 191), Hofmann (1989: 464 *s.v.* φίβλα), *LBG*, Lampe (1961), LSJ (*s.v.* φίβλα).

rare — **φίβλον** 'brooch' (only in the plural φίβλα), variant of φίβλα and therefore also from *fībula* 'brooch': inscriptions *SEG* VII.371.ii.3 etc. (II AD); *SEG* II.776.i.8 etc. (III AD). LSJ suppl.

Deriv. of loan
VI AD – Byz. — **φιβλόω** 'fasten with a pin', 'transfix', from *fībula* 'pin' via φίβλα + -όω.
Literature: Hesych. as gloss ε 1644, 2504 (V/VI AD); Malal. 5.13.20, 6.20.27 (VI AD).
Post-antique: numerous. *LBG*, Sophocles (1887).
Notes: forms derivatives ἐμφιβλόω, συμφιβλόω. Binder (2000: 190–1), Hofmann (1989: 465), Immisch (1885: 368), Lampe (1961), LSJ (*s.v.* φιβλόομαι, though the active occurs). See §4.6.1, §10.2.2 H.

φιβουλ-: see φιβλ-.

foreign — **φιδει(ϊ)ούσσωρ** 'surety', from *fidēiussor* 'guarantor': Antec. in Latin script 3.20.pr. *fideiussores* etc. (VI AD); later in Greek script. Zilliacus (1935a: 188–9). See §7.3 n. 36.

Direct loan
V AD – Byz.

φιδεικομ(μ)ισ(σ)άριος (-α, -ον) 'left in trust', 'recipient of a legacy paid at the discretion of the main heir', and a kind of praetor, from *fideicommissārius* 'concerning *fideicommissum*'.

Documents: *P.Cair.Masp.* 67151.54, 67312.25 (both VI AD).

Literature: Thüngen 2016: A5 etc. (V AD); Just. *Nov.* 1.1.1 etc., but in Latin script 108.2, *Codex* 1.3.45.6 etc. (VI AD); Lyd. *Mag.* perhaps p. 128.20, in Latin script p. 78.5 acc. pl. *fideicommissarios* (VI AD); Antec. in Latin script 1.14.1 *fideicommissarian* etc. (VI AD).

Post-antique: common in legal texts. *LBG.*

Notes: Avotins (1989, 1992), Daris (1991a: 115), Hofmann (1989: 466), Zilliacus (1935a: 188–9), Meinersmann (1927: 63), LSJ suppl. See §4.2.2, §7.2.1, §7.3 n. 36, §10.2.1, §10.2.2 B.

Direct loan
IV AD – Byz.

φιδε(ι)κόμ(μ)ισ(σ)ον, φιδικόμισσον, φειδικόμισος (-ου, τό) 'legacy paid at the discretion of the main heir', from *fideicommissum* 'legacy paid at the discretion of the main heir'.

Documents: tachygraphy in Menci 2000: 290 (VI AD).

Literature: Gregorius Nazianzenus, *Testamentum*, Pitra 1868: 156.3 (IV AD); Thüngen 2016: A8 etc. (V AD); Hesych. as lemma φ 269 (V/VI AD); Just. *Codex* 1.5.18.20 etc. but in Latin script 1.3.45.33, *Nov.* 1.1.1 etc. but in Latin script 107.1 etc. (VI AD); Antec. in Latin script 1.14.1 *fideicommisson* etc. (VI AD).

Post-antique: common in legal texts. *LBG.*

Notes: Menci (2000: 290), Avotins (1989, 1992), Hofmann (1989: 466), Zilliacus (1935a: 188–9), Immisch (1885: 357–8), Lampe (1961), LSJ suppl. See §4.2.4.1 n. 55, §7.3 n. 36, §10.2.1, §10.2.2 B.

φιδειούσσωρ: see φιδειϊούσσωρ.

name

Φιδῆλις, from *fidēlis* 'trustworthy': probably a legion's name in II AD inscriptions from Ephesos, e.g. *I.Ephesos* 36a.11, 36b.10. Hofmann (1989: 466).

foreign

φιδουκιάριος 'fiduciary', from *fīdūciārius* 'fiduciary': Antec. in Latin script 1.19. pr. *fiduciarioi* etc. (VI AD); later in Greek script. *LBG.*

not Latin?

Φιλιτιανοί, meaning uncertain, may be from the saint's name *Fēlīciānus* (Sleumer 1926) or a Greek formation meaning 'inhabitants of Philae'. Commentaries on papyri *P.Cair.Masp.* 67057.1.9 (VI AD) and *P.Oxy.* 2480.82 (VI AD), Hofmann (1989: 466), *LBG*, LSJ.

non-existent?

φιλογερμανικός 'loyal to Germanicus', from φιλο- 'fond of' + the name *Germānicus*: perhaps inscription *CIRB* 1123.4 (I AD). LSJ.

Deriv. of loan
I BC – V AD

φιλόκαισαρ, φιλοκαίσαρος, φιλόκεσαρ (gen. -αρος/-ου, ὁ) 'loyal to Caesar', 'loyal to the emperor', from φιλο- 'fond of' + *Caesar* via Καῖσαρ.

Inscriptions: common, e.g. *IG* XII.IV.II.568.1 (I BC); *IG* II/III².III.3535.11 (I AD); *IG* V.I.59.10 (II AD); *IG* V.I.547.15 (III AD); *CIRB* 67.3 (V AD).

Coins: ΒΑΣΙΛΕΥΣ ΜΕΓΑΣ ΑΓΡΙΠΠΑΣ ΦΙΛΟΚΑΙΣΑΡ in Judaea, Head 1911: 808, cf. 809 (I AD).

Literature: Philo Judaeus, *Legatio ad Gaium* 37 etc. (I BC/AD).

Notes: Hofmann (1989: 140 *s.v.* Καῖσαρ), LSJ. See §4.6.2, §8.1.5, §9.1 n. 4, §10.2.2 D.

Loan compound I AD	**φιλοκλαύδιος** (-ον) 'friend of Claudius', from φιλο- 'fond of' + name *Claudius*. Inscriptions: e.g. *SEG* III.740.6 (I AD); *SEG* XXVII.521.3 (I AD). Coins: ΒΑΣΙΛ. ΗΡΩΔΗΣ ΦΙΛΟΚΛΑΥΔΙΟΣ in Judaea, Head 1911: 808 (I AD). Notes: inscriptions only from Cos and Calymna. Use continues into reign of Nero (Segre 1952: no. 111.12). LSJ. See §4.5, §8.2.1, §9.1 n. 4, §10.2.1, §10.2.2 D; cf. Κλαύδιος.
rare	**φιλοκόμοδος** 'friend of Commodus', from φιλο- 'fond of' + the name *Commodus*: Hdn.Hist. 1.17.3 (II/III AD); occasional Byzantine texts. LSJ, *LBG*.
rare	**φιλονέρων** 'friend of Nero', from φιλο- 'fond of' + the name *Nero*: inscription Segre 1952: no. 111.11 (I AD); perhaps originally present on other inscriptions but later effaced (e.g. *IG* XII.IV.II.1143.11, I AD). LSJ.
Deriv. of loan I BC – Byz.	**φιλορώμαιος, φιλορώμεος** (-α, -ον) 'friend of the Romans', from φιλο- 'fond of' + *Rōma* 'Rome' via Ῥωμαῖος. Inscriptions: e.g. *IG* XII.VI.I.349.4 (I BC); *CIRB* 31.1 (I BC/AD); *SEG* XLVI.940.i.1 etc. (I AD); *I.Stratonikeia* 189.3 (II AD); *CIRB* 1250.4 (III AD); *SEG* XLVIII.993.4 (V AD). Coins: ΒΑΣΙΛΕΥΣ ΜΑΝΝΟΣ ΦΙΛΟΡΩΜΑΙΟΣ at Edessa, Head 1911: 814 (II AD); ΑΥΡ. ΚΑΡΡΗΝΩΝ ΦΙΛΡΩΜΑΙΩΝ ΚΟΛΩΝΙΑ at Carrhae, Head 1911: 814 (II/III AD). Literature: e.g. perhaps Diodorus Siculus 29.22.1 (I BC); Jos. *Vit.* 345 (I AD); Hdn. *Pros.Cath.* III.1.133.19, 228.20, prescribing the accent φιλορώμαιος (II AD); Themistius, Ἐπὶ τῆς εἰρήνης Οὐάλεντι 132c Downey and Schenkl (IV AD); Agathias, Keydell 1967: 136.17 (VI AD). Post-antique: numerous with ῥωμαῖος meaning 'Greek', forming derivative φιλορωμαιότης 'love of Greeks' (*LBG*). Notes: LSJ, LSJ suppl. See §2.4, §4.6.2, §4.6.3, §5.3.2 n. 25, §8.1.5, §9.1 n. 4, §10.2.2 D, §10.3.2.
rare	**φιλοτιβέριος** 'friend of Tiberius', from φιλο- 'fond of' + the name *Tiberius*: Philo Judaeus, *Legatio ad Gaium* 37 (I BC/AD). LSJ. **φιμινάλια**: see φεμινάλια.
foreign	**φισκάλιος** 'of the treasury', from *fiscālis* 'of the treasury': Antec. in Latin script 1.25.1 *fiscalia* etc. (VI AD); later in Greek script. Hofmann (1989: 467), Zilliacus (1935a: 188–9), *LBG*. See §9.5.6 n. 68. **φισκῖνα**: see πισκεῖνα.
Direct loan I AD – Byz.	**φίσκος** (-ου, ὁ) 'basket', 'crate', 'imperial treasury', from *fiscus* 'basket', 'imperial treasury'. Documents: e.g. *O.Petr.Mus.* 147.9 (I AD); *P.Hever* 64.29 (II AD); *P.Iand.* VII.145.5 (III AD); perhaps *P.Oxy.* 1551.17 (IV AD). Inscriptions: common, e.g. *IG* V.II.516.16 (I AD); *IG* II/III².I.1100.4 etc. (II AD); *I.Ano Maked.* 138.6 (III AD); *IGPorto* 53.1 (IV AD). Literature: e.g. Artemidorus, *Onirocriticon* 4.59.52 (II AD); Philostratus, *Vitae sophistarum* 2.614.21 Kayser (II/III AD); Eus. *HE* 9.10.11 (IV AD); Nil. 2.178.16 (V AD); Hesych. as lemma φ 561 (V/VI AD); Just. *Nov.* 112.2.1 (VI AD); Antec. 3.1.5, but in Latin script 1.25.1 *fiscon* etc. (VI AD).

Post-antique: numerous, forming derivative φισκόομαι 'be punished by confiscation'. *LBG* (*s.v.* φίσκον), Zervan (2019: 198), Triandaphyllidis (1909: 127).

Notes: forms derivative φισκοσυνήγορος. Avotins (1992), Daris (1991a: 115), Mason (1974: 5, 97), Hofmann (1989: 467), Zilliacus (1935a: 188–9), Meinersmann (1927: 63–4), Immisch (1885: 358), Lampe (1961), LSJ, LSJ suppl. See §4.1.1, §4.2.4.1 n. 51, §4.6.2, §10.2.1, §10.2.2 D.

Deriv. of loan VI AD – Byz. **φισκοσυνήγορος** (-ου, ὁ), an official, calque of *advocātus fiscī* formed from *fiscus* 'imperial treasury' via φίσκος + συνήγορος 'advocate'.

Documents: *Stud.Pal.* VIII.1028.2 (VI AD); *P.Freer* 1+2.210 (VI AD); perhaps *P.Cair.Masp.* 67057.2.23 (VI AD).

Literature: Hesych. as lemma φ 562 (V/VI AD); Just. *Codex* 1.33.5.9 (VI AD); Gloss. Ps.-Cyril. 472.11.

Post-antique: survives, forming derivatives φισκοσυνηγορία 'administration of taxes', φισκοσυνηγοράτον 'tax office', etc. *LBG*, Zervan (2019: 198).

Notes: Filos (2010: 244, 251), Daris (1991a: 115), Hofmann (1989: 467 *s.v.* φισκος), Cavenaile (1952: 199), Immisch (1885: 358), LSJ. See §4.6.2, §10.2.2 D.

φιτιᾶλις: see φετιάλιος.

Φλαβιάλιος: see Φλαουιάλιος.

rare **φλαβίλλιον** 'fan', from *flābellum* 'fan' + -ιον: Athenaeus 14.647f (II/III AD). Hofmann (1989: 467), *TLL* (*s.v. flābellum* 832.28–9), LSJ.

Φλαβυάλιος: see Φλαουιάλιος.

φλάγελλα: see φραγέλλη.

φλαγέλλιον: see φραγέλλιον.

rare **φλάγελλον** 'whip', from *flagellum* 'whip': Edict.Diocl. 10.3 (IV AD). Lauffer (1971) also restores it at 10.18, where the right reading is φραγέλλιον (*q.v.*) (*SEG* XXXVII.335.iii.31). Byzantine φραγέλλον 'whip' (*LBG*, Triandaphyllidis 1909: 124) is probably a separate development. Hofmann (1989: 467–8), LSJ suppl. See §4.3.2.

φλαγελλόω: see φραγελλόω.

not ancient? **φλαγιτάτωρ** 'creditor insistently demanding repayment', from *flāgitātor* 'creditor insistently demanding repayment': probably no ancient examples. Zilliacus (1935a: 188–9).

foreign **φλάμα** (τά), said by DH *AR* 2.64.2 (I BC) to be Latin term for items worn by flamens, is perhaps *flāminia*, neut. pl. of *flāminius* 'of a flamen'. Hofmann (1989: 469).

rare **φλᾶμεν, φλαμέντας, φλαμήν, φλάμονες, φλάμινες, φλαμίνιοι**, a kind of priest, from *flāmen* 'flamen' and perhaps *flāminius* 'of a flamen': usually marked, e.g. DH *AR* 2.64.2 (I BC); Plut. *Mor.* 274c and *Marc.* 5.6 (I/II AD); App. *BC* 1.8.65 (I/II AD); inscriptions e.g. *IG* II/III².III.5206.1 (IV AD); *SEG* VI.588.4. Famerie (1998: 201–3), Strobach (1997: 201), Freyburger-Galland (1998: 140–1), Mason (1974: 4, 97), Hofmann (1989: 469, 470), LSJ (*s.v.* φλαμέντας), LSJ suppl. (*s.v.* φλαμέντας).

not Latin?   **φλαμία** 'spear' in *Acta Thomae* 165 = Bonnet 1903: 278.8 (III AD) is suggested by Hofmann (1989: 470) as from *framea* 'Germanic spear' (originally Germanic). Lampe (1961).

non-existent   **φλαμινάλιος** is cited by Mason (1974: 97) as from *flāminālis* 'former flamen' on the basis of an abbreviation on inscription *IG* II/III².III.5206.1 (IV AD) that probably stands for φλᾶμεν. LSJ suppl. (*s.v.* φλαμέντας).

                  φλάμινες: see φλᾶμεν.

foreign   **φλαμινίκα** transliterating *flāminica*, a priestess: Plut. *Mor.* 285a (I/II AD). Mason (1974: 97), Hofmann (1989: 470), LSJ (*s.v.* φλαμέντας).

                  φλαμίνιοι: see φλᾶμεν.

not ancient   **φλάμμουλα** transliterating *flammula* 'little flame': interpolation in Dsc. 4.133 RV. *TLL* (*s.v. flammula* 875.21–3), Sophocles (1887).

foreign   **φλαμμουλάριος**, apparently transliterating unattested **flammulārius* 'standard-bearer': Lyd. *Mag.* p. 74.6 (VI AD). Diethart (1993: 225–6), Zilliacus (1935a: 224–5), *TLL* (*s.v. flammulārius*), *LBG* (*s.vv.* φλαμμουλάριος, φλαμπουριάρης), Triandaphyllidis (1909: 129). See §8.1.7.

rare   **φλάμμουλον** 'red banner', from *flammula* 'red banner' (*TLL s.v.* 875.16–21) or perhaps *flammeolum* 'bridal veil': Lyd. *Mag.* p. 18.25, *Mens.* 1.41.6 (VI AD); perhaps old scholion to *Od.* 11.579 as gloss on δέρτον 'membrane that contains the bowels', but given the difference in meaning that could be a different word; frequently in Byzantine texts (with derivatives φλαμμούλιον 'banner', φλαμμουλίσκιον 'streamer', etc.). Modern φλάμπουρο 'flag' etc.: Babiniotis (2002), Andriotis (1967), Meyer (1895: 69–70). Zilliacus (1935a: 224–5), *LBG*, Zervan (2019: 198), Triandaphyllidis (1909: 130), Lampe (1961).

                  φλάμονες: see φλᾶμεν.

Direct loan
IV–VI AD   **Φλαουιάλιος, Φλαυιάλιος, Φλαουειάλιος, Φλαβυάλιος, Φλαβιάλιος** (-ου, ὁ), a military rank, from *Flāviālis* 'Flavian'.
         Documents: *Chrest.Wilck.* 424.i.9 = i.3 (IV AD); perhaps *P.Kellis* I.15.2 (IV AD); *SB* 4779.3 (IV AD?); *P.Pintaudi* 36.5 (V/VI AD); *CPR* XXIV.20.2 (V/VI AD); *P.Paramone* 13.1 (VI AD); *BGU* II.369.5 (VI AD); *P.Lond.* I.113(1).103 (VI AD).
         Inscriptions: perhaps *I.North Galatia* 450.7 (V–VI AD?).
         Notes: Scharf (1996), Daris (1991a: 115), Hofmann (1989: 470), Zilliacus (1935a: 226–7), Meinersmann (1927: 64), *LBG*. See §4.2.5, §10.2.1, §10.2.2 C.

not ancient?   **φλασκίον** 'flask', perhaps from *flascō* 'flask' (*TLL*) + -ιον: as gloss in scholia to *Od.* 2.349d (ἀμφιφορεύς καλεῖται τὸ παρὰ ἰδιώταις λεγόμενον φλασκίον), 2.353a. Hofmann (1989: 470), *LBG*, Triandaphyllidis (1909: 121), Meyer (1895: 70 *s.v.* φλάσκα), Andriotis (1967 *s.vv.* φλάσκα, φλασκί), Lampe (1961), LSJ (*s.v.* φλάσκη).

non-existent?   **φλάσκων** 'flagon', from *flascō* 'flask' (*TLL*): perhaps (emendation) Hesych. α 7549 as gloss that is itself glossed (V/VI AD). Hofmann (1989: 470 *s.v.* φλασκίον), *LBG*, LSJ (*s.v.* φλάσκη).

Φλαυιάλιος: see Φλαουιάλιος.

φλέμινα: see φλιμέλιον.

foreign **φλεξεντιής**, perhaps from *flexuntēs* (archaic term for Roman cavalry): stated by Hesych. φ 599 (v/vi ad) to be Latin for a kind of cavalry. Hofmann (1989: 470–1), Hahn (1906: 13), Immisch (1885: 340, reading φλεξέντης).

rare **φλιμέλιον**, *φλέμινα* 'blood-swelling on horses' feet', from *flēmina* 'swelling around the ankles' (itself from φλεγμονή 'inflammation'): *Hippiatr.Berl.* (Apsyrtus) 51.1, marked (iii/iv ad?); unmarked in later parts of *Hippiatr.* Fischer (1979), Hofmann (1989: 471), *DÉLG* (s.v. φλέμινα), Frisk (1954–72: II.1028), Beekes (2010 s.vv. φλέμινα, φλιμέλια), *LBG* (s.vv. φλεμίνα, φλέμινα), LSJ.

not ancient **φλόκκος** 'tassels', cited by Meyer (1895: 70) as from *floccus* 'tuft of wool': no ancient examples. Andriotis (1967 s.v. φλόκος) gives an Italian derivation. Triandaphyllidis (1909: 122).

φλοός: see αἰρίσφλως.

φλουβινάριον: see πουλβινάριον.

φλουμα-: see πλουμα-.

φλοῦς: see αἰρίσφλως.

not ancient? **φλῶρος** 'white', cited by Meyer (1895: 70) as from *flōrus* 'light-coloured': probably no ancient examples.

φλῶς: see αἰρίσφλως.

foreign **φόδερε** transliterating inf. of *fodiō* 'dig': Plut. *Fab.* 1.2 (i/ii ad). Sophocles (1887).

foreign **φοίδερα** transliterating pl. of *foedus* 'treaty': Procop. *Bell.* 3.11.4, 8.5.14 (vi ad); occasionally later. *LBG*.

rare **φοιδερατικός** 'connected with allies', from *foederātus* 'bound by treaty to Rome' + -ικός: Just. *Nov.* 147.2 (vi ad); Ath.Schol. in Latin script 20.6.2 etc. (vi ad); perhaps Malal. 14.40 (vi ad); Byzantine texts. Avotins (1992), Hofmann (1989: 471), Zilliacus (1935a: 226–7), *LBG*, *TLL* (s.v. unattested **foederāticus*, which is not claimed to have ever existed), Lampe (1961), LSJ suppl. See §8.1.7.

Direct loan v ad – Byz. **φοιδερᾶτος** (-ου, ὁ) 'bound by a treaty', 'ally', from *foederātus* 'ally bound by treaty'.
Inscriptions: *SEG* LI.920.3 (vi ad).
Literature: Nil. 1.284.1 (v ad); Malchus frag. 11.2 Cresci, marked (v/vi ad); Malal. 14.23 etc. (vi ad); Just. *Codex* 1.5.12.71 etc., *Nov.* 103.3.1 etc. (vi ad); Procop. *Bell.* 3.11.2 etc. (vi ad).
Post-antique: numerous. Zilliacus (1935a: 188–9, 226–7), Triandaphyllidis (1909: 130).
Notes: Avotins (1989, 1992), Hofmann (1989: 471), Lampe (1961), LSJ suppl. See §4.1.1, §4.2.4.1 n. 51, §10.2.1, §10.2.2 N.

φοκάριον: see φωκάριον.

φολβεῖνον: see πουλβῖνον.

φολερόν: see φολλερόν.

φόλης: see φόλλις.

Direct loan
II AD – Byz.

φολιᾶτον, φουλιᾶτον (-ου, τό), a type of perfumed oil, from *foliātum* 'perfume made from aromatic leaves'.
  Inscriptions: Edict.Diocl. 36.88 (IV AD).
  Literature: Galen VI.427.4 Kühn etc. (II AD); Orib. *Ecl.* 51.8.8 etc. (IV AD); Aëtius 16.147.1 etc. (VI AD); *Hippiatr.Camb.* 69.4.
  Post-antique: survives in medical texts. *LBG*.
  Notes: Hofmann (1989: 471–2, merging this with φολιᾶτος), Sophocles (1887 *s.v.* φουλιᾶτον), LSJ (*s.v.* φουλιᾶτα), LSJ suppl. (*s.vv.* φολιᾶτον, φουλιᾶτα). See §4.2.4.1 n. 55, **§6.5**, §8.2.2, §10.2.1, §10.2.2 L.

not ancient?

φολιᾶτος 'bearing foliage', from *foliātus* 'bearing foliage': alchemist, Berthelot and Ruelle 1888: 318.7. Hofmann (1989: 471–2, merging this with φολιᾶτον), LSJ suppl.

φόλις: see φόλλις.

non-existent?

φολλατώριον 'fuller's shop', from unattested **follātōrium*: papyri perhaps *P.Lond.* II.191.5 (II AD); perhaps *P.Erl.* 99.26 (II AD). Sidro and Maravela (forthcoming), Daris (1991a: 115), Hofmann (1989: 472), Meinersmann (1927: 64), *TLL* (*s.v. follātōrium*), LSJ suppl. See §8.1.7 n. 34.

rare

φολ(λ)ερόν, a coin, from *follis*, a coin (*TLL s.v.* 1017.17–73): Malal. 16.12 (VI AD); occasionally later. *LBG* derives it from *follāris*, which is probably a transliteration of φολλερόν: *TLL*. Hofmann (1989: 472), *LBG*, Sophocles (1887), *TLL* (*s.v. follis* 1017.71–2), Lampe (1961).

Direct loan
IV AD – modern

φόλλις, φόλις, φόλης (-εως, ὁ) 'bellows', a coin, a tax, or a sum of money equal to 12,500 denarii, from *follis* 'bag', 'purse', 'bellows', a coin, a sum of money (*TLL*).
  Documents: e.g. *SB* 15158.6 etc. (III/IV AD); *P.Cair.Isid.* 126.8 (IV AD); perhaps *Stud.Pal.* VIII.1213.3 (V AD); *P.Oxy.* 2196.11 etc. (VI AD).
  Inscriptions: *SEG* XXXIV.1243.25 etc. (V AD); Šašel and Šašel 1986: no. 2040A.8; *MAMA* VII.566.7.
  Literature: e.g. Epiph. *Mens.4* 82.49 (IV AD); *Anthologia Graeca* 9.528.3 (IV AD); Zosimus, *Historia nova* 2.38.4 Paschoud (V AD?); Hesych. as part of gloss κ 3201 (V/VI AD); Malal. 17.7 (VI AD); *V.S.Aux.* 7.8 (VI AD).
  Post-antique: numerous. *LBG*, Zervan (2019: 199), Triandaphyllidis (1909: 104, 125). Modern φόλα 'poison', 'patch': Babiniotis (2002), Andriotis (1967). Modern dialectal φόλ'τα 'blister' (Andriotis 1974: 585), φόλλος, φολλίτσι 'bellows' (Meyer 1895: 70).
  Notes: Meyer (1895: 70) argues that only meaning 'bellows' is Latinate, with coin sense coming from ancient Greek φολίς 'horny scale' (cf. modern φολίδα 'scale', Babiniotis 2002); Kahane and Kahane (1972–6: 532–3) see coin sense as Latinate. Bagnall (1985: 17–18), Binder (2000: 260), Menci (2000: 291), Daris (1991a: 115), Hofmann (1989: 472–3), Viscidi (1944: 42), Zilliacus (1935a: 188–9, 1937: 334), Meinersmann (1927: 64), *TLL* (*s.v. follis* 1017.43–53, 69–73), Lampe (1961 *s.v.* φόλις), LSJ, LSJ suppl. See §4.2.5, §10.2.1, §10.2.2 G.

rare	**φοράριος** on inscription *I.Sinope* 114.4 (I/II AD) may come from unattested *forārius* and mean 'shopkeeper'; the editor's equation with post-antique φουρνάριος (*q.v.*) is unlikely. Hofmann (1989: 473), LSJ suppl.
rare	**φορειά** 'filth', apparently from *foria* 'diarrhoea': Hdn. *Pros.Cath.* III.1.291.15 (II AD). Hofmann (1989: 473), LSJ. See §5.3.2 passage 10.
	φόρκες: see φοῦρκα.
	φόρμα: see φόρμη.
Direct loan with influence **III–VI AD**	**φορμαλ(ε)ία, φορμαρία, φωρμαρία, φρουμαρία** (-ας, ἡ) 'list of supplies', 'receipt', from *fōrmula* 'list' with influence from -ία. Documents: e.g. *P.Oxy.* 1115.12 (III AD); *P.Turner* 46.3 etc. (IV AD); *P.Flor.* III.377.11 (VI AD); *SB* 15956.8 (VI AD). Notes: after III AD always spelled -ρία. Daris (1991a: 115, with derivation from *fōrmālis*), Hofmann (1989: 474, 480–1), Zilliacus (1935a: 188–9), Meinersmann (1927: 64, 65), Palmer (1945: 53), *LBG*, LSJ, LSJ suppl. See §4.2.3.1 n. 38, §4.4, §6.2, §9.2, §10.2.1, §10.2.2 O.
rare	**φόρμη, φόρμα, φώρμη, φούρμη** 'quality', 'class', 'cobbler's last', from *fōrma* 'form': papyrus *P.Mich.* XIV.680.11 (III/IV AD); Edict.Diocl. 8.9 etc. (IV AD). The same Latin may, via a different and later borrowing, be the basis of Byzantine φόρμα 'rule', 'figure', 'form' (*LBG*) and modern φόρμα 'pattern' (Meyer 1895: 71), but φόρμα is usually derived from Italian *forma* (Babiniotis 2002; Andriotis 1967). Daris (1991a: 115), Hofmann (1989: 481–2), LSJ suppl.
foreign	**φόρμικα** 'ant', from *formīca* 'ant': Hesych. as lemma φ 777 (V/VI AD). Immisch (1885: 341), Hofmann (1989: 474 *s.v.* φόρμιξ), *LBG*.
	φορν-: see φουρν-.
name	**φόρον, φόρος** 'marketplace', 'one's proper place of jurisdiction', from *forum* 'marketplace': in generic sense as part of phrases in legal texts, where it is probably semantic extension of φόρος 'tribute' (because it appears in Greek script and never unambiguously neuter), e.g. Just. *Codex* 2.2.4 φόρου παραγραφή = *fori praescriptio*. Also as part of names of specific forums, e.g. NT Acts 28:15 (I AD); inscription *I.Ephesos* 1534.2 (IV/V AD); Malal. 7.1 (VI AD); *P.Lond.* III.992.13 (VI AD); *P.Cair.Masp.* 67312.7 (VI AD). Binder (2000: 246–7), Leclercq (1997: 298–9), Avotins (1989, 1992), Daris (1991a: 116), Mason (1974: 6, 97), Hofmann (1989: 475), Zilliacus (1935a: 188–9), Meinersmann (1927: 64), *LBG* (*s.v.* φόρος), Triandaphyllidis (1909: 123), Zervan (2019: 199–200), Kahane and Kahane (1972–6: 535), Meyer (1895: 70–1), LSJ, LSJ suppl. (*s.vv.* φόρον, φόρος B). See §9.3 n. 25.
foreign	**φόρτις** transliterating *fortis* 'strong': Plut. *Mor.* 319a (I/II AD). Sophocles (1887).
foreign	**φορτοῦνα** transliterating *fortūna* 'fortune': Lyd. *Mens.* 4.100 etc. (VI AD); Byzantine texts. Modern φουρτούνα 'storm at sea' comes from Italian: Babiniotis (2002), Andriotis (1967). *LBG*.
	φοσατ-: see φοσσατ-.

Direct loan
II AD – Byz.

φόσσα (-ας/-ης, ἡ) 'ditch', from *fossa* 'ditch'.
Documents: O.Claud. inv. 8208, in Cuvigny 1998: 90 (II AD).
Literature: Plut. *Fab.* 1.2, marked (I/II AD); implied by Luc. *Hist.Conscr.* 15 (II AD) as being used by a contemporary; *Hippiatr.Berl.* (Apsyrtus) 99.6 (III/IV AD?); Hesych. as gloss β 1299 (V/VI AD).
Post-antique: numerous. *LBG*, Triandaphyllidis (1909: 131).
Notes: forms derivatives φοσσεύω, φοσσίον. Hofmann (1989: 475), Zilliacus (1935a: 226–7), Hahn (1907: 708 n. 114, on Lucian). See §9.4 passage 53, §10.2.1, §10.2.2 J.

rare

φοσ(σ)ατεύω, φωσ(σ)ατεύω 'encamp', from *fossātum* 'ditch' (*TLL s.v. fosso* 1214.5) via φοσσᾶτον + -εύω: Malal. 12.21 (VI AD); Byzantine texts. Hofmann (1989; 476 *s.v.* φοσσᾶτον), *TLL* (*s.v. fosso* 1214.43), *LBG*, Lampe (1961).

Direct loan
V AD – modern

φοσ(σ)ᾶτον, φωσ(σ)ᾶτον, φουσ(σ)ᾶτον (-ου, τό) 'boundary', 'ditch', 'camp', 'army', from *fossātum* 'ditch' (*TLL s.v. fosso* 1214.5).
Inscriptions: *SEG* IX.356.36 (VI AD); *I.Syria PAES* 785¹.6.
Literature: John Chrysostom, *PG* LXII.168.20–6 etc., marked (IV/V AD); Agath. *Arm.* 86.21 (V AD); Hesych. as lemma φ 805 (V/VI AD); Malal. 18.60 (VI AD); Procop. *Aed.* 3.6.23, marked, part of place name (VI AD); scholion to Eur. *Ph.* 442 as gloss. Unverified example (II AD) in Zilliacus (1937: 322, 334).
Post-antique: very common, forming derivative φοσσατικῶς 'with an army'. *LBG*, Zervan (2019: 200), Triandaphyllidis (1909: 131), Daris (1989: 116). Modern φουσ(σ)άτο 'army': Babiniotis (2002), Andriotis (1967), Meyer (1895: 72); cf. Katsanis (2007: 804) on further loans into Albanian and Romanian.
Notes: evidently unfamiliar until V AD, so Hesych. entry probably composed before that. Forms derivative φοσσατεύω. Kramer (1996b, 2011: 353–63), Binder (2000: 219), Daris (1989: 116), Hofmann (1989: 475–6), Viscidi (1944: 18), Zilliacus (1935a: 226–7, 1937: 334), Meinersmann (1927: 64), Immisch (1885: 360), *TLL* (*s.v. fosso* 1214.8–11, 18), Lampe (1961), LSJ and LSJ suppl. (*s.v.* φόσσατον). See §4.2.4.1 n. 55, §10.2.1, §10.2.2 C.

rare

φοσσεύω, φωσσεύω 'besiege', from *fossa* 'ditch' via φόσσα + -εύω: Malal. 12.35.18 etc. (VI AD); occasional Byzantine texts. Probably source of παραφοσσεύω. Hofmann (1989: 476–7), Zilliacus (1935a: 226–7), *LBG*, Triandaphyllidis (1909: 131), Lampe (1961).

rare

φοσσίον 'storage pit', from *fossa* 'ditch' via φόσσα + -ιον: as gloss in old scholia to Demosthenes 8.61a (τοὺς θησαυροὺς σιροὺς ἐκάλουν οἱ Θρᾷκες καὶ οἱ Λίβυες, ἃ νῦν φοσσία ἰδιωτικῶς), 61b; occasional Byzantine texts. Modern dialectal φοσσίν 'pit': Andriotis (1974: 585). Hofmann (1989: 475 *s.v.* φόσσα), *LBG*.

φουάλικλον: see φούλλικλον.

rare

φουγίων, πουγίων 'dagger', from *pūgiō* 'dagger': unpublished ostracon O.Dios inv. 403.9 (II AD); papyrus *BGU* I.40.3 (II/III AD). Schirru (2013: 316), Daris (1991a: 116), Hofmann (1989: 477), Meinersmann (1927: 64), LSJ. Cf. βοῦγλιν.

φουλβίν, φουλβῖνα(ν), φουλβῖνον: see πουλβῖνον.

φουλιᾶτον: see φολιᾶτον.

φοῦλκα: see φοῦρκα.

φουλκίζω: see φουρκίζω.

not ancient	**φοῦλκον** 'wedge' (as a battle formation), allegedly from unattested **fulcum*: no ancient examples. Zilliacus (1935a: 144–5, 226–7), *LBG*, Lampe (1961).
foreign	**φούλλικλον** transliterating *folliculus* 'inflated ball' (presumably as otherwise unattested variant **folliclum*): Athenaeus 1.14f (II/III AD). Binder (2000: 157), Hofmann (1989: 477), *TLL* (*s.v. folliculus* 1014.78, 1015.12–15), Sophocles (1887 *s.v.* φουάλικλον), LSJ.
rare	**φούλλων** (ὁ) 'fuller', 'launderer', from *fullō* 'fuller', 'launderer': Edict.Diocl. 22.1 (IV AD); Diethart (1998: 176) suggests that φώλων on an undated inscription may be the same word. Hofmann (1989: 477), LSJ suppl.
non-existent	**φουλλωνικός** from *fullōnicus* 'for fulling': superseded restoration instead of φουλλώνων on inscription *IG* VII.23.B3 = Edict.Diocl. 22.1. (IV AD).
not ancient	**φουμίζω** 'boast vainly', from *fūmus* 'smoke', 'empty talk' (*TLL s.v. fūmus* 1544.3) + -ίζω: no ancient examples. Hofmann (1989: 477), *LBG*, Lampe (1961).
rare	**φουμῶσος** 'smoked' (of cheese), from *fūmōsus* 'smoky': Athenaeus 3.113d (II/III AD). Hofmann (1989: 478), LSJ.
Direct loan **II AD – modern**	**φοῦνδα, ποῦνδα** (-ης, ἡ) 'money belt', from *funda* 'strap', 'sling'. Documents: *P.Hamb.* 1.10.34 etc. (II AD); *P.Warr.* 18.13 (III AD); *SB* 9834.b42 (III/IV AD). Inscriptions: Reinach 1906: 104 no. 17.4 (II/III AD). Literature: *Anonymus Bobiensis* as gloss p. 35.32 De Nonno (V AD?); with *ventralis* in glossaries, e.g. Gloss. *Herm.L.* 21.36. Post-antique: limited survival in original meaning, but became Byzantine φοῦνδα/φοῦντα 'tassel'. *LBG*, Triandaphyllidis (1909: 122). Modern φούντα 'tassel': Babiniotis (2002), Andriotis (1967). Notes: may form derivative φούνδιον. Daris (1991a: 117), Hofmann (1989: 478), Meinersmann (1927: 64), Meyer (1895: 71 *s.v.* φοῦντα), LSJ, LSJ suppl. See §10.2.1, §10.2.2 H.
rare	**φουνδάριον**, a textile object, apparently from *funda* 'strap' via φοῦνδα + -άριον: unpublished ostracon O.Dios inv. 747.13 (II AD).
non-existent?	**φουνδάτωρ**, meaning uncertain, perhaps from *fundātor* 'founder': perhaps inscription Heberdey and Wilhelm 1896: 151 no. 256.2. Hofmann (1989: 478). For φουνδάτωρ 'soldier armed with a sling' see φουνδίτωρ.
rare	**φούνδιον**, perhaps 'sling' or 'purse', apparently from *funda* 'sling' (via φοῦνδα?) + -ιον: papyrus *P.Mich.* VIII.478.47 (II AD). Editor *ad loc.*, Daris (1991a: 116), *LBG* (*s.v.* φοῦνδιν).
foreign	**φουνδίτωρ, φουνδάτωρ** transliterating *funditor* 'soldier armed with a sling': Lyd. *Mag.* p. 72.22 (VI AD). Zilliacus (1935a: 226–7), *LBG* (*s.v.* φουνδάτωρ).

not ancient   **φοῦνδος** 'farm', from *fundus* 'farm': no ancient examples. Zilliacus (1935a: 188–9), *LBG*.

not ancient   **φουνεράριος** 'funerary', from *fūnerārius* 'of funerals': no ancient examples. Zilliacus (1935a: 188–9), *LBG*.

not ancient   **φουνερατίκιος** 'concerned with funerary expenses', from *fūnerātīcius* 'concerned with funeral expenses': no ancient examples. Zilliacus (1935a: 188–9), *LBG*.

     φοῦντα: see φοῦνδα.

not ancient?   **φοῦντος** 'bottom', probably from *fundus* 'bottom': alchemist, Berthelot and Ruelle 1888: 336.20. *LBG*, Meyer (1895: 71), Andriotis (1967 *s.v.* φοῦντο).

rare   **φοῦρκα, φοῦλκα, φόρκες** 'forked frame for a cart', 'prop shaped like a two-pronged fork', from *furca* 'fork': Edict.Diocl. 15.9 (IV AD); Plut. *Cor.* 24.10, *Mor.* 280f, both marked (I/II AD); Hesych. as lemma φ 771 (V/VI AD). Means 'gallows', 'cross for crucifixion' in Byzantine texts (*LBG*, Zervan 2019: 201, Triandaphyllidis 1909: 124; modern φούρκα 'gallows', Babiniotis 2002, Andriotis 1967), and derivative φουρκίζω (*q.v.*) suggests that meaning for antiquity, but there are no certainly ancient examples with that meaning: papyrus *P.Sijp.* 61.4, often dated to VI AD, may be from VII AD. Editor of *P.Sijp.* 61 *ad loc.*, Binder (2000: 171–2), Hofmann (1989: 478–9), Meyer (1895: 71), Lampe (1961), LSJ suppl.

rare   **φουρκίζω, φουλκίζω** 'hang on the gallows', from *furca* 'fork' (via φοῦρκα?) + -ίζω: Malal. 18.13, 119 (VI AD); Byzantine texts. Byzantine derivatives φούρκισις 'hanging', φουρκισμός 'hanging'. Modern φουρκίζω 'take with a pitchfork': Babiniotis (2002). Hofmann (1989: 478 *s.v.* φουρκα), Zilliacus (1935a: 188–9), *LBG* (*s.v.* φουλκίζω), Meyer (1895: 71), Lampe (1961 *s.vv.* φουλκίζω, φουρκίζω, φουσκιάζω).

foreign   **φούρκιφερ** transliterating *furcifer* 'slave punished with the *furca*': Plut. *Cor.* 24.10, *Mor.* 280e–f (I/II AD). Strobach (1997: 201), *LBG*.

     φούρμη: see φόρμη.

not ancient?   **φουρνάκιον** 'small oven', from *fornax/furnax* 'oven' via φούρναξ + -ιον: probably no ancient examples. Hofmann (1989: 479 *s.v.* φουρναξ), *LBG*, LSJ suppl.

rare   **φουρνάκιος** 'baked in the oven', from *furnāceus* 'baked in the oven': Athenaeus 3.113a, 3.113b (II/III AD). Hofmann (1989: 479), LSJ.

rare   **φο(υ)ρνακοναῖον**, perhaps 'bakery' and if so from *fornax/furnax* 'oven': ostracon *O.Krok.* 11.333.8 (I/II AD).

rare   **φούρναξ, φόρναξ** 'kiln', 'oven', from *fornax/furnax* 'oven', 'kiln': perhaps papyrus *P.Rein.* 11.108.4 (VI AD); Epiph. *Pan.* 1.347.29, 348.21, marked (IV AD). Capron *et al.* (2004: 212), Daris (1991a: 116), Hofmann (1989: 479), Cavenaile (1951: 400), *LBG*, Lampe (1961).

not ancient   **φουρνάριος** 'baker', from *furnārius* 'baker' (or *furnus* 'oven' via φοῦρνος + -άριος): no ancient examples, though cf. *s.v.* φοράριος. Zilliacus (1935a: 188–9), *LBG*, Andriotis (1967 *s.v.* φούρναρης).

not ancient?	**φουρνέλλον** 'oven', 'furnace', from *furnus* 'oven' (via φοῦρνος) or a related word: no securely ancient examples. Babiniotis (2002) and Andriotis (1967) derive modern φουρνέλο 'hole for putting explosives in a rock' from Italian *fornello*. *LBG* (*s.v.* φουρνέλον), LSJ suppl.
foreign	**Φουρνικάλια** is stated by Plut. *Mor.* 285d (I/II AD) to be a Roman festival; no Latin equivalent attested, but **Furnicālia* has been conjectured. Hofmann (1989: 479), Sophocles (1887).
not ancient	**φουρνίκιος** 'baked in the oven', variant of φουρνάκιος and hence ultimately from *furnāceus* 'baked in the oven': epitome of Athenaeus, 11.1 p. 25.10, 13 Peppink, in the passage where the main text of Athenaeus has φουρνάκιος (*q.v.*). *LBG*.
rare	**φουρνίτης** 'baked in the oven', from *furnus* 'oven' via φοῦρνος: Galen XIII.264.15 Kühn (II AD). Hofmann (1989: 480 *s.v.* φοῦρνος), *LBG*, LSJ (*s.v.* φουρνάκιος).
non-existent?	**φουρνῖτις**, meaning uncertain, perhaps feminine of φουρνίτης and therefore ultimately from *furnus* 'oven': only as a conjecture. Hofmann (1989: 480 *s.v.* φοῦρνος), LSJ (*s.v.* φουρνάκιος).
rare	**φουρνοειδής** 'oven-like', from *furnus* 'oven' via φοῦρνος + -ειδής 'looking like': Zosimus alch., Berthelot and Ruelle 1888: 173.13 etc. (III/IV AD). Hofmann (1989: 480 *s.v.* φοῦρνος), *LBG* (*s.v.* φουρνοειδῶς), LSJ.
rare	**φουρνοπλάστης** 'potter', from *furnus* 'oven' via φοῦρνος + πλάστης 'moulder': as gloss on ἱπνοπλάθης, Timaeus Sophista, *Lexicon Platonicum* ι 8 Valente (IV AD). Probably coined as calque of ἱπνοπλάθης. Hofmann (1989: 480 *s.v.* φοῦρνος), LSJ. See §2.2.1.
Direct loan **I AD – modern**	**φοῦρνος** (-ου, ὁ) 'oven', from *furnus* 'oven'. Documents: perhaps *P.Rein.* 11.108.4 (VI AD), see Capron *et al.* 2004: 212. Inscriptions: Edict.Diocl. 14.12 (φούρνων at 9.20 is probably a different word: Lauffer 1971: 247, 253) (IV AD). Literature: e.g. Erot. *Voc.Hipp.* 78.1 as gloss (I AD); Cyran. 3.36.36 (II AD?); Evangelium Thomae, *De infantia Jesu* Gd.16.1 = Burke 2010: 443.2 (II AD?); Athenaeus 3.113c (II/III AD); Zosimus alch., Berthelot and Ruelle 1888: 246.8 (III/IV AD); Orib. *Col.* 12.σ.29 (IV AD); *Apophth.Patr.* 14.28.20 (V AD); Hesych. as gloss ι 774 (V/VI AD); Aëtius 8.63.125 (VI AD); as gloss in scholia to Ar. *Av.* 1001, *V.* 139b, 837, *Nu.* 96a, Aes. *Pr.* 365c., etc. Post-antique: common, forming derivatives φουρνάριος 'baker', φουρνάριον 'oven', etc. (*LBG*). Zervan (2019: 201), Triandaphyllidis (1909: 124). Modern φούρνος 'oven' and derivatives: Babiniotis (2002), Andriotis (1967, 1974: 586), Meyer (1895: 71–2). Notes: forms derivatives φουρνίτης, φουρνοειδής, φουρνοπλάστης. Binder (2000: 142–3), Hofmann (1989: 480), Zilliacus (1935a: 188–9), Lampe (1961), LSJ, LSJ suppl. See §2.2.1, §4.2.4.1 n. 51, §5.2.3, §8.2.3, §10.2.1, §10.2.2 I.
foreign	**φούρτι** '(legal action) about theft', from *furtī* (gen. of *furtum* 'theft'): Antec. in Latin script 2.1.16 *furti* etc. (VI AD); later in Greek script. *LBG* (*s.vv.* φούρτη, φοῦρτον, φοῦρτος). See **§7.2.2** passage 28.

foreign | **φούρτιβος** 'stolen', from *furtīvus* 'stolen': Antec. in Latin script 2.6.2 *furtivon* etc. (VI AD); later in Greek script. Zilliacus (1935a: 188–9), Triantaphyllides (1892: 276), *LBG*. See §9.5.6 n. 68.

φουσᾶτον: see φοσσᾶτον.

Direct loan
VI AD – Byz. | **φοῦσκα** (-ας, ἡ) 'mixture of vinegar and water', from *pōsca/pūsca* 'mixture of vinegar and water'.
Literature: *Hippiatr.Par.* (Pel.) 164 (V AD?); Aëtius 3.81.1 etc. (VI AD); Alex. Trall. II.199.17 etc. (VI AD).
Post-antique: survives, forming derivative φουσκάριον 'shop where sour wine is sold' (*LBG*). Sophocles (1887). Unrelated to Byzantine φούσκα 'bladder' (*LBG*) from φύσκη 'large intestine'.
Notes: Hofmann (1989: 480), LSJ. See §4.2.3.1, §10.2.1, §10.2.2 I.

rare | **φουσκάριος** 'seller of vinegar-and-water mixture', from *pōscārius* with presumably a similar meaning (*TLL*); papyrus *SB* 12703.1.6 (VI AD); occasionally later. Diethart (1998: 176), Daris (1991a: 116), Meinersmann (1927: 65), *LBG*, Lampe (1961), LSJ suppl.

foreign | **φοῦσκος** transliterating *fuscus* 'dark-skinned': Lyd. *Mag.* p. 168.13 (VI AD). Sophocles (1887).

φουσσᾶτον: see φοσσᾶτον.

φραγγέλλιον: see φραγελλιον.

φραγγελλόω: see φραγελλόω.

rare | **φραγγέλλωσις** 'whipping', from the Latin source of φραγελλόω via φραγελλόω + -σις: Ps.-Epiph. *PG* XLIII.461c (IV AD?); Byzantine texts. Hofmann (1989: 469 *s.v.* φλαγελλοῦν), *LBG*, Lampe (1961).

φραγγελόω: see φραγελλόω.

rare | **φραγέλλη, φλάγελλα** 'whip', from *flagellum* 'whip': papyrus *P.Oxy.* 2339.10 (I AD); scholion to Ar. *Ach.* 724 (ἱμάντες δέ, λώρους λέγει, φραγέλλια· τὸ γὰρ παλαιὸν φραγέλλαις ἔτυπτον οἱ λογισταὶ τοὺς τῆς ἀγορᾶς); Byzantine texts. Binder (2000: 252), *DÉLG* (*s.v.* φραγέλλιον), *LBG* (*s.v.* φράγελλα), LSJ, LSJ suppl. (*s.vv.* φραγέλλη, φλάγελλα). Cf. φραγέλλιον.

Direct loan with
suffix
I AD – modern | **φραγέλλιον, φλαγέλλιον, φραγγέλλιον** (-ου, τό) 'whip', from *flagellum* 'whip' + -ιον.
Documents: *P.Lond.* II.191.11 (II AD).
Inscriptions: perhaps *SEG* VII.372.3 etc. (II AD); Edict.Diocl. 10.18 in *SEG* XXXVII.335.iii.31 (IV AD); *I.Chr.Asie Mineure* I.290.4 (IV AD).
Literature: e.g. NT John 2:5 (I AD); Gregorius Nazianzenus, *PG* XXXV.1117c (IV AD); Geront. *V.Mel.* 2.44.23 (V AD); Hesych. as gloss μ 364, σ 1190 (V/VI AD); Romanus Melodus, *Cantica* 51.11.7 Grosdidier de Matons (VI AD); as gloss in scholia to Luc. *Cal.* 12, Ar. *Ach.* 724; commentary on biblical passage. Unverified example (III AD) in Zilliacus (1937: 323, 334).
Post-antique: numerous. *LBG* (*s.v.* φραγέλιον), Zervan (2019: 202). Modern φραγγέλ(λ)ιο, φραγγέλι 'whip': Babiniotis (2002), Andriotis (1967), Meyer (1895: 72).

Notes: in *I.Chr.Asie Mineure* I.290.4 φραγέλλια σιδαρᾶ cannot be whips and are probably tools for levelling top of measure filled with grain (Cuvigny 2017: 106–13). Perhaps meaning 'sapling' in *P.Lond.* II.191.11 (*BL* VIII.175). Manganaro (1992: 283–5), Binder (2000: 252), Daris (1991a: 115 *s.v.* φλαγέλλιον), Hofmann (1989: 467 *s.v.* φλαγελλον), Cavenaile (1952: 196), Zilliacus (1937: 334), Cameron (1931: 235, 246), Meinersmann (1927: 64), *DÉLG*, Beekes (2010), Sophocles (1887 *s.v.* φλαγέλλιον), *TLL* (*s.v.* φλαγέλλιον), Lampe (1961), LSJ (*s.vv.* φραγέλλιον, φλαγέλλιον), LSJ suppl. (*s.vv.* φραγέλλιον, φλαγέλλιον). See §4.1.1 n. 15, §4.3.2, §4.6.1, §8.17 n. 34, §9.3 n. 21, §10.2.1, §10.2.2 M; cf. φλάγελλον, φραγέλλη, φραγελλόω.

φραγελλίτης: see φραγηλίτης.

Direct? loan with suffix **I AD – modern**	**φραγελλόω, φλαγελλόω, φραγγελ(λ)όω** 'whip' could be from *flagellō* 'whip' or from *flagellum* 'whip' (via φραγέλλιον?) + -όω. Literature: e.g. NT Mark 15:15 (I AD); *Acta Pauli et Theclae* 21 = Lipsius 1891: 249.10 (II AD); *Test.XII* 12.2.3 (III AD or earlier); Gregorius Nazianzenus, *PG* XXXVI.332c (IV AD); Agath. *Arm.* 20.16 (V AD); Romanus Melodus, *Cantica* 36.15.4 Grosdidier de Matons (VI AD). Post-antique: numerous; Byzantine pres. φραγελ(λ)ίζω is probably back-formation from aorist ἐφραγέλ(λ)ωσα. *LBG* (*s.vv.* φραγελλίζω, φλαγελλόω), Sophocles (1887 *s.v.* φλαγελλόω). Modern φραγγελλώνω 'whip': Babiniotis (2002). Notes: forms derivative φραγγέλλωσις. Bartalucci (1995: 121), Hofmann (1989: 468–9), Zilliacus (1935a: 188–9, 1937: 334), *DÉLG* (*s.v.* φραγέλλιον), Lampe (1961 *s.vv.* φλαγελλόω, φραγελλόω), LSJ. See §4.3.1, §4.6.1, §9.2, §9.3 n. 21, §10.2.1, §10.2.2 O, §10.3.1.
not ancient?	**φραγηλίτης, φραγελλίτης**, a kind of church security guard, from *flagellum* 'whip' via φραγέλλιον + -ίτης: inscription *I.Tyr* 10.3. *DÉLG* (*s.v.* φραγέλλιον), *LBG*, LSJ suppl.
not ancient?	**φράξο(ς)** 'ash tree', from *fraxinus* 'ash': probably no ancient examples. *LBG* (*s.vv.* φράξον, φράξος), Meyer (1895: 72), Andriotis (1967).
foreign	**φρᾶτερ**, from *frāter* 'brother': as part of title φρᾶτερ ἀρουᾶλις 'member of the Arval Brethren' (usually acc. φρᾶτρεμ ἀρουᾶλεμ), inscriptions e.g. *MkB* 2.1 (1875–6) 18 no. 106.12 (I AD); *I.Ephesos* 3034.5 (II AD). As part of *fratres patrueles*, Antec. in Latin script 3.2.1 etc. (VI AD). Drew-Bear (1972: 228), Mason (1974: 7, 97), Hofmann (1989: 480), *DÉLG*. See §7.3 passage 32.
not Latin?	**φρατριάζω, φατριάζω** 'conspire', with Byzantine φ(ρ)ατριάρχης, φ(ρ)ατριαστής (*LBG*): perhaps from *frāter* 'brother' (*TLL s.v.* φρατριάζω), but a Greek derivation is also possible (*DÉLG s.v.* φράτηρ, Beekes 2010 *s.v.* φράτηρ, LSJ). Lampe (1961). See §8.1.7 n. 34.
not ancient	**φραυδάτωρ** 'swindler', from *fraudātor* 'swindler': no ancient examples. Zilliacus (1935a: 188–9).
not ancient	**φριγγιλάρι**, a bird, from *fringilla* 'chaffinch': no ancient examples. Meyer (1895: 72).
rare	**φριγιδάριον, φριγδάριον** 'cold room at the baths', from *frīgidārium* 'cold room': inscription *IGBulg.* V.5599.8 (II AD). LSJ suppl.

not ancient	**φροντάριον** 'forehead-ornament', from *frontālia* 'forehead-ornament': no ancient examples (papyrus *SB* 12942 is post-antique). Daris (1991a: 116), LSJ suppl.
non-existent	**φρουκτουάριος** 'person with right of profit', from *frūctuārius* 'usufructuary': cited as ancient loan by Zilliacus (1935a: 188–9) but probably part of οὐσουφρουκτουάριος (*q.v.*).
	φρουμαρία: see φορμαλεία.
Direct loan **II–IV AD**	**φρουμεντάριος** (-α, -ον or -ου, ὁ) 'concerned with victualling', as masc. subst. an official, from *frūmentārius* 'of the corn supply'. Documents: perhaps *P.Michael.* 9.B4 (I AD); *P.Mich.* IX.562.2 (II AD); *P.Coll. Youtie* II.74.5 (III AD); *P.FuadUniv.* 14.5 (III AD); perhaps *P.Oxy.* 43r.2.11 etc. (III AD, see LSJ *s.vv.* φρουμεντάριος, φορμαλεία); *SB* 2253.2 (III/IV AD); *O.Ashm.Shelt.* 81.2 (III/IV AD). Inscriptions: e.g. *I.Pergamon Asklepieion* 106.2 (I/II AD); *F.Delphes* III.IV.98.5 (II AD); *IG* X.II.1.207.6 (III AD). Literature: Eus. *HE* 6.40.2 (IV AD); Lyd. *Mag.* p. 6.27 etc., marked (VI AD). Post-antique: minimal survival. *LBG.* Notes: may form derivative σουφρουμεντάριος. Paschoud (1983), Daris (1991a: 116), Mason (1974: 5, 9, 98), Hofmann (1989: 481), Zilliacus (1935a: 226–7), Meinersmann (1927: 65), *DÉLG*, Lampe (1961), LSJ, LSJ suppl. See §4.2.2, **§8.2.1**, §10.2.1, §10.2.2 D, §10.3.2.
rare	**φωκαρία** 'housekeeper', 'concubine', from *focāria* 'kitchen maid', 'concubine': papyrus *BGU* II.614.13 (III AD). Daris (1991a: 116), Hofmann (1989: 481), Meinersmann (1927: 65), LSJ suppl. See §6.2 n. 13, §12.2.1.
Direct loan **II AD**	**φωκάριον, φοκάριον** (-ου, τό) 'concubine', from *focāria* 'concubine'. Documents: *P.Princ.* II.57.9 (II AD); *Pap.Choix* 6.8 (II AD); *BGU* II.600v.4 (II AD). Notes: Gilliam (1968: 96–7), Daris (1991a: 116), Hofmann (1989: 481 *s.v.* φωκαρία), Cavenaile (1951: 400–1, 1952: 197), LSJ suppl. See §4.2.3.1, §9.2, §10.2.1, §10.2.2 N, §12.2.1.
	φώλων: see φούλλων.
	φωρμαρία: see φορμαλεία.
	φώρμη: see φόρμη.
	φωσ(σ)-: see φοσσ-.

X

not ancient	**χάρτα** 'papyrus', from *charta* 'papyrus' (itself from χάρτης 'papyrus'): no ancient examples. Zilliacus (1935a: 176–7).
not Latin?	**χαρταρέα** 'tax on papyrus', perhaps from unattested **chartārea*: inscription *SEG* XL.1133.8 (III AD); not *ILS* 9470.6, which has Greek χαρτηρά. Beekes (2010 *s.v.* χάρτης) has a Greek derivation. Mason (1974: 99), LSJ.

not Latin?	**χαρτάριος**, 'keeper of archives' or 'papyrus-seller', perhaps a variant of χαρτουλάριος (*q.v.*) or perhaps from *chartārius* 'papyrus-maker/-seller' or from χάρτης + -άριος: inscription *I.Smyrna* 542.3 (I/II AD); perhaps papyrus *BGU* II.466.12 (II/III AD). Editor of inscription *ad loc.*, Harrauer (2006: 139), Hofmann (1989: 482–3), Meinersmann (1927: 65), *DÉLG* (*s.v.* χάρτης), LSJ suppl. See §6.1.
not Latin?	**χαρτ(ι)ατικόν** 'payment for an official document' may be from *chartiāticum* 'money for buying papyrus' or *vice versa*. Hofmann (1989: 483), Zilliacus (1935a: 220–1), *DÉLG* (*s.v.* χάρτης), Frisk (1954–72: II.1075), Beekes (2010 *s.v.* χάρτης), *LBG*, LSJ (*s.v.* χαρτιατικά), LSJ suppl. (*s.vv.* χαρτατικόν, χαρτιατικά).
	χαρτουλάριον: see χαρτουλάριος.
Direct loan **V AD – Byz.**	**χαρτουλάριος, καρτουλάριος** (-ου, ὁ) 'registrar', 'archivist', from *chartulārius* 'keeper of public archives' (*TLL*). Documents: common, e.g. *O.Douch.* IV.405.3 (IV/V AD); perhaps *SB* 16344.4 (V AD); *P.Oxy.* 3804.239 (VI AD). Inscriptions: e.g. *I.Cret.* IV.489.5 (V/VI AD); *I.Ephesos* 1323.8 (VI AD). Literature: e.g. Agath. *Arm.* 128.18 (V AD); Nil. 3.105.1 (V AD); Just. *Nov.* 8.7 etc., but in Latin script 117.11 (VI AD); Ath.Schol. 1.2.15 (VI AD). Post-antique: common, forming derivative χαρτουλαρεύω 'be registrar'. *LBG*, Zervan (2019: 205–6), Triandaphyllidis (1909: 127). Notes: commentary to *P.Oxy.* 3960.21 suggests some examples may really be a neuter χαρτουλάριον 'secretariat'. Avotins (1992), Hofmann (1989: 483), Zilliacus (1935a: 178–9, 220–1), Meinersmann (1927: 65), *DÉLG* (*s.v.* χάρτης), Frisk (1954–72: II.1075), Beekes (2010 *s.v.* χάρτης), *TLL* (*s.v.* *chartulārius* 1002.43–6), Lampe (1961), LSJ, LSJ suppl. See §4.2.4.1 n. 50, **§6.1**, §10.2.1, §10.2.2 D.
rare	**χ(ε)ιρομανίκιον** 'cuff', 'sleeve', 'long glove', from χείρ 'hand', 'arm' + *manicae* 'cuffs', 'sleeves' (via μανίκιον?): papyrus *P.Münch.* III.1.142.13 (VI AD). Filos (2010: 244, 251), Daris (1991a: 116). Cf. μάνικα.
rare	**χειρομάνικον** 'sleeve', from χείρ 'arm' + *manicae* 'cuffs', 'sleeves': Orion, *Etymologicum* p. 192.39 Sturz, as gloss (V AD); Byzantine texts (often derived from Orion). *LBG* gives definition 'arm-splint', which is unlikely in Orion. See **§2.2.1** with n. 22; cf. μάνικα.
rare	**χειρομάππιον** 'towel', from χείρ 'hand' + *mappa* 'towel' via μαππίον: papyrus *P.Princ.* II.82.43 (V AD). Filos (2010: 251), Daris (1991a: 116), Hofmann (1989: 261 *s.v.* μάππα), LSJ.
Deriv. of loan **V AD – Byz.**	**χερνιβόξεστον** (-ου, τό) 'washbasin', from χέρνιψ 'water for washing hands' + *sextārius* 'pint measure' via ξέστης. Documents: *P.Wash.Univ.* I.59.13 (V AD); *P.Amst.* I.87.8 (V/VI AD); Maravela-Solbakk 2009: 139.1 (V/VI AD); perhaps *P.Prag.* II.178.1.19 (V/VI AD); *Stud.Pal.* XX.151.10 (VI AD); *SB* 15300.4 (VI AD). Literature: probably Gloss. Ps.-Philox. 202.31 (cf. *CGL* VI.86 *s.v.* *aquiminale*).

Post-antique: numerous. *LBG* (*s.v.* χερνιβούξεστον), Sophocles (1887 *s.v.* χερνιβόξεστα).

Notes: Maravela-Solbakk (2009: 139–40), Filos (2010: 244, 251), Diethart (1988: 68–9), Daris (1991a: 117), LSJ, LSJ suppl. See §4.6.2, §8.2.2, §9.2, §10.2.2 M.

χιρομανίκιν: see χειρομανίκιον.

not Latin? **χορταρῖνος,** meaning uncertain, perhaps from *chōrs*, variant of *cohors* 'farmyard', 'cohort', perhaps via *cohortālīnus/cōrtālīnus*, an official (*TLL*), or a Greek formation from χορτάριον 'hay': *O.Did.* 463.4 (II/III AD) with commentary.

χορτάριος: see χωρτάριος.

χόρτη: see κοόρτη.

χορωνός: see κορώνη.

χουλιάριν: see κοχλιάριον.

Χρηστιανός: see Χριστιανός.

Deriv. of loan
III AD – Byz.

Χριστιανίζω 'become Christian', from *Chrīstiānus* 'Christian' via Χριστιανός + -ίζω.

Literature: e.g. Origen, *Contra Celsum* 3.75.46 Borret (II/III AD); Gregorius Nazianzenus, *Epistulae* 11.6 Gallay (IV AD); *ACO* II.I.II p. 118.6 (V AD); *ACO* III p. 8.9 (VI AD).

Post-antique: survives.

Notes: Sophocles (1887), Lampe (1961). See §4.6.1, §10.2.2 O.

Deriv. of loan
III AD – modern

Χριστιανικός (-ή, -όν) 'Christian', from *Chrīstiānus* 'Christian' via Χριστιανός + -ικός.

Documents: *P.Lips.* 1.43.13 (IV AD); *P.Cair.Masp.* 67004.8 (VI AD).

Literature: common, e.g. *Act.Scillit.* 117.3 (II/III AD); Porphyry, *Contra Christianos* frag. 88.6 (III AD); Gregorius Nyssenus, *PG* XLVI.825c (IV AD); *ACO* I.I.III p. 60.35 (V AD); *ACO* III p. 23.38 (VI AD).

Post-antique: common. Sophocles (1887). Modern Χριστιανικός 'Christian': Babiniotis (2002), Andriotis (1967).

Notes: adverb Χριστιανικῶς 'in a Christian manner' considered separate word by Lampe (1961). Avotins (1992), Hofmann (1989: 484 *s.v.* Χριστιανός), LSJ. See §4.6.1, §8.2.3 n. 51, §10.2.2 O, §10.4.2.

Deriv. of loan
II AD – modern

Χριστιανισμός (-οῦ, ὁ) 'Christianity', from *Chrīstiānus* 'Christian' via Χριστιανός + -σμός.

Inscriptions: *I.Chr.Égypte* 615.1.

Literature: common, e.g. Ignat. *Ep.* 2.10.1 (I/II AD); Celsus, Ἀληθὴς λόγος 1.1 Bader (II AD); Origen, *Exhortatio ad martyrium* 12 Koetschau (II/III AD); Eus. *PE* 1.1.1 (IV AD); Soz. 6.28.1 (V AD); *ACO* III p. 21.12 (VI AD).

Post-antique: common. Sophocles (1887). Modern Χριστιανισμός 'Christianity': Babiniotis (2002).

Notes: Lampe (1961). See §4.6.1, §8.2.3 n. 51, §10.2.2 O, §10.4.2.

not ancient? **Χριστιανοκατήγορος** 'opponent of the Christians', from *Chrīstiānus* 'Christian' via Χριστιανός + κατήγορος 'accuser': Ps.-John Chrysostom, *PG* LV.692.38. *LBG*.

rare	**Χριστιανομερῖται**, a Jewish sect friendly to Christianity, from *Chrīstiānus* 'Christian' via Χριστιανός + μερίτης 'sharer': *Narratio de rebus Persicis* 245a = Bratke 1899: 44.1 (v/vi AD). Lampe (1961).
Direct loan **I AD – modern**	**Χριστιανός, Χρηστιανός, Χρηστυανός** (-οῦ, ὁ) 'Christian', from *Chrīstiānus* 'Christian'.
	Documents: e.g. *P.Oxy.* 3119.14 (III AD); *P.Lond.* VI.1919.17 (IV AD); *P.Oxy.* 3149.3 (V AD); *P.Münch.* I.8.35 (VI AD).
	Inscriptions: e.g. Asdracha 1995: 289 no. 118.3 (II/III AD); *MAMA* X.8.5 etc. (III AD); *I.Chr.Bulgarien* 36.4 (IV AD); *SEG* II.752.3 (V AD); *I.Estremo Oriente* 55.8 etc. (VI AD).
	Literature: very common, e.g. NT Acts 11:26 (I AD); Luc. *Peregr.* 13 (II AD); Porphyry, *Contra Christianos* frag. 39.9 (III AD); Eus. *HE* 4.17.11 (IV AD); *ACO* II.1.II p. 156.25 (V AD); *ACO* III p. 64.24 (VI AD).
	Post-antique: very common. Sophocles (1887). Modern Χριστιανός 'Christian': Babiniotis (2002), Andriotis (1967).
	Notes: forms derivatives Χριστιανίζω, Χριστιανικός, Χριστιανισμός, Χριστιανότης, Χριστιανομερῖται, Χριστιανῶς, ψευδοχριστιανός. Kittel *et al.* (1932–79 *s.v.* χρίω), Hofmann (1989: 484), Lampe (1961), LSJ. See §4.2.4.1 n. 51, §4.6.1, §6.4, §8.2.3 n. 51, §9.3 nn. 21 and 25, §10.2.1, §10.2.2 N, **§10.4.2**, §10.5, §12.2.2.
Deriv. of loan **IV AD – Byz.**	**Χριστιανότης** (-τητος, ἡ) 'Christianity', from *Chrīstiānus* 'Christian' via Χριστιανός + -ότης.
	Documents: *P.Kellis* I.48.4 (IV AD).
	Literature: *ACO* I.I.VII p. 129.18 (V AD); *Carth.* 375.4 (V AD).
	Post-antique: numerous. *LBG*.
	Notes: *LBG*. See §4.6.1, §10.2.2 O.
rare	**Χριστιανῶς** 'in a Christian fashion', from *Chrīstiānus* 'Christian' via Χριστιανός: an occasional alternative to Χριστιανικῶς, Porphyry, *Contra Christianos* frag. 39.29 (III AD); Eus. *HE* 6.19.7 (IV AD). *LBG*, LSJ (*s.v.* χριστιανός).
	χρούστη: see κρούστη.
rare	**χῶρος, κῶρος** 'north-west wind', from *caurus/cōrus* 'north-west wind': NT Acts 27:12 (I AD); Lyd. *Ost.* 43 (VI AD); bilingual glossaries, e.g. Gloss. *Herm.L.* 11.26, Gloss. *Herm.Mp.* 295.15; implied by a gloss in Hesych. χ 880 (V/VI AD). The aspiration is probably a Greek addition by association with χῶρος 'place', and therefore Latin *chorus* on inscription *IG* XIV.1308, from Rome, suggests that this form could have been more current in the Greek of Rome than is now apparent. Hemer (1989: 140–1), Leclercq (1997: 300–1), Hofmann (1989: 484), Sophocles (1887), Blass *et al.* (1979: §5 n. 6), LSJ. See **§9.3**.
rare	**χωρτάριος, χορτάριος** 'member of a cohort', from *chōrtālis*, variant of *cohortālis* 'of a cohort': documents *SB* 8247.19 (I AD); *O.Claud.* II.266.6 (II AD). *LBG* (*s.v.* χορτάριος) has a different interpretation. Daris (1991a: 117), Mason (1974: 8, 100), Cavenaile (1951: 401). Cf. κοορτάλιος.
	χώρτη: see κοόρτη.

Ψ

name ψευδαντωνῖνος 'pseudo-Antoninus', from ψευδ- 'false' + name *Antōnīnus*: as name, Dio Cassius 78.32.4 etc. (II/III AD). *LBG*, LSJ. Cf. Ἀντωνεῖνος.

rare ψευδοχριστιανός 'false Christian', from ψευδο- 'false' + *Chrīstiānus* 'Christian' via Χριστιανός: Thdt. *Orthod.* 132.25 (V AD); *Vita S. Marinae* 6.56 Clugnet (VI AD). *LBG*, Lampe (1961).

ψίκι: see ὀψίκιον.

Ω

ὠάν, ὤας: see ὄουαν.

not Latin? ὠᾶτος 'egg-shaped', from *ōvātus* 'egg-shaped': Byzantine term for a room in Constantinople. Meaning 'tub', not necessarily Latinate: Her.Mech. *Stereom.* 2.21.1. LSJ (*s.v.* ὤατον), *LBG*, Sophocles (1887), Lampe (1961).

ὠκία: see οὐγγία.

Ὠκτόβριος: see Ὀκτώβριος.

ὠνκία: see οὐγγία.

ὤπτι, ὠπτίων: see ὀπτίων.

ὠραιῶν: see ὀρατίων.

ὠράριον: see ὀράριον.

ὠρατίων: see ὀρατίων.

foreign ὠράτωρ transliterating *ōrātor* 'orator': Plut. *Mor.* 276a (I/II AD). Strobach (1997: 201), Hofmann (1989: 486), *LBG*.

ὠρδενάριος, ὠρδινάριος: see ὀρδινάριος 1.

ὠρδινᾶτος: see ὀρδινᾶτος.

ὠρεῖον, ὤρριον: see ὄρριον.

non-existent ὤρνα 'voting-urn', from *urna* 'urn': superseded reading of Dio Cassius 59.28.8 (II/III AD). Sophocles (1887). Cf. οὖρνα.

ὠστιάριος: see ὀστιάριος.

foreign ὤστιον, ὤστια transliterating *ōstium* 'door': DH *AR* 3.44.4 (I BC); scholion to Ar. *Pl.* 330. Hofmann (1989: 487).

ὠφέλ(λ)ιον: see ὀφέλλιον.

4

HOW WERE LATIN WORDS INTEGRATED INTO GREEK? SPELLING AND INFLECTION

There are many different ways that a word from one language can be adopted into another language's inflectional system. It can become an unanalysable, uninflected unit (e.g. English 'patois' and 'macramé', which have no plurals), or retain the inflection it had in the source language (e.g. English 'index' when its plural is the Latinate 'indices'), or be altered only to the extent of acquiring an inflection from the borrowing language (e.g. English 'index' when its plural is the Anglicized 'indexes'), or be more significantly changed during the borrowing process (e.g. English 'parsnip', from Latin *pastinaca* and/or French *pasnaie* with influence from 'neep').[1] Such alterations during borrowing are distinct from the further changes that may also take place after borrowing, when a loanword typically evolves along with other words in the borrowing language (e.g. English 'bishop', which comes ultimately from *episcopus* but shows the effects of having been part of English for more than a thousand years). Established loanwords may also form derivatives that never existed in the source language (§2.4).

Latin loanwords in Greek almost always underwent some degree of assimilation: they never retained a functioning Latin inflectional paradigm, and although a few ended up indeclinable, the vast majority took normal Greek endings.[2] But most loanwords were not altered more than necessary to fit into a Greek paradigm. Significant changes such as the addition of suffixes or changes in form to resemble existing Greek words affected only a small minority of loanwords – but that minority included all the verbs.

Because Latin and Greek were written in different alphabets, even writing the loanword in the Greek alphabet involved an additional level of adaptation. That adaptation almost always took place, not only for loanwords but also for codeswitches: single words and short phrases explicitly marked as foreign usually appeared in Greek script. (This is true of papyri and inscriptions as well as literature and therefore can be guaranteed to be ancient practice, but it had some exceptions, for which see §7.1.[3]) Latin script was normally reserved for longer chunks of Latin, ones designed to be read and understood by people who knew Latin, and even such longer passages of Latin were sometimes written in Greek script.[4] The Greek avoidance of Latin script is particularly striking in view of the fact that Latin writers often used Greek script for Greek codeswitches in Latin texts.[5] This difference between Greek and Roman practice probably reflects a different knowledge base: most educated Latin speakers knew the Greek alphabet, but

---

[1] *OED s.vv.*

[2] That is, loanwords never retained functional Latin inflections, but isolated Latin endings did occur; see §7.2, §7.3. The extent to which Latin words were integrated into Greek may have to do with the specific relationship between those two languages rather than general tendencies of Greek, for many Hebrew and Aramaic words appear in the Septuagint and New Testament with unintegrated, indeclinable forms (e.g. Ἰσραήλ, Χερούβ, Ἐμμανουήλ; see Danker *et al.* 2000 *s.vv.*), as do many English loanwords in modern Greek (Stathi 2002: 317–19).

[3] But it no longer applies in modern Greek, where English codeswitches and even loanwords often appear in Roman script (Stathi 2002: 315).

[4] E.g. J. N. Adams (2003: 40–63), Dickey (2016: 121–7, 151–3, 161–6).

[5] There are some uncertainties about exactly where and how much Latin writers used Greek script, since papyrus evidence is less extensive for Latin than for Greek and scripts were sometimes changed during medieval transmission, but it is nevertheless possible to tell that the practice was widespread; see e.g. O'Sullivan (2018).

most educated Greek speakers did not know the Roman alphabet.

The topics treated in this chapter have been the subject of extensive scholarly investigation, almost always without distinction between loanwords and codeswitches. The picture that emerges from that investigation is complex and in places rather murky. Although there is no getting around the fact that Greek speakers were not entirely consistent in the way they handled Latin words, a sharper and clearer view of their practices emerges when one sets the codeswitches aside and focusses on loanwords.

4.1 WRITING LATIN WORDS IN GREEK SCRIPT

Greek spellings of Latin loanwords were usually not transliterations of the Latin spellings, but representations in the Greek alphabet of the way the words were pronounced; indeed until the sixth century AD most Greek speakers responsible for deciding how to spell Latin words probably did not know the Latin alphabet and therefore had no idea how a Roman might write a Latin word.[6] And because Greek did not have exactly the same sounds as Latin, the representation was approximate even when the person writing the word knew exactly how a Latin speaker would pronounce it – which of course he or she often did not. Greek speakers wrote Latin sounds with the letters representing the nearest Greek sound to the one they were

aiming at; we cannot know whether they then pronounced the words with any distinctively Latin sounds or used the usual Greek phonetic system, though the latter is more likely in most contexts.

The pronunciation of both Latin and Greek changed considerably during the long period during which they were in contact, with the result that the sound represented by a particular letter of the Latin alphabet sometimes had very different representations in the Greek of different periods. The spellings of loanwords often reflected pronunciation at the time of borrowing, but with ongoing linguistic contact spellings could also be updated to reflect later changes in Latin pronunciation.

4.1.1 Outline of transcription practices

The usual equivalents employed by Greek speakers writing Latin words are listed below. This simplified overview omits much interesting variation and is intended merely as an indication of the most common practices, not as any kind of definitive list of possibilities.[7] The vowel equivalents apply only to vowels that were normally pronounced; Latin vowels that could be omitted in pronunciation due to syncope generally disappeared in Greek spelling.[8] Many consonants fluctuated between being written single or double, regardless of whether the Latin spelling had a single or a double consonant.[9]

---

[6] In this respect the factors affecting the spelling of Latin words in Greek script are different from those affecting the spelling of Greek words in Latin script, where the original Greek spelling could have played a greater role. Latin authors were using Greek words from the earliest evidence we have for Latin literature, and they established spelling conventions that became widespread among Romans (e.g. αι = *ae*, οι = *oe*, ου = *u*, υ = *u/y/i*, θ = *t/th*, φ = *p/ph/f*, χ = *c/ch*, ζ = *s/ss/z*: see Leumann (1977: §20, 85, 135.3, 165, 181b), or for a more complex and chronologically nuanced set of equivalents Biville (1990–5: II.381–3, 395, 407–20). Such conventions may sometimes have influenced Greek speakers' spellings of Latin words; J. N. Adams (2003: 44–53) discusses a few transliterations probably done by people with knowledge of Latin spelling, but these are entire Latin texts written in

Greek script (on such transliterated texts see also Wouters 1976) rather than loanwords.

[7] For more detailed information see Binder (2000), García Domingo (1979: 45–88), Gignac (1976), Sallés Verdaguer (1976–7), Leclercq (1993, 1997), Meinersmann (1927: 104–14), Wessely (1903).

[8] E.g. φίβλα (*fibula*), ἀκίσκλος (*acisculus*). Binder (2000: 153–214), Gignac (1976: 309–10), Leumann (1977: §101–7), Schirru (2013: 312–13), Dieterich (1898: 38–40, 73–4). Note that in this book Latin vowel quantities are marked only where directly relevant to the discussion and when source words are indicated in the Lexicon.

[9] E.g. ἀννῶνα or ἀνῶνα (*annona*), Ἀπρίλιος or Ἀπρίλλιος (*Aprilis*). Binder (2000: 109–10), Gignac (1976: 155–6), García Domingo (1979: 80–2).

Conventional spelling in Latin alphabet	Most common spelling(s) in Greek alphabet
a	α (ἄλη ← *āla*)
b	β (βίρρος ← *birrus*)[10]
c	κ (κάγκελλος ← *cancellus*)
d	δ (δεκουρίων ← *decuriō*)
e (short)	ε or ι (ῥεπούδιον or ῥιπούδιον ← *repudium*)[11]
e (long)	η, ι, or ε (βισήλεκτος, βισίλεκτος, or βισέλεκτος ← *bis ēlēctus*)[12]
f	φ (φίσκος ← *fiscus*)
g	γ (γράδος ← *gradus*)
h	not written[13]
i (short)	ι, ει, η, or ε (κιρκίτωρ, κερκείτωρ, or κερκήτωρ ← *circitor*)[14]
i (long)	ι, ει, or η (σκρίνιον, σκρείνιον, or σκρήνιον ← *scrīnium*)
i (consonantal)	ι or ει (Ἰούλιος or Εἰούλιος ← *Iūlius*)
k	κ (Καλάνδαι ← *Kalendae*)
l	λ (Λατῖνος ← *Latīnus*)[15]
m	μ (Μάρτιος ← *Mārtius*)
n (not before c or g)	ν (νοτάριος ← *notārius*)
n (before c or g)	γ or ν (κάγκελλος or κάνκελλος ← *cancellus*)
o (short)	ο or ω (πρόξιμος or πρώξιμος ← *proximus*)
o (long)	ω, ο, or ου (πωμάριον or πομάριον ← *pōmārium*, σάπων or σάπουν ← *sāpō*)[16]
p	π (πάλλιον ← *pallium*)
qu	κου, κυ, or κο (κουιντάνα, κυιντάνα, or κοιντάνα ← *quīntāna*)[17]
r	ρ (Ῥώμη ← *Rōma*)
s	σ (σάγος ← *sagum*)
t	τ (τίρων ← *tīrō*)
u (short)	ου, ο, or ω (κουστωδία, κοστωδία, or κωστωδία ← *custōdia*)[18]

[10] In late texts Latin *b* was sometimes spelled υ when it followed *a* (e.g. σταῦλον, variant of στάβλον ← *stabulum*), because the Greek diphthong αυ was developing towards the modern Greek pronunciation 'av' at the same time that β was devoping in the direction of 'v'. Cf. Gignac (1976: 68–70).

[11] Cf. Binder (2000: 218–20).

[12] Cf. Binder (2000: 96–8, 270).

[13] Latin words beginning with *h* are now sometimes written with a rough breathing in Greek and sometimes with a smooth breathing, but this choice is strictly editorial (sometimes influenced by Byzantine scribes' etymological awareness or lack thereof): in antiquity breathings were very rarely written. As aspiration tended to be lost in both Latin and Greek most loanwords were probably pronounced without *h*.

[14] Binder (2000: 117–35) examines in detail the use of ε.

[15] Sometimes *r* and *l* are interchanged, usually by dissimilation: e.g. ἀκκουβιτάλιον or ἀκκουβιτάριον (*accubitale*), φραγέλλιον or φλαγέλλιον (*flagellum*). Gignac (1976: 102–7, 1981: 49–50), Schirru (2013: 316), Dieterich (1898: 122–3).

[16] Binder (2000: 220–3) examines in detail the use of ου.

[17] The most common is κου; κο seems to be used mainly before ι, perhaps because of the familiarity of the digraph οι in Greek. Some words containing *qu* use multiple spellings while others are notably consistent, e.g. κουαδράριος (*quadrātārius*), κυαιστιωνάριος (*quaestiōnārius*). Gignac (1976: 225–6), Binder (2000: 107–9), Leumann (1977: §52b), García Domingo (1979: 73–5), Meinersmann (1927: 110–12), Schwyzer (1939: 158), Dieterich (1898: 74).

[18] Binder (2000: 137–52) examines in detail the use of ο.

u (long)	ου, ο, or ω (προκουράτωρ, προκοράτωρ, or προυκωράτωρ ← *prōcūrātor*)
v (= consonantal *u*)	ου or β (οὐετερανός or βετερανός ← *veterānus*)
x (before vowels)	ξ (ἐξάκτωρ ← *exāctor*)
x (before consonants)	ξ, κσ, or simplification of cluster (ἐξκέπτωρ, ἐκσκέπτωρ, or ἐξέπτωρ ← *exceptor*) [19]
ae	αι or ε (αἰράριον or ἐράριον ← *aerārium*) [20]
oe	οι (φοιδερᾶτος ← *foederātus*)
au	αυ, α, or αου (Αὔγουστος, Ἄγουστος, or Ἀούγουστος ← *Augustus*) [21]
ev	εβ, εου, or ευ (βρέβιον, βρέουιον, or βρέυιον ← *brevia*)

Often particular transcriptions are characteristic of specific chronological periods, places, or text types; these partly reflect differences in pronunciation, but the relationship between spelling and pronunciation is not always straightforward. For example, Latin *v* (consonantal *u*) was originally pronounced like English 'w' and was therefore written ου in Greek during the Republic and early Empire (e.g. οὐετερανός 'veteran' from *veterānus*, a loan that first appears in the first century AD). Later, Latin *v* came to sound more like our 'v', and at the same time Greek β (which had originally represented a sound like our 'b') also started to be pronounced more like our 'v', so Greek speakers used β to represent Latin *v* (e.g. βήναβλον 'throwing-spear' from *vēnābulum*, a loan that first appears in the fifth or sixth century AD).[22] Words that had been borrowed before this change could be spelled either way in later centuries; thus οὐετερανός was often spelled βετ(ε)ρανός in inscriptions, but the spelling with ου persisted with almost complete consistency in papyri of all periods, suggesting that in that type of Greek the loanword had become so established that its spelling was unaffected by the changing pronunciation of the original in Latin. Words borrowed after this change were usually spelled with β, but even in such words ου was occasionally used owing to patterns established by earlier borrowings. For example *vēlārium* 'curtain' appears to have been borrowed in the fourth century AD but usually appears on papyri as οὐηλάριον, probably by association with *vēlum* 'covering', which had been borrowed by the second century AD and was always spelled with ου- in papyri (see §3.2 *s.vv.* βηλάριον and βῆλον, forms found in literature).

Byzantine legal texts often use a fundamentally different kind of Latin spelling, transliterating the spellings of Latin words without regard for their sounds; in this system not only are the Latin vowel quantities irrelevant, but Latin *h* can become Greek *v* owing to the graphic similarity of the two in late Roman capitals.[23] The beginnings of this system can be seen in a sixth-century

---

[19] Binder (2000: 227–8).

[20] Binder (2000: 100–1).

[21] Binder (2000: 106–7, 215–16).

[22] There is no single date for the change in spelling: the β spelling first appears in papyri during the first century AD and gradually becomes more common over subsequent centuries. See Gignac (1976: 68–9), García Domingo (1979: 70–3), Binder (2000: 102–6), Schwyzer (1939: 158). Schirru (2013: 310–11) claims that the difference between ου and β is not chronological but sociolinguistic, with higher-register borrowings taking the spelling ου and lower-register ones β; the possibility is interesting, but the argument is circular since there is no external reason to suppose that the words spelled with ου in fact belonged to a higher register. The most detailed treatment is that of Zilliacus (1935b), which provides much interesting information but treats any Latin word appearing in a Greek papyrus as being a transcription of contemporary Latin pronunciation. Codeswitches and new loanwords were indeed transcriptions of the Latin pronunciation, but established loanwords had established Greek pronunciations that probably developed in line with contemporary Greek changes rather than being tied to either the original Latin pronunciation or subsequent changes in Latin phonetics. The distinction between newly introduced Latin words and long-established loanwords may account for some of the spelling variation that Zilliacus sees as being connected to the position of the *v* in the Latin word – but further research would be needed to establish the facts.

[23] See §3.2 *s.vv.* ἐξιβιτόριος, ἐρεδιτάριος, ὀνοράριος, προϊβιτόριος, προνερεδεγεριτεύω; on Byzantine transcriptions more generally Dain (1930), Van der Wal (1983: 50–2).

tendency to use ε for Latin *e* regardless of its quantity, but the full-blown version does not develop until after A D 600.

4.1.2 *Utility for scholarship*

The Greek spellings of Latin words offer important insights into the pronunciation of both Greek and Latin, and those insights have long been enthusiastically exploited by scholars; indeed the spellings of Latin words in Greek texts have to date been much more thoroughly studied than other features of those words. Work on the spellings of loanwords usually focusses on inscriptions or papyri, since in those text types we can be confident of knowing the original ancient spellings.[24] Although more could still be done, the present work is not the place to attempt it, and the outline given here is intended primarily to indicate where readers can turn for further information.

The most important works on what Latin words tell us about Greek pronunciation are those of Gignac and García Domingo. Gignac's study of the phonology of Greek papyri in the Roman and Byzantine periods (1976) uses transcriptions of Latin words as clues to the pronunciation of Greek, to assist in identifying both overall trends in the evolution of Greek pronunciation and regionalisms in Egyptian pronunciation that may be due to influence from the Egyptian language.[25] García Domingo's massive study of Latin words in the Hellenistic age (1979) uses inscriptions containing transcribed Latin words to extract information on Greek pronunciation of that period.

The main work on what the Greek forms of Latin words tell us about Latin pronunciation has been done by Binder (2000) and García Domingo (1979). The former uses all types of evidence from all periods and attempts to recover non-standard late Latin forms, while the latter uses inscriptions and focusses on the Hellenistic period. The Latin words in Hellenistic Greek inscriptions are often used by Latinists, because they offer information

about Latin pronunciation (and therefore sometimes about Latin etymology) at a period for which direct Latin evidence is scarce.[26] Particular attention has been paid to the use of ει to represent Latin *ī* in early inscriptions, since it often mirrors the use of *ei* for particular examples of *ī* in Latin of the same period; although by the time of most papyri ει and ι were frequently interchanged regardless of the quantity of the original Latin vowel, at an early period the alternation can be demonstrated to be meaningful.[27]

Although the results of all this research are considerable, they are much more modest than those of Biville's work (1990–5) on the phonetics of Greek loanwords in Latin. In addition to obtaining information about the pronunciation of both Greek and Latin from the Latin forms of Greek words, Biville dated the original borrowings of loanwords (even ones apparently borrowed long before their first surviving attestations) by the different Latin forms of Greek loanwords borrowed at various periods. She also used those forms to establish whether certain contentious words were in fact borrowings from Greek. I am not in a position to judge how solidly the Greek loanwords in Latin actually support the conclusions she draws, but Binder (2000: e.g. 267–73) is right to be more cautious in drawing conclusions from the forms of Latin loanwords in Greek. It is clear that during the many centuries through which Latin and Greek remained in contact, the spellings of early borrowings were sometimes influenced by later contact (cf. §4.1.1).

The material gathered in the Lexicon portion of the present work may be useful for further research in this area, but care should be taken in using it for this purpose. Since the main purpose of the Lexicon lemmata is to allow users to find the words they are looking for, many different kinds of spellings are included: original ancient spellings, spellings invented by editors, and spellings invented by lexicographers and other scholars. Many of the modern spellings have been heavily influenced by awareness of words' etymologies and of the Latin spellings of the source words;

[24] Binder (2000) and Sallés Verdaguer (1976–7) include data from all text types.

[25] Gignac (1976: e.g. 217–26, 246–7, 253–6). Schirru (2013) also examines spellings in papyri.

[26] E.g. Leumann (1977: §146c), Allen (1978: 41).

[27] E.g. J. N. Adams (2003: 48–50), García Domingo (1979: 49–52).

they are completely unsuitable for use as data on ancient pronunciation.

4.2 THE ASSIMILATION OF LATIN NOUNS AND ADJECTIVES INTO GREEK DECLENSIONS

Certain Latin and Greek declensions had obvious similarities. These originated from a common inheritance of Indo-European inflectional patterns and were reinforced in the minds of bilingual speakers by a significant body of obviously related vocabulary, much of it the result of early borrowing from Greek to Latin: pairs like ἐπιστολή/*epistula* 'letter', ταῦρος/*taurus* 'bull', and λέων/*leo* 'lion' provided models for the assimilation into Greek of Latin nouns in -*a*, -*us*, and -*o*. Usually, therefore, Latin nouns and adjectives acquired regular inflections in Greek following predictable patterns. Nevertheless, some words did not follow the models available, and some others belonged to paradigms not well supplied with models, leading to unpredictable Greek forms.[28] Whichever Greek paradigm a loanword ended up in, however, it was normally adopted directly into that paradigm, without the addition of affixes or folk-linguistic influence; for the exceptions see §4.3, §4.4, and §4.5.

4.2.1 *Distinguishing between nouns and adjectives*

The borrowing process involved considerable fluidity between nouns and adjectives, with the result that many Latin adjectives ended up as nouns in Greek. Often that process was complete by the time of our earliest Greek evidence, so that Latin adjectives appear to have been borrowed as nouns. Sometimes, however, a Latin word first appeared in Greek as an adjective and was substantivized only later. Such later development seems to follow the usual Greek patterns for

substantivization and is probably unconnected to the words' Latin origins (cf. §12.2.1).

The earliest Latin adjectives borrowed, the names of the Roman months, constitute a special case of the substantivization process: when the month names first entered Greek they functioned primarily as adjectives, but by late antiquity they were primarily nouns owing to a change in idioms for expressing dates. Speakers using Kalends, Nones, and Ides found adjectives more convenient (e.g. καλάνδαις Ἰανουαρίαις 'on the January Kalends'; πρὸ μιᾶς ἡμέρας νωνῶν Ἰανουαρίων 'one day before the January Nones', Plut. *Mor.* 319b). But in the modern system of counting days progressively from the beginning to the end of the month, which began in the fifth century AD, the noun involved was always masculine μείς/μήν 'month'.[29] Therefore in dates like τὴν πρώτην ἡμέραν τοῦ μηνὸς Ἰανουαρίου 'the first day of the month of January', the word 'month' did not need to be expressed, resulting in formulations like τὴν πρώτην Ἰανουαρίου 'the first of January' (Lyd. *Mens.* 3.17.3).

Since Greek adjectives can always function as nouns, but Greek nouns very rarely function as adjectives, loanwords with endings that could belong to either category can be considered adjectives if they functioned as such at any point after being borrowed. The pool of loanword adjectives is much smaller than the pool of nouns (§10.3.1) but more regular in its inflection and therefore shows the adaptation process more clearly.

4.2.2 *Adjectives*

Latin first/second-declension adjectives ending in -*us*, -*a*, -*um* normally became Greek first/second-declension adjectives. These ended in -ος in the masculine and -ον in the neuter, but in the feminine there were three possibilities: native Greek adjectives with stems ending in ι, ε, and ρ normally formed feminines in -α, native adjectives

---

[28] The main work on the morphology of Latin loanwords in Greek is the dissertation of Filos (2008), which contains far more detailed information than can be provided here; as it unfortunately remains unpublished I am grateful to the author for allowing me to report a few of its findings (as cited below). Other significant discussions of loan-

word morphology are García Domingo (1979: 89–99), Meinersmann (1927: 114–19), and Döttling (1920).

[29] For the use of Roman dating formulae in Greek see Solin (2008) and Sijpesteijn (1979); for the fifth-century shift Solin (2008: 266).

with other stem terminations normally formed feminines in -η, and a group made up mainly of compound adjectives lacked a separate feminine entirely and used masculine forms instead (two-termination adjectives). Lexicographers, who need to assign loanword adjectives to one of these three groups in order to include them in dictionaries, normally assume that loanwords took the feminines suggested by their forms unless there is clear evidence to the contrary. But often there is no evidence in either direction, because many loanword adjectives are unattested in the feminine. This situation probably leads to distortion particularly with adjectives traditionally considered to belong to the two-termination group, such as καταφρακτάριος, -ον 'armoured' (*catafractarius*) and σκουτουλᾶτος, -ον 'with a checked pattern' (*scutulatus*), because in Roman-period Greek that group was disappearing: native words that had previously lacked a separate feminine often appear with one in documentary papyri (Gignac 1981: 105). It is therefore very likely that some or all of the loanword adjectives traditionally considered to be two-termination in fact formed separate feminines. Unfortunately, however, they are rarely attested agreeing with feminine nouns, particularly in inscriptions and papyri (cf. Filos 2008: 247), and therefore it is impossible to be certain on this point.

Adjectives that would be expected to form feminines in -α, however, are unproblematic; many of these are attested in the feminine, always with the expected endings, and the unattested ones probably did not deviate from that pattern. The loanwords in this category are ἐκστρανήιος 'unrelated' (*extraneus*), ἐξτραορδινάριος 'unusual' (*extraordinarius*), Ἰανουάριος 'January' (*Ianuarius*), Ἰούλιος 'July' (*Iulius*), Ἰούνιος 'June' (*Iunius*), Καπετώλιος 'Capitoline' (*Capitolius*), καυσάριος 'dismissed because of illness' (*causarius*), κιβάριος 'of the household' (*cibarius*), κουαιστώριος 'of a quaestor' (*quaestorius*), Μάϊος 'May' (*Maius*), Μάρτιος 'March' (*Martius*), μιλιάριος 'of a thousand' (*miliarius*), ὀνοράριος 'honorary' (*honorarius*), ὀρδινάριος 2 'regular' (*ordinarius*), πραιτώριος 'praetorian' (*praetorius*), ῥούσιος 'reddish' (*russeus*), σπούριος 'bastard' (*spurius*), Φεβρουάριος 'February' (*Februarius*), φιδεικομμισσάριος 'left in trust' (*fideicommissarius*), and φρουμεντάριος 'concerned with victualling' (*frumentarius*).

Most loanword adjectives that would be expected to form feminines in -η either do so or are unattested in the feminine. The loanwords in this group are ἀνισᾶτος 'flavoured with aniseed' (*anesatus*), Αὐγουσταλιανός 'pertaining to the Augustalis' (*Augustalianus*), Αὔγουστος 2 'of Augustus' (*Augustus*), ἀψινθᾶτος 'flavoured with wormwood' (probably *absinthiatus*), βένετος 'blue' (*venetus*), βόνος 'good' (*bonus*), γάλβινος 'greenish-yellow' (*galbinus*), δουκιανός 'pertaining to the *dux*' (*ducianus*), ἐμαγκιπᾶτος 'emancipated' (*emancipatus*), κλασσικός 'naval' (probably *classicus*), κομιτιανός 'of a count' (*comitianus*), κουμουλᾶτος 'heaping' (*cumulatus*), Λαδικηνός 'Laodiccan' (*Laodicenus*), Λατῖνος 'Latin' (*Latinus*), μυρσινᾶτος 'with myrtle' (*myrsinatus*), Ναυατιανός 'Novatianist' (*Novatiani*), οὐετερανός 'veteran' (*veteranus*), παγανικός 'civilian' (probably *paganicus*), πεξός 'brushed' (*pexus*), περεγρῖνος 'foreign' (*peregrinus*), πληγᾶτος 'wounded' (*plagatus*), πούβλικος 'public' (*publicus*), πραιτέριτος 'in arrears' (*praeteritus*), πραιτωριανός 'praetorian' (*praetorianus*), πριβᾶτος 'private' (*privatus*), Σαβελλιανός 'Sabellian' (*Sabelliani*), Σευηριανός 'Severian' (*Severiani*), σοῦμμος 'highest in rank' (*summus*), στατοῦτος 'fixed' (*statutus*), and τρακτός 'bleached' (*tractus*).

Three adjectives whose feminines should have ended in -η, however, could nevertheless form feminines in -α: λεγίτιμος 'based on law' (*legitimus*), πρῖμος 'first' (*primus*), and στολᾶτος 'wearing a *stola*' (*stolatus*). This variation is probably due to the influence of the original Latin feminine ending -a, particularly as στολᾶτος occurs only, and πρῖμος mainly, as part of longer phrases (§7.3).

Latin first/second-declension adjectives did not all end in -*us*, -*a*, -*um*; some ended in -*er*, -*era*, -*erum* or -*er*, -*ra*, -*rum*. One of each of these types was borrowed into Greek, both becoming first/second-declension adjectives in -ρος, -ρα, -ρον: *asper, aspera, asperum* became ἄσπρος, ἄσπρα, ἄσπρον 'white', and *sacer, sacra, sacrum* became σάκρος, σάκρα, σάκρον 'sacred'.[30]

---

30 Ἄσπρος probably had a feminine in -η in addition to the one in -α, owing to internal Greek tendencies (Gignac 1981: 113–15).

Latin third-declension adjectives also became Greek first/second-declension adjectives, usually by substituting the common Greek adjective endings -ιος, -ία, -ιον for Latin -is, -e. Thus castrensis, castrense became καστρήσιος, καστρησία, καστρήσιον 'of the camp', and similarly ἀννάλιος 'yearly' (annalis), Ἀπρίλιος 'April' (Aprilis), ἰλλούστριος 'noble' (illustris), κιρκήσιος 'of the circus' (circensis), Κοιντίλιος 'July' (Quintilis), κομιτατήσιος 'belonging to the imperial court' (comitatensis), κονσουλάριος 'consular' (consularis), Μουτουνήσιος 'of Mutina' (Mutinensis), πατριμωνάλιος 'belonging to the imperial property' (patrimonialis), περσονάλιος 'personal' (personalis), and Ῥωμανήσιος (an architectural construction, Romanensis).[31] But diloris 'having two epaulettes' dropped the i to become δίλωρος. Month names in -er, -is, -e followed a similar pattern, so that September, October, November, and December became the regular first/second-declension adjectives Σεπτέμβριος, Ὀκτώβριος, Νοέμβριος, and Δεκέμβριος.[32] Latin third-declension adjectives with other endings do not seem to have been borrowed into Greek.

In late Greek -ιος and -ιον were often shortened to -ις and -ιν, a change that also affected Latin loanwords.[33] When the loanword in question was originally a third-declension adjective in -is, there is sometimes a temptation to see Greek -ις as a direct continuation of Latin -is, but that identification is usually wrong. It is probably right, however, for the comparatively early form Αὐγουστᾶλις in the title σοδᾶλις Αὐγουστᾶλις: Augustalis 'of Augustus' normally appears in Greek as the perfectly regular Αὐγουστάλιος, but the Latin ending seems

to assert itself when the word is part of a fixed phrase (§7.3).[34]

Thus all loanword adjectives, whatever their declension in Latin, ended up as first/second-declension adjectives in Greek apart from the occasional preservation of a Latin ending in a fixed phrase. As far as we can tell, the resulting loanword adjectives behaved like native Greek adjectives of the same types except that a few formed Latinate feminines in -α where -η would be expected, primarily in longer phrases.

4.2.3 First-declension nouns

Latin first-declension nouns and first/second-declension adjectives substantivized in the feminine were normally borrowed into the Greek first declension. But whereas Latin had only one first-declension paradigm, with all nominatives singular ending in -ă, Greek had five: feminines in -η (by far the most common paradigm), feminines in -α, -ας (paradigm used when the last letter before the ending was ι, ε, or ρ), feminines in -α, -ης, masculines in -ης (the most common paradigm for first-declension masculines), and masculines in -ας (masculine paradigm used when the last letter before the ending was ι, ε, or ρ). These were declined identically in the plural but differed in the singular: feminines in -η had nom. -η, gen. -ης, dat. -ῃ, acc. -ην; feminines in -α, -ας normally had -ᾱ, -ᾱς, -ᾳ, -ᾱν but sometimes -ᾰ, -ᾱς, -ᾳ, -ᾰν; feminines in -α, -ης had -ᾰ, -ης, -ῃ, -ᾰν; masculines in -ης had -ης, -ου, -ῃ, -ην; masculines in -ας had -ᾱς, -ου, -ᾳ, -ᾱν. The distinction between ᾱ and ᾰ eventually became inaudible, probably during the early centuries of the Roman period, and since the ancients did not use macrons that distinction had never been visible in writing. But a difference between nouns that had originally ended in -ᾱ and ones that had originally ended in -ᾰ often remained audible in the accent, since forms in -ᾰ tended to take different accents from forms in -ᾱ (e.g. θάλαττᾰ versus ἡμέρᾱ).

How were Latin loanwords distributed among these paradigms? That question is harder to answer than one might expect, because most of the evidence is unreliable: on a question like this, editions and even manuscripts of literary texts cannot be guaranteed to reflect the practices of the original writers. Evidence from papyri and

---

[31] For the disappearance of -n- in -ensis see §6.7. Cf. Palmer (1945: 14, 31), García Domingo (1979: 98–9), Freyburger-Galland (1998: 141–2).

[32] This development may have been assisted by analogy with the other month names, which at the time they were borrowed into Greek were Ἰανουάριος, Φεβρουάριος, Μάρτιος, Ἀπρίλιος, Μάϊος, Ἰούνιος, Κοιντίλιος, and Σεξτίλιος. It could also be relevant that originally the month names occurred mainly in the feminine (agreeing with Καλάνδαι, Νῶναι, or Εἰδοί: §4.2.1).

[33] Gignac (1981: 115).

[34] Augustalis also occasionally has first-declension forms reflecting (though not acutally including) a nominative Αὐγουστάλης; these occur only when it is substantivized, and only in early inscriptions.

inscriptions is more reliable, but many nouns do not appear there in the right forms to make clear which paradigm they followed. Only well-preserved, unabbreviated forms in the singular are helpful, and determining a word's paradigm often requires two such forms, a nominative or accusative singular and a genitive or dative singular.

Therefore along with looking at the data it is useful to consider what we might expect Greek speakers to have done with first-declension Latin words, and here scholars have traditionally seen two main possibilities. If speakers followed the models offered by pre-existing equivalents like ἐπιστολή/*epistula* and ποιητής/*poeta*, most Latin first-declension nouns should have become feminines in -η or masculines in -ης, according to their original genders; feminine -α, -ας and masculine -ας should be used only for stems ending in ι, ε, or ρ, while feminine -α, -ης should not be used at all. But if speakers simply imported Latin nominatives into Greek and declined them according to the paradigm they best fitted, the Latin nominative -ă should have put the majority of first-declension loanwords into the Greek paradigm in -α, -ης.

4.2.3.1 *Feminines*

Ancient scholars seem to have considered the paradigm in -α, -ης the correct one for Latin first-declension feminines. In a passage that may go back to the second-century AD grammarian Herodian, the Byzantine scholar Choeroboscus appears to say that when Αὐγούστα is a place name it follows the paradigm in -α, -ας, but when

it is a common noun meaning 'empress' it follows the paradigm in -α, -ης because (in that sense only?) it is Latinate and therefore must have a nominative in -ă.[35]

4 Περὶ δὲ τοῦ Αὐγούστα λέγουσιν ὅτι ὤφειλεν Αὐγούστη εἶναι ἡ εὐθεῖα διὰ τοῦ -η, τὸ γὰρ -τ- τῷ -η χαίρει, οἷον χαίτη ἐλάτη Ἀφροδίτη μελέτη ἀρετή τελευτή· καὶ κατ' ἄλλον δὲ κανόνα ὤφειλεν Αὐγούστη εἶναι, ἐπειδὴ τὰ εἰς -ος ἀρσενικὰ ποιοῦντα κατ' ἰδίαν θηλυκά, τουτέστι μὴ ὄντα κοινὰ τῷ γένει (διὰ τὸ ὁ φιλόσοφος καὶ ἡ φιλόσοφος), ἔχοντα πρὸ τοῦ -ος σύμφωνον μὴ τὸ ρ, εἰς -η ποιοῦσι τὸ θηλυκόν, οἷον σοφός σοφή, καλός καλή, κάλλιστος καλλίστη, ἄριστος ἀρίστη, μέγιστος μεγίστη· οὕτως οὖν καὶ ἀπὸ τοῦ Αὔγουστος Αὐγούστη ὤφειλε γενέσθαι τὸ θηλυκόν, ἀλλ' ἔτρεψε τὸ -η εἰς τὸ -α βραχὺ δηλονότι Ἰταλικῶς· τὸ γὰρ ὄνομα Ἰταλικόν ἐστιν. ὅθεν ἀξιοῦσι τὸ μὲν κύριον ὄνομα Αὐγούστα λέγειν (ὅτι ἐκτείνει τὸ -α καὶ προσθέσει τοῦ -ς ποιεῖ τὴν γενικήν, οἷον Αὐγούστα Αὐγούστας, ὥσπερ Ἀθηνᾶ Ἀθηνᾶς, Διοτίμα Διοτίμας, Φερετίμα Φερετίμας, Δωρικῶς δηλονότι τραπέντος τοῦ -η εἰς -α μακρόν), τὸ δὲ ἐπὶ τῆς βασιλίδος Ἰταλικόν ἐστι, καὶ διὰ τοῦτο τρέπει τὸ -α εἰς -η ἐν τῇ γενικῇ, οἷον Αὐγούστης, ὥσπερ Μοῦσα Μούσης, ἅμαξα ἁμάξης, ὡς τοῦ -α συνεσταλμένου ὄντος.

And concerning Αὐγούστα they say that the nominative should have been Αὐγούστη with an -η, for τ tends to take -η, as in χαίτη, ἐλάτη, Ἀφροδίτη, μελέτη, ἀρετή, and τελευτή. And it should have been Αὐγούστη by another rule also, since masculines ending in -ος that form separate feminines, that is not being of common gender (this specification is added because of φιλόσοφος, which can be either masculine or feminine), if they have a consonant other than ρ before the -ος, form the feminine in -η, as σοφός σοφή, καλός καλή, κάλλιστος καλλίστη, ἄριστος ἀρίστη, and μέγιστος μεγίστη. Therefore in the same way too the feminine from Αὔγουστος should have been Αὐγούστη, but it changed the -η to short -α [i.e. the form in -ă is irregular], clearly in the Latin fashion; for the noun is Latin. And that's why people think it right to pronounce the proper name Αὐγούστα (because it lengthens the -α and makes its genitive by adding -ς, that is Αὐγούστα Αὐγούστας, like Ἀθηνᾶ Ἀθηνᾶς, Διοτίμα Διοτίμας, and Φερετίμα Φερετίμας, with the -η turning into long -α clearly in the Doric fashion), but the word for 'empress' is Latin, and because of this it turns

---

35 Choeroboscus, *Prolegomena et scholia in Theodosii Alexandrini canones, Grammatici Graeci* IV.I 305.7–22, cf. Hdn. Κλισ.Ὀνομ. III.II.752.34–753.13. The distinction between ᾱ and ă was certainly inaudible in Choeroboscus' day but perhaps still perceptible to some people in Herodian's. It is notable that Choeroboscus does not consider the possibility of declension with -ă, -ᾱς, like μοῖρα; in Classical Greek all nouns declined that way had ι, ε, or ρ before the ending, but so did all nouns declined with -ᾱ, -ᾱς, the pattern that he here admits for the place name. Numerous places bore the name *Augusta*, including the city Augusta Emerita (now Mérida in Spain), which was mentioned by Greek writers as early as Strabo. Surviving literature does not clearly follow Choeroboscus' rules for inflecting this word.

the -α to -η in the genitive, that is Αὐγούστης, like Μοῦσα Μούσης and ἅμαξα ἁμάξης, because the -α is short.

But only four Latin loanwords can be verified to have joined the paradigm in -α, -ης, and even they did not always follow it with complete consistency. Only three of these had been first-declension nouns in Latin: Αὐγοῦστα 'empress' (*Augusta*), ταβέλλα 'writing tablet' (*tabella*), and τοῦρμα 'troop' (*turma*).[36] The fourth, κλάσσα 'fleet', came from third-declension *classis* (§4.2.5) and therefore cannot have been attracted into this paradigm by the quantity of the -*a* in the nominative singular. In modern Greek the paradigm in -α, -ης has been replaced by the one in -α, -ας, and that process had already begun in the Roman period.[37] No doubt the pressures that caused native Greek words to move out of this paradigm also made it difficult for loanwords to move in, but two facts suggest that the gradual dissolution of the paradigm in -α, -ης is not the main reason for its rare use by loanwords. Adoption into this paradigm was clearly not impossible for loanwords borrowed in the Roman period, since it happened with the four just mentioned; three of those were borrowed in the first century AD and one (Αὐγοῦστα) perhaps as late as the third. Conversely, no word borrowed during the Hellenistic period can be verified to have joined this paradigm; that applies even to proper names, which at that period are better attested in

inscriptions than are the loanwords in this study (García Domingo 1979: 89–90). The conclusion can only be that despite Choeroboscus' views, the quantity of Latin -*a* did not normally determine which first-declension paradigm a Latin loanword followed.

Latin feminines ending in -*ia*, -*ea*, and -*ra* would on any theory be expected to use the paradigm in -α, -ας, and that is what happened to such nouns whenever a consistent outcome can be verified. The loanwords in this group are ἀγραρία 'garrison' (*agraria*), βικαρία 'office of deputy' (*vicaria*), βικία 'vetch' (variant of βικίον, *vicia*), δουκηναρία '200,000 sesterces' (*ducenaria*), κεντουρία 'century' (*centuria*), κλεισούρα 'narrow pass' (*clausura*), κολωνία 'colony' (*colonia*), κορριγία 'thong' (*corrigia*), κουβικουλαρία 'chamberlain' (probably *cubicularia*), κουστωδία 'guard' (*custodia*), οὐγγία 'ounce' (*uncia*), παρατοῦρα 'distinctive dress' (*paratura*), πεδατοῦρα 'watchman's allotted area' (*pedatura*), προβατωρία 'imperial letter of commendation' (*probatoria*), σαβούρα 'ballast' (*saburra*), φαμιλία 'family' (*familia*), and φασκία 'bandage' (*fascia*).[38]

Feminines with endings other than -*ia*, -*ea*, or -*ra*, if they did not join the paradigm in -α, -ης, would be expected to join the one in -η. But only five words consistently did so, and each is a special case in one way or another. Ῥώμη 'Rome' (*Roma*) and βυκάνη 'trumpet' (*bucina*) were borrowed very early; κοόρτη 'cohort' came from third-declension *cohors* and thus did not end in -*a* in Latin; βεττονική 'betony' (*vettonica*) and δελματική 'Dalmatian tunic' (*dalmatica*) looked like substantivizations of Greek adjectives in -ικός, -ική, -ικόν. There is no evidence of Latin loanwords joining the paradigm in -η without such special circumstances. In fact, nine words that would have been expected to do so instead joined the paradigm in -α, -ας: κατήνα 'chain' (*catena*), κουιντάνα (a tax, *quintana*), πανίκουλα 'tumour' (*panicula*), πίλα 2 'pier' (*pila*), πραῖδα 'loot' (*praeda*), ῥόγα 'distribution of wages' (*roga*), σίτλα 'bucket' (*situla*), στρᾶτα 'street' (*strata*), and φοῦσκα 'mixture of

---

[36] Native Greek words in this paradigm had recessive accents, but Choeroboscus' discussion of Αὐγοῦστα (passage 4 above) implies that Latin loanwords perhaps did not. If the place name and the word for 'empress' had had different accents, Choeroboscus might have mentioned that difference, since it would have helped to distinguish the meanings. Moreover, in the Byzantine manuscript tradition Αὐγοῦστα is normally accented on its second syllable regardless of meaning, and since it was still in active use in Byzantine Greek, that accent is likely to be real (§5.1). (In modern Greek Αυγούστα survives both as a personal name and as a word for 'empress', and it still has the accent on the second syllable in both senses: personal communication from Stephanie Roussou.) It is thus unlikely that the Byzantines pronounced this word Αὔγουστα: when the -α is short, the correct written accent is probably Αὐγοῦστα. (The *u* is short in Latin, but a Greek speaker would probably have considered it long for purposes of accentuation: §5.2.3.)

[37] Gignac (1981: 6), Horrocks (2010: 285–6).

[38] Note also φορμαλεία (*formula*) with an extra vowel (§4.4), and ἀπαλαρέα (*epularis*) (§4.2.5). The quantity of the final -α is unknown, and late borrowings could not meaningfully have either quantity. García Domingo (1979: 89–90), Freyburger-Galland (1998: 138–9).

vinegar and water' (*posca*). It therefore seems that the paradigm in -α, -ας was preferred for Latin loanwords whatever their stem terminations. Regardless of whether the -α was long or short (we do not know, and in late borrowings it cannot meaningfully have been either), this outcome is unexpected, because it violates the rules followed by native Greek words.

What was the reason for that preference? Internal Greek tendencies cannot explain it, since the paradigm in -η never disappeared and is still productive in modern Greek. Nor could there have been some kind of association between the -α, -ας paradigm and Latin in the minds of Greek speakers: Latin third-declension nouns that joined the Greek first declension seem to have preferred the other paradigms. The determining factor was probably the Latin first-declension paradigm taken as a whole, since that did not include any endings in -*e*. In addition to a nominative in -*ă* and accusative in -*ăm*, the Latin singular had a genitive and dative in -*ae* and ablative in -*ā*. These forms would have been matched much better by Greek genitive -ας and dative -ᾳ than by -ης and -η, and that match in vowel quality seems to have made more difference in paradigm choice than the rule about ι, ε, and ρ.

So far we have considered only the feminines that seem to follow one paradigm fairly consistently. Most feminines, however, cannot be verified to follow a particular paradigm, either because there is too little evidence or because the evidence is inconsistent. When one considers all available evidence, inconsistency is common: many feminines appear with nominatives/accusatives in both -η/-ην and -α/-αν, and/or with genitives/datives in both -ης/-η and -ας/-ᾳ. But most of that evidence comes from literature, and in particular most of the forms with η come from literature. And since the forms with α usually violate the rules followed by native Greek words, both Byzantine scribes and modern editors might have corrected α to η in the paradigms of nouns whose stems do not end in ι, ε, or ρ. García Domingo's (1979: 89–90) examination of Latin words in Hellenistic Greek inscriptions found no first-declension feminine forms with η at all; all attestations in the singular, including those of proper names, had α. Filos' (2008: 145) examination of Latin words in Greek papyri found that more than

80% of singular forms had α and less than 20% η.[39] Therefore it is unlikely that the declension of feminines was as inconsistent as the literary evidence suggests. On the basis of the non-literary evidence only five first-declension feminine loanwords can be verified to have a fluctuating declension: ἄλη (*ala*), ἀννῶνα (*annona*), κέλλα (*cella*), ματρῶνα (*matrona*), and μανδήλη from third-declension neuter *mantele* (§4.2.5).[40] Even these may have had stable declensions within the practice of particular times, places, or speakers.

Latin first-declension feminines did not all end up in the Greek first declension; they could also move to other paradigms. Some became second-declension neuters, probably because the nominative singular ending -*a* was reinterpreted as a neuter plural: βικίον 'vetch' (*vicia*), δελματικόν 'Dalmatian tunic' (*dalmatica*), καμίσιον 'shirt' (probably *camisia*), probably καράκαλλον 'hood' (*caracalla*), καροῦχον 'carriage' (variant of καροῦχα, *carruca*), κούρκουμον 'halter' (*curcuma*), λουκάνικον 'sausage' (*lucanica*), μέμβρανον 'parchment' (variant of μεμβράνα, *membrana*), μεμόριον 'grave monument' (*memoria*), ὀξύγγιον 'tallow' (*axungia*), σπόρτουλον (a payment, *sportula*), φαλκίδιον 'heir's minimum portion' (*Falcidia*), and φωκάριον 'concubine' (*focaria*).[41] Two, *averta* 'backpack' and *abolla* 'cloak', remained in the first declension but could take either masculine or feminine endings (ἀβερτή and ἀβερτής, ἀβόλλης and ἀβόλλα). These may have originally been borrowed in one of the many forms in which first-declension masculines and feminines were indistinguishable, leading to a use in Greek with the 'wrong' gender, sometimes corrected by speakers with knowledge of Latin.[42] Less explicably, two feminines transferred to the third declension and kept their original gender (*caliga* 'boot' became κάλιξ and *fabrica* 'workshop' φάβριξ),[43]

---

[39] Gignac (1981: 6–11) and Meinersmann (1927: 115) make similar observations.

[40] Nouns of Greek origin also sometimes fluctuated between -η- and -α- in Roman-period papyri (Gignac 1981: 3–13).

[41] Some of these also have feminine variants. Cf. Schirru (2013: 317), Cavenaile (1952: 197), Tod (1904: 202).

[42] Cf. Schirru (2013: 320–2). Note also masc. (usually) ἁρματοῦρα from fem. *armatura*.

[43] Both also had first-declension variants in Greek.

while one (*faba* 'beans') became a third-declension neuter (φάβα, gen. φάβατος). Several became second-declension masculines: κάμπανος 'steelyard' (*campana*), καράκαλλος 'hood' (variant of καράκαλλον, *caracalla*), κούκκουμος 'jar' (variant of κούκκουμα, *cucuma*), and λίβερνος (a ship, *liburna*).[44]

4.2.3.2 Masculines

Latin first-declension masculines were much rarer than the feminines, and only five were borrowed into Greek. None of these had *i*, *e*, or *r* before the ending, so they might have been expected to join the first-declension masculine paradigm in -ης, but in fact they all joined the one in -ας. Thus *collega* 'colleague' became κολλήγας, *maiuma* (a festival) may have become Μαιουμᾶς, *scriba* 'scribe' became σκρίβας, *subadiuva* 'under-assistant' became σουβαδιούβας, and *verna* 'home-born slave' became βέρνας. Their declensions do not always match those of native Greek words in -ας: -ς is occasionally omitted in the nominative singular, and the genitive singular is often a Doric -α rather than -ου.[45]

A number of loanwords that had not been first-declension masculines in Latin shifted to that declension in Greek; these all joined the paradigm in -ης. Univerbations and Latin–Latin compounds sometimes resulted in Latin words ending in *-is* (§4.5), which in Roman-period Greek sounded like -ης and therefore could be assimilated into the first-declension masculine paradigm. Thus *summa rudis* 'chief instructor at a gladiatorial school' and *secunda rudis* 'deputy chief instructor' became σουμμαρούδης and σεκουνδαρούδης respectively, consistently inflecting like first-declension nouns in -ης. Such assimilation was especially likely for Latin words with *t* before the ending, as words in *-tis* could easily be attracted into the large group of Greek masculines

in -της.[46] Thus the titles *ab actis*, *a secretis*, and *cura palatii* became ἀβάκτης, ἀσηκρῆτις/-ης, and (with the addition of -ς) κουροπαλάτης.[47] Some words from other Latin declensions also became first-declension masculines in -ης, especially when they could thereby end in -της. Third-declension *Quirites*, *Quiritium* 'Roman citizens' and *quadrans*, *quadrantis* 'quarter' became Κυιρῖται and κοδράντης, and second-declension *boletus* 'mushroom' became βωλήτης.

The readiness with which these words joined the paradigm in -ης shows that that paradigm was in principle an attractive one for loanwords: why was it not used by any that had in Latin been first-declension masculines? As in the case of feminines, the frequent appearance of *a* and total absence of *e* in the Latin declension must have played a role. (The occasional omission of -ς in the nominative singular must also be due to influence from the Latin form.) In a Greek context words that followed the paradigm in -ας without a preceding ι, ε, or ρ would have seemed Doric, and that appearance probably triggered the Doric genitive in -α.[48]

4.2.3.3 Conclusions

First-declension loanword nouns diverged from normal Greek patterns more than loanword adjectives did. The influence of the original Latin endings led all first-declension masculines and most feminines to join paradigms that had α

---

[44] Cf. Schirru (2013: 319–24); for similar gender changes affecting Greek loanwords in Latin, see André (1968).

[45] For omission of -ς see e.g. οὐέρνα (= βέρνας) in *MAMA* I.26: Ἀσκληπιάδης οὐέρνα τοῦ Σεβ(αστοῦ) Ἀσκληπιάδη πατρὶ καὶ Μομίᾳ μητρὶ σὺν τοῖς ἀδελφοῖς μνήμης χάριν. For the Doric genitive see e.g. Gignac (1981: 12), Meinersmann (1927: 115).

[46] For the general Greek tendency to use the -της suffix as an ending for compounds see Schwyzer (1939: 451–2), Chantraine (1933: 314–17).

[47] The first two of these are often indeclinable. Titles without a *t* before the *-is* acted differently: ἀβρέβις was always indeclinable, and *a commentariis* became ἀκομενταρήσιος (§4.4).

[48] In late varieties of koiné Greek the genitive in -α was also used for some native masculines in -ας, and indeed it eventually became the normal genitive for that paradigm (Gignac 1981: 12–14; Horrocks 2010: 286). But the use of -α for Latin masculines starts too early to be simply part of that shift (García Domingo 1979: 90–1). Many of the earliest Greek speakers to interact with the Romans spoke Doric, and that dialect therefore played a significant role in establishing Greek–Latin equivalencies in the earliest period of contact (Risch 1976: 884–5); nevertheless that early role does not by itself explain the treatment of first-declension masculines, since other loanwords did not end up with Doric forms.

throughout the singular, while words that shifted to the Greek first declension from other Latin declensions usually joined paradigms that had η in at least some forms. The influence of the original forms also sometimes led masculine nouns to omit -ς in the nominative singular. The quantity of Latin *ă* was noticed by scholars but seems to have had little effect on loanwords' assignment to paradigms, even at a period when distinctions of quantity were still audible.

4.2.4 Second- and fourth-declension nouns

The Latin second and fourth declensions merged in Greek, so that loanwords from both normally joined the second declension. Such loanwords behaved like regular Greek second-declension nouns apart from some fluctuation in gender. For Latin first- and third-declension nouns that joined the Greek second declension, and Latin second-declension nouns that completely left that declension in Greek, see §4.2.3.1 and §4.2.5.

4.2.4.1 Second declension

Latin second-declension masculines in -*us* (both nouns and substantivized adjectives) normally became Greek second-declension masculines in -ος.[49] These were very frequent, especially nouns in -άριος,[50] which were more common than all

other types of -ος noun put together.[51] Latin second-declension masculines in -*r* showed a wide range of different forms in Greek, with no consistency between one word and the next and little consistency even in representations of the same word. The most common word in this group, *magister*, normally became μάγιστρος or took another second-declension form such as μαγίστερος or μαγίστορος, but it could also take third-declension

us), κουβικουλάριος (*cubicularius*), κυαιστιωνάριος (*quaestionarius*), λαγκιάριος (*lancearius*), λανάριος (*lanarius*), λεγεωνάριος (*legionarius*), λεκτικάριος (*lecticarius*), λεντιάριος (*lintearius*), ληγατάριος (*legatarius*), λιβερνάριος (perhaps **liburnarius*), λιβράριος (probably *librarius*), μακελλάριος (*macellarius*), μαρμαράριος (*marmorarius*), μονητάριος (*monetarius*), νοτάριος (*notarius*), νουμεράριος (*numerarius*), ὀρδινάριος 1 (*ordinarius*), ὀρριάριος (*horrearius*), ὀστιάριος (*ostiarius*), πιμεντάριος (*pigmentarius*), πλουμάριος (*plumarius*), προπινάριος (*popinarius*), ρεφερενδάριος (*referendarius*), ρητιάριος (*retiarius*), ριπάριος (*riparius*), σαγιττάριος (*sagittarius*), σαλγαμάριος (*salgamarius*), σαλτάριος (probably *saltuarius*), σηκρητάριος (*secretarius*), σηρικάριος (*sericarius*), σησκουπλικάριος (*sesquiplicarius*), σικάριος (*sicarius*), σιλεντιάριος (*silentiarius*), σιλιγνάριος (*siliginarius*), σκουτάριος (*scutarius*), σκρινιάριος (*scriniarius*), στατιωνάριος (*stationarius*), ταβελλάριος (*tabellarius*), ταβλάριος (probably *tabularius*), τεσσαράριος (*tesserarius*), φακτιωνάριος (*factionarius*), χαρτουλάριος (*chartularius*). The -άριος was often shortened to -άρις as part of a general late Greek development (Gignac 1981: 25–7).

[51] Ἀδριανός (*Hadrianus*), ἀκίσκλος (*acisculus*), ἀστᾶτος (*hastatus*), Αὔγουστος 1 (*Augustus*), βενετιανός (*venetianus*), βέρεδος (*veredus*), βιόκουρος (*viocurus*), βίρρος (*birrus*), βισήλεκτος (*bis electus*, §4.5), Γερμανικός (*Germanicus*), δηποτᾶτος (*deputatus*), δομεστικός 1 (*domesticus*), Δομιτιανός (*Domitianus*), ἠβοκᾶτος (*evocatus*), κάγκελλος (*cancellus*), Καισαριανός (*Caesarianus*), κάλτιος (*calceus*), κάμπος (*campus*), κανδιδᾶτος (*candidatus*), κάστελλος (probably *castellus*), καστρησιανός (*castrensianus*), κηρίολος (*cereolus*), κίρκος (*circus*), κουριῶσος (*curiosus*), κωδικίλλος (*codicillus*), ληγᾶτος 1 (*legatus*), λιβέλλος (*libellus*), λιμιτάνεος (*limitaneus*), λοῦδος (*ludus*), μαγιστριανός (*magistrianus*), μισσίκιος (*missicius*), μόδιος (*modius*), μοῦλος (*mulus*), νούμερος (*numerus*), νοῦμμος (*nummus*), ὄγκινος (*uncinus*), ὀρδινᾶτος (*ordinatus*), Οὐαλεντινιανοί (*Valentiniani*), παγανός (*paganus*), πᾶγος (*pagus*), παλατῖνος 1 (*Palatinus*), πᾶλος (*palus*), πάστιλλος (*pastillus*), πατρίκιος (*patricius*), πραιπόσιτος (*praepositus*), πραίφεκτος (*praefectus*), πριμικήριος (*primicerius*), πριμίπιλος (*primipilus*), πριμισκρίνιος (*primiscrinius*), προμῶτος (*promotus*), πρόξιμος (*proximus*), ρέος (*reus*), σάλιος (*Salius*), σεκουνδοκήριος (*secundicerius*), σηστέρτιος (*sestertius*), τίτλος (*titulus*), τριβοῦνος (*tribunus*), φασίολος (*phaseolus*), φίσκος (*fiscus*), φοιδερᾶτος (*foederatus*), φοῦρνος (*furnus*), Χριστιανός (*Christianus*).

---

[49] Cf. García Domingo (1979: 91–2). No second-declension feminines were borrowed.

[50] Ἀκισκλάριος (*aciscularius*), ἀκουάριος (*aquarius*), ἀκτουάριος (*actuarius*), ἀννωνάριος (probably *annonarius*), ἀργεντάριος (*argentarius*), ἀρκάριος (*arcarius*), ἀστιάριος (perhaps *hastiarius*), αὐράριος (*aurarius*), βαλλιστάριος (*ballistarius*), βαρβαρικάριος (*barbaricarius*), βενεφικιάριος (*beneficiarius*), βερεδάριος (*veredarius*), βηξιλλάριος (*vexillarius*), βικάριος (*vicarius*), βουκελλάριος (*buccellarius*), βουρδωνάριος (*burdonarius*), βρακάριος (*bracarius*), γαλεάριος (*galearius*), γουνάριος (*gunnarius*), δουκηνάριος (*ducenarius*), δουπλικάριος (*duplicarius*), δρακονάριος (*draconarius*), δρομεδάριος (*dromadarius*), ἐσσεδάριος (*essedarius*), ἰσικιάριος (perhaps *isiciarius*), καβαλλάριος (probably *caballarius*), καγκελλάριος 1 (*cancellarius*), καλιγάριος (*caligarius*), καμψάριος (probably *capsarius*), κανονικάριος (*canonicarius*), καπικλάριος (*capiclarius*), κελλάριος (*cellarius*), κεντηνάριος (*centenarius*), κλαβικουλάριος (*clavicularius*), κλιβανάριος (*clibanarius*), κολλεκτάριος (*collectarius*), κομμερκιάριος (*commerciarius*), κονδιτάριος (*conditarius*), κορνικουλάριος (*cornicularius*), κουαδράριος (*quadratarius*)

forms such as μαγίστωρ or μαγίστηρ.[52] *Signifer* 'standard-bearer' and *imaginifer* 'standard-bearer' usually joined the third declension as σίγνιφερ and ἰμαγίνιφερ, but in both cases a few second-declension forms are also attested.[53] The only second-declension Latin noun in *-er* that consistently had a Greek second-declension form is *aegri*, plural of *aeger* 'ill', which became αἶγροι.

Why was there so much variation? It is tempting to assume that the unfamiliar concept of a second-declension nominative in *-r* caused practical difficulties in adaptation, and that *aegri* was easier because it was borrowed in the plural, which did not have the problematic *-r* ending. But no such practical difficulties seem to have affected the borrowing of Latin adjectives: there the masculine second-declension ending *-er* was consistently converted to -ρος (§4.2.2). Moreover clear models for the equivalence between Latin and Greek second-declension nouns in *-r* existed, for example *ager* 'field' and ἀγρός, *Alexander* and Ἀλέξανδρος. Probably the real reason for the variation was the influence of the original nominative in *-r*. In the first declension such influence from original forms appeared to be stronger for nouns than for adjectives, so it may be relevant that *aeger* is normally an adjective in Latin.

Latin second-declension neuters in *-um* normally became Greek second-declension neuters in -ον. These were common, though not as common as the masculines, and again the majority shared a single suffix: loanword neuters in -ιον[54] were more numerous than all other types.[55]

Some second-declension nouns changed genders when borrowed.[56] Most easily explicable are the words for types of wine, which sometimes shifted from neuter to masculine to reflect the genders of the Latin and Greek words for 'wine': *vinum* was neuter but οἶνος masculine. Thus *Falernum* 'Falernian wine' became Φαλέρνος and Φαλερῖνος, and *mustum* 'must' became μοῦστος – though *conditum* 'spiced wine' remained neuter as κονδῖτον (cf. terms in *-atum*, §6.5). Words for money sometimes changed from masculine to neuter, perhaps to reflect the gender of words for

(*Capitolium*), κελλάριον (*cellarium*), κεντηνάριον (*centenarium*), κερβικάριον (perhaps *cervicarium*), κιβάριον (*cibaria*, pl.), κίτριον (perhaps *citrum*), κολλήγιον (*collegium*), κομέτιον (*comitium*), κομμεντάριον (*commentarium*), κομμονιτώριον (*commonitorium*), κονσιστώριον (*consistorium*), λέντιον (*linteum*), λουσώριον (*lusorium*), μαγκίπιον 1 (perhaps *mancipium*), μανδήλιον (perhaps *mantelium*), μηνσώριον (*mensorium/missorium*), μιλιάριον (*miliarium*), μουνικίπιον (*municipium*), ὀράριον (*orarium*), ὅρριον (*horreum*), ὁσπίτιον (*hospitium*), ὀφφίκιον (*officium*), ὀψίκιον (*obsequium*), παλάτιον (*palatium*), πάλλιον (*pallium*), πανάριον (*panarium*), πατριμώνιον (*patrimonium*), πεκούλιον (*peculium*), πλουμάκιον (*plumacium*), πλουμίον (perhaps *plumeum*), πραισίδιον (*praesidium*), πραιτώριον (*praetorium*), πριβιλέγιον (*privilegium*), πριγκίπια (pl., *principia*, pl.), πωμάριον (*pomarium*), ῥεπούδιον (*repudium*), σαλάριον (*salarium*), σαλιβάριον (*salivarium*), σιλέντιον (*silentium*), σιλίγνιον (probably *siligineum*), σκουτάριον (perhaps *scutarium*), σκρίνιον (*scrinium*), σόλιον 2 (*solium*), σουδάριον (*sudarium*), στιπένδιον (*stipendium*), συμψέλλιον (*subsellium*), σωλάριον (*solarium*), τρούλλιον (perhaps *trullium*), φιβλατώριον (*fibulatorium*). The -ιον was often shortened to -ιν as part of a general late Greek development (Gignac 1981: 25–9). Cf. García Domingo (1979: 93).

[52] Gignac (1981: 23–4), cf. Cavenaile (1952: 200–1), Psaltes (1913: 181). Binder (2000: 255–6) argues that μάγιστρος must have been borrowed from a variant *magistrus*; such variants probably existed, both for *magister* and for other nouns in *-er*, but if Greek speakers had encountered those nouns mainly through variants in *-rus*, the Greek loans would have consistently ended in -ρος rather than showing such variety.

[53] Cf. Gignac (1981: 24). First-declension nom. pl. σιγνιφέραι and ἰμαγινιφέραι also appear (Lyd. *Mag.* pp. 70.11, 72.8). Cf. the names Γλάβερ (García Domingo 1979: 92) and Νίγερ (Leclercq 1997: 296, 306); also Byzantine names (Psaltes 1913: 181).

[54] Αἰράριον (*aerarium*), ἀμικτώριον (*amictorium*), ἀρμάριον (*armarium*), ἄτριον (*atrium*), βενεφίκιον (*beneficium*), βηλάριον (*velarium*), διάριον (*diarium*), ἰσίκιον (*isicium*), Καπετώλιον

[55] Ἀκκούβιτον (*accubitum*), ἄκτα (pl., *actum*), ἀλιμέντα (pl., *alimentum*), βάκλον (*baculum*), βέρβον (*verbum*), βῆλον (*velum*), βήναβλον (*venabulum*), βήξιλλον (*vexillum*), βιατικόν (*viaticum*), βότον (*votum*), βουκκελλᾶτον (*buccellatum*), δέκρετον (*decretum*), δηπόσιτον (*depositum*), δίγεστον (*digesta*, pl.), δωνατίουον (*donativum*), δωράκινον (*duracinum*), ἐξπέδιτον (*expeditum*), ἤδικτον (*edictum*), ἰνστιτοῦτα (pl., *instituta*, pl.), ἴντυβον (*intubum*), ἰούγερον (*iugerum*), ἰοῦγον (*iugum*), κάστρον (*castrum*), κίτρον (*citrum*), κομμέντον (*commentum*), κομπρόμισσον (*compromissum*), κονδῖτον (*conditum*), λανᾶτον (*lanatum*), ληγᾶτον (*legatum*), μανδᾶτον (*mandatum*), μητᾶτον (*metatum*), πάκτον (*pactum*), παλλίολον (*palliolum*), πριμίπιλον (*primipilum*), ῥέσκριπτον (*rescriptum*), ῥοσᾶτον (*rosatum*), σάλγαμον (*salgama*, pl.), σαξίφραγον (*saxifragum*), σήκρητον (*secretum*), σίγνον (*signum*), σπέκλον (*speculum*), σπικᾶτον (*spicatum*), στάβλον (*stabulum*), φάκτον (*factum*), φιδεικόμμισσον (*fideicommissum*), φολιᾶτον (*foliatum*), φοσσᾶτον (*fossatum*).

'money' (*nummus* versus ἀργύριον and χρήματα): *denarius* became δηνάριον and *assarius* ἀσσάριον.[57] Words with other meanings also sometimes changed gender between masculine and neuter (in both directions), perhaps because Greek speakers originally encountered them in forms where the genders were not distinguishable.[58]

4.2.4.2 Fourth declension

Latin fourth-declension masculines, which were indistinguishable from second-declension masculines in the nominative and accusative singular, often became second-declension masculines in Greek: γράδος 'stepped pedestal' (*gradus*), κᾶσος 'occasion' (*casus*), κῆνσος 'assessment for taxes' (*census*), κόνβεντος 'assembly' (*conventus*), μαγίστρατος 'magistrate' (*magistratus*), οὐσούφρουκτος 'usufruct' (*usus fructus*), and τρακτᾶτος 'administration' (*tractatus*). Some, however, became second-declension neuters:

ἐξέρκετον 'army' (*exercitus*), κομιτᾶτον 'staff' (*comitatus*), and πρόκεσσον 'procession' (*processus*). Others appeared in Greek with both genders: κομιᾶτον or κομιᾶτος 'leave of absence' (*commeatus*), σάλτον or σάλτος 'forest' (*saltus*), τιρωνᾶτον or τιρωνᾶτος 'body of recruits' (*tironatus*).[59] Only one fourth-declension feminine was borrowed, and that became a second-declension feminine: Εἰδοί 'Ides' from *Idus*, a word that normally occurred with adjectives and whose gender would therefore have been particularly evident.

4.2.5 Third-declension nouns

Latin third-declension nouns took a wide variety of forms, a few of which had obvious equivalents among the Greek paradigms. Such equivalents produced stable, predictable patterns of assimilation followed by the majority of words for which they were available. Thus nouns ending in -ō, -ōnis were normally assimilated into the Greek third-declension paradigm in -ων, -ωνος/-ονος; these could be either masculine or feminine in Latin and kept the same gender in Greek.[60] Most had -*i*- before the -ō in Latin, resulting in a distinctive group of loanwords in -ιων: ἀδιτίων 'act of taking possession of an inheritance' (*aditio*), ἀδνοτατίων 'imperial decision on a petition' (*adnotatio*), βηξιλλατίων 'troop' (*vexillatio*), δεκουρίων 'decurion' (*decurio*), δηληγατίων 'annual declaration by the state of the amount of tax to be paid' (*delegatio*), ἐμαγκιπατίων 'emancipation' (*emancipatio*), ἐξκουσατίων 'grounds for being excused' (*excusatio*), ἰνδικτίων 'period of fifteen years' (*indictio*), κεντουρίων 'centurion' (*centurio*), κογνιτίων 'judicial investigation' (*cognitio*), λαργιτίων 'distribution of gifts' (*largitio*), μουλίων 'muleteer' (*mulio*), ὀπτίων 'assistant' (*optio*), ὀρδινατίων 'order' (*ordinatio*), παπυλιών 'tent' (*papilio*), προφεσσίων 'declaration' (*professio*), στατίων 'station' (*statio*),

---

[56] Binder (2000: 241) argues that when Latin neuters ended up as Greek masculines, the gender change must have happened within Latin before the words were borrowed, since the Latin neuter gender is not continued in Romance and therefore was suffering attrition before the end of antiquity. This explanation may well be right for some late borrowings, but in early ones such as Φαλέρνος (I AD) the Romance loss of the neuter gender can scarcely be relevant: some Latin neuters must have changed gender during the borrowing process, just as some masculines and feminines did.

[57] Other explanations have also been proposed for these words: Cavenaile (1952: 196–7) suggests that ἀσσάριον comes from *as* 'penny' + -άριον and δηνάριον has assimilated to diminutives in -άριον, García Domingo (1979: 93–4) sees a neuter Latin source for δηνάριον, and Cameron (1931: 238–9) thinks the form of ἀσσάριον was influenced by δηνάριον. But if the explanation proposed here is right, it would also account for two third-declension words for money that shifted from masculine neuter: *semis* → σιμίσιον, *tremis* → τριμήσιον (§4.2.5).

[58] Masculine to neuter: κάρρον (*carrus*), κούμουλον (*cumulus*), μόδιον (a variant of μόδιος, *modius*), πουλβῖνον (*pulvinus*). Neuter to masculine: γαῖσος (*gaesum*), λάρδος (*laridum*), σάγος (*sagum*), σκάμνος (*scamnum*). Variants with the Latin gender are also attested for some members of each group. Sometimes both genders were used already in Latin: βάλτιον/βάλτιος (*balteus/balteum*), λῶρος/λῶρον (*lorum/lorus*). Feminine ἑβίσκος (*hibiscum*) looks like a shift from neuter to feminine under the influence of the Greek word for the same plant, ἀλθαία, but the feminine is attested in Latin too (*TLL s.v. hibiscum* 2691.16–18). Cf. Schirru (2013: 319).

[59] On all these groups see Gignac (1981: 25), García Domingo (1979: 96–7), Diethart (2006).

[60] Cf. Palmer (1945: 119–21, but note that his sharp division between agent nouns in '-ων and place names in -ών does not match our data), Cavenaile (1952: 194), Chantraine (1933: 159–65), Gignac (1981: 48), García Domingo (1979: 94), Psaltes (1913: 182–3), Freyburger-Galland (1998: 139–40). The difference in quantities in the oblique cases was less apparent to speakers than it looks to us, given the late Greek merger of o and ω.

and ταβελλίων 'notary' (*tabellio*). There are also a few exceptions: the -*i*- tended to change to -ε- in λεγεών or λεγιών 'legion' (*legio*) and ῥεγεών or ῥεγιών 'district' (*regio*), *praedelegatio* 'advance instructions about taxes' probably became second-declension προδηληγᾶτον, and the Latin source of κολλητίων 'filing clerk' is unknown. Nouns without the -*i*- assimilated in the same way: βουρδών 'mule' (*burdo*), κάρβων 'coal' (*carbo*), κέντρων 'rag' (*cento*), μερμίλλων 'gladiator' (*murmillo*), πραίκων 'herald' (*praeco*), σάπων 'soap' (*sapo*), σκρίβων 'officer of the imperial bodyguard' (*scribo*), and τίρων 'recruit' (*tiro*). The only borrowing in -*ō* that adhered more closely to the Latin by not adding -ν in the nominative is the unusually early legal term ὀπινίω 'legal opinion' from *opinio* (III AD), which had acquired the -ν by the sixth century.

Latin nouns in -*or*, -*ōris* normally assimilated into the Greek third-declension paradigm in -ωρ, -ορος;[61] these were masculine in both Latin and Greek. Most had -*t*- before the -*or* in Latin, and more than half of those had -*a*- before the -*t*-, resulting in a large group of loanwords in -(ά)τωρ: ἀδιούτωρ (a title, *adiutor*), βιάτωρ 'agent' (*viator*), βυκινάτωρ 'trumpeter' (*bucinator*), δηλάτωρ 'accuser' (*delator*), δηληγάτωρ (an official, *delegator*), δησέρτωρ 'deserter' (*desertor*), δικτάτωρ 'dictator' (*dictator*), ἐξάκτωρ 'tax collector' (*exactor*), ἐξκέπτωρ 'clerk' (*exceptor*), ἐξκουβίτωρ 'soldier of the imperial guard' (*excubitor*), ἐξπλωράτωρ 'scout' (*explorator*), ἰμπεράτωρ 'commander' (*imperator*), ἰουράτωρ 'sworn witness' (*iurator*), καμπιδούκτωρ 'drill-master' (*campidoctor*), κηνσίτωρ (an official, *censitor*), κιβαριάτωρ (an official, perhaps **cibariator*), κιρκίτωρ 'inspector of frontier posts' (*circitor*), κομάκτωρ 'collector of money' (*coactor*), κονδούκτωρ 'contractor' (*conductor*), κορρήκτωρ (an official, *corrector*), κουαίστωρ (a title, *quaestor*), κουράτωρ 'curator' (*curator*), μανδάτωρ 'guarantor' (*mandator*), μητάτωρ 'measurer' (*metator*), νωμενκλάτωρ 'name-reminder' (*nomenclator*), ὀπινάτωρ (an official, *opinator*), ὀψωνάτωρ 'caterer' (*obsonator*), πραίτωρ

(a title, *praetor*), προβοκάτωρ (a gladiator, *provocator*), προκουράτωρ 'administrator' (*procurator*), προτήκτωρ (a title, *protector*), ῥογάτωρ (an official, *erogator*), σεκούτωρ (a gladiator, *secutor*), σενάτωρ 'senator' (*senator*), σπεκουλάτωρ (a role, *speculator*), στάτωρ (a role, *stator*), στράτωρ 'groom' (*strator*), and τεστάτωρ 'maker of a will' (*testator*). Nouns without the -*t*- assimilated in the same way: ἀντικήνσωρ 'teacher of law' (*antecessor*), δηφήνσωρ (a title, *defensor*), δισκούσσωρ 'auditor' (*discussor*), κήνσωρ 'censor' (*censor*), κούρσωρ 'courier' (*cursor*), πρίωρ (a title, *prior*), and σουκκέσσωρ 'relief' (*successor*). Two other third-declension words in -*r* also joined the Greek third declension and retained their masculine gender: Καῖσαρ, Καίσαρος 'emperor' (*Caesar, Caesaris*) and αὔγουρ, αὔγουρος 'augur' (*augur, auguris*).[62] But masculine *carcer, carceris* 'prison' joined the second declension as κάρκαρον/κάρκαρος.

Third-declension masculines and feminines in -*x* became third-declension nouns in -ξ, retaining their original genders and the original stem-final consonants of the oblique cases: βίνδιξ, βίνδικος (a title, *vindex, vindicis*); δούξ, δουκός 'duke' (*dux, ducis*); κῶδιξ, κώδικος 'book' (*caudex, caudicis*); λῶδιξ, λώδικος 'blanket' (*lodix, lodicis*); μάτριξ, μάτρικος 'list' (*matrix, matricis*); ποντίφεξ, ποντίφικος (a priestly title, *pontifex, pontificis*); ῥήξ, ῥηγός '(western) king' (*rex, regis*).[63] Likewise *manceps, mancipis* became μάγκιψ, μάγκιπος 'contractor' and the title *princeps, principis* became πρίγκεψ, πρίγκιπος, retaining their masculine genders.

By contrast, third-declension masculines in -*is* (both nouns and substantivized adjectives) normally became second-declension masculines in -ιος, though a few also had nominatives in -ις.[64] These loans fell into two groups. Ones that had originally ended in -*ensis* came to end in -ήσιος

---

[61] Cf. Palmer (1945: 118–19), Chantraine (1937: 89–91), Gignac (1981: 48), Buck and Petersen (1945: 302), Psaltes (1913: 182), Freyburger-Galland (1998: 140). The inversion of vowel quantities was less apparent to speakers than it looks to us, given the Greek merger of o and ω.

[62] Cf. García Domingo (1979: 95).

[63] Also ἅλιξ 1, probably really declined ἅλληξ, ἅλληκος, from *hallex, hallecis*, perhaps with change of gender. Cf. Freyburger-Galland (1998: 139).

[64] These may reflect the original Latin nominative, but they may also simply be reflections of the general late Greek use of -ις for -ιος (Gignac 1981: 25–7). Gignac (1981: 49–50) counts this nominative -ις as a third-declension form and therefore believes that some Latin -*is* nouns genuinely fluctuated between the second and third declensions, but there is very little evidence for these nouns taking other third-declension forms.

(for the loss of -n- see §6.7): Αὐγουστήσιοι (a Jewish group, Augustensis), κομμενταρήσιος 'secretary' (commentariensis), κουιντανήσιος (a role, quintanensis), perhaps πορταρῆσις 'gate-keeper' (*portarensis), and φαβρικήσιος 'armourer' (fabriciensis). Ones in -alis could become loanwords in -άλιος: κηνσουάλιος (an official, censualis), μεμοριάλιος 'clerk' (memorialis), ὀφφικιάλιος (a title, officialis), φετιάλιος (a priest, fetialis), and Φλαουιάλιος (a rank, Flavialis). But many of those, as well as the nouns in -aris, ended up joining the large group of loanwords in -άριος, owing to analogical pressure from that group and the tendency for confusion between l and r (§4.1.1 n. 15): κοντουβερνάλιος/κοντουβερνάριος 'comrade' (contubernalis), perhaps κουροπερσονάριος (a role, cura personalis, cf. §4.5), πριγκιπάλιος/πριγκιπάριος 'officer' (principalis), πριμιπιλάριος (a rank, primipilaris), σιγγλάριος (a role, singularis), σχολάριος 'one of the imperial guards' (scholares), and φαμιλιάριος 'member of the household' (familiaris). Follis 'bag', however, joined the Greek third declension as φόλλις, φόλλεως. A few masculines in -is changed gender to become second-declension neuters: canalis became κανάλιον 'culvert', bessalis became βήσαλον 'brick', (lapis) specularis became σπεκλάριον 'transparent stone', and the coin names semis and tremis became σιμίσιον and τριμήσιον (§4.2.4 n. 57).

Third-declension feminines in -is were less often borrowed. Two joined the first declension, a route perhaps suggested by the third-declension adjectives in -is (§4.2.2). Thus classis became κλάσσα 'fleet' and the substantivized feminine of epularis 'pertaining to feasts' became ἀπαλαρέα 'bread-basket'.[65] Cassis, cassidis 'helmet' appeared both as third-declension κασσίς, κασσίδος and as first-declension κασσίδα, κασσίδας.

Third-declension masculines not belonging to one of the groups already mentioned were assimilated in a variety of ways not predictable from their endings. Comes, comitis 'count' became third-declension masculine κόμης, but limes, limitis 'frontier' became second-declension neuter λιμιτόν.[66] Aborigines 'original inhabitants of Italy' became third-declension Ἀβοριγῖνες, but ordo, ordinis 'order' became second-declension

ὄρδινος. Quadrans, quadrantis 'quarter' joined the first declension as κοδράντης. The Greek borrowing of vigil, vigilis 'watchman' is traditionally given today as οὐίγουλ, but it is attested only in the genitive plural οὐιγούλων/βιγούλων and therefore could have belonged to practically any paradigm. Feminines, though rarer, also show diversity: cohors, cohortis joined the first declension as κοόρτη 'cohort', while moles, molis became second-declension μῶλος 'breakwater'.

Third-declension neuters normally became second-declension neuters in -ον, regardless of their original Latin endings in the nominative singular. This shift probably occurred via their plurals, which in Latin all ended in -a and looked like the plurals of second-declension neuters in -um; sometimes the stem of the Greek word demonstrably comes from the plural (or oblique cases of the singular) rather than from the nominative singular, as in κάπιτον (pl. κάπιτα) 'ration allowance' from caput (pl. capita) and μίλιον (pl. μίλια) 'mile' from mille (pl. milia). Most of the third-declension neuters borrowed were i-stems in Latin (probably because most were substantivized adjectives) and therefore had plurals in -ia; the i was usually retained in Greek, so these loanwords normally ended up as neuters in -ιον, a loanword group that was already large because of the borrowing of Latin neuters in -ium. Thus ἀκκουβιτάλιον 'couch cover' (accubitale), ἀστίλιον 'shaft' (hastile), βραχιάλιον 'bracelet' (bracchiale), βρέβιον 'list' (breve), ἐξεμπλάριον 'sample' (exemplar), κολλάριον 'collar' (collare), κοχλιάριον 'spoon' (cochlear), μιλιαρήσιον (a coin, miliarense), πραικόκκιον 'little apricot' (praecox), σουβαλάριον 'water-bag' (subalare), ταλάριον 'sandal fastened at the ankles' (talare), τριβουνάλιον 'tribunal' (tribunal), and φακιάλιον 'facecloth' (faciale). But κάμπιστρον 'loincloth' (campestre) and πραίσεντον 'troops serving in the imperial palace (praesens) did not have the ι in Greek, perhaps suggesting that they were borrowed via oblique cases of the singular rather than the plural. A few neuters simply remained plural and never formed a singular at all: βρουμάλια 'festival of the winter solstice' (Brumalia), Σατορνάλια 'Saturnalia' (Saturnalia), φεμινάλια 'trousers' (feminalia). Mantele 'hand towel' must have been borrowed in the singular, for it became first-declension μανδήλη.

[65] Cf. Binder (2000: 260–1).
[66] Gignac (1981: 49), Psaltes (1913: 183).

Some words that had belonged to other declensions in Latin transferred to the third declension in Greek. Two feminines in -ξ came from the first declension, κάλιξ 'boot' from *caliga* and φάβριξ 'workshop' from *fabrica*. Two masculines in -ων came from the second declension, πάτρων 'patron' from *patronus* and κόλων 'colonist' from *colonus*. And two third-declension neuters came from other declensions: φάβα, φάβατος 'beans' from first-declension feminine singular *faba*, and ἄρμα, ἄρματος 'weapons' from second-declension neuter plural *arma*.

4.2.6 Poetic forms

Latin loanwords occasionally appear in mock-epic forms when used in hexameter poetry. Πέρνα 'ham' (*perna*) appears as πτέρνη at *Batrachomyomachia* 37. Λιμιτόν 'frontier' (*limes*) occurs as λιμίτοιο on inscription *SEG* VIII.296.1, the title δομεστικός 1 (*domesticus*) as δομεστίκοιο in Dorotheus, *Visio Dorothei* 86, and ὀράριον 'kerchief' (*orarium*) as ὠραρίοιο in Dorotheus, *Visio Dorothei* 332. Λοῦδος 'gladiatorial school' (*ludus*) appears as λούδοισιν on a prose inscription discussed by Papanikolaou (2019). It is tempting to suggest that such forms demonstrate that the words concerned were thoroughly integrated and had long been part of Greek, but the *Batrachomyomachia* passage is the first attestation of πέρνα.

4.3 LATIN WORDS THAT ACQUIRED GREEK SUFFIXES AS PART OF THE BORROWING PROCESS

Some loanwords appear to have been borrowed with the aid of suffixation, and the use of this device was heavily dependent on the part of speech to which the loanword belonged: all verbs were formed with suffixes, but only 7% of directly borrowed nouns and 2% of adjectives used them. For more information on the particular suffixes used, see §4.6.1.

4.3.1 Verbs

Greek speakers only rarely formed new verbs by direct borrowing from Latin (§10.3.1); most Greek verbs of Latin origin were derivatives of loanwords (for whose formation see §4.6.1).

Nevertheless, the twelve verbs that probably were directly borrowed are sufficient to reveal what the borrowing process was. A single form of the Latin verb was selected, either the present stem or the perfect passive participle (i.e. the supine stem), and a Greek verb-forming suffix was added; the resulting stem could be inflected as a regular Greek verb in all tenses, with the addition of augments and endings as needed.[67] The suffix used was most often -εύω, but -ίζω also appears three times and -όω once. The verb with -όω, φραγελλόω 'whip' (probably *flagello* or *flagellum*), is the earliest, attested from the first century; σκουτλόω 'decorate with *opus sectile*' (probably *scutula*) may be another example from the same century, if it is not a derivative of σκούτλα. Βυκινίζω 'blow the trumpet' (probably *bucino* or *bucina*), Σαβελλίζω 'hold Sabellian views' (*Sabellius*) and τρακταΐζω 'handle' (*tracto*) come from the third, fourth, and fifth centuries respectively. In the fourth century -εύω emerges with δηληγατεύω 'assign as tax to be paid' (probably *delego*), followed in the fifth by ῥογεύω 'pay in kind' (*erogo*), μητατεύω 'commandeer' (probably *metor*), and τρακτεύω 'administer' (*tracto*); in the sixth these are joined by ἀδιτεύω 'take possession of an inheritance' (*adeo*), ἐξκουσεύω 'excuse' (*excuso*), ἐξπελλεύω 'collect taxes' (*expello*), and κομφιρματεύω 'confirm' (*confirmo*).[68]

---

[67] This kind of borrowing process, i.e. one in which a suffix is necessary, is known as 'indirect insertion' (Wichmann and Wohlgemuth 2008: 97–9). Horrocks (2010: 380) observes that at a much later period in the history of Greek the borrowing of Turkish words followed a pattern strikingly similar to that of Latin words in antiquity: verbs were rarely borrowed, and when such borrowing did occur the borrowed verbs 'were standardly formed by the addition of the productive -ίζω [-'izo] to the Turkish past-tense stem formed with the suffix /-di-/ (with vowel harmony): e.g. *kavur-mak* [ka(v)urmak], 'to roast', past-tense stem *kavur-du-*, producing Greek καβουρντίζω/καβουρδίζω'. Kahane and Kahane (1982: 152) report that Byzantine Greek borrowed Old French verbs in the infinitive and added -ίζω or -ιάζω. For the use of -εύω and -ίζω for loanwords note also Browning (1983: 41), Mandilaras (1973: 67–8), Meinersmann (1927: 119).

[68] There is a possible example in the second century, πραιδεύω if that comes from *praedor* rather than from *praeda* via πραῖδα. Further possible examples are from the fourth century ὀψικεύω, if that comes from *obsequor* rather than *obsequium* via ὀψίκιον, and from the fifth ληγατεύω, if that comes from *lego* rather than *legatum* via ληγᾶτον. Cf. Psaltes (1913: 316–21), Burgmann (1991: 68).

4.3.2 Nouns

By far the most common suffix attached to nouns during borrowing was -ιον, which was used to borrow at least twenty-two loanwords.[69] Although this figure is small in comparison to the hundreds of nouns that were borrowed without any suffix, it is not negligible and represents eight times as many borrowings as any other nominal suffix, indeed twice as many as all other nominal suffixes combined. Moreover -ιον is not used in the same way as the other suffixes; they tended to perform specific functions by creating words that clearly belonged to particular semantic categories (-ία forming abstract nouns; -τωρ, -ίτης, and -ᾶς forming agent nouns, etc.), while the addition of -ιον rarely makes a discernible difference to a word's meaning. Of course, -ιον was extremely common on native roots in post-Classical Greek and had a wide range of uses.[70] It is therefore possible that Greek speakers added it to Latin words simply because they were in the habit of adding it to Greek words. Nevertheless, scholars have occasionally suggested that there must have been a particular reason for the frequency of -ιον in the derivation process of Latin loanwords, namely that -ιον was (sometimes) added to allow the accent to remain on the same syllable in Greek as it had occupied in Latin.[71] Thus for example *flagéllum* 'whip' if borrowed without a suffix might most naturally have been accented φλάγελλον (attested once), but by forming φραγέλλιον speakers caused the

Greek accent to match the Latin one. Likewise *sólea* 'sandal' if borrowed as σολεα would probably have been accented σολέα (not attested in that sense), but the suffixed form σόλιον kept its accent on the same syllable as in Latin.

Unfortunately, this explanation for the addition of -ιον does not work for the majority of verifiable examples. Often the addition of -ιον results in an accent that does not match the Latin one, when the accents would have matched without the suffix: ἰντύβιον 'endive' from *íntubum*, καμπάγιον 'boot' from *cámpagus*, κομόδιον 'gratuity' from *cómmodum*, παλλιόλιον 'small cloak' from *pallíolum*, καννίον (a kind of container) from *cánna*, μαντίον (a garment) from *mántus*, πουλλίον 'chicken' from *púllus*.[72] And often the accent matches with -ιον but would probably also have matched without it: ἀμπούλλιον 'flask' from *ampúlla*, βαστέρνιον 'enclosed litter' from *bastérna*, βράκιον 'trousers' from *brácae*, καρακάλλιον 'hood' from *caracálla*, λαγήνιον 'little flagon' from *lagéna*, σκουτέλλιον 'dish' from *scutélla*.[73] Therefore accentuation does not explain the prevalence of -ιον.

A previously unnoticed complication is that many Latin words appear in Greek both with and without -ιον. Sometimes only one form was well established and the other rare, but often both versions appear to be integrated loanwords. In those cases either version can be earlier. The expected and more common pattern is that words

---

[69] Certainly borrowed with -ιον: ἀμπούλλιον (*ampulla*), βαστέρνιον (*basterna*), βεστίον (*vestis*), βουκκίον (*bucca*), βράκιον (*bracae*), καμπάγιον (*campagus*), καννίον (*canna*), καρακάλλιον (*caracalla*), κομόδιον (*commodum*), κουκούλλιον (*cucullus*), κουσούλιον (*casula*), λαγήνιον (*lagena*), μαντίον (*mantus*), μαππίον (*mappa*), μαρούλιον (*amarus*), παλλιόλιον (*palliolum*), πουλλίον (*pullus*), σκουτέλλιον (*scutella*), σκούτλιον (*scutula*), σόλιον 1 (*solea*), σουβλίον (*subula*), φραγέλλιον (*flagellum*). Probably or perhaps borrowed with -ιον: ἀλίκιον (*alicula*), ἰντύβιον (*intubum*), καλίγιον (*caliga*), καπίστριον (*capistrum*), κασίδιον (*cassis*), κεντώνιον (*cento*), κίτριον (*citrum*), κουκκούμιον (*cucuma*), λαμνίον (*lamina*), πατέλλιον (*patella*), πλουμίον (*pluma*), ῥαίδιον (*raeda*), σιλίγνιον (*siligo*). On the use of -ιον with Latin loanwords in Greek see Schirru (2013: 317–19), Filos (2008: 326–8), Palmer (1945: 86), Cavenaile (1952: 195–7), Cameron (1931: 233).

[70] Petersen (1910), Palmer (1945: 79–83, 84–6), Chantraine (1933: 54–77), Buck and Petersen (1945: 46).

[71] Hofmann (1989: iii, 405), Filos (2008: 115).

[72] Of course, we do not always know what the accents of ancient Greek words were (see §5), but these accents are certain, for the first four because they follow an invariable rule of ancient accentuation (nouns of more than three syllables ending in -ιον are recessive: Probert 2003: 83) and for the last three because they survive into modern Greek and are compatible with a variable rule of ancient accentuation (words of three syllables ending in -ιον may be recessive or paroxytone if the first syllable is heavy: Probert 2003: 93–4). For the Byzantine evidence for accentuation of Latin words in -ιον see Psaltes (1913: 271–2).

[73] The accents of all these except βράκιον are certain because they follow the invariable rule mentioned in the previous note; βράκιον is probable because it follows the rule that words of three syllables ending in -ιον are generally recessive if the first syllable is light (Probert 2003: 93). But the modern Greek form βρακί suggests that the ancient accent may have been βρακίον, in which case it would not have matched the Latin. The accents of most other loanwords in -ιον are not certain.

first appear without the suffix and later with it, in which case it is likely that the existing loanword formed a derivative in -ιον without further reference to Latin; examples include third-century βουρδών and sixth-century βουρδώνιον (*burdo* 'mule'), first-century κάγκελλος and fifth-century καγκέλλιον (*cancellus* 'latticed barrier'), and second-century κάστελλος and fifth-century καστέλλιον (*castellus* 'fort') (§4.6.1). But sometimes the form with -ιον is earlier and the form without appears to have been reborrowed directly from Latin: *mappa* 'napkin' appears in the third century as μαππίον and in the sixth as μάππα, *ampulla* 'flask' in the second century as ἀμπούλλιον and in the third as ἀμποῦλλα, *bracae* 'trousers' in the second century as βράκιον and in the fourth as βράκαι, *cassis* 'helmet' (stem *cassid-*) in the third century as κασίδιον and (probably) in the fourth as κασσίς, *palliolum* 'small cloak' in the first century as παλλιόλιον and in the second as παλλίολον.[74] This pattern suggests that there was nothing inherently difficult about the words borrowed with -ιον: those words cannot have needed the suffix in order to assimilate into Greek, since they could also be borrowed without it.

One motivation for adding -ιον may have been a sense on the part of Greek speakers that Latin loanwords not referring to people ought to end in -ιον. The practice of adding -ιον during borrowing began in the first century AD, and the stock of Latin loanwords available at the start of that century could easily have given speakers such a sense. At that point Greek had borrowed from Latin thirty-one nouns not referring to people, eleven of which (35%) ended in -ιον; no other identifiable termination accounted for more than three.[75] That distribution might well have

encouraged Greek speakers to add -ιον to new Latin loanwords.

Other suffixes (for which see also §4.6.1) were occasionally used to make Greek nouns from Latin words. At least two agent nouns seem to have been formed with -τωρ: ἀρμικούστωρ 'person in charge of weapons' (*armicustos*), δισέκτωρ 'quarry engineer' (*deseco*), and perhaps κιβαριάτωρ (an official) if that comes directly from *cibaria*. Two words for festivals used -ειος substantivized in the neuter plural: Ἀντώνεια 'Antonine festival' (*Antonius*) and Σευήρεια 'Severan games' (*Severus*). Two Egyptian honorific months (which functioned as nouns rather than adjectives from the moment of their creation, unlike the Roman months in §4.2.1) were formed with a fluctuating suffix -ῆος/-ειος, and one with -ιεύς: Γαιῆος '(month) of Gaius' (*Gaius*), Δρουσιλλῆος '(month) of Drusilla' (*Drusilla*), and Δρουσιεύς '(month) of Drusus' (*Drusus*). Two abstract nouns were probably formed with -ία: Ῥωμανία 'Roman empire' (*Romanus*) and προπριεταρία 'ownership' (*proprietarius*).[76] At least one borrowing used -άριον, σικάριον 'dagger' (*sica*) – perhaps also σκουτάριον 'shield' (*scutum*?), οὐδωνάριον 'sock' (*udo*?), and πιλάριον 'eye-salve' (*pilum*?). Two may have used -ίτης, though both could be derivatives of loans rather than direct borrowings: βεστιαρίτης 'clothes-person' (probably *vestiarius*), σιλιγνίτης '(bread) from siligo' (perhaps *siligo*). Other suffixes account for at most one loanword each: -ᾶς in βουκκᾶς 'biscuit-baker' (*bucca*), -εῖον in κουβουκλεῖον 'bedroom' (*cubiculum*), perhaps -ίδιον in κασίδιον 'helmet' (*cassis*, if the etymology is not *cassid-* + -ιον), and perhaps -ις in σίλιγνις 'flour from siligo' (*siligo*, if it is not a derivative of σιλίγνιον). The adjective-forming suffix -ικός, substantivized in the neuter, seems to have been used to form καλανδαρικά 'new year's allowances' from some word related to *Kalendae*.

---

[74] Only occasionally does the form without -ιον seem to be back-formed from the existing loanword rather than reborrowed from Latin: *caracalla* 'cloak with hood' appears in the third century as καρακάλλιον and in the fourth as καράκαλλον.

[75] The nouns borrowed before I AD not referring to people are: 1) ending in -ιον, ἀσσάριον, ἄτριον, δηνάριον, διάριον, Καπετώλιον, κομέτιον, κοχλιάριον, μίλιον, ὀξύγγιον, παλάτιον, πωμάριον; 2) ending in -(ε)ία, κεντουρία, κολωνία, οὐγγία; 3) ending in -ων, κέντρων, λεγεών; 4) with other endings, βυκάνη, γαῖσος, Εἰδοί, Καλάνδαι, κάμπιστρον, κοδράντης, λωρῖκα, μόδιος, νοῦμμος, Νῶναι,

πέρνα, Ῥώμη, σάγος, σηστέρτιος, Φαλερῖνος. Also existing at this period, but obviously Greek derivations from loanwords and therefore probably not relevant, are δικτατωρεία, πατρωνεία, Ῥωμαῖα.

[76] Perhaps the effect of -ία on *proprietarius* should be regarded as one of influence rather than suffixation, as with the feminine abstracts from adjectives in -*ius* (§4.4), but since *proprietarius* was a noun the process must have been slightly different.

4.3.3 Adjectives

The ubiquitous adjective-forming suffix -ικός was used to borrow at least one loanword, λαργιτιωναλικός 'related to distribution of gifts' from *largitionalis*. Two more may have been thus formed: καβαλλαρικός 'horse-drawn', if it comes from *caballaris*, and κελλαρικός 'of a cellar', if from *cellarius*. The suffix -ειος, which in substantivized form assisted in the creation of several loanword nouns, appears in Γερμανίκειος 'of Germanicus' (*Germanicus*) and probably in Νερώνειος 'of Nero' (*Nero*).

4.4 LOANWORDS WHOSE FORMS WERE FURTHER INFLUENCED BY GREEK WORDS

Some loanwords were re-formed in Greek under the influence of pre-existing Greek words, a process known as 'folk etymology' or 'popular etymology'.[77] Although these have attracted much attention for the evidence they offer that Greeks tried to make foreign words look and sound 'more Greek', they are not very common.

Most loanwords that show influence from other words do so only sporadically, in one or two attestations out of many. Occasionally the influenced form is confined to a literary text and is likely to be a deliberate creation of that text's author. Thus πέρνα 'ham', from *perna*, takes the form πτέρνη in the *Batrachomyomachia* under the influence of epic words in πτ-, and Ἀβοριγῖνες 'original inhabitants of Italy', from *Aborigines*, appears as Βορείγονοι in Lycophron's *Alexandra*, apparently influenced by Βορέας 'north wind' and/or βόρειος 'of the north wind' and γονή 'offspring, family'.

More often the sporadic influenced forms occur in documents and inscriptions, where they are less likely to be deliberate choices made in the full awareness of the word's usual form. Thus δελματική 'Dalmatian tunic' (*dalmatica*) may be spelled δερματική by association with δέρμα 'skin', δηνάριον 'denarius' (*denarius*) may be spelled δυνάριον under the influence of δύναμις 'power',

δουπλικάριος 'soldier receiving double pay' (*duplicarius*) may be spelled διπλοκάριος under the influence of διπλόος 'double', λεγεωνάριος 'legionary' (*legionarius*) may be spelled λογιωνᾶρις by association with λόγος 'account', μαντίον 'short cloak' (*mantus*) may be spelled μανδύον under the influence of μανδύα 'cloak', μεμόριον 'grave monument' (*memoria*) may be spelled μνημόριον by association with μνημεῖον 'memorial', πριμιπιλάριος 'senior centurion' (*primipilaris*) may be spelled πρινπιλάριος under the influence of πρίν 'before', and τεσσαράριος 'officer who distributes the watchword' (*tesserarius*) may be spelled θεσσάριος under the influence of θέσις 'setting'.[78] Such words show individual Greek speakers struggling with unfamiliar words and trying to fit them into a more familiar pattern, but the fact that the Greek-influenced spellings did not catch on more widely shows that the majority of speakers did not feel a strong need to use them.

In about 3% of borrowings, however, a Greek-influenced form did catch on and became the loanword's main or even its only form. In such words the Greek word responsible for the influence was normally one close to the new loanword both in form and in meaning. Thus *popinarius* 'keeper of a cook-shop' became προπινάριος under the influence of προπίνω 'drink to', *clausura* 'closure' became κλεισούρα 'narrow pass' under the influence of κλείω 'close', *marmorarius* 'marble-mason' became μαρμαράριος under the influence of μάρμαρος 'marble', and *plagatus* 'wounded' became πληγᾶτος under the influence of πληγή 'blow'.

Previously borrowed Latin loanwords, which of course were often close to new ones in form and meaning, could also exercise such influence. Thus in the fourth century the title *a commentariis* became ἀκομενταρήσιος under the influence of the third-century borrowing κομμενταρήσιος, in the fifth century *antecessor* 'teacher of law' became ἀντικήνσωρ under the influence of fourth-century κήνσωρ 'censor' (and of ἀντί), and in the

77 For the phenomenon see §2.3; for previous work on its application to Latin loanwords in Greek e.g. Filos (2019), Mason (1974: 8), Cavenaile (1951: 403), Viscidi (1944: 8), Cameron (1931: 232), Meinersmann (1927: 120), Triandaphyllidis (1909: 106–9).

78 See Cavenaile (1951: 403), who offers additional examples, not all necessarily due to folk etymology. For the reasons to be cautious about attributing too many features to this cause, see (in a discussion of Latin borrowings from Greek) Biville (1990–5: II.420–2).

sixth century *siliginarius* 'seller of siligo' became σιλιγνάριος under the influence of second-century σιλίγνιον. (Σιλίγνιον may also have influenced second-century σιλιγνίτης '(bread) from siligo' and σίλιγνις 'flour from siligo', but those are probably derivatives rather than direct borrowings.) According to the sixth-century antiquarian John Lydus (see §9.5.5 passage 74), προβατωρία 'imperial letter of commendation' often became πριβατωρία under the influence of πριβᾶτος 'private' – but πριβατωρία is not otherwise attested, suggesting that the influence visible to us may be much less than existed in antiquity.

Influence based on words less closely connected to the new loanword was also possible. *Bucina* 'trumpet' became βυκάνη under the influence of μηχανή 'contrivance', which had been borrowed into Latin as *machina* and therefore offered a model equivalence for that suffix, and *cento* 'patchwork' often became κέντρων under the influence of κέντρον 'goad'.

Influence could also occur when the beginning or end of a loanword resembled a common Greek prefix or suffix. *Augusteus* 'Augustan' and *Caesareus* 'Caesarian' became Αὐγούστειος and Καισάρειος probably under the influence of -ειος, *Augusteum* 'temple of Augustus' became Αὐγουστεῖον perhaps under the influence of -εῖον, *subsellium* 'low seat' became συμψέλλιον under the influence of σύν, and *praedelegatio* 'advance instructions about taxes' may have become προδηληγᾶτον under the influence of πρό.[79] Words beginning with Latin *prō-* are spelled προ- more often than πρω-, no doubt in part because of the influence of the Greek prefix; note in particular προβοκάτωρ (a type of gladiator, borrowed in the second century from *provocator*), προτήκτωρ (a title, borrowed in the third century from *protector*), and προφεσσίων ('declaration', borrowed in the second century from *professio*), which are attested early enough that the original quantity might have been audible when the word was borrowed. The effect of ἀντί on *antecessor* has already been noted. Adjectives in *-ius*, *-ia*, *-ium* substantivized in the

feminine to form abstractions in -ία were probably influenced by the abstract-forming suffix -ία: δουκηναρία '200,000 sesterces' (*ducenarius*) and πληναρία 'completeness' (*plenarius*). Likewise -ία probably caused the addition of -(ε)ι- when *formula* 'list' became φορμαλεία.

Two examples are particularly interesting. *Sextarius* 'pint measure' underwent a major change to become ξέστης, probably with an unattested original borrowing *ξεστάριον and removal of what looked like the suffix -άριον. *Falernus* 'Falernian' could be applied to anyone or anything from a particular region; its most notable use was for the famous Falernian wine. When first borrowed into Greek, *Falernus* became Φαλερῖνος under the influence of -ῖνος; later it was borrowed again without influence as Φαλέρνος. The new borrowing largely replaced the old one in reference to people and places, but in reference to the wine Φαλερῖνος and Φαλέρνος coexisted for centuries. On the fourth-century Edict of Diocletian not only is the wine called Φαλερῖνος in Greek, but the Latin has become *Falerinus* to match; this suggests a strong awareness of the suffix and its existence in both languages, but a less strong awareness of normal Latin usage.[80]

4.5 COMPOUNDS AND UNIVERBATIONS CREATED DURING THE BORROWING PROCESS

A further 2% of borrowings come from Latin words that entered Greek only as part of larger conglomerations. Technically speaking some of these are univerbations, that is, phrases fused into a single word that largely preserves the original forms of the component parts, like English 'subpoena' from Latin *sub poena*, 'sinecure' from Latin *sine cura*, and 'adieu' from Middle French *a dieu*. Others are compounds, that is, formations at least one of whose elements

---

[79] Probably also κερβικάριον (*cervical*) with influence from -άριον, perhaps Νερώνειος (*Neroneus*) with influence from -ειος; ἀκκουβιτάλιον, βραχιάλιον, κοντουβερνάλιος, πριγκιπάλιος, and φακιάλιον have variants in -άριον/-άριος that could be due to the influence of -άριον/-άριος.

[80] Edict.Diocl. 2.7. The Edict also names several other wines, and they do not all end in *-īnos*, nor do they all match between the two languages: there are matches between (genitive singular) *Piceni* and Πικήνου (2.1a), *Tiburtini* and Τιβουρτίνου (2.2), *Aminnei* and Ἀμιννέου (2.4), *Saiti* and Σαΐτου (2.5), and *Surrentini* and Σουρρεντείνου (2.6), but not between *Sabini* and Σαβινησίου (2.3). Many of these lines have variant readings, including in 2.7 Φαλέρνου but not *Falerni*.

appears in a special combining form, such as ἀρχι-, φιλο-, -νίκης, or -άρχης. Some compounds apparently formed within Greek are made up of two Latin elements, and these can be difficult to distinguish from univerbations and from compounds formed in Latin and then borrowed into Greek. Sometimes the way the elements are joined reveals the original formation process, for Latin tended to link the elements of a compound with -i-, Greek tended to use -o-, and univerbations did not add linking vowels.[81] Thus *campidoctor* was compounded in Latin and then borrowed into Greek as καμπιδούκτωρ 'drill-master', κουροπερσονάριος was compounded in Greek from *cura* and (probably) *personalis*, and σουμμαρούδης was a univerbation of *summa rudis*. But sometimes speakers altered borrowed compounds in ways that obscured their original formations: the Greek borrowing of *secundicerius* 'functionary of the second rank' was normally spelled σεκουνδοκήριος as if the compound had been formed in Greek, and the Greek result of the phrase *cura palatii* 'person in charge of the imperial residence' could be spelled either κουροπαλάτης (a compound) or κουραπαλάτης (a univerbation). Fortunately the key distinction among the directly borrowed Latin loanwords in Greek is not between compounds and univerbations, but between Latin–Latin and Greek–Latin formations, which were used very differently.

All the indubitable univerbations and Latin–Latin compounds among the directly borrowed loanwords are titles or occupational terms. (The possible exception, οὐσούφρουκτος 'usufruct', may have been univerbated before borrowing.) The reason for this prevalence of titles and occupational terms is probably that imperial-period Latin speakers very often formed such terms with two-word phrases. Thus most titles that became univerbated loanwords in Greek are also attested as titles in Latin: ἀβάκτης comes from *ab actis*, ἀκομενταρήσιος from *a commentariis* (with influence from κομμενταρήσιος), ἀσηκρῆτις from *a secretis*, βισήλεκτος from *bis electus*, κουροπαλάτης probably from *cura palatii*, σεκουνδαρούδης from *secunda rudis*, and σουμμαρούδης from

summa rudis.[82] Ἀβρέβις, ἀννούμερος, and κουροπερσονάριος, however, have no attested Latin equivalents. For ἀννούμερος one can suppose that a title *a numero* or *a numeris* might have existed without leaving traces visible to us, and the source of κουροπερσονάριος could be *cura personalis* or *cura personarum*, even if we are not aware of the use of either phrase as a title – but a Latin equivalent of ἀβρέβις would have to be *a brevibus*, which in Greek would have produced the unattested *ἀβρεβιβους. Therefore ἀβρέβις was probably created within Greek on the analogy of ἀβάκτης, using *a* + *breve*. That in turns suggests that ἀννούμερος and κουροπερσονάριος might also be Greek creations; like ἀβρέβις, they come from the late antique period, when such a move would have been possible.

By contrast the hybrid Greek–Latin compounds are rarely titles. There are only four such compounds among the directly borrowed loanwords, and their existence is not normally acknowledged. Because compounds are typically created from elements of the language in which the compound is formed, the appearance of a Latin word as part of a hybrid compound is often taken as proof that that Latin word had already been integrated into Greek (e.g. Viscidi 1944: 8). Typologically, however, such an argument is unsound: it is perfectly possible, and not even particularly uncommon, to form a hybrid compound with a word taken directly from another language (§2.4). The four hybrid loanwords of this type all have the Greek element first and the Latin second, though that could be coincidental: φιλοκλαύδιος 'friend of Claudius' from φιλο- + the name *Claudius*, ὁλοκόττινος (the name of a coin) from ὁλο- + *coctum* (*aurum*) + -ινος, προμάξιμον (a garment) from πρό + *maximum*, and περιστερόπουλλος 'small dove' from περιστερά + *pullus*. A potential fifth example could be ἔμπλουμος 'tapestry woven', if that is not derived via πλουμίον. Although both elements of σουβρικοπάλλιον are originally Latinate,

---

[81] Filos (2010: 231–2), Schwyzer (1939: 438).

[82] For more detailed discussion of these and rarer Latin univerbations in Greek, see Filos (2006, 2008: 425–38, 446–51). For the *ab* titles in Latin itself (c. 100 different titles occurring c. 750 times in total), Väänänen (1977) and *TLL* (s.v. ā, ab 22.81–23.46). For Latin univerbations in Byzantine Greek, Psaltes (1913: 186–7).

the second is much more likely than the first to have been considered a Greek word by the people who first used this compound (§4.6.2), so it may have been a hybrid in the minds of its creators. (For the more numerous hybrid compounds formed from previously borrowed loanwords, which can have the Latin and Greek in either order, see §4.6.2).

4.6 DERIVATIVES OF LOANWORDS

Traditionally, studies of Latin loanwords in Greek have not distinguished words taken from Latin by direct borrowing from those formed within Greek from previously borrowed loans. Treating those two groups together avoids the problem that some words' formation processes are unknown, but it severely reduces one's ability to understand how Greek speakers interacted with Latin and its vocabulary. There is a fundamental difference between creating a new word by applying a familiar suffix to a familiar word that happens to have been borrowed several centuries previously, and creating a new word by taking it from another language, even if one may also add a familiar suffix in the latter situation. Therefore it is worth making the attempt to distinguish internal Greek derivations (taking 'derivation' in its broadest sense of forming new words from existing ones by any process, including both suffixation and compounding) from the other Latinate words. And some are easily distinguishable: for example βηλόθυρον 'curtain at door', which first appears in the sixth century, is clearly a Greek compound of the second-century loanword βῆλον 'curtain' (*velum*) and native θύρα 'door', while ταβλίζω 'play dice', which appears in the fourth century, is obviously a Greek combination of the first-century loanword τάβλα 'dice-board' (*tabula*) and the suffix -ίζω. As these examples suggest, the key factor in the identification of derivatives is the existence of an earlier, or at least contemporary, loanword as the basis of the derivation.

4.6.1 Derivation by suffixation

Most loanword derivatives in Greek are formed with suffixes. The majority are nouns, and the suffix most often used is -ιον (for which see §4.3.2). As we have already seen, -ιον was often applied

during the initial borrowing process, perhaps because it was very common among early loanwords (particularly ones not referring to people), giving Greek speakers the idea that Latin loanwords not referring to people ought to end in -ιον. That idea may also have supplied some of the motivation for the addition of -ιον to previously borrowed loanwords, for sometimes there was no obvious difference in meaning or usage between the derivative and the original loan, both of which might coexist for centuries. For example, ξέστης 'pint' (*sextarius*) and its derivative ξεστίον 'pint' both seem to have designated the same measure, both occur in the same kinds of ancient texts, and both survived into the modern period.[83] But some other words with no obvious difference in meaning do show a difference in usage. Thus σάπων (*sapo*) is the normal term for 'soap' in literary texts, but only its derivative σαπώνιον appears in papyri; κάστελλος 'fort' (*castellum*) occurs in papyri while its derivative καστέλλιον does not; λεκτείκα 'litter' (*lectica*) appears in all text types, but its derivative λεκτίκιον occurs only in literature. A few seem to have a different meaning from the original loan, for example κονδούκτωρ 'contractor' (*conductor*) versus its derivative κονδουκτόριον 'board of contractors' and μάγκιψ 'contractor' (*manceps*) versus its derivative μαγκίπιον 1 'bakery'.[84] Occasionally

---

[83] Similarly βίρρος and βίρριον 'hooded cloak' (*birrus*), βουρδών and βουρδώνιον 'mule' (*burdo*), δελματική and δελματίκιον 'Dalmatian tunic' (*dalmatica*), κάγκελλος and καγκέλλιον 'lattice' (*cancellus*), κέλλα and κελλίον 'room' (*cella*), κέντρων and κεντώνιον 'rag' (*cento*), κούκκουμα and κουκκούμιον 'jar', 'kettle' (*cucuma*), λανᾶτον and λανάτιον 'wool garment' (*lanatum*), λῶδιξ and λωδίκιον 'blanket' (*lodix*), λῶρος and λωρίον 'thong' (*lorum*), νοῦμμος and νούμμιον 'coin' (*nummus*), ῥαῖδα and ῥαίδιον 'carriage' (*raeda*), σάγος and σαγίον 'blanket' (*sagum*), though of course one cannot rule out the original existence of distinctions no longer visible today.

[84] Also perhaps λᾶμνα 'metal plate' versus λαμνίον 'little metal plate' (*lamina*), μανδήλη 'towel' versus μανδήλιον 'little towel' (*mantele*), μάτριξ 'list' versus ματρίκιον 'register' (*matrix*), πατέλλα 'dish' versus πατέλλιον 'little dish' (*patella*), σέλλα 'seat' versus σελλίον 'little seat' (*sella*), σίτλα 'bucket' versus σιτλίον 'little bucket' (*situla*), σκάμνος 'bench' etc. versus σκαμνίον 'seat' etc. (*scamnum*), ταβέρνα 'shop' versus ταβέρνιον 'small shop' (*taberna*), τάβλα 'tablet' etc. versus ταβλίον 'tray' etc. (*tabula*), τρούλλα 'ladle' versus τρούλλιον (a dish, perhaps *trulla*), though when the only difference is that the form in -ιον is traditionally interpreted as a diminutive, that difference could be an illusion.

the derivative replaces the original loanword, as with λωρίκιον 'corselet', which appeared in the third century AD, the last in which λωρῖκα (*lorica*) is clearly attested. And often it is uncertain whether a form in -ιον is in fact a derivative rather than a direct borrowing from Latin with the aid of a suffix (cf. §4.3.2).

Most other nominal suffixes changed words' meanings in predictable ways. Abstract nouns were usually formed with -(ε)ία, which produced first-declension feminines: δικτατωρεία 'dictator-ship' from δικτάτωρ (*dictator*), ἐξακτορία 'office of tax collector' from ἐξάκτωρ (*exactor*), κομακτορία 'bank' from κομάκτωρ (*coactor*), κουρατορία 'office of curator' from κουράτωρ (*curator*), παγαρχία 'district under a pagarch' from παγάρχης (ultimately *pagus*), πατρωνεία 'patron-age' from πάτρων (*patronus*), ῥιπαρία 'office of water-watchman' from ῥιπάριος (*riparius*). Some, however, were formed with -ότης or -σις, result-ing in third-declension feminines: μαγιστρότης 'office of the *magister*' from μάγιστρος (*magister*), πατρικιότης 'patriciate' from πατρίκιος (*patricius*), σκάλωσις 'scaffolding' from σκάλα (*scalae*), σκούτλωσις 'chequered work' from σκουτλόω (ultimately *scutula*), Χριστιανότης 'Christianity' from Χριστιανός (*Christianus*). A few used -(σ)μός to form second-declension masculines: οὐγκιασμός 'measurement in twelfths' from οὐγγία (*uncia*), Χριστιανισμός 'Christianity' from Χριστιανός (*Christianus*).[85] Agent nouns were most often created with -(ι)της, which resulted in first-declension masculines some of which were eventually borrowed back into Latin,[86] but -ᾶς is used in παστιλλᾶς 'confectioner' from πάστιλλος

(*pastillus*), and the borrowed Latin suffix -άριος also occurs.[87] Feminine counterparts of masculine titles and occupational terms were often taken directly from Latin or formed by changing a sec-ond-declension -ιος to -ία (Αὐγοῦστα 'empress' from *Augusta*, πατρικία 'wife of a patrician' from πατρίκιος (*patricius*), κουβικουλαρία 'chamberlain' either from *cubicularia* or via κουβικουλάριος from *cubicularius*), but feminines could also be formed by adding -ισσα to a masculine, as in κομήτισσα 'countess' from κόμης (*comes*) and πατρώνισσα 'patroness' from πάτρων (*patronus*).[88] The suf-fixes -άριον, as in μουλάριον 'mule' from μοῦλα/μοῦλος (*mula/mulus*), probably οὐδωνάριον 'sock' from οὐδών (*udo*), and perhaps πιλάριον 'eye-salve' from πίλα 1 (*pila*); -ίδιον, in φασκίδιον 'bandage' from φασκία (*fascia*); -ᾶτον, in κιτρᾶτον 'citron drink' from κίτρον (*citron*); and perhaps -ις, probably in σίλιγνις 'flour from siligo' from σιλίγνιον (*siligineum*) were occasionally used, as was a substantivization of the adjective-forming suffix -ικός in καλανδικά 'new year's allowances' from Καλάνδαι (*Kalendae*).[89] One derived noun was apparently formed with two suffixes added simultaneously: πατελλίκιον 'little dish' from πάτελλα (*patella*) with both -ικός and -ιον.

Adjectives were also formed from loan-words by suffixation. The usual suffix was -ικός: ἀννωνικός 'concerning the grain supply' from ἀννῶνα (*annona*), ἀρκαρικός 'of the treasurer' from ἀρκάριος (*arcarius*), δουκικός 'pertaining to the *dux*' from δούξ (*dux*), probably καβαλλαρικός 'horse-drawn' from καβαλλάριος (*caballarius*), per-haps κελλαρικός 'of a cellar' from κελλάριον (*cel-larium*), perhaps κλασσικός 'naval' from κλάσσα (*classis*), perhaps παγανικός 'civilian' from παγανός (*paganus*), πατρωνικός 'of a patron' from πάτρων (*patron*), πλουμαρικός 'tapestry

85 For -(ε)ία (originally two abstract-forming suffixes -ία and -εία, but after the Hellenistic merger of ει and ι effect-ively functioning as one) see Palmer (1945: 52–4, 70–7), Chantraine (1933: 78–90); for -ότης Palmer (1945: 115–16), Chantraine (1933: 293–8); for -σις Palmer (1945: 102–7), Cavenaile (1952: 198), Chantraine (1933: 275–89); for -(σ)μός Palmer (1945: 99–102), Chantraine (1933: 138–47).

86 βυκανητής 'trumpeter' (βυκάνη ← *bucina*), ἐξπελλευτής 'tax collector' (ἐξπελλεύω ← *expello*, later probably → *expelleuta*), κελλαρίτης 'cellarer' (κελλάριον or κελλάριος ← *cellarium* or *cellarius*, later probably → *cellarites*), πωμαρίτης 'fruiterer' (πωμάριον ← *pomarium*), Ῥωμαϊστής 'actor of Latin comedies' (Ῥωμαΐζω?, ultimately ← *Roma*), σταβλίτης 'stableman' (στάβλον ← *stabulum*), τρακτευτής (a title, τρακτεύω ← *tracto*, later probably → *tracteuta*); per-

haps also βεστιαρίτης 'clothes-person' (βεστιάριον? ← *ves-tiarius*); with different meaning σιλιγνίτης '(bread) from siligo' (σιλίγνιον ← *siligineum?*). Palmer (1945: 110–15), Cavenaile (1952: 193, 198), Chantraine (1933: 310–20).

87 For -ᾶς and its variable declension see Olsson (1925), Palmer (1945: 49–50), Cavenaile (1952: 194), Chantraine (1933: 31–2), Gignac (1981: 16–21); for -άριος see §6.1.

88 Palmer (1945: 93), Cavenaile (1952: 195), Chantraine (1933: 109–10), Filos (2008: 311–15).

89 For -άριον see §6.3; for -ίδιον Palmer (1945: 86–7), Cave-naile (1952: 196), Chantraine (1933: 68–72); for -ᾶτον §6.5; for -ις Chantraine (1933: 111–15).

woven' from πλουμάριος (*plumarius*), Ῥωμαϊκός 'Roman' from Ῥωμαῖος (ultimately *Roma*), φαμιλιαρικός 'of a servant' from φαμιλιάριος (*familiaris*), Χριστιανικός 'Christian' from Χριστιανός (*Christianus*). There are also examples with -αῖος, as ξεστιαῖος 'of a pint' from ξεστίον (ultimately *sextarius*), Ῥωμαῖος 'Roman' from Ῥώμη (*Roma*); -ινος, as κίτρινος 'yellow' from κίτρον or κίτριον (*citrum* or *citrium*), probably μεμβράϊνος 'made of parchment' from μεμβράνα (*membrana*); -ιακός, as ἀννωνιακός 'belonging to the grain supply' from ἀννῶνα (*annona*), Καπετωλιακός 'Capitoline' from Καπετώλια (*Capitolius*); -ίς, as Καπετωλίς 'Capitoline' from Καπετώλιος (*Capitolius*) or Καπετώλιον (*Capitolium*), Λατινίς 'Latin' from Λατῖνος (*Latinus*), Ῥωμαῖς 'Roman' from Ῥωμαῖος (ultimately *Roma*); -ωτός, as καγκελλωτός 'latticed' from κάγκελλος (*cancellus*); and perhaps -(ε)ιος in Καισάρειος perhaps from Καῖσαρ (*Caesar*).[90] There is also a derivative adverb, Ῥωμαϊστί 'in Latin' from Ῥωμαῖος with -στί.

Derivation via suffixes was particularly important for creating verbs, since Latin verbs were not often borrowed directly (§4.3.1, §10.3.1). The earliest verbs derived from loanwords come from the first century BC and use -εύω: πατρωνεύω 'be patron' from πάτρων 'patron' (*patronus*) and δικτατωρεύω 'be dictator' from δικτάτωρ 'dictator' (*dictator*).[91] Starting in the first century AD there are also derivatives in -ίζω, namely βακλίζω 'beat' from βάκλον (*baculum*), perhaps βυκινίζω 'blow the trumpet' from βυκάνη (*bucina*), Ῥωμαΐζω 'speak Latin' from Ῥωμαῖος (ultimately *Roma*), ταβλίζω 'play dice' from τάβλα (*tabula*), Χριστιανίζω 'become Christian' from Χριστιανός (*Christianus*), and these are later joined by ones in -έω and -όω, namely παγαρχέω 'hold the office of pagarch' from παγάρχης (ultimately *pagus*), παστιλλόω 'make into a paste' from πάστιλλος (*pastillus*), probably σκουτλόω 'decorate with *opus sectile*' from σκούτλα (*scutula*), φασκιόω 'bandage up' from φασκία (*fascia*), φιβλόω 'fasten with a pin' from φίβλα (*fibula*), and perhaps φραγελλόω 'whip' from φραγέλλιον (*flagellum*).[92]

4.6.2 *Derivation by compounding or prefixation*

Greek speakers often formed new words by compounding and/or adding prefixes. Although linguists usually consider those two processes to be fundamentally different, in Greek it is difficult to distinguish meaningfully between a prefix and a word often used as the first element of compounds, and therefore in Greek contexts 'compounds' traditionally include words formed with prefixes. Three types of compound (in that sense of 'compound') were formed in Greek from Latin loanwords: ones with a Greek first element and a loanword as the second, ones with the loanword first and the Greek second, and ones where both elements came from Latin. The third group is very small, so the vast majority of the loanword compounds are 'hybrids' involving elements from both Greek and Latin.[93] Hybrid compounds are common in English, for example 'television' from

---

[90] For -ικός see Palmer (1945: 35–7), Cavenaile (1952: 197), Chantraine (1933: 385–96); for -αῖος Palmer (1945: 19–21), Chantraine (1933: 46–9); for -ινος Palmer (1945: 29–30), Chantraine (1933: 200–3), Schwyzer (1939: 490–1); for -ιακός Palmer (1945: 34), Cavenaile (1952: 197), Chantraine (1933: 393); for -ίς (a high-register suffix often considered to form nouns rather than adjectives, though in our data the words concerned often function as adjectives) Palmer (1945: 91–2), Chantraine (1933: 335–48); for -ωτός Palmer (1945: 45); for -(ε)ιος Palmer (1945: 21–2), Chantraine (1933: 49–53).

[91] Later examples: ἀγραρεύω (ἀγραρία ← *agraria*), ἀννωνεύομαι (ἀννῶνα ← *annona*), δηλατορεύω (δηλάτωρ ← *delator*), perhaps δηληγατεύω (δηληγατίων ← *delegatio*?), ἐξακτορεύω (ἐξάκτωρ ← *exactor*), κουρατορεύω (κουράτωρ ← *curator*), probably ληγατεύω (ληγᾶτον ← *legatum*?), perhaps μητατεύω (μητᾶτον ← *metatum*?), probably ὀψικεύω (ὀψίκιον ← *obsequium*?), πακτεύω (πάκτον ← *pactum*), probably πραιδεύω (πραῖδα ← *praeda*?). Palmer (1945: 134–7), Cavenaile (1952: 197–8). Cavenaile divides loanwords in -εύω into two groups: ones forming part of juridical language, which added -εύω to the supine stem, and ones forming part of military language, which added -εύω to the root of the verb. This distinction does not fit our loanword data, but rare and foreign juridical verbs are in fact very likely to be formed from the supine stem (Dain 1930: 106; Burgmann 1991: 68).

[92] For -ίζω see Palmer (1945: 140–3), Cavenaile (1952: 198); for -όω Palmer (1945: 131–4); for -έω Palmer (1945: 124–31).

[93] For more information on Latin–Greek hybrid compounds in Greek see Filos (2010, 2008: 358–425), cf. Cavenaile (1952: 199); for the formation of Greek compounds more generally, see Sommer (1948), Schwyzer (1939: 425–55). Modern Greek still forms hybrid compounds freely, now often with English loanwords (Stathi 2002: 321).

the ultimately Greek 'tele-' 'at a distance' and ultimately Latin (via French) 'vision', but English is notable for having borrowed a high percentage of its vocabulary from several different foreign languages. Often both elements of our hybrid compounds have been part of English for so long that it scarcely makes sense to think of the compounds as hybrids: 'churchwarden', for example, combines an etymologically Germanic 'church' with an etymologically French 'warden', but from the perspective of English speakers there is no real difference between that formation and the Germanic + Germanic one that produced 'churchyard'. In some other languages such as French or German, however, a lower percentage of borrowed vocabulary makes hybrids rarer. In Greek hybrids make up more than a quarter of all derivative loanwords, and (including both the derivatives and the hybrids formed as part of the borrowing process, for which see §4.5) 5% of all loanwords.

Many of the hybrid compounds are words for measures. Like many languages (cf. English 'half-mile', 'half-pint', 'half-inch' and 'two-mile', 'two-pint', 'two-inch'), Greek used a predictable system of compounds to indicate the quantity of a wide variety of measures. Thus δραχμή 'drachma' formed ἡμίδραχμον 'half-drachma', δίδραχμον 'two drachmae', τρίδραχμον 'three drachmae',

τετράδραχμον 'four drachmae', etc.; ὀβολός 'obol' formed ἡμιωβέλιον 'half-obol', διώβολον 'two obols', τριώβολον 'three obols', etc.; πούς 'foot' formed ἡμιπόδιον 'half-foot' and τριπόδιον 'three-foot', τάλαντον 'talent' formed ἡμιτάλαντον 'half-talent' and τριτάλαντον 'three talents', etc. There was a widespread tendency for such compound forms to attach -ον or -ιον to the root of the simplex noun (cf. Chantraine 1933: 57), but this rule was by no means absolute: τριπόδιον had an alternative form τρίπους, μνᾶ 'mina' formed ἡμιμναῖον 'half-mina' etc., and πῆχυς 'cubit' formed ἡμίπηχυς 'half-cubit' etc. Many such forms also had matching adjectives in -(ι)αῖος: διδραχμιαῖος 'worth two drachmae', τετραδραχμιαῖος 'of four drachmae', ἡμιωβελιαῖος 'worth half an obol', διωβολιαῖος 'weighing two obols', τριωβολιαῖος 'weighing three obols', ἡμιποδιαῖος 'half a foot broad', ἡμιταλαντιαῖος 'in which the prize is half a talent', τριταλαντιαῖος 'holding three talents', ἡμιπηχυαῖος 'half a cubit long'.

Therefore measuring units borrowed from Latin, such as οὐγγία 'ounce' or 'twelfth', μόδιος 'peck', ξέστης 'pint', and ἀσσάριον 'penny', could automatically form a whole range of hybrid compounds, as illustrated in Figure 1. Indeed so well established were the principles governing the way quantities of measures could be expressed that

	οὐγγία 'ounce'	μόδιος 'peck'	ξέστης 'pint'	ἀσσάριον 'penny'
ἡμι- 'half'	ἡμιούγκιον, (ἡμιουγκιαῖος)		ἡμίξεστον	(ἡμιασσάριον)
δι- 'two'	διούγκιον	(διμόδιον)	(δίξεστον)	
τρι- 'three'	τριούγκιον	τριμόδιον	(τρίξεστον)	
τετρα- 'four'	τετραούγκιον	(τετραμόδιον)	τετραξεστιαῖος	(τετράσσαρον)
πεντα- 'five'	(πενταούγκιον)	(πενταμόδιον), (πενταμοδιαῖος)	πενταξεστιαῖος	
ἑξα- 'six'	ἑξαούγκιον		ἑξάξεστος, ἑξαξεστιαῖος	
ἑπτα- 'seven'	(ἑπταούγκιον)			
ὀκτα- 'eight'	(ὀκταούγκιον)		(ὀκτάξεστος), (ὀκταξεστιαῖος)	(ὀκτασσαριαῖος)
ἐννα- 'nine'	ἐνναούγκιον			
δεκα- 'ten'	(δεκαούγκιον)		(δεκαξεστιαῖος)	

Figure 1 Compounds of loanwords for measurements (including in parentheses terms too rare to be considered loanwords)

such compounds could easily have been created spontaneously, with exactly the same meanings, by many different speakers. Nevertheless, compounds that occur repeatedly in the same form are more likely to have been spreading among Greek speakers as loanwords than to have been spontaneously re-created by each user.

Prepositions, which frequently appear as the first elements of Greek–Greek compounds, also occur in Greek–Latin ones. Σύν 'with' appears in συνουετρανός 'fellow veteran' from οὐετερανός (*veteranus*), συγκελλάριος 'comrade' from κέλλα (*cella*), and the ecclesiastical title σύγκελλος from κέλλα (*cella*). Παρά 'beside' forms παράτιτλον 'marginal scholion' from τίτλος (*titulus*), and ἐν 'in' forms ἔμπλουμος 'tapestry woven' (perhaps via πλουμίον from *pluma*, but a direct borrowing is also possible).

Numerous other Greek terms can occur as the first elements of hybrid compounds. Ἀρχι- 'chief' forms ἀρχισταβλίτης 'chief stableman' from σταβλίτης (ultimately *stabulum*), and πρωτο- 'first' forms πρωτοπατρίκιος 'first patrician' from πατρίκιος (*patricius*). Φιλο- 'fond of' produces φιλορώμαιος 'friend of the Romans' from Ῥωμαῖος (ultimately *Roma*) and φιλόκαισαρ 'loyal to Caesar' from Καῖσαρ (*Caesar*). Μήτηρ 'mother' appears in μητροκολωνεία 'mother-colony' from κολωνία (*colonia*), ὕδωρ 'water' in ὑδρορόσατον 'rose water' from ῥόσατον (*rosatum*), and χέρνιψ 'water for washing hands' in χερνιβόξεστον 'washbasin' from ξέστης (*sextarius*). Some compounds are adjectival: ἰσοκαπετώλιος 'equivalent to Capitoline' from ἴσος 'equal' and Καπετώλια (*Capitolius*), λινόπηξος 'of combed linen' from λίνον 'linen' and πεξός (*pexus*).

These examples suggest that the Greek–Latin hybrid compounds were formed like other Greek compounds, and the same applies to the less numerous Latin–Greek hybrids. These include Καπετωλιονίκης 'victor in the Capitoline games' from Καπετώλια (*Capitolius*) + -νίκης, λωροτόμος 1 'strap-cutter' from λῶρος (*lorum*) + -τόμος, παγάρχης 'pagarch' from πᾶγος (*pagus*) + -άρχης, the title φισκοσυνήγορος from φίσκος (*fiscus*) + συνήγορος, βηλόθυρον 'curtain at door' from βῆλον (*velum*) + θύρα, and three terms for 'Dalmatian tunic with

hood', all composed from δελματική (*dalmatica*) + μαφόρτης and its variants (δελματικομαφόρτης, δελματικομαφόρτιον, δελματικομαφόριον).

The sole Latin–Latin compound to be formed from a loanword is σουβρικοπάλλιον 'outer cloak', whose second element is clearly the previously borrowed πάλλιον 'mantle' (*pallium*).[94] The first half is more doubtful; it probably comes from *subricula* or *sublica*, one of which is probably also the source of the rare σουβρίκιον 'hood' and σουβρικός. It is possible that the compound was formed using one of these rare Greek forms, but more likely that the first element was taken directly from Latin.

There is also an interesting group of compounds beginning with a Latinate ἀπο- meaning 'former' or 'belonging to the class of' and translating Latin *ex*, but none of these is frequent enough to count as a loanword.[95]

4.6.3 Derivatives of derivatives

The derivation processes could be combined more or less indefinitely, since derivatives that became established as loanwords were then available for creating further derivatives. Thus Ῥωμαῖος 'Roman', itself a derivative of Ῥώμη 'Rome' by suffixation, produced further derivatives both by compounding (φιλορώμαιος 'friend of the Romans') and by suffixation (Ῥωμαΐζω 'speak Latin', Ῥωμαϊστί 'in Latin', etc.). Likewise παγάρχης 'pagarch', a derivative of πᾶγος 'district' by compounding, produced παγαρχέω 'hold the office of pagarch' and παγαρχία 'district under a pagarch' by suffixation, while σταβλίτης 'stableman', derived from στάβλον 'stable' by suffixation,

---

94 This compound is likely to have been created in Greek, not only because it is not attested in Latin, but also because the linking vowel is Greek -o- rather than Latin -i-; see §4.5.

95 They are ἀποδρακωνάριος 'former standard-bearer', 'person belonging to the class of standard-bearers'; ἀποκόμης 'former count'; ἀποπροτήκτωρ 'former protector', 'person belonging to the class of protectors'. For this use of ἀπό see Filos (2006: 53–7, 2008: 438–50), *DGE* (s.v. ἀπό B.VIII.2), *LBG* (s.v.), *P.Herm.Landl.* (pp. 13, 51–2), Kruit (1994: 84–5), Lewis (1960: 186–7), Cervenka-Ehrenstrasser (1996: 92). In Latin these senses of *ex* are post-Classical but not terribly late; see Väänänen (1973) and *TLL* s.v. *ex* 1102.10–55. This *ex* is sometimes said also to appear as ἐξ- in loanwords, but the only example of that, ἐξκεντυρίων 'former centurion' from *ex centuriōne* or an unattested **excenturiō*, is uncertainly attested.

produced ἀρχισταβλίτης 'chief stableman' by compounding. The longest chain of derivatives may have started with ξέστης 'pint', from which ξεστίον 'pint' was derived by suffixation, from which ξεστιαῖος 'of a pint' probably arose with the addition of a further suffix, and from that by compounding τετραξεστιαῖος 'holding four pints', πενταξεστιαῖος 'holding five pints', and ἑξαξεστιαῖος 'holding six pints'.

4.7 CONCLUSIONS

Latin loanwords were normally integrated into Greek both by being written in Greek letters and by inflecting according to the pattern of a regular Greek declension. Their Greek spellings typically reflected pronunciation, rather than transliterating their Latin spellings, and therefore provide important evidence for the pronunciation of both Latin and Greek at different periods. But such evidence must be used with care: spellings are often variable, and as time passed the Greek spelling of a Latin loanword borrowed earlier could be (but was not always) updated to reflect changes in Latin pronunciation. Therefore the pronunciation reflected by a Greek spelling is not necessarily that of Latin speakers contemporary with the Greek writer who produced that spelling, nor necessarily that of the Latin speakers from whom the loanword was originally borrowed.

Most nouns joined the Greek paradigm closest to their original Latin paradigm, without any further alteration. Often the changes involved were minimal, as when second-declension nouns in -us and -um and fourth-declension nouns in -us joined the Greek second declension, and when third-declension nouns belonging to a paradigm with an obvious equivalent in the Greek third declension joined that equivalent paradigm. But third-declension masculines in -is and third-declension neuters of all types normally joined the Greek second declension, and some others shifted paradigms individually. There was some fluctuation in the declensions of loanwords, particularly ones that in Latin had belonged to the second declension in -r. Most loanword nouns inflected exactly like native Greek words belonging to the paradigm they had joined, but anomalies caused by influence from their Latin forms are sometimes attested. The most significant such anomaly occurred in the first declension, where many loans from the Latin first declension took endings with -α despite having stem terminations that in the case of native Greek words would have led to endings with -η. That this anomaly was caused by the influence of the Latin first-declension paradigm is suggested by loanwords from other Latin declensions that shifted into the Greek first declension: these were far more likely to take endings with -η than were loans from the Latin first declension. Most loanword nouns retained their original genders, but a substantial minority changed gender (often, but not always, with an identifiable reason) or appeared in Greek with more than one gender.

Latin adjectives often became nouns in Greek, taking the appropriate noun paradigm. Those that remained adjectives all joined the Greek first/second-declension adjective paradigm, regardless of how they had declined in Latin. Adjectives were more likely than nouns to follow regular Greek patterns; masculine forms in -r were absorbed without difficulty, and only a few feminines took endings in -α where -η would be expected, usually as part of longer phrases. Widespread lack of attestation in the feminine makes it uncertain how many of the loanword adjectives traditionally assigned to the two-termination category really belong there.

The process of direct absorption into a Greek paradigm worked only for nouns and adjectives; verbs could be borrowed only with the aid of a suffix such as -εύω. Some nouns and adjectives also acquired a suffix as part of the borrowing process, though in their case the borrowing would have been possible without it. By far the most common suffix used to borrow Latin nouns was -ιον, perhaps in part because so many loanword nouns ended in -ιον for other reasons that Greek speakers could have developed an expectation that certain kinds of Latin loanwords ought to end in -ιον.

The forms of some loanwords were further influenced by Greek words or affixes (folk etymology), as when *sextarius* 'pint measure' became ξέστης. Such influenced forms were normally sporadic variants, but in about 3% of borrowings they became the standard forms of the words concerned. Early Latin loanwords some-times exercised influence of this type on later borrowings.

Some Latin words entered Greek only as part of compounds or univerbations. Univerbations and Latin–Latin compounds created as part of the borrowing process are all titles and occu-pational terms; most of these already existed in Latin, but some may have been created by Greek speakers using elements taken directly from Latin. At least four hybrid Greek–Latin compounds were also created within Greek using a Latin element that had not been previ-ously borrowed.

Once loanwords had been borrowed into Greek they could form derivatives either by suf-fixation (again the most common suffix was -ιον) or by compounding, normally resulting in hybrid compounds. Particularly notable among the com-pounds is a set of words for measures. The deriva-tives could then form further derivatives more or less *ad infinitum.*

5

HOW WERE LATIN LOANWORDS ACCENTED IN GREEK?

The accentuation of Latin words in Greek is a vexed issue: did such words retain their Latin accents, or were they re-accented to fit Greek patterns? Of course, because of the flexible nature of the Greek accent and the similarity between Greek and Latin accent rules many Latin words came with accents that already fitted Greek patterns, but what happened to Latin accents that did not? The question has been debated for over a century without agreement being reached; as the accent question is of some importance as evidence of loanwords' integration, and has not previously been seen in that light, it is worth reviewing both the debate and the evidence here.

5.1 THE BASIC FACTS

In discussing Latin and Greek the term 'accent' refers to a syllable more prominent than others in the same word; the way that prominence is perceived varies and can involve pitch, loudness, duration, and/or vowel quality.[1] Every Latin word had an accent on one of its last three syllables; although these were very rarely written we can be reasonably sure of knowing where they were, because the position of the Latin accent is almost completely predictable from rules spelled out by ancient writers (e.g. Quintilian 1.5.30–1). Greek words also had an accent on one of the last three syllables, but the position of the Greek accent was not fully predictable; as a result there are some Greek words of whose accentuation we are uncertain.

Information on the accents of ancient Greek words is preserved in a variety of ways. Our main source of such information is the accent marks in Byzantine manuscripts, since Greek accents were regularly written from around the late ninth century onwards. In determining where to put

the accents Byzantine scribes mainly used their native-speaker intuitions, for the position of the accent has normally remained constant all the way to modern Greek.[2] For words that had not survived as part of the spoken language, and for whose accentuation Byzantine scribes therefore had no intuitions, they assigned accents based on instructions given in the ancient grammatical texts on accentuation. Some fragments and epitomes of those grammatical texts are still extant today, allowing us to consult them directly, and some words appear with accent marks on ancient papyri. A few ancient words have survived into spoken (usually dialectal) modern Greek without being attested in the Byzantine manuscript tradition; for these the modern accent can provide a clue to the ancient one.

For some words, unfortunately, we have none of these types of information. Words that occur only on inscriptions, ostraca, and/or documentary papyri normally reach us without any information on their ancient accentuation, and because it is customary in modern editions to accent every word of a Greek text, editors usually feel obliged to provide accents for such words. Since many Latin loanwords occur only in such non-literary sources, modern scholars have produced more arguments than one might expect on the question of how Latin loanwords in Greek were accented.

The background to those arguments is the accent rules in the two languages. In Latin, the accents of two-syllable words fell on the first syllable; in words of three or more syllables the

---

[1] See e.g. Probert (2019: 27–8).

[2] For the preservation of the ancient accent position in modern Greek, and the exceptions to that rule, see e.g. Holton *et al.* (2019: 223), Hatzidakis (1892: 418–40). For more information on the evidence for ancient Greek accentuation, including several further types of evidence that are not relevant for loanwords, see Probert (2006: 15–52).

accent fell on the penultimate (next to last) syllable if that syllable was heavy,[3] otherwise on the antepenultimate (third syllable from the end). Only monosyllables were accented on the final syllable. In Greek, the main accent rule was that if the last syllable contained a long vowel or diphthong,[4] the accent had to fall on one of the last two syllables: it could fall on the antepenultimate only if the last syllable had a short vowel. Therefore the Greek and Latin accent rules directly conflicted for words with a light penultimate syllable and a long vowel in the final syllable, such as *cĕntŭrĭō*, which in Latin had to be accented *centúrio* but in Greek could not be accented **κεντούριων*.[5] All available evidence suggests that in such words Greek speakers changed the accents of Latin words to fit Greek patterns.[6]

The positions of Greek accents were also influenced by a large number of less absolute rules, or tendencies; scholarly arguments focus on the extent to which such tendencies caused Latin loanwords to change their accents. Certain terminations were associated with particular accentuation: for example, adjectives ending in -ικός were accented on the final syllable, nouns ending in -σύνη were accented on the penultimate syllable, and nouns of more than three syllables ending in -ιον were recessive (accented as far from the end of the word as the rules allowed), as were first-declension nouns ending in short -α (Probert 2003: 82–3, 86). And when a new accent was needed, for example at the creation of a new word that did not involve one of the suffixes with characteristic accentuation, that new accent was most often recessive; recessive accentuation was common for loanwords because it functioned as a default accentuation in Greek, that is, the most common accent position, especially for words not belonging to any specific morphological class for which a different accent pattern was normal (Probert 2006: 128–44).

The differences between Latin and Greek accents were not only about position; there were also differences in the type of prominence a syllable could have. It is often said that Latin accents were stress accents and Greek accents were pitch accents. This distinction is an oversimplification (Probert 2019: 27–35), but there was evidently some kind of difference, for whereas Latin always had only one kind of accent, Greek originally had two. Greek grammarians distinguished between acute and circumflex accents, in that the acute indicated a rise in pitch and the circumflex a rise followed by a fall (they also had a grave sign, but that essentially indicated an unaccented syllable). This distinction was nearly always observed when accents were written in antiquity and in the Byzantine period; it is still used today in writing ancient (but not modern) Greek, although the distinction between acute and circumflex ceased to be audible well before the end of antiquity. Various rules dictated when an accent was written acute or circumflex (§5.2.3), and there is no evidence that anyone writing in Greek ever exempted Latin loanwords from such rules.

5.2 SCHOLARLY ARGUMENTS

5.2.1 *Assuming diachronic stability*

For most of the twentieth century prevailing views on the accentuation of Latin loanwords were based on those of Wackernagel

---

[3] A heavy syllable is one containing a long vowel or diphthong, and/or ending in a consonant; Latin syllable division principles mean that a vowel followed by two consonants usually, but not always, forms the nucleus of a syllable ending in a consonant, while a vowel followed by only one consonant usually, but not always, forms the nucleus of a syllable ending in a vowel.

[4] For this purpose the diphthongs αι and οι usually counted as short vowels if they appeared at the very end of a word. For more information on the Greek accent see Probert (2003, 2006).

[5] An additional complication is that this accent rule was not absolute in Greek: the genitives of ι-stems such as πόλις (e.g. πόλεως, πόλεων) are accented on the antepenultimate despite having a long vowel in their final syllables. (There is a historical reason for this exception, for πόλεως was created by quantitative metathesis from πόληος and the accent reflects this earlier form; πόλεων is presumably accented by analogy with πόλεως.) In theory it is possible that the prior existence of forms such as πόλεως and πόλεων could have led speakers to accept Latin forms such as **κεντούριων*, and over time an influx of Latin loans with such accents could then have led to a change in the rules governing Greek accents. But as there is no evidence that any of this actually happened, the complication is purely a theoretical one.

[6] In modern Greek adaptations of loanwords from English, accents that do not fit the obligatory rules for Greek accents are usually changed, but not always: see Stathi (2002: 315).

(1926: 56–8) as reformulated by Schwyzer (1939: 395). Wackernagel's original argument had two parts: that Latin words generally kept their Latin accents when borrowed into Greek (e.g. *guttátus* becoming γουττᾶτος), and that certain classes of words changed their accents. He identified three such classes: words with accents not allowed by the Greek rules, which ended up with a recessive accent in Greek (e.g. *centúrio* becoming κεντουρίων); words with endings that could be equated to Greek suffixes normally accented on the final syllable, which ended up with a final accent in Greek (e.g. *domésticus* becoming δομεστικός); and words that changed the position of the accent and ended up with recessive accents in Greek for no obvious reason (e.g. *Augústus* becoming Αὔγουστος).[7] Schwyzer, who in the context of a comprehensive grammar could offer only a very condensed discussion of the topic, endorsed Wackernagel's view but simplified it in a way that focussed on the first part, the principle that most loanwords did not change their accents when borrowed into Greek. Later scholars then tended to accept that principle without always appreciating the limits within which it applied.

Towards the end of the century Clarysse (1997: 178–9) proposed a reversal of Schwyzer's principle: Latin loanwords normally acquired new accents in Greek rather than keeping their original accents. Clarysse provided two categories of evidence: the exceptions listed by Wackernagel and Schwyzer and a typological argument that 'most languages' re-accent loanwords. The only examples he gave in support of the typological argument were French and Latin, both of which have a completely fixed accent and therefore do re-accent (integrated) loanwords. But there is an important difference (already pointed out by Wackernagel) between such a fixed accent, which effectively forces loanwords to be re-accented if they are not to sound strikingly foreign, and the more flexible Greek accent, which allows retention of the original accent of many loanwords. To have any validity, a typological argument on this point would need to look at what happens to the accents of loanwords in languages that,

like Greek, do not have a fixed accent. English is such a language, and in English loanwords sometimes keep their original accents and sometimes change them: for example American 'garáge' preserves the original accentuation of this French loanword, while British 'gárage' does not.[8]

Although Clarysse's argument was explicitly framed as a reversal of the earlier principle, it was in fact effectively the same as Wackernagel's view: when an accented suffix or some other rule of Greek accentuation made the original accent of a Latin word seem alien in Greek, the accent was changed to fit the Greek rules, but 'if the Greek rules allowed the Latin accent to stay on the same place as in the original language, then the place of the accent did not as a rule change, why should it' (Clarysse 1997: 178). This was effectively Wackernagel's original view differently expressed, but from it Clarysse drew a prescriptive principle to guide editors, namely that one can simply apply the rules of Greek accentuation to loanwords. The effect of this is that instead of investigating the particular Greek rule (or tendency) involved and finding out whether it seemed to be responsible for shifting the accents of loanwords, as one would have to do to apply Wackernagel's principle as a prescriptive rule, one can simply assume that all loanwords had the accents that their suffixes most commonly bore in Greek. As a prescriptive rule, therefore, Clarysse's principle is significantly easier for papyrologists to apply than Wackernagel's – and perhaps more importantly, at least for Clarysse's purposes, it can be generalized to loanwords from languages such as Egyptian where the original position of the accent is less clear than in Latin. If correct, therefore, Clarysse's prescriptive principle would represent a major improvement for papyrologists.

Despite these tempting characteristics, Clarysse's reformulation was immediately challenged by Radt (1998), who pointed out that in Byzantine manuscripts of Strabo the accentuation of Latin personal and place names very

---

[7] Wackernagel's examples were λούκουντλος, μάκελλον, Σέκουνδος, and Κούαρτος, none of which I would consider a loanword and which may not all have the accents he proposed.

[8] The situation within French itself is complex (see e.g. Dell 1984; Ladd 2008: 59–60; Van der Hulst 2010: 20–1, 25–6), but it usually resulted in final-syllable stress on French loanwords in English. However, many loanwords originally pronounced with such stress later moved the accent to an earlier syllable (C. Barber 1997: 130–2; Svensson 2009).

often shows a striking correlation with the original Latin accent. Such correlation suggests an underlying principle that the original accent does not move unless forced to do so by a fairly strong tendency in Greek.

Radt's view was in turn challenged by Kramer (1998b), who pointed out that manuscript practice is often inconsistent: the words cited by Radt as having manuscript accents correlating with the original Latin accent also have, in other manuscripts, accents that do not match the Latin. Kramer asserted that the only reason editors pay more attention to the Latinate than to the non-Latinate accents is the influence of Wackernagel's principle. He also argued that when Latin loanwords survive into modern Greek they tend to have been re-accented, giving three examples of this re-accentuation: ἄμπουλλα from *ampúlla*, λίβελλος from *libéllos*, and βουρδών from *búrdo*. (The last of these involves one of the accented suffixes Wackernagel discusses, and the other two could fit into Wackernagel's category of words that become recessive for no apparent reason, though there is no good evidence that they in fact had during antiquity the accents Kramer gives them.) He therefore concluded that one can reformulate Clarysse's principle in stronger terms: all loanwords in Greek simply followed the Greek accent system, with no reference whatsoever to their original accentuations, and had a tendency to be recessive when no other Greek rule intervened (Kramer 1998b: 134).

Radt (1999) replied to this by pointing out that when manuscripts disagree about accentuation there is a very good reason to prefer the Latinate readings: Byzantine scribes had a tendency to apply the Greek accent system to everything and did not themselves know Latin or its accent system, so while they might easily apply a non-Latin accent by mistake, the only reason they were likely to apply a Latin accent is that it was in the exemplar being copied.

Kramer (2001b) responded with more examples of Latin loanwords that survive into modern Greek with non-Latinate accents: Αὔγουστος from *Augústus*, κάγκελλο from *cancéllus*, ἄπληκτον from *applícitum*, words with suffixes -ανός and -ικός from *-ánus* and *´-icus*. Again

these fit perfectly with Wackernagel's principle as originally formulated.[9]

After a few years' pause the subject was taken up again by Probert (2006: 132–6), who had a different goal: not establishing a prescriptive rule for accenting loanwords, but investigating the default recessive accentuation of Greek. Probert observed that we have explicit testimony from an ancient grammarian that at least some Latin loanwords preserved their original accentuation: a statement that 'Italian' (i.e. Latin) words with the suffix -ερνος were accented on the penultimate syllable (§5.3.2 passage 6). As Probert observed (2006: 133), this is not the accent the usual Greek rules would predict. Probert's main concern, however, was not with Latin words that retained their original accentuation but with ones that were re-accented; she concluded that when re-accentuation occurred, it followed the accentuation of the suffix if that suffix had a strong accentual tendency in Greek, and otherwise it followed the default recessive accentuation.

5.2.2 *Assuming diachronic change*

All these scholars assumed that the way Greek speakers accented Latin words remained stable over time, but there was also a separate set of discussions by other scholars starting from the opposite premise: that early borrowings must have been adapted differently from later ones. The clearest exponent of this view is Mihăescu (1993: 344–8), who maintained that words borrowed before the fourth century AD were usually re-accented to fit Greek accentual patterns, while those borrowed later usually kept their Latin accents. Mihăescu supported his argument with examples of words in each category,

[9] Kramer also published a combined version of his 1998b and 2001b arguments as Kramer (2011: 139–50). In addition to the points mentioned above, he claimed in all three articles that the Latin accent could not have been preserved in Greek because the difference in nature between the Latin stress accent and the Greek pitch accent would have meant that Greek speakers did not perceive Latin accents as accents. This argument can be dismissed, however, because in the first century AD the Roman writer Quintilian clearly equated Greek accents with Latin ones (1.5.22–4, 29).

but not with evidence for the dates at which they were borrowed, and when such evidence is found it does not always fit his theory.[10] He chose the fourth century as the transition point not on the basis of evidence for when the words concerned were actually borrowed, but because his explanation for the change in accentuation practice is that it was linked to the loss of distinctive vowel quantity, which he dated to the fourth century. Mihăescu's view is not isolated: similar ideas can also be found in Bartoli (1912: 987–94) and Filos (2014: 322).[11] Moreover the existence of such a shift in the Greek treatment of Latin accents may be implied by a generally acknowledged change in the accentuation of Greek words in -ικος: in antiquity such words were regularly accented -ικός, but in modern Greek a recessive accent is often used, a fact traditionally explained with reference to large numbers of Latin borrowings in '-icus.[12] The change in the accentuation of -ικος is usually dated to the Byzantine period, however, and the putative shift in the way Greek handled Latin loanwords is also sometimes presented as Byzantine. Moreover some of the ancient loanwords appear to have changed their accents between ancient and modern Greek (e.g. modern βετεράνος 'veteran', which has a 'Latinate' accent that was probably not present on ancient οὐετερανός, borrowed by the first century AD), a possibility that greatly complicates the picture.[13]

The evidence so far presented for a change in the Greek treatment of Latin accents does not suffice to prove that there was such a change, let alone that it occurred in the fourth century. Although the re-accentuation of the -ικος suffix is highly suggestive, there has been no serious attempt to demonstrate that it was really connected to Latin influence, and the connection cannot be assumed without further investigation: the accentuation of at least one other suffix also changed between ancient and modern Greek, and in that case Latin influence was clearly not involved.[14] At the same time the idea of a change in the treatment of Latin accents cannot be dismissed out of hand, since it is common for loanwords adopted early in a given language-contact situation to be more thoroughly adapted to the phonology of the borrowing language than ones adopted later, once increasing bilingualism and an influx of other loanwords has accustomed the speakers of the borrowing language to the sound patterns of the donor language.[15] This typological picture means that any shift in the Greek treatment of loanword accents may be unconnected to the loss of distinctive vowel quantity, and therefore that there is no particular reason to date it to the fourth century (rather than, e.g., the Byzantine period, or indeed the second century). In fact even if the shift is indeed connected to the loss of distinctive vowel quantity that would not necessarily date it to the fourth century, since the date of that loss is disputed. What is needed is a rigorous examination of the evidence, focussing on words whose accentuation can be clearly established both for Byzantine and for modern Greek (and that have the same accent at both periods) and whose original borrowing dates can be ascertained with reasonable confidence. There is no space for such a study in the present work, but it is hoped that someone will conduct one soon: such research might enable real progress on the thorny question of how to accent loanwords in papyri.

5.2.3 *Acute or circumflex?*

While the scholarly debates just outlined focus on the position of the accent, there is also a debate about the form of some accents. In pronunciation,

---

[10] Mihăescu (1993: 348) lists as examples of words borrowed before the fourth century Αὔγουστος, κάγκελλον, γέμελλος, γέμελλα, and πέδικλον; according to my evidence (§3.2), only the first actually belongs in that category.

[11] But Binder (2000: 13–14) rejects Mihăescu's view.

[12] E.g. Tonnet (2003: 105), who cites βλάχικος, ψεύτικος, αλλιώτικος. The idea that Latin influence was behind the accent shift appears to go back to Hatzidakis (1892: 428), who considered but ultimately rejected it, pointing out that there were not very many Latin loanwords with this suffix; Meyer, however, endorsed it (1895: 76).

[13] Psaltes (1913: 304–5, cf. 293–4) locates the accent shift from -ιανός to -ιάνος in the Byzantine period and attributes it to Italian influence.

[14] The ancient -ία suffix became -ιά during the Byzantine period, when the ι ceased to be pronounced as a vowel and therefore could no longer take the accent: Scheller (1951), cf. Browning (1983: 77), Horrocks (2010: 169).

[15] See e.g. Thomason and Kaufmann's borrowing scale (Thomason 2001: 70–1). For a diachronic shift in the way modern Greek handles certain loanwords from English, see Stathi (2002: 305).

the distinction between acute and circumflex disappeared during (or perhaps even before) the Roman period, but in writing accents (at least on ancient Greek) it has been maintained to the present day. Modern scholars accenting Greek words must therefore decide not only where to put the accent, but which accent mark to use. In doing so they normally follow the rules laid down by ancient grammarians, which specify that a circumflex can appear only on a long vowel and only on one of the last two syllables of a word; if the penultimate syllable has a long vowel and is accented, the accent must be circumflex if the final syllable contains a short vowel and acute if the final syllable contains a long vowel, whereas if the final syllable has a long vowel and is accented, the accent can be either circumflex or acute – one has to learn the particular form involved to know which.

The difficulty here is how to evaluate vowel quantity in loanwords. Some scholars argue that the quantity that matters is the Latin one, so that if the name *Iūcŭndŭs* becomes Ἰουκουνδος while keeping the accent on the penultimate syllable, that accent must be an acute because the vowel is short: Ἰουκούνδος (Solin 2015: 289). But it is far from clear that Greek speakers would have agreed with this argument. In Greek the sound spelled ου existed only as a long vowel during the period when vowel length was still a meaningful concept,[16] and therefore at that period pronouncing a short ου would have involved introducing a sound not otherwise present in Greek. Of course, unfamiliar sounds do sometimes enter languages via loanwords, and if that happened with short ου in Greek it would be important evidence for a significant phonological impact of Latin on Greek – but without any evidence that it did actually happen, one cannot simply assume that impact of such significance occurred. Later, of course, the vowel length distinction was lost along with the distinction in pronunciation between acute and circumflex accents; after that point Greek speakers writing accents used the grammarians' rules to determine which accent to write as well as where to write it. Those rules do not mention any

situations in which ου could count as short, and therefore writers following the rules undoubtedly would have treated it as long and written Ἰουκοῦνδος. Although these arguments are not normally stated explicitly, many editors must agree with them, for they usually put a circumflex on ου derived from Latin *ŭ*.[17] For example, LSJ has μοῦστος (*mŭstum*) and φοῦρνος (*fŭrnus*), the LSJ supplement has βοῦλβα[18] (*vŭlva*) and ἰοῦγον (*iŭgum*), DGE has βοῦλβα, Lampe (1961) has ἰοῦγον and φοῦρνος, and LBG has βοῦλβα and μοῦστος.[19] But the practice is not universal, for the LSJ supplement also has κουκκούλλος (*cucŭllus*).

Even more difficulties arise when the accented vowel is α, ι, or υ, since these letters could be used both for long and for short vowels in Greek. For example, Latin participles in *-atus* had a long *a*, including *cumulātus*, *dēputātus*, and *lēgātus*, which became Greek κουμουλατος, δηπουτατος, and ληγατος – with a long α or with a short one?[20] We can tell from the Byzantine use of these words that the accent remained on the penultimate syllable, but by that time both the acute/circumflex pronunciation distinction and the distinction between long and short α had been lost, so Byzantine scribes and the editors of Byzantine texts display uncertainty about the accent (Psaltes 1913: 136–7; Dain 1930: 111). There was no pre-existing group of Greek words in -ατος with a consistent vowel quantity that might have

---

[16] The Boeotian dialect may be an exception to this generalization, but I know of no Latin loanwords borrowed into Boeotian.

[17] Further difficulties arise in the (rare) forms where the ου is in the final syllable; counting it long can result in accents like αὐρικαισωρίβους (*auricaesoribus*), which is a gross violation of the Latin accent rules, and as the forms concerned are inevitably codeswitches they may well not have had accents violating the Latin accent rules. Nevertheless it is usual to print αὐρικαισωρίβους (e.g. Lauffer 1971: 191, DGE).

[18] This accentuation assumes that the -α is short, as in Latin. An additional problem with the accentuation of first-declension loanwords is that the quantity of final -α is usually unknown (§4.2.3.1).

[19] Ἰουκουνδος itself, being a name, is not in these lexica, but Solin's point was made in reaction to the accentuation Ἰουκοῦνδος in the *Lexicon of Greek Personal Names*.

[20] I am grateful to Erich Trapp and Panagiotis Filos for illuminating discussion on the issues in this paragraph, and in particular to Professor Trapp for explaining the rationale behind the accentuation in LBG, which follows the majority practice of editors of the texts on which it is based but imposes consistency on the treatment of words in -ατος.

influenced the quantity of the α in these loan-words, and we have no other indications of the quantity that the vowel had in ancient Greek. Moreover, for many loanwords the quantity question is not even meaningful; as the distinction between long and short α was lost before the end of antiquity, words borrowed after that loss cannot really have had either vowel quantity in Greek. Yet putting either accent on them entails making a statement about the quantity of the α, for in this context an acute indicates short α just as clearly as a circumflex indicates long α.

Modern scholars tend to treat the question of accent shape differently from that of accent position: for the position of the accent they generally follow the practice of Byzantine manuscripts, but for its shape they often standardize so that all words that historically share a particular suffix accent that suffix in the same way. There is a good reason for this distinction, for the position of the accent was a real linguistic feature in Roman-period and Byzantine Greek, and we know that a single suffix could have different accents in different words: the Byzantine manuscript tradition indicates that while *centúriō* became κεντουρίων, *légiō* became λεγεών.[21] But in the same period the acute/circumflex distinction was not a real linguistic feature, just a graphic convention. Ancient and Byzantine scribes chose between acute and circumflex accents by applying Herodian's rules and making their best guess at the quantities of vowels whose quantities were no longer audible; their best guess about quantity does not have any more authority behind it than our best guess, whereas their instinct about the position of the accent usually does. And the principle behind Herodian's rules is that words with the same suffix normally have the same accentuation; standardization in the shape of accents applied to a particular suffix is part of following those rules.

Unfortunately, however, scholars do not agree about how (or sometimes even whether) to standardize accent shape. Overall the circumflex is more popular than the acute for -ατος in ancient texts, but there is considerable variation. For example, the LSJ supplement has δηποτᾶτος and ληγᾶτος, *LBG* has δεπουτάτος, κουμουλάτος, and λεγάτος, *DGE* has δηπουτᾶτος, Lampe (1961) has δηπουτᾶτος but ληγάτος, Cervenka-Ehrenstrasser (2000: 237) has δηπουτᾶτος, Daris (1991a) has δηπουτᾶτος and κουμουλᾶτος, Sophocles (1887) has δηπουτᾶτος, κουμουλᾶτος, and ληγᾶτος, and Meyer (1895: 38) has ληγᾶτος. LSJ (which does not contain these three words) almost always has -ᾶτος but uses an acute on Γαισάται from *gaesātī* (compare the *TLL*'s Γαισᾶται).

5.3 ANCIENT EVIDENCE

There is in fact some ancient evidence for the accentuation of Latin loanwords, though it has been overlooked by almost all scholars in both these debates: one accented papyrus containing a Latin loanword, and several relevant pronouncements by ancient grammarians.

5.3.1 Accented papyrus

The accented form κορρηκτῶρι (a title in the dative singular) occurs on a sixth-century documentary papyrus fragment (P.Vindob. G 21595.6, Benaissa 2011: 241). This is the Latin accent (*corrēctórī*), and the spelling with ω reflects the Latin quantity of the accented vowel. The expected Greek form would have been κορρήκτορι, like ῥήτορι 'orator', σημάντορι 'commander', or ἀμύντορι 'defender' (Probert 2003: 88); the Greek and Latin accents coincided in the nominative (*corréctor* vs ῥήτωρ) but not in the oblique cases, and the vowel quantities never coincided. By the sixth century there was no longer any difference in pronunciation between o and ω, but the writer of this papyrus probably knew what he was doing in using ω, as the fragment contains no spelling mistakes. The circumflex indicates that the writer considered the final -ι to be short: it is not the Latin dative singular ending but the Greek one, as would be expected for a loanword that had been part of Greek for two centuries by the time this papyrus was written.

Papyri containing accents are normally literary texts, composed in forms of Greek that would have been difficult to comprehend at the time the papyrus was written; the accents were provided

---

[21] Cf. Wackernagel (1926: 57). This particular inconsistency cannot be due to the dates at which the words were borrowed, as both κεντουρίων and λεγεών were probably borrowed in the first century BC.

to help the reader divide up words in *scriptio continua* and to disambiguate potentially misleading clusters of letters. Documentary papyri were written in varieties of Greek more familiar to their intended readers and therefore rarely contain any accents, so this papyrus is unusual.[22] And the reason for the unusual accent must have to do with the word κορρηκτῶρι, not the text more generally, for this fragment does not include any other accents: the accented syllables of twelve other words are clearly visible and do not bear accent marks.

Κορρήκτωρ is rare in papyri; the only other example comes from the fourth century (κορρηκτορος, *P.Oxy.* LXIII.4385.9). Therefore the purpose of the accent here may have been to help the reader identify the word, though documentary papyri often contain rare words that are left unaccented and it is hard to see how else a reader might have been tempted to divide the words in this line.[23] Another possibility is that the accent was meant to help the reader identify the form as a dative, rather than the nominative κορρήκτωρ – though given that the word was preceded by an article in the dative and an adjective in the dative, a Greek speaker would probably have been expecting the noun also to be in the dative. A third possibility, unlikely but perhaps not to be completely ruled out, is that the writer was a stickler for what he saw as the correct pronunciation of this title, i.e. pronunciation with the Latin accent, and that he wrote the accent in order to cause the recipient to pronounce κορρηκτῶρι that way when reading the text out loud. If the first or second possibility is right, this papyrus is evidence that κορρηκτῶρι normally had a Latinate accent in the sixth century, but if the third is right, the papyrus may be evidence that the accent was disputed. Regardless of the motivation for the accent mark, however, it must show that two centuries after this word was borrowed at least some Greek speakers pronounced it with a Latinate accent in an oblique case. The papyrus also shows that Greek speakers used circumflex accents on loanwords in circumstances where they would have used a circumflex on a native Greek word.

5.3.2 *Herodian's pronouncements*

The second-century (AD) grammarian Herodian was the main ancient authority on accentuation. His works are largely lost in their original form, but a long epitome by the writer now known as 'pseudo-Arcadius' includes pronouncements about the accents of a number of Latin words and names, which are underlined in the quotations below.[24] In two passages an explicit distinction is made between the accentuation of Latin loanwords and that of native Greek words with similar terminations; in both cases the loanwords preserve their Latin accents.

> 5 Τὰ εἰς ΝΑ μονογενῆ βαρύνεται· *Κύννα* (ἡ πόρνη), Ἄννα, γέννα, χλαῖνα, εἰ μὴ κατὰ πάθος γένοιτο, Ἀθηνᾶ, μνᾶ. τὰ δὲ Ἰταλικὰ προπερισπῶνται· <u>Σαβῖνα</u>, <u>Φαυστῖνα</u>, <u>Ἰουστῖνα</u>, <u>Κωνσταντῖνα</u>. (Ps.-Arcadius 237.11–13 Roussou, cf. Hdn. *Pros.Cath.* III.1.256.1–5, 258.18–19)

Words ending in -να, when they have only one gender [i.e. when they are nouns], have recessive accents, as Κύννα (the name of the prostitute), Ἄννα, γέννα, χλαῖνα, unless the -να ending arises from a change, as in Ἀθηνᾶ and μνᾶ. But Latin words [in this category] have a circumflex on the penultimate syllable: Σαβῖνα, Φαυστῖνα, Ἰουστῖνα, Κωνσταντῖνα.

> 6 Τὰ εἰς ΕΡΝΟΣ Ἰταλιωτικὰ παροξύνεται· <u>Φαλέρνος</u>, <u>Πατέρνος</u>. (Ps.-Arcadius 193.12 Roussou, cf. Hdn. *Pros.Cath.* III.1.175.25, followed by more examples taken from Stephanus of Byzantium)

Latin words ending in -ερνος have an acute accent on the penultimate syllable: Φαλέρνος, Πατέρνος.

In a third passage a Latin loan is stated to be an exception to a Greek accentuation tendency, but its Latin etymology is not given as the reason:

> 7 Τὰ εἰς ΣΟΣ δισύλλαβα παραληγόμενα διφθόγγῳ ὀξύνεται, ὅτε ἐπιθετικὰ εἴη, ἢ ἐπὶ πόλεων κεῖται·

---

[22] It is not unique, however: a few other late antique documentary texts contain accents, usually circumflexes (Fournet 1994: 421–2 with n. 34, 2009: 36–7).

[23] The line probably read [τωλα]μπροτατωκορρηκτῶριτ [ησαυγουσταμνικης], i.e. τῷ λαμπροτάτῳ κορρηκτῶρι τῆς Αὐγουσταμνικῆς.

[24] Many more such pronouncements can be found in Lentz's reconstruction of Herodian's works (*Grammatici Graeci* volumes III.I and III.II), but those do not necessarily go back to Herodian (cf. Dickey 2007: 76).

Παισός (πόλις), *Λουσός, Πραισός.* Ἔτι ὀξύνεται καὶ τὰ ἐπιθετικά· *βλαισός.* τὸ μέντοι *Ναῖσος* βαρύνεται, καὶ *Βλαῖσος* (τὸ κύριον) καὶ τὸ γαῖσος (προσηγορικόν, εἶδος δόρατος ὄν). (Ps.-Arcadius 209.5–9 Roussou, cf. Hdn. *Pros.Cath.* III.1.206.16–17, 23, 25–6, 207.1–5)

Two-syllable words in -σος with a diphthong in the penultimate syllable have an acute accent on the final syllable when they are adjectives, or when they are used for cities: Παισός (the city), Λουσός, Πραισός. And the adjectives also have an acute on the final syllable: βλαισός. But Ναῖσος has a recessive accent, and Βλαῖσος (the name) and γαῖσος (a common noun, being a kind of spear).

On the other hand, two passages show Latin words re-accented to follow the Greek tendencies (*Marcéllus* changing to Μάρκελλος and *Rómŭlus* changing to Ῥωμύλος):

8 Τὰ εἰς ΛΛΟΣ πολυσύλλαβα, ὁποίῳ φωνήεντι παραλήγει πλὴν τοῦ Α, προπαροξύνεται· *Μύσκελλος,* Μάρκελλος, *Κύριλλος, Σόφιλλος, δόριλλος.* (Ps.-Arcadius 181.7–9 Roussou, cf. Hdn. *Pros.Cath.* III.1.158.25–7)

Polysyllabic words ending in -λλος, having any vowel except α in the penultimate syllable, have an acute accent on the third syllable from the end: Μύσκελλος, Μάρκελλος, Κύριλλος, Σόφιλλος, δόριλλος.

9 Τὰ διὰ τοῦ ΥΛΟΣ τρισύλλαβα προσηγορικὰ ἢ κύρια, εἰ ἄρχοιτο ἀπὸ φύσει μακρᾶς, παροξύνεται· *κρωβύλος, κηρύλος, Αἰσχύλος,* Ῥωμύλος. (Ps.-Arcadius 184.1–3 Roussou, cf. Hdn. *Pros.Cath.* III.1.163.14–16)

Words of three syllables ending in -υλος, whether common nouns or proper names, if they begin with a syllable containing a long vowel, have an acute accent on the penultimate syllable: κρωβύλος, κηρύλος, Αἰσχύλος, Ῥωμύλος.

Also in this category may be *fória* changing to φορειά, though in this case the Latin etymology is not completely certain:

10 Τὰ γινόμενα ἀπὸ τοῦ ΕΥΩ παροξύνεται· *ἑρμηνεία, βασιλεία, δουλεία, κολακεία, παιδεία* (ἡ παίδευσις, παιδιὰ δὲ τὸ παίγνιον). τὸ δὲ *παρειά* καὶ φορειά (τὸ βοῦρκος) καὶ *ἀρειά* (ἡ ἀπειλή) ὀξύνονται· οὐ γὰρ ἀπὸ τῶν διὰ τοῦ ΕΥΩ. (Ps.-Arcadius 239.5–8 Roussou, cf. Hdn. *Pros.Cath.* III.1.291.7–8, 14–16)

Words derived from verbs in -εύω have an acute accent on the penultimate syllable: ἑρμηνεία, βασιλεία, δουλεία, κολακεία, παιδεία (meaning 'education', but 'game' is παιδιά). But παρειά and φορειά ('mud') and ἀρειά ('threat') have an acute accent on the final syllable; for they are not derived from verbs in -εύω.

In most passages, however, Latin words fit the Greek pattern without changing their accents (*cúmŭlus, Latínus, cámpus, Néro, Népos*):[25]

11 Τὰ εἰς ΛΟΣ ὑπερδισύλλαβα παραληγόμενα τῇ διὰ τοῦ Υ διφθόγγῳ προπαροξύνεται· *δίαυλος, ἴουλος,* κούμουλος, *ὕπουλος.* (Ps.-Arcadius 185.16–17 Roussou, cf. Hdn. *Pros.Cath.* III.1.165.21–3)

Words of more than two syllables ending in -λος with an υ diphthong in the penultimate syllable have an acute accent on the third syllable from the end: δίαυλος, ἴουλος, κούμουλος, ὕπουλος.

12 Τὰ εἰς ΙΝΟΣ τὸ Ι μακρὸν ἔχοντα κύρια ἢ ἐθνικὰ ἢ ἐπιθετικὰ ἢ ὑποκοριστικῶν ἔννοιαν ἔχοντα προπερισπῶνται· *Φιλῖνος, Κρατῖνος, Ἐχῖνος* (τὸ κύριον), Λατῖνος, *Λεοντῖνος, Ῥηγῖνος, Μαμερτῖνος.*

---

[25] There are also a few passages prescribing the accents of Greek derivatives of Latin loanwords, which (as one would expect) always have Greek accentuation: Τὰ εἰς ΜΑΙΟΣ προπερισπᾶται, εἰ μὴ διαστολὴ γένοιτο κυρίου ἢ εἴη σύνθετον· *πυγμαῖος,* Ῥωμαῖος, *Πτολεμαῖος, Ἑρμαῖος.* 'Words ending in -μαιος have a circumflex on the penultimate syllable, unless they are accented differently in order to distinguish them from a proper name or unless they are compounds: πυγμαῖος, Ῥωμαῖος, Πτολεμαῖος, Ἑρμαῖος' (Ps.-Arcadius 166.4–5 Roussou, cf. Hdn. *Pros.Cath.* III.1.133.10–11, 13, 16–17). Ἔτι τὰ διὰ τοῦ ΔΑΙΟΣ προπερισπᾶται· *Ἰουδαῖος, χυδαῖος, Χαλδαῖος.* Ἔτι τὰ διὰ τοῦ ΑΙΟΣ ἐθνικά· *Ἀθηναῖος, Θηβαῖος,* Ῥωμαῖος. 'Also words ending in -δαιος have a circumflex on the penultimate syllable: Ἰουδαῖος, χυδαῖος, Χαλδαῖος. Also ethnics in -αιος: Ἀθηναῖος, Θηβαῖος, Ῥωμαῖος' (Ps.-Arcadius 166.11–13 Roussou, cf. Hdn. *Pros.Cath.* III.1.130.7–8, 132.23). Τὰ ἀπὸ τῶν εἰς ΟΣ δισυλλάβων προπερισπωμένων προπαροξύνεται· *ζῆλος ἀρίζηλος, δοῦλος σύνδουλος, δοῦπος ἐρίγδουπος.* σεσημείωται τὸ *οἰκουρός* καὶ *κηπουρός.* ἔτι καὶ τὰ ὑπερδισύλλαβα· Ῥωμαῖος φιλορώμαιος, *Ἀθηναῖος φιλαθήναιος.* 'Compounds of disyllabic words ending in -ος with a circumflex on the penultimate syllable have an acute on the third syllable from the end: ζῆλος yields ἀρίζηλος, δοῦλος yields σύνδουλος, δοῦπος yields ἐρίγδουπος. But οἰκουρός and κηπουρός are exceptions. The same is true for compounds of words more than two syllables long: Ῥωμαῖος yields φιλορώμαιος, Ἀθηναῖος yields φιλαθήναιος' (Ps.-Arcadius 222.1–4 Roussou, cf. Hdn. *Pros. Cath.* III.1.228.17–20).

(Ps.-Arcadius 197.7–9 Roussou, cf. Hdn. *Pros. Cath.* III.1.183.17–19, 29)

Words ending in -ινος with long ι, whether they are proper names or ethnics or adjectives or have a diminutive sense, have a circumflex on the penultimate syllable: Φιλῖνος, Κρατῖνος, Ἐχῖνος (the name), <u>Λατῖνος</u>, Λεοντῖνος, Ῥηγῖνος, Μαμερτῖνος.

13 Τὰ εἰς ΠΟΣ δισύλλαβα παραλήγοντα διχρόνῳ καταλήγοντι εἰς Μ ἢ Π βαρύνεται· ἵππος, <u>κάμπος</u>, Λάμπος (τὸ κύριον· λαμπός δὲ τὸ ἐπίθετον). τὸ δὲ *καρπός* ὀξύνεται. (Ps.-Arcadius 199.1–3 Roussou, cf. Hdn. *Pros.Cath.* III.1.187.12–13, 15–16)

Words of two syllables ending in -πος with a penultimate syllable having the vowel α, ι, or υ and ending in μ or π have recessive accents: ἵππος, <u>κάμπος</u>, Λάμπος (the proper name; but the adjective is λαμπός). But καρπός has an acute on the final syllable.

14 Τὰ εἰς ΡΩΝ μὴ παραληγόμενα τῇ ΟΙ ἢ ΑΙ διφθόγγῳ, εἰ μὴ τοπικὰ εἴη ἢ πόλει ὁμωνυμεῖ, βαρύνονται· Θήρων, <u>Νέρων</u>, γέρων, τήρων. (Ps.-Arcadius 125.6–7 Roussou, cf. Hdn. *Pros.Cath.* III.1.35.9–11)

Words ending in -ρων that do not have an οι or αι diphthong in the penultimate syllable are accented recessively unless they are place names or identical to city names: Θήρων, <u>Νέρων</u>, γέρων, τήρων.

15 Τὰ εἰς ΩΣ ἁπλᾶ διὰ τοῦ ΤΟΣ κλινόμενα, εἰ μακρᾷ παραλήγοι, ἢ μετοχικὰ ὄντα ὀξύνεται· εὐρώς, ἱδρώς, ἀραρώς, ὑπερδεδιώς. εἰ δὲ ἰαμβικὰ ὑπάρχοι διὰ τοῦ ΤΟΣ κλινόμενα βαρύνεται· γέλως, ἔρως, Νέπως. τὸ δὲ εἴλως ἀπὸ τοῦ ἕλως. (Ps.-Arcadius 232.3–6 Roussou, cf. Hdn. *Pros. Cath.* III.1.244.14–18)

Non-compounded words ending in -ως and declined with a genitive in -τος have an acute accent on the final syllable if they have a long vowel in the penultimate syllable or are participles: εὐρώς, ἱδρώς, ἀραρώς, ὑπερδεδιώς. But iambic words declined with -τος have recessive accents: γέλως, ἔρως, <u>Νέπως</u>. And εἴλως comes from ἕλως.

5.4 CONCLUSIONS

Many loanwords came with a Latin accent that happened to match Greek tendencies; those retained their Latin accentuations in Greek. Some had a Latin accent that was impossible in Greek; those changed their accents. The ones whose Latin accent was unusual but not impossible could follow either path: words in -ῖνα and -έρνος retained their Latin accents, as did γαῖσος, but at least some words in -λλος and -υλος changed their accents. Loanwords could sometimes retain a Latinate accent in oblique cases even when the accentuation of the nominative happened to match Greek tendencies. Therefore there is no mechanical solution to the problem of accentuation for loanwords; it is neither correct to give them all Latin accents nor correct to give them all Greek accents. For each individual word one has to look at all the available evidence before making a decision; sometimes there is not enough evidence to justify either decision properly, but that problem is real and cannot be eliminated by positing rules that did not exist in antiquity.

There is also another difficulty. Both ancient and modern scholars normally treat words in groups by termination, and these groupings seem to allow extrapolation from words whose accents are known to ones about whose accentuation there is no surviving evidence. But such extrapolation is risky, for most accentuation tendencies are universal neither among native Greek words – in Herodian's work most rules are followed by lists of exceptions – nor among loanwords (cf. the variation between κεντουρίων and λεγεών, §5.2.3).

Moreover, there is likely to have been some accentual distinction between codeswitches and loanwords. Parallels from modern languages would suggest that the more integrated a Latin word became in Greek, the greater was the likelihood of its acquiring a Greek accent. But the accents of the non-integrated Latin words are usually irrecoverable: these are precisely the words for which no actual evidence, such as a prescription by an ancient grammarian or appearance in a Byzantine manuscript, is likely to exist.

6

WHICH LATIN SUFFIXES WERE BORROWED INTO GREEK?

Greek is often argued to have borrowed a number of suffixes from Latin, and although borrowed suffixes are not loanwords, such claims require careful attention here for two reasons. If Greek speakers themselves created words with Latin suffixes, some words traditionally considered loanwords may be Greek formations instead. Moreover, suffix borrowing reveals a higher level of linguistic influence than the minimum needed for loanword borrowing and thus provides important information about the linguistic context within which the loanwords were borrowed.[1]

The borrowing of suffixes is not inherently unusual; it has occurred in many modern languages. For example, English borrowed the French suffix -ette from pairs of loanwords like 'cigarette' and 'cigar', and used it to form words such as 'kitchenette' and 'diskette'; although these are not French loanwords in English, they reveal French influence in another fashion and help us understand the way French loanwords have been processed in English.[2] Likewise, Latin occasionally borrowed suffixes from Greek.[3]

6.1 -άριος FROM -ĀRIUS

The clearest case of suffix borrowing is that of -arius, which was indubitably taken from Latin into Greek at an early period, though the Greek version did not function exactly like the Latin.[4] Latin -arius was essentially an adjective-forming suffix with three genders, for example adversarius, -a, -um 'hostile' from adversus 'opposed', necessarius, -a, -um 'necessary' from necesse 'essential', and nefarius, -a, -um 'wicked' from nefas 'wicked act'.[5] The masculine could be substantivized and often designated a person professionally connected with the root word, for example librarius, -i 'scribe' or 'bookseller' from liber 'book', quadrigarius, -i 'charioteer' from quadriga 'four-horse chariot', and sagittarius, -i 'archer' from sagitta 'arrow'. Other meanings for the substantivized masculine were also possible, as with adversarius, -i 'opponent', necessarius, -i 'connection', and denarius, -i 'coin worth ten asses' (from deni 'ten each'). Greek -άριος, however, was almost completely restricted to forming masculine nouns indicating professions or occupations: πλακουντάριος 'cake-maker' from πλακοῦς 'cake', ὑποδηματάριος 'sandal-maker' from ὑπόδημα 'sandal', τυμπανάριος 'drummer' from τύμπανον 'kettledrum', etc.

The borrowing process is fairly easy to ascertain. Greek borrowed many Latin words

---

[1] See Thomason and Kaufmann's borrowing scale (e.g. Thomason 2001: 70–1), where suffix borrowing is associated with level 3, 'more intense contact'.

[2] See OED s.v. -ette, Coleman (1975: 106), and for other borrowed suffixes in English Miller (2012: 177–83, 216–18, 231–2), Durkin (2014: 327–31), Schulte (2019); for the phenomenon more generally Gusmani (1981–3: I.111–38). Pairs of words revealing how the suffix functioned in its original language are only necessary when an existing suffix is borrowed more or less intact; new suffixes can always be created in the borrowing language by resegmentation (e.g. English -thon from 'Marathon', -burger from 'hamburger'), but those are unlikely to match the original suffix well (Gusmani 1981–3: I.116–20, 133).

[3] The best example is -issa from -ισσα, but there are also occasional productive uses of -smus from -σμός and -(is)ta from -(ισ)της (André 1971: 60, 65, 74, 101, 107–10, 130–1). The Latin suffixes -īnus and -(t)icus appear to have been influenced by Greek (André 1971: 131–2).

[4] Filos (2008: 263–74), Palmer (1945: 7, 48–9), J. N. Adams (2003: 495), Cavenaile (1952: 201–2), Cameron (1931: 234), Coleman (2007: 796), Browning (1983: 39), Buck and Petersen (1945: 47), Zilliacus (1937: 312, 334–5), Immisch (1885: 291), Psaltes (1913: 258–60), Sophocles (1887: 36), Dieterich (1928: 111–12), Tonnet (1993: 105). The suffix is still productive in modern Greek, where it is written -άρις or -άρης: Andriotis (1967: 33), Eleftheriades (1993: 3, 64), Meyer (1895: 73–4), Hatzidakis (1892: 183–4).

[5] Leumann (1977: §277), Nichols (1929).

containing -*arius* (§4.2.4.1 n. 50), starting at an early date. By the end of the first century AD there were fifteen loanwords ending in -άριος: ἀρκάριος 'treasurer', βενεφικιάριος (a title), βηξιλλάριος (a military rank), βικάριος 'deputy', γαλεάριος 'soldier's servant', δουπλικάριος 'soldier receiving double pay', Ἰανουάριος 'January', κελλάριος 'cellarer', κορνικουλάριος 'assistant', λεγεωνάριος 'legionary', νοτάριος 'notary', ῥητιάριος (a type of gladiator), σικάριος 'bandit', τεσσαράριος (a military officer), and Φεβρουάριος 'February'. Of these only the month names functioned as adjectives in Greek; the others were all effectively masculine nouns indicating titles or occupations. And in two of them the suffix was easily identifiable because a related word without it had also been borrowed: λεγεωνάριος with λεγεών 'legion' and βηξιλλάριος with βήξιλλον 'cavalry standard'. By the end of the first century AD, therefore, Greek speakers had a set of loanwords that would have made it easy for them to extract a suffix -άριος that formed masculine nouns indicating occupations.

That they did so can be demonstrated by the large group of words indicating professions or occupations that are clearly formed from Greek roots and -άριος. The two earliest date to the first century AD: μηχανάριος 'engineer', 'mechanic', from μηχανή 'machine', and σμαραγδάριος 'emerald-worker' from σμάραγδος 'emerald'.[6] Others quickly followed, including πορθμάριος 'ferryman', from πορθμός 'ferry'; ἀχυράριος, a person with some job involving chaff, from ἄχυρον 'chaff'; σκοπελάριος 'watchtower guard', from σκόπελος 'lookout place'; φαρμαξάριος 'metal-temperer', from φάρμαξις 'treatment of metals'; λακκάριος 'cistern-keeper', from λάκκος 'cistern'; μαγγανάριος 'conjurer', from μάγγανον 'means of charming'; ταρσικάριος 'weaver of Tarsian fabrics', from Ταρσικός 'of Tarsus'; ταπητάριος 'carpet-weaver', from τάπης 'carpet'; νομικάριος, an official, from νομικός 'relating to laws', etc.[7]

Can we be sure that these words really were formed within Greek, as opposed to being additional borrowings from Latin? None is attested in Latin; although Latin words for which no Latin attestations now survive do occasionally turn up in Greek (§8.1.7), they are rare, so when a large group of words exists in Greek but not in Latin, it is unlikely that they are all loanwords for which no Latin evidence survives. Moreover these words are all formed from Greek roots and therefore would have been easier for Greek speakers to create than for Latin speakers. Again, this characteristic is not by itself proof of Greek origin, for Latin speakers were capable of attaching -*arius* to etymologically Greek words, and Greek speakers were capable of borrowing the words thus formed. But when words are both unattested in Latin and formed from Greek roots, and particularly when many words with the same suffix share those characteristics, the conclusion that the suffix was being applied by Greek speakers becomes inescapable.

The fact that -άριος was borrowed into Greek means, of course, that the etymologies of many words in -άριος are uncertain. Words with Greek roots and -άριος cannot automatically be assumed to be Greek formations; some are attested in Latin, and although Latin speakers often borrowed Greek words and could have borrowed ones in -άριος, sometimes it is clear that a particular word was in fact created in Latin. For example, Latin speakers borrowed χάρτης 'papyrus' to form *charta* 'papyrus', of which they made a diminutive *chartula* 'piece of papyrus', from which they formed *chartularius* 'archivist', which Greek speakers then borrowed as χαρτουλάριος 'registrar'. The Latin origin of χαρτουλάριος is clear both from the -ουλ- and from the meaning: had Greek speakers themselves added -άριος to χάρτης, the result would have been χαρτάριος 'papyrus-seller' (which may also be attested). But some other words in -άριος with Greek roots contain no clues

---

[6] Μηχανάριος e.g. *P.Lond.* 1.131*.51 etc. (I AD); cf. Palmer (1945: 7 n. 1), Cavenaile (1952: 201). Σμαραγδάριος e.g. *O.Did.* 343 line 5 (I AD, spelled ζμαρακτάριος).

[7] Πορθμάριος e.g. *O.Amst.* 28.6 (II AD); cf. Cavenaile (1952: 202). Ἀχυράριος e.g. *O.Stras.* I.446.1 (II AD); cf. Cavenaile (1952: 201). Σκοπελάριος e.g. *O.Florida* 6.8 (II AD). Φαρμαξάριος e.g. *O.Claud.* I.15.4 (II AD); cf. editors *ad loc.* and *O.Claud.* IV pp. 12, 260. Λακκάριος e.g. *O.Claud.*

III.446.2 (II AD); cf. *DÉLG s.v.* 1 λάκκος, LSJ. Μαγγανάριος e.g. *P.Oxy.* VII.1050.19 (II/III AD). Ταρσικάριος e.g. *P.Oxy.* XIV.1765.2 (III AD) and *I.Alexandrie imp.* 99.4 (III AD), perhaps already in II AD (*P.Bodl.* 1.27.19); cf. Cavenaile (1952: 201), LSJ, LSJ suppl. Ταπητάριος e.g. *P.Oslo* III.144.6 (III AD); cf. LSJ, *DÉLG s.v.* τάπης, Cavenaile (1952: 201). Νομικάριος e.g. *P.Panop.Beatty* 1.252 (III AD); cf. Cavenaile (1952: 202).

to their etymologies: they may have been created in Latin and borrowed into Greek, or created in Greek and borrowed into Latin, or even created independently in both languages. These include ἀποκρισιάριος 'envoy', ultimately from ἀπόκρισις 'answer' but perhaps via *apocrisiarius* 'envoy'; καμηλάριος 'camel-driver', ultimately from κάμηλος 'camel' but perhaps via *camelarius* 'camel-driver'; and σπαθάριος 'guardsman', ultimately from σπάθη 'broad blade' but perhaps via *spatarius* 'man armed with a broad-bladed sword'.

Words with Latin stems + -άριος can also be problematic. It cannot be assumed *a priori* that all such words were originally formed in Latin, for once the -άριος suffix had become productive in Greek, it could in principle be attached to any Greek word, including those that had originated as Latin loanwords. As we have seen with the Latin–Latin compounds (§4.5), Greek words with multiple Latin components were sometimes constructed by Greek speakers who had borrowed all those components individually. Some words in -άριος with Latin roots must have been formed within Greek, because they not only are unattested in Latin but also contain evidence of the root having been altered within Greek. Thus κελλαρικάριος 'cellarer' can only come from κελλαρικός (formed in Greek by adding -ικός to κελλάριον from *cellarium*, or by adding -ικός directly to *cellarius*) + -άριος, and συγκελλάριος 'comrade' (a calque of *contubernalis*) is almost certainly from σύν 'with' + κέλλα 'room' (from *cella*) + -άριος.[8] Λιβερνάριος 'sailor on a *liburna* ship' probably comes from λίβερνος (from *liburna*) + -άριος, though derivation from unattested *liburnarius* cannot be ruled out. Σαλτάριος 'forester' may be a Greek formation from σάλτον 'forest' (from *saltus*) + -άριος, because although *saltuarius* 'forester' occurs in Latin, the Greek form is usually σαλτάριος rather than σαλτουάριος. Several other words in -άριος with attested Latin equivalents may be Greek formations because the Latin is rare, much later than the Greek, and/or has a different meaning.[9]

Greek speakers were aware that -άριος was a Latin borrowing. In the Byzantine period some earlier texts were rewritten with a systematic effort to eliminate Latin loanwords, and the resulting purge removed not only genuine loanwords, but also words formed by adding -άριος to Greek roots.[10]

It has been suggested that Greek speakers also used -άριος to form adjectives,[11] but the evidence for such use is very weak. The potential examples are all very rare: βωλητάριος 'mushroom-shaped', πανθιωνάριος apparently 'in the form of the Pantheon', and χαλκισκάριος (meaning unknown). But βωλητάριος may come from *boletar* 'vessel for holding mushrooms' + -ιος, and the other two are poorly understood; indeed χαλκισκάριος is probably not an adjective at all.[12]

6.2 -αρία FROM -ĀRIA

Once the suffix -άριος was established for masculine occupational terms a feminine counterpart -αρία emerged. It is unlikely that this suffix was separately borrowed from Latin, for Greek speakers would have had no difficulty in spontaneously forming feminines in -αρία from masculines in -άριος. Indeed Greek occupational terms in -αρία usually have masculine counterparts in -άριος, so that even when they also have Latin equivalents in -*aria* the Greek feminines may be Greek derivatives of the masculines rather than direct borrowings from Latin.[13] I can find only one clear example of this -αρία being applied as

---

[8] A compound of σύν and κελλάριος 'cellarer' (from *cellarius*) is possible but would most likely have meant 'fellow cellarer'. Note also rare βαλνικάριος 'bath attendant' (*balneum* + -ικός + -άριος).

[9] Ἀννωνάριος (ἀννῶνα ← *annona*?), ἀστιάριος (ἄστη ← *hasta*?), ἰσικιάριος (ἰσίκιον ← *isicium*?).

[10] Zilliacus (1937: 334–5), listing ἀποκρισιάριος, βιβλιοθηκάριος, δευτεράριος, ἑβδομάριος, ἑλληνιστάριος, προσμονάριος, and σπαθάριος.

[11] Palmer (1945: 32). Modern Greek has an adjectival suffix -άρης that may go back to -*arius* (Andriotis 1967: 33) but need not be an ancient creation. Enough loanword adjectives in -άριος, -αρία, -άριον survived into the Byzantine period to enable an adjectival suffix to be derived at any point: ἐξτραορδινάριος, καυσάριος, ὀρδινάριος 2, etc.

[12] Cf. LSJ *s.v.* χαλκισκάριον; πανθιωνάριος occurs only at *P.Oxy.* VII.1026.21 and χαλκισκάριος only at *P.Lond.* II.191.8. For βωλητάριος see §3.2.

[13] Thus κουβικουλαρία could come either from *cubicularia* or from κουβικουλάριος; similarly rare κελλαρία and προπιναρία. Probably derived from the masculine, since no Latin feminine is attested, are rare κονδιταρία, μαντηλαρία, and πλουμαρία; probably borrowed directly from Latin, since no Greek masculine is attested, is rare φωκαρία.

a suffix in its own right, without reference to a corresponding masculine, and that is on a Latin root: rare σιλιγνιαρία 'seller of siligo bread' was almost certainly formed from σιλίγνιον + -αρία. This example demonstrates that the suffix could be productive.

There may also be another suffix -αρία, one designating objects and abstractions.[14] Such a suffix is the obvious explanation for three rare words with Greek roots: παραθηκαρία 'receipt for an object entrusted' (παραθήκη 'object entrusted' + -αρία), σκοταρία 'darkness' (σκότος 'darkness' + -αρία), and ἐνδομαρία 'settlement' (ἐνδομέω 'build in' + -αρία). It has also been suggested as a component of five words with Latin roots, but these all have alternative etymologies not involving -αρία. Two are loanwords: δουκηναρία '200,000 sesterces' and πληναρία 'completeness' might come from *ducenti* 'two hundred' + -αρία and *plenus* 'full' + -αρία, but *ducenarius* 'owning or receiving 200,000 sesterces' (borrowed into Greek as δουκηνάριος around the same time as the first attestations of δουκηναρία) and *plenarius* 'complete' are more plausible sources. Three are rare words: ἀργενταρία 'box of silver', ἀρκλαρία 'money chest', and βρακαρία 'trousers' might come from *argentum* 'silver' + -αρία, *arcula* 'casket' + -αρία, and *bracae* 'trousers' + -αρία, but *argentaria* (*cista*) '(chest) for silver' and unattested **arclaria* and **bracaria* have also been suggested. Therefore none of the examples on Latin roots is fully convincing. The three with Greek roots, however, are harder to dismiss: those suggest that Greek speakers could in fact use -αρία as a productive suffix for objects and abstractions.

How was this -αρία created? Given its meaning it cannot be simply a Greek feminine of -άριος, but at the same time Greek speakers could not easily have extracted an independent suffix -αρία from the words they had borrowed from Latin or had derived by adding -ία to borrowings. Those words were ἀγραρία 'garrison', βικαρία 'office of deputy', προπριεταρία 'ownership', ῥιπαρία 'office of water-watchman', and φορμαρία, variant of φορμαλεία 'list of supplies' – plus δουκηναρία and πληναρία if their alternative etymologies are accepted. None of these belonged to a word pair

that would have facilitated extraction of a suffix -αρία as such; that is, none had a relative without the -αρία.[15] But three had well-established relatives in -άριος: βικάριος 'deputy', δουκηνάριος (a title), and ῥιπάριος 'water-watchman'. Once Greek speakers were aware of a suffix -άριος, it would not have been difficult for them to infer from these three pairs the idea that -αρία could be used instead of -άριος for an object or abstraction. That is probably what caused the formation of παραθηκαρία, σκοταρία, and ἐνδομαρία, but there is no evidence that this suffix ever became productive to a significant extent, perhaps because of the inherent ambiguity between it and the other -αρία.

6.3 -άριον FROM -ĀRIUM?

It is debated whether *-arium*, the neuter of *-arius*, was borrowed along with the masculine.[16] Such a borrowing would have been indistinguishable in form from the pre-existing Greek suffix -άριον,[17] and the two would not necessarily have been distinguishable in meaning either: although the original -άριον often had a diminutive force it

[14] Palmer (1945: 76); cf. Filos (2008: 302, 307–9).

[15] Ἀγρός 'field', βῖκος 'jar', ῥιπή 'throwing', φόρμη 'quality', and φορμός 'basket' are irrelevant because their meanings are so different.

[16] Palmer (1945: 13, 83–4) believes that *-arium* was borrowed and eventually caused 'the extinction of the native diminutive suffix -άριον'; cf. Browning (1983: 39), Meyer (1895: 74). But Petersen (1910: 261) believes that the only productive -άριον suffix in Greek was the native one, while Cameron (1931: 234) suggests that *-arium* was not borrowed but native -άριον became more productive because of the importation of *-arius*. Filos (2008: 339, cf. 331–41) argues that the borrowing of Latin words with *-arium* 'revitalised' the use of -άριον, resulting in a suffix with combined ancestry. Tonnet (1993: 105) believes that the question of a Latin origin for -άριον remains open.

[17] For this see Chantraine (1933: 74–5), Petersen (1910: 260–71). In the second century AD Herodian said that the Classical diminutives in -άριον had a short α and the Latin loanwords a long one: τὰ διὰ τοῦ -αριον ὑποκοριστικὰ παρὰ τοῖς παλαιοῖς Ἕλλησι συστέλλει τὸ α, ἱππάριον, φυτάριον, ἡ μέντοι νῦν συνήθεια ἀπὸ τῆς τῶν Ῥωμαίων διαλέκτου πολλὰ ἐπίσταται διὰ τοῦ -αριον ἐκτεταμένα, σουδάριον λέγουσα καὶ κελλάριον (Διχρ. III.II.13.22–5). Soon afterwards, however, the distinction between long and short α was lost, rendering the two suffixes identical in pronunciation as well as in spelling.

was probably not exclusively diminutive,[18] and moreover it is not clear *a priori* what meaning a Greek speaker would have thought -*arium* had. In Latin -*arium* was simply the neuter of the same adjective-forming suffix of which -*arius* was the masculine (§6.1), but the way Greek speakers reinterpreted -*arius* could have affected their view of -*arium*.

Despite these obstacles, some scholars believe they can identify words with a Latinate -άριον suffix, on the grounds that that suffix is the best explanation for Roman-period creations with Greek roots and an -άριον ending that is probably not diminutive. It is sometimes further specified that these words designate implements.[19] The best examples offered are βαλανάριον 'bath towel', γραφιάριον (meaning uncertain), δεξάριον (an ornament), καλαμάριον 'pen-case', μακελλάριον 'provision market', μαλλωτάριον 'sheepskin', and στρατιωτάριον 'sack of military stores'.[20]

A number of Latin loanwords probably acquired -άριον in Greek, and some attempts have been made to determine whether they received a Latinate or a purely Greek (i.e. diminutive) -άριον. The suffix in μουλάριον '(little) mule', οὐδωνάριον 'sock', and σικάριον 'dagger' might be diminutive, and the same applies to σκουτάριον 'shield', if that acquired -άριον at all (it could be a substantivized neuter of *scutarius*). Πιλάριον can refer to an eye-salve, a lead plaster, and a cap; it might be

diminutive in the 'cap' meaning but probably not in the others. But none of these words is certainly diminutive, so conceivably they could all have a Latinate -άριον suffix.[21]

Greek speakers would certainly have been able to identify a suffix -άριον as part of Latinate words. Many Latin loanwords ended in -άριον, not only ones that had ended in -*arium* in Latin but also some that had originally belonged to other paradigms (§4.2.4–5). And the suffix was well represented among early loanwords, with nine borrowed by the end of the first century AD.[22] The first word pair that would have allowed identification of the suffix, κοχλιάριον 'spoon (for eating snails)' and κοχλίας 'snail', was available from the first century BC – though such a pair may not have been needed, since Greek speakers already had the idea that -άριον could be a suffix. Probably the two suffixes simply merged in Greek, producing a single suffix with a wide range of applications. In the Byzantine period words in -άριον were perceived as foreign even if they had Greek roots;[23] that perception suggests that the merged suffix was eventually seen as Latinate.

Strictly speaking, therefore, Greek speakers probably did not borrow -άριον from Latin, but they apparently ended up thinking that they had done so.

---

[18] Petersen (1910: 260–71). In any case diminutives often lost their diminutive force in Hellenistic and Roman-period Greek: late Greek use of an originally diminutive suffix in a non-diminutive sense would not have to come from foreign influence (cf. Psaltes 1913: 271).

[19] Palmer (1945: 84), but note that Petersen (1910: 262–3) thinks the native Greek suffix could be used with this meaning, and some of his examples are too early to be Latinate. Other scholars have suggested very different meanings for the Latinate -άριον: Meyer (1895: 74) says that in modern Greek the descendant of the Latinate -άριον suffix is used particularly for indicating the place where something is, while Andriotis (1967: 33, 34) suggests that all non-diminutive modern Greek nouns in -άριο and many in -άρι derive from the Latinate suffix. Filos (2008: 340) sees the modern Greek descendant of the Latin suffix as referring most often to 'physical objects, body parts and animals', less often to the names of places and buildings and to 'colloquial abstract concepts'.

[20] Palmer (1945: 84); cf. LSJ and LSJ suppl. *s.vv.*, Cervenka-Ehrenstrasser (2000: 270), §3.2 *s.v.* (rare) γραφιάριον.

[21] Also rare ἀμπυλλάριον (meaning uncertain), βουρδωνάριον 'mule', γουβερνάριον 'rudder' (which Palmer 1945: 13, 84 sees as a prime example of the Latinate -άριον suffix, but in which Cervenka-Ehrenstrasser 2000: 217–18 sees the diminutive -άριον, apparently because γουβερνάριον is modelled on *gubernaculum* 'steering-oar', which has a Latin diminutive ending), ἰσικιάριον 'sausage', perhaps κεντρωνάριον 1 'case for κέντρωνες', κεντωνάριον 'patched garment', κρητάριον 1 'piece of chalk', μαππάριον 'napkin', perhaps μουστάριον (meaning uncertain), πουλβινάριον 'little cushion', perhaps προπινάριον 'jug', perhaps σικλάριον (meaning uncertain), τιτλάριον (a kind of writing tablet). But φακιάριον (variant of the loanword φακιάλιον 'facecloth') and its rare derivative σαβανοφακιάριον 'facecloth', cited in this context by Palmer (1945: 84), do not have a suffix at all; they come from *faciale* (§4.2.5, §4.4 n. 79).

[22] Αἰράριον, ἀσσάριον, δηνάριον, διάριον, κιβάριον, κοχλιάριον, πανάριον, πωμάριον, σουδάριον.

[23] Zilliacus (1937: 335) identifies κλινάριον, πλοιάριον, σκευοθηκάριον, στιχάριον, τομάριον, and τροπάριον as having been considered Latin words at that date.

6.4 -ιανός FROM -IĀNUS

The suffix -ianus was a relatively recent creation in Latin, where it emerged in the first century BC by resegmentation of names formed with the older -anus suffix: Aemili-anus (from Aemilius) became Aemil-ianus, Tulli-anus (from Tullius) became Tull-ianus, etc.[24] Among the earliest examples of productive use of -ianus in Latin are Milonianus 'supporter of Milo', Ciceronianus 'supporter of Cicero', and Caesarianus 'supporter of Caesar'. As these examples suggest, -ianus was usually attached to the name of a person to designate partisans, followers, or adherents of that person.

The suffix is generally agreed to have been borrowed into Greek in the first or early second century AD.[25] Χριστιανός 'Christian' was probably the loanword that served as the model (with Χριστός 'Christ', §10.4.2), and the first attestation of the suffix's productive use is probably Justin Martyr's mid-second-century explanation of the internal diversity of Christianity: καὶ εἰσιν αὐτῶν οἱ μέν τινες καλούμενοι Μαρκιανοί, οἱ δὲ Οὐαλεντινιανοί, οἱ δὲ Βασιλειδιανοί, οἱ δὲ Σατορνιλιανοί, καὶ ἄλλοι ἄλλῳ ὀνόματι.[26] 'And some of them are called Marcians, and some Valentinans, and some Basilidians, and some Saturninians, and other groups with other names.' By the time such a passage could be written the suffix must have been productive for quite a while. Another, though less likely, possibility is

that Χριστιανός was not the model for the suffix but its first productive use; in that case the borrowing would date to the first century AD, and the model would be hard to identify (§10.4.2).

As Justin Martyr's list of sects illustrates, -ιανός was very often attached to personal names and used to designate Christian sects and heresies. But a wider range of uses was available to be picked up from the loanwords in -ιανός, which included πραιτωριανός 'praetorian', βενετιανός 'supporter of the blue circus faction', καστρησιανός 'soldier of the frontier guard', etc. This wider range of possibilities was occasionally reflected in Greek formations in -ιανός, such as στρατηλατιανός 'officer of the staff of the στρατηλάτης' (στραηλάτης 'commander' + -ιανός), εἰδωλιανός 'idol-worshipper' (εἴδωλον 'idol' + -ιανός), μαρτυριανοί 'Martyrians' (a sect, from μάρτυς 'martyr' + -ιανός), and ἀνθρωπομορφιανοί 'those who attribute human form to God' (ἀνθρωπόμορφος 'of human form' + -ιανός).[27] The rare Latinism κορτιανός 'member of a cohort', probably formed from co(ho)rtalis + -ιανός or κοόρτη + -ιανός, most likely shows Greek speakers attaching -ιανός to a Latin word other than a name.

6.5 -ᾶτον FROM -ĀTUM

Byzantine and modern Greek have a neuter suffix -ᾶτο(ν) designating items of food and drink, which is generally agreed to derive from Latin -atum, the perfect passive participle neuter ending for first-conjugation verbs.[28] Synchronically, Byzantine and modern words with this suffix are substantivized neuters of adjectives in -ᾶτος (for which see §6.6), but historically the neuter appears to be a separate and earlier borrowing: for several centuries in late antiquity Greek speakers

[24] Leumann (1977: §295.2).

[25] Chantraine (1933: 197), Buck and Petersen (1945: 261), Palmer (1945: 17, 46), André (1971: 101), Blass et al. (1979 §5.2), Browning (1983: 39), J. N. Adams (2003: 419–20, 495), Coleman (2007: 797), Filos (2008: 274–9), Bubenik (2014: 305), Psaltes (1913: 303–5). The accent shift from -iánus to -ιανός was probably caused by the general tendency of Greek adjectives in -νος to be finally accented, though Χριστιανός is effectively a noun (Probert 2003: 94–5). Later in the Roman period -ιανός was commonly used by Greek speakers in Asia Minor to form patronymics and even personal names that were not patronymics (Corsten 2010).

[26] Dialogus cum Tryphone 35.6 Goodspeed; similar concentrations of words in -ιανός can be found e.g. in Eus. HE 4.22.5 and Epiph. Pan. 1.158–9. A possible earlier example of productive use is Λευκολλιανός 'of Lucullus' in the phrase οἱ Λευκολλιανοὶ κῆποι 'the gardens of Lucullus' in Plut. Luc. 39.2. Λευκολλιανός has a Latin base, but the word as a whole may not have been borrowed from Latin, since the Latin for those gardens was horti Luculliani (e.g. Tacitus, Annales 11.32.1).

[27] For στρατηλατιανός see LSJ suppl., Palmer (1945: 46); for εἰδωλιανός Lampe (1961), LBG; for μαρτυριανοί e.g. Epiph. Pan. 1.159.12; for ἀνθρωπομορφιανοί Lampe (1961). These all date to IV AD or later; the only potential early example of -ιανός attached by Greek speakers to a root other than a name is μαγιανός 'magic', which occurs on two first-century papyri (cf. LSJ; LSJ suppl.; Palmer 1945: 46; Browning 1983: 40). But it is more likely that this comes from μαγεία 'magic' + -ανος (with the usual late Greek confusion of ει and ι) than from Μάγος 'Magian' + -ιανός.

[28] Maravela-Solbakk (2010), Meyer (1895: 75), Diethart (1988: 55, 58–9), Hatzidakis (1892: 184). Diethart (2006) discusses other functions of -ᾶτον in Byzantine Greek.

could form nouns in -ᾶτον but not (yet) adjectives in -ᾶτος. The borrowing process for this suffix has previously been inadequately explained; it is challenging to reconstruct because a high percentage of the Greek words involved have multiple possible etymologies.

That the suffix was indeed borrowed can be ascertained from a group of words in -ᾶτον with Greek (or at least non-Latin) roots and no attested Latin equivalents: ἰᾶτον 'drink with honey, wine, and violets' from ἴον 'violet', καρυοφυλλᾶτον 'wine scented with cloves' from καρυόφυλλον 'clove', κουστουμηνᾶτον 'drink made from Crustumerian pears' from κουστούμηνον 'Crustumerian pear', κυδωνᾶτον 'drink made with quinces' from κυδώνιον 'quince', λιβυστικᾶτον 'drink made with *libusticum*' from λιβυστικόν (an herb), σελινᾶτον 'wine flavoured with celery' from σέλινον 'celery', and στυρακᾶτον 'storax wine' from στύραξ 'storax'.[29] Κιτρᾶτον 'citron drink' has a Latin root but no direct Latin equivalent; it must be a Greek derivative of κίτρον from *citrum*. The earliest of these words, σελινᾶτον and perhaps ἰᾶτον, come from the fourth century.[30] By the sixth century the suffix was so popular that one could find lists of beverages composed almost entirely of words using it, such as τῶν δὲ προπομάτων ἄριστόν ἐστι τὸ κονδῖτον καὶ τὸ ἀπιάτον ἢ ἀνισάτον ἢ λιβυστικάτον ἢ ἀψινθᾶτον ἢ κιτράτον ἢ μαστιχάτον 'of the drinks taken before meals the best is spiced wine, and wine flavoured with celery, or wine flavoured with aniseed, or the drink made with *libustikon*, or wine flavoured with wormwood, or the citron drink, or the drink made with mastic' (Alex.Trall. II.341.16–17).

Some Greek words for liquids in -ᾶτον have Latin roots and attested Latin equivalents; these were clearly borrowed from Latin, either as separate words or as the substantivized neuters of borrowed adjectives. They are ῥοσᾶτον 'rose-flavoured wine', from which the Greek compound ὑδρορόσατον 'rose water' was derived; ἀνισᾶτον 'wine flavoured with aniseed' (neuter of ἀνισᾶτος); σπικᾶτον 'embrocation of spikenard'; and φολιᾶτον, a type of perfumed oil.[31]

Others have both Greek roots and attested Latin equivalents; these could in theory be either Latin formations borrowed into Greek or Greek formations paralleled in, or even borrowed into, Latin. They are μυρσινᾶτον 'myrtle wine' and 'myrtle oil' (neuter of μυρσινᾶτος), which could come from *myrsinatus* 'made with myrtle oil' or μυρσίνη 'myrtle' + -ᾶτον; ἀψινθᾶτον 'wine flavoured with wormwood' or 'potion made with wormwood' (neuter of ἀψινθᾶτος), from *apsinthiatum/absentatum* 'wine flavoured with wormwood' or ἀψίνθιον 'wormwood' + -ᾶτον; μαστιχᾶτον 'drink flavoured with mastic', from *mastichatus* 'flavoured with mastic' or μαστίχη 'mastic' + -ᾶτον; and κυμινᾶτον 'preparation of cummin', from *cuminatus* 'with cummin' or κύμινον 'cummin' + -ᾶτον.

In order for the suffix -ᾶτον to have entered Greek, at least one word from this third group must in fact have been borrowed from Latin. Greek speakers began using -ᾶτον in the fourth century, but at that point the only indisputable Latin loans available as models were ῥοσᾶτον, σπικᾶτον, and φολιᾶτον, none of which had a Greek relative without -ᾶτον to allow the suffix to be identified. Moreover the Greek suffix appears to have been applied only to beverages, which neither σπικᾶτον nor φολιᾶτον designated; that would leave only ῥοσᾶτον available as a model, and it is very unlikely that a suffix could have been borrowed from a single word whose formation was opaque. Μαστιχᾶτον and κυμινᾶτον are not early enough to be the model in question: it must have been μυρσινᾶτον and/or ἀψινθᾶτον.

Both μυρσινᾶτον and Latin *myrsinatus* are attested from the fourth century, but the Latin term refers to an oil, not a beverage; on this basis it has been argued that μυρσινᾶτον cannot come from *myrsinatus*.[32] But μυρσινᾶτον too is often used of oil; in fact that is its original and more common sense, with the use for wine being both rarer and

---

[29] Maravela-Solbakk (2010: 261–2).

[30] Σελινᾶτον occurs in the title of Orib. *Col.* 5.23; LSJ attributes it to Philagrius (III–IV AD) because the title introduces an extract attributed to him, but this word may not be part of the quoted material.

[31] Also rare ἀπιᾶτον 'wine flavoured with celery' and πεπερᾶτον 'wine flavoured with pepper' or 'pepper dressing'. Some of these are built on Latin words originally borrowed from Greek, but the spellings indicate derivation via Latin.

[32] Maravela-Solbakk (2010: 260, 264).

later.[33] The best explanation for this situation is that the word was originally borrowed from Latin with its Latin meaning 'myrtle oil', which was later extended to 'myrtle wine' under the influence of the increasing number of words in -ᾶτον designating beverages. Therefore μυρσινᾶτον probably is a Latin loanword – if it had been a Greek formation it would only have meant 'myrtle wine' – but it cannot have been the model from which the suffix was originally borrowed.

Ἀψινθᾶτον must therefore have been the model. In many ways it is perfect for that role, for it designates a beverage and first appears on the Edict of Diocletian, at the very beginning of the fourth century; it is therefore earlier than all the Greek formations in -ᾶτον. The difficulty is that it is also earlier attested than its corresponding Latin; indeed the Edict of Diocletian has *absinthi* in Latin where ἀψινθᾶτου appears in Greek (Edict. Diocl. 2.18), which has been taken as evidence that *apsinthiatum* perhaps did not yet exist at the start of the fourth century.[34] But a word's absence from a text does not demonstrate that the word did not exist at the time of that text's composition, especially when the linguistic knowledge of the writer is suspect – which it is in the case of this section of the Edict, since its composer seems to have been unfamiliar with the usual forms of even well-established Latin words.[35]

Perhaps, therefore, ἀψινθᾶτον comes from *apsinthiatum* and the latter's slightly later attestation is coincidental. But there is also another possibility: ἀψινθᾶτον could be a Greek substantivization of the neuter of ἀψινθᾶτος 'flavoured with wormwood', which is probably first attested in the second century AD. The difficulty with that hypothesis is that most words in -ᾶτον were flavoured wines, and while neuter words for wines made excellent sense in Latin, where they could be felt to agree with an understood *vinum*, Greek words for wines were normally masculine to agree with οἶνος. A neuter suffix designating wines ought, therefore, to be a Latin creation

rather than a Greek one. But perhaps Greek speakers thought of -ᾶτον not as a suffix for wines, but rather as one for beverages, agreeing with neuter πῶμα 'drink'. That interpretation would explain the otherwise rather difficult fact that words in -ᾶτον created within Greek were not all wines, though they were all beverages: ὑδρόροσᾶτον contained no wine at all, and some of the others appear not to have been made primarily from wine. A Greek substantivization of ἀψινθᾶτος might also help to explain the fact that the Latin (usually) has an *i* that the Greek (usually) does not: if this word was borrowed once, it could simply have been taken from a Latin variant without the *i*, but if there were two separate borrowings it would be surprising for both to come from the less common Latin variant. And if ἀψινθᾶτον had been created within Greek it really should have been ἀψινθιᾶτον, for the normal word for wormwood was ἀψίνθιον; ἄψινθος was much rarer.

The likelihood that -ᾶτον was from the start a suffix meaning 'drink prepared with' rather than 'wine flavoured with' could also help explain its startling success in Greek, where for a brief period it seems to have been highly productive. A suffix that only and unambiguously designated beverages was useful, especially for the medical writers (who may well have been responsible for the initial formation of some of the words in -ᾶτον, though the papyri make clear that those words were also used outside medical texts). But Latin *-atum* could have no such unambiguous value: since words in *-atum* were simply neuters of adjectives in *-atus*, they could designate wines, oils (*oleum* was also neuter) and a range of other substances. And since the Latin words for 'beverage' were not neuter,[36] a 'drink prepared with' sense would not have been feasible for *-atum* in any case. The clear restriction of Greek -ᾶτον to beverages was short-lived, however; it came to an end with the borrowing of adjectival -ᾶτος, which introduced into Greek the kind of ambiguities that had always been present in Latin and led to the Byzantine and modern situation where -ᾶτον is used for a range of types of food and drink.

---

[33] Maravela-Solbakk (2010: 259–60).

[34] Therefore both Chantraine (*DÉLG s.v.* ἄψινθος) and Maravela-Solbakk (2010: 257–8, 265) take ἀψινθᾶτον as a Greek formation, with the latter arguing that the Latin is borrowed from the Greek.

[35] In 2.7 *Falerni* is spelled *Falerini*, and in 2.19 *rosati* is spelled *rhosati*.

[36] *Potus* was masculine and *potio* feminine.

6.6 -ᾶτος FROM -ĀTUS

Byzantine and modern Greek have a productive adjectival suffix -ᾶτος derived from the Latin first-conjugation perfect passive participle ending -atus.[37] It is generally thought that the productivity of this suffix does not go back to antiquity (apart from neuters denoting beverages, for which see §6.5), for only one ancient example of -ᾶτος on a Greek root has so far been identified: κυκλᾶτος 'shod', which occurs only once.[38] But there is also an ancient example of -ᾶτος applied by Greek speakers to a Latin root, the rare παρατουρᾶτος 'decorated' derived from παρατοῦρα 'distinctive dress' (from *paratura*). Although this also occurs only once, as a second example of the application of -ᾶτος by Greek speakers it rather changes the overall picture. Both κυκλᾶτος and παρατουρᾶτος come from sixth-century papyri; although the papyrus containing παρατουρᾶτος cannot be more precisely dated, the one containing κυκλᾶτος was written at the very end of that century. Since Byzantine words formed with -ᾶτος started to appear in the seventh century,[39] two examples occurring shortly before the seventh century must represent the beginning of that suffix's productivity, rather than an independent aberration.

By the sixth century there was no shortage of models that would have allowed Greek speakers to identify -ᾶτος as an adjectival suffix. Ἀψινθᾶτος 'flavoured with wormwood' with ἀψίνθιον 'wormwood', μυρσινᾶτος 'with myrtle oil' with μυρσίνη 'myrtle', κουμουλᾶτος 'heaping' with the measure κούμουλον, and πληγᾶτος 'wounded' with πληγή 'blow' would all have made identification of the suffix easy.[40]

Therefore the Byzantine adjectival suffix -ᾶτος was probably borrowed from one or more of these models in the sixth century. Byzantine Greek speakers were aware of the suffix's Latin origin, for when purging texts of Latin loanwords they sometimes also removed words formed with -ᾶτος on a Greek base.[41]

6.7 -ήσιος FROM -ĒNSIS?

Byzantine and modern Greek have a productive adjectival suffix -ήσιος, but there is no consensus about whether its source is Latin -ensis.[42] Greek certainly had the opportunity to borrow -ensis, for already in the first century AD the loanword pair καστρήσιος 'of the camp' (*castrensis*) and κάστρον 'army camp' (*castra*) would have made the suffix identifiable; in the second century that model was joined by κιρκήσιος 'of the circus' (*circensis*) with κίρκος 'circus' (*circus*), and in the fourth century by κομιτατήσιος 'belonging to the imperial court' with κομιτᾶτον 'staff, retinue (especially of the emperor)'. But there are Greek words in -ήσιος going back to the Classical period, even to Hesiod and Homer: βροτήσιος 'mortal' (βροτός), ἐτήσιος 'lasting for a year' (ἔτος), πρυμνήσιος 'of a stern' (πρύμνα), etc.[43] Therefore the suffix cannot simply come from Latin, nor did its use significantly increase owing to the influx of loanwords, for very few new words in -ήσιος were created during the Roman period.[44]

At the same time, the influx of Latin words in -ensis is likely to have affected perceptions of

---

in Greek; nouns are unlikely to have served as models for the borrowing of a clearly adjectival suffix.

[41] Zilliacus (1937: 335), listing γομᾶτος (also πληγᾶτος, which was probably not formed with -ᾶτος).

[42] The origin of -ήσιος is considered uncertain by Palmer (1945: 31) and Andriotis (1967: 119); Latin derivation is favoured by Meyer (1895: 75–6), Psaltes (1913: 305), Costas (1936: 50, 108), Blass *et al.* (1979 §5.2), Bubenik (2014: 305), and Filos (2014: 322); Latin derivation is implicitly rejected by Coleman (2007) and Cavenaile (1952: 199–202), who omit -ήσιος from treatments of borrowed suffixes.

[43] Chantraine (1933: 41–2).

[44] Palmer (1945: 31) found only one new example in Roman-period papyri: ἀρθρήσιος 'jointed' on *P.Oxy.* VII.1060.5 (VI AD), which actually reads αρτερησιε and has been differently interpreted (*Pap.Graec.Mag.* II p. 209). A possible example on a Latin base is κουβουκλείσιος probably derived from *cubiculum* via κουβουκλεῖον, where -είσιος may represent -ήσιος.

---

[37] Palmer (1945: 45–6), Zilliacus (1937: 314, 335), Meyer (1895: 74–5), Sophocles (1887: 37), Coleman (2007: 797), Buck and Petersen (1945: 470), J. N. Adams (2003: 495–6), Psaltes (1913: 302–3), Andriotis (1967: 40–1), Hatzidakis (1892: 184), Tonnet (1993: 105), Eleftheriades (1993: 3, 71, 102).

[38] *P.Cair.Masp.* 67279.18 (vi AD); cf. LSJ *s.v.* κυκλατός. The Greek base is presumably κύκλος 'circle', from the shape of a horseshoe.

[39] E.g. πωγωνᾶτος 'bearded' (πώγων + -ᾶτος); cf. *LBG s.v.*

[40] But the word most often cited as a model for the adoption of -ᾶτος, βαρβᾶτος 'bearded', is too late to be relevant; in antiquity Βαρβᾶτος occurs only as a (rare) personal name. Κανδιδᾶτος 'candidate' and ἀστᾶτος (a military rank), also sometimes offered as models, are exclusively nouns

the suffix -ήσιος. Although not as omnipresent as words with some other suffixes, loanwords in -ήσιος were numerous enough that they must have been noticed: two adjectives in addition to the three just mentioned, plus five or six nouns.[45] Their effect caused some other Latin words to be remodelled during borrowing to end in -ήσιος or neuter -ήσιον: *a commentariis* 'official in charge of records' became ἀκομενταρήσιος, and the coin name *tremis* (gen. *tremissis*) became τριμήσιον (thus reflecting the suffix at least in spelling, though by the time this word was borrowed there was no difference in pronunciation between η and ι).

Latin loanwords in -*ensis* are consistently spelled without the -*n*- in Greek; I cannot find a single occurrence of -ήνσιος in any ancient text, whether documentary, epigraphic, or literary. The loss of -*n*- is usually attributed to the well-known weak pronunciation of *n* before *s* in Latin, but in other loanwords -*ns*- usually entered Greek as -νσ-.[46] The different treatment of -*ns*- in the -*ensis* suffix must be due to Greek speakers immediately equating Latin -*ensis* with their own suffix in -ήσιος: from the beginning, the two suffixes merged. And since there was a relatively small body of earlier Greek words in -ήσιος, most of them not very common, Roman-period Greek speakers probably ended up with the idea that -ήσιος was mainly a Latin suffix, as they did with -άριον.[47] In other words,

the result of the merger between native -ήσιος and -ήσιος from -*ensis* was probably that the latter overwhelmed and absorbed the former.[48]

6.8 -τωρ FROM -*TOR*?

The agent-noun suffix -τωρ is generally considered to have a double source: as an inherited Greek suffix and as one borrowed from Latin.[49] The usual argument is that the inherited suffix, which is found only on a small number of words, had ceased to be productive already in Classical Greek, but in the Roman period new words in -τωρ were formed on Greek roots; as the revival of an obsolete suffix is unlikely without a specific impetus, the obvious explanation is the influence of Latin loanwords in -*tor*, which were borrowed in abundance (§4.2.5). Thus for example θρεπτήτωρ 'nourisher', which occurs in a sixth-century papyrus, seems best derived from θρεπτήριος 'nourishing' + -τωρ, and παραλήπτωρ 'receiver', which is found in several Roman-period texts, appears to come from παραλαμβάνω 'receive' + -τωρ.[50]

But some of the words normally cited as evidence of this revival are attested earlier than has previously been appreciated. Ἀντιλή(μ)πτωρ 'helper', from ἀντιλαμβάνω 'help' + -τωρ, appeared in the second century BC,[51] and

[45] Adjectives Μουτουνήσιος (*Mutinensis*), Ῥωμανήσιος (*Romanensis*); nouns Αὐγουστήσιοι (*Augustensis*), κομμενταρήσιος (*commentariensis*), κουιντανήσιος (*quintanensis*), μιλιαρήσιον (*miliarense*), πορταρῆσις (probably **portarensis*), φαβρικήσιος (*fabriciensis*).

[46] The -*n*- is regularly present (including in papyri: Gignac 1976: 118) in δηφήνσωρ (*defensor*), κῆνσος (*census*), κήνσωρ (*censor*), κηνσίτωρ (*censitor*), and κηνσουάλιος (*censualis*); the only exceptions are μηνσώριον, which had a double source (*mensorium* and *missorium*), and καστρησιανός (*castrensianus*), which was influenced by καστρήσιος. Ἰσικιάριος and ἰσίκιον, though historically they descend from formations beginning *ins*-, are synchronically borrowings of *isiciarius* and *isicium* (*TLL s.vv.*). Schirru (2013: 312) sees a difference in register, with higher-register borrowings preserving the -*ns*- cluster intact and lower-register borrowings dropping the -*n*-, but there is no external evidence for the supposed register difference. Binder (2000: 112–14) does not spot the difference between -*ensis* and other instances of -*ns*-.

[47] Palmer (1945: 31) found in Roman-period papyri and inscriptions only seven words in -ήσιος on Greek roots; in the same texts there are fourteen on Latin roots (twelve

loanwords and two rare words). Zilliacus (1937: 334–5) does not include any words in -ήσιος in the list of words with Greek roots and Latin suffixes that were purged during the Byzantine period for being Latinate, but as the total number of such words was never very large it is possible that they happened not to be in those texts to begin with. Stephanus of Byzantium comments τὸ ἐθνικὸν Ἀκυλήιος ... λέγεται καὶ Ἀκυλεήσιος Ἰταλικῷ τύπῳ 'the ethnic [for Ἀκυληία = Aquileia] is Ἀκυλήιος ... and Ἀκυλεήσιος with the Latin derivation type also occurs' (*Ethnica* α 178) and τὸ ἐθνικὸν Ῥαβεννάτης, παρὰ τοῖς Ἰταλοῖς Ῥαβεννήσιος 'the ethnic [for Ῥάβεννα = Ravenna] is Ῥαβεννάτης, and among the inhabitants of Italy Ῥαβεννήσιος' (ρ 4), where a form in -*ensis* is unattested in Latin (Billerbeck and Neumann-Hartmann 2016: 113).

[48] Filos (2008: 279–89).

[49] Chantraine (1937: 89–91, cf. 1933: 323–9), Palmer (1945: 8, 118–19), Cavenaile (1952: 200), J. N. Adams (2003: 495), Filos (2014: 323), Psaltes (1913: 252–4).

[50] Palmer (1945: 119), Cavenaile (1952: 200), LSJ, *P.Cair. Masp.* 67020r.11.

[51] *UPZ* 1.14.18; note also from the first century BC *BGU* IV.1139.17.

ἐκλήπτωρ 'contractor of works' (ἐκλαμβάνω 'contract' + -τωρ) emerged in the first century BC at the latest.[52] Κτήτωρ 'possessor' (κτάομαι 'possess' + -τωρ) goes back to the first century BC;[53] λεπτοκτήτωρ 'small land-holder' and προκτήτωρ 'previous owner' are both late enough for Latin influence to be unproblematic, but they are more likely to be compounds of κτήτωρ than new formations with -τωρ as has been claimed.[54] Πράκτωρ 'accomplisher' and οἰκήτωρ 'inhabitant' go back to the Classical period.[55] Under these circumstances Latin influence is unlikely to be the whole story, even if it eventually became a contributing factor; the original impetus for the Hellenistic revival of -τωρ was probably that Ionic made more use of -τωρ words than Attic, and that this led to such words being more common in koiné than in Classical Attic.[56]

The earliest Latin loanwords with -τωρ seem to have been borrowed in the first century BC: δικτάτωρ 'dictator', ἰμπεράτωρ 'commander', κομάκτωρ 'collector of money', and στάτωρ (a military functionary), plus from the first century AD βιάτωρ 'agent', κονδούκτωρ 'contractor', κουράτωρ 'curator', σπεκουλάτωρ (a military functionary), and στράτωρ (a military functionary). None of these came with a related term that would have made it easy for Greek speakers to identify -τωρ as a Latin suffix,[57] but a clear model would not have been necessary if Greek speakers recognized the -τωρ in these loanwords as equivalent to their own -τωρ. By the second century Greek speakers were able to add -τωρ to Latin roots, for ἀρμικούστωρ 'person in charge of weapons' must come from *armicustos* + -τωρ and κιβαριάτωρ (an army official) is probably from *cibaria* (perhaps via κιβάριον) + -τωρ; in the third century these were joined by δισέκτωρ 'quarry engineer' from *deseco* + -τωρ.

The chronology of the Latin borrowings confirms the suspicion that they were not the initial catalyst for the revival of -τωρ: the revival predates the borrowings. And there is no evidence that -τωρ was perceived by later Greek speakers as being a Latinate suffix in the way -άριον was.[58] In some respects the situation with -τωρ is likely to have been broadly similar to that with -άριον and -ήσιος: a suffix common on Latin loanwords merged with a pre-existing Greek suffix. But in the case of -τωρ the merger seems to have resulted in a suffix perceived as Greek, whereas in the case of -άριον and -ήσιος the result was apparently perceived as Latin.

6.9 -ἁτωρ FROM -ĀTOR

In the sixth century a suffix -άτωρ seems to have been used on a Greek root to form ἐμβολάτωρ 'collector of dues in connection with grain contributions' from ἐμβολή 'shipment of grain'.[59] The same suffix may appear in two rare Latinate terms, κουσπάτωρ 'prison guard', which at least one Greek speaker considered a Latin word but which has no attested Latin equivalent, and τριομβυράτωρ 'triumvir', which seems to be a remodelling of *triumvir*.[60] This suffix could easily

[52] *O.Stras.* I.786.2, *CPR* XV.15.3, *P.Lond.* II.354.3.

[53] Diodorus Siculus 34/35.2.31. Chantraine (1937: 89) treats this as a new word in Roman-period papyri, where he maintains it means 'owner of land he does not cultivate himself' – but surely this would be a specialization of the already extant κτήτωρ rather than a new creation with a new suffix?

[54] Palmer (1945: 119).

[55] This actually makes them less problematic for the Latin-influence theory than the Hellenistic loans, as they could be survivals of the original -τωρ suffix. Chantraine (1937: 89) treats οἰκήτωρ as a new word in Roman-period papyri, where he maintains it means 'landless peasant' – but surely this would be a specialization of the already extant οἰκήτωρ rather than a new creation with a new suffix?

[56] Fraenkel (1910: 179 n. 2, 221).

[57] Indeed the Greek derivatives of δικτάτωρ, δικτατωρεία 'dictatorship' and δικτατωρεύω 'be dictator', add further suffixes to the whole word rather than to the stem that would be produced by subtracting -τωρ; compare Latin *dictatura* without the -*or*.

[58] Zilliacus (1937: 334–5) does not include any words in -τωρ in the list of words with Greek roots and Latin suffixes that were purged during the Byzantine period for being Latinate; given how common that suffix was, the texts in question must have contained at least some such words.

[59] Buck and Petersen (1945: 302), Chantraine (1937: 91), LSJ suppl., *LBG*; cf. Cavenaile (1952: 200). Attestations of ἐμβολάτωρ include *P.Oxy.* I.126.15, *P.Ant.* II.95.14, *BGU* XVII.2729.5.

[60] Perhaps also in rare ἠβωκάτωρ 'veteran called back into service', which has the wrong meaning to be a straightforward borrowing of *evocator* 'one who orders out troops' and may therefore be a remodelling of *evocatus* using -άτωρ. As ἠβωκάτωρ comes from the third century its formation with -άτωρ would be an isolated phenomenon chronologically, but it is not impossible; several of the loanwords from which the suffix could have been extracted had already been borrowed at that time.

have been extracted from the numerous Latin loanwords in -άτωρ (§4.2.5), for by the sixth century several of these had related loanwords that would have suggested a suffix -άτωρ: κιβαριάτωρ (an army official issuing food and wine to the troops) with κιβάριον 'rations', ρογάτωρ (an official) with ρογεύω 'distribute money', βυκινάτωρ 'trumpeter' with βυκινίζω 'blow the trumpet', ὀψωνάτωρ 'caterer' with ὄψον 'prepared food'. Although only the very beginning of this suffix's development is visible in antiquity, it remained productive in later periods and is probably the ancestor of modern Greek -άτορας.[61]

6.10 -ατίων FROM -ĀTIŌ

There is some evidence for productive use of a suffix -ατίων derived from -atio.[62] Ἀρουρατίων 'tax assessed in proportion to area of land'[63] must come directly from Greek ἄρουρα 'land', since Latin arura is too rare (see TLL) to make it at all likely that there could have been an unattested *aruratio. Two Latinate terms, both too rare to be considered loanwords, may also contain this suffix. Κουρατορατίων (meaning unknown) evidently has a Latin base, but *curatoratio is unattested and would be an unlikely formation; more plausible is a Greek attachment of -ατίων to κουράτωρ 'curator' (from curator), which had been borrowed long before the appearance of κουρατορατίων. Ἀβστινατίων may come from abstineo + -ατίων.

There were plenty of loanwords ending in -ατίων (§4.2.5). By the time ἀρουρατίων appeared in the fourth century (κουρατορατίων emerged in the fifth and ἀβστινατίων in the sixth), Greek speakers had at their disposal at least two loanwords with relatives that would have allowed the identification of a suffix -ατίων: βηξιλλατίων 'troop' with βήξιλλον 'cavalry standard' and βηξιλλάριος (a military rank), ὀρδινατίων 'order' with ὀρδινάριος 2 'regular' and ὀρδινᾶτος 'appointed' (and perhaps ὄρδινος 'order', whose borrowing date is uncertain). Therefore -ατίων was probably borrowed,

but it was not very productive and does not appear to have survived for long.[64]

6.11 -ούρα/-οῦρα FROM -ŪRA?

Byzantine and modern Greek have a productive suffix -ούρα that is generally agreed to come from Latin -ura.[65] But the borrowing may not have taken place during antiquity, for only one ancient example has been proposed: κοπτούρα 'mortar for flour-making', which looks like a Greek formation from κόπτω 'strike' + -ούρα.[66] Κοπτούρα first appears in the second century AD,[67] so even if it does show productive use of -ούρα, it remained isolated for many centuries before the suffix began to be used more generally.

Moreover, it is unlikely that many Greek speakers of the second century AD would have been aware of -ura as a Latin suffix. At that date the only loanword in -ούρα was σαβούρα 'ballast', and there were no related Greek words with σαβ- that might have caused monolingual Greek speakers to identify -ούρα as a suffix – bilingual speakers, of course, might have been aware that σαβούρα came from saburra and did not have an -ura suffix in Latin. The later loanwords with -ούρα were ἁρματοῦρα 'person skilled in the use of the sword', κλεισούρα 'narrow pass', παρατοῦρα 'distinctive dress', and πεδατοῦρα 'watchman's allotted area'. Two of these had relatives that might have enabled the suffix to be identified: ἁρματοῦρα with ἅρμα 'weapons' and κλεισούρα with κλείω 'close', which had influenced the form in which κλεισούρα was borrowed (§4.4). But ἅρμα first appeared in the fifth century, when ἁρματοῦρα was already dying out,

---

[61] Chantraine (1937: 91), Palmer (1945: 119), Costas (1936: 108), Dieterich (1928: 112), Sophocles (1887: 37), Meyer (1895: 75).

[62] Palmer (1945: 120).

[63] See works cited in §3.2 s.v.

[64] Coleman (2007: 796) points out that Byzantine κεφαλητίων 'capitation tax' (cf. LBG s.v. κεφαλιτίων) has a similar Latinate suffix in -τίων, probably independently derived from capitatio 'poll tax'.

[65] Andriotis (1967: 254), Eleftheriades (1993: 3, but cf. 63, 97), Costas (1936: 108), Meyer (1895: 77), Coleman (2007: 797), Filos (2014: 322), Psaltes (1913: 270–1), Sophocles (1887: 37).

[66] Palmer (1945: 66), though Hofmann (1989: 200) favours borrowing from an unattested *coptura. The latter is unlikely because Latin had very few words on the stem of Greek κόπτω: the only such derivative in the TLL is the rare copta, designating a kind of hard cake, which would not have offered Latin speakers much of a basis for forming *coptura.

[67] E.g. P.Mil.Vogl. 11.53.12, Chrest.Wilck. 323.22.

so the only good ancient candidate for the source of the -ούρα suffix is κλεισούρα, which dates to the fifth century. Κλεισούρα is common in Byzantine Greek, where it forms numerous derivatives, and therefore is very likely to have been the source of the Byzantine -ούρα suffix – but it cannot possibly be responsible for κοππούρα.

It is therefore unlikely that a Latinate -ούρα suffix was productive during antiquity; probably another explanation should be found for κοππούρα.

6.12 -ῖνος FROM -*ĪNUS*?

There were three Greek adjectival suffixes in -ινος. One was recessively accented ('-ινος) and used particularly to indicate materials, one was oxytone (-ινός) and used particularly for adjectives of time, and one with a long ι and paroxytone accent (-ῖνος) had a variety of meanings and was fairly common as a way of forming personal names. This last suffix, while basically inherited, is usually thought to be influenced by Latin -*inus* in its use for the ethnics of Greek cities in Magna Graecia, since these were far more likely to end in -ῖνος than ethnics for other Greek cities.[68] Thus Stephanus of Byzantium, writing in the sixth century AD, considered the formation in -ῖνος characteristic of ethnics for cities in Italy: ὁ πολίτης Ἀμπελῖνος ὡς Ἀσσωρῖνος Ἀβακαινῖνος· ὁ γὰρ τύπος τῶν Ἰταλῶν. τῶν δὲ λοιπῶν δυνατὸν Ἀμπελῖται εἶναι. 'The citizen [of Ἄμπελος in Italy is called] Ἀμπελῖνος, like Ἀσσωρῖνος and Ἀβακαινῖνος; for that is the Latin derivation type. But citizens of the other [places called Ἄμπελος, i.e. the ones outside Italy] can be Ἀμπελῖται.'[69]

But many of these ethnics simply could not have been influenced by Latin. For example, Ἀκραγαντῖνος 'of Acragas', Ταραντῖνος 'of Tarentum', Ῥηγῖνος 'of Rhegium', Λεοντῖνος 'of Leontini', and Μεταποντῖνος 'of Metapontum' are all attested in Greek by the fifth century BC, when Rome was a tiny, insignificant settlement far from any of these cities.[70] And those ethnics cannot have been new in the fifth century; they must date back to the cities' foundations or shortly thereafter. Tarentum, Rhegium, and Leontini were founded as Greek colonies in the eighth century BC, Metapontum in the seventh, and Acragas early in the sixth, making the possibility of Latin influence on their ethnics even more remote. While it is true that the Latin ethnics for these cities usually match the Greek ones (*Tarentinus, Reginus, Leontinus, Metapontinus*), that match is more likely to be due to Greek influence on Latin than the reverse. And for Acragas the Latin ethnic is not even a good match: *Acragantinus* is not attested until Lucretius and is clearly just a variant of the earlier and more common *Agrigentinus*, derived from the usual Latin name for Acragas, *Agrigentum* (*TLL s.vv.*).

The cluster of ethnics in -ῖνος from Magna Graecia cannot simply be coincidental, but it also cannot be explained by Latin influence. Influence from another Italic language is unlikely too, for the cities concerned are found all over Magna Graecia, which at the time was an area of tremendous linguistic diversity; their inhabitants were not all in contact with the same other languages. Perhaps the earliest colonists (or the inhabitants of their mother cities, who might also have been behind the creation of the ethnics) used the -ῖνος suffix because of some shared cultural factors or because of the productivity of that suffix in the eighth century BC. Once the pattern of forming ethnics in that region with -ῖνος had been established, later groups of colonists might have been influenced by it in creating their own ethnics.

6.13 -ελλα FROM -*ELLA*?

Βρακέλλαι 'trousers', which occurs on a third-century papyrus, has been suggested as a Greek creation using a borrowed suffix -ελλα.[71] It is

---

[68] Chantraine (1933: 206), Buck and Petersen (1945: 262), Immisch (1885: 271); cf. Schwyzer (1939: 490–1), Blass *et al.* (1979 §5.2). For names in -ῖνος see Chantraine (1933: 205) and note the Attic playwright Κρατῖνος; Herodotus mentions Μυκερῖνος (2.131.1), Εὐπαλῖνος (3.60.3), Βουδῖνος (4.119.1), Πρηξῖνος (7.180), and Ἀτταγῖνος (9.15.4). Psaltes (1913: 296) argues for a different, later (not ancient?) borrowing of -ῖνος. Meyer (1895: 76), Costas (1936: 108), Andriotis (1967: 131), and Eleftheriades (1993: 3) claim feminine-only -ίνα as a modern Greek descendant of a Latin suffix, without discussing the date of borrowing.

[69] *Ethnica* α 279 with the interpretation of Billerbeck (2006: 187); cf. *Ethnica* α 34.

[70] Ἀκραγαντῖνος in Pindar, *Isthmian* 2.17; Ταραντῖνος in Herodotus 3.138; Ῥηγῖνος and Λεοντῖνος in Thucydides 3.86.3; Μεταποντῖνος in Herodotus 4.15.

[71] Cervenka-Ehrenstrasser (2000: 203) and Filos (2010: 226 n. 19) develop the implication of Kramer (1996a: 122); cf. Palmer (1945: 14).

unlikely, however, that Greek speakers would have been able to extract that suffix from the loanwords available to them in the third century. Those were κέλλα 'room', πάτελλα 'dish', σέλλα 'seat', and ταβέλλα 'writing tablet', none of which was part of a pair that would have made it possible to separate -ελλα by identifying a base form of κ-, πατ-, σ-, or ταβ-. Nor, as far as I can tell, are there other Greek words that might provide evidence of a suffix in -ελλα. Under these circumstances there is something to be said for Meinersmann's theory (1927: 12) that βρακέλλαι derives from an unattested Latin *bracellae.

6.14 OTHER SUFFIXES

A number of other Latinate or possibly Latinate suffixes appear in Byzantine and/or modern Greek, but it is not normally claimed that these became productive during antiquity. They are -άλιον, -άνος, -αρίδιον, -άρικος, -ελ(λ)ι, -ήλα/-ίλα, -ούλα, -ούκλα, -ούλι, and -ου(λ)λος.[72] I can find

no evidence that these suffixes were borrowed before the end of antiquity.

6.15 CONCLUSIONS

Five suffixes were extracted from Latin loanwords and became productive in Greek before AD 600: in the first century AD -άριος, in the first or second -ιανός, in the fourth -ᾶτον, and in the sixth -ᾶτος and -άτωρ. Three additional Latin suffixes were very similar to ones already productive in Greek, -άριον, -τωρ, and -ήσιος; in these cases the Latin suffix merged with the native one. Two more, -αρία and -ατίων, show sporadic signs of rare productivity, but not a full acceptance into Greek. Other suffixes, including -οῦρα, -ῖνος, and -ελλα, were probably not borrowed during antiquity.

---

[72] For -άλιον see Filos (2008: 341–7), Petersen (1910: 254–5). For -άνος see Meyer (1895: 73), Andriotis (1967: 23). For -αρίδιον see Filos (2008: 348–52). For -άρικος see Palmer (1945: 16), Meyer (1895: 74). For -ελ(λ)ι see Andriotis (1967: 94), but note that Petersen (1910: 255–6) is sceptical that a suffix -έλλιον existed at all during antiquity,

and Eleftheriades (1993: 57) is sceptical that the source is Latin. For -ήλα/-ίλα see Meyer (1895: 76), Andriotis (1967: 130). For -ούλα see Meyer (1895: 76–7), Andriotis (1967: 253), Palmer (1945: 14), Eleftheriades (1993: 3, 59). For -ούκλα see Meyer (1895: 76), Andriotis (1967: 253), Eleftheriades (1993: 63). For -ούλι see Andriotis (1967: 253), Eleftheriades (1993: 59). For -ου(λ)λος see Filos (2008: 289–300), Bubenik (2014: 305), Andriotis (1967: 253 s.v. -ουλός, cf. s.v. -ούλι), Costas (1936: 108).

7

WHY WERE SOME LATIN WORDS NOT INTEGRATED?

Integration was the norm for Latin words in ancient Greek texts: the vast majority of Latin words appeared in Greek script and with Greek inflections, even when they were otherwise clearly marked as foreign (§4). Nevertheless some texts contain some words in Latin script and/or with Latin inflections, and these exceptions shed further light on the meaning of the integration observed elsewhere.[1]

7.1 THE USE OF LATIN SCRIPT

In the sixth century Latin script was much more used in connection with Greek texts than in previous centuries. In fact so popular was the Latin alphabet at this period that it was sometimes used for entire texts in Greek written by and for Greek speakers.[2] This startling phenomenon demonstrates both that the intended readers of these texts knew the Latin alphabet and that that alphabet had enough prestige to make it worth using for Greek. At the same period, and more relevantly to the current study, legal texts that would previously have been written in Latin began to appear in Greek instead, with certain Latin words in Latin script. This phenomenon is widespread in manuscripts of major sixth-century legal works such as the *Codex* and *Novellae* of Justinian as well as those of lesser-known legal writers such as Athanasius Scholasticus and Theophilus Antecessor; it can

also be seen in a few legal papyri.[3] John Lydus, who wrote about Byzantine government in the sixth century, also used Latin script occasionally for Latin words and phrases. There can be no question that this practice is in principle ancient, but with the exception of the papyri, which provide only a tiny proportion of the evidence, its application in particular cases is mediated by a somewhat unreliable manuscript transmission. Byzantine copyists often changed Latin script to Greek, so that on average late manuscripts contain fewer words in Latin script than do early ones, and modern editors often standardize the resulting inconsistencies between manuscripts by imposing their own regular conventions.

Fortunately two substantial texts with Latin script are available in a form that transmits the original writer's script choices with a fair degree of reliability: a long papyrus fragment and a recent edition of Theophilus Antecessor produced by scholars with a special interest in the script question.[4]

7.1.1 *Latin script in Theophilus Antecessor*

Theophilus' work, composed in AD 533–4, is a 'paraphrase' (effectively a translation) of the Latin *Institutes* of Justinian, the basic introductory textbook for sixth-century students of Roman law. In places it sticks closely to the Latin original,

---

[1] An earlier version of this chapter was published as Dickey (2018).

[2] Feissel (2008); cf. Fournet (2019: 84–6). The texts involved are often ones that in earlier centuries would have been composed wholly or partially in Latin, and it is likely that the use of Greek in Latin script was an intermediate phase between using Latin and openly using Greek; during this phase outsiders who did not know the Latin alphabet would not have been able to tell that the texts were not actually in Latin.

[3] E.g. *P.Cair.Masp.* 67151.

[4] Lokin *et al.* (2010); for the editors' interest see pp. xxiii–xxvi, xlix and Van der Wal (1983). The transmission problem is less acute for Theophilus than for some other writers, because there is a comparatively short interval between the date of the original composition of the work (AD 533–4) and that of the earliest manuscript (c. AD 1000) and there are a large number of useful manuscripts, including several early ones, making it possible to reconstruct an early archetype with unusual precision as well as to observe diachronic trends in alphabet choice.

but elsewhere it expands upon the information provided in the *Institutes,* often in an attempt to provide clarifications of concepts that were not obvious to Greek speakers. As an introductory textbook for students who had to be enabled to cope with the Latin terminology on which Roman law was based, it needed to introduce and define that terminology. Theophilus therefore used many Latin words, both loanwords and code-switches, and his script choices have the potential to reveal to us exactly where he put the boundary between those two types of Latin word – that is, if his distinction between words that belonged in Latin script and words that belonged in Greek script matches our distinction between code-switches and loanwords, for such a match cannot be taken for granted.

At first glance Theophilus' use of the Latin alphabet appears to match the loanword/code-switch distinction very well: long-established loanwords are normally written in Greek script, like κάστρων from *castra* in passage 16, while Latin words not previously attested in Greek texts are normally in Latin script, like *sedetois.*

> 16 Ἐν οἷς δὲ χρόνοις ἐν ἑτέροις διατρίβουσι τόποις ἢ ἐν τοῖς λεγομένοις αὐτῶν SEDETOIS, τουτέστιν ἔνθα διάγειν αὐτοὺς ἀνάγκη, τῶν στρατιωτικῶν ἐν τῷ διατίθεσθαι προνομίων οὐκ ἀπολαύσουσιν. καὶ ὑπεξούσιοι δὲ ὄντες ἀκωλύτως διατίθενται πανταχοῦ μέντοι τὴν ἀκρίβειαν παραφυλάττοντες ἐν ᾧ τῶν κάστρων εἰσὶν ἐκτός. (2.11.pr.)

But when [soldiers] spend time in other places or in their so-called stations, that is, where they are required to remain, they will not enjoy soldiers' privileges in making wills. But even if they are in their fathers' power there is no problem with their making a will anywhere, as long as they observe the proper formalities when they are outside the camp.

But it is not undisputed that what Theophilus' use of the Latin alphabet marks is the synchronic foreignness of Latin words. Indeed a previous study of Theophilus' script choices suggested that what the Latin alphabet marked was not foreignness but technical legal terminology.[5] Of course, the vast majority of the foreign words Theophilus uses are technical legal terms; his work is after

all a law textbook. But *sedetois* 'station' does not look like a legal term, either here or in its other occurrences,[6] and the same can be said for some other words that Theophilus puts in Latin script, for example the underlined words in passage 17.

> 17 Ὁ τρίτος βαθμὸς ἔχει ἐν τοῖς ἀνιοῦσι πρόπαππον προμάμμην, ἐν τοῖς κατιοῦσι προέγγονον προεγγόνην, ἐν τοῖς ἐκ πλαγίου ἀδελφοῦ καὶ ἀδελφῆς υἱὸν καὶ θυγατέρα καὶ ἀκολούθως θεῖον πρὸς πατρὸς θεῖον πρὸς μητρὸς θείαν πρὸς πατρὸς θείαν πρὸς μητρός. ὁ θεῖος ὁ πρὸς πατρὸς Ῥωμαϊστὶ λέγεται PATRUUS, τουτέστιν ὁ τοῦ πατρὸς ἀδελφός, ὅστις Ἑλληνιστὶ λέγεται πατρῷος· ὁ δὲ πρὸς μητρὸς θεῖος καλεῖται AVUNCULUS, τουτέστι τῆς μητρὸς ἀδελφός, ὃς παρ' Ἕλλησι καλεῖται κυρίως μητρῷος· κοινῶς δὲ πᾶς θεῖος λέγεται. ἡ πρὸς πατρὸς θεία λέγεται AMITA, τουτέστι τοῦ πατρὸς ἀδελφή, ἡ δὲ πρὸς μητρὸς MATERTERA, τουτέστι τῆς μητρὸς ἀδελφή· ἑκατέρα δὲ θεία προσαγορεύεται ἤγουν παρά τισι τηθίς. (3.6.3)

The third degree has as ascendants the great-grandfather and great-grandmother, as descendants the great-grandson and great-granddaughter, and as collaterals the brother's and sister's son and daughter; and so also the paternal and maternal uncle and the paternal and maternal aunt. The paternal uncle is called in Latin *patruus*, that is father's brother, which is πατρῷος in Greek, and the maternal uncle is called *avunculus*, that is mother's brother, which is properly called μητρῷος by the Greeks; but commonly they are all called θεῖος. The paternal aunt is called *amita*, that is father's sister, and the maternal one *matertera*, that is mother's sister; but either is called θεία – or indeed, among some people, τηθίς.

It therefore seems very likely that Theophilus used Latin script to signal that a word was Latin, rather than to signal that it was technical legal terminology. But it does not follow from this that the words Theophilus put in Latin script were necessarily always the ones that we would call codeswitches rather than loanwords. In fact Theophilus' script choices cannot match our codeswitch/loanword distinction, for they were not always consistent. Many words alternated between the two scripts, appearing sometimes

---

6 In the Byzantine period it seems to be a military term rather than a legal one (*LBG s.v.* σέδετον).

in the Latin alphabet and sometimes in the Greek one. For example, *mandaton* 'consensual contract' appears 56 times in Latin script and 9 times in Greek script, *peculion* 'personal property' 54 times in Latin script and 14 times in Greek script, *praetor* 'praetor' 47 times in Latin script and 93 times in Greek script, *curator* 'guardian' 4 times in Latin script and 40 times in Greek script, and *patron* 'patron' twice in Latin script and 65 times in Greek script.[7] This variation is not due simply to random chance when a word is common, since some other common terms appear only in Latin script, including *testator* 'maker of a will' (67 occurrences), *pupillos* 'minor', 'ward' (72 occurrences), and *usufructos* 'usufruct' (86 occurrences).

The variation in script choice seems to be linked to the contexts in which the words appear, though many contexts provide no obvious rationale for script choice. The passages where context does give us a clue all involve the use of Latin script and fall into two groups: in most cases there is a particular focus on the term concerned, for example because it is explained or defined, and in others the term concerned is part of a longer Latin phrase (for these see §7.3). For example, Theophilus normally uses Greek script for οὐγγία 'one twelfth', as one would expect from the fact that this word was borrowed into Greek nearly a thousand years before his time. But in passage 18 (in which all instances of this word are underlined) one occurrence is in Latin script – the one in which the word is defined.

18 Ἔστι δὲ ταῦτα· <u>UNCIA</u> τὸ δωδέκατον μέρος τῆς περιουσίας· SEXTANS, τουτέστι τὸ διούγκιον, ὅπερ ἐστὶν ἔκτον μέρος· QUADRANS τὸ τέταρτον, ὅπερ ἐστὶ τριούγκιον· TRIENS τὸ τρίτον, ὃ ποιεῖ τέσσαρας <u>οὐγκίας</u>· QUINCUNX τρίτον δωδέκατον, ὃ ποιεῖ πέντε <u>οὐγκίας</u>· SEMIS τὸ ἥμισυ, ὃ ποιεῖ ἓξ <u>οὐγκίας</u>· SEPTUNX τὸ ἥμισυ δωδέκατον, ὃ ποιεῖ <u>ἑπτὰ</u> <u>οὐγκίας</u>· BES τὸ δίμοιρον, ὃ ποιεῖ ὀκτὼ <u>οὐγκίας</u>· DODRANS τὸ δίμοιρον δωδέκατον, ὃ ποιεῖ ἐννέα <u>οὐγκίας</u>· DEXTANS δίμοιρον ἔκτον, ὃ ποιεῖ δέκα <u>οὐγκίας</u>· DEUNX τὸ δίμοιρον τέταρτον, ὃ ποιεῖ ἕνδεκα <u>οὐγκίας</u>· AS αἱ δώδεκα <u>οὐγκίαι</u>. (2.14.5)

[The names for the divisions of an inheritance] are as follows: *uncia*, the twelfth part of the inheritance; *sextans*, that is, two twelfths, which is a sixth; *quadrans*, a quarter, which is three twelfths; *triens*, a third, which makes four <u>twelfths</u>; *quincunx*, a third and a twelfth, which makes five <u>twelfths</u>; *semis*, half, which makes six <u>twelfths</u>; *septunx*, a half and a twelfth, which makes seven <u>twelfths</u>; *bes*, two thirds, which makes eight <u>twelfths</u>; *dodrans*, two thirds and a twelfth, which makes nine <u>twelfths</u>; *dextans*, two thirds and a sixth, which makes ten <u>twelfths</u>; *deunx*, two thirds and a fourth, which makes eleven <u>twelfths</u>; *as*, twelve <u>twelfths</u>.

Similarly, in passage 19 Theophilus treats the word κωδικίλλος 'codicil' as an integrated loanword, which it probably was since it had entered Greek c. 400 years previously, and writes it in Greek script. But in passage 20 he puts the same word in Latin script because he is explaining it, even though passage 20 comes from later in his work than passage 19.

19 ADEMPTIONA ἤτοι ἀφαίρεσιν τῶν ληγάτων δυνάμεθα καὶ ἐν τῇ αὐτῇ διαθήκῃ ποιεῖν ἰσχυρῶς καὶ ἐν <u>κωδικίλλοις</u>. καὶ ἀδιάφορον εἴτε CONTRARIOIS ῥήμασι γένηται ἡ ADEMPTION εἴτε ἑτέροις. εἶπον γάρ· Τιτίῳ δίδωμι καὶ ληγατεύω ρ′ νομίσματα, εἶτα ἐν τῇ αὐτῇ διαθήκῃ μικρὸν ὕστερον ἢ καὶ ἐν τῷ <u>κωδικίλλῳ</u>, προσθεὶς τὸ NON εἶπον· Τιτίῳ ρ′ νομίσματα NON DO NON LEGO. ἰδοὺ ταῦτα CONTRARIA λέγεται …[8]

We can validly make ademption, that is removal, of legacies both in the same will and in <u>codicils</u>. And it is indifferent whether the ademption is made in the opposite words or in different ones. For [suppose] I said, 'To Titius I give and bequeath 100 *solidi*', and then in the same will a little later, or also in the <u>codicil</u>, having added 'not' I said, 'To Titius I do not give nor bequeath 100 *solidi*.' These are called opposites.

20 Εἴπωμεν λοιπὸν περὶ <u>CODICILLON</u>. <u>CODICILLOS</u> δέ ἐστιν ἐλλιποῦς ἐν διαθήκῃ γνώμης TESTATOROS ἀναπλήρωσις. ἔστι δὲ οὐκ ἄτοπον περὶ τῆς ἀρχαιογονίας τῶν <u>CODICILLON</u> διαλεχθῆναι. (2.25.pr.)

---

8 2.21.pr. The use of Latin for the negative formula *non do non lego*, when the positive is given in Greek as δίδωμι καὶ ληγατεύω, is also notable. Here Theophilus was obliged by the discussion to codeswitch by using *non*, and having done so he then continued in Latin to the end of the formula under discussion (see §7.3 for the treatment of longer phrases, which display some differences from isolated words).

Let us speak next about <u>codicils</u>. A <u>codicil</u> is the filling of a gap in the will-maker's intention [as expressed] in the will. And it is not out of place to talk about the origin of <u>codicils</u>.

This type of alternation, though initially disconcerting, is actually further evidence that Theophilus' script choice was fundamentally governed by his views on which language words belonged to. Theophilus appears to have had a nuanced view of the range of Latin words usable in Greek: he placed them on a continuum from fully established loanwords whose Latin origins only scholars could remember to completely foreign terms not previously seen in Greek. On this continuum stood many partially integrated terms with different degrees of assimilation. The continuum could not be adequately reflected in writing, since only two alphabets were available; therefore Theophilus consistently used Latin script only for words that he consistently saw as foreign, and consistently used Greek script only for words that he saw as fully part of the Greek language. He went back and forth with words that he saw as partially integrated into Greek, depending on how he was thinking about them at the moment of writing. His threshold for considering a term fully part of Greek was very high: even a word like οὐγγία that had been part of the Greek language for a millennium could be treated as foreign when he was thinking about its origins.

There are a few passages where the script choice remains surprising even on this theory, but they too can actually be explained by it. Passage 21 is the first Greek attestation of the term καστρᾶτος 'eunuch by castration', a borrowing of Latin *castratus*. Theophilus defines the term but nevertheless puts it in Greek script.

21 Ὁ εὐνοῦχος ὄνομά ἐστι γενικόν, τέμνεται δὲ εἰς τρία· τῶν γὰρ εὐνούχων οἱ μὲν εἰσὶ σπάδωνες οἱ δὲ <u>καστρᾶτοι</u> οἱ δὲ θλιβίαι. καὶ σπάδωνές εἰσιν οἵτινες διά τι πάθος ἢ ψῦξιν ἐνοχλήσασαν τοῖς γονίμοις μορίοις παιδοποιεῖν κωλύονται, τούτου δὲ ἀπαλλαγέντες παιδοποιοῦσιν. θλιβίαι δὲ οἵτινες ὑπὸ τῆς τροφοῦ ἢ τῆς μητρὸς τυχὸν ἔκθλιψιν τῶν διδύμων ὑπέστησαν. <u>καστρᾶτοι</u> δέ εἰσιν ἐφ' ὧν γέγονεν ἐκτομὴ τῶν γεννητικῶν μορίων. (1.11.9)

Eunuch is a general term which falls into three classes; for some eunuchs are *spadones*, others are *castrati*, others *thlibiae*. Now *spadones* are those that are prevented from begetting children by some derangement or chillness troubling the genital organs, but, when relieved of this, are capable of begetting children. *Thlibiae* are those that have had their testicles crushed by their nurse or by their mother. *Castrati* are those that have had their genital organs excised. (Trans. A. F. Murison in Lokin *et al.* 2010: 93)

The explanation here is probably that Theophilus was not thinking of this word as being Latin when he defined it, simply of its being technical terminology. His point here was to distinguish four technical terms: καστρᾶτος, σπάδων, θλιβίας, and the cover term εὐνοῦχος. All four occurred in both Greek and Latin (*castratus, spado, thlibias, eunuchus*), and three were etymologically Greek, leading the bilingual Theophilus to forget – or at least not to think about the fact that – the fourth, *castratus*, was etymologically Latin.

Passage 22 provides the opposite kind of challenge to our explanation of Theophilus' script choice: a long-standing loanword that would surely have been familiar to all Theophilus' readers and is not the subject of discussion nevertheless appears in the Latin alphabet.

22 Τοῦτο δὲ τὴν ἀρχὴν μόνοις ἐπετράπη στρατιώταις ἐξ αὐθεντίας τοῦτο μὲν Αὐγούστου, τοῦτο δὲ Nerva, οὐ μὴν ἀλλὰ καὶ τοῦ ἀρίστου βασιλέως Τραϊανοῦ. μετὰ γὰρ ταῦτα διάταξις Adrianu δυσφοροῦσι τοῖς <u>veteranois</u> καὶ αὐτοῖς ἐπέτρεψε τὸ διατίθεσθαι ἐν ὑπεξουσιότητι. (2.12.pr.)

Originally, this privilege was granted to soldiers alone, by authority partly of Augustus, partly of Nerva, partly of the excellent emperor Traianus; but afterwards a constitution of Adrianus allowed <u>veterans</u>, who took it ill that they had lost the privilege, also to make a will while in power. (Trans. A. F. Murison in Lokin *et al.* 2010: 315–17)

Here again, closer investigation suggests that the passage is not as much of an exception as it appears. It comes at the end of a discussion of who has the right to make a legally valid will, a matter that was complex for Romans since technically a father retained *patria potestas* over his children as long as he lived and therefore someone whose father was still alive could not legally own anything to bequeath. Before this passage,

Theophilus explained that soldiers and veterans were exceptions to this restriction, in that they could legally own and bequeath some property; in so doing he had to define 'veteran', since for this purpose the precise limits of veteran status were important. As a result, he put *veteranos* in Latin script (2.10.9) and then continued to use that script for it for the rest of the discussion.

Therefore Theophilus' choice of script serves as an indication of his views on the foreignness of words he uses, but not in a way that can be easily equated to our concepts of codeswitches and loanwords. Use of the Greek alphabet means that at the moment of writing Theophilus was not thinking of that word as being foreign, and use of the Latin alphabet means that at the moment of writing Theophilus was thinking of the word's foreign status, but his thoughts depended on a number of factors beyond the ones that we would use when deciding whether to call something an established loanword or a codeswitch. Many of the words for which Theophilus used Latin script were indubitably loanwords.

7.1.2 Latin script before the sixth century

A long papyrus fragment dating probably to the fifth or perhaps to the very early sixth century contains a Greek commentary on Roman law known as the *Scholia Sinaitica*.[9] The writer of this papyrus appears to have used Latin script on the same principles as Theophilus. The words in Latin script are sometimes the topic of an explanation (like *necessaria* in passage 23) and sometimes not (like *r.u.*, which stands for *reuxoria* or *actio rei uxoriae*).

23 Τί ἐστιν NECESSARIA δαπανήματα; NECESSARIA ἐστιν δαπανήματα, ὧν μὴ γινομένων κατεδικάζετο ὁ ἀνὴρ ἐναγόμενος τῇ R U. (16–17)

What are necessary expenses? Necessary expenses are those without which the husband would be convicted if charged with an action for recovery of the dowry.

Even long-established loanwords could appear in Latin script when the writer's focus was on explaining their precise meanings. In passage 24 Latin script is used for *Italia*, which had been part of Greek for a millennium (and probably does not come from Latin, though the writer evidently thought it did).

24 Τῆς ITALIας εἶναι δοκοῦσιν καὶ αἱ νῆσοι τῆς ITALIας. οὐκοῦν ὁ τῆς ITALIας ἐξορισθεὶς εἴργεται καὶ τῶν νήσων αὐτῆς. (38)

The islands of Italy also seem to be part of Italy. Therefore someone banished from Italy is also kept away from its islands.

Overall, the fragment contains thirty-six Latin words other than names and phrases; of these κῶδιξ, πάτρων, and τίτλος appear only in Greek script, Λατῖνος appears in both Greek and Latin script, and the rest appear only in Latin script: *adventicios, cessicios, commiteuo, compensateuo, culpa, dolos, dotalios, emancipatos, excusation, facton, inquisition, instituta, legitimos, mandaton, mora, necessarios, pacteuo, pacton, poena, postumos, potior, praetor, procurator, regula, repudion, responson, retention, reuxoria, stipulation, testamentarios, usucapiteuo, voluptaria*.[10] All the words that appear in Greek script had been borrowed before the *Scholia Sinaitica* were written, but of the thirty-two words that appear only in Latin script, only eight (*emancipatos, excusation, facton, mandaton, pacton, praetor, procurator, repudion*) appear to have been already part of Greek at the time the papyrus was written.

The *Scholia Sinaitica* predate not only Theophilus' work, but also the Justinianic reforms that led to that work. And a similar use of Latin script seems to occur in other, smaller papyrus fragments of pre-Justinianic juridical texts.[11] They therefore demonstrate that the use of Latin script visible in sixth-century legal texts is not original to those texts but comes from the Greek-language legal commentary tradition that

---

[9] Kuebler in Seckel and Kuebler (1927: II.II.461–84), Schulz (1961: 411–13), Corcoran (2017: 103–4), Thüngen (2017). The papyrus, which is now lost, is *TM* 62361 and number 2958 in the Mertens–Pack catalogue. The apparently more recent edition in *FIRA* II: 635–52 reprints an earlier text and is less accurate than Kuebler's version.

[10] That is, these words are always written with at least some of their letters in the Latin alphabet, but other letters may be in the Greek alphabet: see §7.1.3. Τίτλος occurs e.g. at 2, πάτρων at 14, and *Italia* at 38; for the other words see §3.2.

[11] E.g. *P.Ryl.* III.475 and 476, *PSI* XIII.1348, marginalia in *PSI* XIV.1449.

preceded them (§9.5.6). In fact the use of Latin script for Latin words may go back as far as the third century in the legal tradition, for it is apparently used at least once in the fragments of a Greek work attributed to the third-century jurist Modestinus.[12]

Pre-sixth-century texts in other genres almost never use Latin script for single words or short phrases (though longer passages of Latin could always appear in Latin script), but there are some exceptions. The earliest example of which I am aware is a third-century AD inscription from Mylasa containing the line]ἐπανορθῶσαι. *succlam(atum) est*: ἰς αἰῶ[να '… to restore. There was an acclamation, "forever!" …' (*I.Mylasa* 605.55). A study of the manuscript tradition of literary texts suggests that from the fourth century onwards, prose writers not aiming at the highest stylistic levels occasionally used Latin script for short codeswitches; later copyists tended to replace the Latin letters with Greek ones, but the original script is sometimes recoverable.[13]

The sixth-century use of Latin script was therefore not as striking a departure from earlier usage as it now looks. It was probably just an expansion and extension of earlier practice, made more visible to us than that earlier practice by the survival patterns of juridical texts and the preferences of copyists. It follows that sixth-century writers such as Theophilus probably inherited ideas about which Latin words would normally be written in Latin script and which in Greek script: Theophilus was not simply making his own distinctions among Latin terms. Such a tradition would explain why Theophilus appears to have had a very high threshold for treating words as established loans (§9.5.6).

7.1.3 Mixture of scripts within a single word

Words written in Latin script often have Greek endings; for example SEDETOIS 'stations' in passage 16 above has the unambiguously Greek dative plural ending -οις. Greek writers seem sometimes to have had the feeling that Greek script should be used for such endings, prompting them to change alphabets within a single word, as with ITALIας in passage 24.[14] Exactly where in the word these switches occur cannot always be established, for the forms of the Latin and Greek alphabets used by sixth-century legal writers are very similar to one another: some letters would not originally have been identifiable as belonging to a particular alphabet.[15]

In addition to ITALIας, the *Scholia Sinaitica* appear to contain seven other examples of this phenomenon: ἐPACTευσεν (13), COMPENSATεύεται (18), PACTον (21), PROCURATOρα (29), MANDATον (29), DOLον (31), and TESTAMENTARίων (40).[16] But script mixture is the exception rather than the rule in the *Scholia Sinaitica*, for the papyrus also contains at least twenty-six words whose unambiguously Greek endings are written in Latin script, including ones such as the genitive plural title DIFFERENTION (12) where ambiguity within Greek could

---

[12] *Excusationos* at *Dig.* 26.6.2.6. For Modestinus' work and the fact that it was revised after the third century see §9.5.6; the Latin script could come from those revisers or from the sixth-century compilers of the *Digest* rather than from Modestinus himself, and moreover I am not sure what the manuscript authority for it is, the standard edition of the *Digest* being that of Mommsen. In that edition, at least, Modestinus' Latin words are usually in Greek script; compare e.g. ἐξκουσατίονας at 27.1.13.pr.

[13] Crusius (1903: 133–40).

[14] Feissel (2008: 219–20), Zilliacus (1935a: 100–1).

[15] Van der Wal (1983: 33–35), cf. Fournet (2019: 82). In ITALIας the I and α could belong to either script, but the L must be Latin and the ς must be Greek. Modern editors often print in small capitals the words written in Latin script in manuscripts of Greek texts, to reflect the Byzantine copyists' use of uncial script for the Latin and minuscule for the Greek; this convention allows the original ambiguity between alphabets to be preserved for some letters. The editors of Theophilus use small capitals for the entire word, including any Greek letters, and the resulting ambiguities have forced me to replicate their practice in my own quotations from Theophilus; the editors of the *Scholia Sinaitica* distinguish Greek from Latin letters, and therefore in my own quotations from that text I have used small capitals only for Latin letters.

[16] Most of these are disputed by Thüngen (2017: 349–63), who however provides other examples of such mixture (2016). Note also KAPITIS DEMINUTIONA (46), where (the editor appears to believe that) the *k* is in the Latin alphabet but the very use of *k* rather than *c* suggests a Greek spelling. There are also a few places where the papyrus has not been successfully read in a way that makes sense but where editors believe that an alphabet switch occurs, such as INSTIζιι (12).

have been avoided by the use of Greek script, ones such as nominative singular LEGITIMOS (51) where ambiguity with the Latin use of the same ending for a different case could have been avoided by the use of Greek script, and ones such as PACTU (27) where the ending looks very odd in Latin script.

Manuscripts of the major sixth-century legal texts also include words with alphabet shifts. Because these texts were transmitted via the manuscript tradition, however, it is more difficult to be certain how the two alphabets were originally used, for there is little agreement among different manuscripts: the medieval scribes who copied the text gradually increased the number of Greek letters in each word and reduced the number of Latin letters.[17] Older editions sometimes regularized this situation by systematically printing Greek endings in Greek script, but more recent editors tend to print the whole word in Latin script if (some, any) manuscripts have any part of it in Latin.

Two distinctive Greek letters often resist this recent editorial standardization because of the sheer difficulty of putting them into the Latin alphabet; for the same reason their use may go back to the original writers at least some of the time.[18] One is η, which in sixth-century script had exactly the same form as Latin *h*. Many Greek first-declension nominal endings contain η, and Theophilus Antecessor often attached such endings to Latin words: for example, SELLH (1.2.7), POENHN (3.19.19), and ADGNATICHC (3.5.1)[19] all contain a letter that looks like *h* but must in fact be η. Likewise θ is part of many verb endings in Greek, again resulting in mixed script when Latin verbs take Greek endings: ETRADITEUθH, RELEGATEUθOSIN, TRADITEUθENTOS, USUCAPITEUθHSETAI, etc.[20]

The presence of such letters cannot have been a necessary prerequisite for the use of Greek script, for none of the examples of script mixing from the *Scholia Sinaitica* includes them. But the *Scholia Sinaitica* suggest in another way that the presence of θ may have triggered the use of Greek script. The writer frequently refers to the collections of laws known as the *Codex Theodosianus*, *Codex Gregorianus*, and *Codex Hermogenianus*. All these titles were most immediately Latin, but the names involved were etymologically Greek, and it was easy to think of the titles themselves as Greek since both the suffix *-ianus* (§6.4) and the word *codex* (κῶδιξ) had been borrowed into Greek centuries earlier. The *Codex Hermogenianus* nevertheless always appears with the name *Hermogenianus* in Latin script (but κῶδιξ in Greek), and the *Codex Gregorianus* usually appears with the name in Latin script (but κῶδιξ in Greek), while the *Codex Theodosianus* always appears with both the name and the word κῶδιξ in Greek script, probably because of the θ.[21]

7.2 THE USE OF LATIN ENDINGS

Although Latin words in Greek texts normally appear with Greek endings even when they are clearly codeswitches (§2.2.2), there are some exceptions. These fall into two distinct groups: some are typical codeswitches and others so atypical as to be possibly loanwords.

7.2.1 *Codeswitches with Latin endings*

Some of the words in Latin script in the passages just quoted have unambiguously Latin endings (e.g. PATRUUS and AVUNCULUS in passage 17), and Latin endings can even appear on words quoted in Greek script. In passage 25, for example, βρέβεμ is a transcription of *brevem*, accusative of Latin *brevis* 'short'. Greek speakers would have

---

[17] Lokin *et al.* (2010: xxiii–xxiv), Van der Wal (1983: 44), Burgmann (1991: 70).

[18] Van der Wal (1983: 43) argues that the evidence in favour of original use of η is better than the evidence in favour of original use of θ; Burgmann (1991: 70) thinks both may be original.

[19] In ADGNATICHC (ἀδγνατικῆς) the letter before the η is a Latin *c* and the one after the η a Greek ς, which in Theophilus' script looked exactly like Latin *c*. At 3.2.7 the same word is written ADGNATICHS with a Latin *s*; this variation may be a modern editorial choice.

[20] For usage in Theophilus see index of Lokin *et al.* (2010).

[21] The examples are as follows; as these words are very heavily abbreviated, I retain here the editor's ( ) to indicate expansion of abbreviations and [ ] to indicate supplements: ERMOG(ENIANO) κ(ώδικι) 5 (twice), GR(EGORIANU) [κώδικος]) 9, [G]REG(ORIANON) κώδικα 10, G[R]EGO-RIANU 10, Γρεγ(οριανοῦ) κ(ώδικος) 3, Θεοδ(οσιανοῦ) κ(ώδικος) 2, 3, 52.

found this form particularly striking because it ends in -μ, which native Greek words never do.

25 Διὰ τί μικρᾶς Τύχης ἱερὸν ἱδρύσατο Σέρουιος Τούλλιος ὁ βασιλεὺς ἣν βρέβεμ καλοῦσι; (Plut. *Mor.* 281d)

Why did king Servius Tullius establish the shrine of Small Fortune, which they call 'Short'?

This usage cannot be the result of ignorance, nor does it come from the margins of the ancient Greek world, either geographically or chronologically: it was written by Plutarch, who lived in Greece c. AD 100 and was a highly educated native speaker. He composed a very large amount of surviving text, in which he frequently used Latin words. Most are integrated, whether loanwords or codeswitches, but passage 25 is not unique. For example, Plutarch also quotes the Latin accusatives singular πόντεμ (*pontem*), ὄπεμ (*opem*), and ὀνῶρεμ (*honorem*), the accusatives plural δέντης (*dentes*) and φάσκης (*fasces*), the genitives singular οὐιρτοῦτις (*virtutis*), ὀνῶρις (*honoris*), μέντις (*mentis*), and ὀψεκουέντις (*obsequentis*), the nominative singular πότηνς (*potens*), and the ablative singular κάρκερε (*carcere*), all of which have distinctively Latin endings.[22]

All these words are clearly codeswitches, for they are rarely or never found elsewhere, Plutarch does not expect his readers to understand what they mean, and he usually says that they are Latin. And they all have the 'right' endings for their contexts; that is, the Latin ending signals a case that is appropriate for the Greek context, like the accusative in passage 25. In terms of case usage they are classic examples of codeswitching as normally practised by bilingual speakers, and they demonstrate that Plutarch was indeed such a speaker and had command of the Latin inflections. But Plutarch did not always engage in this type of codeswitching; in fact he usually inflected Latin codeswitches as Greek. How did he make the choice between Greek or Latin endings for his codeswitches?

The key seems to be the declensional class of the Latin words concerned. Certain Latin declensions had well-established patterns of equivalence into which large numbers of loanwords fell: the first and second declensions, the fourth declension, and certain types of third-declension words, such as those in -ō, -ōnis (§4.2). Plutarch almost always used Greek endings when he codeswitched with a word belonging to one of those categories, especially the first and second declensions, but he often used Latin endings for words whose Greek equivalents were less straightforward: all the examples quoted above belong to the Latin third declension.[23]

Theophilus had a different system. He used Latin endings only on words for which he also used Latin script, and only for a minority of those words, but nevertheless more often than Plutarch did, and for a wider range of forms. Theophilus produced not only unadapted third-declension forms such as accusatives singular *legem* 'law' (1.2.5) and *heredem* 'heir' (3.9.1),[24] but also unadapted first- and second-declension forms such as accusative singular *custodiam* 'guard' (3.23.3a), nominatives singular *patruus* 'paternal uncle' and *avunculus* 'maternal uncle' (3.6.3), and nominative plural *conventionaliae* 'concerning contracts' (3.18.3), as well as the unadapted fourth-declension accusative *aquaehaustum* 'right to draw water' (2.3.2). It would have been very easy to adapt these latter forms to **custodian*, **patruos*, **avunculos*, **conventionaliai*, and **aquaehauston*, but he did not do so: he apparently wanted to quote these words in conspicuously Latin forms.

Theophilus' choice of endings is much more consistent than his choice of script: most words are always inflected as Greek and some always inflected as Latin, even though the script in which they are written may vary. And his choice

---

[22] *Rom.* 16.6, *Numa* 9.2, *Aem.* 37.2, *Publ.* 12.5, *Mor.* 266f, 318d–e, 322f, 727a.

[23] Whether they all belong to one of the third-declension groups that did not have straightforward equivalents in Greek depends on whether one considers *honorem* and *honoris* to come from *honor* or from *honos*. Words in *-or* typically followed the declension of Greek words in -ωρ (§4.2.5), but it is very likely that Plutarch thought of the nominative as *honos*, the form often preferred by authors he might have used as sources (*TLL s.v. honor* 2916.30–42); in that case it would not have belonged to a declensional type with a straightforward Greek equivalent.

[24] There are also partially adapted third-declension words: *pecus* 'farm animal' has a genitive singular *pecudis* and a genitive plural *pecudum* in Latin, but Theophilus uses *pecus* as a genitive singular and *pecudon* as a genitive plural (both in 4.2.3.pr.).

of endings tends to correlate with the words' frequency: words he uses frequently typically have Greek endings, and rare words are more likely to have Latin endings. Therefore Theophilus' distinction between Latin words quoted with Greek endings and Latin words quoted with Latin endings may come closer to our distinction between loanwords and codeswitches than his distinction between words that appear in Greek script and words that appear in Latin script.[25] But it cannot be exactly the same as our distinction, for words that are rare and marked as foreign often nevertheless have Greek endings (e.g. SEDETOIS in passage 16). It looks as though Theophilus' distinction may fall within our category of codeswitches.

Theophilus' choice of endings was not entirely consistent, and the words that appear with both Greek and Latin endings shed further light on the way those choices were made. In passage 26, for example, the term *ruptum* 'nullified'[26] is used first with a Latin ending and then with a Greek one. This term occurs seventeen times in Theophilus, usually with unambiguous Greek endings and only here with an unambiguous Latin one; the Latin form has almost certainly been triggered by coming after the unadapted phrase *non iure civili factum* (for which see §7.3).

26 Ὥστε οὖν, ὡς καὶ ἤδη εἴρηται, τρία πάθη παρενοχλεῖ ταῖς διαθήκαις· NON IURE CIVILI FAC-TUM, RUPTUM, IRRITON. δυνάμεθα δὲ καὶ τὸ IR-RITON RUPTON καλέσαι καὶ τὸ RUPTON IRRITON (2.17.5)

So therefore, as has already been said, three vices can invalidate wills: not being lawfully made, being nullified, and being frustrated. But we can also call a will that has been frustrated 'nullified' and a will that has been nullified 'frustrated'.

In passage 27 *sententia* 'judicial pronouncement' is used first with a conspicuously Latin ending, then with an ambiguous one that could be either Greek or Latin, and finally with an unambiguously Greek ending. Theophilus uses *sententia* only in this passage, and it looks as though he begins by treating it as foreign before gradually integrating it in the course of the discussion.

27 Τὸ δὲ RESPONSON τέμνεται εἰς δύο, εἰς SEN-TENTIAM καὶ OPINIONA. καὶ τί ἐστι SENTEN-TIA; ἡ αὐτοτελὴς καὶ ἀναμφίβολος ἀπόκρισις, οἷον· Ἔξεστι τόδε ποιεῖν, Οὐκ ἔξεστι τόδε ποιεῖν. OPINION δὲ ἡ ὑπεσταλμένη καὶ μετὰ ἐνδοιασμοῦ προφερομένη ἀπόκρισις, οἷον· Νομίζω ὅτι ἔξεστι τόδε ποιεῖν, Νομίζω ὅτι οὐκ ἔξεστι τόδε ποιεῖν. ἐπετέτραπτο δὲ τούτοις δημοσίᾳ νομοθετεῖν ἤτοι τοὺς νόμους ἑρμηνεύειν· οἵτινες καὶ IURIS CONSUL-TI προσηγορεύοντο, τουτέστιν οἱ περὶ τοῦ νόμου ἐπερωτώμενοι· CONSULERE γάρ ἐστι τὸ ἐρωτᾶν. ὧν αἱ SENTENTIAI καὶ αἱ OPINIONES ταύτην ἔχουσι τὴν αὐθεντίαν ὥστε μὴ ἔχειν παρρησίαν δικαστὴν ταῖς αὐτῶν ἀπειθεῖν ἀποκρίσεσιν, ὥσπερ καὶ βασιλέως βοᾷ διάταξις. (1.2.8)

A *responsum* has two forms: *sententia* and *opinio*. And what is a *sententia*? An absolute and positive answer, as: 'It is lawful to do so-and-so', 'It is not lawful to do so-and-so'. An *opinio*, again, is a non-committal and hesitating answer, as: 'I think it is lawful to do so-and-so', 'I think it is not lawful to do so-and-so'. The jurists were empowered to make law – that is, to explain the laws – with public authority; and they were also designated *iurisconsulti*, that is, persons consulted on the law, for *consulere* means 'to consult'. And their *sententiae* and *opiniones* are of such authority that a judge is not at liberty to disregard their answers; as is indeed laid down by an imperial constitution. (Trans. A. F. Murison in Lokin *et al.* 2010: 23)

It is difficult to be certain to what extent Theophilus' practice in this respect was shared by other writers, but there is some evidence that it was not universal. His contemporary John Lydus seems to have put a Latin ending on *fideicommissarios*, which other writers used with Greek endings and sometimes even in Greek script. In fact Lydus may have followed the principle of consistently using Latin endings on words in Latin script, though the evidence is not extensive.[27]

7.2.2 *Loanwords with Latin endings?*

Codeswitches are inflected to fit their contexts; whether their endings are Greek, Latin, or ambiguous, they indicate a case and number showing how the word fits into its sentence. But

---

[25] Cf. Zilliacus (1935a: 99).

[26] Literally 'broken', neuter singular to agree with an understood *testamentum* 'will'.

[27] I can find only three single-word script switches in Lydus, all second-declension masculines in the accusative plural: *Mag.* p. 16.7 *dominos*, p. 78.5 *tutelarios* and *fideicommissarios*.

Theophilus also uses words with Latin endings in another way: as fixed forms that remain the same irrespective of their contexts. For example, in passage 28 both *commodati* and *furti* are from a Latin perspective genitives, part of the phrases *actio commodati* 'legal action about a loan for use' and *actio furti* 'legal action for theft'. In Greek they seem to have a more independent existence, functioning as nominative or accusative depending on the case of the accompanying article. That article is feminine in order to agree with the Greek equivalent of *actio*, ἀγωγή, which is occasionally expressed with these terms (e.g. ἡ FURTI ἀγωγή, 4.1.14) and may always be implied. Leaving words understood is a normal feature of the syntax of both Greek and Latin, and Theophilus would probably have seen the construction here as an extension of that principle. But it is a significant extension, owing to the frequency with which he uses these terms without ἀγωγή and the fact that ἀγωγή is regularly expressed with other words, as in the double-underlined phrase in passage 28. There is also a clear difference between Theophilus' usage and his Latin model, where *actio* is normally expressed and only occasionally understood.[28] Articles are regularly used in Greek with this type of Latin word; codeswitches, by contrast, often appear without an article (e.g. passages 19, 26, and 27).

28 Διάταξις δὲ τοῦ ἡμετέρου γέγονε βασιλέως, ζητήσεως τοιαύτης ἐπ' αὐτὸν ἀνενεχθείσης, ὥστε κλοπὴν ὑποστάντος τοῦ χρησαμένου ἐξουσίαν εἶναι τῷ δεσπότῃ τοῦ κλαπέντος εἴτε <u>τὴν COMMODATI</u> βούλεται κατὰ τοῦ χρησαμένου κινῆσαι εἴτε <u>τὴν FURTI</u> κατὰ τοῦ κλέπτου, καὶ τῆς

ἑτέρας ἐπιλεχθείσης μὴ δύνασθαι τὸν δεσπότην ἐκ μεταμελείας ἐπὶ τὴν <u>ἑτέραν</u> παραγίνεσθαι <u>ἀγωγήν</u>. ἀλλ' εἰ μὲν ἐπιλέξηται τὸν κλέπτην, ἐλευθεροῦσθαι τὸν χρησάμενον, εἰ δὲ ὁ χρήσας ἔλθῃ κατὰ τοῦ χρησαμένου, αὐτῷ μὲν τῷ χρήσαντι οὐκέτι κατὰ τοῦ κλέπτου <u>ἡ FURTI</u> δοθήσεται, τῷ δὲ χρησαμένῳ ταύτην ἡ διάταξις παρέχει κατὰ τοῦ κλέπτου. τότε δὲ ὁ δεσπότης τοῦ πράγματος κινήσας <u>τὴν COMMODATI</u> ἀπόλλυσι <u>τὴν FURTI</u>, ἡνίκα εἰδὼς ὡς ἐκλάπη τὸ πρᾶγμα τὸ χρησθὲν ἐπελέξατο <u>τὴν COMMODATI</u>. γνοὺς δὲ μετὰ τὴν κατὰ τοῦ χρησαμένου προκάταρξιν εἰ βούλεται καταλιπεῖν <u>τὴν COMMODATI</u> χωρῆσαι δὲ ἐπὶ <u>τὴν FURTI</u>, δίδωσιν αὐτῷ παρρησίαν τοῦτο ποιεῖν ἡ διάταξις ... (4.1.16)

But there is a constitution of our emperor, as a result of a question of this sort being brought to him, to the effect that when something has been stolen from a person who had borrowed it, the owner of the stolen object has the choice whether he wants to bring <u>the *commodati*</u> against the borrower or <u>the *furti*</u> against the thief, and when one has been chosen the owner is not able to change his mind and have recourse to the <u>other action</u>. But if he chooses the thief, the borrower is released [from any obligation], and if the lender proceeds against the borrower, <u>the *furti*</u> will no longer be available to the lender himself, rather the constitution gives it to the borrower to use against the thief. But by bringing <u>the *commodati*</u> the owner of the thing forfeits <u>the *furti*</u> only when he chose <u>the *commodati*</u> knowing that the thing lent had been stolen. But when he finds that out after the beginning of the action against the borrower, if he wants to leave <u>the *commodati*</u> and change to <u>the *furti*</u> the constitution gives him the freedom to do that.

Similarly, in passage 29 the underlined terms are ablatives, giving the source of an obligation. The word 'obligation' (Latin *obligatio*) is sometimes translated into Greek with the feminine noun ἐνοχή and sometimes omitted except for the feminine article, leaving *verbis* to mean '(obligation arising) by words', *re* '(obligation arising) by conduct', *litteris* '(obligation arising) by writing', and *consensu* '(obligation arising) by agreement'.

29 Ἡ δὲ ACCEPTILATION, καθὰ εἴρεται, μόνην διαλύει <u>τὴν VERBIS ἐνοχήν</u>, οὐ μὴν τὰς λοιπάς, οἷον <u>τὴν RE</u> ἢ <u>LITTERIS</u> ἢ <u>CONSENSU</u>· ἀκόλουθον γὰρ ἐνομίσθη εἶναι τὴν ῥήμασι συνισταμένην ἐνοχὴν ἑτέροις δύνασθαι ῥήμασι καταλύεσθαι. εἰ

[28] The equivalent passage in Justinian's *Institutes* (4.1.16 = Krueger 1895: 44) runs *sed nostra providentia etiam hoc in decisionibus nostris emendavit, ut in domini sit voluntate, sive <u>commodati actionem</u> adversus eum qui rem commodatam accepit movere desiderat, sive <u>furti</u> adversus eum qui rem subripuit, et alterutra earum electa dominum non posse ex paenitentia ad alteram venire actionem. sed si quidem furem elegerit, illum qui rem utendam accepit penitus liberari. sin autem commodator veniat adversus eum qui rem utendam accepit, ipsi quidem nullo modo competere posse adversus furem <u>furti actionem</u>, eum autem, qui pro re commodata convenitur, posse adversus furem <u>furti</u> habere <u>actionem</u>, ita tamen, si dominus sciens rem esse subreptam adversus eum cui res commodata fuit pervenit: sin autem nescius et dubitans rem non esse apud eum <u>commodati actionem</u> instituit, postea autem re comperta voluit remittere quidem <u>commodati actionem</u>, ad <u>furti</u> autem pervenire, tunc licentia ei concedatur ...*

δὲ ἑτέρωθέν ἐστι μοί τις ἔνοχος, οἷον ἀπὸ <u>τῆς RE</u>, <u>LITTERIS</u> ἢ <u>CONSENSU</u> ἢ ἀπὸ τῆς NEGOTIORUM GESTORUM ἢ EX TESTAMENTO, βουληθῶ δέ σοι τοῦτο συγχωρῆσαι τὸ χρέος, δύναμαί σε ἐπερωτᾶν οὕτως· Ὁμολογεῖς διδόναι μοι ὅπερ ἐποφείλεις ἐκ τῆσδε τῆς ἀγωγῆς; καὶ σοῦ εἰπόντος Ὁμολογῶ ἡ μὲν προτέρα ἀνῄρηται, τίκτεται δὲ <u>ἡ VERBIS</u>, καὶ λοιπὸν συστάσης <u>τῆς VERBIS</u> ἀκολούθως ἡ ACCEP-TILATION ἐπάγεται. καὶ ἐν ἐκείνῳ μέν ἐστι διαφορὰ SOLUTIONOS καὶ ACCEPTILATIONOS, ὅτι ἡ μὲν SOLUTION πᾶσαν διαλύει ἐνοχήν, ἡ δὲ ACCEPTILA-TION <u>τὴν VERBIS</u>. (3.29.1)

But, as has been said, it is only <u>the obligation</u> <u>*verbis*</u> that acceptilation dissolves, not any of the others, as <u>the obligations *re*</u>, or <u>*litteris*</u>, or <u>*consensu*</u>; for it was reckoned consistent that the obligation created by words should be capable of dissolution by other words. If you are under obligation to me on some other ground, as on <u>a contract</u> <u>*re*</u>, or <u>*litteris*</u>, or <u>*consensu*</u>, or *negotiorum gestorum* or *ex testamento*, and I wish to release you from this debt, I can stipulate with you in these terms: 'Do you engage to give to me what you owe me on such-and-such an action?' and, on your saying 'I engage', the former action is extinguished and <u>the obligation *verbis*</u> arises; and then, <u>the</u> <u>obligation *verbis*</u> being created, acceptilation is consistently applied. There is this difference between *solutio* and acceptilation, that, while *solutio* dissolves every obligation, acceptilation dissolves <u>the obligation *verbis*</u> only. (Trans. A. F. Murison in Lokin *et al.* 2010: 721)

These terms are fairly common in Theophilus. He uses *furti* 62 times, *commodati* 10 times, *verbis* 24 times, *re* 20 times, *litteris* 18 times, and *consensu* 16 times.[29] They can also be found in later legal works, where they appear in Greek script as φούρτι, κομμοδάτι, βέρβις, ῥέ, λίτ(τ)ερις, and κονσένσο(υ), retaining their fossilized Latin endings. Even if these terms were not loanwords in Theophilus' own day, they must have become loanwords soon afterwards. The borrowing of inflected forms that retain their original endings as indeclinable forms in the borrowing language is not unusual in modern languages; compare English 'veto'

(originally an inflected verb form meaning 'I forbid'), 'alibi' (originally an adverb meaning 'elsewhere'), and 're' (originally an ablative meaning 'thing'). It is unusual for ancient Greek, however, and undoubtedly had to do with the specialized nature of legal language in the late antique and Byzantine periods.

7.3 EXPRESSIONS CONSISTING OF MULTIPLE WORDS

Some Latin phrases were borrowed into Greek with univerbation to become one-word loanwords; this process occurred particularly with titles (§4.5). Other Latin phrases appear in Greek texts as multi-word phrases. Of course, since the ancients did not leave spaces between words, the distinction between single words and phrases is most immediately one made by modern editors, but those editorial choices are not without foundation: the Latin expressions that editors choose to print as phrases rather than as single words usually do function differently from the univerbations. They also function differently from individual Latin words found in the same Greek texts, for phrases are much more likely than individual words to appear in Latin script and/or with Latin endings. Of course, most writers never use Latin script at all and therefore put phrases into Greek script. But writers who sometimes use Latin script for individual words use it much more generally for phrases. Theophilus Antecessor, for example, almost always uses Latin script for phrases, and words that he would otherwise put in Greek script appear in Latin script when they are part of longer phrases. In passage 30 he uses πάτρων 'patron' first in Greek script, as would be expected because it was a common word that had entered Greek more than 600 years before his day and was not being explained, and then in Latin script as part of a longer phrase.

30 Ἕκτην ἐπενόησεν ἣν τῷ <u>πάτρωνι</u> καὶ τῇ πατρωνίσσῃ δέδωκε καὶ ἀνιοῦσιν αὐτῶν καὶ κατιοῦσιν, ἣν ὠνόμασεν UNDE LIBERI <u>PATRONI</u> PA-TRONAEQUE ET PARENTES EORUM. (3.9.3)

He invented a sixth type, which he gave to the <u>patron</u> and the patroness and to their older relatives and their descendants, which he called *unde liberi <u>patroni</u> patronaeque et parentes eorum*.

In the *Scholia Sinaitica*, likewise, longer phrases normally appear in Latin script, regardless of the status of the individual words in those phrases. Both Λατῖνος and κολωνία had been established as loanwords for many centuries before the composition of this text, but nevertheless both appear in Latin script in passage 31, where the phrase 'Latin colonies' has a particular meaning beyond those of Λατῖνος and κολωνία in isolation.

31 Ὅπου τις τοῦ οἰκείου ἀδελφοῦ ἀπογραφέντος εἰς τὰς <u>LATINAS COLONIAS</u> ἐπιτροπεύει ἀνήβου ὄντος. (42)

… where someone is the guardian of his own brother, who is a minor and whose registration has been transferred to the <u>Latin colonies</u>.

Writers who never use Latin script also treat phrases differently from single words, by using Latin endings more readily. Plutarch, for example, quotes οὐετέρεμ μεμόριαμ 'ancient memory', ὂκ ἄγε 'do this!', σίνε πάτρις 'without a father', etc.[30] In such a context Plutarch could retain a Latin ending even for μεμόριαμ, a first-declension word that would have been easy to adapt to *μεμορίαν (cf. §7.2.1).

Passage 32 comes from an inscription roughly contemporary with Plutarch; it contains so many Latinate terms that an underlying Latin version can be reconstructed.

32 Γάϊον Ἄντιον Αὖλον Ἰούλιον
Αὔλου υἱὸν Κουαδρᾶτον, δὶς
ὕπατον, ἀνθύπατον Ἀσίας,
σεπτεμουίρουμ ἐπουλώνουμ,
φράτρεμ Ἀρουᾶλεμ, πρεσβευτὴν
καὶ ἀντιστράτηγον Πόντου … (*I.Pergamon* II.440)

Gaius Antius Aulus Julius Quadratus, son of Aulus, twice consul, proconsul of Asia, *septemvir epulonum, frater Arvalis*, propraetorian legate to Pontus …

(Latin version perhaps *Gaium Antium Aulum Iulium Auli filium Quadratum, bis consulem, proconsulem Asiae, septemvirum epulonum, fratrem Arvalem, legatum pro praetore Ponti* …)

This inscription treats Latin material in three different ways. Some words, all titles, are translated: *consul* into ὕπατος, *proconsul* into ἀνθύπατος, *legatus* into πρεσβευτής, and *pro praetore* into ἀντιστράτηγος.[31] Some words, all names belonging to the second declension, are transliterated into Greek with Greek endings: Γάϊον Ἄντιον Αὖλον Ἰούλιον, Αὔλου, Κουαδρᾶτον. And two titles are transliterated into Greek with Latin endings: *septemvir epulonum* 'member of a board of seven men responsible for public feasts' as σεπτεμουίρουμ ἐπουλώνουμ and *frater Arvalis* 'Arval brother' (member of a group of priests) as φράτρεμ Ἀρουᾶλεμ. The reason for the Latin endings must be at least in part that these two titles were phrases: *frater* had a well-established Greek translation, ἀδελφός, and under normal circumstances someone who translated *consul, proconsul*, etc. would also have used ἀδελφός for *frater*. Likewise *epulo* and *Arvalis* both belonged to Latin declensional types that had well-established Greek equivalents (§4.2.5, §4.2.2); someone who could adapt *Auli* to Αὔλου and *Quadratum* to Κουαδρᾶτον would also have been able to adapt *epulonum* to ἐπουλώνων and *Arvalis* to Ἀρουάλιος. But the composer of this inscription chose not to do that, probably because these words were part of fixed phrases, and instead gave them Latin endings.[32]

Again Theophilus Antecessor is particularly revealing. Theophilus commonly uses unadapted phrases such as *non do non lego* in passage 19, *non*

---

[30] *Numa* 13.7, 14.2; *Mor.* 288f. The last example should be *sine patre*, since *sine* takes the ablative; use of the genitive *patris* was probably triggered by the fact that the Greek equivalent of *sine*, ἄνευ 'without', takes a genitive (J. N. Adams 2003: 428). For Plutarch's limited knowledge of Latin see *Demosthenes* 2.2.

[31] These translations are not the author's own; they were standard by the time this inscription was composed (Mason 1974 *s.vv.*).

[32] Other inscriptions handle these phrases other ways. *Frater Arvalis* could be partially translated into ἀδελφὸς Ἀρουᾶλις 'Arval brother', but the fully adapated ἀδελφὸς Ἀρουάλιος does not seem to be attested. *Septemvirum epulonum* could be rendered σεπτέμουιρα ἐπουλώνουμ, with the first word assimilated into the Greek third declension and the second left unassimilated, or ἑπτὰ ἀνδρῶν ἐπουλώνων, literally '(one) of the seven men of the banqueters', with the second word assimilated into the third declension and the first translated. But as far as I can tell there are no examples of inflectional adaptation of both words: *σεπτέμουιρα ἐπουλώνων, the form we would expect given the way most Latin words are treated in Greek, apparently does not occur (Mason 1974: 7, 19, 26, 49, 84, 116, 117; *I.Pergamon* II.436.4, 437.8, 441.4, 451.4; *IGR* III.275.10, IV.383.9; *I.Ephesos* VII.1.3034.4–5). Cf. §4.2.2 on πρῖμος, στολᾶτος, and Αὐγουστᾶλις.

iure civili factum in passage 26, *iuris consulti* in passage 27, *negotiorum gestorum* and *ex testamento* in passage 29, and *unde liberi patroni patronaeque et parentes eorum* in passage 30.[33] The frequency with which such phrases can appear is shown in passage 33.

33 Τί οὖν; ἕξει ὁ <u>PUPILLOS</u> τὴν <u>IN REM</u> ἐπὶ ἐκδικήσει τῶν νούμμων τῶν ὑπ᾽ αὐτοῦ δανεισθέντων. ταῦτα μὲν ἐν ᾧ φαίνονται οἱ νοῦμμοι· εἰ δὲ ὁ λαβὼν <u>MALA FIDE</u> ἐδαπάνησεν αὐτούς, τουτέστιν εἰδὼς ὅτι <u>PUPILLOS</u> ἐστὶν ὁ δανείσας, κατασχεθήσεται τῇ <u>AD EXHIBENDUM</u>. ἐφ᾽ ὧν γὰρ φαινομένων κινεῖται ἡ <u>IN REM</u>, ἐπὶ τούτων κρυπτομένων ἢ <u>MALA FIDE</u> δαπανηθέντων χώρα τῇ <u>AD EXHIBENDUM</u>. εἰ δὲ ἀνηλώθησαν <u>BONA FIDE</u>, τουτέστι τοῦ δανεισαμένου νομίσαντος ἔφηβον εἶναι τὸν δανείσαντα, τότε <u>IN REM</u> κινεῖσθαι οὐ δύναται, οὐδὲ γὰρ φαίνονται οἱ νοῦμμοι, οὔτε μὴν <u>AD EXHIBENDUM</u>, ἐπειδὴ οὐδὲ κρύπτονται οἱ νοῦμμοι οὐδὲ μὴν <u>MALA FIDE</u> δεδαπάνηνται. (2.8.2)

What then? The minor will have the <u>*actio in rem*</u> for recovering the coins he lent. That is, as long as the coins are visible; but if the borrower has spent them <u>in bad faith</u>, that is, knowing that the person who lent them is a minor, he will be liable to the <u>*actio ad exhibendum*</u>. For the proper place of the <u>*ad exhibendum*</u> is for things for which the <u>*in rem*</u> is brought if they are visible, when they are hidden or have been spent in <u>bad faith</u>. But if they have been spent <u>in good faith</u>, that is, with the borrower thinking that the lender is of age, then an <u>*in rem*</u> cannot be brought, for the coins are not visible, nor indeed an <u>*ad exhibendum*</u>, since the coins have been neither hidden nor spent <u>in bad faith</u>.

In this passage all the words in phrases have Latin endings, but the single word *pupillos* has a Greek ending; that pattern is repeated in many other passages. Are phrases simply always codeswitches?[34] But some of these phrases act more like loanwords than like codeswitches: *bona fide*, for example, occurs seventy-one times in this text, in exactly this form,[35] and is also common in later legal writers, who put it in Greek script as βόνα φίδε. *Bona fide* is an important Roman legal concept that has entered other languages as well; in English, for example, 'bona fide' is clearly a borrowing rather than a codeswitch (it is widely used by monolingual English speakers and has an entry in the *Oxford English Dictionary*, which quotes examples going back to 1543). *Mala fide* occurs fourteen times in Theophilus, always in exactly this form, and later often appears as μάλα φίδε; again the same phrase has been borrowed into English (although it is less common than 'bona fide', the *Oxford English Dictionary* gives it an entry with examples going back to 1561). The individual adjectives *bonus* 'good' and *malus* 'bad', and the noun *fides* 'faith', are not otherwise used by Theophilus at all,[36] a fact that makes it very unlikely that he thought of these phrases in terms of their component parts.

In fact the expressions in this passage are strikingly similar to fossilized Latin forms like *furti* or *commodati* (§7.2.2): they occur frequently in a fixed form, neither taking Greek endings nor using different Latin endings in different Greek syntactic contexts as a codeswitch typically would. In this they are very different from φρᾶτρεμ Ἀρουᾶλεμ in passage 32, which has a Latin accusative ending because its Greek context requires an accusative. Here, by contrast, articles are used when needed to show the phrases' syntactic functions: τὴν IN REM, τῇ AD EXHIBENDUM, etc. It is possible that some or all of these phrases are really univerbations in Greek and that Theophilus, who wrote without word division, thought there was no difference at all between fossilized expressions like *furti* and ones like *bona fide*. But it is also possible that Theophilus did make a distinction and

[33] Van der Wal (1983: 38–9) gives a lengthy though incomplete list of such phrases in Theophilus; more can be found in the index to Lokin *et al.* (2010). Cf. Burgmann (1991: 67).

[34] The borrowing of phrases is much rarer than the borrowing of single words, so linguists have a tendency to think of phrases primarily in the context of codeswitches (e.g. Poplack 2018: 142; Matras 2020: 117–18; Myers-Scotton 2006: 259). Nevertheless it is often pointed out that multi-word borrowings exist, and recent work has started to

pay more attention to them (e.g. Zenner and Kristiansen 2014: 7–8; Winter-Froemel 2011: 36; Gusmani 1981–3: I.111).

[35] There is also one example of *bonae fidei* (2.8.2).

[36] He does use *bona* 'goods' as a noun, but that is effectively a different word, as are the various compounds of *fides* that he also employs (*fideicommisson* 'legacy paid at the discretion of the main heir', *fideicommissarios* 'recipient of a legacy paid at the discretion of the main heir', and *fideiussor* 'surety').

considered *bona fide* to be a two-word phrase – but nevertheless treated it as a loanword, to the same extent as he treated *furti* as a loanword.

Borrowing of phrases without full univerbation is, in fact, a reasonably well-attested phenomenon, even if far less common than the borrowing of individual words. English examples include not only 'bona fide' and 'mala fide', but also 'hors d'oeuvre', 'post mortem', and 'ad hoc', which demonstrate their integration by taking English suffixes: plural 'hors d'oeuvres', past tense 'post-mortemed', derivatives 'adhocracy' and 'adhocratic'.[37] Modern Greek dictionaries often include phrases borrowed from other languages, for example in Babiniotis (2002) English γουίντ-σέρφινγκ 'wind surfing', κάντιντ κάμερα 'candid camera', μπόντι-μπίλντινγκ 'body-building', and οφ-δι-ρέκορντ 'off the record'; French σαβουάρ βιβρ *savoir vivre* and τρουα-κάρ *trois quarts*; Portuguese μπόσα νόβα *bossa nova*. Interestingly, though Babiniotis uses Greek script for these and other phrases borrowed from modern languages, he prints Latin phrases in Latin script: for example, *ab urbe condita*, *dies irae* (alphabetized under ντ), *mutatis mutandis*, *sine qua non*, *sui generis*, and *usus norma loquendi*.

7.4 CONCLUSIONS

Imperial-period legal writers sometimes used Latin script for words of Latin etymology, both codeswitches and loanwords; in the sixth century even writers of other genres occasionally used Latin script. The same author could put the same word in different scripts in the course of a single text, depending on how he was thinking about that word at each time: when focussing on a particular word, writers often thought about its etymology and used Latin script even for long-established loanwords, but when focussing on other matters they often put loanwords in Greek script and codeswitches in Latin script. Latin loanwords with Greek endings were sometimes written with the Latin portion in Latin script and the ending in Greek, but Latin script was often used for the ending as well.

Codeswitches could also keep their Latin endings under certain circumstances. Some writers, such as Plutarch, used Latin endings for third-declension nouns that were not easy to assimilate into a Greek declension; the endings fit the codeswitches' Greek contexts. The sixth-century legal writer Theophilus Antecessor used Latin endings more freely, including on codeswitches that would have been easy to integrate into Greek. Theophilus did not always use Latin endings, however; many of his codeswitches have Greek inflections.

Theophilus also used some Latin words in fixed forms, with Latin endings that did not change to fit the context; some of these are frequent and also occur in other texts. These are likely to be loanwords despite their Latin endings.

Some Latin words appear in Greek not as isolated words or as univerbations, but as part of Latin phrases. These are much more likely than single words to take Latin script and/or Latin endings; indeed even well-established loanwords often revert to their Latin forms when they are embedded in longer phrases. Phrases are usually codeswitches, but common ones that regularly appear in a fixed form may be borrowings.

---

[37] *Oxford English Dictionary s.vv.*; note also entries for 'per cent' (with derivatives including 'percentage'), 'a priori' (with derivatives including 'apriorism'), 'sine qua non' (with derivatives including 'sine-qua-nonniness'), 'alter ego' (with derivatives including 'alter-egoism'), 'pro rata' (with derivatives including 'prorate'), 'c'est la vie', 'que sera sera', etc. Lemmata in Berger's dictionary of Roman law (1953) are often phrases, including ones that appear in Greek texts about Roman law.

8

WHEN WERE LOANWORDS USED?

8.1 CHRONOLOGY OF BORROWINGS

The chronology of Latin borrowings into Greek has long appeared to be unproblematically established. It looked as though borrowing began sporadically in the Hellenistic period but remained rare until the fourth century AD, only becoming really common in the sixth.[1] But closer investigation suggests that none of this is right: borrowing began very early and does not appear to have risen at all in late antiquity.

8.1.1 Overall patterns

It has long been obvious that late antiquity is the period when Latin words were most likely to appear in Greek texts.[2] Latin words are ubiquitous in Greek papyri from the fourth century onwards: there are more attested uses of Latin words in fourth-century papyri than there are fourth-century papyrus fragments.[3] Authors of literary texts waited rather longer to reflect the vogue for Latin, but in the sixth century some literature is as full of loanwords as the papyri. Yet this increased usage did not result from increased borrowing; in fact 62% of the 673 Latin words demonstrably borrowed into Greek

in antiquity were borrowed before AD 300. The steady accumulation of borrowings and formation of derivatives from them meant, however, that in each century the Greek language included more Latin loanwords than in previous centuries.[4] Figure 2 illustrates the chronological distribution of new borrowings (words taken directly from Latin either as wholes or in part), new derivatives (words created within Greek from previously borrowed loanwords by compounding or suffixation: §4.6), and the accumulated stock of borrowings and derivatives (from §8.2.1, Figure 7), taking as the date of borrowing or derivation the first secure example of use as a Greek word (i.e. omitting marked, doubtful, and undated attestations; examples datable to a range of two or more centuries are counted in the latest of the centuries to which they might apply).[5]

The data presented in Figure 2 appear also to suggest that the peak period for borrowings was the second century AD. But that peak is likely to be an illusion: many of the words concerned were probably borrowed earlier, even if they did not become visible to us until the second century. When relying on ancient evidence we very rarely see the exact moment of borrowing; instead we see evidence that words have already been borrowed, and therefore the date assignable to a

---

[1] For example, Daris (1991a: 17–18) sees the early fourth century as the turning point at which Greek speakers began to make significant use of Latin words, and Viscidi (1944: 56–7) sees the sixth century as the peak period for Latin borrowings, with more than twice as many borrowings as any other century. Both these scholars include codeswitches as well as loanwords.

[2] E.g. Mason (1974: 11–12), Dubuisson (1985: 140).

[3] Dickey (2003: 256); the figure given there, an average of 1.02 Latin words per fragment, is an underestimate, since it excludes four loanwords that are ubiquitous in papyri (Αὔγουστος, δηνάριον, ἰνδικτίων, οὐγγία) as well as names, which are also very common. See Figure 5 below.

[4] In total there are 147 derivatives and therefore 820 loanwords, but because some words died out before the end of antiquity (§8.2.1), the largest number of loanwords in circulation at any one time was 690 in the sixth century.

[5] Comparison with a similar graph I produced a decade ago (Dickey 2012: 67) will reveal how much my statistics have changed over the course of this project. Unfortunately that earlier article was wrong on quite a few points; it is entirely superseded by this book.

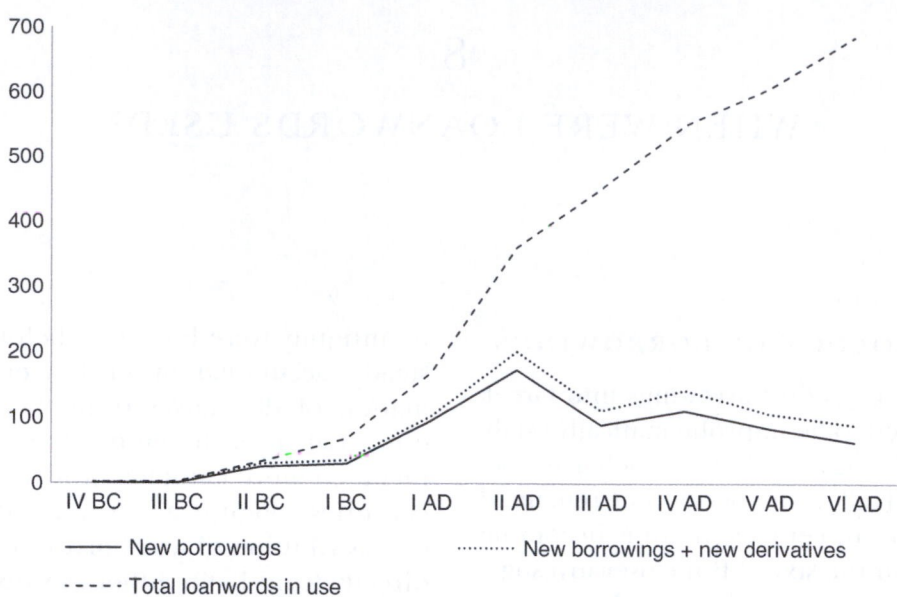

Figure 2 New borrowings and derivatives versus accumulated loanwords; exact numbers in §12.1

borrowing is usually a *terminus ante quem*. For example, the first two attestations of βράκαι 'trousers' are as follows:

34 Ἐσθῆσι δὲ χρῶνται καταπληκτικαῖς, χιτῶσι μὲν βαπτοῖς χρώμασι παντοδαποῖς διηνθισμένοις καὶ ἀναξυρίσιν, ἃς ἐκεῖνοι βράκας προσαγορεύουσιν (Diodorus Siculus 5.30.1 (I BC), possibly quoting Posidonius)

And they wear striking clothing, tunics decorated with all sorts of dyed colours, and trousers, which they call βράκαι.

35 Σχολαστικὸς βράκας ἀγοράσας, ἐπεὶ δὲ στενὰς οὔσας μόγις ὑπεδύσατο, ἐδρωπακίσατο. (Philogelos 64, IV AD)

A learned simpleton bought a pair of trousers; when he could scarcely get them on because they were too tight, he applied a depilatory.

Passage 34 indicates that in the first century BC βράκαι was considered a foreign word, and passage 35 shows that in the fourth century AD it was a loanword. Since those passages are all the evidence available on the early history of βράκαι, we have to date the borrowing to the fourth century, while being aware that it could actually have occurred any time between the first century BC and fourth century AD. And βράκαι is unusual in

that we have evidence of a *terminus post quem* as well as the *terminus ante quem*; usually we have only the latter.

Sometimes the first evidence for a loanword suggests that it had already been part of Greek for a considerable period. For example, the second-century lexicographer Pollux sometimes explains a Classical Greek word by using a loanword, indicating that the loanword had replaced the Classical term in ordinary speech. Thus passages 36–9 indicate that σκάλα 'gangway', πατέλλα 'dish', λίγλα 'spoon', and μανδήλη 'towel' were far from new when Pollux wrote, even though none is certainly attested earlier.

36 Ἀποβάθρα καὶ διαβάθρα, ἣν σκάλαν καλοῦσιν (1.93)

Ἀποβάθρα and διαβάθρα, which they call σκάλα.

37 Τὰς δὲ καλουμένας πατέλλας λεκανίδας ὀνομαστέον, εἰ καὶ ἐξ ἀργύρου εἶεν (6.85)

And the things called πατέλλαι should be named λεκανίδες, even if they are made of silver.

38 Ἐμοὶ δὲ καὶ τὴν καλουμένην λίγλαν μυστίλην ἥδιον καλεῖν ἢ λίγλαν (6.87)

And to me it seems nicer to call the thing known as λίγλα a μυστίλη too, rather than a λίγλα.

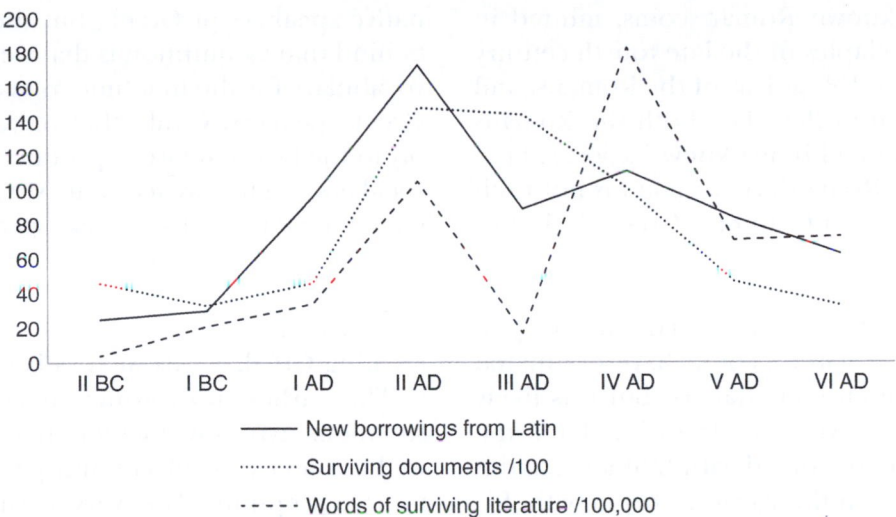

Figure 3 Appearance of new borrowings compared to the amount of surviving Greek literature and documents; numbers and calculations in §12.1

39 Οὕτω δὲ καὶ *νῦν* καλοῦσι τὰ μαλλοὺς ἔχοντα χειρόμακτρα ὡς ἀπὸ τῆς δασύτητος, ὥστ᾽ οὐδὲν ἂν κωλύοι τὰς ὀνομαζομένας <u>μαντήλας</u> οὕτω καλεῖν (7.74)

And even today they call napkins with tufts of wool that (i.e. λάσιον) from their roughness, so that nothing would prevent one from calling the things named <u>μανδήλη</u> that.

The problem of delayed attestation applies to every century, but not to all centuries equally, for the amount of surviving Greek text is unevenly distributed over time. When a particular century is represented by large amounts of surviving text, loanwords are more likely to be preserved than in a century for which the evidence is less abundant. Therefore the borrowing 'peak' in the second century AD is likely to be due mainly to the explosion of evidence in that century, from which we have far more surviving Greek text than from the three previous centuries combined.[6] In fact, a graph of the surviving volume of Greek literature and papyri suggests that the borrowing patterns visible to us could be largely a reflection of the survival pattern of ancient Greek, not of the rate of ancient borrowing (Figure 3). Words may have

been borrowed at a fairly constant rate, or even with a slight decline as time went on.[7]

8.1.2 *The earliest borrowings*

Greek speakers started borrowing from Latin long before the Roman conquest of Greece in the second century BC. In fact the very first borrowings are not directly visible to us; they would have taken place in Italy, where Greek speakers were abundant but from which few early Greek texts are preserved. Greek colonists settled in and around the Bay of Naples starting in the eighth century BC and must have had a word for their rather primitive neighbours to the north soon after the foundation of Rome, even if the earliest secure attestation of Ῥώμη 'Rome' only dates to the second century BC.[8]

---

[6] See §12.1, section on Figure 3. Word counts per century are not available for inscriptions.

[7] Fournet (2019: 75–6) argues that bilingualism became rarer in Egypt over the course of the Empire; if indeed Greek speakers were less likely to interact with Latin speakers and Latin texts in the later centuries, a decline in new borrowings would be expected. It is possible that the large amount of legal Greek surviving from the sixth century also has a distorting effect on our data, but the extent and effects of that distortion are less clear than those of the distortion in the second century (§9.5.6).

[8] There is even some evidence for the presence of Greek speakers in Latium before the foundation of Rome (Peruzzi 1998).

The earliest known Roman coins, minted in Greek-speaking Naples in the late fourth century BC, bear the legend Ῥωμαίων 'of the Romans' and thus indicate that at that date both the Romans and their Greek neighbours knew Ῥωμαῖος as the Greek word for 'Roman'. As Ῥωμαῖος is not itself a direct borrowing but rather a Greek derivative of Ῥώμη, these coins demonstrate that Ῥώμη too must have formed part of the Greek vocabulary (at least in Italy) by that date.[9] The idea of putting the legend in Greek could have originated with the Neapolitan coin-makers, but it is likely that the Romans (who no doubt paid for the minting) at least concurred with that idea, and it may even have been their own to begin with, for Greek was much more widely used than Latin in fourth-century BC Italy. The distinction matters, even if in this case the facts are unknown, because if the early Romans chose to present themselves to the world in Greek, that self-presentation may not have been confined entirely to coinage.[10] Perhaps at this very early period, when elements of Roman culture were first becoming apparent beyond the boundaries of Latium, significant elements of the Greek-language discussion of that culture came from people whose native language was Latin.[11] Romans clearly wrote and spoke in Greek about their own political and social institutions; it is often assumed that most of the vocabulary they used to do so was actually created by native speakers of Greek, but the only evidence behind that assumption is that we usually see that vocabulary for the first time in texts composed by Greek speakers. Could that pattern be due simply to the fact that Greek produced by early Latin speakers is far less likely to survive today than Greek produced by Greek speakers from the same period? We cannot rule out the possibility that Latin speakers not only wrote their first coin legend themselves but also were responsible for creating Greek words such as Ῥώμη and Ῥωμαῖος.

The earliest borrowings in language contact situations typically include personal names as well as names for places and peoples, and Latin is no exception. The very earliest Latin term attested in Greek is the name Λατῖνος, which occurs in Hesiod's *Theogony* as part of an interpolated passage probably added before 510 BC.[12] Latinus was a mythical character, the eponymous early king of Latium, and there is no *a priori* reason why he could not have been invented by the Greeks. In this passage, however, the writer reveals genuine, though slightly garbled, knowledge of the peoples of Italy, indicating that the material in it comes ultimately from an Italian source.[13] Λατῖνος must therefore be a loanword in the *Theogony*, though it need not have been borrowed directly from Latin; it could have come via a third language such as Etruscan. From the third century BC Λατῖνος also appears in the meaning 'Latin', i.e. pertaining to Latium and its people. Other Latin names no doubt appear sporadically from an early period, but names are generally excluded from the present study.[14]

[9] It is nevertheless counted in my statistics as having been borrowed in the second century BC, in order to adhere to consistent criteria for dating borrowings: I have always dated words to the century of their first attestations as integrated loanwords.

[10] Studies of other languages commonly find differences between the linguistic influence of speakers' native language on additional languages they learn ('interference'), and the linguistic influence of a foreign language on speakers' native languages; e.g. Matras (2020: 76–8), Thomason (2001: 66–76), Thomason and Kaufmann (1988: 37–45). For this distinction in Latin, i.e. between the way Latin was affected by Romans who learned Greek and by speakers of Greek (and other languages) who learned Latin, see J. N. Adams (2003: e.g. 27–8, 38, 424–5).

[11] Thus Crawford (1977: 250) 'The early stages of Roman contact with the Greek world saw Rome desperately anxious to explain herself to that world and hence the use of Greek words for Roman institutions which already had roughly the right meaning in the Greek world.'

[12] *Theogony* 1013; for the dating see M. L. West (1966: 49, 397–8, 434–6).

[13] M. L. West (1966: 434–6).

[14] See §12.2.2 for the reasons for this exclusion, the precise definition of 'name' used in applying it, and the justification of that definition; of course by different definitions Ῥωμαῖος and Ῥώμη might also be excluded. The Greek versions of Roman names have been studied elsewhere, e.g. Vallat (2008), Dobias-Lalou (1998), Leclercq (1997), García Domingo (1979), Hanell (1954), Meinersmann (1927: 66–102), and Dittenberger (1872). Corsten (2010) examines Greek names created with the Latinate suffix -ιανός. Roman and Latinate names occurring in Greek inscriptions can be found in the *Lexicon of Greek Personal Names* (Fraser and Matthews 1987–), especially volume IIIA.

The earliest borrowing of a Latin word other than a name is generally thought to be οὐγγία 'one twelfth', 'ounce', which appeared in Sicilian Greek (as ὀγκία) from the fifth century BC.[15] Despite the general agreement among scholars that the source of οὐγγία was Latin *uncia*, it is very difficult to see how a word that had penetrated into Sicilian Greek by that date could actually have originated in Latium. More likely οὐγγία/*uncia* did not originate in Latin *per se* but belonged to a number of languages spoken in the southern half of Italy, and its original adoption by Greek speakers was independent of its original adoption by Latin speakers. If that theory is correct, οὐγγία was not at first a Latin loan, but very soon it effectively became one, for Greek speakers associated it with the Roman weight and its Latin name. The *terminus ante quem* for that association is the third century BC, the date of an inscribed weight found in the Athenian agora. Sicilian and Roman ounces weighed different amounts, and while two earlier weights inscribed with this word (found in Sicily) are on the Sicilian standard, the weight found in Athens is on the Roman standard, meaning that the Greek speakers who produced it used ὀγκία specifically for the Roman ounce. Later Greek writers clearly identified οὐγγία with *uncia*; they changed its spelling to οὐγγία to reflect the quality of the Latin vowel and expanded its meaning to include senses of *uncia* other than 'ounce'.[16]

8.1.3 Polybius and other early literature

More extensive evidence for Latin borrowings starts to appear in the second century BC with the first surviving literary work to focus on Rome, Polybius' *Histories*. Polybius, who lived from c. 200 to c. 118 BC, came from mainland Greece to Rome as a hostage in 167 BC. After spending many years with Scipio Aemilianus and other Roman aristocrats, he eventually wrote the *Histories* as an attempt to explain the Romans' sudden world domination to the inhabitants of Greece. In that work Polybius used some Latin words without explanation, apparently believing that they were already known to his readers. For example, in passage 40 knowledge is assumed not only of Ῥωμαῖος, which had demonstrably been part of Greek for several centuries by the time this passage was written, and of its easily etymologizable Greek derivative Ῥωμαϊκός 'Roman', but also of βυκανητής 'trumpeter' and σάγος 'cloak', which are first attested in this passage.

40 Τούς γε μὴν Ῥωμαίους τὰ μὲν εὐθαρσεῖς ἐποίει τὸ μέσους καὶ πάντοθεν περιειληφέναι τοὺς πολεμίους, τὰ δὲ πάλιν ὁ κόσμος αὐτοὺς καὶ θόρυβος ἐξέπληττε τῆς τῶν Κελτῶν δυνάμεως. ἀναρίθμητον μὲν γὰρ ἦν τὸ τῶν βυκανητῶν καὶ σαλπιγκτῶν πλῆθος. ... πλὴν ἅμα τῷ τοὺς ἀκοντιστὰς προελθόντας ἐκ τῶν Ῥωμαϊκῶν στρατοπέδων κατὰ τὸν ἐθισμὸν εἰσακοντίζειν ἐνεργοῖς καὶ πυκνοῖς τοῖς βέλεσιν, τοῖς μὲν ὀπίσω τῶν Κελτῶν πολλὴν εὐχρηστίαν οἱ σάγοι μετὰ τῶν ἀναξυρίδων παρεῖχον· τοῖς δὲ γυμνοῖς προεστῶσι παρὰ τὴν προσδοκίαν τοῦ πράγματος συμβαίνοντος τἀναντία πολλὴν ἀπορίαν καὶ δυσχρηστίαν παρεῖχε τὸ γινόμενον. (2.29.5–6, 2.30.1–2)

The fact that the enemy was surrounded encouraged the <u>Romans</u>, but on the other hand the good order and loud noise of the force of Celts terrified them. For the quantity of <u>trumpeters</u> and war-trumpeters was innumerable. ... But when the javelin-throwers came forward out of the <u>Roman</u> ranks and hurled javelins thick and fast, as is their custom, the Celts at the back got good protection from their <u>cloaks</u> and trousers; but the naked ones standing in front unexpectedly found themselves in great difficulty without a way out as the situation unfolded.

A number of other Latin words not attested in earlier centuries are also presented as familiar by Polybius: Καπετώλιον 'Capitol', Καπετώλιος 'Capitoline', πατρίκιος 'patrician', βυκάνη 'trumpet', and γαῖσος 'javelin'. But Polybius did not always assume knowledge of the Latin words he deployed; some are explained as if unfamiliar to readers, like δικτάτωρ 'dictator' and μάξιμος 'greatest' in passage 41 and τρὰνς 'across' in passage 42. Δικτάτωρ and some other words thus treated by Polybius were later widely adopted in

---

[15] In early Italy the ὀγκία/*uncia* was one twelfth of the λίτρα/*libra*, which is also sometimes considered a Latin loanword in Greek. For the reasons why I do not consider it one, see §3.2 *s.v.* λίτρα 1.

[16] Something similar happened with νοῦμμος 'coin', which was originally borrowed from another language in the form νόμος, then identified with *nummus*, and eventually re-formed as νοῦμμος (§3.2).

Greek, but others, including μάξιμος and τράνς, were not.[17]

41 Ῥωμαῖοι δὲ <u>δικτάτορα</u> μὲν κατέστησαν Κόιντον Φάβιον, ἄνδρα καὶ φρονήσει διαφέροντα καὶ πεφυκότα καλῶς. ἔτι γοῦν ἐπεκαλοῦντο καὶ καθ᾽ ἡμᾶς οἱ ταύτης τῆς οἰκίας <u>Μάξιμοι</u>, τοῦτο δ᾽ ἔστι μέγιστοι, διὰ τὰς ἐκείνου τἀνδρὸς ἐπιτυχίας καὶ πράξεις. ὁ δὲ <u>δικτάτωρ</u> ταύτην ἔχει τὴν διαφορὰν τῶν ὑπάτων· τῶν μὲν γὰρ ὑπάτων ἑκατέρῳ δώδεκα πελέκεις ἀκολουθοῦσι, τούτῳ δ᾽ εἴκοσι καὶ τέτταρες, κἀκεῖνοι μὲν ἐν πολλοῖς προσδέονται τῆς συγκλήτου πρὸς τὸ συντελεῖν τὰς ἐπιβολάς, οὗτος δ᾽ ἔστιν αὐτοκράτωρ στρατηγός, οὗ κατασταθέντος παραχρῆμα διαλύεσθαι συμβαίνει πάσας τὰς ἀρχὰς ἐν τῇ Ῥώμῃ πλὴν τῶν δημάρχων. (3.87.6)

The Romans appointed as <u>dictator</u> Quintus Fabius, a naturally talented man of exceptional intelligence. Indeed even in our day the men of that family bore the cognomen *Maximus*, which means 'greatest', on account of that man's successes and achievements. A dictator is different from the consuls as follows: twelve lictors attend each of the consuls but twenty-four attend the <u>dictator</u>, and the consuls often need the agreement of the senate to get things done, but the dictator is a general with autocratic powers, upon whose appointment all other offices in Rome (apart from the tribunes) are immediately dissolved.

42 Τρανσαλπῖνοί γε μὴν οὐ διὰ τὴν τοῦ γένους, ἀλλὰ διὰ τὴν τοῦ τόπου διαφορὰν προσαγορεύονται· τὸ γὰρ <u>τρὰνς</u> ἐξερμηνευόμενόν ἐστι πέραν, διὸ τοὺς ἐπέκεινα τῶν Ἄλπεων Τρανσαλπίνους καλοῦσι. (2.15.9)

The Τρανσαλπῖνοι are named not from their race but from their location; for *trans* when translated is 'across', and therefore they call the people across the Alps Τρανσαλπῖνοι.

It is unlikely that Polybius was the first Greek speaker to use the Latin words that appear in his work, even though in most cases that work is our earliest surviving evidence for them (cf. Dubuisson 1985: 16). By the time Polybius arrived in Rome, the Greek speakers of Magna Graecia had been in contact with the Romans for centuries, and Rome itself was full of Greek speakers: educated Romans who spoke Greek as a second language, slaves and captives whose first language was Greek, and free migrants from Greek-speaking areas of southern Italy and Sicily.[18] These people must have already established the necessary terminology to discuss Rome and its major institutions in Greek, either by borrowing words or by creating equivalents with Greek etymologies, for it is simply not possible that when Hannibal was marching through Italy and the senate appointed Fabius Maximus dictator, the Greek speakers of Italy were unable to discuss these events because they had no words for 'senate' or 'dictator'.[19] And Polybius would certainly have picked up whatever Greek terminology existed for discussing Roman concepts, for he associated with a segment of Roman society where Greek was often used as a prestige language. The arguments in favour of Polybius having learned Latin in Rome are excellent (Dubuisson 1985: 9–10), but if he had used *only* Latin he would have been the only person in his circle to do so. It is therefore likely that both the bulk of Polybius' loanwords and the bulk of his (much more numerous) etymologically Greek terms for Roman concepts existed before him – though that does not mean that he made no terminological choices of his own, since there may sometimes have been more than one Greek term in use for a particular Roman concept.

---

[17] The ones later adopted are ἄστᾶτος, δεκουρίων, ἐξτραορδινάριος, κεντουρίων, πραίφεκτος, πρίγκεψ, σάλιος; ones not adopted include Γαισᾶται, ἡμιασσάριον, κοόρτις (though the same Latin word was later borrowed as κοόρτη), κουνίκολος, πάρμη, πάσσον 2, and τριάριος. Βυκανάω and φέρετρον are used without being marked as foreign, but there is no other evidence that Greek speakers knew them. Polybius may also have used the Latin words καλίκιος, κίρκος, λιβέρτος, μιλιάζω, μίλιον, and μόδιος, but their attestation is less certain as they appear only in portions of the work preserved via later writers. On Polybius' Latin words see Dubuisson (1985: 18–53), Langslow (2012: 98–105).

[18] See e.g. J. N. Adams (2003: 9–17), Biville (2002), Holford-Strevens (1993).

[19] Dubuisson (1985: 55–6) argues that such terminology cannot have been standardized in Polybius' day, since multiple Greek terms for the same Roman concept are often attested later and sometimes found even within Polybius' own work. But the existence of multiple terms does not constitute proof that any of them were coined by a particular writer. Langslow (2012: 104–5) suggests that Polybius' terminological variation is not simply inconsistent but often follows systematic patterns, which he might have learned along with the terminology itself.

There is more room for doubt as to whether these terms were already known to Polybius' primary audience, namely Greeks in Greece; clearly these Greeks had had far less history of contact with the Romans than the Greeks in Italy. In this context the distinction Polybius made between words needing explanation as unfamiliar and ones for which no explanation was needed is worth taking seriously, for Polybius came from mainland Greece and knew which words Greeks in Greece would understand. He was not the first historian to write about the Romans in Greek, for Quintus Fabius Pictor had done so in the third century BC; that work (which is now lost) seems to have had considerable success in its day and probably introduced the Greeks to at least some of the Latin words deployed by Polybius. Moreover, by the time Polybius wrote the Romans had solidly conquered and annexed Greece, after having had a presence there for more than half a century, so that the inhabitants of Greece had become used to dealing with Roman army personnel and administrators. It is therefore very likely that the Latin words left unexplained by Polybius were already known to most educated Greeks in Greece, while the ones for which he provided explanations were less familiar. This latter group probably included some words that were current in Italian Greek but not widely known in Greece, and perhaps also some genuinely new importations.

In addition to Polybius, numerous other early writers are thought to have used Latin loanwords, but in most cases their work survives only in the form of quotations, paraphrases, or citations in later authors, making it difficult to be sure that the particular words in question really appeared in those texts.[20] Surprisingly, however, the abstruse poet Lycophron (probably datable to the early second century BC) really does use loanwords: Λατῖνος 'Latin' and Βορείγονοι, which must be a re-formed version of Ἀβοριγῖνες 'original inhabitants of Italy'.[21] An additional

loanword, κέντρων 'rag', is contributed by the technical writer Biton of Pergamon, from the third or second century BC.

8.1.4 Inscriptions and papyri before 100 BC

Greek inscriptions from the third and second centuries BC also use loanwords, but not exactly the same set as Polybius. The loanwords attested in these inscriptions but not in Polybius are ἀσσάριον 'penny', ἄτριον 'entrance hall', δηνάριον (a coin), Εἰδοί 'Ides', Ἰούνιος 'June', Καλάνδαι 'Kalends', Κοιντίλιος 'July', κομέτιον 'assembly', Μάϊος 'May', νοῦμμος 'coin', Νῶναι 'Nones', Ὀκτώβριος 'October', πάτρων 'patron', πατρωνεία 'patronage', Ῥωμαῖα (a set of games), Ῥωμαϊστής 'actor of Latin comedies', σηστέρτιος 'sesterce', and Φεβρουάριος 'February';[22] they also share with Polybius Καπετώλιον, Καπετώλιος, Ῥωμαϊκός, Ῥωμαῖος, and Ῥώμη. Some of the difference between the inscriptional loanwords and those in Polybius probably arises from the topics under discussion, for none of the early inscriptions happens to mention patricians, Roman trumpets, or cloaks. If such topics had been mentioned, it is very likely that Polybius' words πατρίκιος, βυκάνη, and σάγος would have been used. The reverse is more doubtful: if Polybius had wanted to discuss the Roman patronage system, would he have used πάτρων and πατρωνεία? Perhaps not, for overall Polybius (like many authors of Greek literature) had a preference for expressing Roman concepts using pre-existing Greek terms rather than loanwords, even when the pre-existing terms failed to convey the Roman concepts precisely.[23]

Some differences between these two sets of loanwords probably arise from the fact that many of the inscriptions were composed by Latin

[20] For example, Ἀβοριγῖνες in Hellanicus and Myrsilus, κάρκαρον in Sophron and Rhinthon, κίτριον in Phaenias, Ῥωμαῖος in Hellanicus.

[21] The passage containing both these words has sometimes been considered an interpolation, but that theory is inextricably linked with an earlier dating of Lycophron to the third century BC (see e.g. S. West 1984); now that

the later dating is generally accepted the interpolation theory has largely been abandoned (see e.g. Hornblower 2015; Briquel 1989: 109 n. 53). Βορείγονοι (which is conventionally thus cited but appears only in the gen. pl. Βορειγόνων and therefore might instead be third-declension Βορειγόνες) is probably influenced by Βορέας 'north wind' / Βόρειος 'of the north wind' and γονή 'offspring', 'family'. Cf. Hornblower (2015: 446) and Briquel (1989: 109–11 with n. 56), who translates 'gens du Nord'.

[22] Also rare ἰντερκαλάριος and Ῥωμαῖον.

[23] Dubuisson (1985: 54–9); for other ways of expressing 'patron' in Greek see Mason (1974: 195).

speakers. For example, in the second century BC Roman dating terminology is fairly common in inscriptions[24] but completely absent from literature, and Roman currency terms are notably more common in inscriptions than in literature. It looks as though Greek literary writers deliberately expressed time and money in terms their readers would immediately understand, while the authors of inscriptions chose to import Roman forms of expression into Greek. Here a distinction between Greek and Roman inscriptions becomes important, for it was primarily Latin speakers who chose to import these terms into Greek inscriptions.[25] Unfortunately it is not always completely straightforward to separate inscriptions (especially fragmentary ones) by the identities of their authors, and there are some cases that must remain doubtful. Nevertheless a considerable body of inscriptions can be securely attributed to Romans, and these fall into two categories. Some are official government documents, most of which were originally formulated in Latin and then given Greek translations in Rome before being inscribed in Greek-speaking cities.[26] Others, composed either in Greek or bilingually, were set up by private individuals or groups, such as the multilingual Roman traders who settled on Delos starting in 167 BC.[27] Roman dating terminology can be found in inscriptions of both these types, but probably not in any early inscriptions composed by Greeks. In the second century BC the loanwords securely traceable to inscriptions composed by Romans are Εἰδοί, Ἰούνιος, Καλάνδαι, Καπετώλιον, Καπετώλιος, Κοιντίλιος, κομέτιον, Μάϊος, Νῶναι, Ὀκτώβριος, σηστέρτιος, Ῥώμη, Ῥωμαῖος, and Φεβρουάριος. Inscriptions composed by Greeks seem at this period to be primarily or exclusively responsible for ἄτριον, Ῥωμαῖα, Ῥωμαϊκός, and Ῥωμαϊστής.

The question of which loanwords are used is of course only part of the overall picture of how specific documents use Latin; how often loanwords are used also matters, as does the use of Roman names. Figure 4 attempts to capture these additional factors and compare the Greek and Roman use of Latin words in second-century BC Greek, by juxtaposing the complete set of Latin-etymology words in books 1–5 of Polybius[28] with the complete set of Latin-etymology words in the Greek versions of second-century decrees of the Roman senate.[29] Although the totals are higher for Polybius, the density of Latin usage is much higher in the decrees, for books 1–5 of Polybius contain more than thirty times as much Greek text as the remains of the senate decrees:[30] overall the rate of occurrence of Latin words is about

---

[24] In addition to the material discussed here, see Rousset (2008: 80–1, 86–8) on Roman dates in a second-century BC Greek inscription at Delphi.

[25] Cf. J. N. Adams' observations (2003: e.g. 390–3, 470–1) on codeswitching into Latin for dates in otherwise Greek documents, and on Latinate features in Greek translations of Roman official documents, caused not by incompetence but by a desire to produce a version visibly subservient to the original.

[26] There are two main types of government document: decrees of the senate, which were always composed in Latin and translated into Greek, and official correspondence, which was sometimes composed in Greek and sometimes translated from Latin. The earliest preserved senate decree in Greek dates to 189 BC and the earliest official Roman correspondence in Greek to 197–194 BC. For both types see Sherk (1969). For a detailed study of the Latinisms in Greek inscriptions of official Roman documents (including ones not found in Sherk), see García Domingo (1979); note also Horrocks (2010: 141–3), Vaahtera (2001: esp. 48–64), Mason (1974).

[27] On the language of these inscriptions see e.g. J. N. Adams (2003: 642–86), Hasenohr (2008), and Bauzon (2008). Not all traders who identified as Roman or Italian were native speakers of Latin, and in some cases their grasp of Latin was fairly minimal; nevertheless their self-identification had noticeable effects on their inscriptions.

[28] Books 1–5 are the only portions of the *Histories* that survive intact and whose wording can therefore generally be guaranteed to be Polybius' own. The number of personal names was estimated by counting the number of names on every fifth page and multiplying by five; for these purposes 'name' refers to a single word, so an identification of an individual using praenomen, gentilicium, and cognomen counts as three names. Names of places (other than Rome) are excluded on the grounds that their etymologies and the route through which these words reached Greek are too difficult to establish. Names of non-Roman peoples are included only when they have obviously Latinate etymologies, such as Γαισάται and Τρανσαλπῖνοι.

[29] Based on a hand search of texts 1–16 of Sherk (1969); this counts partially preserved words even if only a small portion remains on the stone, but does not count words that are entirely restored. Section C of text 16, which was composed by Greeks, is omitted.

[30] Books 1–5 of Polybius contain approximately 125,000 words of text, while the sixteen decrees contain approximately 4,000 words.

	Polybius' Greek	Romans' Greek
Ῥωμαῖος	544	16
Ῥώμη	61	4
Ῥωμαϊκός	15	
Λατῖνος	11	
Καπετώλιον, Καπετώλιος	5	5
κομέτιον		9
δικτάτωρ, βυκανητής, τριάριος	14	
Καλάνδαι, Νῶναι, Εἰδοί		10
Month names		12
σηστέρτιος, νοῦμμος, ἡμιασσάριον	1	4
σάγος	4	
τράνς	1	
Total excluding names	656 (70% of complete total)	60 (15% of complete total)
Names of tribes	11	
Personal names and derivatives thereof	c. 265	345
Complete total	c. 932	405

Figure 4 Comparison of all the Latin words (loanwords, codeswitches, and names) used in books 1–5 of Polybius with those in Greek translations of decrees of the Roman senate from the second century BC

one for every ten words of text in the decrees and about one for every 134 words of text in Polybius. Some of this difference is due to the fact that personal names are much more common in the decrees (where they make up 85% of the total Latin words) than in Polybius (where they make up only 30% of the total). But even if names are excluded, Latin words are almost three times as frequent in the Roman decrees as in Polybius.

Of the terminology that at this early period seems to have been specifically Roman, most was eventually accepted into Greek. The Roman dating terminology was later used freely by Greek speakers, eventually supplanting the native words: modern Greek month names all come from Latin. Roman currency terms also became widespread in Greek. These shifts were not to be taken for granted, given Greek lexical conservatism, and must be due largely to the influence of official Roman practice, of which these early decrees are only the first sign. As the supreme rulers of the Mediterranean world the Romans wielded considerable influence, and their official inscriptions acted as visible signs of their power.

The Latinizing Greek of their official decrees may have been offensive at first to the educated elite in Greece, but it is unlikely to have bothered all Greek speakers, particularly in regions where Greek was not the original or the majority language. In fact, the language of Roman decrees is known to have been influential in Greek.[31] It is therefore likely that in the surviving second-century BC decrees we can see part of the process that led to the transfer of these loanwords into native speakers' Greek.

Papyri are much less likely than inscriptions to contain Latin words in the second century; indeed what is remarkable is that they have any at all. Egypt only came under Roman control after the battle of Actium in 31 BC, more than a century after the annexation of Greece and more than two centuries after the conquest of Greek-speaking Italy, and therefore in the second century BC Greek speakers in Egypt were not exposed to inscriptions from the Roman senate

[31] Brixhe (2007: 909), Souris and Nigdelis (2007: 898), Dickey (2010b: 209–11), Mourgues (1995: 114–29).

or other linguistic reflections of Roman authority. But the Greek speakers of Egypt nevertheless had contact with Latin long before Actium, both via Greek speakers elsewhere and from their own direct contacts, which even if less intense stretched back for centuries.[32] Even if Romans visiting Ptolemaic Egypt never spoke anything but Greek while in the country, they would have used some Latin terms in that Greek, at the very least names. As a result the early Ptolemaic papyri contain a number of Roman names, along with three loanwords that between them occur four times in papyri datable before 100 BC: Ῥωμαῖος on papyri from 252 and 112 BC, διάριον 'daily wage' on one from 180 BC, and γαῖσος 'javelin' on one from the late second century BC. The first of these was clearly borrowed elsewhere and imported by Greeks or by Romans speaking Greek, and the same may be true of the other two, though it is not impossible that they were borrowed in Egypt.

8.1.5 *The first century* BC

The first century BC saw the Romans increase their presence in Greek-speaking areas already occupied during the second century as well as annexing Egypt. Both loanwords and codeswitches became more frequent, and words that had been presented as unfamiliar in the previous century could now be used as normal Greek words. The treatment of *dictator* offers an example of the difference in the use of certain key terms between the second and first centuries. In the second century δικτάτωρ occured only in Polybius, who used it with restraint (six occurrences in the surviving portions of the work) and carefully explained its meaning. In the first century Diodorus Siculus and the composers of numerous inscriptions used δικτάτωρ without any explanation; Dionysius of Halicarnassus explained it but used it much more freely than his predecessors (fifty-two times) and also employed its derivatives δικτατωρεία 'dictatorship' and δικτατωρεύω 'be dictator'.

As this example suggests, one major source of Latin words in the first century BC is the *Roman Antiquities* of Dionysius of Halicarnassus. Dionysius was far readier to use Latin than most

Greek authors of any period and included almost a hundred different words of Latin origin. Most of these were codeswitches, some of which later became loanwords – but many did not, and indeed some never appear anywhere else in Greek. (See §2.2.3 passage 2 for an example of how Dionysius distinguished loanwords from codeswitches.) The other historian of Rome from this period, Diodorus Siculus, also made use of loanwords but employed many fewer codeswitches than Dionysius. Other first-century BC literary authors using loanwords were the fragmentary grammarian Philoxenus, who used κοχλιάριον 'spoon' and several other terms; the fragmentary botanist Crateuas, who used ὀξύγγιον 'tallow'; and the uncertainly dated *Batrachomyomachia*, which included πέρνα 'ham' (in the mock-epic form πτέρνη). These three terms, which belong to a semantic field and a register very different from that of δικτάτωρ, illustrate that the borrowing of Latin loanwords for food and household items began almost as early as the borrowing of loanwords for key concepts in Roman history and politics (cf. §10.2.3).

Inscriptions also provide good evidence of loanwords in the first century BC. Roman dating terminology is well attested (still primarily in inscriptions composed by Romans), including all the month names. Although some of these are first attested in the first century, they were almost certainly introduced earlier, with their lack of second-century attestation being due to the vagaries of preservation. Αὔγουστος 'August', however, is notable for appearing very soon after that month was renamed from Σεξτίλιος (*IC* II.XI.3 lines 14, 20, from late first century BC), demonstrating that there is not always a time lag between the introduction of a loanword and our first evidence for it. Other terms that first appear in first-century BC inscriptions are ἰμπεράτωρ 'commander', κοδράντης (a coin), κολωνία 'colony', λεγεών 'legion', πατρωνεύω 'be patron', and φιλόκαισαρ 'loyal to Caesar'.

Papyri show a sharp increase in loanwords after the Roman conquest of Egypt in 30 BC. Only one loanword certainly appears in a first-century papyrus earlier than 30 BC: πωμάριον 'orchard', which occurs on a document datable to between 66 and 51. By contrast, at least eleven loanwords appear between 30 and 1 BC, some of

---

[32] See e.g. R. M. Schneider (2018), Cervenka-Ehrenstrasser (2000: 244).

them more than once: βενεφικιάριος (an occupational term), δηνάριον, κάμπιστρον 'loincloth', κεντουρία '(army) century', κομάκτωρ 'collector of money', λεγεών 'legion', λωρῖκα 'corselet', πάτρων, Ῥωμαῖος, Ῥωμαϊκός, στάτωρ (a position in the army), and perhaps κεντουρίων 'centurion' and πατριμώνιον '(imperial) property'. These papyri provide the first attestations for seven of these words, demonstrating that the important role played by papyri in preserving evidence of loanwords began immediately upon the Roman annexation of Egypt. But an additional Latin word that appears in the early Augustan papyri, μωραντι 'delaying' (dative), never occurs anywhere else and was evidently not a loanword – though one would not know that from its use in the papyrus concerned.

Other loanwords introduced in the first century BC are Καισάρειος 'of Caesar', Κυιρῖται 'Quirites', μίλιον 'mile', μόδιος (a measure), παλάτιον 'Palatine Hill', Φαλερῖνος 'Falernian wine', and φιλορώμαιος.

8.1.6 The imperial period

Ninety-two per cent of loanwords first become visible to us in the first century AD or later; even if the early centuries of Greco-Roman contact were crucial in establishing borrowing patterns, the imperial period is when we can best observe them. The factors affecting the borrowing and use of loanwords during the six centuries of the imperial period are complex. They include an increase in the overall status of Latin in late antiquity (see e.g. §9.5.5), the development of a sense on the part of Greek speakers that certain kinds of terminology ought to be Latinate (e.g. §10.2.3), and probably the influence of certain Greek writers who happened to live in Rome (e.g. §9.5.3). Our understanding of these factors is mediated by several different types of evidence, whose quantity and quality fluctuates (§9). These issues will be explored in subsequent chapters.

One question that cannot be explored fully even in subsequent chapters, but that nevertheless needs to be considered, is that of how often loanwords were used during the imperial period. The loanword data used in the present study do not reflect overall frequency of use, only the extent to which particular words were part of the

Greek language at particular periods. Overall frequency has been investigated elsewhere, and in documentary papyri, at least, it is known to display the pattern shown in Figure 5: a slow increase in the late Republic and early Empire, followed by an enormous jump (both in absolute terms and relative to the amount of preserved evidence) in the fourth century AD. This pattern is distinctly different from that produced either by the borrowing of loanwords or by their accumulation (cf. §8.1.1, Figure 2).

Equivalent statistics have not been compiled for literature, but anyone who has read large amounts of late Greek literature is likely to know even without them that literature also shows a sharp increase in Latinisms – not in the fourth century, but in the sixth. As we have seen, neither of these increases can be ascribed to increased borrowing: what caused them? Did Greek speakers use existing loanwords more often, did they codeswitch more, or both? Codeswitching must be part of the answer, for Latin words likely to be codeswitches appear more often in the fourth and sixth centuries than in other centuries. There are two types of such words: ones that were marked by authors as foreign (for example by the use of Latin script, retention of Latin inflections, and/or explanation of their meanings: §2.2.2–3), which are labelled in the Lexicon as 'foreign', and ones that were not (or not always) so marked but did not occur often enough to offer convincing evidence of loanword status (§2.2.1), which are labelled in the Lexicon as 'rare'. The former type occurs primarily in literature, for writers of documents and inscriptions rarely marked words as foreign; the latter type is found in all kinds of Greek texts. These two types have very different distributions, as illustrated in Figure 6. But as that figure shows, neither type of codeswitch has enough of an increase in the fourth century to explain the papyrus data in Figure 5. Therefore the use of existing loanwords must have increased in the fourth century, at least in documentary texts.

8.1.7 Latin words first attested in Greek

One would expect loanwords to appear first in the source language and only later in the borrowing language, but that does not always happen

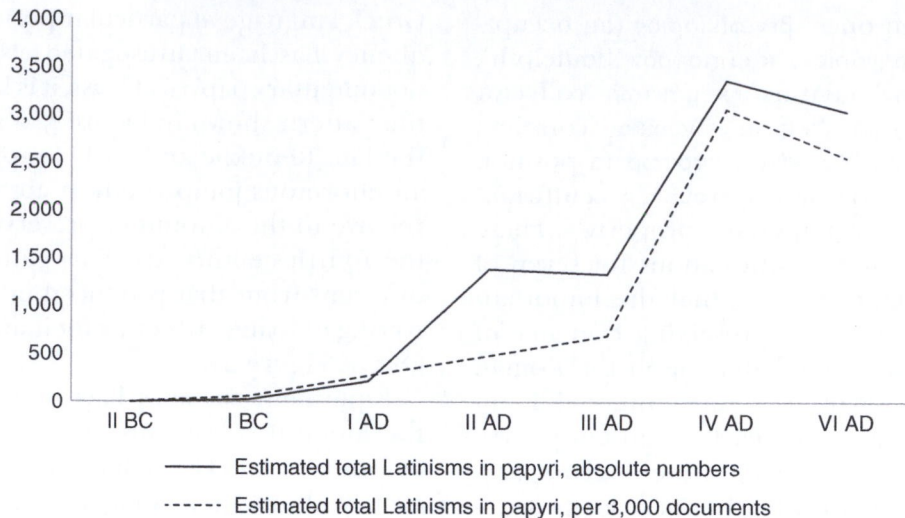

Figure 5 Estimated total occurrences (tokens) of Latin words (both loanwords and codeswitches) in Greek documentary papyri per century, according to Dickey (2003: 256); numbers in §12.1. These statistics omit names and the very common words Αὔγουστος and δηνάριον, whose individual chronological distributions distort the overall picture; they also omit the fifth century, for which the results are uncertain.

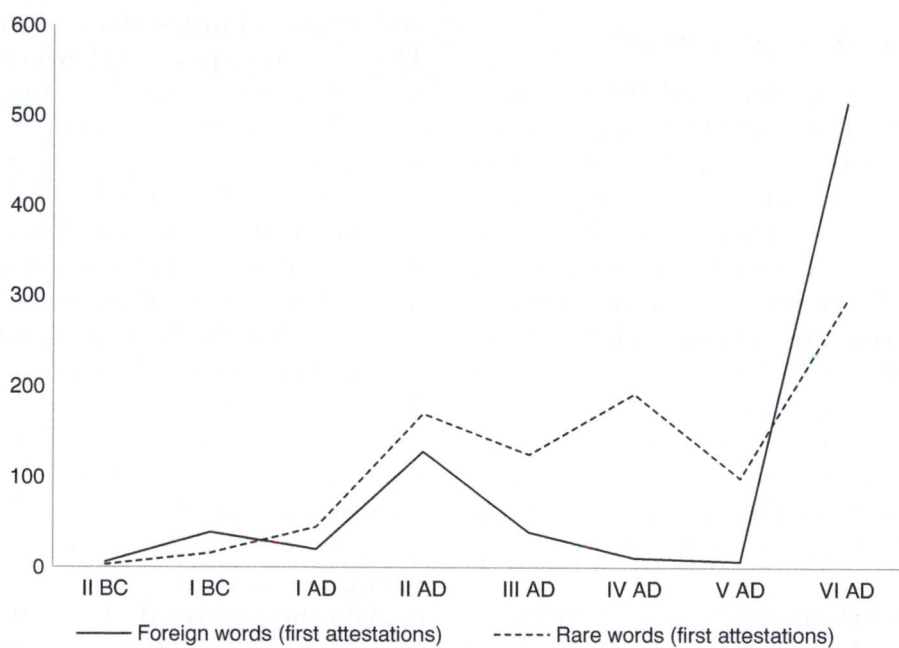

Figure 6 Probable codeswitches by century (omitting undated and very early examples); exact numbers in §12.1

in the surviving evidence, for Greek is in some significant respects better preserved than Latin. The vast numbers of papyri, which contain far more Greek material than Latin, mean that we have much better access to non-literary Greek of the Hellenistic and imperial periods than to non-literary Latin of the same time span. Moreover there is a large body of Greek literature about

Roman history and culture predating the earliest substantially surviving Latin-language equivalents: Polybius, Dionysius of Halicarnassus, and even Plutarch (first and second centuries AD) often provide the earliest surviving discussions of particular elements of Roman history and culture. It is therefore normal for the first attestation of a Latin word to occur not very long before its first appearance as a loanword in Greek: for example *dictator* 'dictator' is attested in Plautus (died 184 BC) and Ennius (died 169 BC), which is about as good as one can get in terms of early appearance in Latin, but those attestations only slightly precede its appearance as δικτάτωρ in Polybius (died c. 118 BC).

In these circumstances it is unsurprising that many early loanwords are attested in Greek before their first appearance in Latin; for example Μάϊος 'May' first occurs in the second century BC but *Maius* 'May' not until the first century BC. Such discrepancies are just accidents of preservation, for the Latin terms were no doubt in use for centuries before their earliest preserved attestation. But at later periods, when there is better Latin evidence, lack of prior Latin attestation is more meaningful. Some later loanwords seem to emerge more or less simultaneously in the two languages, and these often seem to result from an invention or discovery that caused a need for the new word; they suggest that new words could be borrowed more or less immediately in the bilingual empire.

Even for the best-documented periods, however, our evidence for Latin is far from complete, and some Latin words that once existed are now completely unattested in surviving Latin texts; this situation is only to be expected given the loss of almost all ancient Latin documents and a large proportion of the literature. Therefore the *Thesaurus Linguae Latinae* includes occasional entries for words that do not survive in Latin sources but are reconstructable from other evidence, such as Romance descendants and loanwords or codeswitches in other ancient languages.[33] Many of these entries are for words attested only in Greek: *adorator* 'retired soldier' (attested as ἀδωράτωρ),

applicitarus (a title, ἀπλικιτάριος), *armilliger* (a military rank, ἀρμιλλίγεροι), *auricaesor* 'gold-beater' (αὐρικαίσωρ), *bratteolatus* 'decorated with thin gold leaf' (βραττεολᾶτος), *Brumalia* 'festival of the winter solstice' (βρουμάλια), *caballaricus* 'horse-drawn' (καβαλλαρικός), *camela* (a garment, κάμελα, καμελαύκιον), *carraricus* 'of a wagon' (καρραρικός), *centuncularis* (a plant name, κεντουκουλάρις), *cessionarius* (a title, κεσσιωνάριος), *cibariator* 'army official issuing food and wine to the troops' (κιβαριάτωρ), *dulciradix* (a plant name, δουλκιράδιξ), *epularia* 'bread-basket' (ἀπαλαρέα), *equinalis* (a plant name, ἐκυινᾶλις), *exceptarius* 'corn-receiver' (ἐκσκεπτάριος), *excubitum* 'guarding the imperial palace' (ἐξκούβιτον), *excubitus* 'member of the emperor's bodyguard' (ἐξκούβιτος), *exsello* 'unseat' (ἐκσελλίζω), *fenicula* (an object connected with vehicles, φενίκουλα), *flammularius* 'standard-bearer' (φλαμμουλάριος), *garbula* (a kind of boot, γάρβολα), *globa* 'skin' (γλοῦβα), *instrumentarius* 'archivist' (ἰνστρουμεντάριος), *intersedeo* 'sit among' (ἰντερσεδεύω), *lacinaridium* 'shoe' (λακιναρίδιον), *memorarius* (an official, μεμοράριος), *optioprinceps* 'assistant to the chief centurion' (ὀπτιοπρίγκεψ), *patriciatus* 'patrician' (πατρικιᾶτος), *perviaticum* 'toll' (βρεβιατικόν), *pullicrus* (a plant name, πουλλικρούρα), and *ramitarius* (a plant name, ῥαμπτάρια). Sometimes it is clear from the way the Greek term is used that there must really have been a lost Latin original – for example αὐρικαίσωρ appears in the dative plural αὐρικαισωρίβους on a fourth-century inscription – but often the case is doubtful. Some of the Greek words giving rise to such *TLL* entries are probably derivatives rather than direct borrowings, or not ancient, or simply non-existent: it is far from clear that the phenomenon represented by such entries was as common in antiquity as it looks from the *TLL*.[34] Sometimes, as in the case of *foederaticus*

---

[33] The same problem also exists in reverse, with some 'Greek' words attested only in Latin (e.g. Langslow 2000: 80 with n. 9).

[34] Words in the first two of these categories are included in the list above; in the third note e.g. ἀγκέντουμ (*TLL ancentum*), ἀγριλάρια (*TLL agrilaria*), ἐξκεντυρίων (*TLL excenturio*), and φολλατώριον (*TLL follatorium*). Occasionally the *TLL* has entries with lemmata in Greek, not positively asserting that the word in question was part of Latin; a number of words in §3.2 have such *TLL* entries, including βονιτάριος, βουριχάλλιον, βραχιάλιον, γαράριον, διτάριος, δουκικός, δραύκιον, ἐξπελλευτής, ἐξπούγκερος, μαξιλλοπλουμάκιος, ματρίκιον, ματρωνίκιον,

'connected with allies' (φοιδερατικός), the *TLL* expressly states that the 'Latin' lemma is a Greek formation.

Occasionally, lack of attestation in Latin can indicate that a word of Latin etymology was not in fact borrowed from Latin but was created within Greek from Latin elements. For example, πριμοσαγιττάριος 'first archer' and πριμοσκουτάριος 'first shield-bearer' are quoted in Greek as Latin words, but no such terms are attested in Latin and the compounds are formed using the Greek linking vowel -o-; the original Latin forms were probably *primus sagittarius* and *primus scutarius* (cf. §4.5).

8.2 SURVIVAL OF LOANWORDS

Many of the loanwords borrowed during antiquity have survived into the present day as part of modern Greek. But many others disappeared during the Byzantine period, and some even before the end of antiquity. In order to understand the long-term effect that loanwords had on Greek, one needs to know not only when they entered the language, but also when they left.

8.2.1 Survival during antiquity

Ancient Greek sometimes gives the impression of being a language in which obsolescence was impossible, for antiquarian writers gloried in the use of obscure language and took special delight in reviving words that by any normal standard should have counted as dead. Nevertheless some Greek words did disappear during antiquity, and some of those were Latin loanwords. Of course, when dealing with the inherently incomplete evidence of ancient sources it is difficult to be absolutely certain that a word was not used in a particular century, but there are two situations in which one can be reasonably sure that that

was the case. One is when words are completely and permanently unattested after a particular date, and the other is when all occurrences after a particular date mark the word as obsolete or unfamiliar. Examples of the first category include φιλοκλαύδιος 'friend of Claudius', which occurred only during and shortly after the reign of Claudius in the first century AD; Καπετωλιακός 'Capitoline', which was used exclusively of the Capitoline games and therefore vanished with the games themselves after the fourth century AD; and ἀκουάριος 'water-carrier', which was a local term attached to a particular site whose documentation ends after the second century AD. Examples of the second category include the month name Κοιντίλιος, which became obsolete at the end of the first century BC when that month was renamed Ἰούλιος 'July' but which is periodically referred to in later explanations of the renaming; σηστέρτιος 'sesterce' and κομέτιον 'assembly', which were used normally from the second century BC to the third century AD and then vanished until the sixth, when they were treated as foreign; and φρουμεντάριος 'concerned with victualling'. This last term was used normally until the fourth century, does not occur at all in the fifth, and in the sixth appears only in the antiquarian writer John Lydus, clearly marked as obsolete: οἱ καθ' ἡμᾶς λεγόμενοι μαγιστριανοὶ τὸ πρὶν φρουμεντάριοι ἐκαλοῦντο 'the officials that we call μαγιστριανοί were formerly called φρουμεντάριοι'.[35] These two types of obsolete terms between them account for 209 loanwords, a quarter of the 820 that were part of Greek at some point during antiquity. Loanwords began to die out after the first century BC; from that point to the end of antiquity an average of 7% of the ones used in each century vanished after that century, with the exact loss rate fluctuating between 2% and 11% per century. But the losses were greatly outnumbered by new borrowings, so the total stock of loanwords continued to increase throughout antiquity (Figure 7).

ματρωνίκιος, μητροκολωνεία, μιλιάζω, μιλιασμός, μονόμισσα, μονορεκαῦτον, ὀρρεοπραιποσιτία, πατικουρᾶς, πορταρῆσις, πουτιαλογονθρια, προδερέλικτος, φέβερ, φραγέλλιον, φρατριάζω. There are also words whose Greek attestations may suggest an ancient Latin original that has not (yet) been given a *TLL* entry; see McCormick (1981) on **biberaticum* and note also ἀντίπανον and σησαμᾶτος.

[35] *Mag.* p. 6.27–8. Lydus' affection for obsolete terms is such that he uses this term five more times (*Mag.* pp. 98.30, 122.4, 140.12, 194.30; *Mens.* 1.30.10), explaining it on every occasion.

Century	Loanwords inherited from earlier centuries	New loanwords + re-creations/ revivals	Total number of loanwords probably in use	Loanwords that died out after this century, absolute numbers and as percentage of loanwords in use during it	Loanwords borrowed/created in this century that permanently died out before the end of antiquity
IV BC	–	1	1	–	–
III BC	1	2	3	–	–
II BC	3	30	33	–	10
I BC	33	35	68	2 (3%)	11
I AD	66	103	169	8 (5%)	40
II AD	161	201	362	20 (6%)	68
III AD	342	115	457	45 (10%)	28
IV AD	412	139	551	47 (9%)	31
V AD	504	108 + 1	613	14 (2%)	13
VI AD	599	86 + 5	690	79[36] (11%)	10
Total		820 + 6		213	209

Figure 7 Survival, accumulation, and loss of loanwords

A few of the words that died out seem to have been re-created at a later period. In the second century AD παγανικός 'civilian' was a local term specific to one site, whose documentation ended after that century; in the third and fourth it is unattested, and in the fifth it reappeared as a more widely distributed loan. Since παγανικός would have been easy for any Greek speaker to form by adding -ικός to παγανός 'civilian', the chances are excellent that the fifth-century creation was independent of the second-century one. Likewise φασκίδιον, which could easily be formed by adding -ίδιον to φασκία 'bandage', 'strip', appears in documents from the third and fourth centuries with the meaning 'bandage'; in the fifth it is unattested, and in the sixth it appears in literature with the meaning 'belt', 'strap'. Τετραούγκιον, a compound of τετρα- 'four' and οὐγγία 'ounce, twelfth', occurs in the second century meaning 'four ounces' and in the sixth as a legal term meaning 'four twelfths of an estate'. In both these cases the sixth-century formation was probably independent of the earlier one, and the same is probably true of ξεστιαῖος 'of a pint' (ξεστίον 'pint' + -αῖος), which likewise appears only in the second and sixth centuries, though without a change in meaning. Σοῦμμος means 'highest in rank' in papyri and inscriptions from the second, third, and fourth centuries; in the fifth it is unattested, and in the sixth it appears in literature meaning a position in a board game. As σοῦμμος is a direct borrowing rather than a derivative, it could not have been re-created by Greek speakers as easily as the terms just mentioned, but it could have been reborrowed from the original Latin. Αὐγουστεῖον 'Augusteum' refers to a building in Rome until the third century, is unattested in the fourth and fifth, and in the sixth refers to a building in Constantinople: that new meaning is probably not independent of the old one, but it is not a continuation either, more likely a revival.

The vast majority of words that disappear from view and then reappear, however, do not seem

[36] Including 9 whose century of disappearance is uncertain, and 2 (φασκίδιον and ξεστιαῖος) that had died out earlier and been reborrowed, and that are therefore not counted a second time in the total below; unlike the next column, this one includes words that were reborrowed.

to be particularly different in meaning or usage when they return. These are probably continuations of the earlier loans and were very likely still in use during the interval for which they are now unattested. Such temporary absence from visibility is fairly common, affecting 27% of loanwords, and is particularly likely in the fifth century, from which fewer papyri survive than from other centuries. There are 75 loanwords with continuous attestation apart from a gap in the fifth century, as well as 70 with gaps only in one other century.[37] A further 13 have two single-century gaps.[38] It is virtually certain that these words were actually in use during the centuries for which they are unattested, but there is room for doubt about ones with longer gaps in attestation: the 49 loanwords with continuous attestation apart from a single two-century gap, and above all the 12 with even more gaps.[39] I have classified these as

continuations rather than words that died out and were re-created because their later versions are not perceptibly different from the earlier ones, but that evidence is far from conclusive: some or all of these words may in fact have died out and been re-created.

8.2.2 *Loanwords in Byzantine Greek*

Seventy-five per cent of the ancient loanwords survived into Byzantine Greek,[40] where they were joined by further borrowings made during the Byzantine period. Latin loanwords evidently played a significant role in Byzantine language and culture, but there has been considerable debate about exactly what that role was. Byzantine Greek was not a single language, nor even a straightforward diglossia with two sharply distinct registers, but rather a continuum of many registers ranging from ones so low that they remained unwritten (and therefore are not preserved for us) to the most learned, archaizing, and obscure literature, via a host of intermediate stages.[41] Some of the higher registers made heavy use of Latin words: legal texts were full of terminology inherited from Roman law, court ceremonies employed fossilized Latin phrases, the army preserved Roman vocabulary for roles, units, and even commands; and scholars delighted in explaining Latin terms.[42] Most lower registers were also replete with Latin-derived words for everyday objects. Therefore Latin loans were both an essential part of the language and a precious demonstration of the Byzantines' status as the continuation of the Roman empire – but they were also conspicuously non-Attic and as such evidence of the Byzantines' distance from the Classical Greece that they valued so highly. Therefore, although in some contexts Latin words belonged to a high register, in others they were systematically avoided as being

[37] I.e. 21 in the sixth century (reappearing in the Byzantine period, but not necessarily in the seventh century), 20 in the fourth, 24 in the third, 1 in the second, 3 in the first, and 1 in the first century BC. For the purposes of these calculations I have used a different definition of 'attestation' from that used in §8.1.1: here, in order to be sure that statements about lack of attestation are based on sound evidence, I have considered words unattested in a particular century only if there are no examples at all in that century; doubtful and insecurely dated examples count as attestation, as long as they occur later than the first good example. But when determining the date at which words were actually borrowed I excluded doubtful examples and counted insecurely dated ones only in the latest of the centuries from which they might come.

[38] Of the words with two gaps, 2 are unattested in the fourth and sixth centuries, 8 in the third and fifth, 1 in the first and fifth, and 2 in the first century BC and fifth century AD.

[39] The 49 comprise 15 unattested in the fifth and sixth centuries (reappearing in the Byzantine period, but not necessarily in the seventh century), 17 unattested in the fourth and fifth, 15 unattested in the third and fourth, 1 unattested in the first and second, and 1 in the second and first centuries BC. The 12 with more gaps comprise 4 unattested in the fourth, fifth, and sixth centuries; 2 unattested in the third, fifth, and sixth; 1 unattested in the third, fourth, and sixth; 1 unattested in the third, fourth, and fifth; 1 unattested in the second, third, and fifth; 1 unattested in the first, second, and third; 1 unattested in the first centuries BC and AD and the fourth century AD; and κάρρον, which in addition to being unattested in the third, fifth, and sixth centuries seems to disappear during the Byzantine period and reappear only in modern Greek (§8.2.3).

[40] 820 loanwords originally borrowed, of which 213 died out before the Byzantine period but 4 of those were re-created in antiquity and survived, yields 611 loanwords surviving into the Byzantine period.

[41] See e.g. Holton *et al.* (2019: xviii), Horrocks (2010: 212–30), Browning (1983: 5–12).

[42] Biville (2019), Schreiner (2019: 462), Garcea, Rosellini, and Silvano (2019), Kahane and Kahane (1972–6: 516–17, 1982: 132–3), Oikonomedes (1999), Mihăescu (1969), Reichenkron (1961).

stylistically too low. In fact it has been argued that the extreme differences between different registers of Byzantine Greek arose specifically as a reaction to the large numbers of foreign (mainly Latin) words in the lower registers, which some writers avoided on grounds of linguistic purism.[43] This theory is probably an oversimplification, for Greek was capable of an impressive amount of register differentiation even before the Byzantine period. Nevertheless some good evidence has been presented in favour of it, and more investigation would be desirable.

Another disputed point is how many Latin words there really were in Byzantine Greek, and where those words came from. They were not all ancient borrowings, for after AD 600 Greek speakers continued to borrow from Latin – that is, from Latin as distinct from Romance languages such as French and Italian, which also furnished loanwords to the Byzantines.[44] Some of these borrowings arose from continued contact with the West in the seventh century, and others came from medieval Latin after the rise of the Romance languages.[45] What were the proportions of ancient and newer borrowings among the Byzantine loanwords, and how many such loanwords were there in total?

On this point there have been several major studies, which while not completely in agreement converge on a certain general picture. The earliest was that of Triandaphyllidis (1909), who claimed to have found 556 Latin loanwords in Byzantine Greek; if one eliminates those that may not derive from Latin and those that are really variants of other words in the list, Triandaphyllidis' 556 is reduced to a still substantial 520 words.[46] Two hundred and forty of those (46%) are ancient borrowings, and a further 86 (17%) are attested before AD 600 even if they do not seem to be loanwords before that date, leaving 194 (37%) completely new borrowings in the Byzantine period. The second study, that of Kahane and Kahane (1972–6), found 316 Latin loanwords in Byzantine Greek; elimination of words of doubtful etymology and place names reduces that to 312.[47] Of those 312 loanwords, 202 (65%) are ancient borrowings, and a further 51 (16%) are attested before AD 600, leaving 59 (19%) as new arrivals in the Byzantine period.

Most recently Zervan (2019) investigated a corpus of late Byzantine historiography containing 350 loanwords and 170 codeswitches from a wide range of languages. According to my analysis, 129 of the loanwords and 12 of the codeswitches descend from ancient Latin borrowings, for a total of 141 ancient loanwords surviving in this corpus; a further 25 of the loanwords come from Latin and are attested before AD 600, and 78 are new borrowings from Latin in the Byzantine period.[48] The corpus thus contains a total of 244 Latin loanwords: 58% ancient borrowings, 10% attested in antiquity but not fully borrowed then, and 32% purely Byzantine. It also contains 21 new codeswitches from Latin.

These three studies all suggest that there were plenty of Latin loanwords in Byzantine Greek,

---

[43] Kahane and Kahane (1982: 129, 133, 152); cf. Dagron (1969: 55), Mihăescu (1993: 479), Zilliacus (1937).

[44] Triandaphyllidis (1909: 163), comparing the different types of loanwords in Byzantine Greek, calculates a 34% survival rate into modern Greek for the 556 Latin loanwords and compares this to 360 Italian loanwords with a 46% survival rate, 138 Turkish loanwords with a 38% survival rate, 46 French loanwords with a 6.5% survival rate, 37 loans from Slavic languages with a 54% survival rate, and 5 Albanian loans with a 100% survival rate. Cf. Markopoulos (2014).

[45] For Byzantine borrowings from Latin see Kahane and Kahane (1972–6: esp. 588–90, 1982: esp. 150–1), Browning (1983: 67–8), Mihăescu (1993: 334–429, 478–9; 1969 is also of interest, though the words concerned were probably borrowed earlier), Petersmann (1992), Dietrich (1995: 172–3, though many of his examples are actually ancient borrowings), Adrados (2005: 250–2), Katsanis (2007), Diethart (2006, 2008), Zervan (2019).

[46] Triandaphyllidis (1909: 163); the words are listed on pp. 119–32. I cannot be sure that these are all loanwords rather than codeswitches, but Triandaphyllidis considered this question and was convinced that very few were codeswitches (1909: 154–5). I also cannot be sure that all Triandaphyllidis' examples are post-antique, and indeed it seems likely from his literature list (1909: 17–21) that a few examples predate AD 600 – but the vast majority are clearly later.

[47] The Kahanes define Byzantine Greek as starting in the sixth century, so there is some overlap between their 'Byzantine' period and our 'ancient' one.

[48] Zervan's own analysis is somewhat different: he derives 234 of the loanwords from Latin, attributing 160 to ancient and 74 to Byzantine borrowing, and considers there to be 33 Latin codeswitches.

but probably not as many as in late antiquity. Borrowing from Latin continued after AD 600, but most Latin loanwords in Byzantine Greek had started the borrowing process before the end of antiquity, and at least half had been fully borrowed by that point.

Two other studies offer further dimensions to this picture. Tonnet (1993: 102) investigated the percentage of everyday Byzantine vocabulary derived from Latin by examining a sixteenth-century dictionary of basic Greek words useful to travellers in the region. Tonnet concluded that 6.5% of these words were of Latin or Romance origin, without making a further distinction, but many of those are manifestly borrowings from Italian or French rather than Latin. By my calculation 2.8% derive from Latin words borrowed before AD 600. Taking a larger perspective, Mihăescu (1993: 359) found c. 3,000 Latin words in Byzantine Greek, though as he did not specify exactly which words these are, it is impossible to calculate how many are ancient survivals and how many new borrowings.[49] Comparison of this figure with those of Triandaphyllidis, the Kahanes, and Zervan indicates that Mihăescu must have been including codeswitches as well as loanwords. That in turn suggests that Latin codeswitching may have remained common for some time after the end of antiquity.

The present study has identified 611 ancient Latin loanwords that survived into the Byzantine period, but only 39% of those appear among the Byzantine terms identified by Triandaphyllidis, 33% among the Kahanes' terms, and 21% in Zervan's list. What happened to the others? Some, of course, simply died out early in the Byzantine period without a specific reason; after all if the ancient loss rate of 7% per century had continued unchanged in the Byzantine period, a hundred of the ancient loanwords would have disappeared by the middle of the ninth century and another hundred by the middle of the

twelfth. But there are also some specific factors affecting the difference between our data and that of the Byzantine studies. One is genre: those studies all focussed on literature, while ours includes non-literary words found on papyri and/or inscriptions. The use of Greek in Egypt continued after AD 600, but not for very long. Egypt was conquered by the Arabs in the seventh century, with the result that our supply of Greek papyrus evidence dries up in the eighth century. Therefore some loanwords that had survived the end of antiquity only in papyri vanished at that point: for example ἀκκουβιτάλιον 'couch cover', ἀρχισταβλίτης 'chief stableman', κολλητίων 'filing clerk', λεντιάριος 'linen-dealer', παγαρχέω 'hold the office of pagarch', παρατοῦρα 'distinctive dress', παστιλλᾶς 'confectioner', πωμαρίτης 'fruiterer', ῥιπάριος 'water-watchman'. Some of these were not rare in papyri and would not have been likely candidates for natural attrition; their loss has to do with historical rather than linguistic factors.

Some other words that in antiquity occurred primarily or entirely in papyri or inscriptions do turn up occasionally in Byzantine literature, but not often enough to be picked up by the studies just cited. Examples include βαρβαρικάριος 'brocade-maker', βρακάριος 'tailor', ἔμπλουμος 'tapestry woven', καμψάριος 'slave who carries schoolbooks', κολλεκτάριος 'banker', κομόδιον 'gratuity', λοῦδος 'games', σιλιγνάριος 'seller of siligo bread', σιτλίον 'little bucket', and χερνιβόξεστον 'washbasin'. These may not have been as rare in Byzantine speech as they are in Byzantine literature, for many of them refer to things not often mentioned in literature. The same applies to some loanwords that in antiquity are not primarily papyrological or epigraphic, such as βίρρος 'hooded cloak', ἰσίκιον 'dish of mincemeat', σκάλωσις 'scaffolding', συμψέλλιον 'bench', and φεμινάλια 'trousers': the fact that words with such meanings are absent from particular corpora of Byzantine literary texts does not mean that they were not in use in Byzantine conversations. All the words just mentioned must eventually have disappeared, for they are unattested in modern Greek, but some others equally rare in Byzantine texts do appear in modern Greek, demonstrating that such words could survive: for example μανδήλη 'towel', καράκαλλον

---

[49] The figure of 3,000 is clearly intended to include both categories; Adrados (2005: 250) is incorrect to imply that Mihăescu's words are all Byzantine borrowings. Mihăescu (1993: 359) divides these words by semantic field: 785 military terms, 385 public adminstration, 350 legal, 150 plants and animals, 145 clothing, 120 religion and the calendar, 77 weights and measures, 68 court life, 920 other.

'hood', and κάρκαρον 'prison'. Κάρρον 'cart' appears to survive into modern Greek despite not appearing at all (as far as I can establish) in Byzantine texts.

Other loanwords were technical terminology; these appear in Byzantine literature, but only literature belonging to their particular genre, and the technical genres are often omitted from studies of Byzantine vocabulary. The two major groups of words in this category are legal terminology (e.g. ἐμαγκιπατίων 'emancipation', ἐνναούγκιον 'three quarters of an inheritance', ἰνστιτοῦτα 'introduction to Roman law', κανονικάριος 'tax collector', κομφιρματεύω 'confirm', ῥέσκριπτον 'rescript', στιπένδιον 'wages') and medical terminology (e.g. παστιλλόω 'make into a paste', ῥοσᾶτον 'rose-flavoured wine', σπικᾶτον 'embrocation of spikenard', φολιᾶτον, a type of perfumed oil). Most of these were no doubt unfamiliar to non-specialists, but within the relevant disciplines they may have been as familiar as 'adverb' is to modern Classicists.

The total impact of the ancient loanwords on Byzantine Greek was greater than the number of ancient loanwords with Byzantine survivals, for many ancient loanwords had multiple Byzantine descendants. Thus βρουμάλια 'festival of the winter solstice' produced βρουμαλίζω 'celebrate the festival of the winter solstice', βρουμαλισταί 'those who celebrate the winter solstice', and βρουμαλιτικός 'ripening during the winter solstice'. Likewise βένετος 'blue' (a circus faction) produced βενετικός 'blue', βενετοπράσινος 'of the blues and greens', and βενετοφορέω 'wear blue', while κάγκελλος 'latticed barrier or balustrade' produced καγγελίζω 'wriggle', καγκελλοειδῶς 'in the form of a lattice', καγκελλοθυρίς 'latticed gate', and καγκελλοθυρίδιον 'little latticed gate'.[50]

Loanwords did not necessarily remain fixed during the Byzantine period, either in form or in meaning; they developed just as native words did. Additionally, a few loanwords underwent changes specifically related to medieval changes in their Latin source words. For example, medieval *bulla* acquired the meaning 'seal' after AD 600 and

transferred this meaning to the fourth-century loanword βούλλα; the same thing happened when περεγρῖνος came to mean 'pilgrim'. This phenomenon, known as 'continued semantic borrowing', also occurs in modern languages when contact extends over a long period. For example, English borrowed the verb 'present' from French and/or Latin in the thirteenth century, at which period it did not have the meaning 'stage or put on (a play)'; that meaning developed in French in the sixteenth century and soon spread to English (Durkin 2014: 335).

8.2.3 *Survival into modern Greek*

Many ancient loanwords have living descendants, some of which provide central elements of the modern Greek vocabulary (cf. e.g. Kolonia and Peri 2008: 71–4). Modern descendants of ancient Latin loanwords include σπίτι 'house' (ancient ὁσπίτιον), πόρτα 'door' (πόρτα), πουλί 'bird' (πουλλίον), μουλάρι 'mule' (μουλάριον), άσπρος 'white' (ἄσπρος), κίτρινος 'yellow' (κίτρινος), κάμπος 'plain' (κάμπος), βρακί 'underpants' (βράκιον), μαντήλι 'handkerchief' (μανδήλιον), σκαμνί 'stool' (σκαμνίον), φούρνος 'oven' (φοῦρνος), μαρούλι 'lettuce' (μαρούλιον), λουκάνικο 'sausage' (λουκάνικον), κάρβουνο 'coal' (κάρβων), and σαπούνι 'soap' (σαπώνιον). A small modern Greek–English dictionary, the *Collins Greek Dictionary: Essential Edition* (Harper Collins 2019), contains descendants of 79 ancient loanwords, or 10% of the original pool of 820. Some of those loanwords have multiple descendants listed; for example from ancient σκάλα 'stairs' not only modern σκάλα 'stairs', but also σκαλί 'step', σκαλοπάτι 'rung', σκαλώνω 'snag', and σκαλωσιά 'scaffolding'. The total number of words in this dictionary that descend from ancient loanwords is therefore 116, or 1% of its c. 10,400 Greek entries.[51] This probably offers a fairly accurate

---

[50] *LBG s.vv.*; Triandaphyllidis (1909: 111–12) provides additional examples of loanwords that were highly productive in Byzantine Greek, including some with dozens of derivatives.

[51] Απρίλης = Απρίλιος (from ancient Ἀπρίλιος); ασπράδι, ασπρίζω, άσπρο, ασπροπρόσωπος, άσπρος (all from ancient ἄσπρος); αυγουστιάτικος, Αύγουστος (Αὔγουστος 2); βούλωμα, βουλώνω (βούλλα); βρακί (βράκιον); βραχιόλι (βραχιάλιον); Γενάρης = Ἰανουάριος (Ἰανουάριος); γουναράδικο (γουνάριος); Δεκέμβρης = Δεκέμβριος (Δεκέμβριος); δούκας (δούξ); Ιούλης = Ιούλιος (Ἰούλιος); Ιούνης = Ιούνιος (Ἰούνιος); καβαλάρης (καβαλλάριος); καγκελάριος (καγκελλάριος 1); κάγκελο (κάγκελλος); καισαρική (Καῖσαρ); κάλαντα (Καλάνδαι); κάμπος (κάμπος); κανάλι

approximation of the contribution the ancient loanwords have made to the central vocabulary of modern Greek.

This central vocabulary is of course only part of the total current word stock of modern Greek. A more complete picture of the contemporary vocabulary is given in the big Greek–Greek lexicon of Babiniotis (2002), which contains c. 43,600 entries. Those entries include descendants of 81 additional ancient loanwords besides the 79 found in the small dictionary, for a total of 160, or 20% of the original 820. Once again, some have multiple descendants. For example, Babiniotis' lexicon contains not only the five descendants of ancient σκάλα 'stairs' found in the small dictionary, but also five more: σκαλάκι 'little step', σκαλιέρα 'rope ladder', σκαλίτσα 'little stairs', σκαλοπόδαρο 'sides of a ladder', and σκαλωτός 'having steps'. In total 390 of Babiniotis' lemmata are descended from

ancient Latin loanwords, and those make up 1% of the lemmata in the lexicon.[52]

Modern Greek, like modern English, encompasses not only the contemporary version of the language but also several previous centuries. The transition from Byzantine to modern Greek is officially placed in 1453, but in practice scholars investigating the survival of loanwords into modern Greek tend to be thinking of Greek from the nineteenth century onwards. Within that time frame a number of words descended from ancient loans have fallen out of use. Therefore by looking at collections of modern Greek words earlier than Babiniotis' lexicon, such as Andriotis' lexicon (1967) and the collections of early modern dialectal material provided by Meyer (1895), Dieterich (1901), Andriotis (1974), Shipp (1979), and Kahane and Kahane (1972–6), descendants of an additional 75 loanwords not included in Babiniotis (2002) can be found.[53] The total number of ancient loanwords that survived at least as far as the nineteenth century is therefore 235, or 29% of the original 820. The ultimate fate of the ancient loanwords is represented in Figure 8.

This 29% survival rate for ancient loanwords is significantly different from the figure of 10% usually given.[54] Actually that figure never had any validity; it was derived from comparison of the c. 300 nineteenth-century descendants of Latin loanwords collected by Meyer (1895) to the c. 2,900 Latin words that Viscidi (1944: 2) claimed to have identified in Greek texts up to AD 1100. Given the chronological parameters Viscidi used, 10% was never intended as a figure for the survival of strictly ancient material, and it was probably not originally intended as a figure for

(κανάλιον); καντήλι (κανδήλη); κάρβουνο (κάρβων); κάρο (κάρρον); κάστρο (κάστρον); κελάρι (κελλάριον); κελί (κελλίον); κιτρινίζω, κίτρινος (κίτρινος); κόμης (κόμης); κουκούλα (κουκούλλιον); κουρτίνα (κορτίνα); κώδικας, κωδικός (κῶδιξ); λατινικός (Λατῖνος); λουκάνικο (λουκάνικον); λουράκι, λουρί (λωρίον); λουρίδα (λῶρος); Μάης = Μάιος (Μάϊος); μαντηλάκι = μαντιλάκι, μαντήλι = μαντίλι (μανδήλιον); μάπα (μάππα); μαρούλι, μαρουλοσαλάτα (μαρούλιον); Μάρτης = Μάρτιος (Μάρτιος); μάστορας, μαστόρεμα, μαστορεύω (μάγιστρος); μεμβράνη (μεμβράνα); μίλι (μίλιον); μόλος (μῶλος); μουλάρι (μουλάριον); Νοέμβρης = Νοέμβριος (Νοέμβριος); Οκτώβρης = Οκτώβριος (Ὀκτώβριος); ουγκιά (οὐγγία); παλάτι (παλάτιον); πόρτα, πορτάκι (πόρτα); πουλάκι, πουλερικά, πουλί (πουλλίον); πρίγκιπας, πριγκίπισσα (πρίγκεψ); ρήγας (ρήξ); ροδάκινο (δωράκινον); Ρωμαία, ρωμαιοκαθολικός, Ρωμαίος (Ῥωμαῖος); ρωμαϊκός (Ῥωμαϊκός); Ρώμη (Ῥώμη); σαβούρα (σαβούρα); σαπουνάδα, σαπουνόπερα (σάπων); σαπούνι, σαπουνίζω (σαπώνιον); σέλα (σέλλα); Σεπτέμβρης = Σεπτέμβριος (Σεπτέμβριος); σκάλα, σκαλί, σκαλοπάτι, σκαλώνω, σκαλωσιά (σκάλα); σκαμνί (σκαμνίον); σουβλί, σουβλίζω (σουβλίον); σπίτι, σπιτικό, σπιτικός, σπιτονοικοκυρά, σπιτονοικοκύρης (ὁσπίτιον); στάβλος = σταύλος (στάβλον); ταβέρνα (ταβέρνα); ταβερνιάρης, ταβερνιάρισσα (ταβέρνιον); τάβλα (τάβλα); τάβλι (ταβλίον); τίτλος (τίτλος); τρούλος (τροῦλλος); φάβα (φάβα); φασολάδα, φασολάκια, φασόλι (φασίολος); Φεβρουάριος = Φλεβάρης (Φεβρουάριος); φούρναρης, φουρνάρισσα, φούρνος (φοῦρνος); χριστιανή, χριστιανός (Χριστιανός); χριστιανικός (Χριστιανικός); χριστιανισμός (Χριστιανισμός). The sign '=' indicates when two lemmata are variant spellings of the same word; these have been counted only once. This dictionary also contains entries for five words that are attested in antiquity but too rarely to be considered full loanwords at that period: νότα (νότα), πουκάμισο (ὑποκαμίσιον), ράσο (ῥᾶσον), σίκαλη (σήκαλις), υπότιτλος (ὑπότιτλος).

---

[52] The words concerned are marked in the Lexicon as being included by Babiniotis. These figures include 5 ancient loanwords for which it is not completely certain that the modern word is a descendant of the ancient one (marked 'modern?' in the Lexicon); if those are excluded, Babiniotis includes 373 lemmata descended from 156 ancient loanwords.

[53] References are given in §3.2. This figure includes 4 loanwords for which the connection between the ancient and the modern word is not completely certain, marked as 'modern?' in §3.2. Niehoff-Panagiotidis (2019) investigates Latin words that occur in modern dialects but not in Standard Modern Greek.

[54] E.g. Kahane and Kahane (1982: 135).

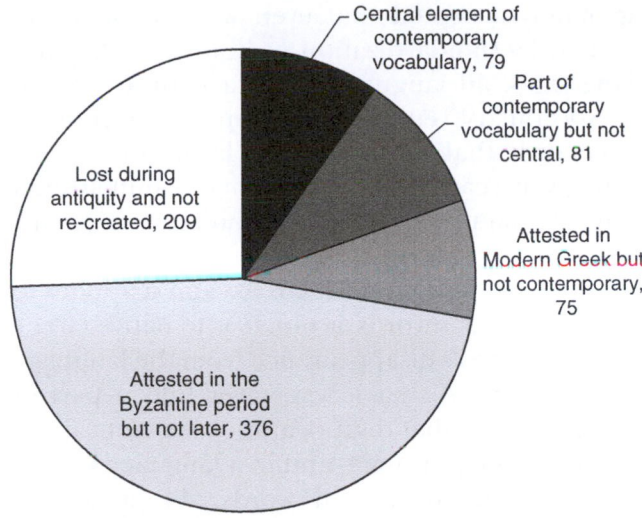

Figure 8 The ultimate fate of the ancient loanwords

the survival of established loanwords rather than codeswitches: although Viscidi never published his corpus, and therefore it cannot be known exactly which words he included, a figure like 2,900 could only be reached by including codeswitches. Codeswitches by their very nature do not survive, and therefore figures for long-term survival have little meaning if codeswitches are included. Moreover many of Meyer's etymologies are doubtful, and he includes words of which no trace can be found in antiquity; only about half his words can be shown to derive from ancient Latin borrowings.[55] Therefore neither Viscidi's figures nor Meyer's are usable for calculating the survival rate of loanwords: the figure of 10% was never based on meaningful data.

The reason survival rates have been so much discussed is that scholars working on ancient and Byzantine Greek have long considered words' survival into modern Greek to be a key indication of their status in antiquity: ancient loanwords with modern Greek descendants are thought to

have been better established in antiquity than ones that disappeared earlier.[56] This idea goes back to the nineteenth century, a period when modern Greek had not yet been standardized and modern parallels for ancient vocabulary were sought in spoken dialects. In the nineteenth and much of the twentieth century Greek was a diglossic language with two radically different varieties: an educated, high-register variety with many archaizing features imitating the Classical language, and a popular, low-register one showing many developments since antiquity. This situation grew out of the extreme range of register variation deployed in Byzantine Greek, which in turn probably had its roots in the significant register variations of late antiquity. Therefore words belonging to a low register could potentially remain in use for many centuries without ever showing up in high-register literature, and words that frequently appeared in such literature might very well not have been part of conversational language at the time those texts were written. Nineteenth-century scholars therefore naturally turned to more popular forms of Greek for information about the language's development. They did not think that they could find that popular language in written texts, both because in a time of diglossia most written texts are more or less influenced by the educated version of the language and because many of the vernacular Greek texts known today had not yet been published.[57] Therefore the obvious place to look for popular language was speech, which (in an age before recording devices) had to be contemporary. For this reason nineteenth-century scholars quite reasonably saw the Greek dialects of their own day as the only real evidence for uneducated usage after the end of the ancient papyri.

But several things have changed since the nineteenth century. Modern Greek is no longer diglossic, not only because the archaizing versions of the language have largely fallen out of use, but also because the traditional oral dialects

---

[55] One hundred and fifty-eight of Meyer's entries descend from words classified in the present study as ancient loanwords. The rest are divided as follows (a few of Meyer's entries pertain to more than one of our entries): 40 rare, 12 foreign, 5 names, 28 not descended from Latin, 3 semantic extensions, 96 not ancient. Cf. Filos (2014: 321), suggesting that c. 200 of Meyer's words come from ancient borrowings. Viscidi himself (1944: 58) calculated that c. 200 of his 2,900 words survived into modern Greek, which would have been a 7% survival rate.

[56] E.g. Meyer (1895: 3), Zillacus (1937: 309), Viscidi (1944: 9), Zervan (2019: 1); counter-arguments in Orioles (1974: 120–1).

[57] Holton et al. (2019: xxxvii–cxv) gives a list of vernacular Greek texts, both literary and non-literary, composed between c. 1100 and c. 1700; many of these were unknown until comparatively recently (p. xvii).

are disappearing: both register extremes are rapidly being replaced by Standard Modern Greek (e.g. Mackridge 2010: 570–5). This standardized language omits many words found in the nineteenth-century dialects, not only because a standardization process inevitably reduces variation, but also due to systematic purging of undesirable vocabulary. Foreign vocabulary was especially likely to be seen as undesirable, and the number of loanwords (especially from Turkish, but also from other languages) has been greatly reduced.[58] Some of the purged vocabulary has been replaced by words with Classical Greek etymologies, including revivals of long-defunct ancient terms (e.g. Mackridge 2010: 575).

As a result, 'survival into modern Greek' now effectively means inclusion in a dictionary of Standard Modern Greek, rather than use in an oral dialect. And since Standard Modern Greek is a partly artificial construct, its relationship to the ancient language is less straightforward than was that of the nineteenth-century dialects. This situation is one reason why modern Greek survival is now often rejected as a criterion for judging the extent to which ancient borrowings were established as loanwords in antiquity, but the rejection tends to be framed in broader terms: a word's long-term survival depends on many factors beside the extent to which it was originally integrated into its language.[59] In fact it is now generally accepted that even without pressures caused by standardization or contact with other languages, all languages have a natural process of vocabulary replacement: some proportion of the words that most speakers know and use in any given year will have vanished a millennium later.[60] That process is the main reason why many native words that were common in ancient Greek are not found in modern Greek, and it applies to established loanwords as much as to native Greek words. A word's disappearance from the language does not mean that it was never fully a part of Greek, even if that disappearance was not caused by deliberate purging – and in a language known to have purged foreign words, disappearance has even less meaning. Equally, the survival into modern Greek of a Latin loanword first attested in antiquity does not mean that that word was thoroughly borrowed in antiquity. Modern Greek survival is not really relevant to understanding the situation in antiquity at all – but it provides a useful illustration of the long-term effect that ancient borrowing from Latin had on the Greek language.

A further complication is that some long-defunct ancient loanwords have been revived in modern Greek.[61] For example, modern δικτατορία 'dictatorship' bears a striking similarity to ancient δικτατωρεία, but the ancient word, designating a Roman office that was obsolete from the beginning of the Empire, disappeared after the fourth century; the modern word has appeared comparatively recently and refers to

---

[58] See e.g. Horrocks (2010: 381, 439, 447), Tonnet (2003: 245–9), Stathi (2002: 303–4), Browning (1983: 16), Contossopoulos (1978: 26). This was not the first purge of foreign vocabulary; for one during the Byzantine period see e.g. Kahane and Kahane (1972–6: 523–5, 1982: 133). Such purges may be part of the explanation for why fewer ancient loanwords now survive than would have been expected had the 7% average loss rate during antiquity simply continued during the Byzantine and modern periods: if that had happened there should have been approximately 272 ancient loanwords left at the start of the nineteenth century and 235 left at the start of the twenty-first century.

[59] E.g. Markopoulos (2014: 84): '[T]he amount of lexical (and structural) borrowings retained in a language long after the completion of a contact situation is dependent on social and political factors, and cannot be utilized to determine the extent of the contact situation. For instance, it is clearly the case that Greek speakers nowadays tend to use a much smaller number of Turkish loanwords than the previous generations, partly because of a campaign to eradicate such influences (mostly in the nineteenth

century), and partly because most of these words are felt obsolete. However, it would constitute a grave methodological mistake to determine the extent of Greek-Turkish bilingualism by taking into account solely the loanwords that survive in Standard Modern Greek of the twenty-first century.'

[60] This process underpins the field of glottochronology, which attempts to supply absolute dates for early phases of languages on the basis of a constant rate of vocabulary replacement. Glottochronology is generally agreed not to work very well, because the rate of vocabulary replacement cannot be relied upon to remain constant, but there is no question that some vocabulary replacement normally occurs; see e.g. parts II and III of Renfrew et al. (2000).

[61] This situation is not unique to loanwords but a general feature of the post-antique development of Greek; see e.g. Eleftheriades (1993: 6–7), Browning (1983: 14), Shipp (1979).

the modern concept of dictatorship. The form of the modern term must come from the ancient loanword, since neither Latin *dictatura* nor any of its equivalents in relevant modern languages has a form like **dictatoria*, but it is not a direct survival of it. Other probable revivals of ancient loanwords are modern δικτατορεύω 'be dictator', Καπιτώλιο 'Capitol', κελλιώτης 'monk who lives in a cell', λεγεωνάριος 'legionary', ματρώνα 'madam', and Σατουρνάλια 'Saturnalia'.

One indication that the modern version of an ancient loanword is a revival rather than survival is lack of attestation for a long period before the modern appearance. But such lack of attestion is not necessarily proof of discontinuity, particularly when the modern word was found in the nineteenth-century dialects, where revivals were unlikely. Therefore modern κάρο 'cart' is probably a survival of κάρρον 'cart', and nineteenth-century dialectal σαλγάμι 'turnip' could be a survival of σάλγαμον 'pickling material', though these words appear to be totally unattested in the Byzantine period. They may have survived for over a thousand years exclusively in subliterary registers, though alternative explanations cannot be completely ruled out.

8.3 COMPARISON WITH GREEK LOANWORDS IN LATIN

How do the borrowing and survival patterns of Latin loanwords in Greek compare with those of Greek loanwords in Latin? The answer is not straightforward, since no collection of Greek loanwords in Latin provides data directly comparable to that in the present study. Indeed the best such collections are those of Weise (1882: 326–544) and Saalfeld (1884), which though enormous (Weise's collection alone contains more than 7,000 words) are almost certainly incomplete, since they predate the discovery of most Latin documents.[62] Moreover Saalfeld's list does not distinguish loanwords from codeswitches, making

it effectively useless for our purposes. Weise, however, divides his words into three groups, one of which probably corresponds roughly to what we would call loanwords; the words in this group can therefore be taken as an (incomplete) corpus of Greek loanwords in Latin.[63] They number 1,252, indicating that there were probably more Greek loanwords in Latin than Latin loanwords in Greek – though probably not exponentially more.

Latin words had a much better chance of long-term survival than Greek ones, for most of the Western Roman empire remained primarily Latin speaking while the language divided itself into the Romance languages and dialects, hundreds of which lasted long enough to be usable by modern scholars.[64] Thus Latin words that died out in one region often persisted in others, resulting in far more overall vocabulary survival than any single Romance language could provide. But most regional varieties of Greek have vanished

---

[62] For continued scholarly reliance on those works see e.g. Biville (1990–5: 1.34 with n. 2). Clackson (forthcoming) provides a complete corpus of Greek words attested or inferable in Latin up to c. 100 BC; it contains 718 words, many clearly codeswitches. He calculates that the *OLD* contains 4,295 Greek words (excluding names), many of which are codeswitches.

[63] The lemmata concerned are those that Weise prints in bold font. He describes them as being words that were totally naturalized into Latin, were used by all speakers, and had no native synonyms ('solche, die dem Volke in Fleisch und Blut übergegangen und total naturalisiert sind, deren fremdes Gepräge daher ganz oder fast ganz verwischt ist; diese bezeichnen meist Kulturobjekte, die den Römern von Haus aus unbekannt, deren Namen ihnen somit gleich mit der Sache zugekommen sind, z. B. *murtus, cupressus, purpura*', 1882: 8) plus words that were used by a majority of speakers despite having native synonyms and that are attested as belonging to the spoken language by their occurrence in inscriptions and/or survival into Romance ('solche, welche sich ebenfalls eingebürgert haben und wenn auch nicht durch alle Schichten der Bevölkerung durchgedrungen sind, so doch von einem großen Teile derselben in der Regel verwendet wurden, obwohl sich meist adäquate römische Ausdrücke entweder von Haus aus daneben vorfinden, oder, besonders auf dem Gebiete der Wissenschaften, durch Übersetzung geschaffen worden sind. Dahin gehören *philosophia* = *sapientia*, *rhetorica* = *ars oratoria* u. a., die mehr dem gebildeten Stande angehören, *petra* = *saxum, lapis*, *nanus* = *pumilio*, *cycnus* = *olor*, die, wie ihr Wiedererscheinen in den romanischen Sprachen beweist, mehr volkstümliche Ausdrücke waren', 1882: 8; further qualified with 'diejenigen … deren Vorkommen in der gesprochenen, lebendigen Sprache des Volks oder der Gebildeten an sicheren Kriterien (inschriftl. Beleg, Übergang in die romanischen Sprachen) einigermaßen deutlich erkennbar war', 1882: 9).

[64] Meyer-Lübke (1935: xxvii–xxxii) lists more than 500 varieties of Romance.

(the Egyptian and Middle Eastern varieties entirely, the Asia Minor and Magna Graecia varieties partially), and therefore in modern Greek we do not have the equivalent of the Romance languages as a group, but only of Italian or another individual Romance language. Moreover the survival of Latin words is traditionally measured by more generous chronological criteria than are traditionally used for Greek: a Latin word is considered to have survived into Romance if it is attested in at least one Romance language or dialect at any point during the medieval or modern periods.[65] If those criteria are used to determine the survival rate into Romance of Weise's corpus of loanwords, that rate is high, at 38% – but such a figure is in no sense comparable to those that we have calculated for Greek.[66] A more comparable figure is the percentage persisting into Italian, and in fact the survival rate into Italian for Weise's corpus of loanwords is 27%, very similar to the 29% survival rate for Latin loanwords in Greek.[67]

[65] See e.g. Meyer-Lübke's etymological dictionary of Romance (1935).

[66] Of a sample consisting of the loanwords on every fifth page of Weise's list (pp. 430, 435, etc.), i.e. 262 words, 99 have an entry in Meyer-Lübke (1935). Clackson (forthcoming) finds a much lower survival rate using a different sample, but he includes codeswitches as well as loanwords.

[67] Of the sample in the preceding note, 70 have a descendant or derivative labelled as Italian by Meyer-Lübke (1935). This fact does not necessarily mean that there are as many Grecisms in Italian as Latinisms in modern Greek, however. Many words of Greek origin in Italian and other modern Romance languages (like many words of Latin origin) are revivals or learned borrowings from the medieval and modern periods rather than direct survivals from antiquity. (See e.g. Stefenelli 1992; Janni and Mazzini 1990.) Kahane and Kahane (1982: 128) state that c. 200 Byzantine Greek words were borrowed into Romance languages during the Middle Ages. Kolonia and Peri (2008: 71) do suggest that the total number of words

8.4 CONCLUSIONS

Latin words began to be borrowed early in the Republican period, and many of the earliest loanwords were probably introduced by Latin speakers, who often communicated with their neighbours in Greek. Most borrowings were probably made before AD 300, but because loanwords normally persisted once introduced, the cumulative effect of borrowing and the formation of derivatives meant that in each century the Greek language contained substantially more loanwords than in previous centuries. Not all loanwords survived, however; a quarter of them died out before the end of antiquity, with an average loss rate of 7% per century.

Most loanwords survived into the Byzantine period, where they produced further derivatives and were joined by some additional borrowings made during that period. Overall, however, both the borrowing rate and the total number of Latin loanwords in use decreased during the Byzantine period. The decrease was largely due to a convergence of historical and cultural factors, but in addition linguistic purists actively tried to suppress the use of loanwords.

Twenty-nine per cent of the ancient loanwords survived into modern Greek, if that period is defined to include the nineteenth-century dialects. Twenty per cent can be found in a large dictionary of contemporary modern Greek, and ten per cent even in a small dictionary. Such dictionaries also include numerous modern derivatives of ancient loanwords. Overall, descendants of ancient borrowings from Latin make up about 1% of the central vocabulary of modern Greek, including many key terms such as 'house', 'soap', 'lettuce', and 'oven'.

of Latin origin in modern Greek is roughly equivalent to the total of words of Greek origin in Italian, but without citing evidence.

9

WHERE WERE LOANWORDS USED?

9.1 OVERALL PATTERNS

Surviving Greek texts can be divided into three main types, which show different borrowing patterns: documents (including documentary papyri, ostraca, and tablets),[1] inscriptions (including graffiti, dipinti, mosaics, and inscribed objects),[2] and literature (including the dictionaries, commentaries, etc. often referred to as 'paraliterary texts').[3] Loanwords also appear on the legends of coins, but not often enough for meaningful patterns to emerge.[4]

Overall, the writers of documents were more likely to use new loanwords than were the authors of literary works: 409 loanwords first appear in documents and only 350 in literature.[5] Adjusting for the fact that our surviving evidence includes far more words of literature than of documents, writers of documentary texts seem to have introduced new loanwords more than ten times as frequently as authors of literary texts.[6] There is no significant distinction in this respect between direct borrowings and derivatives of earlier borrowings: 18% of the loanwords that first appear in documents and 20% of those that first appear in literature are derivatives of earlier borrowings. Therefore the reason for the greater frequency of new loanwords in documents is probably that their composers were readier to use new Latinate words than the authors of literary texts, not simply that they were readier to borrow words from Latin or that they had more opportunity to do so.

These generalizations conceal considerable chronological variation, as illustrated in Figures 9 and 10. Documents, which come primarily from

[1] Technically a 'papyrus' is a fragment of a paper-like substance made from a kind of reed, an 'ostracon' is a piece of broken pottery or (less often) a flake of stone, and a 'tablet' is a piece of wood (sometimes waxed) or metal made into a writing surface. Almost all published documentary papyri and ostraca, and many tablets, can be found on the *Papyrological Navigator*, available at www.papyri.info.

[2] Technically an 'inscription' is carved, usually on stone; a graffito is scratched, and a dipinto is painted. Writing on pottery is traditionally considered to belong to the category of inscriptions if written while the pot was intact, but to the category of ostraca if written after the pot was broken; this distinction corresponds to a meaningful difference in the kinds of texts written. Writing on stone is usually considered to belong to the category of inscriptions, but when a small flake of stone is used like a potsherd it is normally considered an ostracon; again this distinction tends to be meaningful for the kinds of texts written. Many (but by no means all) Greek texts classified as inscriptions can be found on the Packard Humanities Institute's *Searchable Greek Inscriptions* database, available at https://epigraphy.packhum.org. This database also includes curse tablets from Audollent (1904), which I treat as documents.

[3] These texts survive chiefly via the medieval manuscript tradition and occasionally on papyrus; most (including some of the papyrus texts) can be found on the *Thesaurus Linguae Graecae* database (*TLG*), available at http://stephanus.tlg.uci.edu.

[4] See §8.1.2 and §3.2 *s.vv.* Ἀντώνεια, ἀσσάριον, Αὐγούστειος, βότον, ἡμιασσάριον, ἰμπεράτωρ, Καῖσαρ, Καπετώλια, Καπετώλιος, κολωνία, μητροκολωνεία, μονῆτα, πάτρων, Ῥωμαῖος, Ῥώμη, φιλόκαισαρ, φιλοκλαύδιος, φιλορώμαιος; for

more detailed examination of language use on Roman coins, see Zilliacus (1935a: 50–8).

[5] Words that first appear in the same century in both text types are here counted for both types.

[6] As of 22 July 2020 the *TLG* contained 50,669,026 words of literature dated between the second century BC and the sixth century AD (inclusive), and as of 4 June 2021 the *PN* contained 59,701 Greek documents from the same period. Surviving documents vary enormously in length, but as of March 2021 the *Callimachus* site (https://glg.csic.es/Callimachus/DocumentaryPapyriByNumbers.html) reported that a corpus of 57,049 documentary papyri (not identical to our corpus, but mostly overlapping) contained 4,385,285 words, yielding an average document length of 77 words. Our corpus of Greek documents therefore probably contains around 4,596,977 words. It follows that the 409 loanwords that first appear in documents show a rate of around 89 new loanwords per million words used, while the 350 first appearing in literature show a rate of 7 new loanwords per million words used.

Egypt, only begin to be a major source of loanwords in the first century AD, after the Roman conquest of Egypt in the late first century BC. From the fifth century AD the importance of documents as a source of new loanwords diminishes owing to a fall in the quantity of preserved papyri, though in the sixth century the number of new loanwords in documents increases both absolutely and relative to the amount of surviving evidence. Authors of literary texts, by contrast, use new loanwords above all in the fifth and sixth centuries, which between them account for 43% of all loanwords first introduced in literature.

Words introduced in particular text types could, of course, spread to other types in subsequent centuries. The final distribution of loanwords, that is the full range of text types in which each word is attested before the end of antiquity, shows that overall more are found in literature than in documents: 82% of established loanwords

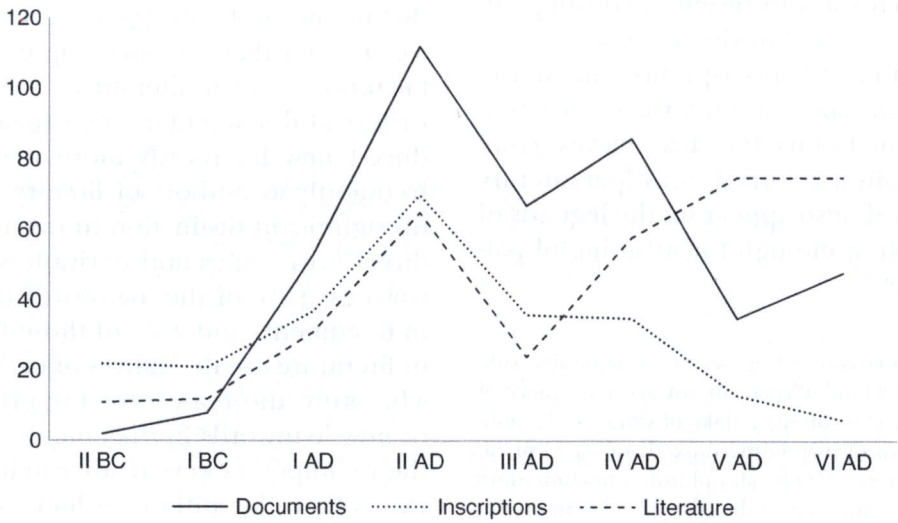

Figure 9 New loanwords (borrowings and derivatives) by text type, absolute numbers per century; numbers and calculations in §12.1

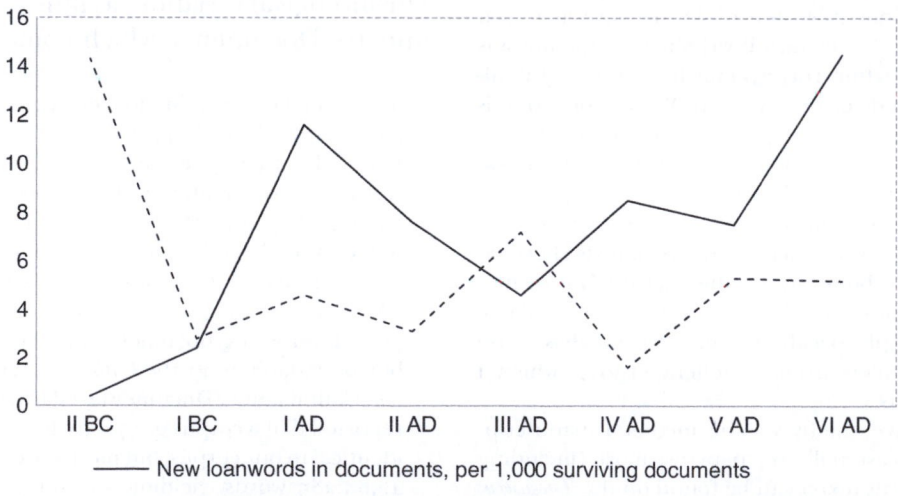

Figure 10 New loanwords by text type, relative to amount of surviving evidence (omitting inscriptions, for which I cannot calculate the chronological distribution of the surviving evidence); numbers and calculations in §12.1

have at least one literary attestation before the end of antiquity, compared to 73% with at least one occurrence in documents. Literary texts are also more likely to incorporate loanwords that originated in other text types than are documents: 48% of the loanwords eventually attested in literature first appeared in documents and/or inscriptions, but only 31% of the loanwords eventually attested in papyri first appeared in literature and/or inscriptions.[7]

As these figures suggest, most loanwords start off in only one text type: only 19% are securely attested in two types in their first century, and only 2% in all three. Although there was a general tendency for words to spread to other types of text after their initial appearance, they did not necessarily or even usually end up in all three: only 36% of loanwords eventually appear in all text types, while 26% remained confined to a single text type throughout antiquity. Of course, some loanwords in this last group failed to spread because they were borrowed in late antiquity and had little time to do so before AD 600, but those seem to be a minority: 62% of the words that never spread beyond a single text type were borrowed or created before AD 400.[8] One might expect the loanwords confined exclusively to one text type to be primarily documentary words, but in fact many are literary words, for reasons that will be explored in §9.5.[9]

Inscriptions present a rather different picture from literature and documents, because they tend to deal only with a limited range of topics. Some types of word, such as titles and occupational terms, are very well represented in the epigraphic material, but many others (such as words for food, beverages, clothing, furniture, animals, and tools) rarely if ever appear on inscriptions (for the major exception, the Edict of Diocletian, see §9.5.1). Inscriptions also tend to use a formal linguistic register and are often formulaic, with the same phrases repeated from inscription to inscription by writers who were evidently not aiming to produce original compositions reflecting their own linguistic resources. As a result fewer loanwords appear in inscriptions: only 245 are first introduced there (compare 409 first introduced in documents and 350 in literature), and only 446 eventually appear there (compare 593 eventually appearing in documents and 672 in literature). The first of these figures could be due in part to the fact that inscriptions are less likely to be dated than documents or literary texts, but the second cannot. Despite all this, inscriptions are a major source of new loanwords in the early period, but their contribution declines steadily after the second century AD (see Figure 9). Derivatives are particularly unlikely to appear in inscriptions: whereas 60% of direct borrowings eventually appear in inscriptions, only 29% of derivatives do so. Derivatives are in general somewhat less likely to spread beyond their original text type than are direct borrowings, but this effect is much more pronounced in inscriptions.[10] This effect could be due to the fact that many derivatives are in the semantic fields poorly represented on inscriptions, as well as to the formal linguistic register of inscriptions: many derivatives are diminutives.

One result of the gradual spread of loanwords among the different text types is that one can see a time lag between words' initial appearance and when they penetrate into a particular text type. On average, across the period from the third to the sixth century, 49% of the loans used for

---

[7] Raw numbers: 672 loanwords eventually attested in literature (including 322 first attested elsewhere), 593 eventually attested in documents (including 184 first attested elsewhere). Statistics in this chapter omit 4 loanwords (3 direct borrowings and 1 derivative) whose first attestations are in coins or indeterminable. Figures for loanwords eventually attested include marked and undatable examples, as long as those are likely to be ancient.

[8] Raw numbers: 158 loanwords first attested in two text types and 15 first attested in three; 295 eventually attested in three types and 215 confined to one type; 133 of that 215 borrowed before AD 400.

[9] Of the 215 loanwords found only in one type of text, 78 (36%) occur only in documents, 18 (8%) only in inscriptions, and 120 (56%) only in literature. The greater contribution of literature in late antiquity is only part of the explanation for this distribution, for of the 133 such loanwords borrowed before AD 400, 62 (47%) occur only in documents, 15 (11%) only in inscriptions, and 56 (42%) only in literature.

[10] I.e., 83% of direct borrowings but 76% of derivatives are eventually attested in literature, and 74% of direct borrowings but 65% of derivatives in documents. Raw numbers: 446 loanwords (403 direct borrowings, 43 derivatives) eventually attested in inscriptions, 672 (560 direct borrowings, 112 derivatives) eventually attested in literature, 593 (497 direct borrowings, 96 derivatives) eventually attested in documents.

the first time in literature were not new to the language as a whole, having appeared in an earlier century in documents and/or inscriptions. In fact 32% had been used in non-literary texts for several centuries. This considerable time lag must be due in part to the lexical conservatism of literature, but that is not the whole explanation, for documentary texts also show a time lag, albeit a smaller one: across the same period, 35% of the loans used for the first time in documents had appeared in an earlier century in literature and/or inscriptions, and 17% had been used in such texts for several centuries before appearing in documents.[11] Probably many loans were borrowed in a particular place and simply took time to diffuse across the empire. (Centuries earlier than the third have much lower percentages of words that were not new to the language as a whole, but that effect must be due at least partly to the way that the explosion of evidence in the second century revealed borrowings that had actually taken place in preceding centuries.[12])

These figures also suggest that at least a third of the loanwords found in papyri from Egypt were not borrowed or created in Egypt but rather spread from other parts of the empire. Of course, our papyrus evidence is incomplete, and it is always not only possible but even likely that words' very first occurrences in documents have not been preserved. But the same applies to other types of evidence. Moreover in the third century we have particularly good evidence for which words had already entered the documentary vocabulary, owing to the large numbers of documents surviving from the second century

(see §8.1.1, Figure 3). And in the third century 29% of the loanwords that first appear in the documentary vocabulary had already appeared somewhere else in the second century or earlier.[13] Therefore the language of the papyri does not reflect an isolated Egyptian situation that can be understood purely on its own terms, but is part of a connected network of Greek speakers who influenced each other.

Loanwords' survival rates differed significantly depending on the text types in which they occur: words attested in literature before the end of antiquity were far more likely to survive into the Byzantine period than ones attested in papyri and/or inscriptions but not literature. Thus 85% of the loanwords attested in literature survived past AD 600, versus 26% of those attested only in papyri and/or inscriptions. And words attested only in literature had an even higher survival rate, with 92% lasting into the Byzantine period.[14] Several factors contribute to this effect. The time lag before loanwords appeared in literature meant that some short-lived terms had already died out before the point at which one would have expected them to be picked up by the authors of literary texts. And a word's occurrence in one work of literature sometimes led authors of other works to employ it as well, so that an ancient author's lexical choices could directly affect those of the Byzantines. This effect was particularly strong with the loanword-rich sixth-century legal texts, which were tremendously influential on later legal writing. Legal terms were especially likely to occur only in literature, a fact that partly explains the high survival rate of exclusively literary words. Another contributing factor is no doubt that Byzantine Greek survives primarily through literature: words that ancient authors knew but did not use in literature (whether because the words themselves belonged to a low register or because the things they designated were not mentioned in literature) may likewise have been avoided by the authors of Byzantine literary texts.

---

[11] Raw numbers for literature: 451 loans first appearing III–VI AD, of which 122 had been borrowed in an earlier century, including 143 borrowed more than one century earlier. Documents: 366 loans first appearing III–VI AD, of which 129 had been borrowed in an earlier century, including 63 borrowed more than one century earlier. In calculating words' first appearances doubtful, marked, and undatable examples are excluded, and texts dated to a range of centuries counted in the last of those centuries, as in §8.1.1. Figures for literature exclude 57 loanwords whose first appearances in literature are not precisely dated or that are always marked in literature.

[12] See §8.1.1. The second century has more loanwords that appear simultaneously in two or three text types (47) than any other century, probably because those words' earlier borrowing and diffusion is not visible to us.

[13] Raw numbers: 29 of 98 loanwords, including 9 that had been borrowed more than one century earlier.

[14] Raw numbers: 572 of 672 loanwords appearing in literature, 37 of 144 appearing only in documents and/or inscriptions, and 111 of 120 appearing only in literature survive.

These factors do not, however, completely suffice to explain the enormous difference in survival rates, and it is likely that a further factor was local and regional variation in loanword choice. Byzantine literature by definition comes from regions where Greek continued to be spoken after the end of antiquity. Therefore only words used in those areas had a reasonable chance of survival; ones restricted to areas where Greek ceased to be spoken, such as Egypt, would naturally have died out. But to what extent was there actually regional variation in loanword usage, and how can we tell?

9.2 LOCAL AND REGIONAL LOANWORDS

Latin is known to have had geographically restricted loanwords from contact with the pre-Roman languages of various provinces; these contributed to the language's regional diversification and eventually to the development of the Romance languages.[15] At first glance one might not expect Greek to have similarly restricted loanwords from Latin, since the two languages were in contact throughout the Greek-speaking world. But the localized loans in Latin are not necessarily found throughout the areas where Latin was in contact with the language from which those loans come, and indeed Latin borrowings from Greek in particular can be characteristic of a specific province or even a particular site rather than the Eastern empire in general.[16] Moreover, although koiné Greek may seem uniform by contrast with the dialects that preceded it, it was perfectly capable of regional variation; indeed numerous studies have found regional features in the koiné of a wide range of places.[17]

It is therefore in principle possible that some Greek borrowings from Latin might also have been geographically restricted, and the obvious place to look for such local or regional terms is the words that occur only in documents and/or inscriptions.

Local terms are easiest to identify when they are restricted to a single site or fairly small region within Egypt, so that their absence from documents found elsewhere in Egypt is conspicuous in comparison to their presence in documents from the site or region where they occur. Most striking are the words unique to Mons Claudianus: ἀκισκλάριος 'stonemason' occurs at least 32 times there, ἀκουάριος 'water-carrier' at least 17 times, and αἴγροι 'ill' at least 5 times, with none of these ever found at any other site. Ἀκίσκλος 'adze' is restricted to Mons Claudianus in that meaning, though it once occurs elsewhere in a different sense, and παγανικός 'civilian' occurs only at Mons Claudianus in the second century AD, though from the fifth century it has a more widespread distribution. Mons Claudianus was an unusual community, with both Greek and Latin speakers thrown together in an isolated quarry in the midst of the Eastern Desert, and its Latin contained Greek loanwords not found elsewhere.[18] That the Greek of Mons Claudianus also contained local loanwords is therefore only to be expected.

But other Eastern Desert sites also have local loans. Berenike, a port on the Red Sea, made frequent use of the occupational term κουιντανήσιος,

---

[15] J. N. Adams (2003: 284–7, 443–59).

[16] J. N. Adams (2003: 443–7).

[17] See e.g. Horrocks (2010: 163–70) on regional pronunciation features in Attica and Egypt; Bubenik (2007) on regional pronunciation, grammatical, and syntactic features in Judaea and Asia Minor; Hoz (1998) on regional features in the Western Mediterranean; Brixhe (1987) and Neumann (1980: 180–1) on regionalisms in Asia Minor; Markopoulos (2014: 87–8) on regionalisms in the koiné of late antiquity; Leiwo (2002, cf. 1995b) on an assortment of features characteristic of (the writing of) the Jewish population of Venusia in Italy; and Leiwo (1995a: 168, 170–1) on Greek words and phrases found only in

Naples, which despite its proximity to Rome continued to use Greek well into the imperial period. Most of these regionalisms are due to language contact, and in the last two examples the contact was with Latin. (Adrados 2005: 187–9 argues that the koiné did not acquire regional features from Latin influence, but without acknowledging these two examples.) Most regionalisms in koiné Greek are not vocabulary items, but note J. N. Adams (2003: 458) on αἴγροι as a regionalism caused by contact with Latin, Zillacus (1937: 314–15, 322–3) on regional variation in the use of Latin loanwords in Greek hagiography, Lowe (1967: 36) on regional words in biblical Greek, and Mason (1974: 9–10) on geographical variation in the use of terms for Roman institutions. Biville (e.g. 1990–5: II.461–2) and Rochette (2010: 285) argue for the existence of a distinct variety of Greek spoken by Romans (not only in Rome, and therefore not purely geographically determined).

[18] J. N. Adams (2003: 444–5).

which is never found elsewhere; κουιντάνα, a tax, may also have been used primarily in and around Berenike. Σουκκέσσωρ '(military) relief' and σουβαλάριον 'water-bag' are found at several Eastern Desert sites but not elsewhere.

Local loanwords seem also to have existed in the more connected communities closer to the Nile. The Hermopolite nome appears to have been exclusively responsible for the title ἀβρέβις and the military rank ἀστιάριος, while the Arsinoite nome had παλλιόλιον 'small cloak'. The region of Antinoöpolis and Antaiopolis had προδηληγᾶτον 'advance instructions about taxes', and the Hermonthis region πορταρῆσις 'gate-keeper'. Oxyrhynchus and its surrounding area had Καπετωλιακός 'Capitoline (of games)' (compare Καπετώλια 'Capitoline games' and Καπετωλιονίκης 'victorious at the Capitoline games', which are widely distributed), and perhaps several other terms: κονδουκτόριον 'board of contractors' and the titles ἀννούμερος and κουροπερσονάριος.[19]

Regional vocabulary specific to Egypt as a whole is more difficult to identify, since most of the Greek surviving from Egypt is documentary and we have so few documentary texts from other regions to serve as comparanda: separating the effects of genre and location is not straightforward. Nevertheless the honorific month names periodically inserted in the Egyptian calendar must have been regional loanwords, as the entire calendar to which they pertained was Egyptian: Γαῖος, Γερμανίκειος (regional only as a month name), Δομιτιανός, Δρουσιεύς, Δρουσιλλῆος, Νερώνειος. Moreover, on semantic grounds it is likely that ῥιπάριος 'water-watchman' and ῥιπαρία 'office of the water-watchman' were specifically Egyptian loanwords. Also likely to be Egyptian are two loans found both on papyri and on inscriptions from Egypt, but not on inscriptions from other regions: ἀρμικούστωρ 'person in charge of weapons' and πραισίδιον 'garrison'. Less certainly, titles and occupational terms frequently

used in papyri and not found elsewhere are likely to have been Egyptian vocabulary, since this type of term so often occurs in funerary inscriptions and in literature that we would expect attestation elsewhere if the words had been used elsewhere. Therefore the following may all have been Egyptian loanwords: ἀρχισταβλίτης 'chief stableman', βισήλεκτος (a title), δίλωρος 'having two epaulettes', κιβαριάτωρ (a military role), κουαδράριος 'stonemason', λιβερνάριος 'sailor on a *liburna* ship', ὀπινάτωρ (a military role), and πωμαρίτης 'fruiterer'.

Not all loanwords now found only or primarily in papyri and ostraca were geographically restricted in antiquity, of course. It is very likely that some were absent from literature or inscriptions only because they designate things inherently unlikely to be mentioned in such texts. Good candidates for this category include ἀκκουβιτάλιον 'couch cover', ἀμικτώριον 'shawl', ἀμπούλλιον 'flask', βακλίζω 'beat', βηλάριον 'curtain', βηλόθυρον 'curtain at door', ἔμπλουμος 'tapestry woven', κάμπανος 'steelyard', κομόδιον 'gratuity', λαγήνιον 'little flagon', λινόπηξος 'of combed linen', παλλίολον 'small cloak', σάλγαμον 'pickling material', σκούτλιον 'dish', σουβρικοπάλλιον 'outer cloak', ταλάριον 'sandal fastened at the ankles', φορμαλεία 'list of supplies', φωκάριον 'concubine', and χερνιβόξεστον 'washbasin'. Some of these words appear in Byzantine texts from outside Egypt, a fact that makes it unlikely that they were used only in Egypt in antiquity.

Even among words of this type, however, some can be suspected of being regionalisms, because they seem to be variants of terms that appear in literature and/or inscriptions from outside Egypt. It is unlikely that such words would be absent from literature simply because of their meanings, and while it is possible that they belonged to a subliterary linguistic register for another reason, geographical restriction is a real possibility. For example, λανᾶτον 'wool garment' is fairly widely distributed, but its close relative λανάτιον, apparently designating the same object, occurs only in documents from Egypt. Of the three words for a Dalmatian tunic with hood, δελματικομαφόρτης and δελματικομαφόρτιον occur both on papyri and on the Edict of Diocletian, but δελματικομαφόριον is found only on papyri. And ἑξαξεστιαῖος 'holding six pints' appears only on papyri, while ἑξάξεστος,

---

[19] Note also πρωτοπατρίκιος, which in papyri occurs only in Oxyrhynchus but is also found once in literature. Rare words often seem to be restricted to a particular place (e.g. βίγλης and δηκέπτος at Mons Claudianus, προπινάριον in the Dakhla oasis), but that could simply be a by-product of their rarity.

which has the same meaning, also appears in literature.

Some words occurring reasonably often in documentary texts but not found elsewhere during antiquity do not have meanings obviously unsuitable for literature or inscriptions and do not look as if they would have belonged to a subliterary register for another reason. These are additional candidates for regional loanwords, though they cannot be certainly identified as such. They include ἐξακτορία 'office of the tax collector', ἰουράτωρ 'sworn witness', πενταξεστιαῖος 'holding five pints', προφεσσίων 'declaration (of birth)', and ταβέλλα 'writing tablet' (apparently designating the same object as the more widespread δέλτος).

If the Greek of Egypt included local and regional loanwords, the chances are good that such loanwords also existed elsewhere in the empire, and indeed likely candidates can be identified from the epigraphic evidence. Thus Αὐγουστήσιοι, the name of a Jewish group, looks very much as if it was local to Rome; κοῦπα 'grave' appears to be confined to Sicily and Italy; and μητροκολωνεία 'mother-colony' may have been specific to the region of Syria and Arabia.

These epigraphic regionalisms all, of course, belong to semantic fields for which epigraphic evidence is plentiful (§9.1). Is there any way to identify non-Egyptian regionalisms in the much larger range of semantic fields under-represented on inscriptions? One group of such regionalisms can probably be found in literature: loanwords with meanings specific to the imperial palace in Constantinople and to that city more generally. Such terms, which must have been used primarily within Constantinople and in its surrounding region, include Αὐγουστεῖον 'Augusteum' (in its second incarnation), κουροπαλάτης 'palace supervisor', πραίσεντον 'troops serving in the imperial palace', πρόκεσσον 'departure of the emperor from the palace', σιλέντιον 'imperial audience', and perhaps τριβουνάλιον (a place in Constantinople).

It may also be possible to find other types of regional loanwords in literature. Indeed, the very fact that a word occurs in literature but never in papyri may in some cases indicate that that word was not in use in Egypt. There is a considerable number of such words: 120 loanwords occur only in literature, notably more than the 78 occurring only in documents. Some of these were borrowed in the fifth and sixth centuries, when the documentary evidence is poor and their absence from such texts may therefore be accidental, but 56 were borrowed before AD 400, when there are plenty of documents. Some of these are technical terminology in fields poorly represented in papyri, such as medicine and Roman history, but others show no obvious reason for being confined to literature; in fact some have exactly the type of meanings that should have caused them to appear in documents. For example, βάκλον 'stick', βράκαι 'trousers', κασσίς 'helmet' (if κάση is an independent borrowing), λάρδος 'salted meat', λωρίον 'thong', λῶρος 'thong', λωροτόμος 1 'strap-cutter', μαρούλιον 'lettuce', ὄγκινος 'hook', ῥαίδιον 'carriage', σαβούρα 'ballast', σκαμνίον 'seat', ταβλίζω 'play dice', and φραγελλόω 'whip' all entered Greek in the fourth century or earlier, are attested in literature in contexts suggesting that they were widely known, and survive at least into the Byzantine period. But they never appear in papyri or ostraca – why not? Perhaps because they were not part of the Greek used in Egypt. Whether they were used everywhere except Egypt or only in particular non-Egyptian regions cannot generally be recovered from our evidence, but *a priori* one might expect some to have had each of these distribution patterns. The survival into the Byzantine period indicates, however, that the areas in which they were used included ones in which Greek continued to be spoken after the end of antiquity.

These regionalisms, like the Latin regionalisms that contributed to the development of the Romance languages, seem to have remained geographically restricted throughout antiquity. It is probable that many more loanwords were temporary regionalisms, geographically restricted for a time before eventually becoming more widely known. After all, many loanwords must originally have been borrowed in a single place and spread outwards from there, and we have seen that that pattern is the best explanation for the tendency of loanwords to originate either in documents or in literature and then to turn up in other text types a century or more after borrowing (§9.1). With some common words we can actually see this process in action: for several centuries after their first appearance in literature they do not occur in documents at all, but then they are frequent, indicating that they have become part of Egyptian Greek. The names of the Roman months are examples of this pattern. These were borrowed in the second and first centuries BC (§8.1.4) but do not appear in documents from Egypt until the second century AD – and then all twelve month names appear at once, making it unlikely that their earlier absence is due simply to accidents of preservation. Other words that seem to have spent several centuries being specifically non-Egyptian vocabulary and then became very much part of Egyptian Greek include κοχλιάριον 'spoon' (five centuries between borrowing and appearance in papyri), πραιδεύω 'plunder' (four centuries), ἀκκούβιτον 'couch' and μόδιος 'peck' (three centuries), and a larger group with a two-century delay, including κῆνσος 'assessment for taxes', πουλβῖνον 'cushion', πραίφεκτος 'prefect', σκουτάριος 'shield-bearer', and τρακτευτής (an official). In some of these cases the thing denoted by the word probably existed in Egypt before the introduction of the word, and in others (such as the Roman months) the thing and the word presumably arrived together.

9.3 THE ACTS OF THE APOSTLES AND REGIONAL VARIATION

The language of the New Testament is distinctive. Some of its differences from other Greek literature have to do with the influence of the Septuagint and other Hebrew and Aramaic source material, but most are usually explained with reference to the moderate educational attainment of its writers, which resulted in their using a type of Greek closer to conversational language than is found in most other literary texts.[20] In this context similarities between the language of the papyri and that of the New Testament are of crucial importance: since the papyri come from Egypt rather than Judaea, and most were not written by Jews or Christians, they demonstrate that many of the distinctive characteristics of New Testament Greek

do not come from the place where it was composed or the people who composed it, but rather from the feature that the New Testament and the papyri have in common, namely writers and audiences with limited education.

Latin loanwords, which are more common in the New Testament than in most Greek literature of its date, fit nicely into this general picture, since the loanwords found in the New Testament normally appear in papyri as well.[21] There are no loanwords that occur in the papyri and the New Testament but not in other Greek literature, presumably because loanwords confined to papyri tend to be either local words, which we would not expect to find in a text composed outside Egypt, or words for things not normally mentioned in literature, which we would not expect to find in any literary text, even the New Testament (§9.2).

The New Testament was written by a diverse group of people, however, and they did not all have the same educational level. The author of the Gospel of Luke seems to have used a more literary Greek than the others; for example, he makes use of the optative mood, which had largely died out in the conversational Greek of the first century AD.[22] The fact that the Gospel of Luke contains fewer Latin loanwords than the other Gospels, and has words of Greek etymology in some passages where the parallel Gospels have

---

[20] See e.g. Blass *et al.* (1979 §3); Moulton and Milligan (1914–29: *passim*); Piñero and Peláez (2003: 121–204), Janse (2007), George (2010).

[21] Loanwords occurring in the New Testament that also turn up both in papyri and in other literary texts are ἀσσάριον, Αὔγουστος, δηνάριον, Καῖσαρ, κεντουρίων, κῆνσος, κολωνία, κουστωδία, λεγεών, λέντιον, μεμβράνα, μίλιον, μόδιος, ξέστης, πραιτώριον, Ῥωμαῖος, Ῥώμη, σουδάριον, σπεκουλάτωρ, τίτλος, φραγέλλιον, Χριστιανός; ones that do not appear in papyri but are attested in literature and/or inscriptions are κοδράντης, οὐά, ῥαῖδα, Ῥωμαϊστί, and φραγελλόω. Marucci (1993: 4–6) gives a slightly different list omitting Αὔγουστος, οὐά, Ῥωμαῖος, Ῥωμαϊστί, Ῥώμη, and Χριστιανός but including λίτρα. See also Hahn (1906: 257–68).

[22] Luke is also notable for displaying more Semitic influence than the other Gospels. Various efforts have been made to reconcile this fact with the higher stylistic register, including that the writer (working before the peak of the Atticist movement in the second century) regarded the Semitic-influenced language of the Septuagint as exemplifying a literary register equal in value to the language of Classical Athens: see L. C. A. Alexander (2005: 231–52), S. Adams (2013); cf. Wifstrand (2005: chapters 1 and 2), Watt (1997).

Latin loanwords, is seen as part of its higher-register style.[23]

It is generally agreed that Acts of the Apostles was written by the same author as the Gospel of Luke, and in most respects this identification can be supported by stylistic analysis, including that the author of Acts also uses the optative and other high-register features.[24] But the use of Latin differs strikingly between the two books, for Acts contains many more Latin words than Luke.[25] And while the few loanwords to appear in Luke are all well attested elsewhere in Greek literature, as well as in papyri, the Latin words of Acts are often rare, found neither in papyri nor in most other literary texts (apart from ones explaining or commenting on Acts). Six words in particular are striking for their total absence from papyri: λιβερτῖνος 'freedman' (Acts 6:9), σημικίνθιον 'belt' (Acts 19:12), σικάριος 'bandit' (Acts 21:38), χῶρος 'north-west wind' (Acts 27:12), εὐρακύλων 'north-east wind' (Acts 27:14), and ταβέρνα 'shop' (Acts

28:15). The contexts in which these occur in Acts are given below as passages 43–7.

43 Ἀνέστησαν δέ τινες τῶν ἐκ τῆς συναγωγῆς τῆς λεγομένης Λιβερτίνων … (Acts 6:9)

And some arose out of the people from the synagogue called 'Freedmen's' … (Narrator's words, about events in Jerusalem. The freedmen in question may have been (descendants of) Jews once enslaved by Romans; see e.g. Bruce (1990: 187).)

44 Δυνάμεις τε οὐ τὰς τυχούσας ὁ θεὸς ἐποίει διὰ τῶν χειρῶν Παύλου, ὥστε καὶ ἐπὶ τοὺς ἀσθενοῦντας ἀποφέρεσθαι ἀπὸ τοῦ χρωτὸς αὐτοῦ σουδάρια ἢ σιμικίνθια καὶ ἀπαλλάσσεσθαι ἀπ' αὐτῶν τὰς νόσους, τά τε πνεύματα τὰ πονηρὰ ἐκπορεύεσθαι. (Acts 19:11–12)

God performed extraordinary miracles through the hands of Paul, so that even when the neck-cloths or belts that had touched his flesh were brought to the sick, their diseases left them and the evil spirits departed. (Narrator's words, about Paul's time in Ephesus; σουδάριον is a Latin loanword. In this passage σουδάρια and σιμικίνθια are usually translated 'handkerchiefs' and 'aprons', but see Strelan 2003.)

45 Οὐκ ἄρα σὺ εἶ ὁ Αἰγύπτιος ὁ πρὸ τούτων τῶν ἡμερῶν ἀναστατώσας καὶ ἐξαγαγὼν εἰς τὴν ἔρημον τοὺς τετρακισχιλίους ἄνδρας τῶν σικαρίων; (Acts 21:38)

So you are not the Egyptian who previously caused a rebellion and led four thousand of the bandits into the desert? (Spoken to Paul by a Roman tribune in Jerusalem)

46 Ἀνευθέτου δὲ τοῦ λιμένος ὑπάρχοντος πρὸς παραχειμασίαν οἱ πλείονες ἔθεντο βουλὴν ἀναχθῆναι ἐκεῖθεν, εἴ πως δύναιντο καταντήσαντες εἰς Φοίνικα παραχειμάσαι λιμένα τῆς Κρήτης βλέποντα κατὰ λίβα καὶ κατὰ χῶρον. Ὑποπνεύσαντος δὲ νότου δόξαντες τῆς προθέσεως κεκρατηκέναι, ἄραντες ἆσσον παρελέγοντο τὴν Κρήτην. μετ' οὐ πολὺ δὲ ἔβαλεν κατ' αὐτῆς ἄνεμος τυφωνικὸς ὁ καλούμενος Εὐρακύλων· συναρπασθέντος δὲ τοῦ πλοίου καὶ μὴ δυναμένου ἀντοφθαλμεῖν τῷ ἀνέμῳ ἐπιδόντες ἐφερόμεθα. (Acts 27:12–15)

Since the harbour was unsuitable for overwintering, most of them formed a plan to put to sea from there, in hopes of reaching and overwintering in Phoenix, a harbour on Crete facing

---

[23] Cf. Blass et al. (1979 §5.1), Orioles (1974: 118), Browning (1983: 40). The Latin words occurring in Luke are ἀσσάριον, Αὔγουστος, δηνάριον (3 times), Καῖσαρ (7 times), λεγεών, μόδιος, and σουδάριον; thus Luke uses Latin words (other than personal names) a total of 15 times. The TLG gives Luke a word count of 19,451 and a lemma count of 2,360, meaning that in terms of tokens there is approximately one Latin word for every 1,300 words of text, and in terms of types approximately one of every 350 words used is from Latin.

[24] See e.g. Bruce (1990: 66–9); for Semitic influence in Acts parallel to that in Luke, see Wilcox (1965). The theory that the two books were written by the same person has occasionally been challenged, and stylistic evidence can be used in that direction too; note in particular Walters (2009). But scholars who see stylistic differences may also choose to argue that an interval of time elapsed between the composition of the two books, during which time the writer's style underwent some changes (see Walters 2009: 15–16).

[25] The Latin words appearing in Acts are εὐρακύλων, Καῖσαρ (9 times), κολωνία, λιβερτῖνος, πραιτώριον, Ῥωμαῖος (11 times), Ῥώμη (5 times), σημικίνθιον, σικάριος, σουδάριον, ταβέρνα, φόρον, Χριστιανός (twice), χῶρος; thus Acts uses Latin words (other than personal names) a total of 37 times. The TLG gives Acts a word count of 18,428 and a lemma count of 2,378, meaning that in terms of tokens there is approximately one Latin word for every 500 words of text, and in terms of types approximately one of every 170 words used is from Latin. For the equivalent statistics for Luke see n. 23. Leclercq (1997: 302–3) notes that Acts also includes more Latin names than other books.

the southwest and <u>northwest wind</u>s. And think-ing, when the south wind blew gently, that they could accomplish this goal, they weighed anchor and sailed along Crete, near the coast. But not long afterwards the tempestuous wind called <u>Εὐρακύλων</u> rushed down from Crete, and since the ship was caught up in the wind and unable to withstand it, we yielded and were carried on by it. (Narrator's words, about Paul's voyage to Rome)

47 Κἀκεῖθεν οἱ ἀδελφοὶ ἀκούσαντες τὰ περὶ ἡμῶν ἦλθαν εἰς ἀπάντησιν ἡμῖν ἄχρι Ἀππίου Φόρου καὶ Τριῶν <u>Ταβερνῶν</u>, οὓς ἰδὼν ὁ Παῦλος εὐχαριστήσας τῷ θεῷ ἔλαβε θάρσος. (Acts 28:15)

And the brothers from there heard about us and came to meet us, as far as the Forum of Appi-us and Three <u>Shops</u>, and when Paul saw them he thanked God and took courage. (Narrator's words, about Paul's arrival in Rome; *Tres Tabernae* was a village on the Appian Way, 33 miles from Rome)

The writer of Acts generally does not mark these rare words as unfamiliar; he appears to think that readers would know them, though the commentaries produced by later Greek writ-ers indicate that that confidence was misplaced. Why? Perhaps we have here further evidence for regional variation, for such a situation is charac-teristic of regionalisms: they are part of normal language for some individuals but not for others, and the people who use the regionalisms may not be aware that other speakers do not use them. And indeed ταβέρνα, λιβερτῖνος, and σικάριος have meanings that would almost inevitably have made them local words of restricted distri-bution. Ταβέρνα must have been a regionalism in the Greek of Rome and its surrounding area: as the Greek version of a Latin place name in a region with many Greek speakers it must have been widely used by Roman Greek speakers.[26] Λιβερτῖνοι, as the name of a particular group of people in Jerusalem, must have been a word local to Judaea; although it is surprising that this group had a Latin name,[27] there can be no meaningful

doubt that it did. Σικάριος was likewise the name of a particular group, rather than a general term for bandits, as Josephus makes clear in passage 48; again it is surprising that such a word should have come from Latin, but evidently it did.[28]

48 Ἀφικομένου δὲ εἰς τὴν Ἰουδαίαν Φήστου συνέβαινεν τὴν Ἰουδαίαν ὑπὸ τῶν λῃστῶν κακοῦσθαι τῶν κωμῶν ἁπασῶν ἐμπιπραμένων τε καὶ διαρπαζομένων. καὶ οἱ <u>σικάριοι</u> δὲ καλούμενοι, λῃσταὶ δέ εἰσιν οὗτοι, τότε μάλιστα ἐπλήθυον χρώμενοι ξιφιδίοις παραπλησίοις μὲν τὸ μέγεθος τοῖς τῶν Περσῶν ἀκινάκαις, ἐπικαμπέσι δὲ καὶ ὁμοίαις ταῖς ὑπὸ Ῥωμαίων σίκαις καλουμέναις, ἀφ' ὧν καὶ τὴν προσηγορίαν οἱ λῃστεύοντες ἔλαβον πολλοὺς ἀναιροῦντες. (Josephus, *Antiquitates Juda-icae* 20.185–6)

And when Festus arrived in Judaea it happened that Judaea was being afflicted by bandits, with all the villages being burned and pillaged. And the men called <u>σικάριοι</u> – these are bandits – were then especially numerous; they used little swords that in size are like Persian swords, but curved and like the weapons called σίκαι by the Romans, from which the bandits took their name, since they killed many people with these weapons.

If λιβερτῖνος and σικάριος were local to Judaea, and ταβέρνα (at least as a place name) was local to the area around Rome, what region might the other words have been characteristic of? Perhaps Rome, for there is evidence that Acts was com-posed by someone who had lived in Rome for sev-eral years. The exact circumstances of the book's composition are unknown, but many scholars take the writer's 'we' (e.g. in passages 46 and 47) at face value, as an indication that he travelled to Rome with Paul.[29] If he did so, he probably

---

[26] Kajanto (1980) offers a good overview of the evidence for native Greek speakers in Rome during the Empire.

[27] It is generally thought that Latin was little used in Roman Judaea; see e.g. Fitzmyer (1970), Rosén (1980: 219–20), Janse (2007: 646). But recent work is challenging this view on the basis of the large number of Latin inscriptions

from the province and the Latin loanwords that entered Semitic languages (usually via Greek); see Isaac (2009), Eck (2000, 2003: 126, 2009: 34–40), Millar (2006b: 164–242 with n. 6 p. 166), Geiger (1996). Bauckham (2002) finds a surprising number of Jews with Roman names in the New Testament.

[28] The source of the name is usually identified (no doubt correctly) as the local Roman administration, but it was also used by the non-Roman inhabitants of Judaea (both in Greek and in Aramaic), in preference to any native term; see e.g. Kittel *et al.* (1932–79: *s.v.*).

[29] See e.g. Bruce (1993: 7–8), Fitzmyer (1998: 49–55), Hemer (1989: 308–64). The difficulty with taking it at face value and extrapolating from it the argument I make

remained there for a considerable period of time, for Acts 28:30 states that Paul taught in Rome for two years. There is then no further information, so the writer could have remained longer in Rome.[30] But even if he left after two years, those years would have provided ample time for his Greek to acquire some features of Roman Greek; these features might have included not only the specific loanwords ταβέρνα, σημικίνθιον, χῶρος, and εὐρακύλων, but also a general tendency to accept Latinisms in Greek. Such a tendency would explain why the writer did not make an effort to suppress the regional loanwords λιβερτῖνος and σικάριος as he had earlier suppressed Latin words when composing the Gospel of Luke. It would also explain why the Greek of Acts has other types of Latin influence as well as loanwords – and has them to a notably greater extent than the Greek of Luke.[31]

Of course, we have not seen conclusive proof that the Greek spoken in Rome did contain local loanwords. But Athenaeus' discussion of δηκόκτα points in that direction (§1), and so does some evidence from Galen (§9.5.3). It is therefore

likely that the influence of that variety of Greek was responsible for the peculiar Latin words in Acts.

9.4 ATTICIZING WRITERS

Famously, many Greek authors of the imperial period – particularly but not exclusively the second century AD – were Atticists. One of the key features of Atticism was avoidance of post-Classical words, and few words were more obviously post-Classical than Latin loanwords. Atticism severely reduced loanword usage in literature, particularly in the works of Atticizing authors.[32] Nevertheless the Atticists also provide key evidence of the penetration of Latin loanwords into the Greek of their day, in two different ways: via the loanwords they accepted and the ones they rejected.

Despite the strictures of Atticism some Latin words were usually considered acceptable: proper names and words for 'Rome' and 'Roman'. The second-century Atticist Lucian, for example, not only used these freely himself (e.g. the underlined words in passage 49) but condemned as ridiculous another author's attempt to avoid them (passage 50). Of course the fact that the other author did try to avoid Roman proper names shows that Lucian's stance was not universal, but equally the fact that Lucian felt free to ridicule that avoidance suggests that he felt able to count on good support for his own position.

49 Ὡς δὲ καὶ εἰς τὴν Ἰταλίαν διεφοίτησεν τοῦ μαντείου τὸ κλέος καὶ εἰς τὴν Ῥωμαίων πόλιν ἐνέπεσεν, οὐδεὶς ὅστις οὐκ ἄλλος πρὸ ἄλλου ἠπείγετο, οἱ μὲν αὐτοὶ ἰόντες, οἱ δὲ πέμποντες, καὶ μάλιστα οἱ δυνατώτατοι καὶ μέγιστον ἀξίωμα ἐν τῇ πόλει ἔχοντες· ὧν πρῶτος καὶ κορυφαιότατος ἐγένετο Ῥουτιλιανός, ἀνὴρ τὰ μὲν ἄλλα καλὸς καὶ ἀγαθὸς καὶ ἐν πολλαῖς τάξεσι Ῥωμαϊκαῖς ἐξητασμένος, τὰ δὲ περὶ τοὺς θεοὺς πάνυ νοσῶν καὶ ἀλλόκοτα περὶ αὐτῶν πεπιστευκώς (Alex. 30)

But when the fame of the oracle came to Italy and burst upon the city of the Romans, there was no one who did not hasten to it, one after the other, some going themselves, some sending messengers – and especially the most powerful and those who had the highest standing in the city. The first

---

here is that if the authors of Luke and Acts are indeed the same person, he would have to have composed Luke before spending a significant amount of time in Rome – but the composition of Luke is normally thought to have taken place several decades after Paul's voyage. If that difficulty is considered insuperable, one could take the traditional alternative interpretation, namely that the passages with 'we' were written not by the author of Acts himself but by a companion of Paul whose work was later incorporated and adapted by the author of Acts. In that version of events the person who originally composed those passages must have ended up in Rome; perhaps the way the author of Acts acquired them was by travelling to Rome himself and encountering their composer.

[30] There is no consensus about the place where Acts was written and/or published; Rome has been suggested (e.g. Bruce 1993: 8), but most scholars remain doubtful that any place can be identified.

[31] Marucci (1993: 6–7) lists twenty-four New Testament usages generally agreed to be Latinate; he finds eleven of these in Acts (in comparison to five in Luke), including ten occurring only in Acts. Marucci (1993: 8–14) also lists usages suggested as partly or possibly Latinate, a few of which I would not accept as being from Latin; he mentions twelve of these as occurring in Acts and seven as occurring in Luke, though the real number is no doubt higher since for common usages Marucci does not give complete lists of references. For non-loanword Latinisms in Acts see also Bruce (1990: 68).

[32] Cf. e.g. Mason (1970).

and foremost of these was <u>Rutilianus</u>, a man who was noble in other respects and had proved his worth in many <u>Roman</u> offices, but who was unhealthy in matters concerning the gods and had formed unusual beliefs about them.

50 Ὑπὸ γὰρ τοῦ κομιδῇ Ἀττικὸς εἶναι καὶ ἀποκεκαθάρθαι τὴν φωνὴν ἐς τὸ ἀκριβέστατον ἠξίωσεν οὗτος καὶ τὰ ὀνόματα μεταποιῆσαι τὰ Ῥωμαίων καὶ μεταγράψαι ἐς τὸ Ἑλληνικόν, ὡς Κρόνιον μὲν Σατουρνῖνον λέγειν, Φρόντιν δὲ τὸν Φρόντωνα, Τιτάνιον δὲ τὸν Τιτανὸν καὶ ἄλλα πολλῷ γελοιότερα. (*Hist.Conscr.* 21)

This writer, on the grounds of being entirely Attic and having purified his language in every detail, thought it right to change even the names of the Romans and to translate them into Greek, for example calling Saturninus Kronios, Fronto Frontis, Titanus Titanios, and others much more ridiculous.

More often, Atticistic scholars mentioned loanwords in order to condemn them or to use them as glosses for the more obscure vocabulary they preferred. Passages 51 and 52 are examples, with the loanwords underlined; note also §8.1.1 passages 36–9.

51 <u>Κοχλιάριον</u>· τοῦτο λίστρον Ἀριστοφάνης ὁ κωμῳδοποιὸς λέγει· καὶ σὺ δὲ οὕτως λέγε. (Phrynichus, *Eclogae* 292)

<u>Κοχλιάριον</u>: Aristophanes the comic poet calls this λίστρον; and you should too!

52 Σωδάριον Ἕρμιππος τὸ ὑφ᾽ ἡμῶν <u>σουδάριον</u>. (Moeris σ 20)

Hermippus used σωδάριον for the thing we call <u>σουδάριον</u>.

Passage 53, from Lucian's condemnation of a lost second-century historical work, offers interesting indirect evidence for the use of loanwords: although the Latin words are not directly named φόσσα can be identified with confidence and πόνς tentatively.[33]

53 Νὴ Δία κἀκεῖνο ὀλίγου δεῖν παρέλιπον· ὁ γὰρ αὐτὸς οὗτος συγγραφεὺς πολλὰ καὶ τῶν ὅπλων καὶ τῶν μηχανημάτων ὡς Ῥωμαῖοι αὐτὰ ὀνομάζουσιν

οὕτως ἀνέγραψεν, καὶ τάφρον ὡς ἐκεῖνοι καὶ γέφυραν καὶ τὰ τοιαῦτα. (*Hist.Conscr.* 15)

By Zeus, I almost left this out: that same writer recorded many of the weapons and engines the way the Romans call them, and he called 'ditch' and 'bridge' and such things the way they do.

The oblique references here would have been much more effective if Lucian's readers recognized the loanwords alluded to than if they did not: did Lucian expect his audience to recognize them? Quite possibly he did, for in passage 54 the reader is apparently expected to know both that Romans greeted each other with *salve* and that *salve* had a connection to *salus* 'health'; as neither of these words was borrowed into Greek readers needed to know some actual Latin to appreciate the allusion fully. It is typical of Atticism that in both passages 53 and 54 the Latin words are evoked without actually using any words that did not have fully Greek etymologies.

54 Ἀλλὰ καὶ ὑμεῖς αὐτοί, εἴ τι κἀγὼ τῆς Ῥωμαίων φωνῆς ἐπαΐω, τοὺς προσαγορεύοντας ἀντιδεξιούμενοι τῷ τῆς ὑγιείας ὀνόματι πολλάκις ἀμείβεσθε. (Lucian, *Pro lapsu* 13)

But also you yourselves, at least if I understand anything of the language of the Romans, often exchange the word for 'health' when you shake hands with those who have greeted you.

Not all second-century Greek authors were Atticists, but even those who were not sometimes expressed discomfort at the need to use loanwords, justifying their use on the grounds that loanwords had become the standard ways of expressing many concepts. The underlined words in passages 55 and 56 are loanwords.

55 <u>Σίλιγνις</u> δ᾽ οὐχ Ἑλληνικὸν μέν, ἑτέρως δ᾽ αὐτὴν ὀνομάζειν οὐκ ἔχω (Galen VI.483.16 Kühn)

<u>Σίλιγνις</u> is not Greek, but I do not have another way of naming it.

56 Παρὸ καὶ διχῶς τοῦ αὐτοῦ πράγματος λεγομένου πειρασόμεθα πρὸς τὰ παρόντα ἁρμοζόμενοι πρόσωπα τὸ μὴ γελώμενον προφέρεσθαι, ὁποῖόν ποτ᾽ ἂν ᾖ κατὰ τὴν φύσιν. οἷον τὸ αὐτὸ ἀρτοφόριον καὶ <u>πανάριον</u> λέγεται, καὶ πάλιν τὸ αὐτὸ σταμνίον καὶ ἀμίδιον καὶ ἴγδις καὶ θυΐα. ἀλλὰ στοχαζόμενοι τοῦ καλῶς ἔχοντος καὶ

---

[33] Hahn (1907: 708 n. 114); on the interpretation of this passage see Vaahtera (2001: 52–3).

σαφῶς καὶ τοῦ μὴ γελᾶσθαι ὑπὸ τῶν διακονούντων ἡμῖν παιδαρίων [καὶ ἰδιωτῶν] <u>πανάριον</u> ἐροῦμεν, καὶ εἰ βάρβαρόν ἐστιν, ἀλλ' οὐκ ἀρτοφορίδα, καὶ σταμνίον, ἀλλ' οὐκ ἀμίδα, καὶ θυΐαν μᾶλλον ἢ ἴγδιν. (Sextus Empiricus, *Adversus mathematicos* 1.234)

Therefore even when the same thing can be said in two different ways, we shall try to fit the persons we are with and say the thing that is not laughed at, whatever it may be in nature. For example, the same object is called ἀρτοφόριον (bread-basket) and <u>πανάριον</u>, and again σταμνίον (chamber pot) and ἀμίδιον are the same, and ἴγδις (mortar) and θυΐα. But aiming at that which is good and clear and at not being laughed at by our servants and by the uneducated, we shall say <u>πανάριον</u>, even if it is foreign, and not ἀρτοφορίς; and σταμνίον rather than ἀμίς, and θυΐα rather than ἴγδις.

Athenaeus' *Deipnosophistae* is particularly revealing in its handling of the tension between Atticism and Latin. The dialogue is set in Rome, hosted by a Roman well versed in both Greek and Latin languages and literatures (1.2c), and includes many Roman characters. One of these, Ulpian of Tyre (whose name is conspicuously Latin), is a fanatical Atticist whose preference for archaic, obscure terms is repeatedly ridiculed by the other characters; Atticism seems to be a running joke in the *Deipnosophistae*. Passage 1 in §1 illustrates Ulpian's indignant response to a fellow diner's use of the Latin word δηκόκτα 'decoction'. The speaker defends himself robustly, arguing not only that the use of foreign loanwords has good Classical precedent but also that the topic itself is Classical, for decoctions were known in the Classical period. Such an argument is of course difficult to make without using the offending word again, and despite his defence of loanwords the speaker appears anxious not to provoke Ulpian further by repeating δηκόκτα. He resorts to a somewhat ambiguous periphrasis clarified by a marked and (ironically) apologetic use of the Latinate word:

57 Ὅτι δὲ καὶ οἱ ἀρχαῖοι οἴδασι τὸ οὕτω λεγόμενον ὕδωρ, ἵνα μὴ πάλιν ἀγανακτήσῃς <u>δηκόκταν</u> μου λέγοντος, δείξω. (3.122e)

And I shall show that the ancients also knew the water that is thus called – I put it this way so that you will not be angry with me for saying <u>δηκόκτα</u> again.

Ulpian makes no objection to this marked usage, and that is part of a pattern: Latin words in the *Deipnosophistae* are often explicitly identified as foreign, and when that occurs no objection is raised to them. Passages 58 and 59 are examples.

58 Ἰσίκια γὰρ ὀνομάζειν αἰδοῦμαι τὸν Οὐλπιανόν, καίπερ αὐτὸν εἰδὼς ἡδέως αὐτοῖς χρώμενον. πλὴν ὁ ἐμός γε συγγραφεὺς Πάξαμος τῶν <u>ἰσικίων</u> μέμνηται, καὶ οὔ μοι φροντὶς Ἀττικῶν χρήσεων. (9.376d)

For I'm ashamed to mention <u>ἰσίκια</u> in front of Ulpian, although I know that he likes to eat them – but my fellow-writer Paxamos mentions <u>ἰσίκια</u>, and I do not care about Attic usages.

59 Τοιοῦτοί τινές εἰσιν, ὦ ἑταῖροι, οἱ Οὐλπιάνειοι σοφισταί, οἱ καὶ τὸ <u>μιλιάριον</u> καλούμενον ὑπὸ Ῥωμαίων, τὸ εἰς θερμοῦ ὕδατος κατεργασίαν κατασκευαζόμενον, <u>ἰπνολέβητα</u> ὀνομάζοντες, πολλῶν ὀνομάτων ποιηταί … (3.98c)

Friends, this is what sophists like Ulpian are like, men who even use the name <u>ἰπνολέβης</u> for the device for preparing hot water that the Romans call <u>μιλιάριον</u>, for they are inventers of all sorts of words …

In passage 60 the same kind of marked usage occurs in the narrator's own voice: the narrator identifies a cake using a Latin word, and then one of the characters uses an obscure term of Greek etymology to discuss the cake with Ulpian. This demonstrates something that might in any case have been suspected from the other examples: the characters' strategies for handling Ulpian's Atticist objections are really the author's strategies for handling his readers' Atticist objections. Evidently Latin words were acceptable as long as they were labelled as foreign, for the Atticists did not object to broad learning or even to multilingualism, but to the inclusion of foreign elements in Greek as if they were Greek words.

60 Ἑξῆς ἐπεισηνέχθη πλακοῦς ἐκ γάλακτος ἰτρίων τε καὶ μέλιτος, ὃν Ῥωμαῖοι <u>λίβον</u> καλοῦσι. καὶ ὁ Κύνουλκος ἔφη· ἐμπίπλασο, Οὐλπιανέ, <u>χθωροδλάψου</u> … (3.126a)

Next was brought in a flat cake made of milk, <u>ἴτριον</u>-cakes, and honey, which the Romans call <u>λίβος</u>. And Cynulcus said, 'Stuff yourself, Ulpian, with <u>χθωρόδλαψον</u> …'

There are a few passages in which Athenaeus' characters use large quantities of conspicuously Latin words without marking them individually as Latin. But in such passages the discussion as a whole is marked as a quotation or paraphrase of a literary work, a marking that appears to have the same distancing effect as labelling individual terms as foreign: no objections are raised by Ulpian. Passage 61, for example, is part of an extended quotation from what is said to be Chrysippus of Tyana's work on bread-making. Nothing is known about Chrysippus of Tyana beyond what Athenaeus tells us, on which basis it is sometimes argued that he must have written a lost work on bread-making around the middle of the first century AD.[34] Sometimes, however, it is suggested that Chrysippus might simply be Athenaeus' invention (Ceccarelli 2000: 286–7). If the work quoted by Athenaeus really existed in the middle of the first century, it had an extraordinary number and density of Latin words for its time. In Athenaeus' own day Latin words were far more widespread in Greek and such a display of Latin erudition would make more sense – though even for this time the density of Latin (underlined words in passage 61) is unusual. Is it possible that Athenaeus invented Chrysippus of Tyana specifically in order to squeeze in a ridiculous number of Latin words without having to apologize for them individually?

61   Χρύσιππος δ' ὁ Τυανεὺς ἐν τῷ ἐπιγραφομένῳ Ἀρτοκοπικῷ εἴδη πλακούντων καὶ γένη τάδε ἀναγράφει· <u>Τερεντῖνον</u>, <u>Κρασσιανόν</u>, <u>Τουτιανόν</u>, <u>Σαβελλικὸν</u> <u>κλοῦστρον</u>, Ἰουλιανόν, Ἀπικιανόν, Κανωπικά, <u>περλούκιδον</u>, Καππαδοκικόν, ἡδύβια, μαρυπτόν, πλίκιον, <u>γουττᾶτον</u>, <u>Μοντιανόν</u>· τοῦτον, φησί, μάξεις ἐξ οἴνου σκληρόν· εἰ δέ σοι τυρίον παρέσται, ἥμισυ μάξεις ἐξ οἴνου καὶ ἥμισυ ἐκ τυροῦ· ἡδονικώτερον γὰρ γίνεται. <u>κλοῦστρον</u> Κυριανόν, <u>κλοῦστρον</u> <u>γουττᾶτον</u>, <u>κλοῦστρον</u> <u>Φαβωνιανόν</u>. <u>μουστάκια</u> ἐξ οἰνομέλιτος, <u>μουστάκια</u> <u>σησαμᾶτα</u>, <u>κλοῦστρον</u> πούριον, γωσλωάνιον, <u>Παυλινιανόν</u>. ἐκ τυροῦ δέ, φησί, γίνεται πλακουντηρὰ τάδε· ἔγχυτος, <u>σκριβλίτης</u>, <u>σουβίτυλλος</u>. (14.647c–d)

[34] Wellmann (1899); cf. the entry 'Chrysippus Tyanensis, Rei Coquinariae Scriptor' in LSJ's list of authors (p. xxi). Luce (2018: 733) reports suggested dates ranging from the second century BC to the first century AD.

Chrysippus of Tyana, in his work entitled Ἀρτοκοπικός, records the following forms and types of cakes: <u>Τερεντῖνον</u>, <u>Κρασσιανόν</u>, <u>Τουτιανόν</u>, <u>Σαβελλικὸν</u> <u>κλοῦστρον</u>, Ἰουλιανόν, Ἀπικιανόν, Κανωπικά, <u>περλούκιδον</u>, Καππαδοκικόν, ἡδύβια, μαρυπτόν, πλίκιον, <u>γουττᾶτον</u>, <u>Μοντιανόν</u>. He says that you knead this last one hard, with wine; and if you have a little cheese, you knead half with wine and half with cheese; for it is tastier like that. Also <u>κλοῦστρον</u> Κυριανόν, <u>κλοῦστρον</u> <u>γουττᾶτον</u>, and <u>κλοῦστρον</u> <u>Φαβωνιανόν</u>. Also <u>μουστάκια</u> with mead, <u>μουστάκια</u> <u>σησαμᾶτα</u>, <u>κλοῦστρον</u> πούριον, γωσλωάνιον, and <u>Παυλινιανόν</u>. And he says that the following cake-like substances are made with cheese: ἔγχυτος, <u>σκριβλίτης</u>, and <u>σουβίτυλλος</u>.

In passage 61 not one of the etymologically Latin words is likely to have been an established loanword in the Greek of Athenaeus' day; in fact most are rarely or never attested elsewhere in Greek, and many are unusual even in Latin. They are not explained, but one does not need to know what they mean in order to follow the passage; probably the cake names were intended as an impressive list of obscurities. In passages such as 58 and 59, however, Athenaeus evidently expected his readers to understand the Latin words he used; the apologies for the use of Latin are on grounds of style, not on grounds of obscurity. In fact those Latin words are likely to have been more comprehensible than their Greek equivalents, both for Athenaeus' characters and for his intended audience. Even outside Rome loanwords had become widespread, and Athenaeus was depicting a conversation in Rome among men who, though Greek speaking, were for the most part Romans by birth or by choice.

9.5 WRITERS USING LARGE NUMBERS OF LOANWORDS

Although the Atticist writers provide much useful information, they are not our main sources of loanwords. The authors with that distinction, unsurprisingly, are ones who positively welcomed an appearance of Latinity in their works. Such authors pose their own problems for us, however, for they codeswitch extensively and do not always make it obvious which Latin words their intended readers would have known.

9.5.1 The Edict of Diocletian

One inscription is exceptional for the range and frequency of the Latin words it includes: the Edict of Diocletian. In AD 301 copies of this lengthy text were set up all over the empire, in Greek in the East and in Latin in the West; although none of these copies survives intact, between them they allow the reconstruction of most of the text, and some sections are preserved in more than one copy. The Edict was produced in an attempt to stem inflation by prescribing maximum prices and a stiff penalty for exceeding them; it therefore lists a huge number of goods and services with their maximum legal prices. This subject matter is unusual for epigraphy and therefore particularly important in revealing the words used in AD 301 for a wide range of everyday objects and activities. The Edict includes at least 80 Latin loanwords, for at least 42 of which it provides the only inscriptional attestation; it also contains at least 80 rarer terms derived from Latin. Many of the latter are not attested anywhere else, and indeed some may never have existed anywhere else, for the Edict's Greek shows Latin influence. Notably Latinate features include the unassimilated dative plural αὐρικαισωρίβους 'gold-beaters' (*auricaesoribus?*), the genitive ὀβιφέρι 'wild sheep' (*oviferi*), the use in one section of σεξτάριος (a transliteration of *sextarius* 'pint measure') rather than the long-established loanword ξέστης, translating *semodialis* 'holding half a peck' as σημοδιαῖος rather than attaching ἡμι- to the established loanword μόδιος 'peck', and giving a Latinate masculine gender to the well-established and otherwise neuter loanwords βάλτιον 'belt' and πουλβῖνον 'cushion'. But the linguistic influence sometimes also went in the other direction, for *Falernum* 'Falernian wine' is spelled *Falerinum* under the influence of Φαλερῖνος (2.7), and *rosatum* 'rose-flavoured wine' is written *rhosatum* under the influence of ῥοσᾶτον (2.19).

The high density of Latinate terms on the Edict is probably due to a combination of factors. Much of its subject matter happens to fall into semantic fields where loanwords were common (§10.2.2–3), but the specific Latin influence on its Greek also resulted in codeswitches.

9.5.2 Historians of Rome

Most of the previous work on Latinisms in Greek literature has focussed on the authors who discussed Roman history and culture: Polybius, Dionysius of Halicarnassus, Diodorus Siculus, Flavius Josephus, Plutarch, Appian, and Dio Cassius.[35] These authors often worked from Latin sources (whether written or oral) and needed to express concepts for which suitable Greek terms did not always exist; they therefore had good reasons to use Latin, and the passages in which they avoided doing so are at least as revealing as the ones in which they did use Latin. Such avoidance was often deliberate, as passage 62 illustrates, but the reasons for it probably varied over time: the earliest historians were probably concerned primarily to make sure their work was easily understandable by its intended audience (§8.1.3), while later ones faced Atticist strictures (§9.4).

62 Ἐβουλεύοντο μὲν καὶ ἥ γε γνώμη συνεγράφετο, οὐ μέντοι καὶ τέλος τι ὡς κεκυρωμένη ἐλάμβανεν, ἀλλὰ <u>αὐκτώριτας</u> ἐγίγνετο, ὅπως φανερὸν τὸ βούλημα αὐτῶν ᾖ. τοιοῦτον γάρ τι ἡ δύναμις τοῦ ὀνόματος τούτου δηλοῖ· ἑλληνίσαι γὰρ αὐτὸ καθάπαξ ἀδύνατόν ἐστι. (Dio Cassius 55.3.4)

[When the Roman senate was inquorate] the senators used to deliberate and their decision used to be written down, but it did not take effect as if it had been ratified [by a full senate meeting]; rather <u>auctoritas</u> was created [by their decision], so that their intention would be clear. For the force of this word indicates something like this – for it is impossible to put it into Greek once and for all [i.e. there is no single Greek word with the meaning of *auctoritas*].

---

[35] For Polybius see Dubuisson (1985: esp. 18–59) and Langslow (2012: 98–105); for Dionysius and Diodorus Hahn (1906: 123–8, 130–1); for Josephus Ward (2007) and Hahn (1906: 236–9); for Plutarch Strobach (1997), De Rosalia (1991), Rochette (2010: 291–2), Setaioli (2007), and Hahn (1906: 239–55); for Appian Famerie (1998: esp. 208–10 on loanwords) and Hering (1935); for Dio Cassius Coudry (2016) and Freyburger-Galland (1997, 1998, 1992, 1984). Note also Wilson (2006) on Aelian; Hahn (1906: 131–4, 235–6, 255–7) on Strabo, Epictetus, and *Periplus Maris Erythraei*; Freeman (1883: 381–5) on Procopius; Dubuisson (1979) and Mason (1974: 15–16) give general overviews.

A study of loanwords is not the place to make further contributions to the study of these authors, because in their case a comparison between loanwords and equivalent Greek expressions is crucial.[36] Loanword usage in such works is also best studied in conjunction with other types of Latin influence, as is usually done in work focussing on individual historians. But this is the place to emphasize that the role played by historians of Rome in loanword adoption was a very small one: the cultural borrowings that entered Greek via this route, such as δικτάτωρ 'dictator', are famous and therefore often the first ones that come to mind when thinking about Latin loanwords, but they made up only a small percentage of the Latin words adopted into Greek (§10.2.2).

9.5.3 Medical writers

The medical writers Dioscorides (I AD), Galen (II AD), Oribasius (IV AD), Alexander of Tralles (VI AD), and Aëtius (VI AD) all used significant amounts of Latin-derived terminology. The density of loanword use in their texts is not high; the large numbers of loanwords and even the fact that some of those words occur many times need to be seen in the context of large bodies of work. Nevertheless it is startling to find significant numbers of loanwords in medical texts, for medicine was an emphatically Greek field and had been since the days of Hippocrates, and the terminology of Latin medical writers was heavily influenced by Greek.[37]

The Latin terminology used by Greek medical writers almost never concerned medical problems; those were discussed using etymologically Greek words.[38] Instead, Latin appeared in the terminology for treatments: the names of plants (e.g. βεττονική 'betony', βικίον 'vetch', κίτρον 'citron'),

measurements (e.g. ἡμιούγκιον 'half-ounce', μόδιος 'peck', ξέστης 'pint'), and medically useful substances (e.g. ὀξύγγιον 'tallow', σάπων 'soap', φαίκλα 'burned wine crust'). Some of these terms were widely used outside medicine, but others look like specifically medical terminology, since they appear primarily or even exclusively in medical texts. Of course, plant names can look like medical terminology by accidents of survival, for many plants were only useful to doctors and therefore were rarely mentioned in non-medical literature. But at least some of these words must have actually been perceived by speakers as technical language, for occasionally we have explicit testimony that certain Latin-derived plant names were seen by later Greek speakers as medical terminology, with native Greek names for the same plants used in non-medical language:

63 Ἐβίσκος· κατὰ ἰατροὺς ἡ μαλάχη, ἡ καὶ ἀλθαία λεγομένη. (*Suda* ε 32)

Ἐβίσκος: doctors' word for mallow, the plant that is also called ἀλθαία.

How did this situation arise? Perhaps because of the influence of Galen's writings. Galen, probably the most important Greek medical writer after Hippocrates, lived in Rome in the second century AD; his works had enormous influence on later medical writers, so that his terminology continued to be employed in the field of medicine regardless of its currency in other types of Greek.[39] Might Galen have borrowed Latin words from his Latin-speaking surroundings and caused them to become medical terminology by incorporating them in his work? Probably not, for two reasons. There is no evidence that Galen actually knew Latin;[40] his presence in Rome does not prove that he spoke the language, since at that date the city was sufficiently bilingual that he would not have needed Latin to live or work there. Moreover Galen was committed to clarity: he wanted readers to understand exactly which ingredients and quantities he was referring to, since the consequences of misunderstanding could be lethal. Therefore he would probably not have introduced foreign words or other

---

[36] On this point see also Mason (1974).

[37] See e.g. Nutton (2012: 160–73), Langslow (2000), J. N. Adams (2003: 356–8), and for the striking absence of Latin in modern Greek medical terminology Ruisinger (2000). Mazzini's study of the language of ancient medicine includes a discussion of Grecisms in Latin medical terminology (Mazzini 1997: I.150–4), but no equivalent discussion of Latinisms in Greek medical terminology. Matters are similar in the closely related field of veterinary medicine (J. N. Adams 1995).

[38] The exception is πανίκουλα 'tumour'.

[39] See e.g. Nutton (2012: 299–317), Guardasole (2004).

[40] Mattern (2013: 139–40), Nutton (2009: 24).

neologisms when well-known alternatives were available.

Indeed, many of Galen's loanwords seem to have been employed precisely because they were already widely known and would therefore enhance clarity. For example, he uses the loan-word κοχλιάριον 'spoonful' nearly seventy times, and clear evidence for that word's currency in the Greek of Galen's day can be found in the works of his Atticist contemporaries:

64 Λίστριον· τὸ ὑπὸ τῶν πολλῶν καλούμενον κοχλιάριον. (Phrynichus, *Praeparatio sophistica* epitome p. 88.5 de Borries)

Λίστριον: the thing that is called κοχλιάριον by most people.

65 Τὸ δὲ κοχλιάριον καλοίης ἂν μυστιλάριον ἢ κοχλιώρυχον. (Pollux 6.87)

And you could call the κοχλιάριον a μυστιλάριον or a κοχλιώρυχον.

Similarly, in naming ingredients Galen often used several different synonyms, one of which was a Latin loanword. Sometimes the way he presents the loanword suggests that he considered it to be the most normal term:

66 ... μετὰ παλαιοῦ στέατος ὑείου. καλεῖται δ' ὑπὸ τῶν πολλῶν ἀξούγγιον τοῦτο. (Galen XII.346.6 Kühn)

... with aged pig's fat; and this is called ὀξύγγιον by most people.

Of course, such words were not specifically medical terminology; that is exactly why Galen used them. But perhaps the 'medical' loanwords were also not specifically medical in Galen's own variety of Greek. We have seen (§1, §9.3) evidence from Athenaeus and the Acts of the Apostles suggesting that some loanwords may have been local to the Greek spoken in the city of Rome. After many decades of hearing and probably speaking that variety of Greek, Galen would have had difficulty preventing himself from being influenced by it when writing – and if some of its vocabulary was unfamiliar to Greek speakers in other parts of the empire, he might not even have been aware of that fact. After all, in using loan-words for the sake of clarity Galen was specifically departing from the traditional literary register

(cf. passage 66 above) to employ words from the spoken language; that is why he was sometimes the first writer to employ loanwords that were evidently not technical medical terminology (e.g. σάπων 'soap', σάρδα 'sardine', φασίολος 'bean'). And in an age before broadcasts and recordings, currency in spoken language was inevitably something that a speaker could only judge from what he heard in his own surroundings. Therefore it is possible that Galen sometimes used a geographically restricted loanword because he considered it the normal Greek term for a particular object, and that owing to his influence that loanword became a technical medical term in later writers. That could be what happened with ἐβίσκος, which was first used as a Greek word by Galen (two earlier writers included it but marked it as Latin), was then so used by later medical writers, and as we have seen (passage 63) was considered to be medical terminology.

Some evidence in favour of this hypothesis is provided by κίτρον 'citron'. The usual Greek word for 'citron' in the imperial period was κίτριον, which Athenaeus' character Democritus uses repeatedly in a long discussion of the fruit (3.83a–85c); although concluding that the word is not Classical, he does not label it as Latin. At the close of that discussion the narrator adds a piece of additional information: the Latin for κίτριον is κίτρον (i.e. *citrum*).

67 Ταῦτ' εἰπόντος τοῦ Δημοκρίτου θαυμάσαντες οἱ πολλοὶ τὴν τοῦ κιτρίου δύναμιν ἀπήσθιον ὡς μὴ πρότερον φαγόντες ἢ πιόντες τι. Πάμφιλος δ' ἐν ταῖς Γλώσσαις Ῥωμαίους φησὶν αὐτὸ κίτρον καλεῖν. (3.85c)

When Democritus had said these things most of the diners, amazed at the power of the citron, ate it up as if they had not previously had anything to eat or drink. And Pamphilus in his 'Rare words' says that the Romans call it *citrum*.

This passage suggests that κίτρον was not a Greek word at all. But Galen had a different view: for him, κίτρον was the normal contemporary term for the citron.[41]

---

[41] Galen may also have used κίτριον, which appears in VI.617.12, VI.618.1, and XII.77.4 Kühn, but caution is needed because those passages have never received a modern critical edition.

68 Μηδικὸν μῆλον, ὃ κίτρον ὀνομάζομεν (Galen, *De victu attenuante* 83.6 Kalbfleisch)

Median apple, which we call κίτρον.

Why did Galen consider κίτρον a normal word, when other Greek speakers thought it was the Latin version of κίτριον? Perhaps because κίτρον was the usual term for this fruit in Rome and κίτριον the usual term elsewhere. Both are Latin loanwords, but κίτρον is closer to the Latin form *citrum*; perhaps the Greek speakers of Rome, who would have been more aware of the Latin form than most Greek speakers elsewhere, borrowed the Latin in a form closer to the original. In any case, the only other ancient texts in which κίτρον appears are medical ones; in all other kinds of literature, documents, and inscriptions κίτριον is used. That distribution suggests that from Galen's time onwards κίτρον was a medical term, and Galen's decision to use it is the most likely reason for that development.

9.5.4 *Hesychius*

Hesychius' lexicon of obscure words includes hundreds of Latin terms, ranging from well-established loanwords to *hapax legomena*. More than 70 Latin words occur as glosses in Hesychius (some appearing more than once), more than 130 occur as lemmata (a few appearing more than once), and at least 8 occur in both roles, appearing as the lemma in (at least) one entry and the gloss in (at least) one other.[42] In general a word's appearance as a gloss is an indication that it was an established loanword, while appearance as a lemma is an indication that it was not (§2.2.1), but as the words that fill both roles suggest, there are some complications. Hesychius' lexicon was not the work of a single individual operating at one point in time; like many ancient lexica it is a composite creation.[43] It was compiled in the fifth or sixth century from earlier sources,

some dating to the second century AD and some perhaps much earlier; during the Byzantine period it then underwent both abridgement and interpolation. Most of the interpolations come from the lexicon of Cyrillus, which was compiled in the fifth century; therefore although Byzantine corruption cannot be completely excluded as the explanation for a surprising passage, the vast majority of the material in Hesychius is certainly ancient. But beyond that general observation no assumptions can be made about the time period to which a particular entry relates, and when the same word appears in different entries it is very likely that they come from different sources.

This situation is partly responsible for the large number of established loanwords that appear as lemmata in Hesychius. Some of these had clearly been borrowed long before the fifth century and were heavily used in imperial-period Greek, such as πάτρων 'patron', παγανός 'civilian', and σκάλα 'stairs'. Probably the entries for these words go back to Hesychius' sources, composed at a time when these words were less familiar to Greek speakers. On the other hand, some loanwords appearing as lemmata had gone out of use in late antiquity and were no longer as familiar to readers as they had been in earlier centuries; examples include βυκανητής 'trumpeter' and δικτάτωρ 'dictator'. The entries for these words could come from later in the tradition, when they had become archaic literary terms. A few of the words that occur as lemmata were probably in use during all the periods from which entries in Hesychius could plausibly be drawn, so that their appearance as lemmata is difficult to explain; for example Λατῖνοι 'Latins' (glossed with Ῥωμαῖοι 'Romans', λ 392). Occasionally different variants of the same word serve as lemma and gloss for the same entry, as with βερεδάριος 'courier', where the older spelling οὐεριδάριος is the lemma and the later βεριδάριος the gloss (ο 1601).

Many of Hesychius' lemmata are not attested anywhere else, making the lexicon an important source for our understanding of the ancient Greek vocabulary. A significant number of these *hapax legomena* lemmata are or could be Latin; examples include ἄβεις 'you have' (*habes*), βούβελα 'beef' (*bubula*), and ἴλαξ 'holm oak' (*ilex*). Although these lemmata are very unlikely

---

[42] These are βερεδάριος, ἐξάκτωρ, καπίστριον, κῆνσος, λέντιον, μάγιστρος, ὅρριον, and φίβλα. One word, λοῦδος, appears in Hesychius but in neither role. Figures are imprecise because sometimes it is impossible to be certain exactly what the words in Hesychius' entries were supposed to be: there are many textual corruptions.

[43] For the history of Hesychius' lexicon see e.g. Dickey (2007: 88–90).

to have been actual loanwords, they are often of interest to scholars working on Latin influence on Greek, for whom Hesychius has long been a valuable source.[44]

9.5.5 *John Lydus*

The sixth-century antiquarian writer John Lydus was an enthusiastic user of Latin words, of which he packed in as many as he could manage. Lydus served in the imperial administration during the first half of the sixth century, a time when the practical utility of Latin was precipitously declining in the East. The Eastern empire had become isolated as the Latin-speaking West was conquered by Germanic speakers; although Justinian reconquered Italy and Sicily in the sixth century they were soon lost again, and most of Europe remained permanently outside the control of Constantinople. Without a substantial body of Latin-speaking imperial subjects Latin effectively became a dead language in the East. A dead language can of course continue to be used for many purposes, as Latin was in the medieval West, but in the West Latin enjoyed several unusual advantages, such as being the language of the Church and the most obvious common language to use for communication between different groups of successors to Roman rule. In the sixth-century East Latin did not have those advantages and rapidly began to disappear. This decline saddened Lydus, whose laments about it provide contemporary testimony not only for Latin's decreasing role in the imperial administration but also about the sharp increase in its social prestige that accompanied that loss of practical utility. Passage 69 offers a view of the relative merits of Latin and Greek that would have been inconceivable in earlier centuries.

69 Νόμος ἀρχαῖος ἦν πάντα μὲν τὰ ὅπως οὖν πραττόμενα παρὰ τοῖς ἐπάρχοις, τάχα δὲ καὶ ταῖς ἄλλαις τῶν ἀρχῶν, τοῖς Ἰταλῶν ἐκφωνεῖσθαι ῥήμασιν. οὗ παραβαθέντος, ὡς εἴρηται, οὐ γὰρ ἄλλως, τὰ τῆς ἐλαττώσεως προὔβαινεν. τὰ δὲ περὶ τὴν Εὐρώπην πραττόμενα πάντα τὴν ἀρχαιότητα διεφύλαξεν ἐξ ἀνάγκης διὰ τὸ τοὺς αὐτῆς οἰκήτορας, καίπερ Ἕλληνας ἐκ τοῦ πλείονος ὄντας,

τῇ τῶν Ἰταλῶν φθέγγεσθαι φωνῇ, καὶ μάλιστα τοὺς δημοσιεύοντας. ταῦτα μετέβαλεν ὁ Καππαδόκης εἰς γραώδη τινὰ καὶ χαμαίζηλον ἀπαγγελίαν, οὐχ ὡς σαφηνείας φροντίζων, ἀλλ᾽ ὅπως πρόχειρα ὄντα καὶ κοινὰ μηδεμίαν ἐμποιοῖ δυσχέρειαν τοῖς κατὰ σκοπὸν αὐτοῦ πληροῦν τὰ μηδαμόθεν αὐτοῖς ἀνήκοντα τολμῶσιν. ... καὶ τί μακρηγορῶ; πάντα παντελῶς διαπέπτωκε μηδεμίαν ἐπίγνωσιν τῶν πρὶν κατορθωμάτων διασῴζοντα. (*Mag.* pp. 238.21–240.1, 240.17–18)

There was an ancient law that all matters being transacted in any way whatsoever by the prefects, and perhaps by the other magistracies as well, be expressed in the language of the Italians [i.e. Latin]. When this law had been sidestepped, as I have stated, since it could not have been otherwise, the process of reduction began to advance. All matters, however, that were being transacted in Europe [i.e. Italy and Sicily] preserved out of necessity the ancient practice on account of the fact that its inhabitants, though they were Greeks for the most part, spoke in the language of the Italians, and especially those who conducted public business. The Cappadocian [an official highly placed in the imperial administration] changed that into a haggish and base idiom [i.e. Greek, or some particular variety of Greek], not because he cared for clarity, as he alleged, but in order that it might be handy and colloquial and cause no difficulty to those who, in accordance with his aim, dared to fill in what from no aspect belonged to them. ... Why, pray, should I speak at great length? Everything has completely collapsed, preserving no cognizance of erstwhile perfections. (Trans. Bandy 1983: 239–41, with my annotations)

Lydus' work on Roman government, Περὶ ἐξουσιῶν or *De magistratibus populi Romani*, was largely antiquarian in nature and aimed to display his knowledge of both the Latin language and Roman history and culture.[45] He therefore used many Latin words, including ones that he clearly did not expect his readers to know. But the readers' ignorance was not always due to the words' never having been borrowed into Greek, for Lydus suggests that some Latin words had indeed been borrowed at one point but then become obsolete. In passage 70, for example, he makes a distinction between the obsolete

---

[44] See e.g. the impressive work of Immisch (1885) and García Domingo (1983: e.g. 254).

[45] E.g. Maas (1992), Bandy (1983), Schamp (2008).

loanword ῥέγεστα[46] and its supposed etymon ῥῆς γέσται (*res gestae*), which had never been part of the Greek bureaucratic language.

70   Νόμος δὲ ἦν (καὶ γὰρ οὐκ ἔστιν, ἄρτι παροφθεὶς ἐξ ἀβελτερίας ἤ, τἀληθὲς εἰπεῖν, κακοδαιμονίας) πάντα διὰ τῶν παρόντων αὐτοῖς χαρτουλαρίων, καὶ αὐτῶν ἀπὸ τῶν ταχυγράφων, ἀναφαίνεσθαι ἐπὶ τῶν λεγομένων ῥεγέστων ἢ κοττιδιανῶν, ἀντὶ τοῦ ἐφημέρων (ῥέγεστα δὲ Ῥωμαῖοι τὰς βίβλους, αἷς ἐνέγραφον τὰ πραττόμενα συνεῖδον ὀνομάζειν, ὅτι ῥῆς γέστας τὰς πράξεις τοῦ πολιτεύματος εἶναι βούλονται), ἔνθεν τοῖς ὅτε δή ποτε ζητοῦσι τὰ ὅτε δή ποτε πεπραγμένα συντόμως περὶ τὴν εὕρεσιν εὐκολία. (*Mag.* p. 164.2–10)

There was a law (for it also does not exist, having been recently disregarded out of stupidity or, truth to tell, misfortune), that all transactions be plainly set forth through the agency of the *chartularii*, who are in attendance upon them (they, too, were from the ranks of the speed-writers), in the so-called *regesta* or *cottidiana*, namely, 'daily registers' (the Romans resolved to call *regesta* the books in which they recorded transactions because they maintain that *res gestae* mean the acts of the government), from which whoever at any time whatsoever sought matters that had been transacted at any time whatsoever could easily find them quickly. (Trans. Bandy 1983: 165)

Lydus was wrong about the etymology of ῥέγεστα: it comes not from *res gestae* but rather from *regesta* 'register', past participle of *regero* 'replace'. This is not his only mistake about Latin[47] – but his knowledge of Greek was sound,

and therefore his comments about the usage of his Greek-speaking contemporaries are of great value today. Passages 71 and 72, for example, tell us that φίβουλα (φίβλα) and σημέντον were the normal terms and κορνουκόπιον and σηγμέντον the special palace terms for the same objects, while passage 73 tells us that ἀπαλαρία was in common use in sixth-century Greek but σατούρα, ἐπουλαρία, and ἐποῦλαι were not. Passage 74 is the only evidence for the variant πριβατωρία – all other surviving sources use προβατωρία, the variant Lydus considered correct – and indicates that the word as a whole was rather more widely used than one might suppose from other evidence. The variant spelling ἀδσηκρῆτις in passage 75 is also attested in an inscription, but without Lydus' testimony we might assume that that spelling was a one-off mistake on the part of the writer of that inscription.

71   Αἱ δέ εἰσι δίπλακες ἀπὸ κόκκου, πρωτείας μετάξης κλωστῆς, χρυσῇ περόνῃ λιθοκολλήτῳ ἀναρπαζόμενοι τοῖς ὤμοις, ἣν ἡμεῖς μὲν φίβουλαν ὡς Ἰταλοὶ καλοῦμεν, κορνουκόπιον δὲ ἰδίᾳ πως ἐν τοῖς βασιλείοις ἔτι καὶ νῦν λέγουσιν (*Mag.* p. 88.9–13)

And these are double-folded mantles dyed scarlet, of first-class spun silk, caught up at the shoulders by a gold brooch set with precious stones, which we call *fibula* as Latin speakers do but which in the palace even today they rather distinctively call *cornucopium*.

72   Ἐν δὲ τῇ βουλῇ χλαμύσι, πορφυραῖς μέν (πῶς γὰρ οὐχί;), πρὸς δὲ τὸ πέρας τῆς ποδήρους ὤας γραμμαῖς τετραγώνοις δι' ὅλου χρυσῷ κοσμουμέναις (σηγμέντα αὐτὰς οἱ τῆς αὐλῆς καλοῦσιν, ἀντὶ τοῦ χρυσόσημα· τὸ δὲ πλῆθος ἐπὶ τῶν ἰδιωτικῶν χλαμύδων σημέντα) (*Mag.* p. 88.19–23)

And in the senate [the emperor wore] cloaks that basically were purple (for how could they not be?), but towards the edge of the border that reached down to his feet they were decorated with square lines entirely in gold (the courtiers call them *segmenta*, which means 'gold embroidery',

---

[46] At least, that was Lydus' view; we have no other ancient evidence for the existence of ῥέγεστα, and it does occur in the Byzantine period, so Lydus' view may not have been right.

[47] See §3.2 *s.vv.* ἀνδαβάτης, βερουτάριος, κάπερε, and κυαιστίων, but note also *Mag.* p. 42.19–24, where Lydus shows an impressive knowledge of Latin by correctly identifying vowel quantities that were no longer audible in his day and had never been represented in writing: παρρικίδας δὲ Ῥωμαῖοι ὁμωνύμως τούς τε γονέων τούς τε πολιτῶν φονέας ἀποκαλοῦσιν, παρέντης ἑκατέρους προσαγορεύοντες. διαφορὰν δὲ ἐπὶ τῆς ἐπωνυμίας ταύτην παρέχουσί τινα· συστέλλοντες γὰρ τὴν πρώτην συλλαβὴν καὶ βραχεῖαν ποιοῦντες τοὺς γονέας, ἐκτείνοντες δὲ τοὺς ὑπηκόους σημαίνουσιν. 'The Romans call both the murderers of parents and the murderers of citizens homonymously *parricidae*, because they call both [parents and citizens] *parentes*.

This, however, is the sort of distinction which they exhibit with regard to the word: namely, by contracting the first syllable and making it short they mean "parents," but by lengthening it they mean "subjects".' (Trans. Bandy 1983: 43) Dmitriev (2018) argues that Lydus knew Latin well but produced erroneous etymologies borrowed from his sources; not all his mistakes are in etymologies, however.

but the people call them *sementa* [when they appear] on the cloaks of private citizens).

73 Ἰστέον δὲ Ῥωμαίοις τὸ κανοῦν ἐπὶ μὲν τῶν ἱερῶν <u>σατούραν</u>, ἐπὶ δὲ τῶν εὐωχιῶν <u>ἐπουλαρίαν</u>, ἣν <u>ἀπαλαρίαν</u> οἱ πολλοὶ ἐξ ἀγνοίας προσαγορεύουσιν· <u>ἐπούλας</u> γὰρ τὰς εὐωχίας Ῥωμαίοις ἔθος καλεῖν. (*Mens.* 1.29.1–4)

One should know that for the Romans a bread-basket is a *satura* at sacrifices but an *epularia* at feasts, the thing that the multitude call ἀπαλαρία out of ignorance. For it was the custom for the Romans to call feasts *epulae*.

74 Καὶ ταύτης μόνης τῆς προσηγορίας μνημονεύουσιν αἱ παρὰ τῶν βασιλέων παρεχόμεναι τοῖς εἰς στρατείαν παριοῦσι <u>προβατωρίαι</u>, οἷον εἰ συστάσεις καὶ ἀποδείξεις (οὐδὲ γὰρ ἁπλῶς τὸ πρὶν ἄδειαν εἶχεν ὁ βουλόμενος ζώνην περιθέσθαι οἵαν οὖν, μὴ πρότερον ἀποδείξας ὡς εἴη πρὸς αὐτὴν ἐπιτήδειος)· προβάρε γὰρ τὸ μετὰ δοκιμῆς ἐπιδεῖξαι τὸ ὑποκείμενον λέγουσιν οἱ Ῥωμαῖοι. νῦν δὲ τὸ πλῆθος αὐτὰς ἐξ ἀμαθοῦς μαντείας τἀληθὲς παραδηλούσης <u>πριβατωρίας</u> καλεῖ (*Mag.* p. 134.4–11)

[A]nd this is the sole designation which is mentioned by the *probatoriae*, that is to say, 'recommendations and proofs', that are granted from the emperors to those to be admitted into service (for in days of old anyone who wanted to put on a belt [i.e. insignia of office] of whatever sort did not simply get permission unless he had previously proved that he was fit for it), for the Romans use *probare* as a term for 'to present the subject with approval'. Nowadays, however, the common people call them *privatoriae* from an illiterate guess, which does hint at the truth. (Trans. Bandy 1983: 135)

75 Ἀβ ἄκτις μὲν ὄνομα τῷ φροντίσματι, σημαίνει δὲ καθ' ἑρμηνείαν τὸν τοῖς ἐπὶ χρήμασι πραττομένοις ἐφεστῶτα, ὡς ἀ πιγμέντις τοὺς ἐπὶ τῶν ἀρωμάτων καὶ <u>ἀ σηκρήτις</u> τοὺς ἐπὶ τῶν σηκρήτων (οὐδὲ γὰρ <u>ἀδσηκρήτις</u> κατὰ τοὺς ἰδιώτας, ἐξ ἀγνοίας μετὰ τοῦ δέλτα στοιχείου τῆς προθέσεως ἐπιβαλλομένης) καὶ ἀ σαβάνις τοὺς ἐπὶ τῶν βαλανείων τῆς αὐλῆς. (*Mag.* p. 162.13–18)

The office has the name *ab actis*, but by way of translation it means 'one who is in charge of transactions pertaining to finances'; as *a pigmentis* means 'those in charge of aromatics'; *a secretis*, 'those in charge of the *secreta*' (certainly not *adsecretis* in accordance with the usage of the uneducated who out of ignorance add on the

preposition coupled with the letter delta); and *a sabanis*, 'those in charge of the baths of the court'. (Trans. Bandy 1983: 163)

Sometimes, however, a word that Lydus seems to treat as unfamiliar was in fact known to other Greek speakers. In passage 76 Lydus quotes κοῦσπος 'wooden foot-fetter' as a foreign word, but in passage 77, which was composed slightly earlier, another writer quotes it as long-established soldiers' slang. Perhaps Lydus was unfamiliar with that particular linguistic register.

76 Κουσπάτωρες, φυλακισταί· <u>κούσπους</u> γὰρ Ῥωμαῖοι τὰς ξυλοπέδας καλοῦσιν, ὡς ἂν εἰ κουστώδης πέδουμ, οἷον εἰ ποδοκάκας καὶ ποδοφύλακας. (*Mag.* p. 72.5–7)

Cuspatores, 'gaolers', for the Romans call wooden fetters *cuspus*, *custodes pedum*, as it were, that is to say, 'foot-binders' and 'foot-wardens'. (Trans. Bandy 1983: 73)

77 Ἐξ αὐτοῦ οὖν ἐπινενόηται ὁ λεγόμενος παρὰ τοῖς στρατιώταις ἕως τῆς νῦν <u>κοῦσπος</u> (Malalas, *Chronographia* 2.17)

From this [Oedipus' infant restraint], therefore, was invented the thing that even today is still called κοῦσπος among soldiers.

Occasionally Lydus puts Latin terms in Latin script (cf. §7.1); as we have his text only via a manuscript of c. AD 900 (Bandy 1983: liii) it is possible that there were originally more examples of Latin script than now survive. Passage 78 is an example.

78 Τοιούτου τινὸς (ἀπείη!) συμβαίνοντος ἀνὰ τὴν πόλιν, οἱ τυχὸν ἐπικαίρως ἐξ αὐτῶν εὑρισκόμενοι βοῶντες τῇ πατρίῳ Ῥωμαίων φωνῇ "OMNES COLLEGIATI CONCURRITE", οἷον εἰπεῖν, "πάντες ἑταῖροι συνδράμετε". (*Mag.* p. 80.17–21)

Whenever some such emergency (may it be absent!) occurs in the city, those of them who chance to be on hand shout in the native speech of the Romans: *Omnes collegiati, concurrite*, that is to say, 'All colleagues, run to the rescue!' (Trans. Bandy 1983: 81)

The exclamation here seems to be a fossilized Latin phrase used by Greek speakers who did not necessarily understand its literal meaning. Such fossilized phrases are well attested in the

Byzantine imperial court in later centuries,[48] but a cry for help does not at first glance seem a plausible context for the preservation of a fossilized phrase. However, this phrase probably needs to be seen in the context of the late antique / early Byzantine army, which used numerous Latin command formulae.[49] There also is a parallel in the English distress call 'Mayday', which comes from French *m'aidez*. It is therefore very likely that in Lydus' day (or, given his conservative tendencies, perhaps in a slightly earlier period) Greek speakers did at least occasionally use a Latin distress call.

9.5.6 *Legal writers*

Given the linguistic situation described by Lydus, it is not at all surprising that over the course of the sixth century the official language of Roman law shifted from Latin to Greek. The linguistic changeover can be followed in the great legal works from the reign of Justinian: the *Codex* (a collection of laws) was published mainly in Latin in 529 and 534, the *Digest* (a collection of jurists' pronouncements) was published mainly in Latin in 533, the *Institutes* (an introduction to Roman law) was published in Latin in 533, Theophilus Antecessor's translation of the *Institutes* was published in Greek in 534, the *Novellae* (laws enacted after the compilation of these works) were published gradually, mainly in Greek, starting in 535; Dorotheus' Greek translation of the *Digest* (now lost) appeared between 536 and 539; and Athanasius' epitome of the *Novellae* was produced in Greek c. 572.[50]

The Greek works among these texts made heavy use of Latin loanwords and codeswitches,[51] both of which they often put in the Latin alphabet (§7.1); most isolated Latin words were given Greek inflections, but some isolated words and most multi-word phrases retained their Latin inflections, sometimes fitting their Greek syntactic contexts and sometimes fossilized (§7.2, §7.3). The result was a peculiar mixture, and it is easy to attribute its strange characteristics to the linguistic shift taking place in the sixth century. But in fact this Latinate legal Greek was probably much older than that, for Greek had long been used as a medium for oral teaching of Roman law in the Eastern empire, as well as for legal arguments in court cases.[52] There are even some surviving pre-Justinianic legal works written in Greek, most notably the fragments of the third-century jurist Herennius Modestinus and the fifth- or very early sixth-century commentary known as *Scholia Sinaitica*, which survives in a long papyrus fragment.[53] These offer insight into what legal Greek was like before the Justinianic reforms and indicate that it was very similar to the legal Greek used after the language shift.

Modestinus' work *De excusationibus* is lost in its original form, but extracts are preserved in the *Digest* of Justinian.[54] These extracts are not

---

[48] E.g. Petersmann (1992: 228–31), Dagron (1969: 38).

[49] Reichenkron (1961: 20–1), Mihăescu (1969), Zilliacus (1935a: 126–67).

[50] E.g. Corcoran (2017), Kaiser (2015), Brandsma (1996: 7–8).

[51] On the Greek of the Justinianic legal works and its incorporation of Latin see e.g. Matino (2013), Feissel (2008: 218–23), Avotins (1989, 1992), Van der Wal (1983), Zilliacus (1935a: 59–112), and Burgmann (1990, 1991: 62), who calculates that in some of them approximately every tenth word is Latin.

[52] On the use of Greek in oral teaching of law see Scheltema (1970, 1967: esp. 57), Corcoran (2017: 101–16), Stolte (2013, 2015: 358–9), Van der Wal (1983: 29), Van Bochove (2019: 219–22), Cribiore (2007: 207–10), Zilliacus (1935a: 80–6). For (often lost) legal texts in Greek before Justinian, Lokin (2013), Tuccillo (2013), Zilliacus (1935a: 67–71, 76–9). For the use of Greek in Roman legal contexts more generally, e.g. Russo Ruggeri (2013), D'Alessio (2013), Biville (2013), J. N. Adams (2003: 383–90), Coles (1966); for language use in other contexts in sixth-century Constantinople, Millar and Adams (2009), Rosellini and Spangenberg Yanes (2019), Nocchi Macedo (2019), Zarini (2019), Mecella (2019), Hemmerdinger (1966); for the role of Latin in Byzantine legal language, Dain (1930), Popescu-Mihuţ (1981), Burgmann (1991), Fögen (1998), Andrés Santos (2006), Matino (2013), Rodríguez Martín (2019), Pedone (2020b).

[53] For the *Scholia Sinaitica* see §7.1.2. A number of shorter papyrus fragments also survive, together forming a considerable body of text; see the forthcoming publication of Dario Mantovani's Redhis project. And some Greek besides that of Modestinus is preserved via the manuscript tradition, for example a few passages in the *Codex Theodosianus* and more in the *Codex* and *Digest* of Justinian (Stolte 2009; Lokin 2013; Tuccillo 2013; Corcoran 2017: 99–101).

[54] On Modestinus and his language see Schulz (1961: 320–4), Masiello (1983), Millar (1999: 102), Liebs (2010: 73),

extensive but nevertheless contain at least twenty Latin words, and the density of Latin terminology is only slightly lower than that of the Justinianic legal works.[55] The *Scholia Sinaitica* fragment contains at least thirty-five isolated Latin words and several longer Latin phrases, and its density of Latin terminology equals that of the Justinianic works.[56] The Latin vocabulary of the *Scholia Sinaitica* is largely the same as that of the Justinianic works: 89% of the Latin words found in the papyrus recur in Theophilus Antecessor or one of the other Greek texts resulting from Justinian's reforms, and one of the papyrus' Latin phrases (κάπιτις δεμινουτίων 'loss of status') also recurs.[57] Modestinus' vocabulary shows more differences, with only 45% of his Latin words recurring in the sixth-century legal works;[58] evidently there was some change over time in precisely which Latin words tended to be used in Greek legal texts,

Lokin (2013: 543–7), Tuccillo (2013: 327), and Corcoran (2017: 99). The original title of the work was Παραίτησις ἐπιτροπῆς καὶ κουρατορίας 'Exemption from tutela and cura', but it is now generally known by the Latin title, meaning 'On excuses'. It has later interpolations, consisting at a minimum of Latin quotations from Roman jurists, and it is conceivable that some of the loanwords now found in the extracts were added by the interpolators. But even the interpolations probably predate the sixth century, as they seem to have been part of the text at the time of the compilation of the *Digest*.

[55] Loanwords ἐξκουσατίων, κάλιξ, καυσάριος, κιβάριον, κουρατορεύω, κουρατορία, κουράτωρ, κωδικίλλος, λεγεωνάριος, ληγατάριος, λιβράριος, πάτρων, πριμιπιλάριος, πριμίπιλον, σαλάριον, συνουετρανός; also rare βεστιάριον, ἰνκόλας, καλκουλάτωρ, ὁρατίων, and perhaps κουρατίων.

[56] Loanwords ἐμαγκιπᾶτος, ἐξκουσατίων, ἰνστιτοῦτα, κῶδιξ, Λατῖνος, λεγίτιμος, μανδᾶτον, πακτεύω, πάκτον, πάτρων, πραίτωρ, προκουράτωρ, ρεπούδιον, τίτλος, φάκτον; also rare ἰγκουισιτίων, πόστουμος, ρετεντίων, ρῆγλα; also foreign ἀδβεντίκιος, *voluptaria*, *dolus*, δοτάλιος, *cessicios*, κομπενσατεύω, κοῦλπα, μόρα, νεκεσσάριος, οὐσουκαπιτεύω, ποῖνα, *potior*, ρεουξορία, ρέσπονσον, στιπουλατίων, τεσταμεντάριος, and perhaps κομμιτεύω. Ἰταλία is also presented as a Latin word, and there are several Latin phrases. See §7.1.2.

[57] The words that do not reappear are *voluptaria*, *cessicios*, *potior*, and ρῆγλα.

[58] The words that do not reappear are βεστιάριον, ἰνκόλας, κάλιξ, καλκουλάτωρ, κιβάριον, λεγεωνάριος, λιβράριος, ὁρατίων, πριμιπιλάριος, πριμίπιλον, συνουετρανός; of these λεγεωνάριος, λιβράριος, and συνουετρανός were loanwords in the third century but had died out by the sixth, while βεστιάριον, ἰνκόλας, καλκουλάτωρ, and ὁρατίων seem never to have been successfully borrowed during antiquity.

but the basic principle that such words were frequently used remained constant. That principle is not surprising at a period when the laws themselves were written in Latin and one of the tasks of Greek-speaking law students was to learn to read and understand legal Latin. One of the goals of the instruction provided in Greek-speaking law schools must have been to teach students the key Latin legal terms and their meanings, a task that could most easily be accomplished by using the actual Latin words that students would encounter when reading the laws for themselves.

Many of the particular Latin words that appear in sixth-century Greek legal writings are not attested earlier, but that in itself is not proof that they had not been part of legal Greek for centuries. Is it possible to identify the ones that had in fact been part of legal Greek earlier, and distinguish them from sixth-century borrowings and codeswitches? The script used can sometimes be helpful; that is, Latin words that legal writers put in Greek script are nearly always well-established loanwords, but Latin words that appear in Latin script may also be established loanwords (§7.1.1). Likewise inflection can be useful, for Latin words to which the legal writers give Latin endings appropriate to their Greek contexts are very likely to be codeswitches, while Latin words that appear with Greek inflections or in fossilized Latin forms could be loanwords (§7.2). Words that appear with complex inflectional patterns significantly removed from their Latin inflections are particularly likely to have been established long before the point at which we first see them. For example, the verbs ἀδιτεύω 'take possession of an inheritance' and ρεπουδιατεύω 'reject an inheritance' come from *adeo* 'take possession of an inheritance' and *repudio* 'reject', via the perfect participles *aditus* and *repudiatus*. They take not only Greek verbal endings, but also augments; moreover they form participles freely and thus take Greek nominal endings as well. Thus in passage 79 *repudiateusēi* has a Greek verb ending, *ēditeusan* has a Greek augment and verb ending, and *aditeusasin*, *repudiateusas*, and *aditeusantes* are participles with Greek nominal endings. Although neither verb is attested before the work from which this passage comes, it is unlikely that either could have been a new creation at the time it was composed, for they had already been adapted to a point where the original Latin verbs were completely unrecognizable.

> 79 Ἐάν τις τελευτήσῃ πολλῶν ὑποκειμένων LEGITIMON προσώπων τοῦ αὐτοῦ βαθμοῦ, καὶ οἱ μὲν ἄλλοι ADITEUSUSIN, εἷς δὲ REPUDIATEUSῃ ἢ κωλυθῇ κληρονομῆσαι ὑπὸ τελευτῆς ἤγουν ἑτέρας αἰτίας (εἰσὶ γὰρ πολλοὶ ὑπὸ τῶν διατάξεων εἰργόμενοι κληρονομεῖν), τὸ τούτου μέρος προσαύξει τοῖς ADITEUSASIN. οἷον τεσσάρων ὄντων οἱ τρεῖς ἠδιτευσαν, ὁ εἷς ἠσθένησεν ἢ REPUDIATEUSAS ἢ τελευτήσας ἢ ὑπὸ νόμου κωλυθεὶς διαδέξασθαι· τὸ τούτου μέρος τοῖς τρισὶν ἐξ ἴσου προσαύξει, εἴτε ζῶσιν οἱ ADITEUSANTES εἴτε καὶ τελευτῆσαι αὐτοὺς συνέβη. (Theophilus Antecessor 3.4.4)

If a man dies, and there are alive a number of statutory persons of the same degree, and all of these except one enter on the inheritance, but the one rejects it, or is prevented from becoming heir by death or some other cause – for there are many persons that are hindered by the constitutions from becoming heirs – then this one's share accrues to those that make entry. For example: there are four of them; three make entry, and one fails, whether because he rejects, or dies, or is prevented by a law from succeeding: this one's share accrues in equal parts to the three that make entry, whether they live or whether it chances that they died. (Trans. A. F. Murison in Lokin *et al.* 2010: 539)

Further evidence that some adaptations we first see in Theophilus' work must predate him comes from a term he specifically labels as obsolete. In later legal Greek ῥεουξορία, a fully inflectable first-declension noun with genitive ῥεουξορίας, was the equivalent of (*actio*) *rei uxoriae* 'legal action for the recovery of the dowry', a phrase fixed in the genitive. Although this word first appears in Theophilus' work, he himself had no interest in it or the concept it represented, mentioning it only to explain that it was no longer current (passage 80). But for at least four centuries before his time the *actio rei uxoriae* had been an important technical term of Roman law, one that would have needed to be discussed in Greek and that must accordingly have had a generally accepted Greek form.[59] It must have been during that period that

the Greek word acquired the very considerable adaptations that we first see in Theophilus. And the fact that this word was already embedded in the Greek legal vocabulary before the concept to which it referred was abolished must in part explain its use by later writers, for Theophilus himself hardly provided much incentive to keep the term alive.

> 80 Καὶ ἡ REUXORIA πάλαι (ἥρμοζε δὲ αὕτη μετὰ διάλυσιν τοῦ γάμου τῇ γυναικὶ κατὰ τοῦ οἰκείου ἀνδρὸς ἐπὶ ἀναλήψει τῶν προικιμαίων πραγμάτων) ἦν τῶν BONA FIDE. ἀλλὰ διάταξις τοῦ ἡμετέρου βασιλέως ταύτην ἀνελοῦσα δέδωκε πρὸς ἀνάληψιν τῆς προικὸς τὴν EX STIPULATU, ὡς οὖσαν πλατυτέραν· καὶ πᾶν τὸ τῆς REUXORIAS δίκαιον ἐπὶ ταύτην μετήγαγε καὶ τούτῳ τῷ θέματι τῶν BONA FIDE τὴν EX STIPULATU ἀπετέλεσεν. (4.6.29)

And formerly the *actio rei uxoriae*, too (which action was open to the wife after the dissolution of the marriage against her husband for the recovery of the property that formed the dowry) was among those *bonae fidei*. But a constitution of our Emperor abolished it and gave the *actio ex stipulatu*, as being more comprehensive, for recovery of the dowry, transferring to it all the legal force of the *actio rei uxoriae* and making the *actio ex stipulatu* in this case *bonae fidei*. (Trans. A. F. Murison in Lokin *et al.* 2010: 827)

Sometimes Theophilus treats the same word very differently in different contexts. In passage 81 he presents two versions of the infinitive of *gero*, one inflected as Greek (*geriteuein*) and one as Latin (*gerere*); both are part of longer phrases written in Latin script.

> 81 PRO HEREDE GERITEUEIN ἐστὶ PRO DOMINO GERERE· οἱ γὰρ παλαιοὶ τῷ HERES ὀνόματι ἀντὶ τοῦ DOMINUS ἐκέχρηντο. (2.19.7)

'To act as heir' means 'to act as owner', for the ancients used to use the word 'heir' instead of 'owner'.

---

59 The Latin goes back at least to the second century, being used e.g. by Gaius, *Institutes* 4.62, and Aulus Gellius, *Noctes Atticae* 4.3.1; cf. Cicero, *De officiis* 3.15.61. The *Scholia Sinaitica* include the term but always abbreviated *r.u.*, a form that seems to reflect the original Latin rather than the Greek univerbation; it is likely that this abbreviation would have been pronounced the way Theophilus' word was written.

This variation is revealing. In Latin *pro herede gero* was a long-established technical legal term,[60] and in Byzantine Greek it would continue as the univerbated loanword προνερεδεγεριτεύω, with the Latin *h* turning into a Greek *ν* owing to graphic confusion between uncial н and ν.[61] Although that loanword is not attested in Greek before Theophilus, it must have already been established (though probably not yet with the misspelling), and that was why he used it: his readers needed to learn the term. But *pro domino gero* was new; in fact it was the explanation of *pro herede gero* provided in the Latin work Theophilus was translating, as shown (with additional context) in passage 82. Therefore Theophilus simply codeswitched into Latin for that phrase. (Of course, there was no real need for the codeswitch at all; the passage would have been clearer had he translated *pro domino gerere* into Greek.) It follows that Theophilus' distinction between *geriteuein* and *gerere* here is probably a distinction between a previously established loanword and his own codeswitch – and as in the case of ῥεουξορία, the loanword continued to be used by later writers. But those writers almost never used the codeswitch; it is clear that they did not simply follow Theophilus' linguistic choices, but rather continued to use the legal Greek that had been established before Theophilus' time and that he also used. This distinction does not mean that Theophilus had no impact at all on later legal Greek, of course – but it does suggest that the usage of later writers can help us identify which elements of Theophilus' language were idiosyncratic and which came from the tradition.

82 Item extraneus heres testamento institutus aut ab intestato ad legitimam hereditatem vocatus potest aut pro herede gerendo vel etiam nuda voluntate suscipiendae hereditatis heres fieri. pro herede autem gerere quis videtur, si rebus hereditariis tamquam heres utatur vel vendendo res hereditarias aut praedia colendo locandove et quoquo modo si voluntatem suam declaret vel re vel verbis de adeunda hereditate, dummodo sciat eum, in cuius bonis pro herede

gerit, testato intestatove obiisse et se ei heredem esse. pro herede enim gerere est pro domino gerere: veteres enim heredes pro dominis appellabant. (Justinian, *Institutes* 2.19.7 = Krueger 1895: 23)

Also an external heir, whether appointed in a will or called to an inheritance fixed by law in a case of intestate death, can become heir either by acting as heir or even by the mere intention to accept the inheritance. And someone is seen to act as heir if he uses things belonging to the inheritance like the heir, by selling things belonging to the inheritance or cultivating or leasing estates, and if he in any way declares his intention to enter into the inheritance, whether in deed or in words, as long as he knows that the person with whose possessions he is acting as heir has died testate or intestate and that he is the heir. For to act as the heir is to act as the owner, since the ancients used to call owners heirs.

Another revealing distinction occurs among the terms for the three basic types of law, according to the classification of the *Institutes*: *ius naturale* 'natural law', *ius gentium* 'law of peoples', and *ius civile* 'civil law'. Theophilus' normal way of handling all three of these was to translate them, using the etymologically Greek phrases φυσικὸν νόμιμον 'natural law', ἐθνικὸν νόμιμον 'gentile law', and πολιτικὸν νόμιμον 'civil law'. For *ius naturale* he used only the translation, never giving the Latin term, but for the other two he informed readers of what the (Greek version of the) Latin was, as shown in passage 83. *Ius gentium* became an adjective ἰουρισγέντιος, with the third-declension genitive plural ending of *gentium* reinterpreted as belonging to the second declension and *ius* fixed in the genitive (probably by analogy with other legal terms such as ἰουρισδικτίων 'jurisdiction' from *iurisdictio* and ἰουρισκονσοῦλτοι 'legal experts' from *iuris consulti*); *ius civile* was less heavily adapted and became ἰουρισκιβίλε.[62] Neither

---

[60] It goes back at least to the early third century, being used e.g. by Ulpian (Just. *Dig.* 11.7.4) and Iulius Paulus (*Pauli Sententiae* 4.8.23).

[61] *LBG*, Van der Wal (1983: 51), Dain (1930: 97–8).

[62] Binder (2000: 258) argues that the use of ἰουρισ- rather than ἰουσ- in these compounds reflects a vulgar Latin nominative *iuris*. But ἰουρισ- was not a nominative, rather a fixed form used as the first half of a compound: the Latin phrase was fundamentally reinterpreted when it became a single word, and that reinterpretation need not have started from a nominative. Moreover Roman legal texts are not good sources for vulgar Latin forms: Roman lawyers tended to use more standard grammar than many

of these forms is attested earlier, but the extensive adaptation of ἰουρισγέντιος suggests that it predates Theophilus, who was perfectly capable of identifying a Latin genitive plural ending in *-ium*.[63] And indeed ἰουρισγέντιος continued to be used in the Byzantine period, but ἰουρισκιβίλε was very rare.[64] It is therefore highly probable that the legal Greek inherited by Theophilus included an established Latin loanword for *ius gentium*, and no established Latin loanword for *ius naturale* – but what about *ius civile*?[65] Probably ἰουρισκιβίλε also predates Theophilus, since it is somewhat adapted, but the evidence is much less conclusive than in the case of ἰουρισγέντιος.

> 83   Ἅπας οὖν δῆμος ἢ ἐγγράφοις κέχρηται νόμοις ἢ ἀγράφοις, καὶ πῇ μὲν ἰδίοις, τουτέστι πολιτικοῖς, πῇ δὲ κοινοῖς, τουτέστι IURISGENTIOIS. ὅσα γὰρ νόμιμα ἑκάστη πόλις ἑαυτῇ συνεστήσατο, μέχρις αὐτῆς ἵσταται, ταῦτα δὲ καὶ IURISCIVILE προσαγορεύεται· ὅσα δὲ ὁ φυσικὸς ἤτοι ἐθνικὸς λόγος μεταξὺ πάντων ἀνθρώπων ἐφηῦρε, ταῦτα

[63] other elements of society, and therefore it is unlikely that they used a non-standard nominative regularly enough to influence Greek speakers.

[63] Theophilus was not only fluent in Latin but even a member of the committee that drafted the Latin *Institutes*; for the implications of his dual involvement in the work see Russo Ruggeri (2016: esp. 18).

[64] Van der Wal (1983: 41) suggests that Theophilus also used a more integrated form *iuriscivilion*, genitive *iurisciviliu*, but I can find no evidence of it in Lokin *et al.* (2010). According to that edition, Theophilus uses ἰουρισκιβίλε in only two forms, nominative/accusative singular *iuriscivile* and nominative/accusative plural *iuriscivilia*, and these both match the endings a Latin speaker would have used on *civile*.

[65] The reason *ius naturale* had not been established in Greek is no doubt that the *Institutes* of Gaius, which was used as the introductory Roman law textbook for centuries until superseded by the *Institutes* of Justinian, divides laws only into *ius civile* and *ius gentium* (1.1); Greek-speaking teachers would therefore not have had much need to discuss *ius naturale*. Theophilus himself probably taught from Gaius' *Institutes* until their replacement by the new textbook caused him to produce his own translation of that. Indeed it is sometimes argued that Theophilus' translation incorporates portions of an older Greek translation of Gaius, as Justinian's *Institutes* incorporates portions of Gaius' *Institutes*; that view may be wrong, but nevertheless the terminology traditionally used to explain Gaius in Greek must had a particular impact on Theophilus' new translation. See Russo Ruggeri (2016: esp. 106–7, 115–55).

παρὰ πᾶσιν ἔθνεσι φυλάττεται καὶ IURISGENTIA προσαγορεύεται. (1.2.1)

Thus every people makes use either of written laws or of unwritten ones, also partly of its own specific laws (that is, civil laws), and partly of ones shared with other peoples (that is, laws of the *ius gentium*). For whatever laws each city has established for itself are in force only within that area, and those are called *ius civile*; but whatever natural or so to speak national reason has discovered among all mankind, those are observed in all nations, and they are called the laws of the *ius gentium*.

It therefore seems likely that at least some of the Latin words first appearing in Theophilus (and potentially also some of those first appearing in other Justinianic legal works) are actually older loans. This conclusion complicates a number of the arguments made in the present work, since it reminds us both that some loanwords may be older than they seem and that there may have been more established loanwords than we can now identify. For example, although from the above discussion it seems likely that ἀδιτεύω, ῥεπουδιατεύω, (προνερεδε)γεριτεύω, ῥεουξορία, and ἰουρισγέντιος were all loanwords borrowed before the sixth century, statistics presented in earlier chapters counted ἀδιτεύω as a sixth-century borrowing and the others as not having been established loanwords at all during antiquity. We have seen that the sharp increase in evidence in the second century AD probably distorts the statistical evidence for the chronology of borrowings (§8.1.1): to what extent might the Justinianic legal reforms have a similarly distorting effect?

The words most likely to have had their apparent histories distorted as a result of the Justinianic reforms are the legal terms whose only ancient occurrences are in sixth-century legal texts.[66] But

[66] Of course, any type of word borrowed at an earlier period might happen to turn up first in these works – but that possibility exists for all texts at all periods (§8.1.1). What is at issue here is a specifically distorting effect resulting from the sudden increase in visibility (to us) of legal Greek when the Justinianic works were created; therefore the words to consider are ones that would clearly have been restricted to that particular genre. Words that also occur in other genres are evidently not thus restricted, and words that are not legal terminology were probably not thus restricted.

not all such terms can be suspected of having originated earlier; *pro domino gerere*, for example, was almost certainly new. The ones likely to pre-date the Justinianic reforms are those that seem to have already been integrated at their first appearance and that demonstrably formed part of Greek legal language after the sixth century.[67] In this group there are 14 words that we have classified as loanwords, 18 classified as rare terms, and 113 classified as foreign (that is, words that never appear in Greek script during antiquity).[68] That is a considerable body of material and might indeed have a distorting effect. In what direction might our view of the ancient loanwords have been distorted?

[67] For this purpose I consider words integrated in the sixth century if they appear in Greek script and/or with Greek inflections (including when the only attestations are in ambiguous forms that could be either Latin or Greek), and I consider them part of later legal Greek if they appear in Greek script with Greek (or at least not conspicuously Latin) inflection at least eight times in relevant *TLG* texts.

[68] Loanwords ἀδιτεύω, ἀδιτίων, ἀννάλιος, δίγεστον, ἐνναούγκιον, ἰνστιτοῦτα, κομφιρματεύω, λεγίτιμος, ὀνοράριος, παράτιτλον, περσονάλιος, ῥέος, στατοῦτος, τεστάτωρ. Rare ἀδγνᾶτος, ἀδεφένδευτος, ἀδμινιστρατίων, δεβίτωρ, ἐξκουσατεύω, ἴγκεστος, καλουμνία, κέρτος, κογνᾶτος, κομπρομισσάριος, κουρατορικός, μανδατωρεύω, μοδεράτωρ, μόρτις καῦσα, περσεκουτίων, προμίττενς, σοῦος, συλληγατάριος. Foreign ἀβιτατίων, ἀβστινατεύω, ἀδεμπτεύω, ἀδιουδικατίων, ἀδρογατίων, ἀδρογάτωρ, ἀδσιγνατεύω, ἀκκεπτιλατίων, ἀκκεσσίων, ἄκτωρ, ἀλτερνατίων, ἀρβιτράριος, βακάντιος, βέρσον, βίτιον, γρατούϊτος, δελίκτον, δεπορτατεύω, δεπορτατίων, δηφηνδεύω, δηφηνσίων, διλιγεντία, διρέκτος, ἐμαγκιπατεύω, ἐξερεδατεύω, ἐξερεδατίων, ἐξερεδᾶτος, ἐξερκιτορία, ἐξερκίτωρ, ἐρεδιτάριος, ἴγκερτος, ἴμφανς, ἰνδέβιτος, ἰνιοῦστος, ἰνστιτουτίων, ἰνστιτοῦτος, ἰντεντίων, ἰντέρδικτον, ἰντερκεσσίων, ἰουρισγέντιος, κάπιτις δεμινουτίων, καῦσα, καυτίων, κομμιτεύω, κομμοδᾶτος, κομφιρματίων, κομφουσίων, κονδεμνατίων, κονδικτίκιος, κοντίνουος, κοντράριος, κοῦλπα, κρεδίτωρ, Λατινότης, λιβερατίων, μενσούρα, μόρα, νεγατόριος, νεκεσσάριος, νοβατεύω, νοβατίων, νόξα, νοξάλιος, ὄπερα, οὖσος, οὐσουάριος, οὐσουκαπιτεύω, οὐσουκαπίων, οὐσουφρουκτουάριος, οὐτίλιος, περμουτατίων, περπετοῦος, πετιτεύω, πιγνερατίκιος, ποῖνα, ποινάλιος, ποσσέσσωρ, ποστλιμίνιον, πουπιλλάριος, ποὐτιλλος, ποῦρος, πραεκάριος, πραετεριτεύω, πραετεριτίων, πραετέριτος, προνερεδεγεριτεύω, προπριετάριος, ῥέ, ῥελεγατεύω, ῥελεγίοσος, ῥεουξορία, ῥεπετιτεύω, ῥεπετιτίων, ῥεπλικατίων, ῥεπουδιατεύω, ῥέσπονσον, ῥοῦπτος, σκρίπτος, σοβρίνη, σοβρῖνος, σούσπεκτος, σπεκιάλιος, στιπουλάνδος, στιπουλᾶτον, τεσταμεντάριος, τεσταμεντιφακτίων, τέσταμέντον, τραδιτεύω, τραδιτίων, τριβοῦτον, τριβουτόριος, φισκάλιος, φούρτιβος.

The overall number of Latin words borrowed would be higher than our figure of 820 if any of those rare and foreign words were in fact loanwords, perhaps as high as 951. The chronology of borrowing suggested in §8.1.1 would clearly be somewhat altered by redating 14 sixth-century loanwords to earlier centuries and adding up to 131 additional loanwords, but the extent of the effect on the overall patterns would depend very much on whether those additional loanwords were borrowed all at the same time or spread out over many centuries. The chances are excellent that they were in fact spread out. Modestinus' treatise demonstrates that in the third century AD there was already a Greek vocabulary for discussing Roman law and that that vocabulary had already incorporated a significant number of loanwords. And the comparison between Modestinus' loanwords and those of the *Scholia Sinaitica* fragment indicates that borrowing continued after the third century, along with some attrition of previously borrowed words. The result was a gradual accretion of legal loanwords over many centuries, a process that no doubt continued during the sixth century before and between the particular texts visible to us. Therefore if some or all of these 145 words were in fact borrowed into Greek before the texts in which we first see them, there is no particular reason to suppose that the overall chronology of borrowing was significantly different from the one now visible to us.

The survival rate within antiquity (§8.2.1) would be higher if these words were counted, since by definition they all survived into the sixth century, and so would the rate of survival into the Byzantine period (§8.2.2). But survival into modern Greek would be somewhat lower (§8.2.3), as comparatively few of these words are still in use. The percentage of loanwords attested in literature would be significantly higher, both in terms of first attestations and in terms of overall attestations (§9.1). The distribution of loanwords by semantic field and by parts of speech (§10.2–3) would also be affected.

9.6 CONCLUSIONS

Writers of documents, inscriptions, and literature all used loanwords, but during the imperial period writers of documents were particularly likely to introduce new ones, both borrowings and derivatives. Most loanwords seem to have started in one text type, and probably also in one geographical region, whence they spread gradually outwards; this spread could take centuries and often was not complete by the end of antiquity. Words attested in literature, particularly if attested only in literature, were far more likely to survive into the Byzantine period than ones found only in documents and/or inscriptions; this pattern is due to a combination of different factors, including regional variation.

Regional variation seems to have existed in many different parts of the Greek-speaking world, whenever new loanwords failed to spread and remained restricted to a particular province, district, or site. Most evidence for local terms comes from documents and inscriptions, but some appears in literature, including indications that some loanwords were specific to the Greek spoken in the city of Rome. Such evidence appears in Athenaeus and may explain peculiar patterns of loanword distribution in the Acts of the Apostles.

Atticizing writers used more loanwords than they are often credited with; although these writers disapproved of treating such words as part of Greek, they were often happy to use them accompanied by an acknowledgement of their non-Attic status. By doing so they sometimes reveal to us that particular loanwords had replaced Attic vocabulary in Roman-period Greek.

Certain texts contain particularly large numbers of loanwords. These include the Edict of Diocletian, which used many loanwords because of the semantic fields into which its subject matter fell and also employed codeswitches; histories of Rome, in which there was a particular need for terminology expressing specifically Roman concepts; medical texts, which probably reflect Galen's use of regional vocabulary specific to Rome; the lexicon of Hesychius, which focussed on words that were obscure at some point during antiquity; and the antiquarian writings of John Lydus. Sixth-century legal texts pose particular challenges, since they include enormous numbers of Latin words whose status as loanwords or codeswitches is difficult to ascertain and that may have been borrowed before the date at which they first become visible to us.

10

WHICH WORDS WERE BORROWED?

Most Latin words were never borrowed into Greek. What factors determined which words Greek speakers chose to adopt into their language? Did they borrow Latin words that represented new concepts? Or ones in particular semantic fields, such as government, where Roman influence was especially powerful? Or did they borrow particular parts of speech? All these factors have been suggested as explanations for borrowings, and each probably played a role, but the overall picture is more complicated than any or indeed all of these theories would suggest.

In considering such questions it is important to distinguish between direct borrowings and derivatives (including compounds). Only the former can tell us what types of words were initially borrowed, but the latter contribute to understanding how Latinate various portions of the Greek vocabulary eventually became.

10.1 CULTURAL BORROWINGS AND CORE BORROWINGS

In studying loanwords it is customary to divide them into cultural borrowings, that is words for new things introduced by contact with another culture, and core borrowings, that is words for things that could already be expressed in the borrowing language.[1] Cultural borrowings are sometimes seen as necessary and core borrowings as unnecessary, but linguistic borrowing is never a necessary or inevitable consequence of the introduction of new concepts. Speakers of any language can create new words or usages without borrowing foreign words, as Greek speakers did with ὕπατος for *consul*, αὐτοκράτωρ for *imperator*, and Σεβαστός for *Augustus*. Even cultural borrowings, therefore, were a choice. Although a detailed comparison of the Roman concepts for

which Greek speakers chose to borrow loanwords with the ones for which they chose to create new terminology using existing Greek words is beyond the scope of the present study, an overview of the extent to which Greek speakers chose borrowing to handle new concepts can be gained from Mason's lexicon of Greek terms for Roman institutions. Of the c. 1,200 entries in that volume, over 85% are re-uses of existing Greek words or new words made from Greek roots, and less than 15% loanwords (Mason 1974: 3).

Mason suggests (1974: 3–8, 115–17) that two factors can be identified as affecting the choice to borrow a Latin word for a Roman concept: loanwords were more likely to be used for some types of concept than others, and the tendency to use loanwords rather than Greek formations increased over time. Mason saw the key feature linking the concepts for which loanwords were more likely to be used as being ideas particularly foreign to Greek speakers. Thus at an early period the Roman magistracies were normally rendered with Greek translations, while the Roman priestly colleges, much more foreign to the Greeks than the magistracies, were rendered with loanwords.[2] But in the late Empire, when neither the priesthoods nor the magistracies seemed foreign, both were often rendered with loanwords. Mason's category of foreign ideas is effectively the same as cultural borrowings, so his findings show that that category is relevant to Greek borrowing patterns. But Mason looked only at loanwords for Roman institutions; when all loanwords are considered, the picture becomes more complicated.

Words for Roman priesthoods and magistracies are clearly cultural borrowings, as are the

---

[1] E.g. Poplack (2018: 59), Matras (2020: 162, 179).

[2] A significant exception to this rule is the early loanword δικτάτωρ for 'dictator', a magistracy for which most Greek-speaking political units had no equivalent and therefore no good translation.

month names and other calendar terms, words for coins and currency units, measurements, gladiatorial vocabulary, and most legal and military terms. Many of the loanwords designating garments, dishes, utensils, foods, and beverages are also likely to be cultural borrowings. Nevertheless, some loanwords appear to have been core borrowings. The clearest examples of these are words for plants and animals that were already known before the Roman conquest, such as βουρδών 'mule' for the animal originally called ἡμίονος, or κίτριον 'citron' for the fruit also called Μηδικὸν μῆλον (§9.5.3). Such loanwords must have duplicated existing Greek vocabulary from the moment they were borrowed.

Other loanwords ended up as core borrowings but probably started off as cultural borrowings; that is, they were originally borrowed in a specific meaning for which there was no earlier Greek word, but their meanings then expanded until they duplicated existing words. For example, *balteum* 'sword-belt' referred to a distinctive item of Roman army gear, and Greek βάλτιον was originally borrowed as the word for that item, but eventually βάλτιον was generalized to refer to any type of belt. It is difficult to establish how many other core borrowings followed such a trajectory, for most words that appear to have duplicated existing vocabulary might in theory have started out with a subtle difference from the native concepts they appear to duplicate. Such a history might for example be posited for βάκλον 'stick', βρέβιον 'list', δηλάτωρ 'accuser', κέλλα 'room', λίγλα 'spoon', μεμβράνα 'parchment', ὁσπίτιον 'house', πόρτα '(city) gate', σουβλίον 'skewer', and στάβλον 'stable'. Often we do not precisely what a loanword's meaning was, nor how that meaning changed over time; for example the numerous words for dishes, containers, and cutlery no doubt often referred to implements of a particular shape or with other distinctive features, but the contexts in which these words are used rarely reveal to us what their shapes or features were, let alone whether or how they changed over time. It is therefore impossible to determine what percentage of the Latin loanwords were core borrowings: about half the loanwords may have ended up designating concepts previously expressed by a native Greek word, but for many of those the equivalence with the native

word cannot be verified, and/or an originally cultural borrowing may have expanded its meaning to become a core borrowing. In fact the number of loanwords that started off as core borrowings has sometimes been argued to be very small: scholars have offered ingenious explanations for how even the terms for common animals, which ought to be the safest examples of core borrowings, might really be cultural borrowings (see the discussion of words for mules in §10.2.2 K).

One reason many scholars want to explain away the apparent core borrowings in Greek is a belief that such borrowing would have been unmotivated and therefore unlikely to occur. But core borrowings are common in language-contact situations; for example, the English speakers who borrowed words like 'beef' and 'pork' from French were not previously unfamiliar with those foods. Nor were the French who took *le weekend* and *le look* from English trying to express new concepts. Other motivations for linguistic borrowing also exist, chief among them being a concept often called 'prestige': words from the other language are perceived as in one way or another more attractive than equivalent native words (e.g. Matras 2020: 162). Scholars often dismiss prestige as a possible motivation for Latin borrowings in Greek, because there is overwhelming evidence that owing to the Greeks' impressive literary and cultural heritage not only Greek speakers but also many Latin speakers considered Greek the more prestigious language. But linguistic prestige can be a complex matter; often different measures of it exist within a single society, and the same linguistic variety may rank differently according to which measure is used. For example, the French also have an impressive literary and cultural heritage, and not only many French speakers but also many English speakers consider French more prestigious than English. But English (like other aspects of Anglo-American culture) nevertheless has a certain cachet in France, and that cachet has led to the adoption of terms like *le weekend* and *le look* – which are in fact prestige borrowings, even though by another measure of prestige they are considered hideously déclassé.[3]

[3] E.g. Gilder (1999), Thody (1995), Beinke (1990), Pergnier (1989); cf. Picone (1996). Cf. Mason (1974: 7–8).

In passage 1 (§1) Cynulcus, defending himself against the charge that in uttering a Latin word he has used hideously déclassé language, begins his response by pointing out that Rome now rules the world. In other words, Roman military and political domination has set up an alternative hierarchy of prestige, one in which Latin loanwords have cachet in Greek. That cachet would have been obvious to everyone involved in the conversation, for they were all demonstrating their appreciation of what Rome had to offer by being there; after all, the conversation is conspicuously set in Rome, not in Athens. The diners who considered Latin words déclassé were therefore not so much like intellectuals in Paris complaining about Anglicisms in French, as like intellectuals at a Francophone dinner in New York making such complaints. As we have seen (§1), Cynulcus goes on to defend his vocabulary on the grounds that it is the normal terminology used in (the Greek spoken in) Rome and that a classical Athenian would also have used it, *mutatis mutandis*. That argument is spelled out in some detail, but the point about prestige is not, because it needs no elaboration. And the patterns of Latin borrowing in Greek show that sometimes Latin did have the kind of prestige needed to introduce core borrowings (see e.g. §9.5.5, §10.2.2 A). Therefore one cannot simply dismiss the possibility of core borrowings on *a priori* grounds: when evidence suggests that a given loanword duplicated a native Greek word from the start, we need to pay attention to that evidence.

10.2 SEMANTIC FIELDS

Latin loanwords have a wide range of meanings and can be found throughout the vocabulary of ancient Greek. Nevertheless they are more common in some semantic fields than in others; for example there are more loanwords relating to dining and to finished items of clothing than to cooking, spinning, or weaving; more loanwords relating to mules than to ships; more loanwords relating to law and government than to mathematics, astronomy, philosophy, and literature. Some of these differences correlate with the extent of Roman cultural impact in different areas; for example the lack of loanwords relating to geometry and athletics, compared to the abundant loanwords relating to engineering and gladiatorial shows, must be due at least in part to different amounts of cultural impact. But not all areas of cultural impact produced loanwords; for example Roman bathing practices, which spread all over the empire and involved specialized buildings, equipment, and activities that all needed to be expressed in Greek, nevertheless seem to have generated very few loanwords. (It is always possible that there were bathing-related loanwords for which evidence no longer survives, but lack of evidence is unlikely to have been systematically concentrated in semantic fields such as shipping, mathematics, or bathing terminology.) Therefore a simple explanation in terms of cultural borrowing is insufficient, and a closer look at the particular semantic fields into which loanwords fall is in order.

10.2.1 Typological comparison of direct borrowings

Linguists working on loanwords in modern languages have developed a set of twenty-two semantic fields that can be used to classify the meanings of loanwords. They have observed that many modern languages are broadly similar to one another in terms of which of these semantic fields are most likely to contain significant numbers of direct borrowings.[4] The fields likely to

---

[4] These come from the Loanword Typology Project, which collected data on 41 different languages from a wide range of language families and parts of the world; see Haspelmath and Tadmor (edd. 2009) and the World Loanword Database (wold.clld.org). Researchers created a list of 1,460 meanings (listed by Haspelmath and Tadmor 2009: 22–34 and based loosely on Buck 1949), divided into 24 categories: the 22 discussed here plus 'the modern world' and 'miscellaneous function words', which were not included in the researchers' final ranking of the semantic fields (Tadmor 2009: 64). The researchers then examined which of those 1,460 meanings were normally expressed by borrowings in each of the 41 languages studied. The meanings are unevenly distributed among the semantic categories, with some categories having considerably more meanings than others, and in consequence the researchers looked not at absolute numbers but at what percentage of meanings in each category were expressed by borrowings. It is impractical to use exactly the same methods here, because only a tiny fraction of the 1,460 meanings are represented by Latin loanwords in Greek, not enough to allow for meaningful comparisons

have the highest percentage of borrowed vocabulary in modern languages are religion, clothing, the house, and law, while the ones likely to have the lowest percentage of borrowed vocabulary are kinship, the body, spatial relations, and sense perception (Tadmor 2009: 64). The semantic distribution of words borrowed from Latin into ancient Greek is significantly but not completely different from this typical modern distribution, as illustrated in Figure 11.[5] Categories where borrowing seems to have been more popular in our data than in modern languages include social and political relations, warfare, food, technology, and language; ones where borrowing seems to have been less popular than in modern languages include religion, agriculture, the house, and law.

Category	Ranking for modern languages	Latin borrowings in ancient Greek
Social and political relations	5	167: ἀβάκτης, Ἀβοριγῖνες, ἀβρέβις, ἀδιούτωρ, ἀδνοτατίων, αἰράριον, ἀκομενταρήσιος, ἀκτουάριος, ἀννούμερος, ἀννῶνα, ἀννωνάριος, Ἀντώνεια, ἄρκα, ἀρκάριος, ἀσηκρῆτις, Αὐγοῦστα, Αὐγουσταλιανός, Αὐγουστάλιος, Αὐγούστειος, Αὔγουστος 1, αὐράριος, βενετιανός, βένετος, βενεφικιάριος, βενεφίκιον, βέρνας, βιάτωρ, βικαρία, βικάριος, βινδίκτα, βίνδιξ, βιόκουρος, βισήλεκτος, βρουμάλια, δέκρετον, δηληγατεύω, δηληγατίων, δηποτᾶτος, δηφήνσωρ, δικτάτωρ, δίλωρος, δομεστικός, δουκηνάριος, δουκιανός, δούξ, ἐκστρανήιος, ἐμαγκιπατίων, ἐμαγκιπᾶτος, ἐξάκτωρ, ἐξκέπτωρ, ἐξπελλεύω, ἤδικτον, ἰλλούστριος, ἰμπεράτωρ, ἰοῦγον, καγκελλάριος, Καῖσαρ, Καισάρειος, Καισαριανός, καμψάριος, κανδιδᾶτος, κανονικάριος, Καπετώλιον, κεντηνάριος, κηνσίτωρ, κῆνσος, κηνσουάλιος, κήνσωρ, κιρκήσιος, κίρκος, κολλήγας, κολλήγιον, κολλητίων, κολωνία, κομάκτωρ, κομέτιον, κόμης, κομιτατήσιος, κομιτᾶτον, κομιτιανός, κομμενταρήσιος, κομμονιτώριον, κόνβεντος, κονδούκτωρ, κονσιστώριον, κονσουλάριος, κοντουβερνάλιος, κορρήκτωρ, κουαίστωρ, κουαιστώριος, κουβικουλαρία, κουβικουλάριος, κουβουκλεῖον, κουράτωρ, κουριῶσος, κουροπαλάτης, κουροπερσονάριος, Κυιρῖται, Λατῖνος, λιμιτόν, λουσώριον, μαγίστρατος, μαγιστριανός, μάγιστρος, Μαιουμᾶς, ματρῶνα, μεμοριάλιος, μουνικίπιον, νωμενκλάτωρ, ὀνοράριος, ὀρδινάριος 2, ὀρδινᾶτος, ὀστιάριος, ὀφφικιάλιος, ὀφφίκιον, ὀψίκιον, παγανικός, παγανός, πάκτον, παλατῖνος, παλάτιον, πατρίκιος, πατριμωνάλιος, πατριμώνιον, πάτρων, περεγρῖνος, πούβλικος, πραιπόσιτος, πραίτωρ, πραιτωριανός, πραιτώριον, πραιτώριος, πραίφεκτος, πριβᾶτος, πριβιλέγιον, πριμικήριος, πρίωρ, προβατωρία, πρόκεσσον, προκουράτωρ, προμῶτος, πρόξιμος, προτήκτωρ, ῥεφερενδάριος, ῥήξ, ῥιπάριος, ῥογάτωρ, Ῥωμανία, Ῥώμη, σαλτάριος, Σατορνάλια, σεκουνδοκήριος, Σευήρεια, σήκρητον, σιλεντιάριος, σιλέντιον, σουβαδιούβας, σοῦμμος, στατιωνάριος, στολᾶτος, τριβουνάλιον, τριβοῦνος, φακτιωνάριος, φαμιλιάριος, φιλοκλαύδιος, φίσκος, φωκάριον
Warfare and hunting	8	112: ἀγραρία, ἄλη, ἀρήνα, ἄρμα, ἀρματοῦρα, ἀρμικούστωρ, ἀστᾶτος, ἄστη, ἀστιάριος, ἀστίλιον, βαλλιστάριος, βήναβλον, βηξιλλάριος, βηξιλλατίων, βήξιλλον, βουκελλάριος, βυκινάτωρ, γαῖσος, γαλεάριος, δεκουρίων, δηληγάτωρ, δησέρτωρ, δουπλικάριος, δρακονάριος, δρομεδάριος, δωνατίουον, ἐξέρκετον, ἐξκουβίτωρ, ἐξπέδιτον, ἐξπλωράτωρ, ἐξτραορδινάριος, ἐσσεδάριος, ἠβοκᾶτος, ἰμαγίνιφερ, καμπιδούκτωρ,

among the different categories. Therefore I have divided all the Latin borrowings among the 22 categories, using the list of meanings for guidance on how the labels for the semantic fields should be interpreted, and have given absolute numbers.

[5] Only direct borrowings are included here, not derivatives, for comparability with the original study, which excluded derivatives (Haspelmath and Tadmor 2009: 13, 15).

κασίδιον, κασσίς, κάστελλος, καστρησιανός, καστρήσιος, κάστρον, καταφρακτάριος, κεντουρία, κεντουρίων, κιρκίτωρ, κλάσσα, κλασσικός, κλιβανάριος, κομιᾶτον, κοόρτη, κορνικουλάριος, κουιντανήσιος, λαγκιάριος, λεγεών, λεγεωνάριος, λιμιτάνεος, λοῦδος, λωρῖκα, μερμίλλων, μητατεύω, μητᾶτον, μητάτωρ, μισσίκιος, νούμερος, ὀπινάτωρ, ὀπτίων, ὀρδινάριος 1, οὐετερανός, οὐίγουλ, πεδατοῦρα, πληγᾶτος, πορταρῆσις, πραῖδα, πραίσεντον, πραισίδιον, πρίγκεψ, πριγκιπάλιος, πριγκίπια, πριμιπιλάριος, πριμίπιλον, πριμίπιλος, προβοκάτωρ, ῥητιάριος, σαγίττα, σαγιττάριος, σεκουνδαρούδης, σεκούτωρ, σενάτωρ, σησκουπλικάριος, σιγγλάριος, σίγνιφερ, σίγνον, σικάριον, σικάριος, σκουτάριον, σκουτάριος, σκρίβων, σουκκέσσωρ, σουμμαρούδης, σπεκουλάτωρ, στατίων, στάτωρ, στράτωρ, σχολάριος, τεσσαράριος, τίρων, τιρωνᾶτον, τοῦρμα, φαβρικήσιος, Φλαουιάλιος, φοιδεράτος, φοσσᾶτον

Clothing and grooming	2	55: ἀβερτή, ἀβόλλης, ἀλίκλιον, ἀμικτώριον, βάλτιον, βαρβαρικάριος, βεστιαρίτης, βεστίον, βίρρος, βλάττα, βράκαι, βρακάριος, βράκιον, βραχιάλιον, γουνάριος, δελματική, δελματικόν, καλιγάριος, καλίγιον, κάλιξ, κάλτιος, καμίσιον, καμπάγιον, κάμπιστρον, καρακάλλιον, καράκαλλον, κέντρων, κολλάριον, κουκούλλιον, κουσούλιον, Λαδικηνός, λανάριος, λανᾶτον, μαντίον, Μουτουνήσιος, μυρσινᾶτος, ὀράριον, παλλιόλιον, παλλίολον, πάλλιον, παρατοῦρα, πεξός, πλουμάριος, πλουμίον, προμάξιμον, σάγος, σάπων, σηρικάριος, σόλιον 1, ταλάριον, φεμινάλια, φίβλα, φιβλατώριον, φολιᾶτον, φοῦνδα
Food and drink	7	52: ἀλιμέντα, ἅλιξ 1, ἀμποῦλλα, ἀμπούλλιον, ἀνισᾶτος, ἀπαλαρέα, ἀψινθᾶτος, βουκκᾶς, βουκκελλᾶτον, βουκκίον, βοῦλβα, ἰσίκιον, κάπιτον, κελλάριος, κιβάριον, κιβάριος, κονδιτάριος, κονδῖτον, κούκκουμα, κοχλιάριον, λαγήνιον, λάρδος, λίγλα, λουκάνικον, μάγκιψ, μακελλάριος, μοῦστος, ὀξύγγιον, ὅρριον, ὀψωνάτωρ, πανάριον, πάστιλλος, πάτελλα, πέρνα, προπινάριος, ῥοσᾶτον, σαλγαμάριος, σάλγαμον, σάρδα, σιλιγνάριος, σιλίγνιον, σκουτέλλιον, σκούτλιον, σουβαλάριον, σπικᾶτον, τρούλλα, φαίκλα, Φαλερῖνος, Φαλέρνος, φοῦρνος, φοῦσκα, φρουμεντάριος
Possession	9	50: ἀδιτεύω, ἀδιτίων, ἀργεντάριος, ἀσσάριον, βιατικόν, βόνος, δηνάριον, δηπόσιτον, διάριον, δισκούσσωρ, δουκηναρία, ἐξεμπλάριον, κάμπανος, κεντηνάριον, κοδράντης, κολλεκτάριος, κομμερκιάριος, κομόδιον, κουιντάνα, κούμουλον, λαργιτίων, λαργιτιωναλικός, λεντιάριος, ληγατάριος, ληγᾶτον, ληγᾶτος, μιλιαρήσιον, μονῆτα, μονητάριος, νουμεράριος, νοῦμμος, ὁλοκόττινος, οὐσούφρουκτος, πεκούλιον, πιμεντάριος, προδηληγᾶτον, προπριεταρία, ῥόγα, ῥογεύω, σαλάριον, σηστέρτιος, σιμίσιον, σπόρτουλον, στιπένδιον, ταβέρνα, τεστάτωρ, τριμήσιον, φαλκίδιον, φιδεικομμισσάριος, φιδεικόμμισσον
Basic actions and technology	12	36: ἀκισκλάριος, ἀκίσκλος, ἀκουάριος, βάκλον, βῆλον, γράδος, δισέκτωρ, κᾶσος, κατήνα, κιστέρνα, κορριγία, κουαδράριος, κοῦπα, λάμνα, λῶρος, μαρμαράριος, μηνσώριον, μιλιάριον, μῶλος, ὀρδινατίων, ὄρδινος, πᾶλος, πίλα 2, Ῥωμανήσιος, σίτλα, σουβλίον, τρακταΐζω, τρακτᾶτος, τρακτεύω, τρακτός, φάβριξ, φάκτον, φασκία, φόλλις, φραγέλλιον, φραγελλόω
The house	3	33: ἀκκουβιτάλιον, ἀκκούβιτον, ἀρμάριον, ἄτριον, βηλάριον, βήσαλον, κάγκελλος, κανδήλη, καννίον, κέλλα, κελλάριον, κερβικάριον, κηρίολος, κορτίνα, λέντιον, λῶδιξ, μανδήλη, μάππα, μαππίον, ὀσπίτιον, παπυλιών, πλουμάκιον, πόρτα, πουλβῖνον, σκάλα, σκάμνος, σόλιον 2, σουδάριον, σπεκλάριον, σπέκλον, συμψέλλιον, σωλάριον, φακιάλιον
Time	13	28: Ἀδριανός, ἀννάλιος, Ἀπρίλιος, Αὔγουστος 2, Γαῖος, Γερμανίκειος, Γερμανικός, Δεκέμβριος, Δομιτιανός, Δρουσιεύς, Δρουσίλληος, Εἰδοί, Ἰανουάριος, ἰνδικτίων, Ἰούλιος, Ἰούνιος, Καλάνδαι, καλανδαρικά, Κοιντίλιος, Μάϊος, Μάρτιος, Νερώνειος, Νοέμβριος, Νῶναι, Ὀκτώβριος, πραιτέριτος, Σεπτέμβριος, Φεβρουάριος

Speech and language	14	27: βρέβιον, βυκάνη, βυκινίζω, κομμεντάριον, κομμέντον, κωδικίλλος, κῶδιξ, λιβέλλος, λιβράριος, μάτριξ, μεμβράνα, νοτάριος, πραίκων, πριμισκρίνιος, ρέσκριπτον, σηκρητάριος, σκρίβας, σκρινιάριος, σκρίνιον, ταβέλλα, ταβελλάριος, ταβελλίων, τάβλα, ταβλάριος, τίτλος, φορμαλεία, χαρτουλάριος
Law	4	25: ἄκτα, ἀντικήνσωρ, βέρβον, δηλάτωρ, δίγεστον, ἐξκουσατίων, ἐξκουσεύω, ἰνστιτοῦτα, ἰουράτωρ, καπικλάριος, κάρκαρον, κλαβικουλάριος, κογνιτίων, κομπρόμισσον, κομφιρματεύω, κουστωδία, κυαιστιωνάριος, λεγίτιμος, μανδᾶτον, μανδάτωρ, ὀπινίω, περσονάλιος, προφεσσίων, ρέος, στατοῦτος
Agriculture and vegetation	6	19: βεττονική, βικίον, βωλήτης, δωράκινον, ἐβίσκος, ἰντύβιον, ἴντυβον, ἰούγερον, κίτριον, κίτρον, κόλων, μαρούλιον, ὀρριάριος, πραικόκκιον, πωμάριον, σαξίφραγον, φάβα, φασίολος, φόσσα
Motion	18	18: βαστέρνιον, βερεδάριος, βουρδωνάριος, καβαλλάριος, κανάλιον, καρούχα, κάρρον, κλεισούρα, κούρσωρ, λεκτεῖκα, λεκτικάριος, λίβερνος, μουλίων, ραῖδα, σαβούρα, σαλιβάριον, σέλλα, στράτα
Religion and belief	1	17: αὔγουρ, Αὐγουστεῖον, Αὐγουστήσιοι, βότον, βούλλα, Καπετώλιος, μεμόριον, Ναυατιανός, Οὐαλεντινιανοί, ποντίφεξ, Σαβελλιανός, Σαβελλίζω, σάκρος, σάλιος, Σευηριανός, φετιάλιος, Χριστιανός
Animals	10	9: βέρεδος, βουρδών, καπίστριον, κούρκουμον, μοῦλα, μοῦλος, περιστερόπουλλος, πουλλίον, στάβλον
Quantity	15	7: κουμουλᾶτος, μιλιάριος, μίλιον, μόδιος, ξέστης, οὐγγία, πρῖμος
Spatial relations	21	4: ὄγκινος, πᾶγος, πληναρία, ρεγεών
Sense perception	22	4: ἄσπρος, γάλβινος, ρούσιος, σκουτουλᾶτος
Kinship	19	3: ρεπούδιον, σπούριος, φαμιλία
The body	20	3: αἶγροι, καυσάριος, πανίκουλα
The physical world	17	3: κάμπος, κάρβων, σάλτον
Emotions and values	16	1: οὐά
Cognition	11	None

Figure 11 Direct borrowings classified according to the categories of Haspelmath and Tadmor (2009: 22–34)

In modern languages at least some of the differences between semantic fields are linked to historical factors that resulted in significant numbers of cultural borrowings in specific categories penetrating into most languages of the world: Christianity, Islam, types of clothing and housing originally developed in Europe, etc. (Tadmor 2009: 64–5). The historical factors affecting ancient Greek were different, though not entirely unrelated. Christianity spread from Greek speakers to Latin speakers rather than the reverse, resulting in the typologically unusual low number of religious loanwords among the Latin contributions to Greek. But centuries of Roman government and Roman military presence left their mark with unusually high numbers of loanwords in the categories of social and political relations and warfare/hunting. At the same time, there are some similarities between the Greek situation and that found in modern languages: words in the categories of spatial relations, sense perception, kinship, the body, and the physical world are unlikely to be borrowed, and words for clothing are very likely to be borrowed.

Can this division into semantic fields tell us more about ancient Greek borrowing practices? Would more detailed analysis reveal not only how Greek speakers compare with speakers of other languages, but more about the factors that might have influenced their own borrowing habits in particular? Perhaps not, for this classification system does not fit the Greek language very well. For example, two of the borrowings listed under 'the physical world', κάμπος 'field' and σάλτον 'forest', are not the normal Greek words for fields and forests: κάμπος is a field used for military purposes, and σάλτον is a forest that forms part of the imperial estate. From a Greek perspective the former is a military term and the latter part of the vocabulary for referring to the emperor and his property; they do not really belong in the 'physical world' category. Likewise ῥεπούδιον 'divorce letter' is classified under 'kinship', because that is where divorce falls in the meaning list for the loanword typology project, but in Greek ῥεπούδιον is part of the vocabulary of law, not of kinship. And βυκάνη 'trumpet' is classified under 'speech and language', because the typologists considered trumpeting primarily a form of communication, but in Greek βυκάνη refers to a Roman army trumpet and belongs to military vocabulary. Many other terms listed above are similarly misclassified from a Greek perspective, and some categories are very broad, obscuring a narrower area in which Latin borrowings are particularly frequent. For example, 'warfare and hunting' combines an area with many loanwords (warfare) and one with very few (hunting).

In order to conduct a deeper and more revealing examination of Greek borrowing practices, as opposed to a broad comparison of how Greek compares to other languages, adjustments to these classifications would be needed. Not only would some words need to be moved from one category to another, but some categories would need to be split up and new ones added. But any such changes would ruin the comparability with other languages that is the point of a typological investigation: since the investigations of other languages all treated divorce as part of kinship and trumpeting as part of speech, whether or not such classifications were really appropriate for the languages concerned, statistical comparisons would become invalid if those meanings were classified differently in Greek. And such comparisons would become impossible if the list of categories itself were different for Greek. Therefore little can be done with the material in Figure 11 apart from the general observations already made.

10.2.2 Internal Greek classification of borrowings and derivatives

To understand Greek on its own terms and identify the semantic fields in which Greek speakers chose to borrow Latin words, one could start from the typological classification and adapt it to fit Greek better. But since the only particular value to the typological classification, its comparability, would be destroyed as soon as any adaptations are made, it is better to start afresh from the Greek data rather than using a pre-existing set of semantic fields.[6] It is important to try to understand which semantic features were shared by significant numbers of loanwords, and then as far as possible to group the borrowings by the shared semantic features most relevant to their borrowing. For example, many borrowings relate to food or to means of transportation, and therefore it is likely that cultural borrowing in those areas created genuine clusters of loanwords. But there are only a few borrowings designating animals: βέρεδος 'fast horse', βουρδών 'mule', μοῦλα 'female mule', μοῦλος 'male mule', περιστερόπουλλος 'small dove', and πουλλίον 'chicken'. And most of these animals were used by the ancients as means of transportation, while the remainder were used as food. Therefore the words for animals were probably borrowed because of being words for means of transportation or for food, not because of being words for animals. It follows that 'animals' is not a meaningful semantic category for Latin loanwords in Greek, and the words concerned should be grouped with transportation or food as appropriate.

It is also worth considering the semantic fields of the loanwords that are derivatives rather than direct borrowings. Although these cannot tell us anything about borrowing tendencies, they contribute to the overall extent to which Greek

---

[6] Such a classification was also attempted by Viscidi (1944: 43), using substantially different data that included both codeswitches and Byzantine material up to AD 1100. He found the following semantic distribution of Latin words: military 431, state 383, law 341, measures 76, calendar 32, court 67, Roman religion 49, Christianity 37, circus shows 78, animals 73, plants 113, clothing 145; other 1,099. As he did not reveal the actual words concerned, however, it is impossible to know exactly how he defined these categories.

vocabulary was Latinate in particular areas. Derivatives do not show exactly the same patterns as direct borrowings, and sometimes the differences are revealing.

In what follows, all 820 Latin loanwords are grouped by semantic field. Words with meanings falling into more than one semantic field are placed in the category that I believe was most relevant to the original borrowing; thus for example οὐγγία means both 'ounce' (suggesting a classification as a measure) and 'one twelfth of an inheritance' in Roman law (suggesting a classification with the legal terminology), but the former meaning is attested earlier and must be the one in which the term was originally borrowed. Sometimes meanings in two classifications appear simultaneously, particularly when a single meaning actually falls into both classifications, as with βάλτιον 'belt'. Because that originally designated a Roman sword-belt, it belonged from the beginning both to military terminology and to the vocabulary of clothing – but nevertheless the military element was probably a more important factor in the borrowing, because βάλτιον was borrowed at a period when Greek speakers were adopting many military words but not yet many words for clothing. Sometimes the reason for putting a word into a particular classification is not obvious from the translation given, and in those cases consultation of the Lexicon (§3.2) will normally reveal the rationale for the classification. But classifications by semantic field are ultimately subjective, and other scholars with a better understanding of the realia behind these words may be able to improve on my decisions. It might therefore be prudent not to put too much reliance in the fine details of the results below – but the general trends are clear enough that changing details would not alter them.

In these groupings loanwords are also divided by the period in which they were borrowed or created: 'early' means words that entered Greek in or before the first century AD, 'middle' ones entering in the second, third, and fourth centuries, and 'late' ones entering in the fifth and sixth centuries. Overall, 55% of direct borrowings are dated to the middle period, with 23% in the early and 22% in the late period (§8.1.1). When the

borrowings in a particular semantic field have a chronological distribution roughly similar to the overall one, borrowing in that field remained fairly constant over time in terms of what percentage of all new borrowings it accounted for. But semantic fields with a different chronological distribution varied over time in what proportion of new borrowings they constituted.

The semantic fields are also compared in terms of the percentage of words that survived into Byzantine and into modern Greek. Here the baseline is the average survival rates discussed in §8.2: overall, 75% of loanwords persisted into the Byzantine period and 29% into modern Greek.

Words referring to useful objects are underlined, and words for roles have a wavy underline; the importance of those features, and of other factors that unite words in different categories, will be discussed in §10.2.3.

A. The emperor, his household, and his property (28 borrowings, or 4% of all borrowings; no derivatives):

Early (4 borrowings = 14%): Αὐγουστεῖον 'Augusteum', Αὔγουστος 1 'emperor', Καῖσαρ 'emperor', παλάτιον 'Palatine, palace'.

Middle (13 borrowings = 46%): Αὐγοῦστα 'empress', δομεστικός 1 (a title), δωνατίουον 'money given to soldiers as a gratuity from the emperor', κομιτατήσιος 'belonging to the imperial court', κομιτᾶτον '(imperial) retinue', κονσιστώριον 'imperial assembly', κουβικουλάριος 'chamberlain', παλατῖνος (a title), πατριμωνάλιος 'belonging to the imperial property, πριβᾶτος 'private (to the emperor)', πατριμώνιον '(imperial) property', σάκρος 'pertaining to the imperial household', σάλτον '(imperial) forest'.

Late (11 borrowings = 39%): ἀδνοτατίων 'imperial decision on a petition', ἐξκουβίτωρ 'soldier of the imperial guard', κομμονιτώριον '(imperial) letter of instruction', κουροπαλάτης 'palace supervisor', πραίσεντον 'troops serving in the imperial palace', προβατωρία 'imperial letter of commendation', πρόκεσσον '(imperial) procession', ῥέσκριπτον 'rescript', σιλέντιον 'imperial audience', σκρίβων 'officer of the imperial bodyguard', σχολάριος 'one of the imperial guards'.

This is the only semantic field in which all the loanwords are direct borrowings, a situation that is probably not accidental. Many of these words had Greek equivalents with the same basic lexical meaning as the Latin words borrowed; for example *sacer* 'sacred' had as Greek equivalents ἱερός and ἅγιος, and therefore when imperial correspondence was referred to in Latin as *sacra*, one might have expected it to be called ἱερά or ἁγία in Greek. Yet σάκρος was created to reflect this meaning of *sacer*. Likewise 'retinue' could have been expressed with ἀκολουθία, 'private' with ἴδιος or οἰκεῖος, and 'forest' with ὕλη. Much of the motivation for these borrowings must have been a feeling on the part of Greek speakers that Latin words were fitting for concepts related to the emperor. And their preference for creating new words in this category by direct borrowing meant that derivatives with meanings in this category were never formed, though these words sometimes formed derivatives with meanings in other categories.

These borrowings are on the whole later than average, meaning that as time went on words connected to the emperor made up a higher and higher percentage of all borrowings. That change is no doubt related to the increasing relevance of the imperial household to Greek speakers after the fourth-century creation of a second imperial capital at Constantinople.

Words in this category have the highest survival rate into Byzantine Greek of any semantic field (96%), but a low survival rate into modern Greek (14%). Both those figures are evidently due to the continuity of the imperial structures into the Byzantine period and their disappearance after that.

B. Law (48 borrowings, or 7% of all borrowings; 7 derivatives, or 5% of all derivatives):

Early (2 borrowings = 4%): ἄκτα 'acts', κουράτωρ 'curator'. No derivatives.

Middle (18 borrowings = 38%): βινδίκτα (a type of manumission), βόνος 'good', ἐξκουσατίων 'grounds for being excused', ἤδικτον 'edict', ἰουράτωρ 'sworn witness', καυσάριος 'dismissed because of illness', κογνιτίων (a type of judicial investigation), κωδικίλλος 'codicil',

ληγατάριος 'legatee', ληγᾶτον 'legacy', ὀπινίω 'legal opinion', πεκούλιον 'personal property', περεγρῖνος 'foreign', προκουράτωρ 'administrator', ῥεπούδιον 'divorce letter', σήκρητον 'court', ταβελλίων 'notary', φιδεικόμμισσον 'legacy paid at the discretion of the main heir'. **Derivatives** (2): κουρατορεύω 'act as curator', κουρατορία 'office of curator'.

Late (28 borrowings = 58%): ἀδιτεύω 'take possession of an inheritance', ἀδιτίων 'act of taking possession of an inheritance', ἀννάλιος 'yearly', ἀντικήνσωρ 'teacher of law', βέρβον 'word', δέκρετον 'decree', δίγεστον 'Digest', ἐμαγκιπατίων 'emancipation', ἐμαγκιπᾶτος 'emancipated', ἐξκουσεύω 'excuse', ἰνστιτοῦτα 'introduction to Roman law', κομπρόμισσον 'arbitrated compromise', κομφιρματεύω 'confirm', κῶδιξ 'book', λεγίτιμος 'based on law', μανδᾶτον 'consensual contract', μανδάτωρ 'guarantor', ὀνοράριος 'honorary', οὐσούφρουκτος 'usufruct', πάκτον 'agreement', περσονάλιος 'personal', προπριεταρία 'ownership', ῥέος 'defendant', στατοῦτος 'fixed', τεστάτωρ 'maker of a will', φάκτον 'action', φαλκίδιον 'minimum portion of an estate reserved by law for the heir(s)', φιδεικομμισσάριος 'left in trust'. **Derivatives** (5): ἐνναούγκιον 'three quarters of an inheritance', ἐξαούγκιον 'half an inheritance', ληγατεύω 'bequeath', πακτεύω 'make an agreement', παράτιτλον 'marginal scholium'.

The questions of how many legal loanwords there really were and exactly when they were borrowed are thorny ones. The criteria used in this study suggest that only 48 Latin terms and 7 derivatives had become established as part of Greek by AD 600, but many more were clearly part of Greek in the Byzantine period, and many of those are first attested before AD 600. From the evidence directly available to us, those additional terms seem to have functioned as codeswitches during antiquity and as loanwords only later, but as we have seen (§9.5.6), our evidence could be distorted by the enormous body of sixth-century legal works and the disappearance of most earlier Greek-language legal material. Therefore the borrowings in this category, which appear to be much later than average, may actually have had a more normal chronological distribution, and more than 48 legal terms may have been borrowed during antiquity. Scholars working on Byzantine Greek often see law as the semantic field with the greatest number of loanwords.[7]

Notable among the legal terms is the high percentage of words concerning inheritance: after Roman citizenship was extended across the empire in AD 212, inheritance rights in Greek-speaking areas became subject to Roman law. Inheritance thus became an area in which ordinary citizens were particularly likely to interact with Roman law, and many of the terms concerned were widely distributed, though others remained confined to legal texts.

Legal loanwords have a very high survival rate into Byzantine Greek (95%), but a low survival rate into modern Greek (16%). Byzantine law was based on the texts established in the sixth century, but that tradition ended with the fall of Byzantium.

C. The military (apart from roles involving proximity to the emperor), including all weapons and armour (106 borrowings, or 16% of all borrowings; 8 derivatives, or 5% of all derivatives):

Early (38 borrowings = 36%): ἄλη 'squadron', βάλτιον 'belt', βηξιλλάριος (a rank), βήξιλλον 'cavalry standard', βυκάνη 'trumpet', γαῖσος 'javelin', γαλεάριος 'soldier's servant', δεκουρίων 'decurion', δουπλικάριος 'soldier receiving double pay', ἰμπεράτωρ 'commander', κάμπος 'field', καστρήσιος 'of the camp', κάστρον 'army camp', κλάσσα 'fleet', κεντουρία 'century', κεντουρίων 'centurion', κομιᾶτον 'leave of absence', κοόρτη 'cohort', κορνικουλάριος 'assistant', κουιντανήσιος (a role), λεγεών 'legion', λεγεωνάριος 'legionary', λίβερνος (a kind of ship), λωρῖκα 'corselet', μισσίκιος (discharged soldier), ὀπτίων 'assistant', οὐετερανός 'veteran', πραισίδιον 'garrison', πραιτωριανός 'praetorian', πριγκίπια 'headquarters', σάγος 'cloak', σίγνον (multiple meanings), σουκκέσσωρ 'relief', σπεκουλάτωρ (a military functionary), στάτωρ (an army position), στράτωρ 'groom', τεσσαράριος 'officer who receives and distrib-

utes the watchword', τοῦρμα 'troop'. **Derivative** (1): βυκανητής 'trumpeter'.

Middle (53 borrowings = 50%): αἴγροι 'ill', ἀρματοῦρα 'military training', ἀρμικούστωρ 'person in charge of weapons', ἀστᾶτος (a rank), ἄστη 'spear', ἀστιάριος (a role), ἀστίλιον 'shaft', βαλλιστάριος 'catapult operator', βηξιλλατίων 'troop', βυκινάτωρ 'trumpeter', βυκινίζω 'blow the trumpet', δηπόσιτον 'soldier's savings', δησέρτωρ 'deserter', δρακονάριος 'standard-bearer', δρομεδάριος 'camel-rider', ἐξπλωράτωρ 'scout', ἠβοκᾶτος 'veteran called back into service', ἰμαγίνιφερ 'standard-bearer', καμπιδούκτωρ 'drill-master', κασίδιον 'helmet', κασσίς 'helmet', κάστελλος 'fort', καστρησιανός 'soldier of the frontier guard', καταφρακτάριος 'armoured', κιρκίτωρ 'inspector of frontier posts', κλασσικός 'naval', λαγκιάριος 'lancer', μητᾶτον 'quarters', μητάτωρ 'measurer', νούμερος (a unit), ὀπινάτωρ (a role), ὀρδινάριος 1 (a rank), πραῖδα 'loot', πραιτώριος 'praetorian', πρίγκεψ (a rank), πριγκιπάλιος 'officer', πριμιπιλάριος (a rank), πριμίπιλον (a concept related to the πριμιπιλάριος), πριμίπιλος (a rank), πρῖμος 'first', σαγιττάριος 'archer', σενάτωρ (a rank), σησκουπλικάριος 'soldier receiving 1.5 times the normal rewards', σιγγλάριος (a role), σίγνιφερ 'standard-bearer', σικάριον 'dagger', σκουτάριος 'shield-bearer', στατίων 'station', στιπένδιον 'wages', τίρων 'recruit', τιρωνᾶτον 'body of recruits', φαβρικήσιος 'armourer', Φλαουιάλιος (a rank). **Derivatives** (6): ἀγαρεύω 'lie in garrison', κιβαριάτωρ (an army official), λιβερνάριος 'sailor on a *liburna* ship', λωρίκιον 'corselet', πραιδεύω 'plunder', συνουετρανός 'fellow veteran'.

Late (15 borrowings = 14%): ἀγραρία 'garrison', ἄρμα 'weapons', βήναβλον 'hunting-spear', βουκελλάριος 'member of armed escort', δηληγάτωρ (an official), ἐξέρκετον 'army', ἐξπέδιτον 'army camp', ἐξτραορδινάριος 'unusual', κλιβανάριος 'armoured cavalryman', λιμιτάνεος 'frontier troops', μητατεύω 'commandeer', πληγᾶτος 'wounded', σαγίττα 'arrow', σκουτάριον 'shield', φοσσᾶτον 'boundary'. **Derivative** (1): καστέλλιον 'fort'.

Military borrowings are on average earlier than borrowings in most other semantic fields, no doubt because the Roman army often served

---

[7] Kahane and Kahane (1972–6: 502, 1982: 129–30) find c. 700 legal loanwords, and Zilliacus (1935a: 99) calls them 'unzählig'.

as a conduit for the early introduction of Latin terminology. Many Greek speakers probably first encountered Latin speakers either when the army arrived in their area or when they themselves joined the army. Interaction with the army did not necessarily take place in Latin, and even joining it did not necessarily mean learning to speak Latin, for many units in the East were primarily Greek speaking. But some Greek-speaking army recruits did learn Latin, and even those who did not were constantly exposed to Latin: all army units included some Latin speakers, and some activities (at a minimum, receiving and responding to orders from the central leadership) were normally carried out in Latin.[8] The direct contact with Latin in this area is also reflected in the higher percentage of direct borrowings as compared to derivatives. An unusually high percentage of the terms in this area describe roles, usually military ranks and duties; some of these had Greek equivalents, but it is likely that the Latin terms were frequent in the Greek spoken within the Roman army, and that they spread outwards from that source.

Military terminology had a lower survival rate than many other semantic fields, probably because of periodic reorganizations that abolished old roles and created new ones. Only 65% of the loanwords in this category lasted into the Byzantine period, and only 19% survived into modern Greek.

D. Other vocabulary of government, including state priesthoods and purely honorary titles (108 borrowings, or 16% of all borrowings; 23 derivatives, or 16% of all derivatives):

Early (21 borrowings = 19%): αἰράριον 'public treasury', ἀννῶνα 'grain supply', αὔγουρ 'augur', Αὐγουστάλιος (a title), βενεφικιάριος (a title), βικάριος 'deputy', δικτάτωρ 'dictator', Καισάρειος (a title), κῆνσος 'assessment for taxes', κολωνία 'colony', κομέτιον 'assembly', κουιντάνα (a tax), κουστωδία 'guard', λιβέλλος 'petition', μουνικίπιον 'self-governing community', πατρίκιος 'patrician', πραιτώριον 'official residence', σάλιος 'Salic priest', φετιάλιος

'fetial priest', φιλοκλαύδιος 'friend of Claudius', φίσκος 'imperial treasury'. **Derivatives** (4): δικτατωρεία 'dictatorship', δικτατωρεύω 'be dictator', φιλόκαισαρ 'loyal to Caesar', φιλορώμαιος 'friend of the Romans'.

Middle (58 borrowings = 54%): ἀβάκτης 'registrar', ἀβρέβις (a title), ἀδιούτωρ (a title), ἀκομενταρήσιος (a title), ἀκτουάριος 'keeper of records', ἀννούμερος (a title), ἀννωνάριος 'official administering the grain supply', βιόκουρος 'person in charge of roads', βισήλεκτος (a title), δηληγατεύω 'assign as tax to be paid', δηληγατίων 'annual declaration by the state of the amount of tax to be paid', δηφήνσωρ (a title), δίλωρος (a title), δουκηνάριος (a title), δούξ (a title), ἐξάκτωρ 'tax collector', ἰνδικτίων 'fifteen-year tax period', Καισαριανός (a title), κανδιδᾶτος (a title), κάπιτον 'ration allowance', κάρκαρον 'prison', κηνσίτωρ (a title), κήνσωρ 'censor', κόμης 'count', κορρήκτωρ (an official), κουαίστωρ 'quaestor', κουαιστώριος 'of a quaestor', κουριῶσος 'inquiry agent', κούρσωρ (a title), κυαιστιωνάριος 'torturer', ληγᾶτος 'deputy', λιμιτόν 'frontier', μαγίστρατος 'magistrate', μαγιστριανός (an official), μάγιστρος (a title), ματρῶνα 'noblewoman', μονῆτα 'mint', ὀρδινάριος 2 'regular', ὀρδινᾶτος (a title), ὀφφικιάλιος (a title), ὀφφίκιον 'official appointment', πᾶγος '(rural) district', ποντίφεξ (a title), πραιπόσιτος (a title), πραίτωρ 'praetor', πραίφεκτος 'prefect', πριμικήριος (a title), προμῶτος 'promoted', προτήκτωρ (a title), προφεσσίων 'declaration (of birth)', ρεγεών '(urban) district', ρήξ '(western) king', ριπάριος 'water-watchman', Ῥωμανία 'Roman empire', σούμμος 'highest in rank', στολᾶτος (a title), τριβοῦνος 'tribune', φρουμεντάριος '(official) concerned with victualling'. **Derivatives** (11): ἀννωνιακός 'belonging to the grain supply', ἀννωνικός 'concerning the grain supply', δουκικός 'pertaining to the *dux*', ἐξακτορεύω 'be a tax collector', ἐξακτορία 'office of the tax collector', μαγιστρότης 'office of the *magister*', μητροκολωνεία 'mother-colony', παγαρχέω 'hold the office of pagarch', παγάρχης 'pagarch', παγαρχία 'district under a pagarch', τρακτευτής (an official).

Late (29 borrowings = 27%): ἀσηκρῆτις 'imperial secretary', Αὐγουσταλιανός 'pertaining to the

---

[8] J. N. Adams (2003: 599–623, 630–4, 760–1), Hatzopoulos (2008: 133–4), Rochette (1997: 147–50), Zilliacus (1935a: 113–70).

Augustalis', βεστιαρίτης (a title), βικαρία 'office of deputy', βίνδιξ (a tax official), δουκιανός 'pertaining to the *dux*', ἐξπελλεύω 'collect taxes', ἰλλούστριος 'noble', ἰοῦγον (a tax assessment unit), καγκελλάριος 1 (a title), κανονικάριος 'tax collector', καπικλάριος 'prison guard', κηνσουάλιος (a tax official), κλαβικουλάριος 'prison guard', κομιτιανός 'of a count', κονσουλάριος 'consular, provincial governor', λαργιτίων 'distribution of gifts', λαργιτιωναλικός 'related to distribution of gifts', μεμοριάλιος (a class of clerk in the civil service), μονητάριος 'coin-maker', πριμισκρίνιος 'chief secretary', πρίωρ (a title), προδηληγᾶτον 'advance instructions about taxes', ρεφερενδάριος (an official), ρογάτωρ (an official), σεκουνδοκήριος (a title), σιλεντιάριος 'silentiary', τριβουνάλιον 'tribunal', χαρτουλάριος 'archivist'. **Derivatives** (8): ἀννωνεύομαι 'have as an allowance', ἐξπελλευτής 'tax collector', πατρικία 'wife of a patrician', πατρικιότης 'patriciate', κομήτισσα 'countess', πρωτοπατρίκιος 'first patrician', ριπαρία 'office of *riparius*', φισκοσυνήγορος (a title).

This is a large, important category in both borrowings and derivatives, and its importance remained roughly constant over time. Many of the terms describe roles and/or are titles. The survival rate into Byzantine Greek is average (75%), but that into modern Greek below average (18%). For more analysis, see §10.2.3.

E. Measures, including calendar terms (34 borrowings, or 5% of all borrowings; 11 derivatives, or 7% of all derivatives):

Early (27 borrowings = 79%): Ἀπρίλιος 'April', Αὔγουστος 2 'August', Γαῖος '(month) of Gaius', Γερμανίκειος '(month) of Germanicus', Γερμανικός '(month of) Germanicus', Δεκέμβριος 'December', Δομιτιανός '(month of) Domitian', Δρουσιεύς '(month) of Drusus', Δρουσιλλῆος '(month) of Drusilla', Εἰδοί 'Ides', Ἰανουάριος 'January', Ἰούλιος 'July', Ἰούνιος 'June', Καλάνδαι 'Calends', Κοιντίλιος 'July', Μάϊος 'May', Μάρτιος 'March', μίλιον 'mile', μόδιος (a measure), Νοέμβριος 'November', Νερώνειος '(month) of Nero', Νῶναι 'Nones', ξέστης 'pint', Ὀκτώβριος 'October', οὐγγία 'ounce', Σεπτέμβριος 'September', Φεβρουάριος 'February'. **Derivative** (1): ἡμίξεστον 'half-pint'.

Middle (7 borrowings = 21%): Ἀδριανός '(month of) Hadrian', ἰούγερον (a land measurement), κεντηνάριον (a weight), κουμουλᾶτος 'heaping', κούμουλον (a measure), μιλιάριον (a measure), μιλιάριος 'of a thousand'. **Derivatives** (6): διούγκιον 'two ounces', ἑξάξεστος 'holding six pints', ἡμιούγκιον 'half-ounce', ξεστιαῖος 'of a pint', ξεστίον 'pint', οὐγκιασμός 'measurement in twelfths'.

Late (no borrowings). **Derivatives** (4): ἑξαξεστιαῖος 'holding six pints', πενταξεστιαῖος 'holding five pints', τετραξεστιαῖος 'holding four pints', τριμόδιον 'vessel holding three pecks'.

The borrowings in this area are strikingly early, with over three quarters of borrowings made before AD 100 and only derivatives appearing in the late period. All the derivatives involve measurements of weight or volume; the calendar terms are all direct borrowings. Most of the calendar terms seem to have been originally imported by Latin speakers writing in Greek (§8.1.4), and other measurements may have been introduced by the Roman provincial authorities. For the derivatives of the measures, see §4.6.2. Words in this category have an unusually high 47% survival rate into modern Greek (67% into Byzantine Greek).

F. Public games and festivals (24 borrowings, or 4% of all borrowings; 6 derivatives, or 4% of all derivatives):

Early (2 borrowings = 8%): μερμίλλων (a kind of gladiator), ρητιάριος (a kind of gladiator). **Derivatives** (3): Καπετώλια 'Capitoline games', Ῥωμαῖα '*ludi Romani*', Ῥωμαϊστής 'actor of Latin comedies'.

Middle (20 borrowings = 83%): Ἀντώνεια 'Antonine festival', ἀρῆνα 'arena', Αὐγούστειος 'festival of Augustus', βενετιανός 'of the blue circus faction', βένετος 'of the blue circus faction', ἐσσεδάριος (a kind of gladiator), κιρκήσιος 'of the circus', κίρκος 'circus', λοῦδος 'gladiatorial school', λουσώριον 'place for games', Μαιουμᾶς 'May day', πᾶλος 'squad of gladiators', προβοκάτωρ (a kind of gladiator), ρούσιος 'of the red circus faction', Σατορνάλια 'Saturnalia', Σευήρεια 'Severan games', σεκουνδαρούδης (a position in a gladiatorial establishment), σεκούτωρ (a kind of gladiator), σουμμαρούδης 'chief instructor in a gladiatorial establishment', φακτιωνάριος 'leader of a circus faction'. **Derivatives** (3): ἰσοκαπετώλιος 'equivalent to Capitoline', Καπετωλιακός 'Capitoline', Καπετωλιονίκης 'victor in the Capitoline games'.

Late (2 borrowings = 8%): αὐράριος 'supporter', βρουμάλια 'festival of the winter solstice'. No derivatives.

The borrowings in this area concentrate in three categories: gladiators, circus factions, and names of festivals. These are all concepts imported by Romans, and to at least some extent by the Roman government authorities, who were often responsible for putting on games and festivals. Words in this category have the lowest survival rate of any semantic field, with only 33% lasting into the Byzantine period and 13% into modern Greek: many festivals and types of entertainment were discontinued before the end of antiquity.

G. Money and finance, apart from taxes and other government finance (28 borrowings, or 4% of all borrowings; 6 derivatives, or 4% of all derivatives):

Early (9 borrowings = 32%): ἀρκάριος 'treasurer', ἀσσάριον 'penny', δηνάριον 'denarius', διάριον 'daily wage', κοδράντης (a coin), κομάκτωρ 'collector of money', νοῦμμος 'coin', σαλάριον 'salary', σηστέρτιος 'sesterce'. No derivatives.

Middle (13 borrowings = 46%): ἀργεντάριος 'banker', βιατικόν 'journey money', δισκούσσωρ 'auditor', δουκηναρία '200,000 sesterces', καλανδαρικά 'new year's allowances', κεντηνάριος 'of 100,000 sesterces', κομόδιον 'gratuity', μιλιαρήσιον (a coin), νουμεράριος 'keeper of accounts', ὁλοκόττινος (a coin), σιμίσιον (a coin), σπόρτουλον (a kind of payment), φόλλις (a coin). **Derivatives** (3): κομακτορία 'bank', νούμμιον 'coin', τετραούγκιον (a coin).

Late (6 borrowings = 21%): κάμπανος 'steelyard', κολλεκτάριος 'banker', κομμερκιάριος 'merchant', ῥόγα 'distribution of wages', ῥογεύω 'pay in kind', τριμήσιον (a coin). **Derivatives** (3): ἀρκαρικός 'of the treasurer', καλανδικά 'new year's allowances', τριούγκιον (a coin).

Ten of the borrowings in this category are the names of coins produced by the Roman authorities, and most of these may have been originally introduced by Latin speakers (§8.1.4). (Two derivatives are also coin names, but as derivatives are Greek formations they are less likely to have originated with Latin speakers.) The directly borrowed coin names may have a different status from the other terms in this category, which show no particular signs of a connection with the Roman government. Survival rates, which do not differ significantly between those two groups, are average into the Byzantine period (74%) and low into modern Greek (18%).

H. Clothing, other wearable items, and textiles (65 borrowings, or 10% of all borrowings; 18 derivatives, or 12% of all derivatives):

Early (9 borrowings = 14%): ἀβόλλης 'thick woollen cloak', κάμπιστρον 'loincloth', κέντρων 'rag', λέντιον 'linen cloth', λῶδιξ 'blanket', παλλιόλιον 'small cloak', πάλλιον 'mantle', πουλβῖνον 'cushion', σουδάριον 'towel'. No derivatives.

Middle (47 borrowings = 72%): ἀβερτή 'backpack', ἀκκουβιτάλιον 'couch cover', ἀλίκλιον (a garment), ἀμικτώριον 'shawl', βαρβαρικάριος 'brocade-maker', βεστίον 'clothes', βηλάριον 'curtain', βῆλον 'covering', βίρρος 'hooded cloak', βλάττα 'purple (wool)', βούλλα 'Roman child's charm', βράκαι 'trousers', βρακάριος 'tailor', βράκιον 'trousers', βραχιάλιον 'bracelet', δελματική 'Dalmatian tunic', δελματικόν 'Dalmatian tunic', καλιγάριος 'boot-maker', καλίγιον 'boot', κάλιξ 'boot', κάλτιος 'shoe', καμίσιον 'shirt', καρακάλλιον 'hood', καράκαλλον 'hood', κερβικάριον 'pillow', κολλάριον 'collar', κουκούλλιον 'hood', λανάριος 'wool-worker', λεντιάριος 'linen-dealer', μανδήλη 'towel', μαππίον 'napkin', Μουτουνήσιος 'from Mutina', ὁράριον 'kerchief', παλλίολον 'small cloak', παπυλιών 'tent', παρατοῦρα 'distinctive dress', πεξός 'brushed', πλουμάκιον 'pillow', πλουμάριος 'tapestry-weaver', σηρικάριος 'silk-worker', σόλιον 1 'slipper', ταλάριον 'sandal fastened at the ankles', φακιάλιον 'facecloth', φασκία 'bandage', φεμινάλια 'trousers', φιβλατώριον (a garment), φοῦνδα 'money belt'. **Derivatives** (11): βίρριον 'hooded cloak', δελματίκιον 'Dalmatian tunic', δελματικομαφόριον 'Dalmatian tunic with hood', δελματικομαφόρτης 'Dalmatian tunic with hood', δελματικομαφόρτιον 'Dalmatian tunic with hood', λωδίκιον 'blanket', οὐδωνάριον 'sock', πλουμαρικός 'tapestry woven', σαγίον 'blanket', σουβρικοπάλλιον 'outer cloak', φασκίδιον 'bandage'.

Late (9 borrowings = 14%): γουνάριος 'furrier', καμπάγιον (a kind of boot), κουσούλιον (a garment), λανᾶτον 'wool garment', μαντίον (a garment), μάππα 'napkin', πλουμίον 'tapestry weaving', προμάξιμον (a garment), φίβλα 'brooch'. **Derivatives** (7): βηλόθυρον 'curtain at door', ἔμπλουμος 'tapestry woven', κεντώνιον 'rag', λανάτιον 'wool garment', λινόπηξος 'of combed linen', μανδήλιον 'little towel', φιβλόω 'fasten with a pin'.

These terms have little or nothing to do with the government. They are concentrated in the middle period and have an average survival rate, with 69% lasting into the Byzantine period and 31% into modern Greek.

I. Food and drink (57 borrowings, or 8% of all borrowings; 15 derivatives, or 10% of all derivatives):

Early (14 borrowings = 25%): κελλάριος 'cellarer', κιβάριον 'rations', κίτριον 'citron', κοχλιάριον 'spoon', Λαδικηνός 'Laodicean', λάρδος 'salted meat', ὀξύγγιον 'grease', πανάριον 'breadbox', πέρνα 'ham', πωμάριον 'orchard', τροῦλλα 'ladle', Φαλερῖνος 'Falernian wine', Φαλέρνος 'Falernian wine', φοῦρνος 'oven'. No derivatives.

Middle (29 borrowings = 51%): ἀλιμέντα 'provisions', ἄλιξ 1 'fish sauce', ἀψινθᾶτος 'flavoured with wormwood', βικίον 'vetch', βουκκᾶς 'biscuit-baker', βοῦλβα 'sow's womb', βωλήτης (a kind of mushroom), δωράκινον (a kind of peach), ἴντυβον 'endive', ἰσίκιον 'dish of mincemeat', κιβάριος 'made of coarse meal', κονδῖτον 'spiced wine', κούκκουμα 'kettle', λαγήνιον 'little flagon', λίγλα 'spoon', λουκάνικον 'sausage', μακελλάριος 'provision-dealer', μαρούλιον 'lettuce', ὀψωνάτωρ 'caterer', πάτελλα 'dish', πιμεντάριος 'spicer', πουλλίον 'chicken', ῥοσᾶτον 'rose-flavoured wine', σάλγαμον 'pickling material', σάρδα 'sardine', σιλίγνιον 'loaf of siligo', σκούτλιον 'dish', φάβα 'beans', φασίολος 'bean'. **Derivatives** (10): ἰσικιάριος 'sausage-maker', κελλαρικός 'of a cellar', κελλαρίτης 'cellarer', κουκκούμιον 'kettle', παστιλλᾶς 'confectioner', πατέλλιον 'little dish', πωμαρίτης 'fruiterer', σίλιγνις 'flour from siligo', σιλιγνίτης '(bread) from siligo', τρούλλιον (a dish).

Late (14 borrowings = 25%): ἀνισᾶτος 'flavoured with aniseed', ἀπαλαρέα 'bread-basket', βουκκελλᾶτον 'flatbread', βουκκίον (a kind of cake), ἰντύβιον 'endive', κονδιτάριος 'maker/seller of spiced wine', μάγκιψ 'baker', μοῦστος 'new wine', περιστερόπουλλος 'small dove', προπινάριος 'keeper of a cook-shop', σαλγαμάριος 'seller of pickled foods', σιλιγνάριος 'seller of siligo bread', σκουτέλλιον 'dish', φοῦσκα 'mixture of vinegar and water'. **Derivatives** (5): κελλαρικάριος 'cellarer', κιτρᾶτον 'citron drink', μαγκίπιον 'bakery', πατελλίκιον 'little dish', ὑδροροσᾶτον 'rose water'.

Like the words for clothing and textiles, these terms must have been introduced through channels largely unconnected to the government. Many refer to useful objects: foodstuffs, containers for food, and other utensils. Their survival rate is slightly above average, with 79% persisting into the Byzantine period and 36% into modern Greek.

J. Architecture and engineering (27 borrowings, or 4% of all borrowings; 7 derivatives, or 5% of all derivatives):

Early (2 borrowings = 7%): ἄτριον 'entrance hall', κάγκελλος 'latticed barrier or balustrade'. **Derivatives** (2): καγκελλωτός 'latticed', σκουτλόω 'decorate with *opus sectile*'.

Middle (21 borrowings = 78%): ἀκισκλάριος 'stonemason', ἀκίσκλος 'adze', γράδος 'stepped pedestal', δισέκτωρ 'quarry engineer', κανάλιον 'culvert', κέλλα 'room', κελλάριον 'cupboard', κορτίνα 'vault', κουαδράριος 'stonemason', κουβουκλεῖον 'bedroom', μαρμαράριος 'marble-mason', ὅρριον 'granary', ὁσπίτιον 'house', πίλα 2 'pier', Ῥωμανήσιος (a kind of architectural construction), σκάλα 'stairs', σπεκλάριον 'transparent stone', στρᾶτα '(paved) street', σωλάριον 'sun terrace', ταβέρνα 'shop', φόσσα 'ditch'. **Derivatives** (3): κελλίον 'room', σκούτλωσις 'decoration with *opus sectile*', ταβέρνιον 'small shop'.

Late (4 borrowings = 15%): βήσαλον 'brick', κιστέρνα 'cistern', μῶλος 'breakwater', πόρτα '(city) gate'. **Derivatives** (2): καγκέλλιον 'lattice', σκάλωσις 'scaffolding'.

Roman engineering techniques had a transformative effect on Greek-speaking cities, which were furnished with aqueducts, paved streets, bridges, arches, and bath-houses. It is therefore interesting that this field does not have more borrowings than it does, and that the borrowings are on average not very early. The survival rate into Byzantine Greek is about average (74%), but that into modern Greek is high (59%), perhaps reflecting the long-term importance of many Roman technologies.

K. Transportation (20 borrowings, or 3% of all borrowings; 7 derivatives, or 5% of all derivatives):

Early (3 borrowings = 15%): κάρρον 'cart', λεκτείκα 'litter', ῥαῖδα 'carriage'. No derivatives.

Middle (13 borrowings = 65%): ἀκουάριος 'water-carrier', βερεδάριος 'courier', βέρεδος 'fast horse', βουρδών 'mule', βουρδωνάριος 'muleteer', καβαλλάριος 'rider', καροῦχα 'carriage', μοῦλα 'female mule', μουλίων 'muleteer', μοῦλος 'male mule', σαβούρα 'ballast', σέλλα 'saddle', στάβλον 'stable'. **Derivatives** (3): καβαλλαρικός 'horse-drawn', ῥαίδιον 'carriage', σταβλίτης 'stableman'.

Late (4 borrowings = 20%): βαστέρνιον 'enclosed litter', καπίστριον 'halter', κούρκουμον 'halter', σαλιβάριον 'bridle'. **Derivatives** (4): ἀρχισταβλίτης 'chief stableman', βουρδώνιον 'mule', λεκτίκιον 'litter', μουλάριον '(little) mule'.

The predominance of land over water transport in the loanwords is striking, for Romans made abundant use of both. Also striking is the large number of words relating to mules, which although certainly important in the Roman period were neither new importations nor the only type of pack animal used. It has been argued that the reason Greek speakers borrowed both βουρδών 'mule' and μοῦλα/μοῦλος 'mule', apparently both at more or less the same time and when they already had the word ἡμίονος 'mule', was that the new pair of words allowed them to make a distinction between the offspring of a female horse and male donkey (μοῦλα/μοῦλος) and that of a male horse and female donkey, a 'hinny' (βουρδών).[9] Although this theory cannot actually be disproven, it is unlikely, because it is not clear that either Greek or Latin actually made such a distinction between the two words;

if Greek speakers had wanted to borrow a word for 'hinny', they would have been more likely to use *hinnus*, which clearly did have that meaning.[10] Another suggested reason for the appearance of μοῦλα/μοῦλος in papyri is that there was a hiatus in the breeding and use of mules in Egypt, leading to the use of a new word when they were reintroduced[11] – but that explanation would not easily account for the borrowing of two Latin words and their use all over the Greek-speaking world. See §10.1.

Words in this category have a high survival rate, with 93% persisting into the Byzantine period and 52% into modern Greek.

L. Medicine (12 borrowings, or 2% of all borrowings; 3 derivatives, or 2% of all derivatives):

Early (1 borrowing = 8%): βεττονική (a plant). No derivatives.

Middle (10 borrowings = 83%): ἐβίσκος 'marsh mallow', κίτρον 'citron', μυρσινᾶτος 'with myrtle', πάστιλλος 'pastille', πραικόκκιον 'little apricot', σαξίφραγον (a plant), σπικᾶτον 'embrocation of spikenard', τρακτός 'bleached (wax)', φαίκλα 'burned wine crust', φολιᾶτον (a kind of oil). **Derivatives** (2): παστιλλόω 'make into a paste', πιλάριον (an eye-salve).

Late (1 borrowing = 8%): πανίκουλα 'tumour'. **Derivative** (1): φασκιόω 'bandage up'.

For analysis of the medical vocabulary see §9.5.3. Words in this category have a high survival rate: 93% persist into Byzantine and 40% into modern Greek.

M. Other tools, furniture, and useful objects (29 borrowings, or 4% of all borrowings; 9 derivatives, or 6% of all derivatives):

Early (5 borrowings = 17%): μεμβράνα 'parchment', συμψέλλιον 'bench', ταβέλλα 'writing tablet', τάβλα 'tablet', φραγέλλιον 'whip'. No derivatives.

Middle (19 borrowings = 66%): ἀκκούβιτον 'couch', ἀμποῦλλα 'flask', ἀμπούλλιον 'little flask', ἄρκα 'chest', ἀρμάριον 'chest', βάκλον 'stick', κανδήλη 'candle', κατήνα 'chain', κηρίολος (an object made of wax), κορριγία

9 Shipp (1979: 170), cf. Immisch (1885: 368).

10 See *OLD s.vv. burdō, hinnus, mūla, mūlus, TLL s.v. burdo.*
11 Cuvigny in *P.Sijp.* p. 195.

637

'thong', λᾶμνα 'metal plate', λῶρος 'thong', ὄγκινος 'hook', σάπων 'soap', σκάμνος 'bench', σκρίνιον 'box', σόλιον 2 'seat', σουβαλάριον 'water-bag', σπέκλον 'mirror'. **Derivatives** (7): λαμνίον 'little metal plate', λωρίον 'thong', σαπώνιον 'soap', σελλίον 'little seat', σκαμνίον 'seat', ταβλίον 'tray', τροῦλλος (a vessel).

Late (5 borrowings = 17%): καννίον (a container), κάρβων 'coal', μηνσώριον 'basket', σίτλα 'bucket', σουβλίον 'skewer'. **Derivatives** (2): σιτλίον 'little bucket', χερνιβόξεστον 'washbasin'.

N. Other roles filled by people (50 borrowings, or 7% of all borrowings; 5 derivatives, or 3% of all derivatives):

Early (8 borrowings = 16%): Ἀβοριγῖνες 'original inhabitants of Italy', βιάτωρ 'agent', κονδούκτωρ 'contractor', Κυιρῖται 'Quirites', νοτάριος 'notary', πάτρων 'patron', σικάριος 'bandit', Χριστιανός 'Christian'. **Derivative** (1): Ῥωμαῖος 'Roman'.

Middle (36 borrowings = 72%): Αὐγουστήσιοι (a Jewish group), βέρνας 'home-born slave', δηλάτωρ 'accuser', δηποτᾶτος 'deputy', ἐκστρανήιος 'unrelated', ἐξκέπτωρ 'clerk', καμψάριος 'slave in charge of clothes', κολλήγας 'colleague', κολλητίων 'filing clerk', κόλων 'colonist', κομμενταρήσιος 'secretary', κοντουβερνάλιος 'comrade', λεκτικάριος 'pall-bearer', λιβράριος 'scribe', Ναυατιανός 'Novatianist', νωμενκλάτωρ 'name-reminder', ὁρριάριος 'granary supervisor', ὀστιάριος 'door-keeper', Οὐαλεντινιανοί 'Valentinians', οὐίγουλ 'watchman', ὀψίκιον 'followers', παγανικός 'civilian', παγανός 'civilian', πραίκων 'herald', πρόξιμος 'deputy', Σαβελλιανός 'Sabellian', σαλτάριος 'forester', Σευηριανός 'Severian', σκρίβας 'scribe', σκρινιάριος 'secretary', σπούριος 'bastard', στατιωνάριος 'member of a foreigners' association', ταβελλάριος 'secretary', ταβλάριος 'registrar', φαμιλιάριος 'member of the household', φωκάριον 'concubine'. **Derivatives** (3): λωροτόμος 'strap-cutter', πατρώνισσα 'patroness', συγκελλάριος 'comrade'.

Late (6 borrowings = 12%): κουβικουλαρία 'chambermaid', κουροπερσονάριος (a role), πορταρῆσις 'gate-keeper', σηκρητάριος 'secretary', σουβαδιούβας 'under-assistant', φοιδεράτος 'ally'. **Derivative** (1): σύγκελλος (an ecclesiastical title).

O. Other (37 borrowings, or 5% of all borrowings; 22 derivatives, or 15% of all derivatives):

Early (8 borrowings = 22%): Καπετώλιον 'Capitol', Καπετώλιος 'Capitoline', κολλήγιον 'council', Λατῖνος 'Latin', οὐά (an exclamation), Ῥώμη 'Rome', τίτλος 'title', φραγελλόω 'whip'. **Derivatives** (6): πατρωνεία 'patronage', πατρωνεύω 'be patron', Ῥωμαΐζω 'speak Latin', Ῥωμαϊκός 'Roman', Ῥωμαῖς 'Roman', Ῥωμαϊστί 'in Latin'.

Middle (17 borrowings = 46%): ἄσπρος 'white', βότον 'vow', βρέβιον 'list', γάλβινος 'greenish-yellow', ἐξεμπλάριον 'sample', κομμεντάριον 'shorthand', κομμέντον 'records', μάτριξ 'list', μεμόριον 'grave monument', ὀρδινατίων 'order', πούβλικος 'public', πραιτέριτος 'in arrears', Σαβελλίζω 'hold Sabellian views', σκουτουλᾶτος 'with a checked pattern', φάβριξ 'workshop', φαμιλία 'family', φορμαλεία 'list of supplies'. **Derivatives** (11): δηλατορεύω 'accuse', κίτρινος 'yellow', κονδουκτόριον 'board of contractors', ὀψικεύω 'accompany', πατρωνικός 'of a patron', ταβλίζω 'play dice', φαμιλιαρικός 'of a servant', Χριστιανίζω 'become Christian', Χριστιανικός 'Christian', Χριστιανισμός 'Christianity', Χριστιανότης 'Christianity'.

Late (12 borrowings = 32%): βενεφίκιον 'gift', κᾶσος 'occasion', κλεισούρα 'narrow pass', κόνβεντος 'assembly', κοῦπα 'grave', ὄρδινος 'order', πεδατοῦρα 'watchman's allotted area', πληναρία 'completeness', πριβιλέγιον 'privilege', τρακταΐζω 'handle', τρακτᾶτος 'administration', τρακτεύω 'administer'. **Derivatives** (5): βακλίζω 'beat', Καπετωλίς 'Capitoline', Λατινίς 'Latin', ματρίκιον 'register', μεμβράϊνος 'made of parchment'.

The overall distribution of loanwords by semantic field is summarized in Figure 12. Words that do not seem to fall into semantic fields where there are significant numbers of other loanwords (i.e. those in groups M, N, and O) often refer to useful objects or to people's roles; the same is true of the words in other categories. Words for objects have a high survival rate, with 87% lasting into the Byzantine period and 68% into modern Greek; their survival rate into modern Greek is higher than for any other category. Words for roles survive at a lower rate, with 67% found in Byzantine and 20% in modern Greek, and the

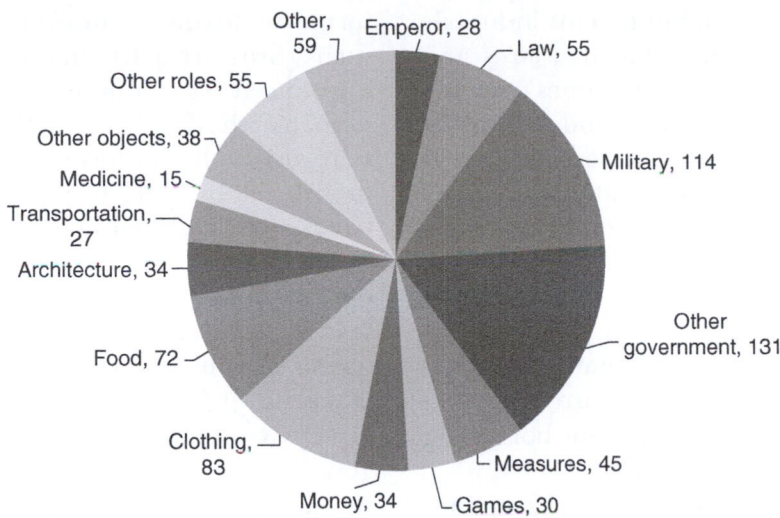

Figure 12 Overall semantic distribution of Latin loanwords
(borrowings and derivatives)

others fall in between, with 80% surviving in Byzantine and 32% in modern Greek.

Further semantic groupings can be identified within these 'other' groups; for example there are eleven words related to Christianity (Χριστιανός 'Christian' (§10.4.2); its derivatives Χριστιανίζω 'become Christian', Χριστιανικός 'Christian', Χριστιανισμός 'Christianity', and Χριστιανότης 'Christianity'; the sect terminology Ναυατιανός 'Novatianist', Οὐαλεντινιανοί 'Valentinians', Σαβελλιανός 'Sabellian', Σαβελλίζω 'hold Sabellian views', and Σευηριανός 'Severian'; and σύγκελλος, an ecclesiastical title). But it is unlikely that the borrowing or creation of these words was significantly facilitated by their semantic fields, even if more loanwords are associated with Christianity than with, for example, worship of the Magna Mater or Mithraism. Christianity's spectacular success among Greek speakers resulted in the creation of large numbers of new Greek words during the Roman period; given this time frame it was practically inevitable that a few would be Latinate.

10.2.3 To what extent are the loanwords connected to Roman political and military power?

Some previous studies of Latin loanwords have claimed that most Latin loanwords in Greek are military, legal, or administrative terms.[12] In our data, however, those semantic fields (sections A–D of the list in §10.2.2) account for only 40% of loanwords.[13] This difference arises partly from paying more attention to papyri, in which loanwords from other semantic fields are more common than in literary sources, and partly from excluding the innumerable codeswitches that literary authors used to explain Roman government and legal terminology; these semantic fields are far less well represented among loanwords than among codeswitches. Nevertheless 40% is still significant, for the military, legal, and administrative fields were important focusses of borrowing.

What those semantic fields have in common is that they are directly connected to the Romans' political and military power over Greek speakers. And scholars who claim that most loanwords belonged to those semantic fields often assert or imply that the linguistic impact of Latin was closely tied to Roman power and rarely extended beyond its limits. Potentially the latter claim could be right even if the specific semantic fields usually invoked to support it make up only 40% of loanwords,

[12] E.g. Garcea (2019: 69), Kaczko (2016: 393), Biville (1992: 234), Brixhe (1987: 107), Reichmann (1943: 2), Chantraine (1937: 88), Costas (1936: 50), Zilliacus (1935a: 170); cf. Binder (2000: 4).

[13] I.e. 43% of borrowings (290 words) and 26% of derivatives (38 words).

639

for there are also other semantic fields indirectly connected to Roman power: the measures and public games, along with the coin names from the money category (i.e. sections E, F, and part of G). Most borrowings in those areas were ultimately due to the Roman authorities, although Greek speakers probably encountered them without any direct contact with the authorities. Adding those fields to the ones directly connected to Roman power, however, accounts for only 50% of loanwords,[14] and therefore while Roman power was evidently an important factor in borrowing, it is simply not the case that Latin linguistic borrowing was largely confined within its limits.

The other half of the loanwords (i.e. sections H–O, and words in G apart from coin names) are a diverse group. Many refer to foods, beverages, clothing, shoes, other textiles, medicine, furniture, means of transportation, building tools, banks, and household utensils. Others refer to people working in those areas, such as muleteers, bankers, and the makers and sellers of specific kinds of foods, beverages, and textiles. The scholars who have previously noticed these loanwords sometimes group them under a general heading of 'daily life',[15] but that label is unsatisfactory for two reasons. A category of loanwords connected to daily life ought to include the ones most common in the lives of imperial-period Greek speakers, but some of these, the measurements and names of coins, do have a connection to Roman power. Moreover a 'daily life' category could suggest that loanwords were borrowed because of a connection to daily life, which is probably not the case, and/or suggest that they were distributed throughout the different areas of daily life, which is certainly not the case (for example, agriculture, water transport, and most basic manufacturing processes are poorly represented).

The real factor uniting most of these loanwords is probably a connection with trade and specialized industry. Many of them (marked with a straight underline in §10.2.2) refer to tools, furniture, textiles, and other useful objects, and such words are particularly likely to have been introduced via commercial contact with the Romans, whether because the objects themselves were originally imported or because they were introduced by specialized workers who moved to Greek-speaking areas and started making them. Indeed there is a striking difference in the number of words for useful objects in these semantic fields (i.e. categories H–O, and G apart from the names of coins), where words for useful objects make up 46% of loanwords, and in the fields directly connected to Roman control (i.e. categories A–D), where words for useful objects make up only 6% of loanwords.[16] The latter figure is very close to the normal frequency of such words in the Greek language as a whole: it is the prominence of useful objects in the semantic fields without any obvious connection to Roman power that is unusual and therefore suggests the influence of trade.[17] It therefore looks as though Latin loanwords spread via two separate channels: the official one of the army and administration, and unofficial one of trade and industry. Both these types of channel seem to have functioned throughout the period for which we have evidence, since borrowings from different periods show up in largely the same percentages in the categories most connected to Roman control and in the categories least connected to that control.

[16] Of the 315 borrowings and 92 derivatives in categories H–O and G apart from coin names, 152 borrowings and 37 derivatives refer to useful objects; of the 290 borrowings and 38 derivatives in categories A–D, 18 borrowings and 1 derivative refer to such objects. Overall, 180 borrowings and 41 derivatives refer to such objects (27% of the 820 loanwords). For these purposes 'object' is defined as tangible, movable, and inanimate; document types do not count as objects but payments and liquids do, on the theory that in antiquity a payment was normally a set of actual coins and liquids were kept in containers.

[17] Statistics for Greek as a whole were calculated by taking a randomly selected group of 2,024 Greek words consisting of the last headword on each page of LSJ (omitting pages on which there are no new entries); 103 of these words, or 5%, refer to useful objects. It could be objected that the two samples are not completely comparable, because borrowings from Latin are usually nouns (§10.3), and words for objects would naturally be more common among a group of nouns than among a group of words of all parts of speech. But the 2,024 Greek words just mentioned include 744 nouns, of which 103 is 14%, still much lower than 46%.

[14] I.e. 53% of borrowings (358 words) and 37% of derivatives (55 words). A few loanwords in other semantic fields may also be connected to Roman power; for example, it is likely that Χριστιανός 'Christian' and σικάριος 'bandit' were originally created by Roman provincial authorities (§10.4.2, §9.3).

[15] E.g. Kahane and Kahane (1972–6: 506, 1982: 130).

Loanwords not designating useful objects very often refer to roles filled by people, such as πάτρων 'patron', οὐετερανός 'veteran', or αἶγροι 'ill' (these are marked with a wavy underline in §10.2.2). Although found in most semantic fields, the words for roles are particularly concentrated in categories directly connected to Roman political and military control. They make up 52% of direct borrowings in categories A–D, but only 27% of borrowings in the areas least connected with Roman control (i.e. H–O, and G apart from the names of coins).[18] Both these figures are much higher than in the Greek language as a whole, where words for people's roles account for only 5% of words.[19] They are also higher than among the derivatives of Latin loanwords, even in the same semantic fields.[20] Why?

The Roman government and Roman army involved many roles that had no exact Greek equivalent and that would therefore not have been completely straightforward to translate, and this issue is likely to have been part of the catalyst for the borrowing of words for roles (cf. §10.1). After all we too refer to Roman officials including centurions, dictators, and consuls by their Latin titles. But the need to express new concepts cannot by itself suffice to explain the extraordinary prevalence of roles among the borrowings connected with Roman political and military control. For one thing, the Roman government and army also had many words for specifically Roman actions, administrative processes, technologies, buildings, and equipment, but those words were much less often borrowed than the ones for roles. Moreover, some of the words concerned would in fact have been easy to translate: αἶγροι 'ill' did not refer to a concept fundamentally unfamiliar

to Greek speakers. And even when the roles were unfamiliar, it would still have been perfectly possible to create words for them within Greek by expanding the meanings of pre-existing words or combining them to make new words. In fact such Greek-etymology words for the Roman roles were often created instead of or alongside borrowings, for example ἑκατοντάρχης for 'centurion', σεβαστός for 'Augustus' and ὕπατος for 'consul'. At an early period those creations were more widely used in Greek than the Latin borrowings, and some remained standard to the end of antiquity; ὕπατος, for example, continued in use and *consul* was never borrowed. But in the middle and particularly the late Empire Latin borrowings became more popular, especially for new roles, roles involving elevated status, and honorary titles. It looks as though imperial-period Greek speakers considered Latin words more desirable as descriptions of roles, particularly high-status ones, than as other kinds of terminology.

That this sense of desirability came from Greek speakers themselves, as opposed to being imposed by the Roman authorities, is suggested by the fact that a number of these words for roles are rare or unattested in Latin and may not actually have been created by Latin speakers before being adopted into Greek. In a few cases we can be sure that Latin titles were created within Greek using elements taken directly from Latin (a process fundamentally different from the formation of Greek derivatives from previously borrowed loanwords, which does not require any knowledge of Latin). For example the title ἀβρέβις must be a Greek formation employing not only Latin words but also Latin title-formation processes, and several other titles were probably created the same way (§4.5). Such formations bear a certain resemblance to modern scientific terminology, which speakers of modern languages often create out of elements taken directly from Latin. And they indicate that imperial-period Greek speakers, like the speakers of the modern languages that today create scientific terms that way, expected certain kinds of terminology to be formed from Latin elements.

Vocabulary in different semantic fields had very different chances of long-term survival, with the survival rate into Byzantine Greek of particular semantic fields ranging from 96% to 31% and that into modern Greek ranging from 59%

---

[18] Of the 290 borrowings in categories A–D, 150 refer to roles; of the 315 borrowings in categories H–O and G apart from coin names, 84 refer to roles. Overall, 245 borrowings refer to roles (36% of the 673 direct borrowings).

[19] Of a sample of 2,024 Greek words (see n. 17 above), 97 refer to roles that could be filled by a person (there are also some words referring to roles filled only by divinities). Such words are of course normally nouns; 97 words for roles make up 13% of the 744 nouns in this sample, still well below the figures for borrowings from Latin.

[20] Of the 38 derivatives in categories most connected to Roman rule, 13 (34%) refer to roles; of the 92 in categories least connected to Roman rule, 12 (13%) do; overall, 27 derivatives refer to roles (18% of the 147 derivatives).

to 13%. The semantic fields directly connected to Roman power all have low survival rates into modern Greek, averaging only 18%; that fact is no doubt connected with the eventual end of the Byzantine empire and consequent loss of the concepts most of these words represented. The semantic fields unconnected to Roman power mostly have higher survival rates into modern Greek, and it has been argued that words in those categories, if they occur in sixth-century papyri (a proxy for having been part of ordinary Greek at the end of antiquity), have a 75% chance of surviving into modern Greek.[21] That claim does not hold true for our data, in which 45% of those words survived into the modern language (37% including ones not attested in sixth-century papyri).[22] The difference is mainly due to the original claim having been made on the basis of an elderly and rather restricted list of loanwords in sixth-century papyri; with a more extensive collection of words appearing in sixth-century papyri, their average survival rate is greatly reduced. Nevertheless, the survival rate for this kind of word is clearly higher than that for terminology connected to Roman power, probably because the end of the Byzantine empire and loss of political independence had less impact on the concepts to which these words referred.

10.3 PARTS OF SPEECH

Previous scholars looking at Latin loanwords have made very different claims about the parts of speech involved: some asserted that only nouns were borrowed, with no verbs or adjectives, while others claimed that even adverbs could be directly borrowed.[23] The situation is complicated by the fact that loanwords do not always belong to the same parts of speech in the borrowing language as they did in the donor language; for example English 'handy' is an adjective, but it has been borrowed into German as *das Handy*, a noun meaning 'mobile telephone' (Matras 2020: 191). The same can happen between Greek and Latin (§4.2.1), but our primary focus here is on the Greek parts of speech.

10.3.1 Direct borrowings

Latin words borrowed into Greek mostly ended up as nouns, but other parts of speech were also represented: overall the direct borrowings are 86% nouns, 12% adjectives, 2% verbs, and one interjection (οὐά).[24] Of course, there is no clear-cut distinction between nouns and adjectives in Greek; not only do they tend to use the same inflections and therefore were classified by ancient grammarians as all being a single part of speech, but Greek adjectives can easily be substantivized to function like nouns. Since nouns very rarely function like adjectives, however, I have normally classified loanwords as adjectives if they are ever used adjectivally in Greek, even if a substantivized use is more common. Words always used as nouns are classified as nouns and assumed to have undergone substantivization during the borrowing process if they are borrowings of Latin adjectives; numerous Latin adjectives were clearly nouns in Greek (§4.2.1).

The predominance of nouns among the loanwords probably has nothing to do with Greek in particular: most languages borrow nouns more readily than other parts of speech. In fact typological studies suggest that for most languages the parts of speech can be arranged in a hierarchy of borrowability, which in descending order runs nouns, adjectives, verbs, prepositions, conjunctions, etc.[25] This hierarchy normally has another

---

[21] Kahane and Kahane (1972–6: 532). The Kahanes' semantic classifications are not, of course, identical to the ones used in this study; the category about which this claim was made is *Wortschatz des Alltags* 'vocabulary of daily life', which has subcategories *Wirtschaft* 'commerce', *Berufe* 'professions', *Siedlung* 'housing', and *Kleidung* 'clothing'. Some of the words that the Kahanes include in these categories have been classified differently in the present study.

[22] Of the 407 words in categories H–O and G apart from names of coins, 175 of which are attested (including uncertain attestations) in sixth-century papyri, 151 survived, including 79 of those in sixth-century papyri.

[23] The first claim was made by Chantraine (1937: 88); for the second see n. 30 below.

[24] Raw numbers: 578 nouns, 82 adjectives, 12 verbs, 1 interjection = 673 borrowings. Rare words likely to have been taken directly from Latin show similar proportions. Clackson's collection (forthcoming) of Greek words in early Latin has a similar distribution: 81% nouns, 11% adjectives, 5% verbs, 3% other.

[25] See e.g. Winford (2010: 176), Tadmor (2009: 61), Matras (2007: 48–62, 2020: 168, 179–81), Appel and Muysken (1987: 170–2) – but note the complexities identified

effect besides ensuring that most loanwords are nouns, for early borrowings, which take place when language contact is low, are typically all nouns, with the other parts of speech only being added (in the order of the hierarchy) as the linguistic contact becomes more intense. But that is not what happened in Greek. Adjectives are among the very first borrowings: Λατῖνος 'Latin' occurs from the third century BC, and the names of the months (which were primarily adjectives when originally borrowed, though over time they shifted to become primarily nouns, §4.2.1) were also borrowed early. In fact adjectives form a higher percentage of early borrowings than they do of later ones: they make up 28% of words borrowed before the end of the first century BC, but only 11% of words borrowed in the fourth, fifth, and sixth centuries AD (see Figure 13). Perhaps the lack of distinction between nouns and adjectives in Greek made adjectives easier than usual for Greek speakers to borrow, but it is also possible that the month names (which appear to have been imported into Greek by Latin speakers, §8.1.4) are a special case, particularly since the lack of equivalent Latin nouns made it difficult to handle these borrowings any other way.[26]

Verbs initially behaved more as the hierarchy would predict, in that they were not borrowed in the early period; they began to appear in the first century AD along with other signs of closer linguistic contact, such as suffix borrowing.[27] But

after that point the borrowing of verbs did not significantly increase; it remained rare throughout antiquity,[28] though not as rare as the borrowing of adverbs, conjunctions, and prepositions, which never occurred at all. It is tempting to explain this situation as resulting from the complex verbal morphology of both Latin and Greek, which would no doubt have made verbs more complicated to borrow than nouns, but that explanation is probably not right: a disinclination to borrow verbs is typologically very common and found in most of the world's languages, regardless of the complexity of their verbal morphology.[29] At most ten Latin verbs seem to have been borrowed directly into Greek, though one was borrowed twice, yielding eleven Greek verbs that may come from Latin verbs: ἀδιτεύω 'take possession of an inheritance' from *adeo*, βυκινίζω perhaps from *bucino*, δηληγατεύω probably from *delego*, ἐξκουσεύω 'excuse' from *excuso*, ἐξπελλεύω 'collect taxes' from *expello*, κομφιρματεύω 'confirm' from *confirmo*, μητατεύω 'commandeer' from *metor*, ῥογεύω 'pay in kind' from *erogo*, τρακτεύω 'administer' and τρακταΐζω 'handle' from *tracto*, and φραγελλόω 'whip' perhaps from *flagello*. The remaining directly borrowed verb seems to come from a Latin noun: Σαβελλίζω 'hold Sabellian views' from *Sabellius*.

It has long been believed that Greek also borrowed Latin adverbs, but actually there is no good evidence of such borrowing. Greek adverbs on Latin stems almost never occur often enough to be considered loanwords; according to the criteria used in this study there is only one loanword

---

by Curnow (2001) and Wohlgemuth (2009). Almond (2017) demonstrates that Greek adjectives could be used in Coptic even though Coptic did not normally have adjectives at all, but less frequently than verbs and much less frequently than nouns.

[26] See §10.3.2 for the way Greek speakers often handled the borrowing of groups of associated words that included a noun. It may be relevant that all the adjectives borrowed before the end of I BC (Λατῖνος 'Latin', Καισάρειος 'of Caesar', Καπετώλιος 'Capitoline', Κοιντίλιος 'July', and the twelve surviving month names) are words that we would capitalize, rather than 'ordinary' adjectives.

[27] For suffix borrowing see §6. Thomason and Kaufmann's scale of linguistic borrowing (Thomason 2001: 70–1) has four levels, running from 'casual contact' at level 1 to 'intense contact' at level 4. Lexical borrowing in which the loanwords are largely nouns and include no conjunctions, pronouns, or particles (i.e. they are all 'content words' rather than 'function words') belongs to level 1. But suffix borrowing belongs to level 3, 'more intense contact'. Other evidence suggests that by the first century

AD 'casual contact' would hardly be the right term for the relationship of Greek and Latin; given political developments at this period we would predict level 3, so the suffix borrowing is typologically to be expected. But the type of lexical borrowing undertaken nevertheless apparently remained at level 1 throughout antiquity.

[28] Borrowing of Latin verbs may have become more common in the Byzantine period. Diethart (2008) identifies c. 350 Latin-origin verbs in *LBG*, 135 of which he derives from Latin verbs, and 135 would make up 5% of the total of c. 2,700 Latinate words he identifies in Byzantine Greek (Diethart 2008: 16). But many of the verbs involved would probably not count as loanwords for the purposes of the present study, so the figures are not directly comparable.

[29] For a superb investigation and explanation of this phenomenon, see Wichmann and Wohlgemuth (2008); cf. Wohlgemuth (2009).

adverb, Ῥωμαϊστί 'in Latin', which is clearly not a borrowing of *Latine* but rather a derivative formed on Ῥωμαῖος 'Roman'. The words normally cited as examples of borrowed adverbs, which are all too rare to be loanwords, are probably also derivatives, since they have corresponding adjectives. For example, πούρως 'absolutely', 'unconditionally' is usually said to come from *pure* 'purely',[30] but it is far more likely to be a derivative of ποῦρος 'absolute', 'unconditional' (a borrowing of *purus*), which is found in the same texts that contain πούρως. Admittedly we find it startling to see πούρως written in Latin script as *puros* (e.g. Theophilus Antecessor 2.14.9), but Latin script does not necessarily indicate direct borrowing. Words with complex Greek inflections could be written in the Roman alphabet when the writer was thinking of the root as Latin (§7.1.1), and it is likely that Greek speakers processed adverbs in -ως as inflectional forms of the corresponding adjectives, so that they could form them at will rather than learning them as individual forms. Thus someone who could form ἠδίτευσαν from ἀδιτεύω (§9.5.6 passage 79) could also form πούρως from ποῦρος. Indeed even today that is how we treat adverbs in -ως for practical purposes, for Greek dictionaries do not normally have separate entries for them: in LSJ κακῶς 'badly' is subsumed under κακός 'bad', ἀληθῶς 'truly' under ἀληθής 'true', and Ῥωμαϊκῶς 'in Roman fashion' under Ῥωμαϊκός 'Roman'.

The direct borrowing hypothesis might in theory be viable for Latinate adverbs that do not have corresponding adjectives in Greek – but the only such adverb that could be ancient, ταυλοειδῶς 'in the form of a tablet' (very rare and not certainly attested before AD 600), also lacks an equivalent Latin adverb from which it could have been borrowed. Indeed no such Latin adverb could have existed, for this form is a Greek compound of a loanword. Probably the lack of a corresponding adjective is just an accident of attestation, and therefore the LSJ supplement reconstructs an adjective *ταβλοειδής from ταυλοειδῶς.[31]

10.3.2 Derivatives of borrowings

Derivatives of loanwords are 67% nouns, 19% adjectives, and 14% verbs, with one adverb (Ῥωμαϊστί 'in Latin').[32] For derivatives there is no typological expectation that nouns should predominate, and the high frequency of nouns among the Greek derivatives may be partly due to the popularity of the suffix -ιον (§4.3.2, §4.6.1).

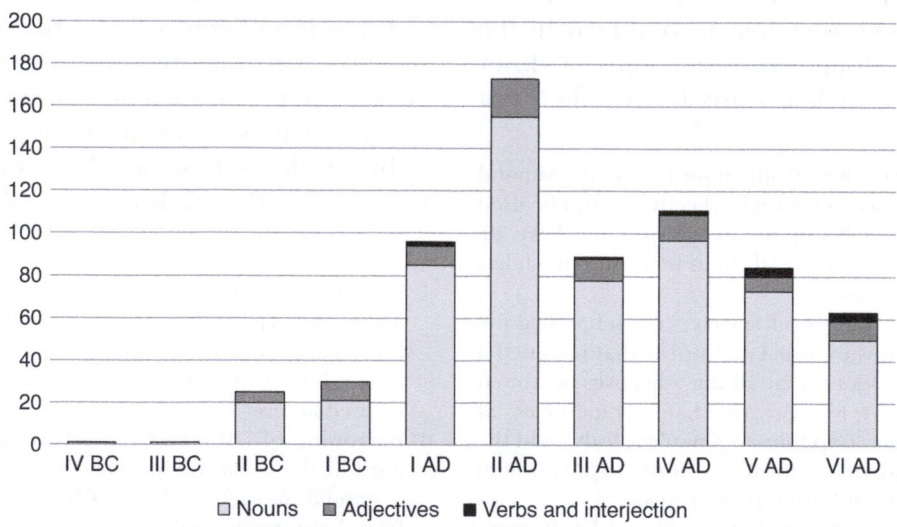

Figure 13 Direct borrowings by century and part of speech; exact numbers in §12.1

<hr />

[30] Triantaphyllides (1892: 270), Zilliacus (1935a: 202), *LBG s.v.* Other adverbs treated this way include βουλγαρίως, διρέκτως, κονφεσσωρίως, νεγατορίως, οὐτιλίως, πουπιλλαρίως, and προκουρατωρίως (Zilliacus 1935a: 180, 184, 196, 202, 214).

[31] Similarly καγκελλοειδῶς, which is definitely not ancient.

[32] Raw numbers: 98 nouns, 28 adjectives, 20 verbs, 1 adverb = 147 derivatives. Rare words likely to be derivatives show similar proportions.

There is also no typological expectation that nouns should be derived earlier than other parts of speech; indeed one might have expected derivative verbs to be more common at the early period when verbs could not be directly borrowed, but if this effect occurred at all, it was minimal (see Figure 14). Greek speakers never formed many verbs on Latin roots, whether by borrowing or by derivation.

Despite the relatively small pool of evidence, some distinct patterns emerge. For most of antiquity Greek speakers had a tendency to borrow nouns and then use native derivation processes to form verbs and adjectives from those nouns, rather than borrowing groups of related words. For example, they borrowed Ῥώμη 'Rome', formed the ethnic Ῥωμαῖος 'Roman' from that rather than borrowing *Romanus*, and then made additional derivatives from Ῥωμαῖος: Ῥωμαῖα (a set of games), Ῥωμαΐζω 'speak Latin', Ῥωμαϊκός 'Roman', Ῥωμαΐς 'Roman', Ῥωμαϊστής 'actor of Latin comedies', Ῥωμαϊστί 'in Latin', and φιλορώμαιος 'friend of the Romans'. Only in the fourth century did words based on the Latin adjectives *Romanus* and *Romanensis* appear: Ῥωμανία 'Roman empire' and Ῥωμανήσιος (a kind of architectural construction), both of which are nouns in Greek. Until a late period, the adjectives directly borrowed were often ones that could not easily have been created in this way, either because Latin had no noun on that stem (e.g.

ῥούσιος 'reddish', γάλβινος 'greenish-yellow', πραιτέριτος 'in arrears') or because the adjective did not simply indicate relationship to the noun (e.g. καυσάριος 'dismissed because of illness', not 'of a cause'; πριβᾶτος 'private', not 'of a private person'; πραιτωριανός 'praetorian', not 'of the praetor'; ἀψινθᾶτος 'flavoured with wormwood', not 'of wormwood'; κιβάριος 'of the household', not 'of food'; φρουμεντάριος 'concerned with victualling', not 'of grain'; ὀρδινάριος 'regular', not 'in order').

This borrowing pattern is particularly visible in the vocabulary for certain Roman offices and social positions, which had a whole set of terms associated with them in each language – but those sets were largely independent of one another. The Latin terminology tended to include a noun for the person, a noun for the position, and an adjective: *dictator* 'dictator', *dictatura* 'dictatorship', *dictatorius* 'of a dictator'; *curator* 'curator', *curatura* 'office of curator', *curatorius* 'of a curator'; *patronus* 'patron', *patronatus* 'position of patron', *patronalis* 'of a patron'. The Greek terminology tended to include a noun for the person, a noun for the position, and a verb: δικτάτωρ 'dictator', δικτατωρεία 'dictatorship', δικτατωρεύω 'be dictator'; κουράτωρ 'curator', κουρατορία 'office or position of curator', κουρατορεύω 'act as curator'; πάτρων 'patron', πατρωνεία 'patronage', πατρωνεύω 'be patron' (also πατρωνικός 'of a patron'). As these examples illustrate, Greek

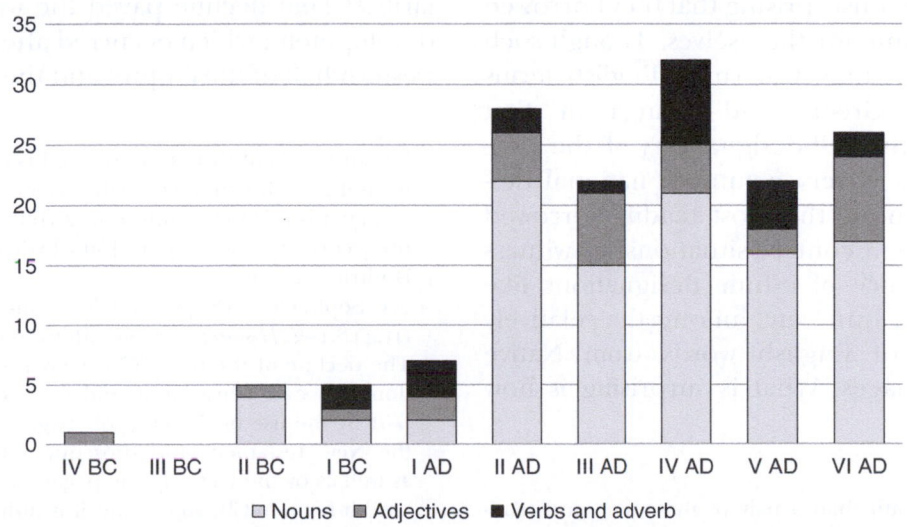

Figure 14 Derivatives of borrowings by century and part of speech; exact numbers in §12.1

speakers normally borrowed only the noun for the person and then used their own derivation processes to create the rest of the terminology.[33] But in the sixth century δουκιανός 'pertaining to the *dux*' was borrowed directly from *ducianus*, even though it seems to have duplicated δουκικός 'pertaining to the *dux*', which had been derived from δούξ 'duke' (from *dux*) several centuries earlier. The increased prestige of Latin in the sixth century is probably relevant here.

10.4 WORDS RELATING TO IDENTITY

One of the more striking results of the borrowing of Latin words was that Greek speakers eventually came to use Latin loanwords to express fundamental aspects of their own identity, even their identity as Greek speakers. How did this situation arise?

10.4.1 'Roman'

One of the most obvious groups of Latin loanwords in Greek is that consisting of words for Rome and the Romans: Ῥωμαῖος 'Roman', Ῥωμαϊκός 'Roman', Ῥώμη 'Rome', Ῥωμαΐζω 'speak Latin', Ῥωμαϊστί 'in Latin', Ῥωμαῖς 'Roman', etc. Words in this group are among the earliest Latin borrowings (§8.1.2) and are frequent in every century. Initially that was only to be expected, for the Greeks had good reason to talk about the Romans, and it is unsurprising that they borrowed the Romans' name for themselves. Though such borrowing is not universal (note English terms like 'German', 'Greek', and 'Hungarian' that do not match the self-designations of the peoples involved) it is very common: national designations are among the most readily borrowed words in language contact situations, as witness the preponderance of ethnic designations like Hopi, Mohegan, Inuit, etc. among the relatively small number of English words from Native American languages. What is surprising is how

the meanings of these terms evolved after they became naturalized into Greek.[34]

Originally, when Roman territory was small and Roman citizens a special group, words meaning 'Roman' referred to these people as distinct from other peoples. For example, when Polybius wrote about Romans in the second century BC, he wrote as an outsider, albeit one who knew the Romans better than most outsiders; he would never have called himself a Roman. But as time went on the Greek world became more and more absorbed into the Roman one. Greek speakers became part of the Roman empire not only by conquest, but also by being given Roman citizenship, which was extended across the empire in AD 212. A second capital, which would eventually become the only capital, was established in Byzantium (Constantinople), and that city came to be called Νέα Ῥώμη 'New Rome', leading to the use of terms such as μεγάλη Ῥώμη 'Great Rome' and παλαιά Ῥώμη 'Old Rome' to designate the Rome in Italy.[35]

Once the Greek-speaking citizens of the empire were as much Roman citizens as the Latin-speaking ones, and once the Eastern capital had as much right to be called 'Rome' as the Western one, it was only natural that Greek speakers began to refer to themselves (among others) as Ῥωμαῖοι. Around the same time the native designation for the Greeks, Ἕλληνες, came to have a pejorative sense and to be associated with paganism and idolatry; it therefore declined in popularity.[36] That decline paved the way for the final development, which occurred after the fall of the western half of the empire and the disappearance

---

[33] Likewise when Latin had a pair of masculine and feminine terms Greek speakers might borrow only the masculine and form the feminine as a derivative: πατρώνισσα 'patroness' comes from πάτρων rather than *patrona*.

[34] For an excellent discussion of the history of these terms' meanings with extensive further references see Rochette (1997: 36–45); for an interesting (but in my view not entirely correct) discussion of John Lydus' use of them, see Dmitriev (2010).

[35] See Sophocles (1887: *s.v.* Ῥώμη) and e.g. Epiph. *Pan.* III.418.1–2, *Historia Alexandri Magni* rec. F 1.2.

[36] The decline of the term Ἕλληνες was associated with the dominance of Christianity and was clearly motivated in part by the use of Ἕλληνες for 'pagans' and 'gentiles' in the New Testament and subsequent Christian writings, as well as by the fact that the pagan emperor Julian then used it for non-Christians. But it is unlikely that the term could have been specialized in this sense had there not by Julian's day been other ways to refer to the Greeks in a non-religious sense.

of Latin from widespread use in the eastern half, when Greek speakers were from their own perspective the only Romans left and the Greek language the only official Roman language. At that point 'Roman' came to mean specifically what we would call 'Greek', both in ethnic and in linguistic terms, and that meaning persisted throughout the Byzantine period. When the Greek language was subdivided into archaizing and evolved forms, the designation 'Roman' was naturally applied to the more evolved form of the language, that is, to demotic Greek. Thus in modern Greek Ρωμιός normally means 'a (modern or Byzantine) Greek person', ρωμιοσύνη 'the (modern) Greek identity', and ρωμαίικα 'the demotic Greek language' (though Ρωμαίος and ρωμαϊκός normally mean 'Roman', and ρωμαϊστί 'in Latin').[37] These modern Greek terms have in turn been borrowed into other modern European languages, so that English 'Romaic' and French *romaïque* also refer to demotic Greek.

10.4.2 'Christian'

The origins of the word Χριστιανός have been debated for over a century; clearly the root is Greek Χριστός and the suffix Latin *-iānus*, but in which language were the two first combined? Is Χριστιανός a borrowing of *Christiānus*, or *vice versa*? The earliest attestations, passages 84–6, are in Greek; although all that can be said with certainty about the date of composition of these passages is that they come from the second half of the first century AD, the events mentioned in the first two passages can be more precisely dated, probably to AD 44 for passage 84 and to AD 60 for passage 85. The context in passage 85 is the interrogation of Paul by King Herod Agrippa II.

84 Ἐγένετο δὲ αὐτοῖς καὶ ἐνιαυτὸν ὅλον συναχθῆναι ἐν τῇ ἐκκλησίᾳ καὶ διδάξαι ὄχλον ἱκανόν, χρηματίσαι τε πρώτως ἐν Ἀντιοχείᾳ τοὺς μαθητὰς Χριστιανούς. (Acts 11:26)

So it was that for an entire year they met with the church and taught a great many people, and it was in Antioch that the disciples were first called 'Christians'. (*NRSV* translation)

85 Ὁ δὲ Ἀγρίππας πρὸς τὸν Παῦλον· Ἐν ὀλίγῳ με πείθεις Χριστιανὸν ποιῆσαι. (Acts 26:28)

Agrippa said to Paul, 'Are you so quickly persuading me to become a Christian?'. (*NRSV* translation)

86 Εἰ δὲ ὡς Χριστιανός, μὴ αἰσχυνέσθω, δοξαζέτω δὲ τὸν θεὸν ἐν τῷ ὀνόματι τούτῳ. (1 Peter 4:16)

Yet if any of you suffers as a Christian, do not consider it a disgrace, but glorify God because you bear this name. (*NRSV* translation)

The earliest evidence for the use of *Christianus* in Latin is slightly later, from the beginning of the second century AD. Passage 87, written c. AD 110, implies that the term (in the form *Chrestianus*) was common in Rome during Nero's persecution of the Christians in AD 64.

87 *Ergo abolendo rumori Nero subdidit reos et quaesitissimis poenis adfecit, quos per flagitia invisos vulgus Chrestianos appellabat.*[38]

Therefore to dispel this rumour Nero fabricated scapegoats and afflicted with particular penalties those whom the masses used to call 'Christians' and hated because of their depravities.

Christianus is also used repeatedly in letters between Pliny and the emperor Trajan, written c. AD 111 (Plin. *Ep. Tra.* 10.96–7). Passage 88 has also been argued to be relevant; although composed c. AD 120, it refers to events that took place in AD 49–51 and can therefore be argued to represent the earliest evidence for *Christianus* in Latin. The argument is tenuous, though, because the passage does not actually contain that word; in order to count the passage as evidence one has to argue that the name *Chrestus* is a back-formation from *Christianus* and therefore implies the prior existence of *Christianus* (Moreau 1950). This argument, while interesting, is unlikely to be right, since *Chrestus* was a proper name in Rome at this period (Montevecchi 1979).

---

[37] Babiniotis (2002); see also *OED s.vv. Romaic, Romaika.*

[38] Tacitus, *Annales* 15.44.2; *Chrestianos* is the manuscript reading but often emended to *Christianos*. There has been considerable discussion of this passage: e.g. Shaw (2015: 80, with further references).

88   *Iudaeos impulsore Chresto assidue tumultuantis Roma expulit* (Suetonius, *Claudius* 25)

[Claudius] expelled from Rome the Jews, who were constantly causing disturbances at the instigation of Chrestus.

On the face of it, this evidence gives chronological priority to Greek, and some scholars have indeed considered Χριστιανός/*Christianus* a Greek formation.[39] But most find it more likely that even if the term was first coined in Antioch in AD 44, it was coined by the Roman authorities and therefore in Latin.[40] Immediately before passage 84 in the text of Acts is a description of the significant expansion of the Christian community in Antioch by the addition of non-Jewish converts, a circumstance that might well have caused the Roman authorities to need a word for this community; a connection between the expansion and the coining of the term is likely, although not made explicit in the text.[41] Moreover, in order for Χριστιανός to have been created within Greek, Greek speakers would have had to have already borrowed the Latin *-ianus* suffix, a requirement that poses difficulties. Although this suffix was certainly borrowed at some point (§6.4), that borrowing process would have required the previous borrowing into Greek of a pair of models that attained widespread currency, so that Greek speakers could see how to split the suffix off from the root (§6). The most likely set of models is Χριστός and Χριστιανός; if Χριστιανός was part of the original model that sparked off the borrowing of the suffix, it must itself have been a loanword. But if Χριστιανός was not part of the original

model but a Greek formation, some other words must have served as the model. What might those have been?

The only possible candidates – that is, the only words in -ιανός attested early enough to be relevant – are Ἡρῳδιανός 'Herodian' with Ἡρῴδης 'Herod' and Καισαριανός 'Caesarian' with Καῖσαρ 'Caesar'.[42] Καῖσαρ is a borrowing of the name (later title) *Caesar*, while Καισαριανός is a borrowing of *Caesarianus*, designating the adherents of Caesar in the civil wars. Καῖσαρ is attested early, but Καισαριανός first occurs in Epictetus, *Dissertationes* 1.19.19, 3.24.117, 4.13.22 (written down not by Epictetus himself but by his pupil Arrian, probably in the early second century) and in Appian, *Bellum civile* 3.13.91 (written c. AD 160 but describing events of 43 BC). In order to act as the catalyst for the borrowing of *-ianus*, Καισαριανός would have had to make significant impact on the consciousness of at least some Greek speakers before AD 44, and it seems unlikely that this happened: the political situation giving rise to Καισαριανός was a relatively short-lived phenomenon, and the term is not attested even once in surviving Greek texts from the relevant period.

Ἡρῳδιανός, designating a group of Jews coupled with the Pharisees, poses many of the same problems as Χριστιανός. It must have been mainly a Greek word, not only because it first appears in Greek (in the New Testament, Matthew 22:16 and Mark 3:6 and 12:13) but because a term of its meaning must have been largely confined to Judaea, where Latin was a minority language (§9.3 n. 27). But it can hardly have been a Greek creation, because if it had been, the *-ianus* suffix would have had to be borrowed even earlier. The only reasonable explanation is that the term was created by the Roman authorities: Ἡρῳδιανός must be a borrowing of *Herodianus*, even if the Latin is unattested at a relevant period. Ἡρῳδιανός was clearly a rare word: the three references in the Gospels seem to be the only relevant attestations, and there is no indication that the group they describe existed outside Judaea. It is very

---

[39] E.g. Blass *et al.* (1979 §5 n. 12), Lifshitz (1962), Spicq (1961), Bickerman (1949), Palmer (1945: 46).

[40] E.g. Townsend (2008), Taylor (1994), Grundmann in Kittel *et al.* (1932–79: IX.529 with n. 298), Peterson (1946), Schwyzer (1939: 490 n. 6), Chantraine (1933: 197), Meillet (1918: 67–8), Debrunner (1917: 162). Mattingly (1958) argues that the term was created in Latin but by Greek speakers; G. Schneider (1993: 478) says it was created by non-Christians but does not specify the language; Slee (2003: 8–9) argues that the term was at first local to Antioch but does not specify which language it was created in; Bile and Gain (2012) argue that either a Greek or a Latin formation is possible.

[41] Or at least not in the usual version of the text; manuscript D does make it explicit with τότε (discussion in Taylor 1994: 75–6, 79).

[42] Some older Greek words look as if they end in -ιανος, but those actually have a suffix -ανος on a stem ending in ι, as Ἀσιανός 'Asian' from Ἀσία 'Asia'; they are not relevant to the suffix borrowing.

unlikely that such a term could have been widely enough known among Greek speakers outside Judaea to result in the borrowing of the -ιανός suffix in Antioch. A much better explanation is that Ἡρωδιανός and Χριστιανός are parallel examples of the same phenomenon: the Roman provincial authorities coined Latin words for troublesome groups, and those 'official' names were then used by Greek speakers as well.[43]

One recent discussion of this term has offered an explanation for why *Christiānus* would originally have been created in Latin (Townsend 2008: 215–16). The disciples sometimes referred to themselves as οἱ τοῦ Χριστοῦ 'those of the Christ' (1 Corinthians 15:23, Galatians 5:24), a term that could not be literally rendered into Latin because of its reliance on the definite article. If the Roman authorities tried to come up with a word for the new group that translated their own name for themselves, *Christiani* might well have been the result of such an effort; once the Romans had established an official term, it could easily have been borrowed back into Greek, perhaps initially by non-Christians who were unfamiliar with the phrase οἱ τοῦ Χριστοῦ.

Efforts to establish the etymology of Χριστιανός sometimes involve an attempt to establish a precise original meaning for the word by identifying a specific word as its model; this can lead to translations such as 'the political partisans of Χριστός', 'the household of Χριστός', 'the worshippers of Χριστός', 'the slaves of Χριστός', etc. But if the word was created in Latin, where the *-ianus* suffix was common, it did not have one single model, and therefore no such specific meaning was intended: *-ianus* indicated relationship in fairly general terms.

Like the words for 'Roman', Χριστιανός and its derivatives (e.g. Χριστιανικός 'Christian', Χριστιανισμός 'Christianity') remained popular throughout the Byzantine period and continue in modern Greek, where Χριστιανός and Χριστιανικός still mean 'Christian' and Χριστιανισμός 'Christianity'. From late antiquity through the nineteenth century, two key features defined the identity of most Greek speakers as opposed to their immediate neighbours – being

Greeks and being Christians. They chose to express both these features with Latin loanwords, thus offering a striking indication of the impact of Latin.

10.5 CONCLUSIONS

Most Latin loanwords originally expressed meanings for which there were no pre-existing Greek expressions, but many eventually ended up competing with and replacing earlier Greek words, and some effectively duplicated existing vocabulary even at the time they were borrowed. Borrowings and derivatives both clustered in certain semantic fields; to a certain extent those fields match the ones in which modern languages are most likely to borrow, but there are also some notable differences from the borrowing patterns of modern languages. Those differences seem to be due mainly to historical factors.

Half the loanwords fall into semantic fields with a direct or indirect connection to Roman political and military power, and a high percentage of those refer to people's roles. Some of these seem to have been motivated by a sense on the part of imperial-period Greek speakers that particular concepts ought to be expressed with Latinate vocabulary. These loanwords are more likely to be direct borrowings (as opposed to derivatives) than other loanwords, and less likely to survive into modern Greek; the first of these tendencies is probably due to an active desire for Latinity on the part of speakers, and the second to historical factors connected to the fall of the Byzantine empire. The other half of the loanwords, many of which refer to useful objects, probably spread through the channels of trade and specialized industry. As their chronological distribution is very similar to that of the first half, loanwords probably entered Greek via both types of channel throughout the period for which we have evidence.

Most loanwords are nouns, but verbs and adjectives were also sometimes borrowed, as was one interjection. Other parts of speech, including adverbs, were probably not borrowed, though adverbs could be formed from loanwords by derivation. Although derivatives were more likely than direct borrowings to be verbs and adjectives, nouns predominated in both groups. Some of

---

[43] Another example of the same phenomenon, with a different suffix, is σικάριος (§9.3).

the distribution of loanwords by parts of speech matches tendencies known from other languages, but some is unusual, including the high percentage of adjectives among early borrowings and the rarity of verbs among derivatives.

A striking illustration of the impact of Latin is provided by two loanwords that together defined the identity of most Greek speakers from late antiquity onwards, Ῥωμαῖος 'Roman' (which eventually came to mean 'Greek') and Χριστιανός 'Christian'. The importance of these words suggests that the impact of Latin was greater than can be measured in purely quantitative terms.

11

OVERALL CONCLUSIONS AND REMAINING QUESTIONS

The role of Latin loanwords in the ancient Greek vocabulary turns out to have been significantly different from the one scholars have long assumed. Loanwords were never very numerous, almost certainly under a thousand even if we allow for missing evidence (§8.2.1, §9.5.6), but they occupied key positions in the vocabulary of ancient Greek (§10.2) and continued to maintain those positions for thousands of years, so that even today their descendants still form part of the central vocabulary of modern Greek (§8.2.3). In these respects the loanwords differ sharply from codeswitches (§2.2), which normally did not survive and tended to occupy more marginal positions in the Greek vocabulary, but which were much more numerous: since codeswitches were not systematically collected for this project, the nearly 1,800 probable codeswitches included in the Lexicon (§8.1.6 with §12.1) represent only part of the surviving evidence and no doubt only a tiny proportion of the codeswitches produced in antiquity.

Borrowing of Latin words began very early, facilitated by the Greek presence in southern Italy (§8.1.2), but most of this early borrowing only becomes visible to us later, owing to the uneven preservation of Greek texts (§8.1.1). Borrowing continued throughout antiquity, as did the formation of Greek derivatives from Latin loans, but did not increase in late antiquity and may even have declined (§8.1.1). The Romans themselves may have played an important role in deciding how they and their distinctive cultural features were represented in Greek, since at an early period they often used Greek to present themselves to the outside world (§8.1.2, §8.1.4). Most of these distinctive cultural features were not in fact represented by loanwords, but by words of Greek etymology, which could always be created or adapted to convey new ideas (§10.1). The motivation for adopting loanwords was never

that they were 'needed' to express concepts that could not be expressed in Greek; borrowing was a choice, and loanwords often ended up duplicating and even displacing older Greek vocabulary (§10.1).

Loanwords spread via two distinct channels, the official ones of government and army and the unofficial ones of trade and industry. Although the words that arrived by the former route are more obvious to us today, those in the latter group were more numerous and tended to survive longer (§10.2.3). Those words are easiest to see in documentary texts, whose writers were readier to use Latinate vocabulary than were the authors of most pre-sixth-century literary texts – though because far more literature than documents survives, more loanwords are preserved for us in literature (§9.1). Papyri began to include loanwords in the second century BC, long before the Roman conquest of Egypt, and immediately reflected the conquest with increased use of Latin in the late first century BC (§8.1.4, §8.1.5). They are particularly rich in loanwords in the later centuries of the Empire: in the fourth century AD there was a huge increase in the frequency with which writers of papyri used established loanwords, accompanied by a smaller increase in codeswitching (§8.1.6). Inscriptions contain fewer loanwords (§9.1), often in a more restricted set of semantic fields, but the Edict of Diocletian is an important exception demonstrating that a wide range of Latinate terminology could in principle appear in epigraphic contexts (§9.5.1). Inscriptions also provide key evidence of early loanword usage (§8.1.4, §8.1.5), as do coins (§8.1.2).

Literary texts include more loanwords, and tell us more about them, than has previously been appreciated. For much of the imperial period Atticist strictures reduced the number of loanwords appearing in literature – the density of loanword usage in ordinary conversation was probably much closer to what we see in papyri than to what we see in literature – but even strict Atticists made some use of loanwords, and often that use is revealing (§9.4). Sometimes our earliest evidence for a borrowing is an Atticist writer's protest against it, even though a word must already have been fairly common in order to draw such a protest (§9.4). Grammarians discussed the inflection and accentuation of loanwords, demonstrating that they considered those words part of Greek (§4.2.3.1, §5.3.2). From those discussions we also learn that loanwords sometimes had slightly anomalous declensions or accentuations because of retaining Latinate features. Evidence from papyri and inscriptions, which unlike most literary texts can be guaranteed to reflect ancient spellings and which (in the case of papyri) occasionally contain ancient accent marks, reinforces both those points (§4.2, §5.3.1).

Literature also reveals that some loanwords were particularly characteristic of certain genres. One such genre is medicine, which had a set of Latinate technical terms probably because of the influence of Galen (§9.5.3). The legal field had the largest body of technical loanwords; although many of these first become visible to us in the sixth century AD, the creation of legal loanwords had started many centuries earlier. There was some turnover in exactly which loanwords the lawyers used, but nevertheless many of those in the sixth-century texts were probably borrowed earlier (§9.5.6).

Variation in loanword usage was not only by genre and register; it could also be geographical. Many loanwords probably started life in one particular place and then spread across the Greek-speaking world, but some failed to spread and remained characteristic of specific localities or regions (§9.2). The Greek spoken in the city of Rome was probably a distinctive variety that incorporated many loanwords, including some not used elsewhere; influence from this variety may explain some unusual features of loanword usage in the New Testament (§9.3) and could be the ultimate source of the Latinate medical terminology (§9.5.3).

For most of antiquity the borrowing process followed certain predictable patterns. The words borrowed were normally nouns or adjectives in Latin, with the adjectives often being substantivized as

part of the borrowing process so that direct borrowings were overwhelmingly likely to be nouns in Greek (§4.2.1, §10.3.1). (Nevertheless, some adjectives remained adjectival in Greek, and a few verbs were also borrowed: §10.3.1, §4.2.2, §4.3.1.) When they needed a set of terminology on a particular topic, Greek speakers tended to borrow a Latin noun and then form their own adjectives and verbs from it rather than borrowing the entire set of terms directly (§10.3.2). Overall, however, there are surprisingly few Greek verbs formed on Latin roots, even by derivation (§10.3.2). Most Latin nouns and adjectives belonged to Latin inflectional categories with obvious Greek equivalents, and Greek speakers normally transferred them into those equivalent categories to produce well-integrated Greek forms – not only when borrowing, but also when codeswitching. A few declensional classes posed more problems; those sometimes resulted in codeswitches retaining their Latin endings (§7.2.1), but loanwords from those classes were nevertheless fully assimilated into Greek inflections, using various methods (§4.2.5). A few nouns changed gender or declensional class during the borrowing process; sometimes semantic or inflectional reasons for these changes can be identified, but not always (§4.2.3, §4.2.4, §4.2.5). Very occasionally a Latin inflected form appears to have become an indeclinable loanword in Greek (§7.2.2). Some Latin words acquired Greek suffixes as part of the borrowing process (§4.3), or were taken directly into Greek compounds; contrary to what has sometimes been argued, the inclusion of a Latin word in a Greek compound does not prove that that word had already been borrowed (§4.5), and the addition of -ιον during borrowing does not indicate that the word in question would have been difficult to borrow without a suffix (§4.3.2). Of course, compounds and other derivatives were also created from already established borrowings, using the normal Greek word-formation processes (§4.6). By the process known as 'folk etymology', pre-existing Greek words (including ones borrowed from Latin) sometimes influenced the forms taken by new loanwords – but that influence was much less common than has previously been alleged (§4.4).

The influx of loanwords (and of Latin names, which began to be borrowed before any other

Latin words and were ubiquitous by the imperial period: §8.1.2, §8.1.4, §9.4) gave imperial-period Greek, especially the varieties used in everyday conversation, a rather Latinate flavour. This flavour was further increased by borrowing Latin suffixes and using them to create large numbers of words that looked Latinate but had never existed in Latin (§6.1, §6.4, §6.5, §6.6, §6.9). Some Latin suffixes merged with older Greek suffixes, leading Greek speakers to perceive all words with those suffixes as Latinate (§6.3, §6.7). By late antiquity Greek speakers felt that certain kinds of words were supposed to come from Latin, and if there was no appropriate Latin word to borrow, they would sometimes create one by using Latin roots and Latin word-formation processes (§4.5).

For most of antiquity the social value of Latinate vocabulary was a complex matter because of competing measures of prestige. From one perspective the prestige of the Classical language gave Latinate words an automatically low status; that perspective led to the avoidance of most loanwords in many literary texts. But another kind of prestige favoured words associated with the Romans, who were the acknowledged masters of the Greek world; that form of prestige led to the loanwords being borrowed in the first place (§10.1). In the sixth century AD the balance between the different measures of prestige shifted, greatly increasing the cachet of Latin; it is probably not coincidental that at the same period Latin lost all its practical utility in the Greek-speaking world. Authors of literary texts reflected that shift both by making much greater use of existing loanwords and by extensive code-switching (§8.1.6). They also sometimes used the Roman alphabet to write words of Latin origin, including some that had been part of Greek for many centuries (§7.1). But before the sixth century, Greek speakers appear to have almost always put Latin words (even unintegrated codeswitches) into the Greek alphabet (§4.1); the only significant exceptions were juridical texts (§7.1.2).

Despite the prestige of Latin among sixth-century Greek speakers, there were probably not very many new borrowings made in that century (§8.1.1), and the rate of borrowing seems to have declined further during the Byzantine period – though the Byzantines did make some new borrowings from Latin (§8.2.2). A quarter

of the ancient loanwords had already died out by the start of the Byzantine period (§8.2.1); attrition was particularly high in the semantic fields of public entertainment and the army, owing to social changes that often made obsolete the concepts to which such words referred (§10.2.2). Many of the rest gradually disappeared during the Byzantine and early modern periods (§8.2.3); the end of the Byzantine empire and consequent disappearance of a Greek-speaking government, army, and legal profession resulted in particularly low long-term survival rates for loanwords in those semantic fields (§10.2.2). Nevertheless, 28% of the ancient loanwords survived at least until the nineteenth century, a survival rate that is probably about the same as that of Greek loanwords in Latin (§8.2.3, §8.3).

Two borrowings in particular show the importance of Latin: Χριστιανός 'Christian' and Ῥωμαῖος 'Roman', which eventually came to mean 'Greek' (§10.4). These terms expressed the two key elements of the identity of late antique Greek speakers, and indeed also of Greek speakers in the Byzantine and early modern periods. The fact that both were conspicuously Latinate shows the extent to which the Roman heritage represented by Latin loanwords had become embedded in the Greek language and its speakers' identities by the end of antiquity, and remained embedded thereafter.

Many questions remain unanswered about Latin influence on Greek, however. Some of the most intriguing may be unanswerable: to what extent were ordinary Greek speakers (as opposed to ancient scholars) aware of the loanwords' Latin etymologies? Did Greek speakers ever pronounce Latin codeswitches or loanwords as in Latin, and if so, under what circumstances? How much codeswitching did the writers of papyrus documents really do – how many of the Latin words that appear once or twice in such texts are actually local loanwords? Other questions are answerable on the basis of surviving evidence, making further research into Latin loanwords highly desirable. For example, when the same item (such as a mule, a centurion, or a date) could be represented both by a loanword and by a word of Greek etymology, what factors influenced the choice between them? Were later borrowings more likely than early ones to retain their Latin accents (§5.2.2)? How (if at all) did the existence of Latin loanwords really contribute to the register differentiation of Byzantine Greek (§8.2.2)? What percentage of the usages complained about by the Atticists are in one way or another Latinate: to what extent was Atticism a reaction to Latin influence? Could a closer study of evidence from Magna Graecia shed more light on the early borrowings and how great a role was played by Greek-speaking Romans? Could a closer study of Greek inscriptions from Rome reveal more about the special features of the variety of Greek spoken there? How much was the native Greek vocabulary affected by semantic extensions due to Latin influence? How much morphological and syntactic influence did Latin have on Greek? Not only these but other questions not yet asked offer excellent opportunities for further research.

12

APPENDICES

12.1 APPENDIX: RAW NUMBERS FOR FIGURES

Figure 2 (§8.1.1)

Century	New borrowings	New derivatives	New borrowings + new derivatives	Total loanwords in use (from Figure 7 in §8.2.1)
IV BC	0	1	1	1
III BC	2	0	2	3
II BC	25	5	30	33
I BC	30	5	35	68
I AD	96	7	103	169
II AD	173	28	201	362
III AD	92	23	115	457
IV AD	109	30	139	551
V AD	85	23	108	613
VI AD	61	25	86	690
Total	673	147	820	

Figure 3 (§8.1.1)

Century	New borrowings from Latin	Surviving documents / 100	Words of surviving literature / 100,000
II BC	25	4,563/100 = 46	383,648/100,000 = 4
I BC	30	3,326/100 = 33	2,144,388/100,000 = 21
I AD	96	4,556/100 = 46	3,372,299/100,000 = 34
II AD	173	14,750/100 = 148	10,475,707/100,000 = 105
III AD	92	14,435/100 = 144	1,657,973/100,000 = 17
IV AD	109	10,081/100 = 101	18,302,562/100,000 = 183
V AD	85	4,691/100 = 47	7,063,461/100,000 = 71
VI AD	61	3,299/100 = 33	7,268,988/100,000 = 73

The 'surviving documents' figure was calculated using the *Papyrological Navigator* (www.papyri .info) on 4 June 2021. I put the language setting on 'ancient Greek' and the date setting on 'strict', recorded the figure for all documents dated to before the end of a given century, and then repeated that process for the previous century and subtracted the latter figure from the former one, so that all documents were counted in the last century of the range to which they are assigned in the *Papyrological Navigator*. The 'words of surviving literature' figure was calculated using the 'statistics' tool of the *Thesaurus Linguae Graecae* (http://stephanus.tlg.uci.edu) on 22 July 2020, again by using the strictest settings, recording a figure for a range of centuries ending in the one under consideration, and subtracting from that figure the equivalent figure for a range ending in the previous century. This method makes the dates of the texts comparable to the dates I have used for the loanwords themselves, since those have been counted in the latest of the centuries to which a date range applies. The figures for documents and literature are kept separate not because it would be impossible to combine them, but because there are so many different ways that they could legitimately be combined, each of which yields a different overall pattern.

Figure 5 ($8.1.6)

Century	Estimated total Latinisms	Estimated total Latinisms per 3,000 documents
II BC	0	0
I BC	22	60
I AD	212	270
II AD	1,380	480
III AD	1,329	690
IV AD	3,365	3,060
VI AD	3,038	2,550

The numbers of estimated total Latinisms are taken directly from figure 10 of Dickey (2003: 256); the estimates per 3,000 documents are taken from the same source but multiplied by 30, as the article gives estimates per 100 documents.

Figure 6 ($8.1.6)

Century	Foreign words	Rare words
Very early	0	1
II BC	5	4
I BC	40	12
I AD	21	44
II AD	127	170
III AD	38	121
IV AD	11	197
V AD	8	104
VI AD	511	292
Undated	5	57
Total	766	1,002

Figure 9 ($9.1)

Century	New words in documents	New words in inscriptions	New words in literature
Very early	0	1	1
II BC	2	22	11
I BC	7	21	12
I AD	52	37	31
II AD	113	73	67
III AD	69	37	23
IV AD	84	33	56
V AD	35	14	77
VI AD	47	7	72
Total	409	245	350

Words that first appear in multiple text types are counted for each of those text types, and four words that do not fall into any of these categories are omitted.

Figure 10 ($9.1)

Century	New words in documents, per 1,000 surviving documents	New words in literature, per 500,000 words of surviving literature
II BC	$2/(4,563/1,000 = 4.56) = 0.4$	$11/(383,648/500,000 = 0.77) = 14.3$
I BC	$7/(3,326/1,000 = 3.33) = 2.1$	$12/(2,144,388/500,000 = 4.29) = 2.8$
I AD	$52/(4,556/1,000 = 4.56) = 11.4$	$31/(3,372,299/500,000 = 6.74) = 4.6$
II AD	$113/(14,750/1,000 = 14.75) = 7.6$	$67/(10,475,707/500,000 = 20.95) = 3.2$
III AD	$69/(14,435/1,000 = 14.44) = 4.8$	$23/(1,657,973/500,000 = 3.32) = 6.9$

IV AD	$84/(10{,}081/1{,}000 = 10.08) = 8.3$	$56/18{,}302{,}562/500{,}000 = 36.61) = 1.5$
V AD	$35/(4{,}691/1{,}000 = 4.69) = 7.5$	$77/(7{,}063{,}461/500{,}000 = 14.13) = 5.4$
VI AD	$47/(3{,}299/1{,}000 = 3.3) = 14.2$	$72/(7{,}268{,}988/500{,}000 = 14.54) = 5.0$

Words that first appear in multiple text types are counted for each of those text types, and four words that do not fall into any of these categories are omitted. For the figures for surviving documents and words of surviving literature, and the method by which they were obtained, see above on Figure 3.

Figure 13 (§10.3.1)

Century	Nouns	Adjectives	Verbs	Interjection
IV BC	0	0	0	0
III BC	1	1	0	0
II BC	19	6	0	0
I BC	21	9	0	0
I AD	85	9	1	1
II AD	155	18	0	0
III AD	81	10	1	0
IV AD	94	13	2	0
V AD	73	8	4	0
VI AD	49	8	4	0

Figure 14 (§10.3.2)

Century	Nouns	Adjectives	Verbs	Adverb
IV BC	0	1	0	0
III BC	0	0	0	0
II BC	4	1	0	0
I BC	2	1	2	0
I AD	2	2	2	1
II AD	22	4	2	0
III AD	16	6	1	0
IV AD	19	4	7	0
V AD	16	2	5	0
VI AD	17	7	1	0

12.2 APPENDIX: WHAT COUNTS AS A WORD?

The statistics in this work have been inevitably affected by numerous decisions about which attestations to group together as variants of the same word, and which to exclude entirely as being proper names. Neither type of decision is straightforward,[1] and both are of particular significance for a study with a quantitative element, since the number of Latin loanwords in Greek depends partly on the decisions made about potential variants; indeed some previous studies could be argued to have significantly inflated the number of loanwords by counting variant spellings as different words. To alleviate the subjectivity involved, in this study such decisions normally follow the lead of LSJ and other major reference works, but since such works do not fully explain the basis of their decisions and usually are not fully consistent, a detailed explanation of the principles behind these decisions is offered here.

12.2.1 Which variants constitute separate words?

Words that share the same form but have different etymologies and different meanings are normally considered separate words. For example, LSJ has four different entries with the lemma νέω: a verb meaning 'swim' (cognate with Latin *no* 'swim'), one meaning 'spin' (cognate with *neo* 'spin'), one meaning 'heap up' (contracted from νηέω), and one that is not a verb (deleted in the Supplement). A loanword inherently has a different etymology from a native word (even if the two share an ancestor in the prehistoric period), so when a Latin loanword happens to take the same form as a pre-existing Greek word with a sharply different meaning, like βικίον 'vetch' (from *vicia*) resembling βικίον 'little jar' (from βῖκος + -ιον), the

---

[1] For an assessment of how difficult it is to distinguish between variants and distinct words even in English, see Durkin (2009: 34–8).

loanword is a new word, not an extension of the old one (§2.3).[2] And when two different Latin words ended up with the same form in Greek, they are separate loanwords: σόλιον 1 comes from *solea* and means 'slipper', and σόλιον 2 comes from *solium* and means 'seat'.[3] But such distinctions cannot be carried back too far in the words' history, for once a pair of homonyms starts to be seen by speakers as a single word, that word can itself be borrowed, yielding a new form that has a single etymology. For example, Latin *clibanarius* 'armoured' probably had a different etymology from *clibanarius* 'using a clay oven', but they were borrowed together as Greek κλιβανάριος 'armoured cavalryman', 'baker', which in consequence is a single word.

Sometimes the same meaning can be expressed by a variety of different forms. When the variation is only in accent and/or word division (e.g. ἀβάκτης or ἀβ ἄκτης 'registrar', ἀσηκρῆτις or ἀ σηκρήτις 'imperial secretary'), the issue is straightforward: that variation is due to modern editors rather than ancient writers, and therefore only one word is involved. Likewise straightforward, despite often going back to the ancient writers, are forms that can be classified as spelling variants. Some such variants are obvious examples of common differences in spelling, such as βένετος and οὐένετος 'belonging to the blue circus faction', κοχλιάριον and κοχλιάριν 'spoon', or ὀράριον and ὡράριον 'kerchief'. Others are less obvious, since ancient misspellings (whether of loanwords or of native Greek words) did not always follow predictable patterns: Αὔγουστος and Ἄκουος 'emperor', βήναβλον and μέναυλον 'hunting-spear', κεντουρία and κεντερυωνέα 'century', κοντουβερνάλιος and κοντουβελάνιος 'comrade', κουκούλλιον and κοῦγλιν 'hood', οὐετερανός and βατρανός 'veteran', etc. Even when misspellings are bizarre, they are normally treated by Greek lexica as variant spellings rather than separate words as long as they do not seem to differ systematically in meaning, gender, suffix, or inflection from the spelling taken as the norm (which may not be the most common

spelling in ancient sources and in some cases is not attested at all in such sources).

More difficulty arises when variants differ in gender. Sometimes both genders were probably inherited from Latin, as in κάστελλος and κάστελλον 'fort' from *castellum/castellus*, but other words seem to have acquired gender variants when borrowed into Greek, for example βικίον, βικία, and βίκος 'vetch' from *vicia*, κάρκαρον and κάρκαρος 'prison' from *carcer*, καρούχα and καροῦχον 'carriage' from *carruca*, κάρρον and κάρρος 'cart' from *carrus*, κούκκουμα and κούκουμος 'jar' from *cucuma*, τίτλος and τίτλον 'title' from *titulus*. When no other differences appear to be correlated with the gender variation, such variants are often treated as belonging to the same word, though lexicographical practice is not consistent on this point. When there could be a difference in meaning, gender variants are normally considered separate words; for example the LSJ supplement separates feminine φωκαρία, which may mean 'housekeeper', from neuter φωκάριον 'concubine', though both come from *focaria*.

Words with identifiably different suffixes and/or different inflections have a stronger claim to be different words than ones that differ only in gender; such words are regularly given different entries in lexica. Thus the *Oxford English Dictionary* has separate entries for 'Londoner' and 'Londonian', even though the definition of the latter is 'a Londoner', and most English speakers would no doubt agree with that decision. LSJ and other Greek dictionaries do the same for Greek, for example with different entries for δελματικομαφόριον, δελματικομαφόρτης, and δελματικομαφόρτιον, which probably all designate the same garment (a Dalmatian tunic with a hood).[4] All three forms are well attested, and therefore it is unlikely that one is simply a mistake for another: Greek speakers probably considered them different words.

Sometimes, however, a form that looks as though it has a different suffix is more likely to be a variant of, or a mistake for, another word than a separate word in its own right. This occurs particularly when the form is rare, as with ἴσικος, variant of ἰσίκιον 'dish of mincemeat', δωνάτιον, variant of δωνάτιουον 'imperial gratuity', and

---

[2] In theory these two could be distinguished by the quantity of the first ι, which is short in the plant name and long in the diminutive, but in practice there was probably no distinction between long and short ι at the time most examples were produced.

[3] LSJ combines these into a single entry, but in so doing violates its normal policy on this issue.

[4] LSJ suppl., spelled δαλμ-.

ἐνξεινπλάρεινον, variant of ἐξεμπλάριον 'sample'. Rare forms can generally be considered variants of better-attested words when there is no evidence to the contrary. Of course, one must be alert to evidence of cases other than the citation form; for example προμῶτος and προμώτης 'promoted' look very different in their nominatives singular but are indistinguishable in the genitive. And they almost always occur in the genitive, so that προμῶτος has only two unambiguous examples and προμώτης one; the division may have been created by speakers' uncertainty in forming cases other than the genitive. As a result of further investigation I have sometimes combined variants that are separated in LSJ (such as common πάτρων 'patron' and rare πατρώνης 'patron'), and often combined words included in LSJ with variants not mentioned there (such as κολωνός 'colonist', variant of κόλων 'colonist').

Variants differing in part of speech can occur when adjectives are used as nouns (substantivized). Many Greek adjectives have well-established substantivized forms with specific meanings; for example ἱερός 'holy' has a substantivized neuter singular ἱερόν 'temple' and a substantivized neuter plural ἱερά 'offerings'. Greek speakers may well have thought of these as three separate (albeit related) words, but LSJ treats them as different forms of a single word; indeed LSJ has a consistent policy of not separating substantivizations from the adjectives from which they were created. This policy results from the same etymological principle as the separation of homonyms with different etymologies: historically, adjectives and their substantivizations are indeed forms of a single word. The *Oxford English Dictionary* also groups such variants together, so that 'private' in the sense of 'low-ranking soldier' can be found under the adjective 'private'. But not all lexica follow this principle; for example, the *Oxford Latin Dictionary* has separate entries for the adjective *privatus* 'private' and its substantivized masculine *privatus* 'private citizen'. Such distinctions introduce significant subjectivity into the division of words, for there can be no clear criteria for deciding which substantivizations count as separate words and which do not; for example, *privatus* also has a substantivized neuter meaning 'private property', and the *Oxford Latin Dictionary* treats this as part of the adjective rather than as a separate word.

In Greek many Latin loanwords appear to fall into adjective–noun groups of this type, but often their histories are less straightforward than those of native Greek substantivizations. Sometimes substantivization had already taken place within Latin, and the noun and adjective were borrowed independently. For example, the Latin adjective *praetorius* 'praetorian' had a substantivized neuter *praetorium* 'headquarters'; the latter was borrowed into Greek as πραιτώριον, followed at a later date by the former, which became πραιτώριος. The Greek noun was therefore not a substantivization of the Greek adjective, and accordingly the LSJ supplement has separate entries for πραιτώριον and πραιτώριος. Something similar occurred with *conditum* 'spiced wine' and *conditus* 'seasoned', which became κονδῖτον and κονδῖτος respectively. On the other hand Καισάρεια 'games in honour of Caesar', Καισάρειον 'temple or shrine of Caesar', Καισάρειος (the name of a month), and Καισάρειος (a title) are probably all substantivizations of Καισάρειος 'of Caesar' as result of a single borrowing of *Caesareus*, and LSJ and the Supplement accordingly group them together under the adjective. Sometimes it is uncertain exactly how the derivation and borrowing processes worked. For example, the adjective *privatus* 'private' had a substantivized neuter *privatum* 'private property' already in the first century BC (*OLD s.v. prīvātus* 1c), but it is not certain whether neuter plural πριβᾶτα 'emperor's private property', first attested in the fourth century AD, comes from the Latin substantive or is a separate substantivization of πριβᾶτος 'private', itself from *privatus* and attested from the second or third century AD. The situation is not helped by the existence of πριβᾶτον 'private bath' (attested from the fourth century AD and connected with (*balneum*) *privatum*) and πριβάτη 'emperor's private property' (attested from the third century AD and connected with (*res*) *privata*). I treat all these as variants of πριβᾶτος, but separation would also be legitimate.

12.2.2 *The problem of names*

Names can be borrowed from one language into another, for example English 'Rome' (from Latin *Roma*, perhaps via French), 'Helen' (from Ἑλένη), and 'David' (from Hebrew דוד). Can they therefore be loanwords? On the one hand, borrowed names can clearly share the defining characteristics of loanwords: they may appear frequently in their new language (§2.2.1), show integration in inflection, pronunciation, and spelling (§2.2.2), remain in use for many centuries (§2.2.3), be employed by monolingual native speakers (§2.2.3), and not be marked as foreign (§2.2.3). On the other hand, names are normally excluded from studies of loanwords, and often even from studies of language contact more generally, either without explanation or on the grounds that they are different from other words.[5] Such a difference certainly exists, but it has not been convincingly argued to prevent names from becoming loanwords.[6] In fact the exclusion of names from loanword studies does not really seem to be based on theoretical considerations at all, but on the practical consideration that most languages have so many names that if included they would overwhelm and bury the other words.

The same consideration affects the inclusion of names in lexica. The *Oxford English Dictionary*,[7] *Oxford Latin Dictionary*, and Greek lexicon of Liddell–Scott–Jones all omit most names, in the interests of having finite numbers of entries. That exceptionally ambitious lexicographical enterprise, the *Thesaurus Linguae Latinae*, was originally intended to be the exception to this rule: the first two volumes published, covering words beginning with A and B, included names on the same basis as other words. But this practice was unsustainable even for the *TLL*, which for letters C and D segregated the names into a separate Onomasticon, and from E onwards effectively omitted them altogether.[8]

Under these circumstances it is clear that even if a theoretical justification is lacking, the current study must omit all or most names. But omission of names is not as straightforward as it sounds, for the boundary between names and other words is not completely clear-cut, and major lexica all have slightly different ways of deciding which side of that boundary individual words fall on. Names readily form derivatives, such as 'Londoner' from 'London' and 'Georgian' from 'George'; these can be as common as the names themselves and indeed constitute a potentially unlimited group, since their formation process is productive enough to allow speakers to create them as needed and be instantly understood. Moreover a loanword may be a name in the borrowing language but not in the source language (such as 'Avon', which comes from a Celtic word for 'river'), or in the source language but not in the borrowing language (such as 'marathon' from the Greek place name Μαραθών). The policy of this study, which is heavily informed by the policies of other lexica as described below, is as follows:

A. Words that function synchronically in Greek simply as the names of individual people, divinities, animals, cities, towns, regions, riv-

---

[5] This exclusion is taken for granted to such an extent that most studies do not even mention it, let alone justify it; for example Haspelmath and Tadmor (2009), offering a comprehensive typological study of loanwords, omit names without discussion. Poplack (2018: 41–2) mentions the exclusion of place names in a way that implies similar treatment of all other types of proper names: she evidently considers the exclusion of personal names so obvious as not to need stating. Matras (2020: 41, 113, 118–19, 173) implicitly provides a justification for such exclusion by arguing that 'unique referents' (a category broader than 'names') behave differently from other vocabulary elements, in that they can automatically be used in any language. But the situation is more complicated than that, for names can in fact be altered or translated: see next note.

[6] Anderson (2007), Coates (2006), Durkin (2009: 266–83). Work has been done on the changes names undergo in bilingual contexts (e.g. Haugen 1953: 191–232; Weinreich 1953: 52–3), sometimes involving antiquity and/or Greek: Mullen (2007, 2013) uses names as evidence for language contact in the Western Roman empire, Kahane and Kahane (1972–6: 548–51, 580–1, 1982: 138–9, 146–7) discuss the Greek use of French and Italian place names in the context of a study of Western loanwords in Byzantine Greek, and J. N. Adams (2003: 369–76) discusses Latin writers codeswitching into Greek for names. For work on Latin names in Greek see §8.1.2 n. 14.

[7] Unless otherwise indicated, all statements about the *OED* refer to the current online version; print versions are sometimes significantly different, and the first edition actually capitalized all lemmata.

[8] In theory the rest of the Onomasticon is still forthcoming, but work on it was postponed indefinitely to improve progress on the main dictionary.

ers, and mountains are excluded, regardless of their etymologies. Thus for example Latin *portus* is a word for 'harbour' also used as a place name (= Ostia), but Greek Πόρτος is attested only as a place name and is therefore excluded. Likewise Σακέρδωτις, a feminine from *sacerdos* 'priest', is excluded because it occurs only as a personal name. When a word is used both as a name and in another sense, as with περεγρῖνος 'foreign' and the personal name Περεγρῖνος, or ῥήγιος 'royal' and the place name Ῥήγιον, the word is included but only the non-name uses are considered.

B. Words that function synchronically in Greek as the names of individual buildings or spaces within a town or city, or as the names of months, festivals, games, or groups of people, as well as the epithets (as opposed to the names) of divinities, are not automatically excluded *qua* names, though they may be excluded for other reasons (see C). Thus for example Αὐγουστεῖον 'Augusteum', Ἰανουάριος 'January', Καπετώλιος 'Capitoline' (an epithet of Zeus), Σατορνάλια 'Saturnalia', Ῥωμαῖα (the games known in Latin as *ludi Romani*), and Χριστιανός 'Christian' are all included.

C. Words that function synchronically in Greek as transparent derivatives of names using the standard productive suffixes, without any extended meanings not evident from the suffix used, are included only if they are common enough to be integrated loan-words. Thus the rarely mentioned sects Κυιντιλλιανός 'Quintillian' and Σεκουνδιανός 'Secundian' are excluded, but the more common Ναυατιανός 'Novatianist', Οὐαλεντινιανοί 'Valentinians', and Σαβελλιανός 'Sabellian' are included. Likewise most ethnics are excluded, but Ῥωμαῖος 'Roman' and Λατῖνος 'Latin' are included.

D. Words that were historically names or derivatives of names but had extended uses in Greek (e.g. ethnic adjectives substantivized to refer to objects) are included, but often only the extended uses are considered. Thus for example δελματική 'Dalmatian tunic' (from *dalmatica* 'Dalmatian tunic' and thus ultimately from *Dalmatae* 'Dalmatians'), Φαλέρνος 'Falernian wine' (from the neuter of *Falernus* 'Falernian'), and φαλκίδιον 'minimum portion of an estate reserved for the heir(s)' (from *Falcidia* with the same sense and thus ultimately from the name *Falcidius*) are included. Likewise Καῖσαρ and Αὔγουστος are included, on the grounds that they functioned as titles rather than names in Greek, and so are their derivatives, except ones that were themselves names in Greek, such as Καισάρεια (the place name 'Caesarea') or Καισαρίων (the name of the son of Julius Caesar and Cleopatra). Ῥώμη 'Rome' is also included, on the grounds that its Greek usage went well beyond the name of a place in Italy, as are its derivatives.

The policies of some major lexica are as follows. The *Oxford English Dictionary* explains its policy on names with 'In common with most British dictionaries, the *OED* has never included entries for names, except where the name has acquired an extended or allusive sense: *wellington boot*, *Honiton lace*, *Armageddon*. The names of fictional characters or beings are only included if there is evidence of extended use: *Svengali*, *munchkin*. On the other hand, the familiarity of many eponyms has concealed their origin in personal names: *boycott*, *mackintosh*.'[9] In practice this policy results in the *OED* having doughnut-like constellations of entries around the names of significant people and places, with no entry for the person or place name itself but entries for all its derivatives. For example there is no entry for 'Elizabeth' as a name or as a monarch, but there is one for 'Elizabeth' in its obsolete sense of a coin of Queen Elizabeth, as well as entries for 'Elizabethan', 'Elizabethanism', and 'Elizabethanize'. Likewise there is no entry for 'London' as the name of a city, but there is one for 'London' in its attributive uses (e.g. 'London fog', 'London Bridge'), as well as entries for 'Londoner', 'Londonese', 'Londonesque', 'Londonian', 'Londonish', 'Londonism', 'Londonize', 'Londonologist', 'London pride', and 'Londony'. 'Chaucer' and 'Spenser' have no entries at all, but 'Chaucerian', 'Chaucerism', and 'Spenserian' do.

---

9 From https://public.oed.com/help/#entries. The non-capitalization of 'wellington' is deliberate: the *OED* entry for that word does not capitalize it. I am grateful to Samantha Schad for drawing my attention to this statement and for illuminating discussion on the *OED*'s policies in this respect.

What kind of entity counts for this purpose as having a name? Among places, the *OED* excludes the names not only of cities, but also of countries, continents, regions, rivers, mountains, and lakes – but it includes the names of seas and oceans ('Mediterranean', 'Atlantic', 'Pacific') and of some particular buildings or spaces within a city ('Pantheon', 'Carfax', 'Capitol', 'curia'). These inclusions make sense, because while the names of e.g. rivers and cities tend to be unique words like personal names ('Thames', 'Nile', 'Rhine', 'Rome', 'Paris', 'Berlin'), the names of oceans and of buildings or spaces within cities do not; they are more often formed from other words, which could be names (e.g. 'Atlantic' ultimately from 'Atlas') but often are not (e.g. 'Pacific', 'Pantheon'). The *OED* also excludes names of people, animals, and ships, but it treats the names of deities inconsistently, including 'Jupiter', 'Zeus', 'Minerva', 'Hercules', 'Thor', 'Christ', 'Jesus', 'Allah', 'Buddha', and 'Brahma', but not 'Athena', 'Apollo', 'Dionysus', 'Odin', 'Isis', 'Osiris', 'Mazda', or 'Ahura Mazda'. Names of constellations are included ('Orion', 'Perseus'), as are months, days of the week, holidays ('Christmas', 'Easter', 'Samhain', 'Rosh Hashanah'), athletic contests ('Olympic games', 'Paralympic'), and foods and beverages named after places ('champagne', 'Bourbon', 'wiener', 'Falernian'). Names of groups distinguished by religion, region, or nationality are also included ('Zoroastrian', 'Muslim', 'Arian', 'Donatist', 'African', 'Canadian', 'English').

The result, of course, is that the *OED* includes a significant number of capitalized words: between 4% and 8% of lemmata are capitalized.[10] Many of these are rare, and an argument could be made that the dictionary might have better suited the needs of users by including the most common personal and place names instead of the rarest derivatives of names. Some other dictionaries do include a selection of names. The *Oxford Latin Dictionary* states its policy as follows (p. vi): 'proper names have been included where their intrinsic importance appears to warrant it, or where their inclusion was thought to help in the understanding of literary texts'. Derivatives of many names are also included, yielding clusters of entries such as *Corinthus* 'Corinth', *Corinthius* 'Corinthian', *Corinthiacus* 'Corinthian', *Corinthiensis* 'Corinthian', and *corinthiarius* 'worker or dealer in Corinthian bronze', or *Nero* 'Nero', *Neroneus* 'Neronian', *Neronianus* 'Neronian', and *Neronia* 'festival of Nero'. This policy results in a higher percentage of capitalized lemmata (10%)[11] and necessitates considerable subjectivity in the choice of names for inclusion, but it avoids the doughnut-shaped clusters of the *OED* and thus arguably produces a more coherent work.

The *Thesaurus Linguae Latinae*, in those volumes from which names are excluded, makes a very different kind of division: not only are the names of people, divinities, cities, regions, and natural features excluded, but also derivatives of such names. Thus there are no entries for *Graecus* 'Greek', *Macedonicus* 'Macedonian', *Italicus* 'Italian', *Iunonius* 'connected with Juno', *Lupercal* 'fertility festival of the Luperci', *Olympias* 'Olympiad', *Palatium* 'imperial residence on the Palatine Hill', etc.[12] This exclusion takes no

---

10 The *OED* is currently undergoing a major revision, and the capitalization rate varies between the revised and unrevised sections. In the most recent print edition of the *OED* (1989, pre-revision), a sample of 1,000 lemmata consisting of the first lemma that is a full word (i.e. excluding letters of the alphabet, prefixes, and suffixes, but not hyphenated words or acronyms) on every tenth page yields 41 capitalized lemmata, and thus a capitalization rate of 4%. In the fully revised sections of the online version (i.e. starting with the letter M), a sample of 500 lemmata consisting of every hundredth lemma yields 42 capitalized lemmata, and thus a capitalization rate of 8%.

11 A sample of 1,000 lemmata, consisting of the first lemma that is a full word (i.e. excluding letters of the alphabet, prefixes, and suffixes) on each of the first 1,000 pages that have at least one new lemma (i.e. excluding pages that consist entirely of lemmata continued from the previous page, and therefore going up to p. 1023), yields 100 capitalized lemmata. There does not seem to be a difference from the *OED* in the type of words capitalized.

12 An exception is made for *latinitas* 'Latinity', *latinizo* 'translate into Latin', and *latino* 'translate into Latin', though *Latinus* and other words on that stem are excluded. The English *praemonenda* (section II A) state, 'Where problems arise over the distinction between proper names and appellatives, each case is decided on its merits', with a note observing, 'Thus examples of *luna*, *musa*, *oceanus* and *ops* referring to deities are placed with the appellatives. Less fortunate was the decision to consign such words as *levita* and *palatium* to the Onomasticon.'

account of the derivatives' meanings and therefore creates some peculiar discrepancies; for example, the month names *Ianuarius, Martius, Maius, Iunius,* and *Iulius* are excluded because of their etymologies, while *Februarius, Aprilis, Augustus, October,* and *December* are included (*Aprilis* and *Augustus* only because they begin with *A,* of course; the *TLL*'s gradual publication process has not yet reached *September* or *November*). The reason for this policy is historical: once a decision had been made to segregate names into the Onomasticon, it made sense to keep all words derived from names with the names from which they were derived. Therefore the original idea was not that *Ianuarius* should be omitted, but that it should be treated with the god's name *Ianus* – but the postponement of the Onomasticon meant that from E onwards words derived from names ended up being simply omitted, whatever their other meanings.[13] Names of festivals, buildings, and spaces within a city are in principle included (though in practice many are excluded for being derivatives of other names): *Kalendae, Idus, Pantheon, Lauretum, curia, forum.*[14]

The Greek lexicon of Liddell–Scott–Jones (LSJ) does not state a policy on inclusion of names, and (as one might expect in a work with such a long and complex history[15]) no consistent policy can be deduced from its practice. There are entries for the names Ὅμηρος, Σαπφώ, Σοφοκλέης, Πλάτων, Σωκράτης, and Ἀπολλόδωρος, but not for Ἡρόδοτος, Θουκυδίδης, Ἀριστοτέλης, Ἱπποκράτης, Περικλῆς, Ἀλκιβιάδης,

or Θεμιστοκλῆς. Names of places are included more often than names of people, but still in fairly unpredictable fashion: there are entries for Ἑλλάς, Ἰθάκη, Ἔφεσος, Ἁλικαρνασσός, Σαλαμίς, and Αἴγινα, but not for Κνωσσός, Σφακτηρία, or Θεσσαλονίκη. Major festivals, games, and months are included: Παναθήναια, Ἴσθμια, Βοηδρομιών. Derivatives of names also appear: along with Ἀθήνη 'Athena' and Ἀθῆναι 'Athens' there are entries for Ἀθήναια 'festival of Athena', Ἀθηναΐζω 'be wise as Athena', Ἀθηναϊκός 'pertaining to Athena', Ἀθήναιον 'temple of Athena', Ἀθηναῖος 'Athenian', Ἀθηναιότης 'quality of being Athenian', and Ἀθηνιάω 'long to be at Athens',[16] while another cluster includes Λάκων 'Laconian', Λακωνίζω 'imitate Lacedaemonian manners', Λακωνικός 'Laconian', Λακώνιον 'female garment', Λακωνίς 'Laconian', Λακωνισμός 'imitation of Lacedaemonian manners', Λακωνιστής 'one who imitates the Lacedaemonians', Λακωνομανέω 'to be mad on Spartan ways', and Λακωνόσημος 'with stripes in Laconian fashion'. Sometimes there are entries for derivatives of names that are not themselves included, as in the *OED*: for example Περίκλειος 'of Pericles', ἀλκιβιάδες (shoes named after Alcibiades), and a cluster of words related to Alexander the Great, who is not himself included.[17]

Overall, however, the percentage of capitalized words in LSJ is 3%, significantly lower than that

---

[13] Statistics on the percentage of words capitalized in the *TLL* would not be meaningful, because the capitalization policies of the *TLL* are very different from those of the other dictionaries examined; for example no capitals are used for *favonius* 'west wind', *latinitas* 'Latinity', or *october* 'October', all of which are capitalized by the *OLD*.

[14] *Pantheon* is *s.v. pantheus* (239.36–54); under *cūria* are names of individual curiae (1482.9–1484.31), and under *forum* names of individual fora (e.g. 1203.36–1204.26).

[15] The 1996 edition of LSJ is effectively a reprint of the ninth edition from 1940 with the addition of a Revised Supplement. The ninth edition incorporates a host of changes added gradually by a variety of editors since the first edition in 1843, which was itself based on a Greek–German lexicon by Franz Passow (1831), which was based on an earlier Greek–German lexicon by Johann Gottlob Schneider from 1797–8. (Preface to LSJ; see also Stray *et al.* 2019.)

[16] Two more derivatives are added in the Supplement, Ἀθηνάδιον 'small image of Athena' and Ἀθηναϊσταί 'guild of worshippers of Athena', for a total of 11 lemmata on the Ἀθην- stem. But even this is a comparatively small proportion of what could have been included. The *Diccionario Griego–Español* (*DGE*) has 34 lemmata on the Ἀθην- stem, adding 19 words not in LSJ or the Supplement (Ἀθηναγόρας, Ἀθηνάγουρον, Ἀθηνάδας, Ἀθηναία, Ἀθήναιος, ἀθηναῖς, Ἀθηναῖς, Ἀθηνακῶν, Ἀθήνιον, Ἀθήνιππος, Ἀθηνίς, Ἀθηνίων, Ἀθηνογένης, Ἀθηνοδίκη, Ἀθηνόδωρος, Ἀθηνοκλῆς, Ἀθηνόκριτος, Ἀθηνοφάνης, Ἀθηνώ) and making into separate lemmata four forms that in LSJ are included under Ἀθῆναι (Ἀθήναζε, Ἀθήνηθεν, Ἀθήνησι, Ἀθήνοθεν). And *DGE* has also been selective, for a search of the *Thesaurus Linguae Graecae* database suggests that at least four additional words on this stem are attested before AD 600: Ἀθηναΐτης, Ἀθήνιος, Ἀθηνόβιος, and Ἀθηνόδοτος.

[17] Ἀλεξανδρίζω 'to be on Alexander's side', Ἀλεξανδριστής 'partisan of Alexander', and Ἀλεξανδροκόλαξ 'flatterer of Alexander'. The name Ἀλέξανδρος has an entry, but the only individual mentioned there is Homer's Paris, who is not relevant to these derivatives.

in the *Oxford Latin Dictionary*.[18] That fact must be the result of its compilers' policies, not of any features in the Greek language itself or in our textual evidence for it, for some other Greek dictionaries have much higher percentages of capitalized entries.[19] The creators of LSJ appear to have been very restrained about including words derived from names, especially derivatives formed with highly predictable suffixes. For example, the suffix -ίτης can be added to any place name to form a noun designating a man from that place, as Ἀβδηρίτης 'man from Abdera', Γαδειρίτης 'man from Cadiz', Ναυκρατίτης 'man from Naucratis', or Συβαρίτης 'man from Sybaris'. LSJ includes these words but omits many others formed on the same principle, including Ἀμβασίτης 'man from Ambason' (*DGE*), Ἀμφιπολίτης 'man from Amphipolis' (*DGE*), Ἀργιλίτης 'man from Argilia' (*DGE*), Ἀρσινοΐτης 'man from the Arsinoite nome' (*DGE*), Ἀσκαλωνίτης 'man from Ascalon' (*DGE*), Γιλδίτης 'man from Gilda' (*DGE*), Ἑρμοπολίτης 'man from Hermopolis' (e.g. *P.Oxy.* LXXII.4903.4), Νικοπολίτης 'man from Nicopolis' (e.g. Plut. *Mor.* 698a), Ὀξυρυγχίτης 'man from Oxyrhynchus' (e.g. *P.Oxy.* XXVII.2476.29), Ταυρομενίτης 'man from Tauromenion' (e.g. Strabo 6.2.6), and Φασηλίτης 'man from Phaselis' (e.g. Polybius 30.9.7). The LSJ supplement adds such words only occasionally and incidentally (e.g. Μεγαλοπολίτης 'citizen of Megalopolis',

added as a further meaning to an existing lemma, and Ὠρείτης 'of Oreus', a title of Apollo); the absence of Ὀξυρυγχίτης and Ἑρμοπολίτης from the Supplement is particularly striking since these words are common in papyri and the editors of the Supplement clearly made a special effort to add words from papyri, even rare ones. Evidently the editors did not feel that such omissions posed a systematic problem.

Another suffix highly productive of capitalized derivatives is -ιανός, plural -ιανοί, which could be added to almost any word to indicate a Christian sect or heresy (§6.4). Examples include Ἀρειανός 'Arian' (i.e. a follower of Arius), Δωνατιανοί 'Donatists' (i.e. followers of Donatus), Ἀδαμιανοί 'Adamites', Ἀετιανοί 'followers of Aëtius', Εὐνομιανοί 'followers of Eunomius', Θεοδοσιανοί 'Theodosians', Κερδωνιανοί 'followers of a dualistic heresy initiated by Cerdon', Κηρινθιανοί 'followers of Cerinthus', Κολλυριδιανοί 'Collyridians', Μακεδονιανοί 'followers of Macedonius', Μελχισεδεκιανοί 'members of sect holding Melchizedek to be or represent a divine power', Νοητιανοί 'followers of Noetus', Σεκουνδιανοί 'Secundians', Σηθιανοί 'Sethians', Σιμωνιανός 'follower of Simon Magus', and Φωτεινιανός 'follower of Photinus' (Lampe 1961). None of these sect names appears in LSJ or in the Supplement; as some are very common and not particularly late, the exclusion is clearly deliberate.

The tacit policy of LSJ and its Supplement therefore seems to be the exclusion not only of most names, but also of most words derived from names. Such capitalized words as are included seem to have been chosen not by any strict application of any criteria such as used by the *OED* or *TLL*, but by following these principles: (1) words important in the Classical literary canon are more worthy of inclusion than rarer or later terms, (2) derivatives of names are sometimes more worthy of inclusion than the names themselves, but (3) derivatives formed using highly productive, transparent derivation processes are generally less worthy of inclusion.

---

[18] A sample of 1,000 lemmata, collected in the same way as for the *OLD* (see n. 11) and going up to p. 1001, yields 31 capitalized lemmata. Again there does not seem to be a difference in the capitalization policy (at least not in the print version of LSJ: the *TLG*'s online version of LSJ de-capitalizes some lemmata that are capitalized in the print version, thereby ending up with an even lower percentage of capitalized lemmata).

[19] *DGE* capitalizes 20% of its lemmata (a sample of 1,000 lemmata, collected in the same way as for the *OLD* and going up to p. 1017, yields 202 capitalized lemmata), but on the other hand *LBG* capitalizes only 2% (a sample of 1,000 lemmata, collected in the same way as for the *OLD* and going up to p. 1001, yields 21 capitalized lemmata). Again there do not seem to be differences in which words are capitalized.

ABBREVIATIONS

More information on the editions of papyri and ostraca can be found in the *Checklist of Editions of Greek, Latin, Demotic, and Coptic Papyri, Ostraca, and Tablets*, J. F. Oates, W. H. Willis, *et al.* (www.papyri.info/docs/checklist). More information on the editions of inscriptions can be found in the *Association internationale d'épigraphie grecque et latine (AIEGL)* epigraphic abbreviation list (https://aiegl.org/grepiabbr.html) and in the bibliography of the Packard Humanities Institute inscriptions site (https://epigraphy.packhum.org/biblio). More information on the editions of literary texts can be found in the *Thesaurus Linguae Graecae Canon of Greek Authors and Works* (http://stephanus.tlg.uci.edu/canon.php).

abl.	ablative
acc.	accusative
ACO	*Acta conciliorum oecumenicorum.* E. Schwartz. Berlin 1925–
Act.Andr.	*Acta Graeca Andreae.* J.-M. Prieur, *Acta Andreae.* Turnhout 1989
Act.Scillit.	*Acta Scillitanorum martyrum.* J. A. Robinson, *The passion of S. Perpetua* (= J. A. Robinson, *Texts and Studies*, I.II). Cambridge 1891: 105–17
Act.Xanth.Polyx.	*Acta Xanthippae et Polyxenae.* M. R. James, *Apocrypha anecdota.* Cambridge 1893: 43–85
ad loc.	*ad locum* '(in commentary/discussion) on that passage'
Adam.	Adamantius Theologus, *De recta in deum fide.* W. H. van de Sande Bakhuyzen, *Der Dialog des Adamantius.* Leipzig 1901
adj.	adjective
AE	*L'Année épigraphique.* Paris 1888–
Aes.	Aeschylus. ***Pr.*** = *Prometheus vinctus*, ***Th.*** = *Septem contra Thebas*
Aëtius	Aëtius Medicus, *Iatricorum.* **Books 1–8:** A. Olivieri, *Aëtii Amideni libri medicinales* (*Corpus medicorum Graecorum*, VIII). Leipzig 1935–50. **Book 9:** S. Zervos, Ἀετίου Ἀμιδηνοῦ

λόγος ἔνατος', *Athena* (= Ἀθηνᾶ σύγγραμα περιοδικόν) 23 (1911): 273–392. **Book 11:** C. Daremberg and C. É. Ruelle, *Oeuvres de Rufus d'Éphèse.* Paris 1879: 85–126, 568–81. **Book 12:** G. A. Kostomoiros, Ἀετίου λόγος δωδέκατος, Paris 1892. **Book 15:** S. Zervos, Ἀετίου Ἀμιδηνοῦ λόγος δέκατος πέμπτος', *Athena* (= Ἀθηνᾶ σύγγραμα περιοδικόν) 21 (1909): 3–144. **Book 16:** S. Zervos, *Gynaekologie des Aëtios*, Leipzig 1901

AfP	*Archiv für Papyrusforschung und verwandte Gebiete*
Agath.	Agathangelus. ***Arm.*** = *Historia Armeniae* (versio Graeca). G. Lafontaine, *La version grecque ancienne du livre Arménien d'Agathange.* Louvain-la-Neuve 1973. ***Greg.*** = *Passio Gregorii Illuminatoris* (rec. altera). G. Garitte, *Documents pour l'étude du livre d'Agathange.* Rome 1946: 23–116
Agora de Palmyre	*L'Agora de Palmyre.* C. Delplace and J. Dentzer-Feydy. Beirut 2005
Agora X	*The Athenian agora*, X: *Weights, measures, and tokens.* M. Lang and M. Crosby. Princeton 1964
Agora XVI	*The Athenian agora*, XVI: *Inscriptions: the decrees.* A. G. Woodhead. Princeton 1997
Agora XVII	*The Athenian agora*, XVII: *Inscriptions: the funerary monuments.* D. W. Bradeen. Princeton 1974
Agora XXI	*The Athenian agora*, XXI: *Graffiti and dipinti.* M. Lang. Princeton 1976
AJP	*American Journal of Philology*
alch.	alchemist
Alex.Trall.	Alexander of Tralles, *Therapeutica* etc. T. Puschmann, *Alexander von Tralles*, I–II. Vienna 1878–9. Cited as vol. III: T. Puschmann, *Nachträge zu Alexander Trallianus.* Berlin 1886

Antec.	Theophilus Antecessor, *Paraphrasis Institutionum* (Lokin *et al.* 2010)		*des Athanasios von Emesa.* Frankfurt 1989
Anton.Hag.		Barsanuph.Jo.	Barsanuphius et Joannes. F. Neyt
V.Sym.Styl.	Antonius Hagiographus, *Vita Symeonis Stylitae senioris.* H. Lietzmann, *Das Leben des heiligen Symeon Stylites.* Leipzig 1908		and P. de Angelis-Noah, *Barsanuphe et Jean de Gaza: Correspondance.* Paris 1997–2002
Apophth.Patr.	*Apophthegmata Patrum, collectio systematica.* J.-C. Guy, *Les apophtegmes des pères: collection systématique.* Paris 1993–2005	BASP	*Bulletin of the American Society of Papyrologists*
		BCH	*Bulletin de correspondance hellénique*
		BGU	*Aegyptische Urkunden aus den koeniglichen* (later *staatlichen*) *Museen zu Berlin: griechische Urkunden.* Berlin
App.	Appian. *BC* = *Bella civilia*		
Ar.	Aristophanes. *Ach.* = *Acharnians,* *Av.* = *Aves,* *Ec.* = *Ecclesiazusae,* *Eq.* = *Equites,* *Nu.* = *Nubes,* *Pl.* = *Plutus,* *Ra.* = *Ranae,* *Th.* = *Thesmophoriazusae,* *V.* = *Vespae*		1895–
		BL	*Berichtigungsliste der griechischen Papyrusurkunden aus Ägypten.* Leiden etc. 1922–
Ast.Soph.	Asterius Sophista, *Commentarii in Psalmos* = *Homiliae in Psalmos.* M. Richard, *Asterii sophistae commentariorum in Psalmos quae supersunt.* Oslo 1956	Callin. V.Hypat.	Callinicus monachus, *Vita sancti Hypati.* G. J. M. Bartelink, *Callinicos: Vie d'Hypatios.* Paris 1971
		Carth.	*Canones Synodi apud Cartaginem.* P.-P. Joannou, *Discipline générale antique,* I.II. Rome 1962: 190–436
Athan.	Athanasius Alexandrinus. *Apol. Const.* = *Apologia ad Constantium imperatorem.* H. C. Brennecke, A. von Stockhausen, and U. Heil, *Athanasius: Werke,* II: *Die 'Apologien',* VIII. Berlin 2006. *Apol.Sec.* = *Apologia contra Arianos sive Apologia secunda.* H. G. Opitz, *Athanasius: Werke,* II.I. Berlin 1940. *Decr.* = *De decretis Nicaenae synodi.* H. G. Opitz, *Athanasius: Werke,* II.I. Berlin 1940. *Ep.Encycl.* = *Epistula encyclica.* H. G. Opitz, *Athanasius: Werke,* II.I. Berlin 1940. *H.Ar.* = *Historia Arianorum.* H. G. Opitz, *Athanasius: Werke,* II.I. Berlin 1940. *Pet.Ar.* = *Petitiones Arianorum.* H. C. Brennecke, A. von Stockhausen, and U. Heil, *Athanasius: Werke,* II: *Die 'Apologien',* VIII. Berlin 2006. *Syn.* = *De synodis Arimini in Italia et Seleuciae in Isauria.* H. G. Opitz, *Athanasius: Werke,* II.I. Berlin 1940.	C.Epist.Lat.	*Corpus epistularum latinarum papyris tabulis ostracis servatarum.* P. Cugusi. Florence 1992–2002
		cf.	indicates that the following material is relevant to the statement made but is not its source; does not indicate whether that material supports or opposes the statement
		CGL	*Corpus glossariorum Latinorum.* G. Goetz. Leipzig 1888–1923
		ChLA	*Chartae Latinae antiquiores.* A. Bruckner, R. Marichal, *et al.* Olten or Dietikon 1954–98
		Chrest.Mitt.	*Grundzüge und Chrestomathie der Papyruskunde,* II.II: *Juristischer Teil, Chrestomathie.* L. Mitteis. Leipzig 1912
		Chrest.Wilck.	*Grundzüge und Chrestomathie der Papyruskunde,* I.II: *Historischer Teil, Chrestomathie.* U. Wilcken. Leipzig 1912
Ath.Mech.	Athenaeus Mechanicus, *De machinis.* R. Schneider, *Griechische Poliorketiker,* I (*Abhandlungen der königlichen Gesellschaft der Wissenschaften zu Göttingen, philologisch-historische Klasse,* N.S. 12 no. 5). Berlin 1912: 7–37	CID	*Corpus des inscriptions de Delphes.* Paris 1977–
		CIG	*Corpus inscriptionum Graecarum.* A. Boeckh. Berlin 1828–77
		CIL	*Corpus inscriptionum Latinarum.* Berlin 1863–
		CIRB	*Corpus inscriptionum Regni Bosporani.* V. V. Struve. Saint Petersburg 1965
Ath.Schol.	Athanasius Scholasticus, *Novellae constitutiones.* D. Simon and S. Troianos, *Das Novellensyntagma*	CISemiticarum II.III	*Corpus inscriptionum Semiticarum,* II.III. Paris 1926

Coll.Herm.	*Colloquia of the Hermeneumata Pseudodositheana.* **C** = Celtis, **H** = Harleianum, **LS** = Leidense–Stephani, **ME** = Monacensia–Einsidlensia, **Mp** = Montepessulana, **S** = Stephani (Dickey 2012–15)
Corinth VIII.I	*Corinth*, VIII.I: *Greek inscriptions 1896–1927.* B. D. Meritt. Cambridge, Mass. 1931
Corinth VIII.III	*Corinth*, VIII.III: *the inscriptions 1926–1950.* J. H. Kent. Princeton 1966
Cos.Indic.	Cosmas Indicopleustes, *Topographia Christiana.* W. Wolska-Conus, *Cosmas Indicopleustès: Topographie chrétienne.* Paris 1968–73
C.Pap.Gr. I	*Corpora papyrorum Graecarum*, I: *i contratti di baliatico.* M. M. Masciadri and O. Montevecchi. Milan 1984
CPR	*Corpus papyrorum Raineri.* Vienna 1895–
Cyran.	Cyranides. D. V. Kaimakes, *Die Kyraniden.* Meisenheim am Glan 1976
Cyr.S.	Cyrillus Scythopolitanus. **Vit.Eu.** = *Vita Euthymii,* **Vit.Sab.** = *Vita Sabae.* E. Schwartz, *Kyrillos von Skythopolis.* Leipzig 1939
Dan.Sket.	Daniel of Sketis. **AA** = *Andronicus et Athanasia,* **AP** = *Anastasia Patricia,* **Eu.** = *Eulogius latomus,* **M.** = *Marcus salus.* B. Dahlman, *Saint Daniel of Sketis: a group of hagiographic texts.* Uppsala 2007
dat.	dative
DÉLG	*Dictionnaire étymologique de la langue grecque: histoire des mots.* P. Chantraine. Paris 1968–80
DÉLG Suppl.	*Supplément to Dictionnaire étymologique de la langue grecque: histoire des mots.* A. Blanc, C. de Lamberterie, and J.-L. Perpillou. Paris 1999
deriv.	derivative
DGE	*Diccionario Griego–Español.* F. R. Adrados and E. Gangutia Elícegui. Madrid 1980–. Online version (which sometimes differs from the printed version) cited from http://dge.cchs.csic.es
DH *AR*	Dionysius of Halicarnassus, *Antiquitates Romanae.* K. Jacoby, *Dionysii Halicarnasei Antiquitatum Romanarum quae supersunt.* Leipzig 1885–1905
DMLBS	*Dictionary of medieval Latin from British sources.* R. E. Latham. Oxford 1975–2013
Dor.Gaz.	Dorotheus of Gaza. **Doct.Div.** = *Doctrinae diversae,* **Ep.** = *Epistulae,* **Vit.Dos.** = *Vita sancti Dosithei.* J. de Préville and L. Regnault, *Dorothée de Gaza: oeuvres spirituelles.* Paris 1963
Dor.Poet. *Visio*	Dorotheus Poeta, *Visio Dorothei.* A. H. M. Kessels and P. W. van der Horst, 'The Vision of Dorotheus (Pap. Bodmer 29): edited with introduction, translation and notes', *Vigiliae Christianae* 41 (1987): 313–59
Dsc.	Dioscorides. **No title** = *De materia medica,* **Eup.** = *Euporista* (Wellmann 1906–14)
ed(d).	editor(s), edition
Edict.Diocl.	Edict of Diocletian. Lauffer 1971 unless otherwise specified
EphraemSyr.	Ephraem Syrus. K. G. Phrantzolas, Ὁσίου Ἐφραίμ τοῦ Σύρου· Ἔργα. Thessaloniki 1988–98
Epict. *Diss.*	Epictetus, *Dissertationes ab Arriano digestae.* H. Schenkl, *Epicteti Dissertationes ab Arriano digestae.* Leipzig 1916
Epiph.	Epiphanius Constantiensis. **Anac.** = *Anacephalaeosis* (spurious). K. Holl, *Epiphanius,* I–III: *Ancoratus und Panarion.* Leipzig 1915–33. **Anc.** = *Ancoratus.* K. Holl, *Epiphanius,* I: *Ancoratus und Panarion.* Leipzig 1915. **Gem.** = *De* XII *gemmis* (Ruelle 1898: 193–9). **Mens.** = *De mensuris et ponderibus.* E. Moutsoulas, 'Τὸ "Περὶ μέτρων καὶ σταθμῶν" ἔργον Ἐπιφανίου τοῦ Σαλαμῖνος', Θεολογία 44 (1973): 157–98. **Mens.4** = *De mensuris et ponderibus, excerptum Graecum 4* (Hultsch 1864: 259–76). **Pan.** = *Panarion.* K. Holl, *Epiphanius,* I–III: *Ancoratus und Panarion.* Leipzig 1915–33. **PG**: see *s.v.* **Theod.** = *Epistula ad Theodosium imperatorem (fragmenta).* K. Holl, *Gesammelte Aufsätze zur Kirchengeschichte,* II. Tübingen 1928: 360–2
Erot. *Voc.Hipp.*	Erotian, *Vocum Hippocraticarum collectio.* E. Nachmanson, *Erotiani vocum Hippocraticarum collectio cum fragmentis.* Gothenburg 1918
esp.	especially

Eur.   Euripides. **Hec.** = *Hecuba*, **Or.** = *Orestes*, **Ph.** = *Phoenissae*

Eus.   Eusebius Caesariensis. **HE** = *Historia ecclesiastica*. G. Bardy, *Eusèbe de Césarée: Histoire ecclésiastique*. Paris 1952–8. **PE** = *Praeparatio evangelica*. K. Mras, *Eusebius Werke*, VIII: *Die Praeparatio evangelica*. Berlin 1954–6. **VC** = *Vita Constantini*. F. Winkelmann, *Eusebius Werke*, I.I: *Über das Leben des Kaisers Konstantin*. Berlin 1975

Eutropius   Eutropius, *Breviarium ab urbe condita* (*Paeanii translatio*). S. P. Lampros, 'Παιανίου μετάφρασις εἰς τὴν τοῦ Εὐτροπίου Ῥωμαϊκὴν ἱστορίαν', *Νέος Ἑλληνομνήμων* 9 (1912): 9–113

Evagr.Schol.
HE   Evagrius Scholasticus, *Historia ecclesiastica*. L. Parmentier and J. Bidez, *The ecclesiastical history of Evagrius with the scholia*. London 1898

Ev.Barth.   *Evangelium Bartholomaei*. N. Bonwetsch, 'Die apokryphen Fragen des Bartholomäus', *Nachrichten von der königlichen Gesellschaft der Wissenschaften zu Göttingen, philologisch-historische Klasse* (1897): 1–42

Ev.Barth.frag.   *Evangelium Bartholomaei, fragmenta*. E. Tisserant and A. Wilmart, 'Fragments grecs et latins de l'Évangile de Barthélemy', *Revue biblique* 10 (1913): 185–90, 321–33

F.Delphes III   *Fouilles de Delphes*, III: *Épigraphie*. Paris 1909–85

fem.   feminine

FHG   *Fragmenta historicorum Graecorum*. K. Müller. Paris 1841–72

FIRA II   *Fontes iuris Romani antejustiniani, pars altera: auctores*. J. Baviera and J. Furlani. 2nd ed., Florence 1940

frag.   fragment

Gel.Cyz.   Gelasius Cyzicenus, *Historia ecclesiastica*. M. Heinemann and G. Loeschcke, *Gelasius: Kirchengeschichte*. Leipzig 1918

gen.   genitive

Geront. *V.Mel.*   Gerontius, *Vita S. Melaniae Junioris*. D. Gorce, *Vie de Sainte Mélanie*. Paris 1962

Gloss. *Herm.*   *Hermeneumata Pseudodositheana*. **A.** = *Amploniana*, **L.** = *Leidensia*, **M.** = *Monacensia*, **Mp.** = *Montepessulana*, **S.** = *Stephani*, **V.** = *Vaticana*. CGL III

Gloss. *Idiom.*   *Idiomata nominativa quae per genera efferuntur*. CGL II.537–48

Gloss. Ps.-Cyril.   Ps.-Cyrillus, *Glossae Graeco-Latinae*. CGL II.213–483

Gloss.
Ps.-Philox.   Ps.-Philoxenus, *Glossae Latino-Graecae*. CGL II.1–212

Gloss. Serv.   *Glossae Servii grammatici*. CGL II.507–36

Hdn.   Herodian the grammarian. **Διχρ.** = Περὶ διχρόνων, **Κλισ.Ὀνομ.** = Περὶ κλίσεως ὀνομάτων, **Μον.Λεξ.** = Περὶ μονήρους λέξεως, **Ὀρθογρ.** = Περὶ ὀρθογραφίας, **Pros.Cath.** = *De prosodia catholica*. A. Lentz, *Grammatici Graeci*, III.I–III.II: *Herodiani Technici reliquiae*. Leipzig 1867–70

Hdn.Hist.   Herodian the historian, *Ab excessu divi Marci*. K. Stavenhagen, *Herodiani ab excessu divi Marci libri octo*. Leipzig 1922

Her.Mech.   Heron Mechanicus. **Def.** = *Definitiones*, **Geom.** = *Geometrica*, **Mens.** = *De mensuris*, **Stereom.** = *Stereometrica*. J. L. Heiberg, *Heronis Alexandrini opera quae supersunt omnia*, IV–V. Leipzig 1912–14. **Pneum.** = *Pneumatica*. W. Schmidt, *Heronis Alexandrini opera quae supersunt omnia*, I. Leipzig 1899

Hes. *Op.*   Hesiod, *Opera et Dies*

Hesych.   Hesychius the lexicographer. **Α–Ο:** K. Latte, *Hesychii Alexandrini Lexicon*. Copenhagen 1953–66. **Π–Ω:** P. A. Hansen, I. C. Cunningham, *Hesychii Alexandrini Lexicon*. Berlin 2005–9

Hieroph.   Hierophilus. **Nut.** = *De nutriendi methodo* (Ideler 1841: 409–17). **Πῶς** = Πῶς ὀφείλει διαιτᾶσθαι (Delatte 1939: 455–66)

Hippiatr.   *Hippiatrica*. **Hippiatr.Berl.** = *Hippiatrica Berolinensia*, **Hippiatr.Camb.** = *Hippiatrica Cantabrigensia*, **Hippiatr.Par.** = *Hippiatrica Parisina*, **Pel.** = Greek translation of Pelagonius. Hoppe and Oder 1924–7

I.Albanie méridionale   *Corpus des inscriptions grecques d'Illyrie méridionale et d'Épire*, III: *Inscriptions d'Albanie*. P. Cabanes and F. Drini. Athens 2016

I.Alexandrie imp. *Recueil des inscriptions grecques et latines (non funéraires) d'Alexandrie impériale (Ier–IIIe s. apr. J.-C.).* F. Kayser. Cairo 1994

I.Anazarbos *Die Inschriften von Anazarbos und Umgebung, 1: Inschriften aus dem Stadtgebiet und der nächsten Umgebung der Stadt.* M. H. Sayar. Bonn 2000

I.Ano Maked. Ἐπιγραφές Ἄνω Μακεδονίας (Ἐλίμεια, Ἐορδαία, Νότια Λυγκηστίς, Ὀρεστίς), 1: Κατάλογος ἐπιγραφῶν. A. Rizakis and G. Touratsoglou. Athens 1985

I.Apameia Pylai *Die Inschriften von Apameia (Bithynien) und Pylai.* T. Corsten. Bonn 1987

I.Aphrodisias and Rome *Aphrodisias and Rome.* J. Reynolds. London 1982

I.Aphrodisias Late Ant. *Aphrodisias in late antiquity: the late Roman and Byzantine inscriptions.* C. Roueché. London 1989

I.Aphrodisias Performers *Performers and partisans at Aphrodisias in the Roman and late Roman periods.* C. Roueché. London 1993

I.Arykanda *Die Inschriften von Arykanda.* S. Şahin. Bonn 1994

I.Assos *Die Inschriften von Assos.* R. Merkelbach. Bonn 1976

I.Beroia Ἐπιγραφές Κάτω Μακεδονίας, 1: Ἐπιγραφές Βεροίας. L. Gounaropoulou and M. V. Chatzopoulou. Athens 1998

I.Byzantion *Die Inschriften von Byzantion, 1: die Inschriften.* A. Łajtar. Bonn 2000

I.Caesarea Maritima *The Greek and Latin inscriptions of Caesarea Maritima.* C. M. Lehmann and K. G. Holum. Boston 2000

I.Callatis *Inscripţiile din Scythia Minor greceşti şi latine = Inscriptiones Scythiae minoris Graecae et Latinae = Inscriptions grecques et latines de scythie mineure, III: Callatis et son territoire.* A. Avram. Bucharest 1999

I.Chr.Asie Mineure *Recueil des inscriptions grecques chrétiennes d'Asie Mineure, 1.* H. Grégoire. Paris 1922

I.Chr.Bulgarien *Spätgriechische und spätlateinische Inschriften aus Bulgarien.* V. Beševliev. Berlin 1964

I.Chr.Égypte *Recueil des inscriptions grecques–chrétiennes d'Égypte.* G. Lefebvre. Cairo 1907

I.Chr.Macédoine *Recueil des inscriptions chrétiennes de Macédoine du IIIe au VIe siècle.* D. Feissel. Paris 1983

I.Chr.România *Inscripţiile greceşti şi latine din secolele IV–XIII descoperite în România.* E. Popescu. Bucharest 1976

I.Cilicie *Inscriptions de Cilicie.* G. Dagron and D. Feissel. Paris 1987

I.Cos Paton *The inscriptions of Cos.* W. R. Paton and E. L. Hicks. Oxford 1891

I.Cos Segre *Iscrizioni di Cos.* M. Segre. Rome 1993

I.Cret. *Inscriptiones Creticae.* M. Guarducci. Rome 1935–50

I.Dacia Rom. *Inscripţiile Daciei Romane = Inscriptiones Daciae Romanae.* Bucharest 1975–

I.Délos *Inscriptions de Délos.* F. Dürrbach. Paris 1926–37

I.Delta *Le Delta égyptien d'après les textes grecs, 1: les confins libyques.* A. Bernand. Cairo 1970

I.Didyma *Didyma, 11: die Inschriften.* A. Rehm. Berlin 1958

I.Eleusis *Eleusis, the inscriptions on stone.* K. Clinton. Athens 2005–8

I.Ephesos *Die Inschriften von Ephesos.* Bonn 1979–84

I.Erythrai Klazomenai *Die Inschriften von Erythrai und Klazomenai,* H. Engelmann and R. Merkelbach. Bonn 1972–3.

I.Estremo Oriente *Iscrizioni dello estremo oriente greco: un repertorio.* F. Canali de Rossi. Bonn 2004

I.Fayoum 11 *Recueil des inscriptions grecques du Fayoum, 11.* É. Bernand. Cairo 1981

IG *Inscriptiones Graecae.* Berlin 1873–

IGBulg. *Inscriptiones Graecae in Bulgaria repertae.* G. Mihailov. Sofia 1956–97

IGChr.Occidentis *Inscriptiones Graecae Christianae veteres occidentis.* C. Wessel. Bari 1989

I.Gerasa *Gerasa: city of the Decapolis.* C. H. Kraeling. New Haven 1938 (inscriptions pp. 355–494, ed. C. B. Welles)

IGLS *Inscriptions grecques et latines de la Syrie.* Paris 1929–

IGNapoli *Iscrizioni greche d'Italia: Napoli.* E. Miranda. Rome 1990–5

Ignat. *Ep.* Ignatius of Antioch, *Epistulae.* P. T. Camelot, *Ignace d'Antioche, Polycarpe*

	de Smyrne: Lettres, Martyre de Polycarpe. 4th ed., Paris 1969
IGPannonia	*Corpus inscriptionum Graecarum Pannonicarum.* P. Kovács. 3rd ed., Debrecen 2007
IGPorto	*Iscrizioni greche d'Italia: Porto.* G. Sacco. Rome 1984
IGR	*Inscriptiones Graecae ad res Romanas pertinentes.* Paris 1906–27
IGUR	*Inscriptiones Graecae urbis Romae.* L. Moretti. Rome 1968–90
I.Hadrianoi Hadrianeia	*Die Inschriften von Hadrianoi und Hadrianeia.* E. Schwertheim. Bonn 1987.
I.Hatshepsout	*Les inscriptions grecques du temple de Hatshepsout à Deir el-Bahari.* A. Bataille. Cairo 1951
I.Heraclea Pontica	*The inscriptions of Heraclea Pontica.* L. Jonnes. Bonn 1994
I.Hierapolis Judeich	*Altertümer von Hierapolis.* C. Humann, C. Cichorius, W. Judeich, F. Winter, *Jahrbuch des kaiserlich deutschen Archäologischen Instituts,* Supplement 4. Berlin 1898 (inscriptions pp. 67–202, ed. W. Judeich)
I.Histria	*Inscripţiile din Scythia Minor greceşti şi latine = Inscriptiones Scythiae Minoris Graecae et Latinae,* I: *Histria şi împrejurimile = Inscriptiones Histriae et viciniae.* D. M. Pippidi. Bucharest 1983
I.Iasos	*Die Inschriften von Iasos.* W. Blümel. Bonn 1985
I.Jud.Western Europe	*Jewish inscriptions of Western Europe.* D. Noy. Cambridge 1993–5
I.Kaunos	*Die Inschriften von Kaunos.* C. Marek. Munich 2006
I.Keramos	*Die Inschriften von Keramos.* E. Varinlioğlu. Bonn 1986
I.Kibyra	*Die Inschriften von Kibyra,* I: *die Inschriften der Stadt und ihrer näheren Umgebung.* T. Corsten. Bonn 2002
I.Kios	*Die Inschriften von Kios.* T. Corsten. Bonn 1985
I.Klaudiupolis	*Die Inschriften von Klaudiu Polis.* F. Becker-Bertau. Bonn 1986
I.Knidos	*Die Inschriften von Knidos.* W. Blümel. Bonn 1992–2019
I.Kos Bosnakis	Ανέκδοτες ἐπιγραφὲς τῆς Κῶ: ἐπιτύμβια μνημεία καὶ ὅροι. D. Bosnakis. Athens 2008
I.Kyzikos	*Die Inschriften von Kyzikos und Umgebung,* I: *Grabtexte.* E. Schwertheim. Bonn 1980
I.Laodikeia Lykos	*Die Inschriften von Laodikeia am Lykos,* I. T. Corsten. Bonn 1997
I.Leukopetra	*Inscriptions du sanctuaire de la Mère des Dieux autochtone de Leukopetra (Macédoine).* P. M. Petsas, M. B. Hatzopoulos, L. Gounaropoulou, and P. Paschidis. Athens 2000
I.Lipára	*Meligunìs Lipára,* XII: *Le iscrizioni lapidarie greche e latine delle isole eolie.* L. Bernabó Brea, M. Cavalier, and L. Campagna. Palermo 2003
ILS	*Inscriptiones Latinae selectae.* H. Dessau. Berlin 1892–1916
I.Magnesia	*Die Inschriften von Magnesia am Maeander.* O. Kern. Berlin 1900
I.Milet	*Milet,* VI: *Inschriften von Milet.* A. Rehm and P. Herrmann. Berlin 1997–2006
I.Mus.Iznik	*Katalog der antiken Inschriften des Museums von İznik (Nikaia).* S. Şahin. Bonn 1979–87
I.Mus.Palermo	*Iscrizioni greche lapidarie del Museo di Palermo.* M. T. Manni Piraino. Palermo 1973
I.Mylasa	*Die Inschriften von Mylasa.* W. Blümel. Bonn 1987–8
inf.	infinitive
I.North Galatia	*The Ankara district: the inscriptions of North Galatia (Regional epigraphic catalogues of Asia Minor,* II). S. Mitchell. Oxford 1982
I.Olbia	*Inscriptiones Olbiae (1917–1965) = Nadpisi Ol'vii (1917–1965).* T. N. Knipovich and E. I. Levi. Leningrad 1968
I.Olympia	*Die Inschriften von Olympia (Olympia: die Ergebnisse der von dem Deutschen Reich veranstalteten Ausgrabung,* V). W. Dittenberger and K. Purgold. Berlin 1896
IOSPE I²	*Inscriptiones Tyrae, Olbiae, Chersonesi Tauricae, aliorum locorum a Danubio usque ad regnum Bosporanum.* B. Latyschev. 2nd ed., Saint Petersburg 1916.
I.Pan du désert	*Pan du désert.* A. Bernand. Leiden 1977

I.Pergamon | *Die Inschriften von Pergamon (Altertümer von Pergamon, VIII.I–II). M. Fränkel. Berlin 1890–5*

I.Pergamon Asklepieion | *Die Inschriften des Asklepieions (Altertümer von Pergamon, VIII.III). C. Habicht. Berlin 1969*

I.Perge | *Die Inschriften von Perge. S. Şahin. Bonn 1999–2004*

I.Perinthos | *Perinthos-Herakleia (Marmara Ereğlisi) und Umgebung: Geschichte, Testimonien, griechische und lateinische Inschriften. M. H. Sayar. Vienna 1998*

I.Pessinous | *The inscriptions of Pessinous. J. Strubbe. Bonn 2005*

I.Philae | *Les inscriptions grecques de Philae. A. Bernand and É. Bernand. Paris 1969*

I.Portes du désert | *Les portes du désert: recueil des inscriptions grecques d'Antinooupolis, Tentyris, Koptos, Apollonopolis Parva et Apollonopolis Magna. A. Bernand. Paris 1984*

I.Priene B–M | *Die Inschriften von Priene. W. Blümel and R. Merkelbach. Bonn 2014*

I.Prusa | *Die Inschriften von Prusa ad Olympum. T. Corsten. Bonn 1991–3*

I.Prusias | *Die Inschriften von Prusias ad Hypium. W. Ameling. Bonn 1985*

I.Salamine | *Salamine de Chypre, XIII: Testimonia Salaminia, II: corpus épigraphique. J. Pouilloux, P. Roesch, and J. Marcillet-Jaubert. Paris 1987*

I.Sardis I | *Sardis, VII: Greek and Latin inscriptions, I. W. H. Buckler and D. M. Robinson. Leiden 1932*

I.Selge | *Die Inschriften von Selge. J. Nollé and F. Schindler. Bonn 1991*

I.Sestos | *Die Inschriften von Sestos und der thrakischen Chersones. J. Krauss. Bonn 1980*

I.Side | *Side im Altertum: Geschichte und Zeugnisse. J. Nollé. Bonn 1993–2001*

I.Sinope | *The inscriptions of Sinope. D. H. French. Bonn 2004*

I.Smyrna | *Die Inschriften von Smyrna. G. Petzl. Bonn 1982–90*

I.Stratonikeia | *Die Inschriften von Stratonikeia. M. Ç. Şahin. Bonn 1981–2010*

I.Syria PAES | *Syria: publications of the Princeton University archaeological expeditions to Syria, III: Greek and Latin inscriptions. E. Littmann, D. Magie, D. R. Stuart, and W. K. Prentice. Leiden 1921–2*

I.Syringes | *Inscriptions grecques et latines des tombeaux des rois ou syringes à Thèbes. J. Baillet. Cairo 1920–6*

I.Thèbes Syène | *De Thèbes à Syène. A. Bernand. Paris 1989*

I.Thespies | *Les inscriptions de Thespies. P. Roesch. 2nd ed., Lyon 2009. www.hisoma.mom.fr/production-scientifique/les-inscriptions-de-thespies*

I.Thrake Aeg. | *Ἐπιγραφὲς τῆς Θράκης τοῦ Αἰγαίου μεταξὺ τῶν ποταμῶν Νέστου καὶ Ἕβρου (Νομοὶ Ξάνθης, Ροδόπης καὶ Ἕβρου) = Inscriptiones antiquae partis Thraciae quae ad ora maris Aegaei sita est (praefecturae Xanthes, Rhodopes et Hebri). L. D. Loukopoulou, A. Zournatzi, M. G. Paris(s)aki, and S. Psoma. Athens 2005*

I.Tomis | *Inscripţiile din Scythia Minor greceşti şi latine = Inscriptiones Scythiae minoris Graecae et Latinae, II: Tomis şi teritoriul său = Tomis et territorium. I. Stoian. Bucharest 1987*

I.Tralleis | *Die Inschriften von Tralleis und Nysa, I: die Inschriften von Tralleis. F. B. Poljakov. Bonn 1989*

I.Tyr | *Inscriptions grecques et latines découvertes dans les fouilles de Tyr, I: inscriptions de la nécropole. J.-P. Rey-Coquais. Paris 1977*

I.Zoora | *Inscriptions from Palaestina Tertia, IA: the Greek inscriptions from Ghor es-Safi (Byzantine Zoora). Y. E. Meimaris and K. I. Kritikakou-Nikolaropoulou. Athens 2005*

JHS | *Journal of Hellenic Studies*

Jos. | Flavius Josephus. **AJ** = *Antiquitates Judaicae*, **BJ** = *Bellum Judaicum*, **Vit.** = *Vita Josephi*

Jo.Scholast. | Joannes Scholasticus, *Synagoga L titulorum*. V. N. Beneshevich, *Ioannis Scholastici synagoga L titulorum*. Munich 1937

JRS | *Journal of Roman Studies*

Jubil. | *Liber Jubilaeorum*. A.-M. Denis, *Fragmenta pseudepigraphorum quae supersunt Graeca*. Leiden 1970: 70–102

Jul.Afric. | Sextus Julius Africanus. **Cest.** = *Cesti*. J.-R. Vieillefond, *Les 'Cestes' de Julius Africanus*, Florence 1970. **Chron.** = *Chronographiae* (Routh 1846: II.221–309)

Just.	Justinian = Flavius Justinianus Imperator. **App.** = *Appendix constitutionum dispersarum* (Kroll and Schöll 1895: 796–803). **Codex** = *Codex Iustinianus*. P. Krüger, *Corpus iuris civilis*, II. Berlin 1914. **Const. Δέδωκεν** = *Constitutio* Δέδωκεν. T. Mommsen, *Corpus iuris civilis*, I. Berlin 1894: part II pp. xviii–xxviiii. **Dig.** = *Digesta*. T. Mommsen, *Corpus iuris civilis*, I. Berlin 1894. **Edict** = *Iustiniani* XIII *edicta quae vocantur* (Kroll and Schöll 1895: 759–95). **Nov.** = *Novellae* (Kroll and Schöll 1895)	= *De ostentis*. C. Wachsmuth, *Ioannis Laurentii Lydi liber de ostentis et calendaria Graeca omnia*. Leipzig 1897
		Macar. see Ps.-Macar.
		Malal. Joannes Malalas, *Chronographia*. I. Thurn, *Ioannis Malalae chronographia*. Berlin 2000
		MAMA *Monumenta Asiae Minoris Antiqua*. London 1928–2013
		Marc.Aurel. Marcus Aurelius Antoninus imperator, Τὰ εἰς ἑαυτόν. A. S. L. Farquharson, *The meditations of the emperor Marcus Antoninus*, I. Oxford 1944
L&S	*A Latin dictionary*. C. T. Lewis and C. Short. Oxford 1879	
LBG	*Lexikon zur byzantinischen Gräzität*. E. Trapp. Vienna 1994–2017	Marc.Diac. Marcus Diaconus, *Vita Porphyrii episcopi Gazensis*. H. Grégoire and M.-A. Kugener, *Marc le Diacre: Vie de Porphyre, évêque de Gaza*. Paris 1930
LBW	*Inscriptions grecques et latines recueillies en Grèce et en Asie mineure (Voyage archéologique en Grèce et en Asie Mineure, fait par ordre du gouvernement français pendant les années 1843 et 1844*, II). P. Le Bas and W. H. Waddington. Paris 1870	Mart.Euph. *Martyrium brevior sanctae Euphemiae*. F. Halkin, *Euphémie de Chalcédoine: légendes byzantines*. Brussels 1965: 37–49
		masc. masculine
Lib.	Libanius. **Ep.** = *Epistulae*, **Or.** = *Orationes*. R. Foerster, *Libanii opera*. Leipzig 1903–22	*MkB* Μουσεῖον καὶ βιβλιοθήκη τῆς Εὐαγγελικῆς σχολῆς, Σμύρνα. Izmir 1873–
		neut. neuter
loc. cit.	*loco citato* 'in the place just mentioned'	Nic. Nicander. **Alex.** = *Alexipharmaca*, **Ther.** = *Theriaca*
LSJ	*A Greek–English lexicon*. H. G. Liddell, R. Scott, H. S. Jones, and R. McKenzie. 9th ed. with revised supplement, Oxford 1996	Nicom. *Exc.* Nicomachus Gerasenus, *Excerpta*. K. Jan, *Musici scriptores Graeci*. Leipzig 1895: 266–82
		Nil. Nilus Ancyranus, *Epistulae*. J.-P. Migne, *PG* LXXIX
LSJ suppl.	*Greek–English lexicon: revised supplement*. P. G. W. Glare and A. A. Thompson. Oxford 1996	nom. nominative
		NRSV *The Holy Bible: new revised standard version*. New York 1989
Luc.	Lucian. **Alex.** = *Alexander*, **Cal.** = *Calumniae non temere credendum*, **Cat.** = *Cataplus*, **D.Deor.** = *Dialogi deorum*, **Demon.** = *Demonax*, **D.Meretr.** = *Dialogi meretricii*, **D.Mort.** = *Dialogi mortuorum*, **Gall.** = *Gallus*, **Hist.Conscr.** = *Quomodo historia conscribenda sit*, **Lex.** = *Lexiphanes*, **Macr.** = *Macrobii*, **Merc. Cond.** = *De mercede conductis*, **Nav.** = *Navigium*, **Peregr.** = *De morte Peregrini*, **Rh.Pr.** = *Rhetorum praeceptor*, **Salt.** = *De saltatione*, **Symp.** = *Symposium*, **Tim.** = *Timon*	NT New Testament
		O.Amst. *Ostraka in Amsterdam collections*. R. S. Bagnall, P. J. Sijpesteijn, and K. A. Worp. Zutphen 1976
		O.Ashm.Shelt. *Greek ostraca in the Ashmolean Museum*. J. C. Shelton. Florence 1988
		O.Bankes *The Bankes ostraka from a box at Kingston Lacy: the Greek texts*. K. A. Worp. Messina 2016
		O.Berenike *Documents from Berenike*. R. S. Bagnall, C. Helms, A. M. F. W. Verhoogt, and R. Ast. Brussels 2000–
		O.Bodl. *Greek ostraca in the Bodleian Library at Oxford and various other collections*. J. G. Tait *et al.* London 1930–64
Lyd.	John Lydus. **Mag.** = *De magistratibus* (Bandy 1983). **Mens.** = *De mensibus*. R. Wuensch, *Ioannis Laurentii Lydi liber de mensibus*. Leipzig 1898. **Ost.**	*O.Brux.* *Au temps où on lisait le grec en Égypte*. J. Bingen. Brussels 1977

O.Claud.	*Mons Claudianus: ostraca Graeca et Latina.* A. Bülow-Jacobsen, H. Cuvigny, J. Bingen, W. E. H. Cockle, W. van Rengen, L. Rubinstein, and F. Kayser. Cairo 1992–2009	*O.Petr.*	Part of *O.Bodl.* I, pp. 82–152
O.Claud.	Ostraca from Mons Claudianus; information from H. Cuvigny	*O.Petr.Mus.*	*Ostraca greci e bilingui del Petrie Museum of Egyptian Archaeology.* M. S. Funghi, G. Messeri, and C. E. Römer. Florence 2012
O.Cret.Chers.	*Greek ostraka from Chersonesos, Crete: ostraca Cretica Chersonesi.* N. Litinas. Vienna 2008	Opp. *C.*	Oppianus Apamensis, *Cynegetica*
		Opp. *H.*	Oppianus Anazarbensis, *Halieutica*
Od.	*Odyssey*	Orib.	Oribasius. **Col.** = *Collectiones medicae,* **Ecl.** = *Eclogae medicamentorum,* **Eun.** = *Libri ad Eunapium,* **Syn.** = *Synopsis ad Eustathium filium.* J. Raeder, *Oribasii collectionum medicarum reliquiae. Corpus medicorum Graecorum,* VI.1.1–VI.1.2. Leipzig 1928–33
O.Did.	*Didymoi: une garnison romaine dans le désert oriental d'Égypte,* II: *les textes.* H. Cuvigny. Cairo 2012		
O.Dios	Ostraca from Dios (Abu Qurayyah); information from H. Cuvigny		
O.Douch.	*Les ostraca grecs de Douch.* H. Cuvigny and G. Wagner. Cairo 1986–2001	*O.Stras.* I	*Griechische und griechisch-demotische Ostraka der Universitäts- und Landesbibliothek zu Strassburg im Elsass.* P. Viereck. Berlin 1923
OED	*Oxford English Dictionary.* Oxford 1989–	*O.Theb.*	*Theban ostraca.* A. H. Gardiner, H. Thompson, J. G. Milne. London 1913
O.Edfou	*Tell Edfou.* B. Bruyère *et al.* Cairo 1937–50	*O.Trim.*	*Amheida: ostraka from Trimithis.* R. S. Bagnall *et al.* New York 2012–
O.Florida	*The Florida ostraka: documents from the Roman army in upper Egypt.* R. S. Bagnall. Durham, N.C. 1976	*O.Waqfa*	*Les ostraca grecs d'Aïn Waqfa (Oasis de Kharga).* H. Cuvigny, A. Hussein, and G. Wagner. Cairo 1993
OGIS	*Orientis Graeci inscriptiones selectae: supplementum Sylloges inscriptionum Graecarum.* W. Dittenberger. Leipzig 1903–5	*O.Wilck.*	*Griechische Ostraka aus Aegypten und Nubien.* U. Wilcken. Leipzig 1899
		O.Xer.	Ostraca from Xeron Pelagos (Feisaleya); information from H. Cuvigny
O.Heid.	*Die griechischen Ostraka der Heidelberger Papyrus-Sammlung.* C. Armoni, J. M. S. Cowey, and D. Hagedorn. Heidelberg 2005	*P.Aberd.*	*Catalogue of Greek and Latin papyri and ostraca in the possession of the University of Aberdeen.* E. G. Turner. Aberdeen 1939
O.Kell.	*Greek ostraka from Kellis.* K. A. Worp. Oxford 2004	*P.Abinn.*	*The Abinnaeus archive: papers of a Roman officer in the reign of Constantius II.* H. I. Bell, V. Martin, E. G. Turner, and D. van Berchem. Oxford 1962
O.Krok.	*Ostraca de Krokodilô.* H. Cuvigny, A. Bülow-Jacobsen, J.-L. Fournet, and B. Redon. Cairo 2005–19		
OLD	*Oxford Latin Dictionary.* P. G. W. Glare. Oxford 1982	*P.Alex.*	*Papyrus grecs du Musée gréco-romain d'Alexandrie.* A. Świderek and M. Vandoni. Warsaw 1964
O.Leid.	*Greek ostraka: a catalogue of the Greek ostraka in the National Museum of Antiquities at Leiden.* R. S. Bagnall, P. J. Sijpesteijn, and K. A. Worp. Zutphen 1980	*P.Alex.Giss.*	*Papyri variae Alexandrinae et Gissenses.* J. Schwartz. Brussels 1969
		Pall.	Palladius Helenopolitanus. **H.Laus.** = *Historia Lausiaca rec.* G. G. J. M. Bartelink, *Palladio: La storia Lausiaca.* Milan 1974. **V.Chrys.** = *Dialogus de vita Joannis Chrysostomi.* P. R. Coleman-Norton, *Palladii dialogus de vita S. Joanni Chrysostomi,* Cambridge 1928
O.Max.	Ostraca from Maximianon (El-Zarqa); information from H. Cuvigny		
O.Mich. III	Part of *P.Mich.* VIII		
O.Oasis Bahria	*Les Oasis d'Égypte à l'époque grecque, romaine et byzantine d'après les documents grecs.* G. Wagner. Cairo 1987	*P.Amh.*	*The Amherst papyri: being an account of the Greek papyri in the collection of the Right Hon. Lord Amherst of Hackney.*

	B. P. Grenfell and A. S. Hunt. London 1900–1
P.Ammon I	*The archive of Ammon Scholasticus of Panopolis*, I: *the legacy of Harpocration.* W. H. Willis and K. Maresch. Opladen 1997
P.Ammon II	*The archive of Ammon Scholasticus of Panopolis*, II: *das Archiv des Aurelius Ammon.* K. Maresch and I. Andorlini. Paderborn 2006
P.Amst.	*Die Amsterdamer Papyri*, I. R. P. Salomons, P. J. Sijpesteijn, and K. A. Worp. Zutphen 1980
P.Ant.	*The Antinoopolis papyri.* C. H. Roberts, J. W. B. Barns, and H. Zilliacus. London 1950–67
Pap.Agon.	*Zehn agonistische Papyri.* P. Frisch. Opladen 1986
Pap.Choix	*Choix de papyrus grecs: essai de traitement automatique.* J. Bingen, A. Tomsin, A. Bodson, J. Denooz, J. D. Dupont, and E. Evrard. Liège 1968
Pap.Graec.Mag.	*Papyri Graecae magicae: die griechischen Zauberpapyri.* K. Preisendanz. 2nd ed., Stuttgart 1973–4
P.Apoll.	*Papyrus grecs d'Apollônos Anô.* R. Rémondon. Cairo 1953
part.	participle
pass.	passive
P.Athen.	*Papyri societatis archaeologicae Atheniensis.* G. A. Petropulos. Athens 1939
P.Bad.	*Veröffentlichungen aus den badischen Papyrus-Sammlungen: griechische Papyri.* Heidelberg 1923–38
P.Bagnall	*Papyrological texts in honor of Roger S. Bagnall.* R. Ast, H. Cuvigny, T. M. Hickey, and J. Lougovaya. Durham, N.C. 2013
P.Berl.Cohen	*Greek documentary papyri from Egypt in the Berlin Aegyptisches Museum.* N. Cohen. Oakville, Conn. 2007
P.Berl.Leihg.	*Berliner Leihgabe griechischer Papyri.* T. Kalén *et al.* Uppsala 1932–77
P.Berl.Moeller	*Griechische Papyri aus dem Berliner Museum.* S. Möller. Gothenburg 1929
P.Berl.Sarisch.	*Berliner griechische Papyri: Christliche literarische Texte und Urkunden aus dem 3. bis 8. Jh. n. Chr.* P. Sarischouli. Wiesbaden 1995
P.Berl.Zill.	*Vierzehn Berliner griechische Papyri.* H. Zilliacus. Helsinki 1941

P.Bingen	*Papyri in honorem Johannis Bingen octogenarii.* H. Melaerts. Leuven 2000
P.Bodl.	*Papyri Bodleianae*, I. R. P. Salomons. Amsterdam 1996
P.Bon.	*Papyri Bononienses.* O. Montevecchi. Milan 1953
P.Bour.	*Les papyrus Bouriant.* P. Collart. Paris 1926
P.Brookl.	*Greek and Latin papyri, ostraca, and wooden tablets in the collection of the Brooklyn Museum.* J. C. Shelton. Florence 1992
P.Cair.Goodsp.	*Greek papyri from the Cairo Museum.* E. J. Goodspeed. Chicago 1902
P.Cair.Isid.	*The archive of Aurelius Isidorus in the Egyptian Museum, Cairo, and the University of Michigan.* A. E. R. Boak and H. C. Youtie. Ann Arbor 1960
P.Cair.Masp.	*Catalogue général des antiquités égyptiennes du Musée du Caire: papyrus grecs d'époque byzantine.* J. Maspero. Cairo 1911–16
P.Cair.Zen.	*Zenon papyri: catalogue général des antiquités égyptiennes du Musée du Caire.* C. C. Edgar. Cairo 1925–40
P.Charite	*Das Aurelia Charite Archiv.* K. A. Worp. Zutphen 1980
P.Col.	*Columbia papyri.* New York or Atlanta, 1929–
P.Coll.Youtie	*Collectanea papyrologica: texts published in honor of H. C. Youtie.* A. E. Hanson. Bonn 1976
P.Corn.	*Greek papyri in the library of Cornell University.* W. L. Westermann and C. J. Kraemer. New York 1926
P.Daris	*Silloge di papiri greci documentari.* S. Daris. Trieste 2015
P.Diog.	*Les archives de Marcus Lucretius Diogenes et textes apparentés.* P. Schubert. Bonn 1990
P.Dubl.	*Greek papyri from Dublin.* B. C. McGing. Bonn 1995
P.Dura	*The excavations at Dura-Europos conducted by Yale University and the French Academy of Inscriptions and Letters: final report*, V.1: *the parchments and papyri.* C. B. Welles, R. O. Fink, and J. F. Gilliam. New Haven 1959
P.Eirene	*Studia Graeca et Latina (papyrologica).* J. Bazant, R. Pintaudi, *et al.* (*Eirene*, vols 34, 40, 46, 52). Prague 1998–
P.Eleph.Wagner	*Les papyrus et les ostraca grecs d'Elephantine.* G. Wagner. Mainz 1998

P.Erl.	Die Papyri der Universitätsbibliothek Erlangen. W. Schubart. Leipzig 1942	P.Graux II	Papyrus Graux, II. H. Cuvigny. Geneva 1995
P.Erl.Diosp.	Ein spätantikes Wirtschaftsbuch aus Diospolis Parva. F. Mitthof. Munich 2002	P.Grenf. II	New Classical fragments and other Greek and Latin papyri. B. P. Grenfell and A. S. Hunt. Oxford 1897
P.Euphrates III	'Documents d'archives romains inédits du Moyen Euphrate (IIIe s. après J.-C.), III'. D. Feissel and J. Gascou, Journal des Savants [no vol.] 2000: 157–208	P.Gron.	Papyri Groninganae: griechische Papyri der Universitätsbibliothek zu Groningen, nebst zwei Papyri der Universitätsbibliothek zu Amsterdam. A. G. Roos. Amsterdam 1933
pf.	perfect	P.Hamb. I	Griechische Papyrusurkunden der Hamburger Staats- und Universitätsbibliothek. P. M. Meyer. Leipzig 1911–24
P.Fam.Tebt.	A family-archive from Tebtunis. B. A. van Groningen. Leiden 1950		
P.Fay.	Fayum towns and their papyri. B. P. Grenfell, A. S. Hunt, and D. G. Hogarth. London 1900	P.Hamb. III	Griechische Papyri der Staats- und Universitätsbibliothek Hamburg. B. Kramer and D. Hagedorn. Bonn 1984
P.Flor.	Papiri greco-egizii: papiri Fiorentini. G. Vitelli and D. Comparetti. Milan 1906–15		
P.Fouad	Les papyrus Fouad I. A. Bataille, O. Guéraud, P. Jouguet, N. Lewis, H. Marrou, J. Scherer, and W. G. Waddell. Cairo 1939	P.Harr.	The Rendel Harris papyri of Woodbrooke College, Birmingham. Cambridge or Zutphen 1936–85
		P.Harrauer	Wiener Papyri als Festgabe zum 60. Geburtstag von Hermann Harrauer. B. Palme. Vienna 2001
P.Freer	'Greek and Coptic papyri in the Freer Gallery of Art'. L. S. B. MacCoull. Dissertation from Catholic University of America, Washington, D.C. 1973	P.Haun. III	Papyri Graecae Haunienses, III. T. Larsen and A. Bülow-Jacobsen. Bonn 1985
P.Freib.	Mitteilungen aus der Freiburger Papyrussammlung. Heidelberg or Bonn 1914–86	P.Heid. IV	Griechische Texte der Heidelberger Papyrus-sammlung. B. Kramer and D. Hagedorn. Heidelberg 1986
P.FuadUniv.	Fuad I University papyri. D. S. Crawford. Alexandria 1949	P.Heid. VII	Fünfundzwanzig griechische Papyri aus den Sammlungen von Heidelberg, Wien und Kairo. A. Papathomas. Heidelberg 1996
PG	Patrologiae cursus completus: series Graeca. J.-P. Migne. Paris 1857–66		
P.Gascou	Mélanges Jean Gascou: textes et études papyrologiques. J.-L. Fournet and A. Papaconstantinou. Paris 2016	P.Herm.	Papyri from Hermopolis and other documents of the Byzantine period. B. R. Rees. London 1964
P.Gen.	Les papyrus de Genève. Geneva 1896–	P.Herm.Landl.	Zwei Landlisten aus dem Hermupolites. P. J. Sijpesteijn and K. A. Worp. Zutphen 1978
P.Genova	Papiri dell'Università di Genova. Milan, Florence, or Rome 1974–		
P.Giss.	Griechische Papyri im Museum des Oberhessischen Geschichtsvereins zu Giessen. O. Eger, E. Kornemann, P. M. Meyer, M. Kotyl. Berlin 1910–	P.Hever	Aramaic, Hebrew and Greek documentary texts from Naḥal ḥever and other sites. H. M. Cotton and A. Yardeni. Oxford 1997
P.Giss.Apoll.	Briefe des Apollonios-Archives aus der Sammlung Papyri Gissenses. M. Kortus. Giessen 1999	P.Holm.	Papyrus Graecus Holmiensis: Recepte für Silber, Steine und Purpur. O. Lagercrantz. Uppsala 1913. Cited from Les alchimistes grecs. R. Halleux. Paris 1981
P.Giss.Univ.	Mitteilungen aus der Papyrussammlung der Giessener Universitätsbibliothek. H. Kling, D. P. Glaue, H. Büttner, et al. Giessen 1924–75		
		P.Iand.	Papyri Iandanae. C. Kalbfleisch, E. Schaefer, L. Eisner, et al. Leipzig 1912–38
P.Got.	Papyrus grecs de la bibliothèque municipale de Gothembourg. H. Frisk. Gothenburg 1929	P.Iand.inv. 653	A sixth-century account of hay. T. Reekmans. Brussels 1962

P.Iand.Zen.	*Die Giessener Zenonpapyri.* P. Schmitz. Paderborn 2007
P.IFAO	*Papyrus grecs de l'Institut français d'archéologie orientale.* J. Schwartz and G. Wagner. Cairo 1971–5
P.Ital.	*Die nichtliterarischen lateinischen Papyri Italiens aus der Zeit 445–700.* J.-O. Tjäder. Lund or Stockholm 1955–82
P.Jena I	*Jenaer Papyrus-Urkunden.* F. Zucker and F. Schneider. Jena 1926
P.Jena II	*Late antique Greek papyri in the collection of the Friedrich-Schiller-Universität Jena.* R. Ast. Bonn 2010
P.Kellis I	*Greek papyri from Kellis,* I. K. A. Worp. Oxford 1995
P.Kellis IV	*The Kellis agricultural account book.* R. S. Bagnall. Oxford 1997
P.Köln	*Kölner Papyri.* B. Kramer, R. Hübner, M. Gronewald, *et al.* Opladen etc. 1976–
pl.	plural
P.Laur.	*Dai papiri della Biblioteca Medicea Laurenziana.* R. Pintaudi. Florence 1976–84
P.Leid.	*Papyri Graeci Musei antiquarii publici Lugduni-Batavi.* C. Leemans. Leiden 1843–85
P.Leid.Inst.	*Papyri, ostraca, parchments and waxed tablets in the Leiden Papyrological Institute.* F. A. J. Hoogendijk and P. van Minnen. Leiden 1991
P.Leipz.	'Die griechischen Papyri der Leipziger Universitätsbibliothek'. *Berichte über die Verhandlungen der königlich sächsischen Gesellschaft der Wissenschaften zu Leipzig, philologisch-historische Classe,* 37: 237–75. C. Wessely. Leipzig 1885
Plin. *Ep. Tra.*	Pliny the Younger, *Epistulae ad Traianum*
P.Lips.	*Griechische Urkunden der Papyrussammlung zu Leipzig.* Leipzig 1906–
P.Lond.	*Greek papyri in the British Museum.* London 1893–1974
P.Lond.Herm.	*A sixth-century tax register from the Hermopolite nome.* R. S. Bagnall, J. G. Keenan, and L. S. B. MacCoull. Durham, N.C. 2011
P.Louvre I	*Griechische Papyri aus Soknopaiu Nesos.* A. Jördens. Bonn 1998
P.Lund II	'Aus der Papyrussammlung der Universitätsbibliothek in Lund, II: griechische Privatbriefe', *K. Humanistiska Vetenskapssamfundet i Lund: Årsberättelse 1936–1937,* VI: 161–72. A. Wifstrand. Lund 1937
P.Lund IV	*Bakchiastexte und andere Papyri der Lunder Papyrussammlung.* E. J. Knudtzon. Lund 1946
Plut.	Plutarch. **Aem.** = *Aemilius Paulus,* **Ant.** = *Antonius,* **Cam.** = *Camillus,* **Cat. Ma.** = *Cato Maior,* **Cor.** = *Coriolanus,* **Fab.** = *Fabius Maximus,* **Luc.** = *Lucullus,* **Marc.** = *Marcellus,* **Mor.** = *Moralia,* **Pomp.** = *Pompeius,* **Publ.** = *Publicola,* **Rom.** = *Romulus*
P.Matr.	*Dieci papyri Matritenses.* S. Daris. Madrid 1990
P.Mert.	*A descriptive catalogue of the Greek papyri in the collection of Wilfred Merton.* H. I. Bell, C. H. Roberts, J. D. Thomas, *et al.* London etc. 1948–67
P.Meyer	*Griechische Texte aus Aegypten.* P. M. Meyer. Berlin 1916
P.Mich.	*Michigan papyri.* Ann Arbor etc. 1931–
P.Michael.	*Papyri Michaelidae: being a catalogue of the Greek and Latin papyri, tablets and ostraca in the library of Mr G. A. Michaïlidis of Cairo.* D. S. Crawford. Aberdeen 1955
P.Mich.Aphrod.	*Settling a dispute: toward a legal anthropology of late antique Egypt.* T. Gagos and P. van Minnen. Ann Arbor 1994
P.Mil. II	*Papiri Milanesi,* II. S. Daris. Milan 1966
P.Mil.Vogl.	*Papiri della R. Università di Milano.* A. Vogliano *et al.* Milan 1937–
P.Münch. I	*Byzantinische Papyri der Bayerischen Staatsbibliothek München.* A. Heisenberg, L. Wenger, and D. Hagedorn. 2nd ed., Stuttgart 1986
P.Münch. III.I	*Griechische Urkundenpapyri der Bayerischen Staatsbibliothek München,* I. U. Hagedorn, D. Hagedorn, R. Hübner, J. C. Shelton. Stuttgart 1986
PN	*Papyrological Navigator,* available at www.papyri.info
P.Naqlun	*Deir El-Naqlun: the Greek papyri.* T. Derda. Warsaw 1995–2008
P.Narm.	*Narmouthis 2006: documents et objets découverts à Médinet Madi en*

	2006. E. Bresciani, A. Delattre, P. Heilporn, A. Martin, A. Menchetti, G. Nachtergael, R. Pintaudi, and F. Silvano. Pisa 2010
P.Neph.	Das Archiv des Nepheros und verwandte Texte. B. Kramer, J. C. Shelton, and G. M. Browne. Mainz 1987
P.Ness. III	Excavations at Nessana, III: non-literary papyri. C. J. Kraemer. Princeton 1958
P.NYU I	Greek papyri in the collection of New York University. N. Lewis. Leiden 1967
P.NYU II	Papyri from the New York University Collection, II. B. E. Nielsen and K. A. Worp. Wiesbaden 2010
P.Oslo	Papyri Osloenses. S. Eitrem and L. Amundsen. Oslo 1925–36
P.Oxf.	Some Oxford papyri. E. P. Wegener. Leiden 1942
P.Oxy.	The Oxyrhynchus papyri. B. P. Grenfell, A. S. Hunt, et al. London 1898–
P.Oxy.Hatz.	'Papyrus letters from Oxyrhynchus'. G. H. Hatzisolis. Dissertation from University of Amsterdam 1994
P.Oxy.Hels.	Fifty Oxyrhynchus papyri. H. Zilliacus, J. Frösén, P. Hohti, J. Kaimio, and M. Kaimio. Helsinki 1979
P.PalauRib.	Papiri documentari greci del fondo Palau-Ribes. S. Daris. Barcelona 1995
P.Panop.	Urkunden aus Panopolis. L. C. Youtie, D. Hagedorn, and H. C. Youtie. Bonn 1980
P.Panop.Beatty	Papyri from Panopolis in the Chester Beatty Library, Dublin. T. C. Skeat. Dublin 1964
P.Paramone	Paramone: Editionen und Aufsätze von Mitgleidern des heidelberger Instituts für Papyrologie zwischen 1982 und 2004. J. M. S. Cowey and B. Kramer. Munich 2004
P.Petaus	Das Archiv des Petaus. U. Hagedorn, D. Hagedorn, L. C. Youtie, and H. C. Youtie. Opladen 1969
P.Petra	The Petra papyri. Amman 2002–
P.Pintaudi	Inediti offerti a Rosario Pintaudi per il suo 65° compleanno. D. Minutoli. Florence 2012
P.Pommersf.	Ein frühbyzantinisches Szenario für die Amtswechslung in der Sitonie: die griechischen Papyri aus Pommersfelden. A. J. B. Sirks, P. J. Sijpesteijn, and K. A. Worp. Munich 1996

P.Prag.	Papyri Graecae Wessely Pragenses. R. Pintaudi, R. Dostálová, and L. Vidman. Florence 1988–
P.Princ.	Papyri in the Princeton University collections. A. C. Johnson, H. B. van Hoesen, E. H. Kase, and S. P. Goodrich. Baltimore or Princeton 1931–42
P.Rain.Cent.	Festschrift zum 100-jährigen Bestehen der Papyrussammlung der Österreichischen Nationalbibliothek, Papyrus Erzherzog Rainer. Vienna 1983
P.Rain. Unterricht	Neue Texte aus dem antiken Unterricht. H. Harrauer and P. J. Sijpesteijn. Vienna 1985
P.Rain. UnterrichtKopt.	Neue Texte und Dokumentation zum Koptisch-Unterricht. M. R. M. Hasitzka. Vienna 1990
P.Rein. II	Les papyrus Théodore Reinach, II. P. Collart. Cairo 1940
pres.	present
Procl.Const. Consol.	Proclus Constantinopolitanus, Homilia consolatoria ad aegrotum. S. Y. Rudberg, 'L'Homélie pseudo-basilienne Consolatoria ad aegrotum', Le Muséon: revue d'études orientales: Tijdschrift voor Oriëntalisme 72 (1959): 301–322
Procop.	Procopius of Caesarea. Aed. = De aedificiis, Arc. = Historia arcana, Bell. = De bellis. J. Haury and G. Wirth, Procopii Caesariensis opera omnia. Leipzig 1962–4
P.Ross.Georg.	Papyri russischer und georgischer Sammlungen. Tbilisi 1925–35
P.Ryl.	Catalogue of the Greek and Latin papyri in the John Rylands Library, Manchester. Manchester 1911–52
P.Sakaon	The archive of Aurelius Sakaon: papers of an Egyptian farmer in the last century of Theadelphia. G. M. Parássoglou. Bonn 1978
P.Sarap.	Les archives de Sarapion et de ses fils: une exploitation agricole aux environs d'Hermoupolis Magna (de 90 à 133 p.C.). J. Schwartz. Cairo 1961
P.Select.	Papyri selectae. E. Boswinkel, P. W. Pestman, and P. J. Sijpesteijn. Leiden 1965
Ps.-Epiph.	see Epiph.

PSI	Papiri greci e latini (Pubblicazioni della Società italiana per la ricerca dei papiri greci e latini in Egitto). Florence 1912–	P.Turner	Papyri Greek and Egyptian edited by various hands in honour of Eric Gardner Turner on the occasion of his seventieth birthday. P. J. Parsons and J. R. Rea. London 1981
PSICom.	(Dai) Papiri della Società Italiana. Comunicazioni Vitelli. Florence 2003–	P.Vars.	Papyri Varsovienses. G. Manteuffel. Warsaw 1935
PSICongr.xxi	Dai papiri della Società Italiana: omaggio al xxi congresso internazionale di papirologia. Florence 1995	P.Vat.Aphrod.	I papiri Vaticani greci di Aphrodito. R. Pintaudi. Rome 1980
P.Sijp.	Papyri in memory of P. J. Sijpesteijn. A. J. B. Sirks and K. A. Worp. Oakville, Conn. 2007	P.Vet.Aelii	Veteranen unter den Severern und frühen Soldatenkaisern: die Dokumentensammlungen der Veteranen Aelius Sarapammon und Aelius Syrion. P. Sänger. Stuttgart 2011
Ps.-Macar.	Spuria attributed to Macarius Aegyptus = Symeon = Macarius Mesopotamius. **Hom.** = Homiliae 7. G. L. Marriott, Macarii anecdota. Cambridge, Mass. 1918: 19–48. **Hom.Spir.** = Homiliae spirituales 50. H. Dörries, E. Klostermann, and M. Kroeger, Die 50 geistlichen Homilien des Makarios. Berlin 1964. **PG**: see s.v. **Serm.** = Sermones 64. H. Berthold, Makarios/Symeon: Reden und Briefe. Berlin 1973	P.Vind.Bosw.	Einige Wiener Papyri. E. Boswinkel. Leiden 1942
		P.Vind.Sal.	Einige Wiener Papyri. R. P. Salomons. Amsterdam 1976
		P.Vind.Sijp.	Einige Wiener Papyri. P. J. Sijpesteijn. Leiden 1963
		P.Vind.Tand.	Fünfunddreißig Wiener Papyri. P. J. Sijpesteijn and K. A. Worp. Zutphen 1976
		P.Vind.Worp	Einige Wiener Papyri. K. A. Worp. Amsterdam 1972
P.Sorb.	Papyrus de la Sorbonne. H. Cadell, J. Gascou, W. Clarysse, and K. Robic. Paris 1966–	P.Warr.	The Warren papyri. M. David, B. A. van Groningen, and J. C. van Oven. Leiden 1941
Ps.-Orib.	see Orib.	P.Wash.Univ. i	Washington University Papyri, i: non-literary texts. V. B. Schuman. Missoula 1980
Ps.-Plut.	see Plut.		
P.Stras.	Griechische Papyrus der Kaiserlichen Universitäts- und Landes-bibliothek zu Strassburg or Papyrus grecs de la bibliothèque nationale et universitaire de Strasbourg. P. Collomp and J. Schwartz. Leipzig 1912–	P.Wash.Univ. ii	Papyri from the Washington University collection, St. Louis, Missouri, ii. K. Maresch and Z. M. Packman. Opladen 1990
P.Tebt.	The Tebtunis papyri. B. P. Grenfell, A. S. Hunt, J. G. Smyly, et al. London 1902–	P.Wisc.	The Wisconsin papyri. P. J. Sijpesteijn. Leiden or Zutphen 1967–77
P.Thead.	Papyrus de Théadelphie. P. Jouguet. Paris 1911	P.Worp	Sixty-five papyrological texts presented to Klaas A. Worp on the occasion of his 65th birthday. F. A. J. Hoogendijk and B. P. Muhs. Leiden 2008
P.Theon.	The family of the Tiberii Iulii Theones. P. J. Sijpesteijn. Amsterdam 1976		
P.Thomas	Essays and texts in honor of J. David Thomas. T. Gagos and R. S. Bagnall. Oakville, Conn. 2001	P.Würzb.	Mitteilungen aus der Würzburger Papyrussammlung. U. Wilcken. Berlin 1934
Ptol.	Ptolemy = Claudius Ptolemaeus Mathematicus. **Geog.** = Geographia. A. Stückelberger and G. Grasshoff, Klaudios Ptolemaios Handbuch der Geographie. Basel 2006. **Harm.** = Harmonica. I. Düring, Die Harmonielehre des Klaudios Ptolemaios. Gothenburg 1930	P.Yadin	The documents from the Bar Kokhba period in the cave of letters. N. Lewis, Y. Yadin, J. C. Greenfield, A. Yardeni, and B. A. Levine. Jerusalem 1989–2002
		q.v.	quod vide 'see that entry/work'
		RÉG	Revue des études grecques
		Rhetor.	Rhetorius Astrologus. **Cap.** = Capitula selecta. F. Cumont, Catalogus codicum astrologorum Graecorum,

VIII.IV: *codicum Parisinorum partem quartem.* Brussels 1921: 115–225. **Plan.** = *De planetarum natura ac vi.* Boll 1908: 213–26

Rom.Mil.Rec. — *Roman military records on papyrus.* R. O. Fink. Cleveland 1971

SB — *Sammelbuch griechischer Urkunden aus Aegypten,* F. Preisigke *et al.* Strasbourg etc. 1915–

Schol.Sinai. — *Scholia Sinaitica.* Seckel and Kuebler 1927: II.II.466–84

SEG — *Supplementum epigraphicum Graecum.* Leiden 1923–

SGDI — *Sammlung der griechischen Dialekt-Inschriften.* H. Collitz and F. Bechtel. Göttingen 1884–1915

sing. — singular

Socr. — Socrates Scholasticus, *Historia ecclesiastica.* P. Périchon and P. Maraval, *Socrate de Constantinople: Histoire ecclésiastique.* Paris 2004–7

Soz. — Sozomenos Salaminius, *Historia ecclesiastica.* J. Bidez and G. C. Hansen, *Sozomenus: Kirchengeschichte.* Berlin 1960

Spomenik — *Spomenik: Srpska kraljevska Akademija.* Belgrade 1888–1942

Studia Pontica III — *Studia Pontica,* III: *recueil des inscriptions grecques et latines du Pont et de l'Arménie.* J. G. C. Anderson, F. Cumont, and H. Grégoire. Brussels 1910

Stud.Pal. — *Studien zur Palaeographie und Papyruskunde.* C. Wessely. Leipzig 1901–24

subst. — substantivized (i.e. used as a noun)

Suppl.Mag. — *Supplementum magicum.* R. W. Daniel and F. Maltomini. Opladen 1990–2

Suppl.Rodio — 'Supplemento epigrafico rodio'. G. Pugliese Carratelli, *Annuario della Scuola Archeologica di Atene e delle Missioni Italiane in Oriente* 30–2 (1952–4): 247–316

s.v. — *sub voce* 'alphabetized under the word'

Syll.[3] — *Sylloge inscriptionum Graecarum,* W. Dittenberger. 3rd ed., Leipzig 1915–24

Syn.Cyr. *Ep.* — Synesius Cyrenensis, *Epistulae.* A. Garzya, *Synésios de Cyrène: correspondance.* Paris 2000

TAM — *Tituli Asiae Minoris.* Vienna 1901–

Test.Abr. — *Testamentum Abrahae.* M. R. James, *The testament of Abraham.* Cambridge 1892

Test.Sal. — *Testamentum Salomonis.* C. C. McCown, *The testament of Solomon.* Leipzig 1922

Test.XII — *Testamenta* XII *Patriarcharum.* M. de Jonge, *The testaments of the twelve patriarchs.* Leiden 1978

Thdr.Anag. — Theodorus Anagnostes = Theodorus Lector. **HE** = *Historia ecclesiastica,* **Tripart.** = *Epitome historiae tripartitae.* G. C. Hansen, *Theodoros Anagnostes: Kirchengeschichte.* 2nd ed., Berlin 1995

Thdr.Heracl. — Theodorus Heracleensis, *Fragmenta in Matthaeum.* J. Reuss, *Matthäus-Kommentare aus der griechischen Kirche.* Berlin 1957: 55–95

Thdr.Pet. — Theodorus Petranus hagiographus, *Vita Theodosii.* H. Usener, *Der heilige Theodosius: Schriften des Theodorus und Kyrillos.* Leipzig 1890

Thdt. — Theodoretus Cyrrhensis. **Ep.Pat.** = *Epistulae, collectio Patmensis.* Y. Azéma, *Théodoret de Cyr: correspondance,* I. Paris 1955. **Ep.Sirm.** = *Epistulae, collectio Sirmondiana.* Y. Azéma, *Théodoret de Cyr: correspondance,* II–III. Paris 1964–5. **Er.** = *Eranistes.* G. H. Ettlinger, *Theodoret of Cyrus: Eranistes.* Oxford 1975. **HE** = *Historia ecclesiastica.* L. Parmentier and F. Scheidweiler, *Theodoret: Kirchengeschichte.* 2nd ed., Berlin 1954. **Is.** = *Commentaria in Isaiam.* J.-N. Guinot, *Théodoret de Cyr: Commentaire sur Isaïe.* Paris 1980–4. **Orthod.** = *Quaestiones et responsiones ad orthodoxos* (dubious attribution). A. Papadopoulos-Kerameus, Θεοδωρήτου ἐπισκόπου πόλεως Κύρρου πρὸς τὰς ἐπενεχθείσας αὐτῷ ἐπερωτήσεις παρά τινος τῶν ἐξ Αἰγύπτου ἐπισκόπων ἀποκρίσεις. Saint Petersburg 1895. **PG** = see *s.v.* Thucydides

Thuc. — Thucydides

TLG — *Thesaurus Linguae Graecae,* http://stephanus.tlg.uci.edu

TLL — *Thesaurus Linguae Latinae.* Munich 1900–

TM — *Trismegistos,* www.trismegistos.org

trans. — translated by

T.Vindol. III — *Vindolanda: the Latin writing tablets, III.* A. K. Bowman and J. D. Thomas. London 2003

UPZ I — *Urkunden der Ptolemäerzeit (ältere Funde),* I. U. Wilcken. Berlin 1927

V.Aesopi — *Vitae Aesopi.* B. E. Perry, *Aesopica,* I. Urbana 1952

V.Dan.Styl. — *Vitae S. Danielis Stylitae* (**A.** = *Vita antiquior,* **Sec.** = *Vita secunda,* **Tert.** = *Vita tertia*) (Delehaye 1923b: 1–147)

Vet.Val. — Vettius Valens. **Anth.** = *Anthologiae,* **App.** = *Appendices.* D. Pingree, *Vettii Valentis Antiocheni anthologiarum libri novem.* Leipzig 1986

V.Luc.Styl. — *Vita sanctae Lucae stylitae* (Delehaye 1923b: 195–237)

V.S.Aux. — *Vita sancti Auxentii.* P. Varalda, *Vita sancti Auxentii.* Alexandria 2017

V.Secundi — *Vita Secundi.* B. E. Perry, *Secundus the silent philosopher.* Ithaca 1964

V.S.Mam. — *Vita sancti Mamantis.* A. Berger, 'Die alten Viten des Heiligen Mamas von Kaisareia', *Analecta Bollandiana* 120 (2002): 241–310

ZPE — *Zeitschrift für Papyrologie und Epigraphik*

← — 'borrowed from'

* — 'the following word is not actually attested'

REFERENCES

Adams, J. N. (1995) *Pelagonius and Latin veterinary terminology in the Roman empire.* Leiden

Adams, J. N. (2003) *Bilingualism and the Latin language.* Cambridge

Adams, J. N. (2007) *The regional diversification of Latin 200 BC – AD 600.* Cambridge

Adams, J. N. (2013) *Social variation and the Latin language.* Cambridge

Adams, J. N., M. Janse, and S. Swain (edd.) (2002) *Bilingualism in ancient society.* Oxford

Adams, S. (2013) 'Atticism, Classicism, and Luke–Acts: discussions with Albert Wifstrand and Loveday Alexander', in S. E. Porter and A. W. Pitts (edd.), *The language of the New Testament: context, history, and development.* Leiden: 91–111

Adrados, F. R. (2005) *A history of the Greek language from its origins to the present,* trans. F. Rojas del Canto. Leiden

Alexander, L. C. A. (2005) *Acts in its ancient literary context: a Classicist looks at the Acts of the Apostles.* London

Alexander, P. J. (1967) *The oracle of Baalbek: the Tiburtine Sibyl in Greek dress.* Washington, D.C.

Allen, W. S. (1978) *Vox Latina: a guide to the pronunciation of Classical Latin.* 2nd ed., Cambridge

Almond, M. (2017) 'An introduction and overview to Greek adjectives in Coptic', in Grossman *et al.* (edd.) 165–94

Amelotti, M., and L. Migliardi Zingale (1977) *Scritti teologici ed ecclesiastici di Giustiniano.* Milan

Anderson, J. M. (2007) *The grammar of names.* Oxford

Andorlini, I. (2001) *Greek medical papyri,* 1. Florence

André, J. (1956) 'Gaulois *sapana,* latin *sapo,* grec σάπων', *Études celtiques,* 7: 348–55

André, J. (1958) *Notes de lexicographie botanique grecque.* Paris

André, J. (1968) 'Les changements de genre dans les emprunts du latin au grec', *Word,* 24: 1–7

André, J. (1971) *Emprunts et suffixes nominaux en latin.* Geneva

Andrés Santos, F. J. (2006) 'Algunos problemas de traducción de la terminología jurídica romana en el imperio bizantino', *Minerva: Revista de filología clásica,* 19: 285–96

Andriotis, N. P. (1967) Ἐτυμολογικὸ λεξικὸ τῆς κοινῆς Νεοελληνικῆς. 2nd ed., Thessaloniki

Andriotis, N. P. (1974) *Lexikon der Archaismen in neugriechischen Dialekten.* Vienna

Angelide, Ch. (1977) 'Τὸ μαρτύριο τῆς ἁγίας Ἰουλιανῆς τῆς ἐκ Νικομηδείας', *Βυζαντινά: ἐπιστημονικὸν ὄργανον κέντρου Βυζαντινῶν ἐρευνῶν φιλοσοφικῆς σχολῆς Ἀριστοτελείου Πανεπιστημίου,* 9: 141–66.

Appel, R., and P. Muysken (1987) *Language contact and bilingualism.* Amsterdam

Asdracha, C. (1995) 'Inscriptions chrétiennes et protobyzantines de la Thrace orientale et de l'île d'Imbros (IIIe–VIIe siècles)', *Ἀρχαιολογικὸν δελτίον,* 49–50: 279–356

Asdracha, C. (1997) 'Inscriptions chrétiennes et protobyzantines de la Thrace orientale et de l'île d'Imbros (IIIe–VIIe siècles)', *Ἀρχαιολογικὸν δελτίον,* 51–2: 333–86

Asdracha, C. (1998) 'Inscriptions chrétiennes et protobyzantines de la Thrace orientale et de l'île d'Imbros (IIIe–VIIe siècles)', *Ἀρχαιολογικὸν δελτίον,* 53.1: 455–521

Ashdowne, R., and C. White (2017) 'Introduction', in R. Ashdowne and C. White (edd.), *Latin in Medieval Britain.* Oxford: 1–58

Audollent, A. (1904) *Defixionum tabellae.* Paris

Audollent, A. (1910) 'Bandeau de plomb avec inscription trouvé a Haïdra (Tunisie)', in [no ed.], *Mélanges offerts à M. Émile Chatelain.* Paris: 545–56

Avotins, I. (1989) *On the Greek of the Code of Justinian: a supplement to Liddell–Scott–Jones together with observations on the influence of Latin on legal Greek.* Hildesheim

Avotins, I. (1992) *On the Greek of the Novels of Justinian: a supplement to Liddell–Scott–Jones together with observations on the influence of Latin on legal Greek.* Hildesheim

Babiniotis, G. (2002) Λεξικό της Νέας Ελληνικής Γλώσσας. 2nd ed., Athens

Backus, A. (2014) 'A usage-based approach to borrowability', in Zenner and Kristiansen (edd.) 19–39

Backus, A., and M. Dorleijn (2009) 'Loan translations versus code-switching', in B. E. Bullock and A. J. Toribio (edd.), *The Cambridge handbook of linguistic code-switching*. Cambridge: 75–93

Bagnall, R. S. (1985) *Currency and inflation in fourth century Egypt*. Chico

Bagnall, R. S. (2009) 'Practial help', in R. S. Bagnall (ed.), *The Oxford handbook of papyrology*. New York: 179–96

Bagnall, R. S., R. Casagrande-Kim, A. Ersoy, and C. Tanrıver (2016) *Graffiti from the basilica in the agora of Smyrna*. New York

Bakker, E. J. (ed.) (2010) *A companion to the ancient Greek language*. Malden

Baldwin, B. (1991) 'Notes on the word ῥόγα', *Eranos*, 89: 121–2

Bandy, A. C. (1983) *Ioannes Lydus: On powers, or the magistracies of the Roman state*. Philadelphia

Barber, C. (1997) *Early modern English*. 2nd ed., Edinburgh

Barber, E. A. (1968) *Greek–English lexicon: a supplement*. Oxford

Barrett, C. K. (1998) *A critical and exegetical commentary on the Acts of the Apostles*, II. Edinburgh

Bartal, A. (1901) *Glossarium mediae et infimae Latinitatis regni Hungariae*. Leipzig

Bartalucci, A. (1995) 'Prestiti latini negli originali e nelle *recensiones* greche degli *Atti dei martiri*', *Koinonia*, 19: 105–24

Bartoli, M. G. (1912) 'Românía e Ῥωμανία', in [no ed.], *Scritti varii di erudizione e di critica in onore di Rodolfo Renier*. Turin: 981–99

Bataille, A. (1956) 'Un inventaire de vêtements inédit', *Eos: Commentarii Societatis philologae Polonorum*, 48.2: 83–8

Bauckham, R. (2002) 'Paul and other Jews with Latin names in the New Testament', in A. Christophersen, C. Claussen, J. Frey, and B. Longenecker (edd.), *Paul, Luke and the Graeco-Roman world: essays in honour of Alexander J. M. Wedderburn*. London: 202–20

Baur, P. V. C., M. I. Rostovtzeff, and A. R. Bellinger (1933) *The excavations at Dura-Europos: preliminary report of fourth season of work*. New Haven

Bauzon, É. (2008) 'L'épigraphie funéraire bilingue des italiens en Grèce et en Asie, aux IIᵉ et Iᵉʳ s. av. J.-C.', in Biville *et al.* (edd.) 109–28

Bean, G. E. (1971) *Journeys in northern Lycia 1965–1967*. Vienna

Bean, G. E., and T. B. Mitford (1970) *Journeys in Rough Cilicia 1964–1968*. Vienna

Beekes, R. S. P. (2010) *Etymological Dictionary of Greek*. Leiden

Bees, N. A. (1941) *Die griechisch-christlichen Inschriften des Peloponnes*. Athens

Beinke, C. (1990) *Der Mythos franglais: zur Frage der Akzeptanz von Angloamerikanismen im zeitgenössischen Französisch*. Frankfurt am Main

Belardi, W. (1958) 'Nomi del centone nelle lingue indoeuropee', *Ricerche linguistiche*, 4: 29–57

Bell, H. I., and W. E. Crum (1925) 'A Greek–Coptic Glossary', *Aegyptus*, 6: 177–226

Bellocchi, M. (2016) 'La commedia: da Epicarmo ad Aristofane', in Cassio (ed.) 320–53

Benaissa, A. (2009) 'Receipt for a gratuity to a *cancellarius*', *AfP* 55: 56–62

Benaissa, A. (2010) 'A Syrian slave girl twice sold in Egypt', *ZPE* 173: 175–89

Benaissa, A. (2011) 'An anonymous *corrector Augustamnicae* of the sixth century', *ZPE* 177: 240–2

Benaissa, A. (2014) 'Three Roman-period papyri in the Beinecke Library', *ZPE* 192: 209–14

Benveniste, E. (1965) 'Termes gréco-latins d'anatomie', *Revue de philologie*, 3rd ser. 39: 7–13

Berger, A. (1953) *Encyclopedic dictionary of Roman law*. Philadelphia

Bernini, A. (2020) 'Un contratto dotale latino-greco: P.CtYBR inv. 4233', *ZPE* 216: 258–64

Berthelot, M., and C.-E. Ruelle (1888) *Collection des anciens alchimistes grecs*, II. Paris

Bickerman, E. J. (1949) 'The name of Christians', *Harvard Theological Review*, 42: 109–24

Bile, M., and B. Gain (2012) 'Une nouvelle étymologie de Χριστιανός? Questions de méthode à propos d'un article récent', *Revue d'études augustiniennes et patristiques*, 58: 141–53

Billerbeck, M. (2006) *Stephani Byzantii Ethnica, volumen* I: α–γ. Berlin

Billerbeck, M., and A. Neumann-Hartmann (2016) *Stephani Byzantii Ethnica, volumen* IV: π–υ. Berlin

Binder, V. (2000) *Sprachkontakt und Diglossie: lateinische Wörter im Griechischen als Quellen für die lateinische Sprachgeschichte und das Vulgärlatein*. Hamburg

Bingen, J. (1966) 'L'Édit du Maximum et les papyrus', in [no ed.], *Atti dell' XI congresso internazionale di papirologia*. Milan: 369–78

Biville, F. (1987) '*Capistrum, feretrum, angistrum*, etc.: emprunts, hybrides et formations héritées, à propos des dérivés médiatifs latins et grecs en -*trum*', in [no ed.], *Études de linguistique générale et de linguistique latine offertes en hommage à Guy Serbat*. Paris: 67–82

Biville, F. (1990–5) *Les emprunts du latin au grec: approche phonétique*. Louvain

Biville, F. (1992) 'Les interférences entre les lexiques grec et latin, et le *Dictionnaire Étymologique* de P. Chantraine', in Létoublon (ed.) 227–40

Biville, F. (2002) 'The Graeco-Romans and Graeco-Latin: a terminological framework for cases of bilingualism', in Adams, Janse, and Swain (edd.) 77–102

Biville, F. (2013) 'Textes et procédures bilingues en droit romain', in Cascione, Masi Doria, and Merola (edd.) 27–85

Biville, F. (2019) 'Le rituel des acclamations: de Rome à Byzance', in Garcea, Rosellini, and Silvano (edd.) 247–63

Biville, F., J.-C. Decourt, and G. Rougemont (edd.) (2008) *Bilinguisme gréco-latin et épigraphie*. Lyon

Blanc, A. (1996) 'Les traductions de 1 *Cor.* 13, 4: à propos du grec περπερεύεσθαι et du latin *perperam*', in M. Dubrocard and C. Kircher (edd.), *Hommage au doyen Weiss*. Nice: 147–67

Blanc, A. (1997) 'Deux adjectifs en -ερος (μαλερός, πέρπερος)', *RÉG* 110: 57–83

Blass, F., A. Debrunner, and F. Rehkopf (1979) *Grammatik des neutestamentlichen Griechisch*. 15th ed., Göttingen

Bogaert, R. (1985) 'Les κολλεκτάριοι dans les papyrus', *Chronique d'Égypte*, 60: 5–16

Bogaert, R. (1992) 'La banque en Égypte byzantine', *ZPE* 116: 85–140

Bogensperger, I. (2017) 'Purple and its various kinds in documentary papyri', in Gaspa *et al.* (edd.) 235–49

Boll, F. (1903) *Sphaera*. Leipzig

Boll, F. (1908) *Catalogus codicum astrologorum Graecorum*, VII: *codices Germanici*. Brussels

Bollini, M. (1975) *Le iscrizioni greche di Ravenna*. Faenza

Bonneau, D. (1984) 'βρέουιον (*breve*), "liste fiscale", dans les papyrus', in [no ed.], *Studi in onore di Cesare Sanfilippo*. Milan: v.109–23

Bonnet, M. (1898) *Acta apostolorum apocrypha*, II.I. Leipzig

Bonnet, M. (1903) *Acta apostolorum apocrypha*, II.II. Leipzig

Bosch, E. (1967) *Quellen zur Geschichte der Stadt Ankara im Altertum*. Ankara

Bourdin, S. (2012) *Les peuples de l'Italie préromaine: identités, territoires et relations inter-ethniques en Italie centrale et septentrionale* (VIIIᵉ–Iᵉʳ *s. av. J.-C.*). Rome

Bovon, F., B. Bouvier, and F. Amsler (1999) *Acta Philippi: textus*. Turnhout

Bowersock, G. W. (1991) 'The Babatha papyri, Masada, and Rome', *Journal of Roman Archaeology*, 4: 336–44

Brandsma, F. (1996) *Dorotheus and his Digest translation*. Groningen

Bratke, E. (1899) *Das sogenannte Religionsgespräch am Hof der Sasaniden* (*Texte und Untersuchungen zur Geschichte der Altchristlichen Literatur* 19.3). Leipzig

Braund, D., and J. Wilkins (edd.) (2000) *Athenaeus and his world: reading Greek culture in the Roman empire*. Exeter

Breccia, E. (1911) *Iscrizioni greche e latine* (Service des antiquités de l'Égypte: Catalogue général des antiquités égyptiennes du Musée d'Alexandrie). Cairo

Briquel, D. (1989) 'Denys, témoin de traditions disparues: l'identification des Aborigènes aux Ligures', *Mélanges de l'École française de Rome: Antiquité*, 101: 97–111

Brixhe, C. (1987) *Essai sur le grec anatolien au début de notre ère*. 2nd ed., Nancy

Brixhe, C. (ed.) (1998) *La koiné grecque antique*, III: *les contacts*. Nancy

Brixhe, C. (2007) 'The Greek of the Roman texts', trans. G. Cox, in Christidis (ed.) 903–10

Browning, R. (1983) *Medieval and modern Greek*. 2nd ed., Cambridge

Bruce, F. F. (1990) *The Acts of the Apostles: the Greek text with introduction and commentary*. 3rd ed., Grand Rapids

Bruce, F. F. (1993) 'Acts of the Apostles', in B. M. Metzger and M. D. Coogan (edd.), *The Oxford companion to the Bible*. New York: 6–10

Bruneau, P. (1988) 'Philologie mosaïstique', *Journal des Savants*, année 1988: 3–73

Brunner, T. F. (1988) 'Ἀμβιτεύειν', *ZPE* 75: 295–6

Brust, M. (2005) *Die indischen und iranischen Lehnwörter im Griechischen*. Innsbruck

Bubenik, V. (2007) 'Eastern koines', in Christidis (ed.) 632–7

Bubenik, V. (2014) 'Language contact', in Giannakis (ed.) II.299–306

Buck, C. D. (1949) *A dictionary of selected synonyms in the principal Indo-European languages*. Chicago

Buck, C. D., and W. Petersen (1945) *A reverse index of Greek nouns and adjectives*. Chicago

Buckler, W. H., W. M. Calder, and C. W. M. Cox (1924) 'Asia Minor, 1924. I – Monuments from Iconium, Lycaonia and Isauria', *JRS* 14: 24–84

Bulić, F., and R. Egger (1926) *Forschungen in Salona*, II: *Der altchristliche Friedhof Manastirine*. Vienna

Burgmann, L. (1990) Ἀθανάσιος Δίγλωσσος: Latina in der Novellenbearbeitung des Athanasios von Emesa', in J. H. A. Lokin and B. H. Stolte (edd.), *Novella Constitutio: studies in honor of Nicholas van der Wal*. Groningen: 57–82

Burgmann, L. (1991) 'Λέξεις ῥωμαϊκαί: lateinische Wörter in byzantinischen Rechtstexten', in Hörandner and Trapp (edd.) 61–79

Burke, T. (2010) *De infantia Jesu evangelium Thomae Graece*. Turnhout

Burton, P. (2002) 'Assessing Latin–Gothic interaction', in Adams, Janse, and Swain (edd.) 393–418

Bussemaker, U. C. (1862) 'Fragmenta poematum rem naturalem vel medicinam spectantium', in [no ed.], *Poetae bucolici et didactici*. Paris: 75–134 of third set of page numbers

Cadell, H. (1974) 'Le renouvellement du vocabulaire au IVᵉ siècle de notre ère d'après les papyrus', in E. Kiessling and H.-A. Rupprecht (edd.), *Akten des XIII. internationalen Papyrologenkongresses*. Munich: 61–8

Caimi, J. (1981) 'Ioannis Lydi *de magistratibus* III 70: note esegetiche e spunti in tema di fiscalità e legislazione protobizantine', in *Miscellanea Agostino Pertusi*, I (= *Rivista di Studi Bizantini e Slavi* 1). Bologna: 317–61

Calder, W. M. (1912a) 'Colonia Caesareia Antiocheia', *JRS* 2: 78–109

Calder, W. M. (1912b) 'Julia-Ipsus and Augustopolis', *JRS* 2: 237–66

Cameron, A. (1931) 'Latin words in the Greek inscriptions of Asia Minor', *AJP* 52: 232–62

Cameron, A. (1976) *Circus factions: blues and greens at Rome and Byzantium*. Oxford

Campanile, E. (1969) 'Note sulle glosse Sicule e sui rapporti linguistici fra Siculo e Latino', in [no ed.], *Studia classica et orientalia Antonio Pagliaro oblata*, I. Rome: 293–322

Cantacuzène, G. (1932) 'Poids inédits trouvés dans la petite Scythie', *Dacia: recherches et decouvertes archéologiques en Roumanie*, 3/4: 602–11

Capron, L., C. Dumoulin, J.-L. Fournet, and G. Husson (2004) '*Corrigenda* aux P. Reinach II', *ZPE* 150: 207–13

Carnoy, A. (1950) 'Le grec moderne σπίτι "maison"', *Παγκάρπεια: Mélanges Henri Grégoire* (= *Annuaire de l'institut de philologie et d'histoire orientales et slaves*, 10). Brussels: II.109–13

Carpinato, C., and O. Tribulato (edd.) (2014) *Storia e storie della lingua greca*. Venice

Carrié, J.-M. (1979) 'Primipilaires et taxe du "Primipilon" à la lumière de la documentation papyrologique', in J. Bingen and G. Nachtergael (edd.), *Actes du XVᵉ Congrès International de Papyrologie, quatrième partie: papyrologie documentaire*. Brussels: 156–76

Cascione, C., C. Masi Doria, and G. D. Merola (edd.) (2013), *Modelli di un multiculturalismo giuridico. Il bilinguismo nel mondo antico: diritto, prassi, insegnamento*. Naples

Cassio, A. C. (2012) 'Intimations of koine in Sicilian Doric: the information provided by the *Antiatticist*', in Tribulato (ed.) 251–64

Cassio, A. C. (2014) 'Lessico "moderno" nei testi greci antichi: storie di continuità e discontinuità', in Carpinato and Tribulato (edd.) 35–48

Cassio, A. C. (ed.) (2016) *Storia delle lingue letterarie greche*. 2nd ed., Florence

Cavenaile, R. (1951) 'Influence latine sur le vocabulaire grec d'Égypte', *Chronique d'Égypte*, 26: 391–404

Cavenaile, R. (1952) 'Quelques aspects de l'apport linguistique du grec au latin d'Égypte', *Aegyptus*, 32: 191–203

Ceccarelli, P. (2000) 'Dance and desserts: an analysis of book fourteen', in Braund and Wilkins (edd.) 272–91

Cervenka-Ehrenstrasser, I. M. (1996) *Lexikon der lateinischen Lehnwörter in den griechischsprachigen dokumentarischen Texten Ägyptens*, I: *A*. Vienna

Cervenka-Ehrenstrasser, I. M. (2000) *Lexikon der lateinischen Lehnwörter in den griechischsprachigen dokumentarischen Texten Ägyptens*, II: *B–Δ*. Vienna

Cervenka-Ehrenstrasser, I. M., and J. Diethart (1997) 'Korr. Tyche 244: O.Amst. 31, 7: "Ein Bund Dörrfische"', *Tyche*, 12: 254

Chantraine, P. (1933) *La formation des noms en grec ancien*. Paris

Chantraine, P. (1937) 'Quelques emprunts du grec au latin', *Revue des études latines*, 15: 88–91

Chantraine, P. (1956) *Études sur le vocabulaire grec*. Paris

Chantraine, P. (1964) 'Grec αἴθριον', *Recherches de papyrologie*, 3: 7–15

Christidis, A.-F. (2007) *A history of ancient Greek: from the beginnings to late antiquity*. Cambridge

Christodoulou, G. A. (1977) *Τὰ ἀρχαῖα σχόλια εἰς Αἴαντα τοῦ Σοφοκλέους*. Athens

Christol, M., and S. Demougin (1990) 'De Lugo à Pergame: la carrière de l'affranchi Saturninus dans l'administration impériale', *Mélanges de l'École française de Rome: Antiquité*, 102: 159–211

Clackson, J. (forthcoming) 'Greek loanwords in early Latin', in J. N. Adams, A. Chahoud, and G. Pezzini (edd.), *A critical guide to the Early Latin language*. Cambridge.

Clarysse, W. (1997) 'Greek accents on Egyptian names', *ZPE* 119: 177–84

Clugnet, L. (1900) 'Vie et récits de l'abbé Daniel, de Scété (VIᵉ siècle)', *Revue de l'orient chrétien*, 5: 49–73, 254–71, 370–406

Clyne, M. (2003) *Dynamics of language contact*. Cambridge

Coarelli, F. (1982) 'L'*Agora des Italiens* a Delo: il mercato degli schiavi?', in F. Coarelli, D. Musti, and H. Solin (edd.) *Delo e l'Italia*. Rome: 119–45

Coates, R. (2006) 'Properhood', *Language*, 82: 356–82

Coleman, R. G. G. (1975) 'Greek influence on Latin syntax', *Transactions of the Philological Society*, 74: 101–56

Coleman, R. G. G. (2007) 'Greek and Latin', in Christidis (ed.) 792–9

Coles, R. A. (1966) *Reports of Proceedings in Papyri*. Brussels

Contossopoulos, N. (1978) *L'influence du français sur le grec: emprunts lexicaux et calques phraséologiques*. Athens

Cook, J. M. (1973) *The Troad: an archaeological and topographical study*. Oxford

Corcoran, S. (2017) 'Roman law and the two languages in Justinian's empire', *Bulletin of the Institute of Classical Studies*, 60: 96–116

Cormack, J. M. R. (1964) 'Inscriptions from Aphrodisias', *Annual of the British School at Athens*, 59: 16–29

Corsten, T. (2010) 'Names in -ιανος in Asia Minor: a preliminary study', in R. W. V. Catling and F. Marchand (edd.), *Onomatologos: studies in Greek personal names presented to Elaine Matthews*. Oxford: 456–63

Costas, P. S. (1936). *An outline of the history of the Greek language, with particular emphasis on the koine and the subsequent periods*. Chicago

Cotton, H. M., R. G. Hoyland, J. J. Price, and D. J. Wasserstein (edd.) (2009) *From Hellenism to Islam: cultural and linguistic change in the Roman Near East*. Cambridge

Coudry, M. (2016) 'Institutions et procédures politiques de la République romaine: les choix lexicaux de Cassius Dion', in V. Fromentin, E. Bertrand, M. Coltelloni-Trannoy, M. Molin, and G. Urso (edd.), *Cassius Dion: nouvelles lectures*. Bordeaux: II.485–518

Cousin, G. (1900) 'Voyage en Carie (suite et fin)', *BCH* 24: 329–47

Crawford, M. H. (1974) *Roman Republican coinage*. London

Crawford, M. H. (1977) Review of Mason (1974), *JRS* 67: 249–50

Cribiore, R. (2007) *The School of Libanius in late antique Antioch*. Princeton

Cromwell, J. (2020) 'Domestic textile production in Dakhleh Oasis in the fourth century AD', in Mossakowska-Gaubert (ed.) 139–52

Cronin, H. S. (1902) 'First report of a journey in Pisidia, Lycaonia, and Pamphylia, II', *JHS* 22: 339–76

Crum, W. E. (1905) *Catalogue of the Coptic manuscripts in the British Museum*. London

Crusius, O. (1903) 'Kleinigkeiten zur alten Sprach- und Kulturgeschichte', *Philologus*, 62: 125–40

Cumont, F., and F. Boll (1904) *Catalogus codicum astrologorum Graecorum*, V.1: *codicum Romanorum partem priorem*. Brussels

Curnow, T. J. (2001) 'What language features can be borrowed?', in A. Y. Aikhenvald and R. M. W. Dixon (edd.), *Areal diffusion and genetic inheritance: problems in comparative linguistics*. Oxford : 412–36

Cuvigny, H. (1998) 'Kainè, ville nouvelle: une expérience de regroupement familial au IIᵉ s. è. chr.', in Kaper (ed.) 87–94

Cuvigny, H. (2002) 'Vibius Alexander, *praefectus* et épistratège de l'Heptanomie', *Chronique d'Égypte*, 77: 238–48

Cuvigny, H. (2005) 'L'organigramme du personnel d'une carrière impériale d'après un ostracon du Mons Claudianus', *Chiron*, 35: 309–53

Cuvigny, H. (ed.) (2006) *La route de Myos Hormos: l'armé romaine dans le désert Oriental d'Égypte*. 2nd ed., Cairo

Cuvigny, H. (2010a) 'Femmes tournantes: remarques sur la prostitution dans les garnisons romaines du désert de Bérénice', *ZPE* 172: 159–66

Cuvigny, H. (2010b) 'Un reçu de rations militaires contre paiement des *publica*', in K. Lembke, M. Minas-Nerpel, and S. Pfeiffer (edd.), *Tradition and transformation: Egypt under Roman rule*. Leiden: 37–51.

Cuvigny, H. (2013) 'Hommes et dieux en réseau: bilan papyrologique du programme "*Praesidia* du désert oriental Égyptien"', *Académie des inscriptions et belles-lettres: comptes rendus des séances*, 2013: 405–42

Cuvigny, H. (2016) 'Une dédicace à Zeus Hèlios Grand Sarapis honorant un *desector* sur un ostracon du Mons Claudianus', in C. Freu, S. Janniard, and A. Ripoll (edd.), *Libera curiositas: mélanges d'histoire romaine et d'antiquité tardive offerts à Jean-Michel Carrié*. Turnhout: 17–21

Cuvigny, H. (2017) Τρισαυγούστιον et φραγέλλιον: contrôle de qualité et mesurage du grain fiscal au IVᵉ s. apr. J.-C. à la lumière de P.Mich. xx 800 et de l'inscription tardive du grenier d'Andriakè (Grégoire, Recueil 290)', *Chiron* 47: 95–114

Cuvigny, H. (2019) 'Poste publique, renseignement militaire et citernes à sec: les lettres de Diourdanos à Archibios, *curator Claudiani*', *Chiron*, 49: 271–97

Cuvigny, H. (2021) '*O.Claud.* IV 873: des "cagneuses" pour la colonne', *Chronique d'Égypte*, 96: 177–8

Cuvigny, H. and K. Lach-Urgacz (2020) "Ορεινὸν κέρμα: monetary circulation in the *praesidia* of the Eastern Desert during the Principate', in T. Faucher (ed.), *Money rules! The monetary economy of Egypt, from Persians until the beginning of Islam*. Cairo: 309–39

Dagron, G. (1969) 'Aux origines de la civilisation byzantine: langue de culture et langue d'état', *Revue historique*, 241: 23–56

Dain, A. (1930) 'La transcription des mots latins en grec dans les *Gloses nomiques*', *Revue des études latines*, 8: 92–113

D'Alessio, R. (2013) 'La *Graeca vox* nella giurisprudenza del Principato', in Cascione, Masi Doria, and Merola (edd.) 119–41

Daniel, R. W. (1986) 'Two rare words', *ZPE* 66: 59–60

Danker, F. W., W. Bauer, K. Aland, B. Aland, W. F. Arndt, and F. W. Gingrich (2000) *A Greek–English lexicon of the New Testament and other early Christian literature*. 3rd ed., Chicago

Daremberg, C., and E. Saglio (1877–1919) *Dictionnaire des antiquités grecques et romains d'après les textes et les monuments*. Paris

Daris, S. (1957) 'Dai papiri inediti della raccolta milanese', *Aegyptus*, 37: 89–103

Daris, S. (1962) 'Varia selecta', *Aegyptus*, 42: 136–40

Daris, S. (1964) 'Note di lessico e di onomastica militare', *Aegyptus*, 44: 47–51

Daris, S. (1970) 'Agraria – Relatoria', *Studia papyrologia*, 9: 35–8

Daris, S. (1991a) *Il lessico latino nel greco d'Egitto*. 2nd ed., Barcelona

Daris, S. (1991b) 'Latino ed Egitto romano', in [no ed.], *Il bilinguismo degli antichi*. Genoa: 47–81

Daris, S. (1991c) 'Spigolature documentarie 24–28', *ZPE* 85: 271–5

Daris, S. (1997) Review of *P.Kellis* I, *Aegyptus*, 77: 139–42

De Cavalieri, F. (1901) *I martirii di S. Teodoto e di S. Ariadne, con un' appendice sul testo originale del martirio di S. Eleuterio*. Rome

De Meyer, L. (1962) 'L'étymologie de *macellum* "marché"', *L'antiquité classique*, 31: 148–52

De Rosalia, A. (1991) 'Il latino di Plutarco', in G. D'Ippolito and I. Gallo (edd.), *Strutture formali dei 'Moralia' di Plutarco*. Naples: 445–59

De Stoop, E. (1911) *Vie d'Alexandre l'Acémète*. Paris

De Visscher, F. (1940) *Les édits d'Auguste découverts a Cyrène*. Brussels

Debrunner, A. (1917) *Griechische Wortbildungslehre*. Heidelberg

Delatte, A. (1939) *Anecdota Atheniensia et alia*, II. Paris

Delehaye, H. (1923a) *Les martyrs d'Égypte*. Brussels

Delehaye, H. (1923b) *Les saints stylites*. Brussels

Dell, F. (1984) 'L'accentuation dans les phrases en français', in F. Dell, D. Hirst, and J.-R. Vergnaud (edd.), *Forme sonore du langage: structure des représentations en phonologie*. Paris: 65–122

Delmaire, R. (1989) *Largesses sacrées et res privata*. Paris

Denis, A.-M. (1970) *Fragmenta pseudepigraphorum quae supersunt*. Leiden

Deroy, L. (1956) *L'emprunt linguistique*. Paris

Di Segni, L., J. Patrich, and K. G. Holum (2003) 'A schedule of fees (*sportulae*) for official services from Caesarea Maritima, Israel', *ZPE* 145: 273–300

Dickey, E. (2003) 'Latin influence on the Greek of documentary papyri: an analysis of its chronological distribution', *ZPE* 145: 249–57

Dickey, E. (2007) *Ancient Greek scholarship*. New York

Dickey, E. (2010a) 'The creation of Latin teaching materials in antiquity: a re-interpretation of P.Sorb. inv. 2069', *ZPE* 175: 188–208

Dickey, E. (2010b) 'Latin influence and Greek request formulae', in Evans and Obbink (edd.) 208–20

Dickey, E. (2012) 'Latin loanwords in Greek: a preliminary analysis', in M. Leiwo, H. Halla-aho, and M. Vierros (edd.), *Variation and change in Greek and Latin*. Helsinki: 57–70

Dickey, E. (2012–15) *The colloquia of the Hermeneumata Pseudodositheana*. Cambridge

Dickey, E. (2016) *Learning Latin the ancient way*. Cambridge

Dickey, E. (2018) 'What is a loanword? The case of Latin borrowings and codeswitches in ancient Greek', *Lingue e linguaggio*, 17: 7–36

Diekamp, F. (1938) *Analecta patristica*. Rome

Diekamp, F., and F. X. Funk (1913) *Patres apostolici*, II. 3rd ed., Tübingen

Dieterich, K. (1898) *Untersuchungen zur Geschichte der griechischen Sprache: von der hellenistischen Zeit bis zum 10. Jahrhundert n. Chr.* Leipzig

Dieterich, K. (1901) 'Zu den lateinisch-romanischen Lehnwörtern im Neugriechischen', *Byzantinische Zeitschrift*, 10: 587–96

Dieterich, K. (1928) 'Die Suffixbildung im Neugriechischen', *Balkan Archiv* 4: 104–67

Diethart, J. (1984) 'Eine verkannte Berufsbezeichnung: βουκ(κ)ας, der "Biskuitbäcker"', *ZPE* 54: 93–4

Diethart, J. (1986) 'Drei Listen aus byzantinischer Zeit auf Papyrus', *Tyche*, 1: 88–90

Diethart, J. (1988) 'Materialien aus den Papyri zur byzantinischen Lexikographie', in Trapp *et al.* (edd.) 47–69

Diethart, J. (1989) 'Corrigenda und Addenda zu Wiener Papyri', *ZPE* 76: 107–14

Diethart, J. (1990a) 'Papyri aus byzantinischer Zeit als Fundgrube für lexikographisches und realienkundliches Material', *Analecta papyrologica*, 2: 81–114

Diethart, J. (1990b) 'Lexikalisches in griechischen Papyri', *Die Sprache*, 34: 190–4

Diethart, J. (1991a) 'Bemerkungen zu Papyri IV: ⟨Korr. Tyche 43–51⟩', *Tyche*, 6: 233–6

Diethart, J. (1991b) 'Die Bedeutung der Papyri für die byzantinische Lexikographie', in Hörandner and Trapp (edd.) 117–21

Diethart, J. (1992) 'Emendationes et interpretationes lexicographicae ad papyrologiam pertinentes', *ZPE* 92: 237–40

Diethart, J. (1993) 'Bemerkungen zu Papyri VI: ⟨Korr. Tyche⟩ 76–113', *Tyche*, 8: 221–7

Diethart, J. (1995a) 'Fünf lexikographisch und realienkundlich wichtige Texte aus Byzantinischer Zeit aus der Wiener Papyrussammlung', *Analecta papyrologica*, 7: 73–91

Diethart, J. (1995b) 'Bemerkungen zu Papyri VIII: ⟨Korr. Tyche⟩ 149–67', *Tyche*, 10: 237–41

Diethart, J. (1998) 'Lexikographische Lesefrüchte: Bemerkungen zu "Liddell–Scott, *Revised Supplement*" 1996', *ZPE* 123: 165–76

Diethart, J. (1999) 'Lexikographische Lesefrüchte II: weitere Bemerkungen zu "Liddell–Scott, *Revised Supplement*" 1996', *ZPE* 128: 177–82

Diethart, J. (2002) 'Lexikographische Lesefrüchte III: weitere Bemerkungen zu "Liddell–Scott, *Revised Supplement*" 1996 und G. W. H. Lampe, *A Patristic Greek Lexicon*', *AfP* 48: 147–55

Diethart, J. (2006) 'Zu neutralen Abstrakta auf -άτον im byzantinischen Griechisch', *Jahrbuch der Österreichischen Byzantinistik*, 56: 13–26

Diethart, J. (2008) 'Beobachtungen zu den lateinischen Zeitwörtern im Griechischen', in Trapp and Schönauer (edd.) 15–36

Diethart, J., and C. Grassien (2004) 'Lesefrüchte zur griechischen und lateinischen Lexikographie', *AfP* 50: 85–98

Diethart, J., and M. R. M. Hasitzka (2001) 'Beobachtungen und Überlegungen zur griechischen, lateinischen und koptischen Lexikographie', *Journal of Juristic Papyrology*, 31: 33–46

Diethart, J., and E. Kislinger (1987) '"Hunnisches" auf einem Wiener Papyrus', *Tyche*, 2: 5–10

Dietrich, W. (1995) *Griechisch und Romanisch: Parallelen und Divergenzen in Entwicklung, Variation und Strukturen.* Münster

Dietz, F. R. (1834) *Scholia in Hippocratem et Galenum*, II. Königsberg

Dindorf, L. (1831) *Ioannis Malalae Chronographia.* Bonn

Dindorf, L. (1870) *Historici Graeci minores*, I. Leipzig

Dindorf, W. (1829) *Aristides*, III. Leipzig

Dittenberger, W. (1872) 'Römische Namen in griechischen Inschriften und Literaturwerken', *Hermes*, 6: 129–55, 281–313

Dmitriev, S. (2010) 'John Lydus and his contemporaries on identities and cultures of sixth-century Byzantium', *Dumbarton Oaks Papers*, 64: 27–42

Dmitriev, S. (2018) 'John Lydus' knowledge of Latin and language politics in sixth-century Constantinople', *Byzantinische Zeitschrift*, 111: 55–70

Dobias-Lalou, C. (1998) 'Sur quelques noms latins en Cyrénaïque', in B. Bureau and C. Nicolas (edd.), *Moussyllanea: mélanges de linguistique et de littérature anciennes offerts à Claude Moussy.* Louvain: 206–12 (non vidi)

Döttling, C. (1920) *Die Flexionsformen lateinischer Nomina in den griechischen Papyri und Inschriften.* Lausanne

Doyle, E. J. (1976) 'Two new fragments of the Edict of Diocletian on maximum prices', *Hesperia*, 45: 77–97

Drew-Bear, T. (1972) 'Some Greek words', *Glotta*, 50: 61–96, 182–228

Dross-Krüpe, K. (2017) 'Χιτών – δαλματική – μαφόρτης – σύνθεσις: common and uncommon garment terms in dowry arrangements from Roman Egypt', in Gaspa *et al.* (edd.) 295–300

Du Cange, C. D. (1883–7) *Glossarium mediae et infimae latinitatis.* Niort

Dubuisson, M. (1979) 'Le latin des historiens grecs', *Les études classiques*, 47: 89–106

Dubuisson, M. (1981) 'Utraque lingua', *L'antiquité classique*, 50: 274–86

Dubuisson, M. (1985) *Le latin de Polybe: les implications historiques d'un cas de bilinguisme.* Paris

Dubuisson, M. (1992a) 'Le grec à Rome á l'époque de Cicéron: extension et qualité du bilinguisme', *Annales: économies, sociétés, civilisations,* 47: 187–206

Dubuisson, M. (1992b) 'Le contact linguistique gréco-latin: problèmes d'interférences et d'emprunts', *Lalies,* 10: 91–109

Dubuisson, M. (2005) 'Le grec de la correspondance de Cicéron: questions préliminaires sur un cas de bilinguisme', *La linguistique,* 41.2: 69–86

Dumont, A., and T. Homolle (1892) *Mélanges d'archéologie et d'épigraphie.* Paris

Dunant, C. (1971) *Le sanctuaire de Baalshamîn à Palmyre,* III: *les inscriptions.* Neuchâtel

Durkin, P. (2009) *The Oxford guide to etymology.* Oxford

Durkin, P. (2014) *Borrowed words: a history of loanwords in English.* Oxford

Durkin, P., and S. Schad (2017) 'The *DMLBS* and the *OED*: medieval Latin and the lexicography of English', in R. Ashdowne and C. White (edd.), *Latin in Medieval Britain.* Oxford: 320–40

Durling, R. J. (1979) 'Lexicographical notes on Galen's pharmacological writings', *Glotta,* 57: 218–24

Eck, W. (2000) 'Latein als Sprache politischer Kommunikation in Städten der östlichen Provinzen', *Chiron,* 30: 641–60

Eck, W. (2003) 'The language of power: Latin in the inscriptions of Iudaea/Syria Palaestina', in L. H. Schiffman (ed.), *Semitic papyrology in context: a climate of creativity. Papers from a New York University conference marking the retirement of Baruch A. Levine.* Leiden: 123–44

Eck, W. (2009) 'The presence, role and significance of Latin in the epigraphy and culture of the Roman Near East', in Cotton *et al.* (edd.) 15–42

Eideneier, H. (1971) 'Einige Ghost-words in der griechischen Papyruslexikographie', *ZPE* 7: 53–60

Eleftheriades, O. (1993) *Modern Greek word formation.* Minneapolis

Ensslin, W. (1926) 'Ein Prozessvergleich unter Klerikern vom Jahre 481 (zu Papyrus Princeton 55)', *Rheinisches Museum,* N.S. 75: 422–46

Ernout, A., and A. Meillet (1979) *Dictionnaire étymologique de la langue latine.* Paris

Esaias (1911) Τοῦ ὁσίου πατρὸς ἡμῶν Ἄββα Ἡσαίου Λόγοι κθ΄. Jerusalem

Evans, T. V., and D. D. Obbink (edd.) (2010) *The language of the papyri.* Oxford

Famerie, É. (1998) *Le latin et le grec d'Appien.* Geneva

Famerie, É. (1999) 'La transposition de *quaestor* en grec', *L'antiquité classique,* 68: 211–25

Faraklas, N. (1968) 'Σκιλλοῦς', Ἀρχαιολογικὸν δελτίον, 23.1: 293–4

Feissel, D. (2003) 'Bulletin épigraphique 580', *RÉG* 116: 668

Feissel, D. (2004) 'Bulletin épigraphique 394', *RÉG* 117: 683–4

Feissel, D. (2008) 'Écrire grec en alphabet latin: le cas des documents protobyzantins', in Biville *et al.* (edd.) 213–30

Feissel, D. (2016) 'Les *breviatica* de Kasai en Pamphylie: un jugement du maître des offices sous le règne de Zenon', in R. Haensch (ed.), *Recht haben und Recht bekommen im Imperium Romanum: das Gerichtswesen der römischen Kaiserzeit und seine dokumentarische Evidenz.* Warsaw: 659–737

Feissel, D., and J. Gascou (1995) 'Documents d'archives romains inédits du Moyen Euphrate (IIIe s. après J.-C.)', *Journal des savants* [no vol.] 1995: 65–119

Feissel, D., and A. Philippidis-Braat (1985) 'Inventaires en vue d'un recueil des inscriptions historiques de Byzance, III: Inscriptions du Péloponnèse', *Travaux et mémoires: Collège de France, Centre de recherche d'histoire et civilisation de Byzance,* 9: 267–395

Ferri, R. (2008) 'New evidence on the meaning of ῥωμαιστής in *IG* XI.2 133: "Actor of Latin Comedies"?', *ZPE* 166: 155–8

Field, F. (1875) *Origenis Hexaplorum quae supersunt.* Oxford

Filos, P. (2006) 'On some Latin univerbations in Greek', *Oxford University Working Papers in Linguistics, Philology and Phonetics,* 11: 43–61

Filos, P. (2008) 'Studies in the morphology of Latin loanwords into Greek: evidence from the papyri'. Dissertation from Oxford University

Filos, P. (2010) 'Greek papyri and Graeco-Latin hybrid compounds', in Evans and Obbink (edd.) 221–52

Filos, P. (2014) 'Latin loanwords in Greek', in Giannakis (ed.) II.320–3

Filos, P. (2019) 'Aspects of folk etymology in ancient Greek: insights from common nouns', in G. K. Giannakis, C. Charalambakis, F. Montanari, and A. Rengakos (edd.), *Studies in Greek Lexicography.* Berlin: 159–81

Finkenstaedt, T., and D. Wolff (1973) *Ordered profusion: studies in dictionaries and the English lexicon.* Heidelberg

Fischer, K.-D. (1979) 'Φλιμέλια und φλέμινα', *Hermes*, 107: 495

Fischer, K.-D. (1980) *Pelagonii Ars veterinaria*. Leipzig

Fischer, K.-D. (2019) 'Einigermassen durchsichtig: Überlegungen zu einer Stelle in Galens Schrift *Über die einfachen Heilmittel*', *Galenos*, 13: 111–13

Fitzmyer, J. A. (1970) 'The languages of Palestine in the first century AD', in *Catholic Biblical Quarterly*, 32: 501–31. Reprinted in S. E. Porter (ed.), *The language of the New Testament: classic essays*. Sheffield: 126–62

Fitzmyer, J. A. (1998) *The Acts of the Apostles: a new translation with introduction and commentary (Anchor Bible)*. New York

Fögen, M. T. (1998) 'Reanimation of Roman law in the ninth century: remarks on reasons and results', in L. Brubaker (ed.), *Byzantium in the ninth century: dead or alive?* Aldershot: 11–22

Forcellini, A., I. Furlanetto, F. Corradini, and I. Perin (1864–1926) *Lexicon totius latinitatis*. 4th ed., Padua

Fournet, J.-L. (1994) 'L'influence des usages littéraires sur l'écriture des documents: perspectives', in A. Bülow-Jacobsen (ed.), *Proceedings of the 20th international congress of papyrologists*. Copenhagen: 418–22

Fournet, J.-L. (2009) 'Esquisse d'une anatomie de la lettre antique tardive d'après les papyrus', in R. Delmaire, J. Desmulliez, and P.-L. Gatier (edd.), *Correspondances: documents pour l'histoire de l'antiquité tardive*. Paris: 23–66

Fournet, J.-L. (2019) 'La pratique du latin dans l'Égypte de l'Antiquité tardive', in Garcea, Rosellini, and Silvano (edd.) 73–91

Fraenkel, E. (1910) *Geschichte der griechischen Nomina agentis auf* -τήρ, -τωρ, -της (-τ-), I. Strasbourg

Franz, J. G. F. (1780) *Scriptores physiognomoniae veteres*. Altenburg

Fraser, P. M., and E. Matthews (1987–) *A lexicon of Greek personal names*. Oxford

Freeman, E. A. (1883) 'Some points in the later history of the Greek language', *JHS* 3: 361–92

Fressura, M. (2021) 'Riedizione del lessico latino-greco P.Vindob. L 27', in A. Ricciardetto, N. Carlig, G. Nocchi Macedo, and M. de Haro Sanchez (edd.), *Le médecin et le livre: hommages à Marie-Hélène Marganne*. Lecce: 143–62

Freyburger-Galland, M.-L. (1984) 'Quelques exemples de l'emprunt linguistique du grec au latin dans le vocabulaire politique de Dion Cassius', *Ktema*, 9: 329–37

Freyburger-Galland, M.-L. (1992) 'Dion Cassius et l'étymologie: *auctoritas* et *Augustus*', *RÉG* 105: 237–46

Freyburger-Galland, M.-L. (1997) *Aspects du vocabulaire politique et institutionnel de Dion Cassius*. Paris

Freyburger-Galland, M.-L. (1998) 'Dion Cassius: problèmes morphologiques posés par les emprunts du grec au latin', in Brixhe (ed.) 137–44

Frisk, H. (1954–72) *Griechisches etymologisches Wörterbuch*. Heidelberg

Frye, R. N., J. F. Gilliam, H. Ingholt, and C. B. Welles (1955) 'Inscriptions from Dura-Europos', *Yale Classical Studies*, 14: 127–213

Gaffiot, F. (1934) *Dictionnaire illustré latin–français*. Paris

Garcea, A. (2019) 'Latin in Byzantium: different forms of linguistic contact', in Garcea, Rosellini, and Silvano (edd.) 43–70

Garcea, A., M. Rosellini, and L. Silvano (edd.) (2019) *Latin in Byzantium*, I: *late antiquity and beyond*. Turnhout

García Domingo, E. (1979) *Latinismos en la koiné: en los documentos epigráficos desde el 212 a. J.C. hasta el 14 d. J.C.* Burgos

García Domingo, E. (1983) 'La penetración del latín en el griego: panorámica desde el siglo VIII a. J.C. hasta el siglo IV d. J.C.' *Cuadernos de filología clásica*, 18: 249–89

Gardner, E. A. (1885) 'Inscriptions copied by Cockerell in Greece, II', *JHS* 6: 340–63

Gardner-Chloros, P. (2009) *Code-switching*. Cambridge

Gardner-Chloros, P. (2010) 'Contact and code-switching', in Hickey (ed.) 188–207

Gascou, J., and K. A. Worp (1988) 'CPR VII 26: réédition', *Tyche*, 3: 103–10

Gaspa, S., C. Michel, and M.-L. Nosch (edd.) (2017) *Textile terminologies from the Orient to the Mediterranean and Europe, 1000 BC to 1000 AD*. Lincoln, Nebr.

Geiger, J. (1996) 'How much Latin in Greek Palestine?', in H. Rosén (ed.), *Aspects of Latin: papers from the seventh international colloquium on Latin linguistics*. Innsbruck: 39–57

Georgacas, D. J. (1958) 'A contribution to Greek word history, derivation and etymology', *Glotta*, 36: 100–122, 161–93

George, C. H. (2010) 'Jewish and Christian Greek', in Bakker (ed.) 267–80

Ghiretti, E. (1996) 'Note sul bilinguismo greco-latino dell'Egitto romano', *Aevum antiquum*, 9: 275–98

Giannakis, G. K. (ed.) (2014) *Encyclopedia of ancient Greek language and linguistics.* Leiden

Gibson, E. P. (1975) 'A unique Christian epitaph from the upper Tembris valley', *BASP* 12: 151–7

Gignac, F. T. (1976) *A grammar of the Greek papyri of the Roman and Byzantine periods,* I: *phonology.* Milan

Gignac, F. T. (1981) *A grammar of the Greek papyri of the Roman and Byzantine periods,* II: *morphology.* Milan

Gilder, A. (1999) *En vrai français dans le texte: dictionnaire franglais–français.* Paris

Gilliam, J. F. (1961) 'Ala Agrippiana and archistator', *Classical Philology,* 56: 100–3

Gilliam, J. F. (1968) '*P.Wisconsin* 14', *BASP* 5: 93–8

Gilliam, J. F. (1976) '*Canaliclarius* and κανανικλάριος (*P.Oxy.* XL 2925)', *BASP* 13: 49–52

Gonis, N. (1998) Review of Cervenka-Ehrenstrasser (1996), *Classical Review,* 48: 217–18

Gonis, N. (2003) Review of Cervenka-Ehrenstrasser (2000), *Classical Review,* 53: 93–4

Gourevitch, D. (1977) '*Stomachus* et l'humeur', *Revue de philologie* 51: 56–74

Grant, A. P. (2009) 'Loanwords in British English', in Haspelmath and Tadmor (edd.) 360–83

Grégoire, H. (1909) 'Rapport sur un voyage d'exploration dans le Pont et en Cappadoce', *BCH* 33: 3–169

Grossman, E., P. Dils, T. S. Richter, and W. Schenkel (edd.) (2017) *Greek influence on Egyptian-Coptic: contact-induced change in an ancient African language.* Hamburg

Guardasole, A. (2004) 'L'héritage de Galien dans l'oeuvre d'Alexandre de Tralles', in J. Jouanna and J. Leclant (edd.), *Colloque 'la médecine grecque antique': actes.* Paris: 219–34

Gusmani, R. (1981–3) *Saggi sull'interferenza linguistica.* Florence

Gusmani, R. (1987) 'Interlinguistica', in R. Lazzeroni (ed.), *Linguistica storica.* Rome: 87–114

Hadei, M. (2016) 'Single word insertions as code-switching or established borrowing?', *International Journal of Linguistics,* 8: 14–25

Hagedorn, D. (1980) 'Lesevorschläge', *ZPE* 40: 85–6

Hagedorn, D. (1986) 'Bemerkungen zu Urkunden', *ZPE* 65: 85–92

Hagedorn, D. (2007) 'Entsprach der Monat Domitianos in Ägypten dem Phaophi oder dem Hathyr?', *ZPE* 159: 261–6

Hagedorn, D., and F. Mitthof (1997) 'Ein Κουρεπιστουλαριος (*cura epistularum*) im Büro des *praeses provinciae Arcadiae*: eine Bemerkung zu P.Mich. XVIII 794', *ZPE* 117: 187–9

Hahn, L. (1906) *Rom und Romanismus im griechisch-römischen Osten, mit besonderer Berücksichtigung der Sprache, bis auf die Zeit Hadrians: eine Studie.* Leipzig

Hahn, L. (1907) 'Zum Sprachenkampf im römischen Reich, bis auf die Zeit Justinians: eine Skizze', *Philologus* suppl. 10: 675–718

Halleux, R., and J. Schamp (1985) *Les lapidaires grecs.* Paris

Hanell, K. (1954) 'Die Form der römischen Eigennamen bei Polybios', *Opuscula Romana,* 1: 66–76

Harrauer, H. (2006) 'Anmerkungen zu Papyri', *Aegyptus,* 86: 139–42

Harrauer, H., and R. Pintaudi (2003) 'Miscellanea di tachigrafia', *Analecta Papyrologica,* 14–15: 117–64

Harrauer, H., and P. J. Sijpesteijn (1988) '20 Bemerkungen zu Papyri', *Tyche,* 3: 111–18

Hasenohr, C. (2008) 'Le bilinguisme dans les inscriptions des *magistri* de Délos', in Biville *et al.* (edd.) 55–70

Haspelmath, M. (2008) 'Loanword typology: steps toward a systematic cross-linguistic study of lexical borrowability', in Stolz, Bakker, and Salas Palomo (edd.) 43–62

Haspelmath, M. (2009) 'Lexical borrowing: concepts and issues', in Haspelmath and Tadmor (edd.) 35–54

Haspelmath, M., and U. Tadmor (2009) 'The loanword typology project and the world loanword database', in Haspelmath and Tadmor (edd.) 1–34

Haspelmath, M., and U. Tadmor (edd.) (2009) *Loanwords in the world's languages: a comparative handbook.* Berlin

Hassall, M., M. Crawford, and J. Reynolds (1974) 'Rome and the eastern provinces at the end of the second century BC', *JRS* 64: 195–220

Hatzidakis, G. N. (1892) *Einleitung in die neugriechische Grammatik.* Leipzig

Hatzitsolis, G. H. (1994) 'Papyrus letters from Oxyrhynchus'. Dissertation from Universiteit van Amsterdam

Hatzopoulos, M. (2008) 'Le grec et le latin dans les inscriptions de Béroia', in Biville *et al.* (edd.) 129–39

Haugen, E. (1950) 'The analysis of linguistic borrowing', *Language,* 26: 210–31

Haugen, E. (1953) *The Norwegian language in America.* Philadelphia

Haupt, M. (1869) 'Excerpta ex Timothei Gazaei libris de animalibus', *Hermes,* 3: 1–30

Hauri-Karrer, A. (1972) 'Lateinische Gebäcksbezeichnungen'. Dissertation from Universität Zürich

Head, B. V. (1911) *Historia numorum.* 2nd ed., Oxford

Heath, J. (1989) *From code-switching to borrowing: foreign and diglossic mixing in Moroccan Arabic.* London

Heberdey, R., and E. Kalinka (1897) *Bericht über zwei Reisen im südwestlichen Kleinasien (Denkschriften der kaiserlichen Akademie der Wissenschaften, philosophisch-historische Classe,* 45.1). Vienna

Heberdey, R., and A. Wilhelm (1896) *Reisen in Kilikien (Denkschriften der kaiserlichen Akademie der Wissenschaften, philosophisch-historische Classe,* 44.6). Vienna

Heitsch, E. (1963) *Die griechischen Dichterfragmente der römischen Kaiserzeit,* I. 2nd ed., Göttingen

Helttula, A. (1994) 'Vessels for mushrooms?', *Arctos,* 28: 7–12

Hemer, C. J. (1989) *The Book of Acts in the setting of Hellenistic history.* Tübingen

Hemmerdinger, B. (1966), 'Les lettres latines à Constantinople jusqu'à Justinien', *Byzantinische Forschungen,* 1: 174–8

Heraeus, W. (1937) *Kleine Schriften von Wilhelm Heraeus,* ed. J. B. Hofmann. Heidelberg

Hering, J. (1935) 'Lateinisches bei Appian'. Dissertation from Universität Leipzig

Herrmann, P. (1985) 'Sühn- und Grabinschriften aus der Katakekaumene im archäologischen Museum von Izmir', *Anzeiger der Österreichischen Akademie der Wissenschaften, philosophisch-historische Klasse,* 122: 248–61

Hickey, R. (ed.) (2010) *The handbook of language contact.* Malden

Hilhorst, A. (1976) *Sémitismes et latinismes dans le pasteur d'Hermas.* Nijmegen

Hock, H. H. (1986) *Principles of historical linguistics.* Berlin

Hofmann, H. (1989) 'Die lateinischen Wörter im Griechischen bis 600 n. Chr.'. Dissertation from Friedrich-Alexander-Universität Erlangen-Nürnberg

Holford-Strevens, L. A. (1993) '*Vtraque lingua doctus:* some notes on bilingualism in the Roman empire', in *Tria lustra = Liverpool Classical Papers,* 3: 203–13

Holton, D., G. Horrocks, M. Janssen, T. Lendari, I. Manolessou, and N. Toufexis (2019) *The Cambridge grammar of medieval and early modern Greek.* Cambridge

Honigmann, E. (1939) *Le synekdèmos d'Hiéroklès et l'opuscule géographique de Georges de Chypre.* Brussels

Hoppe, K., and E. Oder (1924–7) *Corpus hippiatricorum Graecorum.* Leipzig

Hörandner, W., and E. Trapp (1991) *Lexicographica Byzantina.* Vienna

Hörn, J. (1984) 'Latino–Coptica: Erwägungen zu den lateinischen Lehnwörtern des koptischen Wortschatzes', in [no ed.], *Atti del* XVII *congresso internazionale di papirologia.* Naples: III.1361–76

Hornblower, S. (2015) *Lykophron, Alexandra: Greek text, translation, commentary, and introduction.* Oxford

Horrocks, G. (2010) *Greek: a history of the language and its speakers.* 2nd ed., Malden

Horsley, G. H. R. (2007) *The Greek and Latin inscriptions in the Burdur Archaeological Museum.* Ankara

Hoz, J. de (1998) 'Koiné sin Alejandro: Griego y lenguas anhelénicas en el Mediterráneo occidental durante la época helenística', in Brixhe (ed.) 119–36

Hultsch, F. (1864) *Metrologicorum scriptorum reliquiae,* I. Leipzig

Hunger, H. (1967) 'Palimpsest-Fragmente aus Herodians Καθολική Προσῳδία, Buch 5–7: Cod. Vindob. Hist. gr. 10', *Jahrbuch der Österreichischen Byzantinischen Gesellschaft,* 16: 1–33

Husson, G. (1972) 'Carreaux de fenêtres dans les papyrus grecs', *Chronique d'Égypte,* 47: 278–82

Husson, G. (1983) Οἰκία: *le vocabulaire de la maison privée en Égypte d'après les papyrus grecs.* Paris

Husson, G. (1990) 'Houses in Syene in the Patermouthis archive', *BASP* 27: 123–37

Içten, Ç., and H. Engelmann (1992) 'Inschriften aus Ephesos und Umgebung', *ZPE* 91: 283–95

Ideler, J. L. (1841) *Physici et medici Graeci minores,* I. Berlin

Ihm, M. (1907) 'Cabidarius', *Rheinisches Museum* 62: 323–5

Ihnken, T. (1982) 'Küchenlatein in griechischen Papyri', *ZPE* 46: 235–7

Immisch, O. (1885) 'De glossis lexici Hesychiani Italicis', *Leipziger Studien zur classischen Philologie,* 8: 265–378

Irmer, D. (1977) *Palladius: Kommentar zu Hippokrates 'De fracturis'.* Hamburg

Isaac, B. (2009) 'Latin in cities of the Roman Near East', in Cotton *et al.* (edd.) 43–72

Jagić, V. (1917) *Supplementum Psalterii Bononiensis: incerti auctoris explanatio psalmorum Graeca.* Vienna

Janni, P., and I. Mazzini (edd.) (1990) *Presenza del lessico greco e latino nelle lingue contemporanee.* Macerata

Janse, M. (2007) 'The Greek of the New Testament', in Christidis (ed.) 646–53

Jasny, N. (1944) *The wheats of Classical antiquity.* Baltimore

Johnston, D. (ed.) (2015) *The Cambridge companion to Roman law.* Cambridge

Kaczko, S. (2016) 'La *koinê*', in Cassio (ed.) 385–423

Kahane, H., and R. Kahane (1972–6) 'Abendland und Byzanz: Literatur und Sprache. Westliche Einflüsse in Byzanz' in P. Wirth (ed.), *Reallexikon der Byzantinistik.* Amsterdam: I.V.499–I.VI.639

Kahane, H., and R. Kahane (1978) 'The role of the papyri in etymological reconstruction', *Illinois Classical Studies*, 3: 207–20

Kahane, H., and R. Kahane (1982) 'The Western impact on Byzantium: the linguistic evidence', *Dumbarton Oaks Papers*, 36: 127–53

Kaibel, G. (1878) *Epigrammata Graeca ex lapidibus conlecta.* Berlin

Kaimio, J. (1979a) *The Romans and the Greek language.* Helsinki

Kaimio, J. (1979b) 'Latin in Roman Egypt', *Actes du XVᵉ congrès international de papyrologie.* Brussels: III.27–33

Kaiser, W. (2015) 'Justinian and the *Corpus iuris civilis*', in Johnston (ed.) 119–48

Kajanto, I. (1980) 'Minderheiten und ihre Sprachen in der Hauptstadt Rom', in Neumann and Untermann (edd.) 83–101

Kallipolitis/-ou, V./B., and D. Lazaridis/-ou (1946) Ἀρχαῖαι ἐπιγραφαὶ Θεσσαλονίκης. Thessaloniki

Kaper, O. E. (1998) *Life on the fringe: living in the southern Egyptian deserts during the Roman and early Byzantine periods.* Leiden

Karnejev, A. (1894) 'Der Physiologus der Moskauer Synodalbibliothek', *Byzantinische Zeitschrift*, 3: 26–63

Katsanis, N. (2007) 'Greek and Latin: evidence from the modern Greek dialects', in Christidis (ed.) 800–4

Kearsley, R. A., and T. V. Evans (2001) *Greeks and Romans in imperial Asia: mixed language inscriptions and linguistic evidence for cultural interaction until the end of AD III.* Bonn

Keil, J., and Premerstein, A. (1914) *Bericht über eine dritte Reise in Lydien.* Vienna

Keydell, R. (1967) *Agathiae Myrinaei historiarum libri quinque.* Berlin

Kittel, G., G. Friedrich, and O. Bauernfeind (1932–79) *Theologisches Wörterbuch zum Neuen Testament.* Stuttgart

Knackfuss, H. (1924) *Der Südmarkt und die benachbarten Bauanlagen (Milet I.VII).* Berlin

Knibbe, D., H. Engelmann, and B. İplikçioğlu (1993) 'Neue Inschriften aus Ephesos, XII', *Jahreshefte des Österreichischen Archäologischen Institutes in Wien*, 62: 113–50

Koch, P. (1903) 'Die byzantinischen Beamtentitel von 400 bis 700'. Dissertation from Universität Jena

Kolonia, A. and M. Peri (2008) *Greco antico, neogreco e italiano: dizionario dei prestiti e dei parallelismi.* Bologna

Koroli, A. (2016) 'A late antique private letter mentioning textiles and a halter', *Chronique d'Égypte*, 91: 193–8

Kovarik, S. (2007) 'Von Zitronen, Melonen und Pfirsichen: zum Obst- und Gartenbau im spätantiken Ägypten', *AfP* 53: 152–81

Kovarik, S. (2019) 'Korr. Tyche 921', *Tyche*, 34: 250–1

Kramer, J. (1983) 'Etyma romanischer Wörter in griechischen Papyrusurkunden', *ZPE* 51: 117–22

Kramer, J. (1992) 'Roga', *ZPE* 94: 185–90

Kramer, J. (1993) 'Ῥωμαῖοι und Λατῖνοι', in G. W. Most, H. Petersmann, and A. M. Ritter (edd.), *Philanthropia kai Eusebia: Festschrift für Albrecht Dihle.* Göttingen: 234–47

Kramer, J. (1994) 'Zur Rolle von Papyrusbelegen für die Wortgeschichte am Beispiel von *camisia* und καμάσιον/καμίσιον', *AfP* 40: 133–42

Kramer, J. (1995a) 'Κράβατος, κραβάτιον und Verwandtes in den Papyri', *AfP* 41: 205–16

Kramer, J. (1995b) 'T. Varie 3,13: σκάλη "Anlegestelle"', *AfP* 41: 62–5

Kramer, J. (1996a) 'Papyrusbelege für fünf germanische Wörter: ἀρμαλαύσιον, βάνδον, βουρδών, βρακίον, σαφώνιον', *AfP* 42: 113–26

Kramer, J. (1996b) '*Fossatum* im Lateinischen, Griechischen und Romanischen', *Wiener Studien*, 109: 231–42

Kramer, J. (1997) 'Gewürze und Mulsum: zur Bedeutung von κονδῖτος und κονδῖτον in den Papyri', in B. Kramer, W. Luppe, H. Maehler, and G. Poethke (edd.), *Akten des 21. internationalen Papyrologenkongresses.* Stuttgart: I.547–55

Kramer, J. (1998a) 'Bemerkungen zu einer Liste von Haushaltsgegenständen (P. Bodl. I 48)', *AfP* 44: 38–41

Kramer, J. (1998b) 'Von der "Lex Wackernagel" zur "Lex Clarysse": zur Akzentuierung der Latinismen im Griechischen', *ZPE* 123: 129–34

Kramer, J. (1998c) 'Zu Herkunft und Umfeld von ἄπλικτον "Militärlager"', *AfP* 44: 244–52

Kramer, J. (2001a) *Glossaria bilinguia altera.* Munich

Kramer, J. (2001b) 'Zur Akzentuierung lateinischer Wörter in griechischen Papyri', in I. Andorlini, G. Bastianini, M. Manfredi, and G. Menci (edd.), *Atti del XXII congresso internazionale di papirologia.* Florence: II.753–61

Kramer, J. (2002) 'Zur Bedeutung und Herkunft von *caracalla*', *AfP* 48: 247–56

Kramer, J. (2009) 'Ein gallisches Wort in den Papyri: βασκαύλης', *AfP* 55: 330–40

Kramer, J. (2011) *Von der Papyrologie zur Romanistik.* Berlin

Krauss, S. (1899) *Griechische und lateinische Lehnwörter im Talmud, Midrasch und Targum*, II. Berlin

Kreller, H. (1919) *Erbrechtliche Untersuchungen auf Grund der graeco-aegyptischen Papyrusurkunden.* Leipzig

Kretschmer, P. (1912) 'Literaturbericht für das Jahr 1909', *Glotta*, 3: 296–343

Kretschmer, P., and P. Wahrmann (1929) 'Literaturbericht für das Jahr 1926', *Glotta*, 17: 191–271

Kriaras, E. (1968–) *Λεξικό της μεσαιωνικής ελληνικής δημώδους γραμματείας*, 1100–1669. Thessaloniki

Kroll, W., and R. Schöll (1895) *Corpus iuris civilis*, III. Berlin

Krueger, P. (1895) 'Institutiones', in P. Krueger and T. Mommsen (edd.), *Corpus iuris civilis*. Berlin: I.1–56

Kruit, N. (1994) 'Three Byzantine sales for future delivery: *SB* XVI 12401 + 12402, *SB* VI 9051, *P.Lond.* III 997', *Tyche*, 9: 67–88

Ladd, D. R. (2008) *Intonational phonology.* 2nd ed., Cambridge.

Laminger-Pascher, G. (1992) *Die kaiserzeitlichen Inschriften Lykaoniens.* Vienna

Lampe, G. W. H. (1961) *A patristic Greek lexicon.* Oxford

Lanckoroński, K. (1890) *Städte Pamphyliens und Pisidiens*, I: *Pamphylien.* Vienna

Lane, E. (1971) *Corpus monumentorum religionis dei Menis*, I. Leiden

Langslow, D. R. (2000) *Medical Latin in the Roman empire.* Oxford

Langslow, D. R. (2012) 'The language of Polybius since Foucault and Dubuisson', in C. Smith and L. M. Yarrow (edd.), *Imperialism, cultural politics, and Polybius*. Oxford: 85–110

Latte, K. (1952) 'Zur griechischen Wortforschung', *Glotta*, 32: 33–42

Lauchert, F. (1896) *Die Kanones der wichtigsten altkirchlichen Concilien.* Freiburg

Lauffer, S. (1971) *Diokletians Preisedikt.* Berlin

Le Rider, G. (1966) *Monnaies crétoises du Vᵉ au Iᵉʳ siècle av. J.-C.* Paris

Leary, T. J. (1990) 'The "Aprons" of St Paul – Acts 19:12', *Journal of Theological Studies*, 41: 527–9

Leclercq, H. (1993) 'L'apport lexical du latin au grec du Nouveau Testament: le "passage" d'un système d'écriture à l'autre', in L. Isebaert (ed.), *Miscellanea linguistica Graeco-Latina*. Namur: 239–68

Leclercq, H. (1997) 'Le "passage" des noms propres latins dans le grec du Nouveau Testament: une comparaison avec des textes contemporains', *Les études classiques*, 65: 289–308

Lee, J. A. L. (2015) 'The *Sayings of the desert fathers*: their evidence for late koine Greek', *Phronema*, 30: 23–42

Legrand, P.-E., and J. Chamonard (1893) 'Inscriptions de Phrygie', *BCH* 17: 241–93

Leiwo, M. (1995a) *Neapolitana: a study of population and language in Graeco-Roman Naples.* Helsinki

Leiwo, M. (1995b) 'The mixed languages in Roman inscriptions', in Solin, Salomies, and Liertz (edd.) 293–301

Leiwo, M. (2002) 'From contact to mixture: bilingual inscriptions from Italy', in Adams, Janse, and Swain (edd.) 168–94

Lejeune, M. (1993) 'Le nom de mesure λίτρα: essai lexical', *RÉG* 106: 1–11

Lemerle, P. (1935) 'Inscriptions latines et grecques de Philippes (suite)', *BCH* 59: 126–64

Lemerle, P. (1936) 'Le testament d'un Thrace à Philippes', *BCH* 60: 336–43

Létoublon, F. (ed.) (1992) *La langue et les textes en grec ancien: actes du colloque Pierre Chantraine.* Amsterdam

Leumann, M. (1977) *Lateinische Laut- und Formenlehre.* Munich

Lewis, N. (1960) 'Two terminological novelties', *AJP* 81: 186–8

Libertini, G. (1931) 'Sicilia, VII: Catania', *Notizie degli scavi di antichità comunicate alla R. Accademia Nazionale dei Lincei*, 1931: 367–72

Liebs, D. (2010) *Hofjuristen der römischen Kaiser bis Justinian.* Munich

Lifshitz, B. (1962) 'L'origine du nom des chrétiens', *Vigiliae Christianae*, 16: 65–70

Lipsius, R. A. (1891) *Acta Apostolorum apocrypha*, I. Leipzig

Lokin, J. H. A. (2013) 'Alcune note sul bilinguismo nella legislazione romana', in Cascione, Masi Doria, and Merola (edd.) 541–67

Lokin, J. H. A., R. Meijering, B. H. Stolte, and N. van der Wal (2010) *Theophili Antecessoris Paraphrasis Institutionum.* Groningen

López Férez, J. A. (ed.) (2000) *La lengua científica griega: orígenes, desarrollo e influencia en las lenguas modernas Europeas.* Madrid

Loraux, N. (1995) *The experiences of Tiresias: the feminine and the Greek man*, trans. P. Wissing. Princeton

Loring, W. (1890) 'A new portion of the Edict of Diocletian from Megalopolis', *JHS* 11: 299–342

Lowe, A. D. (1967) 'The origin of οὐαί', *Hermathena*, 105: 34–9

Luce, J.-M. (2018) 'Athénée et les gâteaux (14.643e–649c)', in Rougier-Blanc (ed.) II.713–47

Maas, M. (1992) *John Lydus and the Roman past: antiquarianism and politics in the age of Justinian.* London

MacCoull, L. S. B. (1994) 'A further note on *P.Freer* 08.45 (a + b) 300–301', *Analecta papyrologica*, 6: 161–2

Mackridge, P. (2010) 'Modern Greek', in Bakker (ed.) 564–87

Mandilaras, B. G. (1973) *The verb in the Greek non-literary papyri.* Athens

Manfredi, S., M.-C. Simeone-Senelle, and M. Tosco (2015) 'Language contact, borrowing and codeswitching', in A. Mettouchi, M. Vanhove, and D. Caubet (edd.), *Corpus-based studies of lesser-described languages: the CorpAfroAs corpus of spoken Afro-Asiatic languages.* Amsterdam: 283–308

Manganaro, G. (1992) 'Due note tardoantiche', *ZPE* 94: 283–94

Maravela-Solbakk, A. (2009) 'Byzantine inventory lists of food provisions and utensils on an Ashmolean papyrus', *ZPE* 170: 127–46

Maravela-Solbakk, A. (2010) '*Vina fictitia* from Latin into Greek: the evidence of the papyri', in Evans and Obbink (edd.) 253–66

Marek, C. (1993) *Stadt, Ära und Territorium in Pontus-Bithynia und Nord-Galatia.* Tübingen

Markopoulos, T. (2014) 'Language contact in the Byzantine world: facts and ideologies', in Carpinato and Tribulato (edd.) 73–98

Marsden, E. W. (1971) *Greek and Roman artillery: technical treatises.* Oxford

Marucci, C. (1993) 'Influssi latini sul greco del nuovo testamento', *Filologia neotestamentaria*, 6: 3–30

Masiello, T. (1983) *I libri excusationum di Erennio Modestino.* Naples

Mason, H. (1970) 'The Roman government in Greek sources: the effect of literary theory on the translation of official titles', *Phoenix*, 24: 150–9

Mason, H. (1974) *Greek terms for Roman institutions: a lexicon and analysis.* Toronto

Maspero, J. (1912) 'Les papyrus Beaugé', *Bulletin de l'Institut français d'archéologie orientale*, 10: 131–57

Matino, G. (2013) 'Stratigrafia linguistica nella produzione giuridica greca tardoantica e bizantina', in Cascione, Masi Doria, and Merola (edd.) 759–88

Matras, Y. (2007) 'The borrowability of structural categories', in Y. Matras and J. Sakel (edd.), *Grammatical borrowing in cross-linguistic perspective.* Berlin: 31–73

Matras, Y. (2020) *Language contact.* 2nd ed., Cambridge

Mattern, S. P. (2013) *The prince of medicine: Galen in the Roman empire.* Oxford

Matthews, J. (2006) *The Journey of Theophanes.* New Haven

Mattingly, H. B. (1958) 'The origin of the name *Christiani*', *Journal of Theological Studies*, N.S. 9: 26–37

Mayerson, P. (1989) 'The meaning of the word *limes* (λίμιτον) in the papyri', *ZPE* 77: 287–91

Mayerson, P. (1994) 'Ῥουζικόν and ῥόγα in the post-conquest papyri', *ZPE* 100: 26–8

Mazzini, D. I. (1997) *La medicina dei Greci e dei Romani: letteratura, lingua, scienza.* Rome

Mazzucchi, C. M. (1982) *Menae patricii cum Thoma referendario de scientia politica dialogus.* Milan

McCormick, M. (1981) 'Greek hagiography and popular Latin in late antiquity: the case of **biberaticum*–βιβερατικόν', *AJP* 102: 154–63

McDonald, K. (2015) *Oscan in Southern Italy and Sicily.* Cambridge

Mecella, L. (2019) 'Latinismi e cultura letteraria nei frammenti di Pietro Patrizio: per un'indagine sul *De cerimoniis* e sugli *Excerpta historica Constantiniana*', in Garcea, Rosellini, and Silvano (edd.) 361–75

Meillet, A. (1918) Review of A. Debrunner, *Griechische Wortbildungslehre*, in *Bulletin de la Société de linguistique de Paris* 21: 63–8.

Meillet, A. (1930) *Aperçu d'une histoire de la langue grecque.* 3rd ed., Paris

Meinersmann, B. (1927) *Die lateinischen Wörter und Namen in den griechischen Papyri.* Leipzig

Menci, G. (2000) 'Latinismi nei papiri tachigrafici', *Papyrologica Lupiensia*, 9: 277–95.

Merkelbach, R., and S. Şahin (1988) 'Die publizierten Inschriften von Perge', *Epigraphica Anatolica*, 11: 97–169

Mertens, M. (1995) *Les alchimistes grecs*, IV.1. Paris

Mesk, J. (1898) 'Ein unedierter Tractat Περὶ λίθων', *Wiener Studien*, 20: 309–321

Meyer, G. (1895) 'Neugriechische Studien, III: Die lateinischen Lehnworte im Neugriechischen', *Sitzungsberichte der kaiserlichen Akademie der Wissenschaften, philosophisch-historische Classe*, 132: 1–77

Meyer-Lübke, W. (1935) *Romanisches etymologisches Wörterbuch.* 3rd ed., Heidelberg

Micciarelli Collesi, A. M. (1970) 'Nuovi excerpta dall' "Etimologico" di Orione', *Byzantion*, 40: 517–42

Michel, S. (2015) 'Word-formation and folk etymology', in P. O. Müller, I. Ohnheiser, S. Olsen, and F. Rainer (edd.), *Word-formation: an international handbook of the languages of Europe.* Berlin: II.1002–19

Mihăescu, H. (1969) 'Les termes de commandement militaires latins dans le *Strategicon* de Maurice', *Revue roumaine de linguistique*, 14: 261–72

Mihăescu, H. (1981) 'Les termes byzantins βίρρον, βίρρος "casaque, tunique d'homme" et γοῦνα "fourrure"', *Revue des études sud-est européennes*, 19: 425–32

Mihăescu, H. (1993) *La romanité dans le sud-est de l'Europe*, trans. C. Grecescu. Bucharest

Millar, F. (1999) 'The Greek East and Roman law: the dossier of M. Cn. Licinius Rufus', *JRS* 89: 90–108

Millar, F. (2006a) *A Greek Roman empire: power and belief under Theodosius II (408–450).* Berkeley

Millar, F. (2006b) *Rome, the Greek world, and the East, III: the Greek world, the Jews, and the East.* Chapel Hill

Millar, F., and J. N. Adams (2009) 'Linguistic co-existence in Constantinople: Greek and Latin (and Syriac) in the Acts of the synod of 536 CE', *JRS* 99: 92–103

Miller, D. G. (1997) 'The morphological legacy of French: borrowed suffixes on native words in Middle English', *Diachronica*, 14: 233–64

Miller, D. G. (2012) *External influences on English: from its beginnings to the Renaissance.* Oxford

Mitford, T. B. (1939) 'Milestones in western Cyprus', *JRS* 29: 184–98

Mitford, T. B. (1950) 'Some new inscriptions from early Christian Cyprus', *Byzantion*, 20: 105–75

Mitthof, F. (2001) *Annona militaris: die Heeresversorgung im spätantiken Ägypten.* Florence

Mohrmann, C. (1979) *Études sur le latin des Chrétiens*, III. Rome

Montagna, D. M. (1962) 'La lode alla Theotokos nei testi greci dei secoli IV–VII', *Marianum*, 24: 453–543

Montevecchi, O. (1979) 'Nomen christianum', in R. Cantalamessa and L. F. Pizzolato (edd.), *Paradoxos politeia.* Milan: 485–500

Moreau, J. (1950) 'Le nom des Chrétiens', *La nouvelle Clio*, 1–2: 190–2

Mossakowska-Gaubert, M. (2017) 'Tunics worn in Egypt in Roman and Byzantine times: the Greek vocabulary', in Gaspa *et al.* (edd.) 321–45

Mossakowska-Gaubert, M. (ed.) (2020), *Egyptian textiles and their production: 'word' and 'object' (Hellenistic, Roman and Byzantine periods).* Lincoln, Nebr.

Moulton, J. H., and G. Milligan (1914–29) *The vocabulary of the Greek testament illustrated from the papyri and other non-literary sources.* London

Mourgues, J.-L. (1995) 'Écrire aux deux langues: bilinguisme et pratique de chancellerie sous le Haut-Empire Romain', *Dialogues d'histoire ancienne*, 21.2: 105–29

Mullen, A. (2007) 'Linguistic evidence for Romanization: continuity and change in Romano-British onomastics', *Britannia*, 38: 35–61

Mullen, A. (2011) 'Latin and other languages: societal and individual bilingualism', in J. Clackson (ed.), *A companion to the Latin language.* Malden: 527–48

Mullen, A. (2013) *Southern Gaul and the Mediterranean: multilingualism and multiple identities in the Iron Age and Roman periods.* Cambridge.

Mullen, A., and P. James (edd.) (2012) *Multilingualism in the Graeco-Roman worlds.* Cambridge

Müller, C. W., K. Sier, and J. Werner (edd.) (1992) *Zum Umgang mit fremden Sprachen in der griechisch-römischen Antike.* Stuttgart

Murri, R. (1943) 'Ricerche sugli abiti menzionati nei papiri greco-egizi, I', *Aegyptus*, 23: 106–27

Musurillo, H. (1972) *The acts of the Christian martyrs.* Oxford

Muysken, P. (2000) *Bilingual speech: a typology of code-mixing.* Cambridge

Myers-Scotton, C. (2002) *Contact linguistics: bilingual encounters and grammatical outcomes.* Oxford

Myers-Scotton, C. (2006) *Multiple voices: an introduction to bilingualism.* Malden

Nachtergael, G. (2005) 'Papyrologica II', *Chronique d'Égypte*, 80: 229–45

Nagy, G. (2010) *Homer the preclassic.* Berkeley

Naiditch, L. (2000) 'Code-switching and -mixing in Russian–Hebrew bilinguals', in D. G. Gilbers, J. Nerbonne, and J. Schaeken (edd.), *Languages in contact.* Amsterdam: 277–82

Naour, C. (1980) *Tyriaion en Cabalide: épigraphie et géographie historique.* Zutphen

Negroni, A. (2013) '6.1. Le iscrizioni', in D. Rossi and M. Di Mento (edd.), *La catacomba Ebraica di Monteverde: vecchi dati e nuove scoperte.* Rome: 155–319

Neumann, G. (1980) 'Kleinasien' in Neumann and Untermann (edd.) 167–85

Neumann, G., and J. Untermann (edd.) (1980) *Die Sprachen im römischen Reich der Kaiserzeit.* Cologne

Nichols, E. W. (1929) 'The semantics of the termination -ario', *AJP* 50: 40–63

Nicolas, C. (1996) *Utraque lingua. Le calque sémantique: domaine gréco-latin.* Louvain

Niehoff-Panagiotidis, J. (2019) 'I latinismi nella lingua greca moderna', in Garcea, Rosellini, and Silvano (edd.) 465–73

Nimmo Smith, J. (1992) *Pseudo-Nonniani in IV orationes Gregorii Nazianzeni commentarii.* Turnhout

Nivens, R. J. (2002) *Borrowing versus code-switching in West Tarangan (Indonesia).* Dallas

Nocchi Macedo, G. (2019) 'Writing Latin in late antique Constantinople', in Garcea, Rosellini, and Silvano (edd.) 109–28

Nutton, V. (2009) 'Galen's library', in C. Gill, T. Whitmarsh, and J. Wilkins (edd.), *Galen and the world of knowledge.* Cambridge: 19–34

Nutton, V. (2012) *Ancient medicine.* 2nd ed., London

O'Callaghan, J. (1970) 'Sobre PFouad 87 [VIp]', *Studia papyrologica,* 9: 51–60

O'Callaghan, J. (1973) 'El "sudario" en los papiros griegos de época romana', *AfP* 22: 147–50

O'Callaghan, J. (1983) 'La "dalmática" en los papiros griegos', *Analecta sacra Tarraconensia,* 55–6: 285–91

O'Callaghan, J. (1987) 'La palabra "lodix" en los papiros griegos', *Aegyptus,* 67: 183–7

O'Sullivan, N. (2018) 'Manuscript evidence for alphabet-switching in the works of Cicero: common nouns and adjectives', *Classical Quarterly,* 68: 498–516

Odlin, T. (2009) 'Transfer and code-switching: separate territories but common concerns on the border', in L. Isurin, D. Winford, and K. de Bot (edd.), *Multidisciplinary approaches to code switching.* Amsterdam: 337–58

Oikonomidès, N. (1986) 'Silk trade and production in Byzantium from the sixth to the ninth century: the seals of kommerkiarioi', *Dumbarton Oaks Papers,* 40: 33–53

Oikonomidès, N. (1999) 'Administrative language and its public deployment', in E. Chrysos and I. Wood (edd.), *East and West: modes of communication.* Leiden: 47–59

Oliverio, G. (1936) *Documenti antichi dell'Africa Italiana, II.II: Cirenaica: il decreto di Anastasio I° sul'ordinamento politico-militare della Cirenaica.* Bergamo

Olsson, B. (1925) 'Die Gewerbenamen auf -ᾶς in den Papyri', *Aegyptus,* 6: 247–9

Olsson, B. (1926) 'Sprachliche Bemerkungen zu einigen Papyrusstellen', *Aegyptus,* 7: 108–12

Olsson, B. (1935) 'Ἀκατηναριον', *AfP* 11: 219

Orioles, V. (1974) 'Note preliminari ad uno studio sui prestiti latini in greco', *Incontri linguistici,* 1: 109–24

Ormerod, H. A., and E. S. G. Robinson (1914) 'Inscriptions from Lycia', *JHS* 34: 1–35

Orsi, P. (1893) 'Sicilia', *Notizie degli scavi di antichità comunicate alla R. Accademia dei Lincei,* 1893: 276–314

Otto, J. C. T. (1876) *Corpus apologetarum Christianorum saeculi secundi,* I.I. 3rd ed., Jena

Palme, B. (2004) 'Die Löwen des Kaisers Leon', in H. Harrauer and R. Pintaudi (edd.), *Gedenkschrift Ulrike Horak.* Florence: 311–32

Palmer, L. R. (1945) *A grammar of the post-Ptolemaic papyri,* I.I. London

Panagl, O. (2005) 'Volksetymologie und Verwandtes', in D. A. Cruse, F. Hundsnurscher, J. Michael, and P. R. Lutzeier (edd.), *Lexikologie.* Berlin: II.1346–52

Papadopulos-Kerameus, A. (1909) *Varia Graeca sacra.* Saint Petersburg

Papanikolaou, D. (2019) 'Notes on a gladiatorial inscription from Plotinopolis', *Tekmeria,* 14: 203–13

Parássoglou, G. M. (1978) 'Adnotatiunculae I', Ἑλληνικά· Φιλολογικὸν Ἱστορικὸν καὶ Λαογραφικὸν περιοδικὸν σύγγραμμα τῆς Ἑταιρείας Μακεδονικῶν Σπουδῶν, 30: 62–72

Paribeni, R., and P. Romanelli (1914) 'Studii e ricerche archeologiche nell'Anatolia meridionale', *Monumenti antichi,* 23: 6–276

Paris, P., and M. Holleaux (1886) 'Inscriptions d'Oenoanda', *BCH* 10: 216–35

Paschoud, F. (1983) '*Frumentarii, agentes in rebus, magistriani, curiosi, veredarii*: problèmes de terminologie', in [no ed.], *Bonner Historia-Augusta-Colloquium 1979/1981.* Bonn: 215–43

Pease, A. S. (1955) *M. Tulli Ciceronis De natura deorum liber primus.* Cambridge, Mass.

Pedone, M. (2020a) *Apud acta: studi sul processo romano alla luce della documentazione papirologica (IV–VI sec. d.C.).* Turin

Pedone, M. (2020b) 'Intorno ad alcune voci di lessicografia giuridica romea', *Teoria e storia del diritto privato,* 13: 1–27

Peek, W. (1969) *Inschriften aus dem Asklepieion von Epidauros.* Berlin

Pellizzari, A. (2019) 'La lingua degli Ἰταλοί: conoscenza e uso del latino nell'Oriente greco di IV secolo attraverso l'opera di Libanio', in Garcea, Rosellini, and Silvano (edd.) 131–42

Perdrizet, P. (1900) 'Inscriptions de Philippes: les Rosalies', *BCH* 24: 299–323

Pergnier, M. (1989) *Les anglicismes: danger ou enrichissement pour la langue français?* Paris

Peruzzi, E. (1998) *Civiltà greca nel Lazio preromano.* Florence

Petersen, E., and F. von Luschan (1889) *Reisen im südwestlichen Kleinasien,* II: *Reisen in Lykien, Milyas und Kibyratis.* Vienna

Petersen, W. (1910) *Greek diminutives in -ιον: a study in semantics.* Weimar

Petersmann, H. (1992) 'Vulgärlateinisches aus Byzanz', in Müller, Sier, and Werner (edd.) 219–31

Peterson, E. (1946) 'Christianus', in [no ed.], *Miscellanea Giovanni Mercati.* Vatican: I.355–72

Pflaum, H.-G. (1959) 'Lucien de Samosate, *archistator praefecti Aegypti*, d'après une inscription de Césarée de Maurétanie', *École française de Rome: mélanges d'archéologie et d'histoire*, 71: 281–6

Picone, M. D. (1996) *Anglicisms, neologisms and dynamic French.* Amsterdam

Piñero, A., and J. Peláez (2003) *The study of the New Testament: a comprehensive introduction*, trans. D. E. Orton and P. Ellingworth. Leiden

Pinkster, H. (2014) *Woordenboek Latijn/Nederlands.* 6th ed., Amsterdam

Pintaudi, R., and A. Soldati (2021) 'Frammento di tractoria o documento ad essa pertinente (*PL* III/1004)', *Analecta papyrologica*, 33: 47–54

Pisani, V. (1951) 'Miti glottologici', *Paideia*, 6: 291–6

Pisani, V. (1955) Review of Frisk (1954–72), *Paideia*, 10: 278–9

Pitra, J. B. (1868) *Iuris ecclesiastici Graecorum historia et monumenta*, II. Rome

Pitra, J. B. (1884) *Analecta sacra spicilegio Solesmensi parata*, II. Paris

Poccetti, P. (1985) 'Gr. στατάριον / Lat. *statarium* "Sklavenmarkt": Lehnwort oder Bedeutungsentlehnung?', *Glotta*, 63: 172–80

Poccetti, P. (2012) 'Language relations in Sicily: evidence for the speech of the Σικανοί, the Σικελοί and others', in Tribulato (ed.) 49–94

Popescu-Mihuţ, E. (1981) 'Contributions à l'étude des mots latins dans la littérature juridique byzantine', *Revue des études sud-est européennes*, 19: 433–41

Poplack, S. (2018) *Borrowing: loanwords in the speech community and in the grammar.* Oxford

Preger, T. (1901) *Scriptores originum Constantinopolitanarum*, I. Leipzig

Probert, P. (2003) *A new short guide to the accentuation of ancient Greek.* London

Probert, P. (2006) *Ancient Greek accentuation: synchronic patterns, frequency effects, and prehistory.* Oxford

Probert, P. (2019) *Latin grammarians on the Latin accent: the transformation of Greek grammatical thought.* Oxford

Pruneti, P. (1998) 'Da *plumarius* a πλουμάριος: la testimonianza dei papiri', in L. Del Francia Barocas (ed.), *Antinoe cent'anni dopo.* Florence: 145–8

Psaltes, S. B. (1913) *Grammatik der Byzantinischen Chroniken.* Göttingen

Psichari, J. (1889) 'Observations phonétiques sur quelques phénomènes néo-grecs', *Mémoires de la Société de linguistique de Paris*, 6: 303–23

Psichari, J. (ed.) (1892) *Études de philologie néo-grecque: recherches sur le développement historique du grec.* Paris

Pugliese Carratelli, G. (1956) 'Silloge delle epigrafi Acrensi', in L. Bernabò Brea (ed.), *Akrai.* Catania: 151–77

Pugliese Carratelli, G. (1993) 'Epigrafi onorarie di Iasos in Caria', *Rendiconti dell'Accademia nazionale dei lincei, Classe di Scienze morali, storiche e filologiche*, 9th ser., 4: 261–9

Rabe, H. (1896) *Anonymi et Stephani in artem rhetoricam commentaria.* Berlin

Radermacher, L. (1911) 'Kritische Beiträge', *Wiener Studien*, 32: 200–7

Radt, S. (1998) 'Zur Akzentuierung lateinischer Namen im Griechischen', *ZPE* 121: 72

Radt, S. (1999) 'Noch einmal zur Akzentuierung lateinischer Namen im Griechischen', *ZPE* 126: 98

Radt, S. (2010) *Strabons Geographika*, IX. Göttingen

Ramsay, W. M. (1883) 'Unedited inscriptions of Asia Minor', *BCH* 7: 258–78

Ramsay, W. M. (1895–7) *The cities and bishoprics of Phrygia.* Oxford

Ramsay, W. M. (ed.) (1906) *Studies in the history and art of the eastern provinces of the Roman empire, written for the quatercentenary of the University of Aberdeen by seven of its graduates.* Aberdeen

Ramsay, W. M. (1941) *The social basis of Roman power in Asia Minor*, ed. J. G. C. Anderson. Aberdeen

Rapp, C. (2019) 'The use of Latin in the context of multilingual monastic communities in the East', in Garcea, Rosellini, and Silvano (edd.) 93–107

Rea, J. (1980) 'Ordinatus', *ZPE* 38: 217–19

Rea, J. (1990) 'Vestigationes', *ZPE* 82: 126–8

Rea, J. (1992) '*P.Oxy.* XIV 1676.38: from stable to record office?', *ZPE* 91: 81–2

Reichenkron, G. (1961) 'Zur römischen Kommandosprache bei byzantinischen Schriftstellern', *Byzantinische Zeitschrift*, 54: 18–27

Reichmann, V. (1943) *Römische Literatur in griechischer Übersetzung. Philologus* suppl. 34.3, Leipzig

Reinach, T. (1906) 'Inscriptions d'Aphrodisias', *RÉG* 19: 79–150, 205–98

Renan, E. (1864) *Mission de Phénicie.* Paris

Renfrew, C., A. McMahon, and L. Trask (edd.) (2000) *Time depth in historical linguistics.* Cambridge

Rey-Coquais, J.-P. (2002) 'Inscriptions de l'hippodrome de Tyr', *Journal of Roman Archaeology*, 15: 325–35

Rey-Coquais, J.-P. (2006) *Inscriptions grecques et latines de Tyr*. Beirut

Rhoby, A. (2019) 'Latin inscriptions in (early) Byzantium', in Garcea, Rosellini, and Silvano (edd.) 275–94

Ricci, S. de (1903) 'Bulletin épigraphique de l'Égypte romaine, II: Inscriptions grecques (1896–1902), suite', *AfP* 2: 561–71

Risch, E. (1976) 'Entlehnt oder urverwandt?: zum Problem der griechisch-lateinischen Beziehungen', in [no ed.], *Scritti in onore di Giuliano Bonfante*. Brescia: II.883–97. Reprinted in A. Etter and M. Looser (edd.) (1981), *Ernst Risch: kleine Schriften*. Berlin: 576–90

Rizakis, A. (1995) 'Le grec face au latin: le paysage linguistique dans la peninsule balkanique sous l'empire', in Solin, Salomies, and Liertz (edd.) 373–91

Rizakis, A. (2008) 'Langue et culture ou les ambiguïtés identitaires des notables des cités grecques sous l'empire de rome', in Biville *et al.* (edd.) 17–34

Robert, J., and L. Robert (1954) *La Carie: histoire et géographie historique avec le recueil des inscriptions antiques*, II: *le plateau de Tabai et ses environs*. Paris

Robert, J., and L. Robert (1968) 'Bulletin épigraphique', *RÉG* 81: 420–549

Robert, J., and L. Robert (1969) 'Bulletin épigraphique', *RÉG* 82: 424–540

Robert, J., and L. Robert (1970) 'Bulletin épigraphique', *RÉG* 83: 362–488

Robert, J., and L. Robert (1977) 'Bulletin épigraphique', *RÉG* 90: 314–448

Robert, J., and L. Robert (1983) 'Bulletin épigraphique', *RÉG* 96: 76–191

Robert, L. (1936a) Ἀρχαιολόγος, *RÉG* 49: 235–54

Robert, L. (1936b) 'Epigraphica', *RÉG* 49: 1–16

Robert, L. (1943) 'Sur un papyrus de Bruxelles', *Revue de philologie, de littérature et d'histoire anciennes*, 17: 111–19

Robert, L. (1946) *Hellenica* III. Paris

Robert, L. (1955) *Hellenica* X. Paris

Robert, L. (1960a) 'Recherches épigraphiques', *Revue des études anciennes*, 62: 276–361

Robert, L. (1960b) *Hellenica* XI–XII. Paris

Robert, L. (1963) *Noms indigènes dans l'Asie-mineure gréco-romaine*. Paris

Robert, L. (1965) 'Noms de métiers dans des documents byzantins', in [no ed.], Χαριστήριον εἰς Ἀναστάσιον Κ. Ὀρλάνδον, I. Athens: 324–47

Robert, L. (1971) *Les gladiateurs dans l'orient grec.* 2nd ed., Amsterdam

Rochette, B. (1996) 'Sur le bilinguisme dans l'Égypte gréco-romaine', *Chronique d'Égypte*, 71: 153–68

Rochette, B. (1997) *Le latin dans le monde grec.* Brussels

Rochette, B. (1998) 'Le bilinguisme gréco–latin et la question des langues dans le monde gréco-romain: chronique bibliographique', *Revue belge de philologie et d'histoire*, 76.1: 177–96

Rochette, B. (2000) 'La langue des testaments dans l'Égypte du IIIe s. ap. J.-C.', *Revue internationale des droits de l'antiquité*, 3rd ser., 47: 449–61

Rochette, B. (2007) 'L'enseignement du latin dans la partie hellénophone de l'Empire romain: objectifs et méthodes', in Sánchez-Ostiz, Torres Guerra, and Martínez (edd.) 47–63

Rochette, B. (2008) 'Le bilinguisme gréco–latin dans les communautés juives d'Italie d'après les inscriptions (IIIe–VIe s.)', in Biville *et al.* (edd.) 273–304

Rochette, B. (2010) 'Greek and Latin bilingualism', in Bakker (ed.) 281–93

Rodríguez Martín, J.-D. (2019) 'On the use of Latin legal terminology in the Byzantine legal treatise *De actionibus*', in Garcea, Rosellini, and Silvano (edd.) 415–30

Rosellini, M., and E. Spangenberg Yanes (2019) 'L'insegnamento di Prisciano', in Garcea, Rosellini, and Silvano (edd.) 163–81

Rosén, H. B. (1980) 'Die Sprachsituation im römischen Palästina', in Neumann and Untermann (edd.) 215–39

Rostovtzeff, M. I. (1934) *The excavations at Dura-Europos: preliminary report of fifth season of work*. New Haven

Rostovtzeff, M. I., A. R. Bellinger, C. Hopkins, and C. B. Welles (1936) *The excavations at Dura-Europos: preliminary report of sixth season of work*. New Haven

Rostovtzeff, M. I., F. E. Brown, and C. B. Welles (1939) *The excavations at Dura-Europos: preliminary report of the seventh and eighth seasons of work*. New Haven

Rothenhöfer, P. (2020) 'Unter den strengen Augen der Kaiser: ein *sextarium trisaugusteum* mit Kaiserinschrift vom Anfang des 5. Jahrhunderts', *Antiquité tardive*, 28: 289–96

Rougier-Blanc, S. (ed.) (2018) *Athénée de Naucratis, Le banquet des savants, livre XIV*. Bordeaux

Rousset, D. (2008) 'Usage des langues et élaboration des décisions dans le "monument bilingue" de Delphes', in Biville *et al.* (edd.) 71–108

Roussou, S. (2018) *Pseudo-Arcadius' epitome of Herodian's De prosodia catholica.* Oxford

Routh, M. J. (1846) *Reliquiae sacrae.* 2nd ed., Oxford

Ruelle, C.-É. (1898) *Les lapidaires de l'antiquité et du Moyen Age,* II.1: *les lapidaires grecs.* Paris

Ruinart, T. (1689) *Acta primorum martyrum sincera et selecta.* Paris

Ruisinger, M. M. (2000) 'Die Erben des Hippokrates: Anmerkungen zur neugriechischen medizinischen Terminologie', in López Férez (ed.) I.151–63

Rundgren, F. (1957) 'Über einige iranische Lehnwörter im Lateinischen und Griechischen', *Orientalia Suecana,* 6: 31–65

Ruppel, W. (1930) *Der Tempel von Dakke,* III: *die griechischen und lateinischen Inschriften von Dakke.* Cairo

Russo Ruggeri, C. (2013) 'C. 7.45.12 ed il problema della legittimità dell'uso della lingua greca nell'amministrazione della giustizia in età imperiale', in Cascione, Masi Doria, and Merola (edd.) 601–30

Russo Ruggeri, C. (2016) *Studi su Teofilo.* Turin

Saalfeld, G. A. E. A. (1884) *Tensaurus Italograecus: ausführliches historisch-kritisches Wörterbuch der griechischen Lehn- und Fremdwörter im Lateinischen.* Vienna

Sallés Verdaguer, F. (1976–7) 'Estudio fonológico de la transcripción griega de vocablos latinos'. Dissertation from Universidad de Barcelona

Sánchez-Ostiz, Á., J. B. Torres Guerra, and R. Martínez (edd.) (2007) *De Grecia a Roma y de Roma a Grecia: un camino de ida y vuelta.* Pamplona

Sänger, P. (2010) 'Zur Organisation des Sicherheitswesens im kaiserzeitlichen Kleinasien und Ägypten', *Tyche,* 25: 99–122

Sarre, F. (1896) 'Reise in Phrygien, Lykaonien und Pisidien', *Archaeologisch-epigraphische Mittheilungen aus Oesterreich-Ungarn,* 19: 26–57

Sartre, M. (1993) *Inscriptions greques et latines de la Syrie,* XXI: *inscriptions de la Jordanie,* IV: *Pétra et la Nabatène méridionale.* Paris

Šašel, A., and J. Šašel (1986) *Inscriptiones Latinae quae in Iugoslavia inter annos MCMII et MCMXL repertae et editae sunt.* Ljubljana

Savile, H. (1612) Τοῦ ἐν ἁγίοις πατρὸς ἡμῶν Ἰωάννου ἀρχιεπισκοποῦ Κωνσταντινουπόλεως τοῦ Χρυσοστόμου τῶν εὑρισκομένων, VIII. Eton

Schamp, J. (2008) 'Remarques sur Jean le Lydien et le lexique latin à Constantinople', in Trapp and Schönauer (edd.) 37–53

Scharf, R. (1996) 'Zur comitiva Flavialis', *ZPE* 114: 151–2

Scheller, M. (1951) 'Die Oxytonierung der griechischen Substantiva auf -ιᾱ'. Dissertation from Universität Zürich

Scheltema, H. J. (1967) 'Byzantine Law', in *Cambridge Medieval History,* IV.II.XXI: 55–77

Scheltema, H. J. (1970) *L'enseignement de droit des antécesseurs.* Leiden

Schirru, G. (2013) 'Latinismi nel greco d'Egitto', in M. Mancini and L. Lorenzetti (edd.), *Le lingue del Mediterraneo antico.* Rome: 301–32

Schneider, G. (1993) 'Χριστιανός', in H. Balz and G. Schneider (edd.), *Exegetical dictionary of the New Testament,* English version. Grand Rapids: III.477–8

Schneider, R. M. (2018) 'Before the Empire: Egypt and Rome', in Spier *et al.* (edd.) 203–10

Schreiner, P. (2019) 'Latinité cachée à Constantinople (VIe – milieu du XIIIe siècle)', in Garcea, Rosellini, and Silvano (edd.) 447–63

Schubert, P. (1988) 'Κωντοναιτωρ: a ghost word', *ZPE* 75: 173–4

Schulte, M. (2019) 'The semantic development of borrowed derivational morphology: change and stability in French–English language contact', *Diachronica,* 36: 66–99

Schulz, F. (1961) *Geschichte der römischen Rechtswissenschaft.* Weimar

Schwyzer, E. (1922) 'Onomatologisches und Grammatisches aus griechischen Dialektinschriften', *Glotta,* 12: 1–7

Schwyzer, E. (1929) 'Ἐκτράνιος', *Zeitschrift für vergleichende Sprachforschung auf dem Gebiete der Indogermanischen Sprachen,* 56: 309–13

Schwyzer, E. (1931) 'Awest. asparǝnō und byzantin. ἄσπρον: Beiträge zur griechisch-orientalischen Münznamenforschung', *Indogermanische Forschungen,* 49: 1–45

Schwyzer, E. (1939) *Griechische Grammatik,* I. Munich

Scott, K. (1931) 'Greek and Roman honorific months', *Yale Classical Studies,* 2: 199–278

Seckel, E., and B. Kuebler (1927) *Iurisprudentiae Anteiustinianae reliquias.* 6th ed., Leipzig

Segre, M. (1952) 'Tituli Calymnii', *Annuario della Scuola archeologica di Atene* 22/3 = N.S. 6/7: 1–250

Setaioli, A. (2007) 'Plutarch's assessment of Latin as a means of expression', *Prometheus: rivista quadrimestrale di studi classici,* 33: 156–66

Seyrig, H. (1941) 'Antiquités syriennes', *Syria,* 22: 218–70

Shaw, B. D. (2015) 'The myth of the Neronian persecution', *JRS* 105: 73–100

Sherk, R. K. (1969) *Roman documents from the Greek East: senatus consulta and epistulae to the age of Augustus.* Baltimore

Shipp, G. P. (1960) 'Ballista', *Glotta*, 39: 149–52

Shipp, G. P. (1979) *Modern Greek evidence for the ancient Greek vocabulary.* Sydney

Sidro, G., and A. Maravela (forthcoming) '*P.Lond.* II 191 reconsidered', in R. Berardi, S. Coen, G. Iovine, E. E. Prodi (edd.), *Festschrift Daniela Colomo*

Sihler, A. L. (1995) *New comparative grammar of Greek and Latin.* Oxford

Sijpesteijn, P. J. (1979) 'Some remarks on Roman dates in Greek papyri', *ZPE* 33: 229–40

Sijpesteijn, P. J. (1984) '*P.Laur.* IV 177 verso: a note', *ZPE* 55: 160

Sijpesteijn, P. J. (1985) 'Small Byzantine texts', *ZPE* 61: 75–84

Sijpesteijn, P. J. (1987a) 'Κόκχος in *P.Hamb.* I 10,36', *ZPE* 68: 142

Sijpesteijn, P. J. (1987b) 'The "proper name" πρόξιμος/πρώξιμος', *ZPE* 68: 158

Sijpesteijn, P. J. (1987c) 'A small note on *P.Oxy.* XVI 2057', *ZPE* 69: 170

Sijpesteijn, P. J. (1988) 'Short remarks on some papyri, IV', *Aegyptus*, 68: 69–92

Sijpesteijn, P. J. (1991a) 'Short remarks on some papyri, V', *Aegyptus*, 71: 43–51

Sijpesteijn, P. J. (1991b) 'Notes on two papyri', *ZPE* 87: 257–8

Sijpesteijn, P. J. (1992) '*PSI* VIII 955: exit κελλικάριος', *ZPE* 91: 88

Simkin, O. (2012) 'Coins and language in ancient Sicily', in Tribulato (ed.) 162–87

Sirat, C., P. Cauderlier, M. Dukan, and M. A. Friedman (1986) *Le Ketouba de Cologne: un contrat de mariage juif à Antinoopolis* (*Papyrologica Coloniensia*, 12). Opladen

Slee, M. (2003) *The Church in Antioch in the first century* CE*: communion and conflict.* London

Sleumer, A. (1926) *Kirchenlateinisches Wörterbuch.* 2nd ed., Limburg a. d. Lahn

Smith, M. (1971) 'Zealots and *sicarii*: their origins and relation', *Harvard Theological Review*, 64: 1–19

Solin, H. (2008) 'Observations sur la forme grecque des indications calendaires romaines à Rome à l'époque impériale', in Biville *et al.* (edd.) 259–72

Solin, H. (2015) Review of *Lexicon of Greek personal names* VB, in *Arctos*, 49: 288–9

Solin, H., O. Salomies, and U.-M. Liertz (edd.) (1995) *Acta colloquii epigraphici latini.* Helsinki

Sommer, F. (1948) *Zur Geschichte der griechischen Nominalkomposita.* Munich

Sophocles, E. A. (1887) *Greek lexicon of the Roman and Byzantine periods (from* BC *146 to* AD *1100).* New York

Sotiriou, G. (1929) 'Αἱ χριστιανικαὶ Θῆβαι τῆς Θεσσαλίας', Ἀρχαιολογικὴ Ἐφημερίς [no vol.] 1–158

Souris, G., and P. Nigdelis (2007) 'The parallel use of Greek and Latin in the Greco-Roman world', in Christidis (ed.) 897–902

Souter, A. (1949) *A glossary of later Latin to 600* AD. Oxford

Spicq, C. (1961) 'Ce que signifie le titre de chrétien', *Studia theologica*, 15: 68–78

Spier, J., T. Potts, and S. E. Cole (edd.) (2018) *Beyond the Nile: Egypt and the Classical world.* Los Angeles

Stathi, E. (2002) 'Modern Greek', in M. Görlach (ed.), *English in Europe.* Oxford: 301–29

Stefenelli, A. (1992) *Das Schicksal des lateinischen Wortschatzes in den romanischen Sprachen.* Passau

Steigerwald, G. (1990) 'Die Purpursorten im Preisedikt Diokletians vom Jahre 301', *Byzantinische Forschungen*, 15: 219–76

Stein, A. (1915) *Untersuchungen zur Geschichte und Verwaltung Aegyptens unter roemischer Herrschaft.* Stuttgart

Sterrett, J. R. S. (1888a) *An epigraphical journey in Asia Minor.* Boston

Sterrett, J. R. S. (1888b) *The Wolfe expedition to Asia Minor.* Boston

Stolte, B. H. (2009) 'The use of Greek in the Theodosian Code', *Subseciva Groningana*, 8: 147–59

Stolte, B. H. (2013) 'La lingua giuridica del sesto secolo: greco o latino? Un dilemma falso', in Cascione, Masi Doria, and Merola (edd.) 703–12

Stolte, B. H. (2015) 'The law of New Rome: Byzantine law', in Johnston (ed.) 355–73

Stolz, T. (2008) 'Romancisation worldwide', in Stolz, Bakker, and Salas Palomo (edd.) 1–42

Stolz, T., D. Bakker, and R. Salas Palomo (edd.) (2008) *Aspects of language contact: new theoretical, methodological and empirical findings with special focus on Romancisation processes.* Berlin

Stray, C., M. Clarke, and J. Katz (edd.) (2019) *Liddell and Scott: the history, methodology, and languages of the world's leading lexicon of ancient Greek.* Oxford

Strelan, R. (2003) 'Acts 19:12: Paul's "aprons" again', *Journal of Theological Studies*, 54: 154–7

Strobach, A. (1997) *Plutarch und die Sprachen: ein Beitrag zur Fremdsprachenproblematik in der Antike.* Stuttgart

Svensson, A.-M. (2009) 'On the stress-shifting of polysyllabic French loans in English', in C. M. Cain and G. Russom (edd.), *Studies in the history of the English language III: managing chaos.* Berlin: 93–104

Swain, S. (2002) 'Bilingualism in Cicero? The evidence of code-switching', in Adams, Janse, and Swain (edd.) 128–67

Swoboda, H., J. Keil, and F. Knoll (1935) *Denkmäler aus Lykaonien, Pamphylien und Isaurien.* Brünn

Tadmor, U. (2009) 'Loanwords in the world's languages: findings and results', in Haspelmath and Tadmor (edd.) 55–75

Taylor, J. (1994) 'Why were the disciples first called "Christians" at Antioch? (Acts 11, 26)', *Revue biblique*, 101: 75–94

Thody, P. (1995) *Le franglais: forbidden English, forbidden American. Law, politics and language in contemporary France: a study in loan words and national identity.* London

Thomason, S. G. (2001) *Language contact.* Edinburgh

Thomason, S. G. (2003) 'Contact as a source of language change', in B. D. Joseph and R. D. Janda (edd.), *The handbook of historical linguistics.* Malden: 687–712

Thomason, S. G., and T. Kaufman (1988) *Language contact, creolization, and genetic linguistics.* Los Angeles

Thüngen, L. (2016) 'Neuedition von PL II/38 aus einem griechischen Index zu Papinians *Libri definitionum*', *Revue internationale des droits de l'antiquité*, 63: 9–41

Thüngen, L. (2017) 'Anmerkungen zu den *Scholia Sinaitica*', *Revue internationale des droits de l'antiquité*, 64: 313–66

Tischendorf, C. (1876) *Evangelia apocrypha.* 2nd ed., Leipzig

Tod, M. N. (1904) 'A new fragment of the *Edictum Diocletiani*', *JHS* 24: 195–202

Tomber, R. (1998) '"Laodicean" wine containers in Roman Egypt', in Kaper (ed.) 213–19

Tonnet, H. (1993) 'La *corona preciosa* (1527): edition du texte et étude des emprunts latins et néo-latins', in [no ed.], *Emprunts latins et néo-latins (Cahiers Balkaniques*, 19). Paris: 65–107

Tonnet, H. (2003) *Histoire du grec moderne: la formation d'une langue.* 2nd ed., Paris

Townsend, P. (2008) 'Who were the first Christians? Jews, gentiles, and the *Christianoi*', in E. Iricinschi and H. Zellentin (edd.), *Heresy and identity in late antiquity.* Tübingen: 212–30

Trapp, E., and S. Schönauer (edd.) (2008) *Lexicologia Byzantina.* Bonn

Trapp, E., J. Diethart, G. Fatouros, A. Steiner, and W. Hörandner (1988) *Studien zur byzantinischen Lexikographie.* Vienna

Treffers-Daller, J. (2010) 'Borrowing', in M. Fried, J.-O. Östman, and J. Verschueren (edd), *Variation and change: pragmatic perspectives.* Amsterdam: 17–35

Triandaphyllidis, M. A. (1909) *Die Lehnwörter der mittelgriechischen Vulgärliteratur.* Strasbourg

Triantaphyllides, C.-C. (1892) 'Lexique des mots latins dans Théophile et les novelles de Justinien', in Psichari (ed.) 159–277

Triantaphyllopoulos, J. (1966) 'Κουριῶσος (P. Vindob. Sijpesteijn 22ᵛ)', in [no ed.], *Atti dell'XI congresso internazionale di papirologia.* Milan: 249–59

Tribulato, O. (ed.) (2012) *Language and linguistic contact in ancient Sicily.* Cambridge

Tuccillo, F. (2013) 'Brevi note sull' Ἀστυνομικὸς μονόβιβλος', in Cascione, Masi Doria, and Merola (edd.) 323–38

Turner, E. G. (1961) 'Latin versus Greek as a universal language: the attitude of Diocletian', in [no ed.], *Language and society: essays presented to Arthur M. Jensen.* Copenhagen: 165–8

Vaahtera, J. (2001) *Roman augural lore in Greek historiography: a study of the theory and terminology.* Stuttgart

Väänänen, V. (1973) '*Ex* "ancien"', in O. S. Due, H. Friis Johansen, and B. Dalsgaard Larsen (edd.), *Classica et mediaevalia Francisco Blatt septuagenario dedicata.* Copenhagen: 665–74

Väänänen, V. (1977) *Ab epistulis … ad sanctum Petrum: formules prépositionelles latines étudiées dans leur contexte social.* Helsinki

Vallat, D. (2008) 'Interférences onomastiques et péri-onomastiques dans les *Res gestae* d'Auguste', in Biville *et al.* (edd.) 241–57

Van Bochove, T. E. (2019) 'Justinianus latinograecus: language and law during the reign of Justinian', in Garcea, Rosellini, and Silvano (edd.) 199–243

Van der Hulst, H. (2010) 'Word accent: terms, typologies and theories', in H. van der Hulst, R. Goedemans, and E. van Zanten (edd.), *A survey of word accentual patterns in the languages of the world.* Berlin: 3–53

Van der Valk, M. (1971–87) *Eustathii archiepiscopi Thessalonicensis commentarii ad Homeri Iliadem pertinentes.* Leiden

Van der Wal, N. (1983) 'Die Schreibweise der dem Lateinischen entlehnten Fachworte in der frühbyzantinischen Juristensprache', *Scriptorium*, 37: 29–53

Van der Wal, N., and B. H. Stolte (1994) *Collectio tripartita: Justinian on religious and eclesiastical affairs*. Groningen

Van Minnen, P. (1998) 'Notes on papyri', *BASP* 35: 125–33

Versnel, H. S. (1970) *Triumphus: an inquiry into the origin, development and meaning of the Roman triumph*. Leiden

Viscidi, F. (1944) *I prestiti latini nel greco antico e bizantino*. Padua

Volk, R. (1991) 'Einige Beiträge zur mittelgriechischen Nahrungsmittelterminologie', in Hörandner and Trapp (edd.) 293–311

Wackernagel, J. (1916) *Sprachliche Untersuchungen zu Homer*. Göttingen

Wackernagel, J. (1926) Review of J. P. Postgate, *A short guide to the accentuation of ancient Greek*, in *Anzeiger für indogermanische Sprach- und Altertumskunde: Beiblatt zu den indogermanischen Forschungen*, 43: 48–59. Reprinted in Wackernagel's *Kleine Schriften*, II.1188–98

Waelkens, M. (1986) *Die kleinasiatischen Türsteine: typologische und epigraphische Untersuchungen der kleinasiatischen Grabreliefs mit Scheintür*. Mainz am Rhein

Wahrmann, P. (1933) 'Κανναβάριοι, ἀσκομίσθαι', *Glotta*, 22: 42–6

Walde, A., and J. B. Hofmann (1938–54) *Lateinisches etymologisches Wörterbuch*. 3rd ed., Heidelberg

Wallraff, M. (2007) *Oratio funebris in laudem sancti Iohannis Chrysostomi*. Spoleto

Walters, P. (2009) *The assumed authorial unity of Luke and Acts: a reassessment of the evidence*. Cambridge

Walz, C. (1833) *Rhetores Graeci*, v. Stuttgart

Ward, J. S. (2007) 'Roman Greek: Latinisms in the Greek of Flavius Josephus', *Classical Quarterly*, 57: 632–49

Watt, J. M. (1997) *Code-switching in Luke and Acts*. New York

Weinreich, U. (1953) *Languages in contact: findings and problems*. New York

Weise, F. O. (1882) *Die griechischen Wörter im Latein*. Leipzig

Wellmann, M. (1899) 'Chrysippos 21', in G. Wissowa (ed.), *Paulys Real-Encyclopädie der classischen Altertumswissenschaft*. Stuttgart: III.2511

Wellmann, M. (1906–14) *Pedanii Dioscuridis Anazarbei De materia medica libri quinque*. Berlin

Wessely, C. (1902) 'Die lateinischen Elemente in der Gräzität der ägyptischen Papyrusurkunden, I', *Wiener Studien*, 24: 99–151

Wessely, C. (1903) 'Die lateinischen Elemente in der Gräzität der ägyptischen Papyrusurkunden, II', *Wiener Studien*, 25: 40–77

West, M. L. (1966) *Hesiod: Theogony*. Oxford

West, S. (1984) 'Lycophron Italicized', *JHS* 104: 127–51

Whatmough, J. (1949) Review of J. Pokorny, *Indogermanisches etymologisches Wörterbuch*, in *Language*, 25: 285–90

Whatmough, J. (1962) Review of Frisk (1954–72), *Classical Philology*, 57: 241–3

Wichmann, S. and J. Wohlgemuth (2008) 'Loan verbs in a typological perspective', in Stolz, Bakker, and Salas Palomo (edd.) 89–121

Wifstrand, A. (2005) *Epochs and styles: selected writings on the New Testament, Greek language and Greek culture in the post-Classical era*, trans. D. Searby. Tübingen

Wilcken, U. (1924) Review of *PSI* VI, *AfP* 7: 80–6

Wilcox, M. (1965) *The Semitisms of Acts*. Oxford

Wild, J. P. (1964) 'The textile term *scutulatus*', *Classical Quarterly*, 14: 263–6

Wild, J. P., and K. Dross-Krüpe (2017) 'Ars polymita, ars plumaria: the weaving terminology of *taqueté* and tapestry', in Gaspa *et al*. (edd.) 301–20

Wilhelm, A. (1928a) 'Τροφός', *Glotta*, 16: 274–9

Wilhelm, A. (1928b) 'Lateinische Wörter in griechischen Inschriften', *Wiener Studien*, 46: 227–32

Willi, A. (2008) *Sikelismos*. Basel

Wilson, N. G. (2006) 'A note on Latinisms in Aelian', in S. Eklund (ed.), *Συγχάρματα: studies in honour of Jan Frederik Kindstrand*. Uppsala: 211–16

Winford, D. (2003) *An introduction to contact linguistics*. Malden

Winford, D. (2010) 'Contact and borrowing', in Hickey (ed.) 170–87

Winter-Froemel, E. (2011) *Entlehnung in der Kommunikation und im Sprachwandel: Theorie und Analysen zum Französischen*. Berlin

Wohlgemuth, J. (2009) *A typology of verbal borrowings*. Berlin

Woodward, A. M. (1926) 'Excavations at Sparta, 1926', *The Annual of the British School at Athens* 27: 173–54

Worp, K. A. (1982) Review of *P.Wash.Univ.* I, *Bibliotheca Orientalis*, 39: 564–6

Worp, K. A. (2005) 'On the Aureliate of clergy and monks', *ZPE* 151: 145–52

Wouters, A. (1976) '"Latijns grieks" en "grieks latijn": over translitteraties en hun bedoeling', *Hermeneus*, 48: 179–91

Youtie, H. C. (1976) 'P.Cornell inv. 1 11: σουβρικός', *ZPE* 22: 53–6

Zarini, V. (2019) 'L'univers grec et latin d'un poète africain: Corippe et Byzance', in Garcea, Rosellini, and Silvano (edd.) 265–74

Zenner, E. and G. Kristiansen (2014) 'Introduction: onomasiological, methodological and phraseological perspectives on lexical borrowing', in Zenner and Kristiansen (edd.) 1–17

Zenner, E. and G. Kristiansen (edd.) (2014) *New perspectives on lexical borrowing: onomasiological, methodological and phraseological innovations.* Berlin

Zervan, V. (2019) *Die Lehnwörter im Wortschatz der spätbyzantinischen historiographischen Literatur.* Berlin

Zgusta, L. (1980) 'Die Rolle des Griechischen im römischen Kaiserreich', in Neumann and Untermann (edd.) 121–45

Zilliacus, H. (1935a) *Zum Kampf der Weltsprachen im oströmischen Reich.* Helsinki

Zilliacus, H. (1935b) 'Till frågan om det grekiska B:s övergång till spirant', *Eranos*, 33: 63–74

Zilliacus, H. (1937) 'Das lateinische Lehnwort in der griechischen Hagiographie', *Byzantinische Zeitschrift*, 37: 302–44

Zingerle, J. (1930) 'Lexikalische Beiträge', *Glotta*, 19: 72–85

Zuckerman, C. (1988) '*Legio V Macedonica* in Egypt: CPL 199 revisited', *Tyche*, 3: 279–87

INDEX LOCORUM

INDEX OF LATIN WORDS

Latin words are spelled as in the *OLD* (words not in the *OLD* are spelled as in the *TLL*, L&S, or other lexicon where they occur); superscript numbers distinguish Latin homonymns following the *OLD*; bold font indicates loanwords; asterisks indicate unattested words. References are to entries in the Lexicon (§3.2) where the Latin word is mentioned or implied (some Lexicon lemmata are in the Latin alphabet, alphabetized as Greek); as there are many reasons for mentioning Latin words in Lexicon entries, Latin words listed here are not always the source of the Greek words that follow them. Discussions in the main text can be found by following the cross references in the Lexicon entry.

a, ab: ἀ, **ἀβάκτης**, **Ἀβοριγῖνες**, **ἀβρέβις**, **ἀκομενταρήσιος**, **ἀννούμερος**, ἀ πιγμέντις, ἀποκομερκίων, ἀ σαβάνις, **ἀσηκρῆτις**, ἐπὶ βαλανείων, πρωτασηκρήτης

abbas: ἀββᾶ
abeo: ἀβιτώριον
*abitorium: ἀβιτώριον
abolitio: ἀβολιτίων
abolla: **ἀβόλλης**
Aborigines: **Ἀβοριγῖνες**
absinthiatus: **ἀψινθᾶτος**
absolutio: ἀβσολουτίων
absolutorius: absolutorius
abstineo: ἀβστινατεύω, ἀβστινατίων
accensus: ἀκκῆσσος
acceptilatio: ἀκκεπτιλατίων
acceptum: ἄκκεπτον
accessio: ἀκκεσσίων
accipiter: ξιφτέρι
*accubiculum: ἀκκουβίκυλον
accubitale: **ἀκκουβιτάλιον**
accubitalis: ἀκκουβιτάριος
accubitum: ἀκκουβίτιον, **ἀκκούβιτον**
accubitus: ἀκκούβιτος
accumbo: ἀκκουμβίζω, συνακουμβίζω
acies: ἀκία
acinus: ἄκινος
acipenser: ἀκκιπήσιος
aciscularius: **ἀκισκλάριος**
acisculus: ἀκίσκλη, **ἀκίσκλος**
actio: ἀκτίων
actor: ἄκτωρ
actuarius: **ἀκτουάριος**
actum: **ἀβάκτης**, ἄκτα
actus: ἄκτους

acucula: ἀκίκουλα
ad: ad, ἀδνούμιον, ἀδρεσπόνσουμ, ἐνεραδνούμιον
ademptio: ἀδεμπτεύω, ἀδεμπτίων
adeo: adeo, **ἀδιτεύω**
adimo: ἀδεμπτεύω
adipiscor: adipiscor
aditio: **ἀδιτίων**
adiudicatio: ἀδιουδικατίων
adiudico: ἀδιουδικατεύω
adiutor: **ἀδιούτωρ**
adiutorium: ἀειουτώρειν
adiuvo: ἀδιοβάντης
administratio: ἀδμινιστρατίων
admissarius: ἀδμισσάριος
admissionalis: ἀδμισσιονάλιος
adnotatio: **ἀδνοτατίων**
*adnumium: ἀδνούμιον
adoptio: ἀδοπτίων
*adorator: ἀδωράτωρ
adoria: ἀδωρέα
adulter: ἀδουλτέριος
*advenditio: ἀδβενδιτίων
adventicius: ἀδβεντίκιος
*advertor: ἀδουέρτωρ
advocatus: ἀδβοκᾶτος
aedes: αἴδης
aedilicius: αἰδιλίκιος
aedilis: αἰδίλης
aeditor: aeditor
aeger: **αἴγροι**
aequum: αἴκον
aerarium: **αἰράριον**
aerarius: αἰράριος
aes: αἰρίσφλως
aestimatio: αἰστιματίων
aestimatorius: αἰστιματόρια
aestimatus: αἰστιμᾶτος
afratum: ἀφρᾶτον
Africa: Ἀφρική
Africanus: Ἀφρικανός
agentes in rebus: ἀγεντισηρίβους
ager: βασταγάριος
aggestus: ἄγεστα
agminalis: ἀκμινάλιον
agnatio: ἀδγνατίων
agnatus: ἀδγνατικός, ἀδγνᾶτος
agnomen: ἀδνούμιον

ago: ἀγεντισηρίβους, ἄγω, ὂκ ἄγε
agraria: **ἀγραρεύω, ἀγραρία**
*agrilaria: ἀγριλάρια
ala: **ἄλη**
alarius: ἀλάριος
albarius: ἀλβάριος
albatus: ἀλβᾶτοι
albinus: ἀλβῖνος
albucum: ἀλβούκιουμ
albus: ἀλβόμαυρος, ἄλβον, ἄλβος, ἀλφός
algensis: ἀλγενήσιος
alica: ἀλίκιον, ἅλιξ 2
alicula: ἀλίκλα, **ἀλίκλιον**
alienus: ἀλιενονόμινε
alimentarius: ἀλιμεντάριος
alimentum: **ἀλιμέντα**
alium: ἀλλᾶς, ἄλλην, ἄλλιουμ
alius: aliud
allicio: αλ
alligo: ἀλλιγᾶρε
alluvio: ἀλλουβίων
almus: ἄλμα
aloe: ἀλόαμ
altarium: ἀλτάριον
*altarius: ἀλτάριος
alternatio: ἀλτερνατίων
alumen: ἀλοῦμεν
alumnus: ἀλοῦμνος
aluta: ἀλοῦτα
amarus: ἀμᾶρον, **μαρούλιον**
Ambarvalia: Ἀμβαρουία
Ambianensis: Ἀνβιανήσιος
ambio: ἀμβιτεύω, ἀμβιτιάω
ambitio: ἀμβιτιονάριος, ἀμβιτιονεύω, ἀμβιτίων
*ambito: ἀμβιτιάω
ambitus: ἀμβιτεύω, ἀμβίτους
ambulatorius: ἀμβλατώριος
ambulo: ἄμβλα μοῦλα
ami: ἄμμιουμ
amictorium: **ἀμικτώριον**, λεπταμικτόριον
amita: ἄμιτα
amitinus: ἀμιτῖνος
ampulla: **ἀμποῦλλα, ἀμπούλλιον**, ἀμπυλλάριον
ampullacea: ἀμπουλλάκια
amurca: μοῦρκα
anaglypharius: ἀναγλυφάριος
*ancentum: ἀγκέντουμ
ancile: ἀγκίλιον
ancilla: ἀγκίλλα
anclo: ἀγκλία
andabata: ἀνδαβάτης
anesatus: **ἀνισᾶτος**
anesum: ἀνήσουμ
anethum: ἀνήθουμ
angaria: ἀγγαρεία
angario: ἀγγαριεύω
angarius: ἀγγαρεύω, ἀγγάριος
angularis: ἀγγλάριον

angulus: ἄνγλος
annalis: **ἀννάλιος**
annona: **ἀννῶνα, ἀννωνάριος**, ἀννωναρχέω, ἀννωναταμίας, ἀννωνεακόν, ἀννωνέπαρχος, **ἀννωνεύομαι, ἀννωνιακός, ἀννωνικός**, ἀννωνοκάπιτον
annonarius: **ἀννωνάριος**
annualis: ἀννουάλιος
ante: Ἀντίφορος
antecessor: **ἀντικήνσωρ**
*antepannus: ἀντίπανον
antesignanus: ἀντισιγνᾶνος
antilena: ἀντελίνα
Antiochensis: Ἀντιοχήσιος
antiquarius: ἀντικουάριος
Antoninianus: Ἀντωνινιανός
Antoninus: **Ἀντώνεια**, Ἀντωνεῖνος, Ἀντωνινεῖον, ψευδαντωνῖνος
Antonius: **Ἀντώνεια**
apex: ἄπικας
apiastrum: ἀπιάστρουμ
apiatum: ἀπιᾶτον
Apicius: Ἀπίκια, Ἀπικιανόν
apium: ἄπιον
apocrisiarius: ἀποκρισιάριος
apothecarius: ἀποθηκάριος
*applicitarius: ἀπλικιτάριος
applico: ἀπληκεύω, ἀπλικιτάριος, ἀπλίκιτον
Aprilis: **Ἀπρίλιος**
apsinthiatum: **ἀψινθᾶτος**
aqua: ἄκουα
aquaeductus: ἀκιδοῦκτος
aquarius: **ἀκουάριος**
aquila: ἀκυλεής
aquilinus: ἀκύλινον
Aquilo: εὐρακύλων
arbiter: ἄρβιτρος
arbitrarius: ἀρβιτράριος
arbitrium: ἀρβίτριον
arca: **ἄρκα**, ἄρκιον, ἄρκος
arcarius: ἀρκαρικάριος, **ἀρκαρικός, ἀρκάριος**
arcatus: ἀρκᾶτος
*arclaria: ἀρκλαρία
arcuarius: ἀρκουάριος
arcuatus: ἀρκᾶτος
arcula: ἄρκλα, ἀρκλαρία, ἀρκλόλιγκλα
arcus: ἀρκᾶτος
area: ἀερικόν, ἀήρ
arena see *harena*
areola: ἄριλλα
argentarium: ἀργεντάριον, ἀργενταρίτης
argentarius[1]: ἀργενταρία
argentarius[2]: **ἀργεντάριος**, ἀργενταρίτης
argenteus: ἀργέντινος, ἀργέντιος, ἀργεντός
argentum: ἀργενταρία
arma: **ἄρμα**, ἀρμαστατίων, **ἀρμικούστωρ**
armamenta: ἀρμαμέντον
armamentarium: ἀρμαμεντάριον
armarium: **ἀρμάριον**, ἀρμαρίτης

*boletinus: βωλητῖνος

boletus: βωλητάριος, **βωλήτης**, βωλητῖνος, βωλήτιον

*bonitarius: βονιτάριος

bonus: βονιτάριος, **βόνος**

botulus: βότουλος

bracae: **βράκαι**, βρακαρία, βρακέλλαι, **βράκιον**, βράξ, κοντοβράκιον

*bracaria: βρακαρία

bracarius: **βρακάριος**

bracatus: βρακᾶτος

bracchiale: **βραχιάλιον**

bracchiatus: βραχιᾶτος

*bracella: βρακέλλαι

branca: βρεγκάριος

brassica: βράσκη, βράσσικα

*bratteolatus: βραττεολᾶτος

brax: βράξ

breviator: βρεβιάτωρ

brevis: **ἀβρέβις**, βρεβιατικόν, **βρέβιον**, βρέβις

bruma: βροῦμα

brumalis: **βρουμάλια**

brutus: βροῦτος

bubo: βοῦφος

bubula: βούβελα

bubularius: βουβλάρις

bubulcus: Βουβοῦλκος

bucca: βούκκα, **βουκκᾶς**, βουκκίζω, **βουκκίον**, βουκκισμή

buccella: βούκελλα, βουκελλάτης, βουκέλλιον, βουκία

buccellarius: **βουκελλάριος**

buccellatum: **βουκκελλᾶτον**

bucco: βουκκίων

bucina: βουκανιστήριον, βουκονιστήριον, βυκανάω, **βυκάνη**, βυκάνημα, **βυκανητής**, βυκανισμός, **βυκινίζω**, ἐμβυκανάω, ἰβυκηνίζω

bucinator: **βυκινάτωρ**

bucino: βυκανάω, **βυκινίζω**, ἐμβυκανάω

bucinum: βουκανιστήριον, βούκινον

bulbus: βολβός, βούλβους

bulga: βούργια

bulla: βολλωτός, **βούλλα**, βουλλεύω, βουλλίζω, βουλλόω

bullatus: βολλωτός

bullo: βουλλόω

burdo: **βουρδών**, βουρδωνάριον, **βουρδώνιον**, ἱπποβουρδονογένεια, ἱπποβούρδων

burdonarius: **βουρδωνάριος**

burgarius: βουργάριος

burgus: βοῦργος

*burichale: βουριχάλλιον

buricus: βουριχάλλιον, βουριχᾶς, βούριχος

*butina: βυτίνη

*butinum: βούτινον

buttis: βιττιν, βόττης, βοῦττις

byrsa: περεσίκα

*caballaricus: **καβαλλαρικός**

caballaris: **καβαλλαρικός**

caballarius: **καβαλλαρικός**, **καβαλλάριος**, ξυλοκαβαλλάριος

*caballatium: καβαλλάτιον

caballico: καβαλλικεύω

caballus: καβάλλης

cabo: κρισσοκάβων

caepa: κέπα

Caesar: ἀποκαισαρόομαι, **Καῖσαρ**, **Καισάρειος**, Καισαρεύω, Καισαριασταί, Καισαρικός, Καισαρογερμανίκεια, πολυκαισαρίη, **φιλόκαισαρ**

Caesareus: **Καισάρειος**, Καισαρεών, Νεοκαισαρεών

Caesarianus: **Καισαριανός**

Caesariensis: Καισαρήσιος

caesaries: καισάραι

caetra: καίτρεαι

calamarius: καλαμάριον

calcatura: καλκατούρα

calcearius: καλτάριος

calceus: καλίκιος, **κάλτιος**, κάλτοι

calculator: καλκουλάτωρ

calefacio: καλαφάτης

*calefactor: καλαφάτης

Calend-: see Kalend-

caliculus: καλλίκλιον

calidarius: καρδάρι

caliga: καλιγάριον, **καλίγιον**, καλικοφασκία, **κάλιξ**

caligaris: καλιγαρικός

caligarius: καλιγάριον, **καλιγάριος**

caligatus: καλιγᾶτος

callosus: καλλωσόν

calo: calo

calumnia: καλουμνία

*camela: κάμελα, καμελαύκιον

camelarius: καμηλάριος

camella: κάμελα, καμελαύκιον, κάμηλα

camera: καμάρα, κάμελα

camerarius: καμαράριος

camillus: κάμιλλος

camisia: καμισαγοραστής, **καμίσιον**, ὑποκαμίσιον

cammarus: καβουρᾶς

campagus: **καμπάγιον**, κάμπαγος, καμπαγών

campana: καμπανίζω, καμπανιστής, **κάμπανος**

Campanus: Καμπανός

campestre: **κάμπιστρον**

campidoctor: **καμπιδούκτωρ**

campus: **κάμπος**

camum: κάμον

canabae: καύνη

canabarius: κανναβάριος

canaliclarius: καναλικλάριος

canalis: **κανάλιον**

cancellarius: **καγκελλάριος** 1, πρωτοκαγκελλάριος

cancellus: καγκελλάριος 2, **καγκέλλιον**, καγκελλοειδῶς, **κάγκελλος**, **καγκελλωτός**, καγκελοθυρίς, σκαμνοκάγκελος

cancer: κάγκρους

candela: κανδηλάπτης, κανδηλάριον, **κανδήλη**, κανδηλοσβέστης, κανδίλιον, κουκουμοκανδήλη, πολυκάνδηλος, πολυκανδίλιον

candelabrum: κανδηλαῦρον

candidarius: κανδιδάριος

candidatus: **κανδιδᾶτος**

candidus: κάνδιδος

centuncularis: κεντουκουλάρις
centunculus: κέντουκλον, κεντουκουλάρις
centuria: **κεντουρία**
centurio: ἐξκεντορικός, ἐξκεντυρίων, **κεντουρίων**
cera: κήρα
cerealis: κερεάλιος
cerebrum: κέρεβρον
cereolus: **κηρίολος**
ceriolare: κηριολάριον
ceriolarius: κηρουλάριος
cerium: κηρίων
Cermalus: Κερμαλόν
certus: κέρτος
cerula: κηρουλλάριος, κηρούλλιον
cerularius: κηρουλλάριος
cerussa: κηρύσση
cervesia: κερβήσιος
cervical: **κερβικάριον**
cervicarium: **κερβικάριον**
cervulus: Κερβούκολος
cessicius: cessicios
cessio: cessicios, κεσσιωνάριος
cessionarius: κεσσιωνάριος
cetarius: ζητάριος
charta: χάρτα
chartarea: χαρταρέα
chartarius: χαρτάριος
chartiaticum: χαρτιατικόν
chartularius: **χαρτουλάριος**
Christianus: **Χριστιανίζω, Χριστιανικός, Χριστιανισμός,** Χριστιανοκατήγορος, Χριστιανομερῖται, **Χριστιανός, Χριστιανότης,** Χριστιανῶς, ψευδοχριστιανός
cibaria: **κιβαριάτωρ, κιβάριον**
cibariator: **κιβαριάτωρ**
cibarius: **κιβάριος**
cicer: κίκερ
cicuta: κικοῦτα
cingula: κίγκλα
circellus: κιρκιλλίζω, κρικέλλιον, κρίκελλος
circensis: **κιρκήσιος**
circinus: κίρκινος
circito: κιρκητεύω
circitor: **κιρκίτωρ**
circulator: κιρκουλᾶς
circulus: κίρκλος λιξόλας
circus: **κίρκος**
cis: κίστιβερ
cisterna: **κιστέρνα**
citator: κιτάτωρ
citrea: κιτρέα
citreus: κίτρεος, κίτρις
citrium: κιτρειαβολή, κιτρινοειδής, **κίτρινος**, κιτριοειδής, **κίτριον**, κίτρις, ὁλοκίτρινος
citrum: **κιτρᾶτον**, κιτρειαβολή, κιτρινοειδής, **κίτρινος**, κιτριοειδής, **κίτριον**, κίτρις, κιτρόμηλον, **κίτρον**, κιτρόφυλλον, ὁλοκίτρινος
citrus: κίτρος
civilis: ἰουρισκιβίλε
clam: κλάμ

clarus: κλάρος
classicus: **κλασσικός**
classis: **κλάσσα, κλασσικός**, κλάσσις, κλῆσις
Claudianus: Κλαυδιανός
Claudius: Κλαύδιος, **φιλοκλαύδιος**
claustrum: κλῶστρον
clausula: κλαυσουλία
clausura: **κλεισούρα**
clavicularius: καβικλάριος, **κλαβικουλάριος**
clavularius: κλαβουλάριος
clavus: κλαβαρίζω, κλάβιον, κλάβος, μαγκλάβι
clibanarius: **κλιβανάριος**
cliens: κλιέντης
clipeatus: κλιπεᾶτος
clipeus: κλίπεος
cloaca: κλόκιον
clupea: κλοπία
Clusius: Κλούσιος
clustrum: κλοῦστρον, κλουστροπλακοῦς
coactor: **κομακτορία, κομάκτωρ**
cochlear: **κοχλιάριον**
coctus: ὁλοκοτίνιν, ὁλοκοττινοπερίπατος, **ὁλοκόττινος**
coculum: κόκχος
codicarius: κωδικάριος
codicillus: κωδικάριος, κωδικίλλιον, **κωδικίλλος**, κωδικίλλουν, κωδικιλλόω
coemptio: κουηεμπτίων
coeo: κομῖρε
cognata: κογνᾶτα
cognatio: κογνατίων
cognatus: κογνατικός, κογνᾶτος
cognitio: **κογνιτίων**
cognomen: cognomen
cohors: **κοόρτη**, κοόρτις, κορτιανός, χορταρῖνος
cohortalinus: κοορταλῖνος, χορταρῖνος
cohortalis: κοορτάλιος, κορτιανός, χωρτάριος
co-iurator: κουιουράτωρ
collactaneus: collactaneus
collare: **κολλάριον**
collectarius: αἰωνοκολλητίων, **κολλεκτάριος, κολλητίων**
collectio: αἰωνοκολλητίων, **κολλητίων**
collega: **κολλήγας**, κολλήγιος, κολληγίων, συγκολλήγας
collegatarius: κολληγατάριος, συλληγατάριος
collegiatus: κολεγεᾶτος, κολλεγιάτης, κολληγιᾶς
collegium: **κολλήγιον**
collyrium: κολλούριον
colonarius: κολωνάριος
colonia: **κολωνία, μητροκολωνεία**
colonus: Κολονίσιος, **κόλων**, κολωνίτης
colorator: κοροράτωρ
colostra: κλόστρα
colus: κουνοῦκλα
comatus: κομᾶτος
combino: κομβίνευμα, κομβινεύω
comes: ἀντικόμης, ἀποκόμης, **κόμης**, κομητικός, **κομήτισσα**, κομιτοτριβοῦνος, πρωτοκόμης
comissarius: κομισσάριος
comissor: κωμισσᾶτον
comitatensis: **κομιτατήσιος**

comitatus: **κομιτᾶτον**
comitianus: **κομιτιανός**
comitium: **κομέτιον**
commanipularis: κομονοπλάρις
commeatalis: κομιατάλιον
commeatus: **κομιᾶτον**
commentariensis: **κομμενταρήσιος**
commentarium: **ἀκομενταρήσιος, κομμεντάριον**
commentum: **κομμέντον**
commerciarius: **κομμερκιάριος**
commercium: ἀποκομερκίων, κομμέρκιον
commissorius: κομμισσόριος
committo: κομμιτεύω
commodo: κομμοδᾶτος
commodum: κομμοδάριον, **κομόδιον**
Commodus: φιλοκόμοδος
commonitorium: **κομμονιτώριον**
communis: κομμοῦνις
compendiarium: κοπενδάριον
compensatio: κομπενσατίων
compenso: κομπενσατεύω
Compitalia: Κομπιτάλια
compitum: κόμπιτος
compleo: κομπλεύσιμος, κόμπλευτρον, κομπλεύω
completio: κομπλατίων
completus: κομπλατεύω
compromissarius: κομπρομισσάριος
compromissum: **κομπρόμισσον**
comptus: κόμπτον
conamentum: κοναμέντον
concorde: κονκορδιε
concurator: κονκουράτωρ
condemnatio: κονδεμνατίων
condico: *condico*, κονδικτικεύω
condicticius: κονδικτικεύω, κονδικτίκιος
condictio: κονδικτίκιος
condimentum: κουδούμεντον
conditarius: κονδιταρία, **κονδιτάριος**
conditor: κονδίτωρ
conditus: **κονδῖτον**, κονδῖτος 1, κονδῖτος 2, σαλακονδεῖτον
condo: κόνδερε
condominus: κονδωμῆνος
conductio: κονδουκτίων
conductor: κονδουκτορία, κονδουκτορικόν, **κονδουκτόριον**, κονδούκτρια, **κονδούκτωρ**
conductum: κονδοῦκτι
conduma: κονδωμῆνος
confector: κομφέκτωρ
confessorius: κομφεσσόριος
confirmatio: κομφιρματίων
confirmo: **κομφιρματεύω**
confusio: κομφουσίων
congiarum: κογγιάριον
congius: ἡμικόγγιον
coniunctim: κονιοῦγκτιμ
consanguineus: κωνσανγυίναιος
conscriptus: κωνσκρίπτος
consecratio: κωνσεκρατίων
consensus: κονσένσου

consiliarius: κονσιλιάριος
consilium: κωνσίλιον
consistorianus: κονσιστοριανός
consistorium: **κονσιστώριον**
consobrina: κονσοβρῖνα
consobrinus: κονσοβρῖνος, *consororinus*
consolidatio: κονσολιδατίων
consororinus: *consororinus*
Constantianus: Κωνσταντιακός, Κωνσταντιανός
constitutio: κονστιτουτίων
Consualia: Κωνσουάλια
consul: κώνσουλ
consularis: **κονσουλάριος**
consulo: *consulo*
consultatio: κονσουλτατίων
consultus: ἰουρισκονσοῦλτοι
continuo: κοντινουατεύω
continuus: κοντίνουος
contionator: κωντοναίτωρ
contra: κόντρα ταβούλλας
contractus: κοντράκτον
contrarius: κοντράριος
contributarius: ὁμόκηνσος
controversia: κοντροβερσία
contubernalis: **κοντουβερνάλιος, συγκελλάριος**
contubernium: κοντουβέρνιον
contumacia: κοντουμακία
contumax: κοντούμαξ
contus: κοντός
conventio: κομβέντιον, κονβεντίων
conventionalis: κονβεντιονάλιος
conventum: κουβέντα
conventus: κονβενταρχέω, **κόνβεντος**
convicium: κομβίκιον
*coptura: κοπτούρα
copula: κόπλα
corallium: κορωλλικός
corda: κόρδα
corium: κορέλι
cornicen: κορνίκινες, κόρνιξ
cornicularius: **κορνικουλάριος**
cornix: κόρνιξ
cornu: κόρνιξ, κορνουκόπιον
cornutus: κορνοῦτος
corona: κορόλλιον, κορώνη
corrector: **κορρήκτωρ**
correctorius: κορρεκτόριος
corrigia: **κορριγία**
corruda: κορροῦδα
corruptor: κορύπτωρ
cortina: **κορτίνα**
corvus: κόρβος
cottidianus: κοττιδιανός
coxa: κόξα
coxale: κοξάλιον
cras: κρᾶς
Crassianus: Κρασσιανόν
crassus: κράσσος
craticula: κρατίκλη, ῥατίκλα

713

destitor: δεστίτωρ	*Drusilla*: **Δρουσιλλῆος**
destitutor: δεστιτούτωρ	*Drusus*: **Δρουσιεύς**
deunx: *deunx*	*dubius*: δούβιος
deus: δέος	*ducator*: δουκάτωρ
dextans: *dextans*	*ducatus*: δουκᾶτον
diaetarius: διαιτάριος	*ducenarius*: **δουκηναρία**, **δουκηνάριος**
dialis: διάλιος	*ducianus*: **δουκιανός**
diarium: **διάριον**	*ductarius*: δουκτάριον
dico: δίκερε	**dulciradix*: δουλκιράδιξ
dictator: ἀντιδικτάτωρ, **δικτάτωρ**, **δικτατωρεία**, **δικτατωρεύω**	*dulcis*: δούλκις
dictatura: δικτατοῦρα	*duplaris*: δουπλάριος
dies: *dies*	*duplicarius*: **δουπλικάριος**, δουπλικιαρία, συνδουπλικάριος
digesta: **δίγεστον**	*duplicatio*: δουπλικατίων
dilatio: διλατίων	*duplus*: δούπλα
dilatorius: διλατόριος	*dupondius*: διπούνδιον, διπούνδιος
diligentia: διλιγεντία	*duracinus*: **δωράκινον**, μηλοδωράκινον, ῥοδακινέα
diloris: **δίλωρος**	*dux*: **δουκικός**, **δούξ**
dimissorius: διμισσωρία	
directarius: διρεκτάριος	*ebulum*: ἐβούλιον, ἔβουλον
directus: διρέκτος	*edico*: *edico*
direptor: διρέπτωρ	*edictum*: **ἤδικτον**
diribitorium: διριβιτώριον	*edo*: ἔδερε
dirigo: διριγεύω	*effugium*: ἐκφούγιν
discussio: δισκουσσίων	*elecebra*: ἐκλεκέβρα, ἰλλεκέβρα
discussor: **δισκούσσωρ**	*electio*: ἐλεκτίων
disiunctim: δισιοῦνκτιμ	*electus*: **βισήλεκτος**
dispensator: δισπηνσάτωρ	*elix*: ἄλιξ 3
dispositio: δισποσιτίων	*emancipatio*: **ἐμαγκιπατίων**, μαγκιπατίων, μαγκίπιον 2
distribuo: διστριβοῦτος, διστριβούω	*emancipo*: ἐμαγκιπατεύω, **ἐμαγκιπᾶτος**
dito: διτάριος	*emereo*: ἡμέριτος
*divinitatus: διβινιτᾶτος	*emo*: λουδεμπιστής, μάλημπτος
divinus: *divini iuris*	*emptio*: ἔμπτιον, ἐμπτίων
divortium: διβόρτιον	*emptor*: ἔμπτωρ, *familiae emptor*
divus: δίβος	*eo*: *eo*
do: δατόν, δῶ	*epistula*: κουρεπιστουλάριος
dodrans: *dodrans*	*epistularius*: ἐπιστολάριος
dolabra: δολάβρα	*epulae*: ἔπουλαι
dolo: δόλων	*epularis*: **ἀπαλαρέα**, κυθραπαλαρία
dolus: *dolus*	*epulo*: ἐπούλων
domesticus: **δομεστικός** 1, δομεστικός 2	*epulum*: ἔπουλον
domicilium: δομικίλιον	*eques*: ἔκυες
domina: Δόμνα	*equester*: ἐκουέστρης
dominatio: δομινατίων	**equinalis*: ἐκυινᾶλις
dominicus: δομινικός	*equinus*: ἐκουῖνος
dominus: δόμινος	*equisaetum*: ἐκύτιον
Domitianus: **Δομιτιανός**	*equitatus*: ἐκυτᾶτος
donativum: **δωνάτιουον**	*erogatio*: ἠρογατίων, **ῥόγα**
dormitorium: δορμιτώριον	*erogator*: **ῥογάτωρ**
dotalis: δοτάλιος	*erogo*: ῥογάω, **ῥογεύω**
draconarius: ἀποδρακωνάριος, **δρακονάριος**, πρωτοδρακωνάριος	*erraticus*: ἠρράτικος
	ervum: ἔρβουλον
draucus: δραύκιον	*esca*: ἴσκα
dromadarius: **δρομεδάριος**, σουβδρομεδάριος	*Esquilinus*: Ἐσκυλῖνος
dromo: δρομονάριος	*essedarius*: **ἐσσεδάριος**, τεσσεδάρις
dromonarius: δρομωνάριος	*essedum*: ἔσσεδον
drungarius: δρουγγάριος	*Euroaquilo*: εὐρακύλων
drungus: δρουγγαρᾶτον, δρουγγάριος, δρουγγιστί, δροῦγγος	*Eurus*: εὐρακύλων
druppa: δρύππα	*eventum*: ἔβεντον

evocator: ἠβωκάτωρ
evocatus: **ἠβοκᾶτος**, ἠβωκάτωρ
ex: ἐκσημιαφόρος, ἐξκεντορικός, ἐξκεντυρίων
exactor: ἐξάκτης, **ἐξακτορεύω**, **ἐξακτορία**, ἐξακτορικός, **ἐξάκτωρ**
exagium: ἐξάγιον
examino: ἄξαμος
*excenturio: ἐξκεντορικός, ἐξκεντυρίων
*exceptarius: ἐκσκεπτάριος
exceptor: ἐξκεπτορικός, **ἐξκέπτωρ**
exceptorium: ἐσκεπτώριον, σκεπτούριον
excubitor: ἐξκούβιτον, **ἐξκουβίτωρ**
*excubitum: ἐξκούβιτον
*excubitus: ἐξκούβιτος
exculcator: σκουλκάτωρ
excusatio: **ἐξκουσατίων**
excusatus: ἐξκουσᾶτος
excuso: ἐξκουσατεύω, **ἐξκουσεύω**
exemplar: **ἐξεμπλάριον**
exemplum: ἔξεμπλον
exercitor: ἐξερκίτωρ
exercitoria: ἐξερκιτορία
exercitus: **ἐξέρκετον**
exheredatio: ἐξερεδατίων
exheredo: ἐξερεδατεύω, ἐξερεδᾶτος
exhibitorius: ἐξιβιτόριος
exitio: ἐξιτίων
exodiarius: ἐξοδιάριος
*expectoricus: ἐξπεκτορικός
expeditio: πέδιτον
expeditum: **ἐξπέδιτον**
expeditus: ἐξπεδῖτος
expello: **ἐξπελλευτής**, **ἐξπελλεύω**
explicitus: ἔξπληκτος
explorator: **ἐξπλωράτωρ**
expunctio: ἐξπούγγευσις
expunctor: ἐξπούγκτωρ
expungo: ἐξπούγγευσις, ἐξπουγγεύω, ἐξπούγκερος
exsecutor: ἐξεκούτωρ
*exsello: ἐκσελλίζω
extra: ἔξτρα ὄρδινεμ, ἐξτραορδινεύομαι, ἐξτραόρδινος
extraneus: **ἐκστρανήιος**
extraordinarius: **ἐξτραορδινάριος**
exuberantia: ἐξουβεραντία

faba: **φάβα,** φαβάτινος
fabatarium: φαβατάριον
fabatus: φαβᾶτον
fabrica: φαβρική, **φάβριξ**
fabricalis: φαβρικάρεις
fabriciensis: **φαβρικήσιος**
faciale: σαβανοφακιάριον, **φακιάλιον**
facies: φακίης
factio: φακτιω
factionarius: **φακτιωνάριος**
factum: **φάκτον**
facula: φακλεῖον
faecula: **φαίκλα**
faeniculum: φαινοῦκλον, φενίκουλα
falarica: φαλάρικα

falcarius: φαρακράριος
Falcidia: **φαλκίδιον**
Falcidius: Φαλκίδιος
falco: φαλκόνι
Falernus: **Φαλερῖνος**, Φαλερνίτης, **Φαλέρνος**
falsus: φαλσόγραφος, φάλσος
falx: ζάγκλον, φάλκη
fames: φάμης
familia: **φαμιλία**, familiae emptor
familiaris: **φαμιλιαρικός**, **φαμιλιάριος**, φαμιλιαρίς
famosus: φάμωσον
famulus: φάμουλος
far: φάρ
farraceus: φαρράχειος
fascia: **φασκία**, φασκιάριος, **φασκίδιον**, **φασκιόω**
fascinum: φάσκελον
fasciculare: φασικλάριον
fasciola: φασκιόλη
fascis: βαστά, φάσκης, φασκιάρια, φασκίς, φάσκος
faustus: φαῦστος
Favonianus: Φαβωνιανόν
Favonius: Φαβώνιος
favus: φάβος
feber: φέβερ
Februarius: **Φεβρουάριος**
februm: φέβερ
Felicianus: Φιλιτιανοί
felix: φῆλιξ
feminalia: **φεμινάλια**
fenestra: φαινέστρα
*fenicula: φενίκουλα
ferentarius: φερεντάριοι
Feretrius: Φερέτριος
feretrum: φέρετρον
ferio: φέρειν
ferula: φέλλουρα
ferus: φέρι
fetialis: **φετιάλιος**
fibula: ἐμφιβλόω, συμφιβλόω, **φίβλα**, φιβλίον, φίβλον, **φιβλόω**
fibulatorium: ἱμφειβλατώριον, **φιβλατώριον**
fideicommissarius: **φιδεικομμισσάριος**
fideicommissum: **φιδεικόμμισσον**
fideiussor: φιδειϊούσσωρ
fidelis: Φιδῆλις
fiduciarius: φιδουκιάριος
fiscalis: φισκάλιος
fiscus: **φίσκος**, **φισκοσυνήγορος**
flabellum: φλαβίλλιον
flagello: φραγέλλωσις, **φραγελλόω**
flagellum: φλάγελλον, φραγγέλλωσις, φραγέλλη, **φραγέλλιον**,
    φραγελλόω, φραγηλίτης
flagitator: φλαγιτάτωρ
flamen: φλᾶμεν
flaminalis: φλαμινάλιος
flaminica: φλαμινίκα
flaminius: φλάμα, φλᾶμεν
flammeolum: φλάμμουλον
flammula: φλάμμουλα, φλάμμουλον
*flammularius: φλαμμουλάριος

gurgulio: γούργουρας
gutta: γουτάριον
guttarium: γουτάριον
guttatus: γουττᾶτος
gutus: γουτάριον

habena: ἀβῆνα
habeo: habeo, ρατοναβιτεύω
habes: ἄβεις
habitatio: ἀβιτατίων
Hadrianus: **Ἀδριανός**
hallec: ἅλιξ 1
harena: **ἀρῆνα**
harenarius: ἐρανάριος
haruspex: ἀρούσπεξ
hasta: **ἄστη, ἀστιάριος**, ὑσσός
hastatus: **ἀστᾶτος**
hastiarius: **ἀστιάριος**
hastile: **ἀστίλιον**
hebdomadarius: ἑβδομαδάριος
hedera: ἔδερα
helvolus: ἔρβουλος
hemina: ἡμίνα
herba: ἔρβα, ἐρβαρυβία, ἔρβουλον
herbulum: ἔρβουλον
Hercules: Ἡρύκαλον
hereditarius: ἐρεδιτάριος
heres: heres, προνερεδεγεριτεύω
hibiscum: **ἑβίσκος**
hinnuleus: ἰνούλεους
histrio: ἱστρίων
hoc: ὃκ ἄγε
holus: ἁλύσαθρον
honor: ὀνῶρεμ
honorarius: ἰουρισονοράριον, **ὀνοράριος**
horrearius: **ὀρριάριος**
horreum: ὀρρεοπραιποσιτία, **ὀρριάριος, ὄρριον**
*horrianus: ὀρριάνος
hortor: ὀρτάρι
hospes: ὅσπις
hospitium: **ὁσπίτιον**

iaculatorius: ἰακλατόριον
Ianiculum: Ἰανίκολον
ianua: ἰανούα
Ianuarius: **Ἰανουάριος**
Idus: **Εἰδοί**
ilex: ἴλαξ
ilia: ἴλιον
illecebra: ἰλλεκέβρα
illicitus: ἰλλίκιτος
illustris: **ἰλλούστριος**
imaginifer: **ἰμαγίνιφερ**
impedimentum: ἰμπεδιμέντον
impendium: ἰμπένδια
imperator: **ἰμπεράτωρ**
imperium: ἰμπέριον
impero: imperare
impetus: ἔμπετος

in: dies, ἰνποτέστατος, κάπιτον
incertus: ἴγκερτος
incestus: ἴγκεστος
incola: ἰνκόλας
incrementum: ἰγκρεμέντιον
incrusto: ἐγκροστόω
incursus: εἴσκυρσις
indebitus: ἰνδέβιτος
indefensus: ἀδεφένδευτος
index: ἴνδικα
indictio: **ἰνδικτίων**, ἴνδικτος, ὑπερινδικτίονος
indictionalis: ἰνδικτιωνάλιος
indictus: ἴνδικτος
Indicus: Ἰνδικός
induco: ἰνδουκέντα
indulgentia: ἰνδουλγεντία
industria: ἰνδυστρία
infans: ἴμφανς
infero: ἰλλᾶτος
*infibulatorium: ἰμφειβλατώριον
infibulo: ἰμφειβλατώριον
inguinalis: ἰγγυνᾶλις
iniquitas: iniquitas
iniuria: ἰνιουρία
iniustitia: iniustitia
iniustus: ἰνιοῦστος
inquilinus: ἰγκουΐλῖνος
inquisitio: ἰγκουισιτίων
insana: ἰνσᾶνα
inspectio: ἰνσπέσιμον
inspectus: ἴνσπεκτον
institorius: ἰνστιτορία, ἰνστιτουτόριος
instituo: ἰνστιτοῦτος
instituta: **ἰνστιτοῦτα**
institutio: ἰνστιτουτίων
institutorius: ἰνστιτουτόριος
instructus: ἴνστρουκτος
instrumentarius: ἰνστρουμεντάριος
instrumentum: ἰνστρουμεντάριος, ἰνστρούμεντον
intentio: ἰντεντίων
inter: ἰντέρβιβος
intercalarius: ἰντερκαλάριος
intercedo: ἰντερκεδεύω
intercessio: ἰντερκεσσίων
interdico: interdico
interdictio: ἰντερδικτίων
interdictum: ἰντέρδικτον
interrex: ἰντέρρηξ
interrogatorius: ἰντερρογατόριος
*intersedeo: ἰντερσεδεύω
introita: ἰντρόειντα
introitus: ἰντρόειντα, ἰντρόϊτον
intubum: ἴντουβουμ, **ἰντύβιον**, ἰντυβολάχανον, **ἴντυβον**
inula: ἴνουλα
invectus: ἴνβεκτος
inventarium: ἰνβεντάριον, ἰνβέντον
inventum: ἰνβέντον
invicem: invicem
ipse: ἰπσόιουρε

irritus: ἴνριτος
isiciarius: **ἰσικιάριος**
isicium: ἰσικιάριον, **ἰσικιάριος**, ἰσικιομάγειρος, **ἰσίκιον**, ἰσικιοπώλης
isox: ἴσοξ
Italia: Ἰταλία
item: ἴτεμ
iter: iter
iteratio: ἰτερατίων
itinerarium: ἰτινεράριον
iuba: ἰοῦβα
iubeo: κουοδιούσω
iucundus: ἰουκούνδα
iudicialis: ἰουδικιάλιος
iugalis: ἰουγάλιον
iugatio: ἰουγατίων
iugerum: **ἰούγερον**
iugum: **ἰοῦγον**
Iulianus: Ἰουλιανόν
Iulius: Ἰουλιεύς, **Ἰούλιος**
iunior: ἰουνίωρ
Iunius: **Ἰούνιος**
iurator: **ἰουράτωρ**, κουιουράτωρ
iuridicus: ἰουρίδικος
iurisdictio: ἰουρισδικτίων
ius: divini iuris, ἰουρισγέντιος, ἰουρισκιβίλε, ἰουρισκονσοῦλτοι, ἰουρισονοράριον, ἰπσόιουρε, §9.5.6
Iustinianus: Ἰουστινιανός
Iuvenalia: Ἰουβενάλια

Kalendae. **Καλάνδαι, καλανδαρικά, καλανδικά**
kalendaris: **καλανδαρικά**
kalendarium: καλανδάριον
kalendarius: **καλανδαρικά**

labarum: λάβαρον
labellum: λαβέλλιον, λάβελλος
labrum: λάβρα
lacerna: λακέρνιον
lacerta: λακέρδα
lacinaridium: λακιναρίδιον
lacinia: λακιναρίδιον, λακινιά, λακίνιον
lactens: λακτέντον
lacunar: λακωνάριος
lacus: Κούρτιος λάκκος, λάκκος
laena: λαῖνα, ληίνη
lagena: λαγήναρχος, **λαγήνιον**, λάγηνος
lagenarius: λαγηνάριος
lamina: **λᾶμνα, λαμνίον**
lampadarius: λαμπαδάριος
lana: λάϊνος, σαπουλανᾶς
lanarius: **λανάριος**
lanatum: **λανᾶτον**
lanatus: **λανάτιον, λανᾶτον**, λανατουργός
lancea: λαγκία, λαγκίδιον
lancearius: **λαγκιάριος**
lanceo: λαγκεύω
lanceolatus: λαγκιολᾶτος
lanciola: λαγκίολα

lancula: ἀρκλόλιγκλα, λάγκλα, λάγκλιον
lanio: λανιάριος
lanx: λάγκη
Laodicenus: **Λαδικηνός**
Lar: Λάρητες
Larentalia: Λαρενταλία
largitio: **λαργιτίων**
largitionalia: λαργιτιονάλια
largitionalis: **λαργιτιωναλικός**
laridum: λαρδηγός, **λάρδος**
laser: λάσαρον
laterculensis: λατερκουλίσιος
laterculum: λατέρκουλον 1
laterculus: λατέρκουλον 2
Latiaris: Λατιάριος
laticlavius: λατικλάβιος
Latinitas: Λατινότης
Latinus: **Λατινίς, Λατῖνος**
Latium: Λατίνιον, Λάτιον
laureatus: λαυρᾶτον
Lauretum: Λαυρῆτον
laurus: λαῦρος
lautia: λαύτια
laxamentum: λαξαμέντον
lebitonarium: λεβητωνάριον
lectica: **λεκτεῖκα, λεκτίκιον**, λεκτίς
lecticarius: **λεκτικάριος**
lectina: λεκτίνιον
lector: ἀλεκτόριον
lectus[1]: νεόλεκτος
lectus[2]: καταλέκτια
legatarius: **ληγατάριος**, συλληγατάριος
legatio: ληγατίων
legatum: **ληγατεύω, ληγᾶτον**
legatus: **ληγᾶτος** 1
legio: **λεγεών**, λεγιώνη
legionarius: **λεγεωνάριος**
legitimus: **λεγίτιμος**
lego[1]: ἀβστινατεύω, **ληγατεύω**, ληγᾶτος 2
lego[2]: λέγερε
leguminalis: λεγουμενᾶλε
lens: λένς
lenticula: λεντίκουλα
leopardus: λεόπαρδος
lepidus: λέπιδος
lepus: λέπορις
leuga: λεύγη
levir: λέβιρος
lex: λέγες
libellarius: **λιβράριος**
libellensis: λιβελλήσιος
libellus: λιβελλίκιος, λιβέλλιον, **λιβέλλος, λιβράριος**
liber[1, 2]: λίβερ
Liber[3]: Λίβερ
liberatio: λιβερατίων
liberi: λίβεροι
liberta: λιβέρτα
libertas: λιβέρτας
libertinus: λιβερτῖνος

libertus: λιβέρτος
Libitina: Λιβιτίνη
libra: λίβρα, λίτρα 1
librarius: ἀντιλιβράριος, **λιβράριος**
libum: λίβος
liburna: **λιβερνάριος, λίβερνος**, λιβύρνα
*liburnarius: **λιβερνάριος**
Liburnus: λιβέρνιος
lictor: λίκτωρ
lignatio: λιγνατίων
ligo: λιγᾶρε
ligula: ἀρκλόλιγκλα, **λίγλα**, νίγλα
ligurium: λυγγούριον
limbus: λιμβός
limen: limen
limes: **λιμιτόν**, λιμιτοτρόφος
limitaneus: **λιμιτάνεος**
limitotrophus: λιμιτοτρόφος
lingua: λίγγουα
lintearia: λεντιαρία
lintearius: λεντιαρία, λεντιάριον, **λεντιάριος**
linteum: λεντίκιον, **λέντιον**, λεντιυφαντής
linteus: λέντιος
litigator: λιτιγάτωρ
litigiosus: λιτιγίοσος
littera: λίττερα
lituus: λίτυον
locator: λοκάτωρ
loco: λοκᾶτος
lodix: λωδικάριος, **λωδίκιον, λῶδιξ**
lora: λωρόν
loramentum: λωραμέντα
lorica: **λωρῖκα, λωρίκιον**, λωρῖκος
loricarius: λωρικάριος
loricatus: λωρεικάτης
lorum: **λωρίον, λῶρος**, λωρόσοκον, λωροτομέω, **λωροτόμος** 1, λωροτόμος 2
lucanica: **λουκάνικον**
lucar: λοῦκαρ
Lucina: Λουκῖνα
lucius: λούκιος
lucrativus: λουκρατίβος
lucuntulus: λούκουντλος
lucus: λοῦκος
ludarius: λουδάριος
ludio: λυδίων
ludius: λυδός
ludus: λουδεμπιστής, **λοῦδος**, λουδοτρόφος
lumbus: λοῦμβοι
luminare: νουμενάρια
lupa: λούπα
Lupercal: Λουπερκάλιον
Lupercalia: Λουπερκάλια
Lupercus: Λούπερκος
lupinarius: λουπινάριον
lupinum: λούπινον
lupus: λούπης, λοῦπος
lusorius: λουσωρία, **λουσώριον**
lustrum: λοῦστρον

lyncurium: λυγγούριον

Maccus: μακκοάω
macellarius: **μακελλάριος**
macellum: μάκελλος
mafortium: μαφόρτης, στιχομαφόριον
magister: μαγιστρόκηνσος, **μάγιστρος, μαγιστρότης**, πρωτομαΐστωρ
magisterium: μαγιστήριον
magistratus: μαγιστράτη, **μαγίστρατος**
magistrianus: **μαγιστριανός**
magnus: Μάγνος
magulus: μάγουλον
maior: μαίωρ
maiorius: μαιοῦρος
maiuma: Μαιουμάρχης, **Μαιουμᾶς**, Μαιουμίζω
Maius: **Μάϊος**, Μαιουμάρχης, **Μαιουμᾶς**, Μαιουμίζω
malus: μάλημπτος, malus
Mamers: Μάμερτος
mamillare: μαμυλίων
manceps: **μαγκίπιον** 1, μαγκίπισσα, **μάγκιψ**
mancipatio: μαγκιπατίων
mancipium: **μαγκίπιον** 1, μαγκίπιον 2, μαγκίπιον 3
mandatarius: μανδατάριος
mandator: ἀλληλομανδάτορες, **μανδάτωρ**, μανδατωρεύω
mandatum: **μανδᾶτον**
mando: mando
manes: μάνης
mango: ὀνόμαγγων
manicae: μάνικα, μανίκιον, χειρομανίκιον, χειρομάνικον
manicillium: μανικέλλιον
manicium: μανίκιον
manifestus: μανίφεστος
manipularis: μανιπλάριος, μάνιπλος
manipulus: μανίπλον, μάνιπλος
mantele: **μανδήλη, μανδήλιον**, μαντηλαρία, μαντηλάριος
mantelium: **μανδήλιον**
mantica: μάνδιξ
mantus: **μαντίον**, μάντος
manualis: μανουάλιον
manubrium: μανούβριον
*manuclavium: μαγκλάβι
manumissio: manumissio
manumissor: μανουμίσσωρ
manus: μαγκλάβι
mappa: μάπουλον, **μάππα**, μαππάριον, μαππάριος, **μαππίον**, χειρομάππιον
marinus: μαρῖνος, ῥουσμαρῖνον
marita: μαρίτα
maritus: μαρῖτος
*marmarosus: μαρμαρωσσός
marmorarius: **μαρμαράριος**
marmorosus: μαρμαρωσσός
marra: μάρρον
Martenses: Μαρτήσιοι
Martialis: Μαρτιάλιος
Martius: **Μάρτιος**
massa: μάσσα

mastichatus: μαστιχᾶτον
materia: ματερία
materiarius: ματρικάριος
matertera: ματερτέρα
matricarius: ματρικάριος
matricularius: ματρικουλάριος
matrimonium: matrimonium
matrix: **ματρίκιον, μάτριξ**
matrona: **ματρῶνα,** ματρωνίκιον, ματρωνίκιος
matronalis: Ματρωνάλια, ματρωνίκιον, ματρωνίκιος
mattiarius: ματτιάριος
matula: μάτλα
matutinus: ματουτεῖνος
Maurus: μαῦρος
maxilla: μαξίλα, μαξιλλάρι, μαξίλλας, μαξιλλοπλουμάκιος
maxillaris: μαξιλλάρι, μαξιλλάριος
maximus: μάξιμος, **προμάξιμον**
mechanarius: μηχανάριος
medianum: μεδιανόν
medium: μεδιούμ
medius: medius
Megalensia: Μεγαλήσια
melca: μέλκα
meles: μελίνη
melinus: μελίνη
melota: μηλωτή
membrana: **μεμβράϊνος, μεμβράνα**
membranarius: μεμβραϊνάριος
membraneus: **μεμβράϊνος**
membranus: **μεμβράϊνος**
memoralius: μεμοράριος
memorarius: μεμοράριος
memoria: **μεμόριον,** μεμορίτης, μεμοροφύλαξ, οὐέτερεμ μεμορίαμ
memorialis: **μεμοριάλιος**
mens: μέντις
mensa: μενσάδιον, μῆνσα
mensis: μηνσωρων
mensor: μήνσωρ
mensorium: **μηνσώριον**
menstruus: μενστροῦος
mensula: μένσυλα, μήσυλα
mensura: μενσούρα
menta: μέντα
mentagra: μεντάγρα
mentula: μεντούλα
Mercedonius: Μερκηδόνιος
merda: μουρδάρις
metallum: μέταλλον
metator: **μητάτωρ,** προμητάτωρ
metatorius: μητατορικός, μητατώριον
metor: **μητατεύω, μητᾶτον**
metus: μέτους καῦσα
miles: μίλιτες
miliarense: **μιλιαρήσιον**
miliarium: **μιλιάριον**
miliarius: **μιλιάριος**
militaris: militaria

militia: μιλιτία
mille: μιλιάζω, μιλιασμός, **μίλιον**
millenarius: μιλινάριος
mimus: μεῖμος
minimus: minimus
minium: ἀμήνιον, μίνιον
minor: μίνωρ
miscellaneus: μισκελλάνιον
miscellus: μισκέλλας, μίσκελλος
misceo: μισκῆρε
missa: μίσσα
missibilia: μισσιβίλια
missicius: **μισσίκιος**
missorium: **μηνσώριον**
missus: μίσσος
mittendarius: μιττενδάριος
mitto: μονόμισσα
mitulus: μίτλος
mixtus: μίξτος
moderator: μοδεράτωρ
modiarius: μοδιάριος
modiolus: μοδίολος
modius: διμόδιον, μοδιάριος, **μόδιος,** μοδισμός, πενταμοδιαῖος, πενταμόδιον, τετραμόδιον, **τριμόδιον**
mola: μώδα
moles: **μῶλος**
molinarius: μυλινάριος
momar: μῶμαρ
momentarius: μομεντάριος
moneta: **μονῆτα**
monetalis: μονητᾶλις
monetarius: **μονητάριος**
monile: μανιάκης
Montianum: Μοντιανόν
mora: μόρα
morbus: μόρβος
moror: μώρανς
mors: μόρτις καῦσα
mucus: μούκουρα
mula: ἄμβλα μοῦλα, **μοῦλα,** μουλαγόρας, **μουλάριον,** μουλιατρός, μουλικός
mulio: **μουλίων**
mulionicus: μουλιωνικός
mulomedicus: μουλιατρός
mulus: μουλαγόρας, **μουλάριον,** μουλιατρός, μουλικός, **μοῦλος**
mundus: μοῦνδος
munerarius: μουνεράριος
municipium: **μουνικίπιον**
munifex: μουνίφεξ
murcus: μύρκος
murmillo: **μερμίλλων**
murmuro: μουρμουρίζω
murrinus: μόρρια
musarius: μουσιάριος
musculus: μούσκλα
muscus: μούσκουλο
musimo: μοσμονάριος, μούσμων
musmonarius: μοσμονάριος

phaselus: φάσηλος
phaseolus: **φασίολος**
piaculum: πιᾶκλον
picula: πικέλα
picus: πῖκος
pietas: πιετατις
pigmentarius: **πιμεντάριος**
pigmentum: ἀ πιγμέντις
pigneraticius: πιγνερατίκιος
pila¹: πίλα 1, **πιλάριον**
pila²: **πίλα 2**
pilaris: πιλάριος
pilarius: πιλάριος
pilleatus: πιλλᾶτος
pilleus: πίλεος, πιλίον, πῖλος 1
pilum: **πιλάριον**
pilus¹: πῖλος 3
pilus²: πῖλος 2, **πριμίπιλος**
pincerna: πιγκέρνης
piperatus: πεπερᾶτον
piscarium: πισκάριον
piscina: πισκεῖνα
pistor: πιστίκιον
pistrina: πιστρίνη
pistrinarius: πριστινάριος
pistrinum: πιστρῖνον
pius: πίος
plagiarius: πλαγιαρία, πλαγιάριος
plago: **πληγᾶτος**
planipes: πλανιπεδαρία
planta: πλάντρα
planus: πλάνη
plebeius: πλήβειος
plebiscitum: πλεβίσκιτον
plebs: πλῆβις
plecto: πλίκιον
plenarius: **πληναρία**, πληνάριος
plenilunium: πληνιλούνιον
*plintharius: πλινθάριος
pluma: ἐμπλούμιος, **ἔμπλουμος**, εὔπλουμος, ὀρθόπλουμος, πλουμάριον, πλουμαρίσιμος, πλουμίκιον, **πλουμίον**, πλοῦμος
plumacium: μαξιλλοπλουμάκιος, **πλουμάκιον**
plumarius: ὀθονεμπλουμάριος, πλουμαρία, **πλουμαρικός**, **πλουμάριος**, πλουμαρίσιμος, πλουμάρισις, πλουμάρισσα
plumbo: πλουμβατίζω, πλουμβᾶτος
plumeus: **πλουμίον**
plumo: πλουμᾶτος
pluviaticus: πλουβιάτικος
podiolum: ποδηλον
poena: ποῖνα
poenalis: ποινάλιος
polenta: πόλυντρα
politicus: πολιτικοπραιτώριος
pollen: πόλλινος
pomarium: πωμαρικός, **πωμάριον**, **πωμαρίτης**, πωμαριτικός, πωμαρίτισσα

pomarius: πωμάριος, σαπρομωπάριος
pomerium: πωμήριον
pondus: πόνδερε
pons: πόντεμ
pontifex: **ποντίφεξ**
pontificalis: ποντιφικάλιος
pontile: ποντίλιον, πόντιλον, ποντίλωα, ποντίλωμα
popina: προπῖνα, προπινάριον
popinaria: προπιναρία
popinarius: προπιναρία, προπινάριον, **προπινάριος**
popularis: ποπουλάριος
populus: ποπούλους
porcinus: πόρκινος
porcus: πόρκος
porta: ἐξώπορτος, **πόρτα**, πορτᾶς
*portarensis: **πορταρῆσις**
portarius: πορτάριος
*porthmarius: πορθμάριος
porticus: πόρτικος
porto: πόρτακος
Portus: Πόρτος
posca: **φοῦσκα**
poscarius: φουσκάριος
possessio: ποσσεσσίων
possessor: ποσσέσσωρ
postilena: ὀπισθελίνα
postliminium: ποστλιμίνιον
postumus: πόστουμος
potens: πότηνς
potestas: ἰνποτέστατος, ποτέστας
potio: πότιον 1
potior: potior
prae: πραιέναι
praeceptio: πραικεπτίων
praecipuus: πραικίπουος
praeco: **πραίκων**
praecox: **πραικόκκιον**
praecursor: προκουρσάριος
praeda: ἀπραίδευτος, **πραῖδα**, **πραιδεύω**
praedelegatio: **προδηληγᾶτον**
praedicatio: πραεδικατίων
praedispono: προδισπόσιτος
praedium: πραέδιον
praedor: ἀπραίδευτος, **πραιδεύω**
praefectorius: πραεφεκτώριος
praefectura: πρεφεκτορία
praefectus: ἀννωναταμίας, ἀννωνέπαρχος, **πραίφεκτος**
praeiudicialis: πραεϊουδικιάλιος
praeiudicium: πραεϊουδίκιον
praelego: πραιλῆκτος
*praemetator: προμητάτωρ
praepositura: πραιποσιτούρα
praepositus: ἀποπραιπόσιτος, ὀρρεοπραιποσιτία, πραιποσιτεύω, **πραιπόσιτος**
praeposterus: πραεποστέρα
praes: πραῖς
praescribo: πραεσκρίπτος
praescriptio: πραεσκριπτίων

praesens: πραισεντεύω, **πραίσεντον**, πραίσεντος
praesentalis: πραισεντάλιος
praesento: πραισεντεύω
praesidium: πραισιδιάριος, **πραισίδιον**
praestatio: πραεστατίων
praestes: πραιστίτεις
praetentura: πραιτεντούρα
praetereo: πραετεριτεύω, πραετέριτος
praeteritio: πραετεριτίων
praeteritus: πραετέριτος, **πραιτέριτος**
praetexta: praetexta, πραιτεξτᾶτος
praetor: ἀποπραίτωρ, **πραίτωρ**
praetorianus: **πραιτωριανός**
praetorium: πραιτωρίδιον, πραιτωριοκτυπέω, **πραιτώριον**
praetorius: πολιτικοπραιτώριος, **πραιτώριος**
praetura: πραιτούρα
praevaricatio: πραεβαρικατίων
praevaricator: πραεβαρικάτωρ
praevaricor: πραεβαρικατεύω
prandium: πράνδιον
prasinianus: πρασιανός
precarius: πραεκάριος
pressorium: πρισόριον
pridie: πρίδιε
primarius: πριμάριος
primiceriatus: πριμικηρᾶτον
primicerius: **πριμικήριος**
primigenia: πριμιγένεια
primipilaris: **πριμιπιλάριος**
primipilum: **πριμίπιλον**
primipilus: **πριμίπιλος**
primiscrinius: **πριμισκρίνιος**
primitivus: πριμιτῖβος
primogenitus: πριμογένιτος
*primosagittarius: πριμοσαγιττάριος
*primoscutarius: πριμοσκουτάριος
primus: **πριμίπιλον**, **πριμίπιλος**, **πρῖμος**, πριμοσαγιττάριος, πριμοσκουτάριος
princeps: ὀπτιοπρίγκεψ, **πρίγκεψ**
principalis: **πριγκιπάλιος**
principium: **πριγκίπια**
prior: **πρίωρ**
priscus: πρίσκος
privatarius: πριβατάριος
privatianus: πριβατιανός
privatus: πριβατάριος, πριβάτιος, **πριβᾶτος**, πριβατούρα
privilegiarius: πριβιλεγιάριος
privilegium: **πριβιλέγιον**
pro: pro, προδερέλικτος, προνερεδεγεριτεύω
proba: πρόβα
probatio: προβατίων
probatoria: πριβατούρα, **προβατωρία**
probo: προβᾶρε
processus: **πρόκεσσον**
procinctus: procinctus
proculcator: προσκουλκάτωρ
procuratio: προκουρατίων
procurator: **προκουράτωρ**, προκουρατώριος
*prodispono: προδισπόσιτος

profecticius: προφεκτίκιος
professio: **προφεσσίων**
profugus: πρόσφουγος
prohibitorius: προϊβιτόριος
promagister: προμάγιστρος
prometator: προμητάτωρ
promitto: προμίττενς
promotio: προμωτίων
promoveo: **προμῶτος**
pronuntiatio: προνουντιατίων
pronuntio: προνουντιατεύω
prooemium: προοίμιον
propior: propior
proprietarius: **προπριεταρία**, προπριετάριος
proprius: πρόπριος
prosecutoria: προσεκουτωρία
protector: ἀποπροτήκτωρ, **προτήκτωρ**
protelum: πρώτηλα
provincialis: προβιγκάλιος
provocator: **προβοκάτωρ**
proximus: **πρόξιμος**
publico: πουβλικίζω
publicus: πουβλικίζω, **πούβλικος**
pugio: βοῦγλιν, φουγίων
pulcher: πολλαχρός, Ποῦλχερ
pulicaris: πουλικάριος
*pullicrus: πουλλικρούρα
pullus: ὀρνιθοπούλλιον, **περιστερόπουλλος**, **πουλλίον**, ποῦλλος
pulpito: πουλπιτόω
pulpitum: πούλπιτον
puls: πόλτος
pulsator: πουλσάτωρ
pultarius: πολταρίδιον, πολτάριος
pulvinus: πουλβινάριον, **πουλβῖνον**
punctum: ποῦκτον
punga: πουγγίον
pupillaris: βουλγαροπουπιλλάριος, πουπιλλάριος
pupillus: πούπιλλος
purus: πούριον, ποῦρος
pus: πουράτα
puteus: πότιον 2
putialis: πουτιαλογονθρια
putris: ποῦτριν

quadrans: **κοδράντης**, quadrans
quadratarius: **κουαδράριος**
quadratus: κουαδρᾶτος
quadrigarius: κουδριγάριος
quadrum: κόδριν
quadruplicatio: quadruplicatio
quaesitor: κυαισίτωρ
quaestio: κυαιστίων
quaestionarius: κεσσωνάριος, **κυαιστιωνάριος**
quaestor: κουαιστορεία, **κουαίστωρ**
quaestorius: **κουαιστώριος**
quaestus: κυαίστους
quartus: κουάρτος
quasi: κουάσι

statarius: ἀσταταρία, στατάριον 1
statio: ἀρμαστατίων, **στατίων**, στατιωνίζω
stationarius: **στατιωνάριος**
stator[1]: ἀρχιστάτωρ, **στάτωρ**
stator[2]: Στάτωρ
statutus: **στατοῦτος**
stella: στελλάριον
stellionatus: στελλιονᾶτον
sterno: **στρᾶτα**
*stibarius: στειβάριος
stipendiarius: στιπενδιάριος
stipendium: **στιπένδιον**
stipulatio: στιπουλατίων
stipulatus: στιπουλᾶτον
stipulor: στιπουλάνδος
stolatus: **στολᾶτος**
stomachor: στομαχέω
stomachus: στόμαχος
stragulum: στράγλον
strata: **στρᾶτα**
strator: ἀρχιστράτωρ, σουπερστράτωρ, **στράτωρ**
strena: στρήνα
strictoria: στρικτωρία
strictorium: στρικτόριον
strictus: στρικτόν, στρικτός
striga: στρίγλα
strigilis: στρίγλα
stringo: στρικτόν
strix: στρίξ
structor: στρούκτωρ, στρουκτώριον
structorius: στρουκτώριον
stuppa: στουππί, στύβη
stuprum: στοῦπρον
sub: σουβδρομεδάριος, σουφρουμεντάριος
subadiuva: **σουβαδιούβας**
subalare: **σουβαλάριον**
sublica: σουβρίκιον, σουβρικομαφόρτης, σουβρικομαφόρτιον, **σουβρικοπάλλιον**, σουβρικός
suboptio: ὑποπτίων
subricula: σουβρίκιον, σουβρικομαφόρτης, σουβρικομαφόρτιον, **σουβρικοπάλλιον**, σουβρικός
subscribendarius: σκριβηνδάριος, σουβσκριβενδάριος
subsellium: **συμψέλλιον**
subsericus: συψειρικός
subsidiarius: σουβσιδιάριος
subsigno: σουβσιγνᾶτον
substantia: σουβσταντία
substituo: σουβστιτοῦτος
subula: σοῦβλα, σουβλίζω, **σουβλίον**
successio: σουκκεσσίων
successor: **σουκκέσσωρ**
sucinum: σούκινος, σούχινον
sucinus: σούκινος
suda: σοῦδα
sudarium: **σουδάριον**
sudis: σοῦδα
suffragium: σουφράγιον
*suffrumentarius: σουφρουμεντάριος

suggero: σουγγερεύω
suggestio: σουγγεστίων
summa: σομμα, σουμμάρος, **σουμμαρούδης**
summarium: σουμάριον
summarius: σουμμάριος, σουμμάρος
summus: **σοῦμμος**
super: σουπερνούμερος, σουπερστράτωρ
superbus: σούπερβος
superficium: σουπερφίκιον
supernumerarius: σουπερνουμεράριος, σουπερνούμερος
*superstrator: σουπερστράτωρ
supplementum: σουπλημέντα
supplico: σοῦφρα
sura: σούρα
suspectus: σούσπεκτος
suus: σοῦος
*synthecarius: συνθηκάριος
syrellianus: σουρελιανός

tabella: **ταβέλλα**, ταβούλη
tabellarius: **ταβελλάριος**, **ταβλάριος**
tabellio: **ταβελλίων**
taberna: **ταβέρνα**, **ταβέρνιον**, ταβερνοδύτης
tabernarius: ταβερναρία, ταβερνάριος
tabula: κόντρα ταβούλλας, **τάβλα**, **ταβλίζω**, **ταβλίον**, ταβλιόπη, ταβλιστήριον, ταβλιστής, ταβλοδόχος, τάβλον, ταβλοπαρόχιον, ταβλοπάροχος, τάβλωμα, ταβλωτός, ταβούλη, ταυλοειδῶς
tabularium: ταβουλάριον
tabularius: ἀρχιταβλάριος, **ταβλάριος**
tacitus: τάκιτος
talaris: **ταλάριον**
Tarentum: Τερεντῖνον
taurinus: ταυρινᾶς, ταυρίνδα, ταυρίνη
taxatio: ταξατίων
taxo: ταξᾶτος
taxus: τάξος
temperator: τεμπεράτωρ
templum: τέμπλον
temporalis: τεμποράλιος
tendo: τέντα
tensa: θῆσσα
tentorium: τέντριον
Terentius: Τερεντῖνον
termen: τέρμινας, τέρμου
Terminalia: Τερμινάλια
tertianus: τερτιανός
tertiocerius: τερτιοκήριος
tertius: τερτιοδέλματος, τέρτιος
tesserarius: προτεσσαράριος, **τεσσαράριος**, τεσσεδάρις
testamentarius: τεσταμεντάριος
testamentum: τεσταμεντιφακτίων, τεσταμέντον
testator: τεσταμεντάτωρ, **τεστάτωρ**
tetricus: τέτριξ
Tiberis: κίστιβερ, Τίβερις
Tiberius: φιλοτιβέριος
tignum: τίγνον
tina: τίνα

tiro: ναυτοτίρων, τειρωνολογέω, **τίρων**, τιρωνικόν
tironatus: **τιρωνᾶτον**
titulus: **παράτιτλον**, τιτλάριον, **τίτλος**, τιτλόω, ὑπότιτλος, ὑποτίτλωσις
tofus: τοφιών
toga: τόγα, τογατηφόρος
togatus: τογατηφόρος, τογᾶτος
tomentum: τώμεντον
topiarius: τοπιάριος
toral: τοράλλιον
torpedo: τούρπαινα
torquatus: τορκουᾶτος
torqueo: τοῦρτα, τουρτίον
trabea: τραβέα
tractatio: τρακτατίων
tractatus: **τρακτᾶτος**
tracto: **τρακταΐζω**, τρακταϊστέος, τρακταϊστής, **τρακτευτής**, τρακτευτικός, **τρακτεύω**, **τρακτός**, τράκτωμα
tractoria: τρακτωρία
tractum: τρακτόν
traditio: τραδιτίων
trado: τραδιτεύω
tragula: δράγλη, τραγόλας
traho: τρά, **τρακτός**, τράκτωμα
traiecticius: τραεκτίκιος
trans: τράνς
transfero: τρανσλατεύω
translatio: τρανσλατίων
translimitanus: ὑπερλιμιτανός
transversarius: τραουεσσάριν
trecenarius: τρεκινάριος
tremis: **τριμήσιον**
triarius: τριάριος
tribulum: τρίβολος
tribunal: **τριβουνάλιον**
tribunatus: τριβουνᾶτον
tribunicius: τριβουνίκιος
tribunus: ἀποτριβοῦνος, κομιτοτριβοῦνος, **τριβοῦνος**
tribus: τρίβος
tributorius: τριβουτόριος
tributum: τριβοῦτον
tricennalis: τρικενναλικός
triclinium: τρικλίνιον
triens: triens
Trifolinus: τριφύλλινος
trimensis: τριμένσις
triplicatio: τριπλικατίων
triticarius: τριτικάριος
triticum: τρίτικον
triumphalis: τριουμφάλιος
triumphus: θρίαμβος
triumvir: τριομβυρατορία, τριομβυράτωρ, τριούμβουρα
triumviratus: τριομβυρατορία
trixago: τριξαγίνη
trulla: **τροῦλλα**, **τρούλλιον**, **τροῦλλος**, τρυηλίς
trulleus: **τρούλλιον**, **τροῦλλος**
tuba: τοῦβα
tubator: τουβάτωρ
tubicen: τουβίκινες

tubulatus: τουβουλαμέντον
tubulus: τοῦβλον
tufa: τοῦφα, τουφίον
tumba: τοῦμπα
turma: **τοῦρμα**
turmalis: τουρμάλιος
turmarius: τουρμάριος
tutela: τουτέλαε
tutelarius: τουτηλάριος
*Tutianum: Τουτιανόν
tutor: τούτωρ

udo: οὐδών, **οὐδωνάριον**, οὐδώνιον
ultimus: οὔλτιμος
uncia: δεκαούγκιον, **διούγκιον**, **ἐνναούγκιον**, **ἑξαούγκιον**, ἑπταούγκιον, ἡμιουγκιαῖος, **ἡμιούγκιον**, ὀκταούγκιον, **οὐγγία**, οὐγκιαῖος, οὐγκιαρήσιον, **οὐγκιασμός**, οὐγκίον, πενταούγκιον, **τετραούγκιον**, **τριούγκιον**
uncialis: οὐγκιαῖος
uncinatus: οὐγκινᾶτος
uncinus: ὀγκινάρα, **ὄγκινος**
unde: οὔνδε
universitas: universitas
urbanicianus: οὐρβανικιανός
urbanus: οὐρβανός
urbs: οὔρβς
urceolus: ὀρκίολος
urna: γοῦρνα, οὔρνα, ὤρνα
urus: οὖρος
usuarius: οὐσουάριος
usucapio: οὐσουκαπιτεύω, οὐσουκαπίων
usufructuarius: οὐσουφρουκτουάριος
usus: οὖσος, **οὐσούφρουκτος**
ut: ut
uterus: ὄδερος
utilis: οὐτίλιος
utrubi: οὔτρουβι
uxorius: ῥεουξορία

vacantia: βακάντιος
vacantivus: βακάντιβος
vacatio: βακατίων
vador: βαδιάζω
vadum: οὐάδα
vae: οὐαί
vaginarius: βαγινάριος
vagor: βαγεύω
vah: **οὐά**
Valentiniani: **Οὐαλεντινιανοί**
valeo: βάλεας, βαλῆρε
vallaris: οὐαλλάριος
valvoli: βαβοῦλι
vara: οὐάρα
vascellum: βασκέλειον
vasculum: βασκέλειον, βάσκυλον
vasto: βασταγάριος
vates: οὐᾶτις
vectigal: βεκτιγάλιον
vectura: βεκτοῦρα